INDUSTRIAL DEMOCRACY

Also Published in
Reprints of Economic Classics

By SIDNEY & BEATRICE WEBB

The History of Trade Unionism (1894)

INDUSTRIAL
DEMOCRACY

BY

SIDNEY & BEATRICE WEBB

[*1897*] Passfield

69386

REPRINTS OF ECONOMIC CLASSICS

Augustus M. Kelley, Bookseller
New York 1965

Original edition 1897.   Reprinted 1965 from the 1920 edition.

Library of Congress Catalogue Card Number
65 - 18330

PRINTED IN THE UNITED STATES OF AMERICA
by SENTRY PRESS, NEW YORK, N. Y. 10019

INTRODUCTION TO THE 1920 EDITION

THE continued and even increasing demand for this book, though it is more than twenty years old, gives us the opportunity of rewriting the Introduction prefixed to the 1902 edition, and of making certain changes in the Appendices.

We have made no alteration in the text itself (pp. 1-850), which must stand as an analytic description of British Trade Unionism as it was in the last decade of the nineteenth century. Although the details of social organisation are constantly changing, the problems presented to the student remain for long periods essentially the same. It is more instructive to study these problems at a particular phase than to blur the picture by any vain attempt to bring its thousand items down to date. It should be the task of another worker, at some future time, to take a new photograph, possibly at a different angle, with which our own picture may be contrasted.

All that we can usefully do here is to draw attention to the most important changes. The most obvious contrast between the Trade Unionism of 1890 and that of 1920 is the much more influential position in the community that it occupies. When *Industrial Democracy* was published in 1897, some critics ridiculed the idea of attaching even so much importance to the workmen's organisations as to write a book about them. In 1920 the same critics are uneasy in their minds as to whether the despised workmen's

organisations are not destined to swallow up all other
social institutions ! For a measured estimate of the advance
of Trade Unionism, the student is referred to the new
edition of the *History of Trade Unionism*, which has been
extended down to the present year. We have there
described, not merely the fourfold increase in aggregate
membership and the tenfold increase in accumulated funds
during the past thirty years, but also the spread of Trade
Unionism to new fields—to the women wage-earners, to the
great army of agricultural labourers and general workers,
to the clerks and teachers, to various kinds of technicians
and scientific workers, and even to branches of the professions. In the same book will be found an account
of the continued rise of Trade Unionism in legal status
and constitutional importance in the State, together with a
description of the growth in structure and the changes in
thought which have been influencing the Trade Union
world. We do not find that these developments have
rendered obsolete our examination, a quarter of a century
ago, of the problems of the wage-earners' organisations, nor
our analysis of the economic and social effects of Trade
Unionism itself. If we had now to write the book afresh,
after the economic changes resulting from the Great War,
all the figures as to membership and rates of wages would
be vastly different, and more recent examples and illustrations would be added. But—subject to what we have said
in the closing pages of the 1920 edition of the *History of
Trade Unionism*—we believe that the conclusions to which
we came in 1897, as to the place of Trade Unionism in the
community, would hold good of the Trade Unionism of
to-day. In particular, the whole chapter on " The Economic
Characteristics of Trade Unionism " (pp. 703-806), with its
unequivocal demonstration of the essential validity of the
case for Trade Unionism, stands, we think, after more than
a couple of decades of examination by the British economists,
in 1920 unchallenged. The student might usefully consider
to what extent, if any, this analysis of the economics of

Trade Unionism calls for further modifications of the somewhat stereotyped propositions of the economic textbooks as to profits and wages, the rate of interest, and the influences affecting the growth of capital.

We said nothing in 1897 about "the premium-bonus system" and other forms of "payment by results," into which the employers' ingenuity has elaborated the "piecework" that we described (pp. 279-323). Such changes of form and shifts of nomenclature do not, in our judgment, affect the argument that leads the Trade Unionists to accept, and even to prefer, systems of "payment by results," when these are so devised and administered as to exclude Individual Bargaining, and so as to permit of the permanent maintenance of the Standard Rate by Collective Bargaining or some equivalent machinery. The same argument causes them to reject with indignation all the specious attempts that are made—notably in the engineering industry—to introduce varieties of piece-work or of the "premium-bonus system" without allowing the rate or time for each job to be determined in any other way than by the employer's fiat or by Individual Bargaining. The workmen do not always manage to explain the reasons for their decision one way or the other; and they incur much ignorant criticism from people thinking themselves educated whenever they refuse to accept a system of "payment by results"; but in the policy itself the Trade Unions are, in our opinion, entirely justified.[1]

Nor will the reader find in this book any mention of "Scientific Management," "Motion Study," or other new designations given to the improvement of factory processes, usually in conjunction with a "premium-bonus" system, for which the American "Efficiency Engineers" have, during

[1] The various "premium-bonus" systems, and the reasons why their acceptance would, without the fixing of rates for each successive job by some joint authority, or by much more effective Collective Bargaining than the engineering employers can at present bring themselves to agree to, would inevitably undermine the Standard Rate, are examined in *The Works Manager To-day*, by Sidney Webb, 1917.

the present century, made large claims. The attitude of British Trade Unionism to analogous proposals is, however, elaborately explained (pp. 392-429). Employers seem usually unable even to understand the workmen's case. The issue turns essentially on whether or not the employers are prepared to forgo their dictatorship inside their own workshops, and honestly to submit the conditions of employment to an effective joint control, whether by Collective Bargaining or otherwise. In the common prejudice against innovations, which workmen share with persons of higher social grade, there is little that is justifiable. But until the employers in the engineering industry and the building trades offer the workmen some genuine security against an insidious future lowering of rates, as the employers in the cotton trade have learned to do, the economist cannot but hold the Trade Union warranted in resisting any so-called improvement that involves a reversion to Individual Bargaining.[1]

More interesting and promising seem the developments that have taken place since 1897 in the study of Fatigue, in connection with changes in the Normal Day (pp. 324-53), and with the increased amenity of factory conditions; together with the development of "Welfare Work" in industrial employment. We may possibly have here the opening of a new chapter in factory organisation with which we are not yet able to deal.[2]

In an Appendix to the original edition, and in the Introduction to subsequent editions, we described at some length the successive assaults made by the Law Courts upon the legal position conferred upon Trade Unionism by the Acts of 1871-6. This controversy has since been closed, at least for the time being, by the further statutes of 1906 and 1913. We need here do no more than refer to the story of these momentous years, out of which there have emerged, not merely these statutes and quite a new re-

---

[1] Cp. note on preceding page.

[2] Something is said on the subject in *The Works Manager To-day*, by Sidney Webb, 1917, where references are given.

cognition of Trade Unionism by the employers and the
Government Departments, but also the Labor Party, as the
political organisation of the Trade Union world, of which
we had ventured, in 1894, to foretell the coming.[1]

Equally unnecessary is it for us to-day to reprint the
elaborate description, given in the Introduction to previous
editions, of the legislation securing a Legal Minimum Wage
in New Zealand and Australia. What in 1897 we were
almost alone in proposing has, in the last two decades, been
adopted in the United Kingdom, with the general support
of the economists, and almost by common consent, as a
necessary basis of the Policy of the National Minimum. By
the successive Trade Boards Acts of 1908 and 1917, the
Mines (Minimum Wage) Act of 1912, and the Corn Production Acts of 1917 and 1919, a Legal Minimum Wage
has now been prescribed for something like a quarter of all
the wage-earners in the United Kingdom ; for the strongly
combined and relatively well-paid, as well as for the
" sweated " workers ; and actually for more men than women.
What, in fact, has characterised the social history of the
present century has been the unavowed and often per-
functory adoption, in administration as well as in legislation,
of the Policy of the National Minimum, formulated in this
book (pp. 766-84), but elaborated in greater detail in our
work of 1911 on *The Prevention of Destitution.*[2]

In the latter work we have discussed what we did not
foresee in 1897, namely, the sudden adoption of organised
national provision for nearly all the contingencies of the
wage-earners' life. Part of that provision—the securing to all
manual workers, and also to all the humbler employees not
classed as manual workers, of compensation for accidents—
is dealt with in the present volume (pp. 354-91), although
the responsibility for the compensation, now practically
universal, has not yet been assumed by the community as a

[1] *History of Trade Unionism*, original edition, pp. 476-78. See also chaps.
x. and xi. of the 1920 edition.

[2] See the *Cambridge Modern History*, vol. xii. chap. xx., " Social Movements " ;
republished by the Fabian Society under the title of *Towards Social Democracy?*

whole.   This final step has been taken as regards provision
for superannuation (Old Age Pensions Acts of 1906, 1910,
and 1918), though as yet only inadequately, and at too
advanced an age.   What we did not foresee was the bold
application that Mr. Lloyd George was to make of the
Method of Mutual Insurance, by applying it, so far as concerns
medical attendance, sick pay, maternity benefit, and Out of
Work Pay, to nearly the whole of the employed population,
and by transforming it from a voluntary act of thrift to a
sort of compulsory poll-tax payable partly by the employer
and partly by the beneficiary.   This elaborate and costly
scheme of National Insurance has already been more than
once amended, and is plainly not yet in its final form.   So
far, its main effect on the Trade Union Movement has been
to stimulate the enrolment of members and the spread of
organisation among shop assistants, women factory operatives,
agricultural labourers, general workers and other classes
whose response to Trade Unionism had previously been
only sporadic.   Time will show what the total effect will be,
alike on the workmen's organisations and on the public
health.   We have given our criticisms and expressed some
of our misgivings in *The Prevention of Destitution*.[1]

It may be convenient to point out a few other statutory
changes in the United Kingdom between 1897 and 1920.
By a succession of Education Acts, culminating in that of
1918, which is, as yet, only slightly operative, something
has been done to remove the defects to which we referred
(pp. 768-9) ; but we are still very far from a completely
effective enforcement of the National Minimum of Education
and Child Nurture that our Legislature professes to have
adopted.   The serious evil of child labor (pp. 482-89, 768-71),
only slightly mitigated by by-laws as to employment out of
school hours, and by the projected universal modicum of
continuation schooling, has still to be grappled with.   The
long array of Acts and Amending Acts dealing with the

---

[1] See also the Report on the Working of the National Insurance Act, published
as a Supplement of *The New Statesman*.

conditions of employment in factories and workshops
(pp. 771-73) have been consolidated in the Factories and
Workshops Act of 1901 ; but this statute has since been
overlain by Amending Acts and Home Office regulations
all tending in the right direction, but partial, " scrappy," and
confusing. The law and the administration still fail to
secure to all the wage-earners—even to all the women and
young persons—that National Minimum of Sanitation and
Rest which the nation purports to give. Whole classes of
women workers still remain excluded from protection.
Laundries (p. 365) have now been brought under regulation ; but the sections dealing with outworkers (p. 772) and
unhealthy trades (pp. 363-64) continue, in the main, illusory
and inoperative. The numerous exceptions as to overtime
and other relaxations (except in the textile industry) still
hamper administration (pp. 349-51). The Truck Act of
1896 has been found less irksome than the workmen
expected, owing largely to the fact that it has been only
slightly operative.[1] Deductions continue to be made and
fines to be imposed (pp. 315-18, 840) where the wage-earners
are defenceless ; but the spread of Trade Unionism causes a
steady diminution of the evil. The Workmen's Compensation Act of 1897 (pp. 387-91) has now been extended,
but (as the Royal Commission now sitting has discovered)
with many defects, and the serious upheaval of prices has
made the maximum compensation entirely inadequate.
The employers (or, rather, the insurance companies in their
names) have displayed a most fertile ingenuity in raising
quibbles intended to limit the application of the law, but
the highest judicial tribunal has, on the whole, given full
effect to the intention of Parliament, and has, during the
present century, made a badly drafted statute really
operative. It should be added that the actual cost of
compensating for accidents has proved less than was antici-

---

[1] We may correct an erroneous assumption in the footnote on p. 211. The
act proved not to apply to the deduction referred to, and no exemption order
was necessary.

pated : unfortunately, as we suggested (pp. 375-76), much less than it would cost the employers to take all the precautions necessary to prevent them. It remains, therefore, more important than ever, in the interest of the community as a whole, to enforce in all occupations an effective National Minimum of Sanitation and Safety (pp. 375-78, 385-87, 771-73).

One desirable application of the Policy of the National Minimum seemed to us, in 1902, so urgently required for national safety that, in our Introduction to the edition of that year, we drew special attention to the need. Unfortunately, we can, in 1920, repeat what we then wrote. " Perhaps the gravest social symptom at the opening of the twentieth century is the lack of physical vigor, moral self-control, and technical skill of the town-bred, manual-working boy. In the industrial organisation of to-day there are hundreds of thousands of youths, between fourteen and twenty-one, who are taken on by employers to do unskilled and undisciplined work, at comparatively high wages for mere boys, who are taught no trade, who are kept working long hours at mere routine, and who are habitually turned adrift, to recruit the ranks of unskilled labor, as soon as they require a man's subsistence (pp. 482-85, 704-15, 768-69, 811). We see four acute evils arising out of the existence of this class. Ministers of religion deplore the ' hooliganism ' of our great cities. No less serious is the physical degeneracy, which is leading our military advisers to declare that 60 per cent of the adult male population now fail to reach the already low standard of the recruiting sergeant. At the same time, there is a constant deficiency in the supply of highly skilled labor, whilst all educationists agree that it is impossible to give adequate technical training with such voluntary attendance as can be got from lads after ten or twelve hours employment (p. 770). Finally in this suppression of the adult male operative by successive relays of boys between fourteen and twenty-one, we have, as we have shown (pp. 482-89, 768-71), one of the most insidious forms of industrial parasitism.   From the point of view of the community, we cannot afford to regard the growing boy as an independent wealth-producer, to be satisfied by a daily subsistence : he is the future citizen and parent, for whom, up to twenty-one, proper conditions of growth and training are of paramount importance.   Every industry employing boy-labor, and not providing adequate physical and mental training, is using up the stock of the nation, and comes under condemnation as a parasitic trade (p. 771).

" Now, although philanthropists and statesmen have deplored this complex evil, no systematic treatment of it has yet been undertaken.   The Trade Unions, to whom it presents itself primarily as the increase of ' boy-labor,' have found no better device against it than the so-called 'apprenticeship' regulations (pp. 482-89).   But the old system of individual apprenticeship to the master craftsman, with its anomalous restrictions of age and number, and its haphazard amateur instruction, is, as regards nearly all trades, dead and past reviving.   Any attempt to resuscitate it inevitably takes the form of a mere limitation of numbers, or other narrowing of the entrance to a trade—a policy which, as we have demonstrated, does not cure the evil, and is seriously prejudicial to masters and men alike, to the trade itself, and to the whole community (pp. 454-89, 768-71). Unfortunately, this limitation of the number of apprentices has now been embodied in both New Zealand and Victorian law, and we desire therefore to draw pointed attention, not only to the utter futility of this device, but also to the existence of a more excellent way.

" We see no remedy for the grave social evils resulting from the illegitimate use of boy-labor, and the consequent industrial parasitism, except in an appropriate application of the Policy of the National Minimum (pp. 770-71).   The nation must, at any inconvenience, prevent such conditions of employment of boys as are demonstrably inconsistent with the maintenance of the race in a state of efficiency as producers and citizens. As regards youths under twenty-one the community is bound, in its own interest, to secure for them, not as at present, daily subsistence and pocket-money, but such conditions of nurture as will allow of the continuous provision, generation after generation, of healthy and efficient adults. What is required for the ' hooligan ' is adequate opportunity for physical culture and effective technical training, and the systematic enforcement of these by law. This means, we suggest, an extension of the existing ' half-time system.' We see no reason why the present prohibition to employ a boy in a factory or workshop for more than thirty hours in a week should not be extended to all occupations, and at least up to the age of eighteen. The twenty or thirty hours per week thus saved from industrial employment should be compulsorily devoted to a properly organised course of physical training and technical education, which could, under such circumstances, be carried out with a thoroughness and efficiency hitherto undreamt of. Meanwhile employers would remain free to engage boys, but as they could get them only for half-time, they would not be tempted to hire them except for the legitimate purpose of training up a new generation of craftsmen."

We elaborated this proposal in 1911 in *The Prevention of Destitution*, applying it to girls as well as to boys, and urging a genuine extension of education, in addition to mere technical training. But notwithstanding the fact that British trade was, during these years, both more extensive and more prosperous than ever before, no employer would hear of such a thing, and no statesman ever so much as mentioned it. By its neglect of the adolescent the nation continued, year after year, to start a large number of criminals on their careers of alternate crime and imprisonment, which, in the great majority of cases, they begin before they are twenty-one. When the Great War came it was found that something like a third of all our adult men of military age were, to a serious extent, physically degenerate, in innumerable cases demonstrably through neglect in youth.

At last, in 1918, Mr. H. A. L. Fisher, Minister of Education, made a start by incorporating in the Act of that year, not, indeed, our demand for " half-time up to eighteen," but at any rate the beginning of such a scheme, by inducing Parliament to require, from all boys and girls between fourteen and eighteen, at least seven hours per week of continuation schooling, to be taken out of the employer's time. This modest reform was all that the House of Commons would stand ; and this only conditionally on the application of the measure being so long deferred that, even if the Government and the Legislature find sufficient money to provide the schools and the teachers (as looks at present unlikely), the Act cannot possibly be fully in operation before 1930. Much more drastic action is required.

Those who are interested in the current controversies among British Trade Unionists may notice that, in 1897, we did not explicitly mention the issue raised between " organisation by crafts " and " organisation by industries," which has since been made the subject of debate.[1] The considerations adduced in this volume, as to the most effective form of Trade Union organisation (pp. 72-141), indicate that the problem is one of greater complication than can be expressed merely by a contrast between a " craft " and an "industry," beyond which, indeed, the controversy has already passed. But there is a further comment to be made. What lends interest to the controversy is not the immediate practical problems arising from the rivalries between Trade Unions formed on mutually conflicting bases, to which we have sufficiently referred (pp. 104-41), but the advance of thought which the contentions reveal as to the eventual function of Trade Unionism in an essentially Socialist community. When, in 1894, we published the *History of Trade Unionism*, the workmen's organisations, whether by craft or by industry, were looked upon as

[1] See *An Introduction to Trade Unionism*, by G. D. H. Cole, 1916.

related only to the existing capitalist organisation, and as destined to find no place in the Co-operative Common-wealth of To-morrow. Not in this country alone, but generally throughout Europe, working-class opinion and Socialist thought have, on this point, both changed ; and a more highly developed and perfected Trade Unionism now forms, along with the consumers' Co-operative Move-ment, part of the projected organisation of the Socialist Community towards which the world appears to be steadily moving. The contemporary demand for a supersession of " Craft Unionism " by " Industrial Unionism " seems to embody, if not a confusion, at least a mixture of thought. In part, it springs from a desire to overcome the practical inconveniences of rival organisations that we have described (pp. 104-41). In part, however, it represents a stage onward in the progress towards the future Socialist Common-wealth, in which, it is imagined, each " industry " will be controlled by the organisation of the producers (including both brain and manual workers) whom it employs. We suggest, however, that this conception is unduly simplified. We may learn from our experience in the Great War that it is unprofitable to use one and the same form of organisa-tion for both war and peace. Whatever advantage there may be, in the long-drawn-out battle of interests between capitalist employers and manual working wage-earners, in " Industrial Unionism," or even in " One Big Union," there is no reason to assume that, when the capitalist employer has been eliminated, anything like the same organisation would prove the best way of administering a socialised industry. In our judgment, though vocational organisation is destined to play a large, and even an increasing part in the Socialist Commonwealth of the future, this will not take the form of the substitution of the Trade Union for the capitalist employer. What will be called for, in order to secure for the whole community the maximum of effective individual Freedom, will be a more elaborate organisation, in which, not the producers only, but also the consumers, together with the community as a whole (which has its future to safeguard) will all have a place. The participation in industrial management, which is now asked for on behalf of the Trade Unions, is really an adumbration of the influential part to be played in future, not by the Trade Union as we have it to-day, but by the independent organisation of each distinct vocation ; and the problem presented is that the vocational organisation necessarily transcends not only all geographical but also all administrative boundaries. What seems called for is, in due course, a reorganisation of the Vocational World. On this, however, we have written at length, offering our own provisional solution of the problem, in the book entitled *A Constitution for the Socialist Commonwealth of Great Britain* (1920).

SIDNEY AND BEATRICE WEBB.

41 GROSVENOR ROAD, WESTMINSTER,
September 1920.

PREFACE

WE have attempted in these volumes to give a scientific analysis of Trade Unionism in the United Kingdom. To this task we have devoted six years' investigation, in the course of which we have examined, inside and out, the constitution of practically every Trade Union organisation, together with the methods and regulations which it uses to attain its ends. In the *History of Trade Unionism*, published in 1894, we traced the origin and growth of the Trade Union movement as a whole, industrially and politically, concluding with a statistical account of the distribution of Trade Unionism according to trades and localities ; and a sketch from nature of Trade Union life and character. The student has, therefore, already had before him a picture of those external characteristics of Trade Unionism, past and present, which—borrowing a term from the study of animal life—we may call its natural history. These external characteristics—the outward form and habit of the creature— are obviously insufficient for any scientific generalisation as to its purpose and its effects. Nor can any useful conclusions, theoretic or practical, be arrived at by arguing from " common notions " about Trade Unionism ; nor even by refining these into a definition of some imaginary form of combination in the abstract. Sociology, like all other sciences, can advance only upon the basis of a precise observation of actual facts.

The first part of our work deals with Trade Union Structure. In the Anglo-Saxon world of to-day we find that Trade Unions are democracies : that is to say, their internal constitutions are all based on the principle of "government of the people by the people for the people." How far they are marked off from political governments by their membership being voluntary will be dealt with in the course of the analysis. They are, however, scientifically distinguished from other democracies in that they are composed exclusively of manual-working wage-earners, associated according to occupations. We shall show how the different Trade Unions reveal this species of democracy at many different stages of development. This part of the book will be of little interest to those who want simply to know whether Trade Unionism is a good or a bad influence in the State. To employers and Trade Union officials on active service in the campaign between Capital and Labor, or to politicians hesitating which side to take in a labor struggle, our detailed discussions of the relations between elector, representative, and civil servant ; between central and local government ; and between taxation and representation—not to speak of the difficulties connected with federation, the grant of " Home Rule " to minorities, or the use of the Referendum and the Initiative—will seem tedious and irrelevant. On the other hand, the student of democracy, not specially interested in the commercial aspect of Trade Unionism, will probably find this the most interesting part of the book. Those who regard the participation of the manual-working wage-earners in the machinery of government as the distinctive, if not the dangerous, element in modern politics, will here find the phenomenon isolated. These thousands of working-class democracies, spontaneously growing up at different times and places, untrammelled by the traditions or interests of other classes, perpetually recasting their constitutions to meet new and varying conditions, present an unrivalled field of observation as to the manner in which the working man copes with the problem of combining administrative efficiency with popular control.

The second part of the book, forming more than half its total bulk, consists of a descriptive analysis of Trade Union Function : that is to say, of the methods used, the regulations imposed, and the policy followed by Trade Unions. We have done our best to make this analysis both scientifically accurate and, as regards the United Kingdom at the present day, completely exhaustive. We have, of course, not enumerated every individual regulation of every individual union ; but we have pushed our investigations into every trade in every part of the kingdom ; and our analysis includes, we believe, every existing type and variety of Trade Union action. And we have sought to make our description quantitative. We have given statistics wherever these could be obtained ; and we have, in all cases, tried to form and convey to the reader an impression of the relative proportion, statical and dynamic, which each type of regulation bears to the whole body of Trade Union activity. In digesting the almost innumerable technical regulations of every trade, our first need was a scientific classification. After many experiments we discovered the principle of this to lie in the psychological origin of the several regulations : that is to say, the direct intention with which they were adopted, or the immediate grievance they were designed to remedy. Our consequent observations threw light on many apparent contradictions and inconsistencies. Thus, to mention only two among many instances, the student will find, in our chapter on " The Standard Rate," an explanation of the reason why some Trade Unions strike against Piecework and others against Timework ; and, in our chapter on " The Normal Day," why some Trade Unions make the regulation of the hours of labor one of their foremost objects, whilst others, equally strong and aggressive, are indifferent, if not hostile to it. The same principle of classification enables the student to comprehend and place in appropriate categories the seemingly arbitrary and meaningless regulations, such as those against " Smooting " or " Partnering," which bewilder the superficial observer of working-class life. It assists us to unravel the intricate changes of Trade Union policy with regard to such matters as machinery, apprenticeship, and the admission of women. It serves also for the deeper analysis of the division of the whole action of Trade Unionism into three separate and sometimes mutually exclusive policies, based on different views of what can economically be effected, and what state of society is ultimately desirable. It is through the psychology of its assumptions that we discover how significantly the cleavages of opinion and action in the Trade Union world correspond with those in the larger world outside.

It is only in the third part of our work—the last four chapters of the second volume—that we have ventured into the domain of theory. We first trace the remarkable change of opinion among English economists as to the effect of Trade Unionism on the production and distribution of wealth. Some readers may stop at this point, contented with the authoritative, though vague, deliverances favorable to combination among wage-earners now given by the Professors of Political Economy in the universities of the United Kingdom. But this verdict, based in the main upon an ideal conception of competition and combination, seems to us unsubstantial. We have, therefore, laid before the student a new analysis of the working of competition in the industrial field—our vision of the organisation and working of the business world as it actually exists. It is in this analysis of the long series of bargainings, extending from the private customer in the retail shop, back to the manual laborer in the factory or the mine, that we discover the need for Trade Unionism. We then analyse the economic characteristics, not of combination in the abstract in a world of ideal competition, but of the actual Trade Unionism of the present day in the business world as we know it. Here, therefore, we give our own theory of Trade Unionism—our own interpretation of the way in which the methods and regulations that we have described actually affect the production and distribution of wealth and the development of personal character. This theory, in conjunction with our particular view of social expediency, leads us to sum up emphatically in favor of Trade Unionism of one type, and equally emphatically against Trade Unionism of another type. In our final chapter we even venture upon precept and prophecy ; and we consider the exact scope of Trade Unionism in the fully developed democratic state—the industrial democracy of the future.

A book made up of descriptions of fact, generalisations into theory, and moral judgments must, in the best case, necessarily include parts of different degrees of use. The description of structure and function in Parts I. and II. will, we hope, have its own permanent value in sociology as an analytic record of Trade Unionism in a particular country at a particular date. The economic generalisations contained in Part III., if they prove sound on verification by other investigators, can be no more than stepping-stones for the generalisations of reasoners who will begin where we leave off. Like all scientific theories, they will be quickly broken up, part to be rejected as fallacious or distorted, and part to be absorbed in later and larger views. Finally, even those who regard our facts as accurate, and accept our economic theory as scientific, will only agree in our judgment of Trade Unionism, and in our conception of its permanent but limited function in the Industrial Democracy of the future, in so far as they happen to be at one with us in the view of what state of society is desirable.

Those who contemplate scientific work in any department of Sociology may find some practical help in a brief account of the methods of investigation which we have found useful in this and other studies.

To begin with, the student must resolutely set himself to find out, not the ultimate answer to the practical problem that may have tempted him to the work, but what is the actual structure and function of the organisation about which he is interested. Thus, his primary task is to observe and dissect facts, comparing as many specimens as possible, and precisely recording all their resemblances and differences whether or not they seem significant. This does not mean that the scientific observer ought to start with a mind free from preconceived ideas as to classification and sequences. If such a person existed, he would be able to make no observations at all. The student ought, on the contrary, to cherish all the hypotheses he can lay his hands on, however far-fetched they may seem. Indeed, he must be on his guard against being biassed by authority. As an instrument for the discovery of new truth, the wildest suggestion of a crank or a fanatic, or the most casual conclusion of the practical man may well prove more fertile than verified generalisations which have already yielded their full fruit. Almost any preconceived idea as to the connection between phenomena will help the observer, if it is only sufficiently limited in its scope and definite in its expression to be capable of comparison with facts. What is dangerous is to have only a single hypothesis, for this inevitably biasses the selection of facts ; or nothing but far-reaching theories as to ultimate causes and general results, for these cannot be tested by any facts that a single student can unravel.

From the outset, the student must adopt a definite principle in his note-taking. We have found it convenient to use separate sheets of paper, uniform in shape and size, each of which is devoted to a single observation, with exact particulars of authority, locality, and date. To these, as the inquiry proceeds, we add other headings under which the recorded fact might possibly be grouped, such, for instance, as the industry, the particular section of the craft, the organisation, the sex, age, or status of the persons concerned, the psychological intention, or the grievance to be remedied. These sheets can be shuffled and reshuffled into various orders, according as it is desired to consider the recorded facts in their distribution in time or space, or their coincidence with other circumstances. The student would be well-advised to put a great deal of work into the completeness and mechanical perfection of his note-taking, even if this involves, for the first few weeks of the inquiry, copying and recopying his material.

Before actually beginning the investigation it is well to read what has been previously written about the subject. This will lead to some tentative ideas as to how to break up the material into definite parts for separate dissection. It will serve also to collect hypotheses as to the connections between the facts. It is here that the voluminous proceedings of Royal Commissions and Select Committees find their real use. Their innumerable questions and answers seldom end in any theoretic judgment or practical conclusion of scientific value. To the investigator, however, they often prove a mine of unintentional suggestion and hypothesis, just because they are collections of samples without order and often without selection.

In proceeding to actual investigation into facts, there are three good instruments of discovery : the Document, Personal Observation, and the Interview. All three are useful in obtaining preliminary suggestions and hypotheses ; but as methods of qualitative and quantitative analysis, or of verification, they are altogether different in character and unequal in value.

The most indispensable of these instruments is the Document. It is a peculiarity of human, and especially of social action, that it secretes records of facts, not with any view to affording material for the investigator, but as data for the future guidance of the organisms themselves. The essence of the Document as distinguished from the mere literature of the subject is the unintentional and automatic character of its testimony. It is, in short, a kind of mechanical memory, registering facts with the minimum of personal bias. Hence the cash accounts, minutes of private meetings, internal statistics, rules, and reports of societies of all kinds furnish invaluable material from which the investigator discovers not only the constitution and policy of the organisation, but also many of its motives and intentions. Even documents intended solely to influence other people, such as public manifestoes or fictitious reports, have their documentary value if only as showing by comparison with the confidential records, what it was that their authors desired to conceal. The investigator must, therefore, collect every document, however unimportant, that he can acquire. When acquisition is impossible, he should copy the actual words, making his extracts as copious as time permits ; for he can never know what will afterwards prove significant to him. In this use of the Document, sociology possesses a method of investigation which to some extent compensates it for inability to use the method of deliberate experiment. We venture to think that collections of documents will be to the sociologist of the future, what collections of fossils or skeletons are to the zoologist ; and libraries will be his museums.

Next in importance comes the method of Personal Observation. By this we mean neither the Interview nor yet any examination of the outward effects of an organisation, but a continued watching, from inside the machine, of the actual decisions of the human agents concerned, and the play of motives from which these spring. The difficulty for the investigator is to get into such a post of observation without his presence altering the normal course of events. It is here, and here only, that personal participation in the work of any social organisation is of advantage to scientific inquiry. The railway manager, the member of a municipality, or the officer of a Trade Union would, if he were a trained investigator, enjoy unrivalled opportunities for precisely describing the real constitution and actual working of his own organisation. Unfortunately, it is extremely rare to find in an active practical administrator, either the desire, the capacity, or the training for successful investigation. The outsider wishing to use this method is practically confined to one of two alternatives. He may adopt the social class, join the organisation, or practise the occupation that he wishes to study. Thus, one of the authors has found it useful, at different stages of investigation, to become a rent collector, a tailoress, and a working-class lodger in working-class families ; whilst the other has gained much from active membership of democratic organisations and personal participation in administration in more than one department. Participation of this active kind may be supplemented by gaining the intimacy and confidence of persons and organisations, so as to obtain the privilege of admission to their establishments, offices, and private meetings. In this passive observation the woman, we think, is specially well-adapted for sociological inquiry ; not merely because she is accustomed silently to watch motives, but also because she gains access and confidence which are instinctively refused to possible commercial competitors or political opponents. The worst of this method of Personal Observation is that the observer can seldom resist giving undue importance to the particular facts and connections between facts that he happens to have seen. He must, therefore, record what he has observed as a set of separate, and not necessarily connected facts, to be used merely as hypotheses of classification and sequence, for verification by an exhaustive scrutiny of documents or by the wider-reaching method of the Interview.

By the Interview as an instrument of sociological inquiry we mean something more than the preliminary talks and social friendliness which form, so to speak, the antechamber to obtaining documents and opportunities for personal observation of processes. The Interview in the scientific sense is the skilled interrogation of a competent witness as to facts within his personal experience. As the witness is under no compulsion, the interviewer will have to listen sympathetically to much that is not evidence, namely to personal opinions, current tradition, and hearsay reports of facts, all of which may be useful in suggesting new sources of inquiry and revealing bias. But the real business of the Interview is to ascertain facts actually seen by the person interviewed. Thus, the expert interviewer, like the bedside physician, agrees straightway with all the assumptions and generalisations of his patient, and uses his detective skill to sift, by tactful cross-examination, the grain of fact from the bushel of sentiment, self-interest, and theory.   Hence, though it is of the utmost importance to make friends with the head of any organisation, we have generally got much more actual information from his subordinates who are personally occupied with the facts in detail.   But in no case can any Interview be taken as conclusive evidence, even in matters of fact.   It must never be forgotten that every man is biassed by his creed or his self-interest, his class or his views of what is socially expedient.   If the investigator fails to detect this bias, it may be assumed that it coincides with his own!   Consequently, the fullest advantage of the Interview can be obtained only at the later stages of an inquiry, when the student has so far progressed in his analysis that he knows exactly what to ask for.   It then enables him to verify his provisional conclusions as to the existence of certain specified facts, and their relations to others.   And there is a wider use of the Interview by which a quantitative value may be given to a qualitative analysis.   Once the investigator has himself dissected a few type specimens, and discovered which among their obviously recognisable attributes possess significance for him, he may often be able to gain an exhaustive knowledge of the distribution of these attributes by what we may call the method of wholesale interviewing.   One of the most brilliant and successful applications of this method was Mr. Charles Booth's use of all the School Board visitors of the East End of London.   Having, by personal observation, discovered certain obvious marks which coincided with a scientific classification of the East End population, he was able, by interviewing a few hundred people, to obtain definite particulars with regard to the status of a million.   And when results so obtained are checked by other investigations—say, for instance, by the Census, itself only a gigantic and somewhat unscientific system of wholesale interviewing—a high degree of verified quantitative value may sometimes be given to sociological inquiry.

Finally, we would suggest that it is a peculiar advantage, in all sociological work, if a single inquiry can be conducted by more than one person. A closely-knit group, dealing contemporaneously with one subject, will achieve far more than the same persons working individually. In our inquiry into Trade Unionism we have found exceptionally useful, not only our own collaboration in all departments of the work, but also the co-operation, throughout the whole six years, of our colleague and friend, Mr. F. W. Galton. When the members of a group " pool " their stocks of preconceived ideas or provisional hypotheses ; their personal experience of the facts in question, or of analogous facts; their knowledge of possible sources of information ; their opportunities for interviewing, and access to documents, they are better able than any individual to cope with the vastness and complexity of even a limited subject of sociological investigation. They can do much by constant criticism to save each other from bias, crudities of observation, mistaken inferences, and confusion of thought. But group-work of this kind has difficulties and dangers of its own. Unless all the members are in intimate personal communication with each other, moving with a common will and purpose, and at least so far equal in training and capacity that they can understand each other's distinctions and qualifications, the result of their common labors will present blurred outlines, and be of little real value. Without unity, equality, and discipline, different members of the group will always be recording identical facts under different names, and using the same term to denote different facts.

By the pursuit of these methods of observation and verification, any intelligent, hard-working, and conscientious students, or group of students, applying themselves to definitely limited pieces of social organisation, will certainly produce monographs of scientific value. Whether they will be able to extract from their facts a new generalisation, applicable to other facts—whether, that is to say, they will discover any new scientific law—will depend on the possession of a somewhat rare combination of insight and inventiveness, with the capacity for prolonged and intense reasoning. When such a generalisation is arrived at, it provides a new field of work for the ensuing generation, whose task it is, by an incessant testing of this "order of thought" by comparison with the "order of things," to extend, limit, and qualify the first imperfect statement of the law.   By these means alone, whether in sociology or any other sphere of human inquiry, does mankind enter into possession of that body of organised knowledge which is termed science.

We venture to add a few words as to the practical value of sociological investigation.   Quite apart from the interest of the man of science, eager to satisfy his curiosity about every part of the universe, a knowledge of social facts and laws is indispensable for any intelligent and deliberate human action.   The whole of social life, the entire structure and functioning of society, consists of human intervention. The essential characteristic of civilised, as distinguished from savage society, is that these interventions are not impulsive but deliberate ; for, though some sort of human society may get along upon instinct, civilisation depends upon organised knowledge of sociological facts and of the connections between them.   And this knowledge must be sufficiently generalised to be capable of being diffused.   We can all avoid being practical engineers or chemists ; but no consumer, producer, or citizen can avoid being a practical sociologist.   Whether he pursues only his own pecuniary self-interest, or follows some idea of class or social expediency, his action or inaction will promote his ends only in so far as it corresponds with the real order of the universe.   A workman may join his Trade Union, or abstain from joining ; but if his decision is to be rational, it must be based on knowledge of what the Trade Union is, how far it is a sound benefit society, whether its methods will increase or decrease his liberty, and to what extent its regulations are likely to improve or deteriorate the conditions of employment for himself and his class.   The employer who desires to enjoy the maximum freedom of enterprise, or to gain the utmost profit, had better, before either fighting his workmen or yielding to their demands, find out the cause and meaning of Trade Unionism, what exactly it is likely to give up or insist on, its financial strength and weakness, and its hold on public opinion. Common hearsay, or the gossip of a club, whether this be the public-house or a palace in Pall Mall, will no more enable a man intelligently to "manage his own business," than it will enable the engineer to build a bridge. And when we pass from private actions to the participation of men and women as electors, representatives, or officials, in public companies, local governing bodies, or the State itself, the inarticulate apprehension of facts which often contents the individual business man, will no longer suffice. Deliberate corporate action involves some definite policy, communicable to others. The town councillor or the cabinet minister has perpetually to be making up his mind what is to be done in particular cases. Whether his action or abstention from action is likely to be practicable, popular, and permanently successful in attaining his ends, depends on whether it is or is not adapted to the facts. This does not mean that every workman and every employer, or even every philanthropist and every statesman, is called upon to make his own investigation into social questions any more than to make for himself the physiological investigations upon which his health depends. But whether they like it or not, their success or failure to attain their ends depends on their scientific knowledge, original or borrowed, of the facts of the problem, and of their causal connections. Perfect wisdom we can never attain, in sociology or in any other science ; but this does not absolve us from using, in our action, the most authoritative exposition, for the time being, of what is known. That nation will achieve the greatest success in the world-struggle, whose investigators discover the greatest body of scientific truth, and whose practical men are the most prompt in their application of it.

What is not generally recognised is that scientific investigation, in the field of sociology as in other departments of knowledge, requires, not only competent investigators, but a considerable expenditure. Practically no provision exists in this country for the endowment or support from public funds of any kind of sociological investigation. It is, accordingly, impossible at present to make any considerable progress even with inquiries of pressing urgency. Social reformers are always feeling themselves at a standstill, for sheer lack of knowledge, and of that invention which can only proceed from knowledge. There is, we believe, no purpose to which the rich man could devote his surplus with greater utility to the community than the setting on foot, in the hands of competent investigators, of definite inquiries into such questions as the administrative control of the liquor traffic, the relation between local and central government, the population question, the conditions of women's industrial employment, the real incidence of taxation, the working of municipal administration, or many other unsolved problems that could be named. It may be assumed that to deal adequately with any of these subjects would involve an out-of-pocket expenditure for travelling, materials, and incidental outlays of all kinds, of something like £1000, irrespective of the maintenance of the investigators themselves, or the possible expense of publication. To make any permanent provision for discovery in any one department—to endow a chair—requires the investment of, say, £10,000. At present, in London, the wealthiest city in the world, and the best of all fields for sociological investigation, the sum total of the endowments for this purpose does not reach £100 a year.

It remains only to express our grateful acknowledgments to the many friends, employers as well as workmen, who have helped us with information as to their respective trades. Some portions of our work have been read in manuscript or proof by Professor Edgeworth, Professor Hewins, Mr. Leonard Hobhouse, and other friends, to whom we are indebted for many useful suggestions and criticisms. Early drafts of some chapters have appeared in the *Economic Journal*, *Economic Review*, *Nineteenth Century*, and *Progressive Review* in this country ; the *Political Science Quarterly* in New York ;

and Dr. Braun's *Archiv fur Sociale Gesetzgebung und Statistik* in Berlin. They are reproduced here by permission of the editors. A large portion of the book was given in the form of lectures at the London School of Economics and Political Science during 1896 and 1897.

SIDNEY AND BEATRICE WEBB.

41 GROSVENOR ROAD, WESTMINSTER,
LONDON, *November* 1897.

and Dr Beveridge, Mr Max ... der ... phau, and Society in Berlin. The are reproduced are by permission of the editors. A large portion of the book was given in the form of lectures at the London School of Economics and Political Science during 1905 and 1906.

SIDNEY AND BEATRICE WEBB

41 Grosvenor Road, Westminster,
London, November 1906.

INTRODUCTION TO THE 1902 EDITION

(FOURTH IMPRESSION.   FIFTH THOUSAND.)

THE issue of *Industrial Democracy* in a cheaper edition, uniform with the *History of Trade Unionism*, gives us an opportunity of writing a new introductory chapter.

We have practically nothing to add to the descriptive and analytic part of the book.   During the four years which have elapsed since its publication, the Trade Union world has not appreciably changed in structure or function.[1]   The Trade Union "methods" of Mutual Insurance, Collective Bargaining, and Legal Enactment—the multifarious Trade Union "regulations" described in our chapters on the Standard Rate and the Normal Day, New Processes and Machinery, and the Entrance to a Trade—retain their several places in the workmen's constant struggle to uphold and improve the Standard of Life of their class.   But whilst the Trade Union world itself has remained unaltered, the closing years of the nineteenth century have witnessed a gradual change in Trade Union environment, alike in law and in public opinion, which has lately risen, suddenly and dramatically, into public consciousness.   By a series of remarkable legal decisions of the House of Lords, the Trade Unions of the United Kingdom have seen their use of the

---

[1] Trade Union membership and Trade Union funds have, indeed, greatly increased, until, at the present time, there are not far short of two million members, with accumulated funds of nearly four millions sterling.   But these statistical details, including some analysis of the direction of growth, we reserve for the forthcoming edition of the *History of Trade Unionism*, in which we deal also with the principal strikes of the last decade.

Method of Collective Bargaining seriously curtailed.   At the same time, an equally remarkable series of legislative experiments in the Britains beyond the sea have made possible applications of the Method of Legal Enactment hitherto undreamt of.

We must first refer, in order to bring our analysis up to date, to a few statutory changes in the United Kingdom between 1897 and 1902. The minimum age at which children may be employed in factories or workshops (pp. 768-69) is now twelve, and in mines, thirteen ; but practically nothing has been done to prevent other industrial work by children of school age,[1] and we are still very far from any effective enforcement of the National Minimum of Education which our Legislature professes to have adopted.   The serious evil of " boy labor " (pp. 482-89, 768-71) has not been grappled with.   The long array of Acts and Amending Acts dealing with the conditions of employment in factories and workshops (pp. 771-73) have now been consolidated in the Factory and Workshops Act of 1901, which includes a few amendments of detail.   But the law still fails to secure, even to women and children, that National Minimum of Sanitation and Rest which it purports to give.   Whole classes of women workers (p. 772) remain excluded by pedantries of definition.   The numerous exceptions as to overtime and other relaxations still hamper administration (pp. 349-51).   The sections dealing with laundries (p. 365), outworkers (p. 772), and unhealthy trades (pp. 363-64) continue, in the main, illusory and inoperative. We may refer, on this whole subject, to *The Case for the Factory Acts* (London, 1901), edited by Mrs. Sidney Webb.   The objectionable Truck Act of 1896 (pp. 211, 373, 799) has not been amended, but it is right to say that it has been found, in practice, much less irksome to employers or workmen than they severally expected.   This is due to the fact that it has been only slightly operative.

---

[1] See the *Report of the Departmental Committee on the Employment of Children of School Age*, 1901.

The grievances with which the workmen hoped that it would deal (pp. 315-18, 840) have still to be remedied.[1] The Workmen's Compensation Act of 1897 (pp. 387-91) has now been extended to persons employed in agriculture, but not yet to workshop operatives, seamen, carmen, or building workmen engaged on buildings less than thirty feet in height. The employers (or, rather, the insurance companies in their names) have displayed a most fertile ingenuity in raising quibbles intended to limit the application of the law, but the highest judicial tribunal has, on the whole, given full effect to the intention of Parliament, and has made a badly-drafted statute really operative. It should be added that the actual cost of compensating for accidents has proved less than was anticipated—unfortunately, as we suggested (pp. 375-76), much less than it would cost the employers to prevent them. It remains, therefore, more important than ever, not only to extend the Act to the workers at present outside its scope, but also, in the interest of the community as a whole, to enforce in all occupations an effective National Minimum of Sanitation and Safety (pp. 375-78, 385-87, 771-73).

But the changes in the law effected by Parliament during the past four years are of less importance to Trade Unionism than those made by the judges, notably by the House of Lords in its judicial capacity. By a series of unexpected decisions, beginning with Allen *v.* Flood, on the 14th of December 1897, and ending, for the moment, with Quinn *v.* Leathem, on the 5th of August 1901, the highest court of appeal has entirely changed the legal position of Trade Unions. We have, therefore, to consider in what way these decisions affect the conclusions expressed in our Appendix on "The Legal Position of Collective Bargaining" (pp. 853-62).[2]

[1] We may correct an error in the note to p. 211. The Act proved not to apply to the deductions referred to, and no exemption order was necessary.

[2] The principal judgments in these cases have been reprinted in *The Law and Trade Unions : a Brief Review of Recent Litigation specially prepared at the instance of Richard Bell*, M.P. (London, 1901). But the law on the whole subject

The most far-reaching of these decisions, and the one which gives importance to all the others, is that in the case of The Taff Vale Railway Company *v.* The Amalgamated Society of Railway Servants. There had been a dispute between the railway company and many of its employees. A strike took place, which was sanctioned by the governing body of the Trade Union, and was conducted by its authorised officers. It was alleged that, in furtherance of this strike, some of the agents of the Trade Union had committed unlawful acts, and incited others to commit them, to the injury and damage of the railway company. Instead of prosecuting in a criminal court the persons alleged to have been guilty of these offences, the company applied to the Chancery Division of the High Court of Justice for an injunction to restrain from committing such acts, not only certain of the persons implicated, but also the Amalgamated Society of Railway Servants itself. The company also commenced a civil suit against the society in its corporate capacity, claiming a large sum as damages for what were alleged to be its wrongful acts. The society pleaded that, whatever might be the personal liability of individual officers or members, the Trade Union itself could not, in its corporate capacity, be made the object of an injunction, or be sued for damages. It was contended that, under the circumstances described in our *History of Trade Unionism*, the Legislature had deliberately abstained from giving Trade Unions the privileges of incorporation, and had expressly provided against their being sued as corporate bodies. This view had been universally accepted by friends and foes alike. The immunity of Trade Unions from corporate liability for damages had been repeatedly made the subject of official comment, and even of recommendations by Royal Commissions. For twenty years after the Act

---

is now most conveniently to be found in the little volume of annotated statutes and cases, of which we have made use, entitled *Trade Union Law*, by Herman Cohen and George Howell (London, 1901). This gives exact references to the official reports.

of 1871 no action against a Trade Union in its corporate capacity was ever maintained in the English Courts.[1] But on the 22nd of July 1901, the House of Lords decided that the Amalgamated Society of Railway Servants, though admittedly not a corporate body, could be sued in a corporate capacity for damages alleged to have been caused by the action of its officers, and that an injunction could be issued against it, restraining it not merely from criminal, but also from other unlawful acts. Moreover, in their elaborate reasons for their judgment, the law lords expressed the view that not only an injunction, but also a mandamus could be issued against a Trade Union ; that a registered Trade Union could be sued in its registered name ; that even an unregistered Trade Union might be made collectively liable for damages, and might be sued in the names of its proper officers, the members of its executive committee, and its trustees ; that the corporate funds of a Trade Union could be made answerable for costs and damages, even if they were in the hands of trustees ; and that the trustees of Trade Union funds might be joined as parties to a suit against the Trade Union, or might be separately proceeded against for recovery of damages and costs awarded against their Trade Union, whether registered or not. The effect of the judgment, in short, is to impose upon a Trade Union, whether registered or not—although not incorporated for other purposes—complete corporate liability for any injury or damage caused by any person who can be deemed to be acting as the agent of the Trade Union, not merely in respect of any criminal offence which he may have committed, but also in respect of any act, not contravening the criminal law, which the judges may, from time to time, deem wrongful.

[1] In 1892, and again in 1895, civil proceedings were successfully taken by employers against combinations of workmen ; see Trollope and Others *v.* The London Building Trades' Federation and Others, 1892 (mentioned at p. 861), and Pink *v.* The Federation of Trade Unions, etc., 1895. These cases were, however, not seriously defended, not fully argued, and not carried to the highest tribunal.

We do not propose to waste time in discussing whether this judgment of the House of Lords was or was not in accordance with the law of the land on the morning of the decision. There has seldom been an instance in which a judicial decision has so completely and extensively reversed the previous legal opinions, and—we do not hesitate to say —the conscious intention, thirty years before, of Parliament itself. But the case was fully and ably argued, and the decision of the five law lords was unanimous. According to the British Constitution, the view which they have taken of the law is now as definitely the law as if it had been embodied in an Act of Parliament. How does it affect Trade Unionism?

At first sight there would seem little or nothing to complain about. The judgment professes to make no change in the lawfulness of Trade Unionism. No act is ostensibly made wrongful which was not wrongful before. And if a Trade Union, directly or by its agents, causes injury or damage to other persons, by acts not warranted in law, it seems not inequitable that the Trade Union itself should be made liable for what it has done. The real grievance of the Trade Unions, and the serious danger to their continued usefulness and improvement, lies in the uncertainty of the English law, and its liability to be used as a means of oppression. This danger is increased, and the grievance aggravated, by the dislike of Trade Unionism and strikes which nearly all judges and juries share with the rest of the upper and middle classes.

The public opinion of the propertied and professional classes is, in fact, even more hostile to Trade Unionism and strikes than it was a generation ago. In 1867-75, when Trade Unionism was struggling for legal recognition, it seemed to many people only fair that, as the employers were left free to use their superiority in economic strength, the workmen should be put in a position to make a good fight of it against the employers. Accordingly, combinations and strikes were legalised, and some sort of peaceful picketing was expressly authorised by statute. So long as no physical violence was used or openly threatened, the mild tumult and disorder of a strike, a certain amount of harmless obstruction of the thoroughfares, and the animated persuasion of blacklegs by the pickets, were usually tolerated by the police, and not seriously resented by the employers. It all belonged to the conception of a labor disputè as a stand-up fight between the parties, in which the State could do no more than keep the ring. Gradually this conception has given way in favour of the view that, quite apart from the merits of the case, the stoppage of work by an industrial dispute is a public nuisance, an injury to the commonweal, which ought to be prevented by the Government. Moreover, the conditions of the wage contract are no longer regarded only as a matter of private concern. The gradual extension of legislative regulation to àll industries, and its successive application to different classes of workers and conditions of employment, decisively negatives the old assumption of the employer that he is entitled to hire his labor on such terms as he thinks fit. On the other hand, public opinion has become uneasy about the capacity of English manufacturers to hold their own against foreign competition, and therefore resents, as a crime against the community, any attempt to restrict output or obstruct machinery, of which the Trade Unions may be accused. And thus we have a growing public opinion in favour of some authoritative tribunal of conciliation or arbitration, and an intense dislike of any organised interruption of industry by a lock-out or strike, especially when this is promoted by a Trade Union which is believed——often on the strength of the wildest accusations in the newspapers——to be unfriendly to the utmost possible improvement of processes in its trade.

Under the influence of this adverse bias the courts of law have, for the last ten years, been gradually limiting what were supposed to be the legal rights of Trade Unions. There has been, it is true, no attempt to bring back the terrors of the criminal law, the use of which, as an instrument of warfare, is still blunted by the necessity of convincing the common-sense of a jury, not only that the alleged acts were committed, but also that they amounted to a crime, for which (whatever the judge may direct) the jury consider that the defendants ought to be found " guilty." But the employers, as we pointed out four years ago, have discovered a more advantageous weapon than the criminal law. Acts done by officers of Trade Unions have, by aggrieved persons, been made the subject of civil actions for damages, and the judges have declared to be unlawful, though not criminal, many things which had hitherto been regarded as permissible incidents of a strike. Thus, it has been held to be an actionable wrong for a Trade Union to publish a " black list " of non-union firms and " free laborers." [1] Even the most peaceful picketing, without the slightest riot, violence, or coercion, has been held to be actionable, on the ground that it amounted to "watching and besetting," and that this was an annoyance to the employer.[2] But the law, as now interpreted, goes much further than to make a Trade Union answerable in· damages for deeds which would be equally actionable if committed by an individual. Any one man may, whatever motive he may have, lawfully, without molestation or coercion, or "watching and besetting," try to persuade another to do or not to do anything which that other has a right to do or not to do, even though other persons are injured thereby.[3] But it has been held to be an actionable wrong for a couple of men to wait in concert in the street for the purpose of attempting, however quietly and peaceably, to persuade persons not to engage to work for a particular employer.[4] It is probable that it is now an actionable wrong if a Trade Union executive directs or allows any official to try to persuade an employer not to engage, or to discharge, particular blacklegs ; though it is lawful for any one individual to take this step, if he is *bona fide* not acting in

---

[1] Trollope and Others *v.* The London Building Trades' Federation and Others.
[2] Lyons *v.* Wilkins.   [3] Allen *v.* Flood.   [4] Lyons *v.* Wilkins.

concert, express or implied, with any one else.[1]   It has been held to be an actionable wrong for Trade Union officials to try to persuade one firm not to supply another with goods, or not to work up the products supplied by a particular trader, and this, however peaceful and courteous may be the persuasion ;[2] although it is quite lawful for one man to do the same thing.   It would even be lawful for a combination of men, if they happen to be employers desirous of promoting their own trade.   It has been held lawful for a combination of capitalist traders to put the severest pressure of this sort on a trader who stands outside their combination, even to the extent of conspiring, for their own advantage, to drive him out of the business.[3] If a body of workmen aim at the corresponding result their " conspiracy " is actionable.[4]   And though it seems to be still lawful (if there is no breach of contract) for workmen to combine in a refusal to work for a particular firm, without cause assigned—that is, to strike —it is doubtful whether their "conspiracy" is not actionable if their motive for striking is anything else than to improve their own personal conditions of employment. If the judge came to the conclusion that, notwithstanding the workmen's silence, or even their statement to the contrary, they were really striking, not on account of any difference with their employer as to their own wages, but merely in order to put pressure on some other employer, or on some other workmen, with a view to causing the exclusion of these from work, he would very likely hold that such a strike was an actionable wrong against the other employer or workmen, for which these could recover damages.[5]   Even when a strike is lawful, Trade Union officials will now have to be careful how they call the men out.   It is probably actionable if, through the influence of

---

[1] Allen *v.* Flood.   [2] Temperton *v.* Russell.
[3] Mogul S.S. Co. *v.* M'Gregor, Gow, and Co.   [4] Quinn *v.* Leathem.
[5] The "sympathetic strike" or boycott has already been held to be illegal by American courts.   See the remarks of various judges in Temperton *v.* Russell, Lyons *v.* Wilkins, and our note at p. 861.

the official's incitement, some of the workmen strike without notice, or otherwise break their contracts of service, even though the Trade Union official did not intend that they should do so. And if the judges should eventually hold that any particular strike was not warranted, or, though warranted in itself, that wrongful (though not criminal) acts were committed in pursuance of it, which he might have been expected to foresee, the Trade Union official who ordered the strike might very likely be made answerable in damages for the loss suffered by any person through the wrongful acts which he had indirectly but unwillingly caused. In all these cases, wherever a Trade Union official would be liable, the Trade Union itself is now made collectively liable. And it follows from the general law of principal and agent, that whenever any officer of a Trade Union, in the ordinary course of his business, and within the apparent scope of his employment, does anything for which he is liable to be sued for damages, the Trade Union for which he is acting becomes also liable, though he may have acted without orders, or contrary to the general policy of his Trade Union, or even in direct contradiction to the private instructions which he had received from its executive committee. Finally, whenever the Trade Union is liable to be sued, it will be open to the aggrieved person to apply to the Chancery Division of the High Court of Justice for an injunction against the Trade Union and its officials, peremptorily restraining them from committing any of the acts complained of. The issue of such an injunction will be within the discretion of a single Chancery judge, and if it is disobeyed, it can be enforced by summary imprisonment, without trial, for an indefinite period, for what is called " contempt of court."

Such we believe to be now the law, according to the best opinion that a well-informed counsel could give to his client. But so vague and ill-defined, so complicated and uncertain, is the English law on such subjects as conspiracy and libel—indeed, the whole law of torts—to say nothing of that relating to principal and agent, that we cannot pretend that our statement is to be depended on. The very uncertainty is in itself a serious grievance. If a Trade Union executive could know precisely what was the law, it could take care not to infringe it, and might have some chance of compelling its officers to keep within their legal rights. This is now impossible. All that a Trade Union can be sure of is that, whenever the action of any one of its officers causes any injury or loss to any employer, or to any workman outside its ranks, it will be open to any such person, at slight expense, to commence an action against the Trade Union for damages. This will mean, at least, a solicitor's bill. If the action comes into court the Trade Union will know that, though the jury may give a verdict as to the bare facts, the judgment will, in nine cases out of ten, depend practically on the judge's view of the law. And though we all thoroughly believe in the honesty and impartiality of our judges, it so happens that, in the present uncertainty, the very law of the case must necessarily turn on the view taken of the general policy of Trade Unionism. If the judges believed, as we believe, that the enforcement of Common Rules in industry, and the maintenance of a Standard Rate, a Normal Day, and stringent conditions of Sanitation and Safety, were positively beneficial to the community as a whole, and absolutely indispensable to the continued prosperity of our trade, they would no more hold liable, for any damage which, in the conduct of its legitimate purpose, it incidentally caused to particular individuals, a reasonably managed Trade Union than a militant Temperance Society or the Primrose League. But a clear majority of our judges evidently believe, quite honestly, that Trade Unionism—meaning the enforcement of Common Rules on a whole trade—is anomalous, objectionable, detrimental to English industry, and even a wicked infringement of individual liberty, which Parliament has been foolishly persuaded to take out of the category of crimes. Their lack of economic training and their ignorance of economic science is responsible for this state of mind. Unfortunately, their preoccupation with the technical side of their own profession renders it unlikely that they will dispel this ignorance by any careful study of labor problems. When, therefore, they have to decide whether a particular injury, caused by the operations of such a combination, is or is not actionable, they would not be doing their duty, holding the view that they do of its harmfulness, if they did not treat it much more severely than they would if precisely similar acts were committed by associations which they thought to be beneficial to the community—say, for instance, by a combination of capitalist employers, in the course of the fierce and unrelenting competition of international trade. The result is that Trade Unions must expect to find practically every incident of a strike, and possibly every refusal to work with non-unionists, treated as actionable, and made the subject of suits for damages, which the Trade Union will have to pay from its corporate funds.

We do not mean to suggest that every little labor trouble is likely to be followed by a crop of actions against the Trade Union concerned. Employers generally find it too convenient to be on good terms with well-managed Trade Unions to wish to break off friendly negotiations with them. But it will always be open for employers or non-unionist workmen to issue a writ, and in cases of serious dispute it is scarcely likely that they will all forego so easy a means of harassing their opponents. Trade Unions will not all of them find their funds denuded by heavy law costs and damages. It may even be some time before a serious case occurs. But the liability will be always present. It is not too much to say that, except in the most compact and well-disciplined industries, a Union will, so far as its finances are concerned, when fighting is necessary, henceforth have to fight with a halter round its neck.[1]

---

[1] No mere pious declarations in the rules will protect a Trade Union from actions for damages, if wrongful acts are done by the Trade Union itself or by its agents acting within the apparent scope of their authority. The judges will

Ought the law to be amended ?   We say, at once, that Trade Unions would, in our opinion, not be warranted in claiming to have restored that complete immunity from legal proceedings which Parliament intended to confer upon them in 1871-76. We see no valid reason why, *if the law were put into a proper state*, Trade Unions should not be liable to be sued for damages in their corporate capacity, in respect of any injury wrongfully done by them or their agents to other persons.   If, for instance, a Trade Union in its corporate capacity publishes a newspaper, it can hardly claim, as regards actions for libel, to be treated differently from any individual publisher of a newspaper. Nor can we see any justification for such an amendment of the Conspiracy and Law of Property Act, 1875, as would make lawful the only sort of picketing likely to be effective in keeping off blacklegs during a strike.   Moreover, if a Trade Union violates its own rules, or does anything plainly outside their scope, there seems no ground for preventing any dissatisfied member from restraining its action by an injunction.[1]   Finally, if a Trade Union or its official deliberately persuades or induces men to break legally binding existing contracts of service into which they have entered, the Trade Union deserves to pay damages.   So far the recent interpretation of the law must, we think, be accepted.   But Trade Unions have certainly a good claim to have their legal rights and liabilities clearly defined, and precisely and authoritatively set forth.   At present the law is merely a trap in which any one of them may at any moment be caught.   We may go further.   So long as the community decides to let the conditions of the wage-contract be settled by bargaining, both parties must, in common fairness, be left equally free to protect their own interest by combined action, even if such combined action causes damage to the opponent or to others.   It is a mockery of

go behind the rules, if necessary, and form their own conclusion as to the real intentions, purposes, and instructions of the executive committee or general secretary.

[1] Amalgamated Society of Railway Servants for Scotland *v.* The Motherwell Branch of the Society.

justice to tell the workmen that they are allowed to combine, and to strike, in order to exact better terms from their employers, and then to cast them in damages whenever they, in the exercise of this right, and without infringing the criminal law, cause damage to other persons. Every strike, like every other kind of war, necessarily causes damage to other persons—damage which the strikers can clearly foresee, and which the Legislature must as clearly have foreseen when it sanctioned the terms of labor being left to this kind of private war.[1] Moreover, every strike— as public opinion now keenly feels—causes injury to the community as a whole.[2] This may well be a reason for superseding strikes as a method of settling the terms of the contract of service. But it is not fair to the workmen to try indirectly to put down strikes by making the Trade Unions liable for damages for what is incidental to a strike. It is handing them over to the employers with their hands tied. Trade Unions have, therefore, a good claim for an alteration of the law.[3]

[1] " The third section of [the Conspiracy and Protection of Property] Act distinctly legalises strikes in the broadest terms, subject to the exceptions enumerated in the fourth and fifth sections."—Lord Chief-Justice Coleridge in Gibson *v.* Lawson (1891).

[2] Here lurks a danger to the Trade Unions of a revival of the old use of the criminal law against them. It is by no means clear that a conspiracy, neither contemplating nor committing any criminal act, but violating an actionable private right, may not in itself be a criminal offence, if the actionable private right is one in which the public has a sufficient interest. See p. 857.

[3] It may be of service if we submit in precise form the draft of such a bill as Trade Unionists might properly press upon the Cabinet, members of Parliament, and candidates for that position.

A Bill entitled an Act to Amend the Law relating to Trade Disputes

1. No agreement, combination, or conspiracy entered into by or on behalf of an association of employers or a Trade Union in contemplation or furtherance of a trade dispute, and no act committed in pursuance of any such agreement, combination, or conspiracy, shall be actionable, if such act would not be actionable if committed by one person without agreement, combination, or conspiracy of any kind, and if such agreement, combination, or conspiracy would not be indictable as a crime.

2. No act committed, and no agreement, combination, or conspiracy entered into, by or on behalf of an association of employers or a Trade Union in con-

However unlikely it may seem that our present Parliament would consent to effect such an alteration of the law as the Trade Unionists desire, we venture to point out that the existing position is not one that can endure. The two millions of Trade Unionists, comprising probably one-fifth of the national electorate, will certainly not consent to give up the enforcement of Common Rules determining standard minimum wages and other conditions throughout each trade. In this policy they will be supported by all working-class opinion, and will be acting in accordance with the teachings of economic science.[1]   The alternative of free and unfettered Individual Bargaining—in which each workshop has its own peculiar working hours, its own standard of sanitation, and its own arrangements for preventing accidents, exactly as its owner chooses to prescribe, whilst each workman makes his own separate contract for each job with his own employer— has been proved, by a whole century of experience, to lead

templation or furtherance of a trade dispute, shall be actionable by reason only of the motive for which it was committed or entered into, or of there being no lawful excuse or motive for such act, agreement, combination, or conspiracy.

3. No agreement, combination, or conspiracy by or on behalf of an association of employers or a Trade Union in contemplation or furtherance of a trade dispute shall be indictable as a crime if no act itself punishable as a crime is contemplated or committed, whether as means or end, by or in pursuance of such agreement, combination, or conspiracy.

4. The words "trade dispute between employers and workmen" in the third section of the Conspiracy and Law of Property Act of 1875 shall therein have the same meaning as "trade dispute" in this Act.

5. The words "association of employers" and "Trade Union" shall, for the purposes of this Act, both include any association of persons, whether registered or not, which attempts to regulate or influence any or all of the conditions of employment in one or more occupations, and shall also include any alliance, federation, or combination of two or more such associations.

6. The words "trade dispute" shall include any dispute, difference of opinion, or failure of agreement, existing or contemplated, between one or more employers or an association of employers, and one or more workmen or a Trade Union, or any alliance, federation, or combination of any of them, whether registered or incorporated or not, and whether or not such dispute, difference of opinion, or failure of agreement relates to the employment of any of the persons concerned, or to any pecuniary or other interest of any of them, and whether they or any of them belong to the same or different trades or places or societies.

[1] See Part III. Chap. i. "The Verdict of the Economists"; Chap. ii. "The Higgling of the Market"; and Chap. iii. "The Economic Characteristics of Trade Unionism"

to "sweating."   The necessary Common Rules can be enforced only by two methods, Collective Bargaining and Legal Enactment.   If Collective Bargaining, with its inevitable accompaniment of collective abstention from work and occasional stoppages of industry, is, by the judges' interpretation of the law, made impossible, or even costly and difficult, the whole weight of working-class opinion will certainly be thrown in favor of Legal Enactment.   We do not ourselves deprecate this course, but whether Lord Penrhyn and the railway companies, the Shipping Federation and the engineering employers, would see any advantage in it seems to us doubtful.

We pass now to the second great change in Trade Union environment.   Whilst in the United Kingdom the House of Lords has been making the Method of Collective Bargaining virtually inoperative, the Legislatures of the young and vigorous democracies of Australia and New Zealand have been proving how much more elastic, and how much more applicable to modern conditions than has hitherto been supposed, is the alternative Method of Legal Enactment. When we were writing in 1897, the legislation of Victoria and New Zealand was still in its first experimental stage, and but little was known of its actual working (see pp. 246, 488, 770, 776, 814).   It has since been greatly extended in scope as experience has been gained, and it has been carefully described by both official and critical observers. We had ourselves, in 1898, the opportunity of seeing both the Victorian and the New Zealand systems at work, and we spent some time in watching and inquiring, among friends and foes alike, as to the actual results of the experiment. We are more than ever convinced that both Victorian and New Zealand statutes deserve favorable consideration by the employers and the statesmen, no less than by the workmen and the philanthropists of the Mother Country.

The Victorian legislation [1] is less well known in England

---

[1] The best account of the Victorian system and its actual working is the New South Wales Government *Report of Royal Commission of Inquiry into the Work-*

than that of New Zealand. By the Factories and Shops Act, 1896, after a series of vain attempts to put down "sweating" by other means, special "wage boards" were constituted in certain oppressed trades. These were empowered to fix a minimum standard wage for the trade, for both factory and outworkers, by time and by the piece; and also the maximum proportionate number of apprentices or improvers under eighteen years of age, and the minimum to be paid to them. The "Common Rules" thus prescribed for the trade became, in effect, part of the Factory Acts, and were enforced by the factory inspectors, like any other requirements of the Acts, by summary proceedings in the police courts.

This Act only related to six specially sweated trades, and applied only to Melbourne and its suburbs. In 1900, after four years' experience, the law was widened in all directions. The powers of the boards were extended so as to cover practically the whole colony. It was also provided that a board should be formed in any trade or business for which either House of Parliament had passed an approving resolution. It is significant of the appreciation of the law that no fewer than twenty-one more boards were at once constituted, in protected and unprotected industries alike, and many of them at the request of the employers in the trades concerned. This was the case, for instance, with the

---

ing of Compulsory Conciliation and Arbitration Laws (Sydney, 1901), by Judge Backhouse. The laws themselves can be best consulted in the convenient edition of the *Factories and Shops Acts*, by Harrison Ord (Melbourne, 1900). A succinct account of the system, with particulars of recent decisions by the boards, is given by Mrs. W. P. Reeves, in her chapter in *The Case for the Factory Acts* (London, 1901). See also an article by the Hon. W. P. Reeves in the *Economic Journal*, Sept. 1901, entitled "The Minimum Wage Law in Victoria and South Australia"; the annual reports of the Chief Inspector of Factories (Melbourne) for 1896-1900 inclusive; and the evidence given to the Royal Commission at present (December 1901) sitting to inquire into the results of the law. The report of this Commission, to be published shortly, will give us the most authoritative account of the working of the system. It should be added that the Victorian wage board clauses were, in December 1900, enacted almost word for word by the Legislature of South Australia.

boards for the printers (compositors), carriage-builders, cigar-makers, coopers, engravers, saddlers, stonecutters, tanners, and others.

These wage-boards are composed of between four and ten representatives, half elected by the employers and half by the operatives in the particular trade. The board may choose its own chairman, who has a casting vote ; and in many of the trades employers and employed have easily agreed upon a trusted outsider—a judge, a minister of religion, or a responsible government official. In case of disagreement the Government appoints a chairman, choosing usually an outsider of judicial character. The board then sets to work to determine what shall be the standard minimum rate of wages in the trade, and it is interesting to find that, after a more or less protracted but quite friendly " higgling," the representatives have frequently been able to agree on their decision without invoking the chairman's casting vote. The minimum rate thus fixed may be made applicable to any person or class of persons, factory hands or outworkers, by time or by piece ; and it is expressly provided that the board is to take into consideration " the nature, kind, and class of the work, and the mode and manner in which the work is to be done, and the age and sex of the workers, and any matter which may from time to time be prescribed." The board prescribes the maximum number of hours, usually eight, to be worked for the daily wage, and what minimum rate shall be paid for overtime, but does not actually limit the working time (which is limited by law only for women, miners, etc.). Power is reserved to the Chief Inspector of Factories to grant to aged or infirm workers a licence, for twelve months at a time, to work for less than the prescribed rates, and he may also do the same for young improvers without full experience. This provision was added in the 1900 Act, experience having shown both its necessity and its practicability. It should be added that the members of the boards receive from public funds a payment of ten shillings for a full day's session, and five shillings for a half-day's session, the chairman receiving double pay.

Under this Act a legal minimum wage has, in certain trades, been fixed and enforced for five years, and in many other trades for a shorter period. Thus, the minimum weekly wage for tailoresses was fixed, to begin with, at twenty shillings a week, that for shirtmakers at sixteen shillings, and that for adult male boot and shoe operatives at forty-two shillings, these time rates being in each trade also translated into equivalent piecework lists. These wages were considerably above what many of the operatives had previously been receiving, but notwithstanding this fact neither the volume of trade nor the employers' profits appear to have been affected. We could not ascertain that there had been, up to 1898, any diminution of employment in the trades concerned ; on the contrary, the numbers at work had certainly increased. We could find no evidence that prices had risen, and we were informed by employers that they had not done so. Nor were the employers themselves dissatisfied with the result. The explanation of the paradox lies, as we satisfied ourselves, in the very significant fact that, when the employers found themselves compelled to pay a standard wage to all whom they employed, they took care to make the labor as productive as possible—they chose their workers more carefully, kept them fully employed, introduced new processes and machinery, and in every way made the industry more efficient. The effect of stopping competition of wages is, as Mundella from practical experience pointed out over thirty years ago (see p. 723), to concentrate it upon efficiency. The whole experience of the Victorian wage-boards, alike in their successes and in their failures, confirms our analysis of the economic results of the Common Rule (pp. 715-39).[1]

---

[1] It should be stated that this Act, like all factory and sanitary laws, has absolutely failed to become effective among the Chinese. Experience in Victoria, as elsewhere, seems to show that it is impossible to enforce any form of the " National Minimum " on a Chinese population in a white city—a fact of extreme significance in the question of the desirability of their admission or exclusion.

What the Victorian law does is, in effect, to compel employers and workmen to formulate, by common consent, minimum conditions for their own trade, which can be altered when and as required, but which are for the time being enforced by law. No employer is compelled to continue his business, or to engage any workman ; but if he chooses to do so, he must, as a minimum, comply with these conditions, in exactly the same way as he does with regard to the sanitary provisions of the Factory Acts. No workman is compelled to enter into employment or forbidden to strike for better terms, but he is prevented from engaging himself for less than the minimum wage, exactly as he is prevented from accepting less than the minimum sanitation. The law, in fact, puts every trade in which a wage-board is established in the position of the best organised industries in this country, where every firm and every workman finds the conditions of employment effectively regulated (as regards a minimum) by a collective agreement —with the added advantages that in Victoria the enforcement of the Common Rules becomes the business of the professional factory inspector ; that no individual can break away from the agreement ; and that no strikes, picketing, or other disorderly proceedings are ever needed to maintain its operation. This seems to us a distinct advance on the anarchic private war to which the settlement of the conditions of employment is otherwise abandoned.

It is obvious that the Victorian system brings greater advantages to the weaker trades than to those strongly organised. This, to our mind, is one of its merits. The pressing need in the England of to-day is not any increase in the money wages of the better-paid and stronger sections of the wage-earners, but a levelling up of the oppressed classes who fall below the " Poverty Line." The boilermakers in the shipbuilding towns, the Lancashire cotton-spinners, and the Northumberland coalminers may do by their own strength (though not without the cost of constant friction and occasional disastrous wars), as much as or more than any such

law could do for them.   But the unskilled laborers, the operatives whose organisation is crippled by home work, and the
women workers everywhere, can never, in our opinion, by
mere bargaining, obtain either satisfactory Common Rules
or any real enforcement of such illusory standards as they
may get set up.   We think that experience in this and
other countries confirms the economic conclusion that there
is no way of raising the present scandalously low Standard
of Life of these classes, except by some such legal stiffening
as that given by the Victorian law.

We do not suggest that the Victorian law is by any
means perfect.   It is reported, no doubt correctly, that it is
evaded and disobeyed in particular cases, as is also the law
against theft and murder, but this we do not count as a
serious objection to it or any other law.   The Chief Inspector's
licences to work under price are liable to abuse, but honestly
worked as the system now is, we do not regard this exceptional treatment of workers actually incapable of "a fair
day's work" as any drawback.   It is anomalous that the
wage-boards should not be able to frame Common Rules as
to the maximum working hours and the many conditions of
employment other than wages.   More serious is the attempt
to limit the number of apprentices, which—in spite of the
action of Lord James in the English boot and shoe manufacture (pp. 482-89)—we think wholly inexpedient and
prejudicial.   We doubt, moreover, whether it will be found
possible, in the long-run, to work a system of separate
boards for the innumerable separate and often badly defined
trades.   Finally, we object to the retention, as the basis of
the whole law, of the old conception that the amount of the
wage in each trade is a matter for each trade to settle
exclusively for itself, without regard to the interests of the
community.   In our view, the real justification for the interference of the law is the injury to the community as a whole
that results from any form of industrial parasitism—from
the payment, for instance, of wages insufficient for the full
maintenance, under healthy conditions, of the workers and

their families. We should, therefore, have preferred an
explicit statement of this principle by the Legislature, exactly
as is done in the Factory Acts with regard to certain other
conditions of employment, together with a definite statutory
minimum wage and maximum normal day, determined by
physiological considerations, and not to be infringed by any
trade whatsoever.[1] It would then have been possible to
have limited the formation of wage-boards to those occupations in which the operatives were alleged to be working
under conditions in any respect worse than those of the
" National Minimum "—a much more limited task than that
of fixing standard rates in all industries whatsoever—and
to have confined their scope to the comparatively easy duty
of applying the statutory minimum to the particular circumstances of those trades.

It is interesting to notice that, although New Zealand[2]
attacked the problem from the other end, aiming primarily
at preventing strikes, this has worked out, in practice, to
the Victorian solution of enforcing by law certain definite
minimum conditions of employment throughout each trade.
By the Industrial Conciliation and Arbitration Act of 1894,
now superseded by the consolidating Act of 1900, a complete system of industrial tribunals was established, and
empowered to deal with labor disputes of all kinds. Taking
the law as it now stands, we find, in each of the seven
districts into which the Colony is geographically divided, a

---

[1] The obvious difficulties in the way of such a minimum are dealt with at
pp. 774-95.

[2] The latest and most impartial account of the New Zealand system is the
New South Wales *Report of Royal Commission of Inquiry into the Working of
Compulsory Conciliation and Arbitration Laws* (Sydney, 1901), by Judge Backhouse. The Hon. W. P. Reeves (Agent-General in London for New Zealand),
who devised and carried through the Act of 1894, has graphically described its
working in *The Long White Cloud* (London, 1899) and other works ; and in
elaborate detail in his *Experiments of Seven Colonies*, shortly to be published.
See also *A Country without Strikes* and *Newest England*, both by H. D. Lloyd ;
and *Le Socialisme sans Doctrines*, by Albert Métin. For the ablest hostile
criticism of the law, apart from mere theoretical denunciations, the student must
be referred to the series of articles in the *Otago Daily Times* for September 1901,
by Dr. John Macgregor.

local Board of Conciliation, composed of two members elected by the registered Employers' Associations and two by the registered Trade Unions, with a chairman chosen by themselves. In default of election of members or chairman, the Government appoints. This Board does not initiate any proceedings, but deals with any local industrial dispute, whatever the trade, which may be referred to it by a Trade Union, an Employers' Association, or a single employer. Immediately any dispute has been, by either party, so referred to the Board, anything in the nature of a strike or lock-out is expressly prohibited, under penalty of £50. The Board has authority to make full inquiry into the circumstances, except that it cannot compel the production of books. It then makes suggestions for a settlement. If these suggestions are accepted by both parties, they are embodied in an "industrial agreement," which may be made unalterable for any specified term not exceeding three years, and which in any event binds the parties until it is superseded by any new agreement or award. Every such agreement is now enforceable by legal process, with the same effective authority as if it had been enacted as a law. If the parties will not agree the Board is to make a definite "recommendation" as to what, in its opinion, ought to be the settlement. Any dissatisfied party may thereupon, within a month, carry the case to the Court of Arbitration. Failing such an appeal, the Board's "recommendation" becomes binding on the parties as if it were an industrial agreement.

The Court of Arbitration consists of three members appointed by the Government: the president, a judge of the Supreme Court; and two persons recommended by the Employers' Associations and Trade Unions respectively. This Court has the full powers of an ordinary court of justice to investigate any case brought before it by way of appeal from the "recommendation" of a Board of Conciliation; and is free to act according to "equity and good conscience" without being bound by legal pedantries. It makes an award in such terms as it thinks fit, extending, it may be, to a whole trade, either in a specified district or throughout the Colony, and including at its discretion any related or competing industry.   The penalty for breach of the award may be any sum not exceeding £500 on an association, for payment of which the members of the association are made liable individually up to £10 each.   Thus, once any dispute is referred to a Board of Conciliation, either by a Trade Union or an employer, it is certain to lead, either by agreement of the parties, or by their acceptance of the " recommendation " of the Board, or else by the authoritative award of the Court of Arbitration, to the enactment of legally binding " Common Rules " for the trade, which continue in force until they are varied by subsequent proceedings of a similar character.[1]

The evolution of the New Zealand system, from 1894 to 1900, appears to us to be full of instruction.   In its first

---

[1] How extensive is the scope of the authority of these tribunals may be seen from the definition of their sphere.   They are to settle all disputes about "industrial matters," and

" ' Industrial matters ' mean all matters affecting or relating to work done, or to be done by workers, or the privileges, rights, and duties of employers or workers in any industry, not involving questions which are or may be the subject of proceedings for an indictable offence ; and without limiting the general nature of the above definition, includes all matters relating to—

" (*a*) The wages, allowances, or remuneration of workers employed in any industry, or the prices paid or to be paid therein in respect of such employment.

" (*b*) The hours of employment, sex, age, qualification, or status of workers, and the mode, terms, and conditions of employment.

" (*c*) The employment of children or young persons, or of any person or persons, or class of persons in any industry, or the dismissal of or refusal to employ any particular person or persons or class of persons therein.

" (*d*) The claim of members of an industrial union of employers to preference of service from unemployed members of an industrial union of workers.

" (*e*) The claim of members of industrial unions of workers to be employed in preference to non-members.

" (*f*) Any established custom or usage of any industry, either generally or in the particular district affected.

" ' Industry ' means any business, trade, manufacture, undertaking, calling, or employment in which workers are employed.

" ' Worker ' means any person of any age or either sex employed by any employer to do any skilled or unskilled manual or clerical work for hire or reward in any industry."—*Act of* 1900.

form, the law aimed ostensibly and primarily at affording means by which labor disputes could be amicably composed, and, in case of need, compulsorily settled by an award, which might, if certain steps were taken by the parties, be made enforceable by legal process. The local Boards of Conciliation failed, in two-thirds of the cases brought before them, to bring about any settlement, one party or the other promptly carrying the issue to the Court of Arbitration. This seems to have been due partly to the employers' dissatisfaction with the composition of the Boards, to which they had at first refused to elect members. But it soon became evident that the workmen valued the Court of Arbitration more than the Boards, for the very important reason that the award of the Court could be made legally binding on the trade, which was, until 1900, not the case with any decision of a Board. The Trade Unions, at first somewhat cold, became enthusiastic supporters of the Act when they found that, instead of merely preventing strikes, it enabled Common Rules for the industry to be made as legally binding as the Factory Acts. They became, in fact, as Mr. Reeves, the author of the law, admits, "rather too enthusiastic indeed, for they have shown a tendency to make too frequent a use of it." [1] Every trade sought to get its Common Rules embodied in law. This, however, is a rush which will probably exhaust itself as trade after trade finds its conditions settled by an authoritative award, which will, in any case, need amendment only on specific points, and may be made unalterable for a three years' term. The result is, to use the words of a bitter opponent, " it is necessary to put aside altogether the idea that our Act is simply a device for preventing strikes. It is nothing of the kind. It is a device for putting the regulation of trades, occupations, and industries under the control of a statutory court." [2]

Nor do the employers object. At first they usually

---

[1] *The Long White Cloud.*
[2] Dr. John Macgregor, of Wellington, New Zealand.

stood aloof, allowed the Government to appoint their members to the Conciliation Boards in default of election, and practically ignored the Act. But this attitude was given up on better acquaintance with the law and its working. After a time the great majority of employers openly professed their approval of the principle of the Act, and their satisfaction with the Court of Arbitration. One great captain of industry, who had been badly beaten in the Court of Arbitration, and compelled to accept an award which he bitterly resented, candidly confessed to us in 1898 that he had since found that the peace and assurance of peace given by the award, together with the certainty that he was not being undercut by rival employers, quite made up to him the increase of wages he had been compelled to pay. He could now, he said, "sleep at night," confident that there would be no interruption of his business. The enactment of Common Rules for each trade has, in fact, been discovered, in practice, not only to increase productivity, but also to leave unaffected the opportunities of particular employers to reap the full advantage of their position, connection, or capacity. And thus we find, to give only one instance, when the Act of 1900 was before the Legislature, with its express authorisation of the enactment of a Legal Minimum Wage, "the Canterbury Employers' Association," one of the most influential bodies in the Colony, desiring "to impress upon the Government that they are thoroughly in accord with the principles laid down in the Conciliation and Arbitration Act. Any hostility they may have shown in the past was mainly due to the fact that the Act was made to apply to a certain section of the industrial community only. The Government now propose to remove this, and if the Bill now before the House is amended in the direction suggested by the Association, they are strongly of opinion that it would be impossible to conceive of a more useful measure, properly administered, that would prove of such immense benefit to all sections of the industrial community."

It is, however, not strictly accurate to say that the Act

has prevented all strikes. There have been about half a dozen small strikes in New Zealand since 1894, but they have all been among workmen to whom the Act had not, at the time, been applied. If there is no industrial agreement or award in force in any trade, a strike may still occur, but it can be stopped at once if the employer chooses to apply to the local Conciliation Board. The operatives cannot approach the Board except in the capacity of a Trade Union or registered " industrial association," so that, in absolutely unorganised trades, in which the employers prefer not to apply to the Board, disputes may still take place. As, however, any seven workers in any occupation may form a registered association, the case is now of rare occurrence. There has at no time been a strike in contravention of an award under the Act. " It is hardly necessary to point out," writes Judge Backhouse, " that the Act makes no attempt to insist on an employer's carrying on his business, or on a man's working under a condition that he objects to. All it says is that, where a Board or the Court has interfered, the business, if carried on at all, shall be carried on in the manner prescribed ; if the workman works, he shall work under the conditions laid down. There is nothing to prevent a strike in detail ; nothing which will preclude a man from asking for his time [*i.e.* wages earned] and leaving." That is to say, the conditions of employment imposed by the New Zealand Court, like those of the Victorian wageboards, become binding on the employers only as standard minimum conditions, analogous to those of the Factory Acts. By the end of 1901, after seven years' experience of the system, with the one exception of agriculture, all important industries, whether protected by the tariff or not, including coal and gold mining, the mercantile marine, the building, textile, and engineering trades, printing, the railway service, sheep-shearing, meat-freezing, and many minor occupations, have brought themselves voluntarily within the scope of the law. We can only add our personal testimony to that given by every careful investigator into the circumstances of New Zealand, that there is, so far, no evidence of injury to its industrial prosperity; that after seven years' trial, there is no party—scarcely even any section of a party—advocating or desiring the repeal of the law; that it is, on the contrary, almost universally approved of by employers as well as workmen; and that there is every indication that its operation has been of great and enduring benefit to the community as a whole. The world is certainly indebted to New Zealand—and, in particular, to Mr. W. P. Reeves—for an original and highly significant object lesson in labor legislation. It may be added that New South Wales and Western Australia, after elaborate investigation and prolonged discussion, enacted, in 1900-1901, laws following closely the text of that of New Zealand.

The differences between the Victorian and New Zealand systems are full of interest. In Victoria the wage-board, once established, itself takes the initiative, and immediately sets to work, without waiting for a dispute, to frame Common Rules for the whole trade. The New Zealand tribunals cannot themselves initiate proceedings, and must wait until a dispute—which means, in practice, a mere refusal by employer or Trade Union of the other's request—is expressly referred to them. But once any occupation in New Zealand has come under an industrial agreement or an award, though the terms may be indefinitely varied from time to time, some "Common Rules" for the trade will practically always exist. In Victoria, again, the award of the wage-board can never be anything but a minimum. It can contain nothing to prevent an employer from offering better terms, or a Trade Union from striking to get better terms. In New Zealand the law originally contained no mention of a minimum wage, and though this is now expressly authorised by the statute, there is theoretically nothing to prevent the tribunals (like the justices under the Elizabethan statutes) from enacting precise rates or conditions, which would be maxima as well as minima, forbidding employers to offer more, and binding the Trade Union not merely to abstain from a strike, but also to refrain from collectively asking for better terms, or conspiring to obtain them by a concerted refusal to renew contracts of service. In practice, however, the New Zealand awards are always worded as minima, not as maxima—a distinction which we regard as vitally important to the interest of the community, as well as to that of the wage-earners, as the enactment of any maximum discourages efficiency and stops all progress. There is, in fact, no real difference between the Colonies on this point, as it was, from the first, taken for granted in New Zealand that the agreements and awards must take the form only of minimum conditions, seeing that any individual workman above the lowest grade of efficiency could, even with a maximum, always have resorted to the "strike in detail" as a means of enforcing his "rent of ability." The point is, however, of such vital importance that we should prefer to see the tribunal expressly limited to the enactment of minimum, not maximum conditions. A more practical difference between the two Colonies is that, in Victoria, the enforcement of the prescribed minimum becomes the duty of the Government, through its factory inspectors, and breaches of the award are proceeded against, at the public expense, in the police courts. In New Zealand the enforcement of the award is left to the vigilance of the parties concerned, and the necessary legal proceedings are at their own expense, and take place only in the Court of Arbitration. In Victoria each trade must have its own board, which now acts for the whole of that trade throughout the Colony. In New Zealand, though there is provision for the appointment, by way of exception, of special boards for particular cases, this has not been taken advantage of, and each district has its own local board, dealing with all the trades in that district, whilst a single Court of Arbitration deals with all trades all over the Colony. Finally, we have the highly significant difference that, whereas in Victoria the settlement of the conditions of employment is regarded as entirely a matter for the trade concerned, without opportunity of appeal, in New Zealand they are dealt with by tribunals of first instance and a court of appeal, both representing, not the trade concerned, but the community as a whole, and thus charged to have regard to the paramount interest which the public has in the maintenance and progressive advance, alike of the operatives' Standard of Life and of industrial productivity. It is the conscious adoption of this latter principle, by public opinion and the Legislatures of three such important states as New Zealand, New South Wales, and Western Australia, that we regard as the most important feature of these proceedings.

We venture to forecast some of the changes in Trade Union structure and function which will be brought about by these alterations in its environment. First and foremost we anticipate a change among Trade Unionists in their appreciation of the relative merits of Collective Bargaining and Legal Enactment (pp. 253-57). Collective Bargaining necessarily implies the alternative of a collective refusal to come to terms, that is to say, a strike or lock-out. But the decisions of the judges go very far in the direction of making a strike impossible. A Trade Union may, it is true, still lawfully conduct a strike, provided that it is carried out without a breach of the peace ; without threatening any employer that his business will be temporarily brought to a standstill ; without causing any damage to third parties ; without publishing anything that, though true, is technically libellous ; without obstructing the thoroughfare, or "watching and besetting" any place ; and without even any two men trying, in concert, peacefully to persuade a blackleg to remain loyal to his order. There may be a few Trade Unions, such as the Lancashire Cottonspinners, the Northumberland Coalminers, or the shipbuilding Boilermakers which (able as they are to enforce compulsory membership on all persons working at the trade, and so highly skilled as to be incapable of being replaced) could successfully conduct a strike under these conditions, without finding their funds denuded by law expenses and damages. But the vast majority of Trade Unions comprise only a part of the workers in their trades, and in many cases it would be possible, in an emergency, for the employers to get workers of other trades to replace them. With Trade Unions of this kind every strike inevitably leads to proceedings which, though not criminal, may now be held actionable. Moreover, Trade Unions are becoming every day more conscious of the fact that, for the great mass of manual workers who exist below the " Poverty Line," even this amount of collective action is impracticable. To the underfed, badly housed, and overworked man or woman, deprived of the leisure as well as of the strength necessary for organisation—to the isolated outworker or assistant in the small workshop—Collective Bargaining is wholly and for ever out of the question. All these considerations are cutting at the root of that buoyant faith of the older Trade Unionists in the abstract " right of combination," by which they meant the right to a free fight with the employers. On the other hand, the success of the Colonial experiments is rapidly opening the eyes of English employers and workmen to new ways of using the Method of Legal Enactment, and new advantages of its application. For instance, the word " arbitration," has, in the course of four years, completely changed its common meaning. When we wrote our chapter on Arbitration (pp. 222-45) we could still use the term exclusively for a voluntary recourse to a voluntarily chosen tribunal whose award was only voluntarily accepted. Now arbitration in labor disputes has come to mean, in most people's minds, merely a particular form of social machinery by which the conditions of employment can be authoritatively settled, and strikes prevented, whether individual employers or individual workmen like it or not. The interesting differences between the systems of New Zealand and Victoria, with their equally interesting imitations in New South Wales, Western Australia, and South Australia, show how elastic and how closely applicable to the details of each trade and town the once rigid law may be.

Passing now from the " methods " to the " regulations "

of Trade Unionism, we look for even greater changes. Our analysis of these regulations showed that they fell, for all their multifariousness, into two classes—the Device of the Common Rule and the Device of Restriction—classes which are sharply marked off from each other, which rest on absolutely different assumptions, and which are mutually contradictory in their social results. We showed that economic science found nothing to condemn in the Device of the Common Rule; that, in fact, in all regulations based on this principle—notably those relating to the Standard Rate, the Normal Day, and prescribed conditions of Sanitation and Safety—Trade Unionism positively promoted efficiency, stimulated both workmen and employers to greater productivity, and tended constantly to improve both human character and technical processes. On the other hand, we demonstrated that the regulations based on the Device of Restriction—whether of numbers or output, whether in the use of machinery or in transformation of processes—were wholly injurious not only to the trade concerned and to the community as a whole, but also to the manual worker himself. It is to be counted as one of the great merits of British Trade Unionism that it has, during the past hundred years, with practically no outside assistance, been steadily subordinating and discarding the Device of Restriction, which it had inherited partly from the regulations of the Craft Gilds and partly from the instincts of unorganised hired labor; substituting for it, as we proved with reference to trade after trade, its own characteristic invention of the Device of the Common Rule. Already, in 1897, we were able to show that the Device of the Common Rule was, in British Trade Unionism, both the predominant and the growing element, whilst the Device of Restriction lingered only in a minority of trades, in which it was becoming steadily more discredited.

This eminently desirable tendency will now, it is clear, receive a great stimulus. Public opinion so keenly appreciates the danger of German and American rivalry in industry, and international competition is becoming so intense and all-pervading, that every kind of limitation or restriction of productive power is seen to be almost criminal. What with law and popular disapproval, and the better instruction of the workmen themselves, to which Trade Unionism has so much contributed, we expect to see the remnants of the Device of Restriction—especially all forms of Restriction of Numbers—rapidly disappear from the Trade Union world. Restriction of effort, and reluctance to make the most of machinery—already extinct in the trades governed by collectively-agreed-to Standard Lists of Piecework Prices—will linger longest in those occupations in which either timework or competitive piecework survives, and in which the employers refuse or neglect to set their brains to work, in conjunction with the Trade Union officials, to devise more intelligent methods of remuneration. In such trades employers and workmen alike will continue to suffer the consequences of their own stupidity.

On the other hand, the decisive approval which economic science gives to the Device of the Common Rule is reinforced by the growing public appreciation of the national import-ance of preventing every kind of " sweating." As a nation we are becoming keenly conscious of the fact that the existence of whole classes who are chronically underfed, ill-clothed, badly housed, and overworked, constitutes not only a grievance to these unfortunates themselves, but also a serious drain upon the vitality and productivity of the community as a whole. The only effective way to prevent the national loss involved in the existence of " parasitic trades " is seen to be the compulsory extension to them of those Common Rules which the stronger trades have got for themselves. The idea of a compulsorily enforced " National Minimum "—already embodied in our law as regards sanitation and education—is now seen to be appli-cable as regards rest and subsistence. And just at the time when the successful experiments of Victoria and New Zealand have been proving to us that a Legal Minimum

Wage is not at all an impossibility, and that it actually works, and works well, there comes the new Act of the New South Wales Legislature, with its express adoption of the principle, under the very name that we invented for it four years ago. By this statute, passed in December 1901, at the instance of Mr. Bernhard Wise, the Court of Arbitration is empowered to declare that any practice, usage, condition of employment, or industrial dealing shall, with such limitations and exceptions as the Court may declare, become a "Common Rule" for all persons employed in the industry under consideration, to be henceforth obeyed by every employer, and to be enforced by drastic penalties.

One probable application of the policy of the National Minimum seems to us so urgently required for national safety that we give it special prominence. Perhaps the gravest social symptom at the opening of the twentieth century is the lack of physical vigor, moral self-control, and technical skill of the town-bred, manual-working boy. In the industrial organisation of to-day there are hundreds of thousands of youths, between fourteen and twenty-one, who are taken on by employers to do unskilled and undisciplined work, at comparatively high wages for mere boys, who are taught no trade, who are kept working long hours at mere routine, and who are habitually turned adrift, to recruit the ranks of unskilled labor, as soon as they require a man's subsistence (pp. 482-85, 704-15, 768-69, 811). We see four acute evils arising out of the existence of this class. Ministers of religion deplore the "hooliganism" of our great cities. No less serious is the physical degeneracy, which is leading our military advisers to declare that 60 per cent of the adult male population now fail to reach the already low standard of the recruiting sergeant. At the same time, there is a constant deficiency in the supply of highly skilled labor, whilst all educationists agree that it is impossible to give adequate technical training with such voluntary attendance as can be got from lads after ten or twelve hours' employment (p. 770). Finally, in this suppression of the adult male operative by successive relays of boys between fourteen and twenty-one, we have, as we have shown (pp. 482-89, 768-71), one of the most insidious forms of industrial parasitism. From the point of view of the community, we cannot afford to regard the growing boy as an independent wealth-producer, to be satisfied by a daily subsistence : he is the future citizen and parent, for whom, up to twenty-one, proper conditions of growth and training are of paramount importance. Every industry employing boy-labor, and not providing adequate physical and mental training, is using up the stock of the nation, and comes under condemnation as a parasitic trade (p. 771).

Now, although philanthropists and statesmen have deplored this complex evil, no systematic treatment of it has yet been undertaken. The Trade Unions, to whom it presents itself primarily as the increase of " boy-labor," have found no better device against it than the so-called " apprenticeship " regulations (pp. 482-89). But the old system of individual apprenticeship to the master craftsman, with its anomalous restrictions of age and number, and its haphazard amateur instruction, is, as regards nearly all trades, dead and past reviving. Any attempt to resuscitate it inevitably takes the form of a mere limitation of numbers, or other narrowing of the entrance to a trade—a policy which, as we have demonstrated, does not cure the evil, and is seriously prejudicial to masters and men alike, to the trade itself, and to the whole community (pp. 454-89, 768-71). Unfortunately, this limitation of the number of apprentices has now been embodied in both New Zealand and Victorian law, and we desire therefore to draw pointed attention, not only to the utter futility of this device, but also to the existence of a more excellent way.

We see no remedy for the grave social evils resulting from the illegitimate use of boy-labor, and the consequent industrial parasitism, except in an appropriate application of the Policy of the National Minimum (pp. 770-71). The nation must, at any inconvenience, prevent such conditions of employment of boys as are demonstrably inconsistent with the maintenance of the race in a state of efficiency as producers and citizens. As regards youths under twenty-one the community is bound, in its own interest, to secure for them, not as at present, daily subsistence and pocket-money, but such conditions of nurture as will allow of the continuous provision, generation after generation, of healthy and efficient adults. What is required for the "hooligan" is adequate opportunity for physical culture and effective technical training, and the systematic enforcement of these by law. This means, we suggest, an extension of the existing "half-time" system. We see no reason why the present prohibition to employ a boy in a factory or workshop for more than thirty hours in a week should not be extended to all occupations, and at least up to the age of eighteen. The twenty or thirty hours per week thus saved from industrial employment should be compulsorily devoted to a properly organised course of physical training and technical education, which could, under such circumstances, be carried out with a thoroughness and efficiency hitherto undreamt of. Meanwhile employers would remain free to engage boys, but as they could get them only for half-time, they would not be tempted to hire them except for the legitimate purpose of training up a new generation of craftsmen. Finally, we may add that if at any time it should be deemed necessary for the purpose of home defence to have the nation trained to arms, a mere extension of such a half-time system to the age of twenty-one would enable every citizen to be drilled and taught the use of the rifle without the slightest interruption of wage-earning or any segregation in barracks. We suggest that the "citizen-army" of the future will, in the United Kingdom, more probably take this form than that of conscription by ballot or any universal military service for one or two years at a stretch.

SIDNEY AND BEATRICE WEBB.

41 Grosvenor Road, Westminster,
London, *December* 1901.

CONTENTS

PART I

TRADE UNION STRUCTURE

PART II

TRADE UNION FUNCTION

PART II

TRADE UNION FUNCTION—*Continued*

CHAPTER X

CHAPTER XI

CHAPTER XII

CHAPTER XIII

PART III

TRADE UNION THEORY

APPENDICES

PART I

TRADE UNION STRUCTURE

PART I

TRADE UNION STRUCTURE

CHAPTER I

PRIMITIVE DEMOCRACY[1]

IN the local trade clubs of the eighteenth century, democracy appeared in its simplest form. Like the citizens of Uri or Appenzell[2] the workmen were slow to recognise any other authority than "the voices" of all concerned. The members of each trade, in general meeting assembled, themselves made the regulations, applied them to particular cases, voted the expenditure of funds, and decided on such action by individual members as seemed necessary for the common weal. The early rules were accordingly occupied with securing the maintenance of order and decorum at these general meetings of "the trade" or "the body." With this view the president, often chosen only for the particular meeting, was treated with great respect and invested with special, though temporary,

[1] Copyright in the United States of America, 1896, by Sidney and Beatrice Webb.

[2] The early Trade Union general meetings have, indeed, many interesting resemblances, both in spirit and in form, to the "Landesgemeinden," or general meetings of all citizens, of the old Swiss Cantons. The best description of these archaic Swiss democracies, as they exist to-day, is given by Eugène Rambert in his work *Les Alpes Suisses : Études Historiques et Nationales* (Lausanne, 1889). J. M. Vincent's *State and Federal Government in Switzerland* (Baltimore, 1891) is more precise and accurate than any other account in the English language. Freeman's picturesque reference to them in *The Growth of the English Constitution* (London, 1872) is well known.

authority. Thus the constitution of the London Society of Woolstaplers, established 1785, declares "that at every meeting of this society a president shall be chosen to preserve the rules of decorum and good order ; and if any member should not be silent on due notice given by the president, which shall be by giving three distinct knocks on the table, he shall fine threepence ; and if any one shall interrupt another in any debate while addressing the president, he shall fine sixpence ; and if the ·person so fined shall return any indecent language, he shall fine sixpence more ; and should any president misconduct himself, so as to cause uproar and confusion in the society, or shall neglect to enforce a strict observance of this and the following article, he shall be superseded, and another president shall be chosen in his stead. The president shall be accommodated with his own choice of liquors, wine only excepted." [1] And the Articles of the Society of Journeymen Brushmakers, to which no person was to be admitted as a member "who is not well-affected to his present Majesty and the Protestant succession, and in good health, and of a respectable character," provide "that on each evening the society meets there shall be a president chosen from the members present to keep order ; to be allowed a shilling for his trouble ; any member refusing to serve the office to be fined sixpence. If any member dispute on politics, swear, lay wagers, promote gambling, or behave otherwise disorderly, and will not be silent when ordered by the chairman, he shall pay a fine of a shilling." [2]

The rules of every old society consist mainly of safeguards of the efficiency of this general meeting. Whilst political or religious wrangling, seditious sentiments or songs, cursing, swearing, or obscene language, betting, wagering, gaming, or refusing to keep silence were penalised by fines, elaborate and detailed provision was made for the entertain-

---

[1] *The Articles of the London Society of Woolstaplers* (London, 1813).
[2] *Articles of the Society of Journeymen Brushmakers*, held at the sign of the Craven Head, Drury Lane (London, 1806).

ment of the members. Meeting, as all clubs did, at a public-house in a room lent free by the landlord, it was taken as a matter of course that each man should do his share of drinking. The rules often prescribe the sum to be spent at each meeting : in the case of the Friendly Society of Iron-founders, for instance, the member's monthly contribution in 1809 was a shilling " to the box," and threepence for liquor, " to be spent whether present or not." The Brushmakers provided "that on every meeting night each member shall receive a pot ticket at eight o'clock, a pint at ten, and no more." [1] And the Manchester Compositors resolved in 1826 " that tobacco be allowed to such members of this society as require it during the hours of business at any meeting of the society." [2]

After the president, the most important officers were, accordingly, the stewards or marshalmen, two or four members usually chosen by rotation. Their duty was, to use the words of the Cotton-spinners, " at every meeting to fetch all the liquor into the committee room, and serve it regularly round " ; [3] and the members were, in some cases, " forbidden to drink out of turn, except the officers at the table or a member on his first coming into the town." [4] Treasurer

[1] The account book of the little Preston Society of Carpenters, whose membership in 1807 averaged about forty-five, shows an expenditure at each meeting of 6s. to 7s. 6d. As late as 1837 the rules of the Steam-Engine Makers' Society provided that one-third of the income—fourpence out of the monthly contribution of a shilling—" shall be spent in refreshments. . . . To prevent disorder no person shall help himself to any drink in the club-room during club hours, but what is served him by the waiters or marshalmen who shall be appointed by the president every club night." Some particulars as to the dying away of this custom are given in our *History of Trade Unionism*, pp. 185, 186 ; see also the article by Prof. W. J. Ashley on " Journeymen's clubs," in *Political Science Quarterly*, March 1897.

[2] MS. Minutes of the Manchester Typographical Society, 7th March 1826.

[3] *Articles, Rules, Orders, and Regulations made and to be observed by and between the Friendly Associated Cotton-spinners within the township of Oldham* (Oldham, 1797 : reprinted 1829).

[4] Friendly Society of Ironfounders, Rules, 1809. The Rules of the Liverpool Shipwrights' Society of 1784 provided also " that each member that shall call for drink without leave of the stewards shall forfeit and pay for the drink they call for to the stewards for the use of the box. . . . That the marshalmen shall pay the over-plus of drink that comes in at every monthly meeting more than allowed by the

there was often none, the scanty funds, if not consumed as quickly as collected, being usually deposited with the publican who acted as host. Sometimes, however, we have the archaic box with three locks, so frequent among the gilds; and in such cases members served in rotation as "keymasters," or, as we should now say, trustees. Thus the Edinburgh Shoemakers provided that "the keymasters shall be chosen by the roll, beginning at the top for the first keymaster, and at the middle of the roll for the youngest keymaster, and so on until the roll be finished. If any refuse the keymaster, he shall pay one shilling and sixpence sterling."[1] The ancient box of the Glasgow Ropemakers' Friendly Society (established 1824), elaborately decorated with the society's "coat of arms," was kept in the custody of the president, who was elected annually.[2] Down to within the last thirty years the custom was maintained on the "deacons' choosing," or annual election day, of solemnly transporting this box through the streets of Glasgow to the house of the new president, with a procession of ropespinners headed by a piper, the ceremony terminating with a feast. The keeping of accounts and the writing of letters was a later development, and when a clerk or secretary was needed, he had perforce to be chosen from the small number qualified for the work. But there is evidence that the early secretaries served, like their colleagues, only for short periods,

society; and no member of this society is allowed to call for or smoak tobacco during club hours in the club room; for every such offence he is to forfeit and pay fourpence to the stewards for the use of the box."—*Articles to be observed by a Society of Shipwrights, or the True British Society, all Freemen* (Liverpool, 1784), Articles 8 and 9.

[1] *Articles of the Journeymen Shoemakers of the City of Edinburgh* (Edinburgh, 1778)—a society established in 1727.

[2] *Articles and Regulations of the Associated Ropemakers' Friendly Society* (Glasgow, 1836), repeated in the *General Laws and Regulations of the Glasgow Ropemakers' Trade Protective and Friendly Society* (Glasgow, 1884). The members of the Glasgow Typographical Society resolved, in 1823, "that a man be provided on election nights to carry the box from the residence of the president to the place of meeting, and after the meeting to the new president's house."—MS. Minutes of general meeting, Glasgow Typographical Society, 4th October 1823.

and occupied, moreover, a position very subordinate to the president.

Even when it was necessary to supplement the officers by some kind of committee, so far were these infant democracies from any superstitious worship of the ballot-box, that, although we know of no case of actual choice by lot,[1] the committee-men were usually taken, as in the case of the Steam-Engine Makers' Society, " in rotation as their names appear on the books." [2]   " A fine of one shilling," say the rules of the Southern Amicable Union Society of Woolstaplers, " shall be levied on any one who shall refuse to serve on the committee or neglect to attend its stated meetings, . . . and the next in rotation shall be called in his stead." [3] The rules of the Liverpool Shipwrights declared " that the committee shall be chosen by rotation as they stand in the books ; and any member refusing to serve the office shall forfeit ten shillings and sixpence." [4]   As late as 1843 we find the very old Society of Curriers resolving that for this purpose " a list with three columns be drawn up of the whole of the members, dividing their ages as near as possible in the following manner : the elder, the middle-aged and the young ; so that the experience of the elder and the sound

---

[1] The selection of officers by lot was, it need hardly be said, frequent in primitive times.   It is interesting to find the practice in the Swiss " Landesgemeinden."   In 1640 the " Landesgemeinde " of Glarus began to choose eight candidates for each office, who then drew lots among themselves.   Fifty years later Schwyz followed this example.   By 1793 the " Landesgemeinde " of Glarus was casting lots for all offices, including the cantonal secretaryship, the stewardships of dependent territories, etc.   The winner often sold his office to the highest bidder.   The practice was not totally abolished until 1837, and old men still remember the passing round of the eight balls, each wrapped in black cloth, seven being silvern and the eighth gilt.—*Les Alpes Suisses : Études Historiques et Nationales*, by Eugène Rambert (Lausanne, 1889), pp. 226, 276.

[2] *Rules of the Steam-Engine Makers' Society*, edition of 1837.

[3] *Rules of the Southern Amicable Union of Woolstaplers* (London, 1837).

[4] *Articles to be observed by the Association of the Friendly Union of Shipwrights, instituted in Liverpool on Tuesday, 11th November* 1800 (Liverpool, 1800), Rule 19.   The London Sailmakers resolved, in 1836, " that from this evening the calling for stewards shall begin from the last man on the committee, and that from and after the last steward the twelve men who stand in rotation on the book do form the committee."—MS. Minutes of general meeting, 26th September 1836.

judgment of the middle-aged will make up for any deficiency on the part of the young."[1]　In some cases, indeed, the members of the committee were actually chosen by the officers. Thus in the ancient society of Journeymen Papermakers, where each "Grand Division" had its committee of eight members, it was provided that "to prevent imposition part of the committee shall be changed every three months, by four old members going out and four new ones coming in ; also a chairman shall be chosen to keep good order, which chairman, with the clerk, shall nominate the four new members which shall succeed the four old ones."[2]

The early trade club was thus a democracy of the most rudimentary type, free alike from permanently differentiated officials, executive council, or representative assembly. The general meeting strove itself to transact all the business, and grudgingly delegated any of its functions either to officers or to committees. When this delegation could no longer be avoided, the expedients of rotation and short periods of service were used "to prevent imposition" or any undue influence by particular members. In this earliest type of Trade Union democracy we find, in fact, the most childlike faith not only that "all men are equal," but also that "what concerns all should be decided by all."

It is obvious that this form of democracy was compatible only with the smallest possible amount of business. But it was, in our opinion, not so much the growth of the financial and secretarial transactions of the unions, as the exigencies of

---

[1] MS. Minutes of the London Society of Journeymen Curriers, January 1843.

[2] *Rules and Articles to be observed by the Journeymen Papermakers throughout England* (1823), Appendix 18 to Report on Combination Laws, 1825, p. 56. The only Trade Union in which this example still prevails is that of the Flint Glass Makers, where the rules until lately gave the secretary "the power to nominate a central committee (open to the objection of the trade), in whose hands the executive power of the society shall be vested from year to year."—*Rules and Regulations of the National Flint Glass Makers' Sick and Friendly Society* (Manchester, 1890). This has lately been modified, in so far that seven members are now elected, the central secretary nominating four "from the district in which he resides, but open to the objection of the trade."—Rule 67 (Rules, reprinted with additions, Manchester, 1893).

their warfare with the employers, that first led to a departure from this simple ideal. The legal and social persecutions to which Trade Unionists were subject, at any rate up to 1824, made secrecy and promptitude absolutely necessary for successful operations; and accordingly at all critical times we find the direction of affairs passing out of the hands of the general meeting into those of a responsible, if not a representative, committee. Thus the London Tailors, whose militant combinations between 1720 and 1834 repeatedly attracted the attention of Parliament,[1] had practically two constitutions, one for peace and one for war. In quiet times, the society was made up of little autonomous general meetings of the kind described above at the thirty "houses of call" in London and Westminster. The organisation for war, as set forth in 1818 by Francis Place, was very different: "Each house of call has a deputy, who on particular occasions is chosen by a kind of tacit consent, frequently without its being known to a very large majority who is chosen. The deputies form a committee, and they again choose, in a somewhat similar way, a very small committee, in whom, on very particular occasions, all power resides, from whom all orders proceed, and whose commands are implicitly obeyed; and on no occasion has it ever been known that their commands have exceeded the necessity of the occasion, or that they have wandered in the least from the purpose for which it was understood they were appointed. So perfect indeed is the organisation, and so well has it been carried into effect, that no complaint has ever been heard; with so much simplicity and with so great certainty does the whole business appear to be conducted that the great body of journeymen rather acquiesce than assist in any way in it."[2] Again, the protracted legal proceedings of the Scottish Hand-

---

[1] See the interesting *Select Documents illustrating the History of Trade Unionism: I. The Tailoring Trade*, edited by F. W. Galton (London, 1896), being one of the "Studies" published by the London School of Economics and Political Science.

[2] *The Gorgon*, No. 20, 3rd October 1818, reprinted in *The Tailoring Trade* by F. W. Galton, pp. 153, 154.

loom Weavers, ending in the great struggle when 30,000
looms from Carlisle to Aberdeen struck on a single day
(10th November 1812), were conducted by an autocratic committee of five, sitting in Glasgow, and periodically summoning from all the districts delegates who carried back to their
constituents orders which were implicitly obeyed.[1]   Before
the repeal of the Combination Laws in 1824, the employers
in all the organised trades complained bitterly of these " self-
appointed " committees, and made repeated attempts to
scatter them by prosecutions for combination or conspiracy.
To this constant danger of prosecution may be ascribed
some of the mystery which surrounds the actual constitution
of these tribunals ; but their appearance on the scene whenever an emergency called for strong action was a necessary
consequence of the failure of the clubs to provide any constitutional authority of a representative character.

So far we have dealt principally with trade clubs confined
to particular towns or districts.   When, in any trade, these
local clubs united to form a federal union, or when one of
them enrolled members in other towns, government by a
general meeting of " the trade," or of all the members, became impracticable.[2]   Nowadays some kind of representa-

---

[1] Evidence before the House of Commons Committee on Artisans and
Machinery, 1824, especially that of Richmond.

[2] A branch of a national union is still governed by the members in general
meeting assembled ; and for this and other reasons, it is customary for several
separate branches to be established in large towns where the number of members
becomes greater than can easily be accommodated in a single branch meeting-
place.   Such branches usually send delegates to a district committee, which thus
becomes the real governing authority of the town or district.   But in certain
unions the idea of direct government by an aggregate meeting of the trade still so
far prevails that, even in so large a centre as London, resort is had to huge mass
meetings.   Thus the London Society of Compositors will occasionally summon
its ten thousand members to meet in council to decide, in an excited mass
meeting, the question of peace or war with their employers.   And the National
Union of Boot and Shoe Operatives, which in its federal constitution adopts a
large measure of representative institutions, still retains in its local organisation
the aggregate meeting of the trade as the supreme governing body for the district.
The Shoemakers of London or Leicester frequently hold meetings at which the
attendance is numbered by thousands, with results that are occasionally calamitous
to the union.   Thus, when in 1891 the men of a certain London firm had
impetuously left their work contrary to the agreement made by the union with

tive institutions would seem to have been inevitable at this stage. But it is significant to notice how slowly, reluctantly and incompletely the Trade Unionists have incorporated in their constitutions what is often regarded as the specifically Anglo-Saxon form of democracy—the elected representative assembly, appointing and controlling a standing executive. Until the present generation, no Trade Union had ever formed its constitution on this model. It is true that in the early days we hear of [1] meetings of delegates from local

the employers, their branch called a mass meeting of the whole body of the London members (seven thousand attending), which, after refusing even to hear the union officials, decided to support the recalcitrant strikers, with the result that the employers "locked out" the whole trade. (*Monthly Report of the National Union of Boot and Shoe Operatives*, November 1891.) In 1893 the union executive found it necessary to summon at Leicester a special delegate meeting of the whole society to sit in judgment on the London members who had decided, at a mass meeting, to withdraw from the national agreement to submit to arbitration. The circular calling the delegate meeting contains a vivid description of the scene at this mass meeting: "The hall was well filled, and Mr. Judge, president of the union, took the chair. From the outset it was soon found that the rowdy element intended to again prevent a hearing, and thus make it impossible for our views to be laid before the bulk of the more intelligent and reasonable members. . . . If democratic unions such as ours are to have the meetings stopped by such proceedings, . . . if the members refuse to hear, and insult by cock-crowing and cat-calls their own accredited and elected executive, then it is time that other steps be taken." The delegate meeting, by 74 votes to 9, severely censured the London members, and reversed their decision (Circular of Executive Committee, 14th March 1893 : Special Report of the Delegate Meeting at Leicester, 17th April 1893). In most unions, however, experience has shown that in truth "aggregate meetings" are "aggravated meetings," and has led to their abandonment in favor of district committees or delegate meetings.

[1] In the *History of Trade Unionism*, p. 46, we described the Hatters as holding in 1772, 1775, and 1777, "congresses" of delegates from all parts of the country. Further examination of the evidence (House of Commons Journals, vol. xxxvi. ; Place MS. 27,799-68 ; Committee on Artisans and Machinery) inclines us to believe that these "congresses," like another in 1816, comprised only delegates from the various workshops in London. We can discover no instance during the eighteenth century of a Trade Union gathering made up of delegates from the local clubs throughout the country. But though the congresses of the Hatters probably represented only the London workmen, their "bye-laws" were apparently adopted by the clubs elsewhere, and came thus to be of national scope. Similar instances of national regulation by the principal centre of a trade may be seen in the "resolutions" addressed "to the Woolstaplers of England" by the London Society of Woolstaplers, and in the "articles to be observed by the Journeymen Papermakers throughout England," formulated at a meeting of the trade at large held at Maidstone. In the loose alliances of the local clubs in each trade, the chief trade centre often acted, in fact, as the "governing branch."

clubs to adopt or amend the "articles" of their association. A "deputation" from nine local societies of Carpenters met thus in London in 1827 to form the Friendly Society of Operative House Carpenters and Joiners, and similar meetings were annually held to revise the rules and adjust the finances of this federation. It would have been a natural development for such a representative congress to appoint a standing committee and executive officers to act on behalf of the whole trade. But when between 1824 and 1840 the great national societies of that generation settled down into their constitutions, the congress of elected representatives either found no place at all, or else was called together only at long intervals and for strictly limited purposes. In no case do we see it acting as a permanent supreme assembly. The Trade Union met the needs of expanding democracy by some remarkable experiments in constitution-making.

The first step in the transition from the loose alliance of separate local clubs into a national organisation was the appointment of a seat of government or "governing branch." The members residing in one town were charged with the responsibility of conducting the current business of the whole society, as well as that of their own branch. The branch officers and the branch committee of this town accordingly became the central authority.[1] Here again the leading idea was not so much to get a government that was repre-

---

[1] In some of the more elaborate Trade Union constitutions formulated between 1820 and 1834 we find a hierarchy of authorities, none of them elected by the society as a whole, but each responsible for a definite part of the common administration. Thus *The Rules and Articles to be observed by the Journeymen Papermakers* in 1823 provide "that there shall be five Grand Divisions throughout England where all money shall be lodged, that when wanted may be sent to any part where emergency may require." These "Grand Divisions" were the branches in the five principal centres of the trade, each being given jurisdiction over all the mills in the counties round about it. Above them all stood "No. 1 Grand Division" (Maidstone), which was empowered to determine business of too serious a nature to be left to any other Grand Division. This geographical hierarchy is interesting as having apparently furnished the model for most of the constitutions of the period, notably of the Owenite societies of 1833-1834, including the Builders' Union and the Grand National Consolidated Trades Union itself.

sentative of the society as to make each section take its turn
at the privileges and burdens of administration. The seat
of government was accordingly always changed at short
intervals, often by rotation. Thus the Steam-Engine Makers'
rules of 1826 provide that "the central branch of the society
shall be held alternately at the different branches of this
society, according as they stand on the books, commencing
with Branch No. 1, and the secretary of the central branch
shall, after the accounts of the former year have been balanced,
send the books to the next central branch of the society."[1]
In other cases the seat of government was periodically determined by vote of the whole body of members, who appear
usually to have been strongly biassed in favor of shifting it
from town to town. The reason appears in this statement
by one of the lodges of the Ironfounders: "What, we ask,
has been the history of nearly every trade society in this
respect? Why, that when any branch or section of it has
possessed the governing power too long, it has become careless of the society's interests, tried to assume irresponsible
powers, and invariably by its remissness opened wide the
doors of peculation, jobbery, and fraud."[2]

The institution of a "governing branch" had the advantage
of being the cheapest machinery of central administration
that could be devised. By it the national union secured
its executive committee, at no greater expense than a small
local society.[3] And so long as the function of the national

The same geographical hierarchy was a feature of the constitution of the Southern
Amicable Society of Woolstaplers until the last revision of rules in 1892. In only
one case has a similar hierarchy survived. The United Society of Brushmakers,
established in the eighteenth century, is still divided into geographical divisions
governed by the six head towns, with London as the centre of communication.
The branches in the West Riding, for instance, are governed by the Leeds committee, and when in 1892 the Sheffield branch had a strike, this was managed by
the secretary of the Leeds branch.

[1] Rule 19 ; rules of 1826 as reprinted in the Annual Report for 1837.

[2] Address of the Bristol branch of the Friendly Society of Ironfounders to the
members at large (in Annual Report for 1849).

[3] Both the idea of rotation of office, and that of a local governing branch, can
be traced to the network of village sick-clubs which existed all over England in
the eighteenth century. In 1824 these clubs were described by a hostile critic as
"under the management of the ordinary members *who succeed to the several offices*

executive was confined to that of a centre of communication between practically autonomous local branches, no alteration in the machinery was necessary. The duties of the secretary, like those of his committee, were not beyond the competence of ordinary artisans working at their trade and devoting only their evenings to their official business. But with the multiplication of branches and the formation of a central fund, the secretarial work of a national union presently absorbed the whole time of a single officer, to whom, therefore, a salary had to be assigned. As the salary came from the common fund, the right of appointment passed, without question, from the branch meeting to "the voices" of the whole body of members. Thus the general secretary was singled out for a unique position : alone among the officers of the union he was elected by the whole body of members. Meanwhile the supreme authority continued to be "the voices." Every proposition not covered by the original "articles," together with all questions of peace and war, was submitted to the votes of the members.[1] But this was not all. Each branch, in

in rotation ; frequently without being qualified either by ability, independence, or impartiality for the due discharge of their respective offices ; or under the control of a standing committee, composed of the most active and often the least eligible members *residing near the place of meeting.*"—*The Constitution of Friendly Societies upon Legal and Scientific Principles*, by Rev. John Thomas Becher (2nd edition, London, 1824), p. 50.

Comparing small things with great, we may say that the British Empire is administered by a "governing branch." The business common to the Empire as a whole is transacted, not by imperial or federal officers, but by those of one part of the Empire, the United Kingdom of Great Britain and Ireland ; and they are supervised, not by an Imperial Diet or Federal Assembly, but by the domestic legislature at Westminster.

[1] The very ancient United Society of Brushmakers, which dates from the early part of the eighteenth century, retains to this day its archaic method of collecting "the voices." In London, said to be the most conservative of all the districts, no alteration of rule is made without "sending round the box" as of yore. In the society's ancient iron box are put all the papers relating to the subject under discussion, and a member out of employment is deputed to carry the box from shop to shop until it has travelled "all round the trade." When it arrives at a shop, all the men cease work and gather round ; the box is opened, its contents are read and discussed, and the shop delegates are then and there instructed how to vote at the next delegate meeting. The box is then refilled and sent on to the next shop. Old minutes of 1829 show that this custom has remained unchanged, down to the smallest detail, for, at any rate, a couple of generations. It is probably nearly two centuries old.

general meeting assembled, claimed the right to have any proposition whatsoever submitted to the vote of the society as a whole. And thus we find, in almost every Trade Union which has a history at all, a most instructive series of experiments in the use, misuse, and limitations of the Referendum.

Such was the typical Trade Union constitution of the last generation. In a few cases it has survived, almost unchanged, down to the present day, just as its predecessor, the archaic local club governed by the general meeting, still finds representatives in the Trade Union world. But wherever an old Trade Union has maintained its vitality, its constitution has been progressively modified, whilst the most powerful of the modern unions have been formed on a different pattern. An examination of this evolutionary process will bring home to us the transitional character of the existing constitutional forms, and give us valuable hints towards the solution, in a larger field, of the problem of uniting efficient administration with popular control.

We have already noted that, in passing from a local to a national organisation, the Trade Union unwittingly left behind the ideal of primitive democracy. The setting apart of one man to do the clerical work destroyed the possibility of equal and identical service by all the members, and laid the foundation of a separate governing class. The practice of requiring members to act in rotation was silently abandoned. Once chosen for his post, the general secretary could rely with confidence, unless he proved himself obviously unfit or grossly incompetent, on being annually re-elected. Spending all day at office work, he soon acquired a professional expertness quite out of the reach of his fellow-members at the bench or the forge. And even if some other member possessed natural gifts equal or superior to the acquired skill of the existing officer, there was, in a national organisation, no opportunity of making these qualities known. The general secretary, on the other hand, was always advertising his name and his personality to the thousands of members by the printed circulars and financial reports, which became the only link between the scattered branches, and afforded positive evidence of his competency to perform the regular work of the office. With every increase in the society's membership, with every extension or elaboration of its financial system or trade policy, the position of the salaried official became, accordingly, more and more secure. The general secretaries themselves changed with the development of their office. The work could no longer be efficiently performed by an ordinary artisan, and some preliminary office training became almost indispensable. The Coalminers, for instance, as we have shown in our description of the Trade Union world, have picked their secretaries to a large extent from a specially trained section, the checkweigh-men.[1] The Cotton Operatives have even adopted a system of competitive examination among the candidates for their staff appointments.[2] In other unions any candidate who has not proved his capacity for office work and trade negotiations would stand at a serious disadvantage in the election, where the choice is coming every day to be confined more clearly to the small class of minor officials. The paramount necessity of efficient administration has co-operated with this permanence in producing a progressive differentiation of an official governing class, more and more marked off by character, training, and duties from the bulk of the members. The annual election of the general secretary by a popular vote, far from leading to frequent rotation of office and equal service by all the members, has, in fact, invariably resulted in permanence of tenure exceeding even that of the English civil servant. It is accordingly interesting to notice that, in the later rules of some of the most influential of existing unions, the practical permanence of the official staff is tacitly recognised by the omission of all provision for re-election. Indeed, the

[1] *History of Trade Unionism*, p. 291.
[2] *Ibid.* p. 294 ; see also the subsequent chapter on " The Method of Collective Bargaining," where a specimen examination paper is reprinted.

Amalgamated Association of Operative Cotton-spinners goes so far as expressly to provide in its rules that the general secretary " shall continue in office so long as he gives satisfaction." [1]

While everything was thus tending to exalt the position of the salaried official, the executive committee, under whose direction he was placed, being composed of men working at their trade, retained its essential weakness. Though modified in unimportant particulars, it continued in nearly all the old societies to be chosen only by one geographical section of the members. At first each branch served in rotation as the seat of government. This quickly gave way to a system of selecting the governing branch from among the more important centres of the trade. Moreover, though the desire periodically to shift the seat of this authority long manifested itself and still lingers in some trades,[2] the growth of an official staff, and the necessity of securing accommodation on some durable tenancy, has practically made the headquarters stationary, even if the change has not been expressly recorded in the rules. Thus the Friendly Society of Ironfounders has retained its head office in London since 1846, and the Friendly Society of Operative Stonemasons since 1883. The United Society of Boilermakers, which long wandered from port to port, has remained in Newcastle since 1880 ; and finally settled the question in 1888 by building itself palatial offices on a freehold site.[3] Here again

---

[1] Rule 12 in the editions of Rules of 1891 and 1894.

[2] Notably the Plumbers and Irondressers. In 1877 a proposal at the general council of the Operative Bricklayers' Society to convert the executive into a shifting one, changing the headquarters every third year, was only defeated by a casting vote.—*Operative Bricklayers' Society Trade Circular*, September 1877.

[3] Along with this change has gone the differentiation of national business from that of the branch. The committee work of the larger societies became more than could be undertaken, in addition to the branch management, by men giving only their evenings. We find, therefore, the central executive committee becoming a body distinct from the branch committee, sometimes (as in the United Society of Operative Plumbers) elected by the same constituents, but more usually by the members of all the branches within a convenient radius of the central office. Thus the Amalgamated Society of Carpenters gives the election to the members within twelve miles of the head office—that is, to the thirty-five branches in and near Manchester—and the Friendly Society of Ironfounders to the six branches of the

the deeply-rooted desire on the part of Trade Union democrats to secure to each section an equal and identical share
in the government of the society has had to give way before
the necessity of obtaining efficient administration.   In ceasing to be movable the executive committee lost even such
moral influence over the general secretary as was conveyed
by an express and recent delegation by the remainder of the
society.   The salaried official, elected by the votes of all the
members, could in fact claim to possess more representative
authority than a committee whose functions as an executive
depended merely on the accident of the society's offices being
built in the town in which the members of the committee
happened to be working.   In some societies, moreover,
the idea of Rotation of Office so far survived that the
committee men were elected for a short term and disqualified
for re-election.   Such inexperienced and casually selected
committees of tired manual workers, meeting only in the
evening, usually found themselves incompetent to resist, or
even to criticise, any practical proposal that might be brought
forward by the permanent trained professional whom they
were supposed to direct and control.[1]

In face of so weak an executive committee the most
obvious check upon the predominant power of the salaried
officials was the elementary device of a written constitution.
The ordinary workman, without either experience or imagination, fondly thought that the executive government of a
great national organisation could be reduced to a mechanical
obedience to printed rules.   Hence the constant elaboration
of the rules of the several societies, in the vain endeavor to
leave nothing to the discretion of officers or committees.   It
was an essential part of the faith of these primitive democrats
that the difficult and detailed work of drafting and amending

London district.   In the United Society of Boilermakers, down to 1897, the
twenty lodges in the Tyne district, each in rotation, nominated one of the seven
members of which the executive committee is composed.
[1] The only organisation, outside the Trade Union world, in which the executive committee and the seat of government are changed annually, is, we believe,
the Ancient Order of Foresters, the worldwide federal friendly society.

these rules should not be delegated to any particular person or persons, but should be undertaken by "the body" or "the trade" in general meeting assembled.[1]

When a society spread from town to town, and a meeting of all the members became impracticable, the "articles" were settled, as we have mentioned, by a meeting of delegates, and any revision was undertaken by the same body. Accordingly, we find, in the early history of such societies as the Ironfounders, Stonemasons, Carpenters, Coachmakers, and Steam Engine Makers, frequent assemblies of delegates from the different branches, charged with supplementing or revising the somewhat tentative rules upon which the society had been based. But it would be a serious misconception to take these gatherings for "parliaments," with plenary power to determine the policy to be pursued by the society. The delegates came together only for specific and strictly limited purposes. Nor were even these purposes left to be dealt with at their discretion. In all cases that we know of the delegates were bound to decide according to the votes already taken in their respective branches. In many societies the delegate was merely the vehicle by which "the voices" of the members were mechanically conveyed. Thus the Friendly Society of Operative Stonemasons, at that time the largest and most powerful Trade

---

[1] This preference of Trade Unionists for making their own rules will remind the political student that "direct legislation by the people" has an older and wider history with regard to the framing and revising of constitutions than with regard to ordinary legislation. Thus, already in 1779 the citizens of Massachusetts insisted on asserting, by popular vote, that a constitution should be framed, and equally on deciding that the draft prepared should be adopted. In 1818 the Connecticut constitution included a provision that any particular amendment to it might be submitted to the popular vote. In Europe the first constitution to be submitted to the same ordeal was the French constitution of 1793, which, though adopted by the primary assemblies, never came into force. The practice became usual with regard to the Swiss cantonal constitutions after the French Revolution of 1830, St. Gall leading the way in July 1831. See the elaborate treatise of Charles Borgeaud on *The Adoption and Amendment of Constitutions* (London, 1895); Bryce's *The American Commonwealth* (London, 1891); and *Le Referendum en Suisse* by Simon Deploige (Brussels, 1892), of which an English translation by C. P. Trevelyan and Lilian Tomn, with additional notes and appendices, will shortly be published by the London School of Economics and Political Science.

Union, held annual delegate meetings between 1834 and 1839 for the sole purpose of revising its rules. How limited was the power of this assembly may be judged from the following extract from an address of the central executive : " As the delegates are about to meet, the Grand Committee submit to all lodges the following resolutions in reference to the conduct of delegates. It is evident that the duty of delegates is to vote according to the instructions of the majority of their constituents, therefore they ought not to propose any measure unless recommended by the Lodges or Districts they represent. To effect this we propose the following resolutions : that each Lodge shall furnish their delegates with written instructions how to vote on each question they have taken into their consideration, and that no delegate shall vote in opposition to his instructions, and when it appears by examining the instructions there is a majority for any measure, it shall be passed without discussion." [1] The delegate meeting of 1838 agreed with this view. All lodges were to send resolutions for alterations of rules two months before the delegate meeting ; they were to be printed in the *Fortnightly Return*, and discussed by each lodge ; the delegate was then to be instructed as to the sense of the members by a majority vote ; and only if there was no decided majority on any point was the delegate to have discretion as to his vote. But even this restriction did not satisfy the Stonemasons' idea of democracy. In 1837 the Liverpool Lodge demanded that " all the alterations made in our laws at the grand delegate meeting " shall be communicated to all the lodges " for the consideration of our society before they are printed." [2] The central executive mildly deprecated such a course, on the ground that the amendment and passing of the laws would under those circumstances take up the whole time of the society until the next delegate meeting came round. The request, however, was taken up by other

---

[1] *Stonemasons' Fortnightly Return*, May 1836 (the circular issued fortnightly to all the branches by the executive committee).

[2] *Ibid.* May 1837.

branches, and by 1844 we find the practice established of making any necessary amendment in the rules by merely submitting the proposal in the *Fortnightly Return*, and adding together the votes taken in each lodge meeting. A similar change took place in such other great societies as the Ironfounders, Steam-Engine Makers, and Coachmakers. The great bulk of the members saw no advantage in incurring the very considerable expense of paying the coach fares of delegates to a central town and maintaining them there at the rate of six shillings a day,[1] when the introduction of penny postage made possible the circulation of a fortnightly or monthly circular, through the medium of which their votes on any particular proposition could be quickly and inexpensively collected. The delegate meeting became, in fact, superseded by the Referendum.[2]

By the term Referendum the modern student of political institutions understands the submission to the votes of the whole people of any measure deliberated on by the representative assembly. Another development of the same principle is what is called the Initiative, that is to say, the right of a section of the community to insist on its proposals being submitted to the vote of the whole electorate. As a representative assembly formed no part of the earlier Trade Union constitutions, both the Referendum and the Initiative took with them the crudest shape. Any new rule or amendment of a rule, any proposed line of policy or particular application of it, might be straightway submitted to the votes of all the

---

[1] In 1838 a large majority of the lodges of the Friendly Society of Operative Stonemasons voted "that on all measures submitted to the consideration of our Society, the number of members be taken in every Lodge for and against such a measure, and transmitted through the district Lodges to the Seat of Government, and in place of the number of Lodges, the majority of the aggregate members to sanction or reject any measures."—*Fortnightly Return*, 19th January 1838.

[2] It is interesting to find that in at least one Trade Union the introduction of the Referendum is directly ascribed to the circulation in England between 1850 and 1860 of translations of pamphlets by Rittinghausen and Victor Considérant. It is stated in the *Typographical Circular* for March 1889, that John Melson, a Liverpool printer, got the idea of "Direct Legislation by the People" from these pamphlets, and urged its adoption on the union, at first unsuccessfully, but at the 1861 delegate meeting with the result that the Referendum was adopted as the future method of legislation.

members. Nor was this practice of consulting the members confined to the central executive. Any branch might equally have any proposition put to the vote through the medium of the society's official circular. And however imperfectly the question was framed, however inconsistent the result might be with the society's rules and past practice, the answer returned by the members' votes was final and instantly operative. Those who believe that pure democracy implies the direct decision, by the mass of the people, of every question as it arises, will find this ideal realised without check or limit in the history of the larger Trade Unions between 1834 and 1870.

The result was significant and full of political instruction. Whenever the union was enjoying a vigorous life we find, to begin with, a wild rush of propositions. Every active branch had some new rule to suggest, and every issue of the official circular was filled with crude and often inconsistent projects of amendment. The executive committee of the United Kingdom Society of Coachmakers, for instance, had to put no fewer than forty-four propositions simultaneously to the vote in a single circular.[1] It is difficult to convey any adequate idea of the variety and, in some cases, the absurdity of these propositions. To take only those recorded in the annals of the Stonemasons between 1838 and 1839 ; we have one branch proposing that the whole society should go in for payment by the hour, and another that the post of general secretary should be put up to tender, " the cheapest to be considered the person elected to that important office." [2] We have a delegate meeting referring to a vote of the members the momentous question whether the central executive should be allowed " a cup of ale each per night," and the central executive taking a vote as to whether all the Irish branches should not have Home Rule forced upon them. The members, under fear of the coming Parliamentary

---

[1] *Quarterly Report*, June 1860.

[2] The sale of public offices by auction to the highest bidder was a frequent incident in the Swiss " Landesgemeinden " of the seventeenth century. See Eugène Rambert's *Les Alpes Suisses : Études Historiques et Nationales*, p. 225.

inquiry, vote the abolition of all "regalia, initiation, and pass-words," but reject the proposition of the Newcastle Lodge for reducing the hours of labor "as the only method of striking at the root of all our grievances." The central executive is driven to protest against "the continual state of agitation in which the society has been kept for the last ten months by the numerous resolutions and amendments to laws, the tendency of which can only be to bring the laws and the society into disrespect."[1] As other unions come to the same stage in development, we find a similar result. "It appears evident," complains the executive committee of the Friendly Society of Ironfounders, "that we have got into a regular proposition mania. One branch will make propositions simply because another does; hence the absurd and ridiculous propositions that are made."[2] The system worked most disastrously in connection with the rates of contributions and benefits. It is not surprising that the majority of workmen should have been unable to appreciate the need for expert advice on these points, or that they should have disregarded all actuarial considerations. Accordingly, we find the members always reluctant to believe that the rate of contribution must be raised, and generally prone to listen to any proposal for extending the benefits—a popular bias which led many societies into bankruptcy. Still more disintegrating in its tendency was the disposition to appeal to the votes of the members against the executive decision that particular individuals were ineligible for certain benefits. In the United Kingdom Society of Coachmakers, for instance, we find the executive bitterly complaining that it is of no use for them to obey the rules, and rigidly to refuse accident benefit to men who are suffering simply from illness; as in almost every case the claimant's appeal to the members, backed by eloquent circulars from his friends, has resulted in the decision being overruled.[3] The Friendly Society of

---

[1] *Fortnightly Return*, July 1838.
[2] *Ironfounders' Monthly Report*, April 1855.
[3] *United Kingdom Society of Coachmakers' Quarterly Report*, September 1859.

Ironfounders took no fewer than nineteen votes in a single year, nearly all on details of benefit administration.[1] And the executive of the Stonemasons had early occasion to protest against the growing practice under which branches, preparatory to taking a vote, sent circulars throughout the society in support of their claims to the redress of what they deemed to be personal grievances.[2]

The disadvantages of a free resort to the Referendum soon became obvious to thoughtful Trade Unionists. It stands to the credit of the majority of the members that wild and absurd propositions were almost uniformly rejected ; and in many societies a similar fate became customary in case of any proposition that did not emanate from the responsible executive.[3] The practical abandonment of the Initiative ensued. Branches got tired of sending up proposals which uniformly met with defeat. But the right of the whole body of members themselves to decide every question as it arose was too much bound up with their idea of democracy to permit of its being directly abrogated, or even expressly criticised. Where the practice did not die out from sheer weariness, it was quietly got rid of in other ways. In one society after another the central executive and the general secretary—the men who were in actual contact with the problems of administration—silently threw their influence against the practice of appealing to the members' vote. Thus the executive committee of the United Kingdom Society of Coachmakers made a firm stand against the members' habit of overruling its decision in the grant of benefits under the rules. The executive claimed the sole right to decide who was eligible under the rules, and refused to allow discontented claimants to appeal through the official circular. This caused great and recurring discontent ; but the executive committee

---

[1] Report for 1869.

[2] *Fortnightly Return*, 18th January 1849.

[3] The political student will be reminded of the very small number of cases in which the Initiative in Switzerland has led to actual legislation, even in cantons, such as Zürich, where it has been in operation for over twenty years. See Stüssi, *Referendum und Initiative im Canton Zurich*.

held firmly to their position and eventually maintained it. When thirteen branches of the Operative Bricklayers' Society proposed in 1868 that the age for superannuation should be lowered and the office expenses curtailed, the general secretary bluntly refused to submit such inexpedient proposals to the members' vote, on the excuse that the question could be dealt with at the next delegate meeting.[1] The next step was to restrict the number of opportunities for appeals on any questions whatsoever. The Coachmakers' executive announced that, in future, propositions would be put to the vote only in the annual report, instead of quarterly as heretofore, and this restriction was a few years later embodied in the rules.[2] Even more effectual was the enactment of a rule throwing the expense of taking a vote upon the branch which had initiated it, in case the verdict of the society proved to be against the proposition.[3] Another device was to seize the occasion of a systematic revision of rules to declare that no proposition for their alteration was to be entertained for a specified period : one year, said the General Union of Carpenters in 1863 ; three years, declared the Bookbinders' Consolidated Union in 1869, and the Friendly Society of Operative Stonemasons in 1878 ; ten years, ordained the Operative Bricklayers' Society in 1889.[4] Finally, we have the Referendum abolished altogether, as regards the making or alteration of rules. In 1866 the delegate meeting of the Amalgamated Society of Carpenters decided that the executive should "not take the votes of the members concerning any alteration or addition to rules, unless in cases of great emergency, and then only on the authority of the General Council."[5] In 1878 the Stonemasons themselves, who forty years previously had been enthusiastic in their passion for voting on every question whatsoever, accepted a rule

---

[1] *Monthly Circular*, April 1868.
[2] *Quarterly Report*, November 1854 ; Rules of 1857.
[3] *Rules of the Associated Blacksmiths' Society* (Glasgow, 1892), and many others.
[4] *Monthly Report*, October 1889.
[5] *Monthly Circular*, April 1866.

which confined the work of revision to a specially elected committee.

Thus we see that half a century of practical experience of the Initiative and the Referendum has led, not to its extension, but to an ever stricter limitation of its application. The attempt to secure the participation of every member in the management of his society was found to lead to instability in legislation, dangerous unsoundness of finance, and general weakness of administration. The result was the early abandonment of the Initiative, either by express rule or through the persistent influence of the executive. This produced a further shifting of the balance of power in Trade Union constitutions. When the right of putting questions to the vote came practically to be confined to the executive, the Referendum ceased to provide the members with any effective control. If the executive could choose the issues to be submitted, the occasion on which the question should be put, and the form in which it should be couched, the Referendum, far from supplying any counterpoise to the executive, was soon found to be an immense addition to its power. Any change which the executive desired could be stated in the most plausible terms and supported by convincing arguments, which almost invariably secured its adoption by a large majority. Any executive resolution could, when occasion required, thus be given the powerful moral backing of a plebiscitary vote.[1] The reliance of Trade Union democrats on the Referendum resulted, in fact, in the virtual exclusion of the general body of members from all real share in the government. And

[1] Mr. Lecky points out (*Democracy and Liberty*, vol. i. pp. 12, 31, 32) how, in France, "successive Governments soon learned how easily a plebiscite vote could be secured and directed by a strong executive, and how useful it might become to screen or justify usurpation. The Constitution of 1795, which founded the power of the Directors ; the Constitution of 1799, which placed the executive power in the hands of three Consuls elected for ten years ; the Constitution of 1802, which made Buonaparte Consul for life, and again remodelled the electoral system ; the Empire, which was established in 1804, and the additional Act of the Constitution promulgated by Napoleon in 1815, were all submitted to a direct popular vote." The government of Napoleon III., from 1852 to 1870, was ratified by four separate plebiscites. See also Laferrière, *Constitutions de la France depuis 1789;* Jules Clère, *Histoire du Souffrage Universel.*

when we remember the practical subordination of the executive committee to its salaried permanent officer, we shall easily understand that the ultimate effect of such a Referendum as we have described was a further strengthening of the influence of the general secretary, who drafted the propositions, wrote the arguments in support of them, and edited the official circular which formed the only means of communication with the members.

We see, therefore, that almost every influence in the Trade Union organisation has tended to magnify and consolidate the power of the general secretary. If democracy could furnish no other expedient of popular control than the mass meeting, the annual election of public officers, the Initiative and the Referendum, Trade Union history makes it quite clear that the mere pressure of administrative needs would inevitably result in the general body of citizens losing all effective control over the government. It would not be difficult to point to influential Trade Unions at the present day which, possessing only a single permanent official, have not progressed beyond the stage of what is virtually a personal dictatorship. But it so happens that the very development of the union and its business which tends, as we have seen, to increase the influence of the general secretary, calls into existence a new check upon his personal authority. If we examine the constitution of a bank or joint stock company, or any other organisation not formed by the working class, we shall find it almost invariably the rule that the chief executive officers are appointed, not by the members at large, but by the governing committee, and that these officers are allowed a free hand, if not absolute power, in the choice and dismissal of their subordinates. Any other plan, it is contended, would seriously detract from the efficient working of the organisation. Had the Trade Unions adopted this course, the general secretary would have been absolutely supreme. But working-class organisations in England have, almost without exception, tenaciously clung to the direct election of all officers by the general body of members. Whether the post to be filled be that of assistant secretary at the head office or district delegate to act for one part of the country, the members have jealously retained the appointment in their own hands. In the larger trade societies of the present day the general secretary finds himself, therefore, at the head, not of a staff of docile subordinates who owe office and promotion to himself, but of a number of separately elected functionaries, each holding his appointment directly from the members at large.[1] Any attempt at a personal dictatorship is thus quickly checked. There is more danger that friction and personal jealousies may unduly weaken the administration. But the usual outcome is the close union of all the salaried officials to conduct the business of the society in the way they think best. Instead of a personal dictatorship, we have, therefore, a closely combined and practically irresistible bureaucracy.

Under a constitution of this type the Trade Union may attain a high degree of efficiency. The United Society of Boilermakers and Ironshipbuilders (established 1832 ; membership in December 1896, 40,776) is, for instance, admittedly one of the most powerful and best conducted of English trade societies. For the last twenty years its career, alike in good times and bad, has been one of continuous prosperity. For many years past it has dominated all the shipbuilding ports, and it now includes practically every ironshipbuilder in the United Kingdom. As an insurance company it has succeeded in paying, even in the worst years of an industry subject to the most acute depressions, benefits of an unusually elaborate and generous character. Notwithstanding these liberal benefits, it has built up a reserve fund of no less than £175,560. Nor has this prosperity been

---

[1] Even the office staff has been, until quite recently, invariably recruited by the members from the members ; and only in a few unions has it begun to be realised that a shorthand clerk or trained bookkeeper, chosen by the general secretary or the executive committee, can probably render better service at the desk than the most eligible workman trained to manual labor. The Operative Bricklayers' Society, however, lately allowed their executive committee to appoint a shorthand clerk.

attained by any neglect of the militant side of Trade Unionism. The society, on the contrary, has the reputation of exercising stricter control over the conditions of its members' work than any other union. In no trade, for instance, do we find a stricter and more universally enforced limitation of apprentices, or a more rigid refusal to work with non-unionists. And, as we have elsewhere described, no society has more successfully concluded and enforced elaborate national agreements applicable to every port in the kingdom. Moreover, this vigorous and successful trade policy has been consistent with a marked abstention from strikes—a fact due not only to the financial strength and perfect combination of the society, but also to the implicit obedience enforced upon its members, and the ample disciplinary power vested in and exercised by the central executive.[1]

The efficiency and influence of this remarkable union is, no doubt, largely due to the advantageous strategic position which has resulted from the extraordinary expansion of iron-shipbuilding. It is interesting, however, to notice what a perfect example it affords of a constitution retaining all the features of the crudest democracy, but becoming, in actual practice, a bureaucracy in which effective popular control has sunk to a minimum. The formal constitution of the Boiler-makers' Society still includes all the typical features of the early Trade Union. The executive government of this great national society is vested in a constantly changing committee, the members of which, elected by a single district, serve only for twelve months, and are then ineligible for re-election during three years. All the salaried officials are separately elected by the whole body of members, and hold their posts only for a prescribed term of two to five years. Though provision is made for a delegate meeting in case the society desires it, all the rules, including the rates of contribution and

[1] See the enthusiastic description of this organisation in *Zum Socialen Frieden* (Leipzig, 1890), 2 vols., by Dr. G. von Schulze-Gaevernitz, translated as *Social Peace* (London, 1893), pp. 239-243.

benefit, can be altered by aggregate vote ; and even if a delegate meeting assembles, its amendments have to be submitted to the votes of the branches in mass meeting. Any branch, moreover, may insist that any proposition whatsoever shall be submitted to this same aggregate vote. The society, in short, still retains the form of a Trade Union democracy of the crudest type.

But although the executive committee, the branch meeting and the Referendum occupy the main body of the society's rules, the whole policy has long been directed and the whole administration conducted exclusively by an informal cabinet of permanent officials which is unknown to the printed constitution. Twenty years ago the society had the good fortune to elect as general secretary, Mr. Robert Knight, a man of remarkable ability and strength of character, who has remained the permanent premier of this little kingdom. During his long reign, there has grown up around him a staff of younger officials, who, though severally elected on their individual merits, have been in no way able to compete with their chief for the members' allegiance. These district delegates are nominally elected only for a term of two years, just as the general secretary himself is elected only for a term of five years. But, for the reasons we have given elsewhere, all these officials enjoy a permanence of tenure practically equal to that of a judge. Mr. Knight's unquestioned superiority in Trade Union statesmanship, together with the invariable support of the executive committee, have enabled him to construct, out of the nominally independent district delegates, a virtual cabinet, alternately serving as councillors on high issues of policy and as ministers carrying out in their own spheres that which they have in council decided. From the written constitution of the society, we should suppose that it was from the evening meetings of the little Newcastle committee of working platers and rivetters that emanated all those national treaties and elaborate collective bargains with the associated employers that have excited the admiration of economic students. But its unrepresentative character, the short term of service of its members and the practical rotation of office make it impossible for the constantly shifting executive committee to exercise any effective influence over even the ordinary routine business of so large a society. The complicated negotiations involved in national agreements are absolutely beyond its grasp. What actually happens is that, in any high issue of policy, Mr. Knight summons his district delegates to meet him in council at London or Manchester, to concert, and even to conduct, with him the weighty negotiations which the Newcastle executive formally endorses. And although the actual administration of the benefits is conducted by the branch committees, the absolute centralisation of funds and the supreme disciplinary power vested in the executive committee make that committee, or rather the general secretary, as dominant in matters of finance as in trade policy. The only real opportunity for an effective expression of the popular will comes to be the submission of questions to the aggregate vote of the branches in mass meeting assembled. It is needless to point out that a Referendum of this kind, submitted through the official circular in whatsoever terms the general secretary may choose, and backed by the influence of the permanent staff in every district, comes to be only a way of impressing the official view on the whole body of members. In effect the general secretary and his informal cabinet were, until the change of 1895, absolutely supreme.[1]

In the case of the Boilermakers, government by an informal cabinet of salaried officials has, up to the present time, been highly successful. It is, however, obvious that a less competent statesman than Mr. Knight would find great difficulty in welding into a united cabinet a body of district

[1] In 1895, after this chapter was written, the constitution was changed, owing to the growing feeling of the members in London and some other towns, that their bureaucracy was, under the old forms, completely beyond their control. By the new rules the government is vested in a representative executive of seven salaried members, elected by the seven electoral districts into which the whole society is divided, for a term of three years, one-third retiring annually.—*Rules of the United Society of Boilermakers*, etc. (Newcastle, 1895). It is as yet too soon to comment on the effect of this change, which only came into operation in 1897.

officers separately responsible to the whole society, and
nominally subject only to their several district committees.
Under these circumstances any personal friction or disloyalty
might easily paralyse the whole trade policy, upon which the
prosperity of the society depends.   Moreover, though under
Mr. Knight's upright and able government the lack of any
supervising authority has not been felt, it cannot but be
regarded as a defect that the constitution provides no practical control over a corrupt, negligent, or incompetent general
secretary.   The only persons in the position to criticise
effectually the administration of the society are the salaried
officials themselves, who would naturally be indisposed to
risk their offices by appealing, against their official superior,
to the uncertain arbitrament of an aggregate vote.   Finally,
this constitution, with all its parade of democratic form,
secures in reality to the ordinary plater or rivetter little if
any active participation in the central administration of
his Trade Union ; no real opportunity is given to him for
expressing his opinion ; and no call is made upon his
intelligence for the formation of any opinion whatsoever.
In short, the Boilermakers, so long as they remained
content with this form of government, secured efficient
administration at the expense of losing all the educative
influences and political safeguards of democracy.

Among the well-organised Coalminers of the North of
England the theory of " direct legislation by the people "
is still in full force.   Thus, the 19,000 members of the
Northumberland Miners' Mutual Confident Association (established 1863) decide every question of policy, and even many
merely administrative details, by the votes taken in the several
lodge meetings ; [1] and although a delegate meeting is held
every quarter, and by a rule of 1894 is expressly declared to
" meet for the purpose of deliberating free and untrammelled
upon the whole of the programme," its function is strictly
limited to expressing its opinion, the entire list of propositions

---

[1] See, for instance, the twenty-five separate propositions voted on in a single
batch, 9th June 1894.—*Northumberland Miners' Minutes*, 1894, pp. 23-26.

being then "returned to the lodges to be voted on."[1] The executive committee is elected by the whole body; and the members, who retire after only six months' service, are ineligible for re-election. Finally, we have the fact that the salaried officials are themselves elected by the members at large. To this lack of organic connection between the different parts of the constitution, the student will perhaps attribute a certain instability of policy manifested in successive popular votes. In June 1894, a vote of all the members was taken on the question of joining the Miners' Federation, and an affirmative result was reached by 6730 to 5807. But in the very next month, when the lodges were asked whether they were prepared to give effect to the well-known policy of the Federation and claim the return of reductions in wages amounting to sixteen per cent, which they had accepted since 1892, they voted in the negative by more than two to one ; and backed this up by an equally decisive refusal to contribute towards the resistance of other districts. "They had joined a Federation knowing its principles and its policy, and immediately after joining they rejected the principles they had just embraced," was the comment of one of the members

---

[1] Rule 15. We see here a curious instance of the express separation of the deliberative from the legislative function, arising out of the inconvenient results of the use of the Imperative Mandate. The committee charged with the revision of the rules in 1893-1894 reported that "the present mode of transacting business at delegate meetings has long been felt to be very unsatisfactory. Suggestions are sent in for programme which are printed and remitted to the lodges, and delegates are then sent with hard and fast instructions to vote for or against as the case may be. It not unfrequently happens that delegates are sent to support a vote against suggestions which are found to have an entirely different meaning, and may have a very different effect from those expected by the lodges when voting for them. To avoid the mischief that has frequently resulted from our members thus committing themselves to suggestions upon insufficient information, we suggest that after the programmes have been sent to the lodges, lodges send their delegates to a meeting to deliberate on the business, after which they shall return and report the results of the discussion and then forward their votes by proxy to the office. To carry out this principle, which we consider is of the greatest possible interest and importance to our members, no more meetings will be required or expense incurred than under the present system, while on the other hand lodges will have the opportunity of casting their votes on the various suggestions with full information before them, instead of in the absence of this information in most cases, as at present."—Report of 3rd February 1894, in *Northumberland Miners' Minutes*, 1894, pp. 87-88.

of their own executive committee.[1]   This inconsistent action
led to much controversy, and the refusal of the Northumberland men to obey the decision of the special conference, the
supreme authority of the Federation, was declared to be
inconsistent with their remaining members of the organisation.
Nevertheless, in July 1894 they again voted, by 8445 to
5507, in favor of joining the Federation, despite the powerful adverse influence of their executive committee.   The
Federation officials not unnaturally asked whether the renewed application for membership might now be taken to
imply a willingness to conform to the policy of the organisation which it was wished to join.   On this a further vote was
taken by lodges, when the proposition to join was negatived
by a majority of over five to one.[2]

It may be objected that, in this instance of joining the
Miners' Federation, the question at issue was one of great
difficulty and of momentous import to the union, and that
some hesitation on the part of the members was only to be
expected.   We could, however, cite many similar instances
of contradictory votes by the Northumberland men, on both
matters of policy and points of internal administration.   We
suggest that their experience is only another proof that,
whatever advantages may be ascribed to government by the
Referendum, it has the capital drawback of not providing the
executive with any policy.   In the case of the Northumberland Miners' Union, the result has been a serious weakening
of its influence, and, on more than one occasion, the gravest

[1] Report of Conference, 23rd September 1893, in *Northumberland Miners'
Minutes*, 1893.

[2] It should be explained that the Referendum among the Northumberland
Miners takes two distinct forms, the " ballot," and the so-called " proxy voting."
Questions relating to strikes, and any others expressly ordered by the delegate
meeting, are decided by a ballot of the members individually.   The ordinary
business remitted from the delegate meeting to the lodges is discussed by the
general meeting of each lodge, and the lodge vote, or " proxy," is cast as a whole
according to the bare majority of those present.   The lodge vote counts from one
to thirty, in strict proportion to its membership.   It is interesting to note (though
we do not know whether any inference can be drawn from the fact) that the two
votes in favor of the Federation were taken by ballot of the members, whilst
those against it were taken by the " proxy " of the lodges.

danger of disintegration.[1] Fortunately, the union has enjoyed the services of executive officers of perfect integrity, and of exceptional ability and experience. These officers have throughout had their own clearly defined and consistent policy, which the uninformed and contradictory votes of the members have failed to control or modify.

It will not be necessary to give in detail the constitution of the Durham Miners' Association (established 1869), since this is, in essential features, similar to that of the Northumberland Miners.[2] But it is interesting to notice that the Durham experience of the result of government by the Referendum has been identical with that of Northumberland,[3] and even more detrimental to the organisation. The Durham Miners' Association, notwithstanding its closely concentrated 60,000 members, fails to exercise any important influence on the Trade Union world, and even excites complaints from the employers as to "its internal weakness." The Durham coal-owners declare that, with the council overruling the executive, and the ballot vote reversing the decision of the council, they never know when they have arrived at a settlement, or how long that settlement will be enforced on a recalcitrant lodge.

It is significant that the newer organisations which have sprung up in these same counties in direct imitation of the miners' unions give much less power to the members at large. Thus the Durham Cokemen's and Laborers' Association, which, springing out of the Durham Miners' Association in 1874, follows in its rules the actual phrases of the parent organisation, vests the election of its executive committee and officers, not in the members at large, but in a supreme "council."

[1] See, for instance, the report of the special conference of 23rd September 1893, expressly summoned to resist the "disintegration of our Association."— *Northumberland Miners' Minutes*, 1893.

[2] In the Durham Miners' Association the election of officers is nominally vested in the council, but express provision is made in the rules for each lodge to "empower" its delegate how to vote.

[3] This may be seen, for instance, from the incidental references to the Durham votes given in the Miners' Federation Minutes, 1893-1896 ; or, with calamitous results, in the history of the great Durham strike of 1892 ; or in that of the Silkstone strike of 1891. The Durham Miners' Minutes are not accessible to any non-member.

Much the same may be said of the Durham County Colliery Enginemen's Mutual Aid Association, established 1872 ; the Durham Colliery Mechanics' Association, established 1879 ; and (so far as regards the election of officers) the Northumberland Deputies' Mutual Aid Association, established 1887.

If, therefore, democracy means that everything which "concerns all should be decided by all," and that each citizen should enjoy an equal and identical share in the government, Trade Union history indicates clearly the inevitable result. Government by such contrivances as Rotation of Office, the Mass Meeting, the Referendum and Initiative, or the Delegate restricted by his Imperative Mandate, leads straight either to inefficiency and disintegration, or to the uncontrolled dominance of a personal dictator or an expert bureaucracy. Dimly and almost unconsciously this conclusion has, after a whole century of experiment, forced itself upon the more advanced trades. The old theory of democracy is still an article of faith, and constantly comes to the front when any organisation has to be formed for brand-new purposes ;[1] but Trade Union constitutions have undergone a silent revolution. The old ideal of the Rotation of Office among all the members in succession has been practically abandoned. Resort to the aggregate meeting diminishes steadily in frequency and importance. The use of the Initiative and the Referendum has

[1] We may refer, by way of illustration, to the frequent discussions during 1894-1895 among the members of the political association styled the "Independent Labor Party." On the formation of the Hackney Branch, for instance, the members "decided that no president and no executive committee of the branch be appointed, its management devolving on the members attending the weekly conferences" (*Labour Leader*, 26th January 1895). Nor is this view confined to the rank and file. The editor of the *Clarion* himself, perhaps the most influential man in the party, expressly declared in his leading article of 3rd November 1894 : "Democracy means that the people shall rule themselves ; that the people shall manage their own affairs ; and that their officials shall be public servants, or delegates, deputed to put the will of the people into execution. . . . At present there is too much sign of a disposition on the part of the rank and file to overvalue the talents and usefulness of their officials. . . . It is tolerably certain that in so far as the ordinary duties of officials and delegates, such as committee men or members of Parliament, are concerned, an average citizen, if he is thoroughly honest, will be found quite clever enough to do all that is needful. . . . Let all officials be retired after one year's services, and fresh ones elected in their place.'

been tacitly given up in all complicated issues, and gradually limited to a few special questions on particular emergencies. The delegate finds himself every year dealing with more numerous and more complex questions, and tends therefore inevitably to exercise the larger freedom of a representative. Finally, we have the appearance in the Trade Union world of the typically modern form of democracy, the elected representative assembly, appointing and controlling an executive committee under whose direction the permanent official staff performs its work.

CHAPTER II

REPRESENTATIVE INSTITUTIONS

THE two organisations in the Trade Union world enjoying the greatest measure of representative institutions are those which are the most distinctly modern in their growth and pre-eminence. In numbers, political influence, and annual income the great federal associations of Coalminers and Cotton Operatives overshadow all others, and now comprise one-fifth of the total Trade Union membership. We have elsewhere pointed out that these two trades are both distinguished by their establishment of an expert civil service, exceeding in numbers and efficiency that possessed by any other trade.[1] They resemble each other also, as we shall now see, in the success with which they have solved the fundamental problem of democracy, the combination of administrative efficiency and popular control. In each case the solution has been found in the frank acceptance of representative institutions.

In the Amalgamated Association of Operative Cotton-spinners, which may be taken as typical of cotton organisations, the "legislative power" is expressly vested " in a meeting comprising representatives from the various provinces and districts included in the association." [2]   This " Cotton-spinners' Parliament" is elected annually in strict proportion to

---

[1] *History of Trade Unionism*, p. 298 ; see also the subsequent chapter on " The Method of Collective Bargaining."

[2] *Rules of the Amalgamated Association of Operative Cotton-spinners* (Manchester, 1894), p. 4, Rule 7.

membership, and consists of about a hundred representatives. It meets in Manchester regularly every quarter, but can be called together by the executive council at any time. Once elected, this assembly is, like the British Parliament, absolutely supreme. Its powers and functions are subject to no express limitation, and from its decisions there is no appeal. The rules contain no provision for taking a vote of the members ; and though the agenda of the quarterly meeting is circulated for information to the executives of the district associations, so little thought is there of any necessity for the representatives to receive a mandate from their constituents, that express arrangements are made for transacting any other business not included in the agenda.[1]

The actual "government" of the association is conducted by an executive council elected by the general representative meeting, and consisting of a president, treasurer, and secretary, with thirteen other members, of whom seven at least must be working spinners, whilst the other six are, by invariable custom, the permanent officials appointed and maintained by the principal district organisations. Here we have the "cabinet" of this interesting constitution—the body which practically directs the whole work of the association and exercises great weight in the counsels of the legislative body, preparing its agenda and guiding all its proceedings. For the daily work of administration this cabinet is authorised by the rules to appoint a committee, the " sub-council," which consists in practice of the six "gentlemen," as the district officials are commonly called. The actual executive work is performed by a general secretary, who himself engages such office assistance as may from time to time be necessary. In marked contrast with all the Trade Union constitutions which we have hitherto described, the Cotton-spinners' rules do not

---

[1] Rule 9, p. 5. The general representative meeting even resembles the British Parliament in being able itself to change the fundamental basis of the constitution, including the period of its own tenure of office. The rules upon which the Amalgamated Association depends can be altered by the general representative meeting in a session called by special notice, without any confirmation by the constituents.—Rule 45, pp. 27-28.

give the election of this chief executive officer to the general body of members, but declare expressly that "the sole right of electing a permanent general secretary shall be vested in the provincial and district representatives when in meeting assembled, by whom his salary shall be fixed and determined."[1] Moreover, as we have already mentioned, the candidates for this office pass a competitive examination, and when once elected the general secretary enjoys a permanence of tenure equal to that of the English civil service, the rules providing that he "shall be appointed and continue in office so long as he gives satisfaction."[2]

The Amalgamated Association of Operative Cotton-spinners is therefore free from all the early expedients for securing popular government. The general or aggregate meeting finds no place in its constitution, and the rules contain no provision for the Referendum or the Initiative. No countenance is given to the idea of Rotation of Office. No officers are elected by the members themselves. Finally, we have the complete abandonment of the delegate, and the substitution, both in fact and in name, of the representative. On the other hand, the association is a fully-equipped democratic state of the modern type. It has an elected parliament, exercising supreme and uncontrolled power. It has a cabinet appointed by and responsible only to that parliament. And its chief executive officer, appointed once for all on grounds of efficiency, enjoys the civil-service permanence of tenure.[3]

---

[1] Rule 12, p. 6. [2] *Ibid.*

[3] The other branches of the cotton trade, notably the federations of weavers and cardroom hands, are organised on the same principle of an elected representative assembly, itself appointing the officers and executive committee, though there are minor differences among them. The United Textile Factory Workers' Association, of which the spinners form a part, is framed on the same model, a "legislative council," really an executive committee, being elected by the "conference," or representative assembly. (This organisation temporarily suspended its functions in 1896.) Moreover, the rules of the several district associations of the Amalgamated Association of Operative Cotton-spinners exhibit the same formative influences. In the smaller societies, confined to single villages, we find the simple government by general meeting, electing a committee and officers. Permanence of tenure is, however, the rule, it being often expressly provided that the secretary and the treasurer shall each "retain office as long as he gives satisfaction." More than half the total membership, moreover, is

We have watched the working of this remarkable constitution during the last seven years, and we can testify to the success with which both efficiency and popular control are secured. The efficiency we attribute to the existence of the adequate, highly-trained, and relatively well-paid and permanent civil service.[1] But that this civil service is effectively under public control is shown by the accuracy with which the cotton officials adapt their political and industrial policy to the developing views of the members whom they serve. This sensitiveness to the popular desires is secured by the real supremacy of the elected representatives. For the " Cotton-spinners' Parliament " is no formal gathering of casual members to register the decrees of a dominant bureaucracy. It is, on the contrary, a highly-organised deliberative assembly, with active representatives from the different localities, each alive to the distinct, and sometimes divergent, interests of his own constituents. Their eager participation shows itself in constant " party meetings " of the different sections, at which the officers and workmen from each district consult together as to the line of policy to be pressed upon the assembly. Such consultation and deliberate joint action is, in the case of the Oldham representatives at any rate, carried even further. The constitution of the Oldham Operative Cotton-spinners' Provincial Association is, so far as we know, unique in all the annals of democracy in making express provision for the " caucus." [2]

included in two important " provinces," Oldham and Bolton, which possess elaborate federal constitutions of their own. These follow, in general outline, the federal constitution, but both retain some features of the older form. Thus in Oldham, where the officers enjoy permanence of tenure and are responsible only to the representative assembly, any vacancy is filled by general vote of the members. And though the representative assembly has supreme legislative and executive powers, it is required to take a ballot of all the members before deciding on a strike. On the other hand, Bolton, which leaves everything to its representative assembly, shows a lingering attachment to rotation of office by providing that the retiring members of its executive council shall not be eligible for re-election during twelve months.

[1] The nineteen thousand members of the Amalgamated Association of Operative Cotton-spinners command the services of ten permanent officials, besides numerous local officers still working at their trade.

[2] The " caucus," in this sense of the term, is supposed to have been first

The rules of 1891 ordain that "whenever the business to be transacted by the representatives attending the quarterly or special meetings of the Amalgamation is of such importance and to the interest of this association as to require unity of action in regard to voting by the representatives from this province, the secretary shall be required to summon a special meeting of the said representatives by announcing in the monthly circular containing the minutes the date and time of such meeting, which must be held in the council room at least seven days previous to the Amalgamation meeting taking place. The provincial representatives on the amalgamated council shall be required to attend such meeting, to give any information required, and all resolutions passed by a majority of those present shall be binding upon all the representatives from the Oldham province attending the amalgamated quarterly or special meetings, and any one acting contrary to his instructions shall cease to be a representative of the district he represents, and shall not be allowed to stand as a candidate for any office connected with the association for the space of twelve months. The allowance for attending these special meetings shall be in accordance with the scale allowed to the provincial executive council." [1] But even without so stringent a rule, there would be but little danger of the representatives failing to express the desires of the rank and file. Living the same life as their constituents, and subject to annual election, they can scarcely fail to be in touch with the general body of the members. The common practice of requiring each representative to report his action to the next meeting of his constituents, by whom it is discussed in his presence, and the wide circulation

introduced about the beginning of this century, in the United States Congress, by the Democratic Party. See the *Statesman's Manual*, vol. i. pp. 294, 338; Woodrow Wilson, *Congressional Government*, 12th edit. (New York, 1896), pp. 327-330; Lalor's *Cyclopedia of Political Science* (New York, 1891), vol. i. p. 357. The "caucus" in the sense of "primary assembly" is regulated by law in many American States, especially in Massachusetts. See *Nominations for Elective Office in the United States*, by F. W. Dallinger (London, 1897).

[1] Rule 64, pp. 41-42, of *Rules and Regulations for the Government of the Oldham Operative Cotton-spinners' Provincial Association* (Oldham, 1891).

of printed reports among all the members furnish efficient substitutes for the newspaper press. On the other hand, the facts that the representative assembly is a permanent institution wielding supreme power, and that in practice its membership changes little from year to year, give it a very real authority over the executive council which it elects every six months, and over the officers whom it has appointed. The typical member of the "Cotton-spinners' Parliament" is not only experienced in voicing the desires of his constituents, but also possesses in a comparatively large measure that knowledge of administrative detail and of current affairs which enables him to understand and control the proceedings of his officers.

The Coalminers are, as we have elsewhere mentioned, not so unanimous as the Cotton Operatives in their adoption of representative institutions. The two great counties of Northumberland and Durham have unions which preserve constitutions of the old-fashioned type. But when we pass to other counties, in which the Miners have come more thoroughly under the influence of the modern spirit, we find representative government the rule. The powerful associations of Yorkshire, Lancashire, and the Midlands are all governed by elected representative assemblies, which appoint the executive committees and the permanent officers. But the most striking example of the adoption of representative institutions among the Coalminers is presented by the Miners' Federation of Great Britain, established 1887. This great federal organisation, which now comprises two-thirds of the Coalminers in union, adopted from the outset a completely representative constitution. The supreme authority is vested in a "conference," summoned as often as required, consisting of representatives elected by each county or district association. This conference exercises uncontrolled power to determine policy, alter rules, and levy unlimited contributions.[1] From its decision there is no

[1] This was expressly pointed out, doubtless with reference to some of the old-fashioned county unions which still clung to the custom of the Referendum or the

appeal. No provision is made for taking the votes of the general body of members, and the conference itself appoints the executive committee and all the officers of the Federation. Between the sittings of the conference the executive committee is expressly given power to take action to promote the interests of the Federation, and no rule savoring of Rotation of Office deprives this executive of the services of its experienced members.

The "Miners' Parliament," as this conference may not improperly be termed, is in many respects the most important assembly in the Trade Union world. Its regular annual session, held in some midland town, lasts often for a whole week, whilst other meetings of a couple of days' duration are held as business requires. The fifty to seventy members, who represent the several constituent bodies, constitute an exceptionally efficient deliberative assembly. Among them are to be found the permanent officers of the county unions, some of the most experienced of the checkweigh-men and the influential leaders of opinion in the mining villages. The official element, as might be expected, plays a prominent part in suggesting, drafting, and amending the actual proposals, but the unofficial members frequently intervene with effect in the business-like debates. The public and the press are excluded, but the conference usually directs a brief and guarded statement of the conclusions arrived at to be supplied to the newspapers, and a full report of the proceedings— sometimes extending to over a hundred printed pages—is subsequently issued to the lodges. The subjects dealt with include the whole range of industrial and political policy, from the technical grievance of a particular district up to the " nationalisation of mines."[1] The actual carrying out of the

Imperative Mandate, in the circular summoning the important conference of July 1893 : "Delegates must be appointed to attend Conference *with full power to deal with the wages question.*"

[1] Thus the agenda for the Annual Conference in 1894 comprised, besides formal business, certain revisions of rules and the executive committee's report, the Eight Hours Bill, the stacking of coal, the making of Saturday a regular whole holiday, the establishment of a public department to prevent unscrupulous competition in trade, the amendment of the Mines Regulation and Employers'

policy determined on by the conference is left unreservedly
to the executive committee, but the conference expects to be
called together whenever any new departure in policy is
required.   In times of stress the executive committee shows
its real dependence on the popular assembly by calling it
together every few weeks.[1]   And the success with which the
Miners' Federation wields its great industrial and political
power over an area extending from Fife to Somerset and a

Liability Acts, international relations with foreign miners' organisations and the
nationalisation of mines.   It may here be observed that the representatives at
the Federal Conference have votes in proportion to the numbers of the members
in their respective associations.   This practice, often called "proxy voting," or,
more accurately, "the accumulative vote," has long been characteristic of the
Coalminers' organisations, though unknown to any other section of the Trade
Union World.   Thus the rules of the Miners' Federation of Great Britain are
silent as to the number of representatives to be sent to the supreme "Conference,"
but provide "that each county, federation or district vote upon all questions
as follows, viz. : one vote for every 1000 financial members or fractional part of
1000, and that the vote in every case shall be taken by numbers" (Rule 10,
Rules of the Miners' Federation of Great Britain, 1895).   A similar
principle has always been applied at the International Miners' Conferences,
and the practice prevails also in the several county unions or federations.   The
Lancashire and Cheshire Federation fixes the number of representatives to be
sent to its Conferences at one per 500 members, but expressly provides that the
voting is to be "by proxy" in the same proportion.   The Midland Federation
adopts the same rule.   The Yorkshire, Nottinghamshire, Durham, and West
Cumberland associations allow each branch or lodge only a single representative,
whose vote counts strictly in proportion to the membership he represents.   This
"accumulative vote" is invariably resorted to in the election of officers and in all
important decisions of policy, but it is not uncommon for minor divisions to be
taken, unchallenged, on the principle of "one man one vote."   It is not easy to
account for the exceptional preference of the Coalminers for this method of voting,
especially as their assemblies are, as we have pointed out, in practice more
"representative" in their character, and less trammelled by the idea of the
imperative mandate, than those of any other trade but the Cotton Operatives.
The practice facilitates, it is true, a diminution in the size of the meetings, but
this appears to be its only advantage.   In the absence of any system of "proportional representation" it affords no real guide to the relative distribution of
opinion ; the representatives of Yorkshire, for instance, in casting the vote of the
county, can at best express the views only of the majority of their constituents,
and have therefore no real claim to outvote a smaller district, with whose views
nearly half their own constituents may be in sympathy.   If, on the other hand,
the whole membership of the Miners' Federation were divided into fairly equal
electoral districts, each electing a single member, there would be more chance
of every variety of opinion being represented, whilst an exact balance between
the large and the small districts would nevertheless be preserved.

[1] During the great strike in 1893 the Conference met eight times in six
months.

membership numbering two hundred thousand, furnishes eloquent testimony to the manner in which it has known how to combine efficient administration with genuine popular assent.

The great federal organisations of Cotton Operatives and Coalminers stand out from among the other Trade Unions in respect of the completeness and success with which they have adopted representative institutions. But it is easy to trace a like tendency throughout the whole Trade Union world. We have already commented on the innovation, now almost universal, of entrusting the task of revising rules to a specially elected committee. It was at first taken for granted that the work of such a revising committee was limited to putting into proper form the amendments proposed by the branches themselves, and sometimes to choosing between them. Though it is still usual for the revised rules to be formally ratified by a vote of the members, the revising committees have been given an ever wider discretion, until in most unions they are nowadays in practice free to make changes according to their own judgment.[1] But it is in the constitution of the central executive that the trend towards representative institutions is most remarkable, the old expedient of the "governing branch" being superseded by an executive committee representative of the whole body of the members.[2]

[1] There is a similar tendency to disapprove of the Imperative Mandate in the principal Friendly Societies. The *Friendly Societies' Monthly Magazine* for April 1890 observes that "Lodges are advised . . . to instruct their delegates as to how they are to vote. With this we entirely disagree. A proposition till it is properly thrashed out and explained, remains in the husk, and its full import is lost. Delegates fettered with instructions simply become the mechanical mouthpiece of the necessarily unenlightened lodges which send them, and therefore the legislation of the Order might just as well be conducted by post."

[2] Thus the Amalgamated Society of Railway Servants (established 1872) administers the affairs of its forty-four thousand members by an executive committee of thirteen (with the three officers), elected annually by ballot in thirteen equal electoral districts. This committee meets in London at least quarterly, and can be summoned oftener if required. Above this is the supreme authority of the annual assembly of sixty delegates, elected by sixty equal electoral districts, and sitting for four days to hear appeals, alter rules, and determine the policy of the union. A similar constitution is enjoyed by the Associated Society of

This revolution has taken place in the National Union of Boot and Shoe Operatives (37,000 members) and the Amalgamated Society of Engineers (87,313 members), the two societies which, outside the worlds of cotton and coal, exceed nearly all others in membership. Down to 1890 the National Union of Boot and Shoe Operatives was governed by a local executive council belonging to a single town, controlled only by occasional votes of a delegate assembly, meeting, at first, every four years, and afterwards every two years. Seven years ago the constitution was entirely transformed. The society was divided into five equal electoral districts, each of which elected one member to serve for two years on an executive council consisting of only these five representatives, in addition to the three other officers elected by the whole body of members. To the representative executive thus formed was committed not only all the ordinary business of the society, but also the final decision in cases of appeals by individual members against the decision of a branch. The delegate meeting, or "National Conference," meets to determine policy and revise rules, and its decisions no longer require ratification by the members' vote. Although the Referendum and the Mass Meeting of the district are still formally included in the constitution, the complication and difficulty of the issues which have cropped up during the last few years have led the executive council to call together the national conference at frequent intervals, in preference to submitting questions to the popular vote.

Locomotive Enginemen and Firemen (established 1880). It is this model that has been followed, with unimportant variations in detail, by the more durable of the labor unions which sprang into existence in the great upheaval of 1889, among which the Gasworkers and the Dockers are the best known. The practice of electing the executive committee *by districts* is, as far as we know, almost unknown in the political world. The executive council of the State of Pennsylvania in the eighteenth century used to be elected by single-member districts (*Federalist*, No. LVII.), and a similar arrangement appears occasionally to have found a place in the ever-changing constitutions of one or two Swiss Cantons. (See *State and Federal Government in Switzerland*, by J. M. Vincent, Baltimore, 1891.) We know of no case where it prevails at present (Lowell's *Governments and Parties in Continental Europe*, London, 1896).

In the case of the Amalgamated Society of Engineers the constitutional revolution has been far more sweeping. In the various editions of the Engineers' rules from 1851 to 1891 we find the usual reliance on the Mass Meeting, the Referendum and the direct election of all officers by the members at large. We also see the executive control vested in a committee elected by a single district,—the chairman, moreover, being forbidden to serve for more than two years in succession. In the case of the United Society of Boiler-makers we have already described how a constitution of essentially similar type has resulted in remarkable success and efficiency, but at the sacrifice of all real control by the members. In the history of the Boilermakers from 1872 onwards we watch the virtual abandonment in practice, for the sake of a strong and united central administration, of everything that tended to weaken the executive power. The Engineers, on the contrary, clung tenaciously to every institution or formality which protected the individual member against the central executive.[1] Meanwhile, although the very object of the amalgamation in 1851 was to secure uniformity of trade policy, the failure to provide any salaried official staff left the central executive with little practical control over the negotiations conducted or the decisions arrived at by the local branch or district committee. The result was not only failure to cope with the vital problems

[1] In financial matters, for instance, though every penny of the funds belonged to the whole society, each branch retained its own receipts, subject only to the cumbrous annual "equalisation." The branch accordingly had it in its power to make any disbursement it chose, subject only to subsequent disallowance by the central executive. Nor was the decision of the central executive in any way final. The branch aggrieved by any disallowance could, and habitually did, appeal—not to the members at large, who would usually have supported the executive—but to another body, the general council, which met every three years for the express purpose of deciding such appeals. There was even a further appeal from the general council to the periodical delegate meeting. In the meantime the payment objected to was not required to be refunded, and it will therefore easily be understood that the vast majority of executive decisions were instantly appealed against. And when we add that each of these several courts of appeal frequently reversed a large proportion of the decisions of its immediate inferior, the effect of these frequent appeals in destroying all authority can easily be imagined.

of trade policy involved in the changing conditions of the industry, but also an increasing paralysis of administration, against which officers and committee-men struggled in vain. When in 1892 the delegates met at Leeds to find a remedy for these evils, they brought from the branches two leading suggestions. One party urged the appointment, in aid of the central executive, of a salaried staff of district delegates, elected, in direct imitation of those of the Boilermakers, by the whole society. Another section favored the transformation of the executive committee into a representative body, and proposed the division of the country into eight equal electoral districts, each of which should elect a representative to a salaried executive council sitting continually in London, and thus giving its whole time to the society's work. Probably these remedies, aimed at different sides of the trouble, were intended as alternatives. It is significant of the deep impression made upon the delegate meeting that it eventually adopted both, thus at one blow increasing the number of salaried officers from three to seventeen.[1]

Time has yet to show how far this revolution in the constitution of the Amalgamated Society of Engineers will conduce either to efficient administration or to genuine popular control. It is easy to see that government by an executive committee of this character differs essentially from government by a representative assembly appointing its own cabinet, and that it possesses certain obvious disadvantages. The eight members, who are thus transferred by the vote of their fellows from the engineer's workshop to the Stamford Street office, become by this fundamental change of life completely severed from their constituents. Spending all their days in office routine, they necessarily lose the vivid appreciation of the feelings of the man

[1] It is interesting to observe that the United Society of Boilermakers, by adopting in 1895 a Representative Executive, has made its formal constitution almost identical with that of the Amalgamated Society of Engineers. The vital difference between these two societies now lies in the working relation between the central executive and the local branches and district committees ; see the subsequent chapter on " The Unit of Government."

who works at the lathe or the forge. Living constantly in London, they are subject to new local influences, and tend unconsciously to get out of touch with the special grievances or new drifts of popular opinion on the Tyne or the Clyde, at Belfast or in Lancashire. It is true that the representatives hold office for only three years, at the expiration of which they must present themselves for re-election; but there would be the greatest possible reluctance amongst the members to relegate to manual labor a man who had once served them as a salaried official. Unless, therefore, a revulsion of feeling takes place among the Engineers against the institution itself, the present members of the representative executive committee may rely with some confidence on becoming practically permanent officials.

These objections do not apply with equal force to other examples of a representative executive. The tradition of the Stamford Street office—that the whole mass of friendly-society business should be dealt with in all its details by the members of the executive committee themselves—involves their daily attendance and their complete absorption in office work. In other Trade Unions which have adopted the same constitutional form, the members of the representative executive reside in their constituencies and, in some cases, even continue to work at their trade. They are called together, like the members of a representative assembly, at quarterly or other intervals to decide only the more important questions, the detailed executive routine being delegated to a local sub-committee or to the official staff. Thus the executive committee of the National Union of Boot and Shoe Operatives usually meets only for one day a month; the executive committee of the Associated Locomotive Engineers and Firemen is called together only when required, usually not more than once or twice a month; the executive council of the Amalgamated Society of Railway Servants comes to London once a quarter, and the same practice is followed by the executive committee of the National Union of Gasworkers and General Laborers. It is evident that in all these cases the representative executive, whether formed of the salaried officials of the districts or of men working at their trade, has more chance of remaining in touch with its constituents than in the case of the Amalgamated Society of Engineers.

But there is, in our opinion, a fundamental drawback to government by a representative executive, even under the most favorable conditions. One of the chief duties of a representative governing body is to criticise, control, and direct the permanent official staff, by whom the policy of the organisation must actually be carried out. Its main function, in fact, is to exercise real and continuous authority over the civil service. Now all experience shows it to be an essential condition that the permanent officials should be dependent on and genuinely subordinate to the representative body. This condition is fulfilled in the constitutions such as those of the Amalgamated Association of Operative Cotton-spinners and the Miners' Federation, where the representative assembly itself appoints the officers, determines their duties, and fixes their salaries. But it is entirely absent in all Trade Union constitutions based on a representative executive. Under this arrangement the executive committee neither appoints the officers nor fixes their salaries. Though the representative executive, unlike the old governing branch, can in its corporate capacity claim to speak in the name of all the members, so can the general secretary himself, and often each assistant secretary. All alike hold their positions from the same supreme power—the votes of the members ; and have their respective duties and emoluments defined by the same written constitution—the society's rules.

This absence of any co-ordination of the several parts of the constitution works out, in practice, in one of two ways. There may arise jealousies between the several officers, or between them and some of the members of the executive committee. We have known instances in which an incompetent and arbitrary general secretary has been pulled up by one or other of his colleagues who wanted to succeed to his place. The suspicion engendered by the relation of competitors for popular suffrage checks, it may be, some positive malpractices, but results also in the obstruction of useful measures of policy, or even in their failure through disloyalty. More usually the executive committee, feeling itself powerless to control the officials, tends to make a tacit and half-unconscious compact with them, based on mutual support against the criticism of their common constituents. If the members of the committee are themselves salaried officials, they not only have a fellow-feeling for the weaknesses of their brother officials, but they also realise vividly the personal risk of appealing against them to the popular vote. If, on the other hand, the members continue to work at their trade, they feel themselves at a hopeless disadvantage in any such appeal. They have neither the business experience nor the acquaintance with details necessary for a successful indictment of an officer who is known from one end of the society to the other, and who enjoys the advantage of controlling its machinery. Thus we have in many unions governed by a Representative Executive the formation of a ruling clique, half officials, half representatives. This has all the disadvantages of such a bureaucracy as we have described in the case of the United Society of Boilermakers, without the efficiency made possible by its hierarchical organisation and the predominant authority of the head of the staff. To sum up, if there are among the salaried representatives or officials restless spirits, " conscientious critics," or disloyal comrades, the general body of members may rest assured that they will be kept informed of what is going on, but at the cost of seeing their machinery of government constantly clogged by angry recriminations and appeals. If, on the other hand, the men who meet at headquarters in one or another capacity are " good fellows," the machine will work smoothly with such efficiency as their industry and capacity happens to be equal to, but all popular control over this governing clique will disappear.

We see, then, that though government by a representative executive is a real advance on the old expedients, it is likely to prove inferior to government by a representative assembly, appointing its own cabinet and officers. But a great national Trade Union extending from one end of the kingdom to the other cannot easily adopt the superior form, even if the members desire it. The Cotton Operatives enjoy the special advantage of having practically all their membership within a radius of thirty miles from Manchester. The frequent gatherings of a hundred delegates held usually on a Saturday afternoon entail, therefore, no loss of working time and little expense to the organisation. The same consideration applies to the great bulk of the membership of the Miners' Federation, three-fourths of which is concentrated in Lancashire, West Yorkshire, and the industrial Midlands. Even the outlying coalfields elsewhere enjoy the advantage of close local concentration, so that a single delegate may effectively represent the hundreds of lodges in his own county. And it is no small consideration that the total membership of the Miners' Federation is so large that the cost of frequent meetings of fifty to seventy delegates bears only a trifling proportion to the resources of the union. Very different is the position of the great unions in the engineering and building trades. The 46,000 members of the Amalgamated Society of Carpenters in the United Kingdom. for instance, are divided into 623 branches, scattered over 400 separate towns or villages. Each town has its own Working Rules, its own Standard Rate and Normal Day, and lacks intimate connection with the towns right and left of it. The representative chosen by the Newcastle branch might easily be too much absorbed by the burning local question of demarcation against the Shipwrights to pay much attention to the simple grievances of the Hexham branch as to the Saturday half-holiday, or to the multiplication of apprentices in the joinery shops at Darlington. Similar considerations apply to the 497 branches of the Amalgamated Society of Engineers, whose 80,000 members in the United Kingdom are working in 300 different towns. In view of the increasing uniformity of working conditions throughout the country, the concentration of industry in large towns, the growing facilities of travel and the steady multiplication of salaried local officials, we do not ourselves regard the geographical difficulty as insuperable. But it is easy to understand why, with so large a number of isolated branches, it has not yet seemed practicable to constitutional reformers in the building or the engineering trades, to have frequent meetings of representative assemblies.

The tardiness and incompleteness with which Trade Unions have adopted representative institutions is mainly due to a more general cause. The workman has been slow to recognise the special function of the representative in a democracy. In the early constitutional ideals of Trade Unionism the representative finds, as we have seen, absolutely no place. The committee-man elected by rotation of office or the delegate deputed to take part in a revision of rules was habitually regarded only as a vehicle by which "the voices" could be mechanically conveyed. His task required, therefore, no special qualification beyond intelligence to comprehend his instructions and a spirit of obedience in carrying them out. Very different is the duty cast upon the representative in such modern Trade Union constitutions as those of the Cotton Operatives and Coalminers. His main function is still to express the mind of the average man. But unlike the delegate, he is not a mechanical vehicle of votes on particular subjects. The ordinary Trade Unionist has but little facility in expressing his desires ; unversed in the technicalities of administration, he is unable to judge by what particular expedient his grievances can best be remedied. In default of an expert representative he has to depend on the professional administrator. But for this particular task the professional administrator is no more competent than the ordinary man, though for a different reason. The very apartness of his life from that of the average workman deprives him of close acquaintance with the actual grievances of the mass of the people. Immersed in office routine, he is apt to fail to understand from their inconsistent complaints and impracticable suggestions what it is they really desire. To act as an interpreter between the people and their servants is, therefore, the first function of the representative.

But this is only half of his duty. To him is entrusted also the difficult and delicate task of controlling the professional experts. Here, as we have seen, the ordinary man completely breaks down. The task, to begin with, requires a certain familiarity with the machinery of government, and a sacrifice of time and a concentration of thought out of the reach of the average man absorbed in gaining his daily bread. So much is this the case that when the administration is complicated, a further specialisation is found necessary, and the representative assembly itself chooses a cabinet, or executive committee of men specially qualified for this duty. A large measure of intuitive capacity to make a wise choice of men is, therefore, necessary even in the ordinary representative. Finally, there comes the important duty of deciding upon questions of policy or tactics. The ordinary citizen thinks of nothing but clear issues on broad lines. The representative, on the other hand, finds himself constantly called upon to choose between the nicely balanced expediencies of compromise necessitated by the complicated facts of practical life. On his shrewd judgment of actual circumstances will depend his success in obtaining, not all that his constituents desire—for that he will quickly recognise as Utopian,—but the largest instalment of those desires that may be then and there possible.

To construct a perfect representative assembly can, therefore, never be an easy task ; and in a community exclusively composed of manual workers dependent on weekly wages, the task is one of exceptional difficulty. A community of bankers and business entrepreneurs finds it easy to secure a representative committee to direct and control the paid officials whom it engages to protect its interests. Constituents, representatives and officials are

living much the same life, are surrounded by the same
intellectual atmosphere, have received approximately the
same kind of education and mental training, and are constantly engaged in one variety or another of what is
essentially the same work of direction and control.   Moreover, there is no lack of persons able to give the necessary
time and thought to expressing the desires of their class and
to seeing that they are satisfied.   It is, therefore, not
surprising that representative institutions should be seen
at their best in middle-class communities.[1]   In all these
respects the manual workers stand at a grave disadvantage.
Whatever may be the natural endowment of the workman
selected by his comrades to serve as a representative, he
starts unequipped with that special training and that general
familiarity with administration which will alone enable him
to be a competent critic and director of the expert professional.   Before he can place himself on a level with the
trained official whom he has to control he must devote his
whole time and thought to his new duties, and must therefore give up his old trade.   This unfortunately tends to
alter his manner of life, his habit of mind, and usually also
his intellectual atmosphere to such an extent that he
gradually loses that vivid appreciation of the feelings of the
man at the bench or the forge, which it is his function to
express.   There is a certain cruel irony in the problem
which accounts, we think, for some of the unconscious
exasperation of the wage-earners all over the world against
representative institutions.   Directly the working-man
representative becomes properly equipped for one-half of
his duties, he ceases to be specially qualified for the other.
If he remains essentially a manual worker, he fails to cope
with the brain-working officials ; if he takes on the character
of the brain-worker, he is apt to get out of touch with
the constituents whose desires he has to interpret.   It will,
therefore, be interesting to see how the shrewd workmen of

---

[1] In this connection see the interesting suggestions of Achille Loria, *Les Bases
Economiques de la Constitution Sociale* (Paris, 1893), pp. 150-154.

Lancashire, Yorkshire, and the Midlands have surmounted this constitutional difficulty.

In the parliaments of the Cotton-spinners and Coalminers we find habitually two classes of members, salaried officials of the several districts, and representative wage-earners still working at the mule or in the mine. It would almost seem as if these modern organisations had consciously recognised the impossibility of combining in any individual representative both of the requirements that we have specified. As it is, the presence in their assemblies of a large proportion of men who are still following their trade imports into their deliberations the full flavor of working-class sentiment. And the association, with these picked men from each industrial village, of the salaried officers from each county, secures that combination of knowledge, ability, and practical experience in administration, which is, as we have suggested, absolutely indispensable for the exercise of control over the professional experts. If the constituencies elected none but their fellow-workers, it is more than doubtful whether the representative assembly so created would be competent for its task. If, on the other hand, the assembly consisted merely of a conference of salaried officials, appointing one or more of themselves to carry out the national work of the federation, it would inevitably fail to retain the confidence, even if it continued to express the desires of the members at large. The conjunction of the two elements in the same representative assembly has in practice resulted in a very efficient working body.

It is important to notice that in each of the trades the success of the experiment has depended on the fact that the organisation is formed on a federal basis. The constituent bodies of the Miners' Federation and the Amalgamated Association of Operative Cotton - spinners have their separate constitutions, their distinct funds, and their own official staffs. The salaried officers whom they elect to sit as representatives in the federal parliament have, therefore, quite other interests, obligations, and responsibilities than those of the official staff of the Federation itself. The secretary of the Nottinghamshire Miners' Association, for instance, finds himself able, when sitting as a member of the Conference of the Miners' Federation, freely to criticise the action of the federal executive council or of the federal official staff, without in any way endangering his own position as a salaried officer. Similarly, when the secretary of the Rochdale Cotton-spinners goes to the quarterly meeting at Manchester, he need have no hesitation in opposing and, if possible, defeating any recommendation of the executive council of the Amalgamated Association of Operative Cotton-spinners which he considers injurious to the Rochdale spinners. In the form of the representative executive, this use of salaried officers in a representative capacity is likely to tend, as we have seen, to the formation of a virtually irresponsible governing clique. But in the form of a federal representative assembly, where the federal executive and official staff are dependent, not on the members at large but on the assembly itself, and where the representatives are responsible to quite other constituencies and include a large proportion of the non-official element, this danger is reduced to a minimum.

We have now set before the reader an analysis of the constitutional development of Trade Union democracy. The facts will be interpreted in different ways by students of different temperaments. To us they represent the long and inarticulate struggle of unlettered men to solve the problem of how to combine administrative efficiency with popular control. Assent was the first requirement. The very formation of a continuous combination, in face of legal persecution and public disapproval, depended on the active concurrence of all the members. And though it is conceivable that a strong Trade Union might coerce a few individual workmen to continue in its ranks against their will, no such coercive influence could permanently prevail over a discontented majority, or prevent the secession, either individually or in a body, of any considerable number who were seriously disaffected. It was accordingly assumed without question that everything should be submitted to "the voices" of the whole body, and that each member should take an equal and identical share in the common project. As the union developed from an angry crowd unanimously demanding the redress of a particular grievance into an insurance company of national extent, obliged to follow some definite trade policy, the need for administrative efficiency more and more forced itself on the minds of the members. This efficiency involved an ever-increasing specialisation of function.[1] The growing mass of business and the difficulty and complication of the questions dealt with involved the growth of an official class, marked off by capacity, training, and habit of life from the rank and file. Failure to specialise the executive function quickly brought about extinction. On the other hand this very specialisation undermined the popular control, and thus risked the loss of the indispensable popular assent. The early expedients of Rotation of Office, the Mass Meeting, and the Referendum proved, in practice, utterly inadequate as a means of securing genuine popular control. At each particular crisis the individual member found himself overmatched by the official machinery which he had created. At this stage irresponsible bureaucracy seemed the inevitable outcome. But democracy found yet another expedient, which in some favored unions has gone far to solve the problem. The specialisation of the executive into a permanent expert civil service was balanced by the specialisation of the legislature, in the establishment of a supreme representative assembly, itself undertaking the work of direction and control for which the members at large had proved incompetent. We have seen how difficult it is for a community of manual workers to obtain such an assembly, and how large a part is

---

[1] "The progressive division of labour by which both science and government prosper."—Lord Acton, *The Unity of Modern History* (London, 1896), p. 3. "If there be one principle clearer than another, it is this : that in any business, whether of government or of mere merchandising, *somebody must be trusted*. . . . Power and strict accountability for its use, are the essential constituents of good government."—Woodrow Wilson, *Congressional Government* (New York, 1896), 12th edit.

inevitably played in it by the ever-growing number of salaried officers. But in the representative assembly these salaried officers sit in a new capacity. The work expected from them by their employers is not that of execution, but of criticism and direction. To balance the professional civil servant we have, in fact, the professional representative.

This detailed analysis of humble working-class organisations will to many readers be of interest only in so far as it furnishes material for political generalisations. It is therefore important to consider to what extent the constitutional problems of Trade Union democracy are analogous to those of national or municipal politics.

The fundamental requisites of government are the same in the democratic state as in the Trade Union. In both cases the problem is how to combine administrative efficiency with popular control. Both alike ultimately depend on a continuance of general assent. In a voluntary association, such as the Trade Union, this general assent is, as we have seen, the foremost requirement: in the democratic state relinquishment of citizenship is seldom a practicable alternative, whilst the operation of changing governors is not an easy one. Hence, even in the most democratic of states the continuous assent of the governed is not so imperative a necessity as in the Trade Union. On the other hand, the degree of administrative efficiency necessary for the healthy existence of the state is far greater than in the case of the Trade Union. But whilst admitting this transposition in relative importance, it still remains true that, in the democratic state as in the Trade Union, government cannot continue to exist without combining a certain degree of popular assent with adequate administrative efficiency.

More important is the fact that the popular assent is in both cases of the same nature. In the democratic state, as in the Trade Union, the eventual judgment of the people is pronounced not upon projects but upon results. It avails not that a particular proposal may have received the prior authorisation of an express popular vote ; if the results are not such as the people desire, the executive will not continue to receive their support. Nor does this, in the democratic state any more than in the Trade Union, imply that an all-wise government would necessarily secure this popular assent. If any particular stage in the march of civilisation happens to be momentarily distasteful to the bulk of the citizens, the executive which ventures to step in that direction will be no less ruthlessly dismissed than if its deeds had been evil. All that we have said as to the logical futility of the Referendum, and as to the necessity for the representative, therefore applies, we suggest, even more strongly to democratic states than to Trade Unions. For what is the lesson to be learned from Trade Union history ? The Referendum, introduced for the express purpose of ensuring popular assent, has in almost all cases failed to accomplish its object. This failure is due, as the reader will have observed, to the constant inability of the ordinary man to estimate what will be the effect of a particular proposal. *What Democracy requires is assent to results ; what the Referendum gives is assent to projects.* No Trade Union has, for instance, deliberately desired bankruptcy ; but many Trade Unions have persistently voted for scales of contributions and benefits which have inevitably resulted in bankruptcy. If this is the case in the relatively simple issues of Trade Union administration, still more does it apply to the infinitely complicated questions of national politics.

But though in the case of the Referendum the analogy is sufficiently exact to warrant the transformation of the empirical conclusions of Trade Union history into a political generalisation, it is only fair to point out some minor differences between the two cases. We have had occasion to describe how, in Trade Union history, the use of the Referendum, far from promoting popular control, has sometimes resulted in increasing the dominant power of the permanent civil service, and in making its position practically impregnable against any uprising opinion among its constituents. This particular danger would, we imagine, scarcely occur in a democratic state. In the Trade Union the executive committee occupies a unique position. It alone has access to official information ; it alone commands expert professional skill and experience ; and, most important of all, it monopolises in the society's official circular what corresponds to the newspaper press. The existence of political parties fairly equal in knowledge, ability, and electoral organisation, and each served by its own press, would always save the democratic state from this particular perversion of the Referendum to the advantage of the existing government. But any party or sect of opinion which, from lack of funds, education, or social influence, could not call to its aid the forces which we have named, would, we suggest, find itself as helpless in face of a Referendum as the discontented section of a strong Trade Union.

We have seen, moreover, that there is in Trade Union government a certain special class of questions in which the Referendum has a distinct use. Where a decision will involve at some future time the personal co-operation of the members in some positive act essentially optional in its nature—still more where that act involves a voluntary personal sacrifice, or where not a majority alone but practically the whole body of the members must on pain of failure join in it,—the Referendum may be useful, not as a legislative act, but as an index of the probability that the members will actually do what will be required of them. The decision to strike is obviously a case in point. Another instance may be found in the decisions of Trade Unions or other bodies that each member shall use his municipal or parliamentary franchise in a particular manner. Here the success or failure of the policy of the organisation depends not on the passive acquiescence of the rank and file in acts done by the executive committee or the officers, but upon each member's active performance of a personal task. We cannot think of any case of this kind within the sphere of the modern democratic state. If indeed, as Mr. Auberon Herbert proposes, it were left to the option of each citizen to determine from time to time the amount and the application of his contributions to the treasury, the Chancellor of the Exchequer would probably find it convenient, prior to making up the estimates, to take a Referendum as a guide to how much would probably be paid. Or, to take an analogy very near to that of the Trade Union decision to strike, if each soldier in the army were at liberty to leave at a day's notice, it would probably be found expedient to take a vote of the rank and file before engaging in a foreign war. In the modern democratic state, however, as it actually exists, it is not left to the option of the individual citizen whether or not he will act in the manner decided on. The success or failure of the policy does not therefore depend on obtaining universal assent and personal participation in the act itself. Whether the citizen likes it or not, he is compelled to pay the taxes and obey the laws which have been decided on by the competent authority. Whether or not he will maintain that authority in power, will depend not on his original impulsive judgment as to the expediency of the tax or the law, but on his deliberate approval or disapproval of the subsequent results.

If Trade Union history throws doubt on the advantages of the Referendum, still less does it favor the institution of the delegate as distinguished from the representative. Even in the comparatively simple issues of Trade Union administration, it has been found, in practice, quite impossible to obtain definite instructions from the members on all the matters which come up for decision. When, for instance, the sixty delegates of the Amalgamated Society of Engineers met in 1892 to revise the constitution and trade policy of their society, they were supposed to confine themselves to such amendments as had previously received the sanction of one or other of the branches. But although the amendments so sanctioned filled over five hundred printed pages, it was found impossible to construct from this material alone any consistent constitution or line of policy. The delegates were necessarily compelled to exercise larger freedom and to frame a set of rules not contemplated by any one of the branches. And this experience of the Engineers is only a type of what has been going on throughout the whole Trade Union world. The increased facilities for communication, on the one hand, and the growth of representative institutions, on the other, have made the delegate obsolete. Wherever a Trade Union has retained the old ideal of direct government by the people, it has naturally preferred to the Delegate Meeting the less expensive and more thoroughgoing device of the Referendum. For the most part the increasing complication and intricacy of modern industrial affairs has, as we have seen, compelled the substitution of representative institutions. These considerations apply with even greater force to the democratic state.

Trade Union history gives, therefore, little support to the Referendum or the Delegate Meeting, and points rather to government by a Representative Assembly as the last word of democracy.[1] It is therefore important to see whether these Trade Union parliaments have any lesson for the political student. The governing assemblies of even the most democratic states have, unlike Trade Union parliaments, hitherto been drawn almost exclusively from the middle or upper classes, and have therefore escaped the special difficulties of communities of wage-earners. If, however, we assume that the manual workers, who number four-fifths of the population, will gradually become the dominant influence in the electorate, and will contribute an important and increasing section of the representatives, the governing assemblies of the Coal-

[1] " There are two elements co-existent in the conduct of human affairs—policy and administration—but, though the confines of their respective jurisdictions overlap, the functions of each must of necessity be exercised within its own domain by its own hierarchy—the one consisting of trained specialists and experts, intimately conversant with the historical traditions of their own department and with the minutest details of the subjects with which they are concerned, the other qualified by their large converse with whatever is influential and intelligent in their own country or on the European Continent, and, above all, by their Parliamentary talents and their tactful appreciation of public opinion, to determine the general lines along which the destinies of their country should be led."—Speech by the Marquis of Dufferin, *Times*, 12th June 1897.

miners or Cotton Operatives to-day may be to a large extent prophetic of the future legislative assembly in any English-speaking community.

One inference seems to us clear. Any effective participation of the wage-earning class in the councils of the nation involves the establishment of a new calling, that of the professional representative. For the parish or town council it is possible to elect men who will continue to work at their trades, just as a Trade Union branch can be administered by committee-men and officers in full work. The adoption of the usual Co-operative and Trade Union practice of paying travelling expenses and an allowance for the actual time spent on the public business would suffice to enable workmen to attend the district or county council. But the governing assembly of any important state must always demand practically the whole time of its members. The working-man representative in the House of Commons is therefore most closely analogous, not to the working miner or spinner who attends the Coal or Cotton Parliament, but to the permanent and salaried official representatives, who, in both these assemblies, exercise the predominant influence and control the executive work. The analogy may therefore seem to point to the election to the House of Commons of the trained representative who has been successful in the parliament of his trade.

Such a suggestion misses the whole moral of Trade Union history. The cotton or coal-mining official representative succeeds in influencing his own trade assembly because he has mastered the technical details of all the business that comes before it ; because his whole life has been one long training for the duties which he has to discharge ; because, in short, he has become a professional expert in ascertaining and representing the desires of his constituents and in bringing about the conditions of their fulfilment. But transport this man to the House of Commons, and he finds himself confronted with facts and problems as foreign to his experience and training as his own business would be to the banker or the country gentle-man. What the working class will presently recognise is that the duties of a parliamentary representative constitute as much a new business to the Trade Union official as the duties of a general secretary are to the ordinary mechanic. When workmen desire to be as efficiently represented in the Parliament of the nation as they are in their own trade assemblies, they will find themselves compelled to establish a class of expert parliamentary representatives, just as they have had to establish a class of expert trade officials.

We need not consider in any detail what effect an influx of "labor members" of this new type would probably have upon the British House of Commons. Any one who has watched the deliberations of the Coal or the Cotton Parliament, or the periodical revising committees of the other great unions, will have been impressed by the disinclination of the professional representative to mere talk, his impatience of dilatory procedure, and his determination to "get the business through" within working hours. Short speeches, rigorous closure, and an almost extravagant substitution of printed matter for lengthy "front bench" explanations render these assemblies among the most efficient of demo-cratic bodies.[1]

More important is it to consider in what respects, judging from Trade Union analogies, the expert professional representative will differ from the unpaid politician to whom the middle and upper classes have hitherto been accustomed. We have already described how in the Trade Union world the representative has a twofold function, neither part of which may be neglected with impunity. He makes it just as much his business to ascertain and express the real desires of his constituents as he does to control and direct the operations of the civil servants of his trade. With the

[1] These representative assemblies present a great contrast to the Trade Union Congress, as to which see the subsequent chapter on "The Method of Legal Enactment."

entrance into the House of Commons of men of this type, the work of ascertaining and expressing the wishes of the constituencies would be much more deliberately pursued than at present. The typical member of Parliament to-day attends to such actual expressions of opinion as reach him from his constituency in a clear and definite form, but regards it as no part of his work actively to discover what the silent or inarticulate electors are vaguely desiring. He visits his constituency at rare intervals, and then only to expound his own views in set speeches at public meetings, whilst his personal intercourse is almost entirely limited to persons of his own class or to political wire-pullers. Whatever may be his intentions, he is seldom in touch with any but the middle or upper class, together with that tiny section of all classes to whom "politics" is of constant interest. Of the actual grievances and "dim in-articulate" aspirations of the bulk of the people, the lower middle and the wage-earning class, he has practically no conception. When representation of working-class opinion becomes a profession, as in the Trade Union world, we see a complete revolution in the attitude of the representative towards his constituents. To find out what his constituents desire becomes an essential part of his work. It will not do to wait until they write to him, for the working-man is slow to put pen to paper. Hence the professional Trade Union representative takes active steps to learn what the silent members are thinking. He spends his whole time, when not actually in session, in his constituency. He makes few set speeches at public gatherings, but he is diligent in attending branch meetings, and becomes an attentive listener at local committees. At his office he is accessible to every one of his constituents. It is, moreover, part of the regular routine of such a functionary to be constantly communicating with every one of his constituents by means of frequent circulars on points which he believes to be of special interest to them. If, therefore, the professional representative, as we know him in the Trade Union world, becomes a feature of the House of Commons, the future member of Parliament will feel himself not only the authoritative exponent of the votes of his constituents, but also their "London Correspondent," their parliamentary agent, and their expert adviser in all matters of legislation or general politics.[1]

It is impossible to forecast all the consequences that would follow from raising (or, as some would say, degrading) the parliamentary representative from an amateur to a professional. But among other things the whole etiquette of the situation would be changed. At present it is a point of honor in a member of Parliament not to express his constituents' desires when he conscientiously differs from them. To the "gentleman politician" the only alternative to voting as he himself thinks best is resigning his seat. This delicacy is unknown to any paid professional agent. The architect, solicitor, or permanent civil servant, after tendering his advice and supporting his views with all his expert authority, finally carries out whatever policy his employer commands. This is also the view which the professional representative of the Trade Union world takes of his own duties. It is his business not only to put before his constituents what he believes to be their best policy and to back up his opinion with all the argumentative power he can bring to bear, but also to put his entire energy into wrestling with what he conceives to be their ignorance, and to become for the time a vigorous propagandist of his own policy. But if, when he has done his best in this way, he fails to get a majority over to his view, he loyally accepts the decision and records his vote in accordance with his constituents' desires. We imagine that professional representatives of working-class opinion in the House of Commons would take the same course.[2]

[1] "Representatives ought to give light and leading to the people, just as the people give stimulus and momentum to their representatives."—J. Bryce, *The American Commonwealth* (London, 1891), vol. i. p. 297.

[2] It is interesting to notice that in the country in which the "sovereignty of

This may at first seem to indicate a return of the professional representative to the position of a delegate. Trade Union experience points, however, to the very reverse. In the great majority of cases a constituency cannot be said to have any clear and decided views on particular projects. What they ask from their representative is that he shall act in the manner which, in his opinion, will best serve to promote their general desires. It is only in particular instances, usually when some well-intentioned proposal entails immediately inconvenient results, that a wave of decided opinion spreads through a working-class constituency. It is exactly in cases of this kind that a propagandist campaign by a professional debater, equipped with all the facts, is of the greatest utility. Such a campaign would be the very last thing that a member of Parliament of the present type would venture upon if he thought that his constituents were against him. He would feel that the less the points of difference were made prominent, the better for his own safety. But once it came to be understood that the final command of the constituency would be obeyed, the representative would run no risk of losing his seat, merely because he did his best to convert his constituents. Judging from Trade Union experience he would, in nine cases out of ten, succeed in converting them to his own view, and thus perform a valuable piece of political education. In the tenth case the campaign would have been no less educational, though in another way ; and, whichever was the right view, the issue would have been made clear, the facts brought out, and the way opened for the eventual conversion of one or other of the contending parties.

Trade Union experience indicates, therefore, a still further development in the evolution of the representative. Working-

the people " has been most whole-heartedly accepted, the Trade Union practice prevails. The members of the Swiss " Bundesrath " (Federal Cabinet) do not resign when any project is disapproved of by the legislature, nor do the members of the " Nationalrath " throw up their legislative functions when a measure is rejected by the electors on Referendum. Both cabinet ministers and legislators set themselves to carry out the popular will.

class democracy will expect him not only to be able to understand and interpret the desires of his electors, and effectively to direct and control the administrating executive : he must also count it as part of his duty to be the expert parliamentary adviser of his constituency, and at times an active propagandist of his own advice. Thus, if any inference from Trade Union history is valid in the larger sphere, the whole tendency of working-class democracy will unconsciously be to exalt the real power of the representative, and more and more to differentiate his functions from those of the ordinary citizen on the one hand, and of the expert administrator on the other. The typical representative assembly of the future will, it may be suggested, be as far removed from the House of Commons of to-day as the latter is from the mere Delegate Meeting. We have already travelled far from the one man taken by rotation from the roll, and changed mechanically to convey " the voices " of the whole body. We may in the future leave equally behind the member to whom wealth, position, or notoriety secures, almost by accident, a seat in Parliament, in which he can, in such intervals as his business or pleasure may leave him, decide what he thinks best for the nation. In his stead we may watch appearing in increasing numbers the professional representative,—a man selected for natural aptitude, deliberately trained for his new work as a special vocation, devoting his whole time to the discharge of his manifold duties, and actively maintaining an intimate and reciprocal intellectual relationship with his constituency.

How far such a development of the representative will fit in with the party system as we now know it ; how far it will increase the permanence and continuity of parliamentary life ; how far it will promote collective action and tend to increasing bureaucracy ; how far, on the other hand, it will bring the ordinary man into active political citizenship, and rehabilitate the House of Commons in popular estimation ; how far, therefore, it will increase the real authority of the people over the representative assembly, and of the representative assembly over the permanent civil service ; how far, in fine, it will give us that combination of administrative efficiency with popular control which is at once the requisite and the ideal of all democracy—all these are questions that make the future interesting.

CHAPTER III

THE UNIT OF GOVERNMENT

THE trade clubs of the eighteenth century inherited from the Middle Ages the tradition of strictly localised corporations, the unit of government necessarily coinciding, like that of the English craft gild, with the area of the particular city in which the members lived. And we can well imagine that a contemporary observer of the constitution and policy of these little democracies might confidently have predicted that they, like the craft gilds, must inevitably remain strictly localised bodies. The crude and primitive form of popular government to which, as we have seen, the workmen were obstinately devoted, could only serve the needs of a small and local society. Government by general meeting of all the members, administration by the forced service of individuals taken in rotation from the roll—in short, the ideal of each member taking an equal and identical share in the management of public affairs—was manifestly impracticable in any but a society of which the members met each other with the frequent intimacy of near neighbours. Yet in spite of all difficulties of constitutional machinery, the historian watches these local trade clubs, in marked contrast with the craft gilds, irresistibly expanding into associations of national extent. Thus, the little friendly club which twenty-three Bolton ironfounders established in 1809 spread steadily over the whole of England, Ireland, and Wales, until to-day it numbers over 16,000 members, dispersed among 122 separate branches. The scores of little clubs of millwrights and steam-engine makers, fitters and blacksmiths, as if impelled by some overmastering impulse, drew together between 1840 and 1851 to form the great Amalgamated Society of Engineers. The Amalgamated Society of Carpenters and Joiners (established 1860) has, in the thirty-five years of its existence, absorbed several dozens of local carpenters' societies, and now counts within its ranks four-fifths of the organised carpenters in the kingdom. Finally, we see organisations established, like the Amalgamated Society of Railway Servants in 1872, with the deliberate intention of covering the whole trade from one end of the kingdom to the other. How slowly, painfully, and reluctantly the workmen have modified their crude ideas of democracy to meet the exigencies of a national organisation, we have already described.

But it was not merely the workman's simplicity in matters of government that hampered the growth of national organisation. The traditional policy of the craftsman of the English town—the restriction of the right to work to those who had acquired the "freedom" of the corporation, the determined exclusion of "interlopers," and the craving to keep trade from going out of the town—has left deep roots in English industrial life, alike among the shopkeepers and among the workmen. Trade Unionism has had constantly to struggle against this spirit of local monopoly, specially noticeable in the seaport towns.[1]

Down to the middle of the present century the shipwrights had an independent local club in every port, each of which strove with might and main to exclude from any chance of work in the port all but men who had learnt their trade within its bounds. These monopoly rules caused incessant friction between the men of the several ports. Shipwrights out of work in one town could not permanently be kept away from another in which more hands were

[1] It is interesting to note that the modern forms of the monopoly spirit are also specially characteristic of the industry of shipbuilding ; see the chapter on "The Right to a Trade."

wanted. The newcomers, refused admission into the old port society, eventually formed a new local union among themselves, and naturally tended to ignore the trade regulations maintained by the monopolists. To remedy this disastrous state of things a loose federation was between 1850 and 1860 gradually formed among the local societies for the express purpose of discussing, at annual congresses, how to establish more satisfactory relations between the ports. In the records of these congresses we watch, for nearly thirty years, the struggle of the monopolist societies against the efforts of those, such as Glasgow and Newcastle, whose circumstances had converted them to a belief in complete mobility of labor within a trade. The open societies at last lost patience with the conservative spirit of the others, and in 1882 united to form a national amalgamated union, based on the principle of a common purse and complete mobility between port and port. This organisation, the Associated Shipwrights' Society, has, in fifteen years, succeeded in absorbing all but three of the local societies, and now extends to every port in the kingdom. " In these times of mammoth firms, with large capital," writes the general secretary, " the days of local societies' utility have gone by, and it is to be hoped the few still remaining outside the consolidated association of their trade will ere long lay aside all local animus and trivial objections, or personal feeling . . . for the paramount interest of their trade." [1]

The history of the Shipwrights' organisation is typical of that of other port unions. The numerous societies of Sailmakers, once rigidly monopolist, are now united in a federation, within which complete mobility prevails.[2] The Coopers' societies, which in the port towns had formerly much in common with the Shipwrights, now, with one exception, admit to membership any duly apprenticed cooper from

---

[1] *Twelfth Annual Report of Associated Shipwrights' Society* (Newcastle, 1894), p. xi.

[2] *Rules for the Guidance of the Federation of the Sailmakers of Great Britain and Ireland* (Hull, 1890).

another town.   But the main citadels of local monopoly in the Trade Union world have always been the trade clubs of Dublin, Cork, and Limerick.   The Dublin Coopers have, even at the present time, a rigidly closed society, which refuses all intercourse with other unions, and maintains, through an ingenious arrangement, a strict monopoly of this important coopering centre ;[1] and the Cork Stonemasons, who are combined in an old local club, whilst insisting on working at Fermoy whenever they please, will not, as we learn, suffer any mason, from Fermoy or elsewhere, to obtain employment at Cork.

Even in Ireland, however, the development of Trade Unionism is hostile to local monopoly.   Any growing industry is quickly invaded by members of the great English societies, who establish their own branches and force the local clubs to come to terms.   One by one old Irish unions apply to be admitted as branches into the richer and more powerful English societies, and have in consequence to accept the principle of complete mobility of labor.   The famous

---

[1] The arrangement is as follows : The Dublin Coopers do not prohibit strangers from working in Dublin when more coopers are wanted.   On such occasions the secretary writes to coopers' societies in other towns, notably Burton, stating the number of men required.   Upon all such outsiders a tax of a shilling a week is levied as "working fee," half of which benefits the Dublin society, the other half being accumulated to pay the immigrant's return fare.   As soon as work shows signs of approaching slackness, the "foreigner" receives warning that he must instantly depart : it is said that his return ticket is presented to him, with any balance remaining out of his weekly sixpence.   As many as 200 "strangers" will in this way sometimes be paid off, and sent away in a single week.   By this means the Dublin Coopers (*a*) secure absolute regularity of employment for their own members, (*b*) provide the extra labor required in busy times, and (*c*) maintain their own control over the conditions under which the work is done.   The employers appear to be satisfied with the arrangement, which, so far as we have been able to ascertain, is the only surviving instance of what was once a common rule of port unions.   Thus, the rules of Queenstown Shipwrights' Society, right down to its absorption in the Associated Shipwrights' Society (in 1894), included a provision that "no strange shipwright" should be allowed to work in the town while a member was idle.   And the Liverpool Sailmakers' Society (established 1817) has, among the MS. rules preserved in the old minute-book, one providing that "strangers" with indentures should be allowed to work at "legal sail-rooms," but should members be unable to obtain employment elsewhere, then "the stranger shall be discharged and the member be engaged."

"Dublin Regulars," a rigidly monopolist local carpenters' union, claiming descent from the gilds, and always striving to exclude from admission any but the sons of the members,[1] became, in 1890, at the instance of its younger members, one of the 629 branches of the Amalgamated Society of Carpenters and Joiners, bound to admit to work fellow-members from all parts of the world. Among the Irish Shipwrights, too, once the most rigidly monopolist of all, this tendency has progressed with exceptional rapidity. The annual report of the Associated Shipwrights' Society for 1893 records[2] the absorption in that year alone of no fewer than six old Irish port unions, each of which had hitherto striven to maintain for its members all the work of its own port.

But although the growth of national organisation has done much to break down this spirit of local monopoly, we do not wish to imply that it has been completely eradicated. The workman, whether a Trade Unionist or not, still shares with the shopkeeper and the small manufacturer, the old instinctive objection to work "going out of the town." The proceedings of local authorities often reveal to us the "small master," the retail tradesman, and the local artisan all insisting that "the ratepayers' money" should be spent so as directly to benefit the local trade. Trade Unionists are not backward in making use of this vulgar error when it suits their purpose, and the "labor members" of town or county councils can seldom refrain, whenever it is proposed "to send work into the country," from adopting an argument which they find so convincing to many of their middle-class colleagues.[3]

---

[1] See, for instance, the detailed account of it given in the *Report on Trade Societies and Strikes of the National Association for the Promotion of Social Science* (1860), pp. 418-423.

[2] *Twelfth Annual Report of the Associated Shipwrights' Society*, p. xi. (Newcastle, 1894).

[3] During the first eight years of the London County Council (1889-97) several attempts were made to confine contracts to London firms. It is interesting to note that these all emanated from middle-class members of the Moderate Party, and that they were opposed by John Burns and a large majority of the "Labor Members" and Progressives, as well as by the more responsible of the "Moderates."

But if we follow the Labor Member from the council chamber to his Trade Union branch meeting, we shall recognise that the grievance felt by his Trade Unionist constituents is not exclusively, or even mainly, based on the " local protectionism " of the shopkeeper and the small manufacturer. What the urban Trade Unionist actually resists is not any loss of work to a particular locality, but the incessant attempt of contractors to evade the Trade Union regulations, by getting the work done in districts in which the workmen are either not organised at all, or in which they are working at a low Standard Rate. Thus the Friendly Society of Operative Stonemasons incurs considerable odium because the branches in many large towns insert in their local rules a prohibition of the use of stone imported in a worked state from any outside district. But this general prohibition arises from the fact that the practical alternative to working the stone on the spot is getting it worked in the district in which it is quarried. Now, whatever mechanical or economic advantage may be claimed for the latter practice, it so happens that the quarry districts are those in which the Stonemasons are worst organised. In these districts for the most part, no Standard Rate exists, the hours of labor are long and variable, and competitive piecework, unregulated by any common agreement, usually prevails. Moreover, any transference of work from the Stonemasons of large cities where jobs dovetail with each other, to the Stonemasons of quarry villages, entirely dependent on the spasmodic orders for worked stone received by the quarry owner, necessarily involves an increase in the number of Stonemasons exposed to irregularity of work, and habitually " on tramp " from county to county.[1]

----

[1] For instance the " Working Rules to be observed by the Master Builders and Operative Stonemasons of Portsmouth," signed in 1893, by ten master builders and four workmen, on behalf of their respective associations, include the following provision, "That no piecework be allowed and no worked stone to come into the town except square steps, flags, curbs, and landings, and no brick-layers to fix worked stone." The London rules are not so explicit. As formally agreed to in 1892 by the associations of employers and employed, they provide

We may trace a similar feeling in the protests frequently made by the branches of the National Union of Boot and Shoe Operatives, against work being sent into the country villages, or even from a centre in which wages are high, to one working under a lower " statement." That this is not merely a disguised " local protectionism " may be seen from the fact that the Northampton Branch actually resolved in 1888 to strike, not against Northampton employers sending work out of the town, but against a London manufacturer sending his work to Northampton.[1] In 1889, the Executive Council of the same union found itself driven to take action against the systematic attempts of certain employers to evade the wages agreement which they had formally entered into, by sending their work away to have certain processes

that " piecework and subcontracting for labor only shall on no account be resorted to, excepting for granite kerb, York paving and turning." The London Stone-masons, however, claim, as for instance in their complaint in 1894 against the Works Department of the London County Council, that this rule must be interpreted so as to exclude the use in London of stone worked in a quarry district. This claim was successfully resisted by the Trade Union repre-sentatives who sat on the Works Committee. We subsequently investigated this case ourselves, tracing the stone (a long run of sandstone kerb for park railings) back to Derbyshire, where it was quarried and worked. We found the district totally unorganised, the stonemasons' work being done largely by boy-labor, at competitive piecework, without settled agreement, by non-unionists, working irregular and sometimes excessive hours. It was impossible not to feel that, although the London Stonemasons had expressed their objection in the wrong terms and therefore had failed to obtain redress, they were, according to the " Fair Wages " policy adopted by the County Council and the House of Commons, justified in their complaint. Unfortunately, instead of bringing to the notice of the Committee the actual conditions under which the stone was being worked, they relied on the argument that the London ratepayers' money should be spent on London workmen. This argument, as they afterwards explained to us, had been found the most effective with the shopkeepers and small manufacturers who dominate provincial Town Councils. The Trade Unionist members of the London County Council proved obdurate to this economic heresy.

[1] *Shoe and Leather Record*, 28th July 1888. In the same way a general meeting of the Manchester Stonemasons, in 1862, decided to support a strike against a Manchester employer who, carrying out a contract at Altrincham, eight miles off, had his stone worked at Manchester, instead of at Altrincham, as required by the working rules of the Altrincham branch. In this case, the Manchester Stonemasons struck against work coming to themselves at a higher rate per hour than was demanded by the Altrincham masons.—*Stonemasons' Fortnightly Return*, September 1862.

done in lower-paid districts. These employers were accordingly informed, not that the work must be kept in the town, but that, wherever it was executed, the "shop statement" which they had signed must be adhered to. It was at the same time expressly intimated that if these employers chose to set up works of their own in a new place, "they will be at perfect liberty to do so," without objection from the union, even if they chose a low-paid district, "provided that they pay the highest rate of wages of the district to which they go." [1]

We have quoted the strongest instances of Trade Union objection to "work going out of the town," in order to unravel, from the common stock of economic prejudice, the impulse which is distinctive of Trade Unionism itself. It is customary for persons interested in the prosperity of one establishment, one town or one district, to seek to obtain trade for that particular establishment, town or district. Had Trade Unions remained, like the mediæval craft gilds, organisations of strictly local membership, they must, almost inevitably, have been marked by a similar local favoritism. But the whole tendency of Trade Union history has been towards the solidarity of each trade as a whole. The natural selfishness of the local branches is accordingly always being combated by the central executives and national delegate meetings, in the wider interests of the whole body of the members wherever they may be working. Just in proportion as Trade Unionism is strong and well established we find the old customary favoritism of locality replaced by the impartial enforcement of uniform conditions upon all districts alike. When, for instance, the Amalgamated Association of Cotton Weavers, in delegate meeting assembled, finally decided to adopt a uniform list of piecework prices, the members then working at Great Harwood found no sympathy for their plea that such a measure would reduce

[1] The "National Conference" of the Union passed a similar resolution in 1886; *Monthly Report of the National Union of Boot and Shoe Operatives*, January 1887 and February 1889.

their own exceptionally high rates. And although it was foreseen and declared that uniformity would tend to the concentration of the manufacture in the most favorably situated districts, to the consequent loss of the more remote villages, the delegates from these villages almost unanimously supported what was believed to be good for the trade as a whole.[1]

In another industry, the contrast between the old " local protectionism " and the Trade Unionist view has resulted in an interesting change in electioneering tactics. The London Society of Compositors and the Typographical Association have, for the last ten years, used more electoral pressure with regard to the distribution of local work, than any other Trade Union. So long as parliamentary electors belonged mainly to the middle class, a parliamentary candidate was advised by his agent to distribute his large printing orders fairly among all parts of his constituency, and under no circumstances to employ a printer living beyond its boundary. Now the astute agent, eager to conciliate the whole body of organised workmen in the constituency, confines his printing strictly to the best Trade Union establishments, although this usually involves passing over most of the local establishments and sometimes even giving work to firms outside the district. The influence of the Trade Union leaders is used, not to maintain their respective trades in all the places in which they happen to exist, but to strengthen, at the expense of the rest, those establishments, those towns, and even those districts, in which the conditions of work are most advantageous.

We see, therefore, that in spite of the difficulties of government, in spite of the strong inherited tradition of local exclusiveness, and in spite, too, of the natural selfishness of each branch in desiring to preserve its own local monopoly, the unit of government in the workmen's organisations, in complete contrast to the gilds of the master-

---

[1] Special meeting of General Council of Amalgamated Association of Cotton Weavers, 30th April 1892, attended by one of the authors ; see other instances cited in the chapter on " The Standard Rate."

craftsmen, has become the trade instead of the town.[1] Our description of this irresistible tendency to expansion has already to some extent revealed its cause, in the Trade Union desire to secure uniform minimum conditions throughout each industry. In our examination of the Methods and Regulations of Trade Unionism, and in our analysis of their economic working, we shall discover the means by which the wage-earners seek to attain this end, and the reasons which convince them of its importance. In the final part of our work we shall examine how far such an equality is economically possible or desirable. For the moment the reader must accept the fact that this uniformity of minimum is, whether wisely or not, the most permanent of Trade Union aspirations.

Meanwhile it is interesting to note that this conception of the solidarity of each trade as a whole is checked by racial differences. The great national unions of Engineers and Carpenters find no difficulty in extending their organisations beyond national boundaries, and easily open branches in the United States or the South African Republic, France or Spain, provided that these branches are composed of British workmen.[2] But it is needless to say that it has not yet appeared practicable to any British Trade Union even to suggest amalgamation with the Trade Union of any other country. Differences in legal position, in political status, in industrial methods, and in the economic situation between

---

[1] Where at the present day a widespread English industry is without a preponderating national Trade Union, it is simply a mark of imperfect organisation. Thus the numerous little Trade Unions of Painters, and Chippers and Drillers include only a small proportion of those at work in the trades.

[2] The Amalgamated Society of Engineers had, in 1896, 82 branches beyond the United Kingdom, and the Amalgamated Society of Carpenters and Joiners no fewer than 87. About half of these are in the United States or Canada, and most of the remainder in the Australian Colonies or South Africa. The Engineers had one branch in France, at Croix, and formerly one in Spain, at Bilbao, where the United Society of Boilermakers also had a branch until 1894. In the years 1880-82 the United Society of Boilermakers even had a branch at Constantinople. The only other English Trade Union having branches beyond sea is the Steam-Engine Makers' Society, which has opened lodges at New York, Montreal, and Brisbane.

French and English workers—not to mention the barrier of language—easily account for the indisposition on the part of practical British workmen to consider an international amalgamated union. And it is significant that, even within the British Isles, the progress towards national union has been much hampered by differences of racial sentiment and divergent views of social expediency. The English carpenter, plumber, or smith who finds himself working in a Scotch town, is apt to declare the Scotch union in his trade to be little better than a friendly society, and to complain that Scotch workmen are too eager for immediate gain and for personal advancement sufficiently to resist such dangerous innovations as competitive piecework, nibbling at the Standard Rate, or habitual overtime. The Scotchman retorts that the English Trade Union is extravagant in its expenditure, especially at the head office in London or Manchester, and unduly restrictive in its Regulations and Methods. In some cases the impulse towards amalgamation has prevailed over this divergence as to what is socially expedient. The United Society of Boilermakers, which extends without a rival from sea to sea, was able in 1889, through the loyalty of the bulk of its Scottish members, to stamp out an attempted secession, aiming at a national society on the banks of the Clyde, which evoked the support of Scottish national feeling, voiced by the Glasgow Trades Council. In other cases Scotch pertinacity has conquered England. The Associated Shipwrights' Society, the rise and national development of which we have already described, sprang out of the Glasgow Shipwrights' Union, which gave to the wider organisation its able and energetic secretary, Mr. Alexander Wilkie. The British Steel Smelters' Association (established 1886) has spread from Glasgow over the whole industry in the Northern and Midland districts of England. In both these cases the Scotch have " stooped to conquer," the Scottish secretary moving to an English town as the centre of membership shifted towards the south. But in other trades the prevailing tendency towards complete national amalgamation is still baffled by the sturdy Scotch determination—due partly to differences of administration but mainly to racial sentiment—not to be "governed from England."[1] The powerful English national unions of Carpenters, Handworking Bootmakers, Plumbers, and Bricklayers have either never attempted or have failed to persuade their Scottish fellow-workmen to give up their separate Scottish societies. The rival national societies of Tailors are always at war, making periodical excursions across the Border, this establishment of branches in each other's territories giving rise to heated recriminations. In many important trades, such as the Compositors, Stonemasons, and Ironfounders, effective Trade Unionism is as old in Scotland as in England, and the two national societies in each trade, whilst retaining complete Home Rule, have settled down to a fraternal relationship, which amounts to tacit if not formal federation.

Ireland presents a similar case of racial differences, working in a somewhat different manner. Whereas the English Trade Unions have keenly desired union with Scottish local societies, they have, until lately, manifested a marked dislike to having anything to do with Ireland.[2] This has been, in some cases at least, the result of experience.

---

[1] Analogous tendencies may be traced in the Friendly Society movement, though to a lesser extent. The Scottish lodges of the Manchester Unity of Oddfellows have their own peculiar rules. The Scottish delegates to the Foresters' High Court at Edinburgh in 1894, were among the most strenuous opponents of the proposal to fix the headquarters (at present moving annually from town to town) in London or Birmingham. And though exclusively Scottish Orders have never yet succeeded in widely establishing themselves, it is not uncommon for Scottish lodges to threaten secession, as when, in 1889, five Scottish lodges of the Bolton Unity of the Ancient Noble Order of Oddfellows endeavoured to start a new " Scottish Unity " (*Oddfellows' Magazine*, March 1889, p. 70). Such a secession from the Manchester Unity resulted in the " Scottish Order of Oddfellows " which has, however, under 2000 members. There exist also the " St. Andrew's Order of Ancient Free Gardeners of Scotland," with 6000 members, and a " United Order of Scottish Mechanics," with 4000 members, which refuse to merge themselves in the larger Orders.

[2] Scottish branches are declared by Trade Union secretaries to be profitable recruits from a financial point of view, because they are habitually frugal and cautious in dispensing friendly benefits.

From 1832 down to 1840, Irish lodges were admitted to the Friendly Society of Operative Stonemasons, on the same footing as English, whilst the Scotch masons had already their independent organisation. The fortnightly reports during these years reveal constant friction between the central executive and the Irish branches, who would not agree among themselves, and who persisted in striking against members from other Irish towns. At the Delegate Meeting in 1839 the Irish branches had to be specially deprived of the right to strike without prior permission, even in those cases in which the rules allowed to English branches the instantaneous cessation of work to resist encroachments on established customs.[1] But even with this precaution the drain of the Irish lodges upon the English members became unendurable. At length in 1840, the general secretary was sent on a special mission of investigation, which revealed every kind of financial irregularity. The Irish lodges were found to have an incurable propensity to dispense benefits to all and sundry irrespective of the rules, and an invincible objection to English methods of account-keeping. The Dublin lodge had to be dissolved as a punishment for retaining to itself monies remitted by the Central Committee for other Irish lodges. The central executive who, in 1837, had successfully resisted a proposition emanating from a Warwickshire district in favor of Home Rule for Ireland, " as such separation would injure the stability of the society," [2] now reported in its favor. " We are convinced," says the report, " that a very great amount of money had been sent to Ireland for the relief of tramps, etc. . . . to which they had no legal right. . . . However much a separation may be regretted, we feel convinced that until they are thrown more on their own resources, they will not sufficiently estimate the benefits derivable from such an institution to exert themselves on its behalf." [3] The receipts

---

[1] *Rules of the Friendly Society of Operative Stonemasons* (edition of 1839).
[2] Resolutions of the Delegate Meeting 1837.
[3] *Stonemasons' Fortnightly Return*, 2nd January 1840.

from Ireland for the year had been £47 : 10s., whilst the remittances to Ireland had amounted to no less than £545. It is not surprising that the society promptly voted the exclusion of all the Irish branches.

In 1850 the Executive Committee of the Provincial Typographical Association were "reluctantly compelled to declare their conviction that no English executive can successfully manage an Association embracing branches so geographically distant and so materially different in their regulations and their mode of remuneration as those of the sister kingdom." The union thereupon gave up the one Irish branch (Waterford) which had not already insisted on its independence, and refused to entertain any proposals for new ones.[1]   Other societies which, in more recent years, have had Irish branches appear to have found them equally unprofitable, and a source of constant trouble.   The records of the Amalgamated Society of Tailors are full of references to the extravagance and financial mismanagement of its Irish branches.   During the year 1892 no less than four of the principal Irish branches of the society were rebuked by the Executive Council upon this account.   One of these had subsequently to be closed, the Executive stating that its "report is altogether wrong, and does not balance.   The contributions do not average 10d. per member, and the rent of the clubroom is more than the whole income from the branch.   If a satisfactory explanation is not sent at once the branch must be closed." [2]   Finally, in 1896, the Executive of the Associated

---

[1] *Half-Yearly Report of the Provincial Typographical Association*, 31st December 1850.

[2] *Quarterly Report of the Amalgamated Society of Tailors*, April 1892. Report on the Ennis branch.   In this connection the following extract from the proceedings of the High Court of the Ancient Order of Foresters in 1894 will be interesting.   The executive had found it necessary to hold a special investigation into the affairs of the Dublin District; and they recommended the grant of certain advantages upon condition of reform.   This proposal led to a lively debate.   "Were they going," said one prominent Forester, "to encourage extravagant, reckless, and fraudulent mismanagement?   The report presented to them showed distinctly that there had been extravagant, reckless, and fraudulent mismanagement. . . . Not less than £997 had been voted by previous High Courts towards the relief of Dublin Courts. . . . The Order's

Shipwrights' Society reported that it had been compelled "to close the Dublin branch, notwithstanding that the E. C. had instructed both the general secretary and the Humber Delegate to visit them. We have not been able to receive any correct reports from them for some time, and the only word we could get from them was that there was no work and no money, yet when your representatives visited them the officers were so busy working they had not time to convene a meeting of members. . . . Your E. C. offered to have all the idle men sent to ports where employment could be found them, but we are informed where this has been done some of these men, notwithstanding all that has been done for them, refused to pay up their arrears, and rather than pay left their employment and went home. . . . When the branch books were examined it was found they were paying both sick and unemployed benefit to members who were not entitled to it, and the branch officers were receiving salary for work they failed or refused to do. Seeing the Dublin branch entirely ignored the registered rules, your E. C. had no other option but to close the branch. The different branches must deal with these men should they come to their ports."[1]

So strong, however, is the dominant impulse towards the complete union of a trade from one end of the United Kingdom to the other, that it seems, during the last few years, to be slowly overcoming the reluctance of both English and Irish organisations. From 1889 onward, we find such great national unions as the Carpenters, Railway Servants, Engineers, Tailors, and Shipwrights freely opening branches in Irish towns and absorbing the surviving trade clubs of

Chief Official Valuer said ' the members have never done their duty.' That officer thereupon interposed with the remark, ' It was believed that in connection with sickness there was a good deal of malingering.' Another prominent Forester said he would attach the (Dublin) Courts to the Glasgow District. . . . There was only one element of danger, and it was of putting too many Irishmen together."—*Foresters' Miscellany* (September 1894), p. 180.

[1] *The Fifty-eighth Quarterly Report*, July to September 1896, of the Associated Society of Shipwrights, p. 8.

local artisans.[1] The Provincial Typographical Association,
now become the Typographical Association, has, since 1878,
opened sixteen branches in Ireland, and now employs a
salaried organiser for that island, whose efforts have brought
in many recruits. This tendency has been greatly assisted,
especially in the engineering and shipbuilding trades, by the
remarkable industrial development of Belfast. Since 1860
a constant stream of skilled artisans from England and
Scotland have settled in that town, with the result that it
now possesses strong branches of all the national unions of
both countries. With the shifting of the effective centre of
Irish Trade Unionism from Dublin to Belfast has come an
almost irresistible tendency to accept an English or Scottish
government. On the other hand, attempts to unite the
separate local societies of Irish towns in national Trade
Unions for Ireland have almost invariably failed, the Irish
clubs displaying far more willingness to become branches of
British unions than to amalgamate among themselves.[2]

Past experience of British Trade Unionism seems, therefore, to point to the whole extent of each trade within the
British Isles as forming the proper unit of government for
any combination of the wage-earners in that trade. Any
unit of smaller area produces an organisation of unstable
equilibrium, either tending constantly to expansion, or liable
to supersession by the growth of a rival society. But there
is a marked contrast between the union of Scotland with
England, and that effected between either of them and
Ireland. The English and Scottish Trade Unions federate
or combine with each other on equal terms. If complete
amalgamation is decided on, it is frequently the Scotchman,
bringing with him Scotch procedure and Scotch traditions,

[1] The Amalgamated Society of Railway Servants now (1897) possesses no
fewer than 56 Irish branches, the Amalgamated Society of Carpenters and
Joiners 56, the Amalgamated Society of Tailors 35, the Amalgamated Society of
Engineers 19, and the Associated Shipwrights' Society 9.
[2] Almost the only Irish national trade society is the Operative Bakers of
Ireland National Federal Union, formed in November 1889. An Irish Trade
Union Congress has been held annually since 1894.

who is chosen to reign in England, the centre of government being shifted almost automatically to the main centre of the industry.   Union with Ireland invariably means the simple absorption of the Irish branch, and the unconditional acceptance of the English or Scottish rules and organisation.   This is usually brought about by the English or Scottish immigrants into Ireland, aided by sections of Irish members who desire to escape from the weakness of internal dissensions, and to secure the benefits of efficient administration, with the support of a comparatively wealthy and powerful organisation.[1]

Passing now from the boundaries of the autonomous state to the relation between central and local authorities within it, we watch the Trade Unionists breaking away from the traditions of British Democracy.   In the political expansion of the Anglo-Saxon race, the development of local institutions has at least kept pace with the extension of empire.   In the other great organisations of the British working class, which have, equally with Trade Unionism, grown from small local beginnings to powerful corporations of national, or even international extent, the workmen have successfully maintained the complete independence of each local unit.   The Co-operative Movement includes within the British Isles a nominal membership as great as that of Trade Unionism, with financial transactions many times larger in amount.   The 1700 separate Co-operative Societies have united in the colossal business federations of the English and Scottish Wholesale Societies, and in the educational and political federation called the Co-operative Union. But though the Co-operative Movement has gone through many developments since its re-birth in 1844, and has built up a " State within the State," the great federal bodies have

[1] It may not be improper to observe, for English political readers, that the authors are divided in opinion as to the policy of granting Home Rule to Ireland, and are therefore protected against bias in drawing political inferences from Trade Union experience in this respect.   If it is thought that the facts adduced in this chapter tell against Irish self-government, the considerations brought forward in the next chapter may be regarded as making against the policy of complete union with Great Britain.

remained in all cases nothing but the agents and servants of the local societies.[1] And if we turn to a movement still more closely analogous to Trade Unionism, we may watch in the marvellous expansion of the "Affiliated Orders" among the friendly societies, the growth of a world-wide working-class organisation, based on an almost complete autonomy of the separate "lodges" within each "Order."[2] To the members of an Oddfellows' Court or a Foresters' Lodge any proposal to submit an issue of policy to the federal executive would seem an unheard-of innovation. But it is in their financial system that this insistence on complete local autonomy shows itself most decisively. However strongly the qualities of benevolence or charity may prevail among the Foresters or the Oddfellows, it has never occurred to their rich Courts or Lodges to regard their surplus funds as being freely at the disposal of those which were unable to meet their engagements. Each retains and controls its own funds for its own purposes, and its surplus balances are considered as being as much the private property of its own particular members as their individual investments.

To outward seeming the scattered members of a national Trade Union enjoy no less local self-government than those of the Ancient Order of Foresters or the Manchester Unity of Oddfellows. If the reader were to seek out, in some tavern of an industrial centre, the local meeting-place of the Foresters or the Carpenters, the Oddfellows or the Boilermakers, he might easily fail, on a first visit, to detect any important difference between the Trade Union branch and the court or lodge of the friendly society. The Oddfellows who use the club-room on a Monday, the Carpenters who meet there on a Tuesday, the Foresters who assemble on a Thursday, and the Stonemasons or Boilermakers who come

---

[1] *The Co-operative Movement in Great Britain*, by Beatrice Potter (Mrs. Sidney Webb).

[2] See *The Friendly Societies' Movement* (London, 1885) and *Mutual Thrift* (London, 1892), by the Rev. J. Frome Wilkinson, and *English Associations of Working Men*, by Dr. J. Baernreither (London, 1892).

on successive Fridays, all seem "clubs" managing their own affairs. Every night sees the same interminable procession of men, women, and children bringing the contribution money. When the deliberations begin, they all affect the same traditional mystery about "keeping the door," and retain the long pause outside before admitting the nervous aspirant for "initiation"; they all "open the lodge" with the same kind of cautious solemnity, and dignify with strange titles and formal methods of address the officers whom they are perpetually electing and re-electing. But if the visitor listens carefully he will notice, in the Trade Union business, constant references to mysterious outside authorities. The whole branch may show itself in favor of the grant of benefit to a particular applicant, but the secretary will observe that any such payment would have to come out of his own pocket, as the central executive has intimated that the case is not within its interpretation of the rules. The branch treasurer may announce that the balance in hand has suddenly sunk to a few pounds, as he has been ordered by the central office to remit £100 to a branch at the other end of the kingdom. And when a question arises as to some dispute with an employer, the visitor will be surprised to find that this characteristic Trade Union business is not in the hands of the branch at all, but is being dealt with by another outside authority, the "district," on instructions from the general secretary. [1]

Trade Unionism has, in fact, been based from the outset on the principle of the solidarity of the trade. Even the eighteenth-century clubs of handicraftsmen, without national organisation of any kind, habitually contributed their surplus

---

[1] Branch meetings of Trade Unions are private, but it is not impossible for a bona-fide student of Trade Unionism to gain admission as the friend of one of the officials. The authors have attended branch meetings of almost every trade in various industrial centres, and have found their proceedings of great interest, not only as revealing the inner working of Trade Unionism, but also as displaying the marked differences of physique, intellect, and character between the different sections of the wage-earning class, often erroneously regarded as homogeneous. Some of these differences are referred to in the chapter on "The Assumptions of Trade Unionism."

balances in support of each other's temporary needs. When the clubs drew together in a national union, it was assumed, as a matter of course, that any cash in possession of any branch was available for the needs of any other branch. Thus we learn from the resolution of the Stonemasons' Delegate Meeting of 1833, that the several lodges were expected spontaneously to send their surplus monies to the aid of any district engaged in a strike.[1] This archaic trustfulness in the brotherhood of man still contents such a conservative-minded trade as the Coopers, whose " Mutual Association " remains only a loose alliance of local clubs, aiding each other's disputes by voluntary grants.[2] But in the large industries the same spirit soon embodied itself in formal machinery. Among the Stonemasons the primitive arrangement was, it is not surprising to learn, in the opinion of the "Grand Central Committee," "wholly inefficient," each district sending only such funds as it chose, and selecting which out of several districts on strike it would support. The next step, which appears in the first manuscript rules (probably of 1834), was to make each branch " immediately contribute a proportionate share " of the cost of maintaining each strike, fixed by the Grand Committee. Finally, in 1837, we have what has become the typical Trade Union arrangement of a fund belonging, not to the branch, but to the society ; available only for the purposes prescribed by the rules, but within those purposes common to the whole organisation.

It is easy to understand why the Stonemasons, dispersed over the country in relatively small groups, each conscious of its own isolation and weakness in face of the great capitalist contractor, should quickly seize the idea of a common " war-chest." The Carpenters, working under much

---

[1] Circular of "Grand Central Committee," held in Manchester, 28th November 1833, preserved in the records of the Friendly Society of Operative Stonemasons.

[2] See the various " monthly reports " of the Mutual Association of Coopers. A proposal is under discussion to form a central fund, fed by regular contributions for the aid of any branch under attack.

the same circumstances, express this feeling in the following terms : " Although oceans may separate us from each other, our interests are identical ; and if we become united under one constitution, governed by one code of rules, having one common fund available wherever it may be required, we thus acquire a power which, if judiciously exercised, will protect our interests more effectually and will confer greater advantages than can possibly be derived from any partial union." [1] But we may see the same process of financial centralisation at work in trades densely concentrated in a small area. The Cotton-spinners of Oldham and the surrounding towns were, down to 1879, organised as a federation of ten financially autonomous societies, each collecting, expending, and investing its own funds. The great trade struggle of 1877-78 revealed the weakness of this form of organisation. To quote the words of an official of the trade,[2] " The result was that when a strike occurred, some of the branches were on the point of bankruptcy, whilst others were in a good position as regards funds for maintaining the struggle. They soon found out their real fighting strength was gauged, not by the worth of their richest branch, but by the poorest. It was another exemplification of the old law of mechanics that the strength of the chain is represented by its weakest link. After the struggle they remedied the defect by enacting that all surplus funds should be deposited in one common account." Since that time each division of the Lancashire Cotton-spinners has adopted the principle of centralised funds. " We hold," says the General Secretary of the Bolton Spinners, " that where the labour of any number of men is subject to the same fluctuations of trade, when the product of their labour goes into the same market, and when the prices and conditions which regulate their wages are identical, it is imperative upon such men, if they wish to protect their

---

[1] Preface to the *Rules of the Amalgamated Society of Carpenters and Joiners* (Manchester, 1891).

[2] The late John Fielding, secretary of the Bolton Provincial Operative Cotton-spinners' Association, one of the ablest leaders of the Cotton-spinners.

labour, to combine together in one association. It is not sufficient that they shall join separate district societies which in time may boast of possessing a respectable reserve fund entirely under their own control. We have no hesitation in saying that any such accumulated funds are of little use in promoting their purely trade interests." [1]

The paramount necessity of a central fund, available for the defence of any branch that might be involved in industrial war, has become so plain to every Trade Unionist that society after society has adopted the principle of a common purse. But a common purse, as one or two striking instances among successful friendly societies prove, does not, in itself, necessarily involve the establishment of a dominant central executive wielding all administrative power. Where business can be reduced to precise rules, into the carrying out of which no question of policy enters, and no discretion is allowed, experience shows, as we shall presently see, that local branch administration may be as efficient and economical as that of a central authority. But the expenditure of the Trade Union funds is determined, not exclusively by the legislation of its members, but largely by the judgment of its administrators. In all matters of trade protection, whether it be the elaboration of a complicated list of piece-work prices, the promotion of a new factory bill, the negotiation of a national agreement with the associated employers, or the conduct of a strike, it passes the wit of man to prescribe by any written rule the exact method or amount of the expenditure to be incurred. It follows that the larger and most distinctive part of Trade Union administration, unlike the award of friendly benefits, cannot be predetermined by any law or scale, but must be left to the discretion of the executive authority. To vest this discretion absolutely and exclusively in the central executive representing the whole body of members is, it is plain, the only way by which those who have contributed the income can retain

[1] *Annual Report of the Bolton Provincial Operative Cotton-spinners' Association*, 1882.

any control over its expenditure. But this development necessarily entails the withdrawal from the branches of all real autonomy in issues of policy and in the expenditure of their part of the common income. It follows necessarily from the merging of the branch monies into a fund common to the whole society, and from the replenishment of this fund by levies upon all the members alike, that no local branch can safely be permitted to involve the whole organisation in war. Centralisation of finance implies, in a militant organisation, centralisation of administration. Those Trade Unions which have most completely recognised this fact have proved most efficient, and therefore most stable. Where funds have been centralised, and power nevertheless left, through the inadvertence or lack of skill of the framers of the rules, to local authorities, the result has been weakness, divided counsels, and financial disaster.

This cardinal principle of democratic finance has been only slowly and imperfectly learnt by Trade Unionists, and a lack of clear insight into the matter still produces calamitous results in large and powerful organisations. To take, for instance, the Amalgamated Society of Engineers, which was formed for the express purpose of bringing about a uniform trade policy under the control of a central executive. It was intended to secure this result by providing that strike pay should be awarded only by the central executive, leaving the branches to dispense the other benefits prescribed by the rules. But unfortunately this strike pay amounts only to five shillings a week, it being assumed that the member leaving his work will also be receiving the Out of Work donation of ten shillings a week, awarded by his branch. This confusion of trade with friendly benefits has resulted in a serious weakening of the authority of the central executive in matters of trade policy. Whenever the men working in any engineering establishment are dissatisfied with any decision of their employer, they can appeal to their own branch, and, on obtaining its permission, may drop their tools, with the certainty that they will receive at the cost of the whole society the Out of Work benefit of ten shillings a week.[1] The matter will be reported, in due course, by the district committee to the central executive, even if the branch itself does not trouble to apply for permission to pay the additional five shillings a week contingent benefit. But meanwhile, war has been declared, and has actually begun; the local employers may have retaliated with a lock-out, the whole district may even have "come out" in support of their fellow-workmen; and the society may find its prestige and honor involved in maintaining a great industrial conflict without its central executive ever having decided that the point at issue was one which should be fought at all. This, indeed, is precisely what happened in the most disastrous and discreditable of recent trade disputes, the prolonged strike of the Engineers and Plumbers in the Tyneside ship-building yards in 1892, when thousands of men were idle for over three months, not in order to raise the Standard of Life of themselves or any other section of the workers, but because the local Engineers and Plumbers could not agree as to which of them should fit up two-and-a-half inch iron piping. It would be easy for any student of the records of the Amalgamated Society of Engineers to pick out many other cases in which branches have, by paying the Out of Work donation to members refusing work, initiated important trade movements on their own account, without the prior knowledge or consent of the central executive.

This unfortunate confusion between Out of Work benefit and strike pay is not the only ambiguity that perplexes the administrators of the Amalgamated Society of Engineers. Although any authorised dispute is supported

[1] This injurious practice has been greatly strengthened by the fact that the "contingent fund," out of which alone the strike pay could formerly be granted, has often been abolished and subsequently re-established, by votes of the members. During the periods in which the contingent fund did not exist, the society had no other means of resisting encroachments than the award of Out of Work benefit to members who refused to submit to them. But this left the decision to the branch, though the funds which it dispensed were levied equally on the whole society.

from the funds of the society as a whole, it is left to the local members through their district committee to begin the quarrel. This would seem to mean complete local autonomy, and it is cherished as such by the more active branches. But the rule also provides that the resolutions of district committees shall be " subject to the approval " of the central executive, the ultimate veto, though not the direction of the policy, being thus vested in headquarters. The incapacity of the Engineers to make up their minds whether or not they desire local autonomy in trade policy, has more than once placed the society in an invidious and even ludicrous position. Thus, in the autumn of 1895 the Belfast branches, with the confirmation of the central executive, struck for an advance. The federated employers thereupon locked out, not only all the Belfast engineers, but also those on the Clyde. In the negotiations which ensued the central executive naturally represented the society, and eventually arranged a compromise, which was approved by the Clyde branches. The Belfast branches, on the other hand, refused to accept the agreement or to consider the strike at an end, and went on issuing full strike pay, from the funds of the whole society, to all their members. The central executive found itself bitterly reproached by the federated employers for what seemed a breach of faith, and public opinion was scandalised by the lack of loyalty and discipline. Eventually the deadlock was ended by the central executive taking upon itself peremptorily to order the Belfast members to resume work, without waiting for the resolution of the district committee. Whether the central executive had any right to intervene at all, otherwise than by confirming or disallowing a resolution of the district committee, became a matter of heated controversy; and the Delegate Meeting of 1896 not only passed a resolution censuring this action, but also framed a new rule which expressly deprives both the central executive and the district committee of the power of closing a dispute, by making the consent of a two-thirds majority of the local members—some or all of whom must be the very persons concerned—necessary to the closing of a strike.[1] This fanatical attachment of the Engineers to an extreme local autonomy—their persistent assumption that any one section, however small and unimportant, ought to be allowed to draw on the funds of the whole society in support of a policy of which the majority of the members may disapprove—has done incalculable harm to the Amalgamated Society of Engineers. It has been the source of a continuous and needless drain on the society's resources. It has more than once involved thousands of members in a lock-out, when they had no quarrel of their own. It deprives the federated employers of all confidence in those who meet them on the workmen's behalf. And, most important of all, it effectually prevents the society from maintaining any genuine defence of the conditions of its members' employment. National agreements such as are concluded by the United Society of Boilermakers, the Amalgamated Association of Operative Cottonspinners, and the National Union of Boot and Shoe Operatives, by which a general levelling-up of conditions is secured, must necessarily be out of the power of an organisation which cannot give its negotiators the mandate of a common will.

The same conflict between centralisation of finance and the surviving local autonomy of the branches may be traced in the rules of most of the unions in the building trade. Here the tradition has been to require the assent of the whole society, or of the central executive as its representative, before any branch may strike, or even negotiate, for an increase of wages or new trade privileges. But it has been no less firmly rooted in the practice of the building trades, for any branch, or even any individual workman, instantly to cease work, without consulting the central executive, whenever an employer makes an encroachment on the existing Working Rules of that town. In such cases, by the rules of most of the national unions in these trades, strike pay is granted by the branch as a matter of course.

[1] *Rules of the Amalgamated Society of Engineers* (London, 1896), p. 54.

A branch is accordingly expressly authorised to involve the whole society in war, whenever its own interpretation of existing customs is challenged by an employer, even in the minutest particular. We may easily imagine how greatly international hostilities would be increased, if the governor of every colony or out-lying dependency were authorised instantly to declare war, in the name and on the resources of the whole empire, whenever, in his own private judgment, any infringement of national rights had taken place. And although, in the Trade Union instance, each particular branch dispute is usually neither momentous nor prolonged, the result is a captious and spasmodic trade policy, sometimes even ridiculous in its inconsistency, which the central executive has no effective power to check. The Friendly Society of Operative Stonemasons and the Operative Bricklayers' Society have, until recent years, specially suffered from a constant succession of petty quarrels with particular employers, most of which would have been avoided if the point at issue had been made the subject of quiet negotiation by an officer acting on behalf of the whole society.[1] This has been dimly perceived by the leaders of the building trades. Among the Bricklayers and Stonemasons, the traditional right of the branch to strike against encroachments, without authorisation from the central executive, has hitherto been too firmly held to be abolished ; but the newer editions of the rules expressly limit this right to certain kinds of encroachment, and require the branch to obtain the

[1] Sometimes the interpretation placed by two branches on the Working Rules of one or both of them may seriously differ. The Kendal branch of the Friendly Society of Operative Stonemasons had, in 1873, in its Working Rules, a provision requiring employers to provide dinner for men sent to work beyond a certain distance from their homes in the town. A Kendal employer sent members of the Kendal branch to a place twenty miles away which was within the district of another branch having no such rule. The Kendal masons insisted on their employer complying with the Kendal rules, whereupon he replaced them by men belonging to the local branch, who contended that the Kendal rules did not apply to work done in their district. This fine point in interpretation led to endless recrimination between the two branches, and much local friction. Finally the issue was referred to a vote of the whole society, which went against the Kendal branch.—*Fortnightly Return*, October 1873.

authority of the whole society before resisting any other kind of attack. The Amalgamated Society of Carpenters and Joiners has advanced a step further in centralisation of policy. For the last twenty years its rules have expressly forbidden any branch to strike "without first obtaining the sanction of the executive council . . . whether it be for a new privilege or against an encroachment on existing ones."[1] It is no mere coincidence that the Amalgamated Society of Carpenters and Joiners, though younger than many other societies in the building trades, is now the largest and most wealthy of them all.

The difficulties that beset the Amalgamated Society of Engineers and the Operative Bricklayers' Society have been overcome by the United Society of Boilermakers, a union which has found a way to combine efficient administration of friendly benefits with a strong and uniform trade policy. Here the problem has been solved by an absolute separation, both in name and in application, between the trade and friendly benefits. The "donation benefit" for the support of the unemployed is restricted to "a man thrown out of employment through depression of trade or other causes," testified by "a note signed by the foreman or by three full members that are working in the shop or yard he has left," and proved to the satisfaction of the officers of the branch. This benefit cannot be given to a man leaving his employment on a dispute of any kind whatsoever. Strike pay is an entirely separate benefit, awarded, even in the case of a single workman, only by the central executive, and payable only upon its express and particular direction.[2] It follows that, although the branches administer the friendly benefits, they are not allowed to deal in any way with trade matters. If any dispute arises between an employer and his workmen, or even between him and one of his workmen, the case is at once taken up by the district delegate, an officer appointed by and acting for the whole

---

[1] Rule 28, sec. 10 of edition of 1893, p. 66.
[2] *Rules of the United Society of Boilermakers* (Newcastle, 1895).

society, in constant communication with the general secretary at headquarters. No workman may drop his tools, or even give notice to his employer, over any question of trade privileges, except with the prior authorisation of the district delegate ; and to make doubly sure that this law shall be implicitly obeyed, not a penny of benefit may be paid by the branch in any such case, except on the express direction of the central executive.

Nevertheless, the Trade Union branch, even in the most centralised society, continues to fulfil an indispensable function in Trade Union administration. As an association for mutual insurance, for the provision of sick pay, funeral expenses, and superannuation allowance, the Trade Union, like the friendly society, governs its action by definite rules and fixed scales of benefit, which are nowadays settled as an act of legislation by the society as a whole. Even the Out of Work benefit—the " Donation " or " Idle Money," which none but trade societies have found it possible to undertake, is dealt with in the same manner. The printed constitution of the typical modern union prescribes in minute detail what sums are to be paid for sickness or out of work benefit, and attempts to provide by elaborate rules for every possible contingency. The central executive rigidly insists on the rules being obeyed to the letter, and it might at first seem as if nothing had been left for the branch to do. This is very far from being the case. To protect the funds from imposition, local and even personal knowledge is indispensable. Is a man sick or malingering ? Has an unemployed member lost his situation through slackness of his employer's business or slackness of his own energy ? These are questions that can best be answered by men who have worked with him in the factory, know the foreman who has dismissed him, and the employer who has refused to take him on, and are acquainted with the whole circumstances of his life. Here we find the practical utility which has kept the Trade Union branch alive as a vital part of Trade Union organisation.

It serves as a jury for determining, not questions of policy, but issues of fact.[1]

And if for a moment we leave the question of local self-government, and consider all the functions of the branch, we shall recognise the practical convenience of this institution even in the most highly centralised society. It is no small gain in a democratic organisation to have insured the regular meeting together of the great bulk of the members, under conditions which lead directly to the discussion of their common needs. Nor is the educational value of the branch meeting its only justification. In every Trade Union, whether governed by the Referendum or by a Representative Assembly,

[1] The utility of this jury system, if we may so describe the branch function, may be gathered from the experience of other benefit organisations. It is, to begin with, significant that the great industrial insurance companies and collecting societies, with their millions of working-class customers, and their ubiquitous network of paid officials, but without a jury system, find it financially impossible to undertake to give even sick pay, let alone out of work benefit. The Prudential Assurance Company, the largest and best managed of them all, began to do so, but had to abandon it because, as the secretary told the Royal Commission on Friendly Societies in 1873, "after five years' experience we found we were unable to cope with the fraud that was practised." Among friendly societies proper, in which sick benefit is the main feature, it is instructive to find that it is among the Foresters and Oddfellows, where each court or lodge is financially autonomous, that the rate of sickness is lowest. One interesting society, the Rational Sick and Burial Association (established in 1837 by Robert Owen and his "Rational Religionists"), is organised exactly like a national amalgamated Trade Union, with branches administering benefits payable from a common fund. In this society, as we gather, the rate of sickness is slightly greater than in the Affiliated Orders, where each lodge not only decides on whether benefit shall be given, but also has itself to find the money. Finally, when we come to the Hearts of Oak Benefit Society, the largest and most efficient of the centralised friendly societies having no branches at all, and dispensing all benefits from the head office, we find the rate of sickness habitually far in excess of the experience of the Foresters or the Oddfellows, or even of the Rationals, an excess due, according to the repeated declarations of the actuary, to nothing but inadequate provision against fraud and malingering. During the eight years 1884-91, for instance, the "expected sickness," according to the 1866-70 experience of the Manchester Unity of Oddfellows (all districts), was 1,111,553 weeks; the actual weeks for which benefit was drawn numbered no fewer than 1,452,106, an excess of over 30 per cent (*An Enquiry into the Methods, etc., of a Friendly Society*, by R. P. Hardy, 1894, p. 36). "Centralised societies," says the Rev. Frome Wilkinson, "will never be able to avoid being imposed upon; not so, however, a well-regulated branch of an affiliated society with its machinery in good working order" (*The Friendly Societies Movement*, p. 193). See also "Fifty Years of Friendly Society Progress," by the same author, in the *Oddfellows' Magazine* for 1888.

the branch forms an integral part of the legislative machinery. If the laws are made by the votes of the members, it is the branch meeting which is the deliberative assembly, and usually also the polling place. When the society enjoys fully developed representative institutions, the branch becomes at once a natural and convenient electoral division, and supplies, what is so sorely needed in political democracy, a means by which the representative must regularly meet every section of his constituents. In other trades it is common to require that no important alteration of the society's rules shall be put before the Representative Assembly until it has been first discussed, and sometimes voted on, by one or more of the branches. In attending branch meetings we have found most interesting that part of the evening which is taken up with the reports made by the branch representatives on the local Trades Council, on a district or joint committee of the trade, or in the Representative Assembly of the society itself. It has often occurred to us how much it would enliven and invigorate political democracy if the member of Parliament or the Town Councillor had habitually to report to, and discuss with, every section of his constituents, supporters and opponents alike, all the public business in which they were interested. Quite apart, therefore, from any administrative functions, organisation by branches has manifold uses, even in the most centralised society. But these uses have little connection with the problem of centralisation and local autonomy. In all these respects the branches are not separate units of government, but constitute, in effect, a single mass meeting of members, geographically sliced up into aggregates of convenient size.

Thus, in the vexed problem of how to divide administration between central and local authorities, Trade Union experience affords no guide, either to other voluntary associations or to political democracy. The extreme centralisation of finance and policy, which the Trade Union has found to be a condition of efficiency, has been forced upon it by the unique character of its functions. The lavish generosity with which the early trade clubs granted their surplus funds right and left to the clubs in other towns that needed assistance, was not simply an outburst of brotherly unselfishness. Each club had a keen appreciation that a reduction of wages in one centre was likely soon to spread to other towns, as a result either of the competition among the employers, or of the migration among the workmen. And when the various local clubs drew together into a national combination and appointed one salaried officer after another to execute the commands of a central executive, this was not due to any indifference to local self-government or liking for bureaucracy, nor even to any philanthropic impulse to be kind to their weaker brethren, but to a dim recognition of their own dependence upon securing a trade policy uniform from one end of the kingdom to the other. This aspiration has crystallised in the minds of all experienced Trade Unionists into a fixed conviction, which has long since spread to the rank and file. It is obvious that a uniform policy can only be arrived at and maintained by a central body acting for the whole trade. And thus it comes about that the constant tendency to a centralised and bureaucratic administration is, in the Trade Union world, accepted, and even welcomed, by men who, in all the other organisations to which they belong, are sturdy defenders of local autonomy.[1]

[1] This generalisation applies, in its entirety, only to the trade funds and trade policy of the unions. In so far as the friendly society side of Trade Unionism is used only as an adventitious attraction in obtaining members, there is no inherent difficulty in each local branch, in its capacity of " benefit club," fixing its own rates of contribution, retaining its own funds, and administering its own affairs, whilst at the same time forming part, for all trade protection purposes, of a strictly centralised national combination. More usually, however, the friendly society side of Trade Unionism is valued also for the adventitious aid which its accumulating funds bring to the war chest. Thus we find that the national Trade Unions, with very few exceptions, have now centralised not only their trade but also their friendly society resources, the whole of each member's contribution being paid into a common fund available for all the purposes of the society. The result is, accordingly, to concentrate still more authority in the hands of the central executive.

CHAPTER IV

INTERUNION RELATIONS

THROUGHOUT the foregoing chapters we have accepted the current assumption that there is such a thing as a "trade," as to the boundaries of which no question can arise. In the preface to nearly every Trade Union book of rules we find some passage to the following effect : "Every artisan following a given occupation has an interest, in common with all those similarly engaged, in forming rules by which *that particular trade* shall be regulated." But what is a "trade," and how are its limits to be defined ? By the journalist or professional man, every mechanic employed at Armstrong's or Whitworth's would naturally be classed as an engineer ; would be expected to belong to the "Engineers' Trade Union" ; and would at any rate be clearly distinguished from a plumber, a joiner, or a shipwright. Yet the grouping of these mechanics into their several organisations, and the relations of these organisations to each other, are responsible for some of the most serious difficulties of British Trade Unionism.

We had better first state the problem as it appears in some of the principal trades. A single industry will often include sections of workers differing widely from each other in their standard earnings, in the kind and amount of protection called for by their circumstances, and in the strategic strength of their respective positions against the employer, upon which, in the end, their trade policy will depend. Thus a cotton-spinning mill, with 40 pairs of mules, will employ about 90 cardroom operatives, mostly women, the men earning from 18s. to 30s. per week and the women 12s. 6d. to 19s. 6d. ; 40 adult male mule-spinners, earning, by piecework, from 30s. to 50s. per week ; 80 boys and men as piecers, engaged and paid by the mule-spinners at 6s. 6d. to 20s. per week ; and 2 overlookers with weekly salaries of 42s. and upwards. The adjacent cotton-weaving shed, with 800 looms, will employ about 260 male and female weavers, paid by the piece and earning from 14s. to 20s. per week ; 8 overlookers (men), paid by a percentage on the weavers' earnings, and getting 32s. to 42s. per week ; 10 twisters and drawers, earning at piecework 25s. to 32s. per week ; 5 warpers and beamers working by the piece and making from 20s. to 30s. per week ; 3 or 4 tapesizers with a fixed weekly wage of 42s. per week ; a number of children varying from 1 to 50, employed by the weavers as tenters, and paid small sums ; and a manager over the whole with a salary of £200 or £300 per annum.[1]

All these operatives may be engaged by a single employer, work upon the same raw material, and produce for the same market. They have obviously many interests in common. But for all that they do not form a simple unit of government. It is impossible to devise any constitution which would enable these six or more classes of cotton operatives to form an amalgamated union, having a common policy, a common purse, a common executive, and a common staff of officials, without sacrificing the financial and trade interest of one, or even all of the different sections. It suits the well-paid sections, such as the Spinners, Tapesizers, Beamers, Twisters, Drawers, and Overlookers, to pay a high weekly contribution, which would be beyond the means of the Cardroom Operatives and the Weavers. But the manner in which each section desires to apply its funds varies even

---

[1] Compare the still more detailed classification of workers incidentally given in the Board of Trade *Report by Miss Collet on the Statistics of Employment of Women and Girls*, C. 7564, 1894.

more than their amount. The Tapesizers, deriving their strategic strength from their highly specialised skill, the impossibility of replacing them, and the small proportion which their wages bear to the total cost of production, can afford to spend their funds on ample sick and funeral benefits. With a uniform time rate in each district, and few occasions for dispute with their employers, they need no offices or salaried officials whatsoever. It pays the Spinners and Weavers, on the other hand, to maintain a highly skilled professional staff for the purpose of computing and maintaining their earnings under the complicated lists of piecework prices. But the Weavers stand at the disadvantage of needing also a large staff of paid collectors to secure the regular payment of contributions from the girls and married women, who are indisposed to bring their weekly pence to the public-house in which the branch meeting is still frequently held. This applies also to the Cardroom Operatives, but these, working usually at time rates, do not need the weavers' skilled calculator. The Beamers, Twisters, and Drawers, on the one hand, and the Overlookers on the other, have again their own peculiarities. To unite, in any common scheme of contributions and benefits, classes so diverse in their means and requirements, appears absolutely impossible. Still more difficult would it be to provide for the effective representation upon a common executive of sections so different in numerical strength. Not to mention the Tapesizers and Overlookers, who must be completely submerged by the rest, it would be difficult to induce the 19,000 well-paid, well-officered, and well-disciplined Spinners to submit their trade policy to the decision of the 22,000 ill-paid Cardroom Operatives or the 85,000 Weavers, of whom two-thirds are women. On the other hand, the Weavers would not permanently forego the advantage of their overwhelming superiority in numbers, nor would the Spinners allow the Tapesizers an equal voice with themselves. But even if a representative executive could, by some device, be got together, it would not form a fit body to decide the technical questions peculiar to each class.

On each point as it arose, the experts would be in a minority, and the decisions, whatever their justice, would invariably cause dissatisfaction to one section or another. Moreover, quite apart from technical details, the moments of strategic advantage differ from section to section. It may suit the Spinners to move for an advance, at a time when the weaving trade is depressed, and both will be more ready to move than the Overlookers. The Tapesizers, on the other hand, will prefer, to any overt strike, the silent withdrawal of one man after another from a recalcitrant employer, until he is ready to offer the Trade Union terms. It is obvious that a council representing such diverse elements would find it extremely difficult to maintain an active and consistent course. On the other hand, all the sections of Cotton Operatives have manifold interests in common. Every factory act regulating the sanitation, hours of labor, machinery, age of children, and inspection of factories, directly or indirectly concerns every worker in the mill. Such industrial dislocations as Liverpool "cotton corners," or the employers' mutual agreement to reduce stocks by working short time, affect all alike. The policy of the Indian Secretary, the Minister of Education, or the Chancellor of the Exchequer, may, any moment, touch them all on a vital point. If, therefore, the Cotton Operatives are to have any effective voice in regulating these essentially trade matters, their organisation must in some form be co-extensive with the whole cotton industry.

Another instance of these difficulties is presented by the great industry of engineering. A century ago the small skilled class of millwrights executed every kind of engineering operation, from making the wooden patterns to erecting in the mill the machines which had been constructed by their own hands. The enormous expansion of the engineering industry has long since brought about a division of labor, and the mechanics in a great engineering establishment to-day are divided into numerous distinct classes of workers, who are rarely able to do each other's work. The

pattern-makers, working in wood, have become sharply
marked off from the boilermakers and the ironfounders.
The smiths, again, are distinguished from the fitters, turners,
and erectors. Another form of specialisation has arisen with
the increased use of other metals than iron and steel, and
we have brass-founders, brass-finishers, and coppersmiths.
Each generation sees a great development in the use of
machines to make machines, so that a modern engineering
shop, in addition to the time-honored lathe, includes a bewildering variety of drilling, shaping, boring, planing, slotting,
milling, and other machines, attended by wholly new classes
of machine-minders and tool-makers, displaying every grade
of skill. Finally, we have such new kinds of work, with new
classes of specialists, as are involved in the innumerable
applications of iron and steel in modern civilisation, such as
iron ships and bridges, ordnance and armour-plating, hydraulic
apparatus and electric-lighting, sewing-machines and bicycles.
To discover the exact limits of a " trade " in these closely
related but varied occupations is a task of supreme difficulty.
All are working in the same industry, and in the large
establishments of to-day, all may be engaged by a single
employer. The same recurring waves of expansion and
contraction sooner or later affect all alike. On the other
hand, there exist between the separate occupations great
varieties of methods of remuneration, standard earnings, and
strategic position. The strictly - apprenticed boilermakers
(shipyard platers) working in compact groups, at co-operative
piecework, earning sometimes as much as a pound a day,
find it advantageous in good times to roll up, by large subscriptions, a huge reserve fund, to maintain a staff of special
trade officers to arrange their piecework prices at every port,
and to provide handsomely for their recurring periods of
trade depression. At the other end of the scale we have the
intelligent laborer become an automatic machine-minder,
securing relative continuity of low-paid employment by
working any simple machine in any kind of engineering
establishment, and interested mainly in the opening of every

operation to the quickwitted outsider. The pattern-maker again, working in wood, at a high time rate, has little in common with the piece-working smith at the forge. When trade begins to improve, the pattern-makers, followed by the ironfounders, will be busy long before the smiths, fitters, and turners, and, if they wish to recover the wages lost in the previous depression, must move for an advance whilst all the rest of the engineering industry is still on short time. Finally, there is the difficulty of the method and basis of representation. Shall the government be centred in an iron shipbuilding port, where the boilermakers would be supreme, or in an inland engineering centre, when the fitters and turners would have an equally great preponderance? How can the tiny groups of pattern-makers, dispersed over the whole kingdom, get their separate interests attended to amid the overwhelming majorities of the other classes? Any attempt to represent, upon an executive council, each distinct occupation, let alone each great centre, must either ignore all proportional considerations, or involve the formation of a body of impossible dimensions and costliness.

We see, therefore, that within the circle of what is usually called a trade, there are often smaller circles of specialised classes of workmen, each sufficiently distinctive in character to claim separate consideration. The first idea is always to cut the Gordian knot by ignoring these differences, and making the larger circle the unit of government. So fascinating is this idea of " amalgamation " that it has been tried in almost every industry. The reader of the *History of Trade Unionism* will remember the remarkable attempt in 1833-34 to form a national " Builders' Union," to comprise the seven different branches of building operatives. The same years saw a succession of general unions in the cloth-making industry. In 1844, and again in 1863, the coalminers sought to combine in one amalgamated union every person employed in or about the mines, from one end of the kingdom to the other. The " Iron Trades " again were, between 1840 and 1850, the subject of innumerable local projects of amalgamation, in which not only the " Five Trades of Mechanism," but also the Boilermakers and the Ironfounders were all to be included. We need not describe the failure of all these attempts. More can, perhaps, be learnt from the experience of the great modern instance, the Amalgamated Society of Engineers.

It does not seem to have occurred to William Newton, when he launched this famous amalgamation, that any difficulty could arise as to the classes of workers to be included. What he was primarily concerned about was to merge in one national organisation all the various local societies of engineering mechanics, whether pattern-makers, smiths, turners, fitters, or erectors, working either in iron or brass. But " sectionalism " stood, from the very first, in the way. The various local clubs of Smiths and Pattern-makers objected strongly to sink their individuality in a general engineers' union. In the same way, the more exclusive Steam-Engine Makers' Society, in which millwrights, fitters, and turners predominated, refused to merge itself in the wider organisation. To Newton and Allan all these objections seemed to arise from the natural reluctance of local clubs to lose their individuality in a national union. This dislike, as they rightly felt, was destined to give way before the superior advantages of national combination. But subsequent experience has shown that the resistance to the amalgamation was due to more permanent causes. The merely local societies dropped in, one by one, to their greater rival. But this only revealed a more serious cleavage. The present rivals of the Amalgamated Society of Engineers are, not any local engineers' clubs, but national societies each claiming the exclusive allegiance of different sections of the trade. The pattern-makers, for instance, came to the conclusion in 1872 that their interests were neglected in the Amalgamated Society of Engineers, and formed the United Pattern-makers' Association, which now includes a large and increasing majority of this highly skilled class. The Associated Society of Blacksmiths, originally a Glasgow local club, now dominates its particular section of the trade on the Clyde and in Belfast, and has branches in the North of England. The Brass-workers, the Coppersmiths, and the Machine-minders have now all their own societies of national extent. The result has been that the Amalgamated Society of Engineers does not realise Newton's idea as regards any section whatever. The Boilermakers, who refused to have anything to do with amalgamation, and who have persistently put their energy into organising their own special craft, have succeeded, as we have mentioned, in forming one undivided, consolidated, and centralised society for the entire kingdom. Very different is the condition of the engineers. Neither the fitters nor the smiths, the pattern-makers nor the machine-minders, the brass-workers nor the coppersmiths, are united in any one society, or able to maintain a uniform trade policy, even for their own section of the industry. For all this confusion, the enthusiastic adherents of the Amalgamated Society have gone on preaching the one remedy of an ever-wider amalgamation. " The future basis of the Amalgamated Society," urged Mr. Tom Mann in 1891, " must be one that will admit every workman engaged in connection with the engineering trades, and who is called upon to exhibit mechanical skill in the performance of his labor. This would include men on milling and drilling machines, tool-makers, die-sinkers, and electrical engineers, and it would make it necessary to have the requisite staff at the general office to cater for so large a constituency, as there are at least 250,000 men engaged in the engineering and machine trades of the United Kingdom, and the work of organising this body must be undertaken by the A. S. E." [1] Somewhat against the advice of the more experienced officials, successive delegate meetings have included within the society one section of workmen after another. At the delegate meeting of 1892, which opened the society to practically every competent workman in the most miscellaneous engineering establishment, it was even

---

[1] Address to the East End Institute of the Amalgamated Society of Engineers, London, in *Trade Unionist*, 10th October 1891.

urged by some branches that the boundaries should be still further enlarged, so as to permit the absorption of plumbers and ironfounders. This proposal was with some reluctance rejected, but only on the ground that it would have brought the Amalgamation into immediate collision with the 16,278 members of the Friendly Society of Ironfounders (established 1809); and with the compact and militant United Operative Plumbers' Society (established 1848, membership 8758), rivals too powerful to be lightly encountered. Each successive widening of the amalgamation brings it, in fact, into conflict with a larger number of other unions, who become its embittered enemies. The very competition between rival societies which Newton's amalgamation was intended to supersede, has, through this all-inclusive policy itself, been rendered more intense and intractable.

And here it is imperative that the reader should fully appreciate the disastrous effect of this competition and rivalry between separate Trade Unions. The evil will be equally apparent whether we regard the Trade Union merely as a friendly society for insuring the weekly wage-earner against loss of livelihood through sickness, old age, and depression of trade, or as a militant organisation for enabling the manual worker to obtain better conditions from the capitalist employer.

Let us consider first the side of Trade Unionism which has, from the outset, been universally praised and admired, the "ancient and most laudable custom for divers artists within the United Kingdom to meet and form themselves into societies for the sole purpose of assisting each other in cases of sickness, old age, and other infirmities, and for the burial of their dead."[1] Now, whatever weight may be given, in matters of commerce, to the maxim *caveat emptor*—however thoroughly we may rely, as regards articles of personal consumption, on the buyer's watchfulness over his own

---

[1] Preamble to *Rules of the Friendly Society of Ironmoulders* (Manchester, 1809), and to those of many other unions of this epoch.

interests—it is indisputable that, in the whole realm of insurance, competition does practically nothing to promote efficiency. The assumption which underlies the faith in unrestricted competition is that the consumer is competent to judge of the quality of what he pays for, or that he will at any rate become so in the act of consumption. In matters of financial insurance no such assumption can reasonably be maintained. Apart from the dangers of irregularities and defalcations, the whole question of efficiency or inefficiency in friendly society administration is bound up with the selection of proper actuarial data, the collection and verification of the society's own actuarial experience, and the consequent fixing of the due rates of contribution and benefits. When rival societies bid against each other for members, competition inevitably takes the form, either of offering the common benefits at a lower rate, or of promising extravagant benefits at the common rate of subscription. The ordinary man, innocent of actuarial science, is totally unable to appreciate the merits of the rival scales put before him. To the raw recruit the smallness of the weekly levy offers an almost irresistible attraction. Nor does such illegitimate competition between societies work, as might be supposed, its own cure. The club charging rates insufficient to meet its liabilities will, it is true, in the end bring about its own destruction. But the actuarial nemesis is slow to arrive, as many years must elapse before the full measure of the liability for death claims and superannuation allowances can be tested. And when the inevitable collapse comes, the prudent society gains little by the dissolution of its unsound rival. A club which has failed to meet its engagements, and has been broken up, leaves those who have been its members suspicious of all forms of organisation and indisposed to renew their contributions. The payment for some time of high benefits in return for low subscriptions will have falsified the standard of expectation. Those who have lost their money ascribe the failure to the dishonesty or incapacity of the officers, to the workmen's lack of loyalty, to any cause, indeed, rather than to their own unreasonableness in expecting a shilling's worth of benefits for a sixpenny contribution.

In the case of Friendly Societies proper, and in that of Insurance Companies, the untrustworthiness of competition as a guarantee of financial efficiency has been fully recognised by the community, and dealt with by the legislature.[1] Trade Unions, however, have, for good and sufficient reasons, been left outside the scope of these provisions.[2] But, as a matter of fact, competition between Trade Unions on their benefit club side is even more injurious to their soundness than it is to Friendly Societies proper. Dealing as they do, not with a specially selected class of thrifty citizens, but with the whole body of men in their trade ; unable, owing to their other functions, to concentrate their members' attention upon the actuarial side of their affairs ; and destitute of any authoritative data or scientific calculation for such benefits as Out of Work pay, Trade Unions must always find it specially difficult to resist a demand for increase of benefits, or lowering of contribution. If two unions are competing for the same class of members, the pressure becomes irresistible.

The history of Trade Unionism is one long illustration of this argument. In one trade after another we watch the cropping up of " mushroom unions," their heated rivalry

---

[1] It is unnecessary for us to do more than refer to the long series of statutes, beginning in 1786, which provide for the registration, publication of accounts, public audit, and even compulsory valuation of Friendly Societies and Industrial Insurance Companies. By every means, short of direct prohibition, the State now seeks to put obstacles in the way of "under-cutting," and, to use the words of Mr. Reuben Watson before the Select Committee on National Provident Insurance in 1885 (Question 893), discourages "the formation of new societies on the unsound principles of former times." Within the two great "affiliated orders" of Oddfellows and Foresters, which together comprise at least half the friendly society world, the legal requirements are backed by an absolute prohibition to open any new lodge or court without adopting, as a minimum, the definitely approved scale of contributions and benefits. Even with regard to middle-class life assurance companies, Parliament has not only insisted on a specific account-keeping and publication of financial position, but has, since 1872, practically stopped the uprising of additional competitors, by requiring a deposit of £20,000 from any new company before business can be begun.

[2] See the chapter on "The Method of Mutual Insurance."

with the older organisations, and consequent mad race for members ; and finally, after a few years of unstable existence, their ignoble bankruptcy and dissolution. Meanwhile the responsible officials of the older societies will have been struggling with their own " Delegate Meetings " and " Revising Committees," to maintain a relatively sound scale of contributions and benefits. Any attempt at financial improvement will have been checked by the representations of the branch officers that the only result would be to divert all the recruits to their rasher and more open-handed competitors. The records of every important union contain bitter complaints of this injurious competition. The Friendly Society of Ironfounders, for instance, which dates from 1809, is one of the oldest and most firmly established Trade Unions. Its 16,000 members include an overwhelming majority of the competent ironmoulders in England, Ireland, and Wales. For over sixty years it has collected and preserved admirable statistical data of the cost of its various benefits, to provide for which it maintains a relatively high rate of contribution and levies. In August 1891, a leading member called attention to the touting for membership that was going on among his trade in certain districts. " I have now noticed," he concludes, "three distinct societies that enter moulders (ironfounders) who are eligible to join us. They offer, more or less, a high rate of benefit at a low rate of contribution. Whether they are likely to fulfil their promises I leave to the judgment of any thoughtful man who will sit down and compare their rates of contribution and benefits with the statistical figures of our society, as shown continually in the annual reports. Those figures have been arrived at by experience, which is the truest basis of calculation for the future, and I would commend them to the notice of all who set themselves the task of computing the maximum rate of benefit to be obtained at the minimum rate of subscription." [1]   Nor was

[1] Letter from H. G. Percival in the *Monthly Report of the Friendly Society of Ironfounders* (August 1891), pp. 18-21.

this warning unneeded.   When, in the very next month, the
Ironfounders met in delegate meeting to revise their rules,
branch after branch suggested, in order to outstrip the
attractions of their extravagant rivals, an increase of
benefits, without any addition to the contribution.   Thus
Gateshead, Keighley, and Greenwich urged that the Out of
Work benefit should be increased by more than ten per
cent ; Huddersfield and Oldham sought to raise the maximum sum receivable in any one year ; Barrow, Halifax,
and Liverpool asked that travellers should be allowed
sixpence per night instead of fourpence ; Oldham tried
largely to increase the scale of superannuation allowances,
and to raise the Accident Grant from £50 to £100 ;
St. Helens and many other branches demanded a ten per
cent increase of the sick benefit ; whilst Brighton, Keighley,
and Wakefield proposed to raise the funeral money from
£10 to £12.   On the other hand, Chelsea proposed a
reduction of the entrance fee by 33 per cent, whilst
Gloucester sought to lower it by one-half ; Liverpool would
take in men up to the age of 45, instead of stopping at
40 ; and Wakefield suggested the abandonment of any
medical examination at entrance.[1]   Fortunately for the
Ironfounders, their officers, with the statistical tables at
their back, were able to stave off most of these proposals.   But even responsible officials are forced to pay
heed to this reckless competition.   Thus in 1885, when
certain branches of the Steam - Engine Makers' Society,
getting anxious about their old age, suggested that the
provision for the superannuation benefit should be increased,
the central executive demurred to raising the contribution,
pointing out " the keen competition " for membership which
they had to meet, " just as though we were engaged in
commerce.   In every workshop," they continue, " we have
numerous societies to contend with, some of whose members

[1] *Suggestions from Branches of the Friendly Society of Ironfounders . . . for
consideration at the Delegate Meeting to be held in September* 1891 (London,
1891).

think that taking a man from another society and squeezing him into theirs is a valiant act. Many cases will occur to all, but we give one instance. We learned of the Pattern-makers' Association taking members of ours for an entrance fee of 5s., placing them in benefit at once, and even giving them credit for ten years' membership, should they apply for superannuation in the future." [1] These examples enable us to understand why it is that the Trade Unions accumulating the largest reserve funds to meet their prospective liabilities are to be found in the trades in which a single union is co-extensive with the industry. Thus, among the larger organisations, the United Society of Boilermakers with a balance in 1896 of £175,000, or £4 : 7 : 6 per head of its 41,000 members, towers above all other societies in the engineering and shipbuilding trades.

We have dwelt in some detail upon the evils of competition between Trade Unions considered merely as benefit clubs, because this part of their function has secured universal approval. But assuming that the workmen are right in believing trade combination to be economically useful to them—assuming, that is to say, that the institution of Trade Unionism has any justification at all—the case against competition among unions becomes overwhelming in strength. If a trade is split up among two or more rival societies, especially if these are unequal in numbers, scope, or the character of their members, there is practically no possibility of arriving at any common policy to be pursued by all the branches, or of consistently maintaining any course of action whatsoever. "The general position of our society in Liverpool," reports the District Delegate of the Amalgamated Society of Engineers in 1893, " is far from satisfactory, the work of organising the trade being rendered exceptionally difficult, not only by the existence of a large non-union element, but by the existence of a number of sectional societies. Here, as elsewhere, these small and unnecessary organisations

[1] *Steam-Engine Makers' Society ; Executive Council Report on Revision of Rules*, 25th July 1885.

are the causes of endless complications and inconvenience. How many of these absurd and irritating institutions actually exist here I am not yet in a position to say, but the following are those with which I am at present acquainted : Smiths and Strikers (Amalgamated), Mersey Shipsmiths, Steam-Engine Makers, United Pattern-makers, Liverpool Coppersmiths, Brass-finishers (Liverpool), Brass-finishers (Birmingham), United Machine Workers, Metal Planers, National Engineers. All these societies are naturally inimical to our own, yet how long shall we be able to tolerate their existence is another question. . . . The Boilermakers would never permit any section of their trade to organise apart from them ; why we should do so is a question which will assuredly have to be settled definitely sooner or later."[1] The "small and unnecessary organisations" naturally take a different view. The general secretary of the United Pattern-makers' Association, in a circular full of bitter complaints against the Amalgamated Society of Engineers, thus describes the situation : " For the information of those who may not be intimately acquainted with the engineering trade, we may explain that the Pattern-makers form almost the smallest section of that trade—the organised portion being split up into no less than four different sections [societies]—the largest section outside the ranks of the United Pattern-makers' Association belonging to the Amalgamated Society of Engineers. It will be easily understood that this division makes it very difficult for our society to act on the offensive with that promptitude which is often essential to the successful carrying out of a particular movement, as we have to consult with and obtain the co-operation of three societies other than our own ; and as our trade in these societies are in an insignificant minority, it is perhaps only natural that so far as the Amalgamated Society of Engineers is concerned, legislation for the trades that comprise the vast majority of its members should have a priority over a consideration of those questions which concern

[1] " Report of Organising District Delegate (No. 2 division) of Amalgamated Society of Engineers " in *Quarterly Report* for quarter ended March 1893.

so small a handful as the Pattern-makers belonging to their society." [1] An actual example of the everyday working life of a Trade Union branch will show how real is the difficulty thus caused. "Our Darlington members," reports the Pattern-makers' Executive, "have been engaged in a wages movement which has had in one respect a most unsatisfactory termination. The 'Mals' [2] and non-society men pledged themselves to assist our members to get the money up, until the critical moment arrived when notices were to be given in. The non-society element and the 'Mals' then formed an ignominious combination, and declined to go any further in the matter, the Darlington branch of the 'Mals' writing our Secretary to the effect that they would not permit their P.M.'s [Pattern-makers] to strike. They only number three, and the non-society men twice as many, so fortunately they could not do the cause very much injury. The advance was conceded by every firm excepting the Darlington Iron and Steel Works, where our men were drawn out, leaving two 'Mals' and their present allies, the non-society men, at work. Your general secretary wrote the executive committee of the 'Mals' on the subject over three weeks ago, but so insignificant a matter as this is apparently beneath the notice of this august body, as no reply has yet been vouchsafed." [3]

Trade Union rivalry has, however, a darker side. When the officers of the two organisations have been touting for members, and feeling keenly each other's competition, opportunities for friction and ill-temper can scarcely fail to arise. Accusations will be made on both sides of disloyalty and unfairness, which will be echoed and warmly resented by the

---

[1] Circular of United Pattern-makers' Association (on Belfast dispute), 22nd June 1892. The same note recurs in the *Report of Proceedings of the Sixth Annual Meeting* of the Federation of Engineering and Shipbuilding Trades (Manchester, 1896). "As a consequence of their present divided state," said Mr. Mosses, the general secretary of the United Pattern-makers' Association, at this meeting, "they had one district going in for advances, followed in a haphazard fashion by other districts ; and one body of men coming out on strike for the benefit of others who remained at their work."

[2] Members of the Amalgamated Society of Engineers.

[3] *Monthly Report of the United Pattern-makers' Association*, September 1889.

rank and file. Presently some dispute occurs between an employer and the members of one of the unions. These workmen may be dismissed by the employer, or withdrawn by order of their own district committee. The officers of the rival union soon hear of the vacancies from the firm in question. Members of their own society are walking the streets in search of work, and drawing Out of Work pay from the funds. To let these take the places left vacant—to "blackleg" the rival society—is to commit the gravest crime against the Trade Unionist faith. Unfortunately, in many cases, the temptation is irresistible. The friction between the rival organisations, the personal ill-feeling of their officers, the traditions of past grievances, the temptation of pecuniary gain both to the workmen and to the union, all co-operate to make the occasion "an exception." At this stage any pretext suffices. The unreasonableness of the other society's demand, the fact that it did not consult its rival before taking action, even the non-arrival of the letter officially announcing the strike, serves as a plausible excuse in the subsequent recrimi-nations. Scarcely a year passes without the Trade Union Congress being made the scene of a heated accusation by one society or another, that some other union has "blacklegged" a dispute in which it was engaged, and thereby deprived its members of all the results of their combination.[1]

[1] Whenever rivalry and competition for members have existed between unions in the same industry we find numberless cases of "blacklegging." The relations, for instance, between the Amalgamated Society of Engineers, and all the sectional societies, abound in unfortunate instances on the one side or the other. The two societies of Bricklayers have, in the past, frequently accused each other's members of the same crime. The "excursions across the Border" of the English and Scottish societies of Tailors and Plumbers have been enlivened by similar recrimi-nations, which are also bandied about among the several unions of general laborers. The Coalmining and Cotton manufacturing industries are honorably free from this feature. An exceptionally bad case of an established union becoming, through blacklegging, a mere tool of the employers, came to light at the Trade Union Congress of 1892, and was personally investigated by us.

The Glasgow Harbour Laborers' Union, established among the Clyde steve-dores in 1853, had, up to 1889, maintained an honorable record for stability and success. In the latter year it found itself, with only 230 members, menaced with extinction by the sudden uprising of the National Union of Dock Laborers in Great Britain and Ireland, a society organised on the antagonistic idea of including every kind of dock and wharf laborers in a national amalgamation. The small,

The foregoing detailed description has placed the reader in a position to appreciate the disastrous effect of competition between Trade Unions for members. Whilst seriously impairing their financial stability as benefit clubs, this rivalry cuts at the root of all effective trade combination. It is no exaggeration to say that to competition between overlapping unions is to be attributed nine-tenths of the ineffectiveness of the Trade Union world. The great army of engineering operatives, for instance, though exceptional in training and intelligence, and enrolled in stable and well-administered societies, have as yet not succeeded either in negotiating with the employers on anything like equal terms, or in maintaining among themselves any common policy whatsoever. An even larger section of the wage-earning world—that engaged in the great industry of transport—has so far failed, from a similar cause, to build up any really effective Trade Unionism. The millions of laborers, who

---

old-fashioned, and local society, with its traditions of exclusiveness and "privilege," refused to merge itself, but offered to its big rival a mutual "next preference" working arrangement—that is to say, whilst each society maintained for its own members a preferential right to be taken on at the wharves or yards where they were accustomed to work, it should accord to the members of the other society the right to fill any further vacancies at those yards or wharves in preference to outsiders. The answer to this was a peremptory refusal on the part of the National Union to recognise the existence of its tiny predecessor, whose members accordingly found themselves absolutely excluded from work. The National Union no doubt calculated that it would, in this way, compel the smaller society to yield. But at the very moment it had a great struggle on hand, both in Liverpool and Glasgow, with one of the principal shipping firms. Communications were quickly opened up between that firm and the Glasgow Harbour Laborers' Society, with the result that the latter undertook to do the firm's work, and thus at one blow not only defeated the aggressive pretensions of the National Union but also secured its own existence. This line of conduct was repeated whenever a dispute arose between the employers and any Union on the Clyde. When the Blast-furnacemen on strike had successfully appealed to the National Amalgamated Sailors' and Firemen's Union, not to unload Spanish pig iron, the Glasgow Harbour Laborers' Union promptly came to the employers' rescue. During the strike of the Scottish Railway Servants' Union, the same society was to the fore in supplying "scab laborers." Its crowning degradation, in Trade Union eyes, came in an alliance with the Shipping Federation, the powerful combination by which the employers have, since 1892, sought to crush the whole Trade Union movement in the waterside industries. Its conduct was, in that year, brought before the Trade Union Congress, which happened to meet at Glasgow, and the Congress almost unanimously voted the exclusion of its delegates.

must in any case find it difficult to maintain a common organisation, are constantly hampered in their progress by the existence of competing societies which, starting from different industries, quickly pass into general unions, including each other's members. Indeed, with the remarkable exceptions of the coal and cotton industries, and, to a lesser extent, that of house-building, there is hardly a great trade in the country in which the workmen's organisations are not seriously crippled by this fatal dissension.

Now, experience shows that the permanent cause of this competitive rivalry and overlapping between unions is their organisation upon bases inconsistent with each other. When two societies include and exclude precisely the same sections of workmen, competition between them loses half its bitterness, and the solution of the difficulty is only a question of time. We see, for instance, since 1862, the Amalgamated Society of Carpenters and Joiners rapidly distancing its elder competitor, the General Union of Carpenters and Joiners (established 1827). But because the members of both societies belong to identically the same trade, are paid by the same methods, earn the same rates, work the same hours, have the same customs and needs, and are in no way to be distinguished from each other, the branches in a given town find no difficulty in concerting, by means of a joint committee, a common trade policy. And although the existence of two societies weakens the financial position of the one as well as of the other, the identity of the members' income and requirements, and their constant intercourse, tend steadily to an approximation of the respective scales of contribution and benefits. Under these circumstances the tendency to amalgamation is, as we have seen in the preceding chapter, almost irresistible, and is usually delayed only by the natural reluctance of some particular official to abdicate the position of leadership.

The problem which the engineers, the transit workers, and the laborers have so far failed to solve, is how to define a trade. Among the engineers, for instance, there is no general agreement which groups of workmen have interests sufficiently distinct from the remainder as to make it necessary for them to combine in a sectional organisation ; and there is but little proper appreciation of the relation of these sectional interests to those which all engineering mechanics have in common. The enthusiast for amalgamation is always harping on the necessity of union amongst all classes of engineering workmen in order to abolish systematic overtime, to reduce the normal hours of labor, and to obtain recognition of Trade Union conditions from the government. To the member of the United Pattern-makers' Association or of the Associated Blacksmiths, these objects, however desirable, are subordinate to some re-arrangement of the method or scale of remuneration peculiar to his own occupation. The solution of the problem is to be found in a form of organisation which secures Home Rule for any group possessing interests divergent from those of the industry as a whole, whilst at the same time maintaining effective combination throughout the entire industry for the promotion of the interests which are common to all the sections.

Fortunately, we are not left to our imagination to devise a paper constitution which would fulfil these conditions. In another industry we find the problem solved with almost perfect success. We have already described the half-dozen distinct classes into which the Cotton Operatives are naturally divided. Each of these has its own independent union, which carries on its own negotiations with the employers, and would vigorously resist any proposal for amalgamation. But in addition to the sectional interests of each of the six classes, there are subjects upon which two or more of the sections feel in common, and others which concern them all. Accordingly, instead of amalgamation on the one hand, or isolation on the other, we find the sectional unions combining with each other in various federal organisations of great efficiency. The Cotton-spinners and the Cardroom Operatives, working always for the same employers in the same establishments, have formed the Cotton-Workers' Association, to the funds of which both societies contribute. Each constituent union carried on its own collective bargaining and has its own funds. But it agrees to call out its members in support of the other's dispute, whenever requested to do so, the members so withdrawn being supported from the federal fund. The Cotton-spinners thus secure the stoppage of the material for their work, whenever they withdraw their labor, and thereby place an additional obstacle in the way of the employer obtaining blackleg spinners. The Card-room Operatives on the other hand, whose labor is almost unskilled, and could easily be replaced, obtain in their disputes the advantage of the support of the indispensable Cotton-spinners. No federation for these purposes would be of use to the Cotton-weavers, who often work for employers devoting themselves exclusively to weaving, and whose product goes to a different market. But the Cotton-weavers join with the Cotton-spinners and the Cardroom Operatives in the United Textile Factory Workers' Association, a purely political organisation for the purpose of obtaining and enforcing the factory and other legislation common to the whole trade.[1] And it is interesting to notice that the Cotton Operatives not only refrain from converting this strong and stable federation into an amalgamation, but even carry the federal form into the different sections of their industry. The 19,000 Cotton-spinners, for instance, form a single fighting unit, which, for compactness and absolute discipline, bears comparison even with the United Society of Boilermakers. But though the Cotton-spinners call their union an amalgamation, the larger "provinces" retain the privilege of electing their own officers, and of fixing their own contributions for local purposes and special benefits, and even preserve a certain degree of legislative autonomy. The student who derives his impression of these organisations merely from their elaborate separate rules and reports,

[1] This organisation was temporarily suspended in 1896.

might easily conclude that, in the relation between the Oldham or Bolton "province," and the "Representative Meeting" of the Amalgamated Association of Operative Cotton-spinners, we have a genuine case of local and central government. This, however, is not the case. The partial autonomy of the "provinces" of Oldham and Bolton is not a case of geographical, but of industrial specialisation. Each "province" has its own peculiar trade, spinning different "counts" for widely different markets. Each is governed by its own peculiar list of piecework prices, based on different considerations. And though the prevailing tendency is towards a greater uniformity of terms and methods, there is still a sufficient distinction between the Oldham and Bolton trades themselves, and between those of the smaller districts, to make any amalgamation a hazardous experiment. Similar considerations have hitherto applied to the Cotton-weavers, who have, indeed, only recently united into a single body. Differences of trade interests, not easy of explanation to the outsider, have hitherto separated town and town, each working under its own piecework list. These sectional differences resulted, until lately, in organisation by loosely federated autonomous groups. It is at least an interesting coincidence that the increasing uniformity of conditions which, in 1884, permitted the concentration of these groups into the Northern Counties Amalgamated Association of Cotton-weavers, resulted, in 1892, in the adoption, from one end of Lancashire to the other, of a uniform piecework list.

The history of Trade Unionism among the Coalminers also supplies instructive instances of federal action. In Northumberland and Durham the present unions included, for the first ten years of their existence, not only the actual hewers of the coal, but also the Deputies (Overlookers), the Enginemen, the Cokemen, and the Mechanics employed in connection with the collieries. This is still the type of union in some of the more recently organised districts. Both in Northumberland and in

Durham, however, experience of the difficulties of combining such diverse workers has led to the formation of distinct unions for Deputies, Cokemen, and Colliery Mechanics. Each of these acts with complete independence in dealing with the special circumstances of its own occupation, but unites with the others in the same county in a strong federation for general wage movements.[1] And if we pass from the "county federations" which are so characteristic of this industry, to the attempts to weld all coal-hewers into a single national organisation, we shall see that these attempts have hitherto succeeded only when they have taken the federal form. In 1868 and again in 1874 attempts at complete amalgamation quickly came to grief. Effective federation of all the organised districts has, on the other hand, endured since 1863.[2] We attribute this preference for the federal form, not to the difficulty of uniting the geographically separated coalfields, but to the divergence of interests between them. Northumberland, Durham, and South Wales, producing chiefly for foreign export, feel that their trade has little in common with that of the Midland Coalfields, which supply the home market. The thin seams of Somersetshire demand different methods of working, different rates of remuneration, and different allowances, from those in vogue in the rich mines of Yorkshire. The "fiery" mines of Monmouthshire demand quite a different set of working rules from the harmless seams of Cannock Chase.[3] It was, therefore, quite natural that, in 1887, when a demand arose for a strong and active national organisation, this did not take the form of an amalgamated union. The Miners' Federation, which now includes 200,000 members from Fife to Somerset, is composed of separate

---

[1] *The Durham County Mining Federation*, established 1878, includes the Durham Coalminers, Enginemen's, Cokemen's, and Mechanics' Associations. The Northumberland associations have not established any formal federation but act constantly together.

[2] See *History of Trade Unionism*, pp. 274, 287, 335, 350, 380.

[3] See, for instance, the animated discussion on proposed clause to restrict shot-firing, National Conference of Miners, Birmingham, 9th-12th January 1893.

unions, each retaining complete autonomy in its own affairs, and only asking for the help of the federal body in matters common to the whole kingdom, or in case of a local dispute extending to over 15 per cent of the members. Any attempt to draw tighter these bonds of union would, in all probability, at once cause the secession of the Scottish Miners' unions, and would absolutely preclude the adhesion of Northumberland, Durham, and South Wales.[1]

[1] Other industries afford instances of federal union. The compositors employed in the offices of the great London daily newspapers, at specially high wages, and under quite exceptional conditions, have, since 1853, formed an integral part of the London Society of Compositors. But they have, from the beginning, had their own quarterly meetings, and elected their own separate executive committee and salaried secretary, who conduct all their distinctive trade business, moving for new privileges and advances independently of the general body. One or more delegates are appointed by the News Department to represent it at general or delegate meetings of the whole society, whilst two representatives of the Book Department (which comprises nine-tenths of the society) sit on the newsmen's executive committee. There is even a tendency to establish similar relations with the special "music printers." The National Union of Boot and Shoe Operatives presents an example of incipient federation. The union is made up of large branches in the several towns, each possessing local funds and appointing its own salaried officials. In so far as the members belong to an identical occupation, the tendency is towards increased centralisation. But it has become the rule for the members in each town to divide into branches, not according to geographical propinquity, but according to the class of work which they do. Thus, in any town, " No. 1 Branch " is composed exclusively of Rivetters and Finishers, "No. 2 Branch" are the Clickers, and where a separate class of Jewish workers exists, these form a "No. 3 Branch." The central executive is elected by electoral divisions according to membership, and has hitherto usually been composed exclusively of the predominating classes of Rivetters and Finishers. But the Clickers, whose interests diverge from those of their colleagues, have, for some time, been demanding separate representation, which they have now been informally granted by the election of their chief salaried official as treasurer of the whole union. A similar movement may be discerned among the Finishers, as against the Rivetters (now become "Lasters"), and it seems probable that this desire for sectional representation, following on partial sectional autonomy, will presently find formal recognition in the constitution.

The building trades afford an interesting case of the abandonment of the experiment of a general union in favor of separate national societies, which are not at present united in any national federation. The Builders' Union of 1830-34 aimed at the ideal afterwards pursued in the engineering industry. All the operatives engaged in the seven sections of the building trade were to be united in a single national amalgamation. This attempt has never been repeated. In its place we have the great national unions of Stonemasons, Carpenters, Bricklayers, Plumbers, and Plasterers, whilst the Painters and the Builders' Laborers have not yet emerged from the stage of the local trade club. Between the central executives of these societies there is no federal union. In almost every

These examples of success and failure in uniting several sections of workmen in a single unit of government, point to the existence of an upper and a lower limit to the process of amalgamation. It is one of the conditions of effective trade action that a union should include all the workmen whose occupation or training is such as to enable them, at short notice, to fill the places held by its members. It would, for instance, be most undesirable for such inter-changeable mechanics as fitters, turners, and erectors, to maintain separate Trade Unions, with distinct trade policies. And if the Cardroom Operatives could easily " mind " the self-acting mule of the Cotton-spinners, it might possibly suit the latter to arrange an amalgamation between the two societies, just as the Rivetters found it convenient to absorb the Holders-up into the United Society of Boilermakers and Iron Shipbuilders.[1] There appears to be no advantage in carrying amalgamation (as distinct from federation) beyond this point. But there are often serious difficulties in going even thus far. The efficient working of an amalgamated society requires that all sections of the members should be fairly uniform in the methods of their remuneration, the conditions of their employment, and the amount of their standard earnings. Moreover, it may confidently be pre-dicted that no amalgamation will be stable in which the several sections differ appreciably in strategic position, in such a manner as to make it advantageous for them to

town there has, however, grown up a local Building Trades' Federation, formed by the local branches to concert joint action against their common employers, as regards hours of labor and local advances or reductions of wages, both of which are in each town usually simultaneous and identical for all sections. We have elsewhere referred to the difficulties arising from this separate action of each town, and it is at least open to argument whether the building trades would not be better advised to form a national federation to concert a common national policy, having federal officials in the large towns, who would, like the district delegates of the United Society of Boilermakers, represent the whole organisation, though acting in consultation with local committees.

[1] The Holders-up were admitted into the society in 1881, at the instance of the general secretary, who represented that Holders-up were indispensable fellow-workers and possible blacklegs, and must therefore be brought under the control of the organisation, more especially as they were beginning to form separate clubs of their own.

move at different times, or by different expedients. Finally, experience seems to show that in no trade will a well-paid and well-organised but numerically weak section permanently consent to remain in the subordination to inferior operatives, which any amalgamation of all sections of a large and varied industry must usually involve.

Let us apply these axioms to the tangle of competing societies in the engineering trade. The fitters, turners, and erectors who work in the same shop, on the same job, under identical methods of remuneration, for wages approximately equal in amount, and who can without difficulty do each other's work, form, no doubt, a natural unit of government.[1] We might perhaps add to these the smiths, though the persistence of a few separate smiths' societies, and the uprising of joint societies of smiths and strikers, may indicate a different cleavage. With regard to the pattern-makers, it is easy to understand why the United Pattern-makers' Association is now attracting a majority of the men entering this section of the trade. These highly skilled and superior artisans constitute a tiny minority amid the great engineering army ; they usually enjoy a higher Standard Rate than any other section ; and any advances or reductions in their wages must almost necessarily occur at different times from similar changes among the engineers proper. It is even open to argument whether, for Collective Bargaining, the pattern-makers are not actually stronger when acting alone than when in alliance with the whole engineering industry. We are, therefore, disposed to agree with the contention of the United Pattern-makers' Association that "when the interests of our own particular section are concerned, we hold it as the first principle of our Association that these interests can only be thoroughly understood, and effectively looked after, by ourselves." [2] The same conclusions apply,

[1] In 1896, though the Amalgamated Society of Engineers enrolled the unprecedented total of 13,321 new members, all but 1803 of these belonged to the classes of fitters, turners, or millwrights.

[2] Preface to *Rules of the United Pattern-makers' Association* (Manchester, 1892).

though in a lesser degree, to some other sections now included in the Amalgamated Society, and they would decisively negative the suggestion to absorb such distinct and highly organised trades as the Plumbers and Ironfounders.[1]

This conclusion does not mean that each section of the engineering trade should maintain a complete independence. "We quite acknowledge," state the Pattern-makers, "that it would be neither politic nor possible to completely sever our connection with the organisation representative of the engineering trade, and we are always ready to co-operate with contemporary societies in movements which affect the interests of the general body."[2] There are, indeed, some matters as to which the whole engineering industry must act in concert if it is to act at all. A great establishment like Elswick, employing 10,000 operatives in every section of the industry, would find it intolerable to conduct separate negotiations, and fix different meal-times or different holidays for the different branches of the trade. We find, in fact, the associated employers on the North-east Coast expressly com-

---

[1] Our analysis thus definitely refutes the suggestion that the quarrels between the engineers and plumbers, and the shipwrights and joiners respectively, might be obviated by the amalgamation of the competing unions. The two trades overlap in a few shipbuilding jobs, but in nine-tenths of their work it would be impossible for an engineer to take the place of the plumber, or a shipwright that of a joiner, or *vice versâ*. In strategic position the plumber differs fundamentally from the engineer, and the joiner from the shipwright. The engineering and shipbuilding trades are subject to violent fluctuations, which depend upon the alternate inflations and depressions of the national commerce. The building trades, on the other hand, with which nine-tenths of the joiners and plumbers must be counted, vary considerably according to the season of the year, but fluctuate comparatively little from year to year ; and the general fluctuations to which they are subject do not coincide with those of the shipbuilding and engineering industries. By the time that the wave of expansion has reached the building trades, the staple industries of the country are already in the trough of the succeeding depression. It would have been difficult to have persuaded a Newcastle engineer or a shipwright in the spring of 1893, when 20 per cent of his colleagues were out of work, that the plumbers and carpenters were well advised in choosing that particular moment to press for better terms. Finally, we have the almost insuperable difficulty of securing adequate representation for the 9000 plumbers, scattered in every town amid the 87,000 engineers ; and, on the other hand, the 14,000 shipwrights concentrated in a few ports amid the 49,000 joiners spread over the whole country.

[2] Preface to *Rules of the United Pattern-makers' Association* (Manchester, 1892).

plaining in 1890, "of the great inconvenience and difficulty experienced in the settlement of wages and other general questions between employers and employed"; and ascribing the constant friction that prevailed to the "want of uniformity of action and similarity of demand put forward by the various societies representing the skilled engineering labor." Collective Bargaining becomes impracticable when different societies are proposing new regulations on overtime inconsistent with each other, and when rival organisations, each claiming to represent the same section of the trade, are putting forward divergent claims as to the methods and rates of remuneration. The employers were driven to insist that the "deputations meeting them to negotiate . . . should represent all the societies interested in the question under consideration." [1] And when the method to be employed is not Collective Bargaining but Parliamentary action, federal union is even more necessary. If the mechanics in the great government arsenals and factories desire modifications in their conditions of employment, union of purpose among the tens of thousands of engineering electors all over the country is indispensable for success.

So long, however, as the Amalgamated Society of Engineers claims to include within its own ranks every kind of engineering mechanic, and to decide by itself the policy to be pursued, a permanent and effective federal organisation is impossible. Any attempt to combine in the same industry the mutually inconsistent schemes of amalgamation and federation may even intensify the friction. Thus we find, in 1888, to quote again from a report of the

---

[1] Circular of the Iron Trades Employers' Association on the Overtime Question, October 1891. We attribute the practical failure of the Engineering operatives to check systematic overtime, an evil against which they have been striving ever since 1836, to the chaotic state of the organisation of the trade. A similar lack of federal union stood in the way of the London bookbinders in 1893, when they succeeded without great difficulty in obtaining an Eight Hours' Day from those employers who were bookbinders only. In the great printing establishments, such as Waterlow's and Spottiswoode's, they found it practically impossible to arrange an Eight Hours' Day in the binding departments, whilst the printers continued to work for longer hours.

United Pattern-makers' Association, "the sectional societies (on North-east Coast), indignant at the arbitrary manner in which the Amalgamated Society of Engineers had acted, federated together with the avowed object of resisting a repetition of any such behaviour in case of further wages movements, and asserting their right to be consulted before definite action was taken. . . . It is impossible," continues the report, " to dissociate the action of our contemporaries (the Amalgamated Society of Engineers) from their recent unsuccessful attempt at amalgamating the various sectional societies ; and it would seem that they, finding it impossible to absorb their weaker brethren by fair means, had resolved to shatter the confidence they have in their unions by showing them their impotence to influence, of themselves, their relations between their employers and members." [1]   The " Federal Board," thus formed by the smaller engineering societies on Tyneside in antagonism to their more powerful rival, lasted for three years, but failed, it is needless to say, in securing industrial peace.   A more important and more promising attempt has been marred by the persistent abstention of the Amalgamated Society of Engineers.   In 1890, Mr. Robert Knight, the able general secretary of the United Society of Boilermakers, succeeded, after repeated failures, in drawing together in a powerful national federation the great majority of the unions connected with the engineering and shipbuilding industries.   This "Federation of Engineering and Shipbuilding Trades of the United Kingdom " includes such powerful organisations as the United Society of Boilermakers, 40,776 members; the Associated Shipwrights' Society, 14,235 members ; and the Amalgamated Society of Carpenters and Joiners, 48,631 members, who are content to meet on equal terms such smaller unions as the Steam-Engine Makers' Society, 7000 members ; the United Operative Plumbers' Society, 8758 members; the United Pattern-makers' Association, 3636 members; the National Amalgamated Society of Painters and Decorators, and half a dozen more minute

[1] *Monthly Report of the United Pattern-makers' Society*, January 1889.

sectional societies. This federation has now lasted over seven years, and has fulfilled a useful function in settling disputes between the different unions. But as an instrument for Collective Bargaining with the employers, or for taking concerted action on behalf of the whole industry, it is useless so long as the Amalgamated Society of Engineers, with its 87,455 members, holds resolutely aloof. And the Amalgamated Society of Engineers, still wedded to the ideal of one undivided union, cannot bring itself to accept as permanent colleagues, the sectional societies which it regards as illegitimate combinations undermining its own position.[1]

[1] The first numbers of the *Amalgamated Engineers' Monthly Journal*—an official organ started on the accession of Mr. George Barnes to the general secretaryship—shows that thinking members of the Amalgamation are coming round to the idea of federal union with the sectional societies, and others connected with the engineering and shipbuilding industry. Thus Mr. Tom Mann, in the opening number (January 1897, pp. 10-11), declares "that the bulk of the Amalgamated Society of Engineers' men are ashamed . . . of their present powerlessness. . . . Whence comes the weakness? Beyond any doubt it is primarily due to the fact that no concerted action is taken by the various unions. . . . That is, the Amalgamated Society of Engineers has not yet learnt the necessity for forming part of a real *federation* of all trades connected with this particular profession. . . . What member can look back over the last few years and not blush with shame at what has taken place between the Amalgamated Society of Engineers and the Plumbers, and the Boilermakers and Shipbuilders ; and who can derive satisfaction in reflecting upon the want of friendly relations between the Amalgamated Society of Engineers . . . and the Pattern-makers and Shipwrights, and Steam-Engine Makers, etc. ? A fighting force is wanted . . . and this can only be obtained by a genuine federation of societies connected with the trades referred to. . . . The textile workers (cotton) have federated the various societies, and are able to secure united action on a scale distinctly in advance of that of the engineering trades." And in the succeeding issue Mr. John Burns vigorously strikes the same note. "To really prevent this internecine and disintegrating strife, the first step for the Amalgamated Engineers this year is to join at once with all the other unions in [a] federation of engineering trades." Two months later (April 1897, pp. 12-14) comes a furious denunciation of the proposal, signed "Primitive," who invokes the "shades of Allan and eloquence of Newton " against this attempted undoing of their work. "Just because a few interested labor busybodies have got it into their heads that they can run a cheap-jack show for every department of our trade with the same effect as our great combination, we are to drop our arms, pull down our socks, hide our tail under our nether parts, and shout 'peccavi.' . . . Sectional societies for militant purposes are useless, and therefore they only exist—where such is practised—as friendly societies. . . . Amalgamation is our title, our war-cry and our principle ; and once we admit that it is necessary to 'federate' with sectional societies we give away the whole case to the enemy. . . . Federation with trades whose workshop practice is keenly distinct from our own is a good means to a better end.

If now, looking back on the whole history of organisation in the engineering trade, we may be "wise after the event," we suggest that it would have been better if the local trade clubs had confined themselves each to a single section of engineering workmen, and if they had then developed into national societies of like scope. Had this been the case, and could Newton and Allan have foreseen the enormous growth and increasing differentiation of their industry, they would have advocated, not a single comprehensive amalgamation, but a federation of sectional societies of national extent, for such purposes as were common to the whole engineering trade. This federation would have, in the first instance, included a great national society of fitters, turners, and erectors on the one hand, and smaller national societies of smiths and pattern-makers respectively. And as organisation proceeded among the brass-workers, coppersmiths, and machine-workers, and as new classes arose, like the electrical engineers, these could each have been endowed with a sufficient measure of Home Rule, and admitted as separate sections to the federal union. This federal union might then have combined in a wider and looser federation, for specified purposes, with the United Society of Boilermakers, the Friendly Society of Ironfounders, the Associated Shipwrights' Society, and the other organisations interested in the great industry of iron steamship building and equipping.[1]

One practical precept emerges from our consideration of all these forms of association. It is a fundamental condition of stable and successful federal action that the degree of union between the constituent bodies should correspond strictly with the degree of their unity of interest. This will

Federation with trades whose shop practice is similar, whose interests are identical, and who ought to be with us in every fight, is a maudlin means to a general fizzle." The question is now (August 1897) a subject of keen debate in the society.

[1] The several national societies of Carpenters, Plumbers, Painters, Cabinet-makers, etc., would, in respect of their members working in shipbuilding yards, also join this Federation ; whilst they would, at the same time, continue to be in closer federal union with the Bricklayers, Stonemasons, and other societies of building operatives.

be most easily recognised on the financial side. We have already more than once adverted to the fact that a scale of contributions and benefits, which would suit the requirements of one class, might be entirely out of the reach of other sections, whose co-operation was nevertheless indispensable for effective common action. But this is not all. We have to deal, not only with classes differing in the amount of their respective incomes, but also with wide divergences between the ways in which the several classes need to lay out their incomes. The amount levied by the federal body for the common purse must therefore not only be strictly limited to the cost of the services in which all the constituent bodies have an identical interest, but must also not exceed, in any case, the amount which the poorest section finds it advantageous to expend on these services.

But our precept has a more subtle application to the aims and policy of the federal body, and to the manner in which its decisions are arrived at. The permanence of the federation will be seriously menaced if it pursues any course of action which, though beneficial to the majority of its constituent bodies, is injurious to any one among them. The constituent bodies came together, at the outset, for the promotion of purposes desired, not merely by a majority, but by all of them ; and it is a violation of the implied contract between them to use the federal force, towards the creation of which all have contributed, in a manner inimical to any one of them. This means that, where the interests diverge, any federal decision must be essentially the result of consultation between the representatives of the several sections, with a view of discovering the "greatest common measure." These issues must, therefore, never be decided merely by counting votes. So long as the questions dealt with affect all the constituents in approximately the same manner, mere differences of opinion as to projects or methods may safely be decided by a majority vote. If the results are, in fact, advantageous, the disapproval of the minority will quickly evaporate ; if, on the other hand, the results prove to be disadvantageous, the dissentients will themselves become the dominant force. In either case no permanent cleavage is caused. But if the difference of opinion between the majority and the minority arises from a real divergence of sectional interests, and is therefore fortified by the event, any attempt on the part of the majority to force its will on the minority will, in a voluntary federation, lead to secession.

Thus, we are led insensibly to a whole theory of " proportional representation" in federal constitutions. In a homogeneous association, where no important divergence of actual interest can exist, the supreme governing authority can safely be elected, and fundamental issues can safely be decided, by mere counting of heads. Such an association will naturally adopt a representative system based on universal suffrage and equal electoral districts. But when in any federal body we have a combination of sections of unequal numerical strength, having different interests, decisions cannot safely be left to representatives elected or voting according to the numerical membership of the constituent bodies. For this, in effect, would often mean giving a decisive voice to the members of the largest section, or to those of the two or three larger sections, without the smaller sections having any effective voting influence on the result. Any such arrangement seldom fails to produce cleavage and eventual secession, as the members of the dominant sections naturally vote for their own interest. It is therefore preferable, as a means of securing the permanence of the federation, that the representation of the constituent bodies should not be exactly proportionate to their respective memberships. The representative system of a federation should, in fact, like its finances, vary with the degree to which the interests of the constituent bodies are really identical. Wherever interests are divergent, the scale must at any rate be so arranged that no one constituent, however large, can outvote the remainder ; and, indeed, so that no two or three of the larger constituents could, by mutual agreement, swamp all their colleagues. If for instance, it is proposed to federate all the national unions in the engineering trade, it would be unwise for the Amalgamated Society of Engineers to claim proportional representation for its 87,000 members, mainly fitters and turners, as compared with the 10,000 pattern-makers, smiths, and machine-workers divided among three sectional societies. And when a federation includes a large number of very different constituents, and exists for common purposes so limited as to bear only a small proportion to the particular interests of the several sections, it may be desirable frankly to give up all idea of representation according to membership, and to accord to each constituent an equal voice. Hence the founders of the Federation of the Engineering and Shipbuilding Trades exercised, in our opinion, a wise discretion when they accorded to the 9000 members of the Operative Plumbers' Society exactly the same representation and voting power as is enjoyed by the 41,000 members of the United Society of Boilermakers, or by the 49,000 members of the Amalgamated Society of Carpenters. A federal body of this kind, formed only for certain definite purposes, and composed of unions with distinct and sometimes divergent interests, stands at the opposite end of the scale from the homogeneous " amalgamated " society. The representatives of the constituent bodies meet for the composing of mutual differences and the discovery of common interests. They resemble, in fact, ambassadors who convey the desires of their respective sovereign states, contribute their special knowledge to the common council, but are unable to promise obedience to the federal decision, unless it commends itself as a suitable compromise, or carries with it the weight of an almost unanimous consensus of opinion.[1]

The problem of finding a stable unit of government and of determining the relation between superior and subordinate authorities seems, therefore, to be in a fair way of solution

---

[1] We revert to these considerations when, in describing the Trade Union machinery for political action, we come to deal with such federations as the Trade Union Congress and the local Trades Councils.

in the Trade Union world. With the ever-increasing mobility of labor and extension of industry, the local trade club has had to give place to a combination of national extent. So long as the craft or occupation is fairly uniform from one end of the kingdom to the other, the geographical boundaries of the autonomous state must, in the Trade Union world, ultimately coincide with those of the nation itself. We have seen, too, how inevitably the growth of national Trade Unions involves, for strategic, and what may be called military reasons, the reduction of local autonomy to a minimum, and the complete centralisation of all financial, and therefore of all executive government at the national headquarters. This tendency is strengthened by economic considerations which we shall develop in a subsequent chapter. If the Trade Union is to have any success in its main function of improving the circumstances of its members' employment, it must build up a dyke of a uniform minimum of conditions for identical work throughout the kingdom. This uniformity of conditions, or, indeed, any industrial influence whatsoever, implies a certain uniformity and consistency of trade policy, which is only rendered possible by centralisation of administration. So far, our conclusions lead, it would seem, to the absolute simplicity of one all-embracing centralised autocracy. But, in the Trade Union world, the problem of harmonising local administration and central control, which for a moment we seemed happily to have got rid of, comes back in an even more intractable form. The very aim of uniformity of conditions, the very fact that uniformity of trade policy is indispensable to efficiency, makes it almost impossible to combine in a single organisation, with a common purse, a common executive, and a common staff of salaried officials, men of widely different occupations and grades of skill, widely different Standards of Life and industrial needs, or widely different numerical strengths and strategic opportunities. A Trade Union is essentially an organisation for securing certain concrete and definite advantages for all its members—advantages which differ from trade to trade according to its technical processes, its economic position, and, it may be, the geographical situation in which it is carried on. Hence all the attempts at "General Unions" have, in our view, been inevitably foredoomed to failure. The hundreds of thousands of the working class who joined the "Grand National Consolidated Trades Union" in 1833-34 came together, it is true, on a common basis of human brotherhood, and with a common faith in the need for a radical reconstruction of society. But instead of inaugurating a "New Moral World," either by precept or by political revolution, they found themselves as a Trade Union, fighting the employers in the Lancashire cotton mills to get shorter hours of labor, in the Leeds cloth trade to obtain definite piecework rates, in the London building trade to do away with piecework altogether, in Liverpool to abolish the subcontractor, in the hosiery trade to escape from truck and deductions. Each trade, in short, translated "human brotherhood" into the remedying of its own particular technical grievance, and the central executive was quite unable to check the accuracy of the translation. The whole history of Trade Unionism confirms the inference that a Trade Union, formed as it is, for the distinct purpose of obtaining concrete and definite material improvements in the conditions of its members' employment, cannot, in its simplest form, safely extend beyond the area within which those identical improvements are shared by all its members—cannot spread, that is to say, beyond the boundaries of a single occupation. But the discovery of this simple unit of government does not exhaust the problem. Whilst the differences between the sections render complete amalgamation impracticable, their identity in other interests makes some bond of union imperative. The most efficient form of Trade Union organisation is therefore one in which the several sections can be united for the purposes that they have in common, to the extent to which identity of interest prevails, and no further, whilst at the same time each section preserves complete autonomy wherever its interests or purposes diverge from those of its allies. But this is only another form of the difficult political problem of the relation of supreme to subordinate authorities. Whilst the student of political democracy has been grappling with the question of how to distribute administration between central and local authorities, the unlettered statesmen of the Trade Union world have had to decide the still more difficult issue of how to distribute power between general and sectional industrial combinations, both of national extent. The solution has been found in a series of widening and cross-cutting federations, each of which combines, to the extent only of its own particular objects, those organisations which are conscious of their identity of purpose. Instead of a simple form of democratic organisation we get, therefore, one of extreme complexity. Where the difficulties of the problem have been rightly apprehended, and the whole industry has been organised on what may be called a single plane, the result may be, as in the case of the Cotton Operatives, a complex but harmoniously working democratic machine of remarkable efficiency and stability. Where, on the other hand, the industry has been organised on incompatible bases, as among the Engineers, we find a complicated tangle of relationships producing rivalry and antagonism, in which effective common action, even for such purposes as are common to all sections, becomes almost impossible.

Trade Union organisation, if it is to reach its highest possible efficiency, must therefore assume a federal form. Instead of a supreme central government, delegating parts of its power to subordinate local authorities, we may expect to see the Trade Union world developing into an elaborate series of federations, among which it will be difficult to decide where the sovereignty really resides. Where the several sections closely resemble each other in their circumstances and needs, where their common purposes are relatively numerous and important, and where, as a result, individual secession and subsequent isolation would be dangerous, the federal tie will be strong, and the federal government will, in effect, become the supreme authority. At the other end of the scale will stand those federations, little more than opportunities for consultation, in which the contracting parties retain each a real autonomy, and use the federal executive as a convenient, but strictly subordinate machinery for securing those limited purposes that they have in common. And we have ventured to suggest, as an interesting corollary, that the basis of representation should, in all these constitutions, vary according to the character of the bond of union, representation proportionate to membership being perfectly applicable only to a homogeneous organisation, and decreasing in suitability with every degree of dissimilarity between the constituent bodies. Where the sectional interests are not only distinct, but may, in certain cases, be even antagonistic, as, for instance, in industries subject to demarcation disputes, rule by majority vote must be frankly abandoned, and the representatives of societies widely differing in numerical strength must, under penalty of common failure, consent to meet on equal terms, to discover, by consultation, how best to conciliate the interests of all.

PART II

TRADE UNION FUNCTION

INTRODUCTION

"THE chief object of our society is to elevate the social position of our members," is the comprehensive truism by which the ordinary Trade Union defines its function. This simple assertion, of what we may term "corporate self-help," is, in many of the older unions, embellished by rhetorical appeals to the brotherhood of man, and realistic descriptions of the precarious position of the weekly wage-earners. Thus the "main principle" that actuated the "originators" of the Friendly Society of Ironfounders "was that of systematic organisation, and the desire of forming a bond of brotherhood and sympathy throughout the trade, in order that those who, by honest labor, obtained a livelihood in this particular branch of industry might, in their combined capacity, more successfully compete against the undue and unfair encroachments of capital than could possibly be the case by any number of workmen when acting individually." [1] "We are willing to admit," observe the founders of the Amalgamated Society of Engineers, "that whilst in constant employment our members may be able to obtain all the necessaries, and perhaps some of the luxuries of life. . . . Notwithstanding all this, there is a fear always prominent on the mind of him who thinks of the future that it may not continue, that to-morrow may see him out of employment, his nicely-arranged

[1] *Rules of the Friendly Ironmoulders'* [now Ironfounders'] *Society, instituted for the purpose of mutual relief in cases of old age, sickness, and infirmity, and for the burial of their dead:* "Made at Bolton, 19th June 1809. Allowed at Quarter Sessions, 19th July 1809" (Bolton, 1809); see edition of 1891, preface.

matters for domestic comfort overthrown, and his hopes of being able, in a few years, by constant attention and frugality, to occupy a more permanent position, proved only to be a dream. How much is contained in that word continuance, and how necessary to make it a leading principle of our association ! " [1]

But these descriptions of the ultimate objects of working-class organisation afford us little clue to the actual operation of Trade Unionism. The Trade Unionists of our own generation are more explicit. With dry and ungrammatical precision the great modern unions give as their " Objects " long strings of specific proposals, in which are incidentally revealed, with perfect frankness, the means relied upon to achieve these ends. The Amalgamated Association of Operative Cotton-spinners " is formed to secure to all its members the fair reward of their labor ; to provide for the settlement in a conciliatory manner of disputes between employer and employed, so that a cessation of work may be avoided ; the enforcement of the Factory Acts or other legislative enactments for the protection of labor ; to afford pecuniary assistance to any member who may be victimised or without employment in consequence of a dispute or lock-out or when disabled by accident." [2] The Miners' Federation of Great Britain declares that its objects of association " are to take into consideration the question of trade and wages, and to protect miners generally ; to seek to secure mining legislation affecting all miners connected with this Federation ; to call conferences to deal with questions affecting miners, both of a trade, wage, and legislative character ; to seek and obtain an eight hours' day from bank to bank in all mines for all persons working underground ; to deal with and watch all inquests upon persons killed in the mines where more than three persons are killed by any one accident ; to seek

---

[1] The original *Rules and Regulations of the Amalgamated Society of Engineers* (London, 1851), made at Birmingham, September 1850.

[2] *Rules of the Amalgamated Association of Operative Cotton-spinners* (Manchester, 1891).

to obtain compensation where more than three persons are injured or killed in any one accident, in all cases where counties, federations, or districts have to appeal, or are appealed against, from decisions in the lower courts." [1]   The National Union of Boot and Shoe Operatives (established 1874) declares that "The objects of the union are: the establishment of a central fund for the protection of members and advancement of wages ; the establishment of healthy and proper workshops, the employers to find room, grindery, fixtures, fire, and gas, free of charge ; the establishment, as far as practicable, of a uniform rate of wages for the same class of work throughout the union ; to abolish sweaters and control the system of apprentices ; to reduce the hours of labor ; to assist members who are compelled to travel in search of employment ; the introduction of Industrial Co-operation in our trade ; the use of all legitimate means for the moral, social, educational, and political advancement of its members ; also to make provision for the union being represented by a Parliamentary Agent ; to raise funds for the mutual support of its members in time of sickness, and for the burial of deceased members and their wives ; to establish a system of inter-communication with the Boot and Shoe Operatives of other countries." [2]   Finally, we may cite the most prominent and successful of the so-called " new unions," formed in the great uprising of 1889.   The rules of the National Union of Gasworkers and General Laborers state that "The objects of the union are to shorten the hours of labor, to obtain a legal eight hours' working day or forty-eight hours' week ; to abolish, wherever possible, overtime and Sunday labor, and where this is not possible, to obtain payment at a higher rate ; to abolish piecework ; to raise wages, and where women do the same work as men, to obtain for them the same wages as paid the men ; to enforce the provisions of the Truck Acts in their entirety ; to abolish the present system of contracts and agreements between employers and

---

[1] *Miners' Federation of Great Britain—Rules* (Openshaw, 1893).
[2] *Rules of the National Union of Boot and Shoe Operatives* (Leicester, 1892).

employed ; to settle all labor disputes by amicable agreement whenever possible ; to obtain equality of employers and employed before the law ; to obtain legislation for the bettering of the lives of the working class ; to secure the return of members of the union to vestries, school boards, boards of guardians, municipal bodies, and to Parliament, provided such candidates are pledged to the collective ownership of the means of production, distribution, and exchange ; to set aside annually a maximum sum of £200, to be used solely for the purpose of helping to return and maintain members on public representative bodies ; to assist similar organisations having the same objects as herein stated." [1]

We must, however, not look to the formal rules or rhetorical preambles for a scientific or complete account of Trade Union action.   Drafted originally by enthusiastic pioneers, copied and recopied by successive revising committees, the printed constitutions of working-class associations represent rather the aspirations than the everyday action of the members.   More trustworthy data may be obtained from a scrutiny of the cash accounts, or from a close study of the voluminous internal literature of the unions—the monthly, quarterly, and yearly reports of the central executives, the frequent official circulars on particular questions, and the elaborate verbatim notes of conferences and joint committees.   The printed documents circulated by some societies include the diary of their principal trade official, detailing his day-by-day negotiation with employers.[2] Other unions publish to their members periodical reports from their district delegates stationed in the principal industrial centres, containing valuable information as to the movements of trade, graphic accounts of disputes with employers or other societies, and appeals for guidance as to the policy to be pursued.   To the student of sociology this literature— poured out to the extent of hundreds of volumes annually—

---

[1] *Rules of the National Union of Gasworkers and General Laborers of Great Britain and Ireland* (London, 1894).

[2] See the extracts printed in the chapter on " The Standard Rate."

is of fascinating interest. It affords a graphic picture of the actual structure and working of the modern world of manu-facturing industry, with its constant changes of process and shiftings of trade. It lays bare, more completely than any other records known to us, the real nature and action of democratic organisation in the Anglo-Saxon race. And, what is most relevant to our present purpose, it reveals, with all the pathos of success and failure, the working of the various Trade Union Methods and Regulations with the underlying assumptions as to social expediency on which they are based.

But documents, however frank and confidential, are apt to distort facts as well as to display them. A heated recrimi-nation between a local official and the general secretary, a dispute about the wages on a new process, affecting only a tiny minority of the members, or a Parliamentary agitation for a new clause in the Factory Acts will loom large in the proceedings of the year, and may seem to represent the bulk of the union's activity. Meanwhile, the branches may have been engaged in a peaceful but successful maintenance of their old-standing Working Rules, or a new regulation may silently have become habitual, or an old one silently dropped, without this action on the part of the majority of the members rising to the surface in any document whatsoever, public or private. To complete the knowledge yielded by documents, the student must watch the men at work, and discuss the application of particular regulations with em-ployers, managers, and foremen—not omitting the factory inspector and the secretary to the Employers' Association—he must listen to the objections of the small master and the blackleg; above all, he must attend the inside meetings of branches and district committees, where the points at issue are discussed in technical detail with a frank explicitness which is untrammelled either by the prejudices of the rank and file or the fear of the enemy.

This combined plan of studying documents and observing men is the one that we have, during our six years' investigation, attempted to follow. In the ensuing chapters we endeavor to place before the reader an accurate description of the Methods and Regulations actually practised by British Trade Unionism. We shall see the Trade Unionists, from the beginning of the eighteenth century down to the present day, enforcing their Regulations by three distinct instruments or levers, which we distinguish as the Method of Mutual Insurance, the Method of Collective Bargaining, and the Method of Legal Enactment. From the Methods used to enforce the Regulations, we shall pass to the Regulations themselves. These we shall find grouping themselves, notwithstanding an almost infinite variety of technical detail, under seven main heads—the Standard Rate, the Normal Day, Sanitation and Safety, New Processes and Machinery, Continuity of Employment, the Entrance into a Trade, and the Right to a Trade—all of which we examine in separate chapters. This will lead us to the Implications of Trade Unionism—certain practical outgrowths and necessary consequences of Trade Union policy which require elucidadation. Finally, we shall bring into light the Assumptions of Trade Unionism—the fundamental prejudices, opinions, or judgments lying at the root of Trade Union policy—an analysis of which will serve at once to explain and to summarise the various forms of Trade Union action.

In the course of this comprehensive description of Trade Unionism as it is, we shall not abstain from incidentally criticising the various Methods and Regulations, and the different types of Trade Union policy, in respect of the success or failure of Trade Unions to apply them to the facts of modern life. But in this part of our book we carefully avoid any discussion as to the effects of Trade Unionism upon industry, and, above all, we make no attempt to decide whether it has or has not resulted in effectively raising wages, or otherwise improving the conditions of employment. We venture to think that there can be no useful discussion of the economic validity of Trade Unionism until the student has first surveyed its actual contents. Our examination of the theory of trade combination—the possibility, by deliberate common action, of altering the conditions of employment ; the effect of the various Methods and Regulations upon the efficiency of production and the distribution of wealth ; and the ultimate social expediency of exchanging a system of unfettered individual competition for one of collective regulation—in a word, our judgment upon Trade Unionism as a whole—we reserve for the third and final part of this book.

CHAPTER I

THE METHOD OF MUTUAL INSURANCE

IN a certain sense it would not be difficult to regard all the activities of Trade Unionism as forms of Mutual Insurance. Whether the purpose be the fixing of a list of piecework prices, the promotion of a new factory bill, or the defence of a member against a prosecution for picketing, we see the contributions, subscribed equally in the past by all the members, applied in ways which benefit unequally particular individuals or particular sections among them, independently of the amount which these individuals or sections may themselves have contributed. But this interpretation of insurance would cover, not Trade Unionism alone, but practically every form of collective action, including citizenship itself. By the phrase "Mutual Insurance," as one of the Methods of Trade Unionism, we understand only the provision of a fund by common subscription to insure against casualties ; to provide maintenance, that is to say, in cases in which a member is deprived of his livelihood by causes over which neither he nor the union has any control. This obviously covers the "benevolent" or friendly society side of Trade Unionism, such as the provision of sick pay, accident benefit, and superannuation allowance, together with "burial money," and such allowances as that made to members of the Amalgamated Society of Tailors who are prevented from working by the sanitary authorities, owing to the presence of infectious disease in their homes. But it includes also

what are often termed "trade" benefits ; grants for replacing
tools lost by theft or fire, and "out-of-work pay," from the
old-fashioned "tramping card" to the modern "donation"
given when a member loses his employment by the temporary breakdown of machinery or "want of pit room," by
the bankruptcy of his employer or the stoppage of a mill,
or merely in consequence of a depression in trade. "The
simplest and universal function of trades societies," it
was reported in 1860, "is the enabling the workman to
maintain himself while casually out of employment, or
travelling in search of it."[1] On the other hand, our
definition excludes all expenditure incurred by the union as
a consequence of action voluntarily undertaken by it, such
as the cost of trade negotiations, the "victim pay" accorded
to members dismissed for agitation, and the maintenance of
men on strike. These we omit as more properly incidental
to the Method of Collective Bargaining. We also leave to
be dealt with under the Method of Legal Enactment the
provision for the legal aid of members under the Employers'
Liability, Truck, or Factory Acts.

Trade Union Mutual Insurance, thus defined, comprises
two distinct classes of benefit : "Friendly" and "Out of
Work." There is an essential difference between the
insurance against such physical and personal casualties as
sickness, accident, and old age on the one hand, and, on the
other, the stoppage of income caused by mere inability to
obtain employment.

Friendly Mutual Insurance, in many industries the oldest
form of Trade Union activity, has been adopted by practically
every society which has lasted. Here and there, at all times,
one trade or another has, in the first emergence of its
organisation, preferred to confine its action to Collective
Bargaining or to aim at Legal Enactment.[2] But directly

---

[1] *Report of the National Association for the Promotion of Social Science on
Trade Societies and Strikes* (London, 1860), p. xx.

[2] See for the so-called "New Unionism" of 1889, the *History of Trade
Unionism*, pp. 401, 406.

the combination has settled down to everyday life, we find it adding one or other of the benefits of insurance, and often developing into the most comprehensive Trade Friendly Society. For the past hundred years this insurance business has been steadily growing, not only in volume, but also in deliberateness and regularity.

In providing friendly benefits the Trade Union comes into direct competition with the ordinary friendly society and the industrial insurance company. The engineer or carpenter who joins his Trade Union might insure against sickness, old age, and the expenses of burial, by joining the "Oddfellows" and the "Prudential" instead. And from an actuarial point of view the Amalgamated Society of Engineers or Carpenters is not for a moment to be compared with a friendly society of good standing. Unlike the registered friendly society, the Trade Union, even if registered, does not enter into any legally binding contract. A Trade Union cannot be sued ; and the members have individually no legal remedy against it. A member who has paid for a whole lifetime to the sick and superannuation funds may, at any moment, be expelled and forfeit all claim, for reasons quite unconnected with his desire for insurance in old age. Against the decision of his fellow-members there is, in no case, any appeal. Moreover, the scale of contributions and benefits may at any time be altered, even to the extent of abolishing benefits altogether ; and such alterations do, in fact, frequently take place, in spite of all the protests of minorities of old members. And it is no small drawback to the security of the individual member that, in a time of trade depression, just when he himself is probably poorest, he is invariably required to pay extra levies to meet the heavy Out of Work liabilities, on pain of being automatically excluded, and thus forfeiting all his insurance. It is a further aggravation that in any crisis the Trade Union, unlike the friendly society, regards the punctual discharge of its sick and superannuation liabilities as a distinctly secondary consideration. The paramount requisite of an organisation professing to provide against sickness and old age is absolute security that the accumulated funds will be reserved exclusively to meet the growing liabilities. But in a Trade Union there is no guarantee that any of its funds will be reserved for this purpose. During a long spell of trade depression the whole accumulated balance may be spent in maintaining the members out of work. An extensive strike may, at any time, drain the society absolutely dry. The Friendly Society of Operative Stonemasons, for instance, has, during its sixty years' existence, twice been reduced to absolute beggary, in 1841 by a prolonged strike, and in 1879 by the severe depression in trade. A still older and richer union, the Friendly Society of Ironfounders, not only spent every penny of its funds in 1879, but borrowed many thousands of pounds from its members' individual savings to meet the most pressing of its liabilities.[1] This "hole in the stocking" is not mended by any nominal allocation of a certain part of the income, or a specific share of the funds, to the sick or superannuation liabilities. No Trade Union ever dreams of putting any part of its funds legally or effectively out of the control of its members for the time being ; and when a time of stress comes, the nominal allocation offers no obstacle to the "borrowing" of some or all the ear-marked balance for current purposes. Trade Unionists, in short, subscribe their money primarily for the maintenance or improvement of their wages or other conditions of employment : only after this object has been secured do they expect or desire any sick or other friendly benefits, and their rules proceed always on the assumption that such benefits are payable only if and when there is a surplus in hand.

This entire want of legal or financial security has hitherto prevented actuaries from giving serious consideration to the problems of Trade Union insurance.[2] The

---

[1] *History of Trade Unionism*, pp. 157, 334.
[2] This lack of knowledge and absence of serious study has not prevented leading actuaries from denouncing stable and well-managed Trade Unions as

consequence is that the Trade Union scales of contributions and benefits do not rest on any actuarial basis, and represent, at best, the empirical guess-work of the members. Scarcely any attempt has yet been made to collect the data necessary

financially unsound, even on their friendly society side, and inevitably destined to early bankruptcy. Before the Royal Commission of 1867-68, for instance, two of the principal actuaries demonstrated that both the Amalgamated Society of Engineers and the Amalgamated Society of Carpenters were insolvent to the extent of many hundreds of thousands of pounds, and that they were necessarily doomed to collapse. In spite of the patent falsification of these prophecies, and the continued growth in wealth of the great unions, similar denunciations and predictions are still repeated by actuarial authorities ignorant of their own ignorance.

A Trade Union differs fundamentally from a friendly society or insurance company, which undertakes to provide definite payments for a specified premium. A Trade Union is not only free at any time to revise, or even suspend, its benefits; it can, and habitually does, increase its income by levies. Thus, whilst the nominal contribution of the Amalgamated Society of Engineers is a shilling per week, the actual amount received from the members during the ten years 1886-95 averaged, for the whole period, one shilling and twopence halfpenny per week (*Eighth Report by the Chief Labour Correspondent on Trade Unions*, C. 8232, 1896, p. 404), and the rules expressly provide that "when the funds are reduced to £3 per member the contributions shall be increased by such sum per week as will sustain the funds at not less than that amount" (Rule XXV. of edition of 1896, p. 121). A society with such a rule can obviously never become insolvent so long as it retains any members, and chooses to meet its engagements.

But there is another and no less important difference in actuarial position between a Trade Union and a friendly society. A friendly society is rightly deemed unsound if the contributions paid by the members when young do not enable a fund to be accumulated to meet the greatly increased liabilities for sickness, superannuation, and burial as they grow older. A society may have cash in hand, and yet be steering into bankruptcy, if the average age of its members is increasing, or might presently (by a stoppage of recruiting) be found to be increasing. This rapid increase of liabilities with advancing age constitutes what insurance experts denounce as "the vice of assessmentism" — the fallacious assumption that the year's payments can safely be met by the year's levies on the members for the time being. But where membership is universal, the average age, and therefore the liabilities, do not, and cannot, increase. If sick-pay, superannuation, and burial were provided by the State for all citizens, the number of cases year by year would, from an actuarial point of view, remain constant, or would be affected only by the slow and gradual changes in national health. A single trade is, in this respect, in much the same position as the nation, and when a Trade Union habitually includes all the operatives in its industry the percentage of benefit cases is remarkably uniform. Moreover, even in less universal organisations, where the motives for joining are very largely unconnected with friendly benefits, and there is no competing union, the result is practically the same. As a matter of fact, the average age of the members of well-established Trade Unions, so far as this can be ascertained, remains remarkably stable, and seems to increase only with the general improvement in sanitation.

for a more precise computation ; and even such elementary facts as the average age of the members, or the special death rate or sickness rate of the occupation, are often unknown. There is no graduation of contributions according to age, practically no attempt at medical selection of candidates for membership, and a complete uncertainty as to what interest will be received on investments, or whether the funds will be invested at interest at all. In short, the Trade Union, considered merely as a friendly society, does not profess to afford its members any legal security or certain guarantee against destitution in sickness or old age. Its promises of superannuation allowances, and even of sick pay, are, in reality, conditional on there being money left over after providing for other purposes. " The right " [of members to] "any benefit," wrote Daniel Guile, in 1869, in the name of the Ironfounders' Executive, "only exists as long as the Society has power to pay it. Any determination of the exact amount of return a member may rightly expect for a particular amount of contribution rests upon averages of a nature far too abstruse to be entered upon here, and for which, indeed, even the groundwork is wanting." [1] In face of this lack of security, and absence of actuarial basis, it seems at first sight surprising that union after union should add to its purely trade functions the business of an ordinary friendly society. But, as Professor Beesly remarked in 1867, " it is much more economical to depend upon one society combining all benefits, than to contribute to a friendly society for sick and funeral benefits, and to a union for tool and accident benefit and trade purposes." [2] Whether or not the ordinary artisan appreciates the economy effected by " concentration of management and consequent lessening of working expenses," he at any rate realises that it is less irksome to pay to one club than to several. But this hardly explains the persistent advocacy of sick pay and superannua-

---

[1] *Monthly Report of the Friendly Society of Ironfounders*, October 1869.

[2] E. S. Beesly, *The Amalgamated Society of Carpenters and Joiners* (London, 1867), p. 4.

tion allowance by experienced Trade Union officials. Their belief in the advantage of developing the friendly society side of Trade Unionism rests frankly on the adventitious aid it brings to working-class organisation. The benefit club side serves, in the first place, as a potent attraction to hesitating recruits. To the young man just " out of his time " the prospect of securing support in sickness or unemployment is a greater inducement to join the union, and regularly to keep up his contributions, than the less obvious advantages to be gained by the trade combination. " It helps," says Mr. George Howell, " to bind the members to the union when possibly other considerations might interpose to diminish the zeal of the Trade Unionist pure and simple."[1]

Moreover, when, as is usually the case, the whole contribution goes into a common fund, the society gains the advantage of an additional financial reserve, which can be used in support of its trade policy in time of need, and replaced as opportunity permits. Such great Trade Friendly Societies as the Boilermakers', Engineers', Stonemasons', and Ironfounders' have, as we have seen, never hesitated to deplete their balances in order to enable their members to withstand encroachments on their Standard of Life. Thus, the addition of friendly society benefits, bringing, as it does, greatly increased contributions, enables the Trade Union to roll up an imposing reserve fund, which, even if not actually drawn upon, is found to be an effective " moral influence " in negotiations with employers.

We see, therefore, that the friendly society element supplies to Trade Unionism both adventitious attractions and an adventitious support. But this is not all. In a strong and well-organised union, the existence of important friendly benefits may become a powerful instrument for maintaining discipline among the members, and for enforcing upon all the decisions of the majority. If expulsion carries with it the loss of valuable prospective benefits, such, for

[1] *Trade Unionism, New and Old*, by George Howell (London, 1892), p. 102.

instance, as superannuation, it becomes a penalty of great severity. Similarly, when secession involves the abandonment of all share in a considerable accumulated balance, a branch momentarily discontented with some decision of the majority thinks twice before it breaks off in a pet to set up as an independent society. Thus the addition of friendly benefits has been, on the whole, a great consolidating force in Trade Unionism. We can, therefore, quite understand why thoroughgoing opponents of trade combinations have, like the associated employers who came before the Royal Commission in 1867, vehemently denounced the combination of trade and friendly society as illegitimate and dangerous.[1]

Friendly benefits have yet another advantage from the point of view of the Trade Union official. To the permanent salaried officer of a great union, with his time fully occupied by his daily routine, it is no small gain that sick pay and superannuation allowance exercise a great effect in "keeping the members quiet." This was perceived, as early as 1867, by a shrewd friend of the great Amalgamated Societies, the " New Unionism " of that time. " The importance of the principle [of providing all the usual benefits offered by friendly societies] will be best understood," observes Professor Beesly, " by looking at the character and working of the

---

[1] " The combination of trade with benefit purposes was astutely conceived, with a view to increase the strength of trade organisations. The benefit element was first to decoy, and then to control. The lure of prospective benefits having attracted members, the dread of confiscation was to enforce obedience."—*Trade Unionism*, by James Stirling (Glasgow, 1869), p. 43.

There is absolutely no warrant for the accusation—still often repeated—that the use of all the Trade Union funds for strike purposes when the members so decide, amounts, morally if not legally, to malversation. The Chief Registrar of Friendly Societies, questioned on this very point by the Royal Commission on Labor, emphatically upheld the Trade Union practice. " The primary object of the Trade Union," said Mr. Brabrook, " is protection of trade, and all the rest is merely subsidiary. . . . The great bulk of members of Trade Unions know perfectly well that they will not get the benefit in sickness if their money has been previously spent in trade purposes, and they are perfectly willing it should be so spent if emergency or necessity arises " (Questions 1561-3). Mr. J. M. Ludlow, who preceded him in office, entirely confirmed this view. To hypothecate any Trade Union funds for benefit purposes, he added, " might be to the ruin of the Trade Union, and therefore to the ruin of the men who had contributed those funds " (Questions 1783-8).

old-fashioned unions in which it is not adopted. The men combine purely for 'trade purposes.' The subscription is insignificant, sometimes only a penny a week. The members probably belong to the Oddfellows or Foresters for the benefit purposes; and their financial tie to their union being so weak, they join it or leave it with equal carelessness Nevertheless, small as the subscription is, a fund will in course of time be accumulated. There is nothing to do with this fund. There it is, eating its head off, so to speak. The men become impatient to use it; so a demand is made on the employers, irrespective perhaps of the circumstances of the trade. A strike follows. The members live on their fund for a few weeks, and when it is exhausted they give in. Such societies may be called Strike Societies, for they exist for nothing else." [1] "A trade society without friendly benefits," Mr. John Burnett has frequently declared, " is like a standing army. It is a constant menace to peace." And thus we find the employers of this generation abandoning the criticisms of their predecessors in 1867, and reserving their bitterest denunciations for the purely trade society.

With regard to the other branch of their Mutual Insurance business, the Trade Unions occupy a unique position. However imperfectly Trade Unions may discharge the function of providing maintenance for their members when out of work, they undertake here a service which must, in their absence, remain unperformed. No other organisation, whether commercial or philanthropic, has yet come forward to protect the wage-earner against the destitution arising from lack of employment.[2] Experience seems to indicate that Out of

---

[1] E. S. Beesly, *The Amalgamated Society of Carpenters and Joiners*, p. 3 (London, 1867).

[2] Certain experiments have been made since 1894 at Berne, Basle, and St. Gall (Switzerland); at Cologne (Germany); and at Bologna (Italy), in the direction of municipal insurance against unemployment, either voluntary or compulsory. An account of these experiments, which do not appear to have been very successful, will be found in the *Rapport sur la Question du Chômage*, published by the French Government, Conseil Supérieur du Travail (Paris, 1896, 398 pp.); and Circulars 2 and 5 (Series B) of the Musée Social, Paris, containing an elaborate bibliography; to which we can add Charles Raaijmakers, *Verzekering tegen Werkloosheid* (Amsterdam, 1895).

Work pay cannot be properly administered except by bodies of men belonging to the same trade and working in the same establishments. Therefore it is not remarkable that Trade Unions should give most of their attention to the administration of their Out of Work benefits. We find, in fact, that although funeral benefit is almost universal, and accident allowance very widely adopted, these, like insurance of tools, make up in the aggregate a very small proportion of the total expenditure. And though sick pay and super-annuation stand for appreciable sums, it is Out of Work benefit which takes the most important place in the Mutual Insurance business, its limits being extended in many instances, whilst others are cut down.[1] To a middle-class body it would seem natural to give a kind of preferential lien on the funds, to insure the continuance of the weekly allowances to the sick and superannuated members already on the books. A Trade Union not only refrains from taking this course, but actually gives a preference, in effect, to its Out of Work payments, usually continuing them at the full rate, even when its funds are being rapidly exhausted, until it has parted with its last penny. The secret of this bias does not lie altogether in the immense difference in permanence between middle class and working class employment. The main object of the individual member may be to provide against the personal distress which would otherwise be caused to himself and his family by the stoppage of his weekly income. But the object of the union, from the collective point of view, is to prevent him from accepting employment, under stress of starvation, on terms which, in the common judgment of the trade, would be injurious to its interests. This has been recognised from the earliest times as a leading

---

[1] Thus, the *Rules and Regulations of the Operative Bleachers, Finishers, and Dyers' Association* (Bolton, 1891) provide (Rule 24), under the head of sick pay, only for a case not met by the mere friendly society. "Should any member, having his family afflicted with smallpox or other infectious disease and as a consequence be temporarily discharged from following his employment, such member shall be entitled to the ordinary out of work pay. *But if such member become afflicted himself his pay shall cease.*"

object of Out of Work pay.   Already, in 1741, it was remarked that the woolcombers "support one another, insomuch that they are become one society throughout the kingdom.   And *that they may keep up their price*, to encourage idleness rather than labor, if any one of their club is out of work, they give him a ticket and money to seek for work at the next town where a box-club is, where he is also subsisted, suffered to live a certain time with them, and used as before ; by which means he can travel the kingdom round, be caressed at each club, and not spend a farthing of his own or strike one stroke of work.   This has been imitated by the weavers also, though not carried through the kingdom, but confined to the places where they work." [1]

We find the economic result of this tramping system exercising the minds of the Assistant Poor Law Commissioners of 1834.   A leatherdresser " belongs to an incorporated or combined trade ; the directors of this Combination issue tickets to the members.   These tickets are renewed from time to time.   The holder of one goes from place to place, but must not take the same road more than once in six months.   With these intervals he is again and again assisted. . . . This ticket is available in every part of the United Kingdom where a club or lodge of the trade is established.   The individual in question might have had work at £1 per week, but he refused to take it, or indeed 30s. per week ; nothing under £2 would satisfy him ; and when pressed for reasons to account for his refusing such offers—when asked whether it would not be better to get £1 per week than to trust to casual sources of support, he

---

[1] *A Short Essay upon Trade in General*, by a Lover of his Country (London, 1741), quoted in the *History of the Worsted Manufacture in England*, by John James (London, 1857).   How the employers felt the independence thus given to the workers may be inferred from the following advertisement in the *Leicester Herald*, of June 1792 :—" To Master Woolcombers.   The Journeymen Wool- combers in Kendal have left their work, and illegally combined to raise their wages which are already equal to what is paid to the Trade in any part of the Kingdom : they have also granted blanks, or certificates, to E. Hewitson, apprentice to Mr. Pooley ; T. Parkinson, to Mr. Barton ; and W. Wilkinson, to Mr. Strutt, *who without such blanks or certificates must have remained with their masters.*"

replied that he should not like to be ' turned black ' (query—
' returned black ') which would be the case if he worked under
price." [1]

Gradually the Trade Unions themselves make clear the
real object of this system of mutual insurance. In 1844
the Spring Knife Grinders' Protection Society of Sheffield
declare that the " object to be accomplished is to grant relief
to all its members that are out of work ; that none may
have the painful necessity of applying for relief from the
parish, *or comply with the unreasonable demands of our
employers or their servants.*" [2] The Flint Glass Makers
express the same idea. " Our wages depend on the supply
of labor in the market ; our interest is therefore to restrict
that supply, reduce the surplus, *make our unemployed comfortable, without fear for the morrow—accomplish this, and we
have a command over the surplus of our labor, and we need
fear no unjust employer.*" [3] Four years later the Delegate
Meeting of the Amalgamated Engineers resolved to extend
by nine weeks the period during which a member was allowed
to receive continuously the Out of Work allowance. It was
successfully argued that "when bad trade did arrive . . . it
brought with it the absolute necessity of a continuous donation ; for men, who were unemployed for so long a time as
to run through their donation altogether, would be compelled
either to seek parish relief, *or take situations on terms injurious
to the trade.* In the event of their doing the latter, the
Society would exercise but little control over them if it
did not entitle them to some benefit. *For the protection of
the trade, then, it was stated to be absolutely necessary to make
the donation continuous, so that the members of the Society
should be able to resist the inducement of acting contrary to
the general rules of a District.*" [4] Finally, we may cite the

---

[1] *Report of Poor Law Commission* of 1834 ; Appendix, p. 900 *a*.

[2] Manuscript *Rules of the Spring Knife Grinders' Protection Society of Sheffield*
in old account book, dated 1844.

[3] *Flint Glass Makers' Magazine*, opening editorial, No. 1, Sept. 1850.

[4] *Minutes of the Second Delegate Meeting of the Amalgamated Society of
Engineers*, p. 38 (London, 1854). The Constitution and Rules of the Associated

case of the Associated Shipwrights' Society, which has only within recent years systematically adopted regular Out of Work payments. The argument, used by the general secretary at the Delegate Meeting in 1885, which finally decided the matter, was as follows : " It is utterly impossible," Mr. Wilkie told his members, "to secure trade protection when a third or a half of your trade are walking about idle and starving. And unless members of the trade were prepared to buy up, more or less, its surplus labor in the market, it never could have the actual trade protection desired."[1]

This historical explanation of the underlying object of the Out of Work benefit is borne out by the actual practice of to-day. Whilst all the members of a Trade Union are enjoined to do their utmost to find situations for their unemployed brethren, and whilst these are forbidden, under severe penalty, to "refuse work when offered," yet this is always subject to a fundamental condition, so obvious to the Trade Union mind as to need no explicit statement in the rules. A member is not only permitted to refuse job after job if these are offered to him below the " Standard Rate " of remuneration, or otherwise in contravention of the normal terms : he is absolutely forbidden to accept work on any but the conditions satisfactory to his branch. The visitor at a branch meeting of the Engineers or Carpenters will hear members, in receipt of Out of Work pay, report to the branch that they have been offered situations on such and such terms, and ask whether it is considered right that they should accept them. The branch will discuss the question

Ironmoulders of Scotland (Glasgow, 1892) explicitly recognise the use of the Out of Work Benefit as a means of maintaining their standard of wages. " Any member leaving for want of work . . . shall be paid idle benefit . . . but, if leaving on own accord, he shall have no claim to benefit. The phrase ' want of work ' shall refer to all kinds of dismissal without fault of the member —*slackness, underpayment, resisting a reduction of wages, or unjustifiable abuse or ill-treatment from employer or foreman.* . . . ' Own accord ' shall mean all kinds of dismissal for irregularity, absence without leave except from illness, insobriety, and captious or voluntary dismissal." (Rule 30, sec. 4.)

[1] *Address of General Secretary at Delegate Meeting of Associated Shipwrights' Society*, 1885.

from the point of view of the probable effect on the Standard Rate ; and whilst they may permit a maimed or aged member to accept five shillings a week less than the normal wage of the district, they will prefer to keep a fully competent and able-bodied man "on donation," rather than sanction any departure from the Common Rule.[1]

Here we are outside the domain of actuarial science. Even if it should prove possible to reduce to an arithmetical scale of contributions and benefits the loss of income caused by mere slackness of trade, it must always be out of the question to determine what rate of Out of Work benefit can safely be awarded in return for a given subscription, if the acceptance of employment depends on the policy of the society with regard to its Standard Rate. Such a condition takes us out of the category of insurance as provisionally defined above. As understood and administered by all Trade Unions, the Out of Work benefit is not valued exclusively, or even mainly, for its protection of the individual against casualties. In the mind of the thoughtful or experienced Trade Unionist its most important function is to protect the Standard Rate of wages and other normal conditions of employment from being "eaten away," in bad times, by the competition of members driven by necessity to accept the employers' terms.

The reader will now understand why this Mutual Insurance must be regarded, not as the end or object, but as one of the Methods of Trade Unionism. At first sight nothing could appear more simple than the mutual provision of support in order to enable a man to seek work elsewhere, and not be under an absolute compulsion to accept whatever terms an employer may offer. In its economic effect upon the labor market it seems no more than would result from the existence of individual savings in a savings bank. But

[1] The *Rules to be observed by the members of the Bury and District Tape-zers' Friendly Protective Society* (Bury, 1888) provide (p. 7) that "if any member who is out of work and receiving pay make application for a situation or be sent for, and he is offered a less rate of wage than he has been paid before, he shall be at liberty to take it or not, and if he refuse to take it he shall not have his pay stopped."

Trade Unions, as Fleeming Jenkin pointed out, are far more potent in this respect than any savings bank, " because they enable the *community* of workmen to acquire wealth. . . . The individual workman knows that his reserve fund will be nearly useless unless his neighbour has a reserve fund also. If each workman in a strike trusted to his own funds only, the poorer ones must give in first ; and these would secure work, while the richer, after spending a part of their reserve, would find themselves supplanted by the poorer competitors, and the sacrifice made uselessly. A combined reserve fund gives great power by insuring that all suffer alike. The Trade Union, therefore, has a permanent action in raising wages, because it enables men to accumulate a common fund, with which they can sustain their resolution not to work unless they obtain such pay as will give increased comfort." [1] If this collective reserve fund coexists with a common understanding as to the terms without which no member will accept employment, it is obvious that we have a deliberate and conscious use of Mutual Insurance, not to relieve individual distress, but to enforce a Trade Union Regulation.

The Method of Mutual Insurance is pursued, more or less consciously, by every union that gives benefits at all. Until Collective Bargaining was permitted by the employers, and before Legal Enactment was within the workmen's reach, Mutual Insurance was the only method by which Trade Unionists could lawfully attain their end. Hence its high favor with the group of astute officials who led the workmen between 1845 and 1875. Dunning, in fact, expressly gives it as the main method of Trade Unionism. " Singly the employer can stand out longer in the bargain than the journeyman ; and as he who can stand out longest in the bargain will be sure to command his own terms, the workmen combine to put themselves on something like an equality in the bargain for the sale of their labor with their employer. This is the rationale of trade societies. . . . The object in-

[1] " Graphic Representation of the Laws of Supply and Demand," by Fleeming Jenkin, in *Recess Studies* (Edinburgh, 1870), pp. 183-4.

tended is carried out by providing a fund for the support of its members when out of employ, for a certain number of weeks in the year. *This is the usual and regular way in which the labor of the members of a trade society is protected,* that the man's present necessities may not compel him to take less than the wages which the demand and supply of labor in the trade have previously adjusted."[1]

The same view was expressed by William Allan, the first secretary of the Amalgamated Society of Engineers. "We are very little engaged in regulating" rates of wages, he told the Royal Commission in 1867, "they regulate themselves, if I may use the expression. If a member believed," he continued, "that he was not getting a proper rate of wages, the society would encourage him in objecting, that is to say, would pay him his benefit while out of employment. . . . The man would go to the branch to which he belonged, and would there state that he was only receiving a certain rate of wages; if he wished to leave his employment he would ask the question whether under the circumstances he would be entitled to what we call donation, that is Out of Work Benefit, if he left the situation ; and in all probability the society would say, you can leave and we will pay you the benefit. Or they might say, we believe you are getting as much as you ought to expect."[2]

In some small and highly organised trades of skilled handicraftsmen, this method of enforcing Trade Union regulations by Mutual Insurance has tacitly elaborated into an effective weapon, not only of defence, but also of aggression. We may instance the Spanish and Morocco Leather Finishers' Society, a small but powerful union, practically co-extensive with the craft, which has not for fifty years

---

[1] T. J. Dunning, *Trades Unions and Strikes: their Philosophy and Intention* (London, 1860), p. 10. See also Dunning's articles on " Wages of Labour and Trade Societies," in the second, third, and fourth numbers of the *Bookbinders' Trade Circular* (1851) ; *History of Trade Unionism*, p. 179.

[2] *First Report of the Commissioners appointed to enquire into the Organisation and Rules of Trades Unions and other Associations* (London, 1867). Evidence of W. Allan, Questions 787-789.

ordered a formal strike, or in any way overtly " intervened between employer and employed." Nevertheless, it has known how to enforce a detailed uniform price-list in every centre, new or old, in which the trade is carried on ; it has maintained this piece-work list practically unaltered for fifty years, notwithstanding many improvements in processes ; it has, consequently, kept up its members' earnings to certainly more than £2 per week ; and it has successfully enforced a rigid limitation of apprentices, there being nowhere more than one to seven journeymen. Yet no overt collective movement is ever made. If any employer refuses to conform to the regulations, even in the slightest degree, the members leave him one by one, and receive Out of Work benefit, which may continue for thirty-nine weeks.[1] It is usually found, we are told, that an employer remedies any grievance after he has had to put up with a new man every week or two for a few months. In 1845 the Old Smiths' Society, which had suffered severely between 1827 and 1844 from numerous small strikes, removed from their rules all provision for these pitched battles with their employers, in favor of this more silent form of pressure. The preamble to the rules, drawn up by the Delegate Meeting of 1845, adds, " Disputes . . . can only be settled by friendly consultations between both master and man, imbued with the spirit of mutually imparting facts, with a view to render assistance to each other ; if this, in connection with the efforts of mutual and disinterested friends, cannot be accomplished, we say then let men and masters part ; offer no opposition ; the men, however great or small their number, to be supplied with means of existence until they obtain other situations of work from the funds of the society ; and the employers to obtain other men as best they may ; and we contend that this unassuming quiet plan of operations is, according to its number of members, accomplishing, and will continue to accomplish, infinitely more real good to the trade in all its ramifications, at a minimum

---

[1] *Rules to be observed by the Members of the Leeds Friendly Society of Spanish and Morocco Leather Finishers* (Leeds, 1879).

expense to its members, than any other plan of operation by any other society." [1] The same position was aimed at by the Flint Glass Makers in 1850, when their magazine was advocating the use of this nameless weapon which we have christened, for our own convenience, the "Strike in Detail." "As man after man leaves, . . . then it is that the proud and haughty spirit of the oppressor is brought down, and he feels the power he cannot see." [2]

This application of mutual insurance may be made the method of enforcing any Common Rule whatsoever ; and a very effective instrument it is. An employer whose workmen leave him one by one, after due notice, may find little difficulty in filling their places. But if the new-comers, after a brief stay, one by one give notice that they, too, will leave, he is placed in a serious difficulty. He cannot close his doors and appeal for support to his fellow-employers, as there is no strike, and no refusal on the part of the Trade Unionists to accept his terms. Nevertheless, his constant inability to retain any workman for more than a week or two, may easily become so harassing that he will be forced to inquire carefully in what respect his employment falls below the standard of the trade, and to conform to it. The Trade Union, on the other hand, runs no risk of retaliation, and, as only a few men are on the books at any one time, incurs the minimum of expense. As a deliberate Trade Union policy, the Strike in Detail depends upon the extent to which the union has secured the adhesion of all the competent men in the trade, and upon their capacity for persistent and self-restrained pursuit of a common end. It could, accordingly, never become the sole method of any but a small, wealthy, and closely knit society ; but in such a society it may easily, in its coercive effect on the employer, surpass even an Act of Parliament itself.

---

[1] Report on Trade Societies' Rules by Mr. (now the Rt. Hon.) G. Shaw Lefevre in Social Science Association's *Report on Trades Societies and Strikes* (London, 1860).

[2] *Flint Glass Makers' Magazine*, July 1850.

The Strike in Detail is only a more deliberate and self-conscious application of the method of maintaining the standard of life by Mutual Insurance customary among all Trade Unionists. It is impossible to draw any logical distinction between the action of the little union of Leather Finishers and that of the Amalgamated Society of Engineers, as explained by William Allan and T. J. Dunning, or indeed any union which maintains a member in idleness rather than allow him to accept work " contrary to the interests of the trade." The persistent adhesion of Trade Unionists to the Out of Work benefit, and their secondary adoption of what we have called the friendly society business, appear as a perfectly consistent, homogeneous policy the moment the true Trade Union point of view is caught. Any provision which secures the members of the trade against destitution prevents an employer taking advantage of their necessities.[1] Not Out of Work benefit alone, but also sick pay, grants to replace tools or property lost or burnt, burial money for wife or child, and especially accident benefit and superannuation allowance, all serve to enforce the claim of the workman " to be dealt with as an intelligent being, and not merely as a bale of goods or article of merchandise. This," emphatically declares the Friendly Society of Ironfounders, " is, then, the main and central pillar of our organisation. Around it are clustered those monetary benefits that are stated above, and it is from this grand standpoint those benefits must all be estimated : for from this point only it is at all possible to come to a right and fair conclusion as to their real value to individual members." [2]

[1] We may cite a curious small case among the Curriers. The London journeymen curriers have always strenuously resisted the employers' attempts to make them take out shoe hides at an average weight, instead of weighing each one separately. In 1854 certain members represented to the union that their employer had taken advantage of the slackness of work in the winter season to try to enforce this practice upon them ; and that if the union would make them each a loan, they could dispense with sending in their bills to their employer for that week, which would have a good effect as demonstrating their power to stand out. The union readily agreed to lend each man a pound on condition that he drew no wages that week. MS. Minute Book, 1854.

[2] Preface to *Rules to be observed by the Members of the Friendly Society of*

Mutual Insurance, even when considered purely as a Method of Trade Unionism, is by no means beyond criticism. The lack of legal or financial security of the friendly benefits may be worth tolerating by a wage-earner for the sake of the trade as a whole ; but it is none the less an evil on that account. And even the successful Strike in Detail of the Leather Finishers has grave drawbacks, from its own standpoint. No Trade Unionist would deny that the deliberately concerted Common Rules, to which workmen and employers must alike conform, ought to be framed after consideration, not of the desires of one class alone, but from all points of view. The method of Mutual Insurance leaves no place for discussion with the employers. Each party makes up its own mind, relies on its power of holding out, and leaves the issue to depend merely on secret endurance. Frank and full discussion might have revealed facts previously unknown, which would have altered the views of the parties. It might have been discovered that some points most keenly insisted on by one side were regarded as unimportant by the other. The influence of public opinion would have moderated the negotiations. These tendencies make, in Collective Bargaining, for a compromise often representing a real gain to both parties. For all this, the Method of Mutual Insurance allows no place. It is, therefore, not surprising to find that the most highly developed and successful modern organisations make little use of Mutual Insurance as a method of industrial regulation. Among the Coalminers and Cotton Operatives, who together comprise a fifth of the Trade Union world, friendly benefits, and even Out of Work donation, play only the most trifling part. And it is significant that the United Society of Boilermakers, in many

---

Ironfounders (London, 1891). It is interesting to find that this use of Mutual Insurance among workers was elaborately explained and defended in 1819 by the well-known Baptist minister, the Reverend Robert Hall ; see his pamphlets, *An Appeal to the Public on the Subject of the Framework Knitters' Fund* (Leicester, 1819), and *A Reply to the Principal Objections advanced by Cobbett and others against the Framework Knitters' Friendly Relief Society* (Leicester, 1821), both included in his *Works* (London, 1832), vol. iii.

respects the most successful of the great unions, whilst utilising to the full a most elaborate system of Mutual Insurance, keeps the provision against unavoidable casualties entirely distinct from its trade objects. For all that concerns the maintenance and improvement of the conditions of employment the Boilermakers, like the Coalminers and the Cotton Operatives, resort to one or other of the alternative Methods of Trade Unionism, Collective Bargaining, or Legal Enactment.

CHAPTER II

THE METHOD OF COLLECTIVE BARGAINING

THE nature of the Method of Collective Bargaining will be best understood by a series of examples.

In unorganised trades the individual workman, applying for a job, accepts or refuses the terms offered by the employer, without communication with his fellow-workmen, and without any other consideration than the exigencies of his own position. For the sale of his labor he makes, with the employer, a strictly individual bargain.[1] But if a group of workmen concert together, and send representatives to conduct the bargaining on behalf of the whole body, the position is at once changed. Instead of the employer making a series of separate contracts with isolated individuals, he meets with a collective will, and settles, in a single agreement, the principles upon which, for the time being, all workmen of a particular group, or class, or grade, will be engaged. For instance, in a cabinet-making shop, if a new pattern is brought out, the men in the shop hold a brief and informal meeting to discuss the price at which it can be executed, the

---

[1] The phrase "Individual Bargaining" is used incidentally by C. Morrison in his *Essay on the Relations between Labour and Capital* (London, 1854), as equivalent to "what may be called the commercial principle," according to which "the workman endeavours to sell his labor as dearly and the employer to purchase it as cheaply as possible" (p. 9).

We are not aware of any use of the phrase "Collective Bargaining" before that in *The Cooperative Movement in Great Britain* (London, 1891), p. 217, by Beatrice Potter (Mrs. Sidney Webb), where it is employed in the present sense.

rough basis being whether, taking into account the un-
familiarity of the work, and the nature of the task, they can
make no less net wages per hour than they have been
hitherto earning. The foreman has meanwhile been estimat-
ing the job in his own way, on much the same basis as the
men, but probably arriving at a slightly lower figure. The
men's representative talks the matter over with the foreman,
and some compromise is come to, the job standing at that
price for the whole shop. This process differs from that of
a series of individual bargains with the separate workmen, in
that the particular exigencies of each are ruled out of consideration. If the foreman had dealt privately with each
man, he might have found some in such necessity that he
could have driven them to take the job practically at any
price rather than be without work for even half a day.
Others, again, relying on exceptional strength or endurance,
would have seen their way to make the standard earnings at
a piecework rate upon which the average worker could not
even subsist. By the Method of Collective Bargaining the
foreman is prevented from taking advantage of the competition of both these classes of men to beat down the earnings
of the other workmen. The starving man gets his job at
the same piecework rate as the workman who could afford
to stand out for his usual earnings. The superior craftsman retains all his advantages over his fellows, but without
allowing his superiority to be made the means of reducing
the weekly wage of the ordinary worker.

This example of the Method of Collective Bargaining is
taken from the practice of a " shop club " in a relatively
unorganised trade. The skilled artisans in the building
trades afford a typical instance of the second stage. The
" shop bargain " of such a trade as the cabinet-makers merely
rules out the exigencies of the particular workmen in a
single establishment. But this establishment is exposed to
the undercutting of other establishments in the same town.
One employer might have to give exceptional terms to his
" shop club " in a sudden rush of urgent orders, whilst the

workmen in other firms might be virtually at the masters'
mercy owing to bad trade. Directly a Trade Union is
formed in any town, an attempt is made to exclude from
influence on the terms, the exigencies of particular employers
no less than those of particular workmen. Thus in the
building trades we find the unions of Carpenters, Bricklayers,
Stonemasons, Plumbers, Plasterers, and sometimes those of
the Painters, Slaters, and Builders' Laborers obtaining formal
"working rules," binding on all the employers and workmen of the town or district. This Collective Bargaining,
arranged at a conference between the local master builders,
and the local officials of the national unions, settles, for a
specified term, the hours of beginning and ending work, the
minimum rate of wages, the payment for overtime, the age
and number of apprentices to be taken, the arrangements as
to piecework, the holidays to be allowed, the notice to be
given by employers or workmen terminating engagements,
the accommodation to be provided for meals and the safe
custody of tools, and numerous allowances or extra payments
for travelling, lodging, "walking time," "grinding money,"
etc. These elaborate codes, unalterable except by formal
notice from the organisations on either side, thus place on a
uniform footing as regards the hiring of labor the wealthiest
contractor and the builder on the brink of bankruptcy, the
firm crowded with orders and that standing practically idle.
On the other hand, the superior workman retains his freedom
to exact higher rates for his special work, whilst the employer
of superior business ability, or technical knowledge, and the firm
enjoying the best machinery or plant, preserve, it is claimed,
every fraction of their advantage over their competitors.[1]

[1] The number of these "working rules" in force in the United Kingdom
has never been ascertained, but it must be very large, there being scarcely any
town in which one or other of the building trades has not obtained a formal
treaty with its employers. Our own collection of these treaties, in the building
trades alone, numbers several hundreds. Specimens will be found in the *Labour
Gazette* of the Board of Trade for November 1894 ; and in *Le Trade Unionisme
en Angleterre*, edited by Paul de Rousiers (Paris, 1897), pp. 68-70. The British
Library of Political Science, 10 Adelphi Terrace, London, contains these and
other Trade Union documents.

The building trades, in which one town does not obviously compete with another, have hitherto stopped at this stage of Collective Bargaining. Where the product of different towns goes to the same market, we see, in the best organised industries, a still further development. The great staple trades of cotton-spinning and cotton-weaving have ruled out, not merely the exigencies of particular workmen in one mill, or of particular mills in one town, but also those of the various towns over which the industries have spread. The general level of wages in all the cotton-spinning towns is, for instance, settled by the national agreements between the Amalgamated Association of Operative Cotton-spinners and the Master Cotton-spinners' Association. No employer, and no group of workmen, no district association of employers, and no "province" of the Trade Union, can propose an advance or accept a special reduction from the established level of earnings. General advances or reductions are negotiated at long intervals, and with great deliberateness, between the national representatives of each party. Thus we see ruled out, not merely all personal or local exigencies, but also the temporary gluts or contractions of the market, whether in the raw material or in the product. All firms in a district, and all districts in the industry being, as far as possible, placed upon an identical footing as to the rate at which they obtain human labor, their competition takes, it is contended, the form of improving the machinery, getting the best and cheapest raw material, and obtaining the most advantageous market for their wares.

A similar series of collective agreements exists in some other industries. Among the iron-shipbuilders, for instance, a gang of platers will bargain, through their first hand, as to the exact terms upon which they will undertake a job in the building of an iron ship. But the foreman cannot offer, or the men accept terms which in any way conflict with the "district by-laws"—a detailed code regulating hours, overtime, extra allowances, and often also the piecework rates for ordinary work, formally agreed to by the district committee of the Trade Union and the local association of employers. Moreover, the district by-laws, unalterable for a fixed term, exclude the influence of any sudden glut or famine in the labor market, or any temporary fluctuation of the trade of the port. But this is not all. The district by-laws are themselves subject to the formal treaties on such matters as apprenticeship and the standard level of wages concluded between the United Society of Boilermakers and Iron-shipbuilders and the Employers' Federation of Ship-building and Engineering Trades. These treaties, settling certain questions for the whole kingdom, rule out on those points the exigencies of particular localities, and place all ports upon an equality. Thus the collective bargain made by the group of platers on a particular job in one establish-ment of a certain town imports a hierarchy of other collective bargains, concluded by the representatives of the contracting parties in their gradually widening spheres of action.

This practice of Collective Bargaining has, in one form or another, superseded the old individual contract between master and servant over a very large proportion of the industrial field. " I will pay each workman according to his necessity or merit, and deal with no one but my own hands,"—once the almost universal answer of employers— is now seldom heard in any important industry, except in out-of-the-way districts, or from exceptionally arbitrary masters.[1] But it is interesting to notice that Collective Bargaining is neither co-extensive with, nor limited to, Trade Union organisation. A few old-standing wealthy unions of restricted membership have sometimes preferred, as we saw in the last chapter, to attain their ends by the Method of Mutual Insurance, whilst others, at all periods, have been formed with the express design of attaining their ends by the Method of Legal Enactment. On the other

[1] Mr. Lecky observes (*Democracy and Liberty*, vol. ii. p. 361) that collective agreements "are becoming, much more than engagements between individual employers and individual workmen, the form into which English industry is manifestly developing."

hand, whole sections of the wage-earning class, not included in any Trade Union, habitually have their rate of wages and often some other conditions of their employment settled by Collective Bargaining. We do not here refer merely to such cases as the "shop-bargain," which we have just described. The historic strikes of the London building trades in 1859, and the Newcastle engineers in 1871, were both conducted by committees elected at mass meetings of members of the trade, among whom the Trade Unionists formed an insignificant minority.[1]   In the history of the building and engineering trades there are numerous instances of agreements being concluded, on behalf of a whole district, by temporary committees of non-unionists, and where the Trade Unions themselves initiate and conduct the negotiations the agreements arrived at habitually govern in these industries, not the members alone, but the great bulk of similar workmen in the district.   Here and there an eccentric employer may choose to depart from the regular terms, but the great majority find it more convenient to comply with what becomes, in fact, the "custom of the trade."   So thoroughly has the Collective Bargaining been recognised in the building trades, that county court judges now usually hold that the "working rules" of the district are implied as part of the wage-contract, if no express stipulation has been made on the points therein dealt with. Collective Bargaining thus extends over a much larger part of the industrial field than Trade Unionism.   Precise statistics do not exist, but our impression is that, in all skilled trades, where men work in concert, on the employers' premises, ninety per cent of the workmen find, either their rate of wages or their hours of work, and often many other details, predetermined by a collective bargain in which they personally have taken no part, but in which their interests have been dealt with by representatives of their class.

But though Collective Bargaining prevails over a much larger area than Trade Unionism, it is the Trade Union

[1] *History of Trade Unionism*, pp. 210, 299 ; compare pp. 302, 305.

alone which can provide the machinery for any but its most casual and limited application. Without a Trade Union in the industry, it would be almost impossible to get a Common Rule extending over a whole district, and hopeless to attempt a national agreement. If therefore the collective bargain aims at excluding from influence on the bargain, the exigencies of particular firms or particular districts, and not merely those of particular workmen in a single establishment, Trade Union organisation is indispensable. Moreover, it is the Trade Union alone which can supply the machinery for the automatic interpretation and the peaceful revision of the general agreement. To Collective Bargaining, the machinery of Trade Unionism may bring, in fact, both continuity and elasticity.

The development of a definite and differentiated machinery for Collective Bargaining in the Trade Union world coincides, as might be expected, with its enlargement from the workshop to the whole town, and from the town to the whole industry. As soon as a Trade Union properly so called comes into existence with a president and secretary, it becomes more and more usual for these officers to act as the workmen's representatives in trade negotiations. This is the stage in which we find nearly all the single-branched unions, such as those of the Sheffield trades, the Dublin local societies, the Coopers, Sailmakers, and other small and compact bodies of workmen all over the kingdom. Even where the growth of a local union into a national society has necessitated the appointment of a salaried general secretary, giving his whole time to his duties, it is exceptional to find him conducting all, or even the bulk of the negotiations of its members with their employers. In the United Operative Plumbers' Association, for instance, practically the whole of the Collective Bargaining is still conducted by the branch officials, or by representative workmen specially selected as delegates. A further stage is marked by the creation of permanent committees, unconcerned with the ordinary branch administration, to deal solely with local trade questions.

Thus the bulk of the Collective Bargaining of the members of the Amalgamated Society of Engineers was, until 1892, conducted by the society's district committees, each acting for the whole of a local industrial district, in which there are often many branches. These negotiators are, like the branch officials, men working at their trade, and only spasmodically engaged in special business of industrial negotiation. Even disputes of such national importance as the costly and disastrous strikes of the Tyneside engineers of 1891, were initiated and managed by the local district committees and their officials, that is to say, by workmen called from the workshop only for the time required by the society's business. Over more than one-third of the Trade Union world, including such old established and widely extended unions as the Friendly Society of Operative Stonemasons, the Friendly Society of Ironfounders, and the Operative Bricklayers' Society, the workmen have not developed any more specialised machinery for Collective Bargaining than the branch or district committee of men working at their trade, meeting representative employers when occasion arises. This primitive machinery, although a great advance on the " shop-club," has manifest disadvantages. If, as often happens, a personal quarrel or local bitterness is at the bottom of the dispute, the prominent local workman who represents his fellows can hardly escape its influence. And, apart from personal antagonisms and questions of temper, the fact that it is the conditions of his own life that are involved does not conduce to that combination of courage and reasonableness most likely to lead to a lasting settlement. If the negotiator himself is fortunately placed, or would personally be much injured by a strike, he will be tempted to acquiesce in conditions not advantageous to the whole trade. In the reverse case—perhaps the more common—the energetic and active-minded workman, whom his fellows choose to represent them, is apt to find, in the joy of the fight, a relief from the monotony of manual labor. If a strike ensues, it brings to him at any rate the compensation that for a few weeks, or perhaps months, he becomes the paid organiser of the union, overwhelmed, it is true, with anxious and harassing work, but temporarily exchanging a position of passive obedience for one of active leadership.

But, apart altogether from the disturbing influence of the "personal equation," it is obvious that the manual workers will stand at a grave disadvantage if they do not command the services of an expert negotiator. Unfortunately for his interests, the workman has an inveterate belief in what he calls a "practical man"—that is, one who is actually working at the trade concerned. He does not see that negotiation is in itself a craft, in which a man must have had a special training before he can be considered a "practical" man for the business in hand. The proper adjustment of the rate of remuneration in a given establishment requires, to begin with, a wide range of industrial and economic knowledge. Unless the workman's negotiator is accurately acquainted with the rates and precise conditions prevailing in other establishments and in other districts, he will be unable to criticise the statements which will be made by the employer, and incapable of advising his own clients whether their demand is a reasonable one. Without some knowledge of the economic conditions of the industry, the state of trade, the number of orders in hand or to be expected, and the condition of the labor market, his judgment of the opportuneness or strategic advantage of the men's demand will be of no value. The mechanic kept working for fifty or sixty hours a week at one narrow process in a single establishment would be an extraordinary genius if he could acquire this information. Nor would a knowledge of the facts alone suffice. The best kit of tools will not make a man a good carpenter without that training in their use which experience alone can give. The quick apprehension and mental agility which make up the greater part of the art of using facts are not fostered by days spent in physical toil. Finally, the perfect negotiator, like the perfect carpenter, attains his expertness only by incessant practice of his art.   Here again, the workman is at a special disability compared with the captain of industry.   The making of bargains and agreements, which occupies only an infinitesimal fraction of a workman's life and thought, makes up the daily routine of the commercial man.

These considerations have slowly overcome the workman's objections, and have, in the most powerful unions, together comprising over a third of the aggregate membership, caused the bulk of the Collective Bargaining to be gradually transferred from the non-commissioned officers to the salaried civil service of the movement.   Especially in the piecework trades has the amateur negotiator most clearly demonstrated his inefficiency.   When the workman's remuneration depends on a combination of many different and constantly changing factors—the novelty of the pattern, the character of the material, the variations in the machinery, the speed of the engine—success in bargaining demands, in addition to all the other qualifications, a special aptitude for quickly seizing the net result of proposed changes in one or more of the factors.   It is in the piecework trades therefore that we find the machinery for Collective Bargaining in its most highly developed form.   The great staple industries of cotton, coal, and iron, together with boot and shoe-making, and the hosiery and lace trades, have especially developed elaborate and complicated organisations for Collective Bargaining which have excited the admiration of economic students all over the world.

We must here plunge into a maze of complicated technical detail relating to these industries, each of which has developed its machinery for Collective Bargaining in its own way, and we despair of making the reader understand either our exposition or our criticism unless he will keep constantly in mind one fundamental distinction, which is all-important.   This vital distinction is between the making of a new bargain, and the interpreting of the terms of an existing one.   Where the machinery for Collective Bargaining has broken down, we usually discover that this distinction has not been made ; and it is only where this fundamental distinction has been clearly maintained that the machinery works without friction or ill-feeling. Let us consider first the interpretation of an existing bargain. Directly a general agreement or formal treaty has been concluded in any trade between the general body of employers, on the one hand, and the general body of workmen on the other, there arises a practically incessant series of disputes as to the application of the agreement to particular cases. Thus, as we shall see, the highly elaborate and precisely detailed lists of the English Cotton-spinners do not prevent, in one or other of the thousands of mills to which they apply, the almost daily occurrence of a difference of opinion between employer and operative as to the wages due. Similarly the unanimous agreement of a " uniform statement " in the boot and shoe trade leaves open endless questions as to the classification of the ever-changing patterns called for by the fashion of each season. The determination of the " county average " of the Northumberland or Durham coalminer leaves it still to be determined what tonnage rate should be fixed for any particular seam, in order that the workmen may earn the normal wage. The point at issue in these cases is not the amount per week which the workmen in any particular establishment should be permitted to earn—for that has, in principle, already been settled—but the rate at which, under the actual conditions of that establishment, and the class of goods in question, the piecework price must be computed in order that the average earnings of a particular section of workmen shall amount to no more and no less than the agreed standard. This, it will be seen, is exclusively an issue of fact, in which both the desires and the tactical strength of the parties directly concerned must be entirely eliminated. For conciliation, compromise, and balancing of expediencies, there is absolutely no room. On the other hand, it is indispensable that the ascertainment of facts should attain an almost scientific precision. Moreover, the settlement should be automatic, rapid, and inexpensive. The ideal machinery for this class of cases would, in fact, be a peripatetic calculating-machine, endowed with a high degree of technical knowledge, which could accurately register all the factors concerned, and unerringly grind out the arithmetical result.

When we come to the settlement of the terms upon which a new general agreement should be entered into, an entirely different set of considerations is involved. Whether the general level of wages in the trade should be raised or lowered by 10 per cent ; whether the number of boys to be engaged by any one employer should be restricted, and if so, by what scale ; whether the hours of labor should be reduced, and overtime regulated or prohibited,—are not problems which could be solved by even the most perfect calculating-machine. Here nothing has been decided, or accepted in advance by both parties, and the fullest possible play is left for the arts of diplomacy. In so far as the issue is left to Collective Bargaining there is not even any question of principle involved. The workmen are frankly striving to get for themselves the best terms that can permanently be exacted from the employers. The employers, on the other hand, are endeavouring, in accordance with business principles, to buy their labor in the cheapest market. The issue is a trial of strength between the parties. Open warfare—the stoppage of the industry—is costly and even disastrous to both sides. But though neither party desires war, there is always the alternative of fighting out the issue. The resources and tactical strength of each side must accordingly exercise a potent influence on the deliberations. The plenipotentiaries must higgle and cast about to find acceptable alternatives, seeking, like ambassadors in international conference, not to ascertain what are the facts, nor yet what is the just decision according to some ethical standard or view of social expediency, but to find a common basis which each side can bring itself to agree to, rather than go to war. Finally, however wise may be the decision come to, the acceptance and carrying out of the collective bargain ultimately arrived at, depends upon the extent to which the negotiators express the feelings and command the confidence of the whole class affected. All these considerations must be taken carefully into account in the formation of successful machinery for Collective Bargaining.

The most obvious form of permanent machinery for Collective Bargaining is a joint committee, consisting of equal numbers of representatives of the employers and workmen respectively. This may almost be called the " orthodox " panacea of industrial philanthropists. For over thirty years, since the experiments of Sir Rupert Kettle and Mr. Mundella, employers and workmen have been persistently urged to adopt the form of a " board of arbitration and conciliation," consisting of representatives of each side, and with or without an impartial chairman or an umpire. Such a joint committee, it has been supposed, could thrash out in friendly discussion all points in dispute, and arrive at an amicable understanding. In intractable cases, the umpire's decision would cut the Gordian knot. Readers of the *History of Trade Unionism* will remember how eagerly this idea was taken up by the organised workmen in certain great industries, and how, in coalmining and iron and steel in particular, it has since enjoyed the favor both of employers and employed. We need not stop to describe all the cases in which this form of machinery has, from time to time, been adopted. We shall best understand its operation by considering a couple of leading instances, the " joint boards " of the boot and shoe trade, and the " joint committees " of the Northumberland and Durham coalminers.

The great machine industry of boot and shoe-making has been provided, for some years past, with a formal and elaborate constitution, mutually agreed to by employers and employed, and expressly designed " to prevent a strike or lock-out, and to secure the reference of all trade disputes to arbitration." [1] The machinery for Collective Bargaining thus

[1] *Rules for the Prevention of Strikes and Lockouts, etc.*, 16th August 1892,

established puts into concrete form all the aspirations of enthusiastic advocates of " industrial peace." We have first a " local board of conciliation and arbitration " in every important centre of the trade. To this board, formed of an equal number of elected representatives of the local employers and the local Trade Unionists, must be referred " every question, or aspect of a question, affecting the relations of employers and workmen individually or collectively." If the board cannot agree, the question goes to an impartial umpire, acceptable to both sides. Issues affecting the whole industry were, until 1894, dealt with by a national conference of great dignity and importance. Nine chosen leaders of the Federated Associations of Boot and Shoe Manufacturers of Great Britain met, in the council chamber of the Leicester Town Hall, an equal number of elected representatives of the National Union of Boot and Shoe Operatives. These elaborate debates, conducted with all the ceremony of a State Trial, were presided over by an eminent and universally respected solicitor, sometime mayor of the town. If no agreement could be arrived at, the conference enjoyed the services, as umpire, of no less an authority than Sir Henry (now Lord) James, formerly Attorney-General, before whom, sitting as a judge, the issue was elaborately reargued by the spokesmen of each side. Finally as a means of influencing the public opinion of the trade, there were published, not only the precise and authoritative decisions of the conference or the umpire, but also a verbatim report of all the proceedings.[1]

We can imagine how this elaborate and carefully thought out machinery for Collective Bargaining would have

appended to Report of Conference, 1892. These rules, which are signed by three employers and three workmen, on behalf of their respective associations, consist of fifteen clauses defining the constitution and method of working both of the " Local Board of Conciliation and Arbitration," and of the " National Conference." They will be found in the Board of Trade *Report on Strikes and Lockouts of* 1893, C, 7566 of 1894, pp. 253-257.

[2] The "transcript of the shorthand writers' notes" of the Conference of August 1892, and the subsequent trial before the umpire, forms a volume of 152 pages of rich material for the student of industrial organisation.

delighted the heart of the enthusiastic believers in " boards of conciliation and arbitration." Nor need it be contested that it has been the means of effecting many peaceful settlements in the industry. But we do not think that any one conversant with the trade, or any student of the voluminous reports of the proceedings, will deny that the boards have been the cause of endless friction, discontent, and waste of energy among workmen and employers alike. Scarcely a quarter passes without the operatives, in some district or another, revolting against their local board ; condemning or withdrawing their representatives ; and even occasionally refusing to obey the award of the umpire.[1] The employers are, on their side, no better satisfied than the men, and in 1894 the national conference was brought to an end by the secession of the federated manufacturers, and their resolute refusal to submit the issues to arbitration. The result was a stoppage in 1895 of practically the entire industry from one end of the kingdom to the other, which was only brought to an end by the half-authoritative interference of the Board of Trade.[2]

If we examine this general discontent we find it taking different forms among the workmen and the employers respectively. The operatives complain that, when a general agreement has been concluded they cannot get any speedy or certain enforcement of it through the local boards. Thus, the Bristol representative at the annual delegate meeting in 1894, complained bitterly of the dilatory way in which his local board acted in its interpretation work. Questions " had been hanging about from six to nine months from the board to the umpire. Decisions had been given by the umpire on boots after a delay of eight or nine

[1] The local boards, of which twelve were in existence at the end of 1894, date from 1875. The Stafford Board was dissolved in 1878, and the Leeds Board in 1881. The years 1891-94 saw no fewer than seven dissolutions, and the important centres of Stafford, Manchester, and Kingswood still remain without boards. The National Conference, established in August 1892, met five times in the next three years, the sittings being suspended on the withdrawal of the employers in December 1894.

[2] See the *Labour Gazette*, April and May 1895.

months. . . . In one case in the factory where he worked a boot was sent to the arbitration board, and thence to the umpire. The decision arrived at by the latter was in favor of the men. There was something like seven shillings each due to two or three men on that particular boot. But one of them had left the town in the interim, and the result of the delay was that he was practically swindled out of the seven shillings. New samples had been introduced at the beginning of the year, and the shoes had been made under protest, at a price the employers had quoted, till the end of the season. Then, perhaps, when the season was ended, they got a decision in their favor, face to face with all the difficulties of getting back the money due to them. . . . This continual delay sickened the whole of them in Bristol, and although there had not been a ballot taken on the question of arbitration in Bristol, he felt sure there were over ninety per cent of the men opposed to it." [1]

The Kingswood Local Board broke up in 1894, the umpire resigning his post in disgust. Discussion had proceeded upon a "statement" for "light" boots, and points in dispute were submitted to the umpire by the board. The bulk of the manufacturers thereupon flatly refused to send any samples of the boots in question, and thus made it impossible for the umpire to decide the cases submitted to him.[2] This produced the greatest possible irritation among the men, who urged that, as the employers had failed to submit to the umpire's award, the operatives' claim should be adopted. These cases might be indefinitely multiplied from all the centres of the industry. But delay is not the only objection brought by the operatives against the working of the local boards. When at last the umpire's decision has been given it has often failed to command the assent, and sometimes even to secure the obedience of the workmen. This arises, we believe, from the class of umpire whom it has been

[1] Report of the Edinburgh Conference, May 1894 (the delegate meeting of the National Union of Boot and Shoe Operatives).
[2] *Shoe and Leather Record*, 30th November 1894.

necessary to choose. The questions of interpretation necessarily turn, not on any general principle, but on extremely technical trade details, which are unintelligible to any person outside the industry.[1] In the absence of any paid professional expert, permanently engaged for precisely this work, the umpire has in practice to be chosen from among the employers, the board usually agreeing upon a leading manufacturer in another district. This reliance on the unpaid service of a non-resident increases the delay. But what is more important is, that however generally respected such an umpire may be, it is inevitable that, when his award runs counter to the claim of the operatives, these should accuse him of class bias. The alternative of choosing one of the officials of the union would, it need hardly be said, be equally distasteful to the employers.

The discontent of the employers is directed chiefly to another feature of the organisation. The work of the local boards is so laborious and incessant that the great magnates of the industry cannot spare time to attend. On questions of interpretation, they would be willing to leave the business to their managers or smaller employers. But besides questions of interpretation the local board have perpetually brought before them disputes which turn upon the admission of what the employers regard as " new principles." If the local board, with the concurrence of its employer-members, decides the issue, all the other employers in the district, some of whom may be " captains of industry " on a huge scale, find a new regulation made binding on them in the conduct of what they regard as " their own business." If on the other hand the local board remits such issues—virtually the

[1] Thus the umpire for the Norwich Local Board had to award rates to be paid in the following cases, remitted from a single meeting. (1) " A woman's 5ths if changed from self-vamp to calf vamp ; (2) a girl's 4ths if changed from self-vamp to glacé kid vamp ; (3) a woman's 4th's ditto ; (4) a girl's kid button levant seal vamp or golosh ; (5) a girl's glacé kid one finger strap ; (6) a woman's kid elastic mock button front shoe sew-round." The award, which is equally unintelligible to the general reader, will be found in the *Shoe and Leather Record Annual* for 1892-93, p. 121.

conclusion of new general agreements——to the national conference, all the employers in the kingdom find themselves
in a similar predicament. Moreover, in a publicly conducted
national conference, formed of equal numbers from each
party, neither the representative workmen nor the representative employers dare concede anything to their opponents, or
even submit to a compromise. The result is that every
important issue is inevitably remitted by the conference to
the umpire. Lord James has accordingly found himself in
the remarkable position of imposing laws upon the entire
boot and shoe-making industry, prescribing for instance, not
only a minimum rate of wages, but also a precise numerical
limitation of the number of boy-learners to be engaged by
each employer, the conditions under which alone a wholesale
trader may give work out to sub-contractors, and the extent
to which employers shall themselves provide workshop
accommodation, and the date before which such premises
shall be in use. This, it is obvious, goes beyond Collective
Bargaining. The awards of Lord James amount, in fact,
to legislative regulation of the industry, the legislature in
this case being, not a representative assembly acting on
behalf of the whole community, but a dictator elected by the
trade.[1]

It is therefore not surprising to find the employers
quickly protesting against so drastic and far-reaching
an arrangement. But it was one to which they had explicitly and unreservedly pledged themselves. They had
promised, by the rules of the 16th August 1892, that
"every question or aspect of a question affecting the
relations of *employers and workmen* individually or collectively
should in case of disagreement be submitted for settlement,"
first to the local board, then to the national conference, and

[1] It is a minor grievance of the employers that no distinguished lawyer
can be found to give the unpaid and laborious service of an umpire, who is not
also a politician. It is impossible for the employers to avoid the suspicion
that any politician will be unconsciously biassed in favor of the most numerous
section of the electors. See the significant quotation given in the footnote at
p. 240.

finally, if need be, to the umpire.   That this promise was not confined to questions of interpretation is made manifest by the express mention in the same document of the settlement of disputes involving " new principles."   In the long discussion which led up to the signing of the rules, they had, in fact, successfully pleaded for adopting " honestly and unreservedly arbitration pure and simple, and for every dispute, and under all conditions." [1]   In their anxiety to remove every chance of a stoppage of their industry, they had overlooked the fundamental distinction between questions of the interpretation of an existing contract and questions as to the terms of a new settlement.   If they had listened to the warning of the able editor of their own trade organ, they would not have made this blunder.   The very month before the conference of 1892 he was urging exactly the distinction upon which we insist.   " Employers," he wrote, " have never contended that arbitration would settle every conceivable kind of dispute between capital and labor. But they have contended that *where certain established principles are already recognised by both sides, the adjustment of details can better be settled by arbitration than in any other way.* . . .   It must be obvious that, whatever the future may bring, employers could not now prudently allow every dispute with their workmen to be settled by a third person.   To say nothing of the question of boy labor which is now at issue, a number of others may be mentioned regarding which the employer could not consent to surrender any portion of his discretion or responsibility." [2]   The subsequent events quickly proved that this view of the state of mind of the average employer was correct, and that the chosen representatives of the Federated Associations of Boot and Shoe Manufacturers had failed to understand the words which they were, with all solemnity, using.   When the

---

[1] Speech of Mr. Gale, a leading employer. Third day of Conference, August 1892.   The men had wished to exclude any question of a general reduction of wages, whereupon the employers had insisted that no exception whatever should be made.

[2] *Shoe and Leather Record*, July 1892.

workmen brought up cases of actual disputes that had arisen about boy labor, machinery, the " team system," and the employment of non-unionists, the employers protested that they had never meant such questions as these to be discussed at all. The president had, of course, no alternative but to hold them bound to their explicit agreement, and to overrule their protests. After prolonged ill-feeling, the associated employers revolted, and withdrew their representatives from the national conference, alleging first of all, that the workmen had in some cases refused to abide by the award of the umpire, and further, that the national conference had become " a legislative tribunal for the trade." [1]

Thus experience of the working of the elaborate machinery for Collective Bargaining provided in the boot and shoe industry has revealed many imperfections. Some of these have been avoided in our second example, the conciliation boards and the joint committees of the Northumberland and Durham coalminers. Here we have, to begin with, a clear distinction maintained between the machinery for interpretation and that for concluding a new agreement. The earnings of the miners in both counties are determined ultimately by general principles [2] applicable to the whole of each county, which are revised at occasional conferences of representative

[1] Manifesto of Federated Associations of Boot and Shoe Manufacturers of Great Britain, 20th December 1894. For documents and exact particulars of the dispute which thereupon arose, see *Labour Gazette*, April and May 1895 ; also the *Shoe and Leather Record*, and the Monthly Reports of the National Union of Boot and Shoe Operatives from October 1894 to June 1895. We have here dealt with the matter, not on its merits, but only in so far as it illustrates the machinery for collective bargaining. The agreement brought about by the Board of Trade on 19th April 1895, which now governs the industry, expressly excludes four specified subjects from discussion by the local boards and makes no provision for a national conference. But so far as we understand the document, no distinction is even now made between questions of interpretation and questions as to the terms of a new agreement. Both kinds of questions are, as before, to be decided where necessary by the umpire.

[2] These general principles include a normal standard wage, with a corresponding normal tonnage rate, applicable to the whole county. This is called the " County Average," a somewhat misleading phrase as the normal rate is not, and has long not been, a precise " average " of the actual earnings of all the miners in the county, and is now only a conventional figure upon which percentages of advance or reduction are based.

workmen and employers.[1] Neither in Durham nor in Northumberland has this board of conciliation anything to do with the interpretation of the formal agreement from time to time arrived at, or with the incessant labor involved in its application. Its meetings, held only at rare intervals, command the presence of the greatest coal-owners in the county, and of the most influential miners' leaders specially elected for the purpose. The board deliberates in private, and publishes only its decisions. Resort to the umpire, or in Northumberland to the casting vote of the chairman, is rare, the usual practice being for a frank interchange of views to go on until a basis of agreement can be found. On the other hand, all questions of interpretation or application are dealt with by another tribunal, which goes on undisturbed even when one or other party has temporarily withdrawn its representatives from the board of conciliation. In marked distinction from the conciliation board, the "joint committee" in each county meets frequently, and is engaged in incessant work. But this committee is expressly debarred from dealing with "such as may be termed county questions, or which may affect the general trade,"[2] and is rigidly confined to the application of the existing general agreement to particular mines or seams.[3]

[1] In Durham this conference is, since February 1895, called "The Board of Conciliation for the Coal Trade." The rules of that date provide for eighteen representatives of each side, with an umpire to be mutually agreed upon, or in default nominated by the Board of Trade. In Northumberland, the corresponding "Board of Conciliation" now consists of fifteen on each side, with an independent chairman having a casting vote, to be nominated, in default of agreement, by the Chairman of the Northumberland County Council. The name and constitution of these boards are frequently varied in minor details.

[2] *Durham Miners' Joint Committee Rules*, November 1879.

[3] Owing to the great differences in the ease and facilities with which the coal is got in different mines and different seams of the same mine, it is impossible, consistently with uniformity in the rate of payment for the whole work done, to apply any identical tonnage rate throughout the county. When it is found that the men in any mine constantly earn per day an amount which departs appreciably from the normal (the so-called "County Average"), the employer or the workmen appeal for a readjustment of the tonnage rate in that particular instance. It must be counted as a grave defect in the miners' organisations outside Northumberland and Durham that no systematic arrangements exist for this adjustment of the standard wage to the particular circumstances of each mine or seam.

For deliberateness and impartiality this tribunal leaves nothing to be desired. The members, all of whom are practically acquainted with the industry, do not directly represent either of the parties concerned in any dispute, and have no other interest than that of securing uniformity in the application of a common agreement. The chief disadvantage of the tribunal is that which we have already seen complained of in the local boards of the boot and shoe trade. For deciding mere issues of fact, as to the circumstances of a particular seam or pit, a joint committee is necessarily a cumbrous, expensive, and dilatory machine. Every case involves the journeying to Newcastle of witnesses on both sides, and their examination by all the members of the committee. This consumes so much time that cases frequently stand in the agenda for several months before being reached, a fact which leads to great dissatisfaction to those concerned.[1] Moreover, it is often impossible to come to any decision without personal inspection of the seam, and difficult cases are therefore constantly referred for decision to one employer and one workman, with power to choose an umpire. This results in a more precise ascertainment of facts, but increases the delay and expense. Finally, there is in such cases no guarantee that the decisions, arrived at by different sets of people, will preserve that exact uniformity which it is the special function of the tribunal to enforce.

Thus, the much-advertised expedient of a single joint committee of employers and employed to deal with all questions that arise between them, has not proved a wholly

---

In Lancashire, Derbyshire, and other districts of the Miners' Federation, for instance, there is no better protection of the standard wage than pit-lists, prescribing tonnage rates for individual collieries. No machinery exists for ensuring uniformity (of the rate of pay for the amount of work) between these lists, or even for revising their rates to meet the changing circumstances of particular seams. If a miner finds he is earning a very low amount per day, he applies to his lodge meeting for permission to leave and receive strike benefit. More or less informal negotiations may then be opened with the mine manager, who often fixes a new rate, in consultation either with the group of miners themselves, or with the lodge officials, or in some instances with salaried agents of the union.

[1] This is especially the case in Durham, where the number of mines dealt with is very large.

satisfactory machinery for Collective Bargaining. The expediency of having separate machinery for the essentially different processes of interpreting an existing agreement and concluding a new one is, we think, clearly demonstrated. For one of these two processes, the application and interpretation of an existing agreement, a joint committee is a cumbrous and awkward device. A better solution of the problem has been found in the Lancashire cotton trade. The cotton operatives, like the Northumberland and Durham coalminers, have distinguished, clearly and sharply, between the formation of a new general agreement and the application of an existing agreement to particular cases. But they have done more than this. Unconsciously and, as it were, instinctively, they have felt their way to a form of machinery for Collective Bargaining which uses the representative element where the representative element is needed, whilst on the other hand it employs the professional expert for work at which the mere representative would be out of place.

We will first describe the machinery for the interpretation of an existing agreement. The factors which enter into the piecework rates of the Lancashire cotton operatives are so complicated that both the employers and the workpeople have long since recognised the necessity of maintaining salaried professional experts who devote their whole time to the service respectively of the employers' association and the Trade Union. The earnings of a cotton-spinner, for instance, depend upon the complex interaction of such factors as the "draw" of the mule, the number of its spindles, and the speed with which the machinery works. To compute the operative's earnings, even with the aid of the elaborate printed tables known as the "List," entails no ordinary amount of arithmetical facility. But it is especially the custom of allowing the operative compensation for defective material or old-fashioned machinery and the employer a corresponding allowance for improvements, which has thrown the collective bargaining, as regards interpretation, entirely into the hands of professional experts. Thus, if an Oldham operative finds his earnings falling below the current figure, either because the raw cotton is inferior or the machinery obsolete, or if an employer speeds up his engine or introduces improvements, the experts on each side visit the mill, and confer together as to the net effect of the change. If the deficiency in earnings is considered to be due to imperfection in the raw material, or to the old-fashioned character of the machinery, the employer is required to add a specified percentage to the normal piecework rate, so that the workman may not suffer. On the other hand, if the employer has effected special improvements, by which the product is augmented, without increasing the strain on the operative, he is allowed to deduct a corresponding percentage from the "List" price. The cotton-weavers have what is essentially the same machinery for calculating the characteristic technical details of their trade.

The importance and complication of the duties thus entrusted to the salaried officials of the cotton-spinners' and cotton-weavers' unions has led to the adoption of an interesting method of recruiting this branch of the Trade Union Civil Service. The Cotton-weavers, in 1861, subjected the candidates for the then vacant office of general secretary to a competitive examination.[1] This practice was adopted by the Cotton-spinners, and is now the regular way of selecting all the officials who are to concern themselves with the intricate trade calculations. The branches retain the right of

[1] Mr. Thomas Birtwistle, the successful candidate on this occasion, was, after over thirty years' honorable service of his Trade Union, appointed by the Home Secretary an Inspector in the Factory Department, as the only person competent to understand and interpret the complicated methods of remuneration in the weaving trade. His son, brought up in the Trade Union office, has since also been appointed a factory inspector. The successful candidate at the Bolton Cotton-spinners' examination in 1895 was, after two years' service as Trade Union Secretary, engaged in a similar capacity by the local Master Cotton-spinners' Association. So far as we know, this is the first instance of a Trade Union official transferring his services from the operatives to the employers, and it throws an interesting light on the transformation of the "labor leader" into the professional accountant. The bulk of the daily work of the Trade Union officials in the cotton industry consists, in fact, in securing the uniform observance of a collective agreement, a service which, like that of a legal or medical professional man, could, with equal propriety, be rendered to either client.

nominating the candidates, and the members, acting through their Representative Assembly, their right of election. But between the day of nomination and that of election all the candidates submit to a competitive examination, conducted by the most experienced officers of the unions. A fairly stiff paper is set in the arithmetic and technical calculations required in the trade, and each candidate writes an essay. But a prominent part is played by an oral examination, in which the examiners assume the part of employers, cross-question the candidates one by one on the alleged grievances of which they are supposed to have come to complain, and do not refrain, in order to test their wits and their good temper, from adopting the bullying manners of the worst employers. The marks gained by all the candidates are printed in full detail, the name of the glib-tongued " popular leader " being sometimes followed by the comment of " entirely wrong " or " not worked " in all his arithmetical calculations, and by infinitesimal marks for spelling, writing, and conduct under cross-examination. The result is usually the election of the candidate who has obtained the highest marks, but the Representative Assembly occasionally exercises its discretion in giving a preference to a candidate of known character or good service, who has fallen a few marks behind the best examinee.[1]

---

[1] OPERATIVE COTTON-SPINNERS' PROVINCIAL ASSOCIATION OF BOLTON AND DISTRICT.

Offices : 77 St. George's Road, Bolton.

Examination Paper for Candidates applying for situation of Gen. Sec. of the above Association.

25th January 1895.

Subject I.—Calculations.

1. Find the number of stretches put up in a week, and the price per 100 required to produce a gross wage of £3 : 9 : 7 per pair of mules, from the following particulars :—Number of spindles in one mule, 1090. From 56½ hours, deduct 2¼ hours for cleaning and accidental stoppages, and one hour and ten minutes for doffing. Speed of each mule, 4 stretches in 75 seconds.

2. Taking the stretches as ascertained by the previous question to be each

It is to this method of selection that we attribute the remarkable success of the officials of the Cotton Trade Unions in obtaining the best possible terms for their members. We regard it as a great disadvantage to the Trade Union world that the system has not hitherto spread to other unions. It seems to us to combine the advantages of competitive examination and popular selection, and it ensures the union against the serious calamity of finding itself saddled with an incompetent officer.

This part of the machinery for Collective Bargaining among the Cotton Operatives—the meeting of the salaried professional experts on each side—deals, as we have said, only with questions of interpretation, that is, the application

$64\frac{1}{2}$ inches long, how many hanks would the week's production amount to, and what price per 1000 hanks would be required to bring out the wage previously given?

3. Assuming the standard price paid for producing a certain count of yarn to be 12s. 7d. per 100 lbs., what would the price be after a reduction of 7.9 per cent, and what percentage would it require to bring back the reduced price to the original amount?

4. Divide .3364502 by .001645.

5. Extract the square root of 80's counts to three places of decimals, and then ascertain the required turns per inch for both twist and weft, the assumed standard being the square root of the counts, multiplied by $3\frac{1}{8}$ for weft, and $3\frac{5}{8}$ for twist.

6. If good fair Egyptian cotton is advanced from $4\frac{5}{16}$ths to $4\frac{3}{8}$d. per lb., what would be the rate per cent of the increase? Also what would be the amount of the broker's commission on a sale of 1000 bales of 480 lbs. each, at one-quarter of one per cent, and what would be the difference in his commission as between selling at one price and the other?

7. An upright shaft runs at the rate of 80 revolutions per minute, and has on it a wheel with 70 teeth driving a wheel with 40 teeth on the line shaft. Over each pair of mules there is on the line shaft a drum 40 inches in diameter driving a counter pulley 16 inches in diameter. On the counter shaft is a drum 30 inches in diameter, driving a rim-pulley 15 inches in diameter. Give the revolutions of the rim shaft per minute.

8. Assuming a rim shaft to be making 680 revolutions per minute, with a 20-inch rim, a $11\frac{1}{2}$-inch tin roller-pulley, a 6-inch tin roller, and spindle wharves $1\frac{3}{8}$ths of an inch in diameter, what will be the number of revolutions of the spindles per minute, after allowing $\frac{1}{16}$th of an inch each to the diameter of the tin roller and spindle wharves for slipping of bands?

II.—*Writing, Composition, and Spelling.*

Compile an essay on Trade Unions, with special reference to their useful features. The essays must not exceed about 1200 words, and the points taken

to particular jobs, or particular processes, of the existing general agreements accepted by both sides. When it comes to concluding or revising the general agreement itself—a matter in which not one firm or operative alone is interested, but the whole body of employers and workmen—we find the machinery for Collective Bargaining taking the form of a joint committee composed of a certain number of representatives of each side. Thus the Cotton-spinners, whilst leaving to the arbitrament of the secretaries of the district union and district employers' association all questions relating to particular mills or particular workmen, revise the details of their lists in periodical conferences in which the leading employers of the district concerned arrange the matter with the leading trade union officials and representative operatives. And when the point at issue is not the alteration of the technical details of the list, but a general reduction or advance of wages by so much per cent throughout the trade, or a general shortening of the working time, we see the matter

into consideration will be handwriting, spelling, composition, and the clear concise marshalling of whatever facts or arguments are adduced.

III.—Oral Examination.

Each candidate will be examined separately as to his capacity for dealing orally with labour disputes. On this point they will have to formulate what they consider would be a complaint requiring immediate attention, and the examiners will question them, and possibly urge some arguments against the views advanced.

Candidates will be allowed from ten in the forenoon to five in the afternoon to complete their examination in the two first subjects, with one hour for dinner. Candidates will not be allowed to refer to any books or papers. The third subject (oral examination) will not be taken until Sunday, the 27th instant, at 1 o'clock.

THOMAS ASHTON, ⎱
JAS. MAWDSLEY, ⎰ *Examiners.*

Thirteen candidates in all entered for this examination. The examiners allowed a maximum of 50 marks for each sum, and 100 marks each for writing, spelling, composition, and oral examination, making 800 marks the maximum attainable. The number of marks obtained by the candidates varied from 195 to 630. The post was finally given to the second candidate in the list (610 marks), who was an old and esteemed officer of the union, and whose second place at the examination was chiefly due to his obtaining lower marks for handwriting than the most successful candidate.

discussed between appointed representatives of the whole body of the employers, attended by their agents and solicitors, and the central executive of the Amalgamated Association of Operative Cotton-spinners as representing all the district unions.

In the case of the English Cotton-spinners the lists of prices have been so carefully and elaborately worked out that even district conferences are of only occasional occurrence. The general policy of both employers and operatives is against any but rare and moderate variations of the standard earnings. Such questions as hours of labor and sanitation do not, among the Cotton Operatives, for reasons that we shall explain in a subsequent chapter, fall within the sphere of the Method of Collective Bargaining. The joint conferences of the whole trade take place therefore only in momentous crises, and are accompanied by all the solemnity and strenuousness of an assembly on whose decision turns the question of peace or war.

It is interesting to see one of these momentous conferences at work. The historic all-night sitting which settled the great Cotton-spinners' dispute of 1893, and concluded the agreement which has since governed the trade, was vividly described by one of the leading Trade Union officials who took part in it. The employers had demanded a reduction of 10 per cent, whilst the men had urged that it would be better to reduce the number of hours worked per week. The stoppage had lasted no less than twenty weeks, practically every mill in the whole industry being closed. Feeling on both sides had run high, but after frequent negotiations and incessant newspaper comment, the points at issue had been narrowed down, and both parties felt the need of bringing the struggle to an end. To escape the crowd of reporters the place of meeting was kept secret, and fixed for 3 P.M. at a country inn, to which the whole party journeyed together in the same train.

"On the employers' side was Mr. A. E. Rayner, looking all the better for his holiday at Bournemouth. With him were some sixteen or seventeen others, amongst whom were Mr. Andrew, Mr. John B. Tattersall, and Mr. James Fletcher of Oldham. There was also Mr. John Fletcher, Mr. R. S. Buckley, and Mr. Smethurst of the Ashton district, who took with them Mr. Dixon to keep them in countenance. Mr. Sidebottom of Stockport also gave a kind of military flavor to his colleagues, whilst Mr. John Mayall of Moseley attended to look in and lend some dignity to the occasion, in which he was assisted by Mr. W. Tattersall, secretary of the federation. On the operatives' side Mr. Ashton, Mr. Mellor, and Mr. Jones did duty for Oldham ; Mr. Wood, Mr. Rhodes, and Mr. Carr represented the Ashton district ; whilst the general business was attended to by Mr. Mullin, Mr. Mawdsley, Mr. Fielding, and some dozen others, whilst Mr. D. Holmes, Mr. Wilkinson, and Mr. Buckley had a watching brief for the winders and reelers. Perhaps we ought not to omit mentioning that the employers had brought with them Mr. Hesketh Booth, clerk to the Oldham magistrates, who was counterbalanced by Mr. Ascroft, another Oldham solicitor, who had accompanied the cardroom hands.

" Those whose names we have mentioned, with others, made up a party of between thirty and forty, and after taking a few minutes to straighten themselves up after leaving the train, they settled down to business. Mr. A. E. Rayner was unanimously voted to the chair. . . . Both sides had prepared and got printed a series of proposals, and the employers had . . . them printed side by side on the same sheet. In many of them there was nothing to differ about except the wording, as the idea aimed at was the same in both cases. But the clause dealing with the reduction was the first, and in their sheets the employers had left the amount out, whilst the operatives had put in $2\frac{1}{2}$ per cent. The employers wished the discussion on this point to be deferred to the end of the meeting, but feeling that unless a settlement could be arrived at on this, the whole of the time spent on the other clauses would be wasted, the operatives insisted it should be taken first. The employers then retired, and after being absent some time, returned and offered to accept a reduction of 3 per cent. The operatives then retired, and after a prolonged absence, offered to recommend the acceptance of sevenpence in the pound.[1] Then came an adjournment for tea, and further discussion on the same subject followed, which was, however, carried on by means of deputations from one section to the other, as it was found that much better progress was made by this system than by all being together, with its concomitant long speeches, which generally came to nothing. This point ultimately disposed of in favour of the sevenpence, some minor clauses were got through, the next discussion being on the arrangement of intervals between the times when wages can be disturbed. This discussion brought up the time to after ten o'clock, and everybody was tired and anxious to be going home. . . . But as there seemed to be every prospect of being able to ultimately agree, it was considered that they should not run the risk of rendering the meeting useless by separating. In order to give the jaded men an opportunity for freshening up, an adjournment for half an hour was therefore agreed to, during which cold remains of the tea vanished. This, combined with a smoke and a stroll in the open air, put everybody right, and when business was resumed it went on swimmingly. There was little said by the employers over their clause, that union operatives must work amicably with non-union men, and another affirming that in any proposal to change the rate of wages the state of trade for the three previous years must be taken into account. . . . When this work was done the remaining clauses which affirm the desirability of (employers and operatives) working together for the promotion of measures conducive to the general interests of the trade, were soon gone through, and at nearly four o'clock in the morning the jaded disputants rushed off to get a little change of air whilst the agreement was being picked out from piles of papers and put together in proper form. At this stage a little diversion was occasioned by the arrival of a cab con-

[1] Equal to 2.916 per cent.

taining a reporter of one of the Manchester papers, who, after hunting all over South-east Lancashire for the meeting-place, had at last found the right spot. This bit of enterprise having been rewarded by about six lines of something, he rushed off back to catch his paper. Just after five (after fourteen hours) the documents were in shape, and the requisite signatures attached, and with a few, evidently heart-felt congratulatory remarks from the chairman, and a vote of thanks having been given to him, the proceedings closed." [1]

The machinery for Collective Bargaining developed by the Cotton Operatives, in our opinion, approaches the ideal. We have, to begin with, certain broad principles unreservedly agreed to throughout the trade. The scale of remuneration, based on these principles, is worked out in elaborate detail into printed lists, which (though not yet identical for the whole trade) automatically govern the actual earnings of the several districts. The application, both of the general principles and of the lists, to particular mills and particular workmen, is made, not by the parties concerned, but by the joint decision of two disinterested professional experts, whose whole business in life is to secure, not the advantage of particular employer or workmen by whom they are called in, but uniformity in the application of the common agreement to all employers and workmen. The common agreements themselves are revised at rare intervals by representative joint committees, in which the professional experts on both sides exercise a great and even a preponderating influence. The whole machinery appears admirably contrived to bring about the maximum deliberation, security, stability, and promptitude of application. And whilst absolutely no room is left for the influence upon the negotiations of individual idiosyncrasies, temper, ignorance of fact, or deficiency in bargaining power, whether on the side of the employer or

[1] "How matters were arranged," *Cotton Factory Times*, 31st March 1893 ; see *Labour Gazette*, May 1893. The formal treaty, known as the "Brooklands Agreement," will be found in the Board of Trade *Report on Wages and Hours of Labour*, Part II., Standard Piece Rates, 1894, C, 7567, p. 10.

the operative, the uniform application of an identical method of remuneration throughout the whole trade leaves the able capitalist or energetic workman free to obtain for himself the full advantage of his superiority.[1]

The reader who has had the patience to follow the foregoing exposition will have seen that, taking the Trade Union world as a whole, the machinery for Collective Bargaining must be regarded as extremely imperfect. We do not here discuss whether Collective Bargaining is, or is not, economically advantageous to the workmen or to the community. We may, however, assume that it is desirable, if it exists, that it should be carried on without friction. And if for the moment we take the Trade Union point of view, and assume the expediency of a Common Rule, excluding the influence of particular exigencies, it is essential that this Common Rule should be wisely and deliberately determined on, uniformly applied, and systematically enforced. This demands machinery which, over the greater part of the Trade Union world, has not yet been developed. Throughout the great engineering and building trades, and indeed, in nearly all the timework trades, Collective Bargaining, though practically universal, is carried on in a haphazard way with the most rudimentary machinery, and usually by amateurs in the craft of negotiation. The piecework trades have, in the main, been forced to recognise the importance of commanding the services of salaried professionals to deal with their complicated lists of prices. Only among the Cotton-spinners and Cotton-weavers, however, do we yet find any arrangement for ensuring, by a technical examination, for continuity of expert

---

[1] The United Society of Boilermakers, whose hierarchy of agreements we have described, has, in effect, similar machinery for Collective Bargaining. New agreements are concluded at meetings with the employers, in which the expert salaried officials are associated, at any rate in form, with representative workmen. The machinery for interpretation consists, in effect, of a joint visit by salaried officials representing respectively the associated employers and the Trade Union. "They had tried a joint committee on the Tyne," said Mr. Robert Knight, "but the employers could not spare the time, for all their local disputes mostly required visiting, and so they came to prefer a reference to a delegate who was their representative, and he met the men's delegate with the best results."—*Newcastle Leader* "*Extra*" *on Conciliation in Trade Disputes* (Newcastle, 1894), p. 15.

services. Finally, we see the whole machinery for Collective Bargaining seriously hampered, except in two or three trades, by the failure to make the vital distinction between interpreting an existing wage contract, and negotiating the terms upon which a new general agreement should be entered into. We must, in fact, conclude that, among the great unions only the Cotton-spinners, Cotton-weavers, and the Boilermakers, and, to a lesser extent, the North of England and Midland Iron-workers [1] and the Northumberland and Durham

---

[1] For the rules, history, and working of these Boards, see *Industrial Conciliation*, by Henry Crompton; *Industrial Peace*, by L. L. F. R. Price (London, 1887); Sir Bernhard Samuelson's paper in February 1876 before the British Iron Trade Association; the evidence before the Royal Commission on Labor, 1892, particularly that of Messrs. Whitwell and Trow, Group A, 14,974 to 15,482; and the summary of the rules at p. 368 of the Parliamentary Paper, c. 6795, xii. Reports of their proceedings are given in the monthly *Ironworkers' Journal*, the organ of the Iron and Steel Workers of Great Britain. Though these Boards have repeatedly been described, their observers have, in our opinion, dealt rather with the formal than with the real constitution, and with the aspirations rather than with the actual results of the organisation. An important but scarcely noticed element in the problem is the fact that a certain proportion of the workmen are themselves employers of subordinate labor. Exactly what classes of workmen—puddlers, millmen, mechanics, enginemen, laborers, etc.—are entitled to vote in the election of representatives, and how effectively all the different grades are actually represented on the Boards, has never been described. It is reported that a large number of the cases dealt with by the Midland Board at any rate, concern differences, not between a firm and its wage-earners, but between a manual-working sub-contractor and his subordinates, the latter not being represented on the Board. With regard to the actual results of the Boards, the student would have to investigate whether the rates fixed from time to time did not operate rather as maxima than as minima; whether, that is to say, the incompleteness and lack of authority of both the employers' and the workmen's organisations did not lead to many firms taking advantage of the awards of the Board to stave off larger demands from their workmen, whilst at other times using their own strategic position to compel the men to accept lower terms than the Board was awarding. In January 1893, for instance, one of the union officials deplored, in a meeting of the members, "the private reductions which they had submitted to all round," in contravention of the rates fixed by the Midland Board (*Ironworkers' Journal*, January 1894). Some years later the men's dissatisfaction led to the following manifesto: "Amongst large numbers of the workmen there is a growing opinion that the Board is unsatisfactory, and that it would be to the workers' interests to dissolve it. It is stated that employers only appeal to the Wages Board when it suits them, and that they ignore its principles and rules, when by so doing they can take undue advantage of their workmen, so that the maintenance of the Wages Board is only beneficial to the employer and prejudicial to the interests of the workmen. . . . Even the employer section fear to enforce adherence to its rules because of giving offence to those employers who simply look upon the Board as a convenience for imposing

Miners, can be said to be adequately equipped with efficient machinery for Collective Bargaining.

The foregoing analysis of the Method of Collective Bargaining, and of the machinery by which it is carried out, will have revealed to the student two of its incidental characteristics, which to some persons appear as fatal evils, and to others merely as the "defects of its qualities." The keen Individualist will scent an element of compulsion in the so-called "voluntary" agreements governing the conditions of a whole trade. The ardent advocate of "industrial peace" will fail to discover any guarantee that the elaborate negotiations between highly-organised classes will not end in a declaration of war instead of a treaty of agreement.

That some measure of compulsion is entailed by the Method of Collective Bargaining no Trade Unionist would deny. Trade Unionists, as we have explained, value Collective Bargaining precisely because it rules out of account the particular exigencies of individual workmen or establishments. With this exclusion of exigencies there comes necessarily a certain restriction on personal idiosyncrasy, which some would describe as a loss of liberty. When, for instance, the employers and workmen in a Lancashire town collectively settle which week shall be devoted to the annual "wake," even the exceptionally industrious cotton-spinner or weaver finds himself bound to keep holiday, whether he likes it or not. It is impossible to make common arrangements for numbers of men without running counter to the desires of some of them. The wider the range of the Common Rule, and the more perfect is the machinery for its application and enforcement, the larger may be the minority which finds itself driven to accept conditions which it has not desired. It follows that the Trade Union must provide, in its consti-

unjust conditions upon their workmen." (Official Circular from the Executive Council of the Associated Iron and Steel Workers of Great Britain, 10th August 1896, in *Ironworkers' Journal*, September 1896). For analogous cases under the North of England Board, the student should investigate the action of the Stockton Malleable Iron Company (see *Ironworkers' Journal*, January 1894), and that of the Barrow Steel Works (*Ibid.* January 1896).

tution, some means of securing the obedience of all its members to the regulations decided upon by the majority. The rules of all unions, from the earliest times down to the present day, contain clauses empowering the fining of disobedient members, the alternative to paying the fine being expulsion from the union. We have already pointed out that the development of the friendly society side of Trade Unionism incidentally makes this sanction a penalty of very real weight, and one which can be easily enforced. To this pecuniary loss may, moreover, be added the incidents of outlawry. When a union includes the bulk of the workmen in any industry, its members invariably refuse to work alongside a man who has been expelled from the union for "working contrary to the interests of the trade." In such a case expulsion from the union may easily mean expulsion from the trade. But whilst the Trade Union has thus most drastic punishments at its command, the individual member is habitually protected from tyranny or caprice by an elaborate system of appeals, which ensure him against condemnation otherwise than according to the positive laws of his community. This disciplinary system is, of course, usually applied to men who deliberately undermine the Common Rule by accepting lower terms than those collectively agreed to.[1] But it is also used against workmen who break the agreement in the other direction. " To give one illustration," said the general secretary of the United Society of Boilermakers, to the Royal Commission on Labor, " we had a case

[1] The Trade Unionist feeling against men who work "under price" is expressed in the following quotation from the *Amended General Laws of the Amalgamated Society of Cordwainers* (London, 1867), one of the most ancient of unions :—

" A scab is to his trade what a traitor is to his country, and though both may be useful to one party in troublesome times, when peace returns they are detested alike by all ; so when help is wanted a scab is the last to contribute assistance, and the first to grasp a benefit he never labored to procure ; he cares only for himself, but he sees not beyond the extent of a day ; and for momentary and worthless approbation would betray friends, family, and country. In short, he is a traitor on a small scale—he first sells the journeymen and is himself afterwards sold in his turn by his master, until at last he is despised by both and deserted by all. He is an enemy to himself, to the present age, and to posterity."

at Hartlepool a short time since, where a vessel was in for repairing, and the men knew that the vessel was in a hurry, and thought there was a very good chance to get an advance in their wages, so they went to their foreman, and made a demand for 2s. a week advance. The foreman, knowing the arrangement between our association and the employers' association, refused to give the advance, and at once wired to me at Newcastle, and by the orders of the council I sent back to say that the employer was to give the men the advance as asked for, because we did not want to stop the work, as the ship was in a hurry, and we wanted to get her off. The employer gave the men the advance as asked for, and we at once sent to the firm requesting the firm to tell us the amount of money they had paid to the men as advances of wages on that job. When the job was completed those particulars and details were sent to us at Newcastle, and also the names of the men who were engaged upon the job, and who had made the demand. As soon as that was done our council ordered the members who received the money to refund that again to the Society, and we sent a cheque from the head office to that firm equal to the amount of the advances given." [1] In another case men knowing that their employer was under a time limit for the completion of a ship made a sudden demand for a rise. Precisely the same action was taken by the union, and the men were also fined " for dishonorable behaviour to employer under contract to deliver."

[1] Royal Commission on Labor, Group A, Question 20,718. The frequency with which this disciplinary power is exercised may be judged from an extract from the *Monthly Report* for May 1897, referring only to a single district. The list is not usually published.

"The following members have been dealt with by the committee during April :—

F. F., foreman, holding two jobs at Heyes, 40s.

T. B., rivetter, doing plater's work, 10s.

E. T., plater, neglecting his work through drinking, 10s.

J. J., rivetter, doing plater's work, 20s.

H. R., excessive overtime, 30s.

T. C., using abusive language to Strike Secretary, 10s.

R. D., using disgusting and obscene language to Mr. W. H., foreman, 10s."

In the world of modern industry this submission of the personal judgment to the Common Rule extends far beyond the range of those who, by Trade Union membership, may be considered to have agreed to forego an individual decision. When the associated employers in any trade conclude an agreement with the Trade Union, the Common Rule thus arrived at is usually extended by the employers, as a matter of course, to every workman in their establishments, whether or not he is a member of the union.[1] This universal application of a collective bargain to workmen who have neither personally nor by representatives taken any part in it, is specially characteristic of the Sliding Scale. In the ironworks of the North and Midlands the awards of the accountants engaged by the joint committees of employers and workmen habitually govern every wage contract in the establishments concerned, however distasteful the whole proceeding may be to a particular section of workmen. The position of the South Wales coalminers is even more striking. Not a third of the 120,000 men are even professedly members of any Trade Union, or in any way represented in the negotiations, and of the organised workmen a considerable proportion, forming three separate unions, each covering a distinct district, expressly refused to agree to the 1893 Sliding Scale, and withdrew their representatives from the joint committee. Nevertheless, the whole of the 120,000 men, with infinitesimal special exceptions, find their wages each pay-day automatically determined by the accountant's award. In this case the associated employers, in alliance with a minority of the workmen, enforce, upon

[1] This practice has recently received authoritative official confirmation. Certain boot manufacturers in Bristol and Northampton, whilst holding themselves bound to give to members of the National Union of Boot and Shoe Operatives the terms specified in the collective agreements, claimed the right to pay what they liked to the non-unionists they employed. On the issue being referred, at the instance of the Trade Union, to the Permanent Secretary of the Board of Trade as umpire, he decided that the decisions of the Local Boards were, unless expressly restricted, applicable to unionists and non-unionists alike, although the latter were in no way parties to the agreement. See Award of 6th May 1896, in *Labour Gazette*, May 1896.

an apathetic or dissentient majority, under pain of exclusion from the industry or exile from the district, a method of remuneration and rates of payment which are fiercely resented by many of them. In instances of this kind it is the employers who are the instruments of coercion. In other industries we find the Trade Union, acting in alliance with the Employers' Association, putting its own forms of pressure on dissentient employers, who refuse to join the association, or to conform to the arrangements agreed to by the industry as a whole. The records of the local boards in the boot and shoe trade contain many appeals from the representatives of the Associated Employers to the National Union of Boot and Shoe Operatives, in which the union is incited to use all its influence to compel rival firms to conform to the trade agreements. Here a majority of workmen, at the instance of, and in alliance with a majority of employers, practically force a minority of both masters and men to accept the Common Rules which have commended themselves to the main body of the trade. In short, experience shows that any successful attempt to arrange common terms in a highly-developed modern industry, inevitably leads, however "voluntary" may be the basis of the associations concerned, to a virtually compulsory acquiescence in the same terms, if not throughout the whole trade, at any rate by many firms and many workmen who have in no sense willingly agreed to them.

This compulsion takes a more obvious form when it is a question of providing the cost of the machinery by which the common arrangements are made and applied. In the South Wales coalfield, where, as we have seen, the Silding Scale is practically universal, a compulsory deduction of sixpence per annum is made by the employers from the earnings of about 40,000 men, whether or not they individually agree with the Sliding Scale, or are members of any Trade Union. In the Rhondda Valley, and in a few other districts, the compulsion goes a step farther. The employers compulsorily deduct a few pence per month from their workmen's earnings, as the contribution to the Trade Union. A certain agreed percentage is retained by the employer and his clerks for their trouble, and the balance is handed over to the agents of the men's unions. By far the largest and most important miners' union in South Wales has no other subscription than this compulsory deduction in the employer's pay office, and is without any lodges, branch officials, or other organised machinery. To all intents and purposes, therefore, Trade Union membership, summed up, as it is, in this enforced contribution to maintain officials with whom the employers can negotiate, is, over a large part of the South Wales coalfield, absolutely compulsory.[1]

But whilst the compulsory Trade Unionism of the South Wales coalfields, as enforced by the employers, extends to the collective arrangements, and to payment for their cost, it makes no provision for ensuring that the apathetic or dissentient workers shall have any opportunity of expressing their desires, or of taking any part in controlling their own side of the business. As most of the men from whom the Sliding Scale pence are deducted are not even nominally on the roll of any Trade Union, they are never troubled to vote on any question, and the working-men members on the Sliding Scale committee, representing the small minority of men on the books of the

---

[1] A similar compulsory membership characterises the manufactured iron trade. The Midland Iron and Steel Wages Board decided that employers should compulsorily collect from all their operatives the contribution due in respect of the men's share of the Board's expenses. Some employers neglected to do this, and on complaint made by the Operatives' Secretary, the Chairman of the Board held that all employers were bound to make the deduction (*Ironworkers' Journal*, March 1895). The North of England Manufactured Iron Board adopts the same practice. The Truck Act of 1896 forbids any such deduction, and, in order to enable it to be continued, Mr. Trow, the Operatives' Secretary, moved and carried a resolution that the Home Secretary should be asked to make an order excluding their trade from the scope of the Act (*Ironworkers' Journal*, March 1897). The Midland Board unanimously joined in the application on the express ground, as stated by the Chairman, that the Act "might have the effect of preventing them deducting the contributions of the men to the Wages Board" (*Ironworkers' Journal*, April 1897). It will be interesting to see whether the Home Secretary extends his sanction to the principle of compulsory contribution, by complying with the request, and issuing an order exempting the whole trade from the Truck Act.

several unions, conclude such agreements with the employers, and make such disposition of the compulsory deductions, as seem best in their own eyes, or in those of their immediate constituents. We have, in fact, in this remarkable case, an instance of collective administration without democratic control. In another case in the same industry, where collective action and compulsory payment is enforced by the law, provision is at least made for a ballot to be taken. We have described elsewhere [1] how long and persistently the Miners' Trade Unions have fought to obtain the right to have their own agent at the pit mouth, to see that their members are not defrauded in the computation of their tonnage earnings ; and we have also pointed out how invaluably these checkweighers have served as union officials.[2] By the Coal Mines' Regulation Act of 1887 it was enacted that, whenever a mere majority of the workers in any coal pit, to be ascertained by a ballot vote, decided to appoint a checkweigher, the amount of his wages should be shared among all the workers in the pit who were paid according to the weight of coal gotten, and that it should be compulsorily deducted from their earnings, whether they voted for the appointment or against it.

More generally, however, it is left to the Trade Union to take such steps as it can to enforce the common trade agreements, and to collect for itself the expenses involved. This may be effected in two ways. Following the example of the South Wales Coal-owners, the Trade Union may enforce, throughout the whole trade, an agreement concluded between a section of the employers and the employed, levying a compulsory tax for the purpose upon all persons

---

[1] *History of Trade Unionism*, pp. 289, 453.

[2] Among the amendments of the law now sought by the Miners' Federation is one enabling the hewers in any mine to appoint an assistant checkweigher, at the expense of the whole pit, to act whenever " the said checkweigher is acting in any other capacity for or on behalf of the workmen of the colliery." " What they wanted to do," explained the Yorkshire representatives at the Miners' Conference in 1896, " was to make it so that the men employed at any colliery could appoint an assistant checkweigher to look after the work when the weigher was away on association business."

at work. Thus the old close corporation of Dublin Coopers, whilst allowing strangers to work, does not admit them to membership, but insists that they shall obey all the regulations of the union, and contribute weekly to its funds so long as they work in the town. But this "taxation without representation" is alien to working class sentiment, and the almost universal practice of Trade Unionism is to expect every member of the trade to bear his share, not only in the cost of its administration, but also in the work of its government. "We contend," declare the Flint Glass Makers, "that it is the imperative duty of men who live by a trade to support, protect, and keep it in a respectable condition. Men who refuse to subscribe to the funds of a Trade Union never can be looked upon by those who are members of such a union with that feeling of satisfaction and respect which makes one happy in the thought that unity of action is the aim of all for the good of each other."[1] Hence we have, not only compulsory acceptance of the trade customs but also compulsory membership of the Trade Union concerned. In old days, when any Trade Union action was a criminal offence, this compulsion easily passed into personal violence.[2] But British Trade Unionists now content themselves with the more peaceful method practised by the employers. An employer habitually refuses to engage any workman who does not agree to his workshop rules, or to those adopted by the employers' association. In the same way, the Trade Unionist will, if he can, refuse to accept work in an establishment where he is obliged to associate with non-unionists; "working beside a non-unionist," say the Flint

[1] Address of Central Committee, *Flint Glass Makers' Magazine*, May 1889.

[2] In the *History of Trade Unionism* we have described the practice of "rattening," for which some of the Sheffield trade clubs were, up to 1867, unhappily notorious. In the early part of the century the trade clubs of Dublin and Glasgow had an equally evil reputation for personal violence (see *History of Trade Unionism*, pp. 3, 31, 79, 149, 154, 242). With the growth of legal freedom for Trade Unions to employ peaceful, and really more effective, sanctions, this resort to summary lynch law has died out. We know personally of no instance in which, during the present generation, physical violence has been used to compel Trade Union membership.

Glass Makers, "is bad enough to a man of brain and principle, without having to suffer the indignity of being compelled to assist him in his labor. . . . This being so we do not hesitate to say that before an employer engages a unionist, he ought to clear all the non-unionists off the premises. Where we have demanded this, it has been done." This is put even more definitely by the Coal-miners. The minutes of the Derbyshire Miners record, for instance, under date of 1892, "that this Executive Committee recommend our members, where the majority are union men, to use every legal effort to induce others to join, and failing this we advise our members neither to work nor ride with them, but that due notice of their intention to take such actions be given to the management in each case before being put into practice." [1]

There is a strange delusion in the journalistic mind that this compulsory Trade Unionism, enforced by refusal to work with non-unionists, is a modern device, introduced by the "New Unionists" of 1889. Thus Mr. Lecky states as a fact [2] that the establishment of monopolies, and the exclusion, "often by gross violence and tyranny," of "non-unionists from the trades they can influence" is specially marked "among the New Unionists." But any student of Trade Union annals knows that the exclusion of non-unionists is, on the contrary, coeval with Trade Unionism itself, and that the practice is far more characteristic of its older forms than of any society formed in the present generation. The trade clubs of handicraftsmen in the eighteenth century would have scouted the idea of allowing any man to work at their trade who was not a member of the club. And at the

---

[1] Minutes of Executive Meeting, Derbyshire Miners' Association, July 1892. It is an incident of this refusal, on the part of the employer or on that of the wage-earner, to consent to work with persons of whose conduct he disapproves, that employers seek to insist on "character notes," workmen classify firms into "fair" and "unfair," and the associations on both sides circulate to their members "blacklists" of the men who have made themselves objectionable, towards the employers in the one case, and towards their fellow workmen in the other.

[2] *Democracy and Liberty*, vol. ii. p. 348.

present day it is especially in the old-fashioned and long-established unions that we find the most rigid enforcement of membership. Among the Coalminers it is the men of Northumberland, Durham, and the West Riding of Yorkshire, strongly combined for a whole generation, who have set the fashion of absolutely refusing to "ride" (descend in the cage) with non-unionists.[1] In the best organised industries indeed, whether great or small, such as the Boilermakers, Flint Glass Makers, Tape-sizers, or Stuff-pressers—the very aristocracy of "Old Unionists"—the compulsion is so complete that it ceases to be apparent. No man not belonging to the union ever thinks of applying for a situation, or would have any chance of obtaining one. It is, in fact, as impossible for a non-unionist plater or rivetter to get work in a Tyneside shipyard, as it is for him to take a house in Newcastle without paying the rates. This silent and unseen, but absolutely complete compulsion, is the ideal of every Trade Union. It is true that here and there an official of an incompletely organised trade may protest to the public, or before a Royal Commission, that his members have no desire that any workman should join the union except by his own free will. But, however *bonâ fide* may be these expressions by individuals, we invariably see such a union, as soon as it secures the adhesion of a majority of its trade, adopting the principle of compulsory membership,

---

[1] For an extreme instance of this boycott of non-unionists, see the remarkable letter of William Crawford, the leader of the Durham miners, given in full, at p. 280 of the *History of Trade Unionism*, and written, we believe, about 1870. "Regard them," said Crawford, "as unfit companions for yourselves and your sons, and unfit husbands for your daughters. Let them be branded, as it were, with the curse of Cain, as unfit to mingle in ordinary, honest, and respectable society." But this extension of the ostracism from the workplace to the home, from industrial relations to social life, is repugnant to British working-class sentiment, and has never extensively prevailed. However illogical may be the distinction, there is a general feeling, now spreading, we think, to other classes of society, that it is inexpedient to extend social ostracism beyond the sphere of the offence. Business men habitually deal with others of known bad character in private life, so long as their commercial dealings are unobjectionable. On the other hand, English society does not refuse to meet at dinner statesmen of good private character, whose public acts it deems in the last degree unscrupulous. The more logical policy advocated by Crawford is regarded as fanaticism.

and applying it with ever greater stringency as the strength of the organisation increases.

Whatever we may think of these various forms of compulsion, it is important to note that they are in no way inconsistent with the old ideal of "freedom of contract"—the legal right of every individual to make such a bargain for the purchase or sale of labor as he may think most conducive to his own interest,—and that they are, in fact, a necessary incident of that legal freedom.

When an employer, or every employer in a district, makes the Sliding Scale a condition of the engagement of any workman, the dissentient minority are "free" to refuse such terms. They may, in the alternative, break up their homes and leave the district, or learn another trade. The wage-earners cannot be denied a similar freedom. When a workman chooses to make it a condition of his acceptance of employment from a given firm, that he shall not be required to associate with colleagues whom he dislikes, he is but exercising his freedom to make such stipulations in the bargaining as he thinks conducive to his own interest. The employer is "free" to refuse to engage him on these terms, and if the vast majority of the workmen are of the same mind, he is "free" to transfer his brains and his capital to another trade, or to leave the district. But to any one not obsessed by this conception of "freedom," it will be obvious that a mere legal right to refuse particular conditions of employment is no safeguard against compulsion. Where practically all the competent workmen in an industry are strongly combined, an isolated employer, not supported by his fellow capitalists, finds it absolutely impossible to break away from the "custom of the trade." The isolated workman who objects to Trade Unionism finds himself in the same predicament. The coal-hewer in a Northumberland village has no more real freedom of choice as to whether or not he will join the union than a Glamorganshire miner has about working under the Sliding Scale. The workmen's case for Trade Unionism and the employers' case against it both proceed on the same assumption.[1] *Wherever the economic conditions of the parties concerned are unequal, legal freedom of contract merely enables the superior in strategic strength to dictate the terms.*   Collective Bargaining does not get rid of this virtual compulsion : it merely shifts its incidence.   Where there is no combination of any kind, the strategic weakness of the individual wage-earner, unable to put a reserve price on his labor, forces him to accept the lowest possible terms.   When the workmen combine the balance is redressed, and may even incline, as against the isolated employer, in favor of the wage-earner. If the employers meet combination by combination, the compulsion exercised upon individual capitalists or individual wage-earners may become so irresistible as to cease to be noticed.   In the most perfected form of Collective Bargaining, compulsory membership becomes as much a matter of course as compulsory citizenship.

If, indeed, we examine more closely the common arguments against this virtual compulsion, we shall see that the customary objection is not directed against the compulsion itself, but only against the persons by whom it is exercised, or the particular form that it takes.   The ordinary middle-class man, without economic training, is wholly unconscious of there being any coercion in an employer autocratically deciding how he will conduct " his own business." [2]   But the very notion of the workmen claiming to decide for themselves under what conditions they will spend their own working days strikes him as subversive of the social order.   The ardent Trade Unionist, on the other hand, resents the " tyranny " of the employer's workshop rules, but sees no harm in a strong union relentlessly enforcing its will on the capitalists, without deigning to consult with them beforehand.

---

[1] This assumption is examined in detail in our chapter on " The Higgling of the Market."

[2] " The capitalists or master class . . . think the internal arrangements of their establishments, hours, mode of payment or contract no more the affairs of the public than the routine of a man's own household."—" Trade Unions and their Tendencies," by Edmund Potter, F.R.S., *Social Science Association Transactions*, 1860, p. 755.

The modern compromise between these diametrically opposite views, and one now attracting a growing share of public approval, is the settlement of the conditions, neither by the workmen nor by the employers, but by collective agreement between them. It is this feeling that accounts for the ever-increasing favor for Boards of Conciliation and Arbitration and joint committees of all sorts. Public opinion, that is to say, accepts as inevitable the submission of the individual to the Common Rule, and seeks merely to ensure that this submission should be based upon due representation of the persons directly concerned. The most fervent advocates of this Collective Bargaining between the representatives of employers and employed welcome, in the interests of Industrial Peace, the application of these collective agreements over whole districts of an industry, and for specified long terms, though this necessarily involves the compulsory acquiescence of individual firms and individual workmen who would have preferred to make separate bargains. And thus we come, step by step, to the remarkable proposal of the Chairman of the Royal Commission on Labor, the Duke of Devonshire, himself a great employer, concurred in by seven other eminent members, that Trade Unions and Employers' Associations, extending over whole trades, should be encouraged to become definitely incorporated bodies, expressly authorised to conclude collective agreements for their constituents, and empowered to secure the compliance of all their members with these new trade laws by legally enforcible penalties, " every member of a (duly registered) association being during membership held to be under a contract with the association for observance of the collective agreement," the association being given " the right to recover damages from those of its members who infringed the collective agreement." [1]

---

[1] See the Report, signed by the Duke of Devonshire, the Right Honorable Leonard Courtney, M.P., and six other members, C, 7421, p. 117. This proposal is further examined in our chapter on "The Implications of Trade Unionism."

But the essential reasonableness of English public opinion sets limits to all these forms of legal freedom of contract and economic compulsion, whether it is the capitalist's "freedom of enterprise," the wage-earner's "freedom of combination," or the freedom of representative joint committees to decide what shall be the customs of the trade. When it becomes obvious that individual capitalists are using their strategic advantage to compel the wage-earners to accept conditions patently dangerous to life, health, or character, middle-class opinion supports legislation to curb their greed. When a group of workmen strike against machinery, or to enforce some obviously anti-social regulation, they find themselves deserted by the general body of Trade Unionists, frequently thwarted by other members of their trade, and even condemned by the executive of their own union. And when the Duke of Devonshire and Mr. Leonard Courtney proposed, in the Royal Commission on Labor, to give increased power of trade regulation to free associations of employers and employed, they were met by the objection that such joint agreements in particular trades might easily become prejudicial to the interests of other industries or of the general body of consumers. At the root of all these instinctive qualifications of logical doctrines, there lies a half-conscious admission that neither employers nor employed are morally free to ignore the interest of the community as a whole. This reveals to us an inherent shortcoming of every attempt to determine the conditions of industry by mere contract between capitalists and workmen. Even in the most perfected forms of Collective Bargaining, when each of the parties is fully represented, and the agreement arrived at really expresses the combined desires of both, there is no guarantee that the terms are such as will be conducive to the welfare of the community.

We have left to the last what is usually regarded as the capital drawback to the Method of Collective Bargaining, even in its most perfect development. In the machinery adopted by the Lancashire Cotton Operatives, for instance, there is no provision for the contingency of a failure to come to an agreement. In such a contingency the bargaining simply comes to an end, and we have that deliberate collective refusal on the part of the employers to give work, or on the part of the operatives to accept work, which is known as a "lock-out" or a "strike." These cessations of work are, in our view, necessarily incidental to all commercial bargaining for the hire of labor, whether individual or collective, just as the customer's walking out of the shop, if he does not consent to the shopkeeper's price, is incidental to retail trade.[1] This, we need hardly observe, is a very different matter from the ignorant assumption that there is some necessary connection between strikes and Trade Unions. We have already noted the existence of Trade Unions which prefer the Method of Mutual Insurance to that of Collective Bargaining, and do not therefore engage in strikes at all; and we shall elsewhere instance Trade Union organisations whose operation is confined to the Method of Legal Enactment. On the other hand, long before a Trade Union comes into existence in any industry Collective Bargaining, as we have already explained, prevails in a more or less elaborate form; and, with Collective Bargaining, the inevitable resort to concerted refusal to work. It is a matter of simple history that strikes have been far more numerous in industries which have practised Collective Bargaining without Trade Unionism, than in those in which durable combinations have existed.[2] The influence of Trade Unions on strikes is indeed exactly similar to their influence on Collective Bargaining. The elaboration of the "shop

[1] The bitterest opponents of Trade Unionism admit this. "Strikes, I consider," said a leading employer in 1860, "as the action and the almost inevitable result of commercial bargaining for labor. They will always exist."—"Trade Unions and their Tendencies," by Edmund Potter, F.R.S., *Social Science Association Transactions*, 1860, p. 756.

[2] We need only remind the reader of the incessant "pit strikes" of the Northumberland and other coalfields prior to the miners' organisation in permanent Trade Unions; of such angry insurrections as those of the Luddites in 1811 and the "plug riots" of 1842; and of the perpetual series of "shop disputes" that still go on among those handicrafts which have not advanced in organisation beyond the "shop bargain."

bargain " into the local " working rules," and of these again into the national agreement has naturally been accompanied by a similar extension of the " shop dispute," into a local strike, and of this again into a general stoppage of the industry.   In this connection we may quote the Royal Commission on Labor, " that when both sides in a trade are strongly organised and in possession of considerable financial resources, a trade conflict, when it does occur, may be on a very large scale, very protracted and very costly.   But just as a modern war between two great European States, costly though it is, seems to represent a higher state of civilisation than the incessant local fights and border raids which occur in times or places where governments are less strong and centralised, so, on the whole, an occasional great trade conflict, breaking in upon years of peace, seems to be preferable to continued local bickerings, stoppages of work, and petty conflicts." [1]

But whether or not we accept this flattering analogy, it is impossible to deny that the perpetual liability to end in a strike or a lock-out is a grave drawback to the Method of Collective Bargaining.   So long as the parties to a bargain are free to agree or not to agree, it is inevitable that, human nature being as it is, there should now and again come a deadlock, leading to that trial of strength and endurance which lies behind all bargaining.   We know of no device for avoiding this trial of strength except a deliberate decision of the community expressed in legislative enactment.   One favourite panacea, incidentally referred to in our account of the boot and shoe trade—the reference of the dispute to an impartial arbitrator—we reserve for a separate chapter.

[1] Fifth and Final Report of the Royal Commission on Labor, 1894, C, 7421, p. 36.   Mr. Lecky echoes this report.   " There can be little doubt that the largest, wealthiest, and best-organised Trade Unions have done much to diminish labor conflicts."—*Democracy and Liberty*, vol. ii. p. 355.

CHAPTER III

ARBITRATION

THE essential feature of arbitration as a means of determining the conditions of employment is that the decision is not the will of either party, or the outcome of negotiation between them, but the fiat of an umpire or arbitrator. It is distinguished from that organised negotiation between Trade Unions and Employers' Associations which we have termed Collective Bargaining, in that the result is not arrived at by bargaining at all, the higgling between the parties being, in fact, expressly superseded. On the other hand, it is not Legal Enactment, though it bears some resemblance to this form, because the award is not obligatory on either of the parties. Their refusal to accept it, or their ceasing to obey it, even if they have promised to do so, carries with it no coercive sanction.

These characteristics of arbitration, as a method of settling the conditions of employment, come to the front on every typical occasion. We see the employers and workmen at variance with each other. Negotiations, more or less formally carried on, proceed up to a point at which a deadlock seems inevitable. To avert a stoppage of the industry, both parties agree to "go to arbitration." They adopt an impartial umpire, either to act alone or with assessors representing each side. Each party then prepares an elaborate "case," which is laid before the new tribunal. Witnesses are called, examined, and cross-examined. The umpire asks for such additional information as he thinks fit. Throughout the proceedings the utmost latitude is allowed. The "reference" is seldom limited to particular alternatives, or expressed with any precision.[1] The umpire, in order to clear up points, is always entering into conversation with the parties. Practically no argument, however seemingly irrelevant, is excluded; and evidence may be given in support of claims founded on the most diverse economic theories. Finally, the umpire gives his award in precise terms, but usually without stating either the facts which have influenced him or the assumptions upon which he has made up his mind. The award—and this is an essential feature—carries with it no legal sanction, and may at any moment be repudiated or quietly ignored by any capitalist or workman.[2]

[1] Thus the operatives may be asking for an Eight Hours' Day, the dismissal of an unjust foreman, and the abolition of sub-contracting, whilst the employers urge a reduction of wages and the more regular attendance of the men. The umpire's award may include any or all of these points, and might conceivably decide all in favour of the respective claimants.

[2] A list of the principal works on arbitration will be found at p. 323 of our *History of Trade Unionism*. Mention should have been made among them of the report on *Industrial Conciliation and Arbitration* prepared by Carroll D. Wright for the Massachusetts Labor Bureau (Boston, 1881); and J. S. Jeans's *Conciliation and Arbitration in Labour Disputes* (London, 1894) can now be added. The most important recent publications have been made on the Continent. We may cite, in particular, the bulky volume of the French "Office du Travail," entitled *De la Conciliation et de l'arbitrage dans les Conflits Collectifs entre patrons et ouvriers en France et à l'étranger* (Paris, 1893); the numerous reports and pamphlets by Julien Weiller of Mariemont, Belgium; and *Conseils de l'industrie et du travail* by Charles Morisseaux (Brussels, 1890). The English experience is well discussed by Dr. von Schulze-Gaevernitz in *Zum Socialen Frieden* (Leipzig, 1890), translated as *Social Peace* (London, 1893).

The student should note that there has been, until quite recently, no clear distinction drawn between Collective Bargaining, Conciliation, and Arbitration. Much of what is called Arbitration or Conciliation in the earlier writings on the subject amounts to nothing more than organised Collective Bargaining. Thus, the classic work of Mr. Henry Crompton (*Industrial Conciliation*, London, 1876) describes, as "conciliation," the typical cases in which representative employers and workmen meet to bargain on behalf of the trade. The Nottingham hosiery board, established in 1860, often described as a model of arbitration, was, in effect, nothing more than machinery for Collective Bargaining, no outsider being present, the casting vote being given up, and the decisions being arrived at by what the men called "a long jaw." In 1868 Mr. Mundella observed in a lecture, ' It is well to define what we mean by arbitration. The sense in which we use the word is that of an arrangement for open and friendly bargaining . . . in

Yet arbitration has one characteristic feature in common with the higgling of employers and workmen which it supersedes. The arbitrator's award is a general ordinance, which, in so far as it is accepted, puts an end to Individual Bargaining between man and man, and thus excludes, from influence on the terms of employment, the exigencies of particular workmen, and usually also those of particular firms. It establishes, in short, like Collective Bargaining, a Common Rule for the industry concerned. We can therefore understand why the Trade Unionists from 1850 to 1876 so persistently strove for arbitration, and so eagerly welcomed the gradual conversion of the governing classes to a belief in its benefits. At a time when the majority of employers asserted their right to deal individually with each one of their "hands," habitually refused even to meet the men's representatives in discussion, and sought to suppress Collective Bargaining altogether by the use of ambiguous statutes and obsolete law, it was an immense gain for the Trade Unions to get their fundamental principle of a Common Rule adopted.[1] During the last twenty years arbitration has greatly increased in popularity among the public, and each ministry in succession prides itself on having attempted to facilitate its application. Whenever an industrial war breaks out, we have, in these days, a widespread feeling among the public that both parties should voluntarily submit to the decision of an impartial arbitrator. But however convenient this solution may be to a public of consumers, the two combatants seldom show any alacrity in seeking it, and can

which masters and men meet together and talk over their common affairs openly and freely."—*Arbitration as a Means of Preventing Strikes*, by A. J. Mundella (Bradford, 1868).

[1] Arbitration was accordingly opposed by the more clear-sighted of the opponents of Trade Unionism. "Our main objection," said one of the leading critics, "both to arbitration and conciliation, as palliatives of Unionism, is that they sanction, nay necessitate, the continuance of the system of combination, as opposed to that of individual competition. . . . In so doing we lend the authority of public recognition to the pestilent principle of combination, and sanction the substitution of an artificial mechanism for that natural organism which Providence has provided for the harmonious regulation of industrial interests."—*Trade Unionism*, by James Stirling (Glasgow, 1869), p. 50.

rarely be persuaded to agree to refer their quarrel to any outside authority. Although arbitration has been preached as a panacea for the last fifty years, the great majority of " captains of industry " still resent it as an infringement of their right to manage their own business, whilst the leaders of the organised workmen, once enthusiastic in its favor, now usually regard it with suspicion. The four years, 1891-95, saw, in Great Britain, four great industrial disputes in as many leading industries. But neither in cotton manufacture nor in coal-mining, neither in the great machine industry of boot-making nor in engineering, could the capitalists and workmen agree to let their quarrels be settled by an impartial umpire. What happened in each of these instances—and they were typical of many others—was the breaking off of Collective Bargaining, a prolonged stoppage and trial of endurance, ending, not in arbitration but in a resumption of Collective Bargaining, and the conclusion of a fresh agreement under new and more favorable auspices.

At first sight this disinclination of workmen or employers to submit their claims to an impartial tribunal appears perverse and unreasonable. Business men, it is said, almost invariably refer disputes between themselves to more or less formal arbitration, and would never dream of stopping their own industry, or drying up the source of their own profits, merely because they could not agree upon an impartial umpire. And if this be true in commercial transactions, where the alternative is nothing worse than an action at law, how much stronger the need must seem when the alternative may easily involve the bankruptcy of capitalists, the semi-starvation of thousands of operatives, and the temporary paralysis, if not the permanent injury, of an important national industry? Unfortunately this taking analogy, drawn from the arbitration between business firms, rests on the old confusion between interpreting an existing agreement and concluding a new one. Commercial arbitrations are invariably concerned with relations already entered into, either by existing contracts or under the law of the land.

No business man ever dreams of submitting to arbitration the terms upon which he shall make new purchases or future sales.[1]   Arbitration in commercial matters is therefore strictly confined to questions of interpretation, both parties resting their claims on a common basis, the existence of which is not in dispute between them.   Now, issues of interpretation of this kind are incessantly occurring between employers and employed, even in the best-regulated industries.   In these cases, as we shall hereafter point out, whilst there is no insuperable objection to arbitration, there is no real necessity to resort to it.   Nor is it for this class of disputes that arbitration is usually proposed.   The great strikes and lockouts which paralyse a whole industry almost invariably arise not on issues of interpretation, but on the proposal of either workmen or employers to alter the terms upon which, for the future, labor shall be engaged.

The position of the employers who object to the fixing of the terms of the wage contract by the fiat of an arbitrator has, from the first, been logical and consistent.   In a weighty article which appeared, twenty years ago, in the official organ of the National Association of Employers of Labor, we find the case stated with perfect lucidity :—

" The sphere of arbitration in trade disputes is strictly and absolutely limited to cases of specific contract, where the parties differ as to the terms of the contract, and are willing, for the sake of agreement and an honorable fulfilment of their engagements, to submit the points in dispute to competent men mutually chosen.   Where there is a basis and instrument of agreement by the parties to which they

---

[1] The frequently cited "Conseils de Prud'hommes" of France (established first at Lyons in 1808, and since greatly developed in all industrial centres) are strictly confined to the settlement of disputes arising out of existing contracts, or (as regards minor matters) the application of the law.   In no case do they presume to fix the rate of wages for future engagements.   They are indeed merely cheap and convenient legal tribunals, which make efforts to compose a dispute before proceeding to pronounce judgment upon it.   For a useful account of these councils, see E. Thomas, *Les Conseils des Prud'hommes, leur Histoire et leur Organisation* (Paris, 1888).   We understand that this is the character also of the similar tribunals which exist in various German States and elsewhere.

wish to adhere, and on which arbiters have something tangible to decide upon, it is seldom difficult for impartial men to elicit an adjustment fair and equitable to both sides. Arbitration is thus constantly of use in business matters on which differences of view have arisen, and is as applicable to questions between workmen and employers where there is a specific contract to be interpreted as in any other branch of affairs. It is better than going to law, much better than running away from the contract, striking, coercing, and falling into civil damages or criminal penalties, and raising on the back of such unfortunate consequences a blatant and endless protest against 'the labor laws.' But cases in which there are specific contracts absolutely define the sphere of arbitration. To apply the term 'arbitration' to the rate of wages for the future, in regard to which there is no explicit contract or engagement, and all the conditions of which are unknown to employers and employed, is the grossest misnomer that can be conceived. It is certain that neither workmen nor employers could be bound, nor would consent to be bound, even were it possible to bind them, by such arbitrary decrees ; and that the law, therefore, can never give such decrees even any temporary force, unless we are to fall back into the long obsolete tyranny of fixing the rate of wages by Act of Parliament, or by 'King in Council,' or by 'Communal Bureau of Public Safety,' or whatever the supreme power may be." [1]

Thus, from the employers' point of view, the supersession of the higgling of the market by the fiat of an arbitrator is, on its economic side, as indefensible an interference with industrial freedom as a legal fixing of the rate of wages. But an arbitrator's award has additional disadvantages. A law would at any rate be an authoritative settlement, which disposed of the question beyond dispute or cavil. An arbitrator's award, on the other hand, even if it is accepted by the Trade Union, may not commend itself to all the workmen. The employers who accept it may not unnaturally

[1] *Capital and Labour*, 16th June 1875.

feel that they have surrendered their own freedom, without securing any guarantee that the workmen, or some indispensable sections of them, will not promptly commence a new attack on which to provoke a stoppage of the industry. A law, moreover, is a Common Rule, enforced with uniformity on all alike. The arbitrator's award, on the other hand, binds only those firms and those workmen who were parties to it. In almost all industries there are some establishments, and often whole districts, which remain outside the employers' association, and in which masters and men persist in conducting their businesses in their own way. And there is no guarantee that some firms will not break away from the association, and join the ranks of these unfettered outsiders. If the arbitrator's award has secured better terms to the operatives than the masters are unanimously willing to concede, the good and honorable employers are penalised by their virtue. The proceedings of the " Boards of Conciliation and Arbitration " of the boot-making industry contain many complaints by employers that the awards are not enforced on rival firms, who are consequently undercutting them in the market. If our factory or mines legislation had been enforced only on specified good employers, and had left untouched any firm who objected to the regulations, so intolerable an injustice would quickly have led to a repudiation of the whole system.

If we turn from the employers to the Trade Unionists, we find a steadily increasing disinclination among workmen to agree to the intervention of an arbitrator to settle the terms of a new wage contract. This growing antipathy[1] to

---

[1] We may cite as evidence of this antipathy some recent declarations made in the names of the three most powerful organisations in the United Kingdom. It is expressly stated (for instance, in the Derbyshire Miners' Executive Council Minutes of the 2nd of June 1891) that it was the idea that the Royal Commission on Labor was intended to introduce a " huge arbitration system " that determined the whole Miners' Federation steadfastly to refuse to have anything to do with that inquiry. " We are opposed to the system altogether," declared Mr. Mawdsley before that Commission (Group C, Answer 776), on behalf of the Lancashire cotton operatives. And Mr. Robert Knight, giving evidence on behalf of the United Society of Boilermakers (Group A, Answer 20,833), definitely negatived the idea of arbitration, explaining as follows : " I speak from long experience of

arbitration is, we think, mainly due to their feeling of uncertainty as to the fundamental assumptions upon which the arbitrator will base his award. When the issue is whether the "standard earnings" of the Lancashire Cotton-spinners should or should not be decreased by ten per cent, there is no basis accepted by both parties, except the vague admission that the award should not be contrary to the welfare of the community. But this offers no guidance to the arbitrator. Judge Ellison, for instance, acting in 1879 in a Yorkshire coal-mining case, frankly expressed the perplexity of an absolutely open-minded umpire. "It is [he said] for (*the employers' advocate*) to put the men's wages as high as he can. It is for (*the men's advocate*) to put them as low as he can. And when you have done that it is for me to deal with the question as well as I can ; but on what principle I have to deal with it I have not the slightest idea. There is no principle of law involved in it. There is no principle of political economy in it. Both masters and men are arguing and standing upon what is completely within their rights. The master is not bound to employ labour except at a price which he thinks will pay him. The man is not bound to work for wages that won't assist (subsist) him and his family sufficiently, and so forth. So that you are both within your rights ; and that's the difficulty I see in dealing with the question." [1]

But this cold-blooded elimination of everything beyond the legal rights of the parties is neither usual in a wages arbitration, nor acceptable to either side. Each of the parties implicitly rests its case on a distinct economic assumption, or even series of assumptions, not accepted by the other side,

the working of this large organisation that I represent here to-day, and I say that we can settle all our differences without any interference on the part of Parliament or anybody else." The same feeling is shared by smaller societies. "Our experience of arbitration," states the secretary of the North Yorkshire and Cleveland (Ironstone) Miners' Association, "was that we always got the worst of it, and so since 1877 it has been firmly refused."—Joseph Toyn, in *Newcastle Leader* "*Extra*" on *Conciliation in Trade Disputes* (Newcastle, 1894), p. 9.

[1] *Report of South Yorkshire Collieries Arbitration* (Sheffield, 1879), p. 49. The umpire was the Judge of the Sheffield County Court.

and often not expressly stated. The employers will often hold that, in order to secure the utmost national prosperity, wages should rise and fall with the price which they can obtain for their product. Or it may be urged that the wage bill must, under no circumstances, encroach upon the particular percentage of profit assumed to be necessary to prevent capital from leaving the trade.[1] These assumptions would, at one time, have been acquiesced in by many leading workmen, although, perhaps, not by the rank and file. But during the last twenty years, the leaders of the most powerful organisations have definitely taken up the view that considerations of market price or business profit ought, in the interests of the community, to be strictly subordinated to the fundamental question of " Can a man live by the trade ? " It is urged that the payment of " a living wage " ought, under all circumstances, to be a " first charge " upon industry, taking precedence even of rents or royalties, and of the hypothetical percentage allowed as a minimum to capital in the worst times. The skilled mechanic moreover will claim that the length of his apprenticeship warrants him in insisting, like the physician or the barrister, on a minimum fee for his services below which he cannot be asked to descend. The arbitrator's award, if it is not a mere " splitting the difference," must be influenced by one or the other of these assumptions, either as a result of the argument before him, or as the outcome of his education or sympathies. However judicial he may be in ascertaining the facts of the case, the relative importance which he will give to the rival assumptions of the parties can scarcely fail to be affected by the subtle

---

[1] Mr. Mawdsley (Amalgamated Association of Cotton-spinners) is very emphatic on this point. " If we had arbitration we should have much less wages than we are getting now. Arbitrators generally go in for a certain standard of profit for capital—generally speaking, it has been 10 per cent. Mr. Chamberlain has always said that capital ought to have 10 per cent. If the arbitrator went in for 10 per cent in the cotton trade, we should have a very big reduction of wages; and we are not going to have it."—Evidence before Royal Commission on Labor, Group C, Answer 774. We believe the case to which Mr. Mawdsley referred is Mr. Chamberlain's award in the South Staffordshire Iron Trade in 1878.

influences of his class and training. The persons chosen as arbitrators have almost invariably been representative of the brain-working class—great employers, statesmen, or lawyers—men bringing to the task the highest qualities of training, impartiality, and judgment, but unconsciously imbued rather with the assumptions of the class in which they live than with those of the workmen. The workmen's growing objection to arbitration is, we believe, mainly due to their deeply-rooted suspicion that any arbitrator likely to be accepted by the employers will, however personally impartial he may be, unconsciously discount assumptions inconsistent with the current economics of his class.[1]

There is, however, one industry in which, for eight-and-twenty years, arbitration has been habitually resorted to, for the settlement of the terms of new wage contracts. This one exception to the usual dislike of arbitration will, we think, prove the correctness of the foregoing analysis. " The Board of Conciliation and Arbitration for the Manufactured Iron Trade of the North of England," which has existed since 1869, has long been the classical example of the success of arbitration. Besides providing by the machinery of a standing committee for the settlement of interpretation differences, and by half-yearly board meetings for discussing general questions, the rules direct the reference of intractable disputes to an outside umpire. On twenty separate occasions

---

[1] We have collected particulars of no fewer than 240 cases of industrial arbitration, ranging from 1803 to the present day. Excluding mere questions of interpretation, and disputes between workmen themselves, we have found only one case in which, in an arbitration for a new agreement between employers and employed, any person of the wage-earning class has been accepted as umpire. In May 1893 the Northampton Board of Arbitration for the Boot and Shoe Trade appointed Mr. F. Perkins, a working laster, as umpire. (Monthly Report of the National Union of Boot and Shoe Operatives, May 1893).

The arduous and often thankless task of acting as umpire or sole arbitrator is usually undertaken without fee or reward of any kind. Lord James has long given his invaluable services to the boot and shoe trade without remuneration. Dr. Spence Watson, who lately completed his fiftieth arbitration, told us that he had only thrice received any payment whatever, once his railway expenses, once a small fee, and in one case, which involved several weeks' labor, a more substantial payment. The barrister-umpire, called in, in some sense as a professional expert to unravel an intricate case, is occasionally paid.

during the last twenty-eight years this provision has come into operation with regard to the settlement of the conditions of future wage contracts ; and on every occasion the arbitrator's award has been accepted by both employers and employed.

It is an interesting confirmation of the view we have taken that, in this one industry in which arbitration has achieved a continued success, we find the workmen and the employers agreeing in the economic assumptions upon which wages should be fixed, and upon which, therefore, the arbitrator is asked to proceed. It has for more than a generation been traditional among ironmasters that the wages of the operatives ought to vary with the market price of the product.[1] Since the formation of the Board, in 1869, this assumption has been accepted by both parties as the main, and often as the exclusive, rule for the settlement of wages. In the reports of the arbitration proceedings we find both parties constantly reaffirming this principle, each in turn resorting to other considerations only for the sake of argument when the main assumption is for the moment calculated to tell against them. " We entirely agree," declare the operatives in 1877, " that our wages should be regulated by the selling price of iron."[2] Next time it is the employers who assert the same rule. " The eight years sliding-scale arrangement," states their spokesman in 1882, " we believe was the principle of determining wages by the selling price of iron, and it would be extremely difficult, if not dangerous, permanently to depart from that."[3] There is, in fact, as a careful student observes, " a general understanding running throughout the cases and pleadings, both of masters and men, that wages should follow the

[1] See the illustration quoted at pp. 484-486 of the *History of Trade Unionism*. " Old Thorneycroft's Scale," by which puddlers' wages advanced or receded one shilling for each pound sterling per ton in the price of " marked bars," dates, it is said, from 1841 ; see Mr. Whitwell's evidence before Royal Commission on Labor, 1892, Group A.

[2] Report of Arbitration before Mr. (now Sir David) Dale, July 1877, *Industrial Peace*, p. 63.

[3] Report of Arbitration before Mr. (now Sir J. W.) Pease, April 1882, *Ibid.* p. 63.

selling prices of iron." [1]   This was expressly stated by Dr. R. Spence Watson in the letter which accompanied his fifth award as arbitrator for this board.   Whilst observing that " the wages paid in the Staffordshire district, which competes with the North of England in the employment of ironworkers, as well as to some extent in the trade itself, is a factor which cannot be disregarded, [he declares that] in the course of the arguments it was admitted on both sides that . . . the realised price of iron, as shown by the figures taken out by the accountant to the board, may be considered the principal factor in the regulation of wages. . . . It is upon this state-ment [he continues] and these admissions that I am called upon to give my award." [2]

It will be apparent that arbitration on issues of this kind comes really within the category of the interpretation or application of what is, in effect, an agreement already arrived at between the parties.   The question comes very near to being one of fact, answered as soon as the necessary figures are ascertained beyond dispute.   It is therefore not surprising to learn that, during eight of the twenty-eight years of the Board's existence, variations of wages were automatically determined by a formal sliding scale, and that even during the intervals in which no definite scale was adopted the Board itself was able, on eight separate occa-sions, to agree to advances or reductions without troubling the arbitrator at all.   We need not discuss whether the acceptance by employers and operatives alike of the assumption that wages must follow prices is, or is not, advantageous to the workmen, or to the industry as a whole.   But it is evident that the continued success of arbitration in the North of England Iron Board, dealing, as it does, mainly with the interpretation or application of an existing common basis of agreement, affords no guide to other trades in which no such common basis is accepted,

---

[1] *Industrial Peace*, p. 90.
[2] Letter and award of the 28th November 1888 ; *Report of Wages Arbitration before R. S. Watson, Esq., LL.D.* (Darlington, 1888).

and in which the claims of the respective parties rest on opposite assumptions.[1]

But the success of the North of England Manufactured Iron Board, and the more qualified results of similar tribunals in the Midland iron trade, and the Northumberland and Durham coal-mining industry, whilst they give no real support to arbitration as a panacea for strikes, seem at first to open up a new field of usefulness for the arbitrator in the settlement of issues of application or interpretation. These questions of interpretation or application to particular cases are always arising, even in the best-regulated trade, and to provide machinery for their peaceful and indisputable decision is of great importance. Here we have not merely identical assumptions by the two parties, but a precise bargain by which both agree to be bound. Unfortunately it is just in these issues, for which arbitration seems a natural expedient, that its adoption has been found, in practice, most difficult. The application of a general agreement to the earnings of particular individuals, or to the

---

[1] The Midland Iron and Steel Wages Board, which has had an intermittent existence since 1872, was formed on the model of the North of England Board, which it closely resembles. Owing to the inferior organisation of the workmen in Staffordshire and Worcestershire, it has not always worked smoothly, but wage variations have almost always been made by the Board according to a sliding scale, formal or implied, whilst a standing committee applies the general principles to "local questions." See the evidence of Mr. (now Sir B.) Hingley before the Royal Commission on Labor, 1892, and the references given in the preceding chapter.

Among the Northumberland and Durham coalminers, though arbitration as to the terms of new agreements has been repeatedly resorted to, it has been only partially successful in preventing strikes. The Northumberland Miners' Mutual Confident Association went to arbitration on five occasions between 1873 and 1877. But in 1878 the owners forced a reduction without submitting to arbitration, the result being a nine weeks' strike. Between 1879 and 1886 the level of wages was automatically regulated by a sliding scale. In 1887 the employers again insisted on a special reduction, the result being a disastrous strike of seventeen weeks. Since that date alterations in the level of wages have been mutually agreed to by the joint "Wages Committee" without resort to arbitration. The Durham Miners' Association (established 1869) had four arbitrations between 1874 and 1876, and worked under a sliding scale from 1877 to 1889. This did not prevent a six weeks' strike in 1879, terminated by another arbitration. Variations in wages between 1889 and 1892 were mutually agreed to, but in 1892 there ensued the longest and most embittered dispute ever known in the trade.

technical details of particular samples or processes, is at once too complicated, and of too little pecuniary importance, to make it possible to call in an outside arbitrator.[1] The intractable questions, to take one trade as an example, which perplex the local boards in the boot and shoe industry relate only to a few shillings, and frequently concern only one or two workmen. For such issues it is obviously impossible to obtain, either for love or money, the services of any personality eminent enough to command the respect of the whole body of employers and workmen. Where the standard of earnings of large bodies of men, or the prevention of a serious industrial war, are concerned, public spirit will induce men of the calibre of Lord James or Dr. Spence Watson to spend whole days, without fee or reward, in bringing about an adjustment. In commercial arbitrations which involve considerable sums, recourse is had to eminent lawyers, who are paid large fees for mastering the intricate details of each case. This sort of arbitrator is far too expensive a person to be available for the application of general wage contracts to particular cases, and the statesman or philanthropist cannot spare the time. On the other hand, if, as in the boot and shoe trade, recourse is had to some one engaged in the industry, it is difficult to avoid the suspicion of class bias. The big employer from another district, whose services are usually called in, can hardly be expected to content the workmen. The employers, on the

---

[1] Thus, when in 1891, in an arbitration between the West Cumberland Iron and Steel Company and their workmen, the arbitrator (Dr. Spence Watson) was asked to fix the actual rates at which particular men were to be paid, he declined the task as one outside the possible capacity of any arbitrator. "What has always happened," said Dr. Spence Watson, "in every arbitration I have had hitherto? There has been a general question of percentage. . . . The principle of the thing is the thing to leave to arbitration. The detail of the thing, as to how it is to affect this or that or the other, never can be left to arbitration. . . . Already over this matter I have given up several nights to go through these papers and work them in this way and that way, but I have not the knowledge, and you cannot give me the knowledge. . . . Surely the question of individual payment is a question for the manager of the works and the men of the works, and not for a third party."—MS. proceedings. We are indebted to Dr. Spence Watson for permission to examine these and other papers, and for many valuable suggestions and criticisms.

other hand, will not consent to be bound by the decision of an operative.

It is, fortunately, unnecessary for the employers and workmen to get into this dilemma. The correct analogy from the commercial world for all these issues of interpretation is, not the elaborate and costly reference to arbitration, but the simple arrangements for taking an inventory, in connection with a contract of purchase or hire. Instead of calling in an outside authority, eminent enough to be known and trusted by both sides, each party is represented by an inexpensive expert habitually engaged on the particular calculations involved. The two professional men seldom find any difficulty in agreeing upon an identical award. This corresponds exactly to the machinery which is employed with such success in the Lancashire cotton trade. The two secretaries who visit the mill in which any question of interpretation has arisen correspond in all essentials to the two house-agents employed respectively by the owner and the incoming tenant of a furnished house. In the interpretation of wage contracts there is even more justification for this method than in taking an inventory. The object of the house-agent on either side is to get the best terms for his client. But the professional experts who visit a cotton mill, in response to a complaint from operative or employer, are not employed by or responsible to either of the parties directly concerned. And though one represents the associated employers, and the other the combined workmen, both are retained and paid to secure an identical object, namely, absolute uniformity between mill and mill. So far as regards the application to the particular cases of existing general contracts between employers and workmen, arbitration, though possible, is therefore but a clumsy device. The only way of getting an efficient umpire for such technical work would be permanently to employ a professional expert of high standing to give his whole time to the business. But directly an industry is sufficiently well organised to afford the expense of an efficient paid umpire, it can find in the joint meeting of the salaried experts of both sides a far more speedy, economical, and uniform method of settling questions of interpretation than any arbitration could provide.[1]

The reader is now in a position to estimate how far arbitration is likely to serve as a panacea against strikes or lock-outs, or even to become a permanent feature of the most highly organised machinery for Collective Bargaining. In the really crucial instances—the issues relating to the conclusion of a new agreement—habitual and voluntary recourse to an umpire may be expected, we think, only in the unlikely event of capitalists and workmen adopting identical assumptions as to the proper basis of wages. We have seen how unreservedly the best-educated workmen of the North of England accepted, between 1870 and 1885, the capitalists' assumption that it was only fair that wages should vary with the selling price of the product. For twenty years the miners of South Wales have acquiesced in the same doctrine. If this view were to become accepted in other trades, it is conceivable that arbitration would become more popular among them. On the other hand, there is growing up among workmen a strong feeling in favor of a fixed minimum Standard of Life, to be regarded as a first charge upon the industry of the country, and to be determined by the requirements of healthy family life and citizenship. If the capitalists should accept this view, arbitrations might become common, the explicit reference in every case being what conditions were required in the industry to enable the various grades of producers to lead a civilised life. But no such agreement on fundamental assumptions is at present within view. We are therefore

---

[1] In the rare cases in which the two house-agents fail to agree, we understand that the practice is for them privately to refer the matter to another professional, whose decision they both adopt as their own. If in the Lancashire cotton trade, the employers' and workmen's district secretaries do not agree upon an issue of interpretation, it is, in practice, referred to the joint decision of the central secretaries. But on such issues of fact, *if identical principles are thoroughly accepted by both sides*, there is seldom any intractable difference of opinion between professional experts.

constrained not to place any high expectations upon the fiat of an umpire as a method of preventing disputes as to future conditions of labor. Nor can we estimate very highly the practical value of arbitration in the application to particular cases of existing general agreements. In promptitude, technical efficiency, and inexpensiveness the "impartial outsider" is inferior to the joint meeting of the salaried secretaries of either side.

But although arbitration is not likely to supersede Collective Bargaining, or to prevent the occasional breaking off of negotiations, it has great advantages, in all but the best-organised trades, as a means of helping forward the negotiations themselves. The first requisite for efficient Collective Bargaining is for the parties to meet face to face, and in an amicable manner to discuss each other's claim. But this initial step is often one of difficulty. We are apt to forget, in view of the regular negotiations in such highly organised trades as the Cotton Operatives, the Boilermakers, and the Northumberland and Durham Coalminers, how new and unusual it still is for capitalists and workmen to meet on an equal footing, to recognise each other's representative capacity, and to debate, with equal good temper, technical knowledge, and argumentative skill, upon what conditions the employer shall engage "his own hands." Even to-day, in the great majority of trades, the masters would think it beneath their dignity voluntarily to confer with the Trade Union leaders on equal terms; and they would resent as preposterous the idea of disclosing to them their profit and loss accounts, or even the prices they are obtaining for their product. Yet it is upon these facts that they base their demand for a reduction of wages, or their refusal of an advance. The workmen, on the other hand, especially in such half-organised trades, are full of prejudices, misconceptions of the facts, and Utopian aspirations. Under these circumstances, even if the employers consent to meet the men at all, there can be no frank interchange of views, no real understanding of each other's position—in short, no effective negotiation. Recourse to an impartial umpire is one way out of these difficulties. The employer's dignity is not offended by appearing before an eminent jurist or statesman, sitting virtually in a judicial capacity. It is regarded as only natural that the arbitrator should ask for the statistical facts upon which each party bases its case. The mere fact of each having to set forth its claims in precise terms, in a way that can be maintained under cross-examination, is already a great gain. But if the arbitrator is tactful and experienced, he can do a great deal more to bring the parties to agreement. He discovers, by kindly examination, what precisely it is that each party regards as essential, and persuasively puts on one side any irritating reminiscences of past disputes, or theoretic arguments going beyond the narrow limits of the case. In friendly conversation with each side in turn, he draws out the really strong arguments of both, restates them in their most effective form, and in due course impresses them, in the most conciliatory terms, on the notice of the opponent. Those who have read the proceedings before such an experienced arbitrator as Dr. Spence Watson, will, we are sure, agree with us in feeling that his wonderful success as an umpire is far more due to these arts of conciliation than to any infallibility in his awards. In case after case we have been struck by the fact that, long before the end of the discussion, many of the issues had already been disposed of, the points remaining in dispute being so narrowed down by a mutual recognition of each other's case that when the award is at last given each party is predisposed to accept it as inevitable.

In this patient work of conciliation lies the real value of arbitration proceedings. There is no magic in the fiat of an arbitrator as a remedy for strikes or lock-outs. If either party really prefers fighting to conceding the smallest point to its adversary—that is, in those cases in which either employers or the workmen have an overwhelming superiority in strength—there will be no submission to arbitration. If both parties are willing to bargain, and are sufficiently well organised and well educated to be capable of it, no outside intervention will be needed. In those industries, however, where organisation has begun, but has not yet reached the highest form ; where the employers are forced to recognise the power of the men's union, but have not yet brought themselves to meet its officials on terms of real equality ; where the workmen are strong enough to strike, but do not yet command the services of experienced negotiators, the intervention of an eminent outsider may be of the utmost value. It is of small importance whether his intervention takes the form of " arbitration " or " conciliation "—that is to say, whether he is empowered to close the discussion by himself delivering an " award " as umpire, or whether he must wait until he can bring the parties to sign an " agreement " drawn up by himself as chairman. In either case his real business is not to supersede the process of Collective Bargaining, but to forward it. And in view of the usual impossibility of agreeing upon any common assumption as to the proper basis of wages ; in face of the workman's suspicion of the brainworker's training, and the employer's fear [1] of electioneering considerations ; and having regard to the importance of securing universal concurrence in the result, we are inclined to believe that the intervention of the " eminent outsider " will, as a rule, be at once more acceptable and more likely to be successful if he avowedly acts only as a " conciliator." [2]

This inference is supported by the events of the last few years. On three notable occasions outside intervention has been evoked to settle a serious industrial conflict. In 1893 Lord Rosebery, at the express desire of the Cabinet, settled a dispute which had for sixteen weeks stopped the coal

[1] Thus, in the draft rules of a Foreman's Benefit Society, established by some of the leading Tyneside employers, there is a provision for referring to arbitration any dispute between the society and a member. The draft rule significantly adds : " The following cannot be selected as arbitrator : Persons either candidates for or holding political, municipal, or other positions acquired by votes ministers of religion."

[2] " In conciliation the disputants endeavour to convince each other, in arbitration to convince a third party. As in the first case, both sides have equal

trade of the Midlands of England. In 1895 Sir Courtenay Boyle, Permanent Secretary of the Board of Trade, drew up the agreement which terminated the great strike in the boot trade. And Lord James, a distinguished member of the Conservative Ministry of the day, in January 1896 brought about, after protracted negotiations, a settlement of the dispute between the Clyde and Belfast shipbuilders and their engineers. But notwithstanding the official position of these magnates, it is significant that in no case were they asked, and in no case did they attempt, to cut the Gordian knot by the judicial decree of an umpire or arbitrator. It was not their business to inquire into the merits of the case. They were not called upon to make up their minds whether the employers or the workmen were in the right. They had not even to choose between the rival economic assumptions on which the parties rested their respective claims. Their function was to persuade the representatives of both sides to go on negotiating until a basis was discovered on which it was possible for them to agree.

This work of conciliation is, we believe, destined to play a great and for many years an increasing part in the labor struggles of this country. In the present state of public opinion the intervention of an outside " conciliator " is, as regards the imperfectly organised trades, a precursor of regular Collective Bargaining. In many trades the employers themselves are not united in any association : in many others they still haughtily refuse to discuss matters with their workmen. In prolonged disputes public opinion now almost forces the parties to resume negotiations ; and

knowledge of the matter in hand, they must endeavour to show clearly the strong points of the case, and those only. Any attempt at simple advocacy would be thrown away. The appeal must be to acknowledged facts. But, in the second case, advocacy is necessary, and all its many devices—the undesirable as well as the undeniably good. There is a strong antagonism throughout. Arbitration is better than striking or locking out, but inferior to conciliation. Industrial peace in any form is better than industrial war."—" Compulsory or Voluntary Conciliation," by R. Spence Watson, *Ironworkers' Journal*, June 1895.

the intervention of an eminent outsider is found the best lever for Collective Bargaining. His social position or official status secures for the proceedings, even among angry men, a certain amount of dignity, order, and consideration for each other's feelings, whilst it prevents any hasty rupture or withdrawal. So long as Lord Rosebery was willing to go on sitting, it was practically impossible for either the coalowners or the coalminers to stop discussing. But prolonged discussion does not lead to agreement unless the parties get on good terms with each other, and are brought into a friendly mood. It is the conciliator's business to see that this atmosphere of good humour is produced and maintained. The excellent luncheon which Lord Rosebery provided for owners and workmen alike was probably more effective in creating harmony than the most convincing arguments about "the living wage." All this, however, is but preliminary to the real business. We have already described the important part played by a tactful and experienced arbitrator in drawing out the best points in each party's case, restating them in the most persuasive form, and eliminating from the controversy all unnecessary sources of irritation or non-essential differences. The ideal conciliator adds to this a happy suggestiveness and fertility in devising possible alternatives. Throughout the discussion he watches for the particular points to which each party really attaches importance. He has a quick eye for acceptable lines of compromise. At the right psychological moment, when discussion is beginning to be tedious to both sides, he is ready with a form of words. This is the crisis of the proceedings. If the parties are physically and mentally tired, and yet pleased with themselves and no longer angry with their opponents ; if the conciliator is adroit in his drafting, and finds a formula which, whilst making mutual concessions on minor points, includes, or seems to each party to include, a great deal of what each has been contending for, the resolution will be agreed to, if not by acclamation, at any rate after a few minor amendments to save the dignity

of one side or the other ; and almost before some of the
slower-minded representatives have had time to think out all
the bearings of the compromise the agreement is signed, and
peace is secured.

We see, therefore, that outside intervention in wages
disputes may be of the highest value, and we anticipate that
it will, for many years to come, in all but the best-organised
trades, play a great, and even an increasing, part. But its
function will not be that of " arbitration," properly so called,
but rather that of " conciliation," though this will continue
to be sometimes carried on under the guise of arbitration.
Instead of aiming at superseding Collective Bargaining, the
arbitrator will more and more consciously seek to promote
it. In fact, so far from being the crown of industrial organisation, the reference of disputes to an impartial outsider is
a mark of its imperfection. Arbitration is the temporary
expedient of incompletely organised industries, destined to
be cast aside by each of them in turn when a higher stage,
like that of the Cotton Operatives or the Boilermakers, is
attained. The Government of 1896, therefore, did well to
cut down its arbitration bill to a modest " Conciliation Act."
The pretentious legislation of 1867 and 1872, from which
so much was expected, is now simply repealed. The Board
of Trade is empowered, in case of an industrial dispute, " to
inquire into the causes and circumstances of the difference."
It may intervene as the friend of peace, to persuade the
parties to come to an agreement. If a conciliator is desired,
it may appoint one. Finally, if both parties join in asking
that the settlement shall proceed in the guise of arbitration,
and wish the Board of Trade to select the arbitrator for them,
the Board of Trade may accede to their request, as it might
have done without any Act at all ! [1]

[1] The report of the first year's working of this Act, presented to Parliament
in July 1897, shows that 35 applications were made to the Board of Trade. In
7 cases the Board refused to intervene. Of the other 28 cases, 18 were settled
by more or less formal conciliation, and 5 by arbitration, one of which was a
demarcation dispute between different bodies of workmen, and the other 4 were
small local disputes, all in badly-organised trades or districts. Three cases,

The conclusion will disappoint those who see in arbitration, not a subordinate and temporary adjunct to Collective Bargaining, but a panacea for stoppages of industry. The popularity of arbitration has deep roots. At the back of the peremptory public demand for the settlement of any strike or lock-out, there lurks a feeling that in the interests of the whole community neither employers nor workmen ought to be allowed to paralyse their own industry. If one side or the other persists in standing out, we have a clamour for "compulsory arbitration": that is, the intervention of the power of the State. We need not enter into the numerous suggestions that have been made for "State Boards of Arbitration," authoritative intervention by the Board of Trade, or the deposit, by both parties, of sums of money to be legally forfeited upon breach of the award. The authors of such suggestions always find themselves in a dilemma. If resort to this kind of arbitration is still to be voluntary, the liability to penalties or legal proceedings is not calculated to persuade either employers or workmen to come within its toils.[1] If, on the other hand, it is to be compulsory, it will amount to legal enactment of a novel kind. It may well be argued that the community, for the protection of the public welfare, is entitled to step in and

including the notorious strike at Lord Penrhyn's slate quarries, and that of the boot operatives at Norwich, remained intractable, owing to arbitration being refused, twice by the employers and once by both parties.

[1] The following extract from a recent report of so experienced and well-informed a society as the United Textile Factory Workers' Association is significant : " Boards of Conciliation.—Any number of Bills are constantly being introduced on this question, but your Council do not see that any useful purpose can be served by their becoming law. The assumption on which all these proposals are based is that . . . when the return goes down the wages of labor and the profits of capital should go down together. . . . The umpire is never a workman, but always a member of the upper class, whose sympathies and interest lie in the direction of keeping wages down. . . . They believe that the Bills now being brought forward are meant as so many traps with which to catch a portion of the workers' wages, and they have consequently opposed them " (*Report of the Legislative Council of the United Textile Factory Workers' Association* for 1893-94, p. 14). See also the reports of the conferences between the Miners' Federation and the leading coalowners during 1896, in which the workmen's representatives throughout opposed any arbitration scheme by which, as they repeated, " a man can come in and settle what we could not settle among ourselves."

decide the terms upon which mechanics shall labor, and upon which capitalists shall engage them. In such a case the public decision could perhaps best be embodied in the award of an impartial arbitration tribunal, invested with all the solemnity of the State. But here we pass outside the domain of "arbitration" properly so called. The question is then no longer the patching up of a quarrel between capitalists and workmen, but the deliberate determination by the community of the conditions under which certain industrial operations shall be allowed to be carried on. Such an award would have to be enforced on the parties whose recalcitrance had rendered it necessary. This does not imply, as is sometimes suggested, that workmen would be marched into the works by a regiment of soldiers, or that the police would open the gates (and the cashbox) of stubborn employers. All that the award need decree is, that if capitalists desire to engage in the particular industry they shall do so only on the specified conditions. The enforcement of these conditions would become a matter for official inspection, followed by prosecutions for breaches of what would in effect be the law of the land. Here, it is true, we do find an effective panacea for strikes and lock-outs. Although industrial history records plenty of agitations and counter-agitations for and against the fixing by law of various conditions of employment, there has never been either a lock-out or a strike against a new Factory or Truck Act. But by adopting this method of avoiding the occasional breaking off of negotiations which accompanies Collective Bargaining, we should supersede Collective Bargaining altogether. The conditions of employment would no longer be left to the higgling of masters and men, but would be authoritatively decided without their consent in the manner which the community, acting through an arbitrator, thought most expedient. "Compulsory arbitration" means, in fact, the fixing of wages by law.[1]

[1] Such a form of compulsory arbitration is contained in the Factories and Shops Act of 1896 of the Colony of Victoria, which provides (sec. 15) that, "in

order to determine the lowest price or rate which may be paid to any person for wholly or partially preparing or manufacturing either inside or outside a factory, or workroom, any particular articles of clothing, or wearing apparel, or furniture, or for breadmaking, or baking, the Governor in Council may, if he think fit, from time to time appoint a special Board," to consist half of representatives of employers and half of employed. The Board may then prescribe the minimum rates to be paid for particular articles, by piecework for home work, and by either time or piece for factory work. Any employer paying less than the minimum thus fixed is made liable to a fine, and, on a third offence, the registration of his factory or workroom (without which he cannot carry on business) "shall, without further or other authority than this Act, be forthwith cancelled by the Chief Officer." The working of this virtually legal fixing of a minimum wage will be watched with interest by economists. Under the New Zealand Act of 1894, passed by the Hon. W. P. Reeves, now Agent-General for the Colony in London, labor disputes in which Trade Unions are concerned may be referred, first to Public Conciliation Boards, and, failing a settlement, to an Arbitration Court, composed of a Judge of the Supreme Court, with two assessors. This Court may, at its discretion, make its award enforceable by legal process. A fuller account of this Act will be found in our final chapter. The Conciliation and Arbitration Acts of New South Wales (1892) and South Australia (1894) have been practically unsuccessful. ("Quelques expériences de la Conciliation par l'État en Australasie," by Anton Bertram in *Revue d'Économie Politique*, July 1897.)

CHAPTER IV

THE METHOD OF LEGAL ENACTMENT

WE do not need to remind the student of the *History of Trade Unionism* that an Act of Parliament has, at all times, formed one of the means by which British Trade Unionists have sought to attain their ends. The fervor with which they have believed in this particular Method, and the extent to which they have been able to employ it have varied according to the political circumstances of the time. The strong trade clubs of the town handicraftsmen, and the widely extended associations of woollen workers of the eighteenth century relied mainly upon the law to secure the regulation of their trades. So much was this the case that the most celebrated student of eighteenth-century Trade Unionism declares that "the legal prosecution" of transgressors of the law was the chief object [1] of these combinations, and that, in fact, English Trade Unionism "originated with the non-observance of" the statutes fixing wages and regulating apprenticeship. Its fundamental purpose, says Professor Brentano, was "the maintenance of the existing legal and customary regulations of trade. As soon as the State ceased to maintain order it stepped into its place." [2] It is true that later investigation has brought to light some ancient unions, which, springing out of sick clubs, or impetuous

---

[1] Brentano's *Gilds and Trade Unions* (London, 1870), p. clxxiv. (or p. 110 of reprint).

[2] *Ibid.* p. clxxvii. (or p. 113 of reprint).

strikes, adhered to the rival Methods of Mutual Insurance and Collective Bargaining. But Dr. Brentano's generalisation as to the objects and methods of eighteenth-century combinations has, in the main, been confirmed and strengthened. It would have been remarkable if the Trade Unions had not taken this line. Even before the stringent act of 1799 against all workmen's combinations, the very idea of Collective Bargaining was scouted by employers, and strongly condemned by public opinion. On the other hand, the majority of the educated and the governing classes regarded it as only reasonable that the conditions of labor should be regulated by law. Accordingly we find the operatives who objected to the innovations threatening their accustomed livelihood, confidently appealing against their new employers, to Quarter Sessions, Parliament, or the Privy Council. We see the Trade Unions forming committees to put the law in force ; maintaining solicitors to fight their cases in the law courts ; expending large sums in preparing tables of rates, to be enforced by the magistrates ; marshalling evidence before Quarter Sessions in support of these lists ; appearing by counsel at the bar of the House of Commons and before the House of Lords Committees in quest of new legislation, or in opposition to bills of the employers ; and finally organising all the machinery of political agitation, with its showers of petitions, imposing demonstrations in the streets, Parliamentary lobbying, and occasionally, where the members happened, as freemen, to possess the franchise, the swaying of elections.[1]

With the adoption, by Parliament and the law courts, of the doctrine of *laisser faire*, all this machinery fell into abeyance. It soon came to be waste of money to organise petitions, to send up delegates and witnesses, or to pay the fees of solicitors and counsel, only to be met by a *doctrinaire* refusal to go into the merits of the case. From 1800 onward we find every Committee of the House of Commons

---

[1] Illustrations of all these forms of Trade Union activity during the eighteenth century will be found in the *History of Trade Unionism*, pp. 27, 33, 34, 40-54.

reporting in the same strain. " They are of opinion that no interference of the legislature with the freedom of trade, or with the perfect liberty of every individual to dispose of his time and of his labor in the way and on the terms which he may judge most conducive to his own interest can take place without violating general principles of the first import-ance to the prosperity and happiness of the community, without establishing the most pernicious precedent, or even without aggravating, after a very short time, the pressure of the general distress, and imposing obstacles against that distress being ever removed." [1] Debarred alike from overt Collective Bargaining and from Legal Enactment, the Trade Unions of the first quarter of the century fell back on the Method of Mutual Insurance, largely tempered by the use of secret coercion. Those who refused to work "contrary to the interests of the trade" were supported with enthusi-astic generosity, whilst "knobsticks" were boycotted, and even assaulted. When employers retaliated by criminal prosecution, or dismissal of Trade Unionists, the operatives broke out into sullen strikes or angry riots, accompanied by machine breaking and crimes of violence. It was largely the hope of putting an end to this veiled insurrection that induced a landlord Parliament to repeal the Combination Laws, and thus, for the first time, enabled the Trade Unions openly to carry on negotiations with their employers.

Throughout the next quarter of a century Trade Union activity was mainly devoted to building up the machinery for Collective Bargaining.[2] This is easily explained. Whilst the Philosophic Radicals, and indeed much of the educated

---

[1] *Report of Committee on Petitions of Artisans*, 13th June 1811 ; *History of Trade Unionism*, p. 54.

[2] The fact that it was at this stage in their history that the working class combinations forced themselves on the attention of Political Economists and the press, goes far, we think, to account for the common idea that Trade Unionism consists exclusively of Collective Bargaining, with its accompaniments of " sticks and strikes." Between 1824 and 1869, practically all the criticism or de-nunciation of Trade Unionism took the form of homilies about the futility of Collective Bargaining and the wickedness of strikes. Even the Political Econo-mists seem to have been unaware either of the history of the combinations which

public opinion of that generation, worked with the unions in widening and safeguarding their resort to the Method of Collective Bargaining, any idea of regulating by law the conditions of labor of the ordinary workman was regarded by a middle-class electorate as out of the question. Those industries in which there was (owing to the attention of philanthropists or the existence of peculiar grievances) any chance of obtaining special legislation still strove to enforce their Common Rules by the Method of Legal Enactment. The reader of the *History of Trade Unionism* will remember how vigorously and effectively the unions of textile workers supported, between 1830 and 1850, the various "Ten Hours'" bills advocated by Robert Owen and Lord Shaftesbury. The combinations of the coalminers, basing their claims on the unknown horrors of underground life, were even more insistent, from 1843 onward, in demanding successive Mines Regulation Acts. The Hand-loom Weavers and the Stocking-frame Workers long continued pathetically to urge the old arguments in favor of a legal rate of wages, whilst all sections of organised workmen spasmodically attempted to get legal protection for their earnings by an effective prohibition of "truck." But with a House of Commons dominated by employers of labor, the operatives in trades employing only adult males, and free from exceptional grievances, for the most part laid aside their traditional method.

With the enfranchisement of the town artisan in 1867, and the county operative and miner in 1885, we see the relative preference between the three methods again shifting. The case for the legal limitation of the hours of work of adult men was, for instance, explicitly stated at the beginning of the Cotton-spinners' agitation for the Nine Hours' Bill. "We are often told," declared their official manifesto in 1871, "that any legislative interference with male adult labor is

they were criticising, or of the nature and variety of their objects and methods. This lop-sided appreciation of Trade Union purposes and Trade Union methods still lingers in leading articles and popular economic text-books.

an economic error, and it is further urged that as the labor of the working man is his only capital, he should not be restrained in the use or application of it. . . . Now, though at first sight the above reasoning, if reasoning it may be called—seems plausible enough, yet there is a lurking fallacy in it all the more dangerous because of the artful manner in which it is attempted to place the Legislature and the working population in a false position in relation to each other. . . . It is a sound principle of universal law established by the wisdom of more than two thousand years that where in the necessary imperfection of human affairs the parties to a contract or dealing do not stand on an equal footing, but one has an undue power to oppress or mislead the other, law should step in to succour the weaker party. . . . It behoves us as working men to inquire what is wrong in the present factory system, and, if need be, ask the legislature to interfere in our behalf . . . whether the time has not arrived when Parliament should be appealed to to secure a curtailment of the hours of factory labor. . . . If some of our legislators should manifest a disposition to abdicate their legislative functions so far as we are concerned, it may be well to remind them that election day will again come round when their abdication will be accepted." [1]

This change of political conditions explains, not only the increasing demand for new Factory and Mines Acts, additional Railway and Merchant Shipping regulations, and the prevention of accidents and truck, but also the upgrowth, since 1868, of such exclusively political Trade Union organisations as the United Textile Factory Workers' Association, and such predominantly political associations as the Miners' Federation of Great Britain, together with the formation of a general political machinery throughout the Trade Union

[1] Circular signed by the general secretary of the Amalgamated Association of Operative Cotton-spinners, " on behalf of " the delegate meeting, 11th December 1871 ; *History of Trade Unionism*, pp. 295-96. It will be remembered that this Trade Union has always consisted exclusively of men. In our *History of Trade Unionism* we have pointed out how the Nine Hours' agitation was eventually conducted to a successful issue " behind the women's petticoats."

world, in the form of Trades Councils, the Trade Union Congress, and the Parliamentary Committee.

It is probable that no one who is not familiar with Trade Union records has any adequate conception of the number and variety of trade regulations which the unions have sought to enforce by Act of Parliament. The eighteenth-century combinations seem to have limited their aspirations to the fixing of a minimum rate of wages, the requirement of a period of apprenticeship, and the determination of the proper proportion of apprentices to journeymen. With the advent of manufacture on a large scale we see the factory operatives and miners taking up the subjects of sanitation and overcrowding, safety from accidents, and the length of the working day. Besides the universal demand that employers should be made liable for accidents, and forbidden to make any deductions from wages, we have large sections of the Trade Union world demanding an Eight Hours' Day, the prohibition of overtime, and the specifying of definite holidays ; others insisting on the weekly payment of wages, the disclosure of the " particulars " on which the piecework wage is based, and the abolition of all fines and deductions whatsoever. The National Union of Boot and Shoe Operatives ask for the exclusion of alien immigrants, and the compulsory provision of workshop accommodation by the employers ; whilst the Amalgamated Society of Tailors will be content with nothing short of the legal abolition of home work. The Carmen seek, year after year, for an Act of Parliament to enforce their rule that one man shall not be put in charge of two carts ; the Boilermakers, Enginemen, and Plumbers ask that none but certificated craftsmen shall be allowed to hold certain positions ; the Textile Workers want to regulate the temperature and humidity of the spinning-mills and weaving sheds ; whilst the Seamen have a lengthy code of their own extending from an amendment of the laws of marine insurance to the qualifications of a sea-cook, from an improved construction of sea-going vessels to increasing the sum allowed on advance notes, from the enactment of a fixed scale of

manning to the inspection of the ship's medicine chest. Nor
does this enumeration by any means exhaust the list. Every
Parliament sees new regulations of the conditions of employment embodied in the already extensive labor code, whilst
each successive Trade Union Congress produces a crop of
fresh demands.[1] Whether for good or for evil, it appears
inevitable that the growing participation of the wage-earners
in political life, and the rising influence of their organisations,
must necessarily bring about an increasing use of the Method
of Legal Enactment.

But a resort to the law as a means of attaining Trade
Union ends has, from the workmen's point of view, certain
grave disadvantages. Its chief drawback is the prolonged
and uncertain struggle that each new regulation involves.
Before a Trade Union can get a Common Rule enforced by
the law of the land, it must convince the community at large
that the proposed regulation will prove advantageous to the
state as a whole, and not unduly burdensome to the consumers. The workmen's grievance has, therefore, to be
published to the world, to bear discussion in public meetings,
and to meet the criticism of the newspapers. Members of
Parliament must be persuaded to take the matter up, and
made so far to believe in the justice of the claim as to be willing to importune ministers or bore the House of Commons
with the subject. In due course a Royal Commission is
appointed, which hears evidence, collects statistics, and makes
a report. Presently a new Factory or Mines Bill is drafted
by the Home Secretary, and, on the combined advice of

---

[1] See the reports of the various Trade Union Congresses, especially since
1885. It is to be observed that, under the Constitution of the United States,
most of the statutes thus desired by English Trade Unionists, like much of the
legislation already in force, might be held void, as violations of the constitutional
right of freedom of contract. Among the American statutes already disallowed
by the courts on this ground are truck acts, acts requiring weekly or fortnightly
pays, or forbidding coalowners to compute their tonnage rates of wages on
screened coal only, acts prohibiting employers from discharging men merely
because they are Trade Unionists, and a factory act limiting the hours of labor
of adult women. See *Handbook to the Labor Law of the United States* (New
York, 1896), by F. J. Stimson.

Government inspectors, medical experts, sympathetic employers, and, perhaps, a few representative workmen, some kind of clause is inserted to effect, usually not what the Trade Union has been asking for, but the minimum which, in the light of all the evidence, seems indispensable to avert the grossest of the evil. At the committee stage in the House of Commons the clause is pulled to pieces by the spokesmen of the employers on the one hand, and by those of the workmen on the other. But the great majority of the members have, like the minister himself, no direct interest on either side, and speak rather for the general public of consumers anxious to " keep trade in the country " and foster cheapness, than with a view to secure exceptional advantages for the particular section concerned. Thus each step has to be gained by a process of persuasion. To win over in succession the electors, the Members of Parliament, the Ministers of the Crown, and—most difficult task of all—the permanent professional experts, requires, in the officers of a Trade Union, a large measure of statesmanship, and, in the rank and file of the members, a combination of wise moderation, dogged persistency, steadfast loyalty to leaders, and " sweet reasonableness " at a compromise, not usually characteristic of popular movements. At its best the process is a slow one. The Lancashire " Nine Hours' Movement," for instance, attained, perhaps, a more rapid and complete success than any other agitation for factory legislation. Yet it cost the Cotton-spinners four years' expensive and harassing work before the bill reducing the factory day was wrung from a reluctant legislature.[1] On the other hand, the " Nine Hours' Day " of the engineers, gained in 1871 by the Method of Collective Bargaining, was won within six months of the first negotiations with the employers.[2] Nor is the victory ever complete. What Parliament ultimately enacts is never the full measure of what has been asked for. The Cotton Operatives, for instance, did not get their Nine Hours' Day,

[1] *History of Trade Unionism*, pp. 295-298.
[2] *Ibid.* pp. 299-302.

but only a 56½ hours' week. By the Method of Collective Bargaining, on the other hand, Trade Unions have not infrequently gained from employers, at times of strategic advantage, not only the whole of their demands, but also conditions so exceptional that they would never have ventured to embody them in a legislative proposal. We shall hereafter see how this consideration deters strong Trade Unions, like the United Society of Boilermakers and Iron Shipbuilders, from going to Parliament about such unsettled problems as Demarcation of Work or the Limitation of Apprentices, on which they feel that they can exact better terms than would be conceded to them by the community as a whole. But taking merely the hours of labor we may note how, whilst Parliament has not yet been converted even to an Eight Hours' Day for Miners, the coal-hewers of Northumberland and Durham have long since secured by Collective Bargaining a working day for themselves of less than 7 hours, and a working week which never exceeds 37 hours.

At first sight, it may seem strange that, in face of all these difficulties and disadvantages, the Trade Unions should so persistently, and even increasingly, seek for legislative regulation of their respective industries. The explanation is that, however tedious and difficult may be the process of obtaining it, once the Common Rule is embodied in an Act of Parliament, it satisfies more perfectly the Trade Union aspirations of permanence and universality than any other method. It is, as we have shown, as yet rare for a Trade Union to have been able to establish by the Method of Collective Bargaining anything like uniform conditions throughout the whole country. Such prominent and wealthy unions, for instance, as the Amalgamated Society of Engineers and the Amalgamated Society of Carpenters, find themselves compelled to recognise hours of labor varying, in different towns, from 48 to 57 per week in the one case, and from 41 to 60 in the other.[1]

[1] The Grays and Woolwich Arsenal branches of Engineers among others, stand at 48 hours, whilst the Vale of Leven branch works 57. Among the

But even where any Trade Union rule exists, either national or local, there are, as we have mentioned, always some extensive districts, and some important establishments, in which the rule is either not recognised at all, or is systematically evaded. An Act of Parliament, on the contrary, applies uniformly to all districts, whether the Trade Union is strong or non-existent, and to all employers, whether or not they belong to the Employers' Association. It corresponds, in fact, to the ideal form of Collective Bargaining, a National Agreement made between a Trade Union including every man in the trade, and an Employers' Association from which no firm stands aloof. Like such an agreement it excludes, from influence on the wage-contract, the exigencies, not only of particular workmen or particular establishments, but also those of particular districts. But it goes a stage farther in this direction. A National Agreement, however stable, is always liable to be changed, in accordance with the relative strength of employers and employed, at each of the successive inflations and depressions which characterise modern industry. The Cotton-spinners, for instance, whose standard earnings are determined by an exceptionally stable National Agreement, have, during the last twenty years, agreed to twelve alterations of this standard, five times upward and seven downward. But once any part of the conditions of employment has been deemed of sufficient importance to the community to be secured by law, it is beyond the reach of even the most extreme commercial crises. In the blackest days of 1879, when many cotton manufacturers were reduced to bankruptcy and the operatives suffered a reduction of twenty per cent of their wages, no one ever suggested that the expensive statutory requirements as to the sanitation of the factory, or the fencing of dangerous

Carpenters, taking the mid-winter hours, the Middleton branch works 41½ hours, the Bury branch 43½, and those of Prestwich and Radcliffe 44, whilst Yarmouth, Yeovil, and many Irish branches are still at 60. See *Statistics of Rates of Wages, etc.*, published by the A.S.E. in 1895, and the *Annual Report of the Amalgamated Society of Carpenters* for 1894. Compare, too, the *Reports on Wages and Hours of Labour*, published by the Board of Trade, C, 7567, 1894.

machinery should be relaxed. In our *History of Trade Unionism* we have shown [1] how seriously, in these years, the Nine Hours' Day of the engineering and building trades secured by Collective Bargaining, was nullified by the practice of systematic overtime. But neither inflation nor depression has, as a matter of fact, led to any alteration since 1874 in the length of the Cotton-spinners' Normal Day, which the Factory Act in effect prescribes. The Common Rule embodied in an Act of Parliament has, therefore, the inestimable advantage, from the Trade Union point of view, of being beyond the influence of the exigencies of even the worst times of depression. And, if we may judge from the history of the last fifty years, such a rule is more apt to " slide up " than to " slide down." Once any regulation has been adopted, it becomes practically impossible altogether to rescind it, whilst the movement of public opinion, notably on such matters as education, sanitation, safety, and shorter hours of labor, has been steadily in favor of increased requirements in the normal Standard of Life.[2] These characteristics of the Method of Legal Enactment have, as we shall see in subsequent chapters, an important bearing on the kind of Regulations which the Trade Unionists seek to enforce by this particular Method. But before we consider the rules themselves, we have first to describe the nature and extent of the Trade Union machinery for using the method.

The Trade Unions have not yet developed, for their application of the Method of Legal Enactment, even so much formal machinery as they possess for the Method of Collective Bargaining. This backwardness, is, in the main, to be attributed to the difficulty of the task. The dominant tendency in Trade Union· history is, as we have seen, to

---

[1] Page 333.

[2] This " partiality," however, is not an inherent attribute of the Method of Legal Enactment. Its existence during the present generation is, we hold, due to the shifting of political power from the middle class, who had become opponents of any restriction of competition, to the wage-earners, who have continued to believe in regulation.

make the trade throughout the country the unit of organisation. But to bring any proposal effectively before the legislature, that is to say, to persuade members of Parliament to take the matter up, Trade Union leaders must convert, not the employers and workmen in their own industry wherever carried on, but the electors of particular constituencies, to whatever trade they belong. An organisation according to localities has, therefore, to be superposed upon an organisation according to trades.

Two great industries—cotton and coal—have been able to surmount this difficulty, and these alone have as yet developed any effective political machinery. The powerful unions of Cotton Operatives, for instance, three-fourths of whose 132,000 members are to be found in ten constituencies within twenty miles of Bolton, have, during the past twenty-five years, constructed a special organisation for obtaining and enforcing the legislative regulations which they desire. The five societies of Spinners, Weavers, Cardroom Operatives, Beamers, and Overlookers are federated in the United Textile Factory Workers' Association, which carries on no Collective Bargaining, and possesses no insurance side, but has for its sole object " the removal of any grievance . . . for which Parliamentary or Governmental interference is required." [1] The Representative Assembly [2] of this federation, consisting of nearly 200 delegates from a hundred local branches, amalgamates all sections of the Cotton Operatives into one solid union for their common political purposes. But it is the Federal Executive,[3] appointed annually by this Representative Assembly, that governs the Parliamentary policy and organises the political force of the Trade. This Cabinet, composed in the main of the salaried officials of the separate unions, meets regularly throughout the year, exclusively for political business. At these private meetings, held in the parlor of a Manchester

---

[1] Rules of 1890.
[2] Called the " General Council."
[3] Called the " Legislative Council."

public-house, all rhetoric and formality is banished, and the complaints of the constituents are discussed with cynical shrewdness. If they appear to admit of any legislative or administrative remedy, the president and secretary—who are invariably leading officials of the Spinners and the Weavers respectively—are directed to take the matter up. These officers are wise enough to call in expert assistance. There is usually some eminent lawyer representing a Lancashire constituency, who is glad to put his brains freely at the disposal of so influential an organisation. A clause or a bill is drafted, and communications are opened up with the Home Office. Once certain of the technical accuracy and administrative feasibility of the proposals, the Federal Executive opens a vigorous political campaign. Public meetings are organised, at which the local members of Parliament, or in default, the opposition candidates, are impartially invited to preside. By these meetings not only the 300,000 persons employed in or about the cotton mills, but also the other electors, and the Parliamentary candidates themselves, are patiently educated. It is no small help in this process that the Cotton Operatives have what is virtually their own organ in the press, and that their leading officials write, in addition, much of the " labor news " in the provincial newspapers. When the Parliamentary session opens, the struggle is transferred to the lobby of the House of Commons. It is perhaps a fortunate chance that the present general secretary of the Spinners belongs to the Conservative party, whilst the general secretary of the Weavers is a staunch adherent of the Liberals. No member for a cotton constituency, to whichever party he may belong, escapes the pressure. Meanwhile, in order to smooth the way for legislation, the employers will have been approached with a view to arriving at some common policy which the trade, as a whole, can press on the Government. The millowners, for instance, will be persuaded not to oppose increased factory regulation, on consideration of the operatives joining them to stop a threatened Indian import duty, or combining in support of " the rehabilitation of silver." When a general election comes near an urgent appeal is issued to all the 132,000 members, reminding them that they should vote only for those candidates, of whatever political party, who promise to support the trade programme. No one can read the frequent circulars, the minutes of the conferences with employers and members of Parliament, the reports of the public meetings, dinners to factory inspectors and deputations to the Home Office, the leading articles in the *Cotton Factory Times*, and the " questions to candidates " for election in Lancashire constituencies, without admitting that the Cotton Operatives have known how to construct a political machine of remarkable efficiency. The result is that the legislative regulation of the Cotton trade has been carried to a point far in advance of any other industry, whilst the law is enforced with a stringent regularity unknown in other districts.[1]

In the case of the Cotton Operatives the close observer may suspect that the political machinery is better than the material out of which it is made. Absorbed in chapels and co-operative stores, eager by individual thrift to rise out of the wage-earning class, and accustomed to adopt the views of the local millowners and landlords, the Cotton Operatives, as a class, are not remarkable for political capacity. In the interest that they take in public affairs they are behind the coalminers of the North and Midland districts of England. Among these underground workers the instinct for democratic politics is so keen that they have, for over twenty years, sent their own officials to represent them in the House of Commons. Like the Cotton Operatives they have exceptional political opportunities, four-fifths of the whole membership being massed in a relatively small number of Parliamentary constituencies. These advantages are, however, largely neutralised by the fact that they are, for political purposes, divided

---

[1] The meetings of the United Textile Factory Operatives' Association were temporarily suspended in 1896, the officials stating that the time was inopportune for any further extension of factory legislation.

into two hostile factions, the Miners' Federation on the one hand, and the county unions of Northumberland and Durham on the other.

The miners of Northumberland and Durham were, for over a generation, the pioneers and energetic leaders of the movement in favor of the legal regulation of the conditions of labor in the mine. We need not again describe the machinery of the active legal and Parliamentary campaigns between 1843 and 1887. From the appointment of the "Miners' Attorney-General" down to the death of Alexander Macdonald, the promoters of the successive Mines Regulation Acts drew their strongest support from the two Northern counties. We have described elsewhere[1] the curious combination of industrial circumstances and economic theories which have brought the Northumberland and Durham unions to a standstill as regards the legal regulation of their trade. They still nominally retain a separate political machinery under the name of the National Union of Miners.[2] But the effective political influence of the miners of these counties is now expressed mainly by their three officials having seats in the House of Commons. These members, in conjunction with the leading local officials of the Northumberland and Durham Unions, object to the extension of legal regulation, and actively oppose the Eight Hours' Bill.

The great bulk of the miners have, however, retained their belief in the Method of Legal Enactment, and are to-day even more persistent than their fathers in demanding its further application. The Miners' Federation of Great Britain (established 1887, and now counting 200,000 members), which we described in our chapter on "The Unit of Government," is essentially a political organisation. It deals, it is true, also with Collective Bargaining, in so far as anything

---

[1] *History of Trade Unionism*, pp. 284-292, 377-380.

[2] This federal body, formed by Alexander Macdonald exclusively for Parliamentary purposes, once included practically all the miners' unions in the kingdom, and was, in its time, the most influential political organisation in the Trade Union world. To-day it is confined to the two unions of Northumberland and Durham, and retains only a shadowy separate existence.

approaching to a National Agreement is concerned.   But all
the ordinary business of Mutual Insurance and Collective
Bargaining is performed by the separate county unions, and
nine-tenths of the federal work relates, like that of the United
Textile Factory Workers' Association, to matters in which
legislative or governmental interference is required.   Like the
Cotton Operatives, too, the Miners' Federation acts through a
Representative Assembly and an Executive which is virtually
a cabinet of the salaried officials of the constituent Unions.
It is a matter of common knowledge that this organisation
exercises great political power, and it is, in Parliamentary
influence, second only to the United Textile Factory Workers'
Association.   In one respect it is even stronger.   Owing to
the loyalty of the miners to their leaders, and to their democratic fervor, the Parliamentary and local elections in mining
constituencies may be said to be entirely controlled by the
miners' organisations.   No candidate can be elected who
does not support their programme.   It is in the manipulation of both political parties in the House of Commons that
the Miners fall behind the Cotton Operatives.   The Miners'
Federation has, in the first place, to struggle against the very
serious obstacle presented by the resolute hostility of the
Northumberland and Durham unions.   In the Parliament of
1892-95 if Mr. Pickard or Mr. Woods proposed some measure
desired by the Miners' Federation, he was pretty sure to be
answered not by an employer, but by Mr. Burt or Mr.
Fenwick, speaking for the miners of the two Northern
counties.   The fact too, that all the miners' representatives
in the House of Commons are loyal supporters of one political
party interferes, to some extent, with their influence both with
that party and with its opponents.   And although this great
federation can count among its officials men of ability,
experience, and unquestioned integrity, we are inclined to
doubt whether the general level of technical and economic
knowledge among them is quite as high as that of the staff
of the Cotton Operatives, recruited as the latter is by
competitive examination.   It is, perhaps, due to this fact that

the Miners' officials do not as yet realise the necessity of expert legal and Parliamentary counsel in their deliberations, and make far less use than the Cotton Operatives of outside help. They have no intercourse with the Government Mines Inspectors, and, unlike the Cotton Operatives, they do not enjoy the advantage of constantly meeting, on terms of easy equality, the salaried officers of the employers' associations. Moreover, they have no organ of their own in the press, and they seldom contribute to other newspapers. Strong in their numbers and their concentrated electoral power, the Miners have, in fact, hitherto somewhat suffered from their isolation. But notwithstanding all these drawbacks, the steady improvement and progressive elaboration of the Mines Regulation Acts, in the face of powerful capitalist opposition, bears eloquent testimony to the past and present effectiveness of the Miners' political organisations.

No trade society other than those connected with cotton and coal has developed any effective machinery for obtaining the legal regulations which are demanded by its members. This is, in some cases, to be attributed to the absence, among the rank and file, of any keen desire for special Acts of Parliament. Some powerful unions, like the United Society of Boilermakers, which enforces a rigid limit on the number of apprentices, are comparatively indifferent to the law as an instrument for obtaining the conditions of labor that they desire. But there are other trades which feel, even more strongly than the Cotton Operatives and Miners, their dependence on the Method of Legal Enactment as the only effective way of securing what they consider fair conditions of employment. Not to mention such modern organisations as those of the Gasworkers and Seamen, whose objects are mainly legislative, we watch old-established unions like the Amalgamated Society of Tailors, the several societies of cutlery workers of Sheffield, and the Hosiers of the Midland counties all basing their aspirations on the legal regulation of homework, and the prohibition of insidious forms of truck." Typical "old unionists" like the Ironfounders,

Stonemasons, and Engineers are constantly voting by large majorities in favor of drastic legal enactments providing for the better sanitation of their workplaces, for additional pre-cautions against accidents, for the compulsory compensation of those who suffer through negligence, for the adoption in all public contracts of the Standard Rates of Wages, and last, but in recent years not least, for the suppression of overtime, and the maintenance of a Legal Day.   And yet it is not too much to say that, as regards all these points, the organised Trade Unions, with their hundreds of thousands of electors, exercise, to-day, practically no appreciable influence on the House of Commons and, unlike the Cotton Operatives and Miners, have not learnt either to supplement the efforts of sympathetic philanthropists, or to strengthen the hands of willing politicians.   The problem of superposing an organisa-tion according to locality upon one according to trades, has, in fact, proved too complicated for Trade Union statesman-ship.

We shall best understand this failure by considering first the difficulties that prevent any single trade from attaining political influence, and then the kind of organisation by which such difficulties might be overcome.   The typical Trade Union has its members scattered in small groups, each of which makes up a tiny fraction of an electoral constituency. The adult male Cotton Operatives of Oldham practically dominate the local electorate, but the Oldham Plumbers number only 69, and the Oldham Carpenters only 152 —contingents too small to be able to impress their views on Parliamentary candidates.   At Morpeth again, the Coal-miners have, for over twenty years, been able to actually return one of their own officials as the member.   But the Morpeth Tailors number only five, and are thus practically helpless.   Even in London, where the Amalgamated Society of Tailors dominates its own skilled branch of the trade, its two thousand members are spread over sixty constituencies. It is evident that the only way by which the men engaged in such widely dispersed industries as building and tailoring can force their grievances on an ignorant public or a reluctant Parliament, is by combined action among the different trades of each constituency. Even the Engineers, who are in certain centres aggregated in large numbers, are politically weakened in their own strongholds by their division into sectional societies. And joint action is even more clearly necessary in the case of the great number of little local trades, which have not the compensation of numerous branches and a large aggregate membership. Now, the long and varied experience of the Cotton Operatives and, to a lesser extent, that of the Coalminers prove that if a political federation is to be successful, three conditions are absolutely indispensable. There must, in the first place, be a vigorous central executive, to which is entrusted the entire direction of all the proceedings. In effective connection with this central committee, there must be local organisations in the various constituencies, always prompt to obey the directions of the leaders, and to subordinate other interests to the main object. Finally, the central committee must not only have in its service an adequate staff of able men as officials, but must also know how to command, either for love or money, and be willing frequently to use, the professional advice of trained experts in law, in Parliamentary procedure, in administration, and in what may be called general politics.

It may at first be thought that, in the annual Trade Union Congress, the Parliamentary Committee, and the local Trades Councils, the Trade Union world possesses a political machinery fulfilling these elementary conditions. There is a Representative Assembly, to which nearly every organised trade sends delegates. This assembly has nothing to do with Mutual Insurance or Collective Bargaining, and deals exclusively with the political interests of the Trade Union world. It elects a Cabinet of thirteen members, on which sit some of the ablest salaried officers of the movement. The duty of this " Parliamentary Committee " is expressly defined to be " to watch all legislative measures directly affecting the question of Labor, to initiate such legislative action as Congress may direct, and to prepare the programme for the Congress." [1] Finally there exist, in over a hundred towns, which together elect a third of the House of Commons joint committees of the local Trade Union branches, formed " to watch over the general interests of Labor—political and social—both in and out of Parliament." [2] But a short examination of the constitution and working of this organisation will, we think, make clear that, whatever outward resemblances to an effective political machine it may possess, it lacks all the essential conditions of efficiency and success.

Let us, to begin with, take the Parliamentary Committee upon which, to follow the analogy of the Cotton Operatives should fall the duties of formulating a national Trade Union programme, of guiding the deliberations of the Trade Union Congress, of directing the necessary political campaign throughout the constituencies, and finally, of conducting the desired measures through Parliament. But the Parliamentary Committee has, for the last twenty years, had practically no means of fulfilling these functions. The central executive of the unions, from whom alone any responsible statement of the trade grievances and proposals can be obtained, seldom dream of communicating their desires to the Parliamentary Committee. This has naturally followed from the fact that there is no central staff able to cope with such proposals as have from time to time come in. [3] For all the Parliamentary and other business of the Trade Union world as a whole there is provided only a single secretary, who is usually one of the " Labor Representatives " in the House of Commons

[1] Amended Standing Orders, drawn up by Parliamentary Committee November 1894.

[2] Rules of the London Trades Council, revised March 1895. The Manchester and Salford Trades Council (established 1866) declares that its objects are "to watch over the social and political rights and interests of Labor, local and national, but not of party political character. Its duties shall be to direct the power and influence possessed by its constituents, in promoting and supporting such measures as may appear likely to increase the comfort and happiness of the people, and generally to assist in securing the ends for which Trade Unions were called into existence." (Report for 1890.)

[3] *History of Trade Unionism*, pp. 356-358, 470-474.

with prior duties to his own constituency. For the last five years the occupant of the post has been a salaried official of his own union, busily occupied with its particular sectional interests. The Parliamentary Committee admittedly pays only for the leavings of his time and attention, a large part of the salary of £200[1] going, in fact, to the son or friend who does the routine office work during his frequent absences from London. It is therefore impossible for the Parliamentary Committee to investigate grievances, or to form an independent judgment on technical proposals. The members of the Committee are, no doubt, severally quite competent to deal with their own trades, but for the Committee as a whole to act on this assumption necessarily means its implicit acceptance of the technical proposals of any one of its members. As regards the vast majority of unrepresented trades the Committee has absolutely no means of ascertaining, either what is complained of, or what remedies are practicable. Nor does it ever occur to the Parliamentary Committee to attempt to make up for this deficiency by seeking expert or professional advice, for which Congress has never been asked to provide funds. We despair of making any middle-class student realise the strength and persistency of this disinclination of Trade Unionists to call in outside counsel. A Board of Railway Directors or a Town Council do not imagine that they are bartering their independence or impairing their dignity when they consult an engineer or a solicitor, or when they employ an actuary or a Parliamentary draughtsman. Though they are themselves what the Trade Unionists would call " practical men " they invariably commit even their own proposals to professional experts to be critically examined and put into proper form. But owing, we believe, to a combination of sturdy independence, naïve self-complacency, and an extremely narrow outlook on affairs, the Parliamentary Committee, like most Trade Union organisations, apparently regard themselves as competent to be their own solicitors, their own actuaries, and even their own Parliamentary

---

[1] Raised, in 1896, to £300.

draughtsmen.[1] It is unnecessary to add that, in each capacity, they attain the proverbial result.

Any idea of intellectual leadership of the Trade Union world has accordingly long since been abandoned by the Parliamentary Committee. This has entailed the degeneration of the Trade Union Congress. The four or five hundred members coming from all trades and parts of the kingdom are largely unknown to each other and new to their work. Each delegate brings to the meeting his own pet ideas and legislative projects. In order to make such a Representative Assembly into a useful piece of democratic machinery, the first requisite is a strong " Front Bench " of responsible leaders, who have themselves arrived at a definite and consistent policy. But this, as we have seen, is beyond the capacity of the Parliamentary Committee in its present lack of information, staff, and expert counsel. What happens, in fact, is that a few stock resolutions are moved by members of the Committee, but nine-tenths of the time of Congress is given to the casual proposals sent in by the rank and file. These are not examined or reported on by the Parliamentary Committee, or even referred for consideration to special committees elected for the purpose. They appear higgledy-piggledy in the agenda of the Congress sitting as a whole, the order in which they are discussed being decided by lot.[2] The bewildered delegates, fresh from the bench or the mine, find themselves confronted with a hundred and fifty heterogeneous proposals, some containing highly technical amendments of the statutes relating to particular trades, others being mere pious aspirations for social amelioration, and others, again, involving far-reaching changes in the economic and political constitution of the country. All these come before Congress with equal authority ; are explained in five-

---

[1] We have already mentioned that the United Textile Factory Workers' Association is honorably distinguished among Trade Unions for its freedom from this defect. The Co-operative and Friendly Society Movements have, to a large extent, learnt a similar lesson.

[2] Some improvement has been made in this respect during the last year or two, the notices of motion being now classified according to their subjects.

minute speeches ; and as regards four out of every five, get passed without inquiry or discrimination.[1]   Instead of a deliberative assembly checking and ratifying a programme prepared, after careful investigation, by a responsible Cabinet, the Trade Union Congress is now an unorganised public meeting, utterly unable to formulate any consistent or practical policy.

In the absence alike of an effective central executive, and of any definite programme, it is of minor import that the joint committees which should act in the several constituencies are themselves inefficient, and completely divorced from the other parts of the machine.   We do not need to repeat our detailed description and working of the Trades Councils.[2]   It is obvious that if such Councils are to be of any use in influencing the constituencies, they must receive the confidence and support of the central executive of each trade, and strictly co-ordinate all their political action with that of the Parliamentary Committee.   But for reasons on which we have elsewhere dwelt, the central executives of the national trade societies view with suspicion and jealousy the very existence of local committees over whose action they have no control.   The Parliamentary Committee, which ought to exercise that control, has, in the absence of a real programme and of anything like an office staff, for many years given up all attempts to direct, or even to influence, the bodies through which alone it could conduct an effective electoral campaign. Without leadership, without an official programme, and without any definite work, the Trades Councils have become, in effect, microscopic Trade Union Congresses, with all the deficiencies of unorganised public meetings.   Their wild and inconsistent resolutions, no less than their fitful and erratic action, have naturally increased the dislike of the central executives, and of the salaried officials who dominate the Parliamentary Committee.   Since 1895 they have even been excluded from participation in the Trade Union Congress.   Thus

---

[1] *History of Trade Unionism*, pp. 467-470.
[2] *Ibid.* pp. 440-444, 466, 467.

there is now no working connection between the central committee and the organisations in the several constituencies.

We see therefore that, notwithstanding a great parade of political influence, the Trade Union world, as a whole, is really without an organised machinery for using the Method of Legal Enactment. This outcome of thirty years' effort may well lead to doubts whether it is practicable to construct efficient machinery for the political business of the whole Trade Union world. Some persons may suggest that the experience of the Cotton Operatives and the Coalminers points rather to the development of separate political machinery for each great group of industries. On this assumption we should have political federations of the Engineering and Shipbuilding trades, of the various branches of the Clothing Trade, of the Building and Furniture Trades, and perhaps even of the Transport Workers and the General Laborers. But whether the machinery for using the Method of Legal Enactment covers the whole Trade Union world, or is confined to particular sections, it will not be possible for it to obtain even such success as has been won by the Cotton Operatives and the Coalminers without a radical change in spirit, if not also in form. It may safely be predicted that no Parliamentary organisation of the Trade Union world will be politically effective until the narrow limits of its action are definitely recognised, and until the separate functions of the Central Federal Executive, the Representative Assembly, and the Local Councils are clearly understood, and placed in proper co-ordination with each other.

Let us first consider the importance of recognising the narrow limits within which such political influence must be exercised. We have here, in fact, a particular application of the principles upon which, as we showed in our chapter on " Interunion Relations," any combined action must be based. The paramount condition of stable federation is, as we have suggested, that the constituent bodies should be united only in so far as they possess interests in common, and that in respect of all other matters they should retain heir independence. The Trade Union Congress is a federation for obtaining, by Parliamentary action, not social reform generally, but the particular measures desired by its constituent Trade Unions.[1] These all desire certain measures of legal regulation confined to their own particular trades, and they are prepared, if this limitation is observed, to back up each other's demands. On many important subjects, such as Freedom of Combination, Compensation for Accidents, Truck, Sanitation, "the Particulars Clause," the weekly payment of wages, and the abolition of disciplinary fines, they are united on general measures. But directly the Congress diverges from its narrow Trade Union function, and expresses any opinion, either on general social reforms or party politics, it is bound to alienate whole sections of its constituents. The Trade Unions join the Congress for the promotion of a Parliamentary policy desired, not merely by a majority, but by all of them ; and it is a violation of the implied contract between them to use the political force, towards the creation of which all are contributing, for the purposes of any particular political party. The Trade Unionists of Northumberland and Durham are predominantly Liberal. Those of Lancashire are largely Conservative. Those of Yorkshire and London, again, are deeply impregnated with Socialism. If the Congress adopts the Shibboleths, or supports the general policy of any of the three parties which now—on questions outside Trade Unionism—divide the allegiance of British workmen, its influence is at once destroyed. The history of the Trade Union Congress during the last twenty years emphatically confirms this view. Whether it is "captured" by the Liberals (as in 1878-85) or by the Socialists (as in 1893-94); whether it is pledged to Peasant Proprietorship or to Land Nationalisation ; whether it declares in favor of Bimetalism or the "Nationalisation of the means of production,

---

[1] In the course of our subsequent analysis of the Trade Union Regulations themselves, and in our final survey, we shall discover the political programme for the Trade Union world. See the chapters on "The Economic Characteristics of Trade Unionism" and "Trade Unionism and Democracy."

distribution, and exchange," it equally destroys its capacity for performing its proper work, and provokes a reaction which nullifies its political influence.

Once this limitation were understood and definitely recognised it would become possible to weld the separate parts of the existing Trade Union organisation into a political machinery of considerable influence. The first requisite would be a central federal committee, meeting exclusively for the definite political purposes which we have indicated. To this Parliamentary Committee the central executive of each national trade would bring its particular grievances, with the remedies proposed, just as the Weavers' executive submits to the United Textile Factory Workers' Association its objections to over-steaming and its proposals for the abolition of this practice. On no account must any proposal be taken up by the Parliamentary Committee which had not received the express endorsement of the central executive of the trade concerned. Any departure from this rule would bring the federal committee into conflict with its real constituents, and deprive it of all guarantee that the proposal had been accepted by the bulk of the members most directly to be affected. But this endorsement would not in itself suffice. The Parliamentary Committee, acting in conjunction with the officers of the trade concerned, would have to take expert advice as to the extent of the grievance, the practicability of the remedy proposed, and the best form in which it could be put. The approved legislative proposals of the several trades could then be marshalled into a precise and consistent Parliamentary programme, from which all vague aspirations or rhetorical claptrap would be excluded. When the programme for the year had, after careful investigation and thought, at last been framed, it would have to be presented to a Representative Assembly of all the trades. In emphatic contrast with the practice of the present Trade Union Congress, it should be made a cardinal rule that no proposition for political action should be brought before the Assembly, unless it had first been submitted to the Parlia mentary Committee for investigation and report. With such a rule the delegates from each trade would find before them the proposals which had been sent up by their executives, couched in the best possible language, and recommended to the delegates of the other trades by the cumulative authority of the officials of the industry concerned, the skilled political staff of the Parliamentary Committee itself, and the legal and administrative experts who had been consulted. At this stage, discussion by all the trades would serve to reveal any latent divergence of interest or policy which would militate against the electoral success of even a perfectly devised programme. But such an assembly would fulfil a much more important purpose than merely amending and ratifying an official programme. It would enable the leaders to explain the several items, and demonstrate to the whole Trade Union world their necessity, adequacy, and consistency with the common interests of all Trade Unionists.

The programme once settled, the work of political agitation would begin. Here the Parliamentary Committee would have to be supplemented by a local federation in each constituency. This local body would naturally be formed, like the present Trades Councils, of representatives from all the Trade Union branches in the constituency, or in the town. It would be vital to its efficiency and success that the central executives of the several trades should regard its constitution as of national importance to them ; urge their branches to elect their most responsible members ; and give them every encouragement to contribute their quota of the local expenses from the society's funds. It goes without saying that these local councils must, no less strictly than the Trade Union Congress, avoid all bias in favor of one or other political party, and confine themselves rigidly to Trade Union objects. But their proceedings must be subject to a yet narrower limit. Unlike the existing Trades Councils, they must realise that it is no part of their business to frame the Parliamentary programme even in matters on which all their constituent branches are unanimous. This follows from the fact that each trade must be dealt with as a national unit.   Before the Engineers or the Tailors can hope to get any amendment of the law relating to their trade, all the branches from one end of the kingdom to the other must be prepared to back up an identical demand ; and the demand must be formulated in terms capable of being pressed upon Ministers and the administrative experts. This identity and precision can only be secured by central action.   The work of the local Trades Councils must, therefore, as regards all Parliamentary action, be executive only. Both in order to retain the confidence of the central executive of each trade, and to function properly as a part of the political machine, the local councils would have rigidly to confine themselves to pushing the official Trade Union programme for the time being.   If any of their members wanted this programme altered, he could bring his proposal forward in the local branch of his own union, have it voted upon by his fellow-tradesmen, and get it sent up to his own central executive.   If it was not a matter on which his own Trade Union could be induced to take action, it would most assuredly not be fit for adoption by a federation of Trade Unions.   The local Trades Council would, without interfering with general policy, find abundant occupation in organising and educating the local Trade Unionist electors ; in carrying out the frequent instructions received from the skilled political staff of the Parliamentary Committee in watching and criticising the action of the Parliamentary representatives of the constituency, to whatever party they belonged ; in supplementing and supervising the local work of the mines, factory, and sanitary inspectors ; and, wherever it was thought fit, in conducting a municipal campaign.   For all elections to local bodies, it could, of course, frame its own programme.   Here it would have to act as its own Representative Assembly.   Like the Trade Union Congress the Trades Council would have to elect and to trust a responsible cabinet ; to restrict it to a Trade Union as distinguished from a general political programme ; to provide it with officers and funds adequate to its task ; to expect that it should act only after inquiry and expert or professional advice ; and above all, to insist that it should keep itself free from suspicion of acting in the interests of any particular party.

We are thus brought back, at each stage of the organisation, to the paramount need of intellectual leadership. Without concerted federal action between the trades, no progress can be made in carrying out their desires for the use of the Method of Legal Enactment. Without a central committee really directing and concentrating the action of the local councils, no electoral campaign can ever be effective. Without a " Front Bench " of responsible leaders, no Representative Assembly can ever formulate a consistent programme, or rise above the dignity of a public meeting. The great officials of the leading trades must realise that it is their duty, not merely to stir up their own branches to feeble and fitful agitation for the particular legal reforms that they desire themselves, but to get constructed the federal organisation which alone can secure their accomplishment. In this federal organisation they must themselves take the leading part. For this work they are at present, with all their capacity and force, usually quite unfit. Each man knows his own trade, and the desires of his own union, but is both ignorant and indifferent as to the needs or desires of every other trade. Before they can form anything like a Cabinet with a definite and consistent policy, they must learn how to frame a precise and detailed programme which shall include the particular legislative regulations desired by each trade, whilst avoiding the Shibboleths of any political party. Nor is this an impossible dream. At one period, as we have elsewhere described,[1] the Trade Union world possessed, in " the Junta " and their immediate successors, an extremely efficient Cabinet, which both led the Trade Union Congress and directed the action of the Trades Councils. In close communication with the executives of the great trades, and

[1] *History of Trade Unionism*, pp. 215-283.

making unstinted use of expert counsel, this Junta prepared a reasoned and practicable programme; explained it to representative gatherings by which it was ratified; and enlisted the Trades Councils in an organised electoral campaign in its support. The result was seen in the memorable Parliamentary triumphs of 1871 and 1875. With the passing away of the Junta, and the breach between the Parliamentary Committee and its unpaid counsellors, this effective leadership came insensibly to an end. If the machinery is again to become effective, the Parliamentary Committee must realise that its duty is to lead both the Trade Union Congress and the Trades Councils; to formulate its own policy; to provide itself with an adequate salaried staff; and, above all, to make the fullest possible use of professional experts. With the creation of a strongly centralised, and thoroughly equipped political federation confining its work exclusively to Trade Union objects, the organised trades might reasonably hope to obtain the same measure of success in the detailed legal regulation of the conditions of their labor, as that achieved by such " old Parliamentary hands " as the Coalminers and the Cotton Operatives, whilst these latter unions would find their power to obtain further regulation in their own trades indefinitely increased by the effective support of the whole Trade Union world.[1]

---

[1] The degeneration of the whole political machinery has, during the last few years, become so obvious to the leading Trade Unionists, that spasmodic attempts at reform have been made. We cannot, in this analytical volume, go into the details of the story of how the Parliamentary Committee of 1895, by the casting vote of its chairman, imposed a brand new constitution on the Trade Union Congress. We need only remind the reader that by the new Standing Orders, which were held to govern the Cardiff Congress before they were adopted, the Parliamentary Committee brought in three important innovations. No Trade Unionist could be elected as a delegate unless he was either a paid official of his own union, or else still working at his original trade. The Trades Councils were excluded from all representation or participation in the Congress. And, most important of all, the method of voting in Congress was changed from the ordinary practice of Representative Assemblies to a system of voting by trades. These alterations, it will be seen, do not proceed along the lines which we have suggested. There is no proposal to increase the efficiency or strengthen the staff of the Parliamentary Committee, or to co-ordinate the several parts of

the political machine. Instead of intellectual leadership being provided, we see an attempt merely to silence or exclude the troublesome elements. We need not dwell upon the first of the alterations, aimed, as it was, merely at one or two influential delegates whose exclusion was desired by the dominant officials. By abruptly turning out the Trades Councils, who actually initiated the Congress twenty-seven years before, and had ever since taken a vigorous part, the Parliamentary Committee cut adrift the very bodies upon which any effective Trade Union campaign in the constituencies must depend. The Trades Councils, thus " outlawed " from the Trade Union world, are now centres of bitter hostility to the salaried officials of the great trades ; sources of dissension and political weakness, instead of being valuable supports and allies. But the most important and, as we think, most injurious change was that effected in the method of voting. Prior to 1895, though the Unions were allowed to send delegates in proportion to their membership and contribution to the Congress funds, each delegate had an individual vote, and no proxy voting was allowed. In this way, the larger unions could, if they chose to send their full number of dele-gates, exercise their due proportion of voting power. But the officials of some powerful societies found the arrangement inconvenient. In some cases their societies demurred to the expense of sending more than three or four delegates, and thus failed to secure a proportionate influence. In other cases when the full number of delegates was sent, some of these insisted on exercising an independent judgment, and voted according to their own political sympathies, or in response to appeals from the smaller trades. In the absence of any leadership of the Congress as a whole, independence degenerated into anarchy. To the practical officials of the Coal and Cotton industries, the flighty and irresponsible behaviour of the Congress appeared likely to militate against the success of the particular technical measures promoted by their own unions. It does not seem to have occurred to them that it might be their duty to put their brains into the business ; to come forward as the Cabinet of the Congress, formulating a con-sistent policy for the Trade Union world as a whole ; and boldly to appeal for the confidence and the pecuniary support by which alone any policy could be carried into effect. The investigation and co-ordination of the needs of the several trades would have involved, instead of an occasional pleasant jaunt to London, a good deal of hard thinking, and many tedious consultations with experts of all kinds. It was easier to put themselves in a position mechanically to stop the passing of any resolution which seemed likely to be injurious to their trades. The four representatives of the coal and cotton industries on the committee, therefore, insisted on the adoption of the so-called " proxy voting " used by the Miners' Federation in their own conferences. Under this system each trade as a whole is accorded the number of votes to which its aggregate membership entitles it, but is not required to send more than a single delegate. If more than one are sent, they may decide among themselves how the vote of the trade shall be cast, and may even entrust their voting cards to one among their number, and leave the Congress. It is obvious that this mechanical system of voting tends to throw the entire power in the hands of the officials. In fact, already at the Congress of 1895, one society, enjoying forty-five votes, sent only its general secretary to represent it, and as this economical practice leaves the voting power of the union unimpaired, it will certainly be adopted by others. By this system the officers of the great unions have secured their own permanent re-election on the Parliamentary Committee, and, whenever needed, the power to reject any proposal before Congress, without incurring either the " intolerable toil of thought," which due consideration of the needs of the smaller trades would involve, or the trouble of any intellectual leadership of the Congress as a whole.

It will henceforth be less than ever necessary for the officials of the great trades to intervene in the debates, or to seek to guide the less experienced sections of the Trade Union world. Already at Cardiff signs were not wanting that in future Congresses we shall see the big officials, holding the pack of voting cards allotted to their own unions, listening contemptuously to the debating of the smaller trades, and silently voting down any proposition which displeases them.

But the new Standing Orders do more than destroy the value of the Trade Union Congress as a deliberative assembly, and deprive it of its functions as a representative gathering through which the policy and programme of the Parliamentary Committee might be explained to the Trade Union world. The new system of voting contravenes, in the worst possible way, the principles of representation which we have, in our chapter on "Interunion Relations," deduced from the nature of federal association, and is therefore fraught with the gravest danger to the stability of the Congress. The Congress, including as it does, many divergent, and even opposing interests, can never be more than a loose federation for the limited purposes which its several sections have really in common. Its decisions ought therefore to be arrived at, not by mere majority vote, but by consultation between the sections, with a view of discovering the "greatest common measure." But under the present system the Miners' Federation and the United Textile Factory Workers' Association together number a third of the membership represented at the Congress, whilst so long as they act in conjunction with the Amalgamated Societies of Engineers and Carpenters, and the National Union of Boot and Shoe Operatives, they constitute an absolute majority of any possible Congress. To give to five trades an absolute majority over the combined forces of all the rest, must, if persisted in, either extinguish any chance of energetic political co-operation by the others, or else lead to these forming a new federation of their own.

CHAPTER V

THE STANDARD RATE

AMONG Trade Union Regulations there is one which stands out as practically universal, namely, the insistence on payment according to some definite standard, uniform in its application. Even so rudimentary a form of combination as the " shop club " requires that all its members shall receive, as a minimum, the rate agreed upon with the foreman for the particular job. The organised local or national union carries the principle further, and insists on a Standard Rate of payment for all its members in the town or district. The Standard Rate, it should be observed, is only a minimum, never a maximum. The Friendly Society of Operative Stonemasons, for instance, agrees (1897) with the London Central Master Builders' Association that all its able-bodied members shall receive not less than tenpence halfpenny per hour. But the Society has no objection to an employer offering a particular stonemason, whose skill or character is valued, any higher rate that he may choose. The Amalgamated Society of Tailors, in conjunction with the Master Tailors' Association of the particular town, settles a " log " fixing the payment for each kind of garment. But this does not prevent West End master tailors, with the full sanction of the union, paying some members far above the London log rates. In fact, though there are certain seeming exceptions with which we shall deal separately, we know of no case in which a Trade Union forbids or discourages its members from receiving a higher rate of remuneration, for the work actually performed, than the common Standard Rate fixed for the whole body.

But although the Standard Rate is a minimum, not a maximum, the establishment of this minimum necessarily results in a nearer approximation to equality of rates than would otherwise prevail. Trade Union officials who have had to construct a piecework list, or to extend such a list from one shop to the whole town, or from one town to the whole trade, know that, in order to secure a standard list of prices, they have had to pare down the rates hitherto enjoyed by particular shops or even particular towns. It is exactly this willingness on the part of the more fortunately situated sections of the trade to forego, for the sake of a Standard Rate, the higher rates which happen, by some accident, to have become current for a particular line of work, that makes uniformity possible. We have already cited, in describing how Trade Unionism breaks down local monopoly, the case of the Cotton-weavers, who discovered that, in order to secure a uniform list of piecework prices—meaning, to the majority of members, an advance of wages—one or two districts had to consent to a positive reduction of the rates they had hitherto enjoyed.[1] The powerful society of Flint Glass Makers has recently afforded us an even more striking example. When in 1895 the Flint Glass Makers concerted with their employers a uniform "catalogue of prices" for all the glass works in Yorkshire, the York branch, which enjoyed higher rates than any other in the county, at first vehemently protested. A uniform list, they urged, "was impracticable, unless by some section of us making enormous sacrifices"; and its enforcement would involve the "edifying spectacle of a Trade Union compelling its members to work at a reduced wage, when neither they nor the employer desired it."[2] Notwithstanding this protest, the members of the union

---

[1] See the chapter on "The Unit of Government."

[2] Letter from T. Mawson, a member of the York branch, in the *Flint Glass Makers' Magazine*, October 1895; vol. ii. No. 8, pp. 427, 428.

approved the preparation of the uniform list, which was submitted to general meetings of all the Yorkshire branches. The issue was thus put before the York members, and though it was made clear that the new list would involve a reduction of their own earnings, the feeling in favor of uniformity was so strong that, as the general secretary records, out of a total of eighty-four members in the branch at the time, " the vote against the catalogue was only the miserable total of nine." [1]

This conception of a Standard Rate is, as we need hardly explain, an indispensable requisite of Collective Bargaining. Without some common measure, applicable to all the workmen concerned, no general treaty with regard to wages would be possible. But the use of a definite standard of measurement is not merely an adjunct of the Method of Collective Bargaining. It is required for any wholesale determination of wages upon broad principles. The most autocratic and unfettered employer spontaneously adopts Standard Rates for classes of workmen, just as the large shopkeeper fixes his prices, not according to the higgling capacity of particular customers, but by a definite percentage on cost.[2] This conception of a consistent standard of measurement the Trade Union seeks to extend from establishments to districts, and from districts to the whole area of the trade within the kingdom.

This Trade Unionist insistence on a Standard Rate has been the subject of bitter denunciation. The payment of "bad and lazy workmen as highly as those who are skilled and industrious," [3] " setting a premium on idleness and incapacity,"

---

[1] Address of the Central Secretary of the Society, in the *Flint Glass Makers' Magazine*, October 1895 ; vol. ii. No. 8, pp. 447-451.

[2] Practical convenience and the growth of large establishments have, no doubt, much to do with the adoption of uniformity. The little working master, or small employer, could know personally every workman, and adjust without much difficulty a graduated rate of wages. But the modern employer of labor on a large scale cannot be bothered with precisely graduated special rates for each of his thousand " hands." It suits him better to adopt some common principle of payment, simple of application by his clerks and easily comprehended by the workmen.

Measures for putting an End to the Abuses of Trade Unions, by Frederic Hill (London, 1868), p. 3. So persistent is this delusion that Mr. Lecky, writing "destructive to the legitimate ambition of industry and merit," that "worst kind of Communism, the equal remuneration of all men," are only samples of the abusive rhetoric of capitalists and philosophers on the subject. Even as lately as 1871 a distinguished economist poured out the following tirade against the assumed wickedness of the Trade Unions in this respect : " Not yet, but in course of time, as economic principles become popularly understood, we shall see Trade Unions purged of their most erroneous and mischievous purpose of seeking an *uniform rate of wages without regard to differences of skill, knowledge, industry, and character*. There is no tenet of Socialism more fatal in its consequences than this insidious and plausible doctrine—a doctrine which, if acted upon rigidly for any length of time by large classes of men, would stop all progress. Put in plain language it means that there shall not be in the world any such thing as superior talent or attainment ; that every art and handicraft shall be reduced to the level of the commonest, most ignorant, and most stupid of the persons who belong to it." [1]

Such criticisms are beside the mark. A very slight acquaintance with Trade Unionism would have shown these writers that a uniform Standard Rate in no way implies equality of weekly wages, and has no such object. For good or for evil, the typical British workman is not by any means a Communist, and the Trade Union regulations are, as we shall see, quite free from any theoretic " yearnings for equal division of unequal earnings."

The misapprehension arises from a confusion between the rate of payment and the amount actually earned by the workman. What the Trade Union insists on, as a necessary condition of the very existence of Collective Bargaining, is a Standard *Rate* of payment for the work actually performed. But this is consistent with the widest possible divergence

in 1896, naïvely echoes the charge against the Trade Unions by implying that "they insist on the worst workman being paid as much as the best."—*Democracy and Liberty*, vol. ii. p. 385.

[1] Presidential Address of William Newmarch at Social Science Congress of 1871 (*Transactions of Social Science Association*, 1871, p. 117).

between the actual weekly incomes of different workmen. Thus we have the significant fact that the Standard Rate insisted on by the great majority of Trade Unionists is, not any definite sum per hour, but a list of piecework prices. The extent to which these piecework lists prevail throughout the country is seldom realised. Even those who have heard of the elaborate tonnage rates of the Ironworkers, Steel-smelters, and Coalminers, and the complicated cotton lists, which together govern the remuneration of a fourth of the Trade Union world, often forget the innumerable other trades, in which (as with the Tailors, Bootmakers, Compositors, Coopers, Basketmakers, Brushmakers) lists of prices, signed by employers and employed, and revised from time to time, date from the very beginning of the century.[1] When, as in all these cases, the Standard Rate takes the form of a schedule of piecework prices, it is clear that there can be no question of equalising the actual earnings of different workmen. One basketmaker or one coalminer may be earning two pounds a week, whilst another, receiving the same Standard Rate and working the same number of hours, may get less than thirty shillings ; and another, putting in only half-time, may have only ten or fifteen shillings for his week's income.

Nor can it be assumed that in the industries in which the Trade Union rate is not based on piecework, but takes the form of a definite standard wage per hour, this necessarily implies equality of remuneration. Even where workmen in such trades put in the same number of hours, their weekly incomes will often be found to differ very materially. Thus, whilst ordinary plumbing, bricklaying, and masonry is paid for at uniform rates per hour, directly the job involves any special skill, the employer finds it advantageous to pay a higher rate, and the Trade Union cordially encourages this practice. The superior bricklayer, for instance, is seldom

---

[1] These piecework lists can now be conveniently studied in the admirable selection published by the Labor Department of the Board of Trade as Part II. of the Report on Wages and Hours of Labor, 1894 [C, 7567,-1].

employed at the Standard Rate, but is always getting jobs
at brick-cutting (or " gauge work "), furnace-building, or sewer
construction, paid for at rates from ten to fifty per cent
over the standard wage.　In all industries we find firms with
special reputations for a high class of production habitually
paying, with full Trade Union approval, more than the
Trade Union rate, in order to attract to their establishment
the most skilful and best conducted workmen.　In other
cases, where the employer rigidly adheres to the common
rate, the superior workman finds his advantage, if not
actually in higher money earnings, in more agreeable
conditions of employment.　In a large building the
employer will select his best stonemasons to do the carving,
an occupation not involving great exertion and consistent
with an occasional pipe, whilst the common run of workmen
will be setting stones under the foreman's eye.　The best
carpenters, when not earning extra rates for " staircasing "
or " handrailing," will get the fine work which combines
variety and lightness, and is done in the workshop, leaving
to the rougher hands the laying down of flooring and other
heavy mechanical tasks.　These distinctions may seem
trivial to the professional or business man, who to a large
extent controls the conditions under which he works.　But
no workman fails to appreciate the radical difference in
net advantageousness between two different jobs, one involving exposure to the weather, wear and tear of clothing,
monotonous muscular exertion, and incessant supervision,
and the other admitting a considerable share of personal
liberty, agreeably diversified in character, and affording scope
for initiative and address.　Though there may be in such
cases equality in the number of shillings received at the end
of the week, the remuneration for the efforts and sacrifices
actually made will have been at very different rates in the
two cases.

We do not wish to obscure the fact that a Standard
Rate on a timework basis does, in practice, result in a nearer
approach to uniformity of money earnings than a Standard

Rate on a piecework basis. Nor is there any doubt that a considerable section of the wage-earning class have a deeply-rooted conviction that the conscientious, industrious, and slow mechanic ought in equity to receive no less pay than his quicker but equally meritorious neighbour ; more especially as the normal earnings of even the quickest mechanic do not amount to more than is demanded for the proper maintenance of his household. It is often assumed that this conviction has produced, in the Trade Union world, a fundamental objection to piecework. Had this been the case, it would have been strange that we should have had to quote, as typical instances of Unions strongly enforcing a Standard Rate, so many trades in which piecework universally prevails. The annexed table will show that, whilst certain important trades enforce time wages, a large majority of organised trades either insist on, or willingly accept, piecework remuneration.[1] By an analysis of this table we shall prove that this remarkable divergence of view arises, almost exclusively, from the character of the operations performed. What the Trade Unionists are aiming at, in the one case as in the other, is, as we have explained, uniformity in the *rate* of remuneration. In some industries this can be maintained only by insisting on time wages. In others, covering, as it happens, a far larger number of organised workmen, time wages would produce just the opposite result, and the Trade Unionists accordingly insist, with equal determination, on payment by the piece.

---

[1] Though payment by the piece is as old as the relation of employer and wage-earner, the first serious study of this method of remuneration appears to be that of Marx (*Capital*, part iv. ch. xxi.), who draws attention, as usual, to the valuable glimpses of its working afforded by the official reports of the Inspectors of Factories and the Children's Employment Commission. For further information see the careful analysis of Mr. D. F. Schloss, in his *Methods of Industrial Remuneration* (London, 1st edition, 1891 ; 2nd edition, 1894) ; and his exhaustive Reports to the Labor Department of the Board of Trade on Profit-sharing, Gain-sharing, and Co-operative Contracts respectively. But neither Karl Marx nor Mr. Schloss, nor any other writer known to us, seems to have perceived the explanation of the difference in the attitude towards piecework between the different Trade Unions.

Tables showing with regard to all the Trade Unions in the United Kingdom having more than 1000 members (those of unskilled laborers and transport workers being omitted), whether they systematically enforce piecework or time wages respectively, or whether they willingly recognise both methods of remuneration.[1]

I.—Trade Unions which insist on Piecework

	Membership in 1894.
Coalminers (including Miners' Federation, Durham, Northumberland, South Wales, Forest of Dean, and West Bromwich)	322,000
Cleveland Ironstone Miners	3,700
Amalgamated Association of Operative Cotton-spinners .	18,250
Northern Counties Association of Cotton-weavers . .	83,600
Amalgamated Society of Lacemakers, Nottingham . .	3,500
Amalgamated Society of Tailors (and Scottish ditto) .	19,500
National Union of Boot and Shoe Operatives . .	44,000
Amalgamated Society of Boot and Shoe Makers . .	4,300
Associated Iron and Steel Workers	6,700
Flint Glass Makers' Society	2,150
Yorkshire Glass Bottle Makers	2,450
Sheffield File Cutters	1,700
Amalgamated Wire Drawers	1,600
British Steel Smelters	2,400
South Wales Tinplate Workers	6,000
Staffordshire Hollow Ware Pressers (Potters) . .	1,350
Kidderminster Carpet Weavers	1,400
Hosiery Workers' Federation	3,900
Felt Hat Makers	3,150
Cigar Makers	1,250
United Society of Curriers	1,100
16 other Societies	39,000
49 Trade Unions	573,000

[1] The printed table is summarised from one including every Trade Union in the United Kingdom which has as many as 1000 members (omitting those of general laborers and transport workers). Its total of 1,003,000 represents nine-tenths of the Trade Union world (with the same omission), the remaining tenth, which is dispersed in hundreds of tiny unions, being similarly divided. Of the 111 principal organisations we see that 49, having 57 per cent of the aggregate membership, actually insist on piecework, whilst 73 out of the 111, having 71 per cent of the aggregate membership, either insist on piecework, or willingly recognise it. The unions which fight against piecework number 38, having only 29 per cent of the aggregate membership.

It is interesting to compare this analysis of Trade Union artisans with the rough estimate made by the Labor Department for the whole wage-earning population.

II.—Trade Unions which willingly recognise, in various Departments, both Piecework and Timework

United Society of Boilermakers and Iron-shipbuilders . 39,650
Associated Shipwrights' Society 13,750
Amalgamated Brassworkers' Society 5,100
Associated Blacksmiths' Society 2,350
Sailmakers' Federation 1,250
Spindle and Flyer Makers, Lancashire . . . 1,150
Amalgamated Card and Blowing Room Operatives . . 22,200
Typographical Association, London Society of Compositors,
    Scottish and other Compositors' Unions . . 31,000
Bookbinders (two societies) 4,350
Mutual Association of Coopers 6,000
Cabinetmakers (three societies) 7,100
Six other Societies 6,100

       24 Trade Unions 140,000

III.—Trade Unions which insist on Timework

Amalgamated Society of Engineers . . . 78,450
Friendly Society of Ironfounders 15,200
United Pattern-makers' Association 3,150
United Society of Brassfounders . . . 2,750
Amalgamated Society of Carpenters (and two other societies) 58,000
Friendly Society of Operative Stonemasons (with Scottish ditto) 25,000
Operative Bricklayers' Society (and another society) . . 26,700
National Union of Operative Plasterers . . . 8,500
United Society of Operative Plumbers . . . 8,150
Amalgamated Society of Lithographic Printers . . 2,550
Bradford Dyers 2,700
Bakers (English, Scottish, and Irish) . . . 8,950
United Kingdom Society of Coachmakers . . . 5,700
18 other Societies 44,200

       38 Trade Unions 290,000

The first thing we notice in these tables is that, among the trades in which piecework is either insisted on by the

Excluding agriculture and domestic service, about 33 per cent of the male wage-earners in the United Kingdom are supposed to be engaged in piecework trades, and 67 per cent in timework trades. It seems probable, therefore, that among Trade Unionists a larger percentage work by the piece than among the workers in unorganised trades.

men, or readily accepted by them, we find the largest and the most powerful Trade Unions. The Miners and Cotton Operatives, who would instantly strike against any attempt to introduce time wages, are only paralleled in the strength and extent of their Trade Unions by the Boilermakers and Iron-shipbuilders, who adopt piecework as the basis of the greater part of their wage contracts. And so far is piecework from being objected to by Trade Union officials, that we find, in these trades, that the preponderating part of the Trade Union machinery, including the ablest and most influential officials, has been called into existence for the express purpose of dealing with piecework lists. The district delegates of the Boilermakers, the secretaries of the Cotton Operatives, the investigators of the Boot and Shoe Operatives, and the checkweigh-men of the Coalminers spend their whole lives in arranging remuneration on a piecework basis.

On the other hand, though the time workers are in the minority, we have among them some very strong unions, such as the Stonemasons, the Bricklayers, and the Plumbers, who have always vehemently denounced piecework as the bane of their trades. How can we explain this divergence?

On asking a leading official of the Cotton-spinners' union why he objected to time wages, he replied that, in his opinion, it was only the system of piecework remuneration that had saved his trade from the evils of sweating. The work of a cotton-spinner, he explained, varies in intensity (and his product in quantity) according to the number of spindles which he has to attend to, and the speed at which the machinery runs, conditions over which the operative has no control. Owing to the introduction of mules bearing an increased number of spindles, and the constant " speeding up " of the machinery, the amount of work placed upon the operative is steadily, though often imperceptibly, increased.[1]

[1] " It would be a mistake if we imagined that labor had become easier compared with former times. As far as a comparison can be made, the opposite is the case. A handloom weaver can work 13 hours per day ; to let a six-loom weaver work 13 hours is a physical impossibility. The nature of the work has entirely changed. In place of muscular exertion there is now the minding of the

If he were paid by the hour or the day, he would need, in order to maintain the same rate of remuneration for the work done, to discover each day precisely to what degree the machinery was being "speeded up," and to be perpetually making demands for an increase in his time wages. Such an arrangement could not fail to result in the employer increasing the work faster than the pay.

Under a system of payment by the amount of yarn spun, the operative automatically gets the benefit of any increase in the number of spindles or rate of speed. An exact uniformity of the rate of remuneration is maintained between man and man, and between mill and mill. If any improvement takes place in the process, by which the operative's labor is reduced, the onus of procuring a change in the rate of pay falls on the employer. The result is, that so effectually is the cotton-spinner secured by his piecework lists against being compelled to give more work without more pay, that it has been found desirable deliberately to concede to the employers, by lowering the rates as the number of spindles increases, some share of the resulting advantages, in order that the Trade Union may encourage enterprising mill-owners in the career of improvement. The cotton-weavers have a similar experience. The weaver's labor depends upon the character of the cloth to be woven, involving a complicated calculation of the number of "picks," etc. Time wages would leave them practically at the employers' mercy for all but the very easiest work. But by a highly technical and complex list of piecework rates, every element by which the labor is increased effects an exactly corresponding variation in the remuneration. Only under such a system could any uniformity of rate be secured.

In another great class of cases piecework is preferred by

machine, *i.e.* mental strain. Those who have observed the mulespinner in Oldham in the midst of the whirling of 2500 spindles, or the female worker in Burnley environed by four or six shuttles, working at the speed of 200 picks per minute, know what a higher degree of mental application is here demanded."— *The Cotton Trade in England and on the Continent*, by Dr. G. von Schulze-Gaevernitz (London, 1895), pp. 126, 127.

the workmen, with the same object of securing a Standard
Rate, but under entirely different conditions. The coalminers have, in some counties, had a long experience of
both time wages and piecework, with the result that, where-
ever there is a strong Trade Union, piecework is insisted on for
all hewers. The explanation is to be found in the circumstances under which the work is done. Employers have
found it impossible to supervise by foremen or managers the
numerous hewers scattered in the recesses of the mine. The
only possible alternative to paying the hewers at piecework
rates, was to let out the different parts of the mine to
working contractors, who engaged hewers by the hour to
work alongside them. This was the notorious " Butty
System," against which the organised hewers have persistently
struggled. It was found that, whatever was the customary
standard of daily time wages, the " Butty Master," who set
the pace, was always increasing the quantity of work to be
done for those wages by himself putting in an unusual
intensity of effort. It is obvious that, under this system, the
ordinary hewer lost all security of a Standard Rate. It paid
the Butty Master to be always " speeding up," because he
received the product, not of his own extra exertion alone,
but of that of all his gang. The only method by which the
ordinary hewers could secure identity of rate was to dispense
with the Butty Masters, and themselves work by the piece.

We shall find exactly the same preference for piecework
wages in other trades among men who work under a sub-
contractor, or in subordination to another class of workmen
paid by the piece. The strikers, for instance, who work with
smiths paid by the piece, were themselves formerly paid time
wages. In most parts of the country they have now been
successful in obtaining the boon of a piecework rate proportionate to that of the smiths, so that they are secured
extra remuneration for any extra spurt put on by the smith.
Another large class of workmen in a somewhat similar
position have not been so fortunate. The shipyard " helpers,"
who work under the platers (iron-shipbuilders), are paid by

the day, whilst the platers receive piecework rates. The first object of any combination of helpers has always been to secure piecework rates, in order that their remuneration might bear some proportion to the rapidity and intensity of work, the pace being set by the platers. But owing to the strength of the Boilermakers' Union, to which the platers belong, the helpers have never been able to attain their object.[1] The iron and steel industries afford numerous other instances in which workers paid by the day are in subordination to workers paid by the piece. In all these cases, the subordinate workers desire to be paid by the piece, in order that they may secure a greater uniformity in the rate of payment for the work actually done.

Coming now to the trades in which piecework is most strongly objected to by the operatives, we shall find the argument again turning upon the question of uniformity of the rate of remuneration. The engineers have always protested that the introduction of piecework into their trade almost necessarily implied a reversion to Individual Bargaining. The work of a skilled mechanic in an engineering shop differs from job to job in such a way as to make, under a piecework system, a new contract necessary for each job. Each man, too, will be employed at an operation differing, if only in slight degree, from those of his fellows. If they are all working by the hour, a collective bargain can easily be made and adhered to. But where each successive job differs from the last, if only in small details, it is impossible to work out in advance any list of prices to which all the men can agree to adhere. The settlement for each job must necessarily be left to be made between the foreman and the workman concerned. Collective Bargaining becomes, therefore, impossible. But this is not all. The uncertainty as to the

---

[1] See, for the Boilermakers' or Platers' Helpers, the paper by J. Lynch, in the *Report of the Industrial Remuneration Conference* (London, 1885), and the discussion at the Trade Union Congress of 1878. Many of the helpers are now members of the National Amalgamated Union of Labor and other laborers' unions ; see the evidence given on their behalf before the Royal Commission on Labor, 17th May 1892, Group A.

time and labor which a particular job will involve makes it impossible for the foreman, with the best intentions in the world, to fix the prices of successive jobs so that the workman will obtain the same earnings for the same effort. And when we remember the disadvantage at which, unprotected by collective action, the individual operative necessarily stands in bargaining with the capitalist employer, we shall easily understand how the Amalgamated Society of Engineers should have been led to declare that, under this system of settling a special price for each job, " it is well known that piecework is not a bargain, but a price dictated by the employer and lowered at will." And the report adds that " the system has often been made the instrument of large reductions of wages, which have ended in the deterioration of the conditions of the workmen. . . . If an expert workman, by his skill and industry, earns more than his neighbour, and much more than his daily wages come to, a reduction is at once made, and made again until eventually the most expert is only able, by intense application and industry, to earn a bare living, whilst the less skilful is reduced below living prices." [1]

We could cite from the reports of the great national unions of the Engineers, Ironfounders, and Carpenters innumerable similar protests against piecework in their trades, all based upon the proved impossibility of maintaining a Standard Rate, if each job has to be separately priced. It

[1] *Abstract Report of the Council's* (of the A. S. E.) *Proceedings*, September 1860 to April 1862, pp. 24-26.

This process of fixing a piecework rate for all the men, by the speed of an exceptionally expert workman under special pressure, has been more than once unconsciously revealed by employers. Already in 1727, in a manual entitled *The Duty of a Steward to his Lord*, by Edward Laurence, naïve directions are given how to achieve this object. "Also if any new sort of work is to be done, not mentioned in the following particulars, the Steward's best way is to hire a *good* labourer *and to stand by him the whole day* to see that he does a good day's work, and then to measure the same, in order to know what it is worth." The efficacy of piecework, as an expedient for reducing wages was described in a letter to the *Times* in 1852 by Charles Walker and Sons, an engineering firm. " When work which has been done daywork is put on the piece, the employer usually regulates the piecework price *a little under the price of it at daywork*, knowing

is, however, more interesting to watch the same conviction being gradually borne in upon the mind of an exceptionally able employer. In 1876, William Denny, the well-known Clyde shipbuilder, who had put his whole establishment on piecework rates, delivered a remarkable lecture on the advantages of this method of remuneration, alike to the employer and to the workmen, specially commending the intensity of competition which it secured. He was utterly unable to understand why the workmen objected to a system which, in giving an "increase of from 25 to 50 per cent in his wages—and this increase my experience confirms as a rule—puts at once within his power a more comfortable and easy style of living, combined with an opportunity of saving, which, if he is a sober and careful man, will enable him to enjoy a pleasant old age, and even to lay by sufficient money to enable him to refuse on his own account any rate of payment which he deems insufficient." [1]

Notwithstanding all these allurements, the Trade Unions persisted in their objection. After ten years' further experience of the working of piecework, William Denny at last perceived the real root of the men's protest. In an interesting letter written in 1886 he describes his own conversion :—

At the time I published my pamphlet *The Worth of Wages*, I was under the impression piecework rates would regulate themselves as I then assumed time wages did. A larger experience of piecework has convinced me that, excepting in cases where rates can be fixed and made

---

how production is increased by it. But he finds that men do work in quantity far beyond what they have been doing daywork, earning often 10s. per day, when at daywork they had done much less than half the work at 5s. 6d. per day. So much, indeed, is this the case, that manufacturers have made it a private rule that men for their extra work should earn 'time and quarter' or 'time and third,' and *have reduced the price accordingly ;* that is, where 5s. was the man's day pay, the price should be so arranged that ultimately he should earn 6s. 3d. or 6s. 8d. per day. This method we do not quite agree with, and we believe it has made men complain " (*Times*, 9th January 1852). Thus the employer not only gets the advantage of an increased output upon the same fixed capital, but actually contrives also insidiously to alter, to his own profit, the proportion between the muscular energy expended by the workman and the amount of food which the latter obtains.

[1] *The Worth of Wages*, by William Denny (Dumbarton, 1876).

a matter of agreement between the whole body of the men in any works and their employers, piecework prices have not a self-regulating power, and are liable, under the pressure of heavy competition, to be depressed below what I would consider a proper level. You must understand there is a broad and very real distinction in piecework between the kind of work which can be priced in regular rates and that in which contracts are taken by the men for lump jobs of greater or less extent. In the former kind of piecework it is easily possible for the rates to be effectively controlled by the joint efforts of the employers and the workpeople, as it is in the case of time wages. In the latter, owing to there being no definite standard, it is quite possible that the prices may be raised too high for competitive efficiency, or depressed to too low a point to recoup the workmen for the extra exertion and initiative induced by the very nature of piecework. In such work as that of rivetters, iron fitters, and platers and in much of carpenters' work standards of price or rates can be arranged or controlled, and the workers are not likely to endure any arrangement they may consider inequitable. They are indeed much more likely by insisting on uniform rates for a whole district to do injustice to the more intelligent and energetic employers, who, by introducing new machinery and new processes, are directly influential in drawing work to their districts. It is evident that if piecework rates are not reduced so as to make the improvements in machinery and methods introduced by such employers fully effective in diminishing cost of production, there will be a tendency on their part to abandon these attempts, with diminished chances of work for their districts. In the case of such improvements it is possible to reduce rates without in any way reducing the effective earnings of the work-people. I may say that in our own experience we have almost invariably found our workers quite willing to consider these points fairly and intelligently. Frequently they themselves make such suggestions as materially help us to reduce cost of production. Such cases of invention and helpfulness on their part are rewarded directly through our awards scheme of which you have particulars.

In the second kind of piecework, involving contracts which cannot be arranged by rates and controlled by the whole body of the workers, the prices are necessarily a matter of settlement between individual workmen and small groups of workmen and their foreman. Here it depends upon the control exercised by the heads of the business whether this kind of piecework drifts into extravagances, or into such reductions of contract prices as either to reduce them to less than the value of time wages or to so little above time wages that they do not compensate the men for their extra exertions. We have found in testing such piecework that the best method is to compare the earnings made by these piece-workers in a given period with the time wages which they would have received for the same period ; and it is the duty of one of our partners to control this section of the work, and he does it almost invariably to he advantage of the men. Our idea is that the men should be able to average from 25 to 50 per cent more wages on such piecework within a given time than their time wages would amount to. There are occasional and exceptional cases where the results are less or more favourable. Where they are less favourable, we consider them to be not only a loss to the men, but disadvantageous to ourselves ; and our reason for this is very clear, as unless the men feel that their exertions produce really better wages, and that increased exertions and better arrangements of work will produce still further increases of wages, there is an end to all stimulus to activity or improvement.

I know an instance in which a well-meaning foreman, desirous of diminishing the cost of the work in his department, reduced his piece-work prices to such a point that he not only removed all healthy stimulus to activity from his workmen, but produced among them serious discontent. Our method of piecework analysis and control enabled us to discover and remedy this before serious disaffection had been produced. I know another instance in which a foreman, while avoiding the mistake I have just mentioned, gave out his contracts in such small and scattered portions, and under such conditions as to the way in which the work was to be done and as to the composition of the co-partneries formed by the men, that he not only reduced their earnings to very nearly time rates, but created very serious disaffection among them. He was in the habit of forcing the men to take into their co-partneries personal favourites of his own, who very naturally became burdens upon those co-partneries. As soon as our returns and inquiries revealed to us these facts, we insisted that the contracts entered into with the men should be of a sufficient money amount to enable them to organise themselves and their work efficiently. We removed the defective arrangements above referred to, and laid down the principle that their co-partneries were to be purely voluntary. We were enabled by these means, and without altering a single price, to at once raise their earnings from a level a little above what they could have made on time wages to a very satisfactory percentage of increase and to remove all discontent. These two instances will show you how necessary it is in this kind of piecework that there should be a direct control over those who are carrying it out. When the heads of a business are absentees or indifferent the most effective way in which the workmen can control such piecework would be by taking care that the standard of time wages was always kept perfectly clear and effective, and that regular comparisons per hour on piecework were made. Such comparisons would immediately enable them to arrive at a correct conclusion as to whether the prices paid them were sufficiently profitable.

There is besides a mixed kind of piecework in which skilled workmen employ laborers at time wages to do the unskilled portion of their work for them. Here, too, some kind of control is required, as instances occasionally occur in which the skilled workmen treat their laborers, either intentionally or unintentionally, with harshness. I have even known an instance in which such piecework contractors reduced their laborers' time wages on the pay day without having given them any previous notice. On the other hand, there are instances in which these laborers behaved in an unreasonable and unfair spirit to the skilled workmen who employ them.

In conclusion, I would say that the method of piecework is one which cannot be approved or condemned absolutely, but is dependent upon the spirit and the way in which it is carried out for the verdict which should be passed upon it. It is imperative in such kinds of piecework as by their nature cannot be reduced to regular rates that either the employer should take the responsibility of safeguarding his workmen's interests, or that the workmen themselves should, by such a method as I have suggested, obtain an effective control over them.

There are besides conditions in which even piecework rates of a general nature may become instruments of very great hardship. I mean instances in which the workers are incapable of effective resistance, and in which employers are either themselves ground down under the force of a competition with which they are unable to cope, or in which, while the employers possess extreme powers of position and capital, they are deficient in any corresponding sense of responsibility to their workpeople. I hope the day is not far distant in which an absentee employer would be looked upon with as much contempt and disapproval as are absentee landlords. If such a healthy public opinion should ever become dominant, it is to be hoped it will be most active in influencing those employers whose works are conducted in great part or wholly upon the piecework method.[1]

We have, in this able explanation, a frank admission of the whole case of the Amalgamated Society of Engineers against the introduction of piecework into their trade. No Trade Unionist could have expressed more forcibly than Denny has done the impossibility of a uniform rate under a system of individual piecework bargains. It is true that Denny trusted to the personal intervention of an enlightened and benevolent employer to mitigate the evil. But we need not wonder that the workmen have hesitated to admit a system which avowedly involves the complete surrender of their position. Moreover, it is at least doubtful whether the good employer, who protected his workmen against his own

[1] *Life of William Denny*, by A. B. Bruce (London, 1889), p. 113; see the article on Denny (who lived from 1847 to 1887) in the *Dictionary of Political Economy*.

foreman's zeal to lower the expense of production, would long survive in competition with his less scrupulous rivals, who drove the sharpest possible bargain with their hands.

It is interesting to observe that the hint thrown out by William Denny, as to the importance of workmen systematically checking all the piecework earnings by the standard time rate, has since been followed up by the Amalgamated Society of Engineers. In some cases, piecework is now recognised by the union, even in highly organised districts, on the understanding that every man in the shop shall draw every week time and a quarter wages, *whatever his production has been*. If at the end of a job there is a balance due to him, he is allowed to receive it. Now, it is obvious that under this arrangement it is possible to maintain something like a uniform rate. The natural tendency of the foreman to reduce the rates is checked by his knowledge, first, that in no case will it profit him to make the piecework price work out at less than time and a quarter, even for the slowest men in the shop ; and secondly, that, unless the piecework prices work out sufficiently above that minimum to furnish a real incentive for extra exertion, the operatives, secure in any event of time and a quarter wages, would quietly drop back to time-work speed. Such a method of remuneration cannot, however, be classed as piecework proper. It is rather a high scale of time wages, with a bonus on extra output.[1]

The considerations which converted William Denny from his enthusiasm for competitive piecework apply, not only to the various departments of the engineering and shipbuilding trades, but also to the work of carpenters, plumbers, stonemasons, and bricklayers. In all these trades there is so much difference between job and job that piecework is inconsistent with Collective Bargaining. The work of the plumber engaged to lay pipes, of varying sizes, in all kinds of situations, can obviously be estimated only by the time

---

[1] For other varieties of "bonus on output," see the acute discriminations of Mr. D. F. Schloss in *The Methods of Industrial Remuneration*, 2nd ed. (London, 1894).

employed. The masons, chiselling stones of varied hardness, different shapes, and more or less free from troublesome flaws, could not possibly frame a list of piecework rates which would yield identical wage to identical effort. The same is true of the multifarious work of the carpenter and joiner. When we come to the actual erection of houses, in brick or stone, it may, at first sight, seem as if uniformity was more possible. But if we watch the line of bricklayers or stonemasons working side by side at building a wall, or putting up the carcase of a house, we shall see that it would be impossible precisely to reckon up the work accomplished by any individual among them. Nor has this ever been attempted by the most exacting employer. " Piecework," in putting up walls or houses, has, indeed, been the subject of long and bitter controversy among the bricklayers. But piecework in this trade has always meant, not the payment of each individual workman by the piece, but the letting out of a sub-contract for the whole job to a " piecemaster," who gets it done by bricklayers *at time wages*. This system of sub-contract, mistermed " piecework " to the confusion of outsiders, is objected to for the same reason as the coal-miners allege against the " Butty System." The working sub-contractor forces the pace in order to gain the advantage, not of his own extra exertion alone, but also that of his gang. It is, in fact, a fraudulent attempt to obtain piece-work exertion whilst paying only time wages. And as the system, in the opinion of the experts, almost inevitably tends to the " scamping " of the work by the sub-contractor or piece-master, it has long since been given up by respectable builders, and is now usually prohibited in architects' specifications.

In marked contrast with the Trade Unions, such as the Cotton Operatives and Coalminers, which insist on piece-work, and with those, such as the Bricklayers and Stone-masons, which insist on timework, stand those societies which accept with seeming indifference either method of remunera-tion. The various Trade Unions of the compositors, in all parts of the country, have, for over a century, formally recognised both the "scale" of piecework rates and the "stab" or time wages. In the numerous revisions of the collective agreements between employers and employed, the compositors have constantly striven to maintain a standard rate. "Speaking generally," reports the Revision Sub-Committee to the London Society of Compositors in 1890, "our desire has been to so amend the scale as to place all compositors as far as possible on an equality, no matter what class of work they may be engaged upon, or whether employed as piece or 'stab hands—allowance, of course, being made for the varying capabilities of those employed."[1] Although the work of a compositor includes many different varieties, these, unlike certain engineering operations, are all capable of fairly precise enumeration in a "scale" extending to between 30 and 40 pages octavo. Thus, piecework is in no way inconsistent with Collective Bargaining, or the maintenance of a Standard Rate, and is therefore not objected to. On the other hand, the compositor is not liable to be "speeded up," nor yet over-driven by machinery or a zealous foreman, so that there is no reason to object to time wages, if the employer prefers this system.[2] As a matter of fact most straightforward setting-up

[1] Report of Sub-Committee appointed to revise the London Scale of Prices, 1890.

[2] The system of payment by the piece was apparently universal in British printing offices in the eighteenth century. The introduction of "establishment," or time wages, was an innovation of the employers at the beginning of the present century, consented to by the operatives with much reluctance, and denounced by some of them as leading to reduction of rates. (See Place MSS. 27,799-99/103.) The acceptance of both systems of remuneration has involved the enactment of various subsidiary rules to check unfair wages calculated to depress rates. Thus employers are not allowed to change from one system to another without due notice, as otherwise the operative would be required to do all difficult composition by the piece, the "fat" (or profitable work) being given out at time wages. Elaborate arrangements are made for the fair distribution of "the fat," the "clicker" who hands out the "copy" to the different compositors being appointed and frequently paid by the "chapel," the ancient organisation of the workmen in each printing office. Many disputes have arisen from employers attempting to withhold "the fat" from the piecework compositors; or, on the other hand, to use the pieceworkers to force the pace of the timeworkers. Compositors' unions therefore prefer that the employer should confine himself to one system or the other.

In 1876 a joint committee of the Glasgow master printers and their compositors decided that the "clicking system," or fair sharing of the "fat," was

of ordinary book matter and daily newspaper work is done by the piece, whereas corrections and special jobs difficult of calculation are done by " stab " men.

The other leading instance of an impartial acceptance of both piecework and time wages is offered by the United Society of Boilermakers and Iron-shipbuilders. Here the bulk of the work in building new ships is done by the piece, at rates settled, as we have already mentioned, between the district committee of the union and the particular firms or the local employers' association. On the other hand, repairing work, which cannot be classified in advance, is done at time wages. Thus the by-laws for the Mersey district declare that " piecework of any description is not allowed on repair jobs in either wet or dry docks ; and no man shall be in any way compelled to put in any given number of rivets, or tasked as to other work, which he shall do during the day ; but in all cases, the principle of a fair day's work for a fair day's pay be faithfully and honorably carried out by every member of this Association." [1] We see the same distinction unconsciously influencing another trade, the Tinplate Workers, who, less fortunate than the Boilermakers, have not succeeded in organising their whole trade into a single society. The General Union of Tinplate Workers, with Liverpool for its headquarters, whose work is mainly connected with shipbuilding, and is so diverse as to render it difficult, if not impossible, to construct any piecework list, insists on time wages. On the other hand, the National Amalgamated Tinplate Workers' Union, with its headquarters at Wolverhampton, which comprises mainly the artificers of sheet metal pots and pans, has a regular list of prices, and prefers to work by the piece. So closely does this difference of policy coincide with difference of work that the Manchester Branch of the General Union (the shipyard society), which

equivalent to an addition to a farthing per 1000, this advance being conceded to the compositors in shops where that system did not prevail.—*MS. Minutes of Glasgow Typographical Society*, 12th December 1876.

[1] *By-laws for the Mersey District United Society of Boilermakers and Iron shipbuilders* (Liverpool, 1889).

finds itself by exception employed in the fashioning of pots and pans, refuses to abide by the principle of time work followed by the port branches, and elects to work by the piece. In both cases the aim is the same, namely the maintenance of a Standard Rate. But the difference of policy between the two societies, arising, as can be seen, from the difference in their respective tasks, is not clearly understood by either, and is the subject of constant friction between them. And so it happens that (forgetting the example of its own Manchester Branch) the General Union of Tinplate Workers accuses the National Amalgamated Tinplate Workers' Union of betraying the central position of Trade Unionism by not insisting on time wages. On the other hand, the latter society, confident in its piecework lists, sees no reason why it should not establish branches of pieceworkers in the ports, where time work has hitherto prevailed, and where piecework would probably break down all Collective Bargaining.

This instance indicates how unconscious particular Trade Unions may be of the principles upon which their empirical action has really been based. The same unconsciousness sometimes leads to a persistence in whichever method of remuneration has been customary, long after the circumstances have changed. Thus the Cabinetmakers, among whom Collective Bargaining in any elaborate form has practically disappeared, might possibly have maintained their organisation if they had, like the Bricklayers and Stonemasons, insisted on reverting to time wages. At the beginning of this century, the Cabinetmakers had elaborate lists of prices, collectively agreed to between employers and employed ; and we have ample evidence of the efficiency with which the contemporary cabinetmakers' unions conducted their Collective Bargaining. In consequence of the great changes in and multiplication of patterns, and the alteration of processes, the lists have long since been obsolete, and no one has yet found it possible to classify the innumerable jobs now involved in the manufacture of furniture. " Estimate work," " lump work," and other forms of the individual bargain accordingly prevail.　So strong, however, has been the tradition and custom of piecework in the trade that none of the various unions which have from time to time arisen during the last half century have been able to stand out for time wages.　Collective action accordingly now seldom rises higher than the " shop bargain," and even this frequently breaks down.

Another instance of a customary adherence to a traditional method of remuneration is to be found in the Ironfounders' and Engineers' rigid refusal to recognise piecework even on those jobs which involve the constant repetition of precisely the same operation.　We have already explained why the bulk of the work in an engineering shop cannot be done at piecework rates consistently with Collective Bargaining.　But with the enormous expansion of the trade, and the application of machinery to particular processes, a considerable section of engineers and " machine moulders " have long found themselves turning out a constant succession of identical articles for which it would be quite practicable to frame a uniform piecework list which would allow of Collective Bargaining.　So strong, however, was the traditional feeling of the mechanics against piecework (meaning " estimate work " and Individual Bargaining) that the Amalgamated Society of Engineers positively refused, down to 1892, to allow any employer to introduce any piecework whatsoever, with the consequence that establishment after establishment became closed to the union.　At last, at their quinquennial " Parliament " in 1892, the Engineers decided to permit the formation of piecework lists, in the cases in which they were practicable, and appointed salaried officers to carry out this new form of Collective Bargaining.　The Friendly Society of Ironfounders still refuses to take this step, with the result that the automatic machine process of casting has fallen to a separate class of workmen, who are not eligible for membership to this old-established union.

We are now in a position to come to some general conclusion as to the attitude which Trade Unions take up with regard to piecework and time work. It is not true that Trade Unions object to piecework as such ; in fact, a majority of Trade Unionists either willingly accept, or else positively insist on, that system of remuneration. Nor is it true that employers universally prefer piecework. The members of the great race of sub-contractors in all industries are always trying to employ time workers, in order to obtain for themselves the fullest possible advantage of their own driving power. In the same way, employers whose machinery is rapidly improving complain of the inequity of the piecework system, as being apt to deprive them of part of the advantage of an increase in the speed of working. What the capitalist seeks is to get more work for the old pay. Sometimes this can be achieved best by piecework, sometimes by time work. Workmen, on the other hand, strive to obtain more pay for the same number of working hours. For the moment, at any rate, the individual operative can most easily secure this by piecework. But not even for the sake of getting more pay for the same number of hours' work will the experienced workman revert to the individual bargain, with all its dangers. Accordingly the Trade Unions accept piecework only when it is consistent with Collective Bargaining, that is, when a standard list of prices can be arrived at between the employers on the one hand, and the representatives of the whole body of workmen on the other. As a matter of fact this is practicable, so far as concerns anything above mere unskilled laboring, in a majority of the organised industries, in which, therefore, piecework prevails by consent of both masters and men. It is, indeed, impossible to decide whether Trade Unionism has, on the whole, favored or discouraged the substitution of piecework for time wages. On the one hand, every increase in Trade Union organisation, and especially every extension of the class of salaried Trade Union officials, has made more possible the arrangement of definite piecework lists. This process is now extending from trade to trade. The very establishment of these lists has, on the other hand, lessened the employers' desire to introduce piecework, whilst to any method of remuneration involving individual bargaining, such as "estimate" or "lump" work, the Trade Unions have shown implacable hostility.

And just as the fundamental idea of the Standard Rate has enabled us to understand the Trade Union attitude towards piecework, so, too, we shall find it throwing light upon various minor regulations of particular Trade Unions. Various unions of operatives working at time wages have from time to time attempted to secure a real, as distinguished from a nominal identity in the rate of remuneration, by fixing, not merely the minimum money wage, but also the maximum amount of work to be done for that wage. Some of these rules have obtained notoriety as classic instances of the folly and perversity of Trade Unions. The fifth by-law of the Bradford Lodge of the Laborers' Union of 1867 was quoted before the Trade Union Commission as follows: "You are strictly cautioned not to outstep good rules by doing double the work you are required, and causing others to do the same, in order to gain a smile from the master."[1] And the following rule of the Leeds Lodge of the Bricklayers' Laborers' Union was at the same time given: "Any brother in the Union professing to carry any more than the common number, which is eight bricks, shall be fined one shilling, to be paid within one month, or remain out of the benefit until such fine be paid."[2] Nor were such rules entirely confined to unskilled laborers. The Manchester Bricklayers' Association were stated, in 1869, to have a rule providing that "Any man found running or working beyond a regular speed shall be fined 2s. 6d. for the first offence, 5s. for the second, 10s. for the third, and if still persisting, shall be dealt with as the Committee think proper."[3] The Friendly Society of Operative Stonemasons adopted, in 1865, the following rule:

---

[1] Evidence of Mr. A. Mault, Secretary of the Manchester Builders' Association. Q. 3120.

[2] *Ibid.* Q. 3122.

[3] W. T. Thornton, *On Labour* (London, 1869), pp. 350, 351.

" In localities where that most obnoxious and destructive
system generally known as ' chasing ' is persisted in, lodges
should use every effort to put it down. Not to take less
time than that taken by an average mason in the execution
of the first portion of each description of work is the practice
that should be adopted among us as much as possible ; and
where it is plainly visible that any member or other individual is striving to overwork or ' chase ' his fellow-workmen, thereby acting in a manner calculated to lead to the
discharge of members or a reduction of their wages, the party
so acting shall be summoned before the lodge, and if the
charge be satisfactorily proved a fine shall be inflicted." [1]

These and similar regulations, widely advertised by the
Trade Union Commission of 1867-69, met with universal
condemnation. It does not seem to have been perceived
that, however bad were their secondary results, they were, in
their inception, a necessary protection of any Standard Rate
upon a time-work basis. It is a necessary incident of the
collective bargain that one man should not underbid another ;
and this underbidding can as easily take place by the offer
of more work for the same hour's wage, as by the offer of
the normal amount of work for a lower hourly wage. By
underbidding in the hourly rate, this would be lowered for
all. It follows equally that by underbidding in point of the
intensity of effort, this would, in the same way, soon be
raised for all. But the workmen's by-laws were designed
also to meet a more insidious attack. Many pushing foremen, in building contracts, intent on getting the utmost work
out of their men, were accustomed to bribe particular workmen with beer, or by the promise of a slightly increased rate
of pay, to work at exceptional speed, with the object of
" pulling on " all the other workmen to the same speed.
These " bell horses," as they were termed by the workmen,
were, in fact, used to increase the intensity of the work beyond the normal standard tacitly implied in the collective

[1] Rule 11, Class 2, p. 31, in *Laws of the Friendly Society of Operative
Stonemasons* (Bolton, 1867).

bargain, much in the same way as the pieceworking Butty Master forced the speed of the time-working coal hewer. The practice was, in fact, a method of obtaining extra work from the whole gang, whilst paying only one or two men in the gang for the extra exertion involved. When done without the men's knowledge, the practice amounted to a fraudulent evasion of the bargain.

Such practices on the part of employers and their foremen would quickly have rendered a Standard Rate and Collective Bargaining impossible, and it was not unnatural that the workmen should have adopted regulations in their own defence. The coal hewers and the strikers, exposed, as we have seen, to being similarly " driven," met the attack by insisting on themselves receiving piecework rates. The cotton-spinners and cotton-weavers protected themselves against the constant "speeding up" of the machinery by elaborating their piecework lists. The builder's laborer whose fetch and carry work could hardly be paid by the piece could find no other expedient than fixing by collective agreement the maximum task as well as the minimum wage.

But if the use of " bell horses " is a fraud on the men, the regulations devised to check this practice may easily work out so as to be a fraud on the employer. He has, in effect, contracted for his labor at an all-round rate, on the assumption that he receives a normal average of work. In the group of workmen there will, of course, be some of average speed, together with a few quicker men, and a few slower. Any regulations which tend to restrict the quick workers necessarily lower the average of the whole, upon which the collective bargain has by implication been based.

This practice of " levelling down " the quantity of labor is seen at its worst when it is used as a weapon not of defence but of aggression. It is one thing to prohibit individual workmen from allowing themselves to be used as a means of exacting unpaid extra labor from their fellows. It would be quite another matter if Trade Unions, unable to raise the sum of their wages, advocated to all their members an insidious diminution of their energy without notice to the employer. This might be as much a fraudulent alteration of the implied bargain as the practice of the Butty Master. We know of one case of this nature, the so-called "go canny" policy, adopted for a short time by the National Union of Dock Laborers in Liverpool. The employers had steadfastly refused to increase the remuneration for their low-paid work, and the men found themselves powerless to obtain what they considered a living wage. In desperation they adopted the expedient of not putting any energy into their work. In this somewhat remarkable case the laborers alleged that they were only following the practice of the commercial man. "There is no ground for doubting," observed the report of their executive committee, "that the real relation of the employer to the workman is simply this—to secure the largest amount of the best kind of work for the smallest wages ; and, undesirable as this relation may be to the workman, there is no escape from it except to adopt the situation and apply it to the common-sense commercial rule which *provides a commodity in accordance with the price.* . . . The employer insists upon fixing the amount he will give for an hour's labor without the slightest consideration for the laborer ; there is, surely, therefore, nothing wrong in the laborer, on the other hand, fixing the amount and the quality of the labor he will give in an hour for the price fixed by the employer. *If employers of labor or purchasers of goods refuse to pay for the genuine article, they must be content with shoddy and veneer.* This is their own orthodox doctrine which they urge us to study."[1]

From the old standpoint of a purely competitive individualism, it is not easy to deny the men's right to sell an adulterated form of labor if they think it to their advantage

---

[1] *Report of Executive of the National Union of Dock Laborers in Great Britain and Ireland*, 1891 (Glasgow, 1891, pp. 14-15). The men quoted the following sentence from Jevons's *Primer of Political Economy:* "The employer, generally speaking, is right in getting work done at the lowest possible cost ; and if there is a supply of labor forthcoming at lower rates of wages, it would not be wise in him to pay higher rates."

to do so. If, as in the instance cited, the men openly proclaim their intention, there is no question of fraud ; and they may, from this point of view, fairly claim to be acting like an exceptionally honest trader who, whilst selling shoddy goods, does not pretend that they are anything else. The employers may retaliate by dismissal. The men may, in return, persuade their successors to adopt the same method. The quarrel becomes a "struggle for existence," in which the "fittest" in these arts of war may survive.

We have, however, come to believe that in such internecine struggles the interests of the community as a whole almost inevitably suffer. In spite of the protests of John Bright, successive Parliaments have prohibited the adulteration of commodities. But adulteration of labor is infinitely more injurious to the community. We have, in fact, in this case a striking illustration of the utter fallacy of the statement that "labor is a commodity, . . . an article saleable and purchaseable," which could not logically be treated "as anything else."[1] We cannot separate the quantity or quality of the day's work from its effect upon the health and character of the human being who is rendering it. The sub-contractor's practice of "driving," the constant pressure upon a man to work always at the very top of his speed, will quickly break down the health of the worker, and impoverish the nation by producing premature old age. On the other hand, systematic loitering will destroy the character and efficiency of even the most resolute worker. In adulterating the product, you adulterate the man. To the unskilled laborers of a great city, already demoralised by irregularity of employment and reduced below the average in capacity for persistent work, the doctrine of "go canny" may easily bring about the final ruin of personal character. It was an instinctive appreciation of this truth which led the responsible Trade Union officials unhesitatingly to denounce the new departure of the

[1] Speech of the well-known capitalist opponent of Trade Unions, Edmund Potter of Manchester, Social Science Association's *Report on Trade Societies and Strikes*, 1860, p. 603.

Liverpool dock laborers. It remains, so far as we know, a unique instance in Trade Union annals.[1]

When we turn from time workers to pieceworkers, we find the subsidiary regulations called into being to defend the Standard Rate wholly free from any objectionable character, beyond a certain inevitable complexity. The first series of these is concerned with accuracy of measurement. Employers have always claimed the right of making, by their agents or themselves, all the calculations involved in preparing their pay sheets, and they have expected the operatives implicitly to accept their figures. Against this contention the Trade Unions have persistently and successfully struggled. In all the cases in which the operative is unable easily to check the computation, it is obvious that such an arrangement left the Standard Rate entirely at the master's mercy. " In weighing how was the collier to obtain justice? He was at the bottom of the pit, and could not see the master's nominee at the top—and so again there arose the cry of being cheated in weight. For years this was a bone of contention ; and in revising the Inspections (Mines Regulation) Act of 1860, the delegates of the men prevailed upon the Government to insert a clause, ordering that coal should be duly weighed by a just steelyard at the pit's mouth, and that the men might, at their own cost, appoint a checkweigh-man who should not further interfere with the working but to see and take an account of the men's work. Opposition to this clause was strongly offered by the delegates of the employers . . . the masters did not want a weighing clause at all. . . . A compromise was submitted to. The weighing clause was incorporated with another clause—the 29th—with a rider

---

[1] It is only fair to Trade Union officials to say that the two enthusiasts who, in despair of otherwise benefiting the unfortunate laborers, initiated this policy, did not belong to the ranks of the workmen—a fact which the reader of their able and ingenious argument will already have perceived. They were shortly afterwards formally excluded, as middle-class men, from the Trade Union Congress at Glasgow in 1892. When, in 1896, it was suggested that a similar policy should be adopted by the International Federation of Ship, Dock, and River Workers, it was opposed by such leaders as Ben Tillett, and rejected by the members' vote.

added to it by the employers, viz. that the checkweigh-man should be selected from persons employed at that colliery." [1]

Without casting any special imputation on coalowners, it may be said that the miners' suspicions have been so far borne out by evidence that Parliament has progressively strengthened the clause thus adopted in 1860. As the law now stands, a simple majority of the miners in any one pit can decide to have a checkweigh-man elected by the pit, and paid by a compulsory stoppage from the earnings of every pieceworker employed, including even those who voted against the proposal. Any person who is or has been a miner may be elected to the post, whether the employer likes it or not, and the law courts insist that he shall be allowed free access to the weighing machines, and given every facility for checking the weights.

A further step in the same direction has been taken at the instance of the powerful unions of cotton operatives. What the coalminers have obtained is the right to have the employers' calculations checked by the men's official. The textile operatives have obtained, not only the publication in advance by the employer of the exact particulars on which he will calculate the piecework earnings, but have also secured the appointment of a Government officer specially charged with seeing that these particulars are correctly stated. [2] The "particulars clause," adopted for cotton-weavers in the Factory Act of the Conservative Government of 1891, and extended to all textile workers by the amending Act of the Liberal Government of 1895, will, in all probability, be applied, within a few years, to all piecework trades in which the computation of earnings lends itself to mistake or fraud. [3]

---

[1] *Transactions and Results of the National Association of Coal, Lime, and Ironstone Miners of Great Britain* (London, 1863), p. vii.

[2] It is much to the credit of the North-East Lancashire Operative Weavers' Association, and to the fair-mindedness of the leading employers, that the veteran official of the weavers' union, who had for a generation fought the men's battles, was, by common consent, marked out as the fittest person to hold this important new office. Mr. T. Birtwistle has fully justified his appointment, and has given universal satisfaction to all parties.

[3] The Factory Act of 1895 empowers the Home Secretary to apply the

By this clause the employer is required to state in writing, before the job is begun, all the particulars (including the rate of payment) required for the precise computation of the operatives' earnings.

But there are other ways of defrauding the pieceworker besides inaccurate calculations. The weight of coal hewn by each miner may be accurately measured at the pit's mouth, but if he is sent to work in a distant or difficult seam, the standard tonnage rate may be very far from securing identical pay for identical effort. The cotton-spinner finds his list of prices a delusion if his mules have to be frequently stopped to repair breakages caused by the bad quality of the raw cotton. And even those who are aware of the coalminers' "county basis," and of the elaborate "cotton lists," seldom realise how technical and how minute are the adjustments which are necessary to attain this end, or how manifold and incessant are the complaints requiring attention. The best way of bringing the facts home to the general reader will, we think, be to give a few extracts from actual proceedings. Thus, the Joint Committee of the Northumberland Coalowners and Miners settled, in a single day, the following as well as many other cases :—

Burradon.—Agreement confirmed. Yard Seam, East Side, until end of current quarter, 1s. 7½d. per ton ; afterwards 1s. 6½d. per ton.

Cramlington, Amelia Pit.—Agreement confirmed: (*a*) Yankee Jack system shall be abolished whenever the owners find it convenient to do so, and upon such abolition the hewing prices in the Low Main and Yard Seams shall be advanced 9 per cent. In the case of the Main Coal Seam the unscreened hewing prices shall be 63 per cent of the present round coal hewing prices, and upon such abolition they shall be advanced 9 per cent.

Walker.—Agreement confirmed. Beaumont and Brockwell Seams. Long wall or broken hewing price shall be paid when 40 yards from commencement of long wall, *i.e.* 40 yards from fast wall side.

New Backworth.—Men request payment for lamps when required to use them in the whole. To be paid extra 1d. per ton in bord and pillar

clause, by mere administrative order, to any piecework trade, and it was so applied in 1897 to manufactures of handkerchiefs, aprons, pinafores, and blouses ; and to those of chains, anchors, and locks.

whole workings, in accordance with county arrangement, when required to use lamps.

Seaton Burn.—Owners desire hewing price for long wall in Bowes' coal in Low Main Seam to be fixed. That standard prices now being paid be reduced 3d. per ton.[1]

Even more diversified are the adjustments of the cotton operatives. Here are some extracts from the diary of the secretary of the Bolton spinners :—

January 5th, 1892.—Mr. Pennington, of the Hindley Twist Company, Hindley, called here this morning. He agreed to weekly pays, and to discontinue the system of one spinner to two pairs of mules. I am to go through the mills on Monday next, and if spinning is not satisfactory, will be made so ; and we are to see in what way the mules can be speeded up so as to give better wages. Work is to be resumed on Thursday morning.

January 6th.—Went to Peake's Place Mill (Messrs. Tristram's), Halliwell, and arranged that the men on the three pairs of mules spinning coarse counts shall receive 2s. 6d. a week extra, until certain alterations and repairs to the mules shall have been made.

January 6th.—Accompanied by Mr. Percival (the secretary of the employers' association), I went to Mr. Robert Briercliffe's Mill, Moses Gate. They have no less rims in stock, so it was agreed that the prices per 100 lbs. for spinning in No. 1 Mill shall be increased 6d. for one month during which the work is to be made satisfactory. The firm have likewise conceded the request of their men, and will adopt payment by indicator. The notice to leave work is consequently withdrawn.

January 8th.—Complaints are to hand from Messrs. M'Connell and Co.'s Sedgwick Mill, Manchester, of bobbins breaking ; being short of doffing tins ; and of the men on six pairs of mules being unable to earn the basis wages.

January 12th.—From our men at Waterloo Mill, Bolton, comes a complaint of the rooms being too cold, and also irregular running of the engine.

January 19th.—Have tested the counts at Melrose Mill, and found the average 2½ hanks wrong. The men are to leave work at breakfast time to-morrow if counts are not put right.

April 7th, 1893.—Mr. Percival and myself, at the request of Messrs James Marsden and Sons, went through their No. 4 Mill to look at the spinning on the counts complained of on Tuesday. We found it below the usual standard at this firm, and Mr. Joseph Marsden undertook to see to its rectification.

---

[1] Proceedings of Joint Committee on 14th November 1891 (*Northumberland Miners' Minutes*, 1891).

April 10th.—Want of window blinds is the complaint from our men at the Parkside Mill, Golborne.

April 18th.—Our members at Messrs. Robert Haworth, Ltd., Castle Hill Mill, Hindley, complain of the overbearing conduct of their over-looker. On investigation, found that they were more to blame than the overlooker.

May 9th.—The drosophore humidifier at Robin Hood, No. 2 Mill, is so detrimental to the health of the men that I am to request the firm not to use it further.

June 12th.—Mr. Percival, Mr. Robinson, and myself went to Howe-bridge Mills to test counts in No. 2 Mill. We found them fully one hank finer than are paid for. The firm promise to put them right, but that is not sufficient for us, as they will be wrong again before the week end. We suggested they should adopt payment by indicator, and the firm subsequently agreed to try a few pairs.[1]

We see the same determination to obtain identical pay-ment for identical effort in the Trade Union regulations enforcing specific additions for extra exertion or incon-venience. Hence the " Working Rules," drawn up in almost every town by the master builders and the several sections of building operatives, include, besides the standard rate for the normal hours and ordinary work, determinate charges for " walking time " beyond a certain distance, and " lodging money " when sent away from home.[2] In trades in which men provide their own steel tools, " grinding money " is a usual extra.[3] When any class of work involves special un-pleasantness or injury to clothing, " black money " or " dirty money " is sometimes stipulated for. Thus, the boilermakers and engineers receive extra rates for jobs connected with oil-carrying vessels. " Men working inside the ballast-tanks or between the deep floors under the engine-beds, after the vessel has been regularly employed at sea, to receive one quarter

[1] These diaries are printed in the Annual Reports of the Bolton Operative Cotton-spinners' Provincial Association.

[2] See, for instance, the *Local Code of Rules for the Guidance of Masons*, signed by the Central Association of Master Builders of London and the Friendly Society of Operative Stonemasons, 23rd June 1892.

[3] " Pattern-makers, millwrights, and machine joiners on dismissal must receive two hours' notice, so as to grind their tools, or be paid two hours in lieu thereof." *London By-laws of the Amalgamated Society of Engineers*, April 1894, clause iv. Rule vi. p. 7.

day, or two and a quarter hours extra for each full day or night, as compensation for the very dirty work." [1] The foregoing are all instances of "extras" charged by Trade Unions of time-workers. But we find a similar list put forward by Trade Unions on a piecework basis. The National Union of Boot and Shoe Operatives prescribes, in minute and technical detail, for a long list of extra pieces of work, to be specially paid for. And a large part of the length and complication of the well-known "scale" of the Compositors is due to their insistence on explicitly defined extra rates for every kind of composition involving more labor than "common matter." It is impossible to convey any adequate idea of the number and variety of the "extras" thus formally agreed to between employers and employed : "bottom notes," "side notes," "under runners," "small chases," "large pages," "pamphlets," "catalogues," "undisplayed broadsheets," "table work," "column work," "parallel matter," "split fractions," "superiors," "inferiors," "slip matter," "interlinear matter," "prefatory matter," "indices," "appendices," and what not. Finally, as if to discourage vain learning, Hebrew, Arabic, and Syriac, and similar languages, together with "pedigrees," are "to be paid double the price of common matter." [2]

We do not think that, after so long and detailed an examination of the Standard Rate, we need weary the reader by any lengthy exposition of the Trade Union regulations prohibiting arbitrary fines and deductions, or any form of "truck." It may seem unreasonable for the workmen to object to the employer's system of maintaining discipline in the factory. But if that system takes the form of imposition of fines for minor offences, and, as is usually the case, the employer puts the fines into his own pocket, it is clear that the average amount of the fines per week is, in effect, an exactly proportionate reduction of the Standard Rate. An employer using this method of enforcing the necessary

[1] Rule VI. of *By-laws for the Mersey District*, United Society of Boiler-makers. 1889.
[2] *The London Scale of Prices for Compositors' Work.* 1891.

discipline finds himself buying his labor cheaper than his competitors, by an amount varying precisely in proportion to the frequency and severity of the penalties which he himself imposes.[1] The same arbitrary character attaches to the once universal system of making the operatives pay for minor breakages, or for incidental requirements of their work. " In the good old times of low wages, irregular work, and poor living," ironically writes an official of the Cotton-spinners, ' operatives used to have to pay for broken bobbins, gas, new brushes, find their own oil-cans, renew parts of their machines that got broken, and no end of other nice little things that made a fair hole in their wages."[2] Against all these practices the Cotton-spinners have long since made good their protest. The Cotton-weavers, of whom a large majority are women, are still occasionally imposed upon, and the rules of their unions accordingly still include a peremptory injunction against submitting to any such deductions. "Never pay, or agree to pay," say, for instance, the Preston rules, " for any shuttles, forks, brushes, or any piece of machinery, matter, or thing belonging to the master, or used in his business in any way whatsoever, except what you may have by sheer negligence wilfully or maliciously broken or destroyed ; and if they stop it from your wages, bring the case before the Committee at their next meeting."[3] But it is not

---

[1] A system of fines may be less objectionable if the money goes to the operatives' sick club, or some other fund for their common benefit. But sick clubs or superannuation funds connected with particular establishments, especially membership is compulsory, are objectionable from the Trade Union point of view on other grounds, notably that of diminishing the operative's independence. This subject is further examined in the chapter on " The Implications of Trade Unionism."

[2] *Cotton Factory Times*, 22nd July 1892.

[3] *Rules of the Preston and District Power Loom Weavers' Association* (Preston, 1891), p. 20.

In piecework trades, the employer seeks to escape paying for any but perfect articles, and usually claims the right to reject, without appeal, any that he chooses. This has led to a whole series of conflicts in different industries. The Trade Unionist contention has been (1) that the operative should not be made to suffer for failures due to the imperfection of material, or defects in the process ; (2) that in any case, if the employer refuses to pay anything for the work on the ground of its imperfection, he should not retain the article for his own profit, but destroy

only such arbitrary charges as fines and deductions, which necessarily vary from mill to mill, that are fundamentally inconsistent with the collective settlement of a Standard Rate. Even such uniform, regular, and definite payments as the "loom rent" of the hand-working weaver of cotton, silk, or carpets, the frame rent of the hosiery worker, and the trough or wheel rent of the Sheffield cutler, have been found, by long and painful experience, to be equally destructive of any definite standard of earnings. This arises from their being continuous and calculated by time, whilst the operative's work is irregular and paid for by the piece. In all these cases rent of the machine is exacted by the employer whether the operative is given work or not. Thus, as the framework knitters allege, when they paid rent for their frames, the employers were tempted to spin out the work over much longer periods than was necessary, doling it out in very small portions in order to keep them paying rent as long as

it; and (3) that there should be some means of appeal against the employer's arbitrary judgment in his own cause. Thus the Potters have fought a long battle for the last sixty years against the condition termed "good from oven," by which the workman is only paid for such articles as come out perfect from the firing oven. As he has no power to select material, and no control over the firing of the oven, this condition throws upon him not only the cost of his own negligence, but also that due to imperfection of raw material, defects of fixed plant, and carelessness of foremen or other operatives. It is a further aggravation that the employer arbitrarily decides which articles should be rejected as imperfect, and was formerly even free to retain and sell those which he had thus escaped paying for. After the great strike of 1836 the Staffordshire Potters succeeded in remedying the latter grievance. It was agreed that articles rejected as imperfect should be broken up, a great temptation being thus removed from unscrupulous employers. But "good from oven" still remains the basis of payment, the Trade Union demand of "good from hand" being still resisted by the employers. In the same way the Glass Bottle Makers, who have several rules in their agreements with their employers defining minutely the circumstances under which men may or may not be charged for spoiled work, have one declaring "that bottles picked out (as spoiled) be not broken down until the men have had an opportunity of inspecting them, but in no case shall they be kept beyond the following day." Article 10 of the *Agreement for* 1895 . . . *between the Yorkshire Glass Bottle Manufacturers' Association, and the Glass Bottle Makers of Yorkshire United Trade Protection Society* (Castleford, 1895).

A particularly aggravated form of the same grievance is resisted by the Friendly Society of Ironfounders, whose members are all paid by time. Notwithstanding this, and the fact that they neither choose the raw material nor direct the process, attempts are from time to time made by employers to make deductions for castings which turn out badly.

possible. And the Macclesfield silk-weavers complain that they are kept always half employed, the giver-out of work finding his advantage in getting it done on as many separate looms as possible, from each of which a full weekly rent is derived. It is easy to see how such a system may open a way for personal tyranny and exaction. It is more to our immediate purpose to notice how incompatible it is with Collective Bargaining and a Standard Rate. If the employer can give out work in unequal quantities to different operatives, but deduct from each an equal sum at the end of the week, no fixed piecework list will secure identical pay for identical work. If A is given thirty pieces to weave, and B only fifteen, both may be paid at the same rate of a shilling per piece, and both may pay the same loom rent of five shillings per week. Yet at the end of the week the net remuneration for weaving one piece will have been to A tenpence and to B eightpence. Thus the rate of payment for identical work will vary from operative to operative, from week to week, and even from firm to firm, according to the way in which, at the uncontrolled discretion of the employers, the work is distributed.[1] A similar objection applies, it will be seen, to the whole system of "truck," or the compulsory purchase by the operatives of commodities or materials supplied by the employers.[2] This is resisted by the unions on the larger

[1] Many minor payments similar in principle to loom rent exist in various industries. Where the operatives are unorganised, and especially if they are women or girls, employers are apt to attempt to charge them for some part of the manufacturing process, or for incidental stores or material. This is sometimes done to avoid the cost and trouble of proper supervision to prevent waste and breakages. In other cases it arises as an incident of a growing specialisation of function. Thus, cotton-weavers used to oil their own looms, but the employers found that it was better done by a professional oiler, who was thereupon employed. Any attempt to deduct even a penny per week per pair of looms to pay his wages is peremptorily stopped by the Weavers' union. Similar developments of specialisation in cotton-spinning might be cited—the uprise of the "strap-piecer" and the "bobbin-carrier" for instance. But no deduction for their wages is permitted by the Cotton-spinners' unions (*Cotton Factory Times*, 10th June 1892). Women woollen weavers are, however, still made to pay the "tuner" of their looms, his work of "setting" the warp and weft being done by the male weavers for themselves.

[2] The Miners' Conference in 1863 made this a special subject of complaint. The truck system still prevails in Scotland and Wales, despite of both equity

ground that it amounts to an insidious enslavement of the wage-earner and his family. But it is also inconsistent with any uniformity in the net rate at which employers obtain their labor, and with definite standard of real income of the wage-earner under such a system, notwithstanding a nominal uniformity of rate, both labor cost and real wages will vary according to the extent of the truck business in each firm, the economy and ability with which this subsidiary store-keeping is managed, and the profit or " loading " which each employer chooses to exact, the latter amounting, in effect, to a fraud upon the workman.[1]

We see, therefore, that the adoption of a Standard Rate —that is, of payment for labor according to some definite standard, uniform in its application—is not by any means so simple a matter as would at first sight appear. Whether we accept payment by the hour or payment by the piece so great are the complications of modern industry, and so ingenious are the devices for evasion, that a long series of subsidiary regulations is found necessary to defend the main position. The whole argument for this series of subsidiary

and law. That no man should be forced, as a condition of work, to spend his money on necessaries for the benefit of his employer is both law and reason. In Scotland . . . the men are only paid by the fortnight, the month, or longer and in the interim tickets for food or clothing are furnished, by which, at certain shops, articles are furnished at an enormous overcharge above a fair market average of cost. In some cases the poor collier rarely sees current coin, all being forestalled betwixt the term of pay and work. . . . Allied to this, in Stafford shire and elsewhere, the butties and doggies, or middlemen, still continue to influence and compel the colliers to spend part of their wages in drink, as a condition of employment. In other cases, in Yorkshire, candles and powder must be purchased of the steward, or some other man, at exorbitant prices above the market rate of profit."—*Transactions and Results of the National Association of Coal, Lime, and Ironstone Miners of Great Britain* (London, 1863), p. xi.

These practices have now been stopped by the miners' unions in all well organised districts. Similar grievances are, however, still complained of in some other trades, where the operatives are powerless to insist on the Truck Acts being obeyed in spirit as well as in the letter.

[1] " Wherever the workmen are paid in goods, or are compelled to purchase at the master's shop, the evils are very great ; much injustice is done to the men and much misery results from it. Whatever may have been the intentions of the master in such a case, *the real effect is to deceive the workman as to the amount he receives in exchange for his labor*."—*On the Economy of Machinery and Manufactures*, by Charles Babbage (London, 1832), p. 255.

regulations rests, it is clear, upon the principal contention. It seems, therefore, worth while to rehearse the Trade Unionist's argument. We have seen that it is a fundamental article of the Trade Union faith that it is impossible, in a system of competitive industry, to prevent the degradation of the Standard of Life, unless the conditions of labor are settled, not by Individual Bargaining, but by some Common Rule. But, without the uniform application of some common standard, collective settlement of these conditions, whether by bargain, arbitration, or law, is plainly impossible.[1] Where employer is competing with employer, each will claim that, if he must forego the chances of Individual Bargaining, he should at any rate be made to pay no more for his labor than his rivals. With this contention the Trade Unionist heartily agrees, and thus we get admitted, as the basis of the Common Rule, the principle of identical pay for identical effort, or, as it is usually termed, the Standard Rate. This, as we have seen, is the very opposite to equality of wages. How accurately this principle of identical pay for identical effort can be applied to the varying capacities of different workmen, or to the varying difficulties of particular tasks, whether it can be most precisely carried into effect by payment by time or payment by the piece, depends upon the character of the process and the intelligence and integrity of the parties. But it is obviously futile to settle, by collective regulation of any kind, a Standard Rate of identical pay for identical effort, if an unscrupulous employer is free to evade this by demanding extra work or additional wear and tear ; by deducting anything from the wage agreed upon ; or by

[1] The dependence of combination among workmen upon the existence of a Standard Rate was well expressed, from the employer's point of view, by Alexander Galloway, the well-known engineer, and friend to Francis Place. "I have always found that in those employments where the wages were uniform . . . there have always been combinations among those men. Now in all those trades where the men have made their own individual engagements, we never see anything like combinations. . . . That which has struck most effectually at the root of all combination among workmen is to pay every man according to his merit, and to allow him to make his own agreement with his employer."—Evidence in *First Report of Committee on Artisans and Machinery*, 1824, p. 27.

obtaining, at the cost of his workmen, by any transaction with them, any other monetary advantage whatever. In short, if the fundamental object of Trade Unionism, the enforcement of a Common Rule, has any justification at all, the principle of the Standard Rate must be conceded, and if a Standard Rate is admitted, the subsidiary regulations which we have described follow as a matter of course.

This general conclusion in favor of a Standard Rate—a point on which every Trade Unionist would unhesitatingly agree—leaves many questions with regard to wages unsettled. One of these is, on what principle, and to what extent, the Standard Rate should, in the same industry, vary from town to town. The employers in the out-of-the-way districts are apt to contend that the workman must put up with a low rate, because of the inferiority of their machinery, their heavy charges for freight, and other local disadvantages. But there seems no reason why the workman should lower his standard of life, and forego his claim to identical pay for identical effort, merely because the capitalist chooses to carry on his business amid unprofitable surroundings. Whether Trade Unionists should go in for equality of nominal wages (a uniform national standard rate), or, making allowance for difference in the cost of living, claim only equality of real wages (involving varying local rates), has never been settled in principle. There are obvious practical difficulties in carrying out the latter idea, as it is impossible to measure with any precision differences in the cost of living in different districts. Accordingly we find most of the " county " unions, especially those of the cotton operatives and coalminers, aiming at a uniform county rate, irrespective of local circumstances. Similarly, the strong old union of hand papermakers, working entirely in a few small provincial towns, easily maintains a uniform rate for the whole industry.[1] But

[1] A uniform Standard Rate is said to have formed one of the principal demands of the great French strike of 1791, which extended to many trades and to all parts of France (Du Cellier, *Histoire des Classes Laborieuses en France*, pp. 320-322 ; Decree of the National Assembly of 14th June 1791).

directly the cost of living becomes appreciably different, even the strongest unions admit variations in local rates. The Journeymen Hatters' Fair Trade Union of Great Britain and Ireland, the old-established society of silk hat makers, has a uniform price list, but allows its London branch to add 10 per cent to the general rates. When we come to the larger and more widely distributed unions, we see the widest possible divergence. Thus the 631 branches of the Amalgamated Society of Carpenters in Great Britain and Ireland recognise no fewer than twenty rates, varying from 5d. per hour in Truro to 10d. per hour in London. Here, as in many other cases, we may well doubt whether even equality of real wages has been attained. Not only has there been no attempt by any large union to secure a national uniform rate, but there is a tendency for officers and executive committees to be apathetic with regard to the process of "levelling up," which would be necessary to obtain equality of real wages. The result is that Trade Unionism cannot be said yet to have progressed beyond the securing of a local Standard Rate. This leaves the workmen exposed to the constant attempts of employers to "level down" the rates in the better-paid districts, in order, as they assert, to meet the competition of the lower-paid districts. Our own idea is that the assumed differences in the cost of living, taking one thing with another, resolve themselves practically into differences in the rent of a workman's dwelling. The expedient of the Hatters seems, therefore, the most practical thing to aim at. There would be many advantages in the enforcement of a uniform Standard Rate in all districts of an industry, treating all provincial towns and urban districts on an equality, but adding a percentage for the exceptional high rents payable in London, and, if necessary, deducting a percentage in respect of the very low rents in a purely agricultural district, in the cases in which, as in the building trades, the industry comprises both town and country. These percentages could be calculated on easily ascertained and undisputed facts.[1]

[1] Instead of a uniform Standard Rate for all the establishments in each town

A more obvious problem with regard to wages must be deferred to a subsequent chapter. We can imagine that the reader has had in his mind an uneasy feeling that we are evading what he conceives to be the crucial point, namely, the share of the joint product to be allotted for the remuneration of the manual labor. But the Trade Union Regulation with which we are dealing—the insistence on a Standard Rate—is not an end but a means : not any particular *sum* of money per week, but a *device* for obtaining for the whole body of competitors something better than they would get by Individual Bargaining. Thus the Sheffield Fork-grinders, the Dock Laborers, the Engineers, and the Steel Smelters all insist on the Standard Rate. But if we look at the weekly earnings for which each trade is fighting, we find

or district, we occasionally find attempts to enforce two or three different rates for what are assumed to be different grades of work. Thus the Scottish Tailors recognise in many towns two, and in Glasgow and Edinburgh three classes of shops, those requiring a better quality of tailoring being compelled to pay a half-penny or even a penny per hour more than the lowest Trade Union rate. The custom is for the employers to classify themselves, the union objecting if any attempt is made, for instance, to get " dress goods " (superfine black broadcloth) made at the second-class rate, or (in Edinburgh and Glasgow) "tweeds" at the third class. In so far as these different rates correspond to real and ascertainable differences in the class of work, they are, it is clear, not inconsistent with the principle of a uniform Standard Rate. In some cases, however, the different rates depend more on the custom and tradition of the various shops than upon any definite difference in the work done. Thus the London branch of the National Union of Boot and Shoe Operatives has long recognised three different " Statements," applying respectively to firms deemed first, second, or third class. An establishment which has hitherto paid the first-class " Statement " is not allowed to do any work at a lower " Statement," for fear this should lead insidiously to the reduction of the rates of the first-class men. On the other hand, there is nothing to prevent a firm, hitherto classed as third or second class, from making at these lower rates goods nearly identical with those usually produced at the first-class " Statement." The result is that the first-class firms are always finding themselves undersold (or at any rate, believing themselves to be under-sold) by enterprising firms on the second-class statement. The employers and the experienced officials of the union have, for ten years, been urging the abolition of these separate " Statements," and the preparation of the uniform list for all London firms, with carefully gradated piecework rates for every kind of boot. Hitherto all attempts at uniformity have broken down, owing mainly to the rooted belief of the union that no reduction of existing rates ought anywhere to be conceded. As a consequence, the first-class employers are said to find a constantly increasing difficulty in maintaining their position in London. The controversy can be best followed in the *Shoe and Leather Record* for the last ten years.

this varying from twenty-four shillings a week up to three times that amount. One thing will be clear, even to the most superficial observer. There is, in the Trade Union world of to-day, absolutely no trace of any desire for equality of wages. The cardroom operatives in a Lancashire Cotton mill, earning from ten to twenty shillings a week, will unhesitatingly come out on strike to assist the cotton-spinners to maintain a Standard Rate, paid out of the products of the combined labor of the two sections, averaging forty shillings a week. The local federations of the building trades, whose members work side by side at the same job, collectively insist, in their treaties with the employers, on half a dozen different rates per hour for the different crafts, the Stonemason habitually getting fifty per cent more than the Builders' Laborer, and the rates, in the present generation, showing no tendency to approximate. Unanimity of Trade Union policy does not, in fact, extend beyond the use of a common device. How much money each trade will claim, no less than how much each will actually receive, depends, in practice, on the traditions, customs, and present opportunities of the particular trade and section concerned. The expectations and aspirations of the operatives, the arguments adduced in justification of their demands, and, to some extent, the particular Trade Union Method employed to enforce them, will, as we shall show in our chapter on the Assumptions of Trade Unionism, depend principally on the Doctrine or Doctrines as to social expediency by which the policy of the particular union is, for the time being, directed.

CHAPTER VI

THE NORMAL DAY

AFTER the Standard Rate, the most universal of the Trade Union Regulations is what we have termed the Normal Day, the determination of a uniform maximum working time for all the members of a craft.[1] This claim to fix the limits of the working day is peculiar to the manual-working wage-earner. Corporations of lawyers, doctors, architects, and other professional brainworkers insist, with more or less stringency, on scales of minimum fees, below which no practitioner is allowed to undertake work. But the conception of a precise Common Rule as to the hours during which an individual shall work is foreign both to the pro-

[1] By the term "Normal Day" we mean the "maximum working day" of Schäffle (*Theory and Practice of Labour Protection*, London, 1893) and Frankenstein (*Der Arbeiterschutz*, Leipzig, 1896), not the elaborately equated "normal day" of Rodbertus (*Der Normalarbeitstag*, Berlin, 1871), varying according to the assumed intensity of labor in different occupations. The latter academic conception has never penetrated to the minds either of English Trade Unionists or German Social Democrats.

From the economic standpoint there has been as yet little scientific investigation of the results of fixing the maximum working day. *The Eight Hours Day*, by Sidney Webb and Harold Cox (London, 1891), and E. L. Jaeger's *Geschichte und Literatur des Normalarbeittages* (Stuttgart, 1892) give the principal references, to which may now be added Hadfield and Gibbins' *A Shorter Working Day* (London, 1892); C. Deneus, *La Journée de Huit Heures* (Ghent, 1893); H. Stephan, *Der Normalarbeitstag* (Leipzig, 1893); Professor L. Brentano's *Ueber das Verhaltniss von Arbeitslohn und Arbeitszeit zur Arbeitsleistung* (Leipzig, 1893), translated as *Hours and Wages in Relation to Production* (London, 1894); John Rae, *Eight Hours for Work* (London, 1894); and Maurice Ansiaux, *Heures de Travail et Salaires* (Paris, 1896).

pertied and to the brain-working class. Nor has it always characterised the wage-earners. The trade clubs of the eighteenth century claimed a legal rate of wages, or a standard list of prices, they insisted on a limitation of apprentices, or sought to enforce the Elizabethan Statutes ; but not until the close of the century do we find any widespread complaints of the length or irregularity of the working day. From the beginning of the present century the demand for a deliberately fixed limit of hours for each day's work, to be arranged either by Collective Bargaining or by Legal Enactment, has spread from one occupation to another, until to-day the great majority of the Trade Unions make the regulation of working hours one of their foremost objects. Nevertheless, there exist even to-day small sections of the working class world who resist any Common Rule as to their hours, and prefer that each individual should be free to labor when and for as long as he may choose. We have, therefore, to seek some explanation, not only of the present popularity of the idea of a Normal Day, but also of its comparatively modern growth, and of its rejection by certain sections of Trade Unionists.

In modern industry the settlement of the hours of labor differs in an essential particular from that of the rate of payment for the work done. In the absence of any form of collective regulation, the rates of wages are determined by Individual Bargaining between the capitalist employer and his several " hands " ; and a distinct and varying agreement as to the amount of remuneration is made with each operative in turn. This is seldom the case with regard to the length and distribution of the working day. In all the numerous industries in which work is not done on the employer's premises, but is still "given out" to be done at home, the manual worker, paid " by the piece," is as free as the author, doctor, or conveyancer, to fix the number of hours, and the exact part of the day or week or year, that he chooses to spend in labor. He has, of course, like the professional man, to suit the convenience of his clients.

He must be on the spot to receive work when it comes, and he must finish it by the time it is required. He must be willing to do extra work in the busy season, and even to turn night into day to cope with a special rush of orders. But subject to this condition, each man can settle for himself the exact hours at which he will begin his work, and the intervals he will allow himself for meals and rest. Unless he is driven, by reason of the low rate at which he is paid, to work "all the hours God made" in order to get bare subsistence, he may break off when he likes to gossip with a friend or slip round to the public-house ; he may, in the intervals, nurse a sick wife or child ; and he can even arrange to spend the morning in his garden, or doing odd jobs about the house. No one acquainted with the daily life of the home-working, skilled craftsman, earning "good money," will ignore the large use that such a man makes of his freedom. For good or for evil his working hours are determined by his own idiosyncrasies. Whether he desires to earn much, or is content with little ; whether he is a slow worker or a quick one ; whether he is a precise and punctual person governing himself and his family by rigid rules, or whether he is "endowed with an artistic temperament," and needs to recover on Monday and Tuesday from the "expansion" of the preceding days—these personal characteristics will determine the limits and distribution of his working time.[1]

[1] The injurious effect upon the personal character of the "average sensual man" of this freedom to stop working whenever he feels inclined, is referred to in our chapter on "The Implications of Trade Unionism." The axiom that the vast majority of the manual workers, like other men, are the better for a certain degree of discipline, would not find ready acceptance among the rank and file of Trade Unionists, and, therefore, can hardly be given as a Trade Union argument in favor of a Normal Day. But the more thoughtful workmen would concur with the dictum of an early admirer of the factory system, that when operatives were "obliged to be more regular in their attendance at their work, they became more orderly in their conduct, spent less time at the ale-house, and lived better at home" (*Memoirs of the Manchester Literary and Philosophical Society*, Second series, London, 1819, vol. iii. p. 129, in a paper "On the Rise and Progress of the Cotton Trade," read in 1815 by John Kennedy). "I always observed," wrote an old compositor in 1859, "that those trades who had settled wages, such as masons, wrights, painters, etc., *and who were obliged to attend*

Very different is the position of the factory operative. Instead of each individual being able to work as he chooses, the whole establishment finds itself, by the nature of things, subject to a Common Rule. In a textile mill, a coal mine, a shipbuilding yard, an engineering firm, or a great building operation it is economically impossible to permit the individual workman to come or go as he feels inclined. Each worker forms part of a complex co-operative process, needing for its proper fulfilment an exact dovetailing of the task of every machine and every " hand " in the work as a whole. To arrange particular hours of labor to suit the varying desires, capacities, and needs of the different operatives, would be obviously incompatible with the economical use of steam power, the full employment of plant, or the highly organised specialisation brought about by division of labor. There is no longer a choice between idiosyncrasy and uniformity. A common standard, compulsory in its application, is economically inevitable. The only question is how and by whom the uniform rule shall be determined. In the absence of collective regulation, whether in the form of Legal Enactment or Collective Bargaining, this uniform rule is naturally made by the employer.[1] And it is a special aggravation of this subordination, that, under the circumstances of the modern capitalist industry, the employer's decision will perpetually be biassed in favor of lengthening the working day. With regard to his domestic servants, the capitalist is free to determine the amount of toil solely with a view of keeping them in the highest possible efficiency. But the same man investing capital in expensive machines, worked by power, finds, even when he pays by the piece, a

regularly at stated hours, were not so much addicted to day drinking as printers, bookbinders, tailors, shoemakers, and those tradesmen who generally were on piecework, *and not so much restricted in regard to their attendance at work* except when it was particularly wanted."—*Scottish Typographical Circular*, March 1859.

[1] " It should always be remembered," remark the Cotton-spinners in 1860 " that anterior to the introduction of factory legislation, the employers *dictated* the hours of labor to their work-people."—*Rules of the Amalgamated Association of Operative Cotton-spinners*, edition of 1860, preface.

positive profit in every additional moment that his costly plant is being employed. Competition is always forcing him to cut down the cost of production to the lowest possible point. Under this pressure other considerations disappear in the passion to obtain the greatest possible " output per machine." [1]

Between these two historic types of the domestic handi-craftsman and the factory operative, there are various intermediate forms in which Individual Bargaining as to the hours of labor is as possible as Individual Bargaining with regard to the rate of payment. In occupations such as agriculture, and even in special departments of the great industries, it is at any rate practicable for an employer to vary the hours of his several workpeople, or, in other words, to make, if he likes, a bargain with each according to his capacity, just as the ordinary capitalist claims to be allowed to pay each man " according to his merit." Where this is the case, the workman's need for a Normal Day depends on considerations strictly analogous to those which cause him to need a Standard Rate. If each workman is free to conclude what bargain he chooses with regard to his working hours, the employer will, it is contended, be able to use the desires or exigencies of particular individuals as a means of compelling all the others to accept the same longer working day.

So far we have considered the Trade Union demand for a Normal Day only in relation to the personal freedom of the operative to take such leisure as he may deem necessary

---

[1] " The great proportion of fixed to circulating capital . . . makes long hours of work desirable. . . . The motives to long hours of work will become greater, as the only means by which a large proportion of fixed capital can be made profitable. When a laborer," said Mr. Ashworth to me, " lays down his spade, he renders useless for that period a capital worth eighteenpence. When one of our people leaves the mill, he renders useless a capital that has cost £100."— Nassau Senior, *Letters on the Factory Act* (London, 1837), pp. 11-14.

" Hence that remarkable phenomenon in the history of modern industry, that machinery sweeps away every moral and natural restriction on the length of the working day." — Marx, *Capital*, Part iv. ch. xv. sec. 3 (vol. ii. p. 406 of *English Translation* of 1887).

or desirable. But to the Trade Unionist, as to the rank and file of the manual working class, the length of the day's work and the amount left over for leisure is of secondary importance beside the vital question of the sum earned. Keen as is the average workman to secure more time to himself, he is far keener to obtain more money to spend. In all timework trades in which Trade Unionism exists the operative gets extra pay for extra hours, usually at a higher rate, whilst the whole race of pieceworkers obviously increase their earnings by working overtime.[1] Every progressive lengthening of the working day would therefore seem to bring with it, as a compensating advantage, a corresponding increase in the weekly income of the wage-earner.[2]

[1] In certain unorganised occupations men, and especially women, are still required to work longer hours to cope with a press of orders without getting any additional payment for the extra labor. But this is seldom the case in trades in which there is any kind of organisation.

[2] This is exactly how it appears to the well-to-do literary man. Thus, Mr. Lecky is much concerned at the diminution of earnings which he supposes to be caused by the Factory Acts. " Take, for example, the common case of a strong girl who is engaged in millinery. For, perhaps, nine months of the year her life is one of constant struggle, anxiety, and disappointment, owing to the slackness of her work. At last the season comes bringing with it an abundant harvest of work, which, if she were allowed to reap it, would enable her in a few weeks to pay off the little debts which weigh so heavily upon her, and to save enough to relieve her from all anxiety in the ensuing year. She desires passionately to avail herself of her opportunity. She knows that a few weeks of toil prolonged far into the night will be well within her strength, and not more really injurious than the long succession of nights that are spent in the ball-room by the London beauty whom she dresses. But the law interposes, forbids her to work beyond the stated hours, dashes the cup from her thirsty lips, and reduces her to the same old round of poverty and debt. What oppression of the poor can be more real and more galling than this ?"—*Democracy and Liberty* (London, 1896), vol. ii. p. 342.

It is interesting to contrast with this imaginary instance the reports of the responsible women officials who are in actual contact with facts, and conversant with the views of the operatives. Writing in 1894, Miss May Abraham (the Senior Woman Factory Inspector) reports that " by dressmakers and milliners . . . legal overtime is almost universally condemned. A dressmaker's assistant, whose legal working day had, for a considerable period, lasted from 8 A.M. to 10 P.M., said to me in the presence of her fellow-workers, ' The overtime exception just spoils the Factory Act.' The chorus of approval with which her remark was endorsed was a clear indication of general discontent, and further experience showed that this had been but one expression of an almost universal feeling. . . . In factories where the payment is by piecework, or in some districts, as in Dublin, where a stipulated sum is allowed for overtime, the weight of hostile

Now, if Trade Unionists believed that this apparent result was the real result,—that freedom to work longer hours invariably, or even usually, meant a corresponding increase of income,—we doubt whether there would have arisen any general movement in favor of limiting the hours of labor. But, rightly or wrongly, Trade Unionists are convinced that irregular or unlimited hours have an insidious influence upon wages, first upon the Standard Rate and ultimately upon the amount earned by each man per week.

This conviction springs from the personal experience of the manual working wage-earner. At any Trade Union meeting where the hours of labor are discussed, it may happen that a young and energetic member will suggest that he would prefer a larger income to increased leisure But one old member after another will get up and explain that as a young married man he had felt the same, but that experience of workshop life had taught him that "what was gained in hours was lost in rates"—an assertion which finds immediate and unhesitating confirmation from the bulk of the meeting. If after the meeting the visitor argues the point with the leading men, and suggests that their personal experience may not warrant so large a generalisation as that a lengthening of hours will necessarily lead to a reduction of the rate of payment per hour or per piece, they will retort by asking, why it is that Royal Commissions and official statistics are always laying bare this almost universal coincidence between long and irregular hours, low rates of pay, and small weekly earnings. Nor will they fail to give an explanation, based on actual experience. "Our members,"

opinion is not so pronounced ; but even here, with the inducement of a supplementary wage, it is only the most unthinking of the workers who favor the system. . . . The consequent effect on the health of the workers is exceedingly injurious . . . I believe . . . that by the workers [the abolition of all overtime] would be welcomed with feelings of the warmest gratitude " (*Report of the Chief Inspector of Factories* for 1893, C. 7368 of 1894, p. 11). This and other reports contain abundant confirmation of Miss Abraham's view. " Could a secret ballot be taken," says Mr. Cramp, one of the Superintending Inspectors, " of all the workers affected by the overtime clauses of the Factory and Workshop Acts, I am convinced that very few would be found voting for its continuance." — *Ibid.* p. 299.

they will say, " look on thirty shillings as a fair week's wage. If they make it, they are content ; if they don't make thirty shillings, they come to the branch and complain. When a master increases the hours, say from fifty-four to sixty, it seems at first a clear gain to the men, who make more money. Presently, on some excuse, the foreman announces a ten per cent cut in rates. The men grumble, but as most of them will still make thirty shillings a week, they put up with a reduction against which they would certainly have come out, if it had meant their only making twenty-seven shillings. After a time the weaker men find they can't keep up their output for such long hours. In a few months, the average weekly earnings of the shop will have dropped, and the men will be wearing themselves out for even less money at the end of the week than they had before. Again and again we have seen this happen, and no amount of middle-class theory will make us believe it is not so."

The Trade Union official who has read his economic text-book will put the argument in more systematic form. When an employer engages a laborer at so much a week, the length of the working day clearly forms an integral part of the wage-contract. A workman who agrees to work longer time for the same money underbids his fellows just as surely as if he offered to work the same time for less money. He sells each hour's work at a lower rate. Among all time-workers, therefore, who are paid by the day, week, or month, the insistence on a Normal Day is a necessary element in the maintenance of their Standard Rate.

Where piecework prevails, or where the time-worker is paid by the hour, the case is, to the Trade Unionist, no less clear. At first sight it would seem that liberty to work for longer hours leaves the Standard Rate unaffected, whilst it increases the amount of the weekly earnings of industrious men. This seems so obvious to the middle-class mind that employers have for generations been honestly unable to understand why a pieceworking Trade Union should concern itself about the hours of labor at all. According to the

Trade Unionists, this is to ignore the plain teaching of economics, as well as the experience of practical men. To them it seems obvious that the actual earnings of any class of workers are largely determined by its Standard of Comfort, that is to say, the kind and amount of food, clothing, and other commodities to which the class has become firmly accustomed.[1] It would not be easy to persuade an English engineer to work at his trade for thirteen shillings a week, however excessive might be the supply of engineers. Rather than do such violence to his own self-respect, he would work as a laborer, or even sweep a crossing. On the other hand, however much in request a Dorsetshire laborer might find himself it would not enter into his head to ask two pounds a week for his work. There is, in fact, the Trade Unionist asserts, in each occupation a customary standard of livelihood, which is, within a specific range of variation, tacitly recognised by both employers and employed. Upon this customary standard of weekly earnings, the piecework or hour rates are, more or less consciously, always based.[2] If there is no limit to the number of hours that each man may work or the employer may require, some exceptionally strong men, able, if only for a few years, to work unceasingly from morning till night, will earn an income far beyond the customary standard of their class. In any bargaining about the Piecework List these large earnings will be quoted by the employer as typical of what every workman might do if only he were industrious, and will be urged as grounds why a reduction

---

[1] This assumption—that the rate of wages of any race or class of wage-earners is largely determined by the standard of expenditure—enunciated by Adam Smith and generally accepted by later economists, will be further examined in our chapter on " The Higgling of the Market " ; and the argument that the bulwark against competitive pressure afforded by this instinctive Standard of Life is enormously strengthened by the Methods and Regulations of Trade Unionism, will be elaborately analysed in the chapter on " The Economic Characteristics of Trade Unionism."

[2] " A price list has always implicitly (and as will be seen sometimes explicitly) a time-basis, *i.e.* it is generally understood that the piece-rates agreed on are such as to enable the average worker with average exertion to earn a certain weekly wage."—Board of Trade (Labor Department) *Report on Wages and Hours of Labour*, Part II., Standard Piece Rates, C. 7567.—I. 1894, p. vii.

in the rate is only reasonable.[1] Nor is this merely a question of successful argument. The exceptional men themselves will not be inclined to hazard, by any dispute, what
is to them ample livelihood, and will oppose any attempt
on the part of the Union to resist reductions or apply for
advances. The hours thus exceptionally worked tend, therefore, insidiously to become customary for the whole trade,
and the piecework rates are gradually lowered so as to yield,
on the longer hours, a weekly income corresponding to the
standard of expenditure to which the class is accustomed.
The ultimate result upon the Standard Rate of leaving the
hours of labor unlimited is accordingly the same in the case
of payment by the piece or hour as it is in the case of payment by the day or week. If, as the Trade Unionists contend, unrestrained competition among the individual operatives
tends to lengthen the working day for all alike, it also insidiously lowers the rate of remuneration for the work done.
The men who have started longer hours gradually find
themselves earning no more than they had formerly done in
the customary day, whilst all the rest discover that they can
only maintain their old wages by similarly increasing their
working time. Thus the whole class gives in return for its
customary livelihood increased labor and energy, involving
greater wear and tear, and the weaker members, unable to
keep up the strain, are forced down to a lower level of subsistence. The same arguments, therefore, which lead the
Trade Unionist to insist on a definite Standard Rate, impel
him, quite apart from any advantage to be gained from
increased leisure and irrespective of the system under which
he is paid, vigorously to uphold the Normal Day.[2]

[1] See the instances cited by the Shipwrights and Coopers in the subsequent
note.

[2] It might, indeed, be urged that the Trade Unionist argument in favor of
collective regulation of the hours of labor, *considered merely as a means of keeping
up the price at which the wage-earner sells each unit of energy*, has a broader
psychological basis than the argument for a Standard Rate itself. If it be true,
as is always asserted both by employers and by Trade Union officials, that the
individual manual worker is far keener to maintain and add to his income than
to preserve or increase his leisure, it seems to follow that a Trade Union which

The Trade Unionist position with regard to the Normal Day is therefore extremely complicated. So long as we fix our attention solely on the proportion between work and leisure, the wage-earners fall, as we have seen, into three classes. To the " hands " employed in a co-operative process, involving the use of costly plant and machinery, and carried on upon a large scale, the fixing of a Normal Day appears the only alternative to leaving their working hours to be determined, and in all probability gradually lengthened, according to the autocratic judgment of their employer. To the domestic handicraftsman, on the other hand, working in his own garret, any collective regulation of the hours of work is a distinct curtailment of his personal liberty, an evil in itself requiring considerable justification before he will be persuaded to adopt it. For the workmen in the intermediate class of industries, in which the length and distribution of the working day can practically vary from individual to individual, the question will depend partly on the extent to which hours of leisure offer any attraction to them, and partly upon the degree to which they realise the perils of Individual Bargaining. Assuming the Trade Unionist position that the wage-earners can obtain better conditions by collective action, all the workmen in the industries standing between the domestic handicraft and the factory system, who desire to protect or increase the amount of their leisure, will naturally come more and more to insist on a Normal Day as a necessary condition of this collective action. But this simple classification by no means disposes of all the variations. With all classes of workers a second and usually more potent consideration enters into the argument, namely, the result of irregular or unlimited hours of labor upon the weekly earnings. To the time-worker paid by the day, week, or month the Normal Day is obviously a part of his bargain for a

insisted on a rigid limitation of working time whilst leaving the rate of pay to the chances of Individual Bargaining, would, in the end, secure for its members a higher level of remuneration for a given expenditure of energy, than a Trade Union which insisted on a Standard Rate, but left the length and intensity of the day's labor to individual agreements.

Standard Rate. The worker by the piece or by the hour will be more or less disposed to insist on Common Rules fixing working time, in the degree that the circumstances of his industry and his personal observations convince him that unregulated hours of labor tend to lower the rate of remuneration of the whole class.[1]

This elucidation of the Trade Union argument gives us the necessary clue both to the historical development of the Hours' Movement and to its present position in the Trade Union world. During the eighteenth century the predominant type of Trade Unionist was the handicraftsman working as an individual producer. The weavers and frame-work knitters, whose combinations to enforce a Standard Rate date from the very beginning of that century, worked in their own homes. Out-work prevailed, too, alongside of the employers' workshop in many other of the organised trades, such as the shoemakers, cutlers, woolcombers, and hatters. And even where workshop industry was the rule the familiar relations between the master workman and the journeymen, the absence of machinery and motive power, and the general slackness of discipline enabled the members of such trade clubs as the sailmakers, coopers, curriers, and calico block-printers to put in attendance at irregular intervals. This practical freedom to leave off at any particular moment, though it was not incompatible with what we should now consider excessive hours of toil, gave the operative a sense of personal liberty which naturally disinclined him to suggest any collective regulation of his working day. Eighteenth-century attempts to impose a Common Rule fixing the hours

---

[1] It will be needless to remind the historical student of the numerous gild ordinances by which the independent master craftsmen of the Middle Ages, though individually at liberty to leave off when they chose, deliberately sought to fix the maximum hours of labor of each trade, mainly in order, as we think, to prevent the working time being insidiously lengthened, and the standard rate of payment undermined, by unfettered competition. Thus the Spurriers, in 1345, fix the maximum working day from dawn to curfew ; the Hatters, Pewterers, and many others in the fourteenth century prohibit night-work ; and the Girdlers, in 1344, forbid work "after none has been wrung" on Saturdays or festival eves.— *Memorials of London and London Life*, by H. T. Riley (London, 1868).

of labor for all the members of a craft are accordingly confined to operatives paid by the day or week, and working on
the premises of their employers.   Thus, the establishment of
a maximum day of fourteen hours (less meal-times) was a
leading demand of that combination of "the Journeyman
Taylors in and about the Cities of London and Westminster,"
which we have cited as one of the earliest Trade Unions.   "'Tis
certain," runs the workmen's petition, "that to work fifteen
hours per day is destructive to the men's health, and especially
their sight, so that at forty years old a man is not capable
by his work to get his bread."   And from the masters'
petition we learn that the men "insist upon and have twelve
shillings and ninepence per week (instead of ten shillings and
ninepence per week, the usual wages), and leave off work at
eight of the clock of night (instead of nine, their usual hour,
time out of mind)." [1]   And turning to other trades, it is
significant that while there is, during the whole of the
eighteenth century, no trace of any hours' movement among
the pieceworking coopers of London, the day-working coopers
of Aberdeen are found, as early as 1732, "entering into
signed associations among themselves, whereby they become
bound to one another under a penalty not to continue in their
masters' service, or to work after seven o'clock at night,
contrary to the usual practice." [2]   The only other cases of
eighteenth-century movements that we know of for regular
or shorter hours occurred among the saddlers and bookbinders

[1] *An Abstract of the Master Taylors' Bill before the Honourable House
of Commons ; with the Journeymen's Observations on each Clause of the
said Bill* (London, 1720).   Similar movements are recorded among the tailors
of Aberdeen in 1720 and 1768 (Bain's *Merchant and Craft Gilds*, p. 261),
and those of Sheffield in 1720 (*Sheffield Iris*, 8th August 1820).   See, for
all these instances, the interesting collection of original *Documents Illustrating
the History of Trade Unionism*, No. I. *The Tailoring Trade*, by F. W.
Galton, published by the London School of Economics and Political Science
(London, 1896).

[2] Bain's *Merchant and Craft Gilds of Aberdeen*, p. 246.   A similar distinction
may be drawn between the pieceworking hatters, who continued to work unlimited
hours in their own homes, and the London hat-finishers, who, working by time
on the employers' premises, struck in 1777 for a reduction of hours.—House of
Commons Journals, vol. xxxvii. p. 192 (18th February 1777).

in the last years of the century,[1] who at that time worked by the day and were in the employers' workshops.

The isolated and exceptional cases of the tailors, hat-finishers, saddlers, and bookbinders emphasise the general indifference relating to the hours of labor which marks eighteenth-century Trade Unionism.[2] This indifference was not wholly due to the greater laxity with regard to hours and workshop discipline possible under a system of individual production. For the protection of their Standard Rate the eighteenth-century handicraftsmen were able to resort to methods no longer open to the modern Trade Unionist. The clubs of town artisans sought to protect their position by the stringent enforcement of the laws requiring a seven years' apprenticeship, and imposing a limit on the number of persons learning the craft. The home-working weavers petitioned Parliament, in some cases successfully, for the legal enforcement of their customary rates of payment. The position of the eighteenth-century Trade Unionist was in many respects analogous to that of the modern solicitor or doctor, who, maintaining his Standard Rate by high educational tests and the exclusion of unauthorised competitors, is unable to understand what justification can be urged for the imposition of a uniform Normal Day.

Very different is the record of the nineteenth century. With the introduction of machinery moved by power, and the rapid development of the factory system, the operatives in the new textile industries lost all individual control over their working day. "Whilst the engine runs," wrote an acute observer of the new industry, "the people must work. Men, women, and children are yoked together with iron and steam. The animal machine—breakable in the best case,

---

[1] See the Saddlers' "Addresses," preserved in the Place MSS., 27,799-112, 114; and Dunning's "Account of the London Consolidated Society of Bookbinders," in the Social Science Association *Report on Trade Societies and Strikes*, 1860, p. 93.

[2] Adam Smith, as Marx pointed out, habitually treated the working-day as a constant quantity.—*Capital*, Part IV. ch. xix. (vol. ii. p. 552 of English translation of 1887).

subject to a thousand causes of suffering, changeable every moment—is chained fast to the iron machine, which knows no suffering and no weariness." Accordingly we find the combinations of the Cotton-spinners, from the very beginning of their history, eagerly supporting the efforts of philanthropists to obtain from Parliament a legal regulation of the hours of labor. The successive Factory Acts thus obtained applied in terms, it is true, only to women and children. But it was obvious to contemporary observers that the whole strength of the agitation came from the men's desire for a legal restriction of their own working day.[1] In 1867 the leaders of the Lancashire Cotton-spinners' unions summoned a delegate meeting expressly " to agitate for such a measure of legislative restriction as shall secure a uniform Eight Hours' Bill in factories, exclusive of meal-times, for adults, females, and young persons ; and that such Eight Hours' Bill have for its foundation a restriction on the moving power." [2] It was, however, impossible to induce the Parliament of these years even to listen to the idea of a direct legal limitation of the hours of adult male workers ; and when, in 1872-74, the Lancashire operatives successfully agitated for a further reduction of the working day, they were astute enough to couch their demand in terms of a mere amendment to the Ten Hours' Act of 1847. Twenty years later we find the recognised organ of the same union declaring that " now the veil must be lifted and the agitation carried on under its true colours. Women and children must no longer be made the pretext for securing a reduction of working hours for men. The latter must speak out and declare that both they and the women and children require

---

[1] Thus, R. H. Greg, citing the Report of the Royal Commission on Factories, vol. i. p. 47 of 1837, observes : " It is obvious, therefore, that the condition of children has been only the cloak for an ulterior object, which object is now frankly avowed to be the same for which the agitation of 1833 took place, namely, the attainment of the Ten Hours' Bill, or a Bill for preventing any factory from working more than ten hours in any one day."—*The Factory Question Considered in Relation to its Effects on the Health and Morals of those employed in Factories, etc.* (London, 1837), p. 17.

[2] *Beehive*, 23rd February 1867 ; *History of Trade Unionism*, p. 295.

less hours of labor in order to share in the benefits arising from the improvements in productive machinery. The working hours cannot be permanently reduced by Trade Union effort. . . . It is only by the aid of Parliament that working hours can be made somewhat uniform." [1] In another great industry the operatives had found themselves equally at the mercy of their employer's decision as to the working day. The coalminers, working underground, can descend and ascend only when the mine manager chooses to leave the shaft free from coal-drawing, and set the men's cage in motion. Hence the coalminers, as soon as they were effectively organised, began to agitate for a fixed working day. Already in 1844-47 we find Martin Jude, the miners' leader, making "an Eight Hours' Bill" one of the foremost objects of the Miners' Association of Great Britain and Ireland, which in those years covered all the English coalfields. From 1863 to 1881 it was, as we have described,[2] an important plank in the programme of Alexander Macdonald. Finally, in 1885 we find the Lancashire Miners' unions expressly insisting that the legal limit should apply to men and boys alike—a demand which was quickly taken up by all the miners' unions except those of Northumberland and Durham.[3]

Meanwhile the transformation of the building and engineering industries was causing the clubs of artisans and mechanics to insist on a definite limit to the working day also in these trades. The growth of large machine-making establishments, and the coming in of the general "contractor" for building operations, both dating from the first quarter of the present century, resulted in the supersession of the small working master, and the massing together of large numbers of workmen, using expensive machinery and plant, and co-operating under strict discipline in a single undertaking. In the great upheaval of the Building Trades in 1833-34, the prohibition of overtime appears as one of

---

[1] *Cotton Factory Times*, 26th May 1893.
[2] *History of Trade Unionism*, pp. 284-289. [3] *Ibid.* pp. 378, 379.

the men's demands, and the Builders' Laborers, in particular, insisted on extra pay for working beyond their regular hours on Saturdays.[1] In 1836 we discover the London Engineers engaged in an eight months' struggle with their employers for the establishment by mutual agreement of a definite Normal Day for the whole trade ; a struggle which ended in the fixing of a Sixty Hours' week, and, for the first time in the engineering trade, the penalising of overtime by extra rates. Before this strike, though the day's work was nominally ten and a half hours, the constant prevalence of overtime, without any extra rate of payment, gave the men no protection whatever against the systematic lengthening of hours by any individual employer.[2] How soon the building operatives secured the same hours is not recorded, but already in 1846 we find the Liverpool Stonemasons demanding a Nine Hours' Day. From this time forward the records of both the engineering and building Trade Unions show the movement for the more strict observance and progressive shortening of the Normal Day to have been continued without intermission. The elaborate treaty concluded in 1892 between the London Building Trade Unions and the associated Master Builders, by which the working time for all building work within twelve miles of Charing Cross was fixed for

[1] See the Masters' Address, 12th June 1833, in *An Impartial Statement of the proceedings of the members of the Trades Union Societies and of the steps taken in consequence by the Master Tradesmen of Liverpool* (Liverpool, 1833). Also the *Statement of the Master Builders of the Metropolis in explanation of the differences between them and the workmen respecting the Trades Unions* (London, 1834). It may be mentioned that the minute books of the Glasgow Joiners, whose secretary was a leading Owenite, contain, between 1833 and 1836, frequent regulations intended to secure the Normal Day. At the general meeting in March 1833, for instance, they formally adopted the working rules of the Scottish National Union, which penalised overtime by " time and a half " rates. In 1836 we find the Society, after a successful strike, insisting, not only on a standard wage of 20s. a week, but also on the total prohibition of overtime for that season. From 1834 onward they were waging constant war on the practice of working by artificial light, securing its prohibition in 1836 after a prolonged strike.

[2] Article by Mr. John Burnett in the *Newcastle Weekly Chronicle*, 3rd July 1875 ; Paper read by William Newton on behalf of the Executive of the Amalgamated Society of Engineers at the Dublin Meeting of the Social Science Association, 1861.

every week in the year, with extra rates intended to penalise all overtime, is only one of the latest of a practically unbroken series of collective agreements.

But though the conception of a Common Rule as to the hours of labor has now spread to all classes of Trade Unionists, whether paid by time or by the piece, handicraftsmen or factory operatives, there is, among the different trades, a marked difference in the intensity with which the demand is pressed upon the employers and the public. Here again our analysis of the Trade Union argument helps us to understand the facts. The Cotton Operatives and Coalminers are the most strenuous advocates of definitely limited and uniform hours of labor. This is not surprising when we remember that, in both these industries, the beginning and leaving off of work depends, not on the will of the operative but on the starting and stopping of the engine ; when we realise further that in both cases the trades are " open " to all comers, and that the Standard Rate is protected neither by the Limitation of Apprentices nor the exclusion of laborers from other occupations. The engineering and building operatives follow at some distance the textile operatives and miners in demanding a strictly defined working day. Almost invariably paid by time, they have recognised that some collective agreement as to the hours of work is a necessary part of their bargain for the sale of their labor.[1] But the economic necessity for uniform hours is

---

[1] We are able to watch the growth of the conception of the Normal Day in some of the handicrafts gradually passing into the system of capitalist establishments carried on upon a large scale. Thus, the Provident Union of Shipwrights of the Port of London, an old trade club which emerged into publicity when the Combination Laws were repealed, resolved, on the 4th of October 1824, "that every member of this Union will not engross a greater share of work than what he can accomplish by working regular hours, viz. : not before six o'clock in the morning, nor later than six in the summer evening ; and that no candle work be performed after the people on the outside have left work, so that every opportunity may be given to those out of employ." And it is instructive to notice that the men's main reason for this innovation was declared to be "that it was necessary to regulate a day's work in consequence of the masters stating, when a man had worked for fourteen or sixteen hours, that they earned 10s. per day, although there was one-half as regarded the number of hours." The same motive shortly afterwards impelled the London Coopers, who are pieceworkers, to make a

with them neither so obvious nor so absolute as in the mine or the cotton-mill ; and in both these industries the unions have relied, for the protection of their Standard Rates, on their traditional policy of insisting on a period of apprenticeship, limiting the number of boys, and excluding " illegal men." With the disuse of apprenticeship, and the impracticability of maintaining a policy of exclusion, the engineering and building Trade Unions are insisting, with ever-increasing urgency, on the rigid enforcement of a definitely limited Normal Day. Where, on the other hand, the unions still rely for the defence of their Standard Rate upon such apprenticeship regulations as are enforced by the United Society of Boilermakers, and, less universally, by the various unions of Compositors, their policy with regard to the Normal Day is more uncertain. In both these trades, as we have seen, timework and piecework are equally recognised by the union. In both cases the union unhesitatingly insists on a definite Normal Day for all work paid for by time. But owing to the existence of other defences of the Standard Rate, and of the practical freedom of these hand workers to arrange their own rate of speed, and the details of their working time, their faith in any uniform Normal Day for pieceworkers partakes rather of the nature of a pious opinion.

With archaic trades this lukewarmness passes into indifference, if not even hostility. The most important, and in many respects the most typical union of this class, is the Amalgamated Society of Boot and Shoe Makers. This small and highly skilled class of handicraftsmen, some of whom still work in their own homes, have been strongly

similar regulation. Hitherto, as the secretary of the union explained, no limit had been set to the working day, and "some strong young men will work from three in the morning till nine at night." The result was that the men "found there was advantage taken by their employers ; and that where there was a difference that was resorted to." And the London Compositors expressly stipulated in the Scale of Prices accepted by the employers in 1810, that the time of beginning work should be formally agreed upon between the master and the "companionship" ; that it should be uniform for all the men ; and that night or Sunday work should be paid for at higher rates.

combined for more than a century, and have, from the first, strictly maintained a Standard List of prices. But working invariably by hand, paid by the piece, and enjoying a customary privilege of coming in and out of the employer's workshop as they thought fit, they have never troubled to settle a Normal Day. Although the trade has been, for half a century, steadily declining before the competition of the machine-made product, the workmen have not been driven to consider the effect of their irregular hours upon their Standard Rate. In olden times they enforced a strict limitation of apprentices, and during the present generation the number of boys who have learnt the trade has been so small [1] that the highly skilled bootmaker, supplying the perfect workmanship called for by a class of rich customers, has maintained what are really monopoly earnings. A somewhat analogous case is that of the United Society of Brushmakers, a strong organisation of skilled handworkers, whose printed lists of prices have been accepted by the employers from 1805 downwards. In this trade, where handwork has always prevailed, the operatives, who are individual producers, have from time immemorial gone in and out of the employer's workshop when they chose. For the protection of their Standard Rate they have clung to their old limitation of apprentices, and have never yet sought to enforce a Normal Day. But it is the Sheffield trades which furnish the great majority of unions indifferent to the Normal Day. Here we have a system of individual production which dates, as regards its main features, from the last century. The employer gives work out, to be done by the operative, either on his own " wheel " at home, or on one temporarily rented in a public "tenement factory." The unions, unable properly to control the Individual Bargains made by their members, who receive and return their work alone, and at irregular intervals,

---

[1] This is due, we think, partly to the current impression that hand shoemaking is rapidly dying out, partly to the abnormal demand for boys at relatively good wages in the enormously expanding machine bootmaking industry, and partly to the relatively high degree of technical proficiency now required to obtain employment at the handmade trade.

struggle fitfully to maintain a Standard Rate by the most archaic regulations on apprenticeship. The practical failure of these regulations, and the constant degradation of the rates, leads the more thoughtful workmen to denounce the whole system of individual production, and to urge its supersession by the factory system, where collective regulation, both of wages and hours, would become possible. But the average Sheffield cutler, accustomed to the apparent personal liberty of his present life, is as yet proof against the economic arguments of his leaders.

The demand for a Common Rule determining the working hours for all the members of a trade is therefore, even in the Trade Union world of to-day, neither so universal nor so unhesitating as the insistence on a Standard Rate of payment. On the other hand, the regulation of hours is less complicated and more uniform than the regulation of wages. The most rigid enforcement of an absolutely uniform Standard Rate is not inconsistent, in well-organised trades, with a very large elasticity, specially devised to meet the highly complex conditions and varying circumstances of modern industry. Any such elasticity with regard to the hours of labor is fatal to the maintenance of a Normal Day. We see this illustrated by the actual working of Trade Union agreements with regard to " Overtime." As soon as the employer was precluded from requiring the attendance of his workmen for as long as he might choose, he very naturally made it a stipulation, in conceding a customary fixed working day, that some provision should be made for emergencies. It might any day become important to him, owing to a sudden rush of pressing orders or similar causes, that some or all of his operatives should give more than the usual hours of work. The Trade Union leaders found no argument against this claim. Moreover they saw their way, as they thought, to making the privilege a source of extra wages to their members. It was generally agreed that the overtime so worked should be paid for at a higher rate— frequently " time and a quarter," or " time and a half." This arrangement appeared a reasonable compromise, advantageous to both parties. The employers gained the elasticity which they declared to be necessary to the profitable carrying on of their business, and were able, moreover, to take full advantage of a busy season. The workmen, on the other hand, were recompensed by a higher rate of payment for the disturbance of their customary arrangement of life, and the extra strain of continuing work in a tired state. The concession involved a deviation from the Normal Day, but the exaction of extra rates would, it was supposed, restrict overtime to real emergencies. For a whole generation accordingly, both employers and workmen regarded the arrangement with complacency.

Further experience of these extra rates for overtime work has convinced nearly all Trade Unionists that they afford the smallest degree of protection to the Normal Day, whilst they are productive of evil consequences to both parties. In spite of the extra rates, employers have, in many trades, adopted the practice of systematically working their men for one or two hours a day overtime, for months at a stretch, and, in some cases, even all the year round. In the engineering and shipbuilding trades in particular, the desire for prompt delivery, in years of good trade, appears to be so great, and the competition for orders is at all times so keen, that each employer thinks it to his advantage to promise to complete the machine, or launch the vessel, at the earliest possible date. The result is that the long hours become customary, and subject to alteration at the will of the employer. Nor has the individual workman any genuine choice. An establishment in which it is a constant practice to work ten or twenty hours a week overtime, does not long retain in employment a workman who prefers his leisure to the extra payment, and who therefore leaves his bench or his forge vacant when the clock strikes.

Whilst the practice of systematic overtime deprives the workman of any control over his hours of labor, the Trade Unionists are beginning to realise that it insidiously affects also the rate of wages. If there is any truth in the economists' assumption that it is the customary standard of life of each class of workers which, in the long run, subtly determines their average weekly earnings, systematic overtime, if paid for as an extra, must, it is clear, tend to lower the rate per hour. That frequent opportunities are afforded for working overtime is, in fact, often given by employers as an excuse for paying a low rate of weekly wages. Where payment is made by the piece, it is usually impossible in practice to distinguish between "time" and "overtime," [1] and in such cases a promise of systematic overtime, enabling the men to make up their total earnings to the old standard, is a common inducement to them to submit to a reduction of their piecework rates. But the timeworker is, in reality, as much at the mercy of the employer as the pieceworker. The promise of "time and a quarter" for the extra hours is a powerful temptation to the stronger men to acquiesce in a reduction of the Standard Rate of payment for the normal working day.

Moreover, when bad times come, and the demand for a particular kind of labor falls off, there is an almost irresistible tendency for the amount of the overtime to increase. The employers see in it a chance of reducing the cost of production by spreading the heavy items of rent, interest on machinery, and office charges over more hours of work.

---

[1] A firm desiring to work overtime has thus a special inducement to introduce payment by the piece, and this has led, in some districts of the engineering trade, to the total destruction of Collective Bargaining.—The *Report specially prepared by the Amalgamated Society of Engineers for the Royal Commission on Labor* (London, 1892), which gives the result of an inquiry made of the branches as to the relative prevalence of Overtime and Piecework in the several towns of the kingdom. It is significant that it is the machine-making centres, Keighley, Colchester, Gainsborough, Ipswich, Lincoln, and Derby that stand out as having the lowest Standard Rates (27s. to 29s. per week). Every one of these branches reports the prevalence of systematic overtime to a large extent, and of piecework. The case would be even stronger if statistics could be obtained from unorganised districts and non-union firms, where competitive piecework and systematic overtime are the invariable accompaniments of low rates. "For many years past," writes Mr. Tom Mann, "it has been the deliberate practice in some of the agricultural machine shops to run a quarter [day] overtime five nights in the week, and in consequence of this the Standard Rate is very low, and the actual working day is one of twelve hours."—*Amalgamated Engineers' Monthly Journal*, January 1897, p. 12.

The workmen are tempted to make up, by extra labor, their drooping weekly earnings. Exactly at the moment when the community needs, perhaps, ten per cent less work from its engineers or its building operatives, a large number of these are pressed and tempted to give ten per cent more work—to the end that nearly twenty per cent of the trade can find no employment whatever! The barrister or the medical man, when the demand for his labor is slack, is not expected or desired to work more hours in the day. The old-fashioned handicraftsman equally reduced his working hours in slack times, and increased them when trade was brisk. In the case of the great machine industries the tendency is, in the absence of a precisely fixed and rigid Normal Day, all in the contrary direction. It is impossible to convince the Trade Unionist of the excellence of an arrangement which periodically results in an extra large percentage of members draining the society's funds by Out-of-Work Pay, at the very moment that other members are working an extra large number of hours overtime. Even the employers are now beginning to object to the arrangement. They feel that it is unbusinesslike to pay higher rates for tired work. And they assert that the men's desire to get these higher rates sometimes leads to dawdling during the day, in order that the overtime may be prolonged.[1]

The necessity for precision and uniformity in the determination of the working hours has been found by experience to be equally absolute where the Normal Day is enforced by the Method of Legal Enactment. The elaborate code which now regulates the hours of labor of women and children in British industry consists of two main divisions, relating respectively to textile manufacture and to other industries, the

---

[1] The really unprofitable character of systematic overtime was detected by a shrewd German lawyer in 1777. Justus Möser relates that when the building operatives worked overtime on his new house, he saw himself thereby defrauded, as the men in the long hours really got through in the aggregate less work in return for the day's pay. "Public authority," he adds, "should here intervene and forbid overtime, which is a fraud on the employer and the customer alike."—"On the Work done in the Hours of Recreation," in *Patriotische Phantasien* (Berlin, 1858), vol. iii. p. 151, noticed in Brentano's *Arbeitszeit und Arbeitsleistung*.

former dating practically from 1833, the latter, it may almost be said, only from 1867. This difference in antiquity is reflected in the varying degree of rigidity attained.

Dealing first with the Normal Day in textile manufactures, the Act of 1833 (which applied, in express terms, only to persons under eighteen years of age) prescribed a maximum of twelve hours a day, less one and a half hours for meals. But it left it open to the discretion of the millowners to have their factories open any hours between 5.30 A.M. and 8.30 P.M., and to fix the meal-times as they chose, whilst time lost through breakdown of machinery might be made up as overtime. The factory inspectors soon found that this elasticity destroyed the efficacy of the law. We need not relate the incidents of the long struggle waged by the Cotton Operatives' unions to secure a genuine limitation of the factory day. One by one the loopholes for evasion were closed up. The right to make up time lost by breakdowns was (as regards mills worked by steam) expressly abolished, the hours of beginning and ending work were definitely prescribed, the times for meals were fixed, all hours were to be reckoned by a public clock. In short, by the Acts of 1847, 1850, and 1874 the right of the millowner to work any extra, or even any different, hours from those prescribed by law, on any excuse whatsoever, has been absolutely taken away. However much the circumstances of one mill or one district may differ from those of another ; whatever may be the nature of their respective trades or the character of their markets ; whether they work with cotton or wool, flax or jute, silk or worsted ; however pressing may be the rush of sudden orders ; whatever time may have been lost by an accident to the boiler ; the precisely determined Normal Day for the protected classes in a textile mill must not be encroached upon, and may not even be temporarily varied to suit the convenience either of employer or operatives. In the case of the textile industry sixty years' experience enabled the Trade Unionists to persuade the expert officials of the Factory Department, and even a reluctant House of

Commons, that however specious may be the arguments for elasticity and qualifications, it is only by the rigid enforcement of precisely fixed and uniform hours that the Normal Day can be really protected.

In other trades, in which factory legislation is of more recent introduction, we see the same lesson in process of being learnt. Between 1860 and 1867 the Ten Hours' Normal Day was introduced for the protected classes in other industries. The Act of 1878 systematically applied it to all non-textile factories and workshops. But the House of Commons could not bring itself to make its uniform rule precise and effective. Endeavors were made, by sanctioning overtime under certain conditions, by enabling the hours of beginning and ending work to be varied, by permitting the prescribed meal-times and holidays to be altered, and by exempting particular processes from particular restrictions, to meet the varying circumstances of different industries. So deeply rooted was the feeling against uniformity that the exceptions and qualifications of the 1878 Act commended themselves even to the Chief Inspector of Factories. In spite of his experience in the textile mills, Mr. Redgrave could welcome with complacency the " undulating and elastic " line of the new Act, " drawn to satisfy the absolute necessities and customs of different trades in different parts of the kingdom," especially mentioning the " extension of hours to meet sudden emergencies, as the case of occupations in which the operatives have to meet regular slack seasons." [1] Twenty years' trial of this " undulating and elastic line " has convinced the officials administering the Act that no such uncertain rule can be maintained. The whole experience of the Factory Department proves that no limitation of the working day can really be enforced, unless there are uniform and definitely prescribed hours before and after which work must not be carried on. The overtime regulations,

[1] *Annual Report of H.M. Chief Inspector of Factories and Workshops*, 1878 (C. 2274 of 1879), p. 5.

hailed as one of the sensible advantages of the Act of 1878, have gone far to neutralise any regulation of hours at all. The report of the Chief Inspector for 1894 is full of complaints by his staff of the impossibility of maintaining the Normal Day in face of the "partial, unsound, and piece-meal privilege" thus given to unfair employers, and of the "modifications" which constitute "a most weakening element in workshop inspection."[1] The knowledge that overtime may be "carried on for forty-eight times in a year is often made," says one inspector, "an excuse for working until 10 P.M. for three or four nights every week in the season."[2] "The steady increase of overtime notices which we receive," declares another, "leads me to infer that . . . occupiers of factories or workshops . . . are exercising those privileges without due regard to the spirit of the law, which only regards overtime as an exceptional contingency, only to be used when exceptional circumstances require it. . . . Overtime employment leads to more undetected evasions of the laws than all the other offences under factory and workshop legislation."[3]

Overtime, in fact, is to-day seldom the "exceptional over-time" contemplated by the Act; but, to use the words of one inspector, merely a means of enabling the employers to "keep their shops open late" on Saturday nights, and of causing "females to be kept" systematically late at work "in dressmaking without a farthing of extra remuneration."[4] "I believe, therefore," officially reports Miss May Abraham, Senior Woman Inspector in 1893, "that although a with-drawal of the overtime exception would meet with protest from employers who have developed its use from an excep-tion into a principle, there are some who would welcome, and many who would be indifferent to such an amendment; that the large class of employers engaged in the textile and

---

[1] *Report of the Chief Inspector of Factories and Workshops*, 1894 (C. 7745 of 1895), pp. 49, 50.
[2] *Ibid.* p. 56 (Mr. Mackie, Assistant Inspector).
[3] *Ibid.* p. 194 (Mr. Dodgson, Inspector).   [4] *Ibid.* p. 191.

allied trades, from whom permission to work overtime has been rigidly withheld, would greet as a measure of justice its withdrawal now from trades logically no more entitled to the exception than their own : and that by the workers its abolition would be welcomed with feelings of the warmest gratitude." [1]   When Mr. Lakeman, after a whole generation of work in London factory inspection, has to account for the long and irregular hours still worked in defiance of the Act, he emphatically declares " that overtime is the root of the mischief, for it has choked the law with partiality and modifications." [2]

We have left to the last what is perhaps the most marked distinction between the Trade Union regulation of the Standard Rate and that of the Normal Day.   Instead of the bewildering variety which characterises the claim to a Standard Rate, where each trade, and each section of a trade, has its own price, we have, with regard to the Normal Day, comparative simplicity and uniformity.   During the last sixty years, the demand for a Normal Day has come in the guise of a succession of waves of popular agitation for a common and uniform reduction of the hours of labor for all trades alike.   The Ten Hours' agitation of the Lancashire Cotton Operatives spread, as we have seen, to the builders, engineers, tailors, and other craftsmen, and resulted, between 1830 and 1840, in the very general adoption of Ten Hours as the Normal Day in the larger towns.   Similarly, the Nine Hours' Movement, started by the Stonemasons in 1846, spread, during the next thirty years, throughout the whole range of industry, and resulted by 1871-74 in the almost universal acceptance of Nine Hours as the Normal Day of artisans, mechanics, and factory workers and the laborers working in association with any of these classes. And it may perhaps be inferred that we stand, at the

---

[1] *Report of the Chief Inspector of Factories and Workshops for* 1893 (C. 7368 of 1894), pp. 11, 12.

[2] *Ibid.* p. 50.   See also the *Opinions on Overtime* (London, 1894), published by the Women's Trade Union League.

present day, in the first years of a similar general move-
ment which will result in the equally widespread adoption of
Eight Hours as the standard working day in all branches of
British industry.[1]

Here at last we do come to something like communistic
feeling among British workmen. The aristocratic shipwright,
pattern-maker, or cotton-spinner, who would resent the idea
that the unskilled laborer or the woman worker had any
moral claim to as high a Standard Rate as himself, readily
accepts, when it comes to a question of hours, the doctrine
of complete equality. The explanation is simple. The most
rigid class distinctions of the wage-earning world have, in
the matter of hours of labor, to bend before the mechanical
necessity for a Common Rule. The same economic influences which make it impossible for each weaver in a mill to
come in and out as he or she chooses, make it convenient,

---

[1] The successive reductions in working hours have been very imperfectly
recorded. At the beginning of the eighteenth century, the ordinary working day
of indoor trades in London seems to have been from 6 A.M. to 9 P.M., whilst men
working out of doors left off at 6 P.M., or at dark. We have described the attempt
of the tailors in 1720 to shorten the day by one hour, and from a rare work in the
Guildhall and Patent Office Libraries, dated 1747 (*A General Description of All
Trades*, Anon.), it would seem that, by the middle of the century, a few other trades
had followed their example. The bookbinders (1787) and saddlers (1793)
secured a further reduction to thirteen hours less meal-times, and in 1794 the
bookbinders gained what would now be called a $10\frac{1}{2}$ hours' day (12 hours less
meal-times). Our impression is that at the opening of the present century this
had become in London the usual working day for all the skilled handicraft trades
working by time. By 1834, at any rate, the London building trades had secured
a ten hours' day and in 1836, the London engineers obtained the same reduction.
Within ten years this became general in most of the large towns, and was adopted
for the textile factories in the celebrated Ten Hours' Bill of 1847. The Nine
Hours' Movement begins with the Liverpool stonemasons in 1846, but does not
become general until 1859-61, nor fully successful until 1871. Meanwhile an
agitation had arisen among the skilled artisans for a Saturday half-holiday. The
building trades had secured a "four o'clock Saturday" in some towns by 1847,
making a $58\frac{1}{2}$ hours' week. By 1861 this had become in London a "two
o'clock Saturday," or $56\frac{1}{2}$ hours a week, an arrangement which was adopted for
the textile factories by the Act of 1874. When, in 1871, the Nine Hours' Day
was won by the engineering and building trades, it took the form of 11 hours less
$1\frac{1}{2}$ hours meal-times, for five days, and six hours less half an hour for breakfast on
Saturday, thus securing 54 hours with a "one o'clock Saturday." In 1890 the
engineering trades on the Tyne and Wear, desiring a more complete half-holiday,
demanded and obtained a "twelve o'clock Saturday" (53 hours). On the great
general revision of hours in the London building trades in 1892, the week was

if not absolutely necessary, for the hours of beginning and
leaving off work to be identical, not for the weavers only,
but also for all the different classes of workpeople employed
in the establishment. And it has been a special feature of
the industrial development of the past thirty years more and
more to include, in a single establishment, not merely different
sections of one trade, but also the most diverse industrial
processes subsidiary to the production of the finished article.
In the leading engineering and shipbuilding yards of the
Tyne and Clyde, or the great works of the railway companies—to cite only a few out of many examples—we find
to-day workmen of a hundred different trades working in a
single establishment whose hours of labor are almost necessarily governed by the same " steam hooter," or factory bell.[1]
Any regulations relating to the length or distribution of
the working day tend, therefore, to be identical for all classes
of operatives.

fixed at 50, 47, and 44 hours according to the season, averaging 48¼ hours
through the year, and always securing the Saturday half-holiday. Finally, we
have the adoption, between 1889 and 1897, of the Eight Hours' Day in over five
hundred establishments, including the Government dockyards and workshops,
nearly all municipal gasworks, and a majority of the London engineering and
bookbinding establishments, together with isolated firms all over the country.

This progressive reduction relates, it need hardly be said, only to the nominal
standard hours of the most advanced districts, and takes no account either of the
prevalence of overtime, or of the lingering of longer hours in other districts. In
the absence of precise and authoritative statistics as to the amount of overtime
worked at different periods per person employed, it is impossible to give any
inductive proof of the lengthening of hours by systematic overtime at the moment
when, owing to a slackening of demand, less of the work is demanded by the
community. But the same tendency may be seen in the recorded changes in the
Normal Day itself. In the extraordinarily busy years of 1871-72 the engineering
employers had agreed with the Trade Unions that the week's work should
be 54 hours, and, on the Clyde, 51 hours only. When the great stagnation
of 1878-79 fell upon the industry, and there was much less engineering work
to be done, the employers decided " that the time has arrived . . . when the
idle hours which have been unprofitably thrown away, must be reclaimed to
industry and profit, by being redirected to reproductive work " (Secret Circular of
the Iron Trades Employers' Association, December 1878). They therefore made
a general attempt to increase the week's work to 57 or 59 hours. A similar
attempt was made in the building trades. For an account of this backwardation
in hours, see *History of Trade Unionism*, pp. 331, 334.

[1] See, for this tendency to an "integration of processes" in competitive industry,
the *Economic Heresies of the London County Council*, by Sidney Webb (London,
1894), a paper read at the Economic Section of the British Association in 1894.

CHAPTER VII

SANITATION AND SAFETY

IN the great establishments of modern industry, where large numbers of manual workers are massed together, the wage-contract implicitly includes many other conditions besides those of the time to be spent in labor, and the rate at which this is to be paid for. The wage-earner sells to his employer, not merely so much muscular energy or mechanical ingenuity, but practically his whole existence during the working day.[1] An overcrowded or badly-ventilated workshop may exhaust his energies ; sewer gas or poisonous material may undermine his health ; badly-constructed plant or imperfect machinery may maim him or even cut short his days ; coarsening surroundings may brutalise his life and degrade his character—yet, when he accepts employment, he tacitly undertakes to mind whatever machinery, use whatever materials, breathe whatever atmosphere, and endure whatever sights, sounds, and smells he may find in the employer's workshop, however inimical they may be to health or safety.

On all these points Individual Bargaining is out of the question. The most ingenious employer would find it impossible to bargain separately with individual workers as

[1] "It matters nothing to the seller of bricks whether they are to be used in building a palace or a sewer ; but it matters a great deal to the seller of labor, who undertakes to perform a task of given difficulty, whether or not the place in which it is to be done is a wholesome and a pleasant one, and whether or not his associates will be such as he cares to have."—*Principles of Economics,* by Professor A. Marshall (London, 1895), 3rd edit. p. 646.

to the temperature of the workshop or the use of the ventilating fan, the fencing of the machinery or the provision of sanitary accommodation : he cannot make any particular concession to a consumptive weaver in the matter of the amount of steam to be injected into the weaving shed, or give special terms to a cautious miner with regard to the construction of the cage or the thickness of the rope on which his life will depend. These conditions are necessarily identical for all the operatives concerned. The issue, therefore, is not whether there shall be a Common Rule excluding the exigencies of particular workers, but by whom and in whose interest that Common Rule shall be made.[1]

The Trade Unionist demands for safe, healthy, and comfortable conditions of work appear to date only from about 1840, and can scarcely be said to have become a definite part of Trade Union policy until about 1871.[2] This long-continued indifference to the risks of accident and disease was, as we need hardly remind the reader, common to all classes. So long as sickness and casualties were regarded as "visitations

---

[1] The individual operative "can quarrel no more with the foul air of his unventilated factory, burdened with poisons, than he can quarrel with the great wheel that turns below" (*The Wages Question*, by Francis A. Walker, New York, 1876, London, 1891, p. 359). "Where a large number of men are employed together in a factory . . . all must conform to the wishes of the majority, or the will of the employers, or the customs of the trade."—*The State in Relation to Labour*, by W. Stanley Jevons (London, 1887), p. 65.

[2] The coalminers, however, always asked for safeguards against the perils of the mine. As early as 1662, it is said that 2000 colliers of Northumberland and Durham prepared a petition to the King, asking, among other things, that the mine owners should be required to provide better ventilation of the pits. Already in 1676, the Government, in the person of the Lord Keeper North, was suggesting that a second shaft ought always to be provided (*The Miners of Northumberland and Durham*, by Richard Fynes, Blyth, 1873). Similar desires were expressed by the earliest of the Miners' unions in 1809 and 1825, and in such pamphlets as *A Voice from the Coalmines, or a Plain Statement of the grievances of the pitmen of the Tyne and Wear* (South Shields, 1825), and *An earnest address and urgent appeal to the people of England on behalf of the oppressed and suffering pitmen of the Counties of Northumberland and Durham* (Newcastle, 1831). In no other industry do we trace any request prior to 1840 for more sanitary conditions of employment (as distinguished from higher wages or shorter hours). Neither in the Parliamentary inquiries of 1824, 1825, and 1838, nor in the numerous investigations of the Commissioners connected with the Factory Acts, Poor Law, or Health of Towns, have we found any evidence that the operatives of that time pressed for healthier conditions of work.

of God," to be warded off by prayer and fasting, effective sanitary regulations were not to be expected either from the workmen's combinations or from Parliament itself.[1] And whilst the theologian was attributing the workman's ill-health to the Act of God, the political economist was assuring him that any unusual risk to health or life, like any extra discomfort, inevitably brought with it substantial compensation in the shape of higher wages. We therefore find that in the comparatively few cases between 1700 and 1840, in which Trade Unions made any complaint of dangerous or insanitary conditions, they brought forward the grievance without any idea of establishing regulations to prevent such conditions for the future, but merely as an argument in favor of the concession of shorter hours or higher wages.[2] We need not follow the gradual disappearance of the theological explanation of disease before the progress of science. Of greater interest to the economic student is the growth of an opinion among the Trade Unionists, that the compensation for insanitary conditions brought about by " the free play of natural forces," was of a totally different character from that prophesied by Adam Smith and his followers. To the intelligent Trade Union official it became increasingly evident that the compensatory effect of bad conditions of employment took the form, not of higher rates

---

[1] Public health legislation dates only from about 1840 ; see Glen, *History of the Law relating to Public Health,* 10th edition (London, 1888). The first general Public Health Act was not passed until 1848.

[2] Thus, when in 1752, the combination of journeymen tailors of London complained that, by their having to work from six in the morning until eight at night, " sitting so many hours in such a position, almost double on the shopboard, with their legs under them, and poring so long over their work by candlelight, their spirits are exhausted, nature is wearied out, and their health and sight are soon impaired," all they asked for was an extra sixpence a day wages (*The Tailoring Trade*, by F. W. Galton, London, 1896, p. 53 ; published by the London School of Economics and Political Science). And when, in 1777, the far-sighted and observant Justus Möser was impressed by the injury to health caused by the conditions under which apprentices and young journeymen were put to work, nothing in the nature of factory legislation occurred to him ; his remedy was a technical institute which should supersede apprenticeship altogether.—" Is not an Institute required for Artisans ? " in *Patriotische Phantasien* (Berlin, 1858), vol. iii. p. 135.

paid by the employer, but of a lower grade of character among the workpeople. When the conditions of safety, health, and comfort in the trade fell below the standard of other occupations, the Trade Union official did not find that his members got higher wages.[1] What happened was that his union was presently made up of workers of coarser fibre, worse character, and more irregular habits. And this result was brought about not entirely, or even mainly, by the refusal of respectable persons to enter trades in which the risks to life, health, and character were exceptionally great. For the great mass of workers, in districts dependent on particular industries, there was practically no choice of occupation, and hence, over large areas of the United Kingdom, physical enfeeblement and moral deterioration became the lot of good and bad alike. Even in the rare cases in which exceptionally strong unions obtained for their members some definite compensation for risk of disease and death, the more thoughtful workmen could not fail to realise that the extra money was no real equivalent for the lives prematurely cut short, the constitutions ruined by disease, or the characters brutalised by coarsening surroundings.

Thus, in the Trade Union world of to-day, there is no subject on which workmen of all shades of opinion, and all varieties of occupation, are so unanimous, and so ready to take combined action, as the prevention of accidents and the provision of healthy workplaces. We do not propose to enumerate, or even to summarise in any detail, the various regulations upon which Trade Unions have insisted for the protection of the life, health, and comfort of their members. These necessarily differ from trade to trade according to the

For over a century economic manuals have reproduced Adam Smith's celebrated analysis of the causes of differences in wages, without any investigation of the facts of industrial life. " There is hardly a grain of truth," wrote Fleeming Jenkin with refreshing originality in 1870, " in the doctrine that men's wages are in proportion to the [un-]pleasantness of their occupation. On the contrary, all loathsome occupations are undertaken by apathetic beings for a miserable hire. . . *The best paid is [also] the most pleasant life."*—" Graphic Representation of the Laws of Supply and Demand," by Fleeming Jenkin, in *Recess Studies* (London, 1870), p. 182.

technical processes and particular grievances of the industry
Sometimes it is the prevention of accidents that is aimed at
Thus, the United Society of Boilermakers has insisted, in
its elaborate agreement with the Ship Repairers' Federation
of the United Kingdom, upon the following clause : " The
employers undertake that, before men are put to work on
[repairing the great tank ships for carrying petroleum in
bulk, in which dangerous vapour accumulates], an expert's
certificate shall be obtained daily to the effect that the tanks
are absolutely safe. Such certificate to be posted in some
conspicuous place." [1] Innumerable other regulations aim at
the removal of conditions injurious to the workers' health
Thus, the various Trade Unions of " ovenmen " (potters'
have for a whole generation protested against being forced
to empty the ovens before these have been allowed to grow
cool, on the express ground that this unnecessary exposure
to a temperature between 170 and 210 degrees Fahrenheit
is seriously detrimental to health. Several strikes have
taken place solely on this point, and the Staffordshire Ovenmen's Union now has a by-law authorising the support of
any member who is dismissed for refusing to work in a
temperature higher than 120 degrees.[2] The Northern
Counties Amalgamated Association of Operative Cotton-
weavers has repeatedly withdrawn its members from weaving sheds into which the employers insisted on injecting an
undue volume of steam, and it succeeded, in 1889, in obtaining a special Act defining the maximum limit to which this
practice might be carried.[3] The carelessness of employers

[1] *Payment for repairs on oil vessels : Agreement between the Ship Repairers
Federation of the United Kingdom and the United Society of Boilermakers*, signed
at Newcastle, 12th January 1894. Similar agreements have been made by the
Amalgamated Society of Engineers (Tyneside District) with the Federation (14th
September 1894), and (Newport and Cardiff District) with the Engineers and
Shipbuilders Employers' Association of Newport and Cardiff, 21st March 1895
and in other seaports.

[2] Information given to us by the officials ; see also Dr. J. T. Arlidge, *The
Pottery Manufacture in its Sanitary Aspects* (London, 1892), p. 17.

[3] Royal Commission on Labor, evidence Group C ; the Cotton Cloth
Factories Act, 1889 (52 & 53 Vict. c. 62), amended by the Factory Acts of 1891
and 1895. See the interesting investigation into the results of this legislation by

with regard to the sanitary condition of the places in which their wage-earners have to work has led to many fitful struggles. Perhaps the most notable, and at the same time significant example is that of the Glasgow tailors. As far back as 1854 we find the union resolving that the members employed in a certain notorious underground cellar "should finish their jobs and leave, until a better workshop was got."[1] In the next year an attempt was made to prohibit all working in underground rooms. The general meeting resolved : "That those employers who have pit-shops at present receive notice to get proper workshops, otherwise the men will be obliged to refuse to work in all shops the same not being above ground."[2] During the following years, the energetic journeymen tailors put into force all the methods of Trade Unionism to attain their end. Mutual Insurance was employed to a remarkable extent, any member choosing to leave an underground workshop being allowed four shillings a week over and above the ordinary Out-of-Work pay. This induced the better class of employers to resume Collective Bargaining, to agree to provide suitable workrooms for their men, and even to submit them to the inspection of the Trade Union officials. But neither Mutual Insurance nor Collective Bargaining availed to put down the evil among the worst employers. The union then turned to the law. An influentially signed memorial was presented to the Town Council in order to obtain a by-law prohibiting the use of underground workshops altogether, and though this request does not appear to have been complied with, the increasing stringency of the sanitary law to some extent served the purpose.[3]

a Home Office Committee of experts, *Report of a Committee appointed to inquire into the working of the Cotton Cloth Factories Act*, 1889 [C, 8348], 1897.

[1] MS. Minutes of Glasgow Tailors' Society, April 1854.

[2] *Ibid.* January 1855.

[3] *Report on Trade Societies and Strikes : National Association for the Promotion of Social Science*, 1860, p. 280, where it is erroneously stated that the clause desired was actually embodied in a local Act of Parliament. We can trace no such provision, and underground workshops are, if properly ventilated, still permitted by law. But the use of premises below the ground-level as dwellings is restricted by the Public Health Acts, and the Factory Act of 1895, sec. 27,

But safety and health are not the only requirements. Many trades enforce a series of regulations designed merely to secure the comfort and convenience of the operatives. In the innumerable " Working Rules " which govern the building trades of the various towns, the Trade Unions generally insist on a clause to compel the employer to provide a dry and comfortable place in which the men may take their meals, lock up their tools in safety, and rest under cover in storms of rain.[1]

It will be unnecessary to give further examples. The long and elaborate code of law which now governs employment in the factory and workshop, the bakehouse and printing office, on sea and in the depths of the mine, is itself largely made up of the Common Rules designed for the protection of the operatives' health, life, or comfort, which have been pressed for by Trade Unions, and have successively commended themselves to the wisdom of Parliament. And the Trade Union Regulations of this class, whether enforced by the Method of Collective Bargaining or by that of Legal Enactment, are constantly increasing in number and variety. Every revision of " Working Rules," or other collective agreements with employers, is made the occasion for new stipulations. Each meeting of the Trade Union Congress sees new proposals under this head formally endorsed by the representatives of other trades. Scarcely a session of Parliament now passes without new Common Rules for the pro-

---

forbids the occupation of any such premises as bakehouses if they were not actually employed as such on 1st January 1896.

[1] Thus, to give only four instances out of our collection of many hundreds, the London Stone Carvers are found insisting, as early as 1876, "that, as a protection from the weather, and to prevent loss of time, all carvers on outdoor jobs to be supplied with tarpaulins or other suitable covering"; the London Plasterers stipulate (1892) that "employers shall provide, where practicable and reasonable, a suitable place for the workmen to have their meals on the works, *with a laborer to assist in preparing them*"; the Nottingham Bricklayers require (1893) "that there shall be a lock-up shop provided for workmen to get their meals in and put their tools in safety"; and the Portsmouth Stonemasons (1893) insist "that suitable shops and mess-houses be erected on all jobs where necessary." All these Working Rules, it will be remembered, are formally agreed to and signed by the representatives of the employers and the Trade Union.

tection of the health or safety of one or other class of operatives being, amid general public approval, added to our Labor Code.[1]

We attribute the rapid development of this side of Trade Unionism to the discovery by the Trade Union leaders that it is the line of least resistance. Middle-class public opinion, which fails as yet to comprehend the Common Rule of the Standard Rate and is strongly prejudiced against the fixing of a Normal Day, cordially approves any proposal for preventing accidents or improving the sanitation of workplaces. The alacrity with which capitalist Parliaments met these requests came as a surprise to the Trade Union officials. To the sweated journeyman tailor at the East End, the fact that he was compelled to labor in an overcrowded workroom seemed less detrimental to his health than the excessive hours of daily toil that were exacted from him. The girls in a London jam factory are still puzzled as to why the Government should compel their employer to provide them with costly sanitary conveniences, and yet permit him to go on paying wages quite inadequate for their healthy subsistence. It cannot be of more urgent importance to the community to insist on sanitary refinements than to secure the fundamental requisites of healthy life and citizenship. Nor is one set of Common Rules less inconsistent with " freedom of enterprise " than the other. With regard to Sanitation and Safety the law has not scrupled to " thrust a ramrod " into the delicate mechanism of British industry, in the shape of rigid rules enforced on all manufacturers alike. Whether a factory be new or old, large or small, in the crowded slums of a manufacturing town or on the breezy uplands of the country side, gaining huge profits for its proprietor or actually running at a loss, the community insists on the observance of uniform rules as to cubic space, ventilation, meal-times, stoppages for cleaning, fire-escapes, doors opening outwards,

---

[1] During the ten years, 1887-1896, there were passed no fewer than thirteen separate Acts relating to the conditions of employment in factories, workshops, mines, shops, or railways, besides several general Public Health Acts.

fencing of machinery, degrees of humidity and temperature, water supply, drainage, and sanitary conveniences, separate for each sex. It is in vain that the manufacturers point out to the House of Commons that these requirements constitute as real and as burdensome an increase in their cost of production as a shortening of the hours of labor, and that the Factory Inspector's requisition for a ventilating fan and the erection of additional sanitary conveniences may result in the actual closing of the oldest and least profitable mills.

It is not easy to find an adequate explanation of this state of mind. Something, we think, is to be attributed to the general fear of infectious disease, which the ordinary middle-class man associates more with overcrowding and defective sanitation than with insufficient food or overtaxed energies. Along with this fear of infection there goes a real sympathy for the sufferers, ill-health and accidents being calamities common to rich and poor. More, perhaps, is due to the half-conscious admission that, as regards Sanitation and Safety at any rate, the Trade Union argument is borne out by facts, and that it is impracticable for the individual operative to bargain about these conditions of his labor. And another factor may come into the decision. There still exists a certain scepticism as to whether the wage-earner is capable of wisely expending any larger wages than will keep body and soul together, or of usefully employing any greater leisure than is necessary for sleep.[1] Ventilating bricks and shuttle-guards, whitewash and water-closets cannot be spent in drink or wasted in betting. Mingled with this economic consideration there is even a subtle element of Puritanism— the vicarious asceticism of a luxurious class—which prefers

---

[1] To the Iron Trades Employers' Association of 1878—an organisation which included the leading captains of British industry—a reduction of wages and a lengthening of hours appeared a positive economic advantage to the community. "It has appeared to employers of labor," said their secret circular urging a return to longer hours of labor and a general reduction of rates of payment, "that the time has arrived when the superfluous wages which have been dissipated in unproductive consumption must be retrenched, and when the idle hours which have been unprofitably thrown away must be reclaimed to industry and profit by being redirected to reproductive work."—*History of Trade Unionism*, p. 331.

to give the poor "what is good for them," rather than that in which they can find active enjoyment.

With public opinion in this state, and a House of Commons predisposed to favor sanitary legislation, it might be imagined that the necessary Common Rules for securing health and safety would have been systematically applied to every industry. This, however, is not the British way of doing things. Neither the permanent officials of the Home Office, nor even the Cabinet Ministers themselves, ever dream of considering it their duty to discover and investigate evils which have not been formally brought to their notice, nor spontaneously to initiate remedial measures which have not been persistently pressed on them by outside agitation. The House of Commons itself has not yet outgrown its traditional attitude of a court, to which suitors must themselves bring petitions if they desire to have their grievances remedied, and must present their case too, in certain prescribed forms, on pain of seeing it, however gross the evil, ignored for many years. The result is that the Common Rules necessary to secure health and safety in particular trades are placed on the Statute Book, not according to the urgency of the need, or the extremity of the evil, but according to the strength of the pressure which is brought to bear. In many individual cases this pressure has come from the philanthropists. The agitations which led to the prohibition of the use of "climbing boys" to clean chimneys (1840),[1]

---

[1] It took over sixty years' agitation to complete this reform. In 1817 a Select Committee exposed the horrors to which the "climbing boy" was exposed. Legislation followed in 1834, when the employment of boys under ten was forbidden, and it was made a criminal offence for a master to send a child up a chimney when it was actually on fire ! This caused the insurance companies to petition against the measure. In 1840 the minimum age for chimney-sweep apprentices was raised to sixteen, and a formal prohibition of their being compelled to ascend chimneys was embodied in the law. This remained largely ineffective until, in 1864, the Chimney Sweepers' Regulation Act punished with imprisonment and hard labor any master who sent a boy up a chimney. The last case of a boy dying in the chimney—once not unusual—occurred in 1875, when another Act was passed increasing the stringency of the law. For a general survey of the progress in this protective legislation, see *The Queen's Reign for Children*, by W. Clarke Hall (London, 1897).

and of the employment of children in theatres (1889), derived their force from the ability with which their advocates appealed to middle-class sentiment. Similar adroit management accounts for Mr. Plimsoll's success in 1876 in extending the Merchant Shipping Acts, though on this occasion the political influence of the organised Trade Unions came effectively into play.[1] The protective rules in the Mines Regulation Acts have, on the other hand, been initiated since 1843 by the Coalminers' leaders themselves, though the direct influence of the Mining Unions has been aided by general public sympathy. But it is in the Common Rules secured by the Cotton Operatives that we see the most striking result of Trade Union pressure. The Factory Acts which their support enabled Mr. Oastler and Lord Shaftesbury to carry between 1833 and 1847 were mainly directed to a limitation of the hours of labor. Since 1870, however, the ingenuity and persistence of the cotton officials have greatly extended the scope of the legal regulation of their trade. The elaborate and detailed provisions of the law as to stoppages for cleaning and protection of machinery, the ventilation of the mills, and the exact space to be allowed between the fixed and moving parts of the mule, the regulation of the temperature and the degree of humidity in the weaving-shed, go far beyond anything that Parliament has yet done in the way of collective regulation of the conditions of labor in the factories and workshops of other trades.[2]

---

[1] *History of Trade Unionism*, p. 356.

[2] This is the more remarkable in that cotton manufacture is an industry in which the margin of profit has long been steadily declining, and has, according to many authorities, now almost vanished. Foreign competition, too, is admittedly keen and increasing. On the other hand, the wholesale slop clothing trade has, during the present generation, expanded by leaps and bounds, and has notoriously produced colossal fortunes. Yet whilst the cotton operatives secure from Parliament refinement after refinement at the cost of their employers, the unfortunate men and women employed by the wholesale clothiers, whose woes were laid bare by the House of Lords Committee on the Sweating System, 1888-90, are still practically excluded from the protection of the Factory Inspector. See "The Lords' Report on the Sweating System," by Beatrice Potter, *Nineteenth Century*, June 1890 ; and Fabian Tract No. 50, *Sweating : its Cause and Remedy* (London, 1893).

On the other hand, the genuine public sympathy with the unfortunate chain and nail worker in the Black Country, with the London "fur-puller" and match-box maker, with the laundress or the dock-laborer, has resulted in nothing but sham legislation of an entirely illusory character.[1] Experience proves, in fact, that public sympathy with the worker's desire for Common Rules securing safe and healthy conditions of work leads to effective regulation cnly when the grievances, besides being graphically and persistently pressed on the House of Commons, are accompanied by proposals for reform which have been worked out in all their technical detail by practical experts. To put it concretely, the factory legislation which each trade has obtained, has, during the last twenty years, varied in stringency and effectiveness, not according to the misery of the workers or the profitableness of the enterprise, but almost exactly with the amount of money which the several unions have expended on official and legal assistance.

So far we have dealt only with the promotion of health or safety by means of specific regulations prescribing the conditions which experience has shown to be necessary to prevent accident or disease. In one direction, however, the Trade Unionists have departed from this, the general line of their policy, and have sought safety in imposing upon the employer, not positive regulations to prevent the evil, but an obligation to pay compensation for it when it has happened. This leads us to the long and bitter controversy connected with "Employer's Liability," in which, during the last twenty years, both workmen and politicians have more than once shifted their ground. To understand the changing features of this controversy, we must examine, in some detail, both its history and its various aspects.[2]

---

[1] On the futility of the laundry clause in the Factory Act of 1895, see the article, "Law and the Laundries," in the *Nineteenth Century*, December 1896, published by the Industrial Sub-Committee of the National Union of Women Workers.

[2] The best account of this difficult subject is the Home Office Memorandum printed as Appendix CLIX. to the Labor Commission Blue Book, C. 7063,

By the common law of England a person is liable, not only for his own negligence, but for that of his servant acting as such. It does not appear that this law was, in old times, made use of by workmen against their employers—probably no one thought of such an insurrectionary proceeding—but in 1837 an action (Priestley *v.* Fowler) was brought against a butcher by one of his assistants to recover compensation for injuries resulting from the overloading of a cart. It was proved that the overloading was due to the negligence of a fellow-servant. On this ground the judges decided that the injured servant could not recover compensation from the common employer. This decision is now deemed by some scientific jurists to have been bad law ;[1] but, good or bad, it founded the distinction which has ever since been made between strangers, to whom the employer is responsible for the negligence of his servants, and the servants themselves.

III. A (1894), pp. 363, 384, and the comments by Sir F. Pollock in the same volume (Appendix clviii. pp. 346-348), with Mr. A. Birrell's *Four Lectures on the Law of Employers' Liability at Home and Abroad* (London, 1897). The Report and Evidence of the Select Committee of 1887 (H. C. No. 285 of 1887) is also important. For a more detailed and technical account of the law and its development, see *Employers and Employed*, by W. C. Spens and R. F. Younger (London, 1887), or *Duty and Liability of Employers*, by W. H. Roberts and G. H. Wallace (London, 1885). The Trade Union view is well given in the pamphlet *Employers' Liability : "Past and Prospective Legislation, with Special Reference to Contracting-Out,"* by Edmond Brown (London, 1896). This is ably criticised in the *Daily Chronicle* pamphlet, *The Workers' Tragedy* (London, 1897). For another point of view, see Mr. Chamberlain's article in the *Nineteenth Century*, November 1892, and his speeches in Parliament during May and July 1897 ; *Miners' Thrift and Employers' Liability*, by G. L. Campbell (Wigan, 1891) ; and *Employers' Liability : What it Ought to Be*, by Henry W. Wolff (London, 1897). The exhaustive report of the French Government "Commission de Travail" for 1892 contains full information on Continental legislation, as to which see the interesting proceedings of the International Congresses on Industrial Accidents, held at Paris, 1889, Berne, 1891, Milan, 1894 (Brussels, 1897); Dr. T. Bödiker's *Die Arbeiterversicherung in den Europäischen Staaten* (Leipzig, 1895) ; and the elaborate bibliography published in Circular No. 1, Series B, of the *Musée Social* (Paris, 1896).

[1] Sir Frederick Pollock remarks, in the Memorandum already cited, "I think the doctrine of the American and English Courts (for it is American quite as much as English) is bad law as well as bad policy. The correct course, in my judgment, would have been to hold that the rule expressed by the maxim *respondeat superior*, whatever its origin or reason, was general. . . . No such doctrine as that of common employment has found place in the law courts of France or of any German State."

The lawyers explained that the workmen must be held implicitly to have contracted to take upon themselves, as part of the risk incidental to their calling, the possible negligence of fellow-employees, for whose action, therefore, the common employer could not fairly be considered liable.

To the manual worker this distinction, for which Lord Abinger was chiefly responsible, seemed an intolerable piece of " class legislation." The workman, injured in the actual performance of his duty, was at least as fit an object for compensation as the chance passer-by. The exception, moreover, destroyed all real responsibility of the largest employers even for their own negligence. In mines and railways, and in the large establishments characteristic of modern industry, the legal " employer " was seldom present or in personal direction of the operations. He might be guilty of the grossest carelessness in choosing his managers ; he might not provide sufficient means for proper appliances ; he might worry his agents to increase the speed of working, deliberately bringing pressure to bear on his superintendents and foremen to increase the output or lower the cost of production, to the hazard of the lives of all concerned. Yet because he did not give the specific order, or direct the use of the particular machine, out of which the accident arose, he escaped all liability for compensation to his injured workmen, on the plea that the negligence was that of their fellow-worker, the manager whom he had put in authority over them.

Under these circumstances, a Trade Union agitation for " employers' liability " was sooner or later inevitable. It was started by Alexander Macdonald, the leader of the coal-miners, whose remarkable career we have traced in our *History of Trade Unionism.*[1] At the conference of miners' delegates at Ashton-under-Lyne in 1858, bitter complaint

[1] See the *History of Trade Unionism*, pp. 284-292 ; the *Report of the Conference of the National Association of Coal, Lime, and Ironstone Miners of Great Britain and Ireland* [at Leeds in 1863] (London, 1864) ; Macdonald's speech in the similar report for 1881 (Manchester, 1881) ; and his speech in *Report of the Eleventh Annual Trade Union Congress* (Bristol, 1878), pp. 17, 18.

was made that many of the collieries were without what would now be considered the most ordinary safeguards against accidents. No real effort was made by the Government to enforce the merely elementary provisions of the Mines Regulation Act of 1842. The frequent mine explosions which marked the years 1860-67, culminating in the terrible catastrophes at the Hartley, Edmunds Main, and Oaks Collieries, where hundreds of miners lost their lives, brought the question of the responsibility of the employer prominently to the front. " How long then," asked the miners at their conference in 1863,"shall such conduct and workings be tolerated? To talk of humanity is nothing, and the law as now carried out is useless. To make the result costly is, then, the only present remedy. . . . When men's lives are held to be sacred their safety will be looked to as a matter of vital importance. At present we ask them to be considered costly, and compensation to be awarded accordingly. Many are alive to costs who are dead to all higher feeling, and these should be dealt with accordingly." [1] It is easy to understand the miners' policy. Their industry was already subject to elaborate Common Rules, which were steadily increasing in number and scope. What was lacking, in the absence of any serious Government inspection, was some means of compelling compliance with the rules. Failure to observe them was *primâ facie* evidence of negligence on the part of the manager of the mine. If the Miners' union could recover damages from the mine-owner whenever an accident occurred in a colliery where the law had not been obeyed, the risk of having to pay out several thousand pounds would, it was argued, induce the employer to take the prescribed precautions against accidents. The proposed right of the operative to sue an employer was merely a practical method of enforcing obedience to the Common Rules regulating the industry. Thus, to Alexander Macdonald, employers' liability presented itself only as one of the instruments of his general policy of obtaining legal

[1] *Transactions and Results of the National Association of Coal etc. Miners of Great Britain* (London, 1863), pp. x.-xiii.

protection for the health and life of the underground workers.

This argument was soon reinforced by another. In 1872 the proposal was, at the instance of the newly-formed Amalgamated Association of Railway Servants, taken up by the Trade Union Congress. Inspired, as the Congress then was, by the able men who were fighting the battle for the workmen's freedom of association, it was eager to denounce all laws which excluded manual workers from the personal rights enjoyed by other classes of the community. To the Parliamentary Committee of these years the wage-earner's disability to recover compensation from his employer, in cases in which a stranger could successfully have sued, seemed another of the invidious disabilities to which the law at that time subjected workmen as such. The lawyer's contention that the wage-earner, by entering into a contract of service, had placed himself in a position different from that of the ordinary citizen, was incomprehensible to them. "There seems to be no sufficient reason," declared the Parliamentary Committee in 1876, "for these exceptions to the general law. Negligence in the employer, or in some person for whose conduct he is ordinarily responsible, and whom he has the power to dismiss, must of course be shown. But if that is shown, why should more be required in the case of a workman than in any other case. The present state of the law takes away a motive for the exercise of careful control and supervision by the employer. It even makes it his interest not to examine too minutely into the way in which his work is carried on, lest he should be held to have personally interfered, and to have become personally liable. The proposed alteration of the law would not be any exceptional legislation in favor of workmen : it would be merely the repeal of an exceptional exclusion of them from the ordinary protection of the law." [1]

[1] Parliamentary Committee's *Report to the Ninth Annual Trade Union Congress*, 18th September 1876, pp. 3, 4 ; see *History of Trade Unionism*, chap. vii. Between 1872 and 1879 no fewer than eight Employers' Liability

The energetic agitation between 1872 and 1880 was entirely based on these two arguments. Almost every session saw the matter brought before Parliament in one form or another ; and each Ministry in succession promised to effect an amendment of the law. At last, in 1880, by the skill and persistence of Mr. Broadhurst, an Employers' Liability Act was passed, which went far to meet the contemporary Trade Union demands. The " doctrine of common employment " was not absolutely abolished ; but an employer was made liable to compensate his injured workmen whenever the accident resulted from the negligence of any superintendent, manager, or foreman, or from obedience to any improper order or rule. A special clause, put in for the benefit of railway servants, made the employer responsible for the negligence of any person in charge of railway signals, points, or engine.

Though the workmen (and, in particular, the miners and railway servants) thus obtained a large measure of the reform they had demanded, experience soon convinced the Trade Unionists that, even to the extent that the 1880 Act went, placing the workman in the same position as the ordinary citizen did practically nothing to secure his safety from accident. The argument that the wage-earner ought to be placed, as regards compensation for accidents, in the same position as any one else, led also to the conclusion that he should be free to enter into any contract as to his legal rights, whether by way of compromising an accident already suffered or by way of compounding, in advance, for any possible accident in the future. The employers accordingly met the new Act by inventing the device since known as " contracting out."

It was decided in 1882, in Griffiths *v.* The Earl of Dudley,[1] that if a workman continued in employment after receipt of a notice that he must forego all his rights under

Bills were introduced in the House of Commons ; see the interesting pamphlet by Mr. C. H. Green, *Employers' Liability : Its History, Limitation, and Extension* (London, 1896), written by an insurance official from an insurance point of view.

[1] 9 Queen's Bench Division, 357.

the Act, and accept, in lieu thereof, a claim on a benefit club to which the employer contributed, he was held to have entered into a contract to relinquish the rights given him by the Act of 1880. The consequences of this decision were soon apparent. It did not suit a large employer to be exposed to the risk of an indefinite liability, or to the worry of being sued for compensation by every aggrieved workman. It became a custom in many collieries, and in some railway and other large undertakings, to establish a special accident fund or benefit society, to which both employer and workmen subscribed, and from which was provided, without litigation, substantial relief in all cases of accident, whether due to proved negligence or not. This enabled the partners or shareholders to satisfy their moral responsibilities to disabled workmen at the least possible expense and trouble to themselves, since their wage-earners directly contributed a portion of the fund, and the total amount of the firm's payment was precisely defined in advance. Such a fund, moreover, tended to attach their workmen permanently to their service by disposing them to abide by the employer's conditions, rather than forfeit, by going elsewhere, their claims on the firm's benefit society. Above all, the existence of such a fund, providing as it did for all accidents whatsoever, enabled the firm confidently to insist that its workmen should "contract out" of the Employers' Liability Act, and thus forego the more limited but legally enforced claims for compensation which they could otherwise make under it.

The vehemence and persistency with which the entire Trade Union world has protested against this practice of "contracting out" has all through been incomprehensible to the middle-class man. To him the whole object of Employers' Liability is compensation to the injured workman or his family. If by a special accident fund this compensation can be provided, not merely for some, but for all accidents whatsoever, and if, moreover, the expense of litigation can thereby be avoided, it seems a clear gain to both parties. What the middle-class man fails to realise is that this is to remit the all-important question of safety of the workman's life to the perils of Individual Bargaining. The Trade Unionists assert that the workman's consent to forego his legal claim is given practically under duress, since a man applying for employment has no free option whether or not he will join the firm's benefit society, and so relieve his employer from that pecuniary inducement to guard against accidents which the Act was intended to afford. Moreover, it is said that this inability of the individual workman to bargain about the conditions of his employment leads, in certain instances, to his being simply defrauded, the benefit of the employer's fund being inferior to what he could obtain by relying on the Act and paying his contributions to an ordinary friendly society. But the fundamental Trade Union objection is that this " contracting out," even if willingly acquiesced in by each individual workman, is against public policy, as defeating the primary purpose of the Act. If the employer, they say, can avoid all liability for negligence by making an annual contribution, fixed in advance, he has no inducement to take precautions against individual accidents. Macdonald's idea of protecting the workman's life by making accidents costly is, in fact, thereby entirely defeated.

For the last fifteen years the Trade Union leaders have, therefore, waged bitter war against " contracting out," [1] and have persistently forced upon Parliament their demand for an express prohibition of the practice. In 1893 the Cabinet was converted to the Trade Union position. Once again the Trade Unionists found all their demands embodied in a Government Bill, which successfully passed the House of Commons. An amendment was inserted by the House of Lords preserving the liberty of contracting out of the Act, but under certain significant new safeguards.[2] In emphatic condemnation of the practice of the London and North-

---

[1] The London and North-Western Railway Company, and all but one of the South-West Lancashire coalowners at present (1897), explicitly compel all their operatives to " contract out."

[2] The House of Lords' Amendment, together with the final discussion upon it, will be found in Hansard's *Parliamentary Debates*, 13th February 1894.

Western Railway Company and the Lancashire Coalowners, the House of Lords declared that "contracting out" was in no case to be made a condition of the workman's being given employment. It was not even to be left any longer to Individual Bargaining. No "contracting out" was to be permitted unless the financial basis of the employer's benefit society had been approved by the Board of Trade as fair to the workmen. But this was not all. No "contracting out" was to be allowed, however favorable to the men might be the consideration offered, unless it had been *collectively* agreed to by the workers in the establishment considered as a whole. For this purpose, elaborate provision was proposed for a "secret ballot" of the workers to be taken under authority of the Board of Trade at intervals of not less than three years ; and a two-thirds majority was to be necessary for consent. Thus, under no circumstances was it to be within the option of an individual wage-earner, acting as an individual, to forego his legal rights. In spite of this remarkable concession to the central position of Trade Unionism—the objection to Individual Bargaining—the majority of the House of Commons, at the instance of its working-men members, preferred to abandon the Bill rather than accept an amendment allowing the detested contracting out under any conditions whatsoever.[1]

The controversy has now been narrowed down to so fine a point that the Trade Union leaders may any day get from

[1] The bitterness with which the Trade Union officials object to "contracting out," and the underlying reason which led them to refuse even the safeguarded provision of the House of Lords' Amendment, are, we think, connected not with "contracting out" as such, but with the existence of employers' benefit societies. An accident fund or benefit society, confined to the workmen in a particular establishment, is, as we shall see in our chapter on "The Implications of Trade Unionism," in many ways inimical to Trade Unionism. Employers' benefit societies are far older than the Act of 1880, and exist in many firms which do not contract out. Moreover, contracting out may take place, as in the South Wales coalmines, with an accident fund common to the whole area, and thus independent of any one employer. Employers' benefit societies cannot therefore be swept away by a side wind. If public opinion is to be led to agree to their prohibition, this must come, like the removal of other deductions from wages, by an amendment of the Truck Acts.

one party or the other the legislation they desire. We are, however, inclined to believe that just as they were disappointed with the Act of 1880, though it gave them practically what they then demanded, so they will find equally unsatisfying any measure on the lines of the Bill of 1893-94, about which they were so enthusiastic. The fact is there is no reason to believe that the mere prohibition of " contracting out " will do anything to diminish the number of accidents. Attempts have been made to prove that the comparatively few undertakings in which contracting out prevails have a higher percentage of accidents than those in which the Act applies. But no statistical evidence yet adduced on the subject will stand examination.[1] It is said, for example, that in Lancashire and Wales, where the coalminers contract out, the proportion of accidents is appreciably higher than in Yorkshire or Northumberland, where they do not. But this was the case also before the Act of 1880 : moreover, the proportion of accidental deaths to persons employed seems to be diminishing more rapidly in Wales and Lancashire than in Northumberland. It is even gravely argued that the London and North-Western Railway Company has eight times as many accidents as the Midland—as if nothing turned on the different definitions of an accident ! The truth is, there is no such difference of pecuniary interest as is supposed between the employer who " contracts out," and the one who remains subject to the Act. In the vast majority of cases the employer does not take the trouble to ask his workmen to bargain away their legal rights ;[2] he protects himself against the worry of litigation by the simpler device of insurance. On payment of a definite annual premium to an ordinary insurance company he is indemnified against any loss by claims under the Act, the

---

[1] A well-known barrister, who has been engaged in between three and four hundred Employers' Liability cases, almost exclusively on the side of the workmen, informed us that his experience has convinced him that the legal liability for compensation had no effect whatever in preventing accidents, at any rate in coalmining.

[2] Thus, in 1891, only 119,122 coalminers, out of 648,450, had contracted

company, to boot, taking all the trouble off his hands. The fear of damages may here and there induce a small master to obey, more promptly than before, the factory inspector's order to guard a driving wheel or fence a lift shaft. But in the great staple industries, insurance against accidents, at a rate of premium which is, in practice, uniform for all the firms in the trade, is becoming almost as much a matter of course as insurance against fire. Thus, even where the workmen retain all their legal rights, the employer has usually no more pecuniary interest in preventing accidents than he has where they have been compelled to contract out of the Act. " Contracting out," with its accompanying contribution to an employer's benefit society, is, in fact, itself only a minor form of insurance.

Insurance stands, therefore, in the way of the Trade Union plan of preventing accidents by making them costly. In the case of ships at sea, this fact has occasionally led philanthropists to suggest that insurance should be prohibited. But insurance is merely a private bargain, often indeed only a co-operative arrangement between friends ; and no such prohibition could possibly be enforced. Besides, insurance is itself only a device for spreading an occasional lump sum payment equally over a number of years : so that the largest establishments prefer to be their own insurers. Here the setting aside of a few hundred pounds a year to form a fund out of which to pay compensation for occasional workmen's accidents is a flea-bite compared with the cost and trouble of adopting the elaborate precautions that might totally prevent their occurrence. This brings us to the economic centre of the whole argument. What has been discovered is, that in the majority of industries it costs less, whether in the form of an annual

---

out, the practice being unknown in Northumberland, Durham, Yorkshire, the Midlands, and Scotland. Of railway companies, only the London and North-Western (compulsorily), and the London, Brighton, and South Coast (optionally), employ this expedient. In other industries we know only very few cases—such as Messrs. Chance's great glass works, and Mr. Assheton Smith's Dinorwic slate quarries—where the men contract out.

premium or in that of an occasional lump sum out of profits, to compensate for accidents than to prevent them.[1]

Considered as a method of preventing industrial accidents, the whole system of employers' liability is an anachronism. When Parliament became convinced that no coal mine could be safely worked without a second shaft, it did not seek to mend matters by conceding to the miners a right of recovering compensation from the mine-owner who worked without such a shaft. What happened was that all mine-owners were peremptorily ordered to have a second shaft, under penalty of heavy fines for each day's neglect to comply with the law. When public opinion demanded that the operatives in a crowded factory should not be exposed to the risk of being burnt to death, the House of Commons never thought of removing this risk by any process of compensation ; it commanded every mill-owner to provide proper fire-escapes, or be punished by the police magistrate. This is the method of our factory, mines, railways, and merchant shipping Acts, and all our public health legislation. " Imagine, for the sake of illustration," wrote Jevons in 1887, " that there is in some factory a piece of revolving machinery which is likely to crush to death any person carelessly approaching it. Here is a palpable evil which it would be

---

[1] Thus, to take only one industry, there can be little doubt that the large number of accidents to railway servants (on an average, over forty every day, a quarter of which are connected with moving vehicles) could, as regards shunters, be at once diminished by the universal adoption of such appliances as automatic couplings ; and that in particular, the almost daily sacrifice of platelayers could be avoided by the rigging-up of temporary signals. But to adopt such precautions throughout the extensive English railway system would be extremely expensive, and possibly irksome.

The trifling amount of the premium that suffices to meet all compensation and costs under the Act of 1880 is, in this connection, very significant. The Iron Trades Employers' Association covers the liability of firms employing 28,000 men in engineering and shipbuilding by a premium varying from fifteen to twenty-seven pence per £100 paid in wages. In the building trade it is four shillings per £100. In Northumberland and Durham the coalowners have a mutual insurance association, to which they pay annually a sum sufficient to meet all damages and costs which any of their members have to pay under the Act of 1880. Their total payments during five years were only £400 a year, a sum which would not have gone far in providing any safeguards in all their collieries. See Evidence before Select Committee on Employers' Liability, 1887 (H. C. No. 285).

unquestionably well to avert by some means or other. But by what means?" And he concluded that there was one "mode of solving the question, which is as simple as it is effective. The law may command that dangerous machinery shall be fenced ; and the executive government may appoint inspectors to go round and prosecute such owners as disobey the law."[1]

This sounds simple ; but it involves two troublesome preliminaries. First, an elaborate technical investigation to ascertain exactly what practical precautions should be adopted ; and, second, to induce a capitalist Parliament to enforce them against negligent employers. In 1872 the latter condition was so hopeless that the Trade Union leaders of that day could see nothing for it but to fall back on the indirect method of making accidents costly to the employer. But public opinion has made a prodigious stride during the last twenty years. Parliament no longer refuses to regulate, in minute detail, the processes of particular industries. Though both the scope and the administration of our industrial legislation still leave much to be desired, it now takes only a few years' agitation for a group of philanthropists or a well-organised Trade Union to get embodied, either in an Act of Parliament or in a "special rule" of the Home Secretary, any well-considered regulation for promoting health or safety which has been approved by the scientific experts. Meanwhile, in one industry after another, the inspection necessary for the enforcement of the law is steadily becoming a reality. By the Coal Mines Regulation Act of 1887 the miners in any pit are enabled to appoint two inspectors of their own, who are empowered to inspect, once a month, every part of the workings, and formally to record their report upon them. In 1858 there were only eleven Government inspectors of mines, all told. By 1896 this number had been increased to thirty-nine (including assistant inspectors), and the service made much

---

[1] *The State in Relation to Labour*, by W. S. Jevons (London, 1887), pp 1-4.

more efficient. In the ten years 1884-1893 over four thousand railway workers lost their lives by accidents without the Board of Trade troubling even to inquire into more than a dozen of the cases ; now, with the appointment of two railway workers as assistant inspectors, about half the fatal accidents that take place are made the subject of elaborate official investigation, with a view of suggesting precautions to prevent their recurrence.[1] In short, the protection of the worker against industrial accidents has now become part of the acknowledged work of Government. An avoidable casualty in a factory or a mine is no longer regarded merely as an injury to the individual, to be atoned for by the payment of money compensation : under modern legislation it is an offence against the community punishable by the magistrate. From this public obligation to provide for health and safety there can obviously be no " contracting out." Nor is it possible for the employer to evade his liability by any payment to an insurance company. The inspector and the magistrate are empowered to see, not only that the fine is paid, but also that the law is complied with. The idea of relying for the protection of life and health upon the chance activity of interested plaintiffs in search of personal compensation, seems, to the modern jurist, archaic. Like murder, theft, and embezzlement, the unnecessary risking of the workers' lives has passed from the domain of civil to that of criminal law.

Let us now leave the arguments used in support of employers' liability by the Trade Union officials, and consider why it secures the suffrages of the rank and file. What the individual workman sees in the proposal is, not so much a vague chance of lessening the risk of accidents, as the certainty of a lump sum down when one occurs, to enable him or his widow to set up a little shop. To the miner or the railway servant it seems an intolerable hardship that his family should be reduced to beggary through no

---

[1] *Report of General Secretary to Annual General Meeting of the General Railway Workers' Union* (London, 1897), pp. 12-17.

fault of his own. What he wants is, not to find out whose fault the accident is—as likely as not it is nobody's fault—but to be compensated for his misfortune. That is also the concern of the community, which has an admitted interest in fulfilling for him that "established expectation" upon which foresight and deliberateness in life depend. Here all inquiries as to whether the accident is caused by the personal negligence of the manager or the carelessness of a fellow-workman, or whether it is the result of a fog or an inexplicable explosion, are quite beside the question. Whether from the standpoint of the community or from that of the injured workman, the notion of making compensation in any way dependent on such considerations is pure inconsequence. Accordingly, wherever the community itself undertakes public services, it is every day compensating more equitably those who suffer bodily injury in the performance of their duties. In the army and navy, the Civil Service, and the police, in the Fire Brigade, and other branches of municipal administration, though the treatment of weekly wage-earners is still far from being as favorable as that of salaried officers, we see constantly a fuller acceptance and more generous interpretation of their right to compensation. Private individuals and corporations sometimes show a sense of the same responsibility. In many particular instances large industrial undertakings will give a "light job," or even a pension, to a clerk or workman disabled in their service. Whenever a sensational accident occurs at sea or in the mine, subscriptions pour in to save the sufferers or their widows and orphans from the workhouse. In short, in all those cases in which public opinion can now be directly appealed to, it is found to be largely in agreement with the workman that it is intolerable for his livelihood to be cut short through no shortcoming or fault in his own character or conduct.

We have said above, parenthetically, that an accident is as likely as not to be nobody's fault. It is necessary to emphasise this, because most accidents are, to use the traditional phrase of the bill of lading, "the act of God."

In the great majority of industrial casualties—probably in three cases out of four—it is impossible to prove that the calamity has been due to neglect on any one's part. A flash of lightning or a storm at sea, a flood or a tornado, irresponsibly claim their victims. The greatest possible care in buying materials or plant will leave undiscovered hidden flaws which one day result in a calamity. In other cases, the accident itself destroys all trace of its own cause. In many, perhaps in most, of the casualties of the ocean or the mine, the shunting yard or the mill, the difficulties in the way of bringing home actual negligence to any particular person are insuperable.[1]

Here, then, we discover a fundamental objection to the doctrine of employers' liability—its irrelevance to the issue between the community and the injured workman, and its practical inapplicability, even as an arbitrary makeshift, to most of the cases it is aimed at. Actual experience indicates that it neither prevents accidents, nor insures their victims. And it has the further drawback that to compel the workman to extract his compensation from the employer is inevitably to plunge him into litigation. Even where compensation can now be recovered the law costs are a serious evil. Moreover, unless the sufferer happens to belong to a strong and wealthy Trade Union, which takes his case up, it is usually quite impossible for him to fight it at all, from lack of both knowledge and funds ; so that he is practically driven to accept any compromise offered by the employer. The Home Office itself admits the failure. In

[1] The proportion of industrial accidents for which actual or constructive negligence by the employer can be shown has been variously estimated at from one-tenth to one-half of the whole. The Employers' Liability Assurance Corporation, which insures employers against their liability under the Act of 1880, found that, in this class of policies, claims were made on them for only 24 per cent of the accidents reported ; and estimated that, in another class of policies, where all accidents whatsoever were insured against, only 3026 out of 26,087 admitted claims (or less than one-eighth) represented accidents for which the employer might have been held legally liable. See evidence before Select Committee on Employers' Liability, 1887 (H. C. No. 285), pp. 4165-4308, and Appendices.

its official memorandum on the state of the law it goes so far as to say, " the truth is that to the workman litigation under the Act of 1880 has more than its usual terrors. It is not merely that litigation is expensive, and that he is a poor man and his employer comparatively a rich one : it is that when a workman goes to law with his employer, he, as it were, declares war against the person on whom his future probably depends ; he seeks to compel him by legal force to pay money ; and his only mode of doing so is the odious one of proving that his employer or his agents—his own fellow-workmen — have been guilty of negligence." Finally, such migratory workers as seamen find legal remedies against their employers absolutely illusory, owing to the impossibility of collecting and keeping together their witnesses, if these are fellow-seamen, during the law's delays.

Let us now examine the question from the employer's point of view. Why should he bear the cost of an accident which is the " act of God," merely because it happens to have occurred on his premises, especially when the same unavoidable calamity which has injured his employees may have crippled, or even ruined, his own business ? And even in the case of accidents due to his own neglect, how can any proportion be depended on between the degree of his culpability and the penalty of adequately providing for all the sufferers ? One accident may involve the payment of a five-pound note to a man who has been laid up for a week with a scalded hand : an exactly similar accident, caused in an exactly similar way, may kill or disable for life a score of people. The most criminal negligence may lead only to a breakdown which hurts nobody, whilst a very venial oversight may make an employer liable to fabulous compensation. Thus there is injustice in making him liable for avoidable accidents, and no justice at all—no sense, in fact—in making him liable for unavoidable ones. Is it to be wondered at that employers resolutely resist Liability Bills in Parliament without regard to party exigencies ?

We now see why the provisions of the Employers'

Liability Act of 1880, like those of the score of Bills which have since been introduced for its amendment, are inadequate and even illusory. It was, no doubt, pleasant to get, under the Act, some pecuniary compensation for a comparatively small class of cases, which would otherwise have remained unprovided for. It would no doubt have been a boon to a larger number of sufferers if the Bill of 1893-94 had been passed. But such measures, however useful they may be to particular sections of wage-earners, deal only with a small proportion of the cases of hardship, and do not discriminate in their favor on any logical or permanently tenable ground.

Abandoning, then, the idea that systematic provision for the sufferers from industrial accidents can be got out of any possible penalties for negligence, however widely the lawyers may stretch the term, what shall we say to the suggestion, as yet scarcely whispered by Trade Unionists, that the law should be so extended as to make provision for sufferers from all industrial accidents, whether due to the proved negligence of any superior or not. Both in Germany and Austria this idea has been already embodied in elaborate schemes of universal provision for accidents, which rank among the most remarkable of social experiments. In England the proposal has appeared as a natural outcome of the Trade Union idea of maintaining the continuity of the worker's livelihood. At the Trade Union Congress of 1877, universal provision for all industrial accidents, the funds to be provided by a tax on commodities, was suggested by a London compositor, as an alternative to the usual employers' liability resolution. It was vehemently denounced by Thomas Halliday, a leader of the coalminers, who said " they wanted no tax upon coal. What they wanted was that their lives and their bodies should be preserved. The best way to secure this was to make the employers responsible, and make them pay the cost. What they wanted was not money, but their lives and limbs preserved." This view was endorsed by Alexander Macdonald and accepted by the Congress amid loud cheers. Thus, the rooted belief in employers' liability as a means of preventing accidents, coupled, perhaps, with the fear of a deduction from wages for compulsory insurance, brushed aside a proposal which deserved more careful consideration. By it we are, indeed, taken outside the domain of anything that can be called employers' liability, however much the phrase may be strained. This involves a reconsideration of the incidence of the burden. To compel employers to incur the liability implied by adequate compensation for all accidents whatsoever, would, whether done directly or by insurance, involve a serious burden upon every enterprise, which would certainly be shifted, though not without friction and expense, on to the customers, in the form of higher prices. What is more, it would fall unequally upon different industries according to their risk, and would thus be transferred unequally to different classes of consumers, not at all in proportion to their ability to bear this new burden, but partly at haphazard, partly in proportion to their actual consumption. At every " repercussion " of the tax, there would be an additional " loading," so that the ultimate charge on the consumer would, as in the case of excise duties on raw materials, far exceed the original sum. As soon as public opinion is prepared to decide that all accidents ought to be compensated for, it will be at once easier, fairer, and more economical to provide the necessary annual sum from public funds, and to raise a corresponding revenue in accordance with the recognised canons of taxation.

Upon the question likely to interest politicians—how soon public opinion will arrive at such a point—all that can be said is that the electors are rapidly becoming aware that accidents are an inevitable part of the cost of modern industry ; indeed, statistically considered, they are not accidents at all, but certainties. And, as we have seen, the public conscience, which has never been perfectly easy on the subject—how could it be in a great mining, manufacturing, and seafaring community like ours ?—grows perceptibly more sensitive from decade to decade. The question cannot be let alone : some solution must be found. At present what stands most conspicuously in the way of public provision for all sufferers from accidents, coupled with factory legislation for their prevention, and criminal prosecutions for the punishment of negligence, is the belief in Employers' Liability. And Employers' Liability, as we have seen, breaks down at every point. The conclusion is obvious.

It would be an incidental, but very advantageous, result of any scheme of public provision that every accident would have its inquest. There would be many gains in extending the present system of public inquiry into casualties. Such an inquiry is now held, (*a*) by the coroner, if death has resulted, or (in the City of London) if there has been a fire ; (*b*) by an officer of the Board of Trade, in cases where a ship has been wrecked or a railway accident involving injury to passengers has occurred ; and (*c*) by an officer of the Home Office in mining accidents. Industrial accidents of every kind must at least be notified to a public office. If a public "inquest" were held, by a duly qualified public officer (with or without a jury), whenever an accident caused loss of life or limb, or other serious bodily harm, to a wage-earner in the course of his employment, the investigation and publicity would probably do much to secure compliance with the Factory or Mines Regulation Acts, and so diminish the number of accidents. If any system of public provision for the sufferers were established, such an inquest would serve a useful purpose in determining whether a casualty had been caused by somebody's negligence or by carelessness on the part of the sufferer himself, or whether it was, in the strict sense, an accident. Where the casualty had arisen from the employer's failure to comply with the law, or from any other gross negligence, a criminal prosecution would naturally follow, any fine imposed thus indirectly reimbursing the State for the expense caused. When the sufferer himself had, by carelessness, brought about his own calamity, his compensation could be wholly or in part withheld, though if death had ensued there would be no public advantage in making his widow and orphans go short of necessary maintenance. The compensation itself should in all cases be payable by the Government out of public funds. Whether there is any practical advantage in the Government, as in Germany and Austria, then levying the amount on corporations of employers (and through them upon the consumers and wage-earners), instead of directly upon the taxpayers as such, seems to us extremely doubtful. Such a system of finance contravenes, like an excise duty on raw materials, all the orthodox canons of taxation. It is perhaps more to the point to say that any attempt to levy an insurance premium upon the workman's weekly wage would, in this country, encounter the unrelenting opposition of the whole Trade Union and friendly society world.[1]

If now we look back on the whole Trade Union argument from the workman's point of view, it is easy, we think, to see running through it one simple idea. Whether we study the regulations imposed by the Collective Bargaining of the iron and building trades, or the elaborate technical provisions of the Factory, Mines, and Merchant Shipping Acts; whether we disentangle the complicated issues of " common employment " or those of " contracting out," we always strike the same root principle, a resolute protest by the manual worker against being required to sell his life or health, in addition to his labor. The individual wage-earner knows that he may always be bribed or terrorised into accepting conditions of employment injurious to health or dangerous to life or limb. He therefore seeks, through his Trade Union, to prohibit Individual Bargaining on these points, and to enforce, in all establishments, those conditions of employment which experience has shown to be necessary for sanitation and safety. It is in vain that the economists

---

[1] See, on this point, the significant Minority Report by Mr. Henry Broadhurst, M.P., in the *Report of the Royal Commission on the Aged Poor*, 1893-95, C. 7684, p. xcviii.

have assured him that extra risks bring higher wages ; or the employers offered him liberal inducements in return for "contracting out" of protective legislation. What the Trade Unionist has, for a whole generation, uniformly answered, is that he will not "coin his blood for drachmas." Hence his persistent hankering after Common Rules, which shall definitely prescribe how much cubic space shall be allowed, what safeguards against accidents shall be adopted, and what provisions shall be made for protection against disease and discomfort. What is remarkable is that, in this resolute determination to lift out of the sphere of "personal freedom" the option to suffer disease, maiming, or death, public opinion has emphatically endorsed the Trade Union view. It is no longer permitted to the sailor to decide whether he will, for extra wages, accept the risk of going to sea in an overloaded ship, or to the cotton operative whether, in order to get employment at all, he will put up with a weaving-shed dripping with steam. We do not now leave it to the white lead worker or the enameller to bargain with their employers as to the extent to which they will risk their health by dispensing with costly precautions ; or allow the coalminer the option of earning high wages by foregoing the elaborate ventilation of an exceptionally perilous pit. And it is not only in the ever-lengthening Factory, Mines, Railways, and Merchant Shipping Acts that this conversion of the public is apparent. The Employers' Liability Act of 1880 was itself a proof that Parliament overrode the lawyers' contention that the workmen must implicitly accept, as part of the wage contract, whatever risk to life or health was incidental to their industry. When, in order to evade this law, employers invented the device of "contracting out," a Liberal House of Commons decided actually to prohibit the risk of accident being made a matter of contract at all, whilst even the Conservative House of Lords resolved that under no circumstances could it be left to Individual Bargaining. Finally, the slackness which has now come over the whole controversy of Employers'

Liability is, we think, to be attributed largely to a half-conscious appreciation by the public that the mere making of accidents costly—a liability which can always be insured against—is not the way to prevent them, and that to foist an illusory liability on the employer for constructive negligence is not the way to provide for the sufferers. As far as the United Kingdom is concerned, the practical conclusion is to prescribe, by definite technical regulations, the precautions against accident and disease which experience and science prove to be necessary ; to punish any breach of these regulations whether any accident has happened or not ; to hold a public inquiry into every serious case of accident, and (as part of the punishment) make the employer pay a forfeit to the State according to the degree of his guilt, whenever the accident has resulted from any breach of the rules or other clear negligence ; and to provide from public funds for the injured workman and his family, however the accident has happened, according to the extent of their needs.

The foregoing analysis of the Trade Union controversy upon Employers' Liability was written in August 1896, and published in January 1897.[1] Since that date the whole situation has been changed by the introduction and passage into law of Mr. Chamberlain's revolutionary "Workmen's Compensation Bill." This measure is admittedly no final solution of the problem, and we prefer, therefore, to leave intact our detailed examination of the position in which the controversy stood in 1896, rather than attempt a hasty reconstruction on the basis of an Act as yet untested by experience.

The measure which the Conservative Government of 1897 has passed as an alternative to the Liberal Govern-

[1] *Progressive Review.*

ment's proposal of 1893-94, seems, in an almost dramatic manner, to give the go-by to all the old controversies.[1] Instead of quibbling over the degree to which the employer's liability for negligence can be stretched, the new law makes him, in most of the great industries of the country, individually liable to compensate his workmen for all accidents suffered by them in the course of their employment, whether caused by negligence or not. Thus, without expressly abolishing the doctrine of "common employment," the law, by securing a certain limited compensation for every accident whatsoever, now puts the workman in an altogether different position from the injured stranger, who can claim only in case of the employer's real or constructive negligence. And although "contracting out" is nominally permitted, provided that the scheme is certified by the Chief Registrar of Friendly Societies as being not less favorable to the workman than his position under the Act, so wide is now the scope of the law and so stringently is this exception guarded, that most of its attractiveness to the employer will have disappeared. The Trade Unionists were, accordingly, well advised in accepting Mr. Chamberlain's bill, notwithstanding its limitations and defects. The right to compensation for all accidents, now granted to about a third of the manual workers, cannot permanently be withheld from the other two-thirds, and the numerous flaws that will certainly manifest themselves in the working of so novel and so far-reaching a statute, may be confidently left to the amending bills to which one Government after another will find itself committed.

The particular employers upon whom the new law imposes a large and indefinite pecuniary liability have, we think, a real grievance. Certain industries have been thus burdened, whilst others, no less liable to accidents,[2] have

---

[1] For a bitter attack on this measure from the Conservative employer's point of view, see J. Buckingham Pope's *Conservatives or Socialists* (London, 1897).

[2] Besides all the processes of agriculture, the building or repairing of houses less than 30 feet high, and all workshop industries, the Act excludes seamen and

been left free. Even within the bounds of a single trade, establishments using one process are made liable to pay compensation for casualties which no care or precaution could prevent, whilst others, using a different process, escape any but the illusory liability of the old law. The novel penalty for accidents to which some employers are thus subjected bears no relation to the degree of their guilt in trying to prevent them ; a casualty due exclusively to the " act of God " will cost them no less than one due to their own personal negligence. In practice the liability to compensation is simply insured against, and employers within the scope of the new Act find themselves saddled with an extra insurance premium, constituting an addition to the cost of production from which other capitalists are exempt.

The two-thirds of the manual workers whom the Act now excludes are suffering from an injustice which cannot easily be redressed on the lines of the present law. It may be practicable to put a liability to pay compensation for all accidents upon a railway company, a coalowner, or the registered occupier of a steam factory. Even in these cases, if the employer neglects to insure, the sufferers in an extensive accident may sometimes find their claims baulked by the firm's bankruptcy. But a large proportion of the excluded workmen are employed by small masters, themselves often little removed from the status of wage-earners, or by migratory contractors of one kind or another, only just living from hand to mouth. Insurance in such cases would be unusual, if not even impossible. Any serious accident in their little industry would, on the one hand, reduce them to bankruptcy, and, on the other, deprive the sufferers of any real chance of extracting compensation from them. Yet the two-thirds of the wage-earners thus employed cannot permanently be denied the compensation for all accidents now granted to the other third. If it is socially expedient to compensate the workers in the great

fishermen ; carmen and drovers and others dealing with horses and cattle ; and such riverside occupations as boatmen and lightermen.

industries for all accidents, there is neither equity nor good sense in withholding a like compensation from those who suffer accidents in other trades.

In our opinion, there must inevitably be a development, either towards the formation of compulsory trade groups, collectively responsible for the accidents occurring in the establishments of their members, or else towards simple State compensation. The former plan, adopted in Germany and Austria, has the economic advantage of making each industry self-supporting, and thus avoiding the disastrous consequences of the growth of "parasitic trades," on which we dwell in the subsequent chapter on "The Economic Characteristics of Trade Unionism." It would, moreover, emphasise the Trade Unionist principle that an industry should be regulated not by the will of individual employers, but by its own Common Rules. Organisation among employers, and therefore Collective Bargaining, would be greatly promoted, with the result that a great impulse would probably be given to Trade Unionism itself. But the necessary regimentation of employers and their control by rigid rules would be extremely distasteful to English capitalists, whilst there would be real difficulty in adapting any such organisation to the remarkable variety, complexity, and mobility of English industry. Simple State compensation avoids all these difficulties, and requires no more regimentation or registration than is already submitted to by every mine or factory owner. If it is desired, as the Marquis of Salisbury declared in the House of Lords in support of Mr. Chamberlain's bill, to create a great life-saving machine, State compensation affords the most effective means to this end. The fact that the Treasury paid for every casualty would change the official bias about dangerous trades, and we should promptly have the Government setting its scientific advisers and factory inspectors to work to devise new means of preventing accidents, to be enforced by the Factories, Mines, Railways, and Merchant Shipping Acts. The public inquests into all serious cases would themselves do much to make the capitalists take every possible precaution, and the Factory Inspector's criminal prosecution of careless employers, which could not be "insured against" or avoided by bankruptcy, would do the rest. Nor would the employers object. Now that Mr. Chamberlain has, in most of our staple trades, made them individually liable for all accidents, a Government which proposed, as the only practicable way of extending compensation to the other industries, to place the liability directly on the State, and to spread its cost impartially over the whole body of income-tax payers (requiring, perhaps, an additional threepence in the pound), might count on the powerful support of the great capitalists in the coal, iron, and railway industries, who would find themselves relieved of the special and exceptional burden now cast upon them.

CHAPTER VIII

NEW PROCESSES AND MACHINERY

A GENERATION ago it was assumed, as a matter of course, by almost every educated person, that it was a cardinal tenet of Trade Unionism to oppose machinery and the introduction of improved processes of manufacture. "Trade Unions," said a well-known critic of the workmen in 1860, "have ever naturally opposed the introduction of machinery, such introduction tending apparently to reduce the amount of manual labor needed, and thus pressing on the majority. No Trade Union ever encouraged invention."[1] In support of this opinion might have been quoted, for instance, the editor of the *Potters' Examiner*, an influential leader of the Potters' Trade Unions, who in 1844 could still confidently appeal to experience in ascribing all the evils of the factory operatives to this one cause. "Machinery," he wrote, "has done the work. Machinery has left them in rags and without any wages at all. Machinery has crowded them in cellars, has immured them in prisons worse than Parisian bastilles, has forced them from their country to seek in other lands the bread denied to them here. I look upon all improvements which tend to lessen the demand for human labor as the deadliest curse that could possibly fall on the heads of our working classes, and I hold it to be the duty of

[1] "Trades Unions and their Tendencies," by Edmund Potter, F.R.S., in the *Transactions of the National Association for the Promotion of Social Science* (London, 1860), p. 761.

every working potter—the highest duty—to obstruct by all legal means the introduction of the scourge into any branch of his trade."

Nowadays we hear no such complaints. When in 1892 Professor Marshall published a careful criticism of Trade Union policy and its results, he deliberately refrained from taking into account or even mentioning, the traditional hostility of Trade Unions to inventions or machinery.[1] And when in 1894, the Royal Commission on Labor reported the result of its three years' elaborate and costly inquiry into the claims and proceedings of the workmen's organisations, it found no reason to repair this significant omission. The Commissioners heard the complaints of employers in every trade, and certainly exhibited no desire to gloss over the faults of the workmen. But if we may trust the summary of evidence embodied in the lengthy Majority Report, resistance to machinery no longer forms part of the procedure of British Trade Unionism. Although the Commissioners analysed the "rules and regulations" of hundreds of separate Trade Unions, in none of them did it discover any trace of antagonism to invention or improvement.[2]

The fact is that Trade Unionism on this subject has changed its attitude. It is quite true that during the first half of the century the Trade Unionist view was that so forcibly expressed in the *Potters' Examiner*. But in 1859 it was noticed by a contemporary scientific observer that neither the Trade Unions in general, nor even those in the same industry, showed any real sympathy with the Northamptonshire bootmakers' strike against the sewing-machine, "deeming it neither desirable nor practical to resist the extension of mechanical improvements, although very sensible of the inconvenience and suffering that are sometimes caused by a rapid change in the nature and extent of the

---

[1] *Elements of the Economics of Industry* (London, 1892), Book VI. ch. xiii. " Trade Unions."

[2] See, in particular, the voluminous analysis of *Rules of Associations of Employers and of Employed*, C. 6795, pp. xii. 513. 1892.

employment afforded in any particular trade."[1] In 1862 the Liverpool Coopers, who had formally boycotted machinery in 1853, resolved " that we permit any member of this society to go to work at the steam cooperage."[2] During this decade the *Monthly Circular* of the Friendly Society of Ironmoulders contains numerous earnest exhortations by the Executive Committee to the members not to resist " the iron man," the new machine for iron moulding. " It may go against the grain," they say in December 1864, " for us to fraternise with what we consider innovations, but depend upon it, it will be our best policy to lay hold of these improvements and make them subservient to our best interests."[3] The United Society of Brushmakers, which had in 1863 and 1867 supported its members in refusing to bore work by steam machinery, and had formally declared that they must " on no account set work bored by steam by strangers,"[4] revised its rules in 1868, and decided " that should any of our employers wish to introduce steam power for boring, no opposition shall be offered by any of our divisions, but each division shall have the discretionary power of deciding the advantage derived from its use."[5] These conversions gain in emphasis and definiteness from decade to decade, until, at the present day, no declaration against innovations or improvements would receive support from the Trade Union Congress or any

[1] " Account of the Strike of the Northamptonshire Boot and Shoe-makers in 1857, 1858, 1859," by John Ball, F.R.S., Irish Poor Law Commissioner and (1855-1858) Under-Secretary of State for the Colonies ; better known as the founder of the Alpine Club. Printed in the *Report of Social Science Association on Trade Societies and Strikes*, 1860, p. 6. The same volume refers (p. 149) to the fact that the organ of the Chainmakers' union " did not hesitate to condemn as foolish the strike of the shoemakers in the Midland Counties against the introduction of machinery."

[2] MS. Minutes of the Liverpool Coopers' Friendly Society, July 1853 and September 1862.

[3] Friendly Society of Ironmoulders, *Monthly Circular*, December 1864.

[4] Annual Report of the United Society of Brushmakers for 1863. See also Report for 1867.

[5] *Rules of the United Society of Brushmakers*, edition of 1869. Such few disputes as have since occurred in this society have arisen (like that at Norwich in 1892) over the exact amount of the piecework rate to be paid on machine work.

similar gathering.[1]   Among all the thousand-and-one rules of existing Trade Unions we have discovered only a single survival of the old irreconcilable prohibition, and that in a tiny local industry, which is rapidly fading away.   The Operative Pearl Button and Stud Workers' Protection Society, established at Birmingham in 1843, and numbering about 500 members, enjoys the distinction of being, so far as we are aware, the only British Trade Union which still prohibits working by machinery.   Its latest " Rules and Regulations " declare " that the system of centering by the engine be annihilated *in toto*, and any member countenancing the system direct or indirect shall be subject to a fine of two pounds.   Any member of the society working at the trade by means of mill-power either direct or indirect, shall be subject to a fine of five pounds." [2]

But every newspaper reader knows that the introduction of machinery still causes disputes and strikes ; and no doubt many excellent citizens still pass by the reports of such disputes as records of the old vain struggle of the handworker against the advance of industrial civilisation.   An examination of the reports would, however, show that the dispute now arises, not on the question whether machinery should be introduced, but about the conditions of its introduction. The change has even gone so far that there are now, as we shall show, instances of trouble being caused by Trade Unions

---

[1] The latest case in which a union has ordered a strike simply against the introduction of machinery into a hand industry is, so far as we know, that of the Liverpool Packing Case Makers' Society in 1886.   The strike failed, and the men have since worked amicably with the machine, and have now become completely reconciled to it on finding, as their secretary informed us, that it had largely increased the trade.

[2] *Rules and Regulations to be observed by the members of the Pearl Button and Stud Workers' Protection Society*, held at the Baptist Chapel, Guildford Street, Birmingham (Birmingham, 1887), Rule 26, p. 14.

We believe that two or three of the old-fashioned trade clubs in branches of the Sheffield Cutlery trades, such, for instance, as the File Forgers and the Tableblade Forgers, still refuse to recognise the new machines which are largely at work in their trades, and which are therefore operated by a new class of workmen. On the other hand, other local unions such as the File cutters, Sawsmiths, and the Pen and Pocket Blade Forgers, have made no objection to the machines, and have encouraged their members to take to them.

putting pressure on old-fashioned employers to compel them to adopt the newest inventions. The typical dispute to-day is a dispute as to terms. The adoption of a new machine, or the introduction of a new process, in superseding an old method of production, usually upsets the rates of wages based on the older method, and renders necessary a fresh scale of payment. If wages are reckoned by the piece, the employers will seek to reduce the rate per piece ; if by time, the workers will claim a rise for the increased intensity and strain of the newer and swifter process. In either case the readjustment will involve more or less higgling, in which the points at issue are seldom confined merely to the amount of remuneration. The degree of difficulty in any such readjustment will depend on the good sense of the parties to the negotiations ; and in this as in other matters good sense has to be acquired by experience. Some industries, cotton-spinning for example, have had a century of experience of readjustments of this kind, which have accordingly become a matter of routine. But in trades in which the use of machinery, and even the factory system itself, are still comparatively new developments, the readjustments are seldom arrived at without a struggle.

As a typical instance of a trade in this stage, take the modern factory industry of boot and shoe manufacture, which is notorious for incessant disputes about the introduction of machinery. In this trade the compact little union of handicraftsmen, working for rich customers, has long since been outstripped by its offshoot, the National Union of Boot and Shoe Operatives, formed exclusively of factory workers, and numbering, at the end of 1896, 37,000 members. We have here an industry which is being incessantly revolutionised by an almost perpetual stream of new inventions and new applications of the old machines. The workmen are noted for their turbulence, want of discipline, and lack of education. The employers, themselves new capitalists without traditions, exposed to keen rivalry from foreign competitors, are eager to take the utmost advantage of every chance. The disputes are endless, and the prolonged conference proceedings, the elaborate arguments before the arbitrators, and the complicated agreements with the employers are all printed in full, affording a complete picture of the attitudes taken up by the masters and the men.

The employers' indictment of the operatives has been graphically summed up by their principal literary spokesman. "It is true," says the editor of the employers' journal, "that objection does not take the form of rattening or direct refusal to work with the machines ; experience has taught the union a more efficacious way of marshalling the forces of opposition. To say openly that labor-saving appliances were objected to would be to estrange that public sympathy without which Trade Unionism finds itself unable to live. So other methods are adopted. The work done by the machines is belittled ; it is urged that no saving of labor is effected by their use ; the men working the machines exercise all their ingenuity in making machine work as expensive as hand labor. There exists among workmen what amounts to a tacit understanding that only so much work shall be done within a certain time, and, no matter what machines are introduced, the men conspire to prevent any saving being effected by their aid. It is of no use to mince words. The unions are engaged in a gigantic conspiracy to hinder and retard the development of labor-saving appliances in this country. The action of their members in failing to exercise due diligence in working new machines is equivalent to absolute dishonesty. It is, indeed, positively painful to any one who has been accustomed to see, for example, finishing machinery running in American factories, to watch English operatives using the same machines. In America the men *work*, they run the machines to their utmost capacity, and vie with each other in their endeavor to get through as much work as possible. But in an English factory they seem to loaf away their time in a manner which is perfectly exasperating. If they run a machine for five minutes at full speed, they seem to think it necessary to stop it and see that no breakage has occurred. Then they walk about the shop, and borrow an oil-can or a spanner, wherewith to do some totally unnecessary thing. This occupies anywhere from five minutes to an hour, and then the machine is run on again for a few minutes ; and if the operator is questioned, he says, 'machines are no good ; I could do the work quicker and better by hand.' And so he could, for he takes care not to allow a machine to beat a shopmate working by hand on the same job, and, in short, does all he can to induce manufacturers to abandon mechanical devices and go back to hand labor. The spirit of comradeship is carried to a ridiculous extent, and no man dare do the best he can, lest his fellow-workmen should be, as he foolishly thinks, injured. . . . It seems to be a settled policy with the men, not to try to earn as much money as possible per week, but as much as possible per job, in other words, to keep the cost of production as high as possible." [1]

Assuming all this to be true in fact—and, so far, at any rate as times of strained relations are concerned, there is no reason to question its accuracy—let us supplement it by two other facts which would hardly have been inferred from it. First, that in the American boot factories which work at such high pressure, the high pressure is invariably paid for by piecework rates. Second, that in England it is the workmen who demand that, in conjunction with the new machines they should be allowed to work by the piece, as they have hitherto been accustomed, and that it is the employers who have resolutely insisted on taking the opportunity of changing to fixed day wages.[2] Here lies the clue to the whole difficulty. We have already explained, in connection with the Cotton-spinners, how piecework is the only possible protection of the Standard Rate for men who are working machines of which

---

[1] *The Shoe and Leather Record*, 19th February 1892.

[2] Thus one of the so-called " Seven Commandments "—the ultimatum of the employers against which the great strike of 1895 took place—was the following. " That the present is not an opportune time for the introduction of piecework in connection with lasting and finishing machinery" (*Labour Gazette*, November 1894). The lasters and finishers have been accustomed to work by the piece ever since the beginning of the factory boot industry.

the rate of speed is always being increased. On such machines payment by the hour, day, or week involves the exacting from the operative an ever-increasing task of work in return for the old wages. In the case of the boot operatives the question is complicated by the fact that the new machines have introduced a new organisation of the factory, the workman steadily becoming less and less of an individual producer, working at his own speed, and more and more a member of a " team," or set of operatives each performing a small part of the process, and thus obliged to keep up with each other. This enforced " speeding up" would be all very well if the old plan of paying by the piece were continued. But when the " more efficient organisation of labor " is coupled with the introduction of a fixed day wage, the workmen see in it an attempt to lower the Standard Rate of remuneration for effort, by getting more labor in return for the old payment.

This position the employers fail even to comprehend. "I know," said the President of the Employers' Association in 1894, "that it will be said it is slavery, pace-making, and driving, and that sort of thing. . . . But the manufacturers contend that that is not so. For instance, when men are put to work in a team, they are waited on hand and foot, and they are never kept waiting for anything, whereas when they have to 'shop' their (own) work a waste of time is involved. That time is saved under the team system."[1] It is part of the brainworker's usual ignorance of the conditions of manual labor that the leaders of the employers could naïvely imagine that, to be " never kept waiting for anything," is an advantage to the man paid a fixed daily wage. To the workman it means being kept incessantly toiling at the very top of his speed for the whole nine hours of the factory day. When this high pressure is demanded for the old earnings, it amounts to a clear attempt to lower the Standard Rate. How this attitude strikes an employer in the same trade,

---

[1] Report of the National Conference between employers and employed, 6th-8th January 1894 ; reprinted in *Monthly Report of the National Union Boot and Shoe Operatives*, January 1894.

conversant with American conditions, may be judged from the following instructive letter written in reply to the editorial first quoted. " Let us take a look into an English machinery-equipped factory. What do we see there? Precisely what you state, only much worse. The workmen, or very often boys, who work on weekly wages, try how little work they can do and how badly they can do that little. They don't seem to care a scrap so long as they get the time over, and are glad when the time comes to clear out of the factory and the day's monotony is over. They are continually meddling with their machines and throwing them out of order. Then the engineer has to be called in. The result is a loss of time, a loss of work, and expense also. *All this to my mind arises from a mistaken policy which English manufacturers adopt in employing so much boy labor and the weekly wages system.* If the piecework system were adopted, and only expert men employed on the machines, better work would be the result, at less cost, and the workman would earn higher wages. Is not that the secret why an American manufacturer can produce his goods at a lower labor cost than similar goods can be produced in this country, while at the same time the American operative is earning much higher wages than his English brother?" [1]

It will not unnaturally be asked why the English employers should wantonly raise difficulties by choosing the awkward moment of the introduction of new machinery, to compel their workmen to abandon the piecework system of remuneration, which has for several generations been customary, and to substitute for it a fixed daily wage. The manufacturers explain that, if piecework rates were conceded in connection with the new machines, and if the scale were calculated on the basis of the workmen's weekly earnings at the old process, the men would very soon so increase their skill and quickness as to earn £3 or £4 per week, instead of the time rate of 26s. as at present. But this, as every cotton manufacturer would recognise, is, economically speaking, no

[1] Letter in *Shoe and Leather Record*, 25th February 1892.

argument at all. The able secretary of the Boot and Shoe Manufacturers' Association has repeatedly urged upon his members that such a result would in no way raise the cost of production per pair of boots, and, on the contrary, would positively lower it, by enormously increasing the output per machine. Unfortunately, such arguments are thrown away on untrained employers, who even when they are contemplating the widest extension of their profits, can seldom view with equanimity the prospect of paying their workmen any larger amount per week than that to which they are accustomed.[1]

The workmen in the factory boot trade, equally untrained in industrial policy, are no less unreasonable than the employers, and on a cognate point. They, too, are so scandalised at the prospect of an increased reward being gained by any one else, that they propose unreasonable and impossible courses in order to prevent it. When, in 1894, the Leicester Branch of the National Union of Boot and Shoe Operatives appointed a committee to draw up a Piecework List for work done in conjunction with the new machinery, these workmen naïvely proceeded on the basis of retaining the "Statement" of piecework rates under the old process, merely deducting, for each article, a percentage estimated to produce a saving to the employer exactly equivalent to the interest he would pay on the cost of the new machinery.[2] Thus, whilst the terms proposed by the

---

[1] An American observer notes the same feeling among German employers. "In Berlin even, I found this narrow-minded begrudging of a working-man's higher earnings. In piecework they reduce the rate of pay of the greater output which brings higher earnings than the general rate. . . . The manufacturers returned to the day rate. . . . because the masters found that the men made too much money under the piecework system."—*The Economy of High Wages*, by J. Schoenhof New York, 1892), p. 400.

The same struggle took place between 1850 and 1860 on the introduction of the factory system and steam power into the Coventry ribbon trade, the operatives demanding piecework rates and the employers insisting on introducing fixed day wages, " partly because the piecework system is a more troublesome one than that of weekly wages, but chiefly because it would work a forfeiture to them of the benefit from the increase of the productiveness of their machinery."—Social Science Association, *Report on Trade Societies and Strikes*, p. 325.

[2] Minutes (in MS.) of the "Piecework Committee," which sat from April to

employers would leave the workmen no incentive to use the new machines, those proposed by the workmen would leave the employers no incentive to introduce them.

The feeling of the workmen in this matter is a superstition from the era of individual production. The operative bootmaker has inherited a rooted belief that the legitimate reward of labor is the entire commodity produced, or its price in the market. This idea was the economic backbone of Owenite Socialism, with its projects of Associations of Producers and Labor Exchanges.[1] In the first number of the *Poor Man's Guardian*, a widely-read journal of 1831, it was expressed in the following verse :—

> Wages should form the price of goods ;
>   Yes, wages should be all,
> Then we who work to make the goods,
>   Should justly have them all ;
> But if their price be made of rent,
>   Tithes, taxes, profits all,
> Then we who work to make the goods,
>   Shall have, just none at all ![2]

When the operative bootmaker proceeds to draft a piece-work list for the new machines, the rates that he proposes really express in figures his economic assumption that " wages should be the price of goods." This state of mind leads him calmly to suggest, in effect, that he should receive the entire net advantage of every new invention. The employer puts in an equally untenable claim to enjoy the whole benefit

September 1894. This Committee was attended by the prominent workmen of the Leicester Branch and the Branch officials. It is only fair to say that when it was seen that the rates proposed worked out to an increase of wages in some cases amounting to as much as 40 per cent, the more experienced officials of the union protested against its proceedings as likely to bring the whole policy of the union into disrepute.

[1] *History of Trade Unionism*, ch. iii.

[2] Place MSS., 27,791-240. The verse is now reprinted in *Dictionary of Political Economy* under "Chartism"; and in the *Life of Francis Place*, by Graham Wallas (London, 1897). The same idea inspired the proposals of Lassalle, and most of the inferences drawn from Karl Marx's *Theory of Value* whilst it still lingers in the declarations and programmes of German Socialism and its derivatives. It is, of course, inconsistent with present economic views as to the "unearned increment," arising from the progress of invention and organisation

of the improvement, and regards the workmen's claim as an attack, not on the community, but on himself. But whatever the employer may desire, the community believes that, in the majority of cases, competition quickly transfers his new gains to the consumer in the shape of reduced prices. In all these contentions, therefore, public opinion is apt to be against the workmen's claim, even to the extent of ignoring their legitimate demand for an increase of earnings commensurate with the greater strain of the new process. The employers have sometimes known how to use this argument with great effect on public opinion. The London Master Builders' Committee complained, in 1859, that the men's argument in favor of a shortening of hours "implied that the benefits to be derived from machinery are not the property of society, of its inventors, of those who apply it, but are to be appropriated by those whose labor it is alleged it will displace." [1]

When the increase in production does not depend on a new machine, but arises merely from a further division of labor, even the experienced leaders of the operatives are honestly unable to conceive how any one can dispute the men's claim to enjoy the whole increase. In 1894 a Bristol firm was charged before the "National Conference" (the central joint-board) "with having introduced a new system of working in Bristol," the so-called "team system," which resulted in the men collectively producing more boots per

of population and capital in dense masses, upon which the modern English Socialist bases his demand for collective ownership of the means of production, and the subordination of the producer to the citizen, and the individual to the community. See Fabian Tract, No. 51, *Socialism, True and False*, and the *Report on Fabian Policy*, presented by the Fabian Society to the International Socialist Congress, 1896 (Fabian Tract, No. 70).

Though the Owenite assumption here referred to was formerly accepted by large masses of English workmen, and though it still lies at the root of the desire for Co-operative Associations of Producers, it cannot be said to characterise the Trade Unionism of the present day, and it will accordingly not be discussed in our chapter on "The Assumptions of Trade Unionism." The student should consult, besides the works of Owen, Hodgskin, Thompson, Lassalle, and Marx, Dr. Anton Menger's *Das Recht auf den vollen Arbeitsertrag.*

[1] *Report on Trade Societies and Strikes, Social Science Association,* 1860, p. 62.

day than before. As the charge was coupled with an alteration from piecework to fixed wages, there would have been some justification for a complaint that the Standard Rate was being imperilled, by the exaction of ever-increasing exertion for a fixed weekly wage. But instead of taking this point, the union claimed that unless the day wage was so fixed that the *cost of each boot to the employer* remained no less than before, the alteration should be regarded as a reduction of wages.[1] The men's case was so prejudiced by this argument that the President (Alderman Sir Thomas Wright) not only rejected their claim, but also went so far as to say that, provided the mere weekly earnings were undiminished, the change of process was not an alteration of conditions, thus altogether ignoring the question of the increased effort and strain involved.

The student of this remarkable series of disputes will not fail to notice that the employers and the workmen both take up positions which are inconsistent with their own arguments. The employers have, in the fullest and most unreserved manner, given in their adhesion to the principle of Collective Bargaining with regard to all the conditions of labor. They have emphasised their adhesion to this principle by insisting on the establishment of a most elaborate machinery for carrying on this Collective Bargaining, of which they make constant use. It is therefore inconsistent of them to claim that any employer has a right to " introduce machinery at any time without notice," and that changes in " the internal

---

[1] The claim and argument will be found in the *Report of the National Conference of the Boot and Shoe Trade*, August 1893. "Supposing," asked the President, "the alteration from piecework to daywork resulted in the worker receiving more money, would you say that was an alteration of which he had a right to complain ? " To this question the obvious answer was that if the new process involved greater exertion or strain than the old, an actual increase of weekly earnings might well mean a lowering of the Standard Rate (of remuneration for effort), and thus involve a grievance to the workmen. But instead of taking this line the men's spokesman said, " I should say that if a particular individual got that money and the employer got eleven dozen of work done at the price of ten dozen provided by the Statement, that that involved a reduction of wages." The same confusion of ideas appears in the cases of "team system " discussed at the National Conference of January 1894.

economy of the factory or the manipulation of the workmen"
are matters for the autocratic decision of each individual
factory owner. It is no doubt a question for each employer
to determine whether or not he will introduce a particular
machine, just as it is for him alone to decide whether or not
he will engage twenty additional workmen. But the regulations and conditions under which the men will be engaged,
or will change their habits of work, are obviously matters
which, on the assumption of Collective Bargaining, cannot be
settled by the will of one party to the wage contract, or even
by the agreement of particular employers and particular
workmen, but must be arranged as a Common Rule by
negotiation between the authorised representatives of both
sides. The employers, moreover, have repeatedly adopted in
their negotiations the principle of the Standard Rate, that
is, the uniform maintenance throughout the trade of identical
payment for identical effort. It is therefore inconsistent of
them to insist on fixed time wages, on a change of process
which must inevitably result in progressively increasing the
intensity of effort imposed on the workmen. Unless there
is some arrangement by which the operatives are ensured
progressively increasing earnings, proportionate to this progressively increasing intensity, the employers are undermining the Standard Rate, that is, insidiously diminishing
the rate of payment for a given amount of effort. The
operatives, on the other hand, whilst recognising that their
very existence as factory bootmakers depends on the supersession of the individual hand bootmaker, are always resenting the further division of labor and the increased use
of machinery. And though they take their stand on the
fundamental principle of maintaining the Standard Rate,
and therefore of insisting on a Piecework Statement, they
yet cannot bring themselves in the new processes to propose
rates which would work out, even at the start, to earnings
equivalent only to their present wages. If the men frankly
asked for an increase in their Standard Rate of so much
per cent, to be worked out in detail by a revision of the

"Statement," the claim would be discussed on its own
merits, as an incident in the perennial higgling between
employers and employed. It may well be that the moment
when profits are being largely increased by a change of
process, is a specially opportune occasion for a rise of wage.
But, when the demand for an advance is disguised in an
assumption that any departure from the old "Statement" is
to be resisted as a positive reduction, the employers get into
a state of inarticulate rage at what seems to them the
intellectual dishonesty of the men's proceedings. If the
operatives desire to maintain the modern Trade Union
principle of the Standard Rate, they must abandon, once
for all, the diametrically opposite assumption that "wages
should be the price of goods," and at once set about the
compilation of a new piecework list applicable to the great
variety of machines and diversity of conditions in the various
factories. Such a list would, no doubt, cost trouble, especially
in view of the survival of many small manufacturers, each
using only one or more of the new machines. But similar
difficulties were met and overcome twenty years ago when
the trade became a factory industry, and American experience
shows that they are not insuperable to-day.[1]

The gradual introduction of composing and distributing
machines into the English printing trade affords an instance
of somewhat similar difficulties in another industry. These
machines began to be used about 1876, but, owing to the
imperfections of the earlier inventions, it was not until the

---

[1] The experience of the English Co-operative Wholesale Society, whose
colossal boot factory remained unaffected by the general stoppage of 1895, is
interesting in showing how an exceptionally able manager, himself once an
operative, has (in anticipation of the agreement of a piecework list for the new
processes) partially solved the problem, by making the weekly wages roughly
proportionate to the increasing output. On a certain "lasting machine" the output varies from 666 pairs per week to as much as 1270, according to the skill
and zeal of the operator. Mr. Butcher has known how to encourage zeal and
skill, by refusing to adhere to the uniform rate per week given by many of the
employers to all their workmen in each process ; paying as much as 40s. to the
principal operator, and (instead of taking on boys) giving 35s. a week even to
his "followers." He declares his intention, on the output rising to 1500 pairs a
week, to increase the wages to £2 : 10s.

last decade of the century that their competition with the old hand compositor came to be seriously felt. The advent of the machine has throughout been most distasteful to the men. But the Compositors' Trade Unions have from the first disclaimed any desire to prevent its introduction, or to forbid the members to work it. Their policy has been to secure the new employment to their own members on terms which protected their Standard Rate. No pretension on their part to receive the whole advantage of the Linotype machine is on record, but it is asserted that they have claimed a share of it. The Chairman of the Linotype Company, speaking to his shareholders in 1893, declared that "Nearly all the offices which have taken the Linotype are union offices—in some cases working by day, and in other cases working by piece. Surely that is sufficient proof that the labor difficulty is not a very serious one. The union [men] have, in my opinion, acted very fairly towards us. All they have said is this : 'Our men think you have an invention which is a great advantage to the trade—saves a great deal of money and labor—and the men should have their fair share of the advantages.' Let the masters pay them fairly, and then I believe there will be no difficulty whatever in introducing this machine."[1] In 1894, the London Society of Compositors was able to come to a satisfactory agreement with the newspaper proprietors, who have up to the present been the chief users of the machine, and it is now at work in the London newspaper offices under conditions formally accepted by both parties.[2]

[1] Speech of the Chairman of the Linotype Company, at the Ordinary General Meeting of Shareholders, Cannon Street Hotel, London, 11th May 1893.

[2] New and amended rules agreed to at a Conference between the Representatives of the London Daily Newspaper Proprietors, and of the London Society of Compositors, held at Anderton's Hotel on 7th June 1894.

Composing machines.

1. All skilled operators—*i.e.* compositors, justifiers, and distributors, as distinct from attendants or laborers—shall be members of the London Society of Compositors, preference being given to members of the Companionship into which the machines are introduced. Distribution to be paid at a minimum rate of 38s. per week of 48 hours, day-work.

2. A Probationary Period of three months shall be allowed, the operator to

Now let us turn from the trades in which the introduction of new machinery is recent enough to be a source of continual friction to those in which this has long ceased to be the case. In the great industries of cotton-spinning and cotton-weaving every part of the machinery employed has, during the last hundred years, been enormously improved. In the early stages of this mechanical progress each step was the subject of furious strife between masters and men, on much the same lines as the battles now being fought in the boot and shoe industry. For the last thirty years, however, the unions have genuinely abandoned all idea of opposing improvements, or of exacting the whole advantage of their introduction. The conditions under which any improvements in machinery shall be introduced have, by common consent, long since been taken out of the hands of the individual employer, or the particular group of operatives. Any change whatsoever in "the internal economy of the factory, or the manipulation of the workmen by the employer"—which, to the new class of boot manufacturers, seems a matter for their own autocratic decision—is, in the cotton industry, referred as a matter of course for prior deliberation and agreement between the expert salaried officials of the Trade Union and the Employers' Association. As the basis of negotiation, the principle of maintaining intact the Standard Rate of payment for a given quantity of effort is unreservedly accepted by both sides. The employers

receive his average weekly earnings for the previous three months. During this period he shall not undertake piecework.

3. In all offices when composing machines are introduced, the operators and case hands shall commence composition simultaneously. . . . Compositors and operators in such offices to be guaranteed two galleys per day of seven working hours on Morning papers, and on Evening papers twelve galleys per week of 42 hours.

4. The scale of prices for machine work shall be, Linotype, $3\frac{1}{4}$d. per one thousand ens for day-work in Evening paper offices, $3\frac{3}{4}$d. per thousand ens for work done in Morning paper offices, $\frac{1}{4}$d. per one thousand extra on all types above brevier; Hattersley, 4d. per one thousand ens for Evening paper work, and $4\frac{1}{2}$d. per one thousand ens for Morning paper work.

This agreement was, in 1896, superseded by a more elaborate one, framed on similar lines.—See *Labour Gazette*, August 1896.

recognise that any increased speed or complexity of the process means increased intensity of effort to the operative, which must therefore be remunerated by progressively increasing earnings. They would never dream of suggesting the substitution of fixed time rates of wages, and they agree, without demur, to a Piecework List which, definitely fixed in advance, completely secures to the workmen these progressive earnings. On the other hand, the operatives have unreservedly abandoned any idea that "wages should be the price of goods." We can imagine the amusement with which such experienced Trade Union officials as Mr. Mawdsley or Mr. Wilkinson would listen to the suggestion that any lowering of the cost per yard to the employer must necessarily be a reduction of wages to the operative. They would reply that, so long as the cotton operative was assured of his Standard Rate, he had no concern with the cost of production at all, except that any reduction resulting from wise administration or improvement of process was positively advantageous to the workmen, by securing for their product an ever-extending market. The Trade Unions of cotton operatives actually meet the innovating employers half-way, by agreeing to a piecework rate which decreases with every rise in the productivity of machinery. The employer therefore knows that every improvement that he can introduce will bring him a real, though not an unlimited, saving in his cost of production. The operatives, on the other hand, have the assurance that the graduated piecework rates, already settled by mutual agreement, after careful consideration by their expert officials, will not only protect their present weekly earnings, but will also immediately remunerate them for any increased effort involved. They have learnt, moreover, by experience, that any consciousness of the increased effort will soon disappear as the closer attention and quicker movement become habitual. It is true that by accepting a lower piecework rate they give up any claim to monopolise for themselves the "unearned increment" of the new invention. On the other hand, they are secured by the employers' concession of a predetermined Piecework List, in all the "rent" of the new dexterity which practice at the new process inevitably produces. Thus, the steadily rising speed of working, which to the boot operative, compelled by his employer to labor at a fixed time wage, is "pace-making and slavery," means to the cotton-spinner a welcome addition to his weekly earnings, and a permanent rise in his Standard of Life.

The United Society of Boilermakers and Iron-ship-builders base their agreements with their employers on similar principles. Thus the internal economy of the vast shipbuilding industry of the North-East coast of England is governed by the following formal treaty as to new appliances, etc. : "Notwithstanding any of the above clauses the shipbuilders are to be entitled to a revision of rates on account of labor-saving appliances, whether now existing and not sufficiently allowed for, or hereafter to be introduced ; for improved arrangements in yards ; for rates to be paid in vessels of new types where work is easier, and for other special cases. The terms of these revisions to be adjusted by a committee representing employers and the Boilermakers' and Shipbuilders' Society. The men shall in like manner be entitled to bring before the said committee any jobs, the rates of which may require revision due to new conditions of working, structural alterations in vessels, or any other cause." This agreement met with some opposition from a section of the workmen, who objected to any allowances being made for machinery, etc. To this complaint the Executive Committee of the union replied : "It is well known to the oldest shipyard plater in our society that he can go into some yards and plate a vessel at 10 per cent per plate less in one yard than he can in another on account of the difference in machinery. The employer therefore who has the best machinery is being paid for his machines through having his work done at a cheaper rate. . . . This is done all over, and rightly so. It is well known to our platers that, on account of the difference of facilities for doing work in the different yards, we have never been able to get a standard list of prices for plating." [1]

We may now sum up what seems to us the outcome of Trade Union experience in dealing with new processes and machinery, and what, judging from the general tendency and the example of the Cotton Operatives, may be expected to become the universal policy. We see, in the first place, that the old attempt of the handicraftsman to exclude the machine has been definitely abandoned. Far from refusing to work the new processes, the Trade Unionists of to-day claim, for the operatives already working at the trade, a preferential right to acquire the new dexterity and perform the new service. In asserting this preferential claim to continuity of employment, they insist that the arrangements for introducing the new process, including not only the rates of wages but also the physical conditions of work, are matters to be settled, not solely by one of the parties to the wage contract, but after discussion between both of them. Moreover, on the principle of Collective Bargaining, the matter is not one which can be left even to agreement between any particular employer and his workpeople, but one which must be settled by negotiation, as a Common Rule to be enforced on all employers and operatives in the particular trade. [2] When this Collective Bargaining takes place, the Trade Union always proceeds on the fundamental assumption that under no circumstances must the "improvement" be allowed to put the operative in any worse position than he was before. The change of technical process, which may revolutionise all the conditions of this working

---

[1] *Monthly Report of the United Society of Boilermakers and Iron-shipbuilders,* January 1895.

[2] This claim, to make the circumstances under which a change of process shall take place a matter for Collective Bargaining, has only lately been admitted, or even comprehended by employers; and the demand would, in many trades, till be regarded as preposterous. Until 1871, indeed, combination for any other objects than improvement in wages or hours was a criminal offence, and it never occurred, even to a good employer, that the most momentous change in the method of working could be a matter for mutual arrangement between his workpeople and himself.

life, is calculated greatly to increase the productivity of his labor, and should, it is claimed, at any rate not be made the occasion of any encroachment on the privileges or advantages which he has hitherto enjoyed. This involves, not only that his weekly earnings shall be maintained, but also that the length of the working day, the amount of physical or mental exertion required by his task, or the discomfort or disagreeableness of his work shall either not be increased, or else that any increase shall be fully paid for by extra rates. It will, moreover, be demanded that any defensive or other regulations, which have hitherto been accepted, shall be continued and made applicable to the new conditions. The pieceworker will expect a definitely settled detailed list of prices ; the timeworker will require any accustomed protection against being " driven " beyond the normal speed, whilst in trades in which apprenticeship has hitherto been regulated a continuance of the regulation will be insisted on.[1] All this merely comes to a demand that the condition and status of the workman should not be deteriorated by the change which is to bring a new profit to the employer. To this there will sometimes be added the further claim which stands, it is obvious, on a different footing, that the wage-earner should receive some of the advantages to be derived from the improvement, and that he should therefore take the opportunity of obtaining, as a condition of his acceptance of the new process, some positive increase in his Standard Rate.

[1] Comfort and habits of life often play an important part in these negotiations, leading sometimes to obstruction, sometimes to encouragement of a change. Thus the Yorkshire Glass Bottle Makers' Society refused in 1875 to work with a new gas furnace, because they declared it would involve a three-shift system ; an objection paralleled by the Northumberland and Durham miners' refusal to shorten the hours of boys, because it will probably involve a change from two to three shifts. In both cases the men assert that the alteration of hours would be inconvenient and unpleasant to them. On the other hand, when in 1876 a new system of " pot-setting " was invented in the glass trade, which was safer and more rapid than the old process, the Yorkshire Glass Bottle Makers' Society passed a resolution demanding its adoption, and insisting on those firms which still retained the old plan paying 2s. per man for the operation, as compared with only 6d. for the new system.—See the Annual Reports of the Yorkshire Glass Bottle Makers' Society for 1875 and 1876.

It is interesting to observe that, with the acceptance of this new policy by the employers, and its complete comprehension by the workmen, it is not the individual capitalist, but the Trade Union, which most strenuously insists on having the very latest improvements in machinery. In the English boot and shoe trade, every improvement is, as we have seen, made the occasion of a prolonged wrangle between employers and workmen. In Lancashire it quickly becomes a grievance in the Cotton Trade Unions, if any one employer or any one district falls behind the rest. The explanation of this difference is obvious. No employer takes any trouble to induce the laggards in his own industry to keep up with the march of invention. Their falling behind is, indeed, an immediate advantage to himself. But to the Trade Union, representing all the operatives, the sluggishness of the poor or stupid employers is a serious danger. The old-fashioned master spinners, with slow-going family concerns, complain bitterly of the harshness with which the Trade Union officials refuse to make any allowance for their relatively imperfect machinery, and even insist, as we have seen, on their paying positively a higher piecework rate if they do not work their mills as efficiently as their best-equipped competitors. Thus, the Amalgamated Association of Operative Cotton-spinners, instead of obstructing new machinery, actually penalises the employer who fails to introduce it! This remarkable difference, in the attitude of both workmen and employers, between the two great English industries of cotton-spinning and bootmaking, goes far to explain their very different standing as regards technical efficiency. The English boot manufacturer is always complaining of the far higher efficiency of the splendidly-equipped factories of Massachusetts and Connecticut. The Lancashire cotton mill, in the amount of output per operative, easily leads the world.

There remains one other type of case to be dealt with, namely that in which the new process, instead of being worked by the old skilled hands, supersedes them by a class of entire novices. As this happens to be the very type which, from its association with tragic episodes in industrial history, strikes the public imagination most forcibly, and has accordingly become a commonplace in the denunciations of our industrial system from the more extreme platforms of social reform, its omission, so far, may have struck the reader as an unexpected oversight. It is possible for the introduction of a new machine or process to annihilate the utility of a workman's skill as completely as the photograph has annihilated the miniature, the railway train the stage coach, or petroleum the snuffers. The heart-rending struggle of the handloom weavers against the power loom is perhaps the best-known instance. Let us follow, step by step, or rather stumble by stumble, the road to ruin of an insufficiently organised trade supplanted by machinery.[1]

When the handicraftsman begins to find his product undersold by the machine-made article, his first instinct is to engage in a desperate competition with the new process, lowering his rate for hand labor to keep pace with the diminished cost of the machine product. This is obviously the "line of least resistance." No newly-devised machine, worked by novices, and not yet perfectly adapted to the process, can convince a skilled handworker that it will ever succeed in turning out as good an article as he can make, or that the saving of time will be at all considerable. The very fact that a lad or a girl at ten or fifteen shillings a week can perform the new process with ease, only confirms him in his attitude of disparagement and incredulity.

[1] The struggle of the small hand industry against the factory system can be best studied at present in Germany and Austria, where the position is being described in detail by scores of competent observers. See, among other studies, Professor Gustav Schmoller's *Zur Geschichte der Deutschen Kleingewerbe im 19th Jahrhundert* (Halle, 1870) ; Dr. Eugen Schwiedland's *Kleingewerbe und Hausindustrie in Oesterreich* (Leipzig, 1894), 2 vols. ; and his two Reports *Ueber eine gesetzliche Regelung der Heimarbeit* (Vienna, 1896 and 1897) ; Dr. Kunc Frankenstein's *Die Deutsche Hausindustrie*, 4 vols. ; the article " Hausindustrie " by Prof. Werner Sombart in Conrad's *Handwörterbuch der Staatswissenschaften*, vol. iv. ; and the magnificent series of monographs on particular trades or districts, published by the " Verein fur Sozial Politik " as *Untersuchungen über die Lage des Handwerks in Deutschland* (Leipzig, 1894-97), 12 volumes.

In such a mood a man does not throw away the skill which is his property and staff of life, to consent to become either a machine-minder at one-half or one-third of his accustomed wages, or else begin life afresh in some entirely new occupation. He confidently pits his consummate skill against the first clumsy attempts of the undeveloped machine, and finds that a slight reduction in the Standard Rate for hand labor is all that seems required to leave his handicraft in full command of the market. His well-intentioned friends, the clergyman and the district visitor, the newspaper economist and the benevolent employer, combine to assure him that this—the Policy of Lowering the Dyke —is what he ought to adopt. But, unfortunately, this is to enter on a downward course to which there is no end. The machine product steadily improves in quality, and falls in price, as the new operatives become more skilled, and as the speed of working is increased. Every step in this evolution means a further reduction of rates to the struggling handworker, who can only make up his former earnings by hurrying his work and lengthening his hours. Inevitably this hurry and overwork deteriorate the old quality and character of his product. The attempt to maintain his family in its old position compels him to sacrifice everything to the utmost possible rapidity of execution. His wife and children are pressed into his service, and a rough and ready division of labor serves to economise the use of the old thought and skill. The work insidiously drops its artistic quality and individual character. In the losing race with the steam engine, the handwork becomes itself mechanical, without acquiring either that uniform excellence or accurate finish which is the outcome of the perfected machine. Presently, the degraded hand product will sell only at a lower price than the machine-made article. The worse the work becomes the more irregular grows the demand. Those select customers, who have remained faithful to the hand product, find, by degrees, that its former qualities have departed, and they one by one accept the modern substitute.

And thus we reach the vicious circle of the sweated industries, in which the gradual beating down of the rate of remuneration produces an inevitable deterioration in the quality of the work, whilst the inferiority of the product itself makes it unsaleable except at prices which compel the payment of progressively lower rates. The handworker, who at the beginning justifiably felt himself on a higher level than the mechanical minder of the machine, ends by sinking, in physique and dexterity alike, far below the level of the highly-strung factory operative. There is now no question of his taking to the new process, which has risen quite beyond his capacity. He passes through the long-drawn-out agony of a dying trade.

This, in main outline, is the story of the handloom weavers in all the branches of the textile industry.[1] We see the same grim evolution going on to-day in the chain and nail trade in the Black Country, and among the unorganised sections of the tailors and cabinetmakers. We need not dilate on the misery to which these unfortunate workers are reduced. But it is important to observe how the interests of the consumers are affected by this " Policy of Lowering the Dyke." It is, in the first place, to be noted that it in no way stimulates the spread of machinery or the perfecting of the new process. The constant yielding of the handworker even diminishes the pressure on his employer to adopt the newest improvements, and positively tempts him to linger on with the old process. So long as he can compete with his rival by another cut off wages, it will not seem worth while to lay out capital and thought in new machinery. Thus, the transition from the old system of production to the improved methods is delayed, to the loss of the consumer for the time being. But what is perhaps of greater importance to the community is the disappearance of any real

[1] "Heartbroken and objectless in their squalid poverty, their insight into the active stirring world beyond them, with its various moving springs and wires, became perverted, and they stuck to their falling trade with a kind of obstinate fatalism."—John Hill Burton, *Political and Social Economy* (Edinburgh, 1849), p. 29.

alternative to the machine product. The degradation of the handworker's craft, resulting, as we have seen, directly from the forcing down of his Standard Rate, deprives the nation of the charm given to the old country stuffs and furniture by their artistic individuality. Even the machine-made product is the worse for the deterioration of the handicraft. It gradually loses the ideal of perfect workmanship and artistic finish, to which the inventor and operative were perpetually striving to approximate. It is, indeed, difficult to discover any advantage whatsoever, either to the handicraftsman or to the community, in a policy which, whilst failing to stimulate the use of labor-saving machinery, neither saves the handworkers from misery, nor preserves to the community what is of value in their handicraft.

Here, then, we have the dramatic instance as it actually occurs ; and certainly the reality is as harrowing as the most fervidly descriptive platform orator can make it appear. And yet its tragedy is incomplete without the final demonstration that the really cruel stages of all this suffering are needless, and are caused not by the iron march of industrial evolution, but simply by the adoption on the part of the workmen and their employers of this " Policy of Lowering the Dyke." We have failed to discover a single instance of supersession by machinery, in which it would not have been possible for the superseded handicraft at least to have died a painless death. There are industries which have been changed by machinery as thoroughly as weaving, but in which, owing to the enforcement of a different policy by the Trade Unions concerned, the handworkers have not only survived, but are to-day busier, more highly paid, and more skilful than ever they were before.

The Amalgamated Society of Cordwainers, an organisation dating from the eighteenth century,[1] had, up to 1857, enjoyed a complete immunity from any invasion by machinery

---

[1] See *History of Trade Unionism*, p. 51, where a circular of 1784 is quoted. The organisation was reformed in 1862, and in 1874 it took the name of the Amalgamated Society of Boot and Shoe Makers.

or new processes. The application of the sewing-machine to bootmaking, and the successive introduction of new inventions led, between 1857 and 1874, to a complete revolution in the trade. At first the rank and file of the workmen bitterly resented the change of conditions, and the employer introducing a new machine was often met by the most unreasonable demands. But the Executive Committee of the Trade Union, whilst maintaining intact the established scale of prices for handwork, steadfastly refused to sanction any resistance to the new processes. On the contrary, it persistently advised all its members who failed to get handwork at the established high rates, to accept employment at the new factories at whatever they could get, and gradually to work out a new piecework list adapted to the altered conditions. In order to secure this fresh " Statement " these members were advised to join hands with the new men whom the factory brought into the trade, and freely to admit them into their branches. Thus, already in 1863, it was resolved "that men employed in the rivetting and finishing peg-work, and those working in factories, be recognised, and can belong to any section, or form sections by themselves." [1] This policy, pressed on the members at every opportunity, was quickly accepted, with the result that the union found itself, in a very few years, composed of two distinct classes of members, handicraftsmen and factory workers. When

---

[1] *The Trade Sick and Funeral Laws of the Amalgamated Society of Cordwainers* (London, 1863). The "rivetters" became a separate class, when, about 1846, rivetting was introduced in place of stitching. See the manifesto of the Leicester shoemakers, quoted by Marx, *Capital*, Part IV. chap. xv. sec. 7 (vol. ii. p. 457 of English translation of 1887). The operatives in the factory boot manufacture are at present divided into the following classes : (1) the " clickers," the men and lads who cut from skins the sections of the boot and uppers ; (2) "rough-stuff cutters," the men who cut the bottom material by knives set in powerful machines ; (3) "fitters," men who place the upper leathers in position for " closing "; (4) "machinists " (often women) who "close " or stitch the uppers ; (5) "lasters," men or boys who place the closed uppers over the last and attach the bottom material (in hand-sewn work these are known as " makers," in " pegged work," now nearly obsolete, they are called " pegmen " or "rivetters "); (6) the "finishers," who blacken the edges, clean the soles, and generally polish up the boot. The two latter classes form a large majority of the whole.

the latter began actually to outnumber their old-fashioned colleagues, it was found convenient, as we have already mentioned, that they should break off, and form a society of their own, the National Union of Boot and Shoe Operatives. The Amalgamated Society of Cordwainers, now again confined to the handicraftsmen, has ever since continued to pursue the same line of policy. It has remained on amicable terms with the new society, neither competing with it for members, nor in any way obstructing its remarkable growth. But what is more important, it has steadfastly refused to allow its own members to compete in cheapness with the new process. If a handmade boot is desired, the old scale for handwork must be paid. Many consequences have resulted from this policy, some of which might not, at first sight, have been expected. As the employers found no way of getting a commoner class of boots made by inferior hand labor at low rates, machinery has gone ahead by leaps and bounds. But it has created an entirely new trade for itself. The keeping up of a high level of price for the handmade article has not destroyed the demand, but has, on the contrary, given it permanence and stability. The employers, finding themselves bound in any case to pay the old scale of rates, have had to concentrate their attention on obtaining the finest possible workmanship, as only in this way were they able to tempt their customers to prefer the necessarily expensive handmade product. Those persons who are prepared to pay well for first-class workmanship find therefore that they can still obtain exactly what they require, and hence remain faithful to the handmade boot. Meanwhile, the handicraftsmen have become a select body, not because they have closed their ranks, but because none but men of long training and exceptional skill can find employment at the recognised scale, or do the highly-finished work which the employers require in return for such high rates. Competition between the handicraftsmen takes, in fact, the form of a continuous elimination of the less skilled among them, who are encouraged, in their youth, to go into the machine trade. The result has been that the skilled hand boot-makers, whilst somewhat diminishing in numbers, have positively improved their scale of prices and average earnings, and more than maintained their level of skill. Finally, notwithstanding a continuous improvement in the efficiency of bootmaking machinery, the handmade boot still remains an ideal to which inventors and factory managers are perpetually striving to approximate their commoner product.

This analysis of the policy of the Amalgamated Society of Boot and Shoe Makers finds a remarkable confirmation in the analogous case of the paper manufacturers. A generation ago this old trade of skilled handworkers, closely combined since the middle of the eighteenth century,[1] was seriously menaced by the rapid spread of machine-made paper. Foreign competition, too, began, on the repeal of the paper duty in 1861, to cut into the trade of the English manufacturers, and the United Kingdom, from being a large exporter of paper, gradually became a large importer. The hand papermakers, who had, from time immemorial, enjoyed wages 15 or 20 per cent higher than those even of skilled artisans in other trades, made no attempt to prevent or to discourage the introduction of paper-making machinery, or even to secure the new work for their own members. The machine-workers were at first admitted to membership of the handworkers' union, but few of them joined, and (as in the analogous case of the boot and shoe operatives) it was afterwards found more convenient for the new class of workmen to form organisations of their own.[2] The highly-paid

---

[1] " Our Society," said the spokesman of the Original Society of Papermakers in 1891, "can go back, according by the records, to 150 or 160 years." Its very archaic rules, preserved in the appendix to the *Report of the Committee on Combinations of Workmen*, 1825, are referred to in the *History of Trade Unionism*, p. 80.

[2] It was stated in evidence in 1874 that " the Society is composed of some 700 men, of whom 420 are employed in vat mills," the former comprising a very large proportion of the entire handmade trade, and the latter only a trifling proportion of the machine trade (*Report of Arbitration on the Question of an Advance in Wages* . . . 10th July 1874, Maidstone, 1874, p. 53). At present (1897) the machinemen are organised in two separate unions, the Amalgamated Society of Papermakers, a strong body in the South of England, and the National

handworkers were incessantly advised to moderate their demands, so as to enable their employers to compete with the new machine mills, which started up in every county. As early as 1864 a leading employer gave them an ominous warning. " When you see . . ." he said, " regular machine mills (such as I intend to stand by, if driven from the vats) rising up around you . . . remember the old fable of 'The Goose with the Golden Eggs' . . . lest . . . you lose the position in which you now stand." [1]   " How can we compete with the machine paper unless wages are reduced ? " asked a millowner in 1891.   " I say the best course for you to adopt," replied the spokesman of the operatives, " is to keep up the quality and the price of handmade paper." [2]   This policy has been consistently pursued by the Trade Union. Far from consenting to lower its members' rates of pay, it has taken every opportunity to raise them.   " We have never had a reduction of wages in the paper trade," declared the men's secretary in 1874. [3]   " In 1839," a leading employer told the arbitrator, " there was an increase of wages, in 1853 a slight modification, in 1854 a slight increase, another increase in 1865, in 1869 a slight increase, when beer money was given instead of beer. . . . So we went on from 1838 to 1872, giving these three or four rises, and, in 1872, a rise of sixpence per day was conceded by the employers without any great fuss"; [4] the pay of a first-class vatman for a " day's work " in a Kentish mill being now 6s. 5d., as compared with 4s. 7d. in 1840. [5]   It is interesting to find the workmen expressly comparing their own attitude with that of the

Union of Paper Mill Workers of Great Britain and Ireland, a weaker society with membership chiefly in the North of England and in Scotland.

[1] *Notes of Proceedings at a Meeting of Paper Manufacturers and Journeymen Papermakers Relative to an Advance in Wages* (Maidstone, 1864), p. 34.

[2] *Report of Arbitration Meeting between Employers and Employed in the Handmade Paper Trade* . . . on 29th January 1891 (Maidstone, 1891), p. 65.

[3] Arbitration Report of 1874, pp. 14, 17.   " Never once in the history of the trade had there been a reduction of the prices."—*Report of Meeting of Employers and Employed* . . . on 15th September 1884 (Maidstone, 1884), p. 18.

[4] Arbitration Report of 1891, pp. 45-46.

[5] See table of rates in the Arbitration Report of 1874, p. 33.

Amalgamated Society of Cordwainers, and justifying it on the same grounds. " There is no doubt," declared their spokesman in 1891, " that handmade paper will continue to hold its own in the market. There are now many branches of industry where machines play a very important part in the production of various goods. . . . [But] if you want a splendid article in those materials, you must have handmade. . . . The same remark applies to the shoemaking trade. Handmade shoemakers now command higher wages than ever they did in the history of the trade. Their services have become much more important and valuable since the introduction of machines, which now manufacture all parts and all kinds of shoes. The people know that if they want a good boot they must have handmade. It seems to me . . . that handmade paper is precisely in the same position. If people want the genuine article they will, notwithstanding the cost, go in for handmade paper." [1] That this policy has, in the paper trade, been attended by success is admitted on all sides. The rigid maintenance of high rates for handmade paper has given the utmost possible encouragement to the introduction of machinery, wherever machinery could possibly be employed. The production of machine-made paper has accordingly advanced by leaps and bounds, to the great advantage of the public in the cheapening of the article for common use. But this enormous increase of production has in no way injured the trade in the superior handmade paper. No attempt is made to compete in cheapness with the machine-made product, the manufacturers, like their operatives, preferring to concentrate their attention on turning out as different a grade of quality as possible. The result has been in the highest degree remarkable. Instead of handmade paper mills having "to be closed all over the country," as was expected in 1860, it was reported to the arbitrator that by 1874 there were actually considerably more vats at work than had ever formerly existed ; that by 1891 the number of vats and the amount of the sales had

[1] Arbitration Report of 1891, p. 10.

still further increased ; and that " the last sixteen years have been the most successful sixteen years that we have ever known in the trade." [1]   All this is fully conceded by the employers. " The masters," declared their spokesman in 1891, " never made such large profits in the old days as they have made since.   I admit [that] my father, for instance, who had a good mill, could only make a bare living." [2]   Meanwhile the speed and continuity of the work has been steadily increased, until the actual output in pounds of paper per man per year in the best-equipped mills is now greater than it has ever been in the history of the craft.   The prosperity of the employers, as their leading representative explained in 1891, " has been due to two causes.   In the first place there has been—and I think the other gentlemen present will bear me out in this—a great increase of sobriety and steadiness on the part of the men.   There was a time when they did not work, sometimes for weeks together, five days a week. . . . That is one great cause to which I attribute our prosperity. . . . The other cause is the introduction of improvements by the masters.   The mills are very different from what they used to be. . . . It is easier for the men to make seven days a week now than it was years ago to make six days. . . . Formerly there were many breakdowns at our mills. . . . All these things have been changed." [3]   We see, therefore, that in spite of the adverse influence exercised, as we shall show in a later chapter, by the Trade Union Restriction of Numbers and the monopoly enjoyed by the old-established employers, the enforcement of a high Standard of Life in the handmade paper trade, far from destroying the livelihood either of masters or men, has been accompanied by a marked advance in their prosperity, and a distinct differentiation between the old product and the new.   The policy of maintaining simultaneously the quality and the price of the hand-

---

[1] Arbitration Report of 1891, p. 30.   [2] *Ibid*. p. 46.
[3] *Ibid*. pp. 50-51.   In the handmade paper trade "a day's work" is a definite quantity of paper, varying according to size and weight.   It has no relation to the period of employment.

made article, whilst it has given a positive encouragement to the introduction of machinery into the trade, has proved, in fact, the salvation of the hand papermaker's craft.

Much the same policy has been pursued by the Amalgamated Association of Operative Cotton-spinners with regard to the introduction of "ring-spinning," an ingenious application of the old "throstle-spinning," which dates from about 1881. By the substitution of the "ring frame" for the "mule," it has been found possible, in the manufacture of certain "counts" of cotton (the coarser "twist" up to about "50's"), greatly to diminish the amount of skill and effort required. What formerly demanded the concentrated attention of a highly-skilled man is now within the capacity of an untrained woman. Had this invention been made fifty years ago, the mule-spinners would undoubtedly have done their utmost to prevent its adoption, and to exclude women from any participation in cotton-spinning. But no such action has been taken, or even suggested. Although the Cotton-spinners' Trade Union, especially in its close alliance with the Weavers and Cardroom Operatives, now exercises a far more effective control over the industry than at any previous period, ring spinning by women has, during the last fifteen years, been allowed to grow up unmolested.[1] It was practically impossible for the adult male spinners, earning two pounds a week, to insist on claiming for themselves work which could be done by women at fifteen shillings a week. But they might have attempted to stave off the innovation by lowering the rates for their own work, and thereby discouraging their employers from making the change. This, as we have seen, was the policy followed two generations ago by the handloom weavers. The Amalgamated Association of Operative Cotton-spinners adopted an entirely different course. When an employer complained that he could no longer compete with rivals who

[1] The ring-frame spinners were even received into the Amalgamated Association of Card and Blowing Room Operatives, with the full assent of the Spinners officials, as being the most suitable textile organisation for them to join

had adopted the ring frame, unless his mule-spinners would accept a lower rate, he was told that under no circumstances could any "lowering of the dyke" be permitted. What he was offered was, as we have described, a revision of the piecework list so arranged as to stimulate him to augment the rapidity and complexity of the mule, in order that the mule-spinners, increasing in dexterity, might simultaneously enlarge the output per machine and raise their own earnings. The cotton-spinners in short, like the hand bootmakers, preferred to meet the competition of a new process by raising their own level of skill, rather than by degrading their Standard of Life. The result has been that, except under certain circumstances, the mule has, up to now, fairly held its own. The number of mule-spinners, like the number of hand bootmakers, remains about stationary, and this without the slightest attempt or desire to close the trade to newcomers. Like the bootmakers, indeed, the mule-spinners are subject to a constant process of selection, the employers naturally refusing to engage, at such high rates, any but the most skilled men.

There is, however, one point, on which the policy of the cotton-spinners with regard to the ring frame, and that of the papermakers with regard to the machine, has fallen short of the policy of the hand bootmakers with regard to the factory system. The Amalgamated Society of Cordwainers did its utmost, as we have seen, to organise the new class of factory workers,[1] so that these could, as quickly as possible, secure a new Standard Rate commensurate with the skill and effort required. This, it will be obvious, is really a necessary corollary of the maintenance of a Standard Rate. The adoption of a new process must, on the whole, be deemed an advantage to the community when it effects a real saving of labor or economy of skill. But it is a very

[1] "That clickers, stuff-cutters, pegmen, finishers, and machinists working at the shoe trade are admitted into society. That all women working at the shoe trade be admitted into the Association upon the same terms, and entitled to the same rights of membership as the men."—Resolution of the National Union of Boot and Shoe Operatives' Conference, 16th September 1872.

different thing when the attractiveness of the new process to the employer is due, not to any real economy of human labor, but to the chance of employing a helpless class of workers at starvation wages. Unless the workers at the new process are paid wages sufficient to maintain them at the required new level of skill and efficiency, the new process must be, in some way, parasitic on the community. To give a concrete instance, if the daughter of a mule-spinner, reared in a comparatively comfortable household, and maintained at home at a cost of fifteen shillings a week, offers her services as a ring-spinner at ten shillings a week, the competition between the mule and the ring frame may reasonably be deemed "unfair." If the woman had to live on the ten shillings, her strength, her capacity of attention, her regularity of attendance, and possibly her respectability, would inevitably degrade. She could, moreover, not bring up, on her wages, a new generation of ring-spinners to replace her. So long as the underpaid worker is otherwise partly maintained— perhaps the most usual case with women and children—the employer is, in effect, receiving a bounty in favor of a particular form of production, and the community has no assurance that the competition between the processes will lead to the survival of the fittest. "Whole branches of manufacture," to use the weighty words of the Poor Law Commission of 1834, "may thus follow the course, not of coal mines or streams, but of pauperism : may flourish like the fungi that spring from corruption, in consequence of the abuses which are ruining all the other interests of the place in which they are established, and cease to exist in the better administered districts in consequence of that better administration."[1] From the point of view of the community, therefore, it is vital that, however low may be the standard of skill and strength required by the new process, there should be maintained such a level of wages as will, at any rate, fully sustain the new operatives at that standard.

---

[1] *First Report of Poor Law Commissioners*, 1834, p. 65 of reprint of 1884 (H. C. 347).

From the point of view of the workers at the old process, it is clearly of the utmost consequence that the new process should get no false stimulus by such a " bounty " as we have described.

This argument, to which we shall recur in our chapter on " The Economic Characteristics of Trade Unionism," is only slowly penetrating into the minds of the mule-spinners. Unlike the Amalgamated Society of Cordwainers, the Amalgamated Association of Operative Cotton-spinners took no trouble to organise their new competitors, the women ring-spinners, to whom the employers were allowed to pay as little as they pleased. After fifteen years' experience, however, this idea is beginning to dawn on the officials of the Cotton-spinners' Union, though no positive action can yet be recorded.[1] But it has never yet occurred to the old-fashioned close corporation of hand papermakers that they are in any way called upon, in their own interest, to assist the comparatively unskilled operatives in the machine paper-mills of the North of England to secure a proper Standard Rate. And the Amalgamated Society of Tailors never dreams of taking steps to organise the ill-paid women of the clothing factories.

We see, then, that where skilled labor is replaced by unskilled, the paramount importance of maintaining the Standard of Life warns off the handworker, both from any claim to work the new process and from any attempt to compete in cheapness with machine work. The hand bootmakers, the hand papermakers, and the cotton mule-

---

[1] Thus, in May 1896, we find the following warning note in the organ of the Amalgamated Association of Operative Cotton-spinners. In the ring-frame spinning, "employers and their agents have practically had the whole field to themselves in the matter of fixing prices and wages, as they have had no opposition from Trade Unions and their officials, and under the circumstances they have taken great care to pay little enough for the labor of the operatives who are employed on the frames. . . . The rapid increase of this class of spinning is preventing the extension of mule-spinning, and so damaging the future prospects of the little piecers of to-day. The Spinners' Union have made a mistake in not paying attention to getting ring-spinners as members of their association, and framing a list of wages to govern this class of labor."--*Cotton Factory Times*, 15th May 1896.

spinners have, in their several ways, discovered another policy, viz. : rigorously to enforce the old high rate of pay for the old work, frankly to abandon to the machine any part of the trade within its scope, and more and more to concentrate attention on maintaining and differentiating the peculiar qualities of their own special article. But this enlightened self-interest requires, from the economic standpoint, to be supplemented by a consideration of the claims of other classes of operatives. The Trade Unionist is beginning to recognise that he has a deep interest in maintaining the Standard Rates of other sections of workers. The logical outcome of Trade Union experience in all these difficult cases seems, indeed, to be a minimum standard of remuneration for effort, whatever the grade of labor, so that, under no circumstances, would any section of workers find itself reduced below the level of complete maintenance.[1] Whenever an employer seeks to substitute a lower for a higher grade of labor, it is only by some such enforcement of a minimum that the community can avoid the pernicious bounty to particular occupations or processes, irrespective of their social advantageousness, that is involved in the labor being partially maintained from other sources than its wages.[2]

---

[1] We must refer the reader for a full explanation of this difficult point of Trade Union theory to our chapter on "The Economic Characteristics of Trade Unionism."

[2] The employers' proposal that one operative should attend to two or more machines falls economically under the head of "speeding up," rather than under that of a change of process, and has therefore been implicitly dealt with in our chapter on "The Standard Rate." The wage-earner's traditional resentment of any labor-saving innovation is here mingled with his even stronger objection to what is commonly an attempt to evade the Standard Rate, by exacting more bodily exertion or mental strain for the same money. Thus the Carmen, paid by time, at a rate for which they are accustomed to mind one horse and cart, strongly protest against one man being required to attend simultaneously to two vehicles. The same feeling influences pieceworkers unless they are sufficiently protected by a Standard List to have confidence that the increase in the day's task and earnings will not be followed by a reduction of rates. The women cotton-weavers of Glasgow, who are practically unorganised, and whose piecework rates, unprotected by any effective list, are always going down to subsistence level, stubbornly refuse to work more than one loom each. The cotton-weavers of Lancashire, on the other hand, whether men or women, relying confidently on their strong Trade Union and their Standard Lists, willingly work as many

looms—two, four, and even six—as they can manage (see " The Alleged Difference between the Wages of Men and Women," by Sidney Webb, *Economic Journal*, December 1891). The employers' attempt to induce engineers to attend to more than one lathe or other machine has led to much friction. In this instance it is not clear to us what is the exact issue. If it is suggested that the engineer should, for the weekly wage hitherto paid for one machine, in future mind two, the case is merely one of an attempted reduction of the Standard Rate, which the men naturally resist. We are unable to gather whether the employers have made it plain that they propose to increase the time wages—say to time and a half—when two machines are minded, or whether they are prepared to establish and bind themselves to adhere to a Standard List of piecework rates, which would automatically secure to the operative an increase in earnings proportionate to the increase in strain. If either of these courses were adopted, we see no reason why the engineers should not, like the cotton-weavers, willingly mind as many machines as they can without undue strain. If the employers claim the right to assign an operative to as many machines as seems fit to them, without arranging special rates with the Trade Union officials, this is simply a denial of the elementary right of Collective Bargaining, and will be fought as such.

CHAPTER IX

CONTINUITY OF EMPLOYMENT

THE Trade Union Regulations which we have described in the foregoing chapters have dealt exclusively with the maintenance and improvement of the conditions of employment: they have left untouched the problem of unemployment. A Standard Rate, a Normal Day, and safe and healthy conditions of work are of no avail if there is no work to be got. "We are willing to admit," said the Engineers of 1851, and the Cloggers of 1872, "that whilst in constant employment our members may be able to obtain the necessaries of life. Notwithstanding all this, there is always a fear prominent in the mind of him who thinks of the future that it may not continue ; that to-morrow may see him out of employment, his nicely-arranged matters for domestic comfort overthrown, and his hopes of being able, in a few years, by constant attention and frugality to occupy a more permanent position, proved only to be a dream. How much is contained in that word 'continuance,' and how necessary to make it a leading principle of our society!"[1] "In a fluctuating trade," say the Tailors, "many who depend for the necessaries of life on their daily toil are often deprived of employment in the most inclement season. They wander through the

[1] Preface to *Rules and Regulations of the Amalgamated Society of Engineers* (London, 1851), and also to *Rules of the Rochdale Operative Cloggers' Society* (Rochdale, 1872). The same sentence occurs, with verbal variations, in other Trade Union rules. (The cloggers make the "clogs," or wooden shoes, commonly worn in the streets by the Lancashire operatives.)

country from city to town, and from town to village, in
search of employment, but, alas, in vain. This continues
until, upon the mind of an honest man, the thought rests
like an incubus, When and how shall I relieve myself of this
degradation ? " [1]

We touch here the "dead point" in our analysis of
Trade Union Regulations. In spite of the vital importance
of the question to men dependent on weekly wages for their
whole livelihood, no Trade Union has hitherto devised a
regulation which secures continuity of livelihood as a condition of employment.

At first sight it would seem as if the best way to obtain
Continuity of Employment would be to require the employer,
as a condition of getting the workman's service at all, to
enter into a contract of hiring for a specified long term.
This is not the course which the Trade Unionists have
followed. Engagements for long terms were once common
in many trades, and farm-servants in some parts of the
country are still engaged for the year. But the mobility
and vicissitudes which characterise modern industry are
hostile to such permanence, and employers have come to
prefer the shortest possible engagements, often insisting on
freedom to discharge their operatives at a few hours' notice.
This tendency, far from being resisted by the Trade Unions,
has invariably been encouraged by them. The Coalminers
of Northumberland and Durham fought hard to get rid of
their "yearly bond"; the Staffordshire Potters in 1866
enthusiastically threw off the "annual hiring"; the "monthly
pays," once common in all occupations, have been replaced
by weekly, or at most, fortnightly settlements; and many
Trade Unions have, at one time or another, expressly prohibited their members from entering into longer engagements,
a prohibition now generally omitted as the practice has
become obsolete.[2]

---

[1] Preamble to *Rules of the Amalgamated Society of Tailors* (Manchester, 1893).

[2] Thus the Scottish Ironmoulders' Society has, since 1838, forbidden engage-

This policy needs no explanation for any one who understands the Trade Union position. The "yearly bond" or annual hiring always meant, in practice, the conclusion of a separate agreement between the employer and each individual workman, and especially when the various terms of service did not expire on a uniform date, was incompatible with Collective Bargaining. Moreover, once the agreement was entered into, the wage-earner found himself, at any rate for the specified term of notice, practically at the mercy of the employer's interpretation of the conditions. The wage contract seldom contains express stipulations with regard to any other points than the amount of remuneration, and perhaps the hours of labor, and it is always implied that the wage-earner binds himself to obey all lawful and reasonable commands of his "master." It is in the wage-earner's power to throw up his job when he likes that his status differs most essentially from that of a slave, and if he foregoes this power, and binds himself for a long term to put up with practically whatever conditions, outside those expressly stipulated for, the employer may choose to impose, it is obvious that the Trade Union loses all power of protecting him against economic oppression.[1] The briefest possible term of service, terminable at a day or a week's notice on either side, has accordingly come to be preferred, for different reasons, by both employers and Trade Unionists.[2] This

ments longer than "from pay to pay," the rule now in force (1892) providing "that no member of this association shall enter into any engagement, either directly or indirectly, for any given time longer than from pay to pay, unless specially authorised by Executive." The United Kingdom Society of Coachmakers, whose rule on the subject dates from 1840, now ordains (1896 edition) that "no member be allowed to article himself under penalty of expulsion." The Tinplate Workers of Glasgow had a rule in 1860 that no member should so engage himself as to prevent his leaving his employer with two weeks' notice ; the Liverpool Painters said one week.—*Report on Trade Societies and Strikes*, by the Social Science Association (London, 1860), pp. 133, 297.

[1] We recur to this aspect of the wage contract in our chapter on "The Higgling of the Market."

[2] It was a special aggravation of the "yearly bond" among the Coalminers that, whilst the workman bound himself for a whole year to hew coal whenever required by a particular employer, that employer did not guarantee to find him continuous employment, and could lay the pit idle whenever he chose

does not mean, as regards the great majority of industries, that the employers are incessantly changing their workmen, or workmen their employers. Wherever costly and intricate machinery is used, and wherever the processes of different workmen are dovetailed one into the other, it pays the employer to retain, even at some sacrifice, the services of the same body of men, accustomed to his business and to each other. In these trades accordingly, a well-conducted workman may rely on retaining his employment so long as his employer has work to be done.

In other industries this absence of any permanent engagement between master and man leaves the employer free to get his work done to-day by one set of workers, and to-morrow by quite another set. Whenever work is " given out " to be done in the workers' own homes, the employer can dole out the jobs as he chooses, sometimes to one family, sometimes to another. A wholesale clothing contractor in East London has thus hundreds of different families looking to him for work, amongst whom his foreman will, each week, arbitrarily apportion his orders. The London Dock Companies maintain what is essentially the same system with regard to their casual labor, the foreman, at certain periods of the day, selecting fresh gangs of men from among the crowd of applicants at the dock gates. Both outworkers and dockers are nominally free to seek work elsewhere, when not engaged by their usual employer. But as they are expected, under pain of being struck off the list, to present themselves to ask for work at certain hours, they practically lose any real chance of obtaining other employment.[1] This extreme discontinuity of employment

(R. Fynes, *The Miners of Northumberland and Durham*, Blyth, 1873). A similar one-sidedness is found in other old contracts of hiring. The chief examples of genuinely bilateral agreements for long terms relate to indoor servants, seamen, and mechanics sent on jobs abroad.

[1] " The Docks," by Beatrice Potter (Mrs. Sidney Webb), in Charles Booth's *Life and Labor of the People* (London, 1889), vol. i. of first edition ; and H. Llewellyn Smith and Vaughan Nash, *The Story of the Dockers' Strike* (London, 1889). This system of engaging casual labor by the hour still prevails in the London docks, but it has, since 1890, been modified by an increase in the

is not confined to unskilled laborers or low-paid home workers. In many skilled handicrafts, where the work is done individually and by the piece, the operative is required to remain in the employer's workshop, or at his beck and call, without being guaranteed either work or pay. "There are firms," reported to the Royal Commission on Labor the representative of the Sheffield trades, "which require their workpeople to present themselves to the managers to receive work at certain times during the day. When they have entered the place in the morning the gates are closed, and whether they have work or not they cannot leave the premises till noon, except by special permit from the firm, and so from noon to evening. . . . I know of a case in the steel trade where the men were expected to be in the firm from 9 A.M. to 6 P.M., if they had but five shillings' worth of work during the week. The men struck against it."[1] The Macclesfield Silk-weavers are in an even worse position. The employers "give out" work to be done in the weavers' own homes, and distribute it so irregularly that a workman may be kept idle for days or even weeks. Nevertheless, as the handloom belongs to the employer, the operative has to pay loom-rent for it week by week with absolute continuity, whether any work has been given to him or not, and he is forbidden by the owner of the loom to use it for any other manufacturer who might offer work.

To capitalists concerned only for present profit, this extreme discontinuity of employment offers several ad-

number of men who are given preferences for employment. The dockers are now divided into three registered classes (permanent men, A list, and B list, each man being numbered in his own class), and one unregistered class (C or casuals). No guarantee of employment is given to any man, but each day's work is allotted, as far as it will go, strictly according to the order of the classes and the numerical order of the men in each class. Thus, the regularity of employment of the preference men has been increased at the expense of making the work of the casual docker less continuous than before. In so far as the change is a step towards the total abolition of the casual system, it must be regarded as an improvement.—See Charles Booth, *Life and Labor of the People*, vol. vii. (London, 1896); and the chapter on "Les Unions de Dockers" in *Le Trade Unionisme en Angleterre*, edited by Paul de Rousiers (Paris, 1897).

[1] Evidence of C. Hobson, Q. 19,029, before Royal Commission on Labor (Group A), 24th March 1892.

vantages. Where the industry is seasonal or otherwise irregular in volume, as in the case of dock labor and the clothing trade, the employer is able, without expense to himself, to expand or contract his working staff in exact proportion to the state of the weather or change of tides or seasons. The giver-out of work can at any moment quadruple his production to fulfil a pressing order, and then drop back to the current demands of a slack season, without incurring factory-rent or other standing charges. The army of men and women standing at his beck and call cost him nothing except for the actual hours that they are at work. And the very existence of such a " reserve army " places each member of it more completely at his mercy with regard to all the conditions of employment. Wherever this " reserve army " exists in conjunction with home-work, or otherwise under circumstances making Individual Bargaining inevitable, the employer can practically dictate terms. How disastrously the whole arrangement operates for the workers concerned has been described by every observer of the sweated trades.

To oppose such a disastrous irregularity of work is a fundamental principle of Trade Unionism. Unfortunately, where the system prevails, the workers are seldom in a position to combine for their own protection. We see a feeble attempt to cope with the evil in the regulation of the Dock, Wharf, and Riverside Laborers' Union, that any man taken on in the London docks shall be guaranteed at least four hours' continuous work. Certain classes of railway servants complain that, whilst they are forbidden by the railway company to take any other employment, they are given only casual and intermittent work, and paid only by the job. To remedy this grievance the General Railway Workers' Union is proposing that it should be enacted by law that every person who is required " to give the whole of his time to the service of the company shall, unless legally dismissed from such service, before his employment is terminated, be entitled to a week's notice, or a week's wages in lieu of notice, and he shall be entitled to full weekly wages while in such employment."[1]   But examples of Trade Union policy on this point must be sought in the more strongly organised trades in which, though so dangerous a discontinuity does not actually exist, there is some danger that it might, if not resisted, insidiously creep in. Thus, the highly-paid compositors in London daily newspaper offices who must stand by waiting for copy to come in, and then work at lightning speed to catch the press, insist on all the men in attendance being guaranteed "a galley and a half"—that is, being paid 5s. 9d. on a morning paper, or 5s. 4½d. on an evening paper—whether they are actually required to do as much work or not.[2]   The old-fashioned union of hand-working Papermakers goes farther, and rigidly enforces the Regulation known as the "Six Days' Custom," which ensures that not less than six days' work, or the equivalent payment, shall be found each week for all the men employed. If an accident occurs, or an engine breaks down, the employer no more thinks of depriving his workmen of their livelihood during the stoppage than he does that of his clerks or manager. He can discharge his men by giving them the customary fortnight's notice, or by paying them the customary forfeit of one guinea, but so long as he retains their services he must pay them at least the agreed minimum of weekly wages.[3]

[1] *General Secretary's Report to Annual General Meeting*, 1897.

[2] The minimum used to be "one galley"; then the rule ran, in mystic phrase, "one galley four hours' work, and extra pay for more than a quarter galley an hour when asked to pull out." We are indebted to Mr. C. Drummond for the following explanation. The newspaper compositors, being paid by the piece, and guaranteed a minimum of work, can do it at their own speed. But in order that the "printer" (*i.e.* manager of the department) may have some control over the time taken, it is agreed that the maximum within which one galley must be completed is four hours, though the compositor will, for his own sake, seldom take so long. It happens very occasionally, when the "printer" is compelled to insist on the utmost possible speed, that he will order the men to "pull out," *i.e.* use every effort. Men working under such an order are entitled to extra pay for all over a quarter of a galley done in an hour.

[3] "That the Six Days' Custom be as follows : Twenty-two post per day and ten on Saturday" (*Rules and Regulations of the Original Society of Papermakers*, Maidstone, 1887), Rule 28. The French papermakers in the eighteenth century

Similarly, the Flint Glass Makers have a binding custom by which the employer is required to find his men a minimum of "eleven moves a week," being thirty-three hours' work, or pay a corresponding amount in wages.[1]

In other trades where work is irregular, the Trade Union objection to its being arbitrarily distributed by the employer—leading, as this does, to the extreme dependence of the wage-earner—has led to regulations for "sharing work." If the workmen know that, however scanty may be the work to be done, it will be fairly distributed among them all, there is much less temptation for the poorer or more grasping members to seek to secure themselves by offering to accept worse conditions of employment.[2]

The most primitive form of sharing work is seen in the "turnway" societies of the Thames watermen, for regulating the "turns," or order in which the men plying at any particular "stairs" serve the passengers who present themselves.[3] What is essentially the same arrangement is presented by the "House of Call" system, under which, among the Tailors, Compositors, Bakers, Upholsterers, and sometimes Joiners and Painters, the employer wanting a

---

required six weeks' notice on either side.—Du Cellier, *Histoire des Classes Laborieuses en France* (Paris, 1860), p. 292.

[1] This custom is recognised in the trade, and is enforced by County Court judges, if the wage contract includes no express stipulation to the contrary. See the cases reported in the *Flint Glass Makers' Magazine*, August 1874 and March 1875, in the Birmingham and Rotherham County Courts.

[2] The growth of the great industry and the world commerce led to a similar development in French Trade Unionism. Du Cellier (*Histoire des Classes Laborieuses en France*, p. 385) notes that, after 1830, the workmen's associations were occupied in devising means to mitigate the evils of unemployment. Where the work was individual in character, the employer was obliged to give the jobs in succession to the several workmen in their order on the roll. Where the work was done in concert, it was shared equally by the whole staff, instead of the number being reduced.

[3] These "turnway societies," incidentally described in Mayhew's *London Labour and the London Poor* (London, 1851), are probably of great antiquity. There were societies of watermen at Rotherhithe in 1789, and of those "usually plying at the Hermitage Stairs" in 1799, whilst already in 1669 we read that "our Gravesend watermen, by some temporary and mean pretences of the late Dutch war, have raised their ferry double to what it was, and finding the sweet thereof, keep it up still" (Thomas Manley's *Usury at Six per Cent Examined*, London, 1669). See the *History of Trade Unionism*, pp. 11, 20.

workman is encouraged or required to send to a place of resort for the unemployed, and the man who has been longest on the list is, if suitable, deputed to fill the vacancy.[1] This arrangement, which is in some trades worked for the mutual convenience of both parties, may degenerate into a refusal to the employer of any power of selection. Thus the Flint Glass Makers insist on the employer taking the member who has been the longest out of work,[2] whether he is competent, or suitable, or not ; and the Silk Hatters expressly arrange so that the employer may not even see the man assigned to him, before he is engaged.[3] This is, in effect, to maintain a craft monopoly, having all the economic characteristics of

---

[1] The Compositors at London, Glasgow, Manchester, etc., use the Trade Union Office for this purpose ; and the Engineers at Manchester keep a "vacant book" in their local office. Most of the smaller trades use particular public-houses as their "House of Call," the publican often himself keeping the register of the unemployed. For incidental descriptions of the "House of Call" system, see *The Tailoring Trade*, by F. W. Galton.

In France the practice of sharing employment was carried so far in some of the incorporated handicrafts that the member who had been longest in continuous work ceded his place in favor of any who had remained a certain time unemployed.—Du Cellier, *Histoire des Classes Laborieuses en France*, p. 289.

[2] *Rules and Regulations of the National Flint Glass Makers' Sick and Friendly Society* (Manchester, 1891). Rule X. is as follows : "When a man falls out of employment the F[actory] S[ecretary] shall inform the D[istrict] S[ecretary] who shall at once write to the C[entral] S[ecretary] for an unemployed certificate ; and when a man is applied for by an employer the F.S. shall apply to the D.S., and should there be no one suitable in the district, he shall write to the C.S. stating what kind of man is wanted, wages, etc., so that there be no mistake as to the man sent to fill the situation. When an employer applies for men the unemployed roll shall be consulted before any promotions be granted either to journeymen or apprentices. Note.—Rule X. is not intended to compel a master to engage any man to whom he has a reasonable objection, the same to be considered by the District Committee." *The Flint Glass Makers' Magazine* contains many references to employers' complaints of this procedure.

[3] The Silk Hatters' custom is so universal that it is only incidentally referred to in the rules. As explained to us by officers of the union it is as follows : "Employers are not allowed to choose, or even to see, workmen whom they engage. A member out of work calls at a hatter's workshop, and sends in a small card (the 'asking ticket'), showing that he is a financial member (*i.e.* not in arrear with his contribution), and what branch of work he does. The journeymen in each workshop take it in turns to attend to such cards. On its being sent in, the man whose turn it is goes in to the employer and asks, 'Do you want a bodymaker ?' (or a shaper, as the case may be). This is called 'asking for' the unemployed member. If the employer says 'yes,' the man is told to come in and commence. If 'no,' his card is returned, and he goes off to the next shop."

a drastic restriction of numbers, with which it is invariably combined.[1]

Any such restriction on the employer's freedom of choice between one workman and another is, however, quite exceptional. More generally, the Trade Union seeks to promote the sharing of work by regulations directed against the greed or selfishness of its own members. Thus the Shipwrights' Provident Union of the Port of London retains to the present day the substance of its original rule of 1824 that "no member shall engross a greater quantity of work than he can accomplish by working the regular hours of the trade, viz. not before or after the recognised working hours per day throughout the year; and that no work be performed inside after the men on the outside of the ship have left work, so that every opportunity may be given to those who are out of employ."[2] The same intention inspires the regulations in many handwork trades against "smooting" or "foxing" or "grassing," that is, working for a second employer after putting in a full day elsewhere. Thus the Manchester Union of Saddlers provides that "no member of this union shall be allowed habitually to work for any other employer than the one by whom he is regularly employed, except there are none out of work in the branch. And no member shall be allowed to obtain any work at this trade whilst in a situation, to do after his working hours for any person except his own employer."[3] And the Wool Shear Benders and Grinders, a tiny Sheffield handicraft, absolutely prohibit their members from working in any other wheel or factory than the one in which they are regularly employed.[4] An

---

[1] We recur to this subject in our chapter on "The Economic Characteristics of Trade Unionism."

[2] Rules of the Shipwrights' Provident Union of the Port of London; see the original wording in a note to the chapter on "The Normal Day."

[3] *Rules of the Union of the Saddlers, Harness Makers, etc.* (Manchester, 1889). Similar rules exist in many other trades, such as the Compositors, Brushmakers, Coachmakers, etc.

[4] The Yorkshire Glass Bottle Makers' Society has a signed agreement with all the employers, which is renewed annually. Among other matters, it provides that "in the event of any furnace being out for repairs, slack trade, or stopped for

extreme case is presented by the Scythe Grinders' Trade Protection Society, which arranges for its members a definite year's engagement, in all cases terminating on the 6th of July (Old Midsummer Day), by which it is understood that no man is ever discharged during the year for slackness of trade, the ebbs and flows of the work of each establishment being shared among the staff with which it started the year. But these are archaic survivals. In the great modern unions any desire to promote the sharing of work by regulations of this type is merged in the general objection to Overtime, and the maintenance of the Normal Day.

The common Trade Union desire to maintain the Normal Day, especially in its manifestations against Overtime and in favor of a Reduction of the Hours of Labor, has at all times been strengthened by the belief that a strict regulation of the working time would incidentally cause employment to be more continuous. Thus, the Amalgamated Association of Operative Cotton-spinners, in supporting Lord Shaftesbury's "Ten Hours' Bill," gave as one of their objects, "a more equitable adjustment or distribution of labor, by means of shortening the hours of labor." [1] And when, in 1872, there was a new movement for reducing the Normal Day, the same idea recurs in the argument that this would "secure

any other cause, the workmen shall, as far as practicable, share the work; provided, nevertheless, that if after a furnace has been out for four months, and there is no probability of its being started again, the master to be at liberty to discharge the surplus workmen."

[1] Circular of 19th January 1845, in Minute Book. Fifteen years later the Cotton-spinners thus referred to their successful agitation : " It should always be remembered that anterior to the introduction of factory legislation, the employers dictated the hours of labor to their workpeople ; and in the various localities those hours varied accordingly, ranging from seventy-four hours and upwards. As, however, in some instances the mills were kept running night and day, we shall certainly be under the mark in assuming that the average hours worked at that time, throughout the country, were 75 per cent per week. It is obvious that sixty people working seventy-five hours per week would produce nearly as much as seventy-five now do working sixty hours, and thus from 20 to 25 per cent of the factory population would be thrown destitute upon the streets. It is equally clear, moreover, that it is the scarcity or redundance of labor in the market which regulates the rate of wages ; and, as under the circumstances we have named, some of the workpeople would be almost worked to death, while those thrown out would be reduced to a state bordering on starvation from the

them moderate but constant employment."[1] In so far as this means only that a reduction of the hours of those in employment would, other things being equal, cause the work to be shared among a larger number of operatives, and so prevent some from being wholly unemployed, the case is, like that of the Shipwrights whose rule we have quoted, merely one of sharing work. As unemployed men have to be maintained somehow, generally by their fellow-members, it may well be more convenient to the whole body that the largest possible number should be employed for the normal hours, than that some should be working abnormally long days, and others walking the streets in search of a job. In times of general depression of trade, or of temporary contraction of demand for a particular industry, such an arrangement seems to the Trade Unionist obviously reasonable. The employer, on the other hand, more than usually eager in bad times to reduce the cost of production, would prefer to lengthen the hours of labor, so as (at time wages) to get more work for the same weekly wage, or (at piece rates) to get a larger output in proportion to his standing charges. Hence we arrive at the paradox that it is generally in times of depression, when the world requires less carpentering or engineering work to be done, that attempts are made to lengthen the Normal Day of those carpenters and engineers who are in employment at all, with the result that the number out of employment is unnecessarily increased. In 1879, for instance, at a time of exceptional contraction of

want of it, the wages of labor would, as a matter of course, from the intense competition to obtain employment, come down to starvation point ; and all our efforts, whether exerted singly or in concert, would be utterly powerless to arrest their downward course. It is clearly then the duty and interest of every worker in the factories of this country to resist, by every legitimate means in his power, not only any attempt to violate the law by overworking women, young persons, and children, but to treat with contempt all overtures by which it is sought to induce him to work more than sixty hours per week, inasmuch as this righteous law is the palladium of his success in his endeavour to improve his social condition." — *Rules of the Amalgamated Association of Operative Cotton-spinners*, edition of 1860, preface.

[1] Circular of 7th January 1872, *ibid*. See, for other examples, *The Eight Hours' Day*, by Sidney Webb and Harold Cox (London, 1891).

business, the Clyde shipbuilders insisted on increasing the working hours from fifty-one to fifty-four per week, and the Manchester builders added from two to three hours to the working week.[1] It is in face of attempts of this sort that the Trade Union Regulations for maintaining the Normal Day seem incidentally to protect the workers from an unnecessary discontinuity of employment.

The reader will see on closer examination that these Regulations, though apparently directed towards Continuity of Employment, are in reality designed primarily to prevent the evils of Individual Bargaining, and to save the workmen, especially in bad times, from falling into personal dependence on the employer or his foreman. Thus the Trade Union objection to the conditions of employment being fixed in advance for long periods completely disappears, as we may learn from the little example of the Scythe-grinders, when this fixing takes place by the Method of Collective Bargaining. The " Working Rules," for which all sections of the building trade persistently struggle, habitually determine the rates of wages, hours of labor, and many other conditions for an indefinitely long period, from which neither employers nor workmen can depart without giving six months' notice. The Miners' Federation in 1893 willingly bound themselves to continue to accept the then existing rates of wages for a year, in return for a corresponding pledge from the associated employers not to seek a reduction during that period. In like manner, the Trade Union objection to the doling out of work in slack seasons ceases when this distribution is made in accordance with any such collective arrangement among the operatives themselves as those that we have just described.[2] *None of these regulations secures, or even attempts*

---

[1] *History of Trade Unionism*, pp. 332-334.

[2] The workers may even resort to the primitive expedient of casting lots ; thus the Rules and Regulations of the Warpers' True Benevolent Sick and Burial Society (Rochdale, 1884) prescribe " that when a mill stops working where our members are employed, and it is obvious that such stoppage will be for some time, when all the men are finishing their work within two days, they shall cast lots whose name shall be first on the list."

to secure, to the workmen a full week's work or a full week's wage for every week in the year. They have little real bearing on Continuity of Employment and are, in substance, only incidents of the Method of Collective Bargaining, required to maintain the Standard Rate and the Normal Day.

There are, in fact, no Trade Union Regulations placing upon the employer the obligation of providing continuous employment for the wage-earners whom he chooses to engage. Wisely or unwisely the Trade Unions have tacitly accepted the position that the capitalist can only be expected to find them wages so long as he can find them work. Continuity of employment becomes, therefore, contingent upon continuity of the consumer's demand, or more precisely, upon an exact adjustment of Supply and Demand. Both employers and workmen wish this adjustment made and continuity secured. But capitalists and manual workers have, with a few exceptions on both sides, advocated diametrically opposite ways of obtaining it. When business becomes slack and sales fall off, the employer's first instinct is to tempt customers by lowering prices. He assumes that, whatever may be the cause of the depression, he can still get orders, and so keep his mills going full time, if only he is enabled to quote a sufficiently low price for his product. For this reduction he looks mainly to the rate of wages. The landlord insists on his fixed rent or royalty, and the mortgagee or debenture holder on his fixed interest. It would be fatal to economise on buildings, machinery, or plant, which must either be kept up to their highest efficiency or replaced earlier than need be at serious cost to himself. It is not worth while, and it is contrary to the brainworker's tradition, to nibble at the salaries of managers or clerks. The conclusion seems inevitable. The alternative to stopping altogether is, whilst the employer temporarily foregoes some of his profits, the workman shall forego some of his wages.

The Trade Unionists entirely dissent from this policy.[1]

[1] Thus, the factory bootmakers, in a time of great depression of trade, emphatically protested against the employers' policy " When in consequence

They point out that, to them, it is not a question of temporarily diminishing surplus profits ; what is at stake is their weekly livelihood, the actual housekeeping of their families and themselves. To the vast majority of workmen, a ten per cent reduction of wages means an actual diminution of food and warmth, an actual privation in the way of clothing and house-accommodation, which they declare to be physically exhausting and detrimental to their industrial efficiency. No manufacturer would think it wise to let his buildings and machinery fall into disrepair, or to reduce the ration and stable accommodation of his horses ; why, asks the Trade Unionist, should he adopt this suicidal policy with regard to the most important factors of his productive efficiency,—the human laborers whom he employs ?[1] If the employer, under the pressure of competition in slack times, tempts the consumer to buy his particular commodity by indefinitely worsening the conditions of employment, he is, in thus deteriorating the physique and character of successive relays of workers, giving away what does not belong to him, the capital value of the human beings in his service.

It is a further aggravation to the Trade Unionist that he believes the sacrifice demanded of him by the employer to be worse than useless. Merely to offer commodities at a lower price in no way increases the world's aggregate demand

of the reckless unscrupulous competition among capitalists we find our commerce becoming less day by day, banks stopping payment, firms which had become bywords in the past for their supposed stability found to be in a state of hopeless insolvency, we protest against that doctrine which would find a panacea for these evils in a general reduction of the wages of the workers or an increase in their hours of labor."—*Monthly Report of the National Union of Boot and Shoe Operatives* (December 1879).

[1] The acceptance by employers of contracts at prices which cannot possibly be made to pay at the existing rates of wages is a subject of constant complaint. The preface to the *Bylaws, Order of Business, and Rules of Order of the Window-Glass Workers of England* (Sunderland, 1886) declares, " Whilst admitting that sometimes pressure is brought to bear on the capitalists or employers, [that] in too many instances, instead of offering any resistance, they accept terms that are disadvantageous to themselves, trusting to their power of remunerating themselves by legally pilfering a portion off each of their workers' weekly earnings ; and there is no limit to the extremes to which labor can be pushed, unless it be that fixed by the Poor-Law authorities and the price paid for their test labor."

for commodities. It may suit the immediate purposes of a single employer, by undercutting his rivals, to engross their trade. It might conceivably suit all the employers in a particular trade, by cheapening their wares, to engross more of the aggregate demand for commodities than would otherwise come their way.[1] But in either case the total demand remains the same, being, in fact, identical with the total product, and all that has happened is a gain in continuity in one direction, balanced by an equivalent loss somewhere else Thus, the Trade Unionist declares a lowering of price to be no real cure for a general depression of trade. When such a policy is adopted all round, the aggregate income of the producers is no greater than it would have been if they had kept up their rates and done less work. The only result is that the workers have to do more work for the same money, and though the wage-earners share, as consumers, in the benefit of the lowered prices, the fact that they only consume a third of the product makes the operation a net loss to their class.[2] If it is retorted that one country may, by a judicious cheapening of its products, engross more than its normal share of the diminished trade of the world, and so keep its own wage-earners employed at the cost of

[1] It must not be forgotten that a fall in the wages of any particular section of workers would, at best, produce a much less than proportionate fall in the retail price of their product. Thus, when the Northumberland coal hewers are urged to submit to a ten per cent reduction, in order to stimulate the demand for their coal, they may well reply that, receiving as they do on an average about 15d. per ton of coal hewn, this ten per cent reduction of wages, which would mean a serious shrinking of their family incomes, could not possibly result in lowering the price to the London consumer to a greater degree than from 24s. to 23s. 10½d. per ton, or by about a half per cent.

The actual variations of price have, in most industries, little connection with variations of wages. "During the last twenty years the retail price of cotton thread has varied from a penny to twopence per spool of 200 yards—that is, 100 per cent—following, more or less closely, the variations of manufacturers' prices. All this time the wages of women workers, who constitute the great majority of operatives in the thread mills, have scarcely varied."—Prof. W. Smart, *Studies in Economics* (London, 1896), p. 259.

[2] In the United Kingdom from three-fifths to two-thirds of the annual product of commodities and services are consumed by the one-fifth of the population above the wage-earning class ; see the reference to official statistics given in *Facts for Socialists* (Fabian Tract, No. 5).

foreigners, the Trade Unionist has the reply that, according to the orthodox Theory of International Trade, any such artificial stimulus to national industry must necessarily be as powerless to increase the total volume of the trade as a Protective Tariff or a system of Bounties on Exports. We shall examine the whole of this argument in our chapter on "The Economic Characteristics of Trade Unionism." It concerns us here only as explaining the persistent Trade Union policy of fighting their hardest against any lowering of wages, and submitting only to superior force.[1]

But certain sections of the Trade Union world do not stop at this negative attitude. They have propounded, as a means of coping with depression of trade, a diametrically opposite policy, which they have done their best to press their employers to adopt. The Cotton Operatives and Coal-miners — trades which we are always having to couple together—have repeatedly met their employers' demands for reduction of wages by an equally confident demand for a restriction of the output. This policy dates from the very beginning of the century. Thus, to quote an official report of 1844, "It can scarcely be credited by one calmly investigating the state of this large body of laborers, that many thousands of them—in fact, the whole of the colliers and miners in Lanarkshire, with a few exceptions, amounting to 16,000 men—have, for many years past (since the repeal of the Combination Laws in 1825), placed themselves under regulations as to the amount of their labor, which, had they been attempted to be enforced by the authority of any government whatsoever, in any country calling itself civilised, would have roused the indignation of every thinking man, as against an act of the most intolerable despotism. And yet

---

[1] In our *History of Trade Unionism* we have described how, for a few years, a small number of unions, mainly in the coal and iron industries, accepted the employers' arguments, and agreed to the celebrated arrangement of the Sliding Scale, which the Coalminers have now practically abandoned. We refer to this method of adjusting wages in our chapter on "The Assumptions of Trade Unionism." Particulars of all known Sliding Scales are given in Appendix II. of the *History of Trade Unionism.*

these regulations were intended by the working colliers . . . for the maintenance of wages at a fair level, for their protection against overwork, and against an overstocking of the market of labor and the market of coal. . . . A certain day's work, called the 'darg,' is fixed, which the colliers themselves allow no one to exceed." [1]

The policy of regulating the output of coal in proportion to the demand for it at the current price has always remained a leading principle of the Coalminers. The " darg," or limit to the day's product of the individual hewer, has at no time extensively prevailed, and is to-day characteristic not of good Trade Union districts, but only of the half-organised Ayrshire and Lanarkshire pits. In England restriction of output has taken the form only of a counter proposal, justifying the miners' refusal to lower wages. [2] When the coalowners have pleaded their accumulating stocks of coal as a reason why wages and prices should be lowered, in order to stimulate demand, the miners have suggested that Supply and Demand

---

[1] Report of Commissioner to inquire into Coalmining, No. 592 of 1844, vol. xvii. p. 31, quoted in J. H. Burton's *Political and Social Economy* (Edinburgh, 1849). In one or two old piecework trades—notably some branches of the Potters and Glass Bottle Makers—a similar limitation of individual output has prevailed under the name of "stint" or "tantum." "In our light metal shops," wrote the secretary of the North of England Glass Bottle Makers' Society in 1895, "the Society has a tantum fixed, which the men are not allowed to exceed : if they do it is paid into the Society, as a reference to the reports will show. . . . I give you a copy of the tantum for light metal in our district as mentioned :—

Reputed Quarts	.	.	.	.	.	110 dozen.
10 oz. Codd's	.	.	.	.	.	105 ,,
5 oz. Codd's .	.	.	.	.	.	115 ,,
Imperial Pints	.	.	.	.	.	115 ,,
Reputed Pints above 12 oz.	.	.	.	115 ,,
Do. under 12 oz., no restriction.						

All bottles made in excess of the above the money is paid into the funds of the Society."—*Report of the Rates of Wages, Lists of Numbers, etc., of the Glass Bottle Makers of Great Britain and Ireland* (Castleford, 1895), p. 49.

[2] *The Rules of the Miners' United Association of the County of Fife* (Dunfermline, 1868) refers in the preamble to " the fearful stocks of coal which have accumulated in the county, which evil stands out like a bold monster, to defy us in having our just rights." The *Articles of Regulation of the Operative Collieries of Lanark and Dumbarton* of 1825 declared " that there should never be allowed to be any stock of coals in the hands of any of the masters."—See Huskisson's *Speeches* (London, 1831), vol. ii. pp. 369, 371.

should be adjusted rather by diminishing the output than by forcing coal upon unwilling buyers. In one recent instance the Trade Union gave a practical illustration of this policy. In March 1892 the Miners' Federation saw its members threatened with a reduction of wages by coal-owners unable to keep up their sales. The men resolved to "take a week's holiday," with the result that the stocks were temporarily diminished, and the reduction was not insisted on.[1]

---

[1] This policy of restricting the output has, under the name of " Limitation of the Vend," long been characteristic of the coal trade. From 1771 to 1844, a period of seventy-three years, there existed, almost continuously, a systematic organisation among the coalowners of the Tyne and Wear for fixing price and output. "The colliery owners met annually and agreed upon what was called the 'basis,' that is, the proportion which each colliery should sell of the total 'vend.' They met monthly, and sometimes fortnightly, to fix what was called the 'issue' for the following month. There was an understanding as to the price at which each colliery should sell. A fine of from 3s. to 5s. per Newcastle chaldron was paid by those who at the end of the year had exceeded their quantity, and this was received by those who were short' (D. A. Thomas). The result was that prices were greatly and continuously raised. It appears that so long as the arrangement effected an actual restriction of the total output, it worked satisfactorily enough to the coalowners. But eventually each coalowner strove, by opening new pits and increasing their capacity, to increase his own "basis." The arrangement then ceased to restrict the total output, and became only one of "sharing work," which came to an end in 1844 by the revolt of the larger collieries, who desired to work their pits to the full capacity. Particulars are to be found in the Reports and Evidence of the Parliamentary Committees of 1800, 1829, 1830, and 1873 on the coal trade (G. R. Porter's *Progress of the Nation*, London, pp. 283-286 of 1847 edition ; Cunningham's *Growth of English Industry and Commerce*, vol. ii. p. 463 ; *Some Notes on the Present State of the Coal Trade*, by D. A. Thomas, M.P., Cardiff, 1896). Mr. Thomas proposes to institute a similar " Limitation of the Vend " for South Wales, urging that if each colliery agreed to produce only its allotted quota of the total output, prices would be automatically maintained, without the need of any concerted action among the sellers as to price, and without actually limiting the total supply below the demand for it at existing prices. This proposal seems to contain, in not providing against a reckless increase in the number and capacity of pits, the same inherent weakness that eventually broke up the Tyne and Wear arrangement.

The coalowners in Westphalia and Pennsylvania have gone farther. The Rhenish Westphalian Coal Syndicate has, since 1893, conducted all sales for the Westphalian coalowners, fixing both price and output. The Coalowners' Association of Pennsylvania, in conjunction with the great railway companies, has an essentially similar arrangement for the supply of anthracite. Sir George Elliot's bold proposal (described in the *Times* of 20th September 1893) of an amalgamation of all the coalmines of the United Kingdom into a single company of £110,000,000, subject to a government control over rises in price, may eventually be adopted in preference to a merely capitalist trust.

For twenty years a similar policy has been urged by the Cotton Operatives at each recurring period of contraction of trade. In the great depression of 1878, when the value of English exports of cotton piece-goods fell no less than 17 per cent below those of 1872, the employers insisted that only by a 10 per cent reduction could they continue their trade. The weavers denied that any such reduction would "remove the glut from an overstocked cloth market," especially in view of the fact that the quantity of piece-goods exported was no less than before, but offered to give way, provided that the employers would, on their side, consent to put all the mills on short time, so as to stop the over-production.[1] Again, in the depression of 1885, the employers pressed for a reduction, and the operatives—this time the spinners—formally offered to "accept a reduction of 10 per cent and four days a week ; 5 per cent and five days ; or full rates with full time." [2] " The employers," as their able secretary explains, " looked upon this as a fallacy, knowing from experience that short time meant increased cost of production." [3]

We do not propose to enter into the complicated economic arguments which are urged for and against this policy of meeting the vicissitudes of demand by a deliberately regulated production.[4] Whatever may be said in favor of Restriction of Output, any systematic use of this device is out of the reach of mere associations of wage-earners. They can, of course, temporarily stop all production by simultaneously refusing to work, as in a strike or in the week's holiday arbitrarily taken by the Miners' Federation in 1892. But

[1] See the Cotton-weavers' manifesto of June 1878, given in the *History of Trade Unionism*, pp. 329, 330.

[2] Minutes of Sub-Committee, Executive Committee, and Representative Meeting of the Amalgamated Association of Operative Cotton-spinners, June 1885.

[3] *Fifty Years of the Cotton Trade*, by Samuel Andrew (Oldham, 1887), p. 10.

[4] The Trade Union position in the controversy of 1878 was ably maintained by Mr. (now the Right Hon.) John Morley, in his *Over Production ; an address delivered at the Trade Union Congress*, 1878 (Nottingham, 1879).

when the industrial machine is in motion, any direct limitation of output is beyond the power of the Trade Union. A
strongly-organised union might insist that no member should
produce more than a given quantity per day (the Coalminers' "darg"), or that all the establishments in the trade
should work only a limited number of hours per week (the
Cotton Operatives' "short time"). But neither of these
expedients has, in practice, any effective result in diminishing
the total amount of production below what the employers
desire. It is always possible to employ more miners in the
pit, to work additional seams, or even to open up new pits.
The millowner puts in additional machines, and directly
prices rise owing to the rumour of restriction, old mills are
reopened and new ones erected. Any attempt on the part
of the wage-earners to limit the output of the individual
operative, though it may cause inconvenience, or increase
the expense of carrying on the industry, has, therefore, no
practical effect in restricting the total amount that will be
produced. Hence, though the English Coalminers and
Cotton Operatives remain firmly convinced that it would be
desirable for their employers to restrict production, they
have taken no steps to effect this restriction by Trade
Union Regulation.[1] The Trade Unionists in short, like
the majority of English employers, have hitherto stood
helpless before the inscrutable ebb and flow of demand, and
have accepted as inevitable the corresponding fluctuations
of work.

Thwarted in their efforts to secure continuity of employment, either from the employer or from the consumer,

---

[1] Restriction of output is, in fact, an employer's device, not a workman's, and
it is usually practised (as in the Coalowners' "Limitation of the Vend" or an
ordinary Trust) without the help of the wage-earners, though occasionally (as in
the "Alliances" of the Birmingham bedstead manufacturers hereafter described)
with the co-operation of the Trade Union. Its economic effect is incidentally
referred to in our chapter on "The Economic Characteristics of Trade Unionism."
We may say at once that, from the workman's point of view, it is of no avail
in maintaining wages unless it is accompanied by the Common Rule of the
Standard Rate, and that with such a Common Rule it is unnecessary and
useless.

particular Trade Unions have turned their force in another direction. If they cannot protect themselves against the fluctuating demands of the capitalist and the consumer, they can at any rate build up barriers against their fellow-workmen. Hence, we find certain sections of the Trade Union world of to-day clinging to the mediæval expedients of apprenticeship and limitation of the recruits to a trade, the exclusion of women, and the maintenance, as against other workmen, of a vested interest in an advantageous means of livelihood.

It is significant that it is only at this point in our analysis of Trade Union regulations that we find ourselves face to face with the idea of " monopoly." The Standard Rate, the Normal Day, and a safe and healthy place of work can be simultaneously enjoyed by the entire wage-earning class of the country. So far from there being any desire that these conditions should be a privilege of any class or section, the Trade Unionists claim that, on any of these points, a successful stand made by one union renders it positively easier for other grades of workmen to put forward similar claims. When the contractors and master builders in any town have been induced to agree to definite Standard Rates for all the bricklayers, stonemasons, and carpenters in their employment, they are predisposed to complete the arrangement by conceding a Standard Rate even to the laborers. And when the leading unions in a town press the Town Council either itself to pay " Trade Union wages," or to compel its contractors to do so, this demand is always intended to apply equally to all classes of wage-earners. Still more is this the case with regard to the Normal Day, which almost inevitably tends, as we have seen, to become identical for all classes of operatives in the same establishment. Finally, all the regulations for securing the sanitation of the workplace and the prevention of accidents necessarily benefit the wage-earners without distinction of grade, merit, or sex. But in the regulations with which we deal in the next two chapters, based upon the idea of a vested interest in a trade, asserted by one set of workmen to the exclusion of others, we have a claim of an entirely different nature, akin to those put forward by the holders of " free-hold offices," ecclesiastical benefices, or Civil Service appointments, when these are threatened with abolition or reorganisation.

CHAPTER X

THE ENTRANCE TO A TRADE

THE trade clubs of eighteenth-century handicraftsmen regarded the limitation of apprentices and the exclusion of
illegal men as the pivot of their Trade Unionism. Down
to 1814 the policy of regulating the entrance into a trade
could claim the sanction of law, and the workmen's organisations did their utmost to prevent the repeal of the Statute
of Apprentices.[1] Notwithstanding the legal opening of
every occupation, the Parliamentary committees of 1824-25
and 1838, and the Royal Commission of 1867 revealed
numerous cases in which Trade Unions sought to regulate
the entrance into their respective trades. It has accordingly
been assumed by many writers that the policy of restricting
numbers forms an integral part of Trade Unionism. In the
following pages we shall examine how far this assumption
holds true of the Trade Unionism of the present day ; we
shall estimate the number of Trade Unions that aim at
restricting the entrance into their trades ; and we shall
analyse the actual working of such regulations in order to
discover how far they succeed in effecting their object. For
the purpose of this analysis it will be convenient to classify
all rules dealing with admission to a trade under the four
heads of Apprenticeship, Limitation of Boy-Labor, Progression within the Trade, and the Exclusion of Women.

[1] *History of Trade Unionism*, pp. 54-56.

(a) *Apprenticeship*

The Trade Union Regulations as to Apprenticeship, unlike those for maintaining the Standard Rate, were not invented by the Trade Unions themselves. They can scarcely be said even to have been modified or developed, like the workmen's policy with regard to new processes and machinery, by Trade Union experience. So far as any system of apprenticeship still lingers in the Trade Union world, this is, in form and in purpose, practically identical with that which prevailed long before Trade Unionism was heard of.[1]

The modern Trade Unionist has, in this matter of apprenticeship, inherited two distinct and contradictory traditions. We have, on the one hand, the remnants of the formal, legal, indentured apprenticeship to the master-craftsman, with its reciprocal obligations between the employer and his apprentices. The master undertook to teach the boys all the mysteries of his craft. The apprentices undertook to serve for a long term for wages below the market rate. As Paley tersely puts it, " instruction is their hire."[2] Round this " apprenticeship to the employer," descended to us from the ordinances made by the master-craftsmen's gilds, there had grown up already in mediæval times a whole series of restrictive conditions, the exaction of fees or premiums

---

[1] With the system of apprenticeship considered as part of the organisation of mediæval industry, we make no attempt to deal. There has been little detailed study either of the facts or of the economic results of this system in the United Kingdom. Adam Smith's celebrated denunciation (*Wealth of Nations*, Book I chap. x. part 2) has been criticised by several of his commentators, notably by Dr. William Playfair in the edition of 1805; see also the latter's pamphlet, *A Letter to the . . . Lords and Commons . . . on the Advantages of Apprenticeships* (London, 1814). The subject has also been dealt with by Dr L. Brentano in his *Arbeitergilden der Gegenwart* (Leipzig, 1871), vol. ii. pp 143-155. A pamphlet, *The Origin, Objects, and Operation of the Apprentice Laws* (London, 1814), preserved in the *Pamphleteer*, vol. iii., gives the master case for freedom. See Dr. Cunningham's *Growth of English Industry and Commerce*, vol. ii. p. 578, etc. ; and *History of Trade Unionism*, pp. 54-56, etc. A recent article, " The Fair Number of Apprentices in a Trade," by C. P. Sanger *Economic Journal*, December 1895, gives useful mathematical formulæ.

[2] *Moral and Political Philosophy*, Book III. part i. chap. xi. (" Apprenticeship ").

rigid limits of age, a definite long term of servitude, and a limitation of the number of apprentices permitted to each employer.[1] These regulations, designed for the double purpose of securing technical training and protecting the craftsmen in their economic monopoly, have their representatives in modern Trade Unionism. On the other hand, we find, alongside this formal apprenticeship, the custom of "patrimony," that is to say, a privilege enjoyed from time immemorial, by the journeymen in certain occupations, of bringing their own sons into the trade, and themselves informally instructing them in the processes of the craft. This "apprenticeship to the journeyman," hitherto undescribed by historian or economist, stands in sharp contrast to the other system. It seems never to have been regulated by law or gild ordinance, and to have rested only on the customs of the workshop. It was, in fact, not a rival system, but a privileged exemption from the operation of the law. The craftsman father could bring his son into the workshop at what age he chose, and for what period he deemed fit. He needed no legal indentures or formal contract. He paid no fee or tax, and was usually subject to no supervision from the authorities of the trade. He could sometimes introduce all his sons in succession, or even simultaneously, without restriction of numbers. Thus, the characteristic idea of apprenticeship to the journeyman has little reference to the well-being of the trade as a whole, but is essentially that of personal privilege, based upon an hereditary vested interest. This tradition of "patrimony," which is still

[1] The "masterpiece," the production of which was a condition of admission to journeymanship, does not seem to have been a feature of English apprenticeship. The "wanderjahre," or customary years of travel from town to town at its close, were likewise unknown, as a regular custom, in this country. These and other differences warn us, in the absence of English evidence, against assuming that apprenticeship in England ran the same course, or led to the same consequences as the system in France, Germany, and the Rhine Valley, as described, for instance, in Levasseur, *Histoire des Classes Ouvrières en France ;* Fagniez, *Études sur l'Industrie et la classe industrielle à Paris ;* Martin-Saint-Léon, *Histoire des Corporations de Métiers ;* Schanz, *Zur Geschichte der Deutschen Gesellenverbände im Mittelalter ;* or Schmoller, *Die Strassburger Tucher und Weberzünft.*

strong in many trades, constantly affects or nullifies, by its laxity, irregularity, and inequality, the deliberate regulation and systematic uniformity aimed at by the system of apprenticeship by legal indentures and its modern derivatives.

We shall best understand the character of these two streams of tradition by examining typical instances of existing Trade Union Regulations in particular industries. By far the best modern example of an effective system of apprenticeship to the employer is that now embodied in the elaborate treaty concluded between the United Society of Boilermakers and Iron-shipbuilders and nearly all the master shipbuilders of the United Kingdom.   Here we have a formal code of rules precisely regulating the admission of apprentices in all the ports of the kingdom. There is, to begin with, a clear distinction between the lad engaged as a " plater's marker " or " rivet boy," who is taught nothing, but is paid full wages, and the apprentice who is taught the trade.   When a boy is taken as an apprentice, which must in any case be before he is eighteen years of age, he enters into formal indentures or written agreement, by which he is bound to serve for five years, at specified low rates of wages, which are, from first to last, far less than he could earn as a rivet boy.   In return, the employer formally contracts to give him adequate instruction as a plater and rivetter.   No apprentice may leave his employer before the expiration of the five years' term of servitude, unless with express permission in writing, and the Trade Union is able to enforce the most rigid boycott of any lad who runs away from his indentures.   The number of apprentices taken by any firm is not to exceed two to every seven journeymen, the ratio being computed on the average number employed during the past five years, with special consideration for rapidly growing establishments and other exceptional cases.   Finally, the engagement of apprentices is left absolutely and exclusively to the employers, no journeyman having any right to bring his own son into the trade otherwise than as an employer's apprentice.[1]

Here, it will be seen, we have a system of apprentice-ship to the employers reproducing, in all essential features, the typical educational servitude of the Middle Ages. To become a boilermaker-apprentice the modern rivet-boy fore-goes often half his actual earnings, and finds himself at the age of twenty-one or twenty-two getting only ten shillings a week. On the other hand, the employer encumbers his yard with a raw lad, who instead of being kept to mere mechanical routine, has to be always trying his hand at work for which he is not yet competent. And once entered on, these reci-procal obligations are practically binding on both parties. The apprentice, it is true, no longer becomes a member of the employer's family, and neither party looks to the law, or to any public authority, to enforce the contract. But these elaborate regulations are much more than mere Trade Union by-laws. A formal treaty signed, not only by a Trade Union practically co-extensive with the industry, but also by nine-tenths of the employers is, to all intents and pur-poses, a coercive law. It is, in fact, practically impossible for any youth to enter the iron-shipbuilding trade in Great Britain except in the way prescribed by the united masters and men.

To see in full force the other stream of tradition—apprenticeship to the journeyman—we must turn from the great modern industry of iron-shipbuilding to the forty or

---

[1] *Memorandum of Arrangement re the Apprentice Question between the Employers and the Committee of the Boilermakers' and Iron-shipbuilders' Society*, 11th October 1893, signed by Col. H. Dyer (of Armstrong's Works, Elswick) as Chairman of the Employers' Committee, and Mr. R. Knight as General Secretary, on behalf of the Trade Union. The United Society of Boilermakers strove, at first, for a ratio of one apprentice to five journeymen, which some employers thought insufficient to keep up the trade (see *Memorandum*, by Mr. J. Inglis, of the firm of A. and J. Inglis, Glasgow; and his Evidence before the Royal Commission on Labor, C. 6194, iii. Group A; more fully explained by him in *The Apprentice Question*, a paper printed in the *Proceedings of the Philosophical Society of Glasgow*, 1894). From Mr. Inglis's latest paper and from Mr. Sanger's article already cited, we gather that the present ratio of two to seven is, according to the best available data, a "fair" one, providing, not only for the maintenance, but also for a normal increase of the trade.

fifty ancient handicrafts composing the Sheffield cutlery trade. Three hundred years ago apprentices in Sheffield were formally indentured to the master craftsman, enrolled at the Court Leet, and at the end of their prescribed term of servitude publicly admitted to the trade. But as far back as 1565 we find existing an exemption of craftsmen's sons from all fees, formalities, and indentures.[1] What was then apparently an exception has to-day become practically the only avenue to employment. Apprenticeship to the employer, now become a capitalist giver-out of work, has almost entirely disappeared. The journeyman, who seldom works on his employer's premises, engages his own boy assistant, who is nowadays never formally indentured or bound for any specified period. Hereditary succession has become the dominant idea. " No journeyman," say the Britannia Metal Smiths, " shall take an apprentice except such be his own or a journeyman's son, who must be under seventeen years of age, but he cannot have an apprentice in addition to his own son or sons."[2] This is put more curtly by the Razor Hafters. " That no boys be admitted to the trade except members' sons."[3]

When the ordinary method of recruiting a trade is for fathers to instruct their own sons, any collective regulation of apprenticeship becomes practically impossible. The father brings in his boy when he finds it convenient, teaches him what he chooses, and pays him anything or nothing as may be arranged between them. The enforcement of a definite period of educational servitude becomes impracticable. Moreover, any effective limitation of the number has to be given up. The commonly accepted ratio of apprentices to adult workmen in modern industry is one boy to every four or five men. But every Sheffield craftsman would feel it an intolerable grievance not to be able to bring his own son

---

[1] *The History of Hallamshire*, by Joseph Hunter (London, 1869), p. 150 see the excellent account of the trade up to 1860 by Frank Hill, in the Social Science *Report on Trade Societies and Strikes* (London, 1860), pp. 521-586.

[2] *Rules of the Britannia Metal Smiths' Provident Society* (Sheffield, 1888).

[3] *Rules of the Razor Hafters' Trade Protection Society* (Sheffield, 1892), p. 6

into his trade. Hence the most restrictive of the Sheffield rules allows each workman of a certain age to have at all times one apprentice of his own. Usually, as with the Scythe Grinders, though the childless journeyman may teach only one son of another member, the happy father has the privilege of bringing all his boys up to his own craft. In some of the Sheffield trades we find the workmen endeavoring to restrict the numbers entering the craft, but the idea of hereditary right to the trade makes these attempts take a peculiar and futile form. The Wool Shear Grinders, the Razor Hafters, and the Edge Tool Forgers[1] among others compel the adult craftsman to wait seven years before he brings in a boy; the Razor Grinders add two years more, making the minimum age thirty; whilst other clubs fix twenty-five or twenty-seven as the age before which "no member shall take an apprentice."[2] In exceptional cases some attempt is also made to get back the old idea of a genuine period of educational servitude, and formal testing of competency. The Britannia Metal Smiths have a rule that "any journeyman having a son or an apprentice shall not leave him to work to himself. If he leave him, he must put him to some other journeyman, to complete his time, unless he first obtain the sanction of a general meeting," and "every boy on completing his apprenticeship shall be reported upon by the men working at the firm as to his abilities, before he is accepted by the Trade. If it be found that the said boy is incompetent as a workman, the Committee shall institute an inquiry, and, if possible, to ascertain the cause, and take the necessary steps to prevent a similar misfortune."[3]

---

[1] *Rules of the Edge Tool Forgers' Union* (Sheffield, 1873), p. 6.

[2] Similar limitations are to be found in gild ordinances. Thus the ordinances of the Gild of the Tailors of Exeter declare that a newly-made freeman shall be allowed to have "the first yeere butt oon seruauant; the second yeere II; the IIIrd III; and a prentise if he be able" (*English Gilds*, by Toulmin Smith, p. 316). And the Ordinances of the Shearmen of London, made in 1350, declare "that no one of this trade shall receive any apprentice if he be not a freeman of the City himself, and have been so for a term of seven years at least." —Riley's *Memorials of London and London Life* (London, 1868), p. 247.

[3] *Rules of the Britannia Metal Smiths' Provident Society* (Sheffield, 1888).

Among the Stonemasons we find a formal apprenticeship to the employer coexisting with the custom of Patrimony.[1] The following detailed description of the way in which the trade is actually recruited at the present day, given to us by a trustworthy and intelligent member of the union, has been confirmed by our own investigations. " The printed Rules of the Stonemasons as to apprentices vary from town to town. Usually they include a limit of one boy to five or six men, and require that, after working three months at the trade, the lad must be actually bound apprentice for a period of five or seven years. Indentures are not insisted on, but some sort of agreement is usual, and these boys are, of course, always 'to the employer.' These rules, which are generally very strictly enforced, apply, however, only to outside ordinary boys who are brought into the trade. In addition to these, every mason is permitted to bring as many of his sons as he likes into the trade, and teach them without any regulations or apprenticeship. Usually the man keeps his son at work as a telegraph boy, or otherwise, until he is sixteen or seventeen years of age, and strong enough to enter the trade and become useful. Then he is brought into the shop and *works for the employer as an improver*. The men always push their sons forward as rapidly as possible, and insist on their getting

Judging by the context the rule applies primarily to employer's apprentices. In some of the Sheffield trades the gradual transformation into factory industries ha led to boys being apprenticed also to the capitalist employer. The number o these apprentices is strictly limited by the Trade Unions, and even here the restriction retains traces of the paternal type. Thus the Britannia Metal Smith have a rule that "no master shall have more than one apprentice at one time *if two or more partners they can have one each ;* and for limited companies, fo the first ten men or fractional part thereof one boy, from eleven to twenty-fiv men two boys, and so raising one boy to every fifteen additional men."

[1] This custom of Patrimony in English trade deserves further study, especiall in reference to its resemblance to the common gild and municipal regulatio permitting the son of a freeman, without other qualification, to take up his ow freedom of the gild or the city on coming of age. We know of no evidenc actually connecting the Trade Union custom with the gild or municipal practice Besides the Stonemasons and the Sheffield trades, traces of the privilege are t be found also among the old unions of Woolstaplers, Millwrights, Coopers Block-printers, Skinners, Beamers, Twisters, and Drawers, Warpers, Spanish an Morocco Leather Finishers, and a few other handicrafts. It was formall abolished by the London Society of Compositors at the revision of their rule

full man's pay the moment they are entrusted with a man's work to do. In point of fact the trade is almost entirely recruited by this means. Very few lads are bound, and very few outside boys enter the trade. The employers are not anxious to have them, because for the first three or four years they earn nothing and spoil a good deal of stone. On the other hand, the men object to them because for the last year or two they are doing a man's work at a good deal below man's pay, while the member's son entering the trade is pushed forward as rapidly as possible, and compelled by the men to demand the man's rate as soon as he is a capable workman, or else leave the shop and go elsewhere. . . . The rule does not in effect amount to any limitation in the number of learners. Men have been known to bring up as many as six or seven sons to the trade, and such a course is not resented by the others. Hence there is no complaint of undermanning the trade ever heard. In Cornwall and some other quarrying districts, where the men are paid piecework, the learners are absolutely confined to sons of members, and they work direct for their father or other workman, and never for the employer. But there is no other limit, and no fixed period of servitude enforced." [1]

in 1879. Continental history reveals what may, perhaps, be an analogous custom, according to which craftsmen's sons were admitted to the freedom of the craft after a shorter period of apprenticeship, an easier test of proficiency, and lower fees ; see, for instance, Du Cellier, *Histoire des Classes Laborieuses en France*, p. 219.

[1] This is one of the instances in which a mere inspection of printed documents, or even a desultory questioning of Trade Union officials, would only mislead the student. There is a common impression that the Stonemasons strictly enforce a long period of educational servitude, and insist on formal indentures. This is frankly stated to any inquirer by the officials of the union. But it does not occur to them to explain that this is not the way in which the trade is actually recruited. Nor do we find any mention of hereditary privilege, or indeed any reference to the regulation of apprenticeship, in any of the editions of the rules issued since the Royal Commission inquiry of 1868. To find any indication of the actual practice we must go back to the earlier rules. The *Laws of the Friendly Society of Operative Stonemasons* (Bolton, 1867) contain, at p. 32, the following clause, elaborated from similar clauses in previous editions : " Boys entering the trade on no occasion to exceed sixteen years of age, and to be legally bound apprentice till twenty-one years of age. No boy to work more than three months without being legally bound. . . . The sons, or step-sons of masons be allowed the scale

The case of the Stonemasons will bring home to the reader the manner in which the Trade Union regulations as to apprenticeship elude any scientific classification. Here we have a trade which seems, at first sight, to be strictly regulated in numbers, age, and fixed period of apprenticeship, all formally defined and rigidly enforced. From this point of view it belongs to the same class as the United Society of Boilermakers. Closer scrutiny reveals, however, the presence, not of formal indentures, reciprocal obligations, fixed period of servitude and limitation of numbers, but of the laxity characterising the hereditary right of all craftsmen's sons to scramble up into journeymen as best they can, insisting all the time on getting the full market rate of wages for boy-labor. Indeed, if we took the extreme case of Cornwall, or other quarrying districts, where the journeyman takes the apprentice, we should have an exact reproduction of the type presented by the Sheffield trades.

We have chosen the Boilermakers, the Sheffield cutlers, and the Stonemasons for special description, because they comprise between them by far the majority of workmen who systematically enforce any apprenticeship regulations at all. All the other trades in which any effective regulation of numbers exists, do not together include as many numbers as the United Society of Boilermakers.[1] But it is among these smaller unions that we find some of the most stringent limitations. Thus, whilst the Boilermakers allow two apprentices to seven journeymen, the Felt Hat Makers[2] and the Flint Glass Cutters[3] have one to five only ; the Lithographic Printers permit one to five, but with a maximum of

of initiation, the same as legal apprentices at the age of eighteen years. . . . No boys to be admitted into this society . . . except they have been legally bound, or are masons' sons or step-sons."

[1] Among them may be mentioned the hand papermakers, gold-beaters, basketmakers, brushmakers, coopers, sailmakers, woolstaplers, calico block-printers, and block-cutters—all characteristically old-fashioned handicrafts.

[2] *Rules of the Amalgamated Society of Journeymen Felt Hatters* (Denton, 1890), p. 26.

[3] *Amended Laws of the United Flint Glass Cutters' Mutual Assistance and Protective Society* (Birmingham, 1887), p. 19.

six in any one firm ;[1] the Flint Glass Makers allow one to six ;[2] the Trimming Weavers of Leek declare that there shall be only one " to every seven going looms " ;[3] and the same ratio of one learner to seven journeymen is prescribed by the Nottingham Lace Trade.[4] The old - established union of Silk Hat Makers declares that any manufacturer " employing three journeymen and having been in business twelve months, shall be entitled to one apprentice, and for ten men, two apprentices ; and one for every ten men in addition to that number," and " that employers' sons be reckoned as other apprentices, and not additional as hereto-fore." [5] Finally, the Yorkshire Stuff Pressers insist that " in any one shop the number of apprentices shall not exceed one to every ten men," [6] and this extreme limitation is also insisted on by our old friends the Pearl Button Makers, though the fact is not mentioned in the rules.

The apprenticeship regulations that we have so far described have one characteristic in common. The elaborate national treaty of the Boilermakers, the stringent exclusiveness of the Pearl Button Makers, the hereditary succession of the Sheffield trades, and the curiously duplex system of the Stonemasons are all actually enforced in their respective trades. It is just this characteristic of reality which makes these instances exceptional in the Trade Union world of to-day. Other unions retain in their books of rules a more or less formal definition of apprenticeship, and a vote of the members would at any time reveal an overwhelming majority theoretically in favor of the strictest regulations of entrance.

[1] *Rules of the Amalgamated Society of Lithographic Printers of Great Britain and Ireland* (Manchester, 1887), p. 26.

[2] *Rules and Regulations of the National Flint Glass Makers' Sick and Friendly Society of Great Britain and Ireland* (Manchester, 1890), p. 19.

[3] *Rules of the Associated Trimming Weavers' Society* (Leek, 1893), p. 5.

[4] *Prices to be paid for various classes of goods in the Levers Branch of the Lace Trade* (Nottingham, 1893), p. 47. The same rule obtains in the other branches of the trade.

[5] *Rules of the Journeymen Hatters' Fair Trade Union of Great Britain and Ireland* (London, 1891), p. 46.

[6] *Rules of the Leeds, Halifax, and Bradford Stuff Pressers' Trades Union Society* (Bradford, 1888), p. 23.

And yet in these same trades we find the actual conditions of entrance so unregulated that the ranks of the Trade Unionists themselves are largely recruited by men who have not come in by the recognised gate. Typical instances are afforded by the printing and engineering industries.

The case of the Compositors is specially significant. We have here a handicraft requiring no small degree of education and manual dexterity, which has ranked, from the outset, as a highly-skilled craft. During the eighteenth century a seven years' term of apprenticeship was universal, and the local trade clubs at the beginning of the present century unhesitatingly excluded from membership and employment any person who presumed to come into the trade through any but the traditional avenue. Nor has the trade become any easier to learn. Neither machinery nor division of labor has yet enabled the capitalist employer to split up the old craft into sections, each calling only for a low grade of skill. Employers and workmen still agree that the only way to attain proficiency is for a boy to be put through a prolonged course of actual technical instruction in a number of separate processes, from deciphering manuscripts to "displaying" advertisements.[1] Accordingly, a large proportion of the best employers in each generation have cordially acquiesced in the attempt made by the Compositors' Trade Unions to maintain the long period of formal servitude, and have often not objected to a reasonable limitation of the number of apprentices. Yet to-day it is probable that a very considerable proportion of the men who obtain work as compositors, and join Compositors' Trade Unions, have undergone no period of educational servitude at all, with or without indentures and have " picked up " such knowledge of the trade as they possess whilst earning a full market rate of wages. What is of even more importance from the Trade Unionist point of view, the attempt to set any limit to the total number of persons entering the trade has totally failed.

---

[1] The most improved machine, the linotype, demands, indeed, an even higher level of skill and a more varied proficiency than that of the compositor at case.

This failure of the Compositors' Trade Unions to carry out their apprenticeship regulations is mainly due to the remarkable spread of the printing industry during the present century. In the case of the Boilermakers the rapid increase of the industry has progressively strengthened the union, and has, in particular, resulted in the actual enforcement of a genuine apprenticeship system. But the development of iron-shipbuilding has taken place almost exclusively in gigantic establishments, carried on by a distinct class of employers. The printing trade, on the other hand, once concentrated in half a dozen towns, has to-day crept into every village, the vast majority of printing offices being tiny enterprises of small working masters. The compositor, moreover, has to deal with a variety of employers, from the London daily newspaper or the great publishers' printer, down to the stationer's shop in a country town or the foreman of a subsidiary department of a railway company, wholesale grocer or manufacturer of indiarubber stamps. When the enterprising workman sets up his hand press in a suburban back street, and takes a boy to help him in his jobbing trade, he is not the kind of employer over whom a Trade Union can exercise any effective control. The Trade Union does not even hear of the numerous instances in which a printing press is set up in the basement of a great advertising manufacturer who chooses to do his own printing on the premises. In all such cases the employment of boy-labor is absolutely unrestricted in numbers, and unregulated by any educational requirements. The standard of quality and speed of working is of the lowest, but the youth who in such shops picks up an elementary acquaintance with " case," presently gets taken on as a cheap " improver " by the little country stationer, and eventually, whether competent or not, drifts to London to pick up casual employment as a journeyman.

With an industry pushing out shoots in this way into all the nooks and crannies of the industrial world, it would tax the ingenuity of the most astute Trade Union official to maintain any effective control over entrance to the craft. Unfortunately for the Compositors, the rules which their local societies have enforced have actually played into the hands of their enemies. Every Compositors' union has persistently striven to maintain something very like the mediæval apprenticeship in its own town, quite irrespective of what was happening elsewhere. The boy who would enter the printing trade in Manchester or Newcastle must be formally " bound " to an employer for seven years, during which he naturally has to forego part of the market rate of wages. He must commence his service at an early age, and complete it with one and the same firm. Nor does he find it easy to become an apprentice at all. Instead of the Boilermakers' ratio of two apprentices to seven journeymen, applied impartially to all firms, the Compositors' unions almost always impose a definite maximum, however large the establishment. Thus, no printing office in Glasgow may have more than ten apprentices ; in Leeds none more than seven ; in Hull none more than three ; and in Manchester, " in order to adjust the balance of supply and demand, and maintain a fair remuneration of labor, the maximum number of apprentices in each recognised office shall be three for the composing room and two for the machine room." [1]   Thus, the great printing establishment of the *Manchester Guardian*, employing over a hundred compositors, is allowed to take no more apprentices than the jobbing master with a dozen men.[2]

This lopsided limitation has had a most unexpected

---

[1] *Rules of the Manchester Typographical Society* (" instituted November 1797 "), Manchester, 1892, p. 35.

[2] The rules of the compositors' unions generally prescribe a ratio of apprentices to journeymen, which, in the case of small masters, is liberal.   The Manchester Typographical Society, for instance, allows a small master, having only two journeymen, to take a couple of apprentices.   But, unlike the apprenticeship regulations in other trades, this ratio is not applied to the large establishments, which are subject to a definite maximum, far below the number that the ratio would allow.   How severely this maximum limits the total number of apprentices in the best Manchester firms may be judged from the fact that twelve of its printing establishments employ half the compositors in the city, having between them 1000 men, and being entitled according to the rule to only sixty apprentices.

result. It might be imagined that Trade Union statesmanship would aim at recruiting the trade from boys brought up in the large establishments, affording systematic training in every branch of the craft, and pervaded, as they usually are, by a strong Trade Union feeling.[1] But the aggregate number of apprentices allowed to such firms is grotesquely insufficient to maintain the trade. When new journeymen are wanted, they have, in three cases out of four, to be drawn from the small establishments, and ultimately from the small towns and rural districts in which neither Trade Unionism nor apprenticeship can be said to exist. Here there is nothing to prevent an unscrupulous employer from taking on as many boys as he chooses, keeping them to the most elementary processes of the craft, and turning them adrift in an untrained state as soon as they begin to ask journeyman's wages. The direct result of the Compositors' "maximum" of apprentices in the large establishments of the strong Trade Union towns is, accordingly, to use, as the chief breeding ground and recruiting ground of the craft, exactly those shops and those districts in which there is the least likelihood of the boys receiving any proper training. Hence we arrive at the paradoxical conclusion that it is the very maintenance of these apprenticeship regulations by the local Compositors' unions that has made the trade now practically an "open" one. As in the country districts any number of boys are, in fact, learning to be compositors, and eventually drifting into the towns, the unions are in a dilemma. If they rigidly maintain their apprenticeship rules, and decline to admit these "illegal men," they find themselves foiled in their negotiations with the employers by the presence of a steadily growing crowd of non-union men, indisposed to

[1] It is interesting to note that there is at least one instance of a Trade Union which consciously adopts this more enlightened policy. The Manchester Union of Upholsterers (now the Manchester Branch of the Amalgamated Society of Upholsterers) has a by-law for the regulation of apprentices which limits the number of lads in small shops and those doing only the cheap common kinds of work to one to six men, while the large shops and those doing high-class work are allowed one to three men.

defer to an organisation from which they are excluded. In order to gain any effective power of Collective Bargaining, the union must make up its mind to admit practically all the men who are actually working at the trade in the particular district, whether they have been apprenticed or not. Nearly all the local Compositors' unions have had periodically thus to "open their books," and take in the "illegal men." And the London Society of Compositors, which includes a third of the Trade Unionist compositors in the United Kingdom, has, since 1879, avowedly admitted to membership any compositor who actually obtains employment in a "fair house" in London, whether he has learnt the trade by apprenticeship or not.[1] The provincial societies still usually profess to confine their membership to men who can produce evidence of having served a seven years' term, but as they all admit without demur any printer who gets employment in the town with a card of membership of any other Compositors' union, including the large open society of the Metropolis, any journeyman whom an employer will engage on the standard piece scale finds no difficulty, whether he has been apprenticed or not, in becoming a fully recognised member of the trade. In short, what is limited is, not the total number of recruits to the trade in the kingdom as a whole, but the proportion of such recruits who receive the educational advantages of the apprenticeship system.

The experience of the Engineers has been no less instructive than that of the Compositors, though in another way. The local trade clubs of smiths and millwrights at the beginning of the present century autocratically excluded from employment all men who could not produce their indentures.[2] Sir William Fairbairn relates how, when in 1811 he obtained a situation as a millwright at Rennie's,

---

[1] "Every compositor working as a journeyman, overseer, storekeeper, reader, or in any other capacity in a fair house . . . shall be eligible as a member."— *Rules of the London Society of Compositors* (London, 1894), p. 6.

[2] Clubs of smiths, millwrights, and "mechanics" took a leading part in the prosecutions and petitions of the 1813 movement to enforce the apprenticeship laws.—*History of Trade Unionism*, pp. 53-56.

the foreman told him that he could not start until he had been accepted by the Trade Union. Failing to produce duly attested indentures, he was refused permission to work, and driven to tramp away from London and seek a situation in a non-unionist district.[1] Similar regulations lasted down to our own day. The Amicable and Brotherly Society of Journeymen Millwrights, a Lancashire Union dating certainly from the beginning of the century, maintained down to 1855 its old by-laws restricting the number of apprentices, and rigidly insisting on proof of servitude. They declare that " any person wishing to join, whose parents have neglected to provide him with a proper indenture, shall be compelled to produce a sworn affidavit, attested by two respectable witnesses, that he has worked at the trade five, six, or seven years, in a millwright's shop, or with a millwright known to the trade, as an apprentice, and he shall pay any sum not less than £3 : 10s., or more than £5, that a general meeting may decide." He shall be " proposed by a free member, and if it afterwards be proved that he was not legally qualified the said member shall be fined £5. Any person bringing a doubtful indenture shall be subject to the same terms of entrance." [2] The same conception underlay the rules of the Amalgamated Society of Engineers for the first thirty years of its existence. The preface to the edition of 1864 declares that " if constrained to make restrictions against the admission into our trade of those *who have not earned a right by a probationary servitude*, we do so, knowing that such

---

[1] *The Life of Sir William Fairbairn*, edited by W. Pole (London, 1877), p. 89 ; *Trade Unionism*, by W. Saunders (London, 1878) ; *History of Trade Unionism*, pp. 75 and 187.

[2] Another old union declared " that one apprentice be allowed to five journeymen ; *nevertheless if the number be complete, the eldest, or next eldest, son of a millwright be allowed to work at the trade* " (*Rules of the Philanthropic Society of Journeymen Millwrights*, 1855). How far the high entrance fees and rigid requirements were intended to provide technical education and restrict the actual numbers entering the trade, and how far they were designed merely to protect the hereditary " vested interest " of the members' sons, is unknown to us. It is quite possible that the millwrights, at the beginning of this century, were, in reality, mainly recruited much in the same way as the stonemasons of to-day : a reference to the privileges of the eldest sons of millwrights, in the preface to Sir W. Fairbairn's *Treatise on Mills and Millwork*, seems to point in this direction.

encroachments are productive of evil, and when persevered in unchecked, result in reducing the condition of the artisan to that of the unskilled laborer, and confer no permanent advantage on those admitted. It is our duty, then, to exercise the same care and watchfulness over that in which we have a vested interest, as the physician does who holds a diploma, or the author who is protected by a copyright."[1] And yet to-day we find the Amalgamated Society of Engineers, and nearly all its sectional rivals, freely admitting to membership any man, whether apprenticed or not, who has worked for five years in an engineering establishment, even if merely as a boy or as a machine minder, and who, at the time of his candidature, is obtaining the Standard Rate of wages for his particular branch of the trade.

This complete collapse of the apprenticeship regulations among the Engineers has not, we think, been due to any unreasonableness in the regulations themselves. Unlike the Compositors, the Engineers have never sought to impose an absolute maximum limit of apprentices, or in any way to discourage the instruction of a proportionate number of boys by the large firms. What they have aimed at in their rules and in their negotiations with employers, has been some such arrangement as that now universally accepted by the iron-shipbuilders. But, less fortunate than the United Society of Boilermakers, the Engineers have found their efforts brought to nought by a progressive disintegration of their old handicraft. We have here, in fact, the typical case of the breakdown of apprenticeship under the influence of the Industrial Revolution. "The millwright of the last century," says Sir William Fairbairn, "was an itinerant engineer and mechanic of high reputation. He could handle the axe, the hammer, and the plane with equal skill and precision ; he could turn, bore or forge with the ease and despatch of one brought up to these trades, and he could set out and cut in furrows of a millstone with an accuracy equal or superior to that of the miller himself. . . . Generally he was a fair arithmetician,

[1] *Rules of the Amalgamated Society of Engineers*, etc. (London, 1864).

knew something of geometry, levelling, and mensuration, and in some cases possessed a very competent knowledge of practical mathematics. He could calculate the velocities, strength, and power of machines : could draw in plan and section, and could construct buildings, conduits, or water-courses, in all the forms and under all the conditions required in his professional practice ; he could build bridges, cut canals, and perform a variety of work now done by civil engineers." [1] So varied a proficiency could only be attained by a long period of educational servitude. The workshops of a great engineering firm of to-day present us with an entirely different spectacle. What the millwright formerly executed with the hammer and the file is now broken up into innumerable separate operations, each of which has its appropriate machine. But this is not all. A distinctive feature of the introduction of machinery into the engineering trade is the remarkable variety and diversity of the " power-moved tools " now required in a large machine shop. A gigantic cotton mill often contains only row after row of a single type of self-acting mule or power loom. An engineering establishment will have in use a long array of different types of drilling, planing, boring, slotting, and milling machines, together with a bewildering variety of applications of the old-fashioned lathe. The precise degree of skill and trustworthiness required to work each of these machines, or even to execute different jobs upon one of them, is infinitely varied. The simple drilling machine or the automatic lathe continuously turning out identical copies of some minute portion of an engine can be tended by a mere boy. Some work executed on an elaborate milling machine, on the other hand, taxes the powers of the most accomplished mechanic. Yet so numerous are the inter-mediate types that the increase in difficulty from each machine to the next is comparatively small. Thus the youth or the laborer who begins by spending his whole day

[1] *A Treatise on Mills and Millwork*, by Sir William Fairbairn (London, 1861), preface.

in "minding" the simplest driller or automatic lathe, may "progress" from one process to another with little further instruction, until, by mere practice on a succession of machines, the sharp boy becomes insensibly a qualified turner or fitter. We need not here discuss whether this "progression" of the more intelligent boys and laborers is not accompanied by the drawback that the majority, from lack of deliberate technical instruction, remain all their lives incapable of any but the simplest routine work. Nor need we dispute the assertion often made that such a "progression" fails, even with the clever and ambitious, to produce an all-round proficiency in mechanical engineering. The fact remains that an ever-increasing number of boys and laborers do climb up this ladder, and become sufficiently competent to obtain employment as fitters, turners, and erectors.

The Amalgamated Society of Engineers has, therefore, during a whole generation, been in a dilemma. Its traditional policy was to exclude the unapprenticed interlopers as "illegal men," and this, on the whole, was the tendency down to 1885. But it found itself powerless to prevent progression within the trade, or to draw a line at any particular machine, in order effectively to separate into distinct classes the "machine-minders" who were "engineers" from those who were "laborers." A Trade Union may conceivably strengthen its position if, by limiting the number of persons learning the trade, it restricts the number of competitors for its particular kind of employment. But once those competitors exist, their presence on the market as non-unionists is fatal to the Method of Collective Bargaining. Hence the Amalgamated Society of Engineers has had to recognise facts and abandon regulations which were being so extensively evaded. For the last ten years each successive delegate meeting has opened the society to new classes of workmen, whether apprenticed or not, until, as we have already mentioned, any adult man who actually obtains employment at the Standard Rate of his particular town and grade, is, in practice, welcomed as a recruit.

We need not enumerate all the trades which stand approximately, with regard to apprenticeship regulations, in the same position as the Engineers and the Compositors. With the important exceptions of the Boilermakers, the Sheffield trades, and the Stonemasons, together with some minor Trade Unions, the whole of the organised workmen in the metal, building, and printing industries belong to this type. The same may be said of the vast majority of the old crafts that have been gradually transformed by the Industrial Revolution. The apprenticeship tradition is still strong, and may often find expression in the rules.[1] In certain towns, or in certain sections of the industry, a real period of educational servitude may still be the customary method of entering the trade. But in some way or another the craft is, as a matter of fact, acquired by unapprenticed men, and there cannot be said to be any real limit to the total number of persons entering the trade. To give some definiteness to our estimate, we may add that we reckon about 500,000 Trade Unionists as belonging to this group of trades.

This leaves a membership of about 900,000, or three-fifths of the whole, in unions which in no way restrict apprenticeship or the learning of their members' occupation by newcomers. We need not dwell on the case of the two

---

[1] Mr. Sanger, in the mathematical article already cited, says, "Roughly speaking, there exist about 100 Trade Unions which have a more or less definite rule for the limitation of the number of apprentices. But the total number of men belonging to the Unions in all probability does not exceed 200,000. I have considered the effect of the rules of each of the Unions separately, and have come to the following conclusions :—

"(1) In the case of 21 Trade Unions whose total membership exceeds 26,500. the rule is such that if carried out strictly it would cause the number of journey-men to decline.

"(2) In the case of 23 Trade Unions, whose total membership exceeds 35,500, the rule is such that if carried out strictly it would not . . . permit the number of journeymen to increase as fast as the male population of England is increasing.

"(3) In the case of 43 Trade Unions, whose total membership exceeds 86,500, the rule is such as to permit the number of journeymen to increase at least as fast as the male population of England.

". . . It must be admitted that at the present time it is not a question of very great practical importance. If a Trade Union has had an unfair rule on this

or three hundred thousand imperfectly organised general laborers, transport workers, and unskilled operatives of all kinds, among whom apprenticeship could never find a place. But among the " open trades " we find some of the strongest and most successful of Trade Unions, notably those of the Cotton Operatives and the Coalminers, who together make up one-fifth of the total membership of the Trade Union world.

The case of the Cotton-spinners is one of peculiar interest. The Amalgamated Association of Operative Cotton-spinners is, as we have already mentioned, one of the strongest, most efficient, and most successful of Trade Unions. In good years and bad alike it has for a whole generation maintained the net earnings of its members at the relatively high level of from 35s. to 50s. a week. During that period it has succeeded in getting the hours of labor reduced, and the conditions of the factory greatly improved. Its success in confining the profits of the capitalist in cotton-spinning to the irreducible minimum is attested by the capitalists them-

point it has rarely been able to actually carry it into effect."—*Economic Journal*, December 1895.

Our own enumeration, based not on what is said but on what is actually done in the various trades, is as follows :—

(1) Membership of Trade Unions actually enforcing apprenticeship regulations :—

(*a*) Really restrictive of numbers . . .	15,000	
(*b*) Not really restrictive of numbers at all (Patrimony restricts choice but not numbers)	25,000	
(*c*) Nominally restrictive, but allowing sufficient recruits to the trades . . .	50,000	
		90,000

(2) Membership of Trade Unions nominally retaining apprenticeship regulations, but effectively open   500,000

(3) Membership of Trade Unions having no apprenticeship regulations :—

(*a*) Transport workers and laborers . .	250,000	
(*b*) Textile, mining, and other occupations .	650,000	
		900,000

1,490,000

selves. Yet no part of the strength and success of this Trade Union can be attributed to a limitation of apprentices, or to any monopoly feature whatsoever. The number of persons learning to be cotton-spinners is, and has always been unrestricted. The trade is usually recruited from the class of " piecers," two of whom work under each spinner, and are paid by him.[1] Thus, instead of the ratio of two apprentices to seven journeymen insisted on by the Boilermakers, or that of one to ten men maintained by the Pearl Button Makers, the Cotton-spinners positively encourage as many as two to each spinner, a ratio which is approximately ten times as great as is required to recruit the trade. Far from there being any scarcity of candidates for employment, the great majority of piecers have to abandon all hope of getting mules, and find themselves compelled to turn to other occupations. Nor is any definite period of service insisted upon. Any man may become a spinner as soon as he can induce an employer to trust him with a pair of mules, and to pay him for his product according to the standard list of piece-work prices.[2] The fact that under these circumstances the Standard Rate of a cotton-spinner has been kept up for a whole generation, and that his average earnings have positively increased, may be for the moment left as an economic problem to those who still retain the old belief that the limitation of numbers and the exclusion of competitors is a necessary part of efficient Trade Unionism.[3]

[1] Occasionally the employer has tried to have only one boy-piecer to two spinners. This system, called "joining" or "partnering," is always resisted by the union, which insists on each spinner having two piecers under him, on the ground that any other arrangement must necessarily involve a diminution of spinners' earnings. The delegate meeting of the Amalgamated Association of Operative Cotton-spinners in December 1878 resolved "that this meeting greatly deplores the system of joining, and pledges itself to use every effort to get that system abolished." Since that date, at the cost of many small strikes, the Lancashire operatives have gained their point, and have now each two piecers.

[2] Once in the trade, he is required to join the Trade Union, but no impediment is placed in his way.

[3] The London Plumbers present an interesting case, economically similar in this respect to the Cotton-spinners. The employers in London do not engage boys or apprentices to assist the men in plumbing, or to learn the trade. The custom is for each plumber to be attended by an adult laborer, known as the

Thus, notwithstanding a strong Trade Union feeling in favor of apprenticeship regulations, these cannot be said to be enforced to-day over more than a small fraction of the Trade Union world, and, with the remarkable exception of the Boilermakers, even this fraction is steadily dwindling. It is especially in such industrial backwaters as Dublin and Cork ; in such homes of the small-master system as Sheffield and Birmingham ; and in such old-fashioned handicrafts as glass-blowing and hat-making, that the archaic apprenticeship regulations linger. Over by far the largest part of the limited field in which apprenticeship once prevailed, the system has gone practically out of use, and restrictive barriers, once supported by universal approval, and fondly kept up by the trade clubs of the eighteenth century, have, during the past hundred years, gradually been swept away. Finally, so far from apprenticeship regulations forming a necessary part of Trade Unionism, a positive majority of the Trade Unionists now belong to occupations in which no shadow of apprenticeship has ever existed.

To explain this state of affairs, we must distinguish between the disuse of apprenticeship as an educational system, and its failure as a method of restricting the entrance into a craft. The abandonment of apprenticeship as a form of technical training is not due to the discovery of any satis-factory alternative. There is, on the contrary, a remarkable consensus of opinion among " practical men," that the present state of things is highly unsatisfactory. But many economic causes have contributed to make obsolete the definite period of educational servitude at wages below the market value of the boy's time. Whatever might be the ultimate effect on the welfare of the trade or the future of the boy, this educational servitude does not now immediately remunerate

---

" plumber's mate." Any employer is at liberty to promote a plumber's mate to be a plumber whenever he chooses, provided only that he pays him the plumber's Standard Rate. Notwithstanding the fact that the number of " plumber's mates," who form the class of learners, is four or five times as numerous as would suffice to recruit the trade, the London branches of the United Operative Plumbers' Society effectively maintain a high Standard Rate.

any of the parties concerned. The employer with a large establishment does not care to be bothered with boys if he has to teach them the whole trade. Even if the thrifty father offers £20 or £30 as a premium, this is no temptation to the capitalist of our own day, paying hundreds of pounds a week in wages alone. He prefers to divide his processes into men's work and boys' work, and to keep each grade permanently to its allotted routine. Now that it is no longer possible for the apprentice to enter his master's household, and all gild discipline has been abolished, the employer feels that he has little control over a boy whom he is legally bound to keep for the stated term. " The advantage," as a great builder remarked to us, " is all on the side of the apprentice." But the boy does not think so. There are to-day so many opportunities for boys to earn relatively high wages without instruction, that they are not easily induced either to enter upon a term of educational servitude at low rates, or to continue on it if they have begun. " The anxiety of the boy to obtain full money as soon as possible is largely responsible," we are told, " for the absence of apprentices." The father, too, is naturally tempted to let his son earn six to fifteen shillings a week either as a tele-graph messenger or errand boy, or as porter in some factory or workshop, rather than forego most of this supplement to the family income in order merely that his son may be called an apprentice instead of a boy.

But it would be unfair to attribute this disinclination to apprenticeship merely to a dislike to sacrifice present income to future advantage. In the industrial organisation of to-day, the workman finds it very difficult, if not in some cases impossible, to place his boy in any occupation in which he will be taught a skilled trade. Even when he can apprentice him, he has little security that the boy's instruction will be attended to. And if we pass from the individual father to the members of the craft in their corporate capacity, we shall see that the system of apprenticeship has lost what was really its main attraction. " No one," said Blackstone,

"would be induced to undergo a seven years' servitude,
if others, though equally skilful, were allowed the same
advantages without having undergone the same discipline."
What the father and the apprentice were willing to pay for
was, not the instruction, but the legal right to exercise a
protected trade.　When this right to a trade could be
obtained without apprenticeship, as, for instance, by way of
"patrimony," father and sons alike have always been eager
to forego its educational advantages.　Whenever a Trade
Union has failed to maintain an effective limitation of
numbers, it very soon gives up striving after any educational
servitude.[1]

In certain exceptional occupations, apprenticeship can
still be made use of to regulate the entrance to the trade.
Where the work is carried on, not by individual craftsmen,
but by associated groups of highly skilled wage-earners, it is
practically within the power of these groups, if supported
by the public opinion of their own community, to exclude
any newcomer from admission.　This "group-system" goes
far, we think, to account for the exceptional effectiveness of
the Trade Union regulations on apprenticeship among the
Boilermakers, Flint Glass Makers, Glass Bottle Makers, and
Stuff Pressers.　If the trade concerned constitutes by itself
only a tiny but indispensable fraction of a large industry,
it will not be worth the employer's while to object to even
unreasonable demands, so long as the Trade Union takes
care to fill each vacancy as it occurs, and ensures him against
any interruption of work.　The proprietor of a cotton mill
is comparatively indifferent to the restrictive rules insisted
on by the Tapesizers, the Beamers, Twisters, and Drawers,

---

[1] It will be noticed that, as among the various forms of apprenticeship that
we have described, the actual educational advantages vary roughly in proportion
to the actual exclusiveness.　The "patrimony" of the Sheffield trades and Stonemasons involves practically little limitation of numbers, and offers, on the other
hand, the very minimum of security for technical instruction.　The real limitations
of the Boilermakers and Flint Glass Makers, on the contrary, whilst they result
in something like a craft monopoly, do give the community in return a genuine
educational servitude, and provide for the constant "selection of the fittest" boys
by the employers.

and even the Overlookers, whose wages form but a trifling percentage of the total cost of production.[1] It is only in the industries in which, by exception, one or other of these conditions prevails, that we see maintained or revived any effective Trade Union limitation of apprenticeship. Over all the rest of the industrial field the barrier is broken down by the stronger forces of the mobility of capital, and the perpetual revolutionising of industrial processes.[2] No Trade Union has been really able to enforce a limitation of apprentices if new employers are always starting up in fresh centres ; if the craft is frequently being changed by the introduction of new processes or machinery ; if alternative classes of workers can be brought in to execute some portion of the operation. These are precisely the conditions which are typical of most of the industries of the present century.

Trade Unions might, it is true, appeal to the law. But apart from the insuperable difficulties of adapting any legally enforced apprenticeship to the circumstances of modern industry, it is easy to see that no revival of the system would gain the support of public opinion. From the point of view of the community the old system has three capital disadvantages. There is no security to the public that the apprentice will be thoroughly and efficiently taught. It is no longer the " master craftsman " who himself instructs the boy and has a direct pecuniary interest in his early proficiency. The scores of apprentices in a modern shipyard

[1] It is to this consideration, we think, that the Patternmakers in engineering establishments, and the Lithographic Printers in the great firms which now dominate that trade, owe their relatively effective position as regards apprenticeship.

[2] The sawyers exhibit a curious evolution. The old hand sawyers of the early part of the century were notorious for the strength and exclusiveness of their Trade Unions. The introduction of the circular saw, driven by steam power, led to the supersession of the old handicraftsmen by a new class of comparatively unskilled workers, who were drawn from the ranks of the laborers, and remained for some years unorganised. With the increasing speed and growing complication of mill-sawing machinery, these mill-sawyers have, in their turn, become a highly specialised class, whom an employer finds some difficulty in supplanting by laborers. The comparative stability which the industry has now attained has enabled these machine workers to establish an effective union, which is gradually enforcing a fixed period of apprenticeship.

are necessarily left mainly to learn their business for themselves, by watching workmen who are indifferent or even unfriendly to their progress, with possibly some occasional hints from a benevolent foreman. In these days of pedagogic science, elaborately trained teachers, and " Her Majesty's Inspectors of Schools," the haphazard relation between the apprentice and his instructors will certainly not commend itself to the deliberate judgment of the community. Moreover, all history indicates that an apprenticeship system must leave outside its scope the large proportion of boys who recruit the vast army of unskilled laborers. In the absence of an apprenticeship system, the abler and more energetic of these succeed, as we have seen, in " picking up " a trade, and in progressing, as adults, according to their capacities. One of the darkest features of the whole history of apprenticeship is the constant necessity, if the system is to be maintained at all, of excluding, from the protected occupations, all " illegal men." We need not weary the reader with mediæval instances.[1] But it will be obvious that the elaborate Apprenticeship Treaty concluded between the Boilermakers and their

---

[1] It is usually forgotten that gild membership, and the right to carry on a skilled craft, at no time extended to the great army of laborers. The case of the Bladesmiths may serve to remind us of the existence of a vast mass of unapprenticed workers. On the 10th October 1408 the masters of the trade of the " Blaydesmiths " in London presented a petition and a code of articles for the government of the trade to the Mayor and Corporation. These articles were read and approved, and they include one, " That no one of the said trade shall teach his journeymen the sec.ets of his trade *as he would his apprentice,* on the pain aforesaid " (namely a fine of 6s. 8d. for the first offence, 10s. for the second, and 13s. 4d. for any further offence). The journeymen alluded to here were no doubt the " strikers " who assisted the smiths in their task.—See Riley's *Memorials of London and London Life* (London, 1868), p. 570.

How large was the proportion of unapprenticed laborers is perhaps roughly indicated by the fire regulations of the Common Council of London in 1667, when the " handicraft companies " of Carpenters, Bricklayers, Plasterers, Painters, Masons, Smiths, Plumbers and Paviours were ordered to elect yearly for each company, 2 Master Workmen, 4 Journeymen, 8 Apprentices and 16 Laborers to form a Fire Brigade (Jupp, *History of the Carpenters' Company,* London, p. 284). There are many occupations to-day in which the number of unskilled laborers exceeds that of the skilled craftsmen ; and it may well be that the gilds at no time included more than a minority even of the adult male workers.—See *History of Trade Unionism,* p. 37 ; Du Cellier, *Histoire des Classes Laborieuses en France* (Paris, 1860), p. 204 ; Mrs. Green, *Town Life in Fifteenth Century,* ii. 103.

employers necessarily closes the door of advancement to the crowd of rivet-boys and platers' helpers in an iron-shipyard, some of whom would otherwise find themselves able to pick up the trade. The Carpet-weavers are driven to prohibit any person, other than a " registered creeler " (the apprentice), " to be at the front of the loom or otherwise doing the work of the weaver,"[1] lest he should insidiously learn the art. The Calico-printers absolutely forbid their " tenters," or laborers, ever to touch the " doctor" (the long knife which adjusts the precise amount of coloring matter), or even to come in front of the machine. Unless a sharp line is drawn, either by law or by custom, between duly apprenticed craftsmen and " illegal men," it is obvious that no apprenticeship system can long exist. Finally, when such a separate class is created, the community can never tell to what extent it is being mulcted for the maintenance of the system. It was, in fact, the cost to the community, and, as he thought, the excessive cost, that led Adam Smith so fervently to denounce the whole apprenticeship system, with its inevitable consequences of monopoly wages and profits. In our own day, it is impossible to calculate how much it costs the community to educate a boilermaker or glassblower. We may infer that we are paying for it in the relatively high wages of these protected trades, but how much we are paying in this way, and upon whom this burden is falling, it is impossible to compute. Undemocratic in its scope, unscientific in its educational methods, and fundamentally unsound in its financial aspects, the apprenticeship system, in spite of all the practical arguments in its favor, is not likely to be deliberately revived by a modern democracy.[2]

[1] *Rules of the Power Loom Carpet-weavers' Mutual Defence and Provident Association* (Kidderminster, 1891).

[2] It may be inferred that technical education, even more than common schooling, is too immediately costly, if not also too remote in its advantages, to be within the means of the great majority of parents. Individual capitalists, who are not necessarily interested in the future welfare even of their own trades, will not bear the expense of teaching a new generation of skilled workmen—whom they may never need to employ. Thus, though Mr. Inglis strongly objected to any limitation of the number of apprentices, he explains why he and other

(b) The Limitation of Boy-Labor

The abandonment of the old period of educational servitude has, in some instances, created a new problem. When the employer finds himself freed from all obligation to teach his boys, and is, on the other hand, obliged to pay them the full market value of their time, he naturally prefers to keep them continuously employed on such routine work as they can best perform. The manufacturing process is therefore subdivided, so that as large a portion as possible shall fall within the competence of boys kept exclusively to one particular task. From the point of the Trade Union, this constitutes a new grievance. It is no longer a case of objecting to an undue multiplication of apprentices, leading in course of time to an unnecessary increase in the number of competent workmen seeking employment. What the men complain of is that the employers are endeavouring, by an alteration of the manufacturing process, to dispense with skilled labor, or, indeed, with adult labor altogether. So far this complaint may appear only another instance of " New Processes and Machinery," a subject sufficiently dealt with in a preceding chapter. If the employer, by any change of process, can bring his work within the capacity of operatives of a lower grade of strength or skill, it is useless, as we have seen, for the superior workers who were formerly employed to resist the change. When, however, the innovation involves, not the substitution of one class of adults for another, but of boys for men, a new argument has to be considered. To the grown-up workmen in a trade, it seems preposterous that they should be thrown out of employment by their youthful sons being taken on in their places. Their aggravation is

employers agreed to the Trade Union restriction. " We have," he says, " our business proper to attend to, and cannot devote all our energies to striving for the greatest good of the greatest number " (*The Apprentice Question*, p. 10). If the community desires to see a constant succession of skilled craftsmen, the community as a whole will have to pay for their instruction. Even with an apprenticeship system, the community, as we suggest above, really paid in the long run.

increased when they see these sons, not taught any skilled craft, but kept, year after year, at the simplest routine work, and discharged in favor of their younger brothers as soon as they begin to ask the ordinary wage of an adult laborer.

To prevent this evil, some Trade Unions, which have given up the requirement of a period of educational servitude, have attempted to enforce a simple limitation of boy-labor. They may make no objection to any number of boys being properly taught their craft, and so rendered competent workmen. Such apprentices would naturally be put first to the simpler processes. But when these simpler tasks are permanently separated from the rest, and handed over to a distinct race of boys, who are not intended to learn the remainder of the work ; when the number of boys so employed is steadily increased, and the number of adult workmen diminished, the change is always fiercely resisted by the Trade Union. We need only describe the leading instance, that of the National Union of Boot and Shoe Operatives. Here the substitution of boys for men has been hotly contested for many years. At first the union sought to meet the case by enforcing the usual apprenticeship regulations. But with the growing use of machinery and subdivision of labor, "any attempt to restrict the entrance by making the conditions not so profitable at first—by making the wage small and the years long"[1]—was broken down by the fact that boys, taking short views of their own advantage, preferred to earn the relatively higher wages of unapprenticed machine-minders. This led, as one of the men's spokesmen declared in 1892, to "the wholesale flooding of the market with boys, and the wholesale discharging of men. . . . I have proof before me of where a number of fathers in this town (Leicester) have been discharged, and their sons set on in their places. . . . We have firms to-day—though we ask for the limitation of 1 boy to 5 men—we have firms in Leicester where they have 5 men to 6 boys, 19 men to

[1] National Conference, 1893 ; proceedings before Umpire.

14 boys, 23 men to 11 boys, 5 men to 21 boys, 13 men to 18 boys, 6 men to 4 boys, 3 men to 9 boys, and 3 men to 1 boy."[1]   The men complained that this state of things not only deprived them of employment, but that it also prevented those who were employed from getting the Standard Rate. "In the town I come from (Norwich)," said another representative, "it is all very well for employers to say, 'I will pay a certain price for your labor.'   But the moment a man asks for the price agreed upon he is discharged, and a boy is put in his place."[2]

The union accordingly asked that the maximum number of boys in any factory should be fixed at the ratio of one to every five journeymen.   The employers did not dispute the facts.   They refused to discuss whether the change was for the public advantage or not.   They fell back on the simple position that the employment of boys was a matter entirely "within the province of the employer, and that it is not a question in which the workmen may rightly interfere." They declared that any limit on the number of boys would be "not only an encroachment on the right of manufacturers to manage their own business in their own way, but also it is impracticable, and cannot be carried out, because of the varying circumstances of the various portions of the trade, and of the various employers and various towns."[3]   The issue was in due course remitted to the umpire, Sir Henry (now Lord) James, in pursuance of the collective agreement described in our chapter on "The Method of Collective Bargaining."   The employers used every argument in defence of their "right" to carry on their own business in their own way.   The men's demonstration of the evils of this excessive use of boy-labor was, however, so overwhelming that the umpire felt bound to admit their contention.   In a remarkable award, dated 22nd August 1892, the principle of restricting, by Common Rule, the proportion of boys to be employed by any manufacturer in the boot and shoe trade

---

[1] National Conference, 1893 ; proceedings before Umpire, 1892, p. 62.
[2] *Ibid*. p. 63.   [3] *Ibid*. pp. 94, 96.

was definitely established, the ratio being fixed at one to three journeymen.[1]

It is not easy to imagine the feelings with which Nassau Senior or Harriet Martineau would have viewed the spectacle of an eminent Liberal lawyer imposing such a restriction on " the right of every man to employ the capital he inherits, or has acquired, according to his own discretion, without molestation or obstruction, so long as he does not infringe on the rights or property of others." [2] Lord James was convinced that he had to cope with a real evil. That a generation of highly-skilled craftsmen should be succeeded by a generation incapable of anything but the commonest routine labor, seemed to him to be a disadvantage, not only to the craftsmen themselves, but also to the community. The competition between the boys and their fathers is, it was argued, an " unfair " one.[3] The wages paid in a boot factory to a boy between thirteen and eighteen, though large in comparison with those given to the old-fashioned apprentice, are far below the sum on which the race of operatives could be

[1] " In the matter of an arbitration between the National Union of Boot and Shoe Operatives, and the National Federation of Associated Employers of Labor in the Shoe Trade, I, the undersigned, having taken upon myself the burden of the said Arbitration, and having heard the parties thereto by themselves and their Witnesses, do now in respect of the matters in dispute submitted to me, adjudge and determine as follows : ' That in respect of the work carried on by Clickers, Pressmen, Lasters, and Finishers, the Employers of Labor in Shoe Factories and Workshops shall in each department respectively be restricted in the employment of boys (under 18) to one boy to every three men employed. And that where the number of men employed shall not be divisible by three, one boy may also be employed in respect of the fraction existing, either less than three, or above each unit of three.

" That whilst the above restriction is general in its *prima facie* application, I further adjudge that it may be inexpedient in certain Factories and Workshops in which the manufacture of goods called ' Nursery Goods,' and other goods of a common quality and of a low price is carried on." Other clauses provided for the adaptation by the Local Boards of the general restriction to such low-class firms, and for the reference of disputes to an umpire.—National Conference, 1892, p. 149.

[2] *Report of the Committee on the State of the Woollen Manufacture in England*, 4th July 1806, p. 12 ; *History of Trade Unionism*, p. 56.

[3] See our chapter on "New Processes and Machinery," for other instances of, in this sense, "unfair" competition ; and our chapter on "The Economic Characteristics of Trade Unionism," for fuller consideration of the results of " parasitic trades."

permanently maintained, and therefore below what may be called the boy's cost of production. An employer carrying on his factory entirely by boy - labor, and yet giving the boys no educational training, is, therefore, enjoying a positive subsidy in aid of just that form of industrial organisation which is calculated to be, in the long run, the most injurious to the community.

But though the excessive multiplication of boy - labor may be a grave social danger, and though Lord James's remedy of limitation is not without precedent,[1] we think that experience points to the impossibility of any Trade Union coping with the evil in this way. Even Lord James's award, with all its decided acceptance of the principle of restriction, gave away the men's case by its exceptions. He refused to bind those employers who "manufactured goods called 'Nursery goods' and other goods of a common quality and of a low price," on the ground that no uniform ratio of boys to men was applicable to their branch of the trade. In this refusal there can be no doubt that he exercised a wise discretion. To have insisted on these "Nursery" manufacturers doing work by adult labor which was actually being performed by boys would have resulted only in their immediate withdrawal from the Federation of Employers, and so from the scope of the award. Thus, these low-class

---

[1] We know of no other instance of the direct limitation of the number of boy workers in a trade by the award of an arbitrator, or even by mutual consent of the employers and men, though the award of Mr. T. (afterwards Judge) Hughes in the case of the Kidderminster Carpet Weavers in 1875, by which the number of boys allowed to actually work on looms was limited to one to five men, was given partly on these grounds (see *Report of Conference of Manufacturers and Workmen before T. Hughes, Esq., Q.C., at . . . Kidderminster, 30th July* 1875. Kidderminster 1875). But there are several instances of regulations by Trade Unions aiming at this end. Thus in 1892 the Brassfounders' Society at Hull succeeded in enforcing a very strict limitation of the number of boys in each shop, in order to stop the competition of excessive boy-labor. The Whitesmiths in the North of England, the Coppersmiths of Glasgow, and the Packing-case Makers in Bradford and other towns have made similar efforts to check the growth of this practice, whilst the Amalgamated Wood Turners' Society of London, in a circular to their employers in 1890, urged that all lads in the trade should be apprenticed for five years, "a system which, when carried out, would be as great a blessing for the lad as for the master, and remove the unfair competition of boy-labor."

manufacturers, together with all small masters and non-associated firms, go on employing as many boys as they choose. The umpire's award, in fact, only applied to those cases in which it was least required. The National Union of Boot and Shoe Operatives accordingly finds itself in much the same position with regard to boy - labor as the Typographical Association does with regard to apprentices. It nominally possesses the power of limiting the number, but this power is only effective in high-class establishments, and not even in all these. The only result of enforcing the limit is thus, not any restriction of the total number of boys in the trade, but merely their concentration in particular districts or particular establishments from which, as they grow up, they overflow to the others. The trade remains, therefore, as overrun as ever, with the added evil that it tends more and more to be recruited from the least educational channels.

In other trades the failure to put any effective restriction on the employment of boy-labor has been even more decided than among the Boot Operatives and the Compositors. The Engineers and Ironmoulders, for instance, have from time to time attempted to enforce a limit of boy - labor. Such regulations can for a time be enforced in strong Trade Union towns, in those branches of the trade which absolutely demand skilled workmen, and in establishments where Trade Unionism has gained a firm hold. But in the meantime the boys, even in Trade Union strongholds, will have been crowding into the workshops of small masters, or of those low-grade establishments which rely almost exclusively on boy-labor. At the same time, as in the analogous case of Trade Union Regulations on apprenticeship, the non-unionist districts will be bringing in an unlimited number of recruits, who have grown up outside Trade Union influence.

It may be objected that this drawback to any limitation of boy-labor relates, not to the regulation itself, but to the method by which it is enforced. If instead of a mere voluntary agreement, the limitation were imposed by law, its universal application would, it may be argued, effectually put a stop to the abuse that is complained of. Such a law would, however, have to be considered from the point of view of those whom it excluded from the trade, as well as from that of those whom it protected. A community which peremptorily limited the number of boys whom employers might engage would find itself under an obligation to provide some other means of maintenance for those who remained over. If the law attempted to distribute the annual supply of boys proportionately over all the industries of the country, it would have to get over the difficulty, which Lord James found insuperable, of framing any Common Rules that could be applied to the different grades of establishments, in all the innumerable varieties of occupation—to say nothing of the complications arising from trades which employ no boys at all, and from others in which boys only are required. Finally, in order to arrive at the necessary adjustment between the total supply of boy-labor and the demand for it, as well as to hit off the happy mean between undue laxness and economic monopoly in any particular trade, it would need to be based upon data as yet absolutely unknown, as to the rate at which each trade was increasing, and the length of the average operative's working life.[1] In short, whilst any legal restriction on the number of boys to be

[1] See "The Fair Number of Apprentices in a Trade," by C. P. Sanger, in *Economic Journal*, December 1895.

The Factories and Shops Act of 1896 (No. 1445) of the Colony of Victoria empowers (sec. 15) a special Board appointed by the Governor, and consisting of equal numbers of employers and employed, to fix, in the Clothing, Bootmaking, Furniture, and Breadmaking industries, " the number or proportionate number of apprentices and improvers under the age of eighteen years who may be employed within any factory or workroom, and the lowest price or rate of pay payable" to them. Any person employing more than the number or proportion so fixed is made liable to fine, and, on a third offence, the registration of his factory or workroom "shall without further or other authority than this Act be forthwith cancelled by the Chief Inspector." If this law is ever put effectively in force, its working will deserve the careful attention of economists.

We should ourselves be inclined to look for a remedy of the evil of excessive boy-labor, not to any Trade Union Regulation, nor yet to any law limiting numbers, but (following the precedent set with regard to children's employment) to a simple extension of Factory Act and educational requirements ; see our chapter on "The Economic Characteristics of Trade Unionism."

employed in a particular industry can scarcely fail to be inequitable, any general restriction on the number of boys to be employed in all trades whatsoever is plainly impossible.

(c) Progression within the Trade

We come now to a small but interesting series of Trade Union Regulations which have hitherto escaped attention. There are some trades which are not recruited from boys at all, but from adult men, who leave their previous work and "progress" to more responsible duties. Thus, the London Builders having practically ceased to employ boys, the Operative Society of Bricklayers is now largely recruited, in the very numerous Metropolitan branches, from young builders' laborers, who are permitted to decide, up to the age of twenty-five, whether they will permanently abandon the hod for the trowel.[1] In this case the progression is practically unregulated by any definite rule. Elsewhere the arrangements are sometimes more elaborate. Thus, the small Manchester Slaters' and Laborers' Society practically admits to membership, as a laborer, any man who is actually working with a slater, and it is from such laborers that the ranks of the slaters are recruited. But although the laborers form a majority of the society, the rules provide for strict regulation of this progression. Any slater's laborer who desires to become a slater must first serve seven years in the lower grade, and then apply to the secretary of the union. A committee of six practical slaters is then appointed, by whom the candidate is examined in all the mysteries of the art. If he passes this ordeal, he is recognised as a slater, and entitled to demand the full slater's pay. The number of laborers so promoted is limited to three in each year.[2]

---

[1] It must be borne in mind that, as part of the defence of the Standard Rate, no laborer is permitted to do *occasional* work as a bricklayer.

[2] *Rules of the Manchester and Salford District Slaters' and Laborers' Society* (Manchester, 1890). The London plumbers, in the absence of boy apprentices,

A more complicated system of progression is to be found in some trades in which the operatives are divided into different grades.   Among the Steel Smelters the subordinates, known as wheel-chargemen, who are recruited from ordinary laborers, perform the onerous task of bringing to the furnace the heavy loads of pig-iron with which it is charged.   The men actually engaged in the smelting operations are divided into three grades, having varying degrees of responsibility for the successful issue of this very costly process, but all alike engaged in severe physical exertion and exposed to excessive heat.   When a vacancy occurs in the third or lowest grade, one of the wheel-chargemen is promoted to fill it.   A vacancy in any of the higher grades must be offered first to any workman of that particular grade who happens to be out of employment.   If no such candidate appears, it is then filled by selection by the employer from the next lower grade.   A precisely similar arrangement is combined with apprenticeship among the Silk-dressers, who are divided into apprentices, third hands, second hands, and first hands.   Among the Flint Glass Makers the hierarchy of grades is even more complex.   An apprentice may become either a " footmaker " or may, if he is competent, skip that grade and become at once a " servitor."   But no " servitor " may become a " workman," and no " footmaker " a " servitor," so long as any man in the higher grade is out of employment.[1]   In the strongly-organised United Society

are, as we have already mentioned, assisted by men known as " plumbers' mates," who have a union of their own.   An employer is free to promote a plumber's mate to be a plumber, whenever he considers him to be worth the plumbers' Standard Rate.   In most parts of the country the " forgers " or smiths in manufacturing establishments are similarly recruited from the strikers who work in conjunction with them, and who are in the same union.

[1] Thus a Flint Glass Maker, advocating a scheme for the absorption of the unemployed, declared that " the servitor that has been waiting for an opportunity to get to the Workman's chair would then get his desire ; the Footmaker that was put to make foot when he was bound apprentice, and is still in that position, although he may be thirty years of age, and perhaps more than that, with a wife and family dependent upon him, and the reason of his still being in that position is not that he has not the ability to be in a higher one, but because there has been no vacancy only where there has been an unemployed man ready to fill it and keep him back."—Letter in *Flint Glass Makers' Magazine*, November 1888.

of Boilermakers this system of progression is curiously worked in with the existence of an inferior grade of operatives, who are freely admitted to the union, but are only permitted to progress under certain conditions. The platers, angle-iron smiths, and rivetters who form the bulk of the society are mostly recruited under the strictly-regulated apprenticeship system which we have described. But there is also another class of members, called "holders up," who are less skilled than their colleagues, and who were only admitted to the union in 1882. A "holder up" may progress to be a plater or rivetter if he becomes competent for their work, but only on condition that no member of the superior grade is out of work in the district in question. Similarly, a plater, rivetter, or angle-iron smith is not allowed to change to another division of the trade so long as any member of that division is seeking employment.

The trades in which this system of regulated progression prevails cannot be said to be entirely "open," as an employer is not permitted to promote a favourite operative in such a way as to leave unemployed any workman of a higher grade. On the other hand, regulated progression differs from apprenticeship, in the total absence of any desire to reduce the number of candidates below that of places to be filled. No obstacle is thus placed in the way of an expansion of trade ; and when bad times return there are more operatives of all classes than there are places to fill. The arrangement is, in fact, merely one for giving to all the members of each grade the utmost possible continuity of employment, at the cost of practically confining the opportunities of individual promotion to the periods of expanding trade.

There are some reasons for expecting this system of regulated progression to become more widely prevalent in British industry. It is specially characteristic of modern trades, and the modern form of business on a large scale. It is adapted to the typical modern device of splitting up a handicraft into a number of separate processes, each of which falls to the lot of a distinct grade of workmen. It is consistent with the decay of apprenticeship, and the "picking up" of each process in turn by the sharp lad and ambitious young mechanic. It goes a long way to secure both the main objects of Trade Unionism, continuity of livelihood, and the maintenance of the Standard of Life. It has no invidious exclusiveness, or attempt at craft monopoly. It lends itself to a combination of all the different grades of workmen in a single industry, whilst enabling each grade to preserve its own feeling of corporate interest. What is even more significant, the system secures to the manufacturing operatives in large industries much the same sort of organisation as has spontaneously come into existence among the great army of railway workers, and in the Civil Service itself. In the graded service of the railway world, whilst there is no fixed rule on the subject, it is usual for the general manager and the directors to fill vacancies in the higher posts by selecting the most suitable candidates from the next lower grade. Newcomers enter, in the ordinary course, at the bottom of the ladder, and progress upwards as vacancies occur. In times of depression, when the staff remains stationary, or has to be reduced, the contraction operates mainly at the bottom. Recruiting for the lowest grade is practically suspended. Higher up, vacancies may remain unfilled and promotion thus be checked, but actual dismissals for want of work are rare, and are only resorted to in cases of absolute necessity. This continuity of livelihood, which prevails largely in great banking corporations, and, indeed, in all extensive business undertakings, is still more characteristic of the British Civil Service. The Postmaster-General, who is by far the largest employer of labor in the country, never dismisses a man for lack of business, and fills practically all the higher grades of his service by promotion from the lower as vacancies occur. The union of competing firms into great capitalist corporations or syndicates, such as those already prevailing in the salt, alkali, and cotton thread trades, and the growth of colossal commercial undertakings under single management, appears likely to bring with it, as a mere matter of convenicnce and discipline, the creation of a similarly graded service in each monopolised industry.

In the case of the Civil Service, as in the Army and Navy, this system of regulated progression is combined with an objectionable feature. Although here and there a man of exceptional ability or influence may be pitch forked into a high post, over the heads of others, the great majority of vacancies in the upper grades are filled by mere seniority, tempered only by the passing over of officers who are notoriously inefficient. No such idea of seniority is to be found in the Trade Union regulations. The manager of a steel works has full liberty to pick out the most competent wheel-chargeman to be a Third Hand. He may fill vacancies in the class of Second Hands from the ablest of the Third Hands, and then choose the very best of the Second Hands to keep up the select group of First Hands on whom the principal responsibility rests.[1] The Silk-dressers leave it absolutely to the employer to pick out, for any vacancy in the higher grades, whichever workman in the lower he may think best qualified for the place. Once a man has been deliberately promoted by his employer to a particular grade, he is entitled, under the Trade Union system of regulated progression as in the Civil Service, to a preference for work of that or any higher class, over any man of an inferior grade. But under these Trade Union regulations the members of any particular grade can urge, as among themselves, no other claim than that of superior efficiency. The very conception of seniority, as constituting a claim to advancement, is foreign to Trade Unionism. Whatever arrangements may be made to protect the vested interests of those already within the circle, there is never any idea of preferring, among the candidates for admission, either those who are oldest or those

---

[1] A short period of service in the lower grade before promotion is sometimes stipulated for in the rules :—

"That no person be allowed to work (as a) second hand before being one year, nor (as a) first hand before being three years at the trade."—*Constitution and Rules of the British Steel Smelters' Amalgamated Association* (Glasgow, 1892), p. 30.

who have served longest. It is a special characteristic of the industrial world, as compared with the more genteel branches of the public service, that such special promotion comes, as a rule, not to the old but to the young; not to the workman grown gray and stiff at his mechanical task, but to the clever young artisan who reveals latent powers of initiative organisation or command.[1] Against such promotion according to merit no Trade Union ever urges a word of objection.

But although the Trade Union world is singularly free from any idea of promotion by seniority, there are, here as elsewhere, traces of what may be called local protectionism, in conflict with the more general class interest. Thus it is a cardinal tenet of the Amalgamated Association of Operative Cotton-spinners that, whilst it is for the operatives to insist on a universal enforcement of the Standard Rate, it is for the employer, and the employer alone, to determine whom he will employ. When a pair of mules are vacant, the mill-owner may entrust them to whomsoever he pleases, provided that the selected person instantly joins the union and is paid according to the " List." But the operatives in the particular mill have not infrequently resented the introduction of a spinner from another mill, even if he is a member of their own union, when there are piecers who have grown up in the service of the firm, and have long been waiting for the chance of becoming spinners. The able officials and leaders of the Amalgamated Association of Operative Cotton-spinners throw their weight against any such feeling on the ground that it is inconsistent with Trade Unionism. The same conflict of the local with the general interest has come up among the Steel Smelters, whose system of regulated progression is so elaborate. At one branch (Blochairn Works, Glasgow) the Wheel-chargemen (there called " helpers ") objected to vacan-

[1] This is, to some extent, the case also in the more business-like branches of the British Civil Service, where the aristocratic tradition is absent. The large graded services of the Post Office, Customs, and Excise are mainly governed by a system of " promotion according to merit," vacancies being filled by selection among the next lower grade, irrespective of seniority.

cies among the Third, Second, or First Hands in their particular
establishment being filled by unemployed men of those
grades, coming from elsewhere. They demanded that the
wheel-chargemen, and the men in other lower grades, should
have a preference for any vacancies that occurred in their
own steelworks. Any such substitution of a vertical for a
horizontal cleavage of the trade would, it is clear, be inconsistent with the regulated progression enforced by the British
Steel Smelters' Amalgamated Association, and would have
seriously hampered the employers' choice of operatives.
The union accordingly refused to recognise the claim of the
Blochairn helpers, and they were eventually excluded from
its ranks.[1]

(d) The Exclusion of Women

So far we have taken for granted that the candidate for
admission to the trade belongs to the male sex. In this we
have followed the ordinary Trade Union books of rules,
which, in nine cases out of ten, have found no need to refer
to the sex of the members. The middle-class Anglo-Saxon
is so accustomed to see men and women engaged in identical
work as teachers, journalists, authors, painters, sculptors,
comedians, singers, musicians, doctors, clerks, and what not,
that he unconsciously assumes the same state of things to
exist in manual labor and manufacturing industry.[2] But in
the hewing of coal or the making of engines, in the building
of ships or the erecting of houses, in the railway service or
the mercantile marine, it has never occurred to the most

---

[1] We need not do more than mention the demand—put forward by the
Enginemen's and the Plumbers' Trade Unions—that the possession of a certificate
of competency, awarded by some public authority, should be made a condition of
practising their respective trades. Regulations of this kind already govern, not
only the learned professions, but also the mercantile marine, and, to a growing
extent, the elementary school service. Protection of the interests of the consumer
may possibly cause them to be extended to some other occupations ; Massachusetts
Law 265 of 1896 requires a certificate for gasfitters.

[2] Similarly, the entrance into industrial occupations of a relatively small number
of middle-class women has given rise to a quite disproportionate impression as to
the extent to which the employment of women has increased ; see the Board of
Trade *Report by Miss Collet on the Employment of Women and Girls*, p. 7.

economical employer to substitute women for men.[1]   And
thus we find that, contrary to the usual impression, nine-
tenths of the Trade Unionists have never had occasion to
exclude women from their organisations.   Even in the
industries which employ both men and women, we nearly
always find the sexes sharply divided in different departments, working at different processes, and performing different
operations.[2]   In the vast majority of cases these several
departments, processes, and operations are mutually com-
plementary, and there is no question of sex rivalry.   In others
we find what is usually a temporary competition, not so
much between the sexes, as between the process requiring
a skilled man, and that within the capacity of a woman
or a boy laborer.   Our chapter on " New Processes and
Machinery " has described the Trade Union policy with regard
to the substitution of unskilled for skilled labor.   The
present section has, therefore, only to treat of the comparatively small number of cases in which, without any
change of process, women attempt to learn the same trade
and perform the same work as men.

The intensity of the resentment and abhorrence with
which the average working man regards the idea of women
entering his trade, equals that displayed by the medical
practitioner of the last generation.   We have, to begin with,
a deeply-rooted conviction in the minds of the most conservative of classes, that, to use the words of a representative
compositor, " the proper place for females is their home."[3]
The respectable artisan has an instinctive distaste for the
promiscuous mixing of men and women in daily intercourse,

[1] The women who worked in coalpits before the Mines Regulation Act of
1842 did the work, not of the coal-hewers, but of boys.   The sweeping prohibition of women working in underground mines happened not to be a Trade
Union demand, for the miners were at the moment unorganised.   It was pressed
for by the philanthropists on grounds of morality.

[2] See "The Alleged Difference between the wages of Men and Women," by
Sidney Webb (*Economic Journal*, December 1891) ; *Women and the Factory
Acts*, by Mrs. Sidney Webb (Fabian Tract, No. 67).

[3] *Report of Proceedings of the Meeting of Delegates from the Typographical
Societies of the United Kingdom and the Continent* (London, 1886), p. 25.

whether this be in the workshop or in a social club.[1] These objections, which often spring from mere old-fashioned prejudice, tend to hide, and in the eyes of progressive reformers, to discredit, the Trade Union objection to a new class of "blacklegs." No employer would dream of substituting women for men, unless this resulted in his getting the work done below the men's Standard Rate. The facts that women have a lower standard of comfort than men, that they seldom have to support a family, and that they are often partially maintained from other sources, all render them, as a class, the most dangerous enemies of the artisan's Standard of Life. The instinctive Trade Union attitude towards women working at a man's trade is exactly the same as that towards men who habitually "work under price," except that it is reinforced in the case of women by certain social and moral prejudices which, in our day, and among certain reformers, are beginning to be considered obsolete. But under the pressure of the growing feeling in favor of the "equality of the sexes" the Trade Unions have, as we shall see, changed front. They began with a simple prohibition of women as women. From this point we shall trace the development of a new policy, based, like that relating to new processes, not on exclusion, but on the

---

[1] As regards many trades, there is much force in this objection. Where men and women work independently of each other, in full publicity, and in comparatively decent surroundings, as is the case with the male and female weavers in a Lancashire cotton mill, there is little danger of sexual immorality. But where a woman or girl works in conjunction with a man, especially if she is removed from constant association with other female workers, experience both in the factory and the mine shows that there is a very real danger to morality. This is increased if the work has to be done in unusual heat or exceptional dress. But the most perilous of relations is that in which the girl or woman stands in a position of subordination to the man by whose side she is working. No one acquainted with the relation between cotton-spinner and piecer can doubt the wisdom, from the point of view of public morality, of the imperative refusal of the Amalgamated Association of Operative Cotton-spinners to allow its members to employ female piecers. Even in the weaving sheds, where the relations between the weavers themselves are satisfactory, the subordination of the women weavers to the male overlooker leads to frequent scandals. The statutory exclusion of women from working in underground mines is, we believe, universally approved.

maintenance of a definite Standard Rate for each grade of labor.

The eighteenth-century trade clubs of hatters, basket-makers, brushmakers, or compositors would have instantly struck against any attempt to put a woman to do any part of their craft.[1] It is interesting that the only case in which we can discover this categorical prohibition still actually existing in a current book of rules of to-day is that of the archaic society of the Pearl Button Makers, whom we have already noticed as extreme in their limitation of apprentices and unique in their peremptory prohibition of machinery. " No female allowed," laconically observes their regulation, " in the capacity of either piecemaker, turner, or bottomer. Any member working where a female does either [process] shall forfeit one pound, and should he continue to do so shall be excluded." [2] In some other small indoor handicrafts, where the work requires no great strength or endurance, employers have, here and there, fitfully sought to teach women the trade. The men, whether organised or not, have done their best to exclude these new competitors, and the employers have not found the experiment sufficiently successful to induce them to continue it.[3]

Wherever any considerable number of employers have resolutely sought to bring women into any trade within their

[1] It will be needless to recall to the reader similar prohibitions by the masters' gilds. Thus the Articles of the London Girdlers (1344) provided "that no one of the said trade shall set any woman to work, other than his wedded wife or his daughter." The "Braelers" (brace-makers) and Leather-sellers of London and the Fullers of Lincoln had the same rule.—Riley's *Memorials*, pp. 217, 278, 547 ; Toulmin Smith's *English Gilds*, p. 180.

[2] *Rules and Regulations to be observed by the Members of the Operative Pearl Button and Stud Workers' Protection Society* (Birmingham, 1887), p. 12.

[3] It has sometimes happened that the women, though acquiring a certain amount of skill in most of the process, have failed in some essential part. Thus when an employer brought his own daughters into the trade of silver-engraving, they were never able, with all his tuition, to pick up the knack of "pointing" their "gravers." The experiment has not been repeated. An attempt was made, some years ago, to teach women to be "twisters and drawers" in a Lancashire cotton mill. The innovation did not, however spread, as the women could never do the "beaming," and it has been abandoned. In this case, by exception, the incident has left its trace in the Trade Union rules. The very exclusive society of "Beamers, Twisters, and Drawers" now provides "That all *male*

capacity, the Trade Unions have utterly failed to prevent them. The most interesting case is that of the compositors.[1] About 1848 the great printing firm of M'Corquodale introduced women apprentices into its letterpress-printing works at Newton-le-Willows in Lancashire, and this example has since been followed by other employers in various towns. There can be no doubt that the male compositors, whether Trade Unionists or not, have been, from first to last, extremely hostile to this innovation, and that they have done their best to prevent it. Down to 1886 all the compositors' Trade Unions expressed, either in their rules or in their practice, this uncompromising policy of exclusion. This policy was justified by the men on the ground that the women worked far below the Standard Rate, and that "unfair" employers made use of them to break down the men's position. In Edinburgh, for instance, the compositors' great strike of 1872-73 was defeated, and the union reduced to impotence by the importation of "female blacklegs," who, as the Board of Trade declares, have "completely revolutionised the trade in that city.[2] In London, where there are probably two hundred women compositors, these set up "1000 ens" of copy for $5\frac{1}{2}$d. to 6d., as compared with a Standard Rate which works out at about $8\frac{1}{2}$d., for work of identical quantity and quality.

The compositors' policy of rigid exclusion from membership failed to keep the women out of their trade. Whenever an employer thought it worth his while to engage women compositors, he ignored the union altogether, and set up a distinct establishment. More than one great London firm has, for instance, a "fair house" in the Metropolis, where

persons wishing to learn the trade of Twisting and Drawing, shall first obtain a shop to work at when he has learned, and procure a certificate from the manager to show that he has engaged him. No youth under sixteen years of age shall be allowed to learn the trade of Twisting and Drawing, and not then, unless there be a vacancy in the mill where he is introduced, and no member out of work on the books."—*Rules of the Blackburn District of the Amalgamated Beamers, Twisters, and Drawers' Association* (Blackburn, 1891), p. 12.

[1] See "Women Compositors," by Amy Linnett, in *Economic Review*, January 1892.

[2] Board of Trade *Third Report on Trade Unions*, C. 5808, 1889, p. 125.

none but Trade Unionists are employed, and another establishment in one of the small towns of the Home Counties, where no Trade Unionist works, and where the employment of women is absolutely unrestricted. Smaller firms employing women take girl apprentices, and rely almost exclusively on female labor.

The futility of the policy of exclusion, combined with the growth of a Socialistic disapproval of trade monopoly, induced the largest compositors' society to alter its tactics. In 1886 we find the able general secretary of the London Society of Compositors (Mr. C. J. Drummond)[1] carrying, at an important conference of all the compositors' Trade Unions, a resolution "that, while strongly of opinion that women are not physically capable of performing the duties of a compositor, this conference recommends their admission to membership of the various Typographical Unions upon the same conditions as journeymen, provided always the females are paid strictly in accordance with scale."[2] This resolution has been acted upon by the London Society of Compositors, the most important of the unions represented, which is now open to women on exactly the same terms as to men.[3]

What the London Society of Compositors has only lately discovered, the Lancashire weavers have, for two generations, unconsciously acted upon. Here there has never been any sex distinction. The various organisations of weavers have, from the introduction of the power-loom, always included women as members on the same terms as men. The piecework list of prices, to which all workers

[1] Now on the staff of the Labor Department of the Board of Trade.

[2] *Report of Proceedings of the Meeting of Delegates from the Typographical Societies of the United Kingdom and the Continent* (London, 1886), pp. 23-25.

[3] It is interesting to trace this change of attitude among the London compositors, partly to a dim and imperfect appreciation of the foregoing argument, and partly also to the growth of Socialist ideas, and the conception of equality of rights ; see the *History of Trade Unionism*, pp. 384, 394. We believe that during ten years only one woman compositor has ever claimed admission to the London Society of Compositors. On it being proved that, employed at Mr. William Morris's Kelmscott Press, she was paid at the Standard Rate, she was promptly enrolled as a member (*Printing News*, October 1892).

must conform, applies to men and women alike. But it is interesting to observe that the maintenance of a Standard Rate has resulted in a real, though unobtrusive, segregation. There is no attempt to discriminate between women's work and men's work as such. The uniform scale of piecework prices includes an almost infinite variety of articles from the plain calico woven on narrow looms to the broad and heavy figured counterpanes which tax the strength of the strongest man. In every mill we see both men and women at work, often at identical tasks. But, taking the cotton-weaving trade as a whole, the great majority of the women will be found engaged on the comparatively light work paid for at the lower rates. On the other hand, a majority of the men will be found practically monopolising the heavy trade, priced at higher rates per yard, and resulting in larger weekly earnings. But there is no sex competition. A woman of exceptional strength, who is capable of doing the heavy work, cannot take advantage of her lower Standard of Life, to offer her services at a lower rate than has been fixed for the men. She is not, as a woman, excluded from what is generally the men's work, but she must win her way by capacity, not by underbidding. On the other hand, though the rates fixed for the lighter work have been forced up to a point that is high relatively to the women's Standard of Life, the wages that can be earned at this grade are too low to tempt any but the weaker men to apply for such looms. In short, the enforcement of a definite Standard Rate, practically unalterable in individual cases, serves, in itself, to prevent sex competition. The candidates for employment tend to segregate into virtually non-competing groups according to their grades of strength and skill.[1]

---

[1] This principle of a classification of work, and strict segregation of the sexes, is now to be found in various other trades. Thus, the very old-fashioned society of goldbeaters sought, down to recent years, absolutely to exclude women. *The Rules of the Goldbeaters' Trade Society* (London, 1875) provided "That no member be allowed to work for a master who employs females on the premises or elsewhere under the penalty of immediate erasure." But this absolute exclusion is now given up in favor of a strict separation between the men's and women's tasks. The later *Rules of the Goldbeaters' Trade Society* (London, 1887) expressly

Precisely the same result has occurred in the hosiery trade, where men and women have for many years belonged to the same organisations and worked side by side. Here the machinery is undergoing a constant evolution, one stage of which affords an interesting example of the relation of men and women workers. At the beginning of 1888 the men working on "circular rib frames" found themselves being ousted by the women working at lower rates. They accordingly demanded, in March 1888, that a uniform rate of 3d. per dozen should be paid to men and women alike. The women protested, saying that if they were to charge the men's price they would be all dismissed. A compromise was agreed to, which allowed the women to work at a farthing per dozen less than the men. This led in May to "the dismissal of the (male) circular rib frame hands from H.'s firm for women to work. The farthing difference as agreed to by the workpeople themselves under the pressure of circumstances created the evil." . . . "It seems to us," continued the Secretary of the Union, "that the simplest and best way of meeting the difficulty will be to agree what frames shall be a man's and what a woman's job." From the June report we see that this suggestion of the Executive Council was adopted by both male and female workers, it being decided that the women should work the "old" machines and the men the "new" ones! This ingenuous proposal was accepted by the women until they found that the "old" machines were, of necessity, being steadily replaced by new ones. Ultimately an agreement was arrived at that the men should work the large, or "eight-head" frames, and the women the small, or "six-head" frames. This segregation of the sexes was secured, not by the exclusion of one sex or the other from either machine, but an ingenious

allow that a member "may work at any shop where females are employed provided he does not assist them or be assisted by them in any part of the work. And the brushmakers, who once strove against women working at all, now seek merely to keep them to their own class of work. "Any member boring p or machine work for women shall be expelled."—*General Trade Rules of t United Society of Brushmakers* (London, 1891), p. 24.

adjustment of the Standard Rate. The women retained their privilege of working at a farthing per dozen less than the men, a concession which gave them a virtual monopoly of their own machine. On the other hand, it was agreed between the union and the employers that, as between the " six-head " frame and the " eight-head " frame, an extra allowance of a farthing per dozen should be paid to compensate for the lesser output of the smaller machine. This prevented the smaller (or women's) machine from encroaching on the work for which the larger (or men's) machine was best fitted. The result has been that, whilst their weekly earnings may differ widely, the women actually obtain the same rate per dozen on their own machine as the men do on theirs, whilst complete segregation of the sexes is secured, and all competition between men and women as such is practically prevented.[1]

The experience of the Lancashire Cotton-weavers and the Leicestershire Hosiers affords, we think, a useful hint to the London Society of Compositors. To complete its policy with regard to women's labor, the latter should not merely admit to membership those women who prove their capacity to do a man's work, but should also take steps to organise the weaker or less efficient female compositors whom this condition excludes. As in the case of alternative processes, the welfare of each party is bound up with the maintenance of the other's Standard Rate. It is easy to see that the women compositors, as a class, stand to lose if the men's employers were to regain the trade from the firms employing women by reducing the men's wages. On the other hand, the men suffer if, owing to the defenceless state of the women and their partial maintenance from other sources, employers are able to obtain their labor at wages positively below what would suffice to keep it in constant efficiency, if the women depended permanently on their wages alone. To prevent any such " bounty " being indirectly paid by other

[1] Amalgamated Hosiery Union, *Monthly Reports* for 1888 ; and personal information in 1893 and 1896.

classes of the community to the employer of female labor, it is necessary that the women should be in a position to maintain a Standard Rate for their own work, even though this may have to be fixed lower than that of the men. Now, Trade Union experience shows that the first condition of the contemporary maintenance of two different Standard Rates, in different grades of the same industry, is that there should be a clear and sharp distinction between them. In the case of the Cotton-weavers this is secured by the different kinds of work, to each of which a definite scale of prices is assigned. The Hosiery Workers accomplish the same result by a differentiation of machine. In the case of the Compositors, though there are many kinds of work for which women have never been found suitable, it is impossible to make any complete classification of men's work and women's work. The only way of preventing individual underbidding by persons of a lower standard of comfort is to segregate the women in separate establishments or departments, and rigidly to exclude each sex from those in which the other is employed in type-setting.[1] If this segregation, which is desirable for moral as well as for economic reasons, were strictly enforced, it would be highly advantageous for the London Society of Compositors to recognise these women, and to organise them either as a " woman's branch," or as an affiliated society. The women could then collectively decide for themselves the standard weekly earnings that ought to be demanded by the ordinary woman compositor, and get a " scale " of piecework prices for women's jobs worked out on this basis. The fundamental necessity for the Compositors, from a Trade Union point of view, is, therefore, not the exclusion of women as women, but the rigid insistence that any candidate for admission into their particular branch of the trade should obtain the Standard Rate. If women are incapable of earning the same piece-work rate as men they are, on this argument, rightly relegated to the easier

---

[1] This need not exclude the employment of a man in the women's department to do laboring or engineering work.

lines of work in which their lower standard of effort can be fully remunerated.

We may now sum up the present Trade Unionist position. The old prohibition of women competitors, against which the women's advocates have so often protested, was as unnecessary as it was invidious. All that is requisite, from a Trade Union point of view, is that the woman's claim for absolute equality should be unreservedly conceded, and that women should be accepted as members *upon precisely the same terms as men.* Nor can the champion of the "equality of the sexes" logically demand from the Trade Unions any further concession. The women's advocates are, in fact, in a dilemma. If they argue that women, though entitled to equality of treatment, may nevertheless work "under price," in order to oust male Trade Unionists from employment, they negative the whole theory and practice of Trade Unionism. If, on the other hand, they ask that women shall be specially privileged to act as blacklegs, without suffering the consequences, they abandon the contention of an equality of treatment of both sexes. Within the world of manual labor, at any rate, "equality" between the sexes leads either to the exclusion of women from the men's trades, or else to the branding of the whole sex as blacklegs.

There is, however, no necessity to get into this dilemma. It is unfair, and even cruel, to the vast army of women workers, to uphold the fiction of the equality of the sexes in the industrial world. So far as manual labor is concerned, women constitute a distinct class of workers, having different faculties, different needs, and different expectations from those of men. To keep both sexes in the same state of health and efficiency—to put upon each the same degree of strain—implies often a differentiation of task, and always a differentiation of effort and subsistence.[1] The Common

---

[1] Professor Edgeworth puts an interesting problem (*Mathematical Psychics*, p. 95). "When Fanny Kemble visited her husband's slave plantations, she found that the same (equal) tasks were imposed on the men and the women, the

Rules with regard to wages, hours, and other conditions by which the men maintain their own Standard of Life are usually unsuited to the women. The problem for the Trade Unionist is, whilst according to women the utmost possible freedom to earn an independent livelihood, to devise such arrangements as shall prevent that freedom being made use of by the employers to undermine the Standard of Life of the whole wage-earning class. The experience of the Lancashire Cotton-weavers and the Leicestershire Hosiers points, we think, to a solution being found in the frank recognition of a classification of work. The essential point is that there should be no under-bidding of individuals of one sex by individuals of the other. So long as the competition of men is virtually confined to the men's jobs, and the competition of women to the women's jobs, the fact that the women sell their labor at a low price does not endanger the men's Standard Rate, and the fact that men are legally permitted to work all night does not diminish the women's chance of employment. In the vast majority of trades, as we have seen, this industrial segregation of the sexes comes automatically into existence, and needs no express regulation. In the very small number of cases in which men and women compete directly with each other for employment, on precisely the same operation, in one and the same process, there can, we believe, be no effective Trade Unionism until definite Standard Rates are settled for men's work and women's work respectively.

This does not mean that either men or women need to be explicitly excluded from any occupation in virtue of their sex. All that is required is that the workers at each operation should establish and enforce definite Common Rules, binding on all who work at their operation, whether they be men or women. The occupations which demanded the

women accordingly, in consequence of their weakness, suffering much more fatigue. Supposing the [employer] to insist on a certain quantity of work being done, and to leave the distribution of the burden to the philanthropist, what would be the most beneficent arrangement—that the men should have the *same fatigue*, or not only *more task*, but *more fatigue ?* "

trength, skill, and endurance of a trained man would, as at present, be carried on with a relatively high Standard Rate. On the other hand, the operatives in those processes which were within the capacity of the average woman would aim at such Common Rules as to wages, hours, and other conditions of labor, as corresponded to their position, efforts, and needs. The experience of the Lancashire Cotton-weavers indicates that such a differentiation of earnings is not necessarily incompatible with the thorough maintenance of a Standard Rate, and also that it results in an almost complete industrial segregation of the sexes. Women are not engaged at the men's jobs, because the employers, having to pay them at the same high rate as the men, find the men's labor more profitable. On the other hand, the ordinary man does not offer himself for the woman's job, as it is paid or at a rate below that which he can earn elsewhere, and upon which, indeed, he could not permanently maintain himself. But there need be no rigid exclusion of exceptional individuals. If a woman proves herself capable of working as well and as profitably to the employer as a man, and is engaged at the man's Standard Rate, there is no Trade Union objection to her being admitted to membership, as in the London Society of Compositors, on the same terms as a man. If, on the other hand, a man is so weak that he can do nothing but the light work of the women, these may well admit him, as do the Lancashire Weavers, at what is virtually the women's rate. The key to this as to so many other positions is, in fact, a thorough application of the principle of the Standard Rate.

CHAPTER XI

THE RIGHT TO A TRADE

AN " overlap " between two trades, leading to a dispute as to which section of workmen has a " right " to the job, may occur in more than one way. A new process may be invented which lies outside the former work of any one trade, but is nearly akin to two or more of them. In such a case, each trade will vehemently claim that the new process " belongs " to its own members, either because the same material is manipulated, the same tools are used, or the same object is effected. But even without a new invention the same conflict of rights may arise. The lines of division between allied trades have hitherto often differed from town to town, and the migration of employers or workmen, or even the mere imitation of the custom of one town by the establishments of another, will lead to serious friction. A new firm may introduce fresh ways of dividing its work, or an old establishment may undertake a new branch of trade. There may even be an unprovoked and naked aggression by a strongly organised class of workmen, upon the jobs hitherto undertaken by a humbler section. In any or all of these ways, the employers may find their desire to allot their work to particular classes of workmen sharply checked by conflicting claims of " right to the trade."

It is in the great modern industry of iron-shipbuilding that we find the most numerous and complicated disputes about " overlap " and " demarcation." The gradual trans formation of the passenger ship from the simple Deal lugger into an elaborate floating hotel has obscured all the old lines of division between trades. Sanitary work, for instance, has always been the special domain of the plumber, and when the sanitary appliances of ships became as elaborate as those of houses, the plumber naturally followed his work. But, from the very beginning of steam navigation, all iron piping on board a steamship, whatever its purpose, had been fitted by the engineer. Hence the plumbers and fitters both complained that "the bread was being taken out of their mouths" by their rivals. We need not recite the numberless other points at which the craftsmen working on a modern warship or Atlantic liner find each new improvement bringing different trades into sharp conflict. The Engineers have, on different occasions, quarrelled on this score with the Boiler-makers, the Shipwrights, the Joiners, the Brassworkers, the Plumbers, and the Tinplate Workers; the Boiler-makers have had their own differences with the Ship-wrights, the Smiths, and the Chippers and Drillers; the Shipwrights have fought with the Caulkers, the Boat and Barge Builders, the Mast and Blockmakers, and the Joiners; the Joiners themselves have other quarrels with the Mill-sawyers, the Patternmakers, the Cabinetmakers, the Upholsterers, and the French Polishers; whilst minor trades, such as the Hammermen, the Ship Painters, and the Red Leaders," are at war all round. Hence an employer, bound to complete a job by a given date, may find one morning his whole establishment in confusion, and the most important sections of his workmen "on strike," not because they object to any of the conditions of employment, but because they fancy that one trade has "encroached" on the work of another. The supposed encroachment may consist of the most trivial detail. The shipwrights admit that the joiners may case (or line with wood) all telegraph connections throughout the ship, except only when these happen to go through cargo spaces, coal bunkers, and the hold. When a joiner passes this magic line even in a job of a few hours,

the whole of the shipwrights will drop their tools. On the
other hand, when the joiners' blood is up, they will all go on
strike rather than see the shipwrights do even a few feet of
what they regard as essentially their own work. Under these
circumstances a task which one man could do in an hour
may stop a whole shipyard. On one occasion, indeed, a
great shipbuilder on the Tyne, finding his whole establishment laid idle by such a quarrel, and utterly unable to bring
the men to reason, finally took off his coat and did the disputed
work with his own hands.[1]

These trivial disputes sometimes blaze up into industrial
wars of the first magnitude. The leading case which took
place on the Tyne a few years ago is thus described by a
great shipbuilder. "For some time before 1890 the division
of work between joiners and shipwrights had led to unpleasant
relations between them, and to interference with the progress
of work. . . . The disputes became so frequent and angry,
when the large amount of Government work came to the
Tyne, that the employers urged the delegates of the two

---

[1] Demarcation disputes, though frequent and serious in certain industries, are
entirely absent from some, and only rarely occur in others. They are, for instance,
practically unknown in the textile trades and the extractive industries, which
together make up a half of the Trade Union world. It is especially in the group
of trades connected with the building and equipping of ships that they are troublesome. They also occur, though to a lesser extent, throughout the engineering
and building trades. Roughly speaking, we may say that they are characteristic
of about one quarter of the whole Trade Union membership. We know of no
systematic description or analysis of this controversy. The student can only be
referred to the materials relating to the particular cases elsewhere cited, especially
the minutes of proceedings of the various joint committees, and to the evidence
given before the Royal Commission on Labor, 45th day. (See Digest for
Group A, vol. iii. C. 6894, x. pp. 48-54.) In earlier ages, when the right to a
continuance of the accustomed livelihood was recognised by law and public opinion,
disputes arising from the encroachments of one craft on the work of another were
habitually settled by what was, in effect, a judicial decree, exactly as if the point
at issue had been the boundary between two landed estates. Thus the apportionment of work between the carpenters and the joiners was a fruitful cause of dispute.
A Committee of the Common Council of the City of London made an elaborate
award in 1632, defining in detail the particular kinds of work to be done by the
Companies of Carpenters and Joiners respectively, "deal coffins" being assigned,
as a knotty question, to both in common.—*The History of the Carpenters' Company*
by Jupp (London, 1848). A similar dispute between the carpenters and joiners
of Newcastle-on-Tyne, who, down to 1589, were combined in a single gild, was

societies to refer their differences to an independent and capable arbitrator, promising that they would, as employers, accept any award that he made. . . . Mr. Thomas Burt, M.P., was proposed by the joiners and accepted by the shipwrights. A very long, patient, and exhaustive inquiry was made into the practices in the Tyne and other places, past and present ; evidence was taken from old hands, delegates, and all who could throw light upon the history of the division of work. . . . After an investigation extending over five and a half months, Mr. Burt issued his award, allotting, out of 168 items in question, 96 to the joiners and 72 to the shipwrights. The joiners . . . disputed the fairness of the findings of the arbitrator they had themselves proposed, and left their employment for fourteen weeks. . . . Many vigorous attempts were made by the employers to induce the joiners to work to the award without success. . . . Ultimately . . . the joiners were called upon by the united trades in the Tyne to submit their contentions absolutely to a Committee or Court com-

---

settled by an award of similar character, "chists for corpses" being, curiously enough, equally made common to the two trades (Beach's Newcastle Companies, pp. 31-33). And, to turn to quite other industries, we find the tanners and whit-tawyers disputing as to the limits of their crafts, "the assize of a white tawyer" being, as Stow declared, "that he make nor tawe no Ledder but Shepe's Ledder, Gotes Ledder, Horses' Ledder, and Hindes Ledder" (Jupp, p. 337), leaving to the tanner the dressing of ox skins, which required the use of bark. The disputes between the London Cordwainers and the "cobelers from beyond sea" raged in 1395 so fiercely that the king "commanded John Fresshe, Mayor of the said city, that the said Cobelers should gain their living as they had done from of old . . . and that it might be declared what of right should belong to the one party and the other." Whereupon, after solemn inquiry, it was ordained, among other things, "that no person who meddles with old shoes shall meddle with new shoes to sell." [Indenture of Agreement between the Cordwainers and the Cobblers, 14th August 1395 ; *Memorials of London and London Life*, by H. T. Riley (London, 1868), pp. 539-541.] This, however, did not bring peace, and in 1409 "our most dread lord the King sent his gracious letters under his Privy Seal unto Drew Barantyn," the then Mayor, which led to renewed inquiry, and a more detailed apportionment of work, assigning to the cobblers the clouting of "old boots and old shoes with new leather upon the old soles, before or behind," but "that if it shall happen that any person desires to have his old boots or bootlets resoled, or vamped and soled, or his galoches or shoes resoled, the same, if it can be done, shall pertain at all times to the said workers called Cordwainers to do it." [Inquisition made for the Regulation of the Cordwainers and the Cobblers, 15th June 1409, *Ibid.* pp. 571-574.] A detailed study of the demarca-tion disputes of former ages would probably be of considerable interest.

posed of one representative from six or seven different trade societies. . . . This Court, at their first meeting, ordered the joiners to resume work on Mr. Burt's award. . . . In January 1891, the plumbers and fitters agreed to appoint representatives to discuss and settle the demarcation of their respective trades . . . owing to the friction that was growing between the two. . . . Conferences between the parties took place : witnesses were examined for the fitters and for the plumbers ; the practice for several years back was carefully investigated ; an agreement was eventually signed by the parties, but . . . it led to disputes . . . the moment it was published, and produced a strike as soon as it was attempted to be worked to. . . . Each of the two parties read the provisions in utter disregard of the other's views and interests, and in equal disregard of the interests of the employers, and . . . disputed points . . . kept the two trades apart for nine weeks. . . . An agreement was arrived at, however, on the 18th June 1891, at a conference between employers, fitters, and plumbers. . . . The Committee met seventeen times . . . settled two sections out of a list of twenty-six, the Chairman giving his decision against the objection of the engineers to the three-inch limit on iron-piping. . . . The fitters rose in a body, charged the Chairman with unfairness, and left the Committee altogether. . . . The other two parties . . . issued an award on the 28th October 1891. The employers were appealed to by the plumbers . . . to put the award into force, and did so, with the result that the fitters left their employment . . . and a second strike ensued on the division of the same work as before in April. . . . After a strike of twelve weeks . . . they [were driven to resume] work upon the award of the Joint Committee. . . . The principal difficulty in composing the disputes has arisen from the variety of the practice in different works and districts. . . . Each society proposes to itself to have the largest possible number of its members employed at the same time . . . and to this end tries to secure the whole of the work it considers belongs to its members according to usage and custom. . . .

The employers' interest is remorselessly sacrificed by the disputants."[1]

It will not, we think, be difficult for the reader to picture, even from this bald narrative, the state of disorganisation and chaos into which these recurring disputes threw the great industries of Tyneside between 1890 and 1893. Within the space of thirty-five months, there were no fewer than thirty-five weeks in which one or other of the four most important sections of workmen in the staple industry of the district absolutely refused to work. This meant the stoppage of huge establishments, the compulsory idleness of tens of thousands of other artisans and laborers, the selling-up of households, and the semi-starvation of thousands of families totally unconcerned with the dispute. Nor was the effect confined, as far as the Trade Unionists were concerned, to these sensational but temporary results. The men were, in fact, playing into the hands of those employers who wished to see Trade Unionism destroyed. The internecine warfare on the Tyne has left all unions concerned in a state of local weakness from which they have by no means yet recovered, and under which they will probably suffer for many years. Their loss of members and of money is the least part of the evil. When one society is fighting another, the whole efficacy of Trade Unionism, as a means of improving the conditions of employment, is, for the moment, paralysed. Even if the angry strife between the two sets of workmen does not lead actually to mutual " blacklegging," it effectively

[1] Extracted from an interesting Memorandum by Mr. John Price, of Palmer and Co., Limited, Shipbuilders and Engineers, Jarrow, which was prepared for the Royal Commission on Labor but was not published by that body.

Among the voluminous pamphlet literature on these disputes the most important documents are the several *Reports of Conferences* between the employers and the several engineering unions in.Newcastle on 9th March, 22nd March, 22nd April, and 26th April 1892 ; the set of *Manifestoes published by the United Operative Plumbers' Association* (Liverpool, 1892) ; the *Report of the Arbitration Proceedings on the question of the apportionment of work to be done by the Ship-wrights and the Joiners* (Newcastle, 1890) ; the publications on the subject by the Shipwrights and the Joiners respectively ; and the *Report of the Proceedings of the Board of Conciliation in revising the award of Mr. Thomas Burt, M.P.* (Newcastle, 1890). The *Newcastle Daily Chronicle* from 1890 to 1893 contains frequent references.

destroys their power of resisting any capitalist encroachment. An employer who desires to beat down his men's terms need only send, on some trivial pretext, for the district delegate of the overlapping trade. The mere rumour that the agent of the rival union has been seen to enter his office will probably excite sufficient apprehension to bring his men to instant submission. Thus, whilst these demarcation disputes cause, to the employers, the wage-earners, and the community at large, all the moral irritation and pecuniary loss of an ordinary strike or lock-out, they must, under all circumstances, weaken all the unions concerned in their struggle for better conditions.

We are, therefore, face to face with an apparently incomprehensible problem. If the workmen have all to lose and nothing to gain by fighting over the demarcation between trades, how is it that their responsible leaders do not peremptorily interfere to prevent such quarrels? The explanation is to be found in the character of the workmen's claims. To them the issue is not one of expediency, but of moral right. "We are fighting this battle," declared the United Pattern-makers' Association in 1889, "on the principle that every trade shall have the right to earn its bread without the interference of outsiders; a principle jealously guarded by every skilled trade . . . and one which we are fully determined shall likewise apply to us." [1] "It is our duty," declared the Amalgamated Society of Engineers, "to exercise the same care and watchfulness over that in which we have a vested interest as the physician does who holds a diploma, or the author who is protected by a copyright." [2] "The machine," says their Tyne District Delegate in 1897, "no doubt is part of the employer's invested capital, but so is the journeyman's skilled labor." [3] The Associated Shipwrights' Society expressly stated in 1893, with reference to a new

---

[1] Circular of United Pattern-makers' Association, 19th December 1889.
[2] Preface to *Rules of the Amalgamated Society of Engineers* (London, 1891), p. 6.
[3] *Amalgamated Society of Engineers' Journal*, March 1897.

dispute on the Clyde, that "while we do not object to any firms dividing their works into departments, or sub-letting portions of the vessels they are building, still we do most respectfully and emphatically contend that no employers should, in suiting their convenience, give away another man's means of living, any more than that no workman would be allowed or justified to go into an employer's office and take his money from his safe and give it to another."[1] "The sacredness of property," writes the Liverpool Delegate of the Engineers in 1897, "is surely applicable to labor, which is as much our property as the lathes are the property of the employer."[2] And if we look through the reports of the unions we have mentioned, or of those in any branch of the building trades, we shall find abundant references, not to the pecuniary advantage of the workmen or the convenience of the employer, but to "our trade rights," or "our universal right and custom," and to a righteous resistance of "encroachment, theft, and confiscation." "Do the Bricklayers aim at extinguishing us altogether?" pathetically remonstrate the Slaters and Tilers. "They roam all over a building from the cellar to the highest point, devouring everything and anything that they choose, no matter what other trade it may belong to—slating, roof-tiling, wall-tiling, floor-tiling, paving, setting stone landings, sills, heads, and steps, plastering, knobbing, whitewashing, etc."[3]

It is, fortunately, unnecessary for us to discuss the workman's initial assumption that it is desirable, in the public

[1] *Minutes of Line of Demarcation Joint-Committee of Shipwrights and Joiners* (Glasgow, 1893), Part II. p. 7, "The Shipwrights' Statement."

[2] *Amalgamated Society of Engineers' Journal*, March 1897.

[3] Correspondence in the *Star*, quoted in *Builder*, 8th April 1893. This sense of wrong is aggravated by an exaggerated consciousness of the pecuniary drain on the union funds involved in the payment of out-of-work benefit to the displaced members. At a branch meeting attended by one of the authors, when a demarcation dispute was under discussion, the fact that the work wrongfully engrossed by the rival trade would have sufficed to take three unemployed members off the books, and so save this great amalgamated union thirty-six shillings a week, was repeatedly adduced as a reason for aggressive action. The aggressive action subsequently cost that same union, at the lowest computation, many thousands of pounds.

interest, for him to be assured of a reasonable continuity of livelihood.[1]   Nor need we here determine whether, if it were possible to secure this end by fencing off each craft from encroachment, the social advantage of this assurance of livelihood would or would not outweigh the drawbacks of the expedient.   It so happens that in the advanced industrial communities of our time, the circumstances are so complex, and so perpetually changing, that it passes the wit of man to define the "right to a trade" in any way that will not produce the most palpable absurdities.

The first attempt is always to base the right on custom. It is natural enough that the workmen in any one town should expect and desire that the prevailing habits of work should be adhered to.   But irrespective of the fact that the "custom of the trade" is found to vary from town to town, and even from establishment to establishment, it is obvious that this affords, of itself, no rule when, as is almost invariably the case, the point at issue is some novel process or some hitherto unfamiliar product.   Each party then interprets the custom in a different way.   It may at first sight seem to be convenient to take, as a guide, the object or purpose of the product.   The shipwrights, in fact, will sometimes claim as their right all that concerns the construction and fitting of ships.   But a modern ship now includes everything that is found in a luxurious hotel; and a shipwright, on this interpretation, would not only have to work in steel as well as in wood, but would also have to be an accomplished engineer, boilermaker, brassfinisher, plumber, joiner, cabinetmaker, French polisher, upholsterer, painter, decorator, and electric light and bell fitter.   And if, in search of some dividing line between these manifestly different crafts, we turn to the tools required, we come to no less incongruous results.   Fifty years ago it would have been admitted without question that it was for the shipwright to use the adze and the mallet, and for the joiner to employ the hammer and the plane.   But the deck of a modern passenger steamer cannot be completed

[1] We recur to this point in our chapter on "Trade Union Assumptions."

without using all these tools, together with others borrowed
from the cabinetmaker and glazier, and machines altogether
unheard of in former times. If each craft is to be confined
to the tools which have characterised it from time immemorial,
the ship would be crowded with workmen each waiting for
the moment to perform his little bit of the common task;
all responsibility for the watertight character of the deck
would be lost, and there would still be altercations as to who
should use the newly-invented machines. Nor does the
material used afford us any dividing line. If this were
accepted, the advance of sanitation, with the disuse of leaden
pipes, would involve the ousting of the whole body of
certificated plumbers, in favor of engineers and bricklayers
destitute of sanitary knowledge. Moreover, in the crucial
instances of demarcation trouble, the material concerned is
common to both parties. Shipwrights, joiners, and cabinetmakers all work in wood; and shipwrights, boilermakers,
engineers, tinplate workers, and plumbers all handle iron.
If the substance fails to afford a dividing line, the disputants
will often fall back on its thickness. The central point in
dispute on the Tyne for two years may, in fact, be said to
have resolved itself into whether the limit of size of the iron
pipes to be fitted by the engineers and the plumbers
respectively, should be $2\frac{1}{2}$ or 3 inches, and whether the
joiners should or should not be confined to wood-work of
$1\frac{1}{2}$ inch thickness.[1] The demarcation disputes between the
boilermakers on the one hand, and the Chippers and Drillers

---

[1] "Mr. Ramsey (Shipwrights).—The question of the thickness of material is
again introduced. I ask is it fair that the joiner trade should have all the say
as to thickness of wood? Is it not a fact that both trades manipulate all thicknesses
of wood in their jobs? We lay and fix any kind of feathered and grooved ceiling
in cargo spaces in the hold of a vessel. . . . We have objected all along to this
Joint Committee dealing with this question of thickness of wood because we consider the principle is not sound. . .

"Mr. Roger (Joiners).— . . . Have we not the same liberty as a trade to
introduce a thickness as the other side has to object to it? . . . We hold we are
not exorbitant in our claim for lining $1\frac{1}{2}$ inches and under. It stands to reason
that joiners are the more competent men to do that class of work. I would like
to ask the other side where, in the ancient shipbuilding from Noah up to fifty
years since, they used nails for fastening. . . . We claim all lining from $1\frac{1}{2}$ inches

on the other, turn chiefly on the size of the holes which each
trade may cut in the iron plates.[1] The doctrine of the right
to the trade thus leads us to the absurd result that a particular task has to be allotted to one trade or another, not
according to its acquaintance with the purpose to be served,
or to its familiarity with the tools or material used, but according to the exact thickness of the pipe or board, or the
precise diameter of the hole in the iron plates, which the
fad, fashion, or science of the hour may prescribe. The
necessity of discovering some line which can be precisely
defined and accurately measured, leads, in fact, to a purely
arbitrary distribution of work, which has the added demerit
of the greatest possible instability.

For all this turmoil the employers have an easy
remedy. " The proper cure," declared the representative of
the Belfast shipbuilders, " is to revert to the old state of
affairs, where the employer selected the men most suited to
do the work " ; or, as the representative of the Tyneside shipbuilders put it, " to uphold the right of an employer to employ
whatever workmen he believes will best serve the purposes
of his trade or business without any regard to trade
societies." And the Scottish shipbuilders declared through
their representative, that "whether a plumber may join
a 2-inch pipe, but not one of $2\frac{1}{4}$ inches, whether a
joiner may dub a plank or a shipwright may plane a rail,
must appear to a disinterested person extremely trivial ; "
and they proposed summarily to " get rid altogether of this
fertile cause of quarrel by abolishing all arbitrary boundaries

and under, simply because it is material we are in the habit of working, and
because it is fastened to the grounds. . . .

" Mr. Wilkie (Shipwrights).— . . . In past years when there was no machinery [the joiners] might have made this claim, but that has all disappeared with
the introduction of machinery. . . . The joiners lay claim to this work because the
vessels carry passengers one way. I hold our claim is far more legitimate, seeing
they carry cargo the other way. . . . Clearly, if it is to be fitted up for cargo it
is shipwrights' work pure and simple."—*Minutes of Line of Demarcation Joint-
Committee of Shipwrights and Joiners* (Glasgow, 1893).

[1] *Report of Proceedings of the Sixth Annual Meeting of the Federation of
Engineering and Shipbuilding Trades* (Manchester, 1896).

between different handicrafts, and leaving it to the master . . . to settle . . . how work is to be distributed. . . ."

To the reader of the foregoing chapters, the Trade Union objection to any such abolition of the boundaries between craft and craft will at once be clear. If there is to be concerted action among the workmen—if, for instance, there is to be any representative machinery for Collective Bargaining,—it is absolutely necessary that the membership of each Trade Union should be precisely defined, so that each workman may know by what collective agreements he is bound.[1] It is, in fact, a condition of any organisation by trades that the lines between the trades, though not necessarily unalterable, should not be wantonly infringed at the mere caprice of a single employer.

But there is a further objection. If an individual employer were free, without encountering any resistance from the Trade Union concerned, to dispense with the services of men to whom he was paying the agreed Standard Rate, and to hand their work over bit by bit to some other sections of workmen, whom he could induce—perhaps actually through their own Trade Union—to work at a lower price, all hope of maintaining a Standard Rate for the more highly skilled unions would be at an end. Unless a Trade Union is to give up its whole case, it is bound, at all hazards, to maintain the principle that the Standard Rate, agreed to by the associated employers, shall be paid, in all establishments, for all the kinds of work to which it was mutually intended to apply.

A solution has therefore to be found which, whilst protecting the employer against the intolerable annoyance of unprovoked stoppages, the worry caused by any friction between trades, and the loss occasioned by "overlap" of work,[2] shall guarantee the Trade Unionists against encroach-

[1] This would obviously be even more necessary than at present if the Duke of Devonshire's proposal to make these collective agreements legally enforcible were adopted ; see the chapter on "The Method of Collective Bargaining."

[2] "A further and most material point in the estimation of the employer, and largely affecting his interest in cheapening and expediting the work, lies in the

ments on their Standard Rate, and prevent any undermining of their organisation. The experience of the last few years points, we think, to the need, if they are to cope with the difficulty, for the development of new structure in the Trade Union world, and for the adoption of a new principle.

When a demarcation dispute now occurs between two well-organised trades, the first attempt of their more reasonable representatives is to come to a mutual agreement as to how the work should be divided between them. Thus the numerous differences between the Boilermakers and the Engineers at Cardiff were amicably settled in 1891 by a formal treaty between the local branches.[1] But such negotiations will, like other Collective Bargaining, occasionally end in a deadlock. Here we have a case for which arbitration would seem to be specially fitted. There is, it is true, no dominant assumption shared by both sides on which the award can be based. But all the trades concerned accept, in principle, the same inconsistent array of different assumptions, and the decision cannot, as we have seen, be other than an arbitrary one. The main requirement, therefore, is that the arbitrator should not be suspected of being influenced by any other assumption than those admitted by

necessity there is that no one trade should, what is called, 'overlap' another. Which means that when one trade takes up a job on which others are to be subsequently engaged before it is completed, the work shall be so divided to each, that each in due rotation shall complete his share before the next commences upon his share, and that when the last has finished his portion the job shall be finished too. This is necessary to secure economy, quickness, and to fix responsibility in the performance of the job."

[1] This treaty is embodied in the "Ports of Cardiff, Penarth, and Barry By-laws" signed by five representatives of the United Society of Boilermakers, five of the Amalgamated Society of Engineers, one of the Steam-Engine Makers' Society, and one of another smaller body of engineers. The preamble is as follows: "For the purpose of more clearly defining and setting forth particular questions in dispute, and in consequence of certain misunderstandings arising between members of the Boilermakers' Society and those of the above-named engineers, respecting their respective claims to particular jobs in connection with the art of boilermaking and iron shipbuilding, we hereby agree that the undermentioned jobs may be worked at in the above ports by the respective parties without let or hindrance." The by-laws consist of five printed pages of technical details, providing for the assignment of certain specified work to the boilermakers and the engineers respectively.

the parties. This points to the establishment of a tribunal by the Trade Unions themselves.

We see such a tribunal arising in the Federation of the Engineering and Shipbuilding Trades, to which we have more than once alluded. During the last seven years innumerable cases of "overlap" and "encroachment" have been quietly disposed of by this tribunal, to the general satisfaction of all concerned. The transformation of the Executive Council of this Federation, formed of the chief salaried officials of fourteen unions, into a supreme court of arbitration in demarcation disputes takes place in the simplest manner.[1] If the Boilermakers of any port make a complaint that the Smiths are encroaching on their trade, neither party is allowed to cause any stoppage of work, and the Federal Executive is summoned to meet at a convenient centre. The officials of the two trades concerned bring up their witnesses and act as advocates. If the council is not satisfied that all the facts have been brought out, two members— say the general secretaries of the Steam Engine Makers' and Shipwrights' societies—are deputed to investigate the dispute on the spot, to consult with the employer, and to

---

[1] The present rule is as follows :—

Dispute between Societies.—If any dispute takes place between any of the societies forming this Federation, unless amicably settled, such dispute shall be referred to a Court of Arbitration selected by the parties affected by the dispute. When a Court is required the parties shall, if possible, mutually agree upon three disinterested referees ; failing this, each party to the dispute shall appoint one or two Arbitrators, who must be Trade Unionists ; the two or four Arbitrators to appoint an Umpire, and, in the event of the Arbitrators failing to agree, his decision shall be final and binding. The Umpire shall not be selected from any trade which may come into conflict with either of the parties to the difference. If a Court of Arbitration is not appointed within one month of an application being made for a reference to arbitration, the Executive shall have power to step in and appoint either Arbitrators or Umpire, as the case might be. The Court, when formed, to decide as to place of meeting, method of procedure, etc. ; each party to pay half of the expenses, unless otherwise ordered by the Court. That when a Court of Arbitration is required by any society in the Federation the Executive of said society shall notify the Secretary of the Federation, who shall then write to the other party affected to appoint an Arbitrator or Arbitrators as the Federation rules prescribe.—*Report of Proceedings of the Fifth Annual Meeting of Federation of Engineering and Shipbuilding Trades* (Manchester, 1895).

report to a future meeting, when a decision is come to. The
ten or twelve experienced Trade Union officials, who thus
adjust the differences between trade and trade, form an
almost ideal body for this purpose. They are free not only
from personal but also from class bias. Whether $2\frac{1}{2}$ inch
iron piping shall be fixed by an engineer or a plumber is
of no consequence to the pattern-maker or the shipwright.
Whether cabin lockers are to be prepared by the cabinetmaker and fixed by the joiner, or whether either trade should
begin and finish the whole job, is a matter of indifference to
the plater or the ironmoulder. Neither directly nor indirectly
have the adjudicators any other interest than that of preventing all stoppage of work by effecting a permanent settlement.
In this task they are aided by the fact that they start with
the same stock of unconscious assumptions as both the
trades concerned. Such arguments as "priority, position,
and purpose," which appear to the aggrieved capitalist as
fantastic and irrelevant as the lawyer's doctrine of "common
employment" does to the injured workman, receive that
serious attention which their iteration on both sides demands.
The adjudicators are steeped in the technical details of the
workshop, from processes and material to the evasions of the
employers and the tricks of the workmen. They possess, in
fact, to the full, the highest possible qualification of a judicial
authority, the unbounded confidence of the disputants, not
only in their knowledge and sympathy, but also in their
absolute impartiality as regards the issues in dispute.
Finally, it is no small advantage that, although their award
has no legal validity, it carries with it a certain latent coercive
authority. It would be difficult, if not impossible, for any
constituent body of the Federation deliberately to disregard
an award to which it had consented, without incurring the
serious penalty of finding its members practically excluded
from employment by a general boycott of the other workmen.[1]

---

[1] We may here remind the reader how, in our chapter on "Interunion Relations," we pointed out that a federation of heterogeneous bodies would not be stable
if based on simple majority rule. It is interesting to notice that the success of

But though a tribunal of this kind may, in demarcation cases, cut the Gordian knot, neither its deliberations nor its awards can permanently command confidence unless it is able to map out some definite and consistent policy, accepted by its litigants and adhered to in all its own decisions. Moreover, it cannot permanently secure industrial peace unless this policy coincides with the interests of the employers and is based on some assumption in which they can agree. Such a policy cannot be found in any doctrine of "the right to a trade," because, as we have shown in the crucial instances of new kinds of work, both parties may, with equal reasonableness, claim that equity is on their side. The solution of the problem is to be found in quite another direction. It is admitted that, within the limits of a single trade and a single union, it is for the employer, and the employer alone, to decide which individual workman he will engage, and upon which particular jobs he will employ him. What each Trade Union asks is that the recognised Standard Rate for the particular work in question shall be maintained and defended against possible encroachment. If the same conception were extended to the whole group of allied trades, any employer might be left free, within the wide circle of the federated unions, to employ whichever man he pleased on the disputed process, so long as he paid him

the Federation of the Engineering and Shipbuilding Trades as a court of arbitration is entirely dependent on its frank abandonment of any idea of representation in proportion to membership. Every union admitted, whether large or small, sends two representatives to the annual meeting, which elects one from each trade—invariably its salaried official—to form the federal executive. It is obvious that if the United Society of Boilermakers or the Amalgamated Society of Carpenters insisted on having twenty times the amount of representation or voting power as the Associated Blacksmiths or the United Pattern-makers, these latter would have no confidence in any award of an executive on which their rivals had so predominant a voice. Unfortunately, this very idea of equality, which has been a condition of the success of this federation, has hitherto stood in the way of the adhesion of the largest society concerned in the engineering and shipbuilding trades. The Amalgamated Society of Engineers, claiming to include within its own ranks all sections of skilled engineering mechanics, has hitherto found it inconsistent with its dignity to associate on equal terms with such smaller sectional societies as the United Pattern-makers' Association and the Associated Blacksmiths. Here again the idea of an all-embracing amalgamation has prevented the effective organisation of the Trade Union world.

the Standard Rate agreed upon for the particular task. The federated Trade Unions, instead of vainly trying to settle to which trade a task rightfully belongs, should, in fact, confine themselves to determining, in consultation with the associated employers, *at what rate it should be paid for*.[1]

If this simple principle were adopted,—say, in the great shipbuilding yards of the North-East coast,—and if it were frankly accepted by the associated employers and the Federation of Engineering and Shipbuilding Trades, the way would clear. The Standard Rate within the unquestioned domain of each particular trade would be determined, as at present, by Collective Bargaining between the associated employers and the Trade Union concerned. But directly any dispute arose as to which trade a job should belong—whether between employer and workman, or between different sections of wage-earners—the Collective Bargaining as to the rate of payment for that job would at once pass out of the hands of both the unions concerned, and would be undertaken, on behalf of the whole body of allied trades, by the Federation. The dispute would, therefore, be referred to the federal officials to negotiate, with the representatives of the associated employers, *a definite Standard Rate for that particular task*. In determining this special rate, they would be guided solely by the character of the work relatively to other operations in the same district. When, as in the notorious disputes between the fitters and plumbers, and the joiners and shipwrights, the earnings of both sets of workmen were practically identical, and the volume of work in

---

[1] This suggested solution has now been tentatively put forward by the young man of exceptional ability who in 1896 became general secretary of the Amalgamated Society of Engineers. Writing on the dispute with the Federation of Engineering Employers as to the employment of laborers on machines, Mr. George Barnes declared that "the whole question from our point of view is really one of wages, and inasmuch as the employers disclaim any intention of invading our territory as skilled mechanics, we believe that a mutually satisfactory solution of the difficulty is to be found in local joint committees, with a reference to the Board of Trade : *such committees to decide—having due regard to class of machines, quality of work, and standard rate of district—upon the wage to be paid*. We shall send in these proposals in proper form."—*Amalgamated Engineers' Monthly Journal*, April 1897.

dispute was of little consequence, the officials of the federated workmen and the associated employers would quickly arrive at an agreed rate. When, as in the more difficult case of a laborer being put to work a new machine, the rates widely diverged, the agreement would involve a longer bargaining. The representative of the associated employers would try to adduce evidence that the work was within the capacity of any general laborer fetched out of the street, and was therefore only worth sixpence an hour. The representative of the federated Trade Unionists would seek to establish that the work really required an engineer's skill or training, and that the particular laborer employed happened to be an exceptional man, who ought to be earning the engineer's rate of tenpence an hour. The advocates on both sides, representing great federations of which the actual disputants formed an infinitesimal proportion, would certainly manage to agree upon a rate for that special work, rather than involve the whole body of their clients in war. Once the special rate for the disputed process was authoritatively determined, the individual employer might engage any workman he pleased *at that rate*, whether he belonged to the Amalgamated Society of Engineers or to the humbler United Association of Machine Workers, or even to the National Laborers' Union. Thus, subject to the Standard Rate for the disputed work being fixed by Collective Bargaining between the associated employers and the federated Trade Unions, any shipbuilder would be at liberty, as between trade and trade, to select which man he pleased to do the work.

For the federated Trade Unions there would remain the further question whether, in the interests of the most perfect organisation, the workman so selected should be transferred from one union to another, or allowed to remain in his old society. If the job was only a temporary one, it would be unnecessary to make any change. If, on the other hand, the task for which he was selected was habitually performed by members of another union, or if it necessitated close companionship with them, it would probably avoid friction if he

were transferred to the roll of the other union. With
this, however, the employers would have nothing to do, and
the particular internal regulations decided upon by the
federation would, as in all other cases, be finally determined
by its constituents.[1]

This solution would not, we think, be objected to by
employers who, like the great captains of industry of
the North-East coast, have become accustomed to dealing with bodies of organised workmen.   It involves no
assumptions other than those to which they have long
since agreed.   The rates for the disputed jobs would be
settled, as they are at present, not by the individual employer or workman, but by collective agreements made by
the associated employers.   The only difference would be
that instead of making that collective agreement with a
single Trade Union, the officials of the associated employers
would deal, as regards the disputed jobs, with officials representing the whole body of Trade Unionists in the district
The employers would be freed from the annoyance of finding
their works stopped by the men's quarrels, and they would
be confirmed in their freedom to allot their jobs in the way
they thought best.

The Trade Unionists, on the other hand, would secure
their fundamental principle of maintaining the Standard
Rate and all the machinery for Collective Bargaining. They
would gain complete protection against any attempt to make
the introduction of a new machine or a new product an

[1] In making these transfers of particular workmen from union to union,
difficulty might arise from the difference in rates of contribution and scales of
benefit between different societies.   This could easily be surmounted, as regards
the workman, by the new society admitting him at once to full benefits, according to his length of membership in the union he leaves.   Mutual arrangements of
this sort already exist for the transfer of members between Scottish and English
unions in the same trade, and some others.   If the unions giving large benefit
demurred to accepting members on these terms, it would be easy for the Federation to smooth the way by giving from federal funds, in respect of each man
officially transferred on demarcation grounds, a sum equal to the accumulated
balance per member possessed by his new colleagues.   Any such question of
financial adjustment between union and union would easily be settled by the
practical good sense of Trade Union officials.

excuse for lowering the rate hitherto paid for a particular grade of skill. On the other hand, they would have frankly to abandon the obsolete doctrine of a "right to a trade." They would have to allow each individual employer complete freedom, provided that he paid the Standard Rates agreed upon for the various kinds of work, to allot them among the trades as he found most convenient, irrespective of past custom. And if the Trade Unions wished to avoid friction among the workmen, and perfect their organisation, they would have to give up all idea of restricting the entrance into the several unions, otherwise than by requiring their recruits to be able to earn the recognised Standard Rate. In both cases, as this and the preceding chapter will have shown, they would only be giving up a principle which the vast majority of unions, over the greater part of the field of British industry, have found it impossible to carry out.

CHAPTER XII

THE IMPLICATIONS OF TRADE UNIONISM

IN the preceding chapters we have attempted systematically to analyse all the current regulations of British Trade Unionism; we have still to set forth and explain certain features of Trade Union policy which are implied in the use of its Methods or are subsidiary to the enforcement of its Regulations.

We will begin with the Method of Mutual Insurance. We have seen how important a part is played, except in a few industries, by the friendly society side of Trade Unionism —how it supplies both adventitious attraction and adventitious support to the workmen's combinations, even when its use as a separate method of enforcing common rules has faded out of sight. Trade Unionists are proud of the great insurance societies which have been built up by their own efforts, and most determinedly oppose any project which seems inimical to their continued prosperity. This affords an explanation of the deadweight of silent opposition which the Trade Unions have hitherto thrown against all competing schemes of insurance. When the rival project is an employer's benefit society, the Trade Unionists object to it for many additional reasons, with which we shall deal in a subsequent part of this chapter. But even when an insurance project is quite unconnected with industrial objects, and takes the impersonal form of a Government Old Age Pension scheme, the Trade Unionists strenuously object to any premium to be levied by way of deduction from their weekly earnings or other form of direct contribution, which would, it is feared, make the workmen less ready to subscribe to a trade friendly society. We find this feeling clearly expressed in Mr. Broadhurst's Minority Report in the Aged Poor Commission of 1895. "The evidence tendered by working class witnesses goes, in my opinion, to show that any scheme involving contributions, otherwise than through the rates and taxes, would meet with much opposition from the wage-earners of every grade. The Friendly Societies and the Trade Unions, to which the working class owe so much, naturally view with some apprehension the creation of a gigantic rival insurance society backed by the whole power of the Government. The collection of contributions from millions of ill-paid households is already found to be a task of great difficulty, intensified by every depression of trade or other calamity. For the State to enter into competition for the available subscriptions of the wage-earners must necessarily increase the difficulty of all Friendly Societies, Trade Unions, and Industrial Insurance Companies, whose members and customers within the United Kingdom probably number, in the aggregate, from eleven to twelve millions of persons. On the other hand, Mr. Charles Booth's proposal for the grant of a pension from public funds, without personal contributions, may secure the hearty support both of the Trade Unions and the Friendly Societies."[1]

So far the Trade Unions stand shoulder to shoulder with the ordinary friendly societies. But when it comes to defining the legal status of the two forms of combination, they at once part company. The friendly societies, confining them-

---

[1] Minority Report of Mr. Henry Broadhurst, M.P. (Friendly Society of Operative Stonemasons), in *Report of the Royal Commission on Aged Poor* (C. 7604), 1895, p. xcix.

This hostility is naturally most marked among members of the great trade friendly societies. The coalminers, who make practically no use of friendly benefits in their Trade Unionism, have always shown themselves willing to encourage the Permanent Relief Funds, through which, by the joint subscriptions of employers and employed, provision is now made for the sufferers from accident within the limits of a given coalfield.

selves strictly to one definite function, have obtained the
privilege, on registration of their rules and submission of
their accounts, of becoming legally incorporated bodies, able
to enter into enforcible contracts with their members and
outsiders, and to sue or be sued in their corporate capacity.
Such complete legalisation does not suit the great trade
societies. Some measure of incorporation they must have,
in order that the money subscribed by all alike may not,
with impunity, be embezzled by those in whose hands it is
placed. But the whole friendly society business of a Trade
Union is, as we have seen in the chapter on " The Method of
Mutual Insurance," only an adventitious adjunct, strictly subordinate to its main function of securing, for its members,
better conditions of employment. In pursuit of these better
conditions the Trade Union must be free, in any emergency,
to use every penny of its funds in the fight. It does not
therefore undertake to maintain all or any of its benefits, if a
majority of the members for the time being wish the cash in
hand to be applied to other purposes. Moreover, it is, as we
explained in the chapter on " The Method of Collective Bargaining," an essential condition of Trade Union action that
the decision of the great mass of the members should be
enforced on individual recalcitrants. A member who persists
in acting in flagrant disobedience to the rules of the association he has joined, whether they relate to friendly benefits
or not, must eventually incur the penalty of expulsion, involving the forfeiture of all claim to future benefit. A Trade
Union would therefore be fatally hampered if it entered into
legally binding contracts to pay particular benefits, or if it
were possible for an aggrieved member to appeal, against
the decision of his fellow-members, to the unfriendly courts
of justice. But this inimical action of discontented members
is not the whole danger. Though combination in restraint
of trade is no longer a criminal offence, it may still, as we
shall see, be made the ground of a civil action for damages.[1]
The indefinite and anomalous state of the law with regard

[1] See the Appendix on " The Legal Position of Collective Bargaining."

to libel and conspiracy leaves open, too, a wide door for harassing proceedings. Already, any agent or official of a Trade Union is liable to be sued by an employer or non-unionist workman, whenever the Trade Union action has, through him, caused loss or damage. If the Trade Union could be sued in its corporate capacity, the members would quickly find the funds which they had subscribed for sick and funeral benefits, attached at the suit of employers aggrieved by a threat to strike, by the libel of an injudicious branch secretary, or by the insolence of a picket. Thus, whilst complete incorporation might protect the individual member against a majority of his fellows, it would put his provision for sickness and old age at the mercy of employers' claims for damages. The insecurity of the friendly society side of Trade Unionism is, in fact, inherent in the conjunction of trade and friendly purposes, and complete legalisation would actually diminish, rather than increase, the likelihood of the funds subscribed for friendly benefits being ultimately applied to meet them.

These considerations explain the peculiar legal status which the Trade Unionists of 1868-71 succeeded in winning for their associations. The Trade Union Act of 1871, whilst giving a duly registered union much the same status as a friendly society so far as the protection of its property was concerned, expressly provided that a Trade Union should not be able to sue, nor be liable to be sued, in respect of any agreement between itself and its members, or with an employers' association or another union. Trade Unions, in fact, have not been clothed with legal personality any further than for the limited purpose of protecting their funds against theft or embezzlement. They are thus in the anomalous position, to quote the Majority Report of the Labor Commission, of exercising "collective action without legal collective responsibility."[1] This peculiar status the Trade Unionists wish to maintain. The Trade Union Minority of

[1] *Fifth and Final Report of the Royal Commission on Labor*, 1894 (C. 7421), par. 149, p. 54.

the Labor Commission resolutely refused to entertain the suggestion "that it would be desirable to make Trade Unions liable to be sued by any person who had a grievance against the action of their officers or agents. To expose the large amalgamated societies of the country with their accumulated funds sometimes reaching a quarter of a million sterling, to be sued for damages by any employer in any part of the country, or by any discontented member or non-unionist, for the action of some branch secretary or delegate, would be a great injustice. If every Trade Union were liable to be perpetually harassed by actions at law on account of the doings of individual members; if Trade Union funds were to be depleted by lawyers' fees and costs, if not even by damages or fines, it would go far to make Trade Unionism impossible for any but the most prosperous and experienced artisans. The present freedom of Trade Unions from any interference by the courts of law—anomalous as it may appear to lawyers—was, after prolonged struggle and Parliamentary agitation, conceded in 1871, and finally became law in 1875. Any attempt to revoke this hardly-won charter of Trade Union freedom, or in any way to tamper with the purely voluntary character of their associations, would, in our opinion, provoke the most embittered resistance from the whole body of Trade Unionists, and would, we think, be undesirable from every point of view."[1]

Passing now to the Method of Collective Bargaining, we notice, in the first place, that it implies the removal of all legal prohibition of combination "in restraint of trade." So long as trade combination was a criminal offence, the Method of Collective Bargaining was not open either to employers or to workmen, and Trade Unionists, when they could not get legislation, had to resort to secret compacts among themselves, resting on the Method of Mutual Insurance. Freedom of combination is now professedly conceded, so far as the criminal law is concerned, but even in England there are

---

[1] *Fifth and Final Report of the Royal Commission on Labor*, 1894 (C. 7421), p. 146.

signs, as will be seen from our appendix on the Legal Position of Collective Bargaining, that, as regards civil liability, Trade Unionists have still a battle to fight. If the recent decisions are upheld, the employers will be able to proceed for heavy damages against any Trade Union official who uses the ordinary arts of bargaining on behalf of his constituents, or who even advises the workmen of a particular firm to refuse the employer's terms. Every strike will bring a shower of writs, ending in bankruptcy proceedings; and Trade Union executives, finding themselves exposed to this harassing persecution, will again become secret conspiracies. If, therefore, Collective Bargaining is to survive as a method of Trade Unionism, Parliament will have to complete the work of 1871-75, and definitely instruct the judges that nothing is to be actionable in labor disputes when done by or in pursuance of a combination of workmen, which would not be actionable if done by a partnership of traders as part of their business, and in the pursuit of their personal gain.

But the workman's freedom of contract, and, still more, his freedom of combination, necessarily involves, as we have seen, his freedom to stipulate with whom he will consent to associate in his labor. This liberty to refuse to accept engagements in establishments where non-unionists are employed, is, in such highly-organised trades as the Northumberland Coalminers or the Lancashire Cotton-spinners, tantamount to compulsory Trade Unionism. And wherever Collective Bargaining is perfected by such formal machinery as the Joint Boards or Joint Committees of the North of England Manufactured Iron Trade, or the Northumberland and Durham Miners, or by such national treaties as those regulating the wages and other conditions of labor of the Boilermakers, hand Papermakers, and factory Boot and Shoe Operatives, the collective regulations become virtually binding throughout the whole trade. The compulsion on the individual, it need hardly be said, is none the less real and effective because it takes an impersonal, peaceful, and entirely decorous form. A plater or rivetter who, because he is out-

side the United Society of Boilermakers, is politely refused
work by every shipbuilder on the North-East coast, is just
as much compelled to join the union, as if membership were,
by a new Factory Act, made a legal condition of employment.

Collective Bargaining thus implies, in its fullest development, compulsory Trade Unionism. It was the recognition
of this fact which led to the remarkable proposal of the Duke
of Devonshire, and some of the most eminent of his colleagues
on the Labor Commission, to enable Trade Unions to enter
into legally binding collective agreements on behalf of all
their members. The great employers of the North of England
find that there is, in their highly - organised industries,
practically no non-unionist minority which they can play off
against the Trade Union, whose officials therefore virtually
speak in the name of all the available workmen. On the
other hand, they have no guarantee that individual branches
or members will loyally abide by the collective agreement
when it is made. It was therefore proposed, by five of the
largest employers of labor on the Commission,[1] that when a
collective agreement had been made between a Trade Union
and an Employers' Association, these bodies should be, in their
corporate capacities, responsible in damages for any breach
by their members, and should be entitled, on the other hand
to recover such damages from the individuals who had infringed the treaty. This suggestion was, as we have mentioned
vehemently objected to by the Trade Unionists, because it

[1] See the "Observations appended to the Report" (C. 7421), pp. 115-119
These were signed, not only by the Duke of Devonshire (himself a great employer
of labor in many industrial undertakings), but also by Sir David Dale of Darling
ton (Ironmaster and Coalowner), Mr. Thomas Ismay (Shipowner), Mr. George
Livesey (Gas Company Director), and Mr. William Tunstill (Railway Director)
They also gained the support of Sir Michael Hicks-Beach, Mr. Leonard Courtney
and Sir Frederick Pollock. This proposal has more than once received the
approval of the *Times*. Thus, in a leading article of the 10th June 1897, relating
to the progress of the Trade Unions, it observed that "at present, though free
from the most serious of the disabilities under which they once labored, they
have no true corporate existence ; they cannot make enforceable contracts ; they
can bind, broadly speaking, their members to nothing. One of the few practical
suggestions which emerged from the stream of loose talk passing through the Labor
Commission was a proposal that this should be altered—a proposal which found
favor with some of the most sober-minded of the members of the Commission."

was incidentally intended to give the Trade Union a legal personality, which would render it liable to be sued in the law courts by any disaffected member or aggrieved outsider. So sweeping a change in Trade Union status was, however, not necessary for the Duke of Devonshire's proposal. His object would have been secured if it had been provided that the Trade Union should be liable to be sued only in respect of collective agreements made with the Employers' Association, and then only for definite penalties specified in such agreements. To this definitely restricted liability no Trade Union need object, provided that it were given, as was contemplated, the corresponding right to recover the penalty from its members in default, and provided that the Employers' Association were made reciprocally responsible to the Trade Union for the defaults of particular employers.

Any such legal enforcement of collective agreements as was proposed by the Duke of Devonshire and his colleagues would, of course, greatly encourage the use of Collective Bargaining as a Method of Trade Unionism. It was, in fact, expressly with the view of facilitating this " substitution of agreements between associations for agreements between individual employers and individual workmen," which the Commissioners had found to be " on the whole, in accordance with the public interest," that so momentous a change was proposed. Trade Unionists would entirely agree that it would " result in the better observance, for definite periods, of agreements with regard to wage-rates, hours of labor, apprenticeship rules, demarcation of work, profit-sharing, and joint insurance schemes." In all but the best organised industries, the workmen's difficulty is, not so much to get better terms granted, as to get them adhered to. Such grievously oppressed trades as the bakers, the tramwaymen, the dock laborers, and almost any section of women workers, may often, by a sensational strike, and the support of public opinion, secure an agreement promising better conditions of employment. But the day after the agreement is signed it begins to crumble away. One employer after another

" interprets " it in his own fashion, and the workers in his establishment, no longer upheld by the excitement of a general strike, and frequently not precisely understanding what is happening, are induced to acquiesce by fear of losing their employment, if not by actual threats of dismissal. If the Trade Union could sue any such employer for damages for breaking the collective agreement, its terms would, for the time being, become, in effect, part of the law of the land. The highly-organised trades would find their advantage rather in the direction of improved discipline among their own members. Until the expiration of the collective agreement at any rate, a recalcitrant minority would find itself confronted, not only by the displeasure of the majority, but also by all the terrors of the law courts.[1] Any such arrangement would therefore greatly strengthen the influence of the Trade Union as a whole, and would, in all industries, tend enormously to the development of such an expert Trade Union Civil Service as is already enjoyed by the Cotton Operatives. Whether this addition to the compulsory character of Collective Bargaining would prove as harmless to the consumers as it would to the great employers ; whether, to use the phrase of Mr. Gerald Balfour, M.P., the Duke of Devonshire's " Socialism by Trade Option " is a safe kind of Socialism for the community to establish ; affords an interesting problem for consideration by economists and statesmen.

The Method of Legal Enactment has implications of its own, which compel us to touch on the wider question of the part taken by the Trade Unionists in the party struggles of politics. We have already described how Mutual Insurance and Collective Bargaining depend on the legal status of the Trade Unions. Freedom of combination, protection for

---

[1] If a Trade Union were made liable for the observance of the agreement for a definite period, it is obvious that no member of the union could be permitted to withdraw for that period, at any rate so far as concerns observing the agreement and contributing towards its expenses. Thus, Trade Union membership would become, in effect, not only universally compulsory, but also irrevocable for a long term. The same would be the case with regard to membership of an employers' association.

Trade Union funds, and liberty to strike have not been gained without political conflicts, in which the Trade Unionists have had to use every means of influencing the legislature. But these questions have involved only certain definite legal reforms, outside the scope of party politics ; and they could, once Parliament was convinced, be finally disposed of.   It is only in connection with the Method of Legal Enactment that the Trade Unions, as such, find it necessary to secure a permanent influence in the House of Commons.   Every year one section or another calls for new regulations to be passed into law, in the form of an amendment of the Factory or Mines, Railway or Merchant Shipping Acts.   The administration of these statutes requires constant supervision, which can only be effectively exercised from the House of Commons.   And with the growth of the public administration of industry, whether central or local, the Trade Unions consider it essential that they should be in a position to secure the strict observance of the standard conditions by the national and municipal employers of labor.

It was, therefore, a vital political necessity that the Trade Unionists should obtain complete electoral rights.   From 1831 to 1884 the banners of the Unions always appeared at the great demonstrations in favor of Parliamentary Reform.   The whole strength of the Trade Union movement was thrown on the side of the ballot, the removal of tests and property qualifications, and everything that promised to facilitate the expression of Trade Union views in Parliament and on local bodies.   Thus, between 1860 and 1885, when the Liberal Party was striving for extensions of the franchise, and the Conservative Party was, with the exception of a few months in the session of 1867, fiercely resisting reform, the Liberal leaders could count on the adhesion of the great bulk of the Trade Unionists.   During these years every prominent Trade Union official belonged to the Radical Wing of the Liberal Party.[1]

---

[1] The revulsion of feeling between 1871 and 1874, caused by the incredible stupidity of the Liberal Cabinet of those years in connection with the criminal

But this alliance with the Liberal Party has proved only temporary. The completion of electoral reform has, since 1885, fallen into the background, the Liberal leaders being indifferent, if not actually hostile, to the Trade Union demands for Manhood Suffrage, Payment of Members, and Payment of Election Expenses, whilst the lukewarm official proposals for Registration Reform have evoked no enthusiasm. Trade Union politics have therefore entered on a new phase. The Trade Unionists, having obtained the vote, now wish to make use of it to enforce, by Legal Enactment, such of their Common Rules as they see a chance of getting public opinion to support. Here they find themselves almost equally balanced between the claims of rival political parties. Judged by past performances, the Conservatives are less unsympathetic to the legal regulation of industry than the Liberals ; whilst the Workmen's Compensation Act of 1897 has placed the Trade Unionists under a fresh obligation to the Conservative Party. On the other hand, the Collectivist wing of the present Liberal Party is beginning, by professions of conversion from " Manchesterism," and large promises of future legislation, to make a special bid for Trade Union support. The leaders on both sides are candidly hostile to the principle of collective regulation, and the Yorkshire Coalminer or Lancashire Cotton-spinner may well doubt whether Sir William Harcourt and Mr. John Morley are any nearer in agreement with him than Mr. Balfour or Mr. Chamberlain. Meanwhile a third party has arisen, to point the moral and compete for the workmen's suffrages. The Socialist candidates are ready to promise

persecution of Trade Unionism, led, as we have described in our *History of Trade Unionism* (pp. 256-280), to an organised revolt, to independent candidatures, and to a certain transference of votes to progressive Conservatives who agreed to satisfy the Trade Union demands. The popular Conservative legislation of 1874-75 (the Trade Union Act and the " Factories (Health of Women) Act "), which embodied a great measure of what the Trade Unionists had been asking for, no doubt detached a large section of workmen from their alliance with Liberalism, especially in Lancashire. But so strong was the impulse towards an extension of the franchise that the leaders, even in Lancashire, made up their quarrel with the Liberal Party, and acted with it until the Reform Bills of 1884-85 were safely passed into law.

the Trade Unionists a systematic and complete regulation of all the conditions of employment. But they show a lamentable deficiency of technical knowledge of the exact regulations required, and they mingle their proposals with revolutionary Shibboleths as to the "nationalisation of the means of production, distribution, and exchange," which the bulk of the Trade Unionists fail even to comprehend. Accordingly, the strong desire of nearly all sections of Trade Unionists for this or that measure of legal enactment does not at present produce much effect on general politics. Unlike their demand for the franchise, it does not, for the moment, attach them, as Trade Unionists, to any political party. But it implies that they would be strongly, and even permanently, drawn to any political leader, of whatever party, who shared their faith in the efficacy of the Common Rule, and who convinced them that he had the technical knowledge, the will, and the Parliamentary power to carry into law such proposals for legal regulation as each trade from time to time definitely demanded.

If now we leave the Methods of Trade Unionism, and pass to its Regulations, we shall see that these, too, have their own implications, and that Trade Unionists oppose or accept certain industrial forms according as these appear to be inimical to Trade Union progress, or the reverse. Foremost among these implications is the strong Trade Union objection to "Home Work," that is, to work being given out by the employer, to be done elsewhere than in the factory or workshop which he provides.[1] In all the industries in which "out-working" prevails to any considerable extent, this

---

[1] Under this head we include all arrangements under which the manual-working wage-earner performs his task elsewhere than in a factory or workshop provided and controlled by his employer. The term "home work" is sometimes used to designate only work taken home by factory workers after the expiration of their factory day (see *Home Work amongst Women*, by Margaret H. Irwin, Glasgow, 1897). On the other hand, the "outworker" may not work in his own home, but (as at Sheffield) on a "wheel" or "trough" rented in a "tenement factory," or (as sometimes among the Scottish hand Shoemakers) in a co-operative workshop rented by a group of workmen or by the Trade Union itself.

objection, steadily growing in intensity for the last half-century, has latterly risen into a crusade. The National Union of Boot and Shoe Operatives [1] and the Scottish Tailors' Society now put the complete abolition of home work in the front of their programme. The English Tailors' Union, though it includes home workers, is scarcely less emphatic. " If," reports the General Secretary, " we cannot altogether abolish this curse we can at least prevent its growth, and wherever there is the slightest sign of the system being introduced into towns where it has hitherto been unknown, it is our duty not to tolerate it for a single minute, but use our utmost endeavors to oppose its introduction, and stamp it out as far as lies in our power in all places where it at present exists." [2]

This vehement objection to home work comes as a surprise to persons unfamiliar with the actual conditions of the wage-earner's existence. One of the principal grievances that Trade Unions are formed to remedy is, as we have seen, the autocratic manner in which the employer, in any unregulated trade, determines at what hours his workshop will open and close, when his workpeople shall take their meals or enjoy their holidays, how fast and how continuously they shall work, and a host of petty regulations, easily passing, with a brutal foreman, into gross personal tyranny. From all this the man or woman working in the home is apparently free. Once the work is taken out of the employer's warehouse, the worker is at liberty to do it when and where and how he pleases, free from the constant supervision and arbitrary meddling of the foreman. Home work has, to the philanthropist, certain sentimental attractions. There is no breaking-up of family life. Husband and wife can work side

---

[1] The National Union of Boot and Shoe Operatives puts high up among its objects the " establishment of healthy and proper workshops, the employers to find room, grindery, fixtures, fire, and gas free of charge."—*Rules of the National Union of Boot and Shoe Operatives* (Leicester, 1892).

[2] *Report of the Fourteenth Conference of Deputies of the Amalgamated Society of Tailors, held in Liverpool,* August 1891 (Manchester, 1891); *Secretary's Report to the Conference,* p. 17.

by side at a common task, whilst the babies frolic around, and the child from school prepares its lessons under the father's eye. No peremptory factory bell summons the wife and mother from her housekeeping or family cares. Cooking the dinner, nursing the baby, teaching the child apprentice—all can be dovetailed into each other, and into the breadwinning craft. The task of every member of the household can be adjusted to their several capacities, even the aged grandfather by the fireside, and the school-girl on her half-holiday, being usefully employed. When illness comes, one member of the family can nurse another, whilst continuing to earn a subsistence. The custom of working at home seems, in fact, to combine all possible advantages. To personal freedom and domestic bliss, there is added the greatest economy of time and the utmost utilisation of capacity.[1]

Unfortunately, the facts of the home worker's life in no way correspond to this Utopian picture. To take work home means, in the words of a boot operative, " to make home miserable."[2] It is conceivable that the highly-educated and well-disciplined journalist, barrister, banker, or stockbroker might find it pleasant to do all his professional work under the eyes of his wife, and amid the playing of his well-bred children. But even he would hardly like to work, eat, and sleep, not to say also cook and wash, in one and the same apartment. The middle-class admirer of home work forgets that the " home " of the ordinary town wage-earner consists of one, or, at most, of two small rooms, and that his work is not done in pen and ink, but in leather, cloth, fur, hot metal, glue, and other substances involving dirt, smells, and effluvia. It is impossible to use, as a workshop, the living room of a family, without submitting to conditions of temperature and atmosphere, crowding and disorder, which are

---

[1] See the description in Dr. Kuno Frankenstein's *Der Arbeiterschutz* (Leipzig, 1896).

[2] *Monthly Report*, National Union of Boot and Shoe Operatives, March 1891.

destructive to health and comfort. All these conditions make the workshop-home positively repulsive to father, mother, and children alike, and every opportunity is sought of escaping from it—the man to the public-house, the woman to gossip with her neighbours, and the children to the streets.[1] Instead of maintaining the integrity of the family, and fostering the domestic virtues, it is accordingly frequently asserted by the most experienced observers that no influence is at the present day more ruinous than home work in its effect on family life and personal character.

Public opinion is, therefore, for reasons of sanitation, family life, and personal character, tending more and more to deprecate any combination of the workshop with the living-room. What has influenced the Trade Unionist is much more the discovery that the custom of home work has a ruinous effect upon wages. In the trades in which this custom prevails, the standard earnings of the home workers are far below the wage customary for equally skilled labor

---

[1] Some glimpse of what home work implies even to a man of very exceptional character, is afforded by the following extract from the Autobiography of Francis Place. (See the *History of Trade Unionism*, chap. ii.) " The consequences of a man and his wife living in the same room in which the man works is mischievous to them in all respects, and I here add, as a recommendation to all journeymen, tradesmen, and other workmen . . . to make almost any sacrifice to keep possession of two rooms, however small and however inconveniently situated as regards the place of their employment. Much better is it to be compelled to walk a mile or even two miles to and from their work to a lodging with two rooms, than to live close to their work with one room. . . . A neat clean room, though it be as small as a closet, and however few the articles of furniture, is of more importance in its moral consequences than any one seems hitherto to have supposed. The room in which we now lived was a front room at a baker's shop. The house had three windows in the front, two in the room and one in a large closet at the end of the room. In this closet I worked. It was a great accommodation to us ; it enabled my wife to keep the room in better order ; it was advantageous, too, in its moral effects. Attendance on the child was not, as it had been, always in my presence. I was shut out from seeing the fire lighted, the room washed and cleaned, and the clothes washed and ironed, as well as the cooking. We frequently went to bed as we had but too often been accustomed to do, with a wet or damp floor, and with wet clothes hanging in the room. Still a great deal of the annoyance and too close an interference with each other in many disagreeable particulars (which having but one room made it inevitable) were removed—happily removed for ever."—Place's MS. Autobiography, quoted in *Labor in the Longest Reign*, by Sidney Webb (London, 1897) ; now included in the *Life of Francis Place* by Graham Wallas (London, 1897).

in the factory industries. The chain and nail workers in the Black Country, the trouser and "juvenile suit" hands in East London, the garret cabinetmakers of Bethnal Green, the cottage bootmakers of the Leicestershire villages, and more noteworthy even than these, the skilled outworking cutlers of Sheffield, were all found, by the House of Lords' Committee on the Sweating System (1890), to be suffering to an extent that could "hardly be exaggerated," from "earnings barely sufficient to sustain existence ; hours of labor such as to make the lives of the workers periods of almost ceaseless toil, hard and unlovely to the last degree ; sanitary conditions injurious to the health of the persons employed and dangerous to the public."[1]   In every one of the trades in which this august Committee reported that "sweating" prevailed, the custom of working in the operatives' own homes was discovered to exist. To the Trade Unionist this close connection between home work and low wages is no mere coincidence. Experience shows that work given out to be done otherwise than on the employers' premises almost invariably becomes the subject

[1] *Report and Evidence of the Select Committee of the House of Lords on the Sweating System* (H. L. 62 of 1890) ; see also "The Lords and the Sweating System," by Beatrice Potter (Mrs. Sidney Webb) in *Nineteenth Century*, June 1890 ; and the references given in Fabian Tract, No. 50, "Sweating, its Cause and Remedy."

It must not be supposed that the custom of "giving out" work to be done in the workers' own homes is a new or an increasing evil. It is, on the contrary, merely the surviving remnant of what was once in many trades the prevailing system. In our *History of Trade Unionism* (pp. 28, 32, 48) we have incidentally described its prevalence in the West of England cloth manufacture, in the hosiery trade, among the Sheffield cutlers, the Spitalfields silk-workers, and the Scottish cotton-weavers. In the early stages of capitalist industry a manufactory, as Du Cellier observes with regard to France, "was not the site but the centre of an industry ; the manufacturer produced the samples and designs . . . but had generally not a single loom working in his own house" (*Histoire des Classes Laborieuses en France*, p. 222). It was an innovation to collect a number of wage-earners in the employer's own workshop, where they worked under constant supervision, and could practise division of labor. In all important industries of Great Britain this has now become the dominant industrial form. It is where the two systems are still competing with each other— where factory and home work co-exist and produce for the same market—that the evil of "sweating" is at its worst.—*Der Arbeiterschutz*, by Dr. Kuno Frankenstein (Leipzig, 1896), p. 492.

of isolated, personal bargaining between the individual wage-earner and the capitalist employer. " To people working *each in their own little shop*," writes Mr. John Burnett, " from early morning until late at night, combination is above all things difficult. . . . One man or one woman can be played off against another, and the prices of labor are thus subject to the daily haggle of workers competing for bread. This is clearly and unmistakably the result of the small workshop system, which is undoubtedly the root of many, if not all the evils from which the nailworkers suffer." [1] The same consequences of " outwork " were noticed by a careful observer of the Liverpool tailors as long ago as 1860. " The work," wrote Mr. (now Sir) Godfrey Lushington, " admits of being done at home, and the operative who engages himself on these terms loses the benefit of the check which the presence of his fellows maintains upon the encroachments of the employer. In such a trade it must always be difficult to establish united action. . . . The common method of reduction is for the employer to produce a garment and say, ' I had this made for 10s. 6d., I cannot pay you 13s. 6d. for a similar article. You too must make it for 10s. 6d. or go elsewhere.' The Society cannot prevent this." [2] Home work, in fact, necessarily involves Individual Bargaining, and makes, moreover, the enforcement of any Common Rule practically impossible.

Finally, experience proves the home worker's " freedom " as to the hours of labor to be delusive. It is true that the Soho tailor can break off when he chooses, and go round to the public-house for a drink ; or the woman " picking peas " in a back alley of Peterborough [3] may get up now and again

[1] *Report to the Board of Trade on the Sweating System* at the East End of London, H. C. No. 331 of 1888.

[2] *Report of the Social Science Association on Trade Societies and Strikes* (London, 1860). Article on the Liverpool Tailors by Mr. (afterwards Sir) Godfrey Lushington, who subsequently became permanent Under-Secretary of State for the Home Department.

[3] One of the principal women's industries in the City of Peterborough is picking dried peas ; sorting by hand the black or defective peas from those of lighter

to gossip with a friend without fear of a foreman's reprimand. But when the rate of pay is so small that even sixteen hours' work does not earn more than the bare day's subsistence, all " free " time disappears ; and to quote again the House of Lords' Committee, " the lives of the workers " become " periods of almost ceaseless toil." This subtle economic compulsion to "work all the hours that God made," is heightened by the ease with which the giver-out of work can demand that the product shall be delivered by a definite time. It is one of the chief attractions of "outwork" to the employers, as they frankly told the House of Lords' Committee, that the utmost possible rapidity in the execution of pressing orders is unfettered by any conception of a normal working day. To meet the spasmodic demands of the "season," thousands of home-working families can, by a word, be automatically compelled to labor all the night through.

The economic effect of home work is thus to undermine the Standard Rate, to destroy the Normal Day, and to abstract, from the total remuneration of the operative, all the advantages of room, fire, light, and sanitary conveniences which would otherwise be provided by the employer. Nor are these insidious effects confined merely to the outworkers. The operatives employed on similar tasks on the employer's premises have to submit to reductions of wages and extensions of hours, under the threat of the diversion of more and more of the business to their out-working competitors.[1] Home work, in fact, makes all Trade Unionism impossible.

Closely related to the Trade Unionists' opposition to Home Work is their rooted objection to the " small master "

color, in order that, when ground into flour, the mass may be as nearly white as possible.

[1] See the cases described from actual experience in " Pages from a Work-girl's Diary," by Beatrice Potter (Mrs. Sidney Webb), in *Nineteenth Century*, September 1888. It is not that the home workers are paid actually lower rates than the workshop hands : a recent Glasgow inquiry again shows this common impression to be erroneous (*Home Work amongst Women*, by Margaret H. Irwin, Glasgow, 1897). The competition of the outdoor with the indoor hands drags down the wages of both.

system. To a certain section of social reformers this seems incomprehensible. The wage-earners are perpetually complaining that they are deprived of access to the means of production, and that rents and profits are monopolised by a relatively small class. The existence, in certain industries, of numerous small establishments would seem to afford, at least to the most energetic workmen, an obvious means of rising to the rank of masters. Yet these " stepping-stones to higher things " are objected to, not so much by the thriftless workman, careless of his future, but by the most thoughtful and experienced Trade Unionists, that is, by exactly the men whose superiority in energy, persistency, and organising power might reasonably be expected to lead to their personal success.

The explanation of this paradox will not be difficult for those who appreciate the Trade Union position. Working men do not combine in order to assist a few of the best among their number to escape out of their class, but for the purpose of raising the class itself. To some shrewd economists it seems even a misfortune to the wage-earning class that they should, as Professor Marshall observes, " every year give over to the ranks of the rich a great number of the strongest and ablest, the most enterprising and far-seeing, the bravest and the best of those who were born among themselves." [1] " What is really important for working men," says Dr. J. K. Ingram, " is, not that a few should rise out of their class—this sometimes rather injures the class by depriving it of its more energetic members. The truly vital interest is that the whole class should rise in material comfort and security, and still more in moral and intellectual attainments." [2]

---

[1] *Inaugural Address delivered at the Ipswich Co-operative Congress* (Manchester, 1889), p. 14.

[2] *Work and the Workman, being an address to the Trade Union Congress at their meeting in Dublin, 16th September* 1880, by J. K. Ingram (Dublin, 1880). It must not be inferred that, because Trade Unions are opposed to the small master system, they have any objection to their members rising to superior positions. The energetic Trade Unionist, often a branch official, is frequently selected for the post of foreman, which he accepts with the full approval of his

Enlightened Trade Unionism, therefore, will judge the small master system according to its effect on the wage-earning class as a whole. On this point there is neither hesitation nor difference of opinion. If we exclude the small master himself, we find a practically unanimous agreement among economists, capitalists, and workmen, that the conditions of employment which the small master offers to his wage-earners are habitually, and in all directions, worse than those of the great establishments. In all that concerns the health, decency, and convenience of the operatives, for instance, there is no comparison between the modern boot-factory and the crowded tenement house or "garden workshop" of the small master. Nor need we weary the reader with quotations to prove that the hours of labor are longer, and the rates of payment lower in the struggling small establishments than in the great capitalist enterprises with which they compete. The very advantages which are causing industry on a large scale to supersede the small master system—the utmost possible application of machinery and division of labor, the obtaining of capital, and raw material on the cheapest terms, the use of the highest inventive and managerial ability—compel the small master, in his desperate struggle for existence, to be perpetually nibbling at wages, and lengthening the hours of labor, both for himself and for those whom he employs. It is a significant fact that the small master system is found to be as characteristic of the sweated trades as Home Work itself. "If we descend to the lower sections of the furniture trade, in which the evils of sweating

---

fellow-members. In some unions, this promotion involves his exchanging an active for an honorary membership, but in the building, engineering, and ship-building trades foremen are welcomed as ordinary members. From foreman the superior man frequently rises to be manager, or even partner, in a large firm; and it would not be difficult to compile a list of great employers of to-day who were, in their wage-earning stage, staunch members of their Trade Unions. To the man of exceptional ability, the system of the Great Industry offers, indeed, more real opportunity of rising to eminence than was before open to him. The proportion of foremen and overlookers to mere manual workers is no doubt smaller to-day than was the proportion of small masters to wage-earners two centuries ago. But the official hierarchy of modern industry affords both a safer and a higher ladder for special talent.

were proved to exist, we may watch the poverty-stricken maker of tables and chairs hawking his wares along Curtain Road, selling direct to the export merchant or to the retail tradesman, or perchance to the private customer. In the manufacture of cheap boots in the Metropolis, of cheap cutlery at Sheffield, of indifferent nails at Halesowen, we meet with this same sorrowful figure—*the small master* or outworker buying his material on credit, and selling his product to meet the necessities of the hour ; in all instances underselling his competitors great and small. Respectable employers, interested in a high standard of production, Trade Unionists keen for a high standard of wage, agree in attributing to this pitiful personage the worst evils of the sweating system." [1]

If then the Trade Unionists declare, to use the words of a Sheffield secretary, that the small masters " are a curse to the trade . . . paying starvation wages to those whom necessity compels to work for them," this is not due to any personal dislike of the small masters, or to any aspersion on their character. It is merely the recognition by Trade Unionists of an economic fact. Thoughtful workmen in the staple trades have become convinced, by their own experience, no less than by the repeated arguments of the economists, that a rising standard of wages and other conditions of employment must depend ultimately on the productivity of labor, and therefore upon the most efficient and economical use of credit, capital, and capacity. In all these respects the small master system stands, by common consent, condemned. When, therefore, we find the whole influence of Trade Unionism constantly acting against this system, and, as one employer naïvely put it to us, " playing into the hands of the great establishments," we must at any rate credit it with the desire so far to promote the utmost possible efficiency of production.

This scientific argument against the small master system

[1] "The Lords and the Sweating System," by Beatrice Potter (Mrs. Sidney Webb), *Nineteenth Century*, June 1890.

appeals chiefly to such enlightened experts as the salaried officials of the Cotton Operatives. What the ordinary workman in other trades sees is, not that the total product per man employed is far less where small establishments prevail, but that, under such circumstances, his own strategic position is seriously weakened. Those better conditions which, as he is convinced, can be secured by enforcing the Common Rule, are put practically beyond his reach. The Operative Bricklayers' Society finds little difficulty in agreeing with the large contractors in London, but is utterly baffled by the host of small jerry-builders in the suburbs, who refuse to conform to fixed conditions of any kind. The Factory Inspector can see that the sanitary conditions of the principal factories are up to the standard, and has little difficulty here in detecting illicit overtime. But without a whole army of assistants it is impossible for him to exercise any check on the myriads of small workshops, which crop up and disappear in our town slums with mushroom-like rapidity. Large establishments, in fact, facilitate both Collective Bargaining itself, and the enforcement of Common Rules however arrived at. And thus we find the small masters frequently complaining that the systematic and uniform arrangements preferred by the great employers "play into the hands" of the Trade Unionists. In 1891, for instance, the small boot manufacturers actually protested against the "capitalist manufacturers' conspiracy" to crush out, by enforcing uniform standards of wages, their smaller competitors. This, explains the employers' editor, "is a ridiculous superstition, but one which we are aware has obtained credence among a certain section of the trade, and is not confined to London. Wherever a Uniform Statement policy has been agreed upon by the leading men of Trades Associations (employers), small manufacturers have raised the cry that it is a conspiracy directed against them by the large houses for sordid ends. The suggestion is too obviously absurd to merit a moment's thought. If small manufacturers cannot continue to exist except by paying less than a proper standard of wages for work done, that is the clearest possible proof that they have no right to exist as such. There is no animus against small manufacturers, but a praiseworthy determination to place all, large and small, upon an equal wage basis ; and he would be a bold man who would dare to find fault with such an arrangement." [1] It is exactly at this "equal wage basis" and similar Common Rules throughout the whole of an industry that Trade Unionism persistently aims. The ablest leaders of the workmen's combinations are therefore instinctively biassed in favor of what we may term a horizontal cleavage of industrial classes, and they are necessarily prejudiced against any interference with this stratification. They are consequently found opposing all vertical cleavages whatever, not merely where, as in the cases of Home Work and Small Masters, these involve worse conditions for the wage-earners, but also in the less noxious forms of employers' benefit societies and profit-sharing.

At first sight nothing seems more kindly and humane on the part of the employer, and less open to objection from the workman's standpoint, than the establishment of a Sick and Burial Club in connection with each large establishment. A few pence per week are stopped from the operatives' earnings, and to the fund thus formed the employer often adds the disciplinary fines, and frequently a substantial contribution from the firm, in whose business the growing capital is invested. To the middle-class philanthropist the workman's sullen hostility to any such arrangement appears "ungrateful." But to any one who has ever understood the assumptions on which the whole Trade Union movement is based, the wage-earner's objection will be clear enough. It is not merely that the workmen feel no guarantee that, in the particular financial arrangements imposed on them, they are getting their money's worth ; nor is the objection due to any doubt as to the security of the fund—to any fear that, just when they need their sick pay or superannuation, the trade may be depressed and the firm bankrupt. What

[1] Editorial in *Shoe and Leather Record*, vol. x. p. 254, 10th April 1891.

the Trade Unionists recognise is that the separate interest thus created cuts them off from their fellow-workmen in other establishments—that a vertical cleavage is set up which interferes with Trade Unionism. We have seen how the fact of the men being compelled to insure against sickness, cost of burial, and old age in the employer's fund renders them indisposed to pay over again to the Trade Union.[1] But there is a more fundamental objection. If, as is usual, a workman forfeits all his benefits should he voluntarily leave the service of the particular firm, there is a strong and growing inducement held out to him to remain where he is, and thus to accept the employer's terms. He loses, in fact, that perfect mobility which, as economists have often pointed out, is a necessary condition of his making the best possible bargain for the sale of his labor. And, to the Trade Unionist, it is a crowning objection that the workman so tied shuts himself out from all the advantages of concerted action with his fellows. Any general adoption of employers' benefit societies would, in fact, go far to render Trade Unionism impossible.

Schemes of profit-sharing are, from a Trade Union point of view, open to similar objections. Unless the Standard Rate and other conditions are rigidly adhered to, the workmen in profit-sharing establishments may easily be losing far more in wages than they gain in "bonus" or share of profit.[2] But it is an even more serious objection that any separate arrangements with particular employers destroy that community of interest throughout the trade on which Collective Bargaining depends. The men employed by a

[1] It was stated at the Annual Conference of Friendly Societies in March 1897 that particulars had been obtained of forty large industrial undertakings, including the Midland Railway Company, in which insurance in the employer's own benefit society was made compulsory on all persons employed, the premium being peremptorily deducted from wages.

[2] Thus, it is unusual for a profit-sharing establishment to afford its operatives larger bonus than 5 per cent on their wages, and few do even as well as this. But except in the most rigidly organised trades, in the strongest Trade Union districts, it is common to find some employers paying several shillings per week below the Standard Rate ; still more, to find Piecework Lists in different establishments varying from 10 to 20 per cent.

specially "benevolent" firm, with a really generous profit-sharing scheme, will not be disposed to join heartily with the rest in any movement for higher wages, lest they should lose the bonus or other privileges which they already enjoy. Yet whilst they stand aloof, contented with their Standard Rate of wages because of these exceptional privileges, it is difficult for the workmen elsewhere to make any effective stand for a higher rate. To the Trade Unionist it seems a very doubtful kindness for an employer to indulge his feelings of philanthropy in such a way as to weaken the capacity of the workmen for that corporate self-help on which their defence against unscrupulous employers depends. Looking at the matter from the Trade Union standpoint, an employer who desired permanently to benefit the workmen in his trade would seek in every way to promote the men's own organisation, and would therefore make his own establishment a pattern to the rest in respect of the strictest possible maintenance of the Standard Rates of wages, hours of work, and other conditions of employment. This would tend to make it more easy for the workmen in other establishments to insist on the same advantages. If he wished to do more for his own workmen, and could afford it, he would scrupulously avoid any departure from the standard methods of remuneration, and any form of benevolence which created any division between his workmen and their fellows. What he would do would be to offer a simple addition to the common Standard Rate, or a simple reduction of the Normal Day without any diminution of earnings. In this way any indirect effect upon the workmen in the other establishments would be in the direction of facilitating their claiming similar advances.

This strong objection of the Trade Unionists to any blurring of the line between the capitalist profit-maker and the manual-working wage-earner, and their preference for the Great Industry, might, at first sight, seem to point towards the desirability of concentrating each trade in the hands of one great employer. But such a concentration of business may, from the Trade Union point of view, easily be carried too far. When in any trade the establishments are all sufficiently large to make it easy for the workmen to combine, the Trade Union fights at the greatest strategic advantage if it is confronted by a number of employers, varying considerably in their pecuniary resources and opportunities for profit-making. Thus, in any coal, engineering, or cotton strike, the circumstances of the employers differ so greatly that, however closely they may be combined, there is a strong tendency for some of them to split off from the rest. Those making exceptional profits will not care obstinately to stand out against the men's demands, and so lose trade which they may never regain, when agreement with the Trade Union would still leave them a handsome surplus. To firms insufficiently supplied with capital, moreover, a long stoppage may easily be more disastrous than anything that the Trade Union asks for. In the private meetings of any employers' association during a strike, these two classes are always pressing for a settlement, and if they fail to persuade their more slow-going and highly-capitalised competitors to accept their view, they are apt at last to make peace on their own account, and so destroy any chance of the employers' successful resistance.[1] If, on the other hand, the whole industry is controlled by a single colossal employer, or if it is distributed among a small number of non-competing employers—especially if the monopoly is in any way protected against new rivals—the Trade Union finds its Methods of Mutual Insurance and Collective Bargaining practically useless. This is the case with the railway com-

---

[1] "I was one of the committee," observed Mr. Samuda, the great London shipbuilder, "for carrying on that contest (the engineers' lock-out of 1851), and the difficulties that existed in maintaining a combination among the masters were enormous, because there were so many masters whose necessities were so great that they could not act to the extent of resisting demands that they thought unjust. It was only men who were thoroughly independent, and who did not care for closing their works, that could stand the difficulty, and face the insolvency that was brought upon weaker houses by resisting the unjust demands of the workmen."—*Evidence before the Royal Commission on Trade Unions*, 1868, Q. 16,805.

panies in the United Kingdom, and some of the grea
capitalist trusts in the United States. Against the unlimited
resources, the secured monopoly of custom, and the absolute
unity of will enjoyed by these modern industrial leviathans
the quarter of a million accumulated funds of the riches
Trade Union, and the clamor of even one or two hundred
thousand obstinate and embittered workmen, are as arrows
against ironclads. In such cases the only available method
of securing a Common Rule is Legal Enactment—difficult
in the face of interests so powerful, for the Trade Unions to
obtain, but once obtained, in so highly organised an industry
easy of application and enforcement. We may therefore
infer that the extreme concentration of industry into trust
and monopolies will lead, either to Trade Union failure and
decay, or else to an almost exclusive reliance on the Method
of Legal Enactment.

When the concentration reaches its most complete form
and industry passes into State Ownership, the Trade Unions
find new considerations entering into their problems
When the employer is the State itself, the strongest and
richest Trade Union is as powerless to stand out for term
as the individual workman. A long strike will bankrupt
dozens of employers and seriously reduce the dividends o
even the wealthiest trust. But if all the workmen in the
Admiralty dockyards stayed out for a year, neither the Civil
Servant manager nor the citizen proprietor would find his
daily income even fractionally diminished. The Trade
Unions are so conscious of this economic helplessness that
they never order a strike in a Government establishment
and they scarcely, indeed, attempt to bargain with so over
whelming an omnipotence. Wherever the State is dominated
by classes or interests who do not share the Trade Union
faith, the Trade Unionists, as such, will therefore be dead
against the extension of State Socialism in their own particular
industries.[1] The case is altered if the conditions of Govern

---

[1] Thus the German delegates to the International Miners' Congress of 189
(held in London) objected to the resolution in favor of the " nationalisation of th

ment employment can be influenced by democratic public opinion. If Parliament were really prepared to insist on the conditions of Government employment being brought into conformity with Trade Union regulations, any extension of the public administration of industry might well secure Trade Union support. At present, however, the Trade Union influence on the conditions of Government employment is, in spite of appearances, extremely ineffective. The Trade Union world, with the exception of the Cotton Operatives and Coalminers, is, as we have pointed out, unable to make its political power felt in Parliament. Nor is the House of Commons, as at present organised, competent, even if it were really willing, effectively to supervise the internal administration of the great public departments. Finally, we have the fact that the present generation of the higher Civil Servants—our real rulers in points of administrative detail—are, for the most part, invincibly ignorant both of industrial organisation and modern economics, and are usually imbued with the crudest prejudices of the Manchester School. It is in vain that Ministry after Ministry avows its intention of abandoning competition wages, and of making the Government a "model employer." The permanent heads of departments have no intention of departing from the "sound" principles which they brought into the service in 1860 or 1870. Hence, a Trade Union secretary will often declare that the Government, instead of being the best, is one of the very worst employers with whom he has to deal.

But even in the most complete and the most perfectly organised Democracy, there would be influences which would

mines," on the express ground that " they in Germany had found that the capitalistic State was the worst possible employer, and the worst enemy and opponent of the workers. There happened to be in Germany some very large State mines, and the conditions of the workers in these mines was infinitely worse than elsewhere. Now the State was indifferent during mining disputes. If it possessed all the mines, it would be as an employer more powerful and more tyrannical than a private employer " (*Daily Chronicle*, 12th June 1897). It is interesting to note that the French and Belgian delegates unanimously supported the resolution, together with a majority of the English (those from Northumberland and Durham alone dissenting), whilst the Germans, though mostly members of the Social Democratic Party, abstained.

prevent the Government, as an employer, giving universal satis
faction to the Trade Unions. Though the working-class vote
would be overwhelming, each section of wage-earners would
find itself a small minority among the rest, and would dis
cover accordingly how difficult it was to force its own
peculiar grievances upon public attention. And, though any
section that was " underpaid " or " overworked " would get
sympathetic support, there would be a strong tendency in
the average man to object to any terms that were out of the
common. Sections of workmen who had, under private
enterprise, been enjoying exceptionally high wages or short
hours, or who had been enforcing strict limitation of
numbers or other monopoly conditions, would find it difficult
to maintain these by appeals to the multitude. The men in
these trades would accordingly, as Trade Unionists, tend
always to be discontented with Government employment.
Thus, public administration of industry under Democratic
control will be most popular among those larger sections of
the wage-earners, who at present suffer from the weakness of
their strategic position, and will remain unpopular among
the smaller and better organised sections, who can now take
advantage of their corporate strength to exact from their
private employers monopoly terms.

These considerations apply with less force to municipal
employment. The Town Council, though more powerful
in Collective Bargaining than any private employer, has
nothing like the omnipotence of the great State Department.
A strike at the municipal gas retorts, or in the workshops of
the Borough Engineer, is a serious matter, which must be
quickly brought to an end, under penalty of the immediate
displeasure of the citizen-consumers. And whilst the Town
Council is weaker than Parliament in strategic position, it is
also more amenable to public opinion. Municipal electoral
machinery has been more thoroughly democratised than
parliamentary, and is therefore easier of access to the local
unions. No great issues of foreign policy, religion, currency
or constitutional reform divide the workmen's ranks. The

moral effect of the Town Council's policy with regard to the conditions of employment is understood by every Trade Unionist. Once the Town Councillors are converted, the permanent officials have no chance of evading or obstructing the decision of the local Representative Assembly. Moreover, the lowlier grades of manual labor contribute a larger proportion of the municipal than they do of the national employees.[1] There is as yet nothing in the municipal service comparable to the great establishments of highly skilled shipwrights and engineers of the national dockyards and arsenals. It is, as we have suggested, far more easy for the Trade Unions to obtain electoral support for a universal " moral minimum," or " fair wages," based on the cost of subsistence, than for any superior conditions, established by trade custom or gained by strategic advantage, in respect of particular sections of workmen. We therefore find the skilled trades less hostile, as Trade Unionists, to the municipal administration of industry than to any extension of State employment, whilst the " sweated trades " and the unskilled laborers clamor for the abolition of the contractor, and the direct employment of labor, as their main hope of salvation.

If, now, we look back on the incidental features of Trade Union policy described in this chapter, we may gain some insight into the kind of social arrangements to which Trade Unionism predisposes the British workman of our own day.

Most fundamental of all considerations to the Trade Unionist is complete freedom of association. This means, that whilst the law must afford full protection to the funds of workmen's associations, it should leave them as much as possible alone ; and that it should, in particular, regard nothing as criminal or actionable if done by or in pursuance

---

[1] Thus, in London in 1891, even after a general improvement of conditions, Mr. Charles Booth found that the great class of " Municipal Labor " came within six of the worst of his eighty-seven occupations, in the percentage of families living in an overcrowded condition.—*Life and Labour of the People*, vol. ix. p. 8.

of a combination of workmen which would not be criminal or actionable if done by a partnership of traders in pursuit of their own gain. But whilst the Trade Unionists insist on their combinations being let alone by the law, they wish to use the law to attain their own particular end—the systematic regulation of the conditions of employment by means of the Common Rule. Hence their desire for a completely demo-cratised electoral system, in which the will of the majority shall really prevail. With regard to the organisation of industry, we see the Trade Unions setting themselves decidedly against any vertical cleavage of society, which interferes with the solidarity of the manual-working wage-earners as against the capitalist employers. This means that Trade Unionists, as such, are not in favor of the " abolition of the wage system," or even of any tampering with it. They would, on the contrary, wish to see simple employment at wages supersede all forms of profit-making by manual workers. They are thus solidly against Home Work, Small Masters, and Profit-Sharing, and in favor of the Great Industry, with its bureaucratic hierarchy of salaried officials. When, however, the Great Industry passes into public administration, Trade Unionists, as such, regard the change with mixed feelings. Government Employment goes far to make two out of their three Methods impracticable, and they have as yet no confidence in the will and capacity of the House of Commons to overcome the hostility to labor of the permanent Civil Service. With local authorities the Trade Unions have a better chance, but even here, though the underpaid and overworked sections welcome municipal employment, the most highly paid unions hesitate to invite the verdict of public opinion on their restrictive regulations and monopoly conditions.

CHAPTER XIII

THE ASSUMPTIONS OF TRADE UNIONISM

So far we have confined ourselves to setting forth and explaining the actual policy of British Trade Unionism, as manifested in the Methods and Regulations of the several Unions, and their direct implications. We have still to examine these Methods and Regulations, together with the policy of Trade Unionism as a whole, in the light of economic science, and from the point of view of the community. But before we pass to this new task it is important to drag into full light the assumptions on which the Trade Unionists habitually base both their belief in Trade Unionism itself and their justification of particular demands. These assumptions, seldom explicitly set forth, will serve at once to explain, and in a sense to summarise, the Methods and Regulations which they inspire.

We have first the typical assumption of all reformers in all ages—the conviction that economic and social conditions can, by deliberate human intervention, be changed for the better.[1] Trade Unionists have never even understood the

---

[1] This belief in the possibility and desirability of deliberately altering the conditions of social life is often regarded as unscientific, if not as impious. Any intentional change is denounced as "artificial"—it being apparently supposed that changes unintentionally produced are more "natural" than others, and more likely to result in the ends we desire. Even Mr. Lecky makes it a matter of reproach to Trade Unionism, modern Radicalism, and other movements which he dislikes, that their policy is "to create a social type different from that which the unrestricted play of social forces would have produced"—a policy which he declares "belongs to the same order of ideas as the Protectionism of the past"

view—still occasionally met with—that there is an absolutely predetermined " Wage-Fund," and that the average
workman's share of the produce depends exclusively on the
arithmetical proportion between the total of this fund and
the number of wage-earners.   They assume, on the contrary,
that the ratio in which the total product of industry is shared
between the property-owners, the brain-workers, and the
manual laboring class respectively, is a matter of human
arrangement, and that it can be altered, effectively and permanently, to the advantage of one class or another, if the
appropriate action be taken.   This assumption we shall
examine in detail in the next chapter.

For the improvement of the conditions of employment,
whether in respect of wages, hours, health, safety, or comfort,
the Trade Unionists have, with all their multiplicity of Regulations, really only two expedients, which we term, respectively, the Device of the Common Rule, and the Device of
Restriction of Numbers.   The Regulations which we have
described in our chapters on the Standard Rate, the Normal
Day, and Sanitation and Safety, are but different forms of one
principle—the settlement, whether by Mutual Insurance,
Collective Bargaining, or Legal Enactment, of minimum conditions of employment, by Common Rules applicable to
whole bodies of workers.   All these Regulations are based
on the assumption that when, in the absence of any Common Rule, the conditions of employment are left to " free
competition," this always means, in practice, that they are
arrived at by Individual Bargaining between contracting
parties of very unequal economic strength.   Such a settlement, it is asserted, invariably tends, for the mass of the

(*Democracy and Liberty*, vol. ii. p. 383).   To any scientific student of sociology
such language is unintelligible.   " To create a social type different from that
which the free play of social forces would have produced " without such " artificial
intervention " is a policy which Trade Unionism shares, not only with fiscal protection, but with all education and invention, the Church of England and the Courts
of Justice, private property and the family, and all other social institutions, good,
bad, or indifferent.   Civilisation itself is nothing but the creation of a social type
different from that which the unrestricted play of social forces would have produced without the deliberate, or " artificial," intervention of man.

workers, towards the worst possible conditions of labor—ultimately, indeed, to the barest subsistence level—whilst even the exceptional few do not permanently gain as much as they otherwise could. We find accordingly that the Device of the Common Rule is a universal feature of Trade Unionism, and that the assumption on which it is based is held from one end of the Trade Union world to the other. The Device of Restriction of Numbers stands in a different position. In our chapter on the Entrance to a Trade we have described how the Regulations embodying this device, once adopted as a matter of course, have successively been found inapplicable to the circumstances of modern industry. The assumption on which they are based —that better conditions can be obtained by limiting the number of competitors—would not be denied by any Trade Unionist, but it cannot be said to form an important part in the working creed of the Trade Union world. In summing up the economic results of Trade Unionism it is on these two Devices of the Common Rule and Restriction of Numbers that we shall concentrate our criticism.

But these initial assumptions as to the need for Trade Unionism and the efficacy of its two devices do not, of themselves, account for the marked divergence between different Unions, alike in the general character of their policy and in the Regulations which they enforce. The universal belief in a Common Rule affords, to begin with, no guidance as to how much wages the members of a particular trade will claim or receive, or how many hours they will consider to be a proper working day. There is, in fact, no "Trade Union Rate of Wages," but many different rates—not even a "Trade Union Working Day," but hours of labor varying from occupation to occupation. This divergence of policy comes out even more strikingly in the adoption or rejection of the Device of Restriction of Numbers, a few trades still making the strict Limitation of Apprentices and the Exclusion of Illegal Men a leading feature of their policy, whilst others throw their trades absolutely open to all comers, and rely exclusively on the maintenance of the Common Rule. This divergence of policy and difference in type between one Trade Union and another comes out strongly in the choice of the Methods by which they enforce their Regulations. The Boilermakers, for instance, rely very largely on Collective Bargaining, whilst the Coalminers get at least as much by Legal Enactment as by any other Method. During the eighteenth century any trade wishing to enforce apprentice-ship regulations turned, as a matter of course, to the law. To-day no union would resort to Parliament on such a point. A hundred and fifty years ago it was especially the skilled craftsmen who wanted their wages fixed by Legal Enactment. At present such favor as is shown to this idea comes almost exclusively from the lowlier grades of labor. On all these points the action of any particular union—the way in which it will seek to use the Device of the Common Rule—is mainly determined by the views of its members as to what is socially expedient. In the wider world of politics we see the electors supporting the policy of one or other political party mainly according as they approve or dis-approve of the general conception of society on which it proceeds. The Trade Unionists, in their narrower sphere of the conditions of employment, are influenced by three divergent conceptions of the principle upon which wages, hours, and other terms of the labor contract ought to be determined. These three assumptions, which we distinguish as the Doctrine of Vested Interests, the Doctrine of Supply and Demand, and the Doctrine of a Living Wage, give us the clue to the conflicting policies of the Trade Union world.

By the Doctrine of Vested Interests we mean the assumption that the wages and other conditions of employ-ment hitherto enjoyed by any section of workmen ought under no circumstances to be interfered with for the worse. It was this doctrine, as we have seen, which inspired the long struggle, lasting down to about 1860, against the introduction of machinery, or any innovation in processes. It is this doctrine which to-day gives the bitterness to demarcation disputes, and lies at the back of all the Regulations dealing with the " right to a trade." [1]   It does more than anything else to keep alive the idea of " patrimony " and the practice of a lengthened period of apprenticeship, whilst it induces the workmen of particular trades to cling fondly to the expedient of limiting the numbers entering those trades, even after experience has proved such a limitation to be impracticable.   But the Doctrine of Vested Interests extends much further than these particular Regulations.   There is scarcely an industry in which it will not be found, on one occasion or another, inspiring the defence of the customary rates of wages or any threatened privilege.   In some cases, indeed, we find the whole argument for Trade Unionism based on this one conception.   The Engineers, for instance, in 1845 supported their case by a forcible analogy.   " The youth who has the good fortune and inclinations for preparing himself as a useful member of society by the study of physic, and who studies that profession with success so as to obtain his diploma from the Surgeons' Hall, or the College of Surgeons, naturally expects in some measure that he is entitled to privileges to which the pretending quack can lay no claim ; and if in the practice of that useful profession he finds himself injured by such a pretender, he has the power of instituting a course of law against him.   Such are the benefits connected with the learned professions.   But the mechanic, though he may expend nearly an equal fortune, and sacrifice an equal portion of his life, in becoming acquainted with the different branches of useful mechanism, has no law to protect his privileges.   It behoves him, therefore,

[1] We see this, for instance, among the Engineers.   " The question as to a turner working the horizontal boring lathe at the Pallion [Works] . . . remains unsettled ; the employers adhering to their right of ' selecting the men and apportioning the work.'   The issue appears to be clean cut, and stated with perfect frankness.   The vested interest—equally with employers—of workmen in a trade by probationary servitude is apparently to be set at naught.   To displace a journeyman, as indicated, in the exercise of the ' right of selecting,' in the manner proposed, is as much a wrong as if the same process was proposed to be adopted with respect to the employer's capital."—Report of Tyneside District Delegate, in *Amalgamated Engineers' Monthly Journal*, May 1897.

on all reasonable grounds, and by all possible means, to secure the advantages of a society like this to himself."[1] The same idea is put with no less clearness by some of the smaller trades. "Considering," say the Birmingham Wireworkers, "that the trade by which we live is our property, bought by certain years of servitude, which gives to us a vested right, and that we have a sole and exclusive claim on it, as all will have hereafter who purchase it by the same means. Such being the case, it is evident it is our duty to protect, by all fair and legal means, the property by which we live, being always equally careful not to trespass on the rights of others. To that end we have formed this Association," etc.[2]

This conception of vested interests is sometimes carried as far by working men as by the powerful organisation which has latterly become distinctively known as "The Trade." Thus the Coopers, whose chief employers then as now were the brewers, were in 1883 keenly resenting the spread of education and temperance, and the threatened measure of "Local Option." "Several Yorkshire towns," remarked their official circular, "have for years until recently been great centres of industry in the export line. These centres of industry are swept away, and nothing I am sorry to say has turned up to replace them, the consequence being that all these men had to obtain blocks elsewhere. There is also the spread of education, an all-powerful influence we are bound to feel, and a blow from which we shall not easily recover. There is also that great Northern baronet, Sir Wilfrid, he too, like Demetrius the Silversmith of Macedonia, and Alexander the Athenian Coppersmith, has wrought us

---

[1] *Rules and Regulations to be observed by the Members of the Journeymen Steam Engine and Machine Makers' and Millwrights' Friendly Society* (Glasgow, 1845). This analogy is repeated in substance in many editions of the rules of the Amalgamated Society of Engineers.

[2] Extract from Address, prefaced to the *Rules and Regulations of the Birmingham Friendly Society of Wire Weavers*, a small union instituted August 1869. The same preamble was used by the Railway Springmakers of Sheffield in the Rules of their Society in 1860; see "Report on Trade Societies' Rules" in the *Report on Trade Societies and Strikes of the National Association for the Promotion of Social Science* (London, 1860), pp. 131-132.

much evil, and from the tone of his speeches means to continue to do so." [1]

It is difficult for middle-class observers, accustomed to confine the doctrine of "vested interests" to "rights of property," to understand the fervor and conviction with which the skilled artisan holds this doctrine in its application to the "right to a trade." This intuitive conviction of natural right we ascribe, in great part, to the long and respectable history of the idea. Down to the middle of the eighteenth century it was undisputed. To the member of a Craft Gild or Incorporated Company it seemed as outrageous, and as contrary to natural justice, for an unlicensed interloper to take his trade as for a thief to steal his wares. Nor was this conception confined to any particular section of the community. To the economists and statesmen of the time the protection of the vested interests of each class of tradesmen appeared a no less fundamental axiom of civilised society than the protection of property in land or chattels. "Our forefathers," said the Emperor Sigismund in 1434, "have not been fools. The crafts have been devised for this purpose that everybody by them should earn his daily bread, and nobody shall interfere with the craft of another. By this the world gets rid of its misery, and every one may find his livelihood." [2] "The first rule of justice," said the Parliament of Paris three hundred and fifty years later, "is to preserve to every one what belongs to him ; this rule consists,

---

[1] Monthly Report of the Mutual Association of Coopers, Feb. 1883. This conception of a "vested interest" in the nation's drinking habits may be paralleled by the attempts made to give the "sanctity of property" to the employer's power of hiring his labor cheap, or working it excessive hours. Thus Sir James Graham, speaking in the House of Commons as a responsible minister of the Crown, solemnly denounced the Ten Hours' Bill of 1844 as "Jack Cade Legislation" (Greville's *Journal of the Reign of Queen Victoria*, vol. ii. p. 236 ; see *The Eight Hours' Day* by Sidney Webb and Harold Cox, London, 1891, p. 240), and a leading Lancashire manufacturer in 1860 publicly argued that "the power of the Trade Union . . . robs (for I can use no milder term) . . . the capitalist of his right to purchase."—"Trades Unions and their Tendencies," by Edmund Potter, a paper printed in the *Transactions of the National Association for the Promotion of Social Science*, 1860, p. 758.

[2] Goldasti's *Constitutions Impériales*, vol. iv. p. 189, quoted by Dr. Brentano, p. 60 ; *History of Trade Unionism*, p. 19.

not only in preserving the rights of property, but still more in preserving those belonging to the person, which arise from the prerogative of birth and of position." [1] " To give to all subjects indiscriminately," argued on that occasion the eminent Advocate-General Séguier, " the right to hold a store or to open a shop is to violate the property of those who form the incorporated crafts." [2]

But this conception of a vested interest in a trade, though it derives sanction among an essentially conservative class from its long and venerable history, does not rest upon tradition alone. To men dependent for daily existence on continuous employment, the protection of their means of livelihood from confiscation or encroachment appears as fundamental a basis of social order as it does to the owners of land. What both parties claim is security and continuity of livelihood—that maintenance of the " established expectation" which is the "condition precedent" of civilised life. And it is easy to trace this social expediency to an elementary observation on personal character. When misfortune arrives in consequence of a man's own act or default, it may well bring the compensation of inducing him to change his habits But when individuals or classes are overwhelmed by disasters which they could have done nothing to avert, experience shows that, though they may be led to passive resignation, they are not stimulated to self-reliance, and they are apt, on the contrary, to be rendered inert or reckless. We do not expect deliberate foresight or persistent industry from a community living on a volcano. [3]   This, indeed, is the

---

[1] Remonstrance by the Parliament of Paris against Turgot's Decrees abolishing the Corvée and the Jurandes ; *Life and Writings of Turgot*, by W. Walker Stephens, p. 132 ; Jobez, *La France sous Louis XVI.* i. 329-331.

[2] Speech of the Advocate Séguier on behalf of the Jurandes at the Lit de Justice for registering Turgot's Decree ; *Life and Writings of Turgot*, by W. Walker Stephens, p. 134 ; *Œuvres de Turgot*, ii. 334-337 ; Foncin, liv. iii. c. ix.

[3] Buckle notices the effect of earthquakes in weakening character ; " men witnessing the most serious dangers which they can neither avoid nor understand, become impressed with a conviction of their inability, and of the poverty of their own resources " (*History of Civilisation*, vol. i. p. 123). Middle-class critics often deplore the " heedlessness " as to the future—the lack of persistent carrying out of a deliberate plan of life—which marks the laborer engaged in a fluctuating

fundamental argument against anything which weakens the feeling of security of private property, that is, against any "shock or derangement being given to the expectation which has been founded on the laws of enjoying a certain portion of good." [1]   And if we pass from the ownership of property to its occupation under contract, we shall recognise the same argument in the agitation long and successfully carried on by Irish and English farmers for a law which should secure them in their "tenant right." It has now been conceded that we cannot expect occupiers of land to exercise the self-sacrifice, foresight, and energy necessary to keep their holdings in the highest possible efficiency, if the results of their work can be arbitrarily confiscated whenever a landlord chooses to exercise his legal right of ejecting a tenant. A similar consideration lies at the base of the universal conviction in favor of a legally regulated currency. Bimetallists and monometallists alike deplore the disastrous effect on national enterprise if, in the absence of a deliberately settled standard of value, the reasonable expectations of merchants and manufacturers are set at naught by currency fluctuations over which they can have no control. We need not weary the reader by citing other instances (such as the law of patents and copyright, the universal practice of compensation for abolition of office, and all the thousand and one claims of persons "injuriously affected," which are sanctioned by the English Lands Clauses Consolidation Acts),[2] whereby the community has deliberately sought to defend particular

trade, and, to some extent, the whole manual labor class. We attribute this characteristic difference between the English middle and working classes largely to the feeling of the weekly wage-earner that he is dependent for the continuity of his livelihood on circumstances over which he has no control, and that he is, by the modern habit of engaging and dismissing workmen for short jobs, made keenly sensible of fluctuations which he can do nothing to avert.

[1] Bentham, *Principles of the Civil Code*, part i. ch. vii. The Whig leaders in 1816 deprecated any discussion by the House of Commons of sinecure offices, and even of excessive salaries, on the ground, as Francis Horner wrote to Lord Holland, that "it is a ticklish thing to begin to draw subtle distinctions about property."—*Memoirs and Correspondence of Francis Horner, M.P.* (London, 1843), vol. ii. p. 386.

[2] *Principles of the Law of Compensation*, by C. A. Cripps, Q.C., 3rd edition (London, 1892).

persons or classes against the evil effect on character that ensues on finding their efforts and sacrifices nullified by circumstances which they were powerless to avert. When we remember this vast network of defence, built up during the present century in protection of the security and continuity of livelihood of brain-workers and property-holders, it is strange that it is just these classes who fail to comprehend the weekly wage-earner's craving for the same boon. "An industrious man," says one of the workmen's spokesmen, "having learnt a trade, or enabled by any honest means to earn a superior living, is equally entitled to an adequate indemnity if his trade or property is interfered with, or rendered less advantageous, as the owner of a water-mill, who has compensation if the water is withdrawn. Every description of property has ample protection, except the poor man's only property, his and his children's industrious habits." [1]

[1] *A Comparative Statement of the Number of Laborers employed in the Execution of the same Quantity of Work if executed by Hand or Machine*, J. Jarrold (Norwich, 1848). Sismondi pointed out in 1834 that "to make a true calculation of what society gains by any mechanical invention there must be deducted from it the loss experienced by all the working men who had been dismissed by it, till they have found an employment as advantageous as the one they had before."—"On Landed Property," in *Revue Mensuelle d'Economie Politique*, February 1834; translated in his *Political Economy and the Philosophy of Government* (London, 1837), page 168.

It is not enough to assert, as is often done, that any recognition of the workman's vested interest in his trade would be incompatible with the industrial mobility which is indispensable to modern society. The community cannot, of course, allow the vested interest of any individual or section to stand in the way of a change which is for the public benefit. This admittedly applies to all vested interests, whether in land, personal property, public offices, or anything else. But when the property owner or the holder of a public office is concerned, the necessary mobility is secured without inflicting loss on the individuals affected, by the simple device of pecuniary compensation. It is difficult to see why persons whose occupations are "injuriously affected" by a railway or other enterprise carried out by Parliamentary powers, should not be compensated for the injury done to their means of livelihood in the same way as the landowner is. This claim to legislative indemnity of displaced workmen was recognised by J. S. Mill. The social advantage derived from the application of new processes and machinery does not, he declares, "discharge governments from the obligation of alleviating, and, if possible, preventing, the evils of which this source of ultimate benefit is or may be productive to an existing generation . . . and since improvements which do not diminish employment on the whole almost always throw some particular class out of it, there cannot be a more legitimate object of the legislator's care

But although the philosophic student may recognise the common origin of all forms of "vested interest" in man's shrinking from the great social evil of a disappointment of "established expectation," he will not so readily admit the virtue of the panacea. It may well be that, as applied to particular forms of personal interest, the remedy may bring with it social evils greater than those which it cures. Thus, public opinion now sides with Turgot and Adam Smith in their denunciation of the evil effects of the close corporations, by which successive generations of craftsmen

than the interests of those who are thus sacrificed to the gains of their fellow-citizens and of posterity" (*Principles of Political Economy*, by J. S. Mill, Book I. chap. vi. sec. 3, p. 62). We are not aware of any case in which this humane principle has been acted upon. It is true that, in the case of workmen displaced by an invention, it would neither be possible nor desirable to pay them lump sums of money. But if they are willing to work the new process, there seems no equitable reason why they should not be kept on at their former wages, even at a considerable temporary loss to the community. The action of the English legislature in awarding compensation for disturbance of vested interests has, indeed, been capricious in the extreme, depending, perhaps, on the momentary political influence of the class concerned. Thus, no compensation was given to the large class of lottery keepers and their servants, either for loss of capital or loss of occupation, when private lotteries were, in 1698, suddenly prohibited. The shipowners and merchants who had invested a large capital in specially designed slave-carrying ships received no compensation when the slave trade was abolished in 1807. On the other hand, when, in 1834, the slaves in the British Colonies were converted into indentured servants, twenty millions sterling were voted to the owners, though no other country, before or after, has taken this course. The owners of Irish Parliamentary Boroughs were compensated when the Union deprived them of these seats, but the owners of English Parliamentary Boroughs, which had equally been recognised sources of income, received nothing when the Reform Bill of 1832 swept them away. In our own day, when a Town Council sets up its own works, and uses public funds to dispense altogether with its former contractors, it pays them no compensation for loss of capital or livelihood. But if the new workshops so much as darken the view from the contractor's windows, the town must pay damages. Parliament gives public authorities full power to ruin, if they can, the private owners of existing gas-works by setting up public electric lighting works, and even to destroy the business of joint-stock cemeteries by starting public burial-grounds. But the House of Commons has jealously refused to permit any Town Council to put up gas-works of its own, whilst any private gas-works are in the field as opponents ; or even to sink its own wells to get a new and entirely different supply of water for the public, without first fully compensating any existing water company, not for taking away any land, works, or water, or infringing any monopoly rights, but simply for loss of income. Whether the holder of an annually granted terminable license to sell intoxicating liquors would or would not be equitably entitled to compensation if Parliament decided for the future not to renew it, is a hotly contested question.

were legally assured of a customary livelihood, whether they kept pace with the times, or jogged along contentedly in the old routine. In exactly the same strain it has been urged by opponents of the institution of private property, that, at any rate, in the form of inherited wealth, it over-reaches its aim, and by securing a livelihood independent of personal exertion, positively counteracts its primary purpose of encouraging each generation to put forth its fullest energies. As against the gilds, modern democracy denies the right of any group or section to monopolise, to the exclusion of less fortunate outsiders, any opportunity of public service. In the same way opponents have argued against private property that, by creating a virtual monopoly of land and capital in the hands of a comparatively small class, the right of exclusive ownership actually hinders whole sections of citizens from that access to the instruments of production by which alone they can exercise their faculties. It is significant that almost the same phrase—"the right to work"—was used by Turgot as an argument against the gilds, and by Louis Blanc as an indictment against private property in capital and land.[1]

It was, however, not these general arguments that induced Parliament to throw over the vested interests of the handicraftsmen. Amid the rush of new inventions, a legal "right to a trade," or a legal limitation of apprentices, whilst it remained an irksome restriction, ceased to safeguard the workman's livelihood. The only remedy for the consequent disturbance of vested interests would have been to have stereotyped the existing industrial order, by the absolute prohibition of machinery or any other innovation. To the statesman, keen on securing the maximum national wealth, any such prohibition appeared suicidal. To the new class of enterprising captains of industry, all restrictions stood in

[1] "The right to work is the property of every man, and this property is the first, the most sacred, and the most inalienable of all" (Introduction to the Law for the Suppression of "Jurandes," *Œuvres de Turgot*, par E. Daire, Paris, 1844, vol. ii. p. 306). This "droit à travailler" preceded by seventy years the "droit au travail" of Louis Blanc.

the way of that free use of their capital from which they could derive private wealth. The dispossessed craftsmen could themselves devise no feasible alternative to *laisser faire*, and no one among the dominant classes thought of any means of compensation. As the Industrial Revolution progressed, the objection to any interference with mobility increased in strength. New armies of workpeople grew up, without vested interests of their own, and accordingly opposed to any conception of society which excluded them from the most profitable occupations. Finally, we have the rise in influence of the great body of consumers, loth to admit that the disappointment of the " established expectation " of particular sections of workers is any adequate ground for refraining from the cheapest method of satisfying their ever-changing desires. The result is that even Trade Unionists feel the Doctrine of Vested Interests to be out of date. It is still held with fervor by the more conservative-minded members of every trade, to whom it fully justifies such restrictive regulations as they are able to maintain.[1] It is naturally strongest in the remnants of the time-honored ancient handicrafts. Those who have troubled to explore the nooks and crannies of the industrial world, which have hitherto escaped the full intensity of the commercial struggle, will have found in them a peculiar type of Trade Union character. Wherever the Doctrine of Vested Interests is still maintained by the workmen, and admitted by the employers—where, that is to say, the conditions of employment are consciously based, not on the competitive battle, but on the established expectations of the different classes— we find an unusual prevalence, among the rank and file, of what we may call the " gentle " nature—that conjunction of quiet dignity, grave courtesy, and consideration of other

[1] Thus, even in 1897 we find an aged compositor writing, " It is useless saying we cannot resist the machine. I say we can and must. Are we to prostrate ourselves before this Juggernaut of a ' higher civilisation,' and be crushed out of existence without a protest ? . . . To live by his own industry is every man's birthright, and whoever attempts to curtail that right is a traitor to the community."—Letter in *Typographical Circular*, February 1897.

people's rights and feelings, which is usually connected with old family and long-established position. But this type of character becomes every day rarer in the Trade Union world. The old Doctrine of Vested Interests has, in fact, lost its vitality. It is still secretly cherished by many workmen, and its ethical validity is, in disputes between different Trade Unions, unhesitatingly assumed by both sides. But we no longer find it dominating the mind of Trade Union leaders, or figuring in their negotiations with employers, and appeals for public support. Whatever fate may be in store for other forms of vested interests, the modern passion for progress, demanding the quickest possible adaptation of social structure to social needs, has effectually undermined the assumption that any person can have a vested interest in an occupation.

When, at the beginning of this century, the Doctrine of Vested Interests was, as regards the wage-earners, definitely repudiated by the House of Commons, the Trade Unionists were driven back upon what we have termed the Doctrine of Supply and Demand. Working men were told, by friends and foes alike, that they could no longer be regarded as citizens entitled to legal protection of their established expectations; that labor was a commodity like any other; and that their real position was that of sellers in a market, entitled to do the best they could for themselves within the limits of the law of the land, but to no better terms than they could, by the ordinary arts of bargaining, extract from those with whom they dealt. It was the business of the employer to buy " labor " in the cheapest market, and that of the workman to sell it in the dearest. It followed that the only criterion of justice of any claim was ability to enforce it, and that the only way by which the workmen could secure better conditions of employment was by strengthening their strategic position against the employer. In the *History of Trade Unionism* we have described how, after the collapse of the Owenite Utopianism of 1833-34, this doctrine came as a new spirit into the Trade Union movement. Thus the Flint Glass Makers, whose strong and restrictive combination dates from 1849, have avowedly based their whole policy upon " Supply and Demand." " When," wrote their chief officer in 1869, " we find Mr. Nasmyth explaining [to the Royal Commission on Trade Unions] the advantage to the employer of a supply of surplus labor, it is easy to understand the consequences to the workmen that an unlimited supply of new hands might have in any market, and their objections to the practice. That the State should enforce any such limitation would certainly be most impolitic. But the conduct of those who refuse to work under a system of an unlimited number of apprentices appears to us precisely similar to that of those employers who insist on it. Both parties are seeking to do the best for their own interests, and neither pretends to consider the interests of those whom their conduct may affect. The masters find it cheaper to employ as many boys as they can, and they leave the displaced workmen to their own resources. The men on their side find it their interest to decline to work with an unrestricted supply of boys, and leave the unemployed youth to do the best they can for themselves. The employer declines all responsibility as to the consequences of displacing a number of middle-aged workmen by boys, on the ground that it is the interest of capital to find the cheapest labor it can. The workmen find it is the interest of their body not to work on such terms. In this battle of interest, in which neither party acknowledge any obligation beyond that of securing their own interests, absolute impartiality appears to us to be the only safe rule of the State. So long as no breach of the general law results, and no legislative restriction exists, the consequences of their conduct must be borne by each party for themselves." [1]

Between 1843 and 1880 the Doctrine of Supply and Demand, though never universally accepted, occupied a dominant place in the minds of most of the leaders of Trade

[1] Editorial in the *Flint Glass Makers' Magazine*, vol. vi. No. 7 (March 1869).

Union thought. Viewed in the light of the workmen's experience of the evils of Individual Bargaining, and of the weakness of merely local unions, it meant the establishment of strong national societies, heaping up great reserve funds, and seeking to control the supply of labor in a whole industry from one end of the kingdom to the other. It involved, moreover, the gradual substitution of a policy of inclusion for that of exclusion. Instead of jealously restricting Trade Union membership to men who had "earned" a right to the trade by a definite apprenticeship under restrictive conditions, the unions came more and more to use all lawful means of enforcing membership on every competent workman whom they found actually working at their trade, however questionable might have been the means by which he had acquired his skill. The policy with regard to apprenticeship underwent, accordingly, a subtle change. The ideas of patrimony, of the purchase and sale of "the right to a trade," and of a traditional ratio between learners and adepts, gradually faded away, to be replaced by a frank and somewhat cynical policy of so regulating the entrance to an industry as to put the members of the union in the best possible position for bargaining with the employers. This conscious manipulation of the labor market, the direct outcome of the Doctrine of Supply and Demand, took different forms in different industries. Among the Flint Glass Makers, for instance, it led to an absolutely precise adjustment, entrance to the trade and progression from grade to grade being so regulated as instantly to fill every vacancy as it occurred, but so as to leave no man in any grade unemployed. "It is," they declared, "simply a question of supply and demand, and we all know that if we supply a greater quantity of an article than what is actually demanded, that the cheapening of that article, whether it be labor or any other commodity, is a natural result."[1] The inference was a strict limitation of boy-labor. "Look to the rule and keep boys back; for this is the foundation of

[1] *History of Trade Unionism*, p. 183.

the evil, the secret of our progress, the dial on which our society works, and the hope of future generations."[1] The Cotton-spinners, accepting the same assumption that their wages must depend exclusively on the strength of their strategic position in the market, find that exactly the opposite policy is the best suited to attain their end. Instead of attempting to restrict the number of boys, they insist that every spinner shall be attended by two piecers, a ratio of learners to adepts ten times as great as is needed to keep up the supply. This regulation is insisted on in all negotiations with the employers, expressly on the ground that only by such an arrangement can the union secure for its members the highest possible remuneration.[2] But the most obvious result of the change of doctrine was a revolution in policy with regard to wages and hours. Under the influence of the Doctrine of Vested Interests, the eighteenth-century Trade Unionists had confined themselves, in the main, to protecting their customary livelihood ; asking advances, therefore, not when profits were large, but when the cost of living had risen. Under the influence of the view that wages should be determined by the strategic position of the combined wage-earners, the Trade Unionists of the middle of the present century boldly asserted a claim, in times of good trade, to the highest possible rates that they could exact from employers eager to fulfil immensely profitable orders. Middle-class public opinion, which had accepted as inevitable the starvation wages caused by Supply and Demand in the lean years, was shocked in 1872-73 at the rumor of coalminers and ironworkers, in those times of plenty, demanding ten shillings or even a pound a day, and faring sumptuously on green peas and champagne. The great captains of industry, though genuinely alarmed at the Trade Union pretensions to share in the

[1] *Flint Glass Makers' Magazine*, September 1857 ; *History of Trade Unionism*, p. 184.

[2] For the economics of this paradox—in our opinion more valid than the position of the Flint Glass Makers—see the subsequent chapter on " The Economic Characteristics of Trade Unionism."

profits of good times, found it difficult to refuse this application of their own Doctrine of Supply and Demand. We find them accordingly arranging, particularly in the coal and iron industries, an intellectual compromise with the Trade Union leaders, which took form in the celebrated device of the Sliding Scale. The Durham and Northumberland coal-owners, and the North of England iron-masters, abandoned, once for all, the theory that wages should be determined by the competition of individual workmen among themselves, or by the skill in bargaining of the individual employer. They thus frankly conceded the central position of Trade Unionism, namely, the advantage of a Common Rule co-extensive with the industry. They gave up, moreover, any claim to take advantage of the glut of labor, which occurs from time to time, and which, under the Sliding Scale, is not admitted as a plea for any reduction of wages. The Trade Unionists, on their side, agreed to forego making any use of the occasional short supply of labor, when they might otherwise have secured an advance. But they also made a more important concession. By agreeing that the rate of wages should automatically vary with the price of the product, they accepted the employers' contention that the workman's income should be determined by Supply and Demand, though it was Supply and Demand applied, not directly to labor, but to the product of labor. In the coal and iron trades, the selling price of the product, as fixed by the competitive market, was taken as a rough index of the average profitableness of the industry for the time being. Thus, the workman's position, as regards his proportion of the product of industry, became that of a humble partner. But he was a partner without any share in the management—without, in particular, any voice in that adjustment of the amount of production to the intensity of demand, upon which the selling price of his product, and therefore his livelihood, necessarily depended. Hence the cry among the coal-miners that no one coal-owner should be allowed, by reckless over-production, to depress the price for the whole trade, and so lower both profits and wages all round. They argued that, if the daily bread of half a million miners' households was to vary automatically with the price of coal—if the workmen, by agreeing to a Sliding Scale, were to forego their right to fight for better terms—then the fixing of the price, as against the consumer, should itself form a part of the general collective agreement upon which the whole industry depended.[1] This would have meant, in fact, a gigantic coal-trust governed by a joint committee of capitalists and workmen, regulating output, prices, and rates of wages, a combination which British coal-owners, despite several attempts, have hitherto failed to establish. The miners, except in South Wales, have therefore abandoned the Sliding Scale, and have now, as we shall presently describe, come under the influence of another doctrine.[2]

Meanwhile, the step which the coal-owners have never been able to take has been taken by most of the Birmingham metal trades. Since 1890 a remarkable series of " Alliances " have been concluded between the Employers' Associations and the Trade Unions of the various sections of the staple industry of Birmingham, based on the idea of a partnership

---

[1] See our chapter on " Continuity of Employment " for a description of the policy of restricting output.

[2] The fall of prices since 1873, to whatever cause it may be attributed, would have made any general adoption of the Sliding Scale disastrous to the wage-earners. Between 1867-77 (taken as par) and 1896, Mr. Sauerbeck's Index Number, representing the general level of prices, has fallen continuously from 100 to 61, the decline having no relation to the extent of business or to the aggregate employers' profits, both of which are much greater now than at any former period. The advocates of a Sliding Scale contemplate, it is true, a periodical revision of the basis. But in a period of falling prices, the onus of making the change would always be on the wage-earners, and even if they overcame this serious obstacle, they would necessarily stand to lose so long as each particular basis was adhered to. In a period of rising prices, as, for instance, between 1850 and 1873, the employers would be at a similar disadvantage. The fact is that, whether we adopt one assumption or another, the rate of wages has no assignable relation to the fluctuations in the price of the product. There seems no valid reason why the wage-earner should voluntarily put himself in a position in which every improvement in productive methods, every cheapening of the cost of carriage, every advance in commercial organisation, every lessening of the risks of business, every lightening of the taxes or other burdens upon industry, and every fall in the rate of interest—all of which are calculated to lower price—should automatically cause a shrinking of his wages.

between employers and workmen to increase the profitableness of the trade as a whole.[1] The terms of the " Alliance " between " the Associated Bedstead and Fender Mount Manufacturers, and those operatives (strip casters, stampers, spinners, turners, burnishers, dippers, and solderers) who are members of the Bedstead and Fender Mount (Operatives) Association," are typical of all these agreements. " The object of the Alliance shall be the improvement of selling prices, and the regulation of wages upon the basis of such selling prices . . . thereby securing better profits to manufacturers and better wages to workpeople." To secure this object the employers and workmen alike agree to combine against any manufacturer who sells below the agreed price, or attempts to reduce wages. " This understanding shall include a pledge on the part of the manufacturers not to employ any but association workpeople (over 21 years of age), excepting by special arrangement with the Operatives' Association," and on the part of the workmen not to work for any but those manufacturers who sell their goods at such prices as are from time to time decided upon by " a Wages Board, to be formed of an equal number of employers and employed." " The first advances of prices would be recommended to the Wages Board whenever it was considered safe to make such advance . . . that is, when all the workpeople have joined their Association, and when all the manufacturers have agreed together to sell at the prices fixed by the Employers' Association. . . . The bonus paid to the members of the Operatives' Association shall be increased at the rate of five per cent advance of bonus upon wages for every ten per cent advance . . . upon present

[1] These " Alliances," which form a significant even though perhaps a temporary industrial development, have elaborate printed agreements, almost identical in their terms. Some idea of the spirit underlying them may be gathered from a pamphlet, *The New Trades Combination Movement, its Principle and Methods*, by E. J. Smith (Birmingham, 1895), on behalf of the employers and from an article by W. J. Davis (Secretary of the National Society of Amalgamated Brassworkers) in the *Birmingham and District Trades Journal* for July 1896. The *Birmingham Daily Post* for the years 1895-96 contains many articles and letters on the subject.

selling prices" (irrespective of changes in the market price of
metal as the raw material).

We have in these Birmingham "Alliances," of which
half a dozen have lately sprung into existence, an exceptionally developed manifestation of the doctrine that the
conditions of employment should be left to Supply and
Demand, or, to put it in another way, should correspond to
the relative strategic position of the parties to the bargain.
Each party naturally does its best, within the limits of the
law, to improve its own position in the market.   The workmen, finding themselves individually powerless to stand out
for better terms, combine in order to strengthen themselves
against the employers.   The employers, on their side, combine
to protect themselves against the workmen.   Finally both
parties, discovering no other way of maintaining the price of
their product, upon which both wages and profits are deemed
to depend, unite their forces in order to exact better terms
from the community for the trade as a whole, and incidentally
to protect themselves against what they choose to consider
the unfair competition of a few individuals among them.   Nor
is such an alliance either so new or so unique as might be
supposed.   The imperfect organisation of employers and
workmen alike, and the absence of a mutual understanding
between them, has hitherto stood in the way of the adoption
of formal or elaborate treaties of this nature.   But a tacit
assumption, acted on by both employers and workmen, may,
in some industries, be as effective in keeping up prices and
excluding competitors as a published treaty.   Thus, the
uniformly friendly relations between the little group of manufacturers of hand-made paper, and the union of the skilled
handicraftsmen employed, are certainly maintained by a half-
conscious compact to hinder new competitors from entering
the trade.[1]   And in such trades as the Plumbers, Basket-

---

[1] Thus, the employers have long allowed the union to limit most strictly the
number of apprentices, even to the point of there being "not a spare hand in the
trade."   The workmen have frequently pointed out how well this suits the
interests of the present employers, alleging that "it would be a great inducement

makers, and many others, it is common to find, in the
" Working Rules," or even in the constitution of the Trade
Union, a regulation inserted at the instance of the employers
which prohibits or penalises work being done directly for
the consumer, or for any class of employers who might
become the business rivals of those who have entered into
the agreement.

We see, therefore, that the Doctrine of Supply and
Demand differs in the most practical way from the Doctrine
of Vested Interests. Instead of being inconsistent with the
facts of modern industry, it seems capable of indefinite
development to meet the changing conditions of the world-
commerce. Far from being antagonistic to the business spirit
of the present century, it falls in with the assumption that
the highest interests of Humanity are best attained by
every one pursuing what he conceives to be his own interest
in the manner, within the limits of the law of the land, that
he thinks best for himself. It is, moreover, merely applying
to the relations of capital and labor the principles which
already govern the business relations of commercial men to
each other. Whether the capitalist can bargain individually
with his workpeople, or is forced by their combination to
deal with them collectively, the Doctrine of Supply and
Demand seems to put the matter on a strictly business
footing. The relation between employer and wage-earner
like that between buyer and seller, becomes, in fact, merely
an incident in the " beneficent private war which makes one
man strive to climb on the shoulders of another and remain
there." [1] Seen in this light, the unsystematic inequality
which is the result of the modern industrial struggle, ha

for capital to enter the trade if labor could be got," but that the Trade Union
regulations made the " vat trade," in effect, " a close corporation. . . . Ther
has long been a mutual agreement between the two parties. . . . There hav
been little disputes from time to time, no doubt, but they have been more in th
nature of family jars than anything else."—*Arbitration on the Question of ar
Advance in Wages* . . ., Rupert Kettle, Esq., Q.C., Arbitrator (Maidstone, 1874)
p. 64.

[1] *Popular Government*, by Sir Henry Maine (London, 1885), p. 50.

important bearings on personal character. If the spirit of self-help causes individuals to combine for their own protection, this conscious co-operation has the advantage of encouraging, not merely energy and persistency, but also that deliberate self-control and subordination of one impulse to another, which lies at the bottom of all voluntary association. We find, in fact, that a complete intellectual acceptance of the Doctrine of Supply and Demand has much the same results upon the attitude of Trade Unionism as it has upon commercial life, and that it throws up, as leaders, much the same type of character in the one case as in the other. Those who know the Trade Union world will have no difficulty in recognising, in certain of its sections, both in corporate policy and in the characters of individual leaders, the same strong, self-reliant, and pugnacious spirit ; the same impatience of sentiment, philanthropy, and idealism ; the same self-complacency at their own success in the fight, and the same contempt for those who have failed ; above all, the same conception of the social order, based on the axiom that " to him that hath shall be given, and from him that hath not shall be taken away even that which he hath." To the idealist who sees in Trade Unionism a great class upheaval of the oppressed against the oppressors, it comes as a shock to recognise, in the Trade Union official of this type, pushing the interests of his own clients at the expense of everybody else, merely another embodiment of the " spirit of the bagman." Nor has the believer in individual self-help any right to complain when the " spirit of the bagman " leads, not to free competition and war, but to close corporations and monopoly. When people discover that they can do better for themselves by uniting to fight some one else than by opposing each other, the very spirit of self-help impels them to combine. If they are individually free to pursue their own interest in the way they think best, it follows that they are free to combine when they think their own interest lies in that direction. " Where combination is possible," Robert Stephenson declared in 1853 with regard to

railways, "competition is impossible." [1]   If the wage-contract
is placed on the same footing as any other commercial
bargain, the pursuit of the individual self-interest may be
expected to work out in practice in the same manner in
that as in other business transactions.   " The more perfect
the competition," said Professor Foxwell in 1888, " the more
certain and strong is the resulting monopoly." [2]   Where, as
in the case of the London water and gas companies, the
American trusts, and the German syndicates, combination
pays better than competition, it will tend gradually to supersede it.   If, as in the Birmingham trades, what is euphemistic-
ally termed an " alliance " between employers and workmen
results in increasing both wages and profits, this strengthening of the common forces against the rest of the community
will, in one form or another, tend to prevail.

But though the Doctrine of Supply and Demand is now
accepted by a large section of the Trade Union world, as
regards the amount of money wages, there is a strong and,
as we think, a growing protest against it.   The assumption
that the conditions of employment should vary according to
the strategic position of each section of the wage-earners,
obviously works out disadvantageously for the weaker
sections.   To the members of the British Steel Smelters'
Association, making as much as a pound a day, the Doctrine
of Supply and Demand seems a reasonable assumption.   The
unorganised laborers by their side, working as hard and as
long for a fifth of the money, are naturally disposed to take
a different view.   To the great army of women workers,
with very few exceptions, the fixing of wages according to
strategic position means, in practice, the barest possible subsistence.   Even in the United Kingdom, after half a century
of improvement, our foremost statistician has computed that

[1] Report of Select Committee on Railway and Canal Bills, 1853, Question
885.
[2] See Professor H. S. Foxwell's suggestive paper contributed to the British
Association in 1888, on "The Growth of Monopoly and its Bearing on the
Functions of the State," published in the *Revue d'Économie Politique*, September
1889.

in 1893 no fewer than 25 per cent of the whole number of adult male workers in the community received for their labor *less* than a pound a week—"that is," Sir Robert Giffen significantly added, "really below the line that one would consider expedient for a minimum subsistence."[1] Nor are the results upon the stronger sections of workmen altogether satisfactory. Though the Doctrine of Supply and Demand gives them high rates of pay in good times, it also brings with it the necessity of submitting, in the alternating periods of contraction, to repeated reductions of wages and lengthening of the hours of labor. There is a growing feeling among Trade Union leaders that fluctuations of this sort are unfavorable to the increase of sobriety, thrift, and deliberateness among the workmen—that a boilermaker, for instance, who earns £300 one year and £50 the next, is less likely to have a comfortable home than a Woolwich Arsenal pattern-maker, receiving a steady wage of thirty-eight shillings a week. There seems, too, a special unreasonableness in determining the hours of labor, not according to the physical strength of the worker or the nature of his task, but according to the strategic position of each section in the competitive labor market. A doctrine which results in the community getting only thirty-seven hours' work a week out of the well-nourished Northumberland coal-hewer, and only thirty-three hours a week out of the highly-paid flint glass maker, whilst forcing the laundry-women to toil for seventy hours, and the chronically underfed chain and nail operatives for eighty hours, stands self-condemned. Finally, there are some of the most vital conditions of employment to which the Doctrine of Supply and Demand is manifestly inapplicable. It is impossible, for instance, to adjust the ventilation, drainage, temperature, sanitary conveniences, and safety of a cotton-mill or an engineering establishment, in proportion to the strategic position of each of the eight or ten different sections of workpeople there employed. These conditions

---

[1] Evidence of Mr. (now Sir) Robert Giffen, Royal Commission on Labor (sitting as a whole), 24th January 1893, Question 6942.

must, in practice, be the same for the piecer and spinner, the boilermaker and his helper. If no other consideration than Supply and Demand entered into the question, it would pay the employer better to silence, by the bribe of higher wages, any minority strong enough to grumble, rather than incur the expense of improving the conditions for the whole establishment.

We reach here a point on which the community has long since become convinced that neither the Doctrine of Vested Interests, nor that of Supply and Demand affords any guide in determining the conditions of employment. In all that concerns the sanitary condition of the workplace, or the prevention of accidents, we are not content merely to protect the " established expectation " of the workmen, nor yet to leave the matter to settle itself according to the strategic position of each section. By common consent the employer is now required, in all this range of conditions, to give his workpeople, not what has been customary, nor yet what they can exact, but what, in the opinion of Parliament and its expert advisers, is necessary for their health and efficiency.

Exactly the same position has been reached with regard to the hours of labor of children in all industries, and to those of adult women in certain industries. The action of the Legislature, from 1847 down to the present day, in fixing the maximum working day for adult women workers, has been based on the assumption that the duration of toil, like the conditions of sanitation and safety, cannot properly be left to Supply and Demand, but must be deliberately determined upon expert evidence of how much factory labor the average woman can do without injury to her health. Nor has Parliament limited this assumption to women and children. By the Railway Servants (Hours of Labor) Act of 1893 it was provided that, whenever the Board of Trade is satisfied that the hours of any railway worker are excessive, or that they do not provide sufficient intervals of uninterrupted rest, the Board may require the railway company to submit, for its approval, a new schedule of hours so framed as to bring the actual hours of work within what the Board may consider to be "reasonable limits," and may compel compliance with the revised schedule under penalty of a fine not exceeding a hundred pounds a day.[1]   To the vast

---

[1] The average public opinion of the propertied classes on these points has been well expressed by the Right Hon. Sir Lyon (now Lord) Playfair, F.R.S., in his essay *On the Wages and Hours of Labor* (London, 1892 ; published by the Cobden Club).   " It is to the interest of all of us that the weak should be protected against the strong ; and hence it is right to enact factory laws to regulate the hours of labor for women and children, and these react without law in shortening the hours of labor of men.   Children are the growing generation of men and women, and their labor should be of a kind that will not stunt their growth.   True, women may be adults [why " may "?] ; and why should we class them with children ?   Because it is to the interest of all of us that female labor should be limited so as not to injure the motherhood and family life of a nation. . . .   It is to the interests of all of us that work should be carried on in normal conditions of health, so that workshops should not maim or stunt humanity.   It is not in the power of individual workmen to protect themselves from defective machinery or bad ventilation ; so it is in the interests of all of us to make laws for their preservation from preventable causes of mortality."   Lord Playfair then proceeds to denounce any interference by the State with regard to the hours of labor or wages of adult men, on the grounds (1) " that it would be impossible for the State to intervene in the management of trade, because, if it did so, it becomes responsible for the success or failure of each particular undertaking," and (2) " that it is, not a theory, but a law of economics surely established, that decline and degradation follow the loss of self-activity."   Lord Playfair nowhere explains why these arguments do not equally negative any State interference with the hours of adult women, or any legal prescription of elaborate and costly sanitary provisions in factories containing only adult men.   Nor does he explain why the same assumption of general wellbeing, upon which he justifies State interference with adult women's hours and adult men's waterclosets, would not equally justify State interference with adult women's wages and adult men's hours.   The whole essay is full of similar jumps from one hypothesis to another, without warning to the reader, or explanation of the reason for the substitution.   It is, in fact, a remarkable instance of the manner in which even a man trained in one science will, in dealing with the subject matter of another in which he has had no systematic training, use the logic of the uneducated.   It is therefore not surprising that, in the very next year after this authoritative deliverance against any State interference with the hours of adult men, it was Lord Playfair himself who piloted through the House of Lords the bill empowering the Board of Trade peremptorily to stop excessive hours of labor among railway servants, and who even resisted an amendment to confine the scope of this protective measure to persons engaged with the movement of traffic (*House of Lords Journals*, vol. cxxv. 1893).   Lord Playfair has, so far as we know, not yet explained why this State intervention in the complicated railway industry has not made the Government "responsible for the success or failure of each particular undertaking" ; nor yet why " decline and degradation " has not followed "the loss of self-activity" among the railway servants.   The change of attitude in England with regard to regulation of the hours of railway servants has been elaborately analysed by Professor Gustav Cohn in two articles on " Die

majority of Trade Unionists the intellectual assumption on which Parliament has acted with regard to the hours of women and railway servants appears to apply all round. The average Trade Unionist unconsciously takes it for granted that the hours of labor, whether fixed by Collective Bargaining or Legal Enactment, ought to be settled without reference to the momentary strategic position of the section concerned. We have already noticed that, with one or two remarkable exceptions, the richer and more powerful sections of the wage-earners put forward no claim to shorter hours of labor than those enjoyed by their less advantageously placed colleagues, and that the successive requests for shorter hours have usually formed part of contemporary general movements extending from one end of the Trade Union world to the other, and based on the plea that the shorter working day proposed was desirable in the interests of physical health and civic efficiency.

When we pass from the circumstances amid which the wage-earner is to work, and the number of hours which he must spend in labor, to the amount of money which he will receive as wages, we find the protest against the Doctrine of Supply and Demand much less universal, and only recently becoming conscious of itself. During the whole of this century middle-class public opinion has scouted the idea that the actual money wages of the operative could possibly be governed by any other considerations than the relative strategic positions of the parties to the bargain. And although the Trade Unionists have never thoroughly accepted this doctrine, even when that of Vested Interests had become manifestly impossible, they have, until recent years, never succeeded in intelligibly setting forth any contrary view. No reader of the working-class literature for the last two hundred years can, however, doubt the existence of an abiding faith in quite another principle. Deep down in their hearts the organised workmen, even whilst holding the

Arbeitszeit der Englischen Eisenbahnbediensten," in the *Archiv fur Eisenbahn-wesen* for 1892 and 1893 respectively.

Doctrine of Vested Interests, or acquiescing in that of Supply and Demand, have always cherished a feeling that one condition is paramount over all, namely, that wages must be so fixed that the existing generation of operatives should at any rate be able to live by their trade. "We ask," say the United Silk Throwers in 1872, "for a fair day's wages for a fair day's work. . . . What is a fair day's wage? Brethren, . . . no one can deny it, the due reward for our labor may be summed up in these words, Shelter, Food, and Raiment both for ourselves, our wives, and our children."[1] Throughout all the negotiations about Sliding Scales, we see constantly emanating from the rank and file of the operatives the demand that the Scale should begin from a minimum below which wages could under no circumstances be reduced. In this they had the support of the ablest working-class thinker of the time. "The first thing," wrote Lloyd Jones in 1874, "that those who manage trade societies should settle is a minimum which they should regard as a point below which they should never go. . . . Such a one as will secure sufficiency of food, and some degree of personal and home comfort to the worker ; not a miserable allowance to starve on, but *living wages*. The present agreements they are going into, on fluctuating market prices, is a practical placing of their fate in the hands of others. It is throwing the bread of their children into a scramble of competition, where everything is decided by the blind and selfish struggles of their employers."[2] "I entirely agree," wrote Professor Beesly, "with an admirable article by Mr. Lloyd Jones in a recent number of the *Beehive*, in which he maintained that colliers should aim at establishing a minimum price for their labor,

---

[1] Preface to *Rules of the United Silk Throwers' Trade and Friendly Society*, "commenced 24th October 1868" (Derby, 1872). In the *Practical Uses and Remarks on the Articles of the Operative Colliers of Lanark, Dumbarton, and Renfrewshire* (Glasgow, 1825), a pamphlet preserved in the Place MSS. (27,805), the phrase occurs, "our aim is lawfully to obtain a bare *living price* for our arduous labor."

[2] "Should Wages be Regulated by Market Price?" *Beehive*, 18th July 1874 ; see also his article in the issue for 4th March 1874, and *History of Trade Unionism*, pp. 325-327.

and compelling their employers to take this into account as the one constant and stable element in all their speculations. All workmen should keep their eyes fixed on this ultimate ideal."[1] For fifteen years this idea of a "Living Wage" simmered in the minds of Trade Unionists. The labor upheaval of 1889 marked its definite adoption as a fundamental assumption of Trade Unionism, in conscious opposition both to the Doctrine of Vested Interests and to that of Supply and Demand. The Match Girls had no vested interests to appeal to, and Supply and Demand, to the crowd of hungry laborers struggling at the dock gates, meant earnings absolutely inconsistent with industrial efficiency. The General Manager of one of the dock companies himself admitted the fact. "The very costume," he told the House of Lords, in which the dock laborers "presented themselves to the work prevents them doing work. The poor fellows are miserably clad, scarcely with a boot on their foot, in a most miserable state; and they cannot run, their boots would not permit them. . . . There are men who come on to work in our docks (and if with us, to a much greater extent elsewhere) who come on without having a bit of food in their stomachs, perhaps since the previous day; they have worked for an hour and have earned 5d.; their hunger will not allow them to continue; they take the 5d. in order that they may get food, perhaps the first food they have had for twenty-four hours. Many people complain of dock laborers that they will not work after four o'clock. But really, if you only consider it, it is natural. These poor men come on work without a farthing in their pockets; they have not anything to eat in the middle of the day; some of them will raise or have a penny, and buy a little fried fish, and by four o'clock their strength is utterly gone; they pay themselves off; it is absolute necessity which compels them. . . . Many people complain of their not working after four, but they do not know the real reason."[2] The result, in fact, of leaving wages

---

[1] *Beehive*, 16th May 1874; *History of Trade Unionism*, p. 326.
[2] Evidence before House of Lords Committee on the Sweating System; *The*

to be settled solely by the relative strategic positions of the parties to the bargain is to drive whole sections of the population to accept earnings so low, and so irregularly discontinuous, as to be wholly insufficient for the maintenance of any muscular strength. It was, we think, this unexpected discovery, made by the House of Lords Committee on Sweating, and by Mr. Charles Booth and his colleagues, that brought public opinion to the aid of the strikers of 1889, and compelled the employers to yield, at any rate for the moment, to demands which neither the Match Girls nor the Dockers had any power to obtain by the strength of their own combinations.

Four years later the same assumption gained world-wide celebrity under Lloyd Jones's own phrase of a " Living Wage." When the members of the Miners' Federation were menaced, in the trade contraction of 1892-93, with a serious reduction of wages, they definitely repudiated the Doctrine of Supply and Demand, and maintained their right, whatever the state of trade, to a minimum sufficient to secure their efficiency as producers and citizens. " They held it as a matter of life and death," said the Vice-President of the Miners' Federation in 1892, " that any condition of trade ought to warrant the working man living. They held that it was a vital principle that a man by his labor should live, and notwithstanding all the teachings of the political economists, all the doctrines taught by way of supply and demand, they said there was a greater doctrine over-riding all these, and that was the doctrine of humanity. They believed that the working-man was worthy of his hire, and held at the present moment that wages were as low as they ever ought to be." [1]   " We have come to the conclusion," repeated the President of the same organisation in 1894, " that prior to 1887 the men were not earning a living wage, that is, they had not sufficient wage at

---

Story of the Dockers' Strike, by Llewellyn Smith and Vaughan Nash (London, 1889), p. 47.

[1] Speech of Sam Woods, M.P., at the Annual Conference of the Miners' Federation of Great Britain, held at Hanley, January 1892, pp. 9-10.

the end of the week to properly feed and clothe their children and pay their way in the world. We think that thirty per cent added on to the rate of wages then paid will secure to the men what we believe to be the rate of wages which will consummate that desirable object." [1]

We can now form a definite idea of the assumption which this generation has set up against the Doctrine of Supply and Demand, and which we have termed the Doctrine of a Living Wage. There is a growing feeling, not confined to Trade Unionists, that the best interests of the community can only be attained by deliberately securing, to each section of the workers, those conditions which are necessary for the continuous and efficient fulfilment of its particular function in the social machine. From this point of view, it is immaterial to the community whether or not a workman has, by birth, servitude, or purchase, acquired a " right to a trade," or what, at any given moment, may be his strategic position towards the capitalist employer. The welfare of the community as a whole requires, it is contended, that no section of workers should be reduced to conditions which are positively inconsistent with industrial or civic efficiency. Those who adopt this assumption argue that, whilst it embodies what was good in the two older doctrines, it avoids their socially objectionable features. Unlike the Doctrine of Vested Interests, it does not involve any stereotyping of industrial processes, or the protection of any class of workers in the monopoly of a particular service. It is quite consistent with the freedom of every wage-earner to choose or change his occupation, and with the employer's freedom to take on whichever man he thinks best fitted for his work. Thus it in no way checks mobility or stops competition. Unlike the Doctrine of Supply and Demand it does not tempt the workmen to limit their numbers, or combine with the employers to fix prices,

---

[1] *Private Minutes of Proceedings at a Joint Conference between Representatives of the Federated Coal-owners and the Miners' Federation of Great Britain and Ireland, Lord Shand in the Chair* (London, 1894); speech of Mr. B. Pickard, M.P., p. 17.

or restrict output. It avoids, too, the evil of fluctuations of wages, in which the income of the workers varies, not according to their needs as citizens or producers, nor yet to the intensity of their exertion, but solely according to the temporary and, as far as they are concerned, fortuitous position of their trade. On the other hand, the Doctrine of a Living Wage goes far in the direction of maintaining "established expectation." Whilst it includes no sort of guarantee that any particular individual will be employed at any particular trade, those who are successful in the competition may feel assured that, so long as they retain their situations, the conditions of an efficient and vigorous working life will be secured to them.[1]

The most obvious drawback of the Doctrine of a Living Wage is its difficulty of application. There is, to begin with, a loss of theoretical perfection in the fact that the indispensable minimum conditions prescribed for each occupation cannot practically be adapted to the requirements of each individual, but must be roughly gauged by needs of the normal type. It may well be that a consumptive weaver or a short-sighted engineer requires, for his continued preservation, atmospheric conditions or elaborate fencing of machinery which would be wasted on the vast majority of his colleagues. It might be found that an exceptionally delicate girl ought not to work more than five hours a day, or that a somewhat backward laborer with a sick wife and a large family could not maintain himself in physical efficiency on the standard wages of his class. But this is not a practical objection. The prescription of certain minimum conditions does not prevent the humane employer from voluntarily granting to any exceptionally unfortunate individuals for whom the minimum is insufficient whatever better terms are physically

---

[1] Thus the Doctrine of a Living Wage does not profess, any more than does the Doctrine of Vested Interests or that of Supply and Demand, to solve the problem of the unemployed or the unemployable. All three doctrines are obviously consistent with any treatment of that problem, from leaving the unemployed and the unemployable to starvation or mendicancy, up to the most scientific Poor Law classification, or the most complete system of state or trade insurance.

possible. What it does prevent is the taking advantage of the strategic weakness of such individuals, and their being compelled to accept positively worse conditions of employment than their stronger colleagues. A more serious difficulty is our lack of precise knowledge as to what are the conditions of healthy life and industrial efficiency. In the matter of sanitation this difficulty has, within the past fifty years, been largely overcome. With regard to the proper limits to be set to the duration of toil, we are every year gaining more information from the doctors and the physiologists, and a Select Committee, called upon to decide upon evidence the maximum working day consistent, in any particular industry, with the healthy existence, home life, and citizenship of the average workman, would arrive, without much difficulty, at a reasonable decision. The case is very different with regard to wages. There are practically no scientific data from which we can compute the needs of particular occupations. The customary standards of life differ from class to class to such an extent as to bear no discoverable relation to the waste and repair involved in the respective social functions of the various grades. It would, it is true, be possible for our imaginary Select Committee to come to some definite conclusion as to the amount of food stuffs, clothing, and house accommodation, without which no family could, in town and country respectively, be maintained in full physical and mental health. But directly we compare the muscular exhaustion of the steel-smelter, plater, or flint glass maker, with the intensity of mental application of the cotton-spinner, engraver, or linotype operator, we have as yet no data from which to estimate the cost of the extra food, clothing, and recreation called for by the greater waste of muscle and nerve of any of these sections, over that incurred by the day laborer or the railway porter. And even if we could come to some conclusion as to the " normal ration " required to keep each trade in health, we should still be unable to decide how much must be added in each case to compensate for irregularity of employment. The stonemasons and the painters, who are rendered idle at every frost, the boilermakers and the engineers, subject to the intense fluctuations of speculative shipbuilding, are in a very different position from the railway servants and municipal employees, whose weekly incomes are practically uninterrupted. There is yet another difficulty. If special wages were fixed to meet the special needs of particular trades, neither the employer nor the community would have any guarantee that the extra sum allowed would be spent in extra nourishment, proper recreation, or insurance against periods of unemployment. Nor are the better-paid sections of the wage-earners at all prepared for any such application of the Doctrine of a Living Wage. All the industries in which the Trade Unions have succeeded in so controlling the conditions of employment as to secure exceptional rates of payment would naturally object to any departure from the Doctrine of Supply and Demand. The plater or rivetter, earning in good times a pound a day, is quite alive to the fact that so large an income cannot be proved to be required to maintain him in full efficiency, especially when he realises how considerable a sum is actually spent by the "average sensual man" in his class on gambling and drink. And, under the capitalist system, his reluctance to give up his position of advantage is justified by the fact, that whatever was saved in wages would merely swell the incomes of the brain-workers and shareholders, whose personal expenditure, and that of their wives, seem to him even more anarchic and wasteful than that of the ordinary working-class family.[1] All these considerations unite to make public opinion slow to apply to money wages the assumption already acted on with regard to the sanitary conditions of employment, and to a large extent accepted with regard to the hours of labor. We

---

[1] There are sound reasons of public policy, as we shall attempt to show in our chapter on "The Economic Characteristics of Trade Unionism," why the better-paid sections should not forego their superior incomes. The Doctrine of a Living Wage, though, as we shall demonstrate, valid as far as regards the establishment of a minimum Common Rule, does not supply a complete theory of distribution.

come, therefore, to the paradox that the Doctrine of a Living Wage, which has profoundly influenced Trade Union policy and public opinion with regard to all the other conditions of employment, finds least acceptance with regard to money wages. Our own impression is that, whilst the Doctrine of Vested Interests is hopelessly out of date, and that of Supply and Demand is every day losing ground, any application of the Doctrine of a Living Wage is likely, for the present, to be only gradual and tentative. In all that concerns Sanitation and Safety it has been already adopted, in principle, by Parliament and public opinion, though the actual securing to every wage-earner of a safe and healthy place of work, irrespective alike of what may have been customary in the trade, and of the employer's fluctuating profits, or demand for labor, is, owing to apathy and ignorance, still only imperfectly accomplished. With regard to the proportion of the day to be spent in toil, public opinion emphatically accepts the same doctrine in the case of children, and, for the most part, in the case of women. The last ten years have seen, moreover, a marked tendency to apply the same principles to the hours of men, and in the case of railway servants the responsibility for preventing labor in excess of what is consistent with industrial efficiency has already been assumed by the Board of Trade. In the matter of wages, public opinion is far more undecided. Under an organisation of industry in which employment is irregular, personal expenditure is uncontrolled, and surplus value accrues to the landlord and capitalist, we cannot expect to see the Doctrine of a Living Wage adopted, with regard to money incomes, by any but those unfortunate classes whose wages are manifestly below the minimum required for full physical efficiency. The events of 1889 and 1893, and the subsequent attention paid to the wages of the lower grades of workers under public bodies, indicate an approach to the view that earnings positively inadequate for industrial efficiency ought, in the public interest, and irrespective of Supply and Demand, to be deliberately brought up to a proper level.

The foregoing exposition of the assumptions of Trade Unionism will have given the reader the necessary clue, both to the historical changes in Trade Union policy from generation to generation, and also to the diversity at present existing in the Trade Union world. As soon as it is realised that Trade Unionists are inspired, not by any single doctrine as to the common weal, but more or less by three divergent and even contradictory views as to social expediency, we no longer look to them for any one consistent and uniform policy. The predominance among any particular section of workmen, or at any particular period, of one or other of the three assumptions which we have described—the Doctrine of Vested Interests, the Doctrine of Supply and Demand, and the Doctrine of a Living Wage—manifests itself in the degree of favor shown to particular Trade Union Regulations. The general faith in the Doctrine of Vested Interests explains why we find Trade Unionism, in one industry, or at one period, expressing itself in legally enforced terms of apprenticeship, customary rates of wages, the prohibition of new processes, strict maintenance of the lines of demarcation between trades, the exclusion of "illegal men," and the enforcement of "patrimony" and entrance fees. With the acceptance of the Doctrine of Supply and Demand we see coming in the policy of inclusion and its virtually compulsory Trade Unionism, Sliding Scales, the encouragement of improvements in machinery and the actual penalising of backward employers, the desire for a deliberate Regulation of Output and the establishment of alliances with employers against the consumer. Finally, in so far as the Doctrine of a Living Wage obtains, we see a new attention to the enforcement of Sanitation and Safety, general movements for the reduction of hours, attempts by the skilled trades to organise the unskilled laborers and women workers, denunciation of Sliding Scales and fluctuating incomes, the abandonment of apprenticeship in favor of universal education, and the insistence on a "Moral Minimum" wage below which no worker should be employed. Above all, these successive changes of faith explain the revolutions which have taken place in Trade Union opinion as to the relation of Labor to the State. When men believe in the Doctrine of Vested Interests, it is to the common law of the realm that they look for the protection of their rights and possessions. The law alone can secure to the individual, whether with regard to his right to a trade or his right to an office, his privilege in a new process or his title to property, the fulfilment of his "established expectation." Hence it is that we find eighteenth-century Trade Unionism confidently taking for granted that all its regulations ought properly to be enforced by the magistrate, and devoting a large part of its funds to political agitations and legal proceedings. When the Doctrine of Vested Interests was replaced by that of Supply and Demand, the Trade Unionists naturally turned to Collective Bargaining as their principal method of action. Instead of going to the State for protection, they fiercely resented any attempt to interfere with their struggle with employers, on the issue of which, they were told, their wages must depend. The Common Law, once their friend, now seemed always their most dangerous enemy, as it hampered their freedom of combination, and by its definitions of libel and conspiracy, set arbitrary limits to their capacity of making themselves unpleasant to the employers or the non-unionists. Hence the desire of the Trade Unionists of the middle of this century, whilst sweeping away all laws against combinations, to keep Trade Unionism itself absolutely out of the reach of the law-courts. The growth of the Doctrine of a Living Wage, resting as this does on the assumption that the conditions of employment require to be deliberately fixed, naturally puts the State in the position of arbitrator between the workman who claims more, and the employer who offers less, than is consistent with the welfare of other sections. But the appeal is not to the Common Law. It is no longer a question of protecting each individual in the enjoyment of whatever could be proved to be his customary privileges, or to flow from identical "natural rights," but of prescribing, for the several sections, the conditions required, in the interest of the whole community, by their diverse actual needs. We therefore see the Common Rules for each trade embodied in particular statutes, which the Trade Unionists, far from resisting, use their money and political influence to obtain. The double change of doctrine has thus brought about a return to the attitude of the Old Unionists of the eighteenth century, but with a significant difference. To-day it is not custom or privilege which appeals to the State, but the requirements of efficient citizenship. Whenever a Trade Union honestly accepts as the sole and conclusive test of any of its aspirations what we have termed the Doctrine of a Living Wage, and believes that Parliament takes the same view, we always find it, sooner or later, attempting to embody that aspiration in the statute law.

The political student will notice that there exists in the Trade Union world much the same cleavage of opinion, upon what is socially expedient, as among other classes of society. All Trade Unionists believe that the abandonment of the conditions of employment to the chances of Individual Bargaining is disastrous, alike to the wage-earners and to the community. But when, in pursuance of this assumption, they take concerted action for the improvement of their condition, we see at once emerge among them three distinct schools of thought. In the special issues and technical controversies of Trade Unionism we may trace the same broad generalisations, as to what organisation of society is finally desirable, as lead, in the larger world of politics, to the ultimate cleavage between Conservatives, Individualists, and Collectivists. The reader will have seen that there is, among Trade Unionists, a great deal of what cannot be described otherwise than as Conservatism. The abiding faith in the sanctity of vested interests ; the strong presumption in favor of the *status quo ;* the distrust of innovation ; the liking for distinct social classes, marked off from each other by corporate privileges and peculiar traditions ; the disgust at the modern spirit of self-seeking assertiveness; and the deep-rooted conviction that the only stable organisation of society is that based on each man being secured and contented in his inherited station of life—all these are characteristic of the genuine Conservative, whether in the Trade Union or the State. In sharp contrast with this character, and, as we think, less congenial to the natural bent of the English workman, we have, in the great modern unions, a full measure of Radical Individualism. The conception of society as a struggle between warring interests; the feeling that every man and every class is entitled to all that they can get, and to nothing more; the assumption that success in the fight is an adequate test of merit, and, indeed, the only one possible; and the bounding optimism which can confidently place the welfare of the community under the guardianship of self-interest—these are typical of the " Manchester School," alike in politics and in Trade Unionism. But in Trade Unionism, as in the larger sphere of politics, the facts of modern industry have led to a reaction. As against the Conservative, the Individualist Radical asserted that " all men are born free and equal, with equal rights to life, liberty, and the pursuit of happiness." But it is now obvious that men are not born equal, either in capacity or in opportunity. There has accordingly arisen, in the Trade Union as in the political world, a school of thought which asserts that a free struggle among unequal individuals, or combinations of individuals, means the permanent oppression and degradation of those who start handicapped, and inevitably results in a tacit conspiracy among the more favored classes to maintain or improve their own positions of vantage at the cost of the community at large. The Collectivist accordingly insists on the need for a conscious and deliberate organisation of society, based, not on vested interests or the chances of the fight, but on the scientifically ascertained needs of each section of citizens. Thus, within the Trade Union movement, we find the Collectivist-minded working-man grounding his regulation of the conditions of employment upon what we have

called the Doctrine of a Living Wage.   In the wider world
of politics we see the Collectivist statesman groping his way
to the similar conception of a deliberate organisation of production, regulation of service, and apportionment of income—
in a word, to such a conscious adjustment of the resources
of the community to its needs as will result in its highest
possible efficiency.   In the Trade Union world the rival
assumptions exist side by side, and the actual regulation of
industry is a perpetually shifting compromise between them.
The political student may infer that, in the larger organisation of society, the rival conceptions of Conservatism, Individualism, and Collectivism will long co-exist.   Any further
application of Collectivism, whether in the Trade Union or
the political world, depends, it is clear, on an increase in our
scientific knowledge, no less than on the growth of new
habits of deliberate social co-operation.   Progress in this
direction must, therefore, be gradual, and will probably be
slow.   And the philosophical Collectivist will, we think, foresee that, whether in the regulation of labor, the incidence of
taxation, or the administration of public services, any stable
adjustment of social resources to social needs must always
take into account, not only the scientifically ascertained conditions of efficiency, but also the " established expectation "
and the " fighting force " of all the classes concerned.

PART III

TRADE UNION THEORY

PART XII

TRADE UNION THEORY

CHAPTER I

THE VERDICT OF THE ECONOMISTS

DOWN to within the last thirty years it would have been taken for granted, by every educated man, that Trade Unionism, as a means of bettering the condition of the workman, was "against Political Economy."[1] This impression was derived, not so much from any explicit declaration of the economists, as from the general view of wages which enlightened public opinion had accepted from them. The Theory of the Wage Fund, in conjunction with closely related theories of the accumulation of capital and the increase of population, seemed definitely to contradict the fundamental assumptions on which Trade Unionism depended. If Political Economy was understood to demonstrate it was plainly impossible, in any given state of capital and population, to bring about any genuine and permanent rise of wages, otherwise than in the slow course of generations, it was clearly not worth while troubling about the pretensions of workmen ignorant of economic science. Accordingly, for the first three quarters of the century we find, beyond the accustomed denunciation of outrages and strikes, practically nothing but a general and undiscriminating hostility to Trade Unionism in the

[1] Even the Christian Socialists, the Positivists, and the champions of labor in Parliament usually regarded the pretensions of Trade Unionism as being in contradiction to the orthodox Political Economy, in which they accordingly did not believe !

abstract, couched in the language of theoretical economics. And although the theory, with all its corollaries, has now been abandoned by economic authority, it still lingers in the public mind, and lies at the root of most of the current middle-class objections to Trade Unionism. We must therefore clear the ground of this obsolete criticism before we can proceed to estimate Trade Union pretensions in the light of the economic science of to-day.

We need not here enter into any detailed history or elaborate analysis of the celebrated Theory of the Wage Fund.[1] As widely popularised by J. R. M'Culloch, from 1823 onward, this theory declared that " wages depend at any particular moment on the magnitude of the Fund or Capital appropriated to the payment of wages compared with the number of laborers. . . . Laborers are everywhere the divisor, capital the dividend." [2] Nor was this statement confined to the truism that the average wages of the wage-receiving class was to be found by dividing the aggregate

[1] The most recent, and in many respects the best, account of this celebrated theory is to be found in *Wages and Capital : an Examination of the Wages Fund Doctrine* (London, 1896), by F. W. Taussig, Professor of Political Economy in Harvard University. *A History of the Theories of Production and Distribution in English Political Economy from 1776 to 1848*, by Edwin Cannan (London, 1893), contains an acutely critical analysis. The fullest exposition of the modern economic view is, perhaps, *The Wages Question : a Treatise on Wages and the Wages Class* (New York, 1876 ; London, 1891), by F. A. Walker. In the *Principles of Economics* (Book VI. ch. ii. page 618 of 3rd edition, London, 1895) Professor Marshall explains in a long note what Ricardo and Mill really meant by their statements on the wage-fund.

[2] Article on " Wages " in *Encyclopædia Britannica* (4th edition, 1823), republished with additions as *A Treatise on the Circumstances which determine the Rate of Wages and the Condition of the Labouring Classes* (London, 1851). A widely read American follower of Ricardo and M'Culloch put the case as follows : " That which pays for labor in every country is a certain portion of actually accumulated capital, which cannot be increased by the proposed action of Government, nor by the influence of public opinion, nor by combinations among the workmen themselves. There is also in every country a certain number of laborers, and this number cannot be diminished by the proposed action of Government, nor by public opinion, nor by combinations among themselves. There is to be a division now among all these laborers of the portion of capital actually there present " (*Elements of Political Economy*, by A. L. Perry, New York, 1866, p. 122). We understand that this work has run through about twenty editions, and is still a popular text-book in the United States. An edition was published in London in 1891.

"fund devoted to their payment" by the number of the laborers for the time being. What was insisted on was that the amount of this "fund" was necessarily predetermined by the economic circumstances of the community at any given time. The amount of the "capital" depended on the extent of the savings from the product of the past. The extent of the fund to be appropriated to the payment of wages depended on how much of that capital was required for plant and materials. Hence the amount of the Wage Fund at any particular moment was absolutely predetermined, partly by the action of the community in the past, and, as suggested by Cairnes, partly by the technical character of the industries of the present.[1] "There is supposed to be," wrote J. S. Mill, "at any given instant a sum of wealth which is unconditionally devoted to the payment of wages of labor. This sum is not regarded as unalterable, for it is augmented by saving and increases with the progress of society ; but it is reasoned upon as at any given moment a predetermined amount. More than that amount it is assumed that the wage-receiving class cannot possibly divide among them ; that amount and no less they cannot but obtain. So that the sum to be divided being fixed the wages of each depend solely on the divisor, the number of participants." [2] It was a plain inference from this view that, whatever might automatically occur in the future if one factor increased faster than the other, the terms of the current bargain for

---

[1] *Some Leading Principles of Political Economy newly expounded* (London, 1874), pp. 199-200.

[2] Mill's review of W. T. Thornton's book *On Labour*, in *Fortnightly Review*, May 1869 ; reprinted in *Dissertations and Discussions* (London, 1875), vol. iv. p. 43.

This conception of a definitely limited wage-fund, all in hand at the beginning of the year, and all replaced at its close, seems to have been derived from the case of the English wheat-growing farmer, who was supposed to calculate, when he had reaped his harvest, how much he could lay out in wages until the next harvest was gathered in. A closer analogy would have been the practice of English Government Departments, such as the Admiralty Shipbuilding yards, which have allotted to them, at the beginning of each financial year, definite sums, theoretically insusceptible of increase, to be expended in wages during the year.

the hire of labor at any particular moment were, as regards
the wage-earning class as a whole, absolutely unalterable,
whether by law or by negotiation. "There is no use," the
workmen were told, "in arguing against any one of the four
fundamental rules of arithmetic. The question of wages is a
question of division. It is complained that the quotient is
too small. Well, then, how many ways are there to make a
quotient larger? Two ways. Enlarge your dividend, the
divisor remaining the same, and the quotient will be larger ;
lessen your divisor, the dividend remaining the same, and
the quotient will be larger."[1] The wage-earners in the
aggregate were at any moment already obtaining all that
could possibly be conceded to them at that moment, and
any gain made by one section of them could only be made
at the expense of their weaker colleagues. Conversely, any
reduction suffered by one section of the wage-earners was
necessarily and contemporaneously balanced by gain to
some other section. "All the capital," declared M'Culloch,
"through the higgling of the market will be equitably
distributed among all the laborers. Hence it is idle to
suppose that the efforts of the capitalists to cheapen labor
can have the smallest influence on its medium price."[2] It
followed with no less logic that any efforts of laborers in
the opposite direction were equally futile. Public opinion

[1] *Elements of Political Economy*, by A. L. Perry, p. 123.

[2] Even after a lifetime of economic study, M'Culloch could deliberately
repeat that "all the wealth of the country applicable to the payment of wages is
uniformly, in all ordinary cases, divided among the laborers. . . . *It is impossible
for the employers of labor artificially to reduce the rate of wages*" (*A Treatise on
the Circumstances which determine the Rate of Wages and the Condition of the
Labouring Classes*, London, 1851, pp. 48-49). "A single rich man may take
advantage of a single poor man by availing himself of the necessities or simplicity
of the latter. But the body of capitalists in any country will always pay away in
wages to the body of working men all the funds which they have applicable to
the employment of labor" (*An Essay on the Relations of Labour and Capital*,
London, 1854, by C. Morrison, p. 18). Fawcett apparently retained the
same view down to his death. "The capital of the country provides its wage-
fund. This wage-fund is distributed amongst the whole wage-receiving population, and therefore the average of each individual's wages cannot increase unless
either the number of those who receive wages is diminished, or the wage-fund is
augmented."—*Manual of Political Economy*, by Henry Fawcett (London, 1869),
pp. 206-207 ; *Life*, by Leslie Stephen (London, 1886), p. 157.

accordingly unhesitatingly refuted Trade Unionism, to use the words of one of the most eminent of modern economists, " with a summary reference to the doctrine of the wage-fund. Strikes could not increase the wage-fund, therefore they could not enhance wages. If they should appear to raise the rate in any trade, this must be due either to a corresponding loss in the regularity of employment or to an equivalent loss, in regularity or in rate, by some other trade or trades occupying a position of economical disadvantage. Hence strikes could not benefit the wages class."[1] But the theory went much further than the mere negativing of strikes and combinations. It left no room for any elevation of the wage-earners even if the improvement justified itself by an increase in productive capacity. If one section of the wage-earners succeeded, by peaceful negotiation or law, in so bettering their own conditions of employment as positively to increase their productive efficiency, this would still bring no greater reward to the class as a whole. Though the increase in the cost of their labor might soon be made up to their employers by its greater product, yet this increased drain on the wage-fund must automatically have depressed the condition, and so lowered the efficiency of other sections, with the result that, though the inequality between the sections would have increased, the aggregate efficiency of the wage-earners as a whole would not have risen. Thus every factory act, which increased the immediate cost of woman or child labor, had to be paid for by a contemporaneous decrease in somebody's wages; and every time a new expense for sanitation or precautions against accidents was imposed on the capitalists, some of the wage-earners had automatically to suffer a diminution of income.[2]

---

[1] *The Wages Question*, by F. A. Walker, p. 387. M'Culloch had expressly observed in his article on "Combinations" in the *Encyclopædia Britannica* (1823) that "nothing but the merest ignorance could make it supposed that wages could really be increased by such proceedings. They depend on the principle which they cannot affect, that is on the proportion between capital and population; and cannot be increased except by the increase of the former as compared with the latter."

[2] It followed logically that bad legislation could not depress, and good

Though public opinion accepted the statical view of the wage-fund as conclusive against the possibility of any general alteration of the terms of the labor contract, this crude conception supplied no answer to the assertion that the workmen in any particular trade might need to defend their own wages against special encroachment, or that they might find it possible, if only at the expense of other sections of wage-earners, to exact better conditions for themselves. But here the Trade Unionists found themselves confronted with the economic " laws " determining the employment of capital. " If," observed M'Culloch, " the wages paid to the laborers engaged in any particular employment be improperly reduced, the capitalists who carry it on will obviously gain the whole amount of this reduction over and above the common and ordinary rate of profit obtained by the capitalists engaged

---

legislation could not raise, the condition of the wage-earners. M'Culloch and Harriet Martineau went this length with regard to Combination Laws and Factory Acts respectively. " Looking generally to the whole of the employments carried on in the country," wrote the former in 1823, and again in 1851, "we do not believe that the Combination Laws had any sensible influence on the average and usual rate of wages. That they occasionally kept wages at a lower rate in some very confined businesses than they would otherwise have sunk to may be true, *though for that very reason they must have equally elevated them in others*" (article on " Combinations " in *Encyclopædia Britannica*, 4th edition, 1823 ; *Treatise on the Circumstances which determine the Rate of Wages*, London, 1851, p. 80). In 1833 Harriet Martineau wrote : " Mrs. Marcet is sorry to find that Mr. E. R[omilly] and I are of the same opinion about the Factory Bill, and I am very glad. She ought to hold the same, namely that legislation *cannot* interfere effectually between parents and children in the present state of the labor-market. Our operations must be directed towards proportioning the labor and capital, and not upon restricting the exchange of the one for the other ; an exchange which *must* be voluntary, whatever the law may say about it. We cannot make parents give their children a half-holiday every day in the year, unless we also give compensation for the loss of the children's labor. The case of those wretched factory children seems desperate ; the only hope seems to be that the race will die out in two or three generations, by which time machinery may be found to do their work better than their miserable selves. Every one's countenance falls at the very mention of the evidence which has lately appeared in the papers " (*Harriet Martineau's Autobiography*, by Maria Weston Chapman, London, 1877, vol. iii. p. 87). It is only fair to add that Harriet Martineau, unlike M'Culloch, was converted by a wider knowledge of the facts of industrial life. She herself records how what she saw in America brought her, not only to appreciate the value of Robert Owen's ideas and to retract her former economic dogmatism, but also to believe that the future possibly lay with a Collectivist organisation of society.—*Ibid.* vol. i. p. 232.

in other businesses. But a discrepancy of this kind could not possibly continue. Additional capital would immediately begin to be attracted to the department where wages are low and profits high, and its owners would be obliged, in order to obtain laborers, to offer them higher wages. It is clear, therefore, that if wages be unduly reduced in any branch of industry, they will be raised to their proper level, without any effort on the part of the workmen, by the competition of capitalists."[1] Similarly, if the laborers insisted on better terms in a particular trade, this must reduce its profitableness to the employers. And capital being assumed to be both mobile and omniscient, it at once began to "flow" out of this less profitable industry, in order to "flow" in to the other trades in which the cost of labor would simultaneously and automatically have been reduced. The laborers who had raised their conditions above the "proper" level found themselves therefore between the horns of a dilemma. If they all wished to be employed at their trade, wages must go back to the old level, and (seeing that part of the previous wage-fund had been diverted away) even temporarily below it. If, on the other hand, they insisted on preserving their newly-won better conditions, it was obvious that only a smaller number of them could find employment, the more so as the portion of the wage-fund invested in that trade would positively have diminished. The displaced workmen, as it was often explained to them, would thus have killed the goose which laid the golden eggs. The few who continued to find full employment at their trade might have gained, but taking the trade as a whole, the men would clearly have lost by the transaction.[2] "And hence the fundamental principle, that there are no means by which wages can be raised,

[1] Article on "Combinations," by J. R. M'Culloch, in *Encyclopædia Britannica*, 4th edition (Edinburgh, 1823), repeated in his *Treatise* of 1851.

[2] If the attempt to get the better conditions were made by means of Mutual Insurance or Collective Bargaining—as the economists always assumed would be the case—it would therefore almost certainly fail, as the displaced workmen would, sooner or later, be driven to compete for employment with those who succeeded in getting work, with the result that things would revert to the old level.

other than by accelerating the increase of capital as compared with population, or by retarding the increase of population as compared with capital, and every scheme for raising wages which is not bottomed on this principle, or which has not an increase of the ratio of capital to population for its object, must be completely nugatory and ineffectual." [1]

And when the Trade Unionists turned from the question of wages to-day, to the possibility of raising them in the following year, middle-class opinion had a no less conclusive answer to their claim. The future wage-fund that would be applicable for the payment of laborers in the ensuing year was, of course, necessarily limited by the available possessions of the community. But within that limit its amount depended on the will of the owners. They might, if they chose, consume any part of it for their own enjoyment, or they might be tempted to abstain from this consumption, and employ a larger or smaller proportion of their total possessions in productive industry. Ricardo had incidentally observed that the "motive for accumulation will diminish with every diminution of profit," [2] and it was assumed without hesitation that, whatever might be the various motives for saving, these motives would be stimulated or depressed according to the rate of interest which might be expected to be gained from the capital so invested. "The higher the rate of profit in any community, the greater will be the proportion of the annual savings which is added to capital, and the greater will be the inducement to save." [3] It thus followed that the rate at which capital, and therefore the wage-fund, would be increased would vary according to profit, rising when the rate of profit rose, and falling when the rate of profit fell. "The greater the proportion of

---

[1] Article on "Wages," by J. R. M'Culloch, in *Encyclopædia Britannica*, 4th edition (Edinburgh, 1823); see his *Principles of Political Economy* (Edinburgh, 1825), part iii. sec. 7.

[2] *On the Principles of Political Economy and Taxation* (London, 1817), p. 136.

[3] Article on the effects of machinery in the *Westminster Review*, January 1826, by W. Ellis, quoted by J. S. Mill (*Principles of Political Economy*, Book IV. chap. iv. p. 441 of 1865 edition).

wages to profits the smaller the tendency to national accumulation."[1] Any rise of wages could, therefore, only be temporary, and must quickly counteract itself, for "an increase in wages reduces the profits, and reduces the inducement to save and extend business, and this again tends to a reduction of wages."[2] Cairnes, in an unguarded moment, went even further. "Profits," he said, "are already at or within a hand's breadth of the minimum . . . below which, if the return on capital fall, accumulation, at least for the purpose of investment, will cease for want of adequate inducement."[3] This automatic check on the wage-earners' pretensions applies, it is clear, to more than the money wages. If by means of a Factory Act they had secured for the future shorter hours or better sanitation, this prospect of a reduction of profits would instantly limit the capitalists' desire to accumulate, and would induce them as a class to spend more of their incomes on personal enjoyment. "There is only a certain produce," wrote one widely-read critic of Trade Unionism, "to be divided between capitalist and laborer. If more be given to the laborer than nature awards, a smaller amount will remain for the capitalist ; the spirit of accumulation will be checked ; less will be devoted to productive purposes ; the wage-fund will dwindle, and the wage of the laborer will inevitably fall. For a time, indeed, a natural influence may be dammed back ; but only to act, ultimately, with accumulated force. In the long run, God's laws will overwhelm all human obstructions."[4] On the

---

[1] *Trade Unionism*, by James Stirling, p. 29.

[2] T. S. Cree, *A Criticism of the Theory of Trades Unions* (Glasgow, 1891), p. 25.

[3] *Some Leading Principles of Political Economy newly expounded*, by J. E. Cairnes (London, 1874), pp. 256-258. This unlucky prophecy was written in that year of colossal business profits, 1873 ! At that date the yield on good "trustee" securities in England was about £4 per £100. It has since fallen (1897) by no less than 25 per cent, yet accumulation and investment have gone on faster than ever.

[4] *Trade Unionism, with Remarks on the Report of the Commissioners on Trades Unions*, by James Stirling (Glasgow, 1869), 2nd edition, 1869 ; new edition, 1889, pp. 26-27. This sapient work was translated into French by T. N. Bernard, and published as *L'Unionisme des Ouvriers en Angleterre*. See also the article by the same author in *Recess Studies* (Edinburgh, 1870).

other hand, if wages remained low, and the rate of profit high, the capitalists would as a class be tempted to limit their personal expenditure, in order to take advantage of the high profits by accumulating as much capital as possible. Thus, as a recent opponent of Trade Unionism quite logically explained, the laborer's "policy should be to make the position of employers as pleasant and profitable as possible, and to coax them into trade, just as a shopkeeper tries to entice customers into his shop."[1] If wages relatively to profits were low one year, they would tend automatically to rise next year; if they were high one year, they would automatically be depressed in the following year.[2]

This theory of the rate of accumulation of capital, taken in conjunction with the Theory of the Wage Fund, appeared finally to dispose of every part of the Trade Union case. But enlightened public opinion had yet another argument to adduce, one which cut at the root, not of Trade Unionism only, but of all genuine improvement of the condition of the present generation of laborers, even if the capitalists actually desired to share their own profits with them. This was the celebrated "principle of population." Malthus had proved

[1] T. S. Cree, *A Criticism of the Theory of Trades Unions*, p. 30.

[2] "While the terms of a particular bargain are of importance to the individual workman and employer concerned, they are not of much importance to the workmen and employers as a whole, *as there is always a compensating action going on which is bringing wages to a true economical point.*"—*Ibid.* p. 10.

"The price of labor, at any given time and place, is not a matter left to the volition of the contracting parties; but is determined for them by a self-adjusting mechanism of natural forces. The amount of capital devoted to production—according to the prevalent strength of the effective desire of accumulation—determines the force of the demand for labor: the number of laborers desirous of employment—in accordance with the prevalent strength of the instinct of population—regulates the supply. All unknown to the capitalist and laborer, the rate of wages is fixed for them, by the natural adjustment of these antagonist forces; the amount of labor demanded by the whole body of capitalists on the one hand, the amount supplied by the whole body of laborers on the other. As Mr. Mill himself has tersely put it, in his *Political Economy*, 'Wages . . . depend on the ratio between population and capital.' When, therefore, the capitalist and the laborer come to divide the product of their joint industry, they find the division ready made to their hand. The profits due to the one, and the wages due to the other, have been apportioned, by the unerring agency of natural influences, and no room is left for cavil or coercion."—"Mr. Mill on Trades Unions," by James Stirling, in *Recess Studies* (Edinburgh, 1870), p. 311.

that human fecundity was, as a matter of fact, far in excess of the actual increase of population, and that the numbers of mankind were kept down by the positive checks of vice and misery, notably by the privations and hardships suffered by the poor. It was the part of wisdom to substitute, for these positive checks, that prudential restraint which delayed marriage or forewent parentage, and the only hope for the laborers lay in a great extension of this prudential restraint, so that the ratio of capital to wage-earners might increase. This hope was at best a faint one, because the prudential restraint would have to extend to the whole wage-earning class, and would have to be maintained with ever-increasing rigor, as the resulting fall in the rate of profit slackened the rate of accumulation. And whatever degree of prudence might animate the wage-earning class at any particular time, it was taken for granted that the rate of increase must habitually rise when wages increased, and fall when wages were reduced. " Thus, if combination were for a time to raise wages, the growth of the wage-fund would be unnaturally retarded, whilst a fictitious stimulus would be given to population by the momentary enrichment of the laboring class. A diminished demand for labor would coincide with an increased supply. The laborer's wages would be forced down to starvation-point ; and his last state would be worse than his first." [1] The ratio of population to capital was, indeed, effectively defended on both sides from any but transitory alteration. If capital fell behind population, wages fell, but this very fall automatically brought about a quickening of accumulation and a slackening of the increase of population. If population fell behind capital, wages rose, but this very rise caused a check to accumulation and a stimulus to the increase of population. " Should a union succeed," said the public opinion of the last generation, " in shutting out competition, and so unnaturally raising wages and lowering profits in some particular trade, a twofold reaction tends to restore the natural equilibrium. An

[1] *Trade Unionism*, by James Stirling, p. 29.

increased population will add to the supply of labor, while a diminished wage-fund will lessen the demand for it. The joint action of these two principles will—sooner or later—overcome the power of any arbitrary organisation, and restore profits and wages to their natural level." [1] " Against these barriers," said Cairnes, " Trade Unions must dash themselves in vain. They are not to be broken through or eluded by any combinations however universal; for they are the barriers set by Nature herself." [2]

So firmly were the various parts of the economist's theory bolted together, that there was only one way in which it was even conceivable that a Trade Union could better the conditions of its members. If the workmen in any trade could, either by law or by an absolutely firm combination extending from one end of the kingdom to another, permanently restrict the numbers entering that trade, they might, it was admitted, gradually force their employers to offer them higher wages. Hence it was habitually assumed that the whole aim and purpose of Trade Unionism was to bring about this position

---

[1] *Trade Unionism*, by James Stirling, p. 27. "In a thickly populated country, which has no vent for its surplus population abroad, Political Economy has but one advice to give to the younger members of the poorer classes. The postponement of, or abstinence from, marriage, or *from giving birth to children*, to a very great extent, is in such a case the only available preventive against the evils of too rapid an increase of numbers."—C. Morrison, *The Relations between Labour and Capital*, p. 51.

[2] *Some Leading Principles of Political Economy newly expounded*, by J. E. Cairnes (London, 1874), p. 338. In contrast with the methods of abstract reasoning, without inquiry into the facts of industry, which were pursued by the economists of the time, may be mentioned the interesting descriptions of the economic circumstances of the Sheffield trades published by Dr. G. Calvert Holland. In his *Mortality, Sufferings, and Diseases of Grinders*, part ii. (Sheffield, 1842), he gives as the result of actual observation (p. 46) that the longer a branch of the Sheffield trades has been in union, and the more perfectly it has been maintained, the higher is the rate of remuneration that the workmen receive, the lower is the degree of fluctuation in the trade, and the greater is the sobriety and thrift of the workers. He adds—" We would even go a step further and contend, that, with few exceptions, the respectability and substantial character of the manufacturers exhibit a strict relation to the same circumstances, viz. the degree to which the branch is associated. The system which gives unlimited play to competition not only lowers wages and degrades the condition of the masses, but ultimately reduces profits, narrows the liberality, and vitiates the moral tone of the manufacturers." Dr. Calvert Holland's observations upon the actual working of industrial competition appear to have been unknown, or at any rate unheeded, by the economists of the time.

of monopoly of a particular service. Such a monopoly was plainly inimical to the interests of the community. The increased drain on the wage-fund automatically depressed the wages of the rest of the wage-earners. Their exclusion from the ranks of the favored trade further intensified their own struggle for employment. Finally, as capital had to receive its normal rate of profit, the consumer found the price of the commodity raised against him. Fortunately, as the economists explained, such anti-social conduct could practically never succeed. Even if the monopolists managed rigidly to exclude new competitors from their trade, the rise in price would attract foreign producers, and lead to an importation of the commodity from abroad. If this were prohibited, the consumer would begin to seek alternatives for a commodity which had become too dear for his enjoyment, and invention would set to work to produce the same result by new processes, employing possibly quite a different kind of labor. One way or another the monopolists would be certain to find their trade shrinking up, so that a mere exclusion of new-comers would no longer avail them. They would find it impossible to maintain their exceptional conditions except by progressively reducing their own numbers, to the point even of ultimate extinction.

With so complete a demonstration of the impossibility of "artificially" raising wages, it is not surprising that public opinion, from 1825 down to about 1875, condemned impartially all the methods and all the regulations of Trade Unionism. To the ordinary middle-class man it seemed logically indisputable that the way of the Trade Unionists was blocked in all directions. They could not gain any immediate bettering of the condition of the whole wage-earning class, because the amount of the wage-fund at any given time was predetermined. They could not permanently secure better terms even for a particular·section, because this would cause capital immediately to begin to desert that particular trade or town. They could not make any real progress in the near future, because they would thereby check the accumulation of capital. And finally, even if they could persuade a benevolent body of capitalists to augment wages by voluntarily sharing profits, the "principle of population" lay in wait to render nugatory any such new form of "out-door relief." "The margin for the possible improvement of [the wage-earners'] lot," emphatically declared Cairnes in 1874, "is confined within narrow barriers which cannot be passed, and the problem of their elevation is hopeless. *As a body they will not rise at all.* A few, more energetic or more fortunate than the rest, will from time to time escape, as they do now, from the ranks of their fellows to the higher walks of industrial life, but the great majority will remain substantially where they are. *The remuneration of labor as such, skilled or unskilled, can never rise much above its present level.*" [1] Trade Unionism was, in fact, plainly "in this dilemma, that whether it fails or whether it succeeds in its immediate object, its ultimate tendency is hurtful to the laborer. If it fails, at once, in forcing higher terms on the employers of labor, the whole cost of the organisation, in money and exertion, is simply thrown away. . . . If, on the contrary, it should attain, for a time, a seeming success, the ultimate result is even worse. Nature's violated laws vindicate their authority by a sure reaction. The presumptuous mortal, who dares to set his selfish will against divine ordinances, brings on his head inevitable retribution ; his momentary prosperity disappears, and he pays, in prolonged suffering, the penalty of his suicidal success." [2]

How far the current conceptions of economic theory

[1] *Some Leading Principles of Political Economy newly expounded* (London, 1874), p. 348.

[2] *Trade Unionism*, by James Stirling, p. 36. "The bitter hostility to trade unions, which at any rate till very recent years, was felt by the 'upper' and enlightened classes, was doubtless chiefly due to dislike of that loss of the more petty delights of power which was involved in the substitution of the relation of buyer and seller of work for the old relation of master and servant, but it was fostered by the 'population and capital' theory of wages, which really made many people believe that associations of wage-earners, however annoying and harmful to employers, must always be powerless to effect any improvement in the general conditions of the employed."—Edwin Cannan, *History of the Theories of Production and Distribution* (London, 1893), p. 393.

really corresponded with the views of the best economists of this period, we cannot here determine. Some of these economists seem to have possessed almost a genius for publishing what they did not mean to say, and the wage-fund theory, even as it appeared to M'Culloch and Nassau Senior, was probably very far from the mechanical figment of the imagination that it now seems to us. And it is only fair to point out that the theory of wages, which to-day fills so large a place in economic thought, formed only an incidental and wholly subordinate part of the teaching of the classic economists. Their minds were directed to other problems : to the evil that was being wrought by industrial and political restrictions, which the generation of statesmen whom they taught have since largely removed. Any fair appreciation of their teaching is, accordingly, as difficult for the democracy of to-day, as a balanced judgment on the Mercantile Theory was to Adam Smith and his immediate followers. Nor was the Wage Fund Theory a mere wanton invention. It expressed in a definite formula certain salient facts of the industry of that generation. The English farm laborer or factory operative was obviously dependent on the wages advanced to him week by week out of his employer's capital. It was a matter of common observation that the number of laborers taken on by the farmer, or of operatives by the mill-owner, depended on the amount of capital that he could command. At a time of rapidly growing population, and manifold new inventions, the utmost possible increase of capital was desirable, whilst the evils of the old Poor Law made almost inevitable the blind adhesion to a crude Malthusianism. The theories of the economists corresponded with the prejudices of the rising middle class, and seemed to be the outcome of every man's experience.

Meanwhile, the economists themselves were undermining the structure which they had hastily erected. Qualification after qualification was introduced, until after the last effort at rehabilitation by Cairnes in 1874, the whole notion of a wage-fund was abandoned. The economic text-books written since that date [1] deal with it, if at all, only as a historical curiosity, and the theory of distribution which has taken its place, far from negativing the possibility of raising the condition of the wage-earners, does not afford even a presumption against wisely-directed Trade Union action. But the discoveries of the economists have penetrated only slowly and imperfectly into the public mind, and most of the current opposition to Trade Unionism is still implicitly based on the old theory. We must therefore, at the risk of wearying the economic student, explain, in some detail, how it breaks down at every point.[2]

Let us consider first the statical notion of a predetermined wage-fund. It does not seem to have occurred to the inventors of this figment that, whatever limit it might set to the advances made to the laborers during the year, it in no way determined the total amount of their remuneration for the year. Even if the farmer's payments for labor up to the harvest had to be restricted to a limited portion of last year's product, this did not prevent him from distributing among the laborers, at Martinmas (the usual end of the yearly hiring), in addition to these advances, some part of the harvest just reaped. As many economists have since pointed out,

---

[1] We may cite, for instance, the economic text-books or treatises of Professors Marshall, Nicholson, Gonner, Mavor, Smart, and Symes.

[2] It is pointed out by Cannan, Taussig, and F. A. Walker, that the Wage Fund Theory was never accepted, to name only writers in English, by W. Thompson, R. Jones, T. C. Banfield, Montifort Longfield, H. D. Macleod, Cliffe Leslie, John Ruskin, or Thorold Rogers in our own country, or by Dr. Wayland, Amasa Walker, Bowen, Daniel Raymond, and Erasmus Peshine Smith in America. It was trenchantly attacked, not only by the Trade Unionists, the Christian Socialists, and the Positivists (see, for instance, T. J. Dunning's *Trade Unions: their Philosophy and Intention* (London, 1860), a work read and praised, but not heeded, by J. S. Mill; J. M. Ludlow's *Christian Socialism* (London, 1851); and the admirable articles on Political Economy by Frederic Harrison in the *Fortnightly Review* for 1867), but also explicitly in the language of abstract economics by Fleeming Jenkin in March 1868, in an article in the *North British Review* ("Trade Unions: how far Legitimate"), and especially by F. D. Longe in 1866, in his *Refutation of the Wages Fund Theory of Modern Political Economy, as enunciated by Mr. Mill and Mr. Fawcett* (London, 1866). The well-known attack by W. T. Thornton, entitled *On Labour, its Wrongful Claims and Rightful Dues, its Actual Present and Possible Future* (London, 1869), and the immediate recantation of the Wage Fund Theory by J. S. Mill, first really attracted economic attention to the subject.

no inconsiderable proportion of the world's laborers, especially in the whaling, fishing, and mining industries, are actually engaged on " shares," and find the amount of the last instalments of their wages for the whole venture both regulated by, and paid out of, the sum of utilities which they have themselves created.[1] Thus, even if there existed any predetermined portion of capital definitely ear-marked as the wage-fund, it would still be only the measure of advances, not of wages ; its amount would throw no light upon the proportion of the income of the community which is obtained by the wage-earning class ; and its limitation would in no wise stand in the way of the year's remuneration of the class as a whole being indefinitely augmented at the end of each year, or on the completion of each undertaking, not out of previously accumulated capital, but actually out of their own product.

But there is, in fact, no such predetermined amount applicable for the payment of wages, still less any fund set apart at the beginning of each year, or any other period. The wage-earners of the world are not, any more than the capitalists of the world, fed for the entire year out of a store of food and other necessaries, or paid out of an accumulated fund of capital, actually in hand at the beginning of the year. Whatever may be the tasks on which the workmen are engaged, they are, as a matter of fact, fed, week by week, by products just brought to market, exactly in the same way as the employer and his household are fed. They are paid their wages, week by week, out of the current cash balances of their employers, these cash balances being daily replenished by sales of the current product. The weekly drawings of the several partners in a firm come from precisely the same fund as the wages of their workpeople. Whether or not any assignable limits can be set to the possible expansion of this source of current income, it will be at once evident that there is no arithmetical impossibility in the workmen obtaining a

[1] This supplies Mr. Henry George (*Progress and Poverty*) with some of his most telling demonstrations of the futility of the wage-fund theory.

larger, and the employers a smaller, proportion of the total drawings for any particular week. If all the hired laborers in the world were, suddenly and simultaneously, to insist on a general rise of wages, there is no mathematical impossibility in the rise being contemporaneously balanced by an equal reduction in the aggregate current drawings of the employers. If the world's current supply of food and other necessaries be supposed to be the limit, what is there to prevent the consumption of the employers and their families from being diminished ? Accordingly we find John Stuart Mill, in his celebrated review of Thornton's book, unreservedly abandoning the very notion of any predetermined wage-fund. " There is no law of nature making it inherently impossible for wages to rise to the point of absorbing, not only the funds which [the employer] had intended to devote to carrying on his business, but the whole of what he allows for his private expenses beyond the necessaries of life. . . . In short, there is abstractedly available for the payment of wages, before an absolute limit is reached, not only the employer's capital, but the whole of what can possibly be retrenched from his private expenditure, and the law of wages on the side of demand amounts only to the obvious proposition that the employers cannot pay away in wages what they have not got. . . . The power of Trade Unions may, therefore, be so exercised as to obtain for the laboring classes collectively both a larger share and a larger positive amount of the produce of labor." [1]

But though it was this statical conception of a definitely limited special wage-fund which gave the educated public its " cocksureness " against the workmen, most of the economists themselves probably laid more stress on what we have termed the dynamic aspect of the theory. If the laborers compelled the employers to agree to give them better terms for the future, this very rise of wages, causing a corresponding fall in profits, would, it was argued, cause such a diminu-

[1] J. S. Mill, *Fortnightly Review*, May 1869 ; *Dissertations and Discussions*, vol. iv. pp. 46, 48.

tion of saving as would presently counteract the rise. Thus it followed that the rate of profit on capital, together with the rate of wages, was, in any given state of mind of the saving class, really unalterable. Any accidental variation in the general rate of profit, whether upward or downward, automatically set up a reaction which continued until the normal was again reached. "Two antagonistic forces," it was said, "hold the industrial world in equilibrio. On the one hand, the principle of population regulates the supply of labor ; on the other, the principle of accumulation determines the demand for it." [1]

Now, before examining this theory point by point, we note that it contains a series of assumptions which were neither explicitly stated nor in any way proved. It takes for granted, in the first place, that Trade Union action must necessarily diminish profits ; an assumption which simply ignores the Trade Union claim—considered at length in the next two chapters—that the enforcement of a Common Rule positively increases the efficiency of industry. Secondly, we have the assumption that a diminution of profits necessarily implies a fall in the rate of interest on capital, thus leaving out of account the possibility that a rise of wages might mean simply an alteration in the shares of different grades of producers, the *entrepreneur* class (and not the mere investor) losing what the manual workers gain. Finally, we have the assumption that the heaping up of material wealth is the only way of increasing the national capital. "The older economists," says Professor Marshall, "went too far in suggesting that a rise in interest (or of profits) at the expense of wages always increased the power of saving ; they forgot that from the national point of view the investment of wealth in the child of the working man is as productive as its investment in horses and machinery. . . . The middle, and especially the professional classes have always denied themselves much in order to invest capital in the education of their children, while a great part of the

[1] *Trade Unionism*, by James Stirling, p. 26.

wages of the working classes is invested in the physical health and strength of their children."[1]

But is it true that the growth of capital depends on the rate of interest, so that "the greater the proportion of wages to profits, the smaller the tendency to national accumulation"?[2] Does the "motive for accumulation" diminish, as Ricardo incidentally declared, "with every diminution of profit"?[3] The great investigators who preceded Ricardo held an exactly opposite view. Sir Josiah Child remarked two centuries ago that the extremely low rate of interest in the Netherlands towards the close of the seventeenth century, far from diminishing accumulation, "was the *causa causans* of all the other causes of the riches of the Dutch people." In countries where the rate of interest was high, he observed that "merchants, when they have gotten great wealth, leave trading, and lend out their money at interest, the gain thereof being so easy, certain, and great ; whereas in other countries, where interest is at a lower rate, they continue merchants from generation to generation, and enrich themselves and the State."[4] "Low interest," he emphatically

---

[1] *Principles of Economics*, 3rd edition (London, 1895), Book IV. chap. vii. pp. 311, 318. The Trade Unionist may very well complain that the economists had, at any rate, no warrant for the definiteness of their assumptions. Even if it be granted that a fall in the rate of interest tends to diminish the amount saved, no reason has been given for the supposition that any particular rise in the rate of wages would necessarily tend to slacken accumulation precisely to such an extent as to cause wages to fall hereafter by the amount of the rise. If, for instance, wages rose generally by 10 per cent, and the cost fell entirely on interest, by how much per cent would the rate be thereby lowered ?   If it lowered the rate from 3 to $2\frac{1}{2}$ per cent, by how much would the amount saved annually be reduced?   If it reduced the amount saved annually from 200 millions to 175 millions, by how much would the general rate of wages be therefore lowered ?   To none of these questions can even an approximate answer be given.   The tacit assumption of the economists that, other things remaining equal, a rise in wages of 10 per cent would necessarily produce such a fall in the rate of interest as would result in such a diminution of the amount annually saved as would cause wages to fall again by at least 10 per cent, will probably be considered by future ages as one of the most extraordinary chains of hypothetical reasoning ever resorted to.

[2] *Trade Unionism*, by James Stirling, pp. 28, 29.

[3] *On the Principles of Political Economy and Taxation* (London, 1817), p. 136.

[4] *A New Discourse of Trade*, 2nd edition (London, 1694), p. 8 ; quoted in *Principles of Economics*, by Professor A. Marshall, Book IV. ch. vii. p. 316 of 3rd edition (London, 1895).

declared, " is the natural mother of Frugality, Industry, and the Arts." [1]   In Adam Smith's opinion a high rate of profit was in many ways positively injurious to national wealth.   " But besides all the bad effects to the country in general," said he, " which have already been mentioned as resulting from a high rate of profit, there is one more fatal, perhaps, than all these put together, but which, if we may judge from experience, is inseparably connected with it.   The high rate of profit seems everywhere to destroy that parsimony which in other circumstances is natural to the character of the merchant.   When profits are high that sober virtue seems to be superfluous, and expensive luxury to suit better the affluence of his situation. . . . Accumulation is thus prevented in the hands of all those who are naturally the most disposed to accumulate ; and the funds destined for the maintenance of productive labor receive no augmentation from the revenue of those who ought naturally to augment them the most. . . . Light come light go, says the proverb ; and the ordinary tone of expense seems everywhere to be regulated, not so much according to the real ability of spending, as to the supposed facility of getting money to spend." [2]   Thus he infers that, after the " profits on stock " or capital " are diminished, stock may not only continue to increase, but to increase much faster than before " ! [3]

[1] *A New Discourse of Trade*, 2nd edition (London, 1694), preface.
[2] Adam Smith, *Wealth of Nations* (London, 1776), Book IV. chap. vii. p. 276 of M'Culloch's edition.
[3] *Ibid*. Book I. chap. ix. p. 42.
The contrary assumption, on which so much of the opposition to Trade Unionism is still based, was, until 1848, more often implied than explicitly stated in economic treatises.   Nassau Senior, who introduced to economics the term " reward of abstinence," nowhere makes the statement that the amount of saving varies with the rate of profit or interest.   " Capitals," he says in one place, " are generally formed from small beginnings by acts of accumulation which become in time habitual," and in the hypothetical example he gives he actually assumes that a decrease in the rate of profit will apply a new stimulus to accumulation (*Political Economy*, p. 192).   M'Culloch, too, regarded the amount of accumulation as depending only on the extent of the margin for saving, not upon the expectation of a high rate of interest or profit.   " The means of amassing capital will be greatest . . . where the net profits of stock are greatest. . . .

The modern economist finds, in the actual facts of industrial life, much that supports this view. It may be true that here and there a capitalist employer, especially a manufacturer or a farmer, will strive harder to increase his capital if he sees the prospect of exceptional profit, than if he can only just pay his way, though on the other side must be set the fact that in this class high profits notoriously lead to extravagant personal expenditure, and that it is, as Adam Smith pointed out, not during periods of high profits, but rather in bad times, that luxuries are retrenched. But there is reason to believe that a large part—in these days perhaps the greater part—of the saving of the world takes place quite irrespective of the rate of interest that can be obtained for the use of the capital. The strongest motives for saving— the desire to provide for sickness and old age, or for the future maintenance of children—go on, as the hoards of the French peasantry show, whether profit or interest is reaped or not. The whole history of popular savings banks demonstrates that what is sought by the great bulk of the investing population is security for their savings, not any particular rate of interest. It is, in fact, within the experience of every savings bank that some depositors, content to get this security only, persist in increasing their deposits over the maximum on which any interest is paid. No reduction in the rate of savings bank interest ever causes anything like a proportionate reduction in the amount of the deposits ; usually, indeed, it causes no visible reduction at all. At the other end of the social scale, though possibly for a different reason, accumulation appears to proceed with equal indiffer-

Give to any people the power of accumulating, and we may depend upon it they will not be disinclined to use it effectively. . . . No instance can be produced of any people having ever missed an opportunity to amass."—*Principles of Political Economy*, 1825, part ii. sec. 2.

Mr. Cannan has drawn our attention to an article by W. Ellis in the *Westminster Review* for January 1826, which contains the first clear expression of the other view. J. S. Mill seems to have been the first systematic economist in England to give definite form to the statement that the rate of accumulation would, in any given state of wealth and habit of mind, vary with the rate of interest to be expected from capital.—*Principles of Political Economy*, Book I. chap. xi.

ence to the rate of profit.   The annual savings of the Astors
and Vanderbilts, the periodical re-investment of income by
the Cavendishes and Grosvenors, the automatic accumula-
tions of the Rothschilds, do not, as a matter of fact, depend
on how much per cent these millionaires expect to get
for their new capital, but on the amount of sheer surplus
over and above their current habits of expenditure.   It is,
to say the least of it, extremely doubtful, as regards all the
large class whose income is greatly in excess of what they
need or desire to spend, whether the amount that they invest
this year will be increased by any prospect that the rate of
interest will be 4 instead of 3 per cent, or diminished if it is
expected that the rate will be only 2 instead of 3 per cent.
Finally, there is a third type of saving where the effect of
any change in the rate of profit is positively in the opposite
direction, the amount of accumulation being increased by a
fall in the rate, and checked by a rise.   A large part of the
saving of the world is done with the motive of obtaining, at
some future time, an income upon which to live without
work.   When a man saves in order to be able to retire from
business or practice ; when it is desired to make provision
for a widow or for daughters ; when the object is what is
popularly known as " founding a family," it is some definite
amount of annual income that is aimed at.   This is especially the case with the professional and upper middle class,
by whom a considerable proportion of the world's accumulation is nowadays made.   If it takes £5000 a year to maintain a family in a country mansion of the accepted stamp,
or if the recognised portion for each daughter is £300 a
year, there is a strong stimulus to go on accumulating until
the necessary capital sum has been reached, and this capital
sum becomes, of course, greater if the rate of interest falls.
No observer of English life can doubt that the recent fall in
the rate of interest on good investments from 4 to $2\frac{1}{2}$ per
cent has, in this way, in many families not only strengthened
the motive to go on working, but also positively stimulated
the accumulation of capital.   " As the rate of interest falls,"

says Professor Smart, " the motive of the richer classes to save rather than to consume grows stronger."[1] And it must not be forgotten that every fall in the rate of interest, by affording new opportunities for its profitable investment in appliances for increasing the productivity of labor, stimulates the desire to invest and presently increases the power to save. Under this head must come, too, the large and ever-increasing form of compulsory saving which is represented by public outlay on permanent works of utility. When a municipality engages in large public works, it does more than find useful investment for savings which would in any case have been made. By making arrangements for repaying the loan within a definite number of years—in England, on an average about thirty—the ratepayers, besides paying the interest, find themselves compelled to put by for the community, out of their individual incomes, before they can begin to save for themselves at all, a sum equal to the annual repayment of debt. It can scarcely be doubted that this compulsory saving, which no individual ratepayer regards as saving at all, is, like taxation generally, to a large extent retrenched from current personal expenditure, and is therefore, to this extent, a clear addition to the capital of the community. Now, the extent to which municipalities will raise loans for public works, to be thus made up by compulsory savings, depends in a very large degree on the rate of interest, rising when that falls and falling when that rises. " Accordingly," concludes Professor Nicholson, " we cannot strictly speak of a particular minimum rate in any society as necessary to accumulation in general ; and if Adam Smith's opinion is well founded, we cannot even say that a rise in the rate of interest will increase, or a fall check accumulation. . . . The growth of material capital depends upon a number of variables, of which the rate of interest is only one, and is, furthermore, *indeterminate in its effect*."[2] To put it con-

---

[1] *Studies in Economics* (London, 1895), p. 297.

[2] J. S. Nicholson, *Principles of Political Economy* (Edinburgh, 1893), p. 394. Sir Josiah Child went so far as to predict that " the bringing down of interest in this kingdom from six to four or three per cent will necessarily, in less than

cretely, it is, to say the least of it, extremely doubtful
whether the accumulated capital of the United Kingdom
would be greater or less at the present time if the rate of
interest on the best security, instead of falling to a little over
2 per cent, had remained at 5 or 6 per cent, the rate at which
Pitt frequently issued Consols.   Still less is it possible for
the economist to predict whether, our national habits being
as they are, the growth in wealth during the next hundred
years would be stimulated or depressed if the rate should
within that period fall even to 1 per cent.   Considering, therefore, that the very poor and the very rich are, as regards
the actual accumulation of material wealth, practically unin-
fluenced either way ; that an increase of wages is likely
positively to increase that highly productive form of the
nation's capital, the physical strength and mental training
of the manual working class ; that the middle class is mainly
bent on securing permanent incomes for future maintenance,
and will therefore be induced to work longer and harder, and
save more, the lower the rate of interest descends ; that a
low rate of interest both stimulates inventions and promotes
their general adoption ; and that municipal and national
enterprise, if favored by a low rate of interest, grows by leaps
and bounds, economists are beginning to assert that a rise of
wages at the expense of profits would probably result, not in
less, but actually in more being produced, and taking all
forms of national wealth into account, that it might be
expected positively to increase the productive capital of the
community in one form or another.   We do not understand
whether Professor Marshall goes this length, but " we may
conclude," he says, " in opposition to [the older economists],
that any change in the distribution of wealth which gives
more to the wage-receivers and less to the capitalists is
likely, other things being equal, *to hasten the increase of
material production*, and that it will not perceptibly retard the
storing-up of material wealth." [1]

twenty years' time, double the capital stock of the nation."—*A New Discourse of
Trade*, 2nd edition (London, 1694), p. 14.
[1] *Principles of Economics*, by Professor A. Marshall, 3rd edition (London,

So far the modern economic criticism of the current middle-class view takes account only of a general bettering of the conditions of labor and a general fall in the rate of profit in all trades. If now we consider the more usual case of an alteration in the profitableness of a particular industry, the modern student finds it equally impossible to come to a dogmatic conclusion against Trade Unionism. The older economists made the convenient assumption that both capital and labor were freely mobile as between one trade and another, and that it was therefore impossible for any important variations between wages and profits in different trades to be of long continuance. Here, again, the popular argument against Trade Unionism ignored the all-important element of time. If the employers in one industry happened to make large profits, additional capital, it was said, would flow into that trade, and the workmen would thus, sooner or later, find the demand for their services increased and their wages raised. But why should the workmen wait? On the economist's own showing, there would be nothing to prevent a combination of all the workmen in the trade taking advantage of the golden opportunity when profits were high, and so increasing their wages as to absorb a large share of this surplus for themselves.[1] There would then be no attraction for additional capital to enter the trade, and therefore no reason why the surplus should not continue to exist, to the benefit of the workmen in that trade. Their wages would have risen relatively to those in other trades, with the result that new workmen would be attracted to it. But it is not easy for men to change their trades

1895), Book IV. chap. vii. p. 311. Some economists are beginning to suggest that the world's stock of capital is largely determined by the world's need of capital —accumulation beyond industrial requirements automatically causing destruction of other capital. See the, on this point, suggestive works of Mr. J. A. Hobson.

[1] " When profits rise in any branch of trade above the usual rate, the masters evidently could, if they chose, afford to make over to the men as additional wages, the whole difference between their old and their new profits. They could do this if they pleased without reducing profits below the previously current and usual rate. And being able to do this it is conceivable that they might by a powerful union be constrained to do it."—W. T. Thornton, *On Labour* (London, 1870), pp. 284, 285.

with advantage, especially among the skilled crafts, and it would take some years before the increased attractiveness of the better-paid trade among boys choosing their occupations caused any appreciable increase in the number of journeymen. Moreover, this would be a clear case in which a Trade Union might by close combination or legal enactment better its conditions of employment without decreasing the amount of work for its own members, and without depriving the rest of the wage-earners of anything that they could otherwise have obtained. All that would then have happened would be that an increase in profits, which would otherwise have gone first to the capitalists, and eventually to the consumers, would have been lastingly secured by a section of the workpeople. Hence the economist's own reasoning seems to bear out the workmen's empirical conclusion, that Trade Union action is most strikingly successful when it takes the form of claiming advances at the moment that trade is profitable.

When we consider the country as a whole, in its competition with other countries, the argument, though more complicated, is equally inconclusive. If the wage-earners of one country obtain, whether by law or by negotiation, better sanitation, shorter hours, or higher wages than their colleagues in other countries, and if these better terms for labor involve a lower rate of profit on capital, it is suggested that capital will "flow" out of the relatively unprofitable country, in order to seek investment abroad. The improvement of the conditions of labor would, under these circumstances, be temporary only, as the resulting diminution of profits would bring about its own cure. To the modern financial expert, actually engaged in international transactions, this contention seems highly problematical. He sees the rates of business profits in different countries remain permanently divergent, two or three times as much being habitually earned by capitalist enterprises in one country, as compared with similar enterprises in another. In spite of the assumed international mobility of capital, even the rates of loan interest in different countries remain very far from equality. And though capital flows here and there from time to time, the expert financier detects nothing in the nature of that promptly - flowing current from low-rate countries to high-rate countries which might be expected to bring the divergence quickly to an end, and which was assumed without evidence by a more theoretic generation. His usual explanation is that, here as elsewhere, it is far more important to the investor of capital to obtain security than to gain an increased rate of interest. This security depends upon a great variety of considerations, among which, in these democratic days, not the least important is the state of mind of the wage-earning class. Hence an improvement in the conditions of employment, made at the cost of the capitalist, far from necessarily driving more capital abroad, as Cairnes imagined, may positively tend to keep it at home. Factory legislation, compulsory sanitation, short hours of labor, a high level of wages, freedom of combination, and generally the habit of treating the wage-earners with consideration, may seem to make capital yield a lower annual return to the investor than might be gained in other countries. But if these things result in political and social stability, if they increase the amenity of life, and especially if they promise to erect a bulwark against revolution and spoliation, the investor will, as a matter of fact, prefer to see his rate of interest gradually decline if the reduction is accompanied by an increase in political security, rather than seek higher gains in more discontented, and therefore less stable communities. Thus the reaction set up by a bettering of the condition of the English workmen at the cost of the capitalist may be quite in the reverse direction to that formerly imagined. But there is another, and, as we think, more important reason for the apparently inexplicable divergence between the rates earned by capital in different countries. Capital does not of itself produce either profit or interest, and can only really be used to advantage when it is employed in conjunction with an efficient organisation of industry, an adequate supply of skilled workmen, and the indispensable element of business ability. It is probable that the profitableness of English industry would be far more endangered by the emigration of all its skilled craftsmen, or the desertion of its genuine captains of industry, than by any merely mechanical investments in foreign lands. An increase of wages, by keeping at home the most energetic and ingenious workmen, who might otherwise have emigrated, thus tends positively to increase profits in England. But the migration of skilled workmen, and still more, that of brain-power, from one country to another, depends on many other motives than the rate of pecuniary reward. Here, again, the reaction set up by a fall in the rate of profit may be quite in the contrary direction to that formerly supposed. If an improvement in the condition of the English working classes adds to the amenity of English life, it may increase the attractiveness of England to the able business man, and so in this way positively increase the profitableness of English industry, and hence the reward of the capitalist and brain-worker, by far more than the improvement has cost. Where the business capacity is to be found, there, in the long run, will be the capital. We need not therefore be surprised to learn that there is absolutely no evidence that the past fifty years' rise in the condition of the English wage-earning class, taken as a whole, has had any effect at all in making the available capital of England less than it would have been made if the rise had not taken place. The exceptionally great fall in the rate of interest which has been so marked a feature of the period, and especially of the last twenty years, is, in fact, a slight indication that the current is nowadays rather in the opposite direction. England may have its Trade Unions, its growing regulation of private industry, and its income-tax and death-duties, but Germany has its revolutionary Social Democracy, France its political instability, the United States its tariff and currency troubles, India its famines, Cuba its chronic rebellion, and South America its revolutions. One of the greatest of the world's international financiers lately remarked, with some surprise, that, in spite of the growing pretensions

of the English legislature and the English Trade Unions to
interfere with private enterprise, and to enforce more liberal
conditions of employment, other countries were showing a
positively increasing desire to remit their savings for investment in English enterprises, and London seemed to be
becoming more attractive than ever to the able business man.

The abstract theories of wages and profits, which public
opinion once thought so conclusive against the Trade
Unionist assumptions, are thus seen, in the light of economic
science, to crumble away.   But there were many educated
men, especially in the world of physical science and natural
history, who never accepted the wire-drawn arguments of the
Wage Fund, but who nevertheless saw, in the "principle of
population," a biological barrier to any real success of Trade
Unionism.   Of what avail could it be for combinations of
workmen to struggle and strive for higher wages, when those
higher wages would only lead automatically to an increase
of population, which must inevitably pull down things again
to the old level?   As one sympathetic friend of progress
regretfully expressed it, it was "the devastating torrent of
children" that blocked the way to any improvement of the
conditions of labor.[1]

Now, it is interesting to observe that, whereas the
Theory of the Wage Fund stood in opposition to every
kind of improvement of the conditions of employment, the
"principle of population" was supposed to negative only an
increase in money wages, or, more precisely, in the amount
of food obtained by the manual workers.   No one suggested that improved conditions of sanitation in the factory
had any tendency to raise the birth-rate ; and it would have
needed a very fervid Malthusianism to prove that a shortening of the hours of labor resulted in earlier marriages.   No
argument could therefore be founded on the "principle of
population" against Trade Union efforts to improve the

---

[1] "If only the devastating torrent of children could be arrested for a few
years it would bring untold relief."—J. Cotter Morison, *The Service of Man*
(London, 1887), preface, p. xxx.

conditions of sanitation and safety, or to protect the Normal Day. And the economists quickly found reason to doubt whether there was any greater cogency in the argument with regard to wages. Malthus and Ricardo had habitually written as if the fluctuations in wages meant merely more or less bread to the laborer's family, and the public assumed therefore that every rise of wages implied that more children would be brought up, and that every fall would result in a diminution. But the wage-earning population, in 1820 as now, included any number of separate grades, from the underfed agricultural laborer of Devonshire, whose wages were only eight shillings a week, to the London millwright who refused to accept a job under two guineas a week. Though it might be true that a rise in wage to the underfed laborer enabled him to bring up more children to maturity, and might even induce him to marry at an earlier age, it did not at all follow that a rise of wages would have the same effect on the town artisan or factory operative, who was already getting more than the bare necessaries of existence. To the one class more wages meant chiefly more food ; to the other it meant new luxuries or additional amenities of life. The economists were quickly convinced that a new taste for luxuries or a desire for additional amenities had a direct effect in developing prudential restraint. M'Culloch himself emphatically declared, on this very ground, that " the best interests of society require that the rate of wages should be elevated as high as possible— that a taste for the comforts, luxuries, and enjoyments of human life should be widely diffused, and, if possible, interwoven with the national habits and prejudices." [1] From the Malthusian point of view, the presumption was, as regards the artisans and factory operatives, always in favor of a rise in wages. For " in the vast majority of instances, before a rise of wages can be counteracted by the increased number of laborers it may be supposed to be the means of bringing into the market, time is afforded for the formation

[1] *Principles of Political Economy*, part iii. sec. 7.

of those new and improved tastes and habits, which are not the hasty product of a day, a month, or a year, but the late result of a long series of continuous impressions. After the laborers have once acquired these tastes, population will advance in a slower ratio, as compared with capital, than formerly; and the laborers will be disposed rather to defer the period of marriage, than, by entering on it prematurely, to depress their own condition and that of their children." In the same way, the presumption was strongly against any reduction of the wages of any classes who were receiving more than bare subsistence. "A fall of wages," continues M'Culloch, "has therefore a precisely opposite effect, and is, in most cases, as injurious to the laborer as their rise is beneficial. In whatever way wages may be restored to their former level after they have fallen, whether it be by a decrease in the number of marriages, or an increase in the number of deaths, or both, it is never, except in . . . exceedingly rare cases . . . suddenly effected. It must, generally speaking, require a considerable time before it can be brought about; and an extreme risk arises in consequence lest the tastes and habits of the laborers, and their opinion respecting what is necessary for their comfortable subsistence, should be degraded in the interim. . . . The lowering of the opinions of the laboring classes, with respect to the mode in which they ought to live, is perhaps the most serious of all the evils that can befall them. . . . The example of such individuals, or bodies of individuals, as submit quietly to have their wages reduced, and who are content if they get only the mere necessaries of life, ought never to be held up for public imitation. On the contrary, everything should be done to make such apathy be esteemed disgraceful."[1] There could not be a more emphatic justification of Trade Union effort. The ordinary middle-class view that the "principle of population" rendered nugatory all attempts to raise wages, otherwise than in the slow course of generations, was, in fact, based on sheer ignorance, not only of the facts

[1] *Principles of Political Economy*, part iii. sec. 7.

of working-class life, but even of the opinions of the very economists from whom it was supposed to be derived.[1] So far were the classic economists from believing it to be useless to raise the wages even of the laborers, that M'Culloch emphatically declared that "an increase of wages is the only, or at all events the most effectual and ready means by which the condition of the poor can be really improved."[2]

The modern student of the population question finds even less ground for apprehension than M'Culloch. The general death-rate of the United Kingdom, like that of all civilised countries, has steadily declined during the past half-century of sanitation, but no connection can be traced between this fall and any rise of wages ; there is, indeed, some slight reason to believe that the death-rate has fallen most among some sections of the wage-earners (for instance, women of all ages) and in some districts (for instance, the great cities) where the rise in wages has been relatively less than elsewhere. But what the fanatical Malthusian most relied on was the increase in births. To him it seemed absolutely demonstrable that, in any given state of the working-class, an increase of wages must inevitably be followed by an increase of births. That the number of

[1] M'Culloch expressly denied that, on a rise in wages, population would naturally increase proportionately to the rise, "as it is sometimes alleged it would. . . . It is not improbable merely, but next to impossible, that population should increase in the same proportion."—Note VI. to his edition of the *Wealth of Nations* (London, 1839), p. 473.

[2] J. R. M'Culloch, *A Treatise on the Circumstances which determine the Rate of Wages* (London, 1851), p. 49.

Nassau Senior also protested against the public view. "Those whose acquaintance with Political Economy is superficial (and they form the great mass of even the educated classes) have been misled by the form in which the doctrine of population has been expressed. . . . Because increased means of subsistence *may* be followed and neutralised by a proportionate increase in the number of persons to be subsisted, they suppose that such *will* necessarily be the case. . . . This doctrine . . . furnishes an easy escape from the trouble or expense implied by every project of improvement. 'What use would it be?' they ask. '. . . If food were for a time more abundant, in a very short period the population would be again on a level with the means of subsistence, and we should be just as ill off as before.' We believe these misconceptions to be extensively prevalent."—Nassau W. Senior, *Political Economy*, 2nd edition, in *Encyclopædia Metropolitana* (London, 1850), p. 50.

marriages went up and down according to the price of wheat was a universally accepted generalisation. But that generalisation, whatever may have been its truth a hundred years ago, has long ceased to have any correspondence with fact. The marriage-rate of the England of this generation, drooping slowly downwards, bears no assignable relation either to the falling prices of commodities, the rising wages of male labor, or the growing prosperity of the country. What is more important, the birth-rate has ceased to have any uniform relation to the marriage-rate. The economists have always looked with longing eyes on the example of France, where the growth of population, and particularly the number of births to a marriage, had, even when J. S. Mill wrote in 1848, shown a steady decline, to which Mill attributed much of the economic progress of the peasant proprietors. This decline in the birth-rate is now seen to be universal throughout North-Western Europe. Our own country is no exception. Down to 1877, the birth-rate of England and Wales had shown no sign of falling off, the rate for each year oscillating about the mean of 35 per thousand. But since 1877 the reduction has been great and continuous, the rate in 1895 being only 30.4 compared with 36.3 in 1876, a fall almost identical with that in France between 1800 and 1850, which filled J. S. Mill with so much hope.[1]

Unfortunately, though the decline in the English birth-rate has now continued for twenty years, there has been as yet no scientific investigation into its cause. It cannot be ascribed to increased poverty or privation of the nation, or of the working-class, for, as compared with previous times, there can be no doubt that the incomes of the English wage-earners have, on the whole, risen ; prices of commodities have fallen ; and the general prosperity of the country has greatly increased.[2] And the impression of statisticians is that the

[1] *Principles of Political Economy*, Book II. ch. vii. p. 178 of edition of 1865. The average birth-rate of France between 1801-10 and 1841-50 fell about 5 per 1000.

[2] For an estimate of this progress see *Labor in the Longest Reign*, by Sidney Webb (London, 1897).

diminution in the birth-rate throughout North-Western Europe has not taken place among the poorest sections of the community. "After the researches of Quetelet in Brussels, Farr in London, Schwabe in Berlin, Villermé and Benoison de Chateauneuf in Paris, it is no longer possible to doubt that the maximum of births takes place among the poorer class, and that poverty itself is an irresistible inducement to an abundant and disordered birth-rate."[1] Such facts as are now beginning to be known point to the conclusion that the fall in the birth-rate is occurring, not in those sections of the community which have barely enough to live on, but in those which command some of the comforts of life—not in the "sweated trades," or among the casual laborers, but among the factory operatives and skilled artisans. We can adduce only one piece of statistical evidence in support of this hypothesis, but that one piece is, we think, full of significance.

The Hearts of Oak Friendly Society is the largest centralised Benefit Society in this country, having now over two hundred thousand adult male members. No one is admitted who is not of good character, and in receipt of wages of twenty-four shillings a week, or upwards. The membership consists, therefore, of the artisan and skilled operative class, with some intermixture of the small shopkeeper, to the exclusion of the mere laborer. Among its provisions is

---

[1] *Population and the Social System*, F. Nitti (London, 1894), pp. 153-162. Adam Smith had observed that poverty "seems even to be favorable to generation" (*Wealth of Nations*, Book I. chap. viii. p. 36). Professor Nitti has his own explanation of the fact : "The long working days of 12, 14, and 15 hours make their intellectual improvement impossible, and compel them to seek their sole enjoyments in those of the senses. Compelled to work for many hours in places heated to a great temperature, often promiscuously with women ; obliged to live upon substances which, if insufficient for nutrition, frequently cause a permanent excitability ; persuaded that no endeavor will better their condition, they are necessarily impelled to a great fecundity. Add to this that the premature acceptance of children in workshops leads the parents to believe that a large family is much rather a good than an evil, even with respect to family comfort. . . . It is clearly to be seen that a very high birth-rate always corresponds with slight wages, long days of work, bad food, and hence a bad distribution of wealth. . . . Nothing is more certain to fix limits to the birth-rate than high wages, and the diffusion of ease." "Poverty," Darwin had observed, "is not only a great evil, but tends to its own increase by leading to recklessness in marriage."—*The Descent of Man* (London, 1871), vol. ii. p. 403.

the " Lying-in Benefit," a payment of thirty shillings for each
confinement of a member's wife.   From 1866 to 1880 the
proportion of lying-in claims to membership slowly rose from
21.76 to 24.72 per 100.   *From 1880 to the present time it
has continuously declined, until it is now only between* 14 *and*
15 *per* 100.

The " devastating torrent of children " in this million of
souls, forming $2\frac{1}{2}$ per cent of the whole population of the
United Kingdom, has accordingly fallen off by no less than
two-fifths, only fourteen being born where formerly twenty-
four would have seen the light.   *The reduction of the birth-rate
in this specially thrifty group of workmen's families has been
more than twice the reduction in the community as a whole.*
The average age of the members has not appreciably changed,
having remained throughout between 34 and 36.   The well-
known actuary of the Society, Mr. R. P. Hardy, watching
the statistics year by year, and knowing intimately all the
circumstances of the organisation, attributes this startling
reduction in the number of births of children to these specially prosperous and specially thrifty artisans entirely to their
deliberate desire to limit the size of their families.[1]

[1] Our own impression, based on ten years' special investigation into English
working-class life, coincides with Mr. Hardy's inference.   There can be no doubt
that the practice of deliberately taking steps to limit the size of the family has,
during the last twenty years, spread widely among the factory operatives and
skilled artisans of Great Britain.   We may remind the reader that the Malthusian
propaganda of Francis Place and J. S. Mill was greatly extended, and for the
first time brought prominently before the mass of the people, by Charles Brad-
laugh, M.P., and Mrs. Annie Besant.   (In chap. iii. of his pamphlet, *Die
künstliche Beschränkung der Kinderzahl als sittliche Pflicht*, 5th edition (Berlin,
1897), Dr. Hans Ferdy gives a careful history of this movement.)   It is at any
rate interesting to note that the beginning in the fall of the birth-rate (1877)
coincides closely with the enormous publicity given to the subject by the prosecution of these propagandists in that very year.

We attribute this adoption of neo-Malthusian devices to prevent the burden
of a large family (which have, of course, nothing to do with Trade Unionism)
chiefly to the spread of education among working-class women, to their discontent
with a life of constant ill-health and domestic worry under narrow circumstances,
and to the growth among them of aspirations for a fuller and more independent
existence of their own.   This change implies, on the part of both husband and
wife, a large measure of foresight, deliberateness, and self-control, which is out
of the reach of the less intelligent and more self-indulgent classes, and difficult
for the very poor, especially for the occupants of one-roomed homes.

Table showing, for each year from 1866 *to* 1896 *inclusive, the number of Members in the Hearts of Oak Friendly Society at the beginning of the year, the number of those who received Lying-in Benefit during the year, the percentage of these to the membership at the beginning of the year, and the birth-rate per* 1000 *of the whole population of England and Wales.* (*From the annual reports of the Committee of Management of the Hearts of Oak Friendly Society, and those of the Registrar-General.*)

| Year. | Hearts of Oak Friendly Society. | | | England and Wales: births per 1000 of the total population. |
	Number of Members at the beginning of each year.	Number of cases of Lying-in Benefit paid during year.	Percentage of cases paid to total Membership at beginning of year.	
1866	10,571	2,300	21.76	35.2
1867	12,051	2,853	23.68	35.4
1868	13,568	3,075	22.66	35.8
1869	15,903	3,509	22.07	34.8
1870	18,369	4,173	22.72	35.2
1871	21,484	4,685	21.81	35.0
1872	26,510	6,156	23.22	35.6
1873	32,837	7,386	22.49	35.4
1874	40,740	9,603	23.57	36.0
1875	51,144	12,103	23.66	35.4
1876	64,421	15,473	24.02	36.3
1877	76,369	18,423	24.11	36.0
1878	84,471	20,409	24.16	35.6
1879	90,603	22,057	24.34	34.7
1880	91,986	22,740	24.72	34.2
1881	93,615	21,950	23.45	33.9
1882	96,006	21,860	22.77	33.8
1883	98,873	21,577	21.82	33.5
1884	104,239	21,375	20.51	33.6
1885	105,622	21,277	20.14	32.9
1886	109,074	21,856	20.04	32.8
1887	111,937	20,590	18.39	31.9
1888	115,803	20,244	17.48	31.2
1889	123,223	20,503	16.64	31.1
1890	131,057	20,402	15.57	30.2
1891	141,269	22,500	15.93	31.4
1892	153,595	23,471	15.28	30.5
1893	169,344	25,430	15.02	30.8
1894	184,629	27,000	14.08	29.6
1895	201,075	29,263	14.55	30.4
1896	206,673	30,313	14.67	

Diagram showing for each of the years 1866–1896 inclusive the birth-rate per 1000 of the total population of England and Wales; and the Lying-in Benefit cases paid by the Hearts of Oak Friendly Society per 100 of its total membership at the beginning of each year.

▬▬▬ Thick black line = birth-rate per 1000 of the total popuation.
·········· Dotted-line = Lying-in Benefit cases per 100 of the membership of the Hearts of Oak.

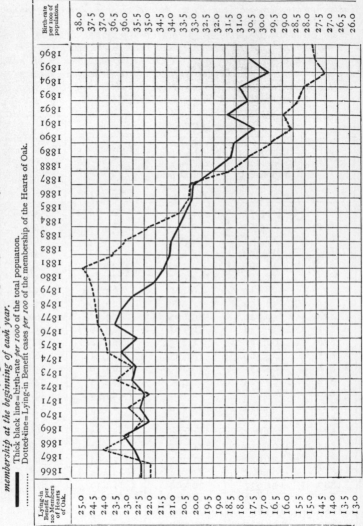

We reach here an aspect of the population question of which Malthus never dreamt, and on which further investigation is imperatively demanded.[1] There are many indications that the danger to be apprehended in North-Western Europe during the coming century is not over-population at all, but a deliberate restriction of population by the more prosperous, more intelligent, and more thrifty sections, brought about by the rise in the Standard of Life itself. This is not the place for any discussion of this momentous fact. For the present we are concerned only with the new light that it throws upon the relation between the increase of population and the rate of wages. Instead of " the principle of population " decisively negativing any possibility of the success of Trade Unionism,

[1] There are indications that the same result is happening in New England. Thus, even as long ago as 1875, it was found that, of 393 working-class families of Massachusetts, those of the skilled mechanics (earning $800 per annum) averaged from one to two children less than those of the laborers (earning less than $700 per annum).

Earnings of 393 families of Massachusetts in 1875, with the number in family, averaged by groups of trades (rearranged).

Trades.	Father's yearly wages.	Number in family.	Wife and children working.	Total earnings of wife and children.	Total yearly earnings of family.
	$			$	$
Skilled workshop handicraftsmen .	752.36	$4\frac{3}{4}$	$0\frac{1}{4}$	69.04	821.40
Metal workers	739.30	$4\frac{1}{2}$	$0\frac{3}{8}$	90.51	829.81
Building trades	721.32	$4\frac{1}{2}$	$0\frac{1}{3}$	73.00	794.32
Teamsters	630.02	$5\frac{1}{2}$	$0\frac{1}{2}$	105.00	735.02
Mill operatives	572.10	5	1	250.35	822.45
Shoe and Leather workers .	540.00	$4\frac{3}{4}$	1	209.00	749.00
Average of these six groups .	659.18	$4\frac{5}{8}$	$0\frac{4}{7}$	132.82	792.00
Metal workers' laborers .	458.09	$5\frac{1}{2}$	$1\frac{1}{6}$	256.08	714.17
Workshop laborers . , .	433.06	$5\frac{9}{10}$	$1\frac{1}{10}$	232.02	665.08
Outdoor laborers . . .	424.12	$6\frac{1}{2}$	$1\frac{1}{3}$	257.93	682.05
Mill laborers . . .	386.04	$6\frac{3}{4}$	$1\frac{1}{2}$	284.08	670.12
Average of these four groups .	425.32	$6\frac{3}{10}$	$1\frac{1}{4}$	257.50	682.88

(*Sixth Report on the Statistics of Labour of Massachusetts*, 1876, p. 71.)

as is still often believed by otherwise well-educated people, the argument is all in the opposite direction. So far as we can draw any inference at all from the facts of English life, there is no reason to believe that a rise in wages, a reduction of hours, or an improvement of the conditions of sanitation and safety among any class of workmen, would cause any increase in the birth-rate of that class; and if the improvement in conditions were to spread to section after section of workers who are now below the level of the skilled artisan, there is every reason to expect that it would result in a positive decline in the birth-rate among those sections.[1] To put the matter concretely, if we could, by Collective Bargaining or Legal Enactment, lift the London dock-laborers into an economic position equal to that of the railway porters, there would not only be no corresponding increase in the number of children born to them, but, in all probability, we should in a very few years find an actual diminution in the size of the average family of the class; and if Trade Unionism could further raise both them and the railway porters to the

---

[1] What is needed is a thoroughly scientific investigation of the subject from all sides. First would come the statistical inquiry as to the exact extent and distribution of the decline in the birth-rate. An analysis of the registrations of births for selected years would show, for instance, whether the birth-rate was uniform among all occupations, or varied from trade to trade; whether it bore any relation to the wage-levels of different industries, or to the average number of rooms occupied by the families in these trades, as tabulated for London by Mr. Charles Booth; or whether it corresponded with the degree of Trade Union membership. A similar analysis of births in the various friendly societies giving " Lying-in Benefit " would be even more suggestive. It would also be possible to use the Trade Union and Friendly Society machinery for taking voluntary censuses of the families of men in different social grades, different trades, or different districts. Such a diagnosis would prepare the way for a physiological inquiry into the means used, and their physical effects, direct and indirect. It would then be for the sociologist to discover the circumstances under the pressure of which these practices were adopted, and what effect they were having on the economic position of various classes, the institution of marriage, family life, and the great social evil of prostitution; most important of all, how sectional restriction of births affected, in extent and character, the breeding ground of subsequent generations. Some preliminary investigations of this sort are being made by students of the London School of Economics and Political Science, but are stopped for lack of funds. We can imagine no way of spending a couple of thousand pounds more likely to be useful to the community than such an investigation. To us it seems, of all problems, the most momentous for the future of the civilised races.

economic position of the "Amalgamated" Engineer, this result would be still more certain and conspicuous.

Accordingly, we do not find any modern economist, however "orthodox" may be his bias, nowadays refuting Trade Unionism by a reference either to the Wage Fund or to the "Population Question."[1] The "Theory of Distribution" which to-day holds the field is of very different character, and one from which the opponent of Trade Unionism can derive little comfort. To begin with, it is declared that wages, like other incomes, depend upon the amount of the aggregate revenue of a community, not upon the amount of its capital. "The labour and capital of the country," says Professor Marshall, "acting on its natural resources, produce annually a certain net aggregate of commodities, material and immaterial, including services of all kinds. This is the true net annual income or revenue of the country; or the National Dividend . . . it is divided up into Earnings of Labor, Interest of Capital, and lastly the Producer's Surplus, or Rent, of land, and of other differential advantages for production. It constitutes the whole of them, and the whole of it is distributed among them; and the larger it is, the larger, other things being equal, will be the share of each agent of production." The extent and character of the industries of the community, and the ever-changing level of wages and prices, are determined by the perpetual play of Supply and Demand, acting through the "law of substitution." "The production of everything, whether an agent of production or a commodity ready for immediate consumption, is carried forward up to that limit or margin at which there is equilibrium between the forces of demand and supply. The amount of the thing, and its price, the amounts of the several factors or agents of production used in making it, and their prices—all these elements mutually

---

[1] Thus, Professor Marshall, though he elsewhere uses expressions which retain traces of the older view, observes, in the latest edition of his *Principles of Economics* (London, 1895), as corrected by the fly-leaf, "it is indeed true that a permanent rise of prosperity is quite as likely to lower as to raise the birth-rate" (p. 594).

determine one another, and if an external cause should alter any one of them, the effect of the disturbance extends to all the others." And the Rent, it will be seen, " is the excess value of the return which can be got by its aid where labor and capital are applied with normal ability up to the margin of profitableness over that which the same labor, capital, and ability would get if working without the aid of any such advantage." Nor is this confined to land rent (or to " a differential advantage not made by man "), for we are elsewhere told " that the rent of land is no unique fact, but simply the chief species of a large genus of economic phenomena ; and that the theory of the rent of land is no isolated economic doctrine, but merely one of the chief applications of a particular corollary from the general theory of demand and supply ; and that there is a continuous gradation from the true rent of those free gifts which have been appropriated by man, through the income derived from permanent improvements of the soil, to those yielded by farm and factory buildings, steam engines, and less durable goods." The result is a constant tendency to equality, but only to equality of remuneration for the marginal use. " Other things being equal, the larger the supply of any agent of production, the further will it have to push its way into uses for which it is not specially fitted, and the lower will be the demand price with which it will have to be contented in those uses in which its employment is on the verge or margin of not being found profitable, and, in so far as completion equalises the price which it gets in all uses, this price will be its price for all uses." [1]

Thus, the effect of perfectly free and unrestrained individual competition among laborers and capitalists is, on the one hand, to secure to their owners the entire differential advantage of all those factors of production which are better than the worst in normal use, and, on the other, to reduce the personal remuneration for all the members of each class

[1] *Principles of Economics*, by Professor Alfred Marshall, 3rd edition (London, 1895), Book VI. chap. i. pp. 588, 591, 609, and chap. ix. p. 705.

of producers to the level of the last, and least advantageously situated, member of that class for the time being. The modern economist tells each class of producers plainly what will happen to their incomes if there is no interference with free competition. The total net produce of the class may be considerable ; the total utility and value of the services of the class as a whole to the employers may be immense ; the consumers themselves may be willing, rather than forego the commodity, to pay a higher price. Nevertheless, if the workmen in that particular class compete freely among themselves for employment, and the employers are unrestrained in taking advantage of this " Perfect Competition," the price with which all the members of the class will have to be content will be set by the last additional workman in the class whose " employment is on the verge or margin of not being found profitable." Under Perfect Competition, " the wages of every class of labor tend to be equal to the produce due to the additional labor of the marginal laborer of that class." [1]

But what the isolated individual wage-earner thus foregoes, the employer does not necessarily gain. For the same reasoning applies, as Professor Marshall points out, to capital in all its mobile forms. The demand-price is determined, not by the total utility of the advantages to be gained by the use of each unit of capital, but by the utility of the last unit of mobile capital, " in those uses in which its employment is on the verge or margin of not being found profitable." Competition among capitalists will force them to cede to the consumer anything above the net advantages of the last, or marginal, unit of mobile capital. Thus, under Perfect Competition, it is on the one hand the landlord, or other owner of the rents or " quasi-rents " of superior instruments of production, and on the other the consumer, in proportion to the extent of his consumption, who is always getting the benefit of that " law of substitution " which pares down the incomes of laborers and capitalists alike, whenever these, in particular

---

[1] *Principles of Economics*, by Professor Alfred Marshall, 3rd edition (London, 1895), Book VI. chap. i. p. 584.

instances, rise above the level for the time being of the equivalent of the marginal use.[1]

All that abstract economics can nowadays tell us about the normal rate of wages is, therefore, that under perfectly free competition it will be always tending, for each distinct and fairly homogeneous class of workman, to be no more than can be got by "the marginal man" of that class, and in so far as labor may be regarded as freely mobile between the different grades, no more than would be given for the "marginal man" of the community as a whole. How much that will be cannot, even on the assumption of perfect completion and frictionless mobility, be determined by any reasoning of abstract economics. "It appears, then, as the conclusion of the argument," sums up our latest systematic writer, "that there is no short and simple rule by which the normal rate of wages in any employment can be determined over a long period or in the long run. We cannot assign with any degree of precision the superior and the inferior limits between which it must lie, and thus we cannot fix upon any point about which the market rates must oscillate."[2]

This necessary indeterminateness of the wage-contract, even under perfect competition, was insisted on by Thornton in 1869, and was thereupon mathematically demonstrated

---

[1] This Theory of Distribution would gain in logical completeness if, after the manner of the classic economists, (1) we could assume that this equivalent of the advantage of the marginal use of capital itself precisely determined, in any community, how much capital would be saved and productively employed—the rate of accumulation being so affected by every variation from the "normal" rate of interest as eventually to counteract the variation; and if (2) we might believe that the amount of the net produce of the marginal laborer determined how many laborers would exist—the increase of population varying in exact correspondence with these "normal" wages. But *as we do not know whether, human nature being as it is, a rise in the rate of interest would on the whole augment the amount of productive capital or decrease it; or whether a rise in wages would increase the birth-rate or diminish it*, both the amount of capital and the number of the population must, as far as abstract economics is concerned for the present be treated as indeterminate; or, rather, as data which, for any particular time and country, the abstract economist can only accept from the statistician.

[2] J. S. Nicholson, *Principles of Political Economy* (Edinburgh, 1893), p. 353

In a comparatively unnoticed paper, Fleeming Jenkin, a physicist of rare power, showed the economists of 1870 that, on their own reasoning, it followed that the rate of wages would vary according as the wage-earners took steps for their own protection or not. In flat contradiction of the current middle-class opinion, he concluded that the case of "the laborer who does not bargain as to his wages . . . is the case of a forced sale, as at a bankruptcy, and of any other sale by auction without a reserved price. . . . The knowledge that goods must be sold, that, in fact, there is no reserved price . . . at once lowers the demand curve while it raises the supply, and by a double action lowers the price. . . . Both in a given market and on an average of years, the power of bargaining will enable a seller to obtain higher prices [than without that power]."[1]

The whole subject was minutely investigated in 1881 by Professor F. Y. Edgeworth, from the mathematical standpoint, in a work which has received too little attention. He sums up his argument as follows. "Suppose a market consisting of an equal number of masters and servants, offering respectively wages and service, subject to the condition that no man can serve two masters, no master employ more than one man ; or suppose equilibrium already established between such parties to be disturbed by any sudden influx of wealth into the hands of the masters. Then there is no determinate, and very generally [no] unique arrangement towards which the system tends under the operation of, may we say, a law of Nature, and which would be predictable if we knew beforehand the real requirements of each, or of the average dealer ; but there are an indefinite number of arrangements à *priori* possible, towards one of which the system is urged, *not* by the concurrence of innumerable (as it were) neuter atoms eliminating chance, but (abstraction being made of custom) by what has been called the Art of Bargaining—higgling dodges and designing

[1] " Graphic Representation of the Laws of Supply and Demand," by Fleeming Jenkin, in *Recess Studies* (Edinburgh, 1870), pp. 173, 175.

obstinacy, and other incalculable and often disreputable accidents." [1]

But competition between individual producers and consumers, laborers and capitalists, is, as the economist is now careful to explain, in actual life very far from perfect, and shows no tendency to become so.[2] Combination, we are told,[3] "is as much a normal condition of modern industry" as competition, as, indeed, on the doctrine of freedom of contract it is bound to be. When wage-earners combine to improve the conditions of their employment, or when employers, on the other hand, tacitly or formally unite to reduce wages,—when, again, a great capitalist undertaking enjoys a virtual monopoly of any kind of employment, abstract economics is frankly incapable of predicting the result. "If," says Professor Marshall, "the employers in any trade act together and so do the employed, the solution of the problem of wages becomes indeterminate. The trade as a whole may be regarded as receiving a surplus (or quasi-rent) consisting of the excess of the aggregate price which it can get for such wares as it produces, over what it has to pay to other trades for the raw materials, etc., which it buys ; and *there is nothing but bargaining to decide the exact shares in which this should go to employers and employed.* No lowering of wages will be permanently in the interest of employers which is unnecessary and drives many skilled workers to other markets, or even to other industries in which they abandon the special income derived from their particular skill ; and wages must be high enough in an average year to attract young people to the trade. This

---

[1] *Mathematical Psychics* (London, 1881), p. 46, by F. Y. Edgeworth, now Drummond Professor of Political Economy in the University of Oxford.

[2] "In practical life such frictional disturbances are innumerable. At no moment and in no branch of production are they entirely absent. And thus it is that the Law of Costs is recognised as a law that is only approximately valid ; a law riddled through and through with exceptions. These innumerable exceptions, small and great, are the inexhaustible source of the undertaker's profits, but also of the undertaker's losses."—*The Positive Theory of Capital*, by E. v. Böhm-Bawerk, translated by W. Smart (London, 1891), p. 234.

[3] *Studies in Economics*, by W. Smart, Adam Smith Professor of Political Economy in the University of Glasgow (London, 1895), p. 259.

sets lower limits to wages, and upper limits are set by corresponding necessities as to the supply of capital and business power. *But what point within these limits should be taken at any time can be decided only by higgling and bargaining.*" [1]

We thus see that it is not only economically permissible, but in the view of our best authorities necessary for self-protection, that the workmen should not simply acquiesce in whatever conditions the employer may propose, but that they should take deliberate steps to protect themselves by " higgling and bargaining," if they are not to suffer lower wages and worse conditions of employment than there is any economic necessity for. " If the workman," says Walker, " from any cause does not pursue his interest *he loses his interest*, whether he refrain from bodily fear, from poverty, from ignorance, from timidity, and dread of censure, or from the effects of bad political economy which assures him that if he does not seek his interest, his interest will seek him." [2] And if the workmen ask how they can strengthen themselves in this higgling and bargaining, how they are most effectually to pursue their own interest, the answer of abstract economics is now, positively, *combination*. " In that contest of endurance between buyer and seller [of labor]," wrote J. S. Mill in 1869, " nothing but a close combination among the employed can give them even a chance of successfully competing against the employers." [3] This was one of the conclusions that most shocked Mill's economic friends of 1869, but it is one which has since become an economic commonplace.[4]   In 1881

---

[1] *Elements of Economics of Industry*, by Professor A. Marshall (London, 1892), p. 341.   " Demand and supply are not physical agencies which thrust a given amount of wages into the laborer's hand without the participation of his own will and actions. The market rate is not fixed for him by some self-acting instrument, but is the result of bargaining between human beings—of what Adam Smith calls 'the higgling of the market.'"—J. S. Mill, *Principles of Political Economy*, Book V. ch. x. sec. 5.

[2] *The Wages Question*, by F. A. Walker (New York, 1876 ; London, 1891), pp. 364, 411.

[3] *Fortnightly Review*, May 1869 ; *Dissertations and Discussions* (London, 1876), vol. iv. p. 42.

[4] " Combination is, in fact, the only way by which the poor can place them-

Professor Edgeworth, in the work which we have already quoted, placed it on the rock of mathematical analysis. Summing up a long mathematical argument as to "the general case in which numbers, natures, and combinations are unequal," he declares that "combination tends to introduce or increase indeterminateness ; and the final settlements thereby added are *more favorable to the combiners* than the (determinate or indeterminate) final settlements previously existing."   In his opinion, in fact, "the one thing from an abstract point of view visible amidst the jumble of catallactic molecules, the jostle of competitive crowds, is that those who form themselves into compact bodies by combination *do not tend to lose, but stand to gain.*" [1]   Nor need the combination amount in any sense to a monopoly. "If, for instance," proceeds Professor Edgeworth, "powerful trade unions did not seek to fix the *quid pro quo*, the amounts of labor exchanged for wealth (which they would be quite competent to seek), but only the rate of exchange, it being left to each capitalist to purchase as much labor as he might demand at that rate, there would still be that sort of indeterminateness favorable to unionists above described." And no trade need refrain, out of consideration for the interests of other trades, from doing the best it can for itself in its negotiations with its own particular employers.   "It is safe to say," observes Professor Taussig, "that in concrete life it happens very rarely, probably never, that a specific rise in wages, secured by strike or trade union pressure or simple agreement, can be shown to bring any off-setting loss in the wages of those not directly concerned. . . . The chances are against any traceable loss which would off-set the visible gain. Certainly an unbiassed and judicious adviser, having the interest of all laborers at heart, would hesitate long before counselling any particular set of laborers against an endeavor

selves on a par with the rich in bargaining."—H. Sidgwick, *Elements of Politics*, ch. xxviii. sec. 2, p. 579 of 2nd edition (London, 1897).

[1] *Mathematical Psychics* (London, 1881), by Prof. F. Y. Edgeworth, pp. 43, 44.

to get better terms from their employers, on the ground that as an ulterior result of success some of their fellows might suffer. If no other objection than this presented itself, he could safely assert that economic science had nothing to say against their endeavors, and much in favor of them." [1] Professor Sidgwick has therefore no difficulty in reciting various typical circumstances under which abstract economics show it to be quite possible for Trade Unions to raise wages, and in concluding that " in all the above cases it is possible for a combination of workmen to secure, either temporarily or permanently, a rise in wages ; whilst in none of them, except the last, has such gain any manifest tendency to be counterbalanced by future loss. And it does not appear that these cases are in practice very exceptional, or that the proposition that ' Trade Unions cannot in the long run succeed in raising wages ' corresponds even approximately to the actual facts of industry," whilst there is really no ground for the conclusion of the older economists " that if one set of laborers obtain an increase of wages in this way, there must be a corresponding reduction in the wages of other laborers." [2] Finally, we have the deliberate judgment of Professor Marshall, cautiously summing up his examination of the arguments for and against Trade Unionism. " In trades which have any sort of monopoly the workers, by limiting their numbers, may secure very high wages at the expense partly of the employers, but chiefly of the general community. But such action generally diminishes the number of skilled workers, and in this and other ways takes more in the aggregate from the real wages of workers outside than it adds to those of workers inside ; and thus on the balance it lowers average wages.[3] . . . Passing from selfish and exclusive action of this

---

[1] *Wages and Capital: an Examination of the Wages Fund Doctrine*, by F. W. Taussig, Professor of Political Economy in Harvard University (London, 1896), pp. 103, 104.

[2] *Principles of Political Economy*, by Henry Sidgwick, Professor of Moral Philosophy at the University of Cambridge (London, 1883), p. 363.

[3] Other authorities doubt whether, on any reasoning of abstract economics, this drawback can be shown necessarily to result. " If," observes Professor Edgeworth, " it is attempted to enforce the argument against Trade Unionism by

sort, we find that unions generally can so arrange their bargaining with employers as to remove the special disadvantages under which workmen would lie if bargaining as individuals and without reserve ; and in consequence employers may sometimes find the path of least resistance in paying somewhat higher wages than they would otherwise have done. In trades which use much fixed capital a strong union may for a time divert a great part of the aggregate net income (which is really a quasi-rent) to the workers ; but this injury to capital will be partly transmitted to consumers, and partly by its rebound, reduce employment and lower wages. . . . Other things being equal, the presence of a union in a trade raises wages relatively to other trades. But the influence which unions exert on the average level of wages is less than would be inferred by looking at the influence which they exert in each particular trade. When the measures which they take to raise wages in one trade have the effect of rendering business more difficult, or anxious, or impeding it in any other way, they are likely to diminish employment in other trades, and thus to cause a greater aggregate loss of wages to other trades than they gain for themselves, and to lower and not raise the average level of wages. . . . The power of unions to raise general wages by direct means is never great ; it is never sufficient to contend successfully with the general economic forces of the age, when their drift is against a rise of wages. But yet it is sufficient materially to benefit the worker, when it is so directed as to co-operate with and to strengthen those general agencies, which are tending to improve his position morally and economically."[1]   No

the consideration that it tends to diminish the total national produce, the obvious reply is that Unionists, as 'Economic men,' are not concerned with the total produce. Because the total produce is diminished it does not follow that the laborer's share is diminished (the loss may fall on the capitalist and the entrepreneur whose compressibility has been well shown by Mr. Sidgwick *Fortnightly Review*, September 1879) ; much less does it follow that there should be diminished that quantity which alone the rational unionist is concerned to increase—the laborer's utility."—*Mathematical Psychics*, p. 45.

[1] *Elements of Economics of Industry*, by Prof. A. Marshall (London, 1892), pp. 407, 408.

economist of the present day can therefore look forward, as the popular advisers of the middle class even within the present generation confidently could, to a time when "the fanatical faith of the working classes in the artificial mechanism of combination will give place to trust in the wiser, because more natural, system of individual competition; and the hiring of labor, like the exchange of commodities, will be set free, to be regulated by the Heaven-ordained laws of Supply and Demand."[1]

Thus, economic authority to-day, looking back on the confident assertions against Trade Unionism made by M'Culloch and Mill, Nassau Senior and Harriet Martineau, Fawcett and Cairnes, has humbly to admit, in the words of the present occupant of the chair once filled by Nassau Senior himself, that "in the matter of [Trade] Unionism, as well as in that of the predeterminate wage-fund, the untutored mind of the workman had gone more straight to the point than economic intelligence misled by a bad method."[2] The verdict of abstract economics is, in fact, decidedly in favor of the Trade Union contention, if only within certain limits. Whether this view of Trade Unionism in the abstract is worth any more, in relation to the actual problems of practical life, than the contrary verdict arrived at by the economists of a preceding generation, is a matter on which opinions will differ. For our own part, we are loth to pin our faith to any manipulation of economic abstractions, with or without the aid of mathematics. We are inclined to attach more weight to a consideration of the processes of industrial life as they actually exist. In the next chapter we shall accordingly seek to follow out the course of that "higgling and bargaining" upon which, as we have seen, the conditions of employment admittedly depend.

[1] *Trade Unionism*, by James Stirling, p. 55.
[2] *Mathematical Psychics* (p. 45), by F. Y. Edgeworth.

CHAPTER II

THE HIGGLING OF THE MARKET

It is often taken for granted that the higgling of the market, in which the workman is interested, is confined to the negotiation between himself and his employer. But the share of the aggregate product of the nation's industry which falls to the wage-earners as a class, or to any particular operative—notably the division of that portion which may be regarded as the "debatable land"—depends not merely on the strength or weakness of the workman's position towards the capitalist employer, but also on the strategic position of the employer towards the wholesale trader, that of the wholesale trader towards the shopkeeper, and that of the shopkeeper towards the consumer. The higgling of the market, which, under a system of free competition and Individual Bargaining, determines the conditions of employment, occurs in a chain of bargains linking together the manual worker, the capitalist employer, the wholesale trader, the shopkeeper, and the customer. Any addition to, or subtraction from, this series of intermediaries between the manual worker and the consumer—the excision of the capitalist employer or of the wholesale or retail trader, the insertion of a sub-contractor at one end or of a "tallyman"[1]

[1] The "tallyman" is a drapery hawker, visiting the houses of his customers, and selling his wares upon a particularly objectionable system of credit. See the article on "Tally System" in Chambers's *Encyclopædia* (London, 1874); and the excellent article under "Tally Trade" in M'Culloch's *Dictionary of*

at the other—will be found, in practice, to materially alter the position of all the parties. We must therefore examine separately the conditions of each of these series of bargains.[1]

It will be convenient to put on one side for the moment any consideration of gluts or scarcities—whether there is a surplus of workmen seeking situations or of vacancies to be filled ; whether manufacturers are heaping up stocks, or are unable to keep pace with the orders they receive ; whether the trader's "turn-over" is falling off or rapidly increasing. These variations in supply and demand will, of course, greatly affect the relative pressure of the forces which determine particular bargains. But fluctuations of this kind, however important they may be to the parties concerned, and however much we may believe them, in the long run, to weight the scales in favor of one class or another, tend only to obscure the essential and permanent characteristics of the several relationships. To reveal these characteristics, we must assume a market in a state of perfect equilibrium, where the supply is exactly equal in quantity to the demand.

We begin with the bargain between the workman and the capitalist employer. We assume that there is only a single situation vacant and only one candidate for it. When the workman applies for the post to the employer's foreman, the two parties to the bargain differ considerably in strategic strength. There is first the difference of alternative. If the foreman, and the capitalist employer for whom he acts, fail to come to terms with the workman, they may be put to some inconvenience in arranging the work of the establish-

---

Commerce and Commercial Navigation (London, 1882), pp. 1357-58 ; also C. S. Devas's *Groundwork of Economics* (London, 1883), note to sec. 213, p. 443.

[1] It is, in our view, one of the most unsatisfactory features of the older economists, that they habitually ignored the actual structure of the industrial world around them, and usually confined their analysis to the abstract figures of "the capitalist" and "the laborer." For a brief description of the main outline of English business structure see the article on "The House of Lords and the Sweating System," *Nineteenth Century*, May 1890, by Beatrice Potter (Mrs. Sidney Webb). A systematic economic analysis of the actual mechanism of English business life is badly needed.

ment. They may have to persuade the other workmen to work harder or to work overtime; they may even be compelled to leave a machine vacant, and thus run the risk of some delay in the completion of an order. Even if the workman remains obdurate, the worst that the capitalist suffers is a fractional decrease of the year's profit.[1] Meanwhile, he and his foreman, with their wives and families, find their housekeeping quite unaffected; they go on eating and drinking, working and enjoying themselves, whether the bargain with the individual workman has been made or not. Very different is the case with the wage-earner. If he refuses the foreman's terms even for a day, he irrevocably loses his whole day's subsistence. If he has absolutely no other resources than his labor, hunger brings him to his knees the very next morning. Even if he has a little hoard, or a couple of rooms full of furniture, he and his family can only exist by the immediate sacrifice of their cherished provision against calamity, or the stripping of their home. Sooner or later he must come to terms, on pain of starvation or the workhouse.[2] And since success in the higgling of the

---

[1] The latest critic of the theory of Trade Unionism denies this inequality, on the ground that whilst the wage-earners must starve if the employers stand out, the employers may be driven into bankruptcy if the workmen revolt (*A Criticism of the Theory of Trades' Unions*, by T. S. Cree, Glasgow, 1891, p. 20). But this very argument assumes " a stoppage of work through a strike "—that is to say, deliberately concerted action among the wage-earners—the very Trade Unionism which the writer declares to be unnecessary.

[2] It is interesting to find this situation clearly seen by an unknown French writer of 1773: "Partout où il y a de très-grandes propriétés, et par conséquent, beaucoup de journaliers, voici comment s'établit naturellement le prix des journées: le journalier demande une somme, le propriétaire en propose un moindre; et comme il ajoute *je puis me passer de vous plusieurs jours, voyez si vous pouvez vous passer de moi vingt-quatre heures*, on sait que le marché est bientôt conclu au préjudice du journalier."—*Éloge de Jean Baptiste Colbert*, par Monsieur P. (Paris, 1773), p. 8. Three years later Adam Smith remarked that "in the long run the workman may be as necessary to his master as his master is to him, but the necessity is not so immediate" (*Wealth of Nations*, London, 1776, Book I. ch. viii. p. 30 of M'Culloch s edition). Du Cellier (*Histoire des Classes Laborieuses en France*) observes that " the struggle in the labor market too often takes place, not between two equal contracting parties, but between a money-bag and a stomach" (p. 324). "In the general course of human nature," remarked the shrewd founders of the American Constitution, "power over a man's subsistence amounts to a power over his will" (*Federalist*, No. lxxix.)..

market is largely determined by the relative eagerness of the parties to come to terms—especially if this eagerness cannot be hid—it is now agreed, even if on this ground alone, " that manual laborers as a class are at a disadvantage in bargaining." [1]

But there is also a marked difference between the parties in that knowledge of the circumstances which is requisite for successful higgling. "The art of bargaining," observed Jevons, "mainly consists in the buyer ascertaining the lowest price at which the seller is willing to part with his object, without disclosing, if possible, the highest price which he, the buyer, is willing to give. . . . The power of reading another man's thoughts is of high importance in business." [2] Now the essential economic weakness of the isolated workman's position, as we have just described it, is necessarily known to the employer and his foreman. The isolated workman, on the other hand, is ignorant of the employer's position. Even in the rare cases in which the absence of a single workman is seriously inconvenient to the capitalist employer, this is unknown to any one outside his office. What is even more important, the employer, knowing the state of the market for his product, can form a clear opinion of how much it is worth his while to give, rather than go without the labor altogether, or rather than postpone it for a few weeks. But the isolated workman, unaided by any Trade Union official, and unable to communicate even with the workmen in other towns, is wholly in the dark as to how much he might ask.

With these two important disadvantages, it is comparatively a minor matter that the manual worker is, from his

[1] *Principles of Economics*, by Professor A. Marshall, 3rd edition (London, 1895), Book VI. ch. iv. p. 649. Professor Marshall adds that "the effects of the laborer's disadvantage in bargaining are therefore cumulative in two ways. It lowers his wages ; and, as we have seen, this lowers his efficiency as a worker, and thereby lowers the normal value of his labor. And in addition it diminishes his efficiency as a bargainer, and thus increases the chance that he will sell his labor for less than its normal value."

[2] W. S. Jevons, *Theory of Political Economy*, 3rd edition (London, 1888), ch. iv. p. 124.

position and training, far less skilled than the employer or his foreman in the art of bargaining itself. This art forms a large part of the daily life of the entrepreneur, whilst the foreman is specially selected for his skill in engaging and superintending workmen. The manual worker, on the contrary, has the very smallest experience of, and practically no training in, what is essentially one of the arts of the capitalist employer. He never engages in any but one sort of bargaining, and that only on occasions which may be infrequent, and which in any case make up only a tiny fraction of his life.

Thus, in the making of the labor contract the isolated individual workman, unprotected by any combination with his fellows, stands in all respects at a disadvantage compared with the capitalist employer. There is an even more serious disadvantage to come. The hiring of a workman, unlike a contract for the purchase of a commodity, necessarily leaves many conditions not precisely determined, still less expressed in any definite form. This indeterminateness of the labor contract is in some respects a drawback to the employer. In return for the specified wage, the workman has impliedly agreed to give work of the currently accepted standard of quantity and quality. The lack of definiteness in this respect leaves him free to skulk or to scamp. But against this the employer protects himself by providing supervision and by requiring obedience to his foreman, if not also by elaborate systems of fines and deductions. Whenever there is any dispute as to the speed of work, or the quality of the output, the foreman's decision is absolute. To the workman, however, the indeterminateness of his contract is a far more fruitful source of personal hardship, against which he has no practicable remedy. When an additional " hand " is taken on in a manufacturing establishment, practically the only point explicitly agreed upon between him and the foreman is the amount of the weekly wage, or possibly the scale of piecework rates. How many hours he shall work, how quickly or how intensely he is to exert himself, what intervals will be allowed for meals, what fines and deductions he will be subject to, what provision is made for warmth and shelter, the arrangements for ventilation and prevention of accidents, the sanitary accommodation, the noise, the smell and the dirt, the foreman's temper and the comrades' manners——all this has to be taken for granted, it being always implied in the engagement that the workman accepts the conditions existing in the employer's establishment, and obeys all his lawful commands. It may be urged that, if the conditions are worse than is customary, the workman will not accept the situation, unless he is offered higher wages. But until he has made his contract and actually begun work, he cannot know what the conditions are, even if he could estimate their disadvantage in terms of money, and stand out for the higher price. Moreover, unless fixed by law or Collective Bargaining, these conditions may at any moment be changed at the will of the employer, or the caprice of the foreman. Thus, when the isolated workman has made his bargain, he has no assurance that it will be adhered to, as regards any element other than the money wage, and even this may be eaten into by unforeseen fines and deductions. On all the other conditions of employment he is, under an unregulated industrial system, absolutely in the hands of the employer for the period of his engagement. The workman may, indeed, give up his situation, and throw himself again on the market, to incur once more the risk of losing his subsistence whilst seeking a new place, and to suffer afresh the perils of Individual Bargaining; but even if he makes up his mind rather to lose his employment than to put up with intolerable conditions, he is not legally free to do so without proper notice,[1] and for his sufferings during this period he has no redress.

Such are the disadvantages at which, when the labor

---

[1] Leaving work without giving the notice expressed or implied in the contract renders the workman liable to be sued for damages; and such actions by the employer against recalcitrant workmen are frequent, especially in the coal-mining industry.

market is in a state of perfect equilibrium, the isolated individual workman stands in bargaining with the capitalist employer. But it is, to say the least of it, unusual, in any trade in this country, for there to be no more workmen applying for situations than there are situations to be filled. When the unemployed are crowding round the factory gates every morning, it is plain to each man that, unless he can induce the foreman to select him rather than another, his chance of subsistence for weeks to come may be irretrievably lost. Under these circumstances bargaining, in the case of isolated individual workmen, becomes absolutely impossible. The foreman has only to pick his man, and tell him the terms. Once inside the gates, the lucky workman knows that if he grumbles at any of the surroundings, however intolerable ; if he demurs to any speeding-up, lengthening of the hours, or deductions ; or if he hesitates to obey any order, however unreasonable, he condemns himself once more to the semi-starvation and misery of unemployment. For the alternative to the foreman is merely to pick another man from the eager crowd, whilst the difference to the employer becomes incalculably infinitesimal. And it is a mistake to suppose that the workman's essential disadvantages in bargaining disappear in times of good trade, or even when employers are complaining of a scarcity of hands. The workman, it is true, need not then fear starvation, for he may rely on finding another employer. But if he refuses the first employer's terms, he still irrevocably loses his day's subsistence, and runs a risk of seeing subsequent days pass in the same manner. Moreover, the tramp after another employer may often mean the breaking up of his home, removal from his friends, dislocation of his children's educa- tion, and all the hundred and one discomforts of migration or exile.[1] The employer, on the other hand, will be induced

---

[1] Thus, in 1896, a year of exceptionally good trade, between five and six hundred members of the Associated Shipwrights' Society obtained advances of railway fares to enable them to move from their homes, where they were un- employed, to other towns where work was to be had ; see *Fifteenth Annual Report of the Associated Shipwrights' Society* (Newcastle, 1897), pp. 164-179.

to offer higher terms, rather than run the risk of foregoing some part of the increased profits of brisk times. But the extent of the " debatable land " is, in these times of high profits, enormously increased, and no one but the employer himself knows by how much. Here the difference in the knowledge of the circumstances becomes all-important, and fatally disadvantageous to the isolated workman. The employer knows about what other firms have been paying for their labor, and to what extent there is a real scarcity of workmen ; hence he can judge how little he need offer to make his place seem worth accepting to the unemployed workman. The isolated workman, on the other hand, has no knowledge whether the scarcity of labor extends beyond his own town, or is likely to be prolonged ; whilst he has not the slightest idea of how much he might stand out for, and yet be taken on. In short, it would be easy to argue that, in spite of the actual rise of his wages in times of good trade, it is just when profits are largest that the isolated workman stands at the greatest economic disadvantage in the division of the " debatable land."

So far the argument that the isolated workman, unprotected by anything in the nature of Trade Unionism, must necessarily get the worst of the bargain, rests on the assumption that the capitalist employer will take full advantage of his strategic strength, and beat each class of wage-earners down to the lowest possible terms. In so far as this result depends upon the will and intention of each individual employer, the assumption is untrue. A capitalist employer who looks forward, not to one but to many years' production, and who regards his business as a valuable property to be handed down from one generation to another, will, if only for his own sake, bear in mind the probable effect of any reduction upon the permanent efficiency of the establishment. He will know that he cannot subject his workpeople to bad conditions of employment without causing them imperceptibly to deteriorate in the quantity or quality of the service that they render. As an organiser of men, he will readily appreciate to how great an extent the smooth and expeditious working of a complicated industrial concern depends on each man feeling that he is being treated with consideration, and that he is receiving at least as much as he might be earning elsewhere. But apart from these considerations of mere self-interest, the typical capitalist manufacturer of the present generation, with his increasing education and refinement, his growing political interests and public spirit, will, so long as his own customary income is not interfered with, take a positive pleasure in augmenting the wages and promoting the comfort of his workpeople. Unfortunately, the intelligent, far-sighted, and public-spirited employer is not master of the situation. Unless he is protected by one or other of the dykes or bulwarks presently to be described, he is constantly finding himself as powerless as the workman to withstand the pressure of competitive industry. How this competitive pressure pushes him, in sheer self-defence, to take as much advantage of his workpeople as the most grasping and short-sighted of his rivals, we shall understand by examining the next link in the chain.

Paradoxical as it may appear, in the highly-developed commercial system of the England of to-day the capitalist manufacturer stands at as great a relative disadvantage to the wholesale trader as the isolated workman does to the capitalist manufacturer. In the higgling of the market with the wholesale trader who takes his product, the capitalist manufacturer exhibits the same inferiority of strategic position with regard to the alternative, with regard to knowledge of the circumstances, and with regard to bargaining capacity. First, we have the fact that the manufacturer stands to lose more by failing to sell his product with absolute regularity, than the wholesale trader does by temporarily abstaining from buying. To the manufacturer, with his capital locked up in mills and plant, continuity of employment is all-important. If his mills have to stop even for a single day, he has irrevocably lost that day's gross income, including out-of-pocket expenses for necessary salaries and maintenance. To the wholesale trader, on the other hand, it is comparatively a small matter that his stocks run low for a short time. His unemployed working-capital is, at worst, gaining deposit interest at the bank, and all he foregoes is a fraction of his profits for the year. Moreover, as the wholesale trader makes his income by a tiny profit per cent on a huge turnover, any particular transaction is comparatively unimportant to him. The manufacturer, earning a relatively large percentage on a small turnover, is much more concerned about each part of it. In short, whilst the capitalist manufacturer is "a combination in himself" compared with the thousand workmen whom he employs, the wholesale trader is "a combination in himself" compared with the hundreds of manufacturers from whom he buys. The disparity is no less great with regard to that knowledge of the market which is invaluable in bargaining. The manufacturer, even if he has a resident agent at the chief commercial centre, can never aspire to anything like the wide outlook over all the world, and the network of communications from retail traders and shipping agents in every town, which make up the business organisation of the wholesale trader. The trader, in short, alone possesses an up-to-date knowledge of the market in all its aspects ; he alone receives the latest information as to what shopkeepers find most in demand, and what native and foreign manufacturers are offering for sale. With all this superiority of knowledge, it is a minor matter that, as compared with the manufacturer, immersed in the organisation of labor and the improvement of technical processes, the wholesale trader is a specialist in bargaining, trained by his whole life in the art of buying in the cheapest and selling in the dearest market.[1]

---

[1] Where, as is the case in many trades, the wholesale trader sends out travellers to visit the retail shopkeepers, the manufacturer is even more dependent on him. For these travellers have great power to "push" one line of goods rather than another, and if any wholesale house has a well-established connection—still more, if its shopkeeping clients are in any way dependent on it—it can seriously injure a particular manufacturer by boycotting

Thus, when the manufacturer negotiates for an order, he is, within certain undefined limits, at the mercy of the wholesale trader. He is told that the price of his product is too high to attract customers ; that the shopkeepers find no demand for it ; that foreign producers are daily encroaching on the neutral markets ; and, finally, that there has just come an offer from a rival manufacturer to supply the same kind of article at a lower price. The manufacturer may doubt these statements, but he has no means of disproving them. He is keenly alive to the fact that his brother manufacturers are as eager as he is to get the order, and some of them, he knows, are always striving to undercut prices. Unless he is a man of substance, able to wait for more profitable orders, or unless his product is a speciality of his own, which no one else makes, he is almost certain to be tempted, rather than lose the business, to accept a lower offer than he meant to. The price he has accepted can only work out in a profit by some lowering of the cost of production. He consults his partners and his foreman as to how this can be effected. Some slight improvement may be possible in the technical process, or a new machine may be introduced. But this takes both time and capital. If neither law nor combination stands in the way, it is far easier to meet the emergency by extracting more work from his operatives for the same pay—by "speeding-up," by lengthening hours, by increased rigor in respect of fines and deductions, or by a positive reduction of time wages or piecework rates. Any idea of introducing better sanitary accommodation or further fencing of machinery is given up, and all the working expenses are reduced to their lowest limit. Whatever reluctance the good manufacturer may have to take this course necessarily disappears when he finds

his product. The manufacturer may, of course, put his own travellers on the road. But it is clearly more economical for the wholesale house to maintain the travellers, so that the little shopkeeper can get all his stock at once, than for the manufacturer of each article to have his own separate staff. The continued existence of the wholesale trader is thus as economically advantageous to all but the largest manufacturers as it is to all but the largest retailers.

his more necessitous or less scrupulous rivals actually fore-stalling him. For just as in every trade there are far-sighted and kindly-disposed employers who feel for their workpeople as for themselves, so there are others in whom the desire for personal gain is the dominating passion, and whose lack of intelligence, or financial "shadiness," shuts them out from any other policy than "grinding the faces of the poor." The manufacturer of this type needs no pressure from the wholesale trader to stimulate him to take the fullest possible advantage of the necessities of his workpeople ; and in face of competition of this kind the good employer has no choice but to yield. Anything, he says to himself, is better for his workpeople than stopping his own mill and driving the trade into such channels.

There is, moreover, another reason that makes the manufacturer yield to the constant nibbling at price, which forms so large a part of the art of the wholesale trader. In order that the manufacturer may make a profit on the year's trading he must obtain for his output, not only enough to cover the outgoings for wages and raw material—the " prime cost " of the finished product—but also the standing charges of the manufactory, termed by Professor Marshall the "supplementary cost." When a manufacturer is pressed to make a bargain at the lowest price, rather than see his mill stand idle, it is the " prime cost " which he thinks of as the minimum that he can accept without loss, since the standing charges will go on anyhow. Each manufacturer in turn prefers to sell at " prime cost " rather than not get an order at all, with the result, as the saying is, of " spoiling the market " for themselves and their rivals alike.[1] The standing charges have to be met somehow, and the harassed employer is forced to turn

---

[1] It was especially this effect of manufacturers' competition to secure orders—the frequent sales at prices covering " prime cost " only—that led to the formation of the remarkable "alliances " in the Birmingham hardware trades described in the chapter on " The Assumptions of Trade Unionism." To secure protection against the resulting constant degradation of price is the usual motive for manufacturers' rings and syndicates. The difference between " prime cost " and " supplementary cost " in English industry is worth further economic and statistical investigation ; see especially the chapter entitled " Cost Taking," in *The New Trades Combina-*

for relief to any possible cutting-down of the expenses of production, wages not excluded. Meanwhile, the wholesale trader sees no possible objection to the reduction he has effected. To him it is of no pecuniary consequence that a large proportion of the manufacturers of a particular article are only just managing to cover its "prime cost," and are thus really losing money, or that the workpeople in the hardest pressed mills or the least fortunate districts are, owing to a worsening of conditions, beginning to degrade in character and efficiency. If the product seriously falls off in quality relatively to the price demanded, he can go else-where ; and he makes, moreover, quite as large a percentage on low-grade goods as on those of standard excellence. And if he thinks about it at all, he regards himself as the representative, not of a particular class of producers, but of the whole world of consumers, to whom it is an obvious advantage that the price should be lowered.

We need not wonder, therefore, at the chronic complaints of manufacturers in every trade, that profits are always being reduced, so that business is scarcely worth carrying on. Even in years of national prosperity, when Income Tax and Death Duties show that vast fortunes are being made some-where, the employers who have no individual speciality, whose output is taken by the wholesale trader, and who are unable to form a "ring" or "alliance" to keep up prices, bitterly complain that it is as much as they can do to cover the "prime cost" of their products, or that, at best, they find themselves earning only the barest interest on capital.[1] For the influences which we have

tion Movement, by E. J. Smith (Birmingham, 1895). For statistics relating to American industry the student may consult the *Report of the Commissioner of Labor in the United States for 1890* (Washington, 1891) and the valuable series of *Reports of Statistics of Manufactures of Massachusetts from 1886 to 1896.* Particulars of English factory usage will be found in *Factory Accounts*, by E. Garcke and J. M. Fells. The only English statistics consist of a brief *Report on the Relation of Wages to the Cost of Production*, C. 6535, 1891.

In his *Principles of Economics*, Book V. chaps. iv. and vii., Prof. Marshall has described the relative influence on exchange value of "prime" and "supple-mentary" cost.

[1] How keenly this pressure is felt by the manufacturers who are exposed to

described affect the higgling of the market when the real demand of the consumers is brisk as well as when it is restricted. They amount, in fact, under a system of free and unregulated competition, to a permanent pressure on manufacturing employers to take the fullest possible advantage of their strategic superiority in bargaining with the isolated workman.

But we should make a mistake if we imagined that the pressure originated with the wholesale trader. Just as the manufacturer is conscious of his weakness in face of the

full competition, may be judged from the following speech from Lord Masham—the Samuel Lister who has made a colossal fortune from his legally protected patents. Having explained why the Manningham Mills had earned less than they were expected to earn, Lord Masham went on to argue that they had earned a great deal more than most other concerns. "Lister & Co. had earned during the eight years it had been a company an average of 4 per cent on the entire capital —that was, throwing debentures, preference shares, and ordinary stock all into one pool. If the money had been invested in agriculture, what would have happened? He had invested the same amount in agriculture, for which he got 2¼ per cent and he bought to receive 3. He had lost as much money nearly in agriculture as he had by his investment in Lister & Co. Then he would go on to cotton. He saw in the *Saturday Review* an article stating that the cotton spinning trade was paying, on the average of a large number of limited companies, 1¼ or 1½ per cent. That looked so outrageous that he could not believe it. He cut the statement out, and sent it to a gentleman who was in the cotton trade, and whose father was in the cotton trade before him. That gentleman sent it back again, saying that it was absolutely true, and he said, 'I will tell you something else—I challenge the whole trade of Lancashire, and I will guarantee that the whole trade of Lancashire is not on the capital invested paying as much as Consols—not the spinning alone, but the whole manufacturing trade of Lancashire.' So much with regard to two industries. Coming to iron, what was the state of the iron trade two or three years ago? Three years ago, at any rate, half the iron concerns in England were standing, and those that were at work were making no profit. They were declaring no dividend, and therefore, if the two good years which they had had just recently were added to the back years, he would guarantee that during the time of Lister & Co. the iron concerns had not made on their capital the 4 per cent that Manningham had. Then he came to another industry, on which he could speak with authority. It was one of the greatest industries in England, and employed over 800,000 persons. If it went on increasing as it had done it would be our greatest industry. He referred to coal. He had been in the coal hole (laughter), and he knew that for several years he made no interest, and he had very nearly as much money invested in it as in Manningham."

This speech was made in January 1897, at a time of roaring good trade, after several years of more than average prosperity, when the aggregate profits of Great Britain as a whole were apparently larger than they had been at any previous period of its history !

wholesale trader, so the wholesale trader feels himself helpless before the retail shopkeeper to whom he sells his stock.
Here the inferiority is not in any greater loss that would
arise if no business were done, for the retailer is impelled to
buy by motives exactly as strong as those which impel the
wholesale house to sell. Nor is it in any difference in bargaining power. In both these respects the wholesale house may
even have the advantage over the shopkeepers. But the
shopkeepers have a closer and more up-to-date knowledge
of exactly what it is that customers are asking for, and,
what is far more important, they can to some extent direct
this demand by placing, before the great ignorant body of
consumers, one article rather than another. They have,
therefore, to be courted by the wholesale trader, and induced
to push the particular "lines" that he is interested in.
There is, however, yet another, and even a more active, cause
for the weakness in strategic position of the wholesale trader.
His main economic function is to "nurse" the small shopkeeper. The little retailer, with a narrow range of clients,
cannot buy sufficient of any one article to enable him to deal
directly with the maker; he cannot, moreover, communicate
with the large number of separate manufacturers whose
products he sells; nor could he spare the capital to pay cash
for his stock. The wholesale trader accordingly acts as his
intermediary. In the large city warehouse, the shopkeeper
finds collected before him the products of all the manufacturers
in the various branches of his trade; he can take as small a
quantity of each as he chooses, and he is given as much
credit as his turnover requires. As long as this state of
things lasts the wholesale trader holds the field. But there
has been, for the last half century, a constant tendency
towards a revolution in retail trade. In one town or one
district after another there grow up, instead of numberless
little shops, large retail businesses, possessing as much
capital and commercial knowledge as the wholesale house
itself, and able to give orders that even the wealthiest
manufacturers are glad to receive. Hence the wholesale

house stands in constant danger of losing his clients, the smaller ones because they cannot buy cheaply enough to resist the cutting prices of their mammoth rivals, and these leviathans themselves because they are able to do without their original intermediaries. The wholesale trader's only chance of retaining their custom is to show a greater capacity for screwing down the prices of the manufacturers than even the largest shopkeeper possesses. He is therefore driven, as a matter of life and death, to concentrate his attention on extracting, from one manufacturer after another, a continual succession of heavy discounts or special terms of some kind. This, then, is the fundamental reason why the manufacturer finds the wholesale trader so relentless in taking advantage of his strategic position. Though often performing a service of real economic advantage to the community, he can only continue to exist by a constant "squeezing" of all the other agents in production.[1]

We come now to the last link in the chain, the competition between retail shopkeepers to secure customers. Here the superiority in knowledge and technical skill is on the side of the seller, but this is far outweighed by the exceptional freedom of the buyer. The shopkeeper, it is true, is

---

[1] The effect of competitive pressure in reducing the percentage of profits to turnover is well seen in the extreme cases in which one or more of the stages are omitted. In the wholesale clothing trade, for instance, there may be, as we have seen, only a single grade of capitalists between the "sweated" woman trouser-hand and the purchasing consumer. This wholesale clothier, though he makes a huge income for himself, extracts only the most infinitesimal sum out of each pair of trousers or "juvenile suit." His success depends upon the fact that he has a colossal trade, dealing every year in millions of garments, and turning over his moderate capital with exceptional rapidity. Even if he were sentimentally affected by the fact that the women to whom his firm gives out its millions of garments earned only six to ten shillings a week, he could not appreciably raise their wages by foregoing his whole profit, seeing that this amounts, perhaps, only to a penny a garment. Or, to take another instance, the original shareholders in the Civil Service Supply Association, who receive profits at the rate of literally hundreds per cent per annum, cannot afford to put any check on their directors' zeal for screwing down the manufacturers, or on their foremen's assiduity in keeping down wages in their own producing departments; for though the profit is colossal, compared with the capital invested, it is derived from tiny percentages on millions of transactions, and, if shared by all the wage-earners concerned in the production and distribution of the articles, would amount to an infinitesimal addition to their weekly wages.

not bound to sell any particular article at any particular time. But he must, on pain of bankruptcy, attract a constant stream of customers for his wares. The customer, on the other hand, is as free as air. He can buy in one shop as well as in another. He is not even bound to buy at all, and may abstain, not only without loss, but with a positive saving to his pocket. He must, in short, be tempted to buy, and to this end is bent all the shopkeeper's knowledge and capacity. Now, with regard to the general run of commodities, the only way of tempting the great mass of consumers to buy is to offer the article at what they consider a low price. Hence a shopkeeper is always on the look-out for something which he can sell at a lower price than has hitherto been customary, or cheaper than his competitors are selling it at. Competition between shopkeepers becomes, therefore, in all such cases entirely a matter of cutting prices, and the old-fashioned, steady-going business, which once contentedly paid whatever price the wholesale trader asked, is driven to look as sharply after "cheap lines" as the keenest trader. It might be suggested that a shopkeeper could equally outbid his rivals if he offered better quality at the same price. But this would be to misunderstand the psychology of the individual consumer.[1] Owing to his lack of technical knowledge, to say nothing of his imperfect means of testing his purchase, the only fact that he can grasp is, with regard to all nondescript commodities, the retail money price, and all temptation must reach his mind through this, the only medium. Under these circumstances, it is easy to understand how the revolution in retail trade, to which we have already referred, plays into the hands of the customer. The mammoth establishments, having a much lower percentage of working expenses to turn over, are able to sell

---

[1] Even the shops which rely on a reputation for quality as their main attraction, do not commit the mistake of merely offering a better article at the same price as is elsewhere charged for common goods. If they did, they would quickly find their customers deserting them. To retain the limited class of well-to-do purchasers who insist on the best quality, a positively higher price must be charged!

at lower prices than the small shops, and they naturally do their utmost to attract customers by widely advertising their cheapness. The customers become used to these low prices, and insist on them as the only condition upon which they will continue to patronise the surviving smaller shops. These, unable to reduce their working expenses, complain piteously to the wholesale houses, who are, as we have seen, driven to supply them on the lowest possible terms, lest they lose their custom altogether.

We thus arrive at the consumer as the ultimate source of that persistent pressure on sellers, which, transmitted through the long chain of bargainings, finally crushes the isolated workman at the base of the pyramid. Yet, paradoxical as it may seem, the consumer is, of all the parties to the transaction, the least personally responsible for the result. For he takes no active part in the process. In the great market of the world, he but accepts what is spontaneously offered to him. He does not, as a rule, even suggest to the shopkeeper that he would like prices lowered. All he does —and it is enough to keep the whole machine in motion— is to demur to paying half a crown for an article, when some one else is offering him the same thing for two shillings. It may be urged that he ought to be ready to pay a higher price for a better quality. As a matter of fact, consumers, whether rich or poor, do strive, in an almost pathetic way, after some assurance of specific quality that would reconcile them to paying the higher price. They recognise that their own personal experience of any article is too casual and limited to afford any trustworthy guidance, and they accordingly exhibit a touching faith in " authority " of one kind or another. Tradition, current hearsay as to what experts have said, and even the vague impression left on the mind by the repeated assertions of mendacious advertisements, are all reasons for remaining faithful to a particular commodity, a particular brand or mark, or even a particular shop, irrespective of mere cheapness. But to enable the consumers to exercise this choice, there must be some easy means of distinguishing between rival wares. It so happens that the bulk of the consumption of the community consists of goods which cannot be labelled or otherwise artificially distinguished. With regard to the vast majority of the purchases of daily life, no one but an expert can, with any assurance, discriminate between shades of quality, and the ordinary customer is reduced to decide by price alone. Nor could he, even on grounds of the highest philanthropy, reasonably take any other course. As a practical man, he knows it to be quite impossible for him to trace the article through its various stages of production and distribution, and to discover whether the extra sixpence charged by the dearer shop represents better wages to any workman, or goes as mere extra profit to one or other of the capitalists concerned. If he is an economist he will have a shrewd suspicion that the extra sixpence is most likely to be absorbed in one form or another of that rent of exceptional opportunity which plays so large a part in industrial incomes. Nor need he, in any particular case, have a presumption against low-priced articles as such, nor even against a fall in prices. The finest and most expensive broadcloth, made in the West of England factories, is the product of worse-paid labor than the cheap " tweeds " of Dewsbury or Batley. Costly handmade lace is, in actual fact, usually the outcome of cruelly long hours of labor, starvation wages, and incredibly bad sanitary conditions, whilst the cheap article, which Nottingham turns out by the ton, is the output of a closely combined trade, enjoying exceptionally high wages, short hours, and comfortable homes. In the same way the great fall in prices, which is so marked a feature of our time, is undoubtedly due, in the main (if not, as some say, to currency changes), to the natural and legitimate reduction of the real cost of production ; to the improvement of technical processes, the cheapening of transport, the exclusion of unnecessary middlemen, and the general increase in intelligence and in the efficiency of social organisation. It follows that the consumers, as consumers, are helpless in the matter. The systematic pressure upon the isolated workman which we have described has reference to them alone, and serves their immediate interests, but it cannot be said to be caused by anything within their volition, or to be alterable by anything which they, in their capacity of consumers, could possibly accomplish.[1]

Such, then, is the general form of the industrial organisation which, in so far as it is not tampered with by monopoly or collective regulation, grows up under "the system of natural liberty." The idea of mutual exchange of services by free and independent producers in a state of economic equality results, not in a simple, but in a highly complex industrial structure which, whether or not consistent with any real Liberty, is strikingly lacking in either Equality or Fraternity. What is most obvious about it is, not any freedom in alternatives enjoyed by the parties concerned,

---

[1] This analysis of the actual working of the modern business organisation, with its constant pressure on the seller, will remind the economic student of Professor Böhm-Bawerk's brilliant and suggestive exposition of the advantage of " present " over " future " goods. At every stage, from the wage-earner to the shopkeeper, it is the compulsion on the seller to barter his " future goods " for " present goods " which creates the stream of pressure. " It is undeniable," says Professor Böhm-Bawerk, " that, in this exchange of present commodities against future, the circumstances are of such a nature as to threaten the poor with exploitation of monopolists. Present goods are absolutely needed by everybody if people are to live. He who has not got them must try to obtain them at any price. To produce them on his own account is proscribed the poor man by circumstances. . . . He must, then, buy his present goods from those who have them . . . by selling his labor. But in this bargain he is doubly handicapped ; first, by the position of compulsion in which he finds himself, and second, by the numerical relation existing between buyers and sellers of present goods. The capitalists who have present goods for sale are relatively few ; the proletarians who must buy them are innumerable. In the market for present goods, then, a majority of buyers who find themselves compelled to buy stands opposite a minority of sellers, and this is a relation which obviously is profoundly favorable to the sellers [that is, the buyers of labor or wares] and unfavorable to the buyers [that is, the sellers of labor or wares]. . . . [This] may be corrected by active competition among sellers [of present goods]. . . . Fortunately, in actual life this is the rule, not the exception. But, every now and then, something will suspend the capitalists' competition, and then those unfortunates, whom fate has thrown on a local market ruled by monopoly, are delivered over to the discretion of the adversary. . . . Hence the low wages forcibly exploited from the workers—sometimes the workers of individual factories, sometimes of individual branches of production, sometimes—though happily not often, and only under peculiarly unfavorable circumstances—of whole nations."—E. von Böhm-Bawerk, *The Positive Theory of Capital* (London, 1891), p. 360.

but the general consciousness of working under pressure
felt by every class of producers. At each link in the chain
of bargainings, the superiority in "freedom" is so over-
whelmingly on the side of the buyer, that the seller feels
only constraint.[1] This freedom of the purchaser increases
with every stage away from the actual production, until it
culminates in the anarchic irresponsibility of the private
customer, "free" alike from all moral considerations as to
the conditions of employment, and from any intelligent
appreciation of the quality of the product. On the other
hand, the impulse for cheapness, of which the consumer is
the unconscious source, grows in strength as it is transmitted
from one stage of bargaining to another, until at last, with
all its accumulated weight, it settles like an incubus on the
isolated workman's means of subsistence.

We pause here for a moment, in our analysis of the
industrial machine, to examine the case of the domestic
servant. The reader will see, from this description of the
higgling of the market, how pointless is the statement—
used as a conclusive argument against the need for Trade
Unionism, or its power to raise wages—of the good wages
enjoyed by domestic servants. There is no analogy between
the engagement of domestic servants to minister to the
personal comfort of the relatively rich, and the wage-contract
of the operative employed by the profit-maker. In the first
place, the conditions of domestic service put employer and

[1] The existence of this feeling of constraint may be inferred from the efforts
which each grade of producers makes to propitiate the buyers. Every form of
bribery is used, from the sweated outworker's "tip" to the "giving-out foreman," the manufacturer's Christmas present to the "buyer" of the wholesale
house, the wholesale trader's dinner to the shopkeepers, and, finally, the cook's
perquisites from the butcher and the dairyman. *It is highly significant that it is
always the seller who bribes, never the buyer.* Sometimes the seller's effort to
escape the pressure takes the form of attempting—usually by giving credit—to
entangle the buyer, so as to destroy his freedom to withhold his custom and
compel him to continue his purchases. Thus, the leather-merchant gives credit
to the boot-manufacturer, the boot-manufacturer to the shopkeeper, and the
shopkeeper to the artisan—the well-understood condition always being that the
buyer in each case continues to deal with the obliging seller, without too closely
scrutinising his prices. We have already mentioned the "tallyman," who finds
his profit in a similar entanglement of the necessitous customer.

employed much more on a par with regard to the bargain than those of industrial wage-labor. The alternative to the well-to-do woman of doing without a servant for a single day is perhaps as disagreeable to her as the alternative to the servant of being out of place; and the worry and inconvenience to the mistress of finding another servant is at least as great as the discomfort to the servant of getting another situation. In capacity of bargaining the servant is normally as good as the mistress, whilst in technical knowledge she is usually vastly superior. In the all-important matter of carrying out the bargain, it is the mistress, with her lack of knowledge, her indifference to details, and her preoccupation with other affairs, whose own ease of body and mind is at the mercy of the servant's hundred and one ways of making herself disagreeable. The personal comfort enjoyed by the servants in a typical middle-class household depends mainly on themselves ; that of the mistress and her family depends to an enormous extent on the goodwill of her servants. But more important than all these considerations is the fact that the conditions of employment of domestic servants in middle or upper-class households are in no way affected by the stream of competitive pressure that weighs down the price of wares and the wages of their producers. As each household works for its own use, and not for sale, the temptation to "undercut" is entirely absent. It does not make an iota of difference to one mistress that another in the same town pays lower wages to her cook or her housemaid. Social pressure acts, in fact, in exactly the opposite direction. Such competition as exists between the households of the well-to-do classes, whether in London or county society, or in the more modest but not less comfortable professional or manufacturers' "set" of a provincial town, takes the form of providing more luxurious quarters and more perfect entertainment for desirable guests, and therefore tends positively to raise the wages spontaneously offered to clever and trustworthy servants. Under these circumstances it might have been predicted that the rise in incomes, the greater desire for domestic comfort, and the growing preoccupation of upper and middle-class women in other things than housekeeping, would have resulted in a marked increase in the wages of servants in private households.[1] So helpless, in fact, are the "employers" in this case that, if cooks and housemaids formed an effective Trade Union, so as to use their strategic advantage to the utmost, middle-class women would be forced to defend themselves by taking refuge behind a salaried official or profit-making contractor—for instance, by resorting to residential clubs, boarding-houses, or co-operatively managed blocks of flats. It is noteworthy that wherever the profit-maker intervenes, the exceptional conditions enjoyed by domestic servants disappear. Notwithstanding the constant demand for servants in private households, the women who cook, scrub, clean, or wait in the common run of hotels, boarding-houses, lodgings, coffee-shops, or restaurants, are as ill-paid, as ill-treated, and as overworked as their sisters in other unorganised occupations.

So far we have mainly concerned ourselves with tracing the stream of pressure to its origin in the private customer. Now we have to consider the equally important fact that, as each class of producers becomes conscious of this pressure, it tries to escape from it, to resist or to evade it. All along the stream we discover the inhabitants of the "debatable land" raising bulwarks or dykes, sometimes with a view of maintaining quiet backwaters of profit for themselves, sometimes with the object of embanking their Standard of Life against further encroachments. It is in

---

[1] It is, we think, somewhat discreditable to English economists that they should have gone on copying and recopying from each other's lectures and text-books the idea that this rise in wages among the domestic servants of the well-to-do classes constituted any argument against the validity of the case for Trade Unionism in the world of competitive industry. We can only attribute it to the fact that male economic lecturers and text-book writers have seldom themselves experienced the troubles of housekeeping, either on a large or on a small scale, whilst the few women economists have hitherto suffered from a lack of personal knowledge of the actual relations between capitalist and workman in the profit-making world.

this deliberate resistance to a merely indiscriminate pressure that we shall find, not only the scope of the Methods and Regulations of Trade Unionism by which certain sections of the wage-earners protect and improve the conditions of their employment, but also the fundamental reason for the analogous devices of the other producing classes—the trade secrets, patents and trade marks, the enormous advertising of specialities, the exclusive franchises or concessions, the capitalist manufacturer's struggle to supersede the trader, and the trader's backstair effort to do without the capitalist manufacturer, together with all the desperate attempts to form rings and trusts, syndicates and "alliances"—by one or other of which is to be explained the perpetual inequality in the profits of contemporary industry, and the heaping up of fortunes in particular trades. If it were not for this deliberate erection of dykes and bulwarks we should find, in all the old-established industries, every manufacturer and trader making only the bare minimum of profit, without which he would not be induced to engage in business at all, and, we may add, every wage-earner reduced to bare subsistence wages, below which he could not continue to exist. But instead of this equality in constraint, with its implication of equality in minimum remuneration, industrial life presents, and has for over two centuries always presented, a spectacle of extreme inequality, alike between classes, trades, and individuals. We do not here refer to the differences of remuneration that are commensurate with differences of personal capacity, whether physical or mental : these, like the differences in advantageousness of different sites and soils, with their equivalent differences of land rent, will, by the economist, easily be put on one side. But it is a matter of common observation that there are, at any moment, huge incomes being gained, now in one trade, now in another, which bear no relation whatever to the relative capacity of the manufacturers or traders concerned, or to the amount of work that they perform. To take only this century, whilst the brewers have always been piling up riches, we see the great fortunes made in cotton and other textiles a hundred years ago succeeded by the fabulous profits of the coal-owners and iron-masters, together with those of the machine-making industry ; the great wealth amassed by the ship-owners and foreign merchants followed by the expansion of the wholesale grocers, the alkali producers, and the sewing-machine manufacturers ; whilst to - day huge gains are admittedly being reaped by the wholesale clothiers and provision dealers, the great soap and pill advertisers, and the bicycle makers.   These times of great fortunes may, as regards any particular trade or any particular firm, last only a few years.   But the experience of the last two centuries furnishes no period in which they did not exist in one quarter or another, and gives us no warrant for assuming that they will, under anything like the existing order of things, ever disappear.   Though each particular case may be temporary only, the phenomenon itself is of constant occurrence.   From the point of view of the community it is, accordingly, not evanescent but permanent.   It may, in fact, be said to be even the most characteristic feature of the present industrial system as compared with any other, and it is one which vitally affects the life of every class.   Without the constant presence of these exceptional profits the indus-trial world would differ as fundamentally from that in which we now exist as a Co-operative Commonwealth or a Socialist State.   In our view, they cannot be philosophically accounted for by any reference to " economic friction " or " lack of mobility " : they are, as we shall now attempt to show, the direct and necessary consequence, under the " system of natural liberty," of the fact that the stream of pressure that we have described impinges, not upon the normal weakness of the isolated individual seller, but upon a series of very unequal dykes and bulwarks, cast up by the different sections of the industrial world.   By passing these briefly in review, we shall be prepared to see, in their due proportion, the devices peculiar to the wage-earning class.

Let us note first one incidental and purely advantageous

effect of the constant pressure on all existing products and in all existing markets. It stimulates the capitalist and brainworker to desire to escape from these closely swept fields, by discovering new products or new markets. The ever-present instinct of every manufacturer or trader is to invent an article which no rival yet produces, or to find customers whom no one yet serves. Here at last he finds a land of real freedom of contract, where he has the same economic liberty to refuse to cheapen his commodity as the buyer has to abstain from gratifying that particular desire. He cannot, of course, actually dictate terms, for the customer may always prefer to go on spending his income as he has hitherto done. But price is settled without reference to fear of competition, and is limited only by the extent and keenness of the demand. Merely to be first in the field in such a case often means a large fortune, which is but the reward for opening up a fresh source of income to producers and of satisfaction to consumers. But the capitalist is keenly conscious of the completeness with which the stream of pressure will presently deprive him of this economic liberty, and he therefore hastens to throw up a dyke before the stream reaches him. Two hundred years ago he turned, like the artisan, to the Government, and applied as a matter of course for a charter, giving him royal authority to exclude " interlopers." When the House of Commons took the view that there should be " no interference of the legislature with the freedom of trade, or with the right of every man to employ the capital he inherits, or has acquired, according to his own discretion," [1] it might have been supposed that all legal dykes and bulwarks against perfect freedom of competition would be brought to an end. But though Parliament has swept away, on this plea, every kind of vested interest of the artisan, it has, throughout the whole century, permitted one section of capitalists after another to entrench

---

[1] *Report on Petitions of the Cotton Weavers*, 1811 ; *Report of the Committee on the State of the Woollen Manufacture in England*, 1806 ; *History of Trade Unionism*, pp. 54, 56.

themselves by laws which excluded other capitalists from competing with them. There has even been lately a recrudescence of Chartered Companies, legally secured in the enjoyment of exceptional privileges.[1] But apart from this accidental result of our growing Imperialism, the century has witnessed the building up of an unparalleled system of railway, gas, water, and tramway monopolies, founded on private Acts of Parliament. Here, it is true, Parliament reserves to itself the right at any time to license another competitor. But the policy throughout has been never to license a new undertaking in competition with one already in the field, however profitably the business may have resulted, unless the new promoters prove that there is a sufficiently large group or section of customers who are still unprovided with the service in question. Thus, it is never admitted even as an argument in favor of a proposed new water company or railway, that the one already in the field is paying 10 per cent dividend. The new promoters do not get their Act unless they convince a committee of each House of Parliament that no existing company is actually supplying the service which they desire to undertake. We do not think that people realise to what an extent the industrial wealth of the country is invested in channels thus legally safeguarded. We roughly estimate that, excluding land and houses, something like one-fourth of the total capital of the United Kingdom is invested under private Acts of Parliament, and in this way protected from the stream of competitive pressure. It is not merely that the privileged capitalists are able to retain the amount of custom with which they first started. They share with the landlords

---

[1] The modern form of charter carefully pays lip-homage to ''freedom of trade.'' But as it usually gives the privileged adventurers the exclusive ownership of land and minerals, the right to levy import and export duties on all traders (which, when the company itself trades, it pays only from one pocket to another), and the power of constructing railways and ports and of making towns and markets, the independent trader (in the Niger Territories, for instance) or the independent miner (in Rhodesia, for instance) does not find his position financially so different from that of the eighteenth-century '' interloper '' as might be supposed.

the unearned increment arising from the mere growth of population. They are even protected against the whole community itself, which is not permitted co-operatively to provide its own railways or water or gas, without first satisfying the monopolist who is in the field. We need not consider whether there was any other way of inducing capitalists to embark in these large, and, at one time, venturesome undertakings, otherwise than by thus according them what is virtually a legal guarantee of protection for their "established expectation." But this deliberate Parliamentary policy of creating and maintaining vested interests as the best means of securing the performance of particular services—this virtual defence against the full stream of competitive pressure enjoyed by a quarter of the whole industrial capital of the community—is in itself an interesting criticism of "the system of natural liberty."

If we pass now to another incidental advantage of the pressure—the incessant attempts of manufacturers to improve their technical processes—we shall find another successful revolt against "the system of natural liberty." If by some new invention, or new machine, the cost of production can be reduced, or a superior article turned out, the manufacturer will be able to yield to the pressure of the wholesale trader, and yet make, at his ease, an increased profit for himself. The effect of the pressure would thus, it would seem, be to give the greatest possible stimulus to improvements in technical processes. But unless the manufacturer can erect some kind of dyke for his improvement, so as to prevent the other manufacturers from adopting the same device, he will very likely find that the invention has been a positive loss to him and them alike. For by the time the principal manufacturers have adopted the improvement, no one among them is any better able to withstand the pressure of the wholesale trader than he was before. The stream of competition will have swept away the whole economic advantage of the new invention by way of reduction of price, to the advantage, first of the traders, and eventually of the customers. But this does not complete the existing manufacturers' discomfiture. To adopt the new invention will have involved an additional outlay of capital, and can scarcely fail to have rendered obsolete, and so destroyed, some portion of their previous possessions. Even at this cost, the adaptation of the old mills to the new requirements leaves much to be desired from the point of view of perfect economy of production. Here is the chance for a new capitalist to build an entirely new mill, equipped with the very latest improvements, and making the utmost of the new invention. The old manufacturers, to whose ingenuity and enterprise the improvement was due, thus find themselves, under a system of free and unregulated competition, placed by it at a positive disadvantage. In this result lies the justification of the Patent Laws, which give the owner of a new invention a legal monopoly of its use for a term of (in the United Kingdom) fourteen years. The present century, and especially the present generation, has seen an enormous extension of patents in every industry, it being now actually rare to find any important manufacturer who does not enjoy one or more of these defences against competition. And though each of them lasts only for fourteen years, capitalist ingenuity has found a way of indefinitely extending their protection. Before one patent runs out, another is secured for some subsidiary improvement in the original invention, which the patentee has, of course, had the best opportunity of discovering, or which he has bought from a needy inventor. The right to manufacture the original invention becomes in due course common to all, but is then of little use to anybody, for the legally protected monopolist of the latest improvement still holds the field. No estimate can be formed of the amount of the capital that is thus by patents legally protected from the pressure of free competition, but its amount is enormous and daily increasing.

We have hitherto dealt with the various forms of legal protection by which the capitalists have succeeded in embanking their profits against the stream of competitive

pressure. We come now to other devices with the same
object. What the manufacturer seeks is in some way to
escape from the penetrating pressure exercised by the
wholesale trader. Stimulated by the desire to secure
increased profits for himself, the trader is always setting
his wits to work to see how he can transform the blind,
impartial pressure of the private customer into a force so
regulated and concentrated as to press always where there
is least resistance. His specialist skill in bargaining, his
trained appreciation of the minutest grades of quality, and
his quick apprehension of improvements in technical processes, enable him so to play off the competing manufacturers
one against the other, as to make them yield up, more
quickly and more completely than would otherwise have
been necessary, the exceptional profits that he discovers them
to be enjoying. Thus, in the typically complete form of
modern business organisation, the wholesale and retail
traders act, virtually, as the expert agents of the ignorant
consumer. The manufacturers are always seeking to relieve
themselves of this expert criticism and deliberately adjusted
pressure on the price or quality of their wares, by entering
into direct relations with the private customer. This is the
economic explanation of the growth, during the present
generation, of the world-wide advertisement of distinctive
specialities, and the consequent development of the use of
trade marks or makers' names. If such an impression can
be created on the minds of consumers that thousands of them
will insist on purchasing some particular article, the manufacturer of that article gains enormously in his strategic
position towards the wholesale trader. It matters not for
this purpose whether the consumer's prejudice is or is not
founded on proved excellence : many a quack medicine gives
as secure a position of vantage as has been won by Cadbury's
Cocoa or Dr. Jaeger's woollens. This enormous development
of "proprietary articles," beginning with patent medicines,
but now including almost every kind of household requisite,
has led to an interesting form of bulwark against the

lowering of prices. The manufacturer of a proprietary article that has once secured the favor of the public, sees little advantage in the cut-throat competition which results in the customer getting it at a lower price. He does not find that appreciably more of his speciality is sold when customers can buy it for elevenpence instead of thirteen-pence-halfpenny. What happens, however, in such a case is that the pressure on the wholesale trader to give special discounts, or otherwise lower the wholesale price, becomes so irresistible, that, presently, the wholesale house finds it practically unremunerative to deal in the article at all, to the consequent loss of the manufacturer. The enterprising proprietor of a distinctive speciality therefore attempts nowadays to fix the price all along the line. For the protection of all parties concerned, he devises what is called an "ironclad contract." He refuses to supply, or withholds the best discount from, any wholesale trader who will not formally bind himself, under penalty, not to sell below a certain prescribed "wholesale price." He may even prescribe a definite retail price, below which no shopkeeper may sell his wares, under penalty of finding the supply cut off. Our own impression is that, where the wholesale trader and the retail shopkeeper continue to be employed at all in the distribution of newly invented commodities, this strictly protected and highly regulated business organisation is already the typical form.[1]

[1] These "ironclad contracts" are not easily seen by persons unconnected with the particular trade, and we do not believe that any one has an adequate idea of their rapid increase, or of the enormous proportion of the total trade to which they now extend. We have had the privilege of studying their operation in one of the largest of English wholesale houses, supplying household requisites of every kind, and itself entering into scores of contracts of this sort. We have now before us the confidential circulars of a manufacturer of well-known specialities, dated 8th June 1896, from which we append some extracts. The circular to retailers, after specifying the wholesale prices and discounts, continues : "To avoid confusion of prices, and also to prevent 'cutting,' and secure a legitimate profit for our customers, we respectfully require all whom we supply not to sell under the prices named below. In the interests of our customers, therefore, *only those will be supplied who have signed an agreement to this effect.*" The circular to the wholesale houses states that there will be paid "a bonus of 5 per cent conditional on goods not being 'cut' below our own quotations to the

But although the shopkeeper prefers regulation of the price of proprietary articles to the ruinous results of free competition in their sale, he greatly dislikes proprietary articles altogether. He is always trying to give a preference to nondescript commodities, of which he can "push" one make rather than another, and thus take advantage of the customer's ignorance to secure larger profits.[1] The manufacturers of proprietary articles retort by appointing their own retail agents on a definite commission, thus bringing into the field the vast number of bakers who sell packet tea, or newsvendors who push a special brand of tobacco. A new product, such as typewriting machines or bicycles, will break away altogether from the typical business organisation, and we see the manufacturers keeping in their own hands both the wholesale and the retail trade, even absorbing also the shipping business and the repairing. When neither patent nor trademark, long-standing reputation nor world-wide advertisement can be used as a bulwark, manufacturers try to protect themselves by rings and other arrangements to fix prices. So obvious is the pecuniary advantage of this course, that it is only the long habits of fighting each other, and the mutual suspicion thus engendered, which prevent a much wider adoption of this expedient by English manufacturers.[2] Finally, we have such bold attempts to abolish

retail trade. . . . This will enable wholesale houses . . . to secure nearly 14 per cent profit, and will, we trust, ensure your continual interest in pushing (the article)." See also an article on "Combination in Shopkeeping" in *Progressive Review*, April 1897.

[1] It is interesting to notice, in this connection, how willingly the Legislature has lent itself, by the comprehensive provisions of the Merchandise Marks Acts, to the legal protection of the security enjoyed by "proprietary articles" against competition either in price or quality. A chemist may make "Condy's Fluid" (the well-known disinfecting solution of permanganate of potash) exactly in the same way as Condy, cheaper than Condy, and better than Condy, but he must not sell, under the only name by which customers will ask for it, any but the article supplied—it may be under an "ironclad contract"—by Condy himself.

[2] We may cite one of the many informal and unknown "rings," which dominate particular branches of manufacture. The English hollow-ware trade, for instance (the manufacture of metal utensils of all kinds) is practically confined to about a dozen firms in and near Birmingham. These have, for many years, united in fixing the prices of all the articles they manu-

competition altogether, by the union of all rivals into a single amalgamation, as have partially or wholly succeeded in the screw, cotton-thread, salt, alkali, and indiarubber tyre industries in this country, and in innumerable other cases in the United States.

In all the foregoing attempts to resist or evade the stream of pressure, the device of the capitalist may be regarded as some form of dyke, tending to maintain prices at a paying level. In other cases we see a different expedient. We have already noticed the fact that, when a new industry springs up, there is nowadays a tendency to prevent any differentiation of productive structure, and to retain all the grades in a single hand. Thus the typewriter and bicycle manufacturers, following in the wake of the great sewing-machine producers, eliminate all the traders. But the telescoping may start also from the other end. Out of the village pedlar in the country, or the little town retailer of cheap boots and clothes, has grown the colossal wholesale clothier of our day, who gives out work to thousands of isolated families all over the country ; sorts and labels in his warehouse their diverse products ; supplies his own retail shops in the different towns ; executes asylum and workhouse contracts ; and ships, on his own account, to Cape Town or Melbourne, the hundreds of thousands of "cheap suits" annually absorbed by the Colonies. Here the characteristic feature is not the keeping up of the price against the consumer, but an exceptionally terrible engine of oppression of the manual-working producer. In all the "sweated industries," in fact, the capitalist's expedient is not to evade the pressure for cheapness, but to find a means of making that pressure fall with all its weight on the worker. We have already described the disadvantageous position of

facture. A uniform wholesale price-list is agreed upon, with three different rates of discount. The firms are classified by common consent, according to the perfection of finish of their wares and the prestige which they enjoy, into three grades, each adhering to its corresponding rate of discount. This "ring" is quite informal, but has for years been well maintained to the apparent satisfaction of its members.

the isolated workman when he bargains with the owner of a mill or a factory. But he has, at any rate, the advantage of knowing what the other workmen are paid, and the invaluable moral support which comes from the companionship of numbers. Moreover, as we have seen, in mills and factories, the Trade Union Methods of Mutual Insurance, Collective Bargaining, and Legal Enactment erect dykes in the form of Common Rules, the economic effects of which we shall presently discuss. But the home-worker is without any of these protections, and finds himself reduced, as a rule, to the barest subsistence wage. And when, as in the slop-clothing trade, these home-workers are mainly drawn from classes without any notion of a definite " Standard of Life "—for Polish Jews and unskilled Englishwomen will do any work, at any price, under any conditions—their wages will be driven even below what would keep the class permanently in working efficiency. Thus, in the so-called " sweating system " the capitalist employer has found a way, not only of evading the downward pressure which the wholesale and retail trader normally exercises upon the manufacturer, but also of escaping the resistance either of combination or legal regulation by which the factory owner seeking to reduce the Standard of Life now usually finds himself confronted. The colossal fortunes which have been, and are still being, made by the wholesale clothiers represent the absorption, by one small section of capitalists, of absolutely the whole of that debatable land lying between the price that a careless consumer, ignorant alike of quality and of the transformation of the industry, will continue to pay, and the wage that half-subsidised women and a stream of outcast Jews from other lands will continue to accept, rather than forego employment altogether.

We have in the foregoing pages briefly indicated some of the principal devices by which almost every section of capitalists, whether manufacturers or traders, nowadays succeed in evading, resisting, or controlling in their own interests the blind coercion which the great mass of uninformed and irresponsible consumers are always unconscientiously exercising. To analyse adequately these various expedients, to discuss how far they increase or diminish the wealth of nations, to discover how they affect national character or are consistent with this or that view of social expediency, would require as detailed an investigation of the actual facts of business organisation as we have undertaken with regard to Trade Unionism. Such an investigation would, we believe, yield results of the utmost value to the community. One thing is clear. Those capitalist dykes and bulwarks, short cuts and artificial floodings, have become so constant and general a feature of the whole "debatable land" of economic bargaining, that any discussion of the relation between consumer and producer, or between capitalist, brain-worker, and manual laborer, which is based on the assumption of a mutual exchange of services among freely competing individual bargainers, is, from a practical point of view, entirely obsolete. We have, in fact, to work out a new scientific analysis, not of any ideal state of "natural liberty," but of the actual facts of a world of more or less complete economic monopolies—legal monopolies, natural monopolies, monopolies arising out of exploiting the prejudices of consumers, and, last but not least, monopolies deliberately constructed by the tacit or formal combination or amalgamation of all the competing interests.[1] But before passing away from this, by the economist, as yet unexplored world,

---

[1] In the *Groundwork of Economics*, sec. 20, p. 33 (London, 1883), Mr. C. S. Devas reminds us that, "in a wise moment," J. S. Mill objected to the abstract methods of his father, and the other economic politicians of that school. "It is not to be imagined possible," Mill said, "nor is it true in point of fact, that these philosophers regarded the few premises of their theory as including all that is required for explaining social phenomena. . . . They would have applied, and did apply, their principles with innumerable allowances. But it is not allowances that are wanted. . . . It is unphilosophical to construct a science out of a few agencies by which the phenomena are determined. . . . *We ought to study all the determining agencies equally, and endeavor, as far as it can be done, to include all of them within the pale of the science, else we shall infallibly bestow a disproportionate attention upon those which our theory takes into account*, while we misestimate the rest, and probably underrate their importance." The quotation is from Mill's *System of Logic*, Book VI., end of chap. viii.

we are compelled to note how it impinges on our own province.[1]

In our analysis of the chain of bargainings which take place between the manual worker and the private customer, and so determine the wages of labor, we demonstrated, not only that the isolated individual workman was at a serious disadvantage in bargaining with the capitalist manufacturer, but also that the capitalist manufacturer himself was to a large extent powerless to offer terms above those prevailing in other establishments. But this latter consideration, as we now see, does not necessarily apply to any but those cases in which there has been no obstruction of the full stream of competitive pressure. If an individual employer is able to ward off this pressure from the price of his product by an exclusive concession or a patent, a trade mark, or even an assured personal connection, or if the whole body of employers can unite in a tacit or formal combination to

[1] These monopolies, it will be observed, are, to a large extent, actually the outcome of legal freedom of contract. If every man is to be free to enter into such contracts as seem to him best in his own interest, it is impossible to deny him the right of joining with his fellow-capitalists to fix prices, regulate production, or actually to amalgamate all competing interests, if this is deemed most advantageous. " Monopoly," says Professor Foxwell, " is inevitable.   . . It is a natural outgrowth of industrial freedom " (" The Growth of Monopoly, and its Bearing on the Functions of the State," in *Revue d'Économie Politique*, vol. iii. September 1889). That this state of things involves the economic compulsion of minorities, the ruin of newcomers by deliberate underselling, and the driving out of the trade of any recalcitrant firm, is, as Mr. Justice Chitty lucidly explained in the case of the Mogul Steamship Co. *v.* Macgregor, Gow, and Co., an inevitable result of legal freedom of contract. The classic economists never made up their minds whether, by a " system of natural liberty," they meant individual freedom of contract, or free competition between individuals. As we have already explained in our chapter on " The Method of Collective Bargaining," these two social ideals are not only not identical, but hopelessly inconsistent with each other. Alike in the world of capital and in the world of labor, individual freedom of contract leads inevitably to combination, and this destroys free competition between individuals. If we desire to maintain free competition between individuals, the only conceivable way would be such a state interference with contracts as would prevent, not only every kind of association, but also every alienation of land and every transfer of small businesses to larger ones, which would in any way cause or increase inequality of wealth or power. Indeed, it would be an interesting point for academic discussion whether free competition among equal units, supposing this to be desired and to be compatible with human nature, can be permanently secured in any other way than by the " nationalisation of the means of production, distribution, and exchange."

regulate the trade, the workpeople in these establishments might, it may be argued, stand some chance of receiving better wages.   And in so far as these partial monopolies are directed by public-spirited philanthropists,—*so long, too, as the exceptional profits remain in the hands of the original capitalists,*—this presumption is borne out by facts.   Such well-known firms as Cadbury, Horrocks, Tangye, and a host of other manufacturers of specialities, are noted for being "good employers," that is, for voluntarily conceding to each grade of labor better terms than similar workers obtain in other establishments.   But in this connection it is important to remember that the standard by which the "good employer" determines the conditions of labor is not any deliberate view of what is required for full family efficiency and worthy citizenship, but a practical estimate of what each grade of workers would obtain from the ordinary employer, working under competitive pressure.   Hence a comparatively small addition to weekly wages, a more equitable piecework list, a larger degree of consideration in fixing the hours for beginning or quitting work, the intervals for meals and the arrangements for holidays, greater care in providing the little comforts of the factory, or in rendering impossible the petty tyrannies of foremen,—any of these ameliorations of the conditions of labor will suffice, without serious inroads on profits, to attract to a firm the best workers in the town, to gain for it a reputation for justice and benevolence, and to give the employer's family an abiding sense of satisfaction whenever they enter the works, or cross the thresholds of their operatives' homes.   To this extent it is true that "the strength of the capitalist is the shield of the laborer." [1]   But this relatively humane relationship is nowadays seldom of long standing.   If the business grows to any size it will very soon be formed into a joint-stock company, in which the old partners may at first retain a large interest, but of which a yearly increasing proportion is transferred to outside shareholders.   These new shareholders, who will have bought in

[1] *Trade Unionism*, by James Stirling (Glasgow, 1869), p. 42.

at a price yielding them no more than the current rate of interest for that class of security, feel that they have no margin of exceptional profit to dispose of. Even if the old partners' families retain large holdings in their ancestral concern, they have, by capitalising their profits, lost their privilege of being benevolent with them ; and the share-holders' meeting, the board of directors, and the salaried general manager inevitably bring in " business principles," and pay no more for labor than they are compelled. And when we pass to the gigantic capitalist corporations, admin-istering legal monopolies, or to the colossal amalgamations more and more dominating the industrial world, we find, in sharpest contrast with the patriarchal employer of economic romance, the daily changing crowd of share and debenture owners, devoid of any responsibility for the conditions of labor, and as uninformed and heedless as the consumer him-self. It is not too much to say that, so far as concerns the personal life of the 50,000 employees of the London and North - Western Railway Company, the 55,000 ordinary shareholders, who own that vast enterprise, are even more ignorant, more inaccessible, and more irresponsible than the millions of passengers whom they serve. The situation is intensified by the fact that, in the absence of law or Collective Bargaining, these great capitalist monopolies can practically dictate their own terms to their workpeople. If, as is now admitted, the isolated workman stands at a serious disadvantage in bargaining with the capitalist manufacturer, what shall we say of the position of the candidate who applies for the situation of porter or shunter to the officer of a great railway company ? Here the very notion of bargaining disappears. This does not mean that such capitalists will necessarily dictate the absolute minimum wage. The corporation decides, in its own interest, what policy it will pursue as regards wages, hours, and other con-ditions. Porters and shunters, plate-layers and general laborers, can be had practically in any number at any price. Whether it pays best to give the lowest wage on which the human animal can temporarily subsist, and be content with a low level of muscular endurance, or whether it is better to pay for superior men, and work them for ninety hours a week, is a question which, in the absence of any interference with "freedom of contract," is settled on much the same principles as actuate a tramway company, deciding whether it is more profitable to wear its horses out in four years or in seven. And once the worker enters the employment of any of these gigantic monopolists, the alternative to submission to his employer's commands is, not merely changing his situation, but finding some new means of livelihood. For a railway servant who leaves without a character, or with a black mark against his name, knows perfectly well that he will seek a situation in vain from any other railway company in the kingdom. Thus it is only in exceptional instances, and then only temporarily, that the wage-earners as a class get any share of the extra profits secured to the capitalists by their dykes and bulwarks. These exceptional profits are quickly capitalised by their owners, and transferred to new shareholders who come in at a premium. The more complete and legally secured is the monopoly, the more certain it is to be disposed of at a price which yields only a low rate of interest—in extreme cases, such as urban waterworks, approximating actually to the return on government securities themselves. On the other hand, the position of the wage-earner is positively worsened, in the colossal capitalist corporations, by the absence of effective competition for his services by rival employers. The difference in strategic position becomes so overwhelming that the wage-contract ceases to be, in any genuine sense, a bargain at all.[1]

Amid all the capitalist devices that we have described, the workmen's efforts to protect themselves against the full

[1] " To assume that the competition between the employer on the one hand, and the wage-earners on the other, when the latter are unorganised and unprotected by law, is a competition between equal units, is so fanciful and contrary to fact, that any conclusions drawn from such an assumption can have little value under present circumstances."—B. R. Wise, *Industrial Freedom* (London, 1892), pp. 13, 15.

stream of competitive pressure will seem comparatively modest. Unlike the promoters of great capitalist undertakings, no section of the wage-earners can nowadays secure from Parliament any exclusive right to perform a certain service. Unlike the owner of a newly-invented machine, a workman cannot even retain a legal monopoly of the most ingenious improvement that he may make in his own share of the productive process, for no country grants a patent to the inventor of a new trick of manual dexterity —perhaps only a novel way of using the fingers—which enormously increases the productivity of industry. Nor can even the most skilled manual laborer in our time assure to himself, like the advertiser of a speciality, or of a legally secured trade mark, the faithful custom of a large body of distant private consumers. And the fact that the wage-earners form the base of the industrial pyramid, and have no weaker class below to whom they can transfer the pressure, shuts them out from such evasions of the stream as we have seen to profit the wholesale clothier. All these dykes and bulwarks are, and must necessarily remain, the exclusive possession of the owners of capital.[1]

The first expedient of the Anglo-Saxon workman is rather an instinct than a method. Over a large part of the

[1] Individual workmen may, of course, become owners of capital, perhaps in the form of sub-contractors, and thus rise out of their class. But this does not affect (unless, indeed, adversely) the economic position of the class itself. It is also claimed by one school of co-operators that associations of wage-earners might entirely supersede the relation of capitalist employer and manual-working wage-earner. Just as a combination of employers or the manufacturers of a proprietary article practically turn the traders into their agents, so an association of workmen might turn the capitalist entrepreneur into a salaried manager working under their orders. This, however, would involve a section of workpeople becoming the owners of the capital with which they work. If this ownership of the instruments of production by associations of producers ever became universal, it would naturally be unnecessary to continue to discuss the economic position of a class of wage-earners. The reasons which, in our opinion, make any such general merging of the positions of capitalist and wage-earner inherently and permanently impossible —the causes which have hitherto prevented such "associations of producers" from becoming even an important part of the British Co-operative Movement— will be found fully stated in *The Co-operative Movement in Great Britain* (London, first edition 1891, second edition 1894), by Beatrice Potter (Mrs. Sidney Webb).

industrial field, the wage-earners cling with stubborn obstinacy to certain customary standards of expenditure. However overpowering may be the strategic strength of the employer, however unorganised and resourceless may be the wage-earners, it is found to be impossible to reduce the wages and other conditions of particular grades of workmen below a certain vaguely defined standard. In the years of worst trade, when thousands of engineers or boilermakers, masons or plumbers, are walking the streets in search of work, the most grasping employer knows that it is useless for him to offer them work in their respective trades at ten or fifteen shillings a week. Sooner than suffer such violence to their feelings of what is fit and becoming to their social position, they will work as unskilled laborers, or pick up odd jobs, for the same, or even lower earnings than they refuse as craftsmen. This stubborn refusal to render their particular class of service for a wage that strikes them as outrageously below their customary standard, does not depend on their belonging to a Trade Union, for it is characteristic of unionists and non-unionists alike, and is found in trades in which no combination exists. Even the dock-laborer, who frantically struggles at the dock-gates for any kind of employment, turns sulky, and discharges himself after a few hours, if he is asked to work for a shilling a day. Nor does it apply only to money wages. The British workman in the building trades, though he is paid by the hour, and often belongs to no union, will accept any alternative rather than let his employer keep him habitually at work for fifteen hours a day. Nor has this conventional minimum any assignable relation to the cost of actual subsistence. The young engineer or plumber, unencumbered by wife or child indignantly refuses to work for a wage upon which millions of his fellow-citizens not only exist, but marry and bring up families. On the other hand, though the London dock-laborer will not go on working at a shilling a day, he willingly accepts irregular work at a rate per hour which taking into account the periods of unemployment incidenta to his occupation, is demonstrably insufficient for sustained physical health or industrial efficiency. This practical check on the employer's power of reducing wages has always been observed by the economists. "Where," observed J. S. Mill, "there is not in the people, or in some very large proportion of them, a resolute resistance to this deterioration—a determination to preserve an established standard of comfort—the condition of the poorest class sinks, even in a progressive state, to the lowest point which they will consent to endure." [1] The classic economists were especially struck by the way in which this determination to preserve an established standard of comfort affected the level of wages in different countries, and among different districts or races in the same country.[2] "Custom," said Adam Smith, . . . "has rendered leather shoes a necessary of life in England. The poorest creditable person of either sex would be ashamed to appear in public without them. In Scotland, custom has rendered them a necessary of life to the lowest order of men, but not to the same order of women, who may, without any discredit, walk about barefooted. In France they are necessaries neither to men nor to women." [3] "The circumstances and habits of

---

[1] J. S. Mill, *Principles of Political Economy*, Book IV. chap. vi. § 1, p. 453. "The habitual earnings of the working classes at large can be affected by nothing but the habitual requirements of the laboring people ; these, indeed, may be altered, but while they remain the same wages never fall permanently below the standard of these requirements and do not long remain above that standard."—*Ibid.* Book V. chap. x. § 5, p. 564.

[2] "In England, for example, the lower classes principally live on wheaten bread and butcher's meat, in Ireland on potatoes, and in China and Hindostan on rice. In many provinces of France and Spain an allowance of wine is considered indispensable. In England the laboring class entertain nearly the same opinion with respect to porter, beer, and cider ; whereas the Chinese and Hindoos drink only water. The peasantry of Ireland live in miserable mud-cabins without either a window or a chimney, or anything that can be called furniture ; while in England the cottages of the peasantry have glass windows and chimneys, are well furnished, and are as much distinguished for their neatness, cleanliness, and comfort, as those of the Irish for their filth and misery. *These differences in their manner of living occasion equal differences in their wages ;* so that, while the average price of a day's labor may be taken at from 20d. to 2s., it cannot be taken at more than 7d. in Ireland, and 3d. in Hindostan."—J. R. M'Culloch, *A Treatise on the Circumstances which determine the Rate of Wages* (London, 1851), p. 32.

[3] *Wealth of Nations*, Book V. chap. ii. art. iv. p. 393.

living prevalent in England," wrote Colonel Torrens, "have long determined that women in the laboring classes shall wear their feet and legs covered, and eat wheaten bread, with a portion of animal food. Now, long before the rate of wages could be so reduced as to compel women in this part of the United Kingdom to go with their legs and feet uncovered, and to subsist upon potatoes, with perhaps a little milk from which the butter had been taken, all the laboring classes would be upon parochial relief, and the land in a great measure depopulated."[1] "These differences in their manner of living," summed up M'Culloch, "occasion equal differences in their wages." But whilst the fact was clearly recognised, no satisfactory explanation of it was given. The only reason for these differences in wages that the classic economists could allege was that the customary "standard of comfort" determined the rate at which the population would increase—that any attempt by the employer to reduce wages below this level would promptly cause fewer children to be born, and thus alter the ratio of workers to wage-fund twenty years hence![2] But this, it is obvious, does not tell us why it is that the workman is able to refuse to accept less to-day, even if population statistics still allowed us to make any such assumption about the birth-rate. If the economists had not been obsessed by the fallacy of a predetermined wage-fund, they would have perceived, in this clinging of each generation to its accustomed livelihood, a primitive bulwark against the innovation of fixing all the conditions of labor by "free competition" among candidates for employment. To the modern observer it is obvious that

[1] *Essay on the External Corn Trade*, by Robert Torrens (London, 1815), p. 58. See other references in Gunton's *Wealth and Progress* (London, 1888), p. 193.

[2] "Even though wages were high enough to admit of food's becoming more costly without depriving the laborers and their families of necessaries ; though they could bear, physically speaking, to be worse off, perhaps they would not consent to be so. They might have habits of comfort which were to them as necessaries, and sooner than forego which they would put an additional restraint on their power of multiplication, so that wages would rise, not by increase of deaths but by diminution of births."—J. S. Mill, *Principles of Political Economy*, Book II. chap. xi. § 2, p. 209 (London, 1865).

the existence, among all the workmen of a particular grade, of an identical notion as to what amount and kind of weekly expenditure constitutes subsistence, is in itself equivalent to a tacit combination. It is, in fact, however it may have come about, an incipient Common Rule, supported by a universal and prolonged refusal to work, which is none the less a strike in that it is unconcerted and undeliberate. If every artisan, without the slightest concert with his fellows, is possessed by an unreasoning prejudice that he and his family must consume wheaten bread, butcher's meat, beer, and tea, instead of living on oatmeal, maize, potatoes, and water, the employer will find it useless to suggest that " any meal is better than none." He quickly discovers that if he offers wages which will provide only the cheaper food, no individual of the class that he requires will accept his situation. He is, in fact, face to face with what is virtually a universal strike. Like all other strikes it may, for one reason or another, presently fail. But as long as it lasts the alternative to the employer of coming to terms with the workman is, not one man's absence from his usual staff, but getting no men at all—not foregoing a fraction of his profits, but shutting up his establishment. It is accordingly plain that, in a class of workmen among whom any such identical notion as to the Standard of Comfort exists, the isolated individual wage-earner bargains at greater advantage than he would if he and his fellows were willing to accept any kind of wages rather than none. The mere existence, among all the workmen competing for a certain class of employment, of an identical notion as to what constitutes their minimum subsistence, amounts, therefore, even without concert or reserve-fund, to a real bulwark against the pressure of competition.[1]

[1] We are unable here to do more than refer to the existence of these popular ideas as to the Standard of Life. How they originate—why, for instance, the English workman should always have insisted on eating costly and unnutritious wheaten bread, or why some classes or races display so much more stubbornness of standard than others, would be a fruitful subject for economic inquiry. We suggest, as a hypothetical classification by way of starting-point, that the races and classes of wage-earners seem to divide themselves into three groups. There are those who, like the Anglo-Saxon skilled artisan, will not work below a

But this primitive bulwark——the instinctive Standard of Life of uncombined resourceless wage-earners——has grave defects. It is, in the first place, a weak bulwark, seldom able to withstand the exceptional pressure of times of adversity, especially as it often fails to cover equally the whole length of the line. Moreover, it is usually weakest in its upper parts, so that the employers, in periods of great pressure, always succeed in planing it down a little. On the other hand, owing to the absence of any deliberate concert, it cannot practically be raised by the workmen's own efforts, even when the pressure is withdrawn, and thus, in the absence of any better protection or of the intervention of some outside force, it is apt to become gradually lower and lower. These defects arise, as we shall see, from (1) the necessary indefiniteness of a merely instinctive Standard of Life, (2) the absence of any material support for the wage-earner's stubbornness, and (3) the impossibility without concerted action of adjusting the workmen's instinctive demands so as to meet the changing circumstances of the industry.

customary minimum Standard of Life, but who have no maximum ; that is to say, they will be stimulated to intenser effort and new wants by every increase of income. There are races who, like the African negro, have no assignable minimum, but a very low maximum ; they will work, that is, for indefinitely low wages, but cannot be induced to work at all once their primitive wants are satisfied. Finally, there is the Jew, who, as we think, is unique in possessing neither a minimum nor a maximum ; he will accept the lowest terms rather than remain out of employment ; as he rises in the world new wants stimulate him to increased intensity of effort, and no amount of income causes him to slacken his indefatigable activity. To this remarkable elasticity in the Standard of Life is, we suggest, to be attributed both the wealth and the poverty of the Jews——the striking fact that their wage-earning class is permanently the poorest in all Europe, whilst individual Jews are the wealthiest men of their respective countries.

The position of the English working-woman in this connection would especially repay inquiry. The poverty-stricken widow, with children depending on her for bread, will accept any rate of wages or any length of hours rather than refuse employment. On the other hand, the well-brought-up daughter of the artisan will obstinately insist on certain conditions of decency, comfort, and "respectability" in her work. But owing to the fact that she so often is not wholly dependent on her wages, she is apt to accept any rate of pay rather than leave a comfortable and well-conducted factory, and employers often complain that no stimulus of piecework or bonus will induce such women-workers to increase their effort beyond a somewhat low maximum.

The lack of definiteness is an essential feature of any merely instinctive standard. What the isolated individual workman feels is that he is entitled to a certain mode of living, a certain vague quantum of weekly expenditure, in return for an equally vague quantum of daily work. Each man translates this for himself into terms of wages, hours, etc., and the translations of thousands of men in different parts of the country inevitably differ among themselves. All engineers, for instance, would agree that fifteen shillings a week was far below their minimum standard. But, in the absence of any concerted action, they would differ among themselves as to whether its money equivalent at a particular time and place was twenty-seven or twenty-nine shillings a week, or whether any given piecework rate was or was not a fair one. Still more indefinite is the workman's instinctive Standard of Life with regard to the length of the working day, meal times, and holidays ; fines and deductions of every kind ; the conditions of over - crowding and ventilation, decency and safety, under which his work is done ; and the wear and tear of nerves, muscles, and clothes to which he is exposed. These differences of translation are the employer's opportunity. By constantly insisting upon taking, as the standard on any point, the lowest translation made by any candidate for employment, he is able gradually to beat all the others down to that level.

It is a no less serious cause of weakness that, in the absence of any collective reserve fund, the isolated individual worker cannot hope to be able to stand out long against an obstinate employer. However strong may be the repugnance to accept what is felt to be less than the standard wage, the workman who has no other resources than the sale of his labor will find himself every day more strongly tempted by necessity to accept something less than he claims. When he is once in employment, his outspoken revolt against any " nibbling " at wages, " cribbing time," or other worsening of the conditions, will be checked, especially in periods of slackness, by his reluctance to " quarrel with his bread and butter."

What the most necessitous man submits to, all the others soon find themselves pressed to put up with. Thus, in the absence of any financial strengthening of the weakest members, the bulwark of a merely instinctive Standard of Life insidiously gives way before employers' importunities.

Finally, whilst the bulwark of a Standard of Life is always yielding under the pressure of severe competition, it does not get systematically built up again in the seasons when the pressure is lightened. To the capitalist the scanty profits of lean years are made up by largely swollen gains in the alternating periods of commercial prosperity. But a wage determined only by an instinctive Standard of Life does not rise merely because the employers are temporarily making larger profits. The "habits and customs" of a people—their ideas of what is necessary for comfort and social decency—may, in the slow course of generations of prosperity, silently and imperceptibly change for the better, but they are unaffected by the swift and spasmodic fluctuations which characterise modern industry. Thus, in years of good trade, when no competent man need remain long unemployed, though the pushing workman may, without a Trade Union, temporarily exact better terms, the class as a whole is apt to get only regular employment at its accustomed livelihood. In the absence of mutual consultation and concerted action, individuals may aspire to a higher standard, but there can be no simultaneous and identical rise, and thus no new consensus of feeling is brought to the aid of the Individual Bargaining of the weaker men.

Trade Unionism, to put it briefly, remedies all these defects of a merely instinctive Standard of Life. By interpreting the standard into precise and uniform conditions of employment it gives every member of the combination a definite and identical minimum to stand out for, and an exact measure by which to test any new proposition of the employer. The reader of our descriptions of the elaborate standard rates and piecework lists, the scales fixing working hours and limiting overtime, and the special rules for sanitation and safety, which together make up the body of Trade Union Regulations, will appreciate with what fervor and persistency the Trade Unions have pursued this object of giving the indispensable definiteness to the Standard of Life of each section of wage-earners. And when we pass from the Regulations of Trade Unionism to its characteristic Methods, we may now see how exactly these are calculated to remedy the other shortcomings of the wage-earners' instinctive defence. By the Method of Mutual Insurance, the most necessitous workman, who would otherwise be the weakest part of the position, is freed from the pressure of his special necessities, and placed in as good a position as his fellows to resist the employer's encroachments. The provision of a common fund enables, in fact, all the members alike to get what the economists have called a "reserve price" on their labor. Thus, the bulwark is made equally strong all along the line. But the Method of Mutual Insurance also carries a stage further this strengthening of the weak parts of the defence. The money saved in good years, when the Out of Work benefit is little drawn upon, will be used to support the members in times of slack trade, when the pressure will be greatest. Thus, the bulwark is specially strengthened against the advancing tide. The Method of Collective Bargaining brings a new kind of support. When the terms of the contract are settled, not separately by the individual workmen concerned, but jointly by appointed agents on their behalf, an additional barrier is interposed between the pressure acting through the employer, and the apprehensions and ignorances of his wage-earners. The conclusion of collective agreements not only excludes, as we have explained, the influence of the exigencies of particular workmen, particular firms, or particular districts, but it also gives the combined manual workers the invaluable assistance of a professional expert who, in knowledge of the trade and trained capacity for bargaining, may even be superior to the employer himself. The Method of Collective Bargaining has the further advantage over reliance on a merely instinctive Standard of Life that the terms can be quickly raised so as to take advantage of any time of rising profits, and indefinitely adjusted so as to meet the requirements of an ever-changing industry. Finally, the Method of Legal Enactment—the use of which by the workmen demands a high degree of voluntary organisation, and above all, an expert professional staff of salaried officers—absolutely secures one element of the Standard of Life after another by embodying them in our factory code, and thus fortifies the workmen's original bulwark by the unyielding buttress of the law of the land.

But this general description of Trade Unionism as the Dyke of a definite Standard of Life, strengthened by the existence of a common purse, the services of expert negotiators, and the protection of the magistrate—though it serves to indicate its place in the higgling of the market —affords too indefinite a mark for useful economic criticism. In the Second Part of this work we laid before the reader an exhaustive analysis of the Regulations imposed by British Trade Unionists, of the Methods by which they seek their ends, and, finally, of the far-reaching views of social expediency upon which the policy of the various sections of the Trade Union world is determined. In this analysis we distinguished between what is universal and what is only partial, and, above all, between the elements that are deepening and extending, and those that are dwindling in scope and intensity. What we have now to do is to follow out the economic effects of each type, and thus enable the reader to form some general estimate of the results upon our industrial development, of the actual content of contemporary Trade Unionism in this country.

CHAPTER III

THE ECONOMIC CHARACTERISTICS OF TRADE UNIONISM

THE economist and the statesman will judge Trade Unionism, not by its results in improving the position of a particular section of workmen at a particular time, but by its effects on the permanent efficiency of the nation. If any of the Methods and Regulations of Trade Unionism result in the choice of less efficient factors of production than would otherwise have been used ; if they compel the adoption of a lower type of organisation than would have prevailed without them ; and especially if they tend to lessen the capacity or degrade the character of either manual laborers or brain-workers, that part of Trade Unionism, however advantageous it may seem to particular sections of workmen, will stand condemned. If, on the other hand, any Trade Union Methods and Regulations are found to promote the selection of the most efficient factors of production, whether capital, brains, or labor ; if they tend to a better organisation of these factors, and above all, if their effect is progressively to increase the activities and improve the character of both brain and manual workers, then, in spite of any apparent contraction of the personal power of the capitalist class, they will be approved by the economist as tending to heighten the faculties and enlarge the enjoyments of the community as a whole.[1]

[1] Here and throughout this chapter we proceed on the assumption that it is desirable for the community to "progress" ; that is to say, that its members should attain, generation after generation, a wider and fuller life by developing

Let us take first the Trade Union Regulations, for, if these have an injurious effect, it is unnecessary to consider by what methods they are enforced. Notwithstanding their almost infinite variety of technical detail these Regulations can, as we have seen, be reduced to two economic devices : Restriction of Numbers and the Common Rule. To the former type belong the ancient Trade Union prescriptions as to Apprenticeship, the exclusion of new competitors from a trade, and the assertion of a vested interest in a particular occupation. The latter type includes the more modern rules directly fixing a Standard Rate, a Normal Day, and definite conditions of Sanitation and Safety.

(a) The Device of Restriction of Numbers

There is a certain sense in which every regulation, whether imposed by law or public custom, laid down by the employer or insisted on by the Trade Union, may be said to restrict the entrance to an occupation. It is inherent in any rule that its enforcement incidentally excludes those who, for one reason or another, cannot or will not conform to it. Thus, a firm which, as a matter of business routine, requires its employees to be regular in their attendance, or to abstain from smoking or drinking at their work, or which

increased faculties and satisfying more complicated desires. When, therefore, for the sake of shortness, we use the phrase " Selection of the Fittest," we mean the fittest to achieve this object of social evolution ; and by the phrase " Functional Adaptation," we mean the adaptation of the individual to an increase in the strength and complexity of his faculties and desires, as distinguished from " Degeneration," the corresponding decrease in faculties and desires. We are aware that this assumption would not command universal assent. The whole Eastern world, for instance, proclaims the opposite philosophy of life ; an Englishman, it is said, " seeks happiness in the multiplication of his possessions, a Hindoo in the diminution of his wants." And there are, if we mistake not, many persons in the Western world whose dislike of modern progress springs, half unconsciously, from an objection to a life which, whilst satisfying more complicated desires, makes increasing demands upon the faculties. To such persons the whole argument contained in this chapter will be an additional reason for disliking the more modern manifestations of Trade Unionism.

systematically dismisses those who fail to attain a certain speed, or repeatedly make mistakes, thereby restricts its employment to operatives of a certain standard of conduct or capacity. Similarly, the universal Trade Union insistence on a Standard Rate of payment for a given quota of work excludes, from the particular occupation those whom no employer will engage at that rate. And when any regulation, either of the employers or of the workmen, is embodied in the law of the land, this new Factory Act automatically closes the occupation to which it applies to all persons who cannot or will not conform to its prescriptions. The kingdom itself may be closed to certain races by a Sanitary Code, with which their religion forbids them to comply. But there is a great distinction in character and results between the incidentally restrictive effects of a Common Rule, to which every one is free to conform, and the direct exclusion of specified classes of persons, whether they conform or not, by regulations totally prohibiting their entrance. In the present section we deal solely with direct attempts to secure or maintain a more or less complete "monopoly" of particular occupations, either by limiting the number of learners, or by excluding, on grounds of sex, previous occupation, or lack of apprenticeship, persons whom an employer is willing to engage, and who are themselves willing to work, in strict conformity with the standard conditions of the trade.

From the standpoint of industrial efficiency, the most obvious characteristic of the Device of Restriction of Numbers is the manner in which it influences the selection of the factors of production. When situations are filled by competitive examination, as for instance in the English Civil Service, it is recognised that any restriction on the number of candidates—still more, any limitation of the candidates to persons of particular families, particular classes, or particular antecedents — lowers the average of quality among the successful competitors. The same consequence results from any restriction which prevents an employer from filling all his vacancies as they occur by selecting the most efficient operatives, wherever he can find them. The mere fixing of a ratio of apprentices to journeymen will exclude from the trade some boys who would otherwise have learnt it, and who might have proved the most capable operatives at the craft. This is certain to be the case if the regulation takes the form of exacting a high entrance fee, or of confining admission to craftsmen's sons. Even without any restrictions on apprenticeship, the requirement that the trade must be entered before a prescribed age, by excluding the quick-witted outsider who desires to change his occupation in after years, necessarily tends to limit the range of the employer's choice, and hence to make the average level of capacity lower in the protected trade than it would otherwise be. And whilst this limitation on the process of selection is injurious even in old-established trades, it becomes plainly more harmful when the question is the choice of men to work a new machine or perform some novel service. The more restricted the field from which the capitalist can pick these new operatives, the lower will be their average level of capacity. Nor is it merely the absence of unemployed workmen that impedes the employer's freedom to select the most efficient man to fill his vacancy. The constant existence of a remnant of unemployed may enable an employer to get a " cheap hand," or help him to lower wages all round ; but the competition of this " reserve army " does little or nothing to promote efficiency. The fact that a man is out of work affords a presumption that he has, for the moment, greater needs, but not that he has greater faculties. To compel employers to fill all vacancies from the unemployed remnant of the trade, in preference to promoting the ablest members of the next lower grade, is often to force them to engage, not the workmen who promise to be the most efficient, but those who have proved themselves below the average in regularity or capacity. On the other hand, if the Restriction of Numbers is carried so far that only one candidate presents himself to fill each vacancy, all selection disappears. Had the regulations of the Flint Glass Makers and the Silk Hatters been enforced with absolute universality every employer in those trades would have found himself compelled, whenever a vacancy occurred in his establishment, either to accept the Trade Union nominee, whatever his character or capacity, or else leave the situation unfilled.

And whilst any limitation of the persons from whom vacancies can be filled insidiously lowers the quality of the recruits, the same influence deteriorates the men already in the trade. When it is known that the master has no chance of getting better workmen, or that his choice will be limited to the unemployed remnant of the trade, the "average sensual man" is apt to lose much of his incentive to efficiency, and even to regularity of conduct. In those trades in which the Device of Restriction of Numbers is effectually practised, an employer habitually puts up with a higher degree of irregularity, carelessness, and inefficiency in his existing staff, than he would if he could freely promote a learner or an assistant to the better-paid situation.

What is not so generally recognised is that, in trades in which the workmen are able to make effective use of the Device of Restriction of Numbers, the brain-workers of the trade are themselves less select, and suffer a similar loss of incentive to efficiency. In such completely organised and old-fashioned trades as glass-blowing and hand papermaking, the policy of limiting the numbers has been so effectively carried out that capitalists who, when trade is brisk and profits large, might desire to set up new works in competition with the old establishments, are actually stopped by the difficulty of obtaining an adequate supply of skilled workmen. Hence, old-fashioned family concerns, with sleepy management and obsolete plant, find the Trade Union regulations a positive protection against competition. This is frequently admitted in the negotiations between masters and men. In 1874, for instance, the spokesman of the hand papermakers put forward this profitable effect of his union's restrictive regulations as a reason why the employers should concede better terms. "If," said he, "the men have good wages, the masters as a rule make large profits, and large profits are inducements which cause fresh capital to be embarked in a trade. If, however, the men have a limit to the supply of labor, no matter what the profits are, fresh capital cannot be introduced, because if a man starts fresh vats he will have no workmen to go on with. The rule as to limiting the supply of labor therefore works both ways. As far as our position in the vat trade is concerned we are like a close corporation. . . . It would be a great inducement for capital to enter the trade if labor could be got, but . . . according to our Rules and Regulations, competition is checked."[1]

From the point of view of the consumer, this use of the Device of Restriction of Numbers by the workmen, and their formation of a close corporation seems, at first sight, analogous to the establishment of a capitalist ring or trust. Both expedients aim at creating a profitable monopoly, for the benefit of those already in the trade, by the exclusion of new competitors. But there is an important difference between the workmen's monopoly and that of the capitalists, in the

---

[1] *Arbitration on the Question of an Advance in Wages.* . . . Rupert Kettle, Q.C., Arbitrator (Maidstone, p. 64, 1874).

Similar conditions seem to have prevailed in the early factory industries of France, after the impulse given by Henry II. (ca. 1550). Towards the end of the seventeenth century the workers in the paper-mills, carpet factories, and manufactories of looking-glasses are described as forming strong though unauthorised corporations, which were encouraged by the employers, and which were recruited exclusively from sons and sons-in-law of the workmen, so as to form virtually a hereditary monopoly. The papermakers were so powerful as to lead to special repressive laws for this industry in 1793 and again in 1796.—Du Cellier, *Histoire des Classes Laborieuses en France* (Paris, 1860), pp. 259, 260, 334 ; and, as regards the papermakers, the articles by C. M. Briquet in the *Revue Internationale de Sociologie*, March 1897.

It is in this exclusion of new capital, and the consequent check to the process of Selection of the Fittest among the employers, that we discover the fundamental objection to the policy of Restriction of Output, which we described in our chapter on " Continuity of Employment." It is, as we explained, impossible for the Trade Union, by any methods or regulations of its own, to limit the aggregate output. But the employers may, and occasionally do effect such a limitation, with or without the co-operation of the Trade Union concerned. In so far as this is effected by preventing or discouraging new capitalist enterprise, it tends to diminish the efficiency of the industry, by checking the " elimination of the unfit " among the employers.

type of industrial organisation that they set up, and in their results upon productive efficiency. A successful Trust loses, it is true, the goad to improvement that comes from the free fight with other competitors. On the other hand, it retains undiminished, and gives full scope to the profit-maker's normal incentive to go on increasing his business and his income. So long as an additional increment of capital promises to yield more than the rate paid to the banker or debenture holder for its use, the capitalist Trust will strive to enlarge its output, and make the utmost possible improvement in its processes. The owners of even the most absolute monopoly do not find it pay to raise the price of their product in such a way as to cause any serious falling-off in the sales ; more commonly, indeed, as in the case of the Standard Oil Company,[1] they get an advantage by actually lowering the price in order to stimulate the demand. They are, in any case, perpetually tempted to engage the ablest brains in the Trust's service, as well as to use the best machines and the latest inventions ; for every cheapening of production that can be effected enures wholly to their own advantage. Hence, however large and disproportionate may be the income drawn by the owners of the Trust, however arbitrary and oppressive may be the social power that it exercises, this capitalist monopoly has at any rate the economic advantage of selecting and organising the factors of production in such a way as to turn out its product at an ever diminishing cost. A close corporation of workmen has, on the contrary, no interest in enlarging its business. The individual operatives who enjoy the monopoly have only their own energy to sell, and they are accordingly interested in getting in return for their definitely limited output as high a price as possible. If they can, by raising price, exact the same income for a smaller number of hours' work, it will positively pay them to leave some of the world's demand unsatisfied. They have nothing to gain by cheapening the

---

[1] See *Wealth Against Commonwealth*, by Henry D. Lloyd (London, 1894); E. von Halle, *Trusts*.

process of production, and they stand actually to lose by every invention or improvement in organisation that enables their product to be turned out with less labor. Any alteration, in short, will be repugnant to them, as involving a change of habit, new exertion, and no pecuniary gain. Rather than forego the utmost possible individual wage, it would even pay them to stop all recruiting, and progressively raise their price as their members drop off one by one, until the whole industry dwindled away.

So far the Device of Restriction of Numbers appears wholly injurious to industrial efficiency. There is, however, one important effect in another direction. If, in the absence of all regulation, the employers are free without let or hindrance to make the best bargain they can with the individual wage-earners, whole sections of the population, men, women, and children, will be compelled to live and toil under conditions seriously injurious to their health and industrial efficiency. Nor is this merely an empirical inference from the history of an unregulated factory system, and from the contemporary facts of the sweated industries. It is now theoretically demonstrated, as we saw in our chapter on " The Verdict of the Economists," that under " perfect competition," and complete mobility between one occupation and another, the common level of wages tends to be no more than " the net produce due to the additional labor of the marginal laborer," who is on the verge of not being employed at all! The Device of Restriction of Numbers manifestly enables the privileged insiders to make a better bargain with their employers—that is to say, to insist on better sanitary conditions, shorter and more regular hours, and, above all, a wage which provides for their families as well as themselves, a more adequate supply of food and clothing. However equivocal may be the device by which this higher Standard of Life is secured, there can be no doubt that, in itself, it renders possible a far higher degree of skill, conduct, and general efficiency than the long hours, unhealthy conditions, and bare subsistence wages which are found prevailing in the unregulated trades. In such a case the Device of Restriction of Numbers must be credited with indirectly preventing evil, and with producing a certain increase of efficiency, as a set-off against the direct weakening of the incentive to improvement that we have been describing. Thus, it is easy to accuse the Glass Bottle Makers of injuring their industry by their drastic Restriction of Numbers. But it is open to them to reply that the very existence of their high level of technical skill depends on their maintaining a high Standard of Life ; that the Restriction of Numbers has been an effective means of maintaining this high standard ; and that without it, their combination would have crumbled away, their lists of Piecework Rates would have been destroyed by Individual Bargaining, and they themselves would have sunk to the low level of the present outcasts of the trade, those incompetent and unorganised workmen who pick up starvation wages by making, in cellars and " crib-shops," the commonest kind of medicine bottles. It was this consideration that induced J. S. Mill to declare that such a " partial rise of wages, if not gained at the expense of the remainder of the working class, ought not to be regarded as an evil. The consumer indeed, must pay for it, but cheapness of goods is desirable only when the cause of it is that their production costs little labor, and not when occasioned by that labor being ill-remunerated. If, therefore, no improvement were to be hoped for in the general circumstances of the working classes the success of a portion of them, however small, in keeping their wages by combination above the market rate would be wholly a matter of satisfaction." [1] Hence, from the point of view of those who regarded Restriction of Numbers as the only means by which wages could be maintained at anything above subsistence level, there was no argument against a Trade Union which adopted this expedient to save its members from slipping into the universal morass. During the fifty years that followed

[1] J. S. Mill, *Principles of Political Economy*, Book V. ch. x. § 5, p. 564.

the repeal of the Combination Laws the Trade Unionists
were incessantly told that "combinations of workmen . . .
always fail to uphold wages at an artificial rate, unless they
also limit the number of competitors." [1] When the Flint
Glass Makers and the Compositors, the Papermakers and
Engineers adopted stringent apprenticeship regulations as
one of the principal devices of their Trade Unionism, in so far
as they were taking the only recognised means of protecting
from a useless degradation their relatively high Standard of
Life, and of maintaining unimpaired their relatively high
level of industrial efficiency, they were but applying the
current teachings of Political Economy.

To sum up, the Device of Restriction of Numbers, by
constantly baulking the free selection of the most capable
manual workers and entrepreneurs ; by removing from both
classes the incentive due to the fear of supersession ; by
stereotyping processes and restricting output ; and by persistently hindering the re-organisation of industry on the
most improved basis, lowers the level of productive efficiency
all round. On the other hand, as compared with "perfect
competition," it has the economic advantage of fencing-off
particular families, grades, or classes from the general degradation, and thus preserving to the community, in these privileged groups, a store of industrial traditions, a high level of
specialised skill, and a degree of physical health and general
intelligence unattainable at a bare subsistence wage. If,
therefore, we had to choose between perfect "freedom of
competition," and an effective but moderate use of the
Device of Restriction of Numbers — between, for instance, the unregulated factory labor of the Lancashire of
the beginning of this century, on the one hand, and the
mediæval craft gild on the other—the modern economist
would hesitate long before counselling a complete abandonment of the old device.

---

[1] J. S. Mill, *Principles of Political Economy*, Book II. chap. xiv. § 6, p. 243
of 1865 edition ; see also p. 229, "Every successful combination to keep up wages
owes its success to contrivances for restricting the number of the competitors."

We are fortunately saved from so embarrassing a choice. In the first place, an effective use of the Device of Restriction of Numbers is no longer practicable. In our chapters on "The Entrance to a Trade" and "The Right to a Trade" we have seen how small and dwindling is the minority of Trade Unions which still rely on this means of protecting their Standard of Life. The ever-growing mobility of capital, and the incessant revolutionising of industrial processes render impracticable, in the vast majority of occupations, any restriction, by the Methods of Mutual Insurance or Collective Bargaining, of the candidates for employment. The steadily-increasing dislike to the Doctrine of Vested Interests makes it every day more hopeless to set up or maintain, by the Method of Legal Enactment, any limitation on the freedom of the competent individual to do any work for which he is positively better fitted, than those by whom it has hitherto been performed. Thus, only an infinitesimal number of Trade Unions actually succeed in limiting the number of persons who become candidates for employment at their occupation. It is true that large sections of the Trade Union world still, as we have seen, cling to the old device. The Compositors, the Engineers, the Ironfounders, the factory Boot and Shoe Operatives, and, in many districts, one or other section of the building trades limit, with more or less stringency, the number of boy-learners in any one establishment. This regulation can, however, only be enforced in establishments or districts over which the Trade Union has exceptional control, and it is entirely nugatory in establishments dispensing with Trade Union labor, and in districts where the skilled workmen are only partially organised. Hence, as we have pointed out in our chapter on "The Entrance to a Trade," these Trade Unions are not, by their apprenticeship regulations, limiting the number of candidates for employment ; they are merely providing, at considerable cost to themselves, that the boys should be trained in the least skilled department of the trade ; initiated into their industrial career by the worst employers and the most indifferent workmen ; and, we may add, brought up with the feelings and traditions of " blacklegs," instead of those of good Trade Unionists. Whatever advantages may be thought to accrue from a systematic and successful Restriction of Numbers, the partial and lopsided application of this device by modern Trade Unions is, we believe, economically as prejudicial to the strategic position of their own members as it is to the interests of the rest of the community.

More effectual in inducing the great majority of Trade Unions to change their tactics has been the discovery—in flat contradiction to J. S. Mill's authoritative dictum—that they can successfully maintain a high Standard of Life, by re-lying exclusively on the Device of the Common Rule. Thus, the Amalgamated Association of Operative Cotton-spinners or the Northumberland Miners' Mutual Confident Association —combinations which have, for a whole generation, success-fully maintained relatively good wages and short hours, together with a high level of sanitation and safety—have never interfered in the employer's free choice of men, what-ever their antecedents, to fill vacancies in their respective trades. In the case of the Cotton-spinners the Trade Union even insists, as we have seen, on there being always ten times as many learners as would suffice to keep up the trade. In so far as the Common Rules governing these industries are enforced by law this may easily be understood. The Device of Restriction of Numbers in no way increases the power of a Trade Union to obtain an Act of Parliament or to press for the rigid application of existing statutes ; it tends, on the contrary, to diminish this power. Any success-ful limitation of numbers necessarily restricts the growth of the industry in question, and thus lessens the electoral area over which it is dominant, whilst the maintenance of a close monopoly alienates the sympathy of the excluded. More paradoxical is the fact that it is not, in practice, found to militate against the maintenance of Common Rules by Collec-tive Bargaining, that a large number of people would like to come into the trade, or even that a crowd of candidates apply for every situation that is vacant. The explanation of this paradox must be sought in the economic characteristics of the Device of the Common Rule.

(b) *The Device of the Common Rule*

We have sufficiently explained, in our chapters on "The Standard Rate," "The Normal Day," and "Sanitation and Safety," that the Device of the Common Rule is, from the workman's point of view, always the enforcement of a minimum, below which no employer may descend, never a maximum, beyond which he may not, if he chooses, offer better terms. This is specially noticeable where the Common Rule is enforced by law. An employer who, for one reason or another, desires to fill his works with the most respectable young women, does not restrict himself to the already high standard of comfort and decency enforced by the Factory Act ; he sees to it that the workrooms are cheerful, warm, and light ; provides dining-rooms and cloak-rooms, hot water, soap, and towels, free from the usual irritating charges ; takes care to prevent any opportunity for the foreman's petty tyrannies ; and strives to make a spirit of kindly consideration pervade the whole establishment. When the Trade Union has to enforce the Common Rule by Mutual Insurance or Collective Bargaining, it never objects to an employer attracting superior workmen to his establishment by adopting a scale of wages in excess of the Standard ; by introducing an Eight Hours' Day ; or by promising to pay full wages during holidays or breakdowns. The mere adoption of a Common Rule, even if it does no more than give definiteness and uniformity to what has hitherto been the average, current, or "fair" conditions of the industry, has therefore the psychological effect of transforming a "mean" into a "minimum" ; and hence of silently setting up, in the eyes of both employers and workmen, a new "mean" between the best and worst conditions prevailing in the trade.[1]

The Device of the Common Rule stands in sharpest contrast, in all that concerns the selection of the factors of production, with the Device of Restriction of Numbers. The enforcement in any industry of a Standard Rate, a Normal Day, and prescribed conditions of Sanitation and Safety does not prevent the employer's choice of one man rather than another, or forbid him to pick out of the crowd of applicants the strongest, most skilful, or best-conducted workman. Hence, the Common Rule in no way abolishes competition for employment. It does not even limit the intensity of such competition, or the freedom of the employer to take advantage of it. All that it does is to transfer the pressure from one element in the bargain to the other—from the wage to the work, from price to quality. In fact, this exclusion, from influence on the contract, of all degradation of price, whether it takes the form of a lower rate of wages, longer hours of labor, or worse conditions of sanitation and safety, necessarily heightens the relative influence on the contract of all the elements that are left. If the conditions of employment are unregulated, it will frequently pay an employer not to select the best workman, but to give the preference to an incompetent or infirm man, a "boozer" or a person of bad character, provided that he can hire him at a sufficiently low wage, make him work excessive and irregular hours, or subject him to insanitary or dangerous conditions. If the employer cannot go below a common minimum rate, and is unable to grade the other conditions of employment down to the level of the lowest and most necessitous wage-earner in his establishment, he is economically impelled to do his utmost to raise the level of

---

[1] The Trade Unionist conception and application of a Standard Rate of remuneration stands, it need hardly be said, at the opposite pole from the mediæval fixing by law of a wage which it was equally an offence to diverge from in either direction. There is no resemblance between the economic effects of fixing a minimum wage, and those of establishing a maximum.

efficiency of all his workers so as to get the best possible return for the fixed conditions.[1]

This is the basis of the oft-repeated accusation brought by the sentimental lady or district visitor against the Trade Union Standard Rate, that it prevents an employer from preferentially selecting an old man, or a physical or moral invalid, when there is a vacancy to be filled. But it is clear that the efficiency of industry is promoted by every situation being filled by the best available candidate. If the old man is engaged instead of the man in the prime of life, the man of irregular habits rather than the steady worker, there is a clear loss all round.[2] From the point of view of the economist, concerned to secure the highest efficiency of the national industry, it must be counted to the credit of the

---

[1] "The consequence is," says Mr. Lecky, of the Trade Union Standard Rate, "that the employer is necessarily driven to employ exclusively the most efficient labor" (*Democracy and Liberty*, vol. ii. p. 347). It is often supposed that this effect of a Standard Rate is confined to Time Wages. But it operates also when (as is the case among the majority of Trade Unionists) the Standard Rate is a Piecework List. Even if the employer pays only in proportion to the work done, it is economically disadvantageous to him and to the community that his premises, machinery, and brain-power should be used short of their maximum capacity. This effect is intensified with every increased use of capital or brain-power in industry. The economic compulsion on the cotton manufacturer to select the most efficient workman to fill a vacancy is as much due to the high cost of machinery as to the high Piecework List.

[2] If all the fully competent workmen are already employed, and the weakling or degenerate is the only candidate for the vacancy, he will be taken on, as constantly happens when business is very brisk, notwithstanding the Standard Rate. But if an old man or an irregular worker is, through philanthropic influence on some employer, or through benevolent favoritism, given a preference, the result is, in practical life, that some more competent workman is left unemployed. Thus, the burden on the philanthropist is not lessened. It may even be increased, for it probably costs more to keep an unemployed workman in the prime of life, with full health and activities, and family obligations, than it does to maintain the aged. Nor does this argument assume, as some may think, any fixed "work fund." Whatever the demand may be for any particular kind of service, efficiency requires that no weakling should be employed until every more competent man is fully occupied. The hypothetical case in which whilst every competent workman in the community is fully employed, there is still some demand unsupplied, but not enough to make it worth while to pay the Standard Rate to one marginal old man or inferior worker, may be abandoned to the casuist. The necessary provision, both for the temporarily unemployed and the permanently unemployable—a problem not created by the enforcement of the Standard Rate— is dealt with in a later part of this chapter.

Device of the Common Rule, that it compels the employer, in his choice of men to fill vacancies, to be always striving, since he cannot get a " cheap hand," to exact, for the price that he has to pay, greater strength and skill, a higher standard of sobriety and regular attendance, and a superior capacity for responsibility and initiative.[1]

But the rigid enforcement of the Device of the Common Rule does more than act as a perpetual stimulus to the selection of the fittest men for employment. The fact that the employer's mind is constantly intent on getting the best possible workmen silently and imperceptibly reacts on the wage-earners. The young workman, knowing that he cannot secure a preference for employment by offering to put up with worse conditions than the standard, seeks to commend himself by a good character, technical skill, and general intelligence. There is, accordingly, under a Common Rule, not only a constant selection of the most efficient candidates, but also a positive stimulus to the whole class to become ever more efficient.[2]

We strike here upon the explanation of the paradox, to which we have referred, that it is not in practice found to militate against the maintenance of Common Rules by Collective Bargaining that a large number of people would like to come into the trade. If a Lancashire millowner or a Northumberland coalowner, tempted by the large number of candidates for employment, were to engage a new cotton-

---

[1] Du Cellier (*Histoire des Classes Laborieuses en France*, Paris, 1860), in referring to the great strikes which prevailed all over France in the spring of 1791 (pp. 320, 321), notes the effect of a Standard Rate in giving a positive advantage to the efficient workman over the inefficient. Most writers in 1860 seem to have assumed that its object was to put the lazy and inefficient workman on a level with his more industrious rival.

[2] The converse has often been pointed out by those who have studied the influence of out-door relief, promiscuous charity, and casual labor. The fact that a man without character, or of irregular habits, can get as easily taken on as a casual dock-laborer, as the unemployed workman with the best possible testimonials, is rightly regarded as exercising a demoralising influence on all London labor. If the dock-companies were compelled to give, say twenty-four shillings a week to every laborer who entered their employment, they would at once begin to pick out only those men on whose regular attendance and faithful service they could rely.

spinner or coal-hewer on any other terms than those customary in the trade, all the other spinners or hewers in his
establishment would instantly "hand in their notices," and
eventually leave his service in a body. No "nibbling at
wages," or other standard conditions, would compensate
such an employer for the loss in efficiency that would be
involved in replacing his whole staff of spinners or hewers
by inexperienced hands. The more "open" is the trade,
and the more attractive are these standard conditions, the
more certain it is that the employers will find it economically
impossible to dispense with the services of the main body
of men already in employment.[1] Where the minimum conditions of employment are fixed and uniform, competition
takes the form of raising the standard of quality, and where
these minimum conditions are relatively high, the successful
candidates, picked as they are, out of a crowd of applicants,
become a very select class, which can be individually
recruited but not collectively replaced. The progressive
raising of the Common Rule, by constantly promoting the
"Selection of the Fittest," causes thus an increasing specialisation of function, creating a distinct group, having a
Standard of Life and corporate traditions of its own which
each recruit is glad enough to fall in with. If we imagine a
community in which each industry was definitely marked
off by its own Common Rule, the strategic strength of the
workmen would be independent of any restriction on the
choice of a trade. The employers in each industry would
be free to pick their workmen where they chose, but, being
unable to go below the minimum wage, or otherwise degrade
the conditions of employment, they would be economically
compelled to select the very best men for the amount of work
required° to satisfy the demand of the consumers. A
newly-arrived workman would equally be free to accept any

---

[1] Hence the rare but prolonged general stoppages of work among the
Lancashire Cotton-spinners require no "picketing." The employers know that
they must have the same body of men back again, and they accordingly do not
open their mills until they have come to terms. The same may be said of the
Coalminers in all well-organised districts.

situation he could get, in whatever trade he chose, but as
he would find no opportunity of ousting a better man by
offering to do his work in an inferior way at a reduced wage,
he would be economically compelled to drop into the
particular occupation in which, under the given distribution
of demand and the given supply of special talent, his
additional labor would produce the greatest addition of
utility.

That the maintenance of a common minimum wage
should, of itself, automatically improve the quality of the
service will, to many readers, seem a paradox. Yet in all
other cases this result of the diversion of competition is an
accepted truism of practical economics. When a middle-
class governing body——a Town Council or a railway company,
for instance——needs a middle-class official, be he doctor or
architect, engineer or general manager, it invariably concentrates the competition on quality by stopping it off price.
The practical experience of business men has taught them
that to engage the doctor or general manager who offers to
come for the lowest salary would be a ruinous bargain.
They accordingly always first fix the salary that they will offer,
determining the amount according to the Standard of Life
of the particular social grade they seek to attract, and they
then pick the best candidate who offers himself at that
salary.[1] The same effect of a fixed price is noticed even in
the sale of wares, though here the fixing of price is seldom
free from some element of monopoly. If rival producers of
goods are precluded, by custom or combination, from " undercutting " each other in the price of their wares, they devote
all their energies to outbidding each other in the quality.
Hence the fact that the accepted price for the morning
newspaper in the United Kingdom has long been uniformly

---

[1] It is interesting to note that the suggestion, often made by inexperienced
" Labor members " of a public body, that it is absurd to offer the customary
high salary for a brain-working post, when there are " plenty of men willing to
do the work for less money," is always held up to derision by their middle-class
colleagues——and, according to the Trade Unionists' own argument, rightly so——
as being a " penny wise and pound foolish " policy.

one penny in no way limits the competition between rival editors. What it does is to concentrate the pressure on a struggle to surpass in excellence of type and paper, prompt and exclusive collection of news, brightness of literary style, and every other form of attractiveness. So overpowering is this impulse among railway companies that, in spite of the strict limitation of the number of competing lines, and their agreements among themselves, the general managers are always trying to outbid each other for public favor in the other ways that are left open to them, and the fact that the three separate railways between London and the North of England agree to charge identical fares is constantly raising the quality of the service in speed, punctuality, and comfort.

But whilst, in the absence of any kind of monopoly, the adoption by all producers of an identical price automatically tends to bring about an improvement in quality, there is, in this as in other respects, a vital distinction between wares and the workmen who produce them. In the case of the wares, the tendency to improvement springs from the effect of the Common Rule in shifting the pressure of competition from price to quality. In the case of the workmen—influenced, as we have seen, in the same way by the mere existence of the Common Rule—we have also to consider the effect on the living human being of improved sanitary conditions, shorter hours of labor, and more adequate wages. If unrestricted individual competition among the wage-earners resulted in the universal prevalence of a high standard of physical and mental activity, it would be difficult to argue that a mere improvement of sanitation, a mere shortening of the hours of labor, or a mere increase in the amount of food and clothing obtained by the workers or their families would of itself increase their industrial efficiency. But, as a matter of fact, whole sections of the wage-earners, unprotected by Factory Act or Collective Bargaining, are habitually crushed down below the level of physiological efficiency. Even in the United Kingdom, at least eight millions of the population—

over one million of them, as Mr. Charles Booth tells us, in London alone—are at the present time existing under conditions represented by adult male earnings of less than a pound a week.[1] The unskilled laborer who is only half fed, whose clothing is scanty and inappropriate to the season, who lives with his wife and children in a single room in a slum tenement, and whose spirit is broken by the ever-recurring irregularity of employment, cannot by any incentive be stimulated to much greater intensity of effort, for the simple reason that his method of life makes him physiologically incapable of either the physical or mental energy that would be involved.[2] Even the average mechanic or factory operative, who earns from 20s. to 35s. per week, seldom obtains enough nourishing food, an adequate amount of sleep, or sufficiently comfortable surroundings to allow him to put forth the full physical and mental energy of which his frame is capable. No middle-class brain-worker who has lived for any length of time in households of typical factory operatives or artisans can have failed to become painfully aware of their far lower standard of nutrition, clothing, and rest, and also of vitality and physical and mental exertion.[3] It has accordingly been pointed out

[1] See Sir R. Giffen's evidence before the Royal Commission on Labor, sitting as a whole, Questions 6942, 6943; Mr. Charles Booth, *Life and Labour of the People*, especially vol. ix. p. 427.

[2] " In England now, want of food is scarcely ever the direct cause of death; but it is a frequent cause of that general weakening of the system which renders it unable to resist disease; and it is a chief cause of industrial inefficiency. . . . After food, the next necessaries of life and labor are clothing, house-room, and firing; when they are deficient the mind becomes torpid, and ultimately the physical constitution is undermined. When clothing is very scanty it is generally worn night and day; and the skin is allowed to be enclosed in a crust of dirt. A deficiency of house-room or of fuel causes people to live in a vitiated atmosphere which is injurious to health and vigor. . . . Rest is as essential for the growth of a vigorous population as the more material necessities of food, clothing, etc." (Professor A. Marshall, *Principles of Economics*, 3rd edit. 1895, pp. 277, 278; see also the interesting series of illustrative facts in *The Groundwork of Economics*, by C. S. Devas, London, 1883). For M'Culloch's remarks, see, among other references, section vii. of his *Principles of Political Economy*, especially as to the " Advantages of a High Rate of Wages."

[3] The rich and the middle-class seldom realise how scandalously low is the standard of daily health among the wage-earners. Apart from actual disease or disablement, the workman and his wife and family are constantly suffering from minor ailments, brought about by unwholesome or deficient food, bad sanitation, the

by many economists, from J. R. M'Culloch to Professor Marshall, that, at any rate so far as the weakest and most necessitous workers are concerned, improved conditions of employment would bring with them a positive increase in production. " A rise in the Standard of Life for the whole population," we are now expressly told, " will much increase the National Dividend, and the share of it which accrues to each grade and to each trade." [1] We see, therefore, that the Device of the Common Rule, so far as the wage-earner is concerned, promotes the action of both forces of evolutionary progress ; it tends constantly to the Selection of the Fittest, and at the same time provides both the mental stimulus and the material conditions necessary for Functional Adaptation to a higher level of skill and energy.

Let us now consider the effects of the Device of the Common Rule upon the brain-workers, including under this term all who are concerned in the direction of industry. When all the employers in a trade find themselves precluded, by the existence of a Common Rule, from worsening the conditions of employment—when, for instance, they are legally prohibited from crowding more operatives into their mills or keeping them at work for longer hours, or when they find it impossible, owing to a strictly enforced Piece-work List, to nibble at wages—they are driven, in their competitive struggle with each other, to seek advantage in other ways.[2] We arrive, therefore, at the unexpected result

lack of sufficient rest or holiday, and absence of medical care. The brain-worker, living temporarily in a wage-earning family, becomes positively oppressed by the constant suffering, of one member or another, from toothache or sores, headache or dyspepsia, and among the women, also from the dragging pains or chronic anæmia brought about by hard work or exposure at improper times. In the "Sweated" industries it is scarcely too much to say that the state of health, which is normal among the professional classes of the present day, is almost unknown.

[1] Professor A. Marshall, *Principles of Economics*, 3rd edit. p. 779.

[2] Thus Mr. Mundella writes of the Standard List of Prices enforced by the Nottingham Hosiery Board : "Formerly, in times of depression, the greatest irregularity prevailed, according to the individual character of the employers. The hard and unscrupulous, trading on the necessities of the workmen, could bring down wages below a reasonable level ; the more considerate must either follow suit or be undersold. Our Board has changed all that. All now pay the

that the insistence by the Trade Union on uniform conditions of employment positively stimulates the invention and
adoption of new processes of manufacture. This has been
repeatedly remarked by the opponents of Trade Unionism.
Thus Babbage, in 1832, described in detail how the invention and adoption of new methods of forging and welding
gun-barrels was directly caused by the combined insistence
on better conditions of employment by all the workmen
engaged in the old process. " In this difficulty," he says,
" the contractors resorted to a mode of welding the gun-
barrel according to a plan for which a patent had been taken
out by them some years before the event. It had not then
succeeded so well as to come into general use, *in consequence
of the cheapness of the usual mode of welding by hand labor*,
combined with some other difficulties with which the patentee
had had to contend. But *the stimulus produced by the combination of the workmen for this advance of wages* induced
him to make a few trials, and he was enabled to introduce
such a facility in welding gun-barrels by roller, and such
perfection in the work itself, that in all probability very
few will in future be welded by hand-labor." [1] " Similar
examples," continued Babbage, " must have presented themselves to those who are familiar with the details of our
manufactories, but these are sufficient to illustrate one of the
results of combinations. . . . It is quite evident that they
have all this tendency ; it is also certain that considerable
stimulus must be applied to induce a man to contrive a new
and expensive process ; and *that in both these cases unless
the fear of pecuniary loss had acted powerfully the improvement would not have been made*." [2] The Lancashire cotton
trade supplied the same generation with a classic instance of

same price, and *the competition is not who shall screw down wages the most, but
who shall buy material best, and produce the best article.*"—*Arbitration as a
Means of Preventing Strikes*, by the Right Hon. A. J. Mundella (Bradford, 1868),
p. 15

[1] C. Babbage, *Economy of Manufactures* (London, 1832), p. 246. The
welding of tubes of all kinds is now invariably done by machinery—a fact which
may be said to have made possible the modern bicycle.

[2] *Ibid.* p 248.

" Trade Union folly " of this kind. Almost every contemporary observer declares that the adoption of the " self-acting " mule was a direct result of the repeated strikes of the Cotton-spinners between 1829 and 1836 to enforce their Piecework Lists, and that many other improvements in this industry sprang from the same stimulus. The *Edinburgh Review* went so far as to say in 1835 that " if from the discovery of the Spinning Frame up to the present, wages had remained at a level, and workers' coalitions and strikes had remained unknown, we can without exaggeration assert that the industry would not have made half the progress." [1] And, coming down to our own day, we have ourselves had the experience of being conducted over a huge steel-works in the North by the able captain of industry who is practically engaged in its administration, and being shown one improvement after another which had been devised and adopted expressly because the workmen engaged at the old processes had, through their powerful Trade Unions, exacted high piecework rates. To the old economist, accustomed to the handicraftsman's blind hostility to machinery, this undesigned result of insistence on high wages seemed a proof of the shortsightedness of Trade Union action. The modern student perceives that the Trade Unions, in insisting on better conditions of employment than would have been yielded by Individual Bargaining, were " building better than they knew." To the wage-earners as a class, it is of the utmost importance that the other factors in production—capital and brain power—should always be

[1] *Edinburgh Review*, July 1835. Similarly, Marx notes that it was not until the employment of women and young children in mines was forbidden that coalowners introduced mechanical traction ; and that, as the Inspectors of Factories report in 1858, the introduction of " the half-time system stimulated the invention of the piecing machine " in woollen yarn manufacture, by which a great deal of child labor was dispensed with (*Capital*, Part LV. chap. xv. sec. 2, vol. ii. p. 390 of English translation of 1887). In the *Proceedings of the Institute of Mechanical Engineers*, 1895 (p. 346), "the great amount of ingenuity which had recently been expended in the charging and drawing of gas-retorts" by hydraulic machinery was described as "the direct result of the labor troubles experienced" since the formation of the Gas Workers' Union, and "it showed what was the general tendency of such troubles."

at their highest possible efficiency, in order that the common
product, on which wages no less than profits depend, may be
as large as possible. The enforcement of the Common Rule
on all establishments concentrates the pressure of competition on the brains of the employers, and keeps them always
on the stretch. " Mankind," says Emerson, " is as lazy as it
dares to be," and so long as an employer can meet the
pressure of the wholesale trader, or of foreign competition,
by nibbling at wages or " cribbing time," he is not likely to
undertake the " intolerable toil of thought," that would be
required to discover a genuine improvement in the productive process, or even, as Babbage candidly admits, to
introduce improvements that have already been invented.
Hence the mere existence of the Common Rule, by debar-
ring the hard-pressed employer from the most obvious source
of relief, positively drives him to other means of lowering
the cost of production. And the fact that the Common
Rule habitually brings to the operatives a greater reward
for their own labor, itself further increases the employer's
incentive to adopt labor-saving machinery. For " the lower
the day wage," we are told, " the smaller the rate of improvement in labor-saving methods and machinery. . . . Where
labor is cheapest, the progress is the slowest." [1] Far from
being an advantage to industry, " the cheapness of human
labor where it prevails is the greatest incentive for the per-
petuation of obsolete methods. . . . The incentive is wanting for replacing, with large capital outlay, old and obsolete
by new and improved machinery. The survival of the
fittest is, therefore, so to speak, the result of a high wage
rate," [2] provided, that is to say, that the high rate is enforced
on all establishments alike. This is now seen even by the
capitalists themselves. " We employers," lately declared one
of the leading captains of English industry, " owe more than,
as a body, we are inclined to admit, to the improvements in
our methods of manufacture *due to the firmness and independ-*

[1] *The Economy of High Wages*, by J. Schoenhof (New York, 1892), p. 276.
[2] *Ibid.* pp. 38, 39.

ence of trade combinations. Our industrial steadiness and enterprise are the envy of the world. The energy and pertinacity of Trade Unions have caused Acts of Parliament to be passed which would not otherwise have been promoted by employers or politicians, all of which have tended to improve British Commerce.[1] . . . Every intelligent employer will admit that his factory or workshop, when equipped with all the comforts and conveniences and protective appliances prescribed by Parliament for the benefit and protection of his workpeople—though great effort, and, it may be, even sacrifice, on his part has been made to procure them—has become a more valuable property in every sense of the word, and a profit has accrued to him owing to the improved conditions under which his workpeople have been placed." [2]

Besides this direct effect in stimulating all the employers, the mere existence of the Common Rule has another, and even more important result on the efficiency of industry, in that it is always tending to drive business into those establishments which are most favorably situated, best equipped, and managed with the greatest ability, and to

[1] A recent instance is afforded by the humble industry of washing clothes. The chairman of the Eastbourne Sanitary Steam Laundry Company, Limited, told his shareholders on 25th January 1897 that "the new Factory Act prevented the hands working so long as they used to do, and the directors had been obliged to provide machinery to enable them to do the work in less time " (*Laundry Record*, 1st March 1897). The extraordinary backwardness of the art of washing clothes, and the difficulty of obtaining skilled, regular, and honest laundry workers, are, we suggest, largely due to the lack of stimulus to employers and of decent conditions for the workpeople, resulting from the absence of Common Rules.

[2] W. Mather, *Contemporary Review*, November 1892. Here Mr. Mather has the economists of to-day on his side. Professor Nicholson cites Thorold Rogers as observing, " that every act of the legislature that seems to interfere with the doctrine of *Laisser Faire*, and has stood the test of experience, has been endorsed because it has added to the general efficiency of labor" (Rogers, *Six Centuries of Work and Wages*, London, 1891, p. 528; Nicholson, *Principles of Political Economy*, Edinburgh, 1893, p. 331). Mr. Mather, who is at the head of a great engineering establishment, is the author of the following interesting pamphlets : *The Forty-eight Hours' Week: a Year's Experiment and its Results at the Salford Iron Works* (Manchester, 1894) ; *A Reply to some Criticisms on Mr. Mather's Report of a Year's Trial of the Forty-eight Hours' Week* (London, 1894).

eliminate the incompetent or old-fashioned employer. This fact, patent to the practical man, was not observed by the older economists. Misled by their figment of the equality of profits, they seem habitually to have assumed that an increase in the cost of production would be equally injurious to all the employers in the trade. The modern student at once recognises that the Device of the Common Rule, from its very nature, must always fail to get at the equivalent of all differential advantages of productive agents above the level of the worst actually required at any given time. When, for instance, the Amalgamated Association of Operative Cotton-spinners secures uniform piecework lists, identical hours of labor, and similar precautions against accident and disease in all English cotton mills, it in no way encroaches upon the extra profits earned by firms of long-standing reputation for quality, exceptional commercial skill, or technical capacity. Similarly, it does nothing to deprive mills enjoying a special convenience of site, the newest and best machinery, valuable patent rights or trade connections, of the exceptional profits due to these advantages. This is still more apparent in the case of the coal-miners, whose Mines Regulation Acts and "county averages" of wages, applying equally all round, necessarily leave untouched the vast incomes derived from the mining royalties of all but the worst mine in use. The very nature of this fundamental device of Trade Unionism—the necessary uniformity of any rule that is to be common to the whole trade—compels it to be fixed with reference to the circumstances, not of the best, but of the worst establishment *at which the Trade Unionists wish to obtain employment.* This does not mean that, in any well-organised trade, the Standard Rate, or other Common Rule, will be fixed so as to enable the economically weakest employers to continue in business. On the contrary, it is a matter of common experience that every time a Trade Union really secures a Common Rule, whether by Collective Bargaining or Legal Enactment, it knocks another nail into the coffin of the least intelligent and worst-equipped employers in the trade.[1] We have already described how the small masters in the boot and shoe industry denounce, as a conspiracy of the great capitalists in the trade, any acceptance of a "uniform statement," or of the high standard of workshop accommodation insisted on by the National Union of Boot and Shoe Operatives. In the building trades, it is the small "jerry masters" who especially protest against the "tyranny" of the "Working Rules," to which the contractor in a large way of business willingly agrees. And in Lancashire, it is in the backward villages, where many of the mills are already shut up, that Factory Acts and Piecework Lists are denounced for the relentless pressure with which they force up the standard of efficiency to the level of Oldham or Bolton.[2]

How far this policy of the "selection of the fittest" among employers can be carried at any particular time is a matter for delicate calculation. It is obviously to the

[1] "We have been working at a loss for years," said a large cotton manufacturer to the Union secretary. "Yes," was the shrewd reply, "you have been losing your little mills and building bigger ones."—*First Prize Essay on Trades Unions*, by "Ithuriel" (Glasgow, 1875), p. 31.

[2] This is a matter of deliberate policy with the modern Trade Union. Thus, the official organ of the Cotton Operatives lately declared, in an article written by a prominent Trade Union official, that "if a firm realises that it cannot manufacture with profit to itself, and it is paying no more than others for labor, it is better that that firm, harsh though the doctrine may seem, should cease to exist, rather than the operatives should accept a reduction in wages and drag the whole trade down with them."—*Cotton Factory Times*, 17th July 1896.

This result is then often pointed to as showing the folly of Trade Union action in "driving capital out of the trade." But, so long as any better-managed, better-equipped, or more favorably situated mill is capable of doing increased business, the amount of effective capital in the trade will not be lessened through the closing of the worst mill. The price remaining the same, and therefore presumably the demand, the same quantity of the product will be produced and sold. All that will have happened will be that the capital in the trade will, on an average, be employed to greater advantage. How much scope there is, in modern industry, for this concentration of business in the most advantageous centres, may be judged from the admirable *Statistics of Manufactures* of Massachusetts from 1886 to 1896, which show that, in the two or three thousand separate establishments investigated, the average business done was only between 50 to 70 per cent of their full productive capacity—in some trades less than half the possible output of the existing plant being made.—See the *Eleventh Report*, Boston, 1897, pp. 99-104, 169.

interest of the Trade Union so to fix the Common Rule as to be constantly "weeding out" the old-fashioned or stupid firms, and to concentrate the whole production in the hands of the more efficient "captains of industry," who know how to lower the cost of the product without lowering the wage. Thus, so long as the more advantageously situated establishments in the trade are not working up to their utmost capacity, or can, without losing their advantage, be further enlarged, the Trade Union could theoretically raise its Common Rule, to the successive exclusion, one after another, of the worst employers, without affecting price or the consumers' demand, and therefore without diminishing the area of employment. By thus "raising the margin of cultivation," and simultaneously increasing the output of the more advantageously situated establishments, this Device of the Common Rule may accordingly shift the boundary of that part of the produce which is economically of the nature of rent, and put some of it into the pockets of the workmen.[1] If, for instance, one employer owns a patent which greatly reduces the cost of production, he will be able, so long as his output amounts only to a portion of the quantity demanded by the public at the old price, to put into his own pocket the entire equivalent of the improvement. But if the Trade Union, by gradually raising its Standard Rate, drives all the other employers one by one out of the trade, and concentrates the whole business into its most advantageous centre, the aggregate cost of production will be thereby greatly reduced. If the increased profit is retained by the monopolist, there is no theoretic reason why the workmen, if they are strong enough, should not encroach on this surplus, until they had reduced it to the current rate of profit of capital. There are, however, practical limits to such a process. However advantageously

---

[1] Ricardo and, more explicitly, J. S. Mill pointed out that anything which increased the output of the more fertile farms would tend to reduce the aggregate rent of agricultural land.—*Principles of Political Economy*, Book IV. ch. iii. § 4, pp. 434-436 of 1865 edition.

situated a particular establishment may be, we do not find that it, in practice, absorbs the whole trade. Considerations of locality and connection, of variety of demand, of the lack of capital, and, above all, the absence of desire or capacity to manage a larger business, set limits to the indefinite extension of even the most advantageously placed firm.[1] And whilst these limits interfere with the concentration of industry, other considerations conspire to hinder the desire of the Trade Union to push to the uttermost its policy of " levelling up." Though it would immediately profit the trade as a whole, and ultimately even its weakest members, the concentration involves, to begin with, a painful wrench for those members who would have to change their methods of working, often alter their habits of life, and sometimes even migrate to a new town. In such trades as the Engineers, the Boot and Shoe Operatives, the Cotton-weavers, and the Compositors, the Trade Union has, for whole generations, been struggling to induce its most apathetic and conservative - minded members to put on the adaptability and mobility of the " economic man." The growth of " uniform lists " and " national agreements " in one trade after another is a sign that this difficulty is, in some cases, being overcome ; whilst part of the increasing preference for the Method of Legal Enactment is, in our view, to be attributed to the fact that it presses uniformly on all districts, and thus positively favors the concentration of each industry in the centres in which it can most advantageously be carried on. It is among the Lancashire Cotton-spinners that this far-sighted policy has been pursued with the greatest persistency, with the result, if we may believe the employers, of transferring to the operatives, in higher wages and better conditions, no small share of each successive improvement in production.

[1] For an expansion of this idea see " The Rate of Interest and the Laws of Distribution," by Sidney Webb, in *Quarterly Journal of Economics*, April 1888. Thus, it cannot be assumed that the cost of the marginal production is equal in good and bad establishments alike. Many other causes than marginal cost of production determine the distribution of business.

This result of the Common Rule—the constant selection of the fittest among the directors of industry, and the concentration of business in the most advantageous centres—is, strangely enough, often made a matter of reproach to Trade Unionism. Thus, even so benevolent an employer as Sir Benjamin Browne, looking back after twenty-six years' experience of the Engineers' fixing of a Nine Hours' Normal Day in 1871, blames the Trade Unions for thereby driving business into the hands of the best-equipped firms. "From this time," he declares, "more was done by large companies and less by small employers, . . . more and more costly and complicated machinery was introduced. . . . The practical effect of the Nine Hours' Movement was to ruin the small employer."[1] But seeing that the aggregate volume of engineering work has admittedly not fallen off —that it has, on the contrary, enormously increased—it cannot but be regarded as an economic gain that this work should be executed where it can be done to the greatest advantage. If, in the absence of a Common Rule, the "small employer," with his imperfect machinery and insufficient capital, with inferior scientific training and inadequate knowledge of the markets, is enabled to divert business from superior establishments by nibbling at wages, requiring systematic overtime, overcrowding his factory, or neglecting precautions against accident, his existence is not only detrimental to the operatives, but also a clear diminution of the nation's productive efficiency. Hence the enforcement of a Common Rule, by progressively eliminating the worst equipped employers and concentrating the whole pressure of competition on securing the utmost possible efficiency of production, tends constantly to the development of the highest type of industrial organisation.[2]

[1] Letter to the *Times* of 11th August 1897.

[2] The student will find an interesting confirmation of much of the preceding analysis, with illustrations drawn from the industry of to-day, in an able address just delivered by a leading employer in the engineering trade. The *Inaugural Address by the President of the Manchester Association of Engineers* (Mr. Joseph Nasmith), published at Manchester (1897), is largely occupied with the means

Thus, the effect of the Common Rule on the organisation of industry, like its effect on the manual laborer, and the brain-working entrepreneur, is all in the direction of increasing efficiency. It in no way abolishes competition, or lessens its intensity. What it does is perpetually to stimulate the selection of the most efficient workmen, the best-equipped employers, and the most advantageous forms of industry. It in no way deteriorates any of the factors of production ; on the contrary, its influence acts as a constant incentive to the further improvement of the manual laborers, the machinery,

by which English employers can best meet foreign competition. He distinguishes three factors of supreme importance, among them being neither low wages nor long hours. " First, the economic effect of improved appliances ; second, the adoption of the best commercial methods ; and third, the fullest development of the skill of all those engaged in an industry, and especially of the leaders. . . . One of the direct consequences of the adoption of the newer methods and appliances has been such a subdivision of some operations as to involve a fresh organisation of labor. Instances will be well known in which the making of a single article, as, for instance, the matrix used in the linotype machine, or the spindles which are made for ring-spinning machines, involves the handling of the article by fifteen or twenty workpeople, each of whom is charged with the performance of one operation, forming possibly a small portion of those which are needed to complete the whole article. This necessitates the design and employment of a large number of machines or appliances, each of which is intended to aid in effecting one of these minor operations, and calling for the attention of a workman *specially trained in its use.* In this way there has been silently worked a revolution which is not always fully appreciated even yet, *and which has had no less an effect than the elevation of the machine tender from a subordinate to an important position in the economy of a workshop.* It is in consequence of the facility of subdivision which the ingenuity displayed in the production of special appliances has brought about, that in all organised industries the labor cost of any article continually tends to decrease. Probably because the economic change which has taken place has only been partially appreciated, we find people still making a great fuss about wages. As a matter of fact the rate of wages is not necessarily a guide to the labor cost of an article, and a wider recognition of this fact would prevent a good deal of trouble. . . . Labor cost and not wages is the determining factor, and there is not necessarily a direct connection between them. Indeed, it may be asserted that they are often in inverse proportion, and that *the more highly organised an industry is, the greater is the tendency for that to be so.* . . . Nothing has so much influence upon this problem as the possibility of making articles in large numbers, and it is in this direction that much remains to be done by engineers. Nothing presents so hopeful a field for the future efforts of constructive engineers as the design and manufacture of machines which will enable the manufacturers to produce all kinds of articles in the greatest possible numbers in any given time. *Wages become a secondary consideration under these circumstances,* and although a change in the rate paid may for a time affect the economic conditions, *it is not long before the skill of the constructor has placed him abreast of the new conditions.*"

and the organising ability used in industry. In short, whether with regard to Labor or Capital, invention or organising ability, the mere existence of a uniform Common Rule in any industry promotes alike the selection of the most efficient factors of production, their progressive functional adaptation to a higher level, and their combination in the most advanced type of industrial organisation.[1] And these results are permanent and cumulative. However slight may be the effect upon the character or physical efficiency of the wage-earner or the employer ; however gradual may be the improvement in processes or in the organisation of the industry, these results endure and go on intensifying themselves so that the smallest step forward becomes, in time, an advance of the utmost importance.

So far the substitution in any trade of the Common Rule for the anarchy of Individual Bargaining would seem to be in every way beneficial. We have now to consider some characteristics which lead to a qualification of this conclusion.

We have to note, in the first place, that the result, though certain, may probably be slow. The passing of a Factory Act enforcing a definite standard of sanitation or a normal day, may be indispensable to prevent the progressive degradation of whole classes of operatives ; by its diversion of the pressure of competition it may re-establish the physique, improve the character, and increase the efficiency of all subsequent generations ; but the very day it comes into operation it will almost certainly raise the cost of labor to the employer, if only for a time. The extension of a uniform Piecework List to all the establishments in an industry may eventually concentrate all the business in the best-equipped

---

[1] The influence of a Common Rule in changing the nature and effects of competition in industry, is, of course, not confined to the relation between employer and workmen. The respective results on the character and efficiency of production, of "complete freedom of enterprise," on the one hand, and of such uniform restrictions as the Adulteration Acts, the by-laws relating to the construction of buildings, or the regulations for the conduct of common lodging-houses on the other, are well worth further study from this point of view.

mills, managed by the most capable employers, and thus positively reduce the cost of production ; but its first effect will probably be to raise that cost in the old-fashioned or outlying establishments not yet dispensed with. Like all permanent changes in personal character or social organisation, the economic effects of the Device of the Common Rule are gradual in their operation, and will not instantly reveal themselves in an improvement of quality or a diminished cost of production.

The response, moreover, in the way of added efficiency will vary from trade to trade. The rapidity with which the response will be given, the extent to which the improvement can be carried, and the particular "curve of diminishing return" that it will describe, will differ in each industry according as its condition at the moment affords more or less scope for the operation of the two potent forces of Functional Adaptation and the Selection of the Fittest, on workmen and capitalists respectively. Thus, the effect of the constant selection among the operatives will vary according to the range of choice which the technical circumstances of the industry permit the employer to exercise. This depends, in practice, for the skilled trades, upon the extent to which the process itself requires the co-operation of boys or other learners, from whom the skilled workers are recruited. Hence, the mule-spinners, attended each by two piecers—ten times the proportion of learners required to keep up the trade—are a far more "selected" class than the skilled hand-working tailors of the West End trade, who need have no boys at all working by their side, and who are largely assisted by women incapable of replacing them. We do not wish to discuss the social expediency of an arrangement, which attracts into an occupation every year thousands of boys, nine-tenths of whom, after they have reached maturity, find themselves skilled in an occupation which they have no chance of following, and which they must perforce abandon, at one period of their life or another, for some new means of livelihood. But whatever may be the consequences of this arrangement to the unsuccessful piecers, its effect on the cotton-spinners, as a class, is to make them a highly selected aristocracy of ability, able to adapt themselves to the progressive complication and "speeding-up" of the machinery. Analogous differences exist between trade and trade in regard to the extent to which Selection of the Fittest can act on the employers, especially as to machinery and location. Thus, the total absence of any form of monopoly in cotton-spinning and cotton-weaving, and the remarkable facility and cheapness with which Lancashire capital can always be obtained for new cotton mills, gives the cotton Trade Unions a special opportunity for increasing the efficiency of the industry, by constantly driving out the weakest firms. A complete contrast to this state of things is presented by such legal or natural monopolies as railways, waterworks, tramways, and gas works, where the Trade Unions have to put up with whatever incompetent Board of Directors or General Manager may happen to hold the field. Nor is the difference between trade and trade any less in regard to the action on the employers of Functional Adaptation. Thus, the factory boot and shoe industry, supplied almost day by day with fresh inventions, and constantly recruited by the upstarting of new businesses, offers obviously more scope for the improvements caused by pressure on the brains of employers, than an industry like English agriculture, where generation often succeeds to generation in the same farm, and economic freedom of enterprise and mobility of capital is comparatively rare. The only direction in which progress could be at all equal as between trade and trade seems to be the improvement of the operatives, brought about by increased food, clothing, and rest. Even in this respect there would be more scope for improvement in an industry carried on by women or unskilled laborers, who are likely to be chronically underfed or overworked, than in a trade employing skilled artisans already earning a high Standard Rate. But once the process of "levelling up" had reached a certain point, this inequality of response would cease to be apparent. At this stage, the increase in efficiency due to improvement in physical health and vigor, like the increase in mental activity made possible by sufficiency of food and rest, might be expected, in all trades, to bear a fairly close relation to the improvement in the workers' conditions, and would probably be subject to much the same limits in all the industries of a particular country. In every other respect trade differs widely from trade in the rapidity and degree with which it responds in the way of added efficiency, to the stimulus of the Common Rule. And this difference between one trade and another, in the potentiality of increased efficiency, bears, it will be obvious, no definite relation to the strategic strength or political power of the operatives. Whether the workers in any particular trade will actually be able to extract from the employers, either by Mutual Insurance, Collective Bargaining, or Legal Enactment, higher wages, shorter hours, or improved sanitation, depends, in practice, on many other circumstances than those affecting the possibilities of increased efficiency. Indeed, if we could admit any generalisation at all on the point, we might infer, from the general " law of diminishing returns," that a trade in which the wage-earners have hitherto been too weak to obtain any Common Rule, would be likely to yield a greater harvest of added efficiency than an old-established, well-organised, and powerful industry, in which the Trade Union had, for generations past, pushed its advantages to the utmost, and so probably exhausted most of the stimulus to increased Functional Adaptation and Selection of the Fittest produced by the use of the Common Rule.

There will, accordingly, be at any particular moment a practical limit to the advantageous raising of the Common Rule. The Selection of the Fittest, whether of employers, workmen, establishments, or districts, can achieve no more than to take the best for the purpose that the community at the time supplies. Functional Adaptation, whether of workmen or employers, or their mutual organisation, can go no

further than the structure for the time being allows. And
though each successive rise in the Common Rule may produce its own increment of additional efficiency, there is a
rapidly decreasing return to each successive application of
pressure. Hence a Trade Union which has, in the first few
years of its complete organisation, succeeded in obtaining
considerable advances in its Standard Rate, sensible reductions of its Normal Day, and revolutionary improvements
with regard to the Sanitation and Safety of its workplaces
—all without injury to the extent and regularity of its
members' employment—may presently find that, in spite of
its perfected organisation and accumulated funds, its upward
course slackens, its movements for further advances become
less frequent or less successful, and, in comparison with the
contemporary gains of other industries, the conditions of
employment will remain almost stationary.

The Trade Unionist has a rough and ready barometer to
guide him in this difficult navigation. It is impossible, even
for the most learned economist or the most accomplished
business man, to predict what will be the result of any particular advance in the Common Rule. So long, however, as
a Trade Union, without in any way restricting the numbers
entering its occupation, finds that its members are fully
employed, it can scarcely be wrong in maintaining its
Common Rules at their existing level, and even, after a
reasonable interval, in attempting gradually to raise them.[1]

When the percentage of workmen out of employment
begins to rise, it is a sign that the demand for their particular
commodity has begun to slacken. This diminution of demand may, as we shall presently see, be due to any one of
an almost infinite number of causes, quite unconnected with
the conditions enjoyed by the operatives. But one of these

---

[1] This assumes, as is nearly always the case, that the wages and other conditions of employment are within the limits of the fullest physiological efficiency.
So long as the family income of the typical skilled mechanic, even in England,
is less than £100 a year, and his hours of labor are more than forty or fifty per
week, the potentiality of improvement in physical and mental efficiency, in family
life and citizenship, no less than in industry, is great.

possible causes is a rise in price, and one of the possible factors in a rise in price is an advance of the Common Rule which does not bring with it, in one form or another, a corresponding increase in the efficiency of the industry. Hence, although it can in no way be inferred that the slackening of demand has been caused by the rise in the level of the Common Rule, rather than to any other of the many possible causes, yet this slackening, however it is caused, must necessarily check any further advance. For assuming the workmen to rely exclusively on the Device of the Common Rule, it will not pay them to obtain a rise of wages, a shortening of hours, or improved conditions of sanitation or safety at the cost of diminishing their own continuity of employment. To put it concretely, whenever the percentage of the unemployed in a particular industry begins to rise from the 3 or 5 per cent characteristic of "good trade," to the 10, 15, or even 25 per cent experienced in " bad trade," there must be a pause in the operatives' advance movement.[1]

[1] The critical reader may retort that, when demand is expanding, a rise in the Common Rule unaccompanied by an increase in efficiency, may check the expansion without actually throwing any men out of work. This might conceivably be the case, if the particular rise in the Common Rule, which outstripped the increase in efficiency, took place before the increased orders for the commodity were given, and if the consequent rise in price merely choked off some or all of a coming increase in demand. This, however, is not the actual sequence of events. What happens first is that the increase in the demand shows itself in the receipt of unusually large orders by the manufacturers. The existing workmen are required to work full time, and then overtime ; most of the unemployed in the trade get taken on ; boys and other learners are promoted and additional men are inquired for ; old establishments are enlarged, and new ones are opened. On this, the Trade Union asks for a rise in wages or a shortening of hours. If this is conceded, and is not followed by increased efficiency, the rise in cost of production and therefore in price can scarcely fail actually to cause some of the men in employment to be discharged. The more completely organised is the trade, the more precise is the index afforded by the percentage of members " on donation."

*(c) The effect of the sectional application of the Common Rule
on the distribution of industry*

We have now to consider the effect of the Device of the
Common Rule, not on the particular trade that practises it,
but on the development of the nation's industry—that is to
say, upon the distribution of the capital, labor, and brain
power of any community among the different occupations
that are open to it.   In the complicated ebb and flow of
the modern world of competitive industry the expansion or
contraction of a particular trade cannot be considered by
itself.   The ordinary manufacturer or operative sees clearly
enough that the growth or decay of his own establishment
is intimately connected with the dwindling or expansion
of other establishments in the same trade.   The economist
detects a similar rivalry between one occupation and
another, even within the same community ; and sees the
area of this competition between distinct classes of workers
indefinitely enlarged by international trade.   Without a full
appreciation of this silent but perpetual struggle between
separate occupations, it is impossible to form any correct
estimate of the influence of any particular factor in the
distribution of industry.

We have, to begin with, the competition between alternative ways of manufacturing the same product.   We need not
dwell on the historic struggles of the handloom weaver and
stocking-frame knitter against the operatives working with
power ; nor recur to the contemporary competition between
handmade clothing and boots, nails and ropes, and the
machine-made articles.   What is more typical of our own
time is the rivalry of one machine-process with another, such
as the innumerable ways of producing steel, or, to take a
simpler instance, the competition in cotton-spinning between
the self-acting mule, worked by men and boys, and the
perfected ring-frame, worked by women.   A new stage in
the competition is seen in the substitution of one material

for another, as, for instance, iron for wood in the making of bedsteads, and steel for iron in railway construction. A step farther brings us to the invention of alternative ways of fulfilling the same desire, exemplified in the rivalry between the railway and the road, the horse and the electric motor. Finally, there is a certain limited sense in which the operatives making entirely unconnected commodities compete for custom, so that, as it is commonly alleged, the seasonal demand for books and pianos fluctuates inversely with that for cricket-bats and bicycles.

So far we have considered the nation as a self-contained community, and we have regarded the customers as choosing only between different products of their own country. Foreign trade brings in a new complication. The English producers of commodities for foreign markets, and those who manufacture, for home consumption, commodities that can be imported from abroad, find their industries expanding or contracting according as the prices of their products rise and fall in other countries as well as at home. This may be clearly seen in the case of English coal. The cargoes from Cardiff and the Tyne go all over the world and find, in many foreign ports, practically no competitors. But how far inland our coals will push into each continent varies with every change of price. In Germany the Silesian and Westphalian mines, in Australasia those of New South Wales, and in South Africa those of the Cape and Natal already supply a large part of the local demand, and the geographical limit at which the use of English coal ceases to be cheaper than the inland supply is seen in practice to be as sensitively mobile as the thermometer. And if we turn to the influence of the import trade, we may watch the area of wheat growing in Great Britain expanding or contracting in close correspondence with the oscillations of the world price of wheat. So far the success of any class of English producers in competing for the world's custom would seem to depend exclusively on their ability to undersell the foreign producers of the same article. But this is only half the truth. The distinctive effect of international trade is to bring into competitive rivalry, without their being conscious of the fact, many other trades within the particular country having no apparent connection with each other. This will be obvious to any one who considers for a moment the relation between exports and imports. Without sounding the depths of the orthodox " Theory of International Trade " or the mysteries of the Foreign Exchanges, it will not be doubted that any increase in our aggregate exports does, in practice, tend to cause at any rate some increase in our aggregate imports. If then, England for any reason increases its export trade—if, for instance, a fall in the cost of production of English machinery, coal, and textiles enables Lancashire and Cardiff increasingly to get the better of their foreign rivals in neutral markets—some increase will certainly reveal itself in our import trade, *not in machinery, coal, and textiles, but in entirely different articles ;* it may be, in American food stuffs and Australian wool, or it may be in German glass wares and Belgian iron. Exactly which articles will be sent to England in increased quantities to pay for the increased foreign purchases of machinery, textiles, and coal, will depend on the relative cheapness of production, both at home and abroad, of all the commodities consumed by England that can also be produced abroad. It may be that food stuffs and wool, glass and iron, can all be produced abroad actually cheaper than they are selling in England. But the increase will tend to occur, not in those commodities in which the difference is least, but principally in those in which the difference is greatest. Hence the expansion or contraction of English production in a particular industry working for the home demand, is affected, not only by the foreign producers of the same commodity for the English market, but also by the expansion and contraction of every English industry working for export, and, yet again, by the conditions existing in all the other English industries that are subject to the competition of imports from abroad. The enormous increase in our imports of food stuffs, and the consequent contraction of

English agriculture, cannot therefore be dissociated from the contemporary increase in our exports : it is the Lancashire cotton-spinner and the Northumberland coal hewer who are most seriously competing with the English farmer. Or, to take another instance, if the jobbing home workers in the Sheffield cheap cutlery trade keep down the price of their product by working long hours, without expensive sanitary precautions, at the starvation wages of cut-throat competition, they may gain by their wretchedness a miserable exemption from the competition of French and German blades in the English market. But the effect of this exemption is to divert the nation's imports into other commodities. The brothers and cousins of the Sheffield cutlers, earning high wages in the Yorkshire glass works and iron furnaces, may therefore find their employment diminished by the persistent influx of German glass and Belgian iron, and they will be entirely unaware that the ebb and flow of their own trades have any connection, either with the expansions and contractions of the export trade of Lancashire on the one hand, or with the cheapness of production of Sheffield cutlery on the other. The same argument applies, it is clear, the other way round. The shrewd officials of the Lancashire Cotton Operatives, working largely for export, are as keenly aware as the employers that in promoting a new Factory Bill, or in resisting a reduction in their Piecework Lists, they must take into account the competition of Massachusetts and Bombay. But neither workmen nor employers in Lancashire realise that in this matter of foreign markets they have to face no less dangerous competitors at their own doors. Though the aggregate volume of our export trade is automatically kept up to a point that will discharge our foreign indebtedness, it does not at all follow that the export of each commodity will remain the same. England in this respect is like one great shop, from which the foreigner will certainly buy some goods. But how he will distribute his purchases among our different products will depend on which of them, relatively to all the others, offers the greatest advantage compared with foreign-made articles. If, without any alteration of the balance of indebtedness, there springs up a new business able by the relative cheapness or attractiveness of its product to command a foreign market, the exports of all our other commodities will tend to be injuriously affected by these new sales. Thus, the development during the last twenty years of a large export trade in ready-made clothing and hardware must have, to some extent, tended to elbow out the elder industries, perhaps those of cotton and wool, some of which would, in the absence of these new competitors, necessarily have expanded to balance the increase in our imports of food stuffs.[1] The Lancashire mule-spinners must therefore

---

[1] This assumes that there has been no addition to the capital, brain power, and labor of the community. It has sometimes been urged that the upgrowth of the wholesale clothing trade in East London has been made possible only by the settlement of Jewish immigrants, and that the newcomers, creating a new export trade, cause an actual addition to our imports, and thus neither diminish employment in other home trades nor restrict any existing export trade. It is, accordingly, suggested that the Jewish immigration is not injurious to the English wage-earners, and that it actually adds to English commercial prosperity.

As a matter of fact, neither the capital nor the brain power, which have created the new export trade in slop clothing, have been provided by the Jewish immigrants, nor is it by any means entirely carried on by immigrant labor. It may be that the opportunity for the trade in its present form arises from the presence of these and other workers of a low Standard of Life ; but the capital and organising capacity have been supplied by our own countrymen ; and must therefore be taken to have been diverted by this opportunity, away from other industries, which find themselves thereby subtly restricted.

If, indeed, the immigrants brought with them their own capital and brain power, and created a new industry exclusively for export, the result would be, as suggested, an addition to our imports, and there would be no tendency to a restriction of the other export trades. But the pinch would then be felt elsewhere. The additional imports would, of course, not be the articles actually consumed by the immigrants, and there would be a shifting of trade, some home industries expanding under the additional demand, others dwindling under the competition of the newly-stimulated imports. The total trade, apart from the immigrants' own production and consumption, would neither be increased nor decreased ; and the total wealth of the nation, apart from the immigrants' own possessions and savings, not affected. The chief importance of the immigration would then lie in its indirect effects on national character and capacity. If the immigrants, like the Polish Jews, brought in a lower Standard of Life, the result might be (besides increasing the overcrowding of the slums) a constant influence for degradation. If, on the other hand, the immigrants, like the Huguenots, introduced a higher Standard of Life, their example might produce a permanent improvement in national character. There is also the obscure question of the effect of the intermixture of races to be considered.

realise that they are competing, not only with the women ring-spinners in Lancashire itself and the mule-spinners in the foreign cotton mills, but also with the English workers in all the trades that produce any article whatsoever for sale to the foreigner.

We come, therefore, to the conclusion that the employers and operatives in any particular industry ought to regard themselves as in the truest sense competing for business, no less than for the supply of capital, brains, and manual labor, with practically every other industry in the country, however unconnected with their own it may seem to be ; and in this competitive struggle the battle, it is obvious, will not always be to the strong, nor the race to the swift. The ebb and flow of business, and hence the distribution of the nation's industry, and the production of one article rather than another, depends on many conditions quite unconnected with the conduct or efficiency of the employers or the workmen concerned, or with their remuneration. A change of taste or fashion, a scientific discovery, the upgrowth of a new class of customers, a mere alteration in the nation's wealth, or in its distribution between classes, a war or a famine, or even a sumptuary law, will make some trades expand and others dwindle, quite independently ot any increase or decrease in the cost at which their products are being turned out. And even if we restrict ourselves to the effect of price in stimulating or contracting the demand for a particular commodity, it will be obvious that its cost of production will vary for many reasons totally unconnected with the requirements of the employers or the conditions of employment of the workpeople concerned. The varying abundance or scarcity of the raw material, the ease and cost with which it can be transported, the discovery of a new ingredient, the invention of a new machine or a new process, a change in the incidence of taxation—all these, and numberless other factors unconnected with the conditions of employment affect cost of production, and therefore price. It is, ot course, this extreme complication of factors — this almost infinite degree of

Plurality of Causes and Intermixture of Effects—that makes it impossible to prove or disprove the efficacy of Trade Unionism by any enumeration of instances. What we have to do is, assuming each trade to be incessantly subjected to the keenest competition of every other trade at home and abroad, to leave on one side all the other influences at work and examine what effect the device of the Common Rule itself exercises upon the distribution of industry.

We have seen, in our analysis of the economic effects of the Common Rule on the industries in which it is applied, that this regulation, with its gradual advance of level, positively tends to diminish the cost of production in those industries. It follows that, other things being equal, they will expand at a greater rate than the unregulated trades. But it is characteristic of the expansion thus caused that it brings incidental advantages to the whole industrial community. The fact that the labor and capital employed in one or more of the nation's industries has become more productive than before does not diminish the aggregate demand or the aggregate purchasing power : on the contrary, it increases it. Any shrinkage in particular trades, due to the partial suppression of their products by the improving industries, will be balanced by at least as much expansion elsewhere, due to the increased purchases of these industries themselves. Moreover, the increased incentive to the invention and perfecting of labor-saving machinery, the added stimulus to the discovery of new markets, new materials, and new ways of satisfying existing desires, which, as we have seen, is an inevitable reaction from the bulwark of the Common Rule, provides the unregulated trades with a stream of ready-made appliances, tested inventions, and new opportunities, which would never have revealed themselves to their own unstimulated brains. Similarly, the general raising of the Standard of Life of any section of wage-earners improves the national stock, from which all occupations draw their recruits.[1]

[1] Thus, the great English factory industry of boot and shoe manufacture, only

But though the regulated industries, by progressively raising the standard of mechanical ingenuity, organising capacity, and physical strength, will have added to the national capital in all its forms, their very superiority makes continuously harder the struggle of the unregulated trades to maintain their position in the world's market. The rapid adoption of new inventions almost inevitably involves the decay and destruction of other trades. Thus, the enormous extension of the use of iron bedsteads—the product of a highly-organised trade—cannot fail to have contracted the manufacture of cheap wooden bedsteads in the sweating dens of the East End "garret masters." This is obvious enough when we consider the substitution of a new commodity for the inferior article which formerly satisfied the same want, or even the satisfaction of one need rather than another, as in the competition between books and bicycles. International trade, as we have seen, causes the same rivalry to exist between industries apparently unconnected with each other. Thus, the lowering of the cost of production of iron bedsteads does not interfere merely with the English production of wooden bedsteads : by its stimulus to the export of iron bedsteads it positively increases the imports into England of entirely different articles, and may, therefore, itself be one of the factors in the contraction of English agriculture, and of the manufacture of the cheaper sorts of glass, cutlery, and wood work.

recently emerging from the quagmire of Home Work, and itself as yet producing hardly any inventions, has been made possible by the amazing mental fertility of Connecticut and Massachusetts, where the well-organised workmen exact wages twice as high as their English rivals. Similarly, the Indian cotton-mills have, without effort of their own, automatically received the inventions which, if we may believe Babbage and the *Edinburgh Review*, owe their very existence to the aggressive Trade Unionism of the Lancashire operatives. And the able Englishmen who began life as artisans, and are now to be found in responsible positions in so many continental factories, are plainly the result of the comparatively high wages and short hours—not to speak of the training in administration—which the English workmen in the regulated trades have derived from their Trade Unionism. In these and many other ways those countries and those industries in which a relatively high standard of life is enforced, are perpetually dispensing to the world, out of their abundance, what their unregulated rivals are unable to produce for themselves.

More important in its detrimental effect on the unregulated trades will be the diversion away from them of the best industrial recruits. In industries unregulated by Common Rules it may suit the immediate profit and loss account of an employer to select, as his foreman, not the man who can most improve the product or the process, but the man who has the greatest capacity for nibbling at wages or cribbing time. The fact that the Common Rules prevent the beating down of wages, the lengthening of hours, or the neglect of precautions against accidents or disease, automatically causes the selection, for the post of foreman or manager, of men who have at their command, in the improvement of machinery and organisation, far more permanent and cumulative ways of reducing the cost of production than taking advantage of the operatives' weakness. The concentration of business in large establishments, which, as we have seen, is one of the results of the Common Rule, directly encourages the enlistment in the industry of men of specialised knowledge and scientific attainments. There is an enormous difference, not as yet adequately realised, between the sort of man who becomes the typical "small master" of the unregulated trades, and the hierarchy of highly-trained organisers, managers, buyers, travellers, agents, chemists, engineers, metallurgists, electricians, designers, and inventors who direct the business of great establishments. This difference in the quality of the recruiting is no less marked among the manual laborers. No operative who is strong enough, or intelligent enough, or regular enough to get into a trade enjoying high wages, short hours, and decent conditions of work will stay in an occupation affording him inferior advantages. The high standard enjoyed by the Lancashire cotton-spinners and engineers, or by the Northumberland miners, causes these trades to draw to themselves the pick of the young men in their respective districts. Hence the final curse of the unregulated trades—they are perpetually condemned to put up with the inferior labor that cannot get employment elsewhere. Every rise in the conditions of life of the factory operative and the coalminer makes it harder for the country district to retain the best boys of the village. Every time the Board of Trade shortens the hours or protects the lives of the railway servant ; each new statute that increases the certainty and amount of his compensation for accident ; every rise in the Standard Rate that public opinion secures to him, indirectly makes the struggle for existence harder for the farmer and the " little master " in the country town.

(d) Parasitic Trades

We have hitherto proceeded on the assumption that the competition between trades is unaffected by anything in the nature of a subsidy or bounty. If the community chooses to give to all the employers in a particular industry an annual bounty out of the taxes, or if it grants to all the operatives in that industry a weekly subsidy from the Poor Rate in aid of their wages, it is obvious that this special privilege will, other things being equal, cause the favored industry to outstrip its rivals. The subsidy or bounty will enable the endowed manufacturers to bribe the public to consume their article, by ceding to them what they have not paid for. An analogous advantage can be gained by the employers in a particular trade if they are able to obtain the use of labor not included in their wage-bill. Under the competitive pressure described in our chapter on " The Higgling of the Market " some of the unregulated trades become, in fact, parasitic. This occurs, in practice, in two distinct ways.

We have first the case of labor partially subsisted from the incomes of persons unconnected with the industry in question. When an employer, without imparting any adequate instruction in a skilled craft, gets his work done by boys or girls who live with their parents and work practically for pocket-money, he is clearly receiving a subsidy or bounty which gives his process an economic advantage over those worked by fully-paid labor. But this is not all. Even if he pays the boys or girls a wage sufficient to cover the cost of their food, clothing, and lodging so long as they are in their teens, and dismisses them as soon as they become adults, he is in the same case. For the cost of boys and girls to the community includes not only their daily bread between thirteen and twenty-one, but also their nurture from birth to the age of beginning work, and their maintenance as adult citizens and parents.[1] If a trade is carried on entirely by the labor of boys and girls and is supplied with successive relays who are dismissed as soon as they become adults, the mere fact that the employers pay what seems a good subsistence wage to the young people does not prevent the trade from being economically parasitic. The employer of adult women is in the same case where, as is usual, he pays them a wage insufficient to keep them in full efficiency, irrespective of what they receive from their parents, husbands, or lovers.[2] In all these instances the efficiency of the services rendered by the young persons or women is being kept up out of the earnings of some other class. These trades are therefore as clearly receiving a subsidy as if the workers in them were being given a "rate in aid of wages." The English farmer pays, it is true, no higher wages, but then he receives in return, since the abolition of the Old Poor Law, only what he pays for: his low Standard of Life involves a low Standard of Work. The employer of partially subsidised woman or child labor gains, on the other hand, actually a double advantage over the self-supporting trades: he gets without cost to himself the extra energy due to the extra food, and he abstracts—possibly from the workers at a rival process,

---

[1] To this, in strictness, should be added their maintenance in old age and their burial. But only a small proportion of the aged wage-earners in the United Kingdom are maintained, and eventually buried, out of their own savings or the assistance of relations. Old age and burial, like education, have already become to a great extent, in the form of charity or the Poor Law, charges upon the community as a whole. See *Pauperism and the Endowment of Old Age* (London, 1892), and *The Aged Poor* (London, 1894), by Charles Booth.

[2] "Women as a rule are supplementary wage-earners."—Charles Booth, *Life and Labour of the People*, vol. ix. p. 205

or in a competing industry—some of the income which might have increased the energy put into the other trade.

But there is a far more vicious form of parasitism than this partial maintenance by another class. The continued efficiency of a nation's industry obviously depends on the continuance of its citizens in health and strength. For an industry to be economically self-supporting, it must, therefore, maintain its full establishment of workers, unimpaired in numbers and vigor, with a sufficient number of children to fill all vacancies caused by death or superannuation. If the employers in a particular trade are able to take such advantage of the necessities of their workpeople as to hire them for wages actually insufficient to provide enough food, clothing, and shelter to maintain them in average health ; if they are able to work them for hours so long as to deprive them of adequate rest and recreation ; or if they can subject them to conditions so dangerous or insanitary as positively to shorten their lives, that trade is clearly obtaining a supply of labor-force which it does not pay for. If the workers thus used up were horses—as, for instance, on an urban tramway—the employers would have to provide, in addition to the daily modicum of food, shelter, and rest, the whole cost of breeding and training, the successive relays necessary to keep up their establishments. In the case of free human beings, who are not purchased by the employer, this capital value of the new generation of workers is placed gratuitously at his disposal, on payment merely of subsistence from day to day. Such parasitic trades are not drawing any money subsidy from the incomes of other classes. But in thus deteriorating the physique, intelligence, and character of their operatives, they are drawing on the capital stock of the nation.[1] And even if the using up is not actually so rapid

[1] The economic position of the slave-owner where, as latterly in the United States and Brazil, the slaves had to be bred for the labor market, closely resembles that of the tramway company using horse-power. So long as the African slave-trade lasted, the importation of slaves being presumably cheaper than breeding them, the industries run by slave labor were economically in much the same position as our own sweated trades—that is to say, supplied with successive relays

as to prevent the " sweated " workers from producing a new
generation to replace them, the trade is none the less
parasitic. In persistently deteriorating the stock it employs,
it is subtly draining away the vital energy of the community.
It is taking from these workers, week by week, more than
its wages can restore to them. A whole community might
conceivably thus become parasitic on itself, or, rather, upon
its future. If we imagine all the employers in all the
industries of the kingdom to be, in this sense, " sweating "
their labor, the entire nation would, generation by generation,
steadily degrade in character and industrial efficiency.[1] And
in human society, as in the animal world, the lower type developed by parasitism, characterised as it is by the possession
of smaller faculties and fewer desires, does not necessarily
tend to be eliminated by free competition.[2] The degenerate
forms may, on the contrary, flourish in their degradation,
and depart farther and farther from the higher type.
Evolution, in a word, if unchecked by man's selective power,

of cheap but rapidly deteriorating labor—and the cheapness of their product,
observed Mill, " is partly an artificial cheapness, which may be compared to that
produced by a bounty on production or on exportation ; or considering the means
by which it is obtained, an apter comparison would be with the cheapness of
stolen goods."—*Principles of Political Economy*, Book III. ch. xxv. § 3, p. 413
of 1865 edition.

[1] The practical agriculturist may see an analogy in the case of land. To the
theoretic economist land often appears as an indestructible instrument of production,
but the agricultural expert knows better. If under complete industrial freedom
the hirers of land sought only to obtain the maximum profit for themselves, it
would pay them to extract for a few years the utmost yield at the minimum outlay. The land so treated would be virtually destroyed as an instrument of production, and could only be brought into cultivation again by a heavy outlay of
capital. But this would not matter to the hirer, if he was free to discard the
worn-out farm when he chose, and to take a fresh one. The remedy in this case
is found in the covenants by which the owner of the land regulates the use of it
by the hirer, so as to ensure that it shall be maintained in complete efficiency.

[2] The apostles of *laisser faire* were sometimes startling in the extent to which
they carried their optimism. Thus, when Harriet Martineau was driven by the
evidence collected by the Factory Commissioners in 1833 to admit that " the case
of these wretched factory children seems desperate," she goes on to add " the
only hope seems to be that the race will die out in two or three generations "
(*Harriet Martineau's Autobiography*, by Maria Weston Chapman, vol. iii. p. 88).
But there was no race of factory children dependent for continuance on its own
reproduction.

may result in Degeneration as well as in what we choose to call Progress.

We might have to accept as inevitable the incidental evils of the parasitic trades if it could be urged that their existence resulted in any positive addition to the national wealth——that is to say, if they utilised capital and found employment for labor that would otherwise have been idle ; or if they fulfilled desires that must otherwise have remained unsatisfied. But this is not the case. We have, to begin with, the fact that the mere existence of any parasitic industry tends incidentally to check the expansion of the self-supporting trades, whether these are regulated or un-regulated. Nor is it only such unprogressive industries as agriculture that suffer. In cotton-spinning, the fact that well-nurtured and respectable young women can be hired at ten or twelve shillings a week is tempting the millowners to substitute the ring-frame for the mule more extensively than would be profitable if the employers had to pay a full sub-sistence wage for their ring-spinners, or if they could get for their ten or twelve shillings a week only such irregular and inefficient workers as could or would permanently live on that income. The fact that the female ring-spinners have been brought up and are partly supported by the mule-spinners themselves, or by other well-paid trades like the engineers, is thus positively throwing more mule-spinners out of work than would otherwise be the case. And there is, as we have seen, a more subtle competition. The fact that the wholesale clothing contractor is allowed to deteriorate and use up in his service the unfortunate relays of sweated out-workers who make his slop clothing, gives him actually a constant supply of vital energy which he need not and does not replace by adequate wages and rest, and thus makes it possible for him to sell his product cheaper, and hence to augment his export trade more than he could have done if his industry were free from social parasitism. And every expansion of this rival export trade tends, as we have seen, to elbow out other sales to the foreigner——it may well be, therefore, to restrict the export, and therefore the manufacture, of hardware, machinery, or textiles.

Nor can it be imagined that there is anything so peculiar in the nature of the products of the "sweated trades," that they could not be just as efficiently supplied to us without their evil parasitism. We venture to assert, on the contrary, that there is no article produced in the whole range of the parasitic trades which could not be manufactured with greater technical efficiency, and with positively less labor, by a highly regulated factory industry. But just as in a single trade the unregulated employer who can get "cheap labor" is not eager to put in machinery, so in the nation, the enterprising capitalists who exploit some new material or cater for some new desire inevitably take the line of least resistance. If they can get the work done by parasitic labor they will have so much the less inducement to devise means of performing the same service with the aid of machinery and steam power, and so much the less interest in adopting mechanical inventions that are already open to them.[1] Thus the parasitic trades not only abstract part of the earnings of other wage-earners, and use up the capital stock of national vigor: they actually stand in the way of the most advantageous distribution of the nation's industry, and thus prevent its

[1] Professor Schmoller observes that "Self-interest in industrial society is like steam in the steam-engine: only when we know under what pressure it is working can we tell what it will accomplish" (*Sendschreiben an Herrn von Treitscke*, Berlin, 1875, p. 37). This is strikingly illustrated by the evil persistence in England, owing to the absence of the pressure of a Standard Rate in the sweated trades, of obsolete and uneconomical processes. "Public attention was directed with some force a short time ago to the wretched condition of the 'nailers' in the Dudley district. In America labor conditions of this kind are impossible owing to the economic circumstances existing, yet nails are made at a labor cost far lower than that common in the Dudley district. The output of a worker in an American nail mill amounts to over $2\frac{1}{2}$ tons per week, while the Staffordshire nailer, working on his old method, only produces 2 cwt. Of what avail is it that the workman in the latter case earn 15s. only, and in the former £6 per week? The labor cost per lb. is in the one case 0.8d. and in the other 0.257d. Thus the earnings are eight-fold greater in the case of the American workman, while the labor cost is only one-third that of the nail produced by the English workman. This is . . . only illustrative of a principle which runs through all industries."— Manchester Association of Engineers, *Inaugural Address by the President, Mr. Joseph Nasmith* (Manchester, 1897), p. 6.

capital, brains, and manual labor from being, in the aggregate, as productive as they would otherwise be. So long as
we assume each industry to be economically self-supporting,
the competition between trades may be regarded as tending
constantly to the most productive distribution of the capital,
brains, and manual labor of the community. Each trade
would tend to expand in proportion as it became more
efficient in satisfying the public desires, and would be limited
only at the point at which some other trade surpassed it in
this respect. Every unit of the nation's capital, like every
one of its capable entrepreneurs and laborers, would tend
constantly to be attracted to the industry in which they
would produce the greatest additional product. If, however,
some trades receive a subsidy or bounty, these parasites will
expand out of proportion to their real efficiency, and will thus
obtain the use of a larger share of the nation's capital, brains,
and manual labor than would otherwise be the case, with the
result that the aggregate product will be diminished, and the
expansion of the self-supporting trades will be prematurely
checked. This tendency of industry to be forced by the
pressure for cheapness, not into the best, but into the lowest
channel, was noticed by the shrewd observers who exposed
the evils of the old Poor Law. "Whole branches of manufacture," they said, "may thus follow the course, not of coal
mines or streams, but of pauperism ; may flourish like the
fungi that spring from corruption, in consequence of the
abuses which are ruining all the other interests of the place
in which they are established, and cease to exist in the
better administered districts, in consequence of that better
administration."[1]

[1] *First Report of Poor Law Commissioners*, 1834, p. 65, or reprint of 1884
(H. C. 347 of 1884). The disastrous effects on agricultural labor of the "rate in aid
of wages" of the old Poor Law have become an economic commonplace. It seems
to be overlooked that what is virtually the same bounty system prevails wherever
work is given out to be done at home. The scanty earnings of women outworkers,
with their intermittent periods of unemployment, inevitably lead to their being
assisted by private charity, if not also from public funds. Thus, a recent investigator in Glasgow reports that "the returns of the Inspectors of the Poor show
that many outworkers, who are in receipt of wages too small to support them,

This condition of parasitism is neither produced by the self-helping efforts of the more fortunate trades to improve their own conditions, nor can it be remedied by any such sectional action. The inadequate wages, excessive hours, and insanitary conditions which degrade and destroy the victims of the sweated trades are caused primarily by their own strategic weakness in face of the employer, himself driven to take advantage of their necessities by the unconscious pressure described in our chapter on " The Higgling of the Market." That weakness, and the industrial inefficiency to which it inevitably leads, are neither caused nor increased by the fact that other sections of wage-earners earn high wages, work short hours, or enjoy healthy conditions of employment. If, as we have argued, these conditions, enforced by the Device of the Common Rule, themselves produce the high degree of specialised efficiency which enables them to be provided, their existence is no disadvantage to the community, nor to any section of it. On the contrary, the resulting expansion of the regulated trades will have reclaimed an additional area from the morass. If, on the other hand, they are not accompanied by a full equivalent of efficiency, their existence in the regulated industries, by increasing cost of production, must be a drawback to these in the competition between trades, and thus positively lessen the pressure on the unregulated occupations and the workers in them.[2] On neither view can the relatively

though working full time, are aided from the rates. Moreover, although to an extent which it is impossible to ascertain, many of the outworkers on low wages are assisted by the churches and by charities. Here evidently part of the wages is paid by outsiders. . . . The cheapness of goods made in such circumstances is balanced by the increase in Poor Rates and in the demands on the benevolent." —*Home Work amongst Women*, by Margaret H. Irwin (Glasgow, 1897).

[2] Thus, in the international competition between trades, the maintenance of wages at high rates by means of Restriction of Numbers is calculated to be disastrous to the trade practising this device. The high price of the labor, coupled with its declining efficiency, can scarcely fail to cause an increase in the price of the product. If this comes into competition with foreign articles, or if a cheap substitute can easily be found, the trade will quickly be checked and the falling off in demand, leading to some workmen losing their employment, will call for increased stringency in excluding fresh learners. The effect of the Restriction of Numbers in any trade, if this is pushed so far as seriously to raise

good conditions exacted by the coalminer or the engineer be said to be in any way prejudicial to the chain and nail maker of the Black Country or the outworking Sheffield cutler, to the sweated shirtmaker of Manchester or the casual dock laborer of an East London slum. Their influence, such as it is, is all in the other direction. The fact that a brother, cousin, or friend is receiving a higher wage, working shorter hours, or enjoying better sanitary conditions is an incentive to struggle for similar advantages.[1]

Unfortunately there is no chance of the parasitic trades raising themselves from their quagmire by any sectional action of their own. It is, for instance, hopeless for the casual dock laborers of London to attempt, by Mutual Insurance or Collective Bargaining, to maintain any effective Common Rules against the will of their employers. Even if every man employed at dock labor in any given week were a staunch and loyal member of the Trade Union, even if the union had funds enough to enable all these men to stand out for better terms, they would still be unable to carry their point. The employers could, without appreciable loss, fill their warehouses the very next day by an entirely new

the price of the product, is, therefore, actually to drive more and more of the nation's capital and labor from the restricted industry, and its progressive dwindling, even to the point of complete extinction, or transfer to another country.

[1] It may be said that one class of parasitic workers—women or child workers —are partly supported from the wages of other operatives, usually better paid ; and that their parasitism is thus made possible by the existence of these better paid operatives, and therefore, in some sense, by Trade Unionism. There is, however, no connection between the two. This kind of parasitism does, indeed, imply a donor of the bounty as well as a recipient, but the existence of differences in income between individuals, or even between classes, is in no way dependent on Trade Unionism. Moreover, there are some cases—such as the relation between home work and casual dock labor in East London—in which two equally low-paid occupations may be said, by their alternate mutual help, to be parasitic on each other. The facility of obtaining "large supplies of low-paid labor," says Mr. Charles Booth, "may be regarded as the proximate cause of the expansion of some of the most distinctive manufacturing industries of East and South London—furniture, boots and shoes, caps, clothing, paper bags, and cardboard boxes, matches, jam, etc. . . . They are found in the neighbourhood of districts largely occupied by unskilled or semi-skilled workmen, or by those whose employment is most discontinuous, since *it is chiefly the daughters, wives, and widows of these men who turn to labor of this kind*."—C. Booth, *Life and Labour of the People* (London, 1897), vol. ix. p. 193.

set of men, who would do the work practically as well.
There is, in fact, for unspecialised manual labor a practically
unlimited "reserve army" made up of the temporarily
unemployed members of every other class. As these
form a perpetually shifting body, and the occupation of
"general laboring" needs no apprenticeship, no combination,
however co-extensive it might be with the laborers actually
employed at any one time, could deprive the employer
of the alternative of engaging an entirely new gang.
The same reason makes it for ever hopeless to attempt,
by Mutual Insurance or Collective Bargaining, to raise
appreciably the wages of the common run of women workers.
Where, as is usually the case, female labor is employed for
practically unskilled work, needing only the briefest experience ; or where the work, though skilled, is of a kind into
which every woman is initiated as part of her general education, no combination will ever be able to enforce, by its
own power, any Standard Rate, any Normal Day, or any
definite conditions of Sanitation and Safety. This is even
more obvious when the parasitic labor is that of boys
or girls, taken on without any industrial experience at all.
Mutual Insurance and Collective Bargaining, as methods of
enforcing the Common Rule, become impotent when the
work is of so unskilled or so unspecialised a character that
an employer can, without economic disadvantage, replace
his existing hands in a body by an entirely new set of
untrained persons of any antecedents whatsoever.

The outcome of this analysis is that the strongest
competitors for the world's custom, and for the use of the
nation's brains and capital, will be the regulated industries
on the one hand, and the parasitic trades on the other—the
unregulated but self-supporting industries having to put up
with the leavings of both home and foreign trade, and a
diminishing quantity and quality of organising capacity and
manual labor.[1] In what proportion a nation's industry will

[1] It may be desirable to observe, in order to prevent possible misunderstanding, that we propose this division of industries into three classes, as a Classification

be divided among the two conquerors will, it is obvious, depend primarily on the extent to which regulation is resorted to. The more widespread and effective is the use of the Device of the Common Rule, the larger, other things being equal, will be the proportion of the population protected from the ravages of "sweating." On the other hand, the more generally the conditions of employment are left to be freely settled by Individual Bargaining, the wider will grow the area of the parasitic trades. And omitting from consideration those industries which are at once unregulated and self-supporting—which succumb, as we have seen, before either victor—it would require delicate economic investigation to estimate the relative advantage, in this day-to-day struggle between industries, of the slow but cumulative stimulus given by the Common Rule, on the one hand, and, on the other, the immediate cheapening of production made possible by parasitism, whether this takes the form of grants in aid of subsistence from persons outside the industry, or of an unremunerated consumption of labor's capital stock. We might infer, from the respective economic characteristics

by Type, not by Definition. "It is determined, not by a boundary line without, but by a central point within ; not by what it strictly excludes, but by what it eminently includes ; by an example, not by a precept" (Whewell, *History of Scientific Ideas*, vol. ii. p. 120 ; Mill, *System of Logic*, vol. ii. p. 276). Here, as elsewhere in Nature, there are no sharp lines of division. The different trades shade off from each other by imperceptible degrees. So far as we are aware, there is no industry that is completely regulated, none that is completely unregulated and self-supporting, and none that is completely parasitic. Mule-spinning, for example, is a highly-regulated industry, but in so far as it is fed with relays of piecers whom it does not support, it is parasitic on other trades. Agriculture, though mainly driven to be self-supporting, is, in some districts, parasitic on occupations with which it is combined, such as fishing or letting lodgings ; and though mainly unregulated, sometimes employs workmen at wages governed by a Standard Rate, or residing in farm cottages, as to which there is some attempt to enforce the Public Health Acts. The parasitic trades themselves usually employ a modicum of organised labor, and their operations are frequently divided between the highly-regulated factory and the unregulated home. It is accordingly impossible to discover whether or not an industry is parasitic by any such operation as dividing the total wages that it pays among the total number of its employees. Any trade is so far parasitic if it employs any labor which is not entirely maintained and replaced out of the wages and other conditions afforded to that particular labor. Our remarks as to parasitic trades apply, therefore, to all industries whatsoever, in so far as they are parasitic.

of these two sources of industrial advantage, that the regulated trades would expand steadily, generation after generation, improving the quality of their products even more rapidly than reducing their price, and thus tending to oust their rivals principally in the more complicated productive processes and the finer grades of workmanship. The parasitic trades, on the contrary, would form a constantly shifting body, cropping up suddenly in new forms and unexpected places, each in succession gaining a quick start in the world's market by the cheapness of its product, often realising great fortunes, but each gradually losing ground before other competitors, and thus individually failing to secure for itself a permanent place in the nation's industry.

Amid all the complications of human society, it is impossible to give inductive proof of any generalisation whatsoever. But the outcome of our analysis is certainly consistent with the main developments of British trade during the nineteenth century, and with its present aspect. If, for instance, we compare the distribution of industry in Great Britain fifty years ago with that of the present day, we are struck at once by the enormous increase in the proportion occupied by textile manufactures (especially cotton), ship-building, machine-making, and coal-mining,[1] as compared with agriculture, and with those skilled handicrafts like watchmaking, silk-weaving, and glove-making, for which England was once celebrated. To whatever causes we may ascribe the success of the former industries, it is at least a striking coincidence that they are exactly those in which the Device of the Common Rule, whether enforced by Collective Bargaining or Legal Enactment, has been most extensively and continuously applied. Equally significant is the fact that the expansion of our manufactures is now taking place, in the main, less in the lower grades of quality than in the higher. Thus, it is in the finer "counts" of

[1] These four great staple industries now contribute three-quarters of the whole exports of British production, and an ever-increasing proportion of our manufactures for home consumption.

yarn, the best longcloth, and the most elaborately figured muslins—not in the commoner sorts of cotton goods—that Lancashire exports find their widest market. In ship-building, the highly complicated and perfectly finished war-ship and passenger liner are the most distinctively British products. And English steam-engines, tools, and machinery are bought by the foreigner in yearly increasing quantities, not because they are lower-priced than many continental manufactures, but because they more than retain their pre-eminence in quality. Coincidently with this expansion in the most skilled parts of our regulated trades has been the gradual ousting, even in the home market, of our manu-factures of the commoner sorts of joinery, glass, paper, and cutlery—all branches in which the English workmen have never been sufficiently organised to enforce a Standard Rate or a Normal Day.[1] We might follow out this coincidence between expansion and regulation still further, pursuing it across the cleavage of handwork *versus* machinery, and not-ing the success of the highly organised Kentish hand paper-makers and Nottingham machine laceworkers, in comparison with the relative weakness before foreign competition of the machine papermakers and hand laceworkers, both of which have always been practically unorganised trades, earning low wages. It is interesting to note that, with the exception of the hand laceworkers, all these weak or decaying industries are carried on by adult men, and therefore debarred from the ordinary form of parasitic subsidy. But the most remarkable decline of an unregulated and self-supporting industry is afforded by British agriculture. The fact that the English farmer has always been able to hire his labor at practically its bare subsistence, and that, unlike the mill-owner, he is free to exact unlimited hours of work, and is

---

[1] In these very industries the more skilled branches of work, producing the finer kinds of glass, cutlery, paper, and furniture, in which the men insist on high standard conditions, have usually suffered comparatively little from foreign inva-sion, in spite of the fact that their old-fashioned unions have retained the Device of Restriction of Numbers, and have thus, as we believe, prevented an expansion of their crafts.

untrammelled by any sanitary requirements, has, we believe, had the worst possible effect on agricultural prosperity. It has, to begin with, deprived the typically rural industry of anything but the residuum of the rural population. For a whole century the cleverest and most energetic boys, the strongest and most enterprising young men, have been drained from the countryside by the superior conditions offered by the industries governed by the Common Rule. It follows that the employer has for generations had very little choice of labor, and practically no chance of securing fresh relays of workers from other occupations. Moreover, though he may reduce wages to a bare subsistence, he can, in the long run, get no more out of the laborers than his wages provide, for it is upon them and their families that he must rely for a continuance of the service. Hence the scanty food and clothing, long hours, and insanitary housing accommodation of the rural population produce slow, lethargic, and unintelligent labor : the low Standard of Life is, as we have mentioned, accompanied by a low Standard of Work. What is no less important, the employers have, of all classes, troubled least about making inventions or improving their processes. If a farmer cannot make both ends meet, his remedy is to get a reduction of rent. The very fact that an agricultural tenant, unlike a mine owner or a cotton manufacturer, is not held rigidly to his bargain with his landlord, and is frequently excused a part of his rent in unprofitable years, prevents that vigorous weeding out of the less efficient, and that constant supersession of the unfit, which is one of the main factors of the efficiency of Lancashire. It is therefore not surprising that, in a century of unparalleled technical improvement in almost every productive process, the methods of agriculture have, we believe, changed less than those of any other occupation. In the rivalry between trades it has steadily lost ground, securing for itself an ever-dwindling proportion of the nation's capital, and losing constantly more and more of the pick of the population that it nourishes. In the stress of international competition it has gone increasingly to the wall, and far from being selected, like such highly regulated trades as coal mining or engineering, for the supply of the world market, it finds itself losing more and more even of the home trade ; not to any specially favored one among its rivals, but to all of them ; not alone in wheat-growing, but in every other branch of its operations. There are, of course, other causes for the decline of English farming, and we are far from pretending to offer a complete explanation of its relatively backward condition, as compared, say, with shipbuilding or machine-making. But the country gentlemen of 1833-1847, who so willingly imposed the Factory Acts on the millowners, and so vehemently objected to any analogous regulations being applied to agriculture, would possibly not have been so eager to support Lord Shaftesbury if they had understood clearly the economic effects of these Common Rules.[1]

[1] Even within a trade the districts in which the Common Rule is rigidly enforced will often outstrip those lacking this stimulus to improvement. Thus, in cotton-spinning Glasgow once rivalled Lancashire, and for the first third of the present century the two districts did not appreciably differ in the extent of their regulation. During the last sixty years the growth of Trade Unionism in Lancashire has led to a constant elaboration, raising, and ever more stringent enforcement of the Common Rules by which the industry is governed. In Glasgow, on the other hand, the operatives' violence and the employers' autocratic behaviour led to serious outbreaks of crime between 1830 and 1837, followed by drastic repression and the entire collapse of Trade Unionism in the textile industry. From 1838 down to the present day the Glasgow cotton manufacturers have, so far as Trade Unionism is concerned, been practically free to hire their labor as cheaply as they pleased, whilst, owing to the lack of organisation, even the Common Rules of the Factory Acts have, until the last few years, been far less rigidly enforced than in Lancashire. It is at least an interesting coincidence that during this period, whilst other manufacturing industries have enormously progressed, Glasgow cotton-spinning has steadily declined in efficiency. A lower grade of labor is now employed, much of it paid only the barest subsistence wage ; the speed of working and output per operative have failed to increase ; improvements in machinery have been tardily and inadequately adopted ; and no new mills have recently been erected. Only a few establishments now remain out of what was once a flourishing industry, and it is doubtful whether all of these will long survive.

Cloth manufacture supplies a similar example. The cloth mills of the West of England have enjoyed the advantage of inherited tradition, and a world-wide reputation for excellence of quality. Since the very beginning of the century the industry has been entirely free from Trade Unionism. Wages have been exceedingly low, and the Factory Inspector has certainly never been instigated to any particular activity. Water-power is abundant and coal cheap, whilst canals and

Unfortunately, the triumphant progress of the regulated trades, as compared with the unregulated but self-supporting industries, does not complete the picture of our industrial life. In the crowded slums of the great cities, in the far out-stretching suburbs and industrial villages which are transforming so much of Great Britain into cross-cutting chains of houses, there are constantly springing up all sorts and conditions of mushroom manufactures—the innumerable articles of wearing apparel, cheap boots and slippers, walking-sticks and umbrellas, mineral waters and sweetstuffs, the lower grades of furniture and household requisites, bags and boxes, toys and knick-knacks of every kind—in short, a thousand miscellaneous trades, none of which can be compared in permanence or extent with any one of our staple industries, but which in the aggregate absorb a considerable proportion of the custom, capital, and organising capacity of the nation. This is the special field of the "small master," driven perpetually to buy his material on credit and to sell his product to meet the necessities of the hour ; of the speculative trader commanding capital but untrained in the technological details of any mechanical industry ; of armies of working subcontractors, forced by the pressure of competition and the absence of regulation to grind the faces of the poor ; and, on the other hand, of the millions of unorganised workers, men, women, and children, who, from lack of opportunity, lack of strength, or lack of technical training, find themselves unable to escape from districts or trades in which the absence of regulation drives them to accept wages and conditions inconsistent with industrial efficiency. We are here in a region seemingly apart from the world of the Great Industry to which our country owes its industrial predominance. These

railways make both Bristol and London accessible. Yet the cloth manufacturers of Gloucestershire, Somersetshire, and Wiltshire have throughout been steadily losing ground before those of Yorkshire and Lancashire. This decline was expressly attributed by one of the most enterprising of them to the lack of stimulus to improvement, manifest alike among the foremen and the employers. Whether our informant would have consciously welcomed the quickening of Functional Adaptation and Selection of the Fittest, brought about by the Common Rules of a strong Trade Union is, however, doubtful !

'sweated trades" seldom enter into direct competition with the highly-organised and self-supporting staple industries. What happens is that one form of parasitism dogs the steps of the other—the wholesale trader or sub-contractor using up relays of deteriorating outworkers, underbids the factory-owner resorting to the subsidised labor of respectable young women. It is refreshing to notice that when one of these sweated trades does get partially caught up into the factory system, and thus comes under Common Rules with regard to Hours of Labor and Sanitation, the factories, even when they pay little more than pocket-money wages to their women operatives, draw slowly ahead of their more disastrously parasitic rivals.[1] But this very competition of subsidised factory labor with deteriorating outworkers makes things worse for these latter. To what depth of misery and degradation the higgling of the market may reduce the denizens of the slums of our great cities is unsounded by the older economists' pedantic phrase of "subsistence level." Unfortunately the harm that the sweater does lives after him. Men and women who have, for any length of time, been reduced, to quote the House of Lords' Committee, to "earnings barely sufficient to sustain existence; hours of labor such as to make the lives of the workers periods of almost ceaseless toil, hard and unlovely to the last degree; sanitary conditions injurious to the health of the persons employed and dangerous to the public,"[2] become incapable of profitable labor. What they can do is to compete fitfully for the places which they cannot permanently fill, and thus not only drag down the wages of all other unregulated labor, but also contribute, by their irregularity of conduct and incapacity for persistent effort, to the dislocation of the machinery of production. But this is not all. No one who has not himself lived among the poor in London or Glasgow, Liverpool or Manchester,

---

[1] In the slop clothing trade, the factories at Leeds and elsewhere, employing girls and women at extremely low wages, but under good sanitary conditions and fixed hours, are steadily increasing.

[2] *Final Report of the Select Committee of the House of Lords on the Sweating System*, 1890.

can form any adequate idea of the unseen and unmeasured injury to national character wrought by the social contamination to which this misery inevitably leads. One degraded or ill-conducted worker will demoralise a family ; one disorderly family inexplicably lowers the conduct of a whole street ; the low-caste life of a single street spreads its evil influence over the entire quarter ; and the slum quarter, connected with the others by a thousand unnoticed threads of human intercourse, subtly deteriorates the standard of health, morality, and public spirit of the whole city. Thus though the morass does not actually gain on the portion of the nation's life already embanked by the Common Rule, we see it perpetuating itself, and, with the growth of population, even positively increasing in area.[1]

(e) The National Minimum

Though Trade Unionism affords no means of putting down industrial parasitism by sectional action, the analysis of the economic effects of the Device of the Common Rule points the way to the solution of the problem. Within a trade, in the absence of any Common Rule, competition between firms leads, as we have seen, to the adoption of practices by which the whole industry is deteriorated. The

[1] Whilst the proportion of those who fall below the level of healthy subsistence has no doubt greatly decreased in the sixty years 1837-1897, there is good reason to believe that their actual number is at least as large as at any previous date. It may even be larger. See *Labor in the Longest Reign*, by Sidney Webb (London, 1897). How extensive is the area occupied by low-paid occupations may be inferred from Mr. Charles Booth's careful summary of his researches into the economic condition of London's 4½ millions. "The result of all our inquiries make it reasonably sure that *one-third of the population are on or about the line of poverty or are below it*, having at most an income which, one time with another, averages twenty-one shillings or twenty-two shillings for a small family (or up to twenty-five or twenty-six shillings for one of larger size), and in many cases falling much below this level. There may be another third who have perhaps ten shillings more, or taking the year round, from twenty-five to thirty-five shillings a week, among whom would be counted, in addition to wage-earners, many retail tradesmen and small masters ; and the last third would include those who are better off."—*Life and Labour of the People*, vol. ix. p. 427.

enforcement of a common minimum standard throughout the trade not only stops the degradation, but in every way conduces to industrial efficiency. Within a community, too, in the absence of regulation, the competition between trades tends to the creation and persistence in certain occupations of conditions of employment injurious to the nation as a whole. The remedy is to extend the conception of the Common Rule from the trade to the whole community, and by prescribing a National Minimum, absolutely to prevent any industry being carried on under conditions detrimental to the public welfare.[1]

This is, at bottom, the policy of factory legislation, now adopted by every industrial country. But this policy of prescribing minimum conditions, below which no employer is allowed to drive even his most necessitous operatives, has yet been only imperfectly carried out. Factory legislation applies, usually, only to sanitary conditions and, as regards particular classes, to the hours of labor. Even within this limited sphere it is everywhere unsystematic and lop-sided. When any European statesman makes up his mind to grapple seriously with the problem of the " sweated trades " he will have to expand the Factory Acts of his country into a systematic and comprehensive Labor Code, prescribing the minimum conditions under which the community can afford to allow industry to be carried on ; and including not merely definite precautions of sanitation and safety, and maximum hours of toil, but also a minimum of weekly earnings. We do not wish to enter here upon the complicated issues of industrial politics in each country, nor to

---

[1] The majority of English statesmen are convinced that France and Germany in giving bounties out of the taxes to the manufacturers of sugar, are impoverishing their respective communities, to the advantage of the consumers—often the foreign consumers—of the sugar. Yet the cost to France and Germany of this policy is merely a definite annual sum, equivalent to the destruction of an iron-clad or two. If we allow an industry to grow up, which habitually takes more out of its workers than the wages and other conditions of employment enable them to repair,—still more, if the effect of the employment is to deteriorate both character and physique of successive relays of operatives, who are flung eventually on the human rubbish-heap of charity or the Poor Law—is not the nation paying to that industry a bounty far more serious in its cost than any money grant ?

discuss the practical difficulties and political obstacles which everywhere impede the reform and extension of the factory laws. But to complete our economic analysis we must consider what developments of the Trade Union Method of Legal Enactment would be implied by a systematic application of the conception of a National Minimum, and how this might be expected to affect the evils that we have described.

One of the most obvious forms of industrial parasitism is the employment of child-labor. The early textile manufacturer found that it paid best to run his mill almost exclusively by young children, whom he employed without regard to what was to become of them when they grew too big to creep under his machines, and when they required more wages than his labor bill allowed. The resulting degeneracy of the manufacturing population became so apparent that Parliament, in spite of all its prepossessions, was driven to interfere. The Yorkshire Woollen Workers were seeking, like the Flint Glass Makers of to-day, to meet the case by reviving the old period of educational servitude. The Calico-printers were aiming, like the National Union of Boot and Shoe Operatives before Lord James, at a simple limitation of the number of boys to be employed.[1] Neither of these expedients was considered practicable. An alternative remedy was found in prohibiting the manufacturer from

[1] *Minutes of Evidence and Report of the Committee on the Petition of the Journeymen Calico-printers*, 4th July 1804, 17th July 1806 ; Hansard's *Parliamentary Debates*, vol. ix. pp. 534-538 ; *History of Trade Unionism*, p. 50. Our analysis of the economic competition between trades enables us to see that no merely sectional measure would be of use against an illegitimate use of boy-labor. For it is not only the adult workers of the particular trade who are injured. In the competition of trade with trade, whether for home or foreign markets, the illegitimate expansion of a bounty-fed industry necessarily implies a relative contraction of other and possibly quite unrelated trades. It is therefore not only, and perhaps not even principally, the adult boot and shoe operatives who are injured by the undue multiplication of boys in the great boot factories ; such trades as the Flint Glass Makers, who succeed in rigidly limiting their own apprentices, and agriculture, which receives the residuum of boys, probably suffer equally, though in a more indirect way, from the fact that the boot and shoe trade receives this subsidy in aid of its own export trade, and thus encourages an increase of foreign imports which happen to come in the form of German glass and American food stuffs.

employing children below a certain age, and requiring him to see that, up to a farther period, they spent half their days at school. The Factory Acts have, as regards children, long since won their way to universal approval, not merely on humanitarian grounds, but as positively conducive to the industrial efficiency of the community. There is, however, still much to be done before the " Children's Charter " can be said effectually to prevent all parasitic use of child-labor. Though children may not be employed in factories until eleven years of age, nor full time until they are thirteen or fourteen, they are allowed to work at other occupations at earlier ages. " In certain districts of England and Wales, if a child of ten has obtained a certificate of previous due attendance [at school] for five years, he may be employed elsewhere than in a factory, workshop, or mine without any farther educational test or condition, *and without any restriction as to the number of hours*" [1] Even if the law with regard to the employment of children in factories were made uniformly applicable to all occupations in all parts of the United Kingdom, the present limits of age are obviously inadequate to prevent parasitism. England has, in this respect, lost its honorable lead in protective legislation, and we ought at once to raise the age at which any boy or girl may enter industrial life to the fourteen years already adopted by the Swiss federal code,[2] if not to the fifteen years now in force in Geneva, and eventually to the sixteen years demanded by the International Socialist and Trade Union Congress of 1896. It is, however, in an extension of the half-time system that we are likely to find the most effective check on child - labor. We have already seen reason to believe that the only way in which proper technical training can now be secured for the great mass of the people

[1] *Report of Departmental Committee appointed to Inquire into the Conditions of School Attendance and Child-Labor*, H. C. No. 311 of 1893, p. 25. In Ireland school attendance is compulsory only in the towns, and hence children of any age may lawfully be employed in the country districts for any number of hours, night or day, otherwise than in factories, workshops, or mines.

[2] Swiss Federal Factory Law of 23rd March 1877.

is by their deliberate instruction in educational institutions. Such instruction can never be thoroughly utilised so long as the youth has to perform a full and exhausting day's work at the factory or the mine.   There is much to be said, both from an educational and from a purely commercial point of view, for such a gradual extension of the half-time system as would put off until eighteen the working of full factory hours, in order to allow of a compulsory attendance at the technical school and the continuation classes.   Any such proposal would, at present, meet with great opposition from parents objecting to be deprived of their children's earnings. Some of the more thoughtful Trade Unionists are, however, beginning to see that such a development of the half-time system, whilst affording the only practical substitute for the apprenticeship training, would have the incidental advantage of placing, in the most legitimate way, an effective check on any excessive use of boy-labor by the employers.[1]   With the contraction of the supply the rate of boy's wages would rise, so that little less might even be earned for the half day than formerly for full time.   Boy - labor, therefore, would become less profitable to the employers, and would tend to be used by them only for its legitimate purpose of training up a new generation of adult workmen.[2]   To prevent parasitism, in short, we must regard the boy or girl, not as an

---

[1] See, for instance, the *Report of the Trade Unionist Minority of the Royal Commission on Labor*, in C. 7421, 1894.   A somewhat analogous arrangement is already in force in Neuchâtel, under its Apprenticeship Law of 1891, and in some other Swiss cantons.

[2] It might even become necessary for the community to pay a premium for the proper technical education of boys in trades in which employers preferred altogether to dispense with them.   Under private enterprise it requires a certain foresight and permanence of interest for individual employers to have any regard for the rearing up of new generations of skilled operatives.   Thus, whilst some of the best shipbuilding establishments in the North of England bestow considerable attention on their apprentices, the rule in the Midland boot and shoe factories is, as we have seen, to teach the boys practically nothing, and the London builders have left off employing boys at all.   It was found that, in 1895, 41 typical London firms in various branches of the building trades, employing 12,000 journeymen, had only 80 apprentices and 143 other "learners" in their establishments.   (See the report of an inquiry into apprenticeship in the London building trades conducted by the Technical Education Board, published in the *London Technical Education Gazette*, October 1895.)

independent wealth-producer to be satisfied by a daily subsistence, but as the future citizen and parent, for whom, up
to twenty-one, proper conditions of growth and education
are of paramount importance. Hence the Policy of a
National Minimum—the prohibition of all such conditions
of employment as are inconsistent with the maintenance of
the workers in a state of efficiency as producers and citizens
—means, in the case of a child or a youth, the requirement
not merely of daily subsistence and pocket-money, but also
of such conditions of nurture as will ensure the continuous
provision, generation after generation, of healthy and efficient
adults.

In the case of adults, parasitism takes the form, if we
may cite once more the unimpeachable testimony of the
House of Lords, of "earnings barely sufficient to sustain
existence ; hours of labor such as to make the lives of the
workers periods of almost ceaseless toil, hard and unlovely
to the last degree ; sanitary conditions injurious to the health
of the persons employed and dangerous to the public." [1]
Each of these points requires separate consideration.

With regard to sanitation, the law of the United Kingdom
already professes to secure to every manufacturing operative,
whether employed in a factory or a workshop, and whether
man or woman, reasonably healthy conditions of employment. In addition to the general requirements of the Public
Health Acts, the employer has put upon him, by the Factory
Acts, as a condition of being allowed to carry on his industry,
the obligation of providing and maintaining whatever is
necessary for the sanitation and safety of all the persons
whom he employs whilst they are at work on his premises.
If the industry is one by its very nature unhealthy, the employer is required to take the technical precautions deemed
necessary by the scientific experts, and prescribed by special
rules for each occupation. So far the Policy of a National
Minimum of Sanitation would seem to be already embodied

[1] *Final Report of the Select Committee of the House of Lords on the Sweating
System*, 1890.

in English law. But appearances are deceptive. Whole classes of industrial wage-earners find themselves entirely outside the Factory Acts, whilst even of those who are nominally included, large sections are, in one way or another, deprived of any real protection. Hence, far from securing a National Minimum of Sanitation and Safety to every one, the law is at present only brought effectively into force to protect the conditions of employment of the strongest sections of the wage-earners, notably the Coalminers and the Cotton Operatives, whilst the weakest sections of all, notably the outworkers of the " sweated trades," remain as much oppressed in the way of sanitation as they are in hours of labor and wages. If it is desired to carry out the Policy of a National Minimum on this point, Parliament will have to make all employers, whether factory-owners, small workshop masters, or traders giving out material to be made up elsewhere, equally responsible for the sanitary conditions under which their work is done.[1]

When we turn from sanitation to the equally indispensable conditions of leisure and rest, English factory legislation is still more imperfect. It has for fifty years been accepted that it is against public policy for women to be kept to manual labor for more than sixty hours a week, and this principle is supposed to be embodied in the law. But here again, the most oppressed classes—the women working day and night for the wholesale clothiers, or kept standing all day long behind the counter of a shop or the bar of a public-house—who are absolutely excluded from the scope of the law. Even where the law applies, it applies least thoroughly in the most helpless trades. We have already described

[1] A beginning has been made by the sections of the Factory Acts of 1891 and 1895 imposing upon persons giving out work to be done elsewhere than on their own premises certain obligations with regard to the sanitary conditions of their outworkers. In their present form, however, these sections are admittedly unworkable, and no serious effort has yet been made to cope with the evils revealed by the House of Lords' Committee on the Sweating System in 1890. See *Sweating, its Cause and Remedy* (Fabian Tract, No. 50), *How to do away with the Sweating System*, by Beatrice Potter (Mrs. Sidney Webb) (Co-operative Union pamphlet), and the *Trade Unionist Minority Report of the Royal Commission on Labor*, in C. 7421, 1894.

how, in all non-textile industries, the overtime provisions destroy the efficacy of the Factory Act,[1] and, in such cases as laundry-workers and dressmakers in small shops, render it practically of no avail. It is one more instance of the irony of English labor legislation that the women in the textile mills have alone secured a really effective limitation of their hours of labor, and this as low as $56\frac{1}{2}$ hours a week, in spite of the fact that they are, of all women workers, the least helpless and, as a class, the best off. And when we pass from women to men, the statute book with regard to the hours of labor is at present a blank, relieved only by the tentative provisions of the Railway Regulation Act of 1893. Before we can be said to have established a National Minimum of leisure and rest, the provisions of the Factory Acts with regard to textile factories will have to be made applicable, with the special modifications appropriate to each particular occupation, to all manual workers whatsoever.

But sanitation and leisure do not, of themselves, maintain the nation's workers in health and efficiency, or prevent industrial parasitism. Just as it is against public policy to allow an employer to engage a woman to work excessive hours or under insanitary conditions, so it is equally against public policy to permit him to engage her for wages insufficient to provide the food and shelter, without which she cannot continue in health. Once we begin to prescribe the minimum conditions under which an employer should be permitted to open a factory, there is no logical distinction to be drawn between the several clauses of the wage contract. From the point of view of the employer, one way of increasing the cost of production is the same as another, whilst to the economist and the statesman, concerned with the permanent efficiency of industry and the maintenance of national health, adequate food is at least as important as reasonable hours or good drainage. To be completely effectual, the Policy of the National Minimum will, therefore, have to be applied to wages.

[1] See a preceding chapter on "The Normal Day."

The proposition of a National Minimum of wages—the enactment of a definite sum of earnings per week below which no employer should be allowed to hire any worker—has not yet been put forward by any considerable section of Trade Unionists, nor taken into consideration by any Home Secretary. This reluctance to pass to the obvious completion of the policy of factory legislation, at once logical and practical, arises, we think, from a shrinking, both on the part of workmen and employers, from having all wages fixed by law. But this is quite a different proposition. The fixing of a National Minimum of Sanitation has not prevented the erection in our great industrial centres of workplaces which, compared with the minimum prescribed by the law, are palatial in their provision of light, air, cubic space, warmth, and sanitary accommodation. And a National Minimum of leisure and rest, fixed, for instance, at the textile standard of $56\frac{1}{2}$ hours' work a week, would in no way interfere with the Northumberland Coalminers maintaining their 37 hours' week, or the London Engineers bargaining for a 48 hours' week. There is even less reason why, with regard to wages, the enactment of a National Minimum should interfere with the higher rates actually existing, or in future obtained, in the tens of thousands of distinct occupations throughout the country. The fact that the Committees of the London County Council are precluded, by its Standing Orders, from employing any workman at less than 24s. a week, does not prevent their engaging workmen at all sorts of higher rates, according to agreement. And if the House of Commons were to replace its present platonic declaration against the evils of sweating by an effective minimum, the superintendents of the various Government departments would still go on paying their higher rates to all but the lowest grade of workmen.

The object of the National Minimum being to secure the community against the evils of industrial parasitism, the minimum wage for a man or a woman respectively would be determined by practical inquiry as to the cost of the food, clothing, and shelter physiologically necessary, according to national habit and custom, to prevent bodily deterioration. Such a minimum would therefore be low, and though its establishment would be welcomed as a boon by the unskilled workers in the unregulated trades, it would not at all correspond with the conception of a "Living Wage" formed by the Cotton Operatives or the Coalminers. It would be a matter for careful consideration what relation the National Minimum for adult men should bear to that for adult women; what differences, if any, should be made between town and country; and whether the standard should be fixed by national authority (like the hours of labor for young persons and women), or by local authority (like the educational qualification for child-labor). To those not practically acquainted with the organisation of English industry and Government administration, the idea will seem impracticable. But, as a matter of fact, the authoritative settlement of a minimum wage is already daily undertaken. Every local governing body throughout the country has to decide under the criticism of public opinion what wage it will pay to its lowest grade of laborers. It can hire them at any price, even at a shilling a day; but what happens in practice is that the officer in charge fixes such a wage as he believes he can permanently get good enough work for. In the same way the national Government, which is by far the largest employer of labor in the country, does not take the cheapest laborers it can get, at the lowest price for which they will offer themselves, but deliberately settles its own minimum wage for each department. During the last few years this systematic determination of the rate to be paid for Government labor, which must have existed since the days of Pepys, has been more and more consciously based upon what we have called the Doctrine of a Living Wage. Thus the Admiralty is now constantly taking evidence, either through the Labor Department or through its own officials, as to the cost of living in different localities, so as to adjust its laborers' wages to the expense of their subsistence. And in our local governing bodies we see the committees, under the pressure of public opinion, every day substituting a deliberately settled minimum for the haphazard decisions of the officials of the several departments.[1] What is not so generally recognised is that exactly the same change is taking place in private enterprise. The great captains of industry, interested in the permanent efficiency of their establishments, have long adopted the practice of deliberately fixing the minimum wage to be paid to the lowest class of unskilled laborers, according to their own view of what the laborers can live on, instead of letting out their work to subcontractors, whose only object is to exact the utmost exertion for the lowest price. A railway company never dreams of putting its situations out to tender, and engaging the man who offers to come at the lowest wage : what happens is that the rate of pay of porters and shunters is deliberately fixed in advance. And it is a marked feature of the last ten years that the settlement of this minimum has been, in some of the greatest industries, taken out of the hands of the individual employer, and arrived at by an arbitrator. The assumption that the wages of the lowest grade of labor must at any rate be enough to maintain the laborer in industrial efficiency is, in fact, accepted by both parties, so that the task of the arbitrator is comparatively easy. Lord James, for instance, has lately fixed, with universal acceptance, a minimum wage for all the lowlier grades of labor employed

---

[1] An interesting survey of the steps taken to secure the payment of the Standard Rate to persons working for public authorities in France, the United Kingdom, Belgium, Holland, Italy, and Switzerland, is given by Auguste Keufer in his *Rapport tendant à rechercher les moyens de parer aux funestes conséquences du système actuel des adjudications* (Paris, 1896, 48 pp.). See also Louis Katzenstein, *Die Lohnfrage unter dem Englischen Submissionswesen* (Berlin, 1896) ; the important *Enquête* of the Communal Council of Brussels into the effect of fixing and of not fixing the rates of wages payable in public contract works, 2 vols. (Brussels, 1896) ; and the *Report of the House of Commons' Committee on the Conditions of Government Contracts* (H. C. 334), July 1897.

In order to put a stop to the practice of engaging learners or improvers without any salary whatsoever, the Victorian Factories and Shops Act of 1896 (No. 1445) enacts (sec. 16) that "no person whatsoever, unless in receipt of a weekly wage of at least two shillings and sixpence, shall be employed in any factory or workroom."

by the North Eastern Railway Company.[1] Indeed, the fixing of a minimum wage on physiological grounds is a less complicated matter, and one demanding less technological knowledge than the fixing of a minimum of sanitation ; and it interferes far less with the day-by-day management of industry, or its productivity, than any fixing of the hours of labor, whether of women or men. To put it concretely, if Colonel Dyer (of Armstrong's) and Mr. Livesey (of the South Metropolitan Gas Works) could for a moment rid themselves of their metaphysical horror of any legal regulation of wages, they would admit that the elaborate Factory Act requirements in the way of Sanitation and Safety, and any limitation of the Hours of Labor, constitute a far greater impediment to their management of their own business in the way they think best than would any National Minimum of wages for the lowest grade of labor. As a matter of fact, what would happen would be the adoption, as the National Minimum, of the wages actually paid by the better establishments, who would accordingly be affected only to the extent of finding their competitors put on the same level as themselves.[2]

More formidable than any *à priori* objection to the National Minimum on the part of employers who would really be unaffected by it, would be the vehement obstruction that any such proposal would meet with from the profit-

---

[1] See his award in the *Labour Gazette* for August 1897.

[2] We desire to emphasise the point that, whatever political objections there may be to the fixing by law of a National Minimum Wage, and whatever practical difficulties there may be in carrying it out, the proposal, *from the point of view of abstract economics*, is open to no more objection than the fixing by law of a National Minimum of Sanitation, or a National Minimum of Leisure, both of which are, in principle, embodied in our factory legislation. Indeed, a minimum wage, since it could in no way interfere with the fullest use of machinery and plant, or otherwise check productivity, would seem to be even less open to economic criticism than a limitation of the hours of labor.

It must not be supposed that the National Minimum of wages would necessarily involve payment by time. There would be no objection to its taking the form of Standard Piecework Lists, provided that these were combined, as they always are in efficient Trade Unions, with a guarantee that, so long as an operative is in the employer's service, he must be provided each week with sufficient work at the Standard Piece Rate to make up the minimum weekly earnings, or be paid for his time.

makers in the parasitic trades. This obstruction would
inevitably concentrate itself into two main arguments. They
would assert that if they had to give decent conditions to
every person they employed, their trade would at once
become unprofitable, and would either cease to exist, or be
driven out of the country. And, quite apart from this
shrinking of the area of employment, what, they would ask,
would become of the feeble and inefficient, the infirm and
the aged, the "workers without a character," or the "poor
widows," who now pick up some kind (that is, some part) of
a livelihood, and who would inevitably be not worth employing at all if they had to be paid the National Minimum
wage?

The enactment of a National Minimum would by no
means necessarily involve the destruction of the trades at
present carried on by parasitic labor. When any particular
way of carrying on an industry is favored by a bounty or
subsidy, this way will almost certainly be chosen, to the
exclusion of other methods of conducting the business. If
the subsidy is withdrawn, it often happens that the industry
falls back on another process which, less immediately profitable to the capitalists than the bounty-fed method, proves
positively more advantageous to the industry in the long
run. This result, familiar to the Free Trader, is even more
probable when the bounty or subsidy takes the form, not of
a protective tariff, an exemption from taxation, or a direct
money grant, but the privilege of exacting from the manual
workers more labor-force than is replaced by the wages and
other conditions of employment. The existence of negro
slavery in the Southern States of America made, while it
lasted, any other method of carrying on industry economically
impossible ; but it was not really an economic advantage to
cotton-growing. The "white slavery" of the early factory
system stood, so long as it was permitted, in the way of any
manufacturer adopting more humane conditions of employment ; but when the Lancashire millowners had these more
humane conditions forced upon them, they were discovered

to be more profitable than those which unlimited freedom of competition had dictated. There is much reason to believe that the low wages to which, in the unregulated trades, the stream of competitive pressure forces employers and operatives alike, are not in themselves any more economically advantageous to the industry than the long hours and absence of sanitary precautions were to the early cotton mills of Lancashire. To put it plumply, if the employers paid more, the labor would quickly be worth more. In so far as this proved to be the case, the National Minimum would have raised the Standard of Life without loss of work, without cost to the employer, and without disadvantage to the community. Moreover, the mere fact that employers are at present paying lower wages than the proposed minimum is no proof that the labor is not " worth " more to them and to the customers ; for the wages of the lowest grade of labor are fixed, not by the worth of the individual laborer, but largely by the necessities of the marginal man. It may well be that, rather than go without the particular commodity produced, the community would willingly pay more for it. Nevertheless, so long as the wage-earner can be squeezed down to a subsistence or, more correctly, a parasitic wage, the pressure of competition will compel the employer so to squeeze him, whether the consumer desires it or not.

It may, however, be admitted that a prohibition of parasitism would have the effect of restricting certain industries. The ablest, best-equipped, and best situated employers would find themselves able to go on under the new conditions, and would even profit by the change. The firms just struggling on the margin would probably go under. It might even happen that particular branches of the sweated trades would fall into the hands of other countries. If the French Government withdrew its present bounties on the production of sugar, some French establishments would certainly be shut up, and the total exports of French sugar, other things remaining equal,

would be diminished. But all economists will agree that
the mere keeping alive a trade by a bounty, whatever other
advantages it may be supposed to have, does not, of itself,
increase the aggregate trade of the country, or the area of
employment. What the bounty does is to divert to sugar
production capital and labor which would otherwise have
been devoted to the production of other articles, presumably
to greater profit, for otherwise the bounty would not have
been required. When the bounty is withdrawn this diversion ceases, and the available capital and labor is re-distrib-
uted over the nation's industry in the more profitable way.
And if it be replied that there will be no demand for these
other articles, the answer is clear. If the bounty-fed sugar
ceases to be exported, the commodities given in exchange
for it cease to be imported, and have to be produced at
home. The capital and labor which formerly produced
sugar is now free to produce the commodities which were
formerly obtained by the export of the sugar. In short, the
aggregate product remaining the same, the aggregate demand
cannot be lessened, for they are but different aspects of one
and the same thing.

Exactly the same reasoning holds good with regard to
what we have called the parasitic trades. Assuming that
the employers in these trades have hitherto been getting
more labor-force than their wages have been replacing, any
effective enforcement of a National Minimum of conditions
of employment would be equivalent to a simple withdrawal
of a bounty. We should, therefore, expect to see a
shrinkage in these trades. But there would be at least a
corresponding expansion in others. Let us, for instance,
imagine that the wholesale clothiers are compelled to give
decent conditions to all their outworkers. It may be that
this will cause a rise in the cost of production of certain
lines of clothing. This will certainly diminish their export
sales, and might even close particular markets altogether.
This check to our export trade will have one of two results.
If our imports go on undiminished, the aggregate of our

exports must, to meet our foreign indebtedness, be made up somehow, and international demand will cause other branches of our export trade to expand. Hence the result of destroying parasitism in the wholesale clothing trade would, on this hypothesis, be to cause a positive increase in the exports, and thus in the number of producers, of such things as textiles, machinery, or coal. But it may be urged that the slackening of the wholesale clothing trade would cause our imports to fall off. In that case there would at last be a gleam of hope for the poor English farmer, whose sales would expand to meet the demand formerly satisfied by foreign food stuffs. Hence it follows that, whatever new distribution of the nation's industry might be produced by the prohibition of parasitism, there is no ground for fearing that the aggregate production, and therefore either the aggregate demand or the total area of employment, would be in any way diminished.[1]

---

[1] It may be interesting to follow out this argument to its logical conclusion. Let us assume a country in which all trades whatsoever are parasitic—that is to say, where every manual worker is working under conditions which do not suffice to keep him permanently in industrial efficiency. In this case an enforcement of a National Minimum would necessarily raise the expenses of production to the capitalist employer (though not the actual labor cost) of all the commodities produced. The economist would nevertheless advise the adoption of the policy. It would be of vital importance, in the economic interests of the community as a whole, to stop the social degradation and industrial deterioration implied by the universal parasitism. The increased cost of production, due to the stoppage of this drawing on the future, would cause a general rise in prices. It is often assumed that such a rise would counteract the advantages of the higher wages. Mr. Herbert Spencer, in the concluding volume of his *Synthetic Philosophy*, naïvely makes this his one economic objection to Trade Unionism. "If," he says, "wages are forced up, the price of the article produced must presently be forced up. What then happens if, as now, Trade Unions are established among the workers in nearly all occupations, and if these unions severally succeed in making wages higher? All the various articles they are occupied in making must be raised in price ; and each trade unionist, while so much the more in pocket by advanced wages, is so much the more out of pocket by having to buy things at advanced rates " (*Industrial Institutions*, London, 1896, p. 536). But this is to assume that the wage-earners purchase as consumers the whole of the commodities and services which they produce. We need not remind the reader that this is untrue. In the United Kingdom, for instance, though the wage-earners number four-fifths of the population, they consume—to take the highest estimate — only between one-third and two-fifths of the annual aggregate of products and services, the remainder being enjoyed by the propertied classes and the brain-workers. Even if a general rise in wages, amounting to say fifty

The question then arises what effect the prohibition of parasitism would have on the individuals at present working in the sweated trades. We need not dwell on the inevitable personal hardships incidental to any shifting of in-industry or change of process. Any deliberate improvement

millions sterling, produced a general rise in prices to the extent of fifty millions sterling, spread equally over all products, it could not be said that the wage-earners as a class would have to bear on their own purchases more than one-third to two-fifths of this additional price. If the rise in price was not spread equally over all commodities and services, but occurred only in those consumed by the other classes, the rise in wages would have been a net gain to the wage-earners. Only in the impossible case of the rise occurring exclusively in the commodities consumed by the wage-earning classes—these commodities being, as we have seen, only one-third to two-fifths of the whole—would that class find its action in raising wages nullified in the simple manner that Mr. Spencer imagines. Hence it is, that even if a rise in the Standard of Life of the whole wage-earning class produces an equivalent general rise in the price of commodities, the result must nevertheless be a net gain to the wage-earners. This process might, theoretically, be carried very far, the ultimate sufferers being the non-working recipients of rent and interest, whose incomes, nominally unimpaired, would purchase progressively less of the annual product. Practically, however, any indefinite rise of wages would be limited by the impossibility of inducing the community of citizen-consumers to sanction, in the interests of the lowliest sections, anything in the way of a legal minimum wage—involving, as this would, a mulcting of the vast majority of the better-off purchasers—which did not commend itself to this majority as being necessary to the public welfare.

Nor can it be inferred that any such general rise in the price of labor, even if it caused a general rise in the price of commodities, would adversely affect the nation's foreign trade. A rise in the price of any one commodity has, almost invariably, an immediate effect upon the volume of the import or export trade *in that commodity*. But if the rise in prices is general and uniform in all the commodities of the community, the aggregate volume of the exports of that community will not be diminished merely by reason of the rise. It is a truism, not only of the academic economists, but also of the practical financiers of all nations, that the imports of our country (together with any other foreign indebtedness) must, on an average of years, be paid for by our exports, taking into account any other obligations of foreigners to us. Any general increase in the cost of labor, such as a rise in the Standard of Life, a general advance of factory legislation, or a universal Eight Hours' Day if we may assume for the sake of argument that this results in a *uniform* rise of prices, would leave our annual indebtedness to foreign countries undiminished, even if it did not increase it by temporarily stimulating imports. Hence it is inferred with certainty that a merely general and uniform rise in prices in one country will not prevent goods to the same aggregate value as before from being exported to discharge that indebtedness. To put it shortly, the mere fact that the manual laborers receive a larger proportion, and the directors of industry or capitalists a smaller proportion of the aggregate product, has no influence on the total volume, or the profitableness to the nation, of its international trade. See Appendix II., in which this question is fully dealt with.

in the distribution of the nation's industry ought, therefore, to be brought about gradually, and with equitable consideration of the persons injuriously affected. But there is no need to assume that anything like all those now receiving less than the National Minimum would be displaced by its enactment.

We see, in the first place, that the very levelling up of the standard conditions of sanitation, hours, and wages would, in some directions, positively stimulate the demand for labor. The contraction of the employment of boys and girls, brought about by the needful raising of the age for full and half time respectively, would, in itself, increase the number of situations to be filled by adults. The enforcement of the Normal Day, by stopping the excessive hours of labor now worked by the most necessitous operatives, would tend to increase the number employed. Moreover, the expansion of the self-supporting trades which would, as we have seen, accompany any shrinking of the sweated industries, would automatically absorb the best of the unemployed workers in their own and allied occupations, and would create a new demand for learners. Finally, the abandonment of that irregularity of employment which so disastrously affects the outworkers and the London dock-laborers, would result in the enrolment of a new permanent staff. All these changes would bring into regular work at or above the National Minimum whole classes of operatives, selected from among those now only partially or fitfully employed. Thus, all the most capable and best conducted would certainly obtain regular situations. But this concentration of employment would undoubtedly imply the total exclusion of others who might, in the absence of regulation, have "picked up" some sort of a partial livelihood. In so far as these permanently unemployed consisted merely of children, removed from industrial work to the schoolroom, few would doubt that the change would be wholly advantageous. And there are many who would welcome a re-organisation of industry which, by concentrating employment exclusively among those in regular attendance, would tend to exclude from wage-labor, and to set free for domestic duties, an ever-increasing proportion of the women having young children to attend to. There would still remain to be considered the remnant who, notwithstanding the increased demand for adult male labor and independent female labor, proved to be incapable of earning the National Minimum in any capacity whatsoever. We should, in fact, be brought face to face with the problem, not of the unemployed, but of the unemployable.

(f) The Unemployable

Here we must, once for all, make a distinction of vital importance : we must mark off the Unemployable from the temporarily unemployed. The case of the workman, normally able to earn his own living, who is unemployed merely because there is, for the moment, no work for him to do, stands on an altogether different plane from that of the man who is unemployed because he is at all times incapable of holding a regular situation, and producing a complete maintenance. Periods of unemployment, if only while shifting from job to job, are, in nearly all trades, an inevitable incident in the life of even the most competent and the best conducted workman. To diminish the frequency and duration of these times of enforced idleness, to mitigate the hardships that they cause, and to prevent them from producing permanent degradation of personal character is, as we have seen, one of the foremost objects of Trade Unionism.[1] But this evil, arising mainly from the seasonal or cyclical fluctuations in the volume of employment for the competent, has no relation to the problem of how to deal with the incompetent. So long as these two problems are hopelessly entangled with each other, and habitually regarded as one and the same thing, any scientific treatment of either of them is impossible.

The problem of the Unemployable is not created by the

[1] We recur to this in our next chapter, "Trade Unionism and Democracy."

fixing of a National Minimum by law. The Unemployable we have always with us. With regard to certain sections of the population, this unemployment is not a mark of social disease, but actually of social health. From the standpoint of national efficiency, no less than from that of humanity, it is desirable that the children, the aged, and the child-bearing women should not be compelled by their necessities to earn their own maintenance in the labor market. But in all other cases, incapacity or refusal to produce a livelihood is a symptom of ill-health or disease, physical or mental. With regard to the principal classes of these Unemployable—the sick and the crippled, the idiots and lunatics, the epileptic, the blind and the deaf and dumb, the criminals and the incorrigibly idle, and all who are actually " morally deficient " —the incapacity is the result of individual disease from which no society can expect to be completely free. But we have a third section of the Unemployable, men and women who, without suffering from apparent disease of body or mind, are incapable of steady or continuous application, or who are so deficient in strength, speed, or skill that they are incapable, in the industrial order in which they find themselves, of producing their maintenance at any occupation whatsoever. The two latter sections—the physically or mentally diseased and the constitutionally inefficient—may, in all their several subdivisions, either be increased or diminished in numbers according to the wisdom of our social arrangements. If we desire to reduce these Unemployable to a minimum, it is necessary, as regards each of the subsections, to pursue a twofold policy. We must, on the one hand, arrange our social organisation in such a way that the smallest possible amount of such degeneracy, whether physical or mental, is produced. We must, on the other hand, treat the cases that are produced in such a way as to arrest the progress of the malady, and as far as possible restore the patient to health.[1]

[1] As regards bodily disease, this twofold policy is now prescribed by the Public Health Acts. To maintain a high standard of health, " common rules "

Now, we cannot here enter into the appropriate social regimen and curative treatment best calculated to minimise the production of the Unemployable in each subdivision, and to expedite the recovery of such as are produced. These physical and moral weaklings and degenerates must somehow be maintained at the expense of other persons. They may be provided for from their own property or savings, by charity or from public funds, with or without being set to work in whatever ways are within their capacity. But of all ways of dealing with these unfortunate parasites the most ruinous to the community is to allow them unrestrainedly to compete as wage-earners for situations in the industrial organisation. For this at once prevents competition from resulting in the Selection of the Most Fit, and thus defeats its very object.[1] In the absence of any Common Rule, it will, as we have seen, often pay an employer to select a physical or moral invalid, who offers his services for a parasitic wage, rather than the most efficient workman, who stands out for the conditions necessary for the maintenance of his efficiency. In the same way, a whole industry may batten on parasitic labor, diverting the nation's capital and brains from more productive processes, and undermining the position of its more capable artisans. And where the industrial parasitism takes the form of irregular employment—as, for instance, among the outworkers in all great cities and the London dock-laborers—its effect is actually to extend the area of the disease. The sum of employment given would suffice to keep in regular work, at something like adequate weekly earnings, a certain proportion of these casual workers. But because it is distributed, as partial employment and partial maintenance, among the entire class, its insufficiency and irregularity demoralise all alike, and render whole sections

as to drainage and water-supply, nuisances, and overcrowding are enforced on every one. To deal with such disease as nevertheless occurs, hospitals are provided. And when it is supposed that the sick contaminate those who are well, isolation and proper treatment are compulsory.

[1] "The main function of competition is that of selection."—Professor Foxwell (in the essay cited on p. 689).

of the population of our large cities permanently incapable of regular conduct and continuous work. Thus, the disease perpetuates itself, and becomes, by its very vastness, incapable of being isolated and properly treated. A dim appreciation of the evil effects of any mixing of degenerates in daily life, joined, of course, with motives of humanity, has caused the sick and the infirm, the imbeciles and the lunatics, even the cripples and the epileptics, to be, in all civilised communities, increasingly removed off the competitive labor market, and scientifically dealt with according to their capacities and their needs. The "Labor Colonies" of Holland and Germany are, from this point of view, an extension of the same policy. To maintain our industrial invalids, even in idleness, from public funds, involves a definite and known burden on the community. To allow them to remain at large, in parasitic competition with those who are whole, is to contaminate the labor market, and means a disastrous lowering of the Standard of Life and Standard of Conduct, not for them alone, but for the entire wage-earning class.[1]

Thus, in our opinion, the adoption of the Policy of a National Minimum of education, sanitation, leisure, and wages would in no way increase the amount of maintenance which has to be provided by the community in one form or another, for persons incapable of producing their own keep. It would, on the contrary, tend steadily to reduce it, both by diminishing the number of weaklings or degenerates annually produced, and by definitely marking out such as exist, so that they could be isolated and properly treated.[2]

---

[1] If the wages of every class of labor, under perfect competition, tend to be no more than the net produce due to the additional labor of the marginal laborer of that class, who is on the verge of not being employed at all, the abstraction of the paupers, not necessarily from productive labor for themselves but from the competitive labor market, by raising the capacity of the marginal wage-laborer, would seem to increase the wages of the entire laboring class.

[2] The persons withdrawn from the competitive labor market, whether as invalids or aged, paupers or criminals, need not necessarily be idle. It would, on the contrary, usually be for their own good, as well as for the pecuniary interest of the community, that they should do such work as they are capable of. But it is of vital importance that their products should not be sold in the open market. If their products are sold, they must inevitably undercut the wares

The exact point at which the National Minimum should be fixed will, however, always be a matter of keen discussion. It will clearly be to the direct advantage of the wage-earning class, and especially to the large majority of self-supporting but comparatively unskilled adult laborers, that the National Minimum should be fixed as high as possible, as this will ensure to them a good wage. Moreover, every trade momentarily hard pressed by foreign competition, whether by way of import or of export trade, will see an advantage to itself in raising the Standard of Life of those who are indirectly its rivals. Even those employers who are already paying more than the minimum will be drawn by their economic interests in this direction. On the other hand, the employers in trades using low-paid labor would resent the dislocation to which a compulsory raising of conditions would subject them, and they would find powerful allies in the whole body of taxpayers, alarmed at the prospect of having

made by self-supporting operatives, who will therefore find their employment rendered less continuous than it would otherwise be, and *who will accordingly be unable to resist the reductions forced upon them by their employers.* This is not, as is often argued, because the institution laborers displace other operatives, but because they lower the price of the product. The psychological effect on the market is even more serious than the direct displacement of custom. Every private manufacturer fears that he may be the one destined to lose his customers to the institution which need not consider cost of production at all ; and this fear supplies the buyers with an irresistible lever for forcing down price. The harm lies in this lowering of the Standard of Life of other classes, not in any mere diversion from them of possible additional custom. Hence there is no economic harm, and nothing but gain, in the inmates of institutions producing for consumption or use inside the institution. This has no tendency to lower prices or wages outside, any more than the fact that sailors at sea wash their own clothes lowers the wages of laundresses on land. And there would be no economic harm in the supported workers performing the whole of some new service for the community, if this was within their capacity, and if it paid better to keep all the more efficient workers employed in other ways. The same would be the case if the service were not new, and if it were, with due consideration for existing workers, wholly taken out of the domain of competitive industry. Thus the time might arrive when all efficient Englishmen would be able to employ their brains and labor to greater advantage than in growing cereals and breeding stock ; and the main processes of agriculture might become, perhaps in conjunction with municipal sewage-farms, abattoirs, and dairies, exclusively Poor Law occupations, producing not for profit but for the sake of providing healthful occupation for the paupers, the infirm, and the aged, and selling their produce in competition only with foreign imports at the prices determined by these.

to maintain in public institutions an enlarged residuum of the Unemployable. The economist would be disinclined to give much weight to any of these arguments, and would rather press upon the statesman the paramount necessity of so fixing and gradually raising the National Minimum as progressively to increase the efficiency of the community as a whole, without casting an undue burden on the present generation of taxpayers.

(g) *Summary of the Economic Characteristics of the Device of the Common Rule*

The preceding analysis of the economic effects of the Device of the Common Rule, first as practised by isolated and separate trades, then as limited by the substitution of alternative processes or alternative products, at home or abroad ; and finally extended, by way of check on the illegitimate use of this substitution, from particular trades to the community as a whole, will have revealed to the student the conditions under which each trade, and the whole body of wage-earners, will obtain the best conditions of employment then and there practicable, and at the same time the manner in which the utmost possible efficiency of the nation's industry will be secured.

We see, to begin with, that the need for the Common Rule is greatest at the very base of the social pyramid.[1] The first necessity for obtaining the greatest possible efficiency of the community as a whole, is so to control the struggle for existence that no section is pushed by it into parasitism or degeneration. In the interests of the economically independent sections of wage-earners, whose labor

[1] On the social importance of not abandoning to themselves those weakest classes of wage-earners who are unable to form strong combinations, see Dr. Heinrich Herkner's *Die Sociale Reform als Gebot des Wirtschaftlichen Fortschrittes* (Leipzig, 1891), ch. x. ; and the reports entitled *Arbeitseinstellungen und Fortbildung des Arbeitervertrages* (Leipzig, 1890), pp. 12, 35, etc.

might be displaced by a parasitic class of workers, no less
than in the interests of the whole community of citizens,
threatened with the growth of degenerate or dependent
classes, it is vitally important to construct a solid basis for
the industrial pyramid, below which no section of wage-
earners, however great the pressure, can ever be forced.
Such an extension of the Device of the Common Rule from
the trade to the whole nation—the enforcement of National
Minimum conditions as to sanitation and safety, leisure and
wages, below which no industry should be allowed to be
carried on—would, we may infer, have the same economic
effect on the industry of the community as the introduction
of the Common Rule has on each particular trade.   Thus it
would in no way prevent competition between trades, or
lessen its intensity.   The consumer would be free to select
whatever product he preferred, whether it was made by men
or by women, by hand or by machinery, by his own countrymen or by foreigners.   The capitalist would be free to
introduce any machinery, to use any process, or to employ
any class of labor that he thought most profitable to himself.
The operative, whether man or woman, would be free to
enter any trade, or to change from one trade to another, as
he or she might be disposed.   All that the community would
require would be that there should be no parasitic labor ;
that is to say, that no employer should be allowed to offer,
and no operative should be permitted to accept, employment
under conditions below the minimum which the community
had decided to be necessary to keep the lowest class in full
and continued efficiency as producers and citizens.   Under
these circumstances the pressure of competition would be
shifted from wages to quality.   Alike between classes, processes, and products, a genuine Selection of the Fittest, un-
handicapped by any bounty, would have free play.   If one
class of operatives superseded another class, it would be
because the successful workers could perform the service
positively better than their rivals, whilst themselves accepting
no subsidy and suffering no deterioration.   The result would

be that, the necessary conditions of health being secured, the struggle for existence would take the form of progressive Functional Adaptation to a higher level, each class seeking to maintain its position by improving its technical capacity.[1]

This National Minimum of conditions for the most helpless and dependent grades of labor can, it is obvious, be obtained only by the Method of Legal Enactment, and it will represent, not the ideal condition which each section strives to attain for itself, but what the bulk of better-off citizens are willing to concede to a minority of less fortunate persons in order to avoid the financial burden and social contamination involved in the growth of parasitic or degenerate classes. But if the maximum income for the workers in each trade, and also the maximum efficiency of the whole industrial machine is to be secured, no section will remain satisfied with these minimum conditions. The greatest possible progress will be obtained by each grade of labor organising itself, and perpetually pushing upwards— seeking by the Device of the Common Rule to divert, within each occupation, the whole force of competition from wages to quality, from remuneration to service, so as to secure always the selection for employment of those individuals who have the most developed faculties, rather than those who have the

[1] To give only two out of many instances, we can imagine nothing more calculated to improve the social position of women, and to render them economically independent of their sexual relationship, than the gradual introduction of a legal minimum wage, below which their employment should not be permitted. Nothing does so much at present to prevent women becoming technically proficient in industry, and to deprive girls of incentive to acquire technical education, than their feeling that they can obtain employment as they are, if only they will accept low enough wages ! The result of the low wages is a deplorably low standard of efficiency, due to lack alike of proper physiological conditions and of stimulus to greater exertions. The improvement in the capacity and technical efficiency of women teachers in the last twenty years, concurrently with the introduction of fixed standards of qualification by the Education Department and, to some extent, the adoption by School Boards of full subsistence wages, is especially significant in this connection. The other instance is that of the casual unskilled laborer of the great cities. At present he knows that he can earn his miserable pittance by transient employment, without a character, without regularity of attendance day by day, and without technical skill. A legal minimum weekly wage would induce the employers to pick their men, and at once set up a Selection of the Fittest for regularity, trustworthiness, and skill.

fewest needs. The object of each section will be to raise its own service to the highest possible degree of specialised excellency, and to differentiate itself to the utmost from the unspecialised and " unskilled " labor, commanding only the National Minimum. In this way, each body of specialists becomes able to insist on its own " rent of ability " or " rent of opportunity." The more open the occupation is to newcomers, and the more attractive are the conditions that are obtained by those who are already employed, the more effective will become the constant Selection of the Fittest. The more progressive is the industry and the more opportunities it provides for technical instruction, the greater will be the Functional Adaptation to a higher level. And so long as this progressive raising of the Common Rule brings with it, either through Functional Adaptation or the Selection of the Fittest, an equivalent increase in the operatives' own productive efficiency, the added wages, or other improvement of conditions, will in themselves constitute a clear addition to the income of the community. And in so far as the maintenance of the Common Rule brings pressure to bear on the brains of the employers, so as to compel them to improve the technical processes of the trade ; and in so far as the progressive raising of the standard concentrates industry in the hands of the most capable employers, in the best-equipped establishments, in the most advantageous sites, the organised wage-earners, in seeking to improve their own conditions, will incidentally have positively added to the resources of the other classes of the community as well as to their own. So far the improvement in the wage-earners' condition need not lead to any rise in the price of commodities. When, however, the operatives in any given industry have exhausted the increased efficiency due to Functional Adaptation and the Selection of the Fittest, whether acting on the employers or on workmen, any further advance of wages will, unless under very exceptional conditions, result in a slackening of the demand for their product. The same result happens in the more frequent case of the advance in wages outstripping for a time the increase in efficiency, or again, even without a rise of wages or of prices, a change of fashion or a new invention may cause the substitution of another grade of labor. In all these cases, the progress of the advance movement of a particular trade will be effectively stopped by an increase in the proportion of its unemployed members. This, indeed, marks the limit of the possible advance in the conditions of any particular trade, beyond which the progressive raising of the Common Rule, whether by the Method of Collective Bargaining or by that of Legal Enactment, fails to achieve its object. Against a positive slackening of the consumers' demand, the producers have no remedy. If, indeed, the wages and other conditions previously enjoyed have been unnecessarily good—if, that is to say, they have been more than enough to maintain the particular degree of specialised intensity of the trade in question—it might theoretically pay the Trade Union to submit to a reduction. In our opinion, this is seldom the case in practice. Even in the relatively well-paid trades, in times of comparative prosperity, the ordinary income of a skilled mechanic—in England, from £80 to £150 per annum —is below the amount necessary for the development in himself, his wife, and his children of the highest efficiency that they are capable of. If the consumers' demand is falling off, and is being diverted to some other process or some other product, the decline can seldom be arrested by any slight fall in price, and the Trade Union may well think that the comparatively small saving in the total cost of production which would be caused by even a 10 or 20 per cent decline of wages, would probably be quite illusory.[1] On the

---

[1] When the slackening of demand for a particular trade is not caused by any substitution, but is the result merely of a universal contraction of the world's industry—due, for instance, to a general failure of crops—there would be no advantage in a reduction of wages, either in a particular trade, or generally of the wage-earners of the world. As any such reduction could not possibly increase the aggregate demand (which is the aggregate product), it would serve no other purpose than to make up, to the capitalists of the world, part of the diminution of income that they would otherwise suffer. Rather than submit to a lowering of the standard conditions of employment it would be better, in such a case,

other hand, there is, as we have shown in our chapter on " New Processes and Machinery," no policy so disastrous for the skilled operatives to pursue as to submit to any reduction of wages, any lengthening of hours, or any worsening of sanitary conditions, that in any way impairs their peculiar specialist efficiency. In the interests of the community as a whole, no less than of their own trade, such of their members as remain in employment must at all hazards maintain un-diminished the high standard of life which alone has per-mitted them to evolve their exceptional talent. What a Trade Union can do, if it finds the demand for its members' services steadily falling off, is to set its expert officials to discover the exact cause of this change of demand. If the decline is not due to a merely temporary depression of trade in general ; if, that is to say, there is going on an actual substitution of process or product which is likely to continue, the first duty of the Trade Union is to make the fact widely known to its own members and the public, so that members may seize every opportunity of escaping from the trade, and so that parents may learn to avoid putting their sons to so unpromising an occupation. The second duty of the threatened trade is to look sharply into the conditions under which the substituted article is being produced, or (in the case of foreign competition) into the conditions of all the export trades of the country. It may be that these are escaping regulation altogether, or that there is a case for demanding a rise in the legal minimum of conditions of employment. The best policy of the threatened trade is, therefore, to throw itself vigorously into the agitation for a general levelling up of the National Minimum. And in this policy they will find themselves increasingly supported by

for the workers of each community to maintain their rate unimpaired, and subsidise their unemployed members. The frequent result of unregulated competition in times of general depression of trade—that the hours of labor of the workers in employment are positively lengthened because of their strategic weakness, and the numbers unemployed thereby *unnecessarily* increased—is an arrangement so insane that it would not be tolerated but for the superstition that the anarchy of "Nature" was somehow superior to the deliberate adjust-ments of science.

public opinion. For if all the occupations enjoying any organisation at all have been pursuing the policy of pushing up their Common Rules and developing their own specialisation, there will have been set up, in the community as a whole, a new conception of what is necessary for the decent existence of any class of workers. In each trade, as we have seen, the enforcement of a Common Rule automatically sets up a new "mean" for the trade, which tends to become a new minimum. Similarly, when a National Minimum has been effectively enforced; and when one occupation after another has raised itself above that minimum to the extent of its particular skill, there will have been created, in the public opinion both of the wage-earners and other classes, not excluding even the employers, a new standard of expenditure for the average working-class family. The psychological establishment of this new standard makes the old minimum, once considered a boon, appear "starvation wages." Hence a growing discontent among the poorest classes of workers, and rising sympathy for their privations, will lead eventually to a rise in the minimum. This rise will be justified to the economists by the increase in efficiency which the enforcement of the legal minimum will have brought about. Thus, the whole community of wage-earners, including the lowest sections of it, may by a persistent and systematic use of the Device of the Common Rule, secure an indefinite, though of course not an unlimited, rise in its Standard of Life. And in this universal and elaborate application of the Common Rule, the economist finds a sound and consistent theory of Trade Unionism, adapted to the conditions of modern industry; applicable to the circumstances of each particular trade; acceptable by the whole body of wage-earners; and positively conducive to national efficiency and national wealth.

(*h*) *Trade Union Methods*

Our survey of the economic characteristics of Trade Unionism would not be complete without some comparison, from an economic standpoint, of the three Methods by which, as we have seen, Trade Unions seek to attain their ends. At first sight this may seem unnecessary. When once a Trade Union Regulation has been successfully enforced upon the employers and workmen in a trade, it can be economically of no consequence whether the Regulation has been obtained by Legal Enactment, or Collective Bargaining, or by the more silent but not less coercive influence that may be exerted by Mutual Insurance. The owners of mining royalties, the lessees of the coal, and the individual hewers will find their faculties and desires affected in exactly the same way, whether the tonnage-rates for the Northumberland coal mines are fixed by law or by the irresistible fiat of the Joint Committee. It is immaterial to the owner of an old-fashioned cotton-mill whether the shortening of hours, or the raising of the minimum cubic space required by each operative, which finally destroys his margin of profit, is enforced by the visits of the Factory Inspector or by those of the secretaries of the Employers' and Operatives' Associations. It might be urged, in short, that it is the Trade Union Regulation itself which influences the organisation of industry, or alters cost of production, profits, or price, not the particular Method by which the Regulation is secured.

But this is to assume that, whether a Trade Union Regulation is supported by one Method or the other, it will be obtained and enforced with equal friction, equal effectiveness, equal universality, and equal rapidity of application to the changing circumstances. Thus, the general reduction of the hours of labor, which characterised the decade 1870 to 1880, had distinctive economic results of its own, whether it was effected by Legal Enactment (as in the textile mills), or by Collective Bargaining (as in the engineering workshops). But the economist cannot overlook the fact that the reduction was, in the one case, secured without any cessation of industry, enforced universally on all establishments in the trade from one end of the kingdom to the other, and rigidly maintained without struggle in subsequent years. In the other case, the reduction of hours cost the community a five months' stoppage of engineering industry in one of its most important centres, and many other struggles.[1] It never became universal, even in the same industry, and it has not been uniformly maintained. On the other hand, the Engineers got the reduction three years sooner than the Cotton Operatives, and have been able, in times of good trade, in well-organised districts, to obtain even further reductions. To complete the economic analysis of Trade Unionism, we have therefore to inquire how far these important differences in the application of the Regulations are characteristic of the several Methods by which they are enforced. In this inquiry, we may leave out the Method of Mutual Insurance, which, in its economic aspect, is hardly distinguishable from imperfect Collective Bargaining, and which, except in a few small trades, may be regarded as an adjunct of the other Methods.[2] The question therefore resolves itself into the manner in which the economic results of the various Trade Union Regulations

---

[1] *History of Trade Unionism*, pp. 299-302.

[2] This omits from consideration the purely Friendly Society side of Trade Unionism. The provision made by wage-earning families against sickness and accident, and the expenses of burial, has an important effect on their well-being, and cannot be ignored by the economist. But in this respect, as we have seen in our chapter on "The Method of Mutual Insurance," the Trade Unions amount to no more than small offshoots from the great Friendly Society movement, and (as regards death benefit) of the equally extensive system of "industrial insurance." In the United Kingdom, these provide, in the aggregate, many times more sick and funeral benefit than the whole of the Trade Unions put together. The economic results of this form of saving, like that of mere individual hoarding or deposit in a savings bank, are, therefore, in no way characteristic of Trade Unionism. The Trade Union, as we have seen, is a bad form of Friendly Society, and if it had to be considered exclusively as a Friendly Society, its total lack of actuarial basis and absence of security would bring upon it the severest condemnation. The main benefit provided by the Trade Union is, however, not sick pay or funeral money, but the Out of Work Donation, and this, as we have pointed out, must be regarded, not as an end in itself, but as a means of maintaining or improving the members' conditions of employment—as a method, that is, of supporting the Trade Union Regulations.

are modified, according as they are enforced by Collective Bargaining or Legal Enactment.

Confining ourselves to the circumstances of this country at the present time, we see that to obtain and enforce a Trade Union Regulation by the Method of Collective Bargaining necessarily involves, as we described in a previous chapter, the drawback of occasional disputes and stoppages of work. The seven hundred or more strikes and lock-outs annually reported to the Board of Trade [1] represent a considerable amount of economic friction. The laying idle of costly and perishable machinery and plant, the dislocation of business enterprise, the diversion of orders to other countries, the absorption in angry quarrels of the intellects which would otherwise be devoted to the further development of our industry—above all, the reduction to poverty and semi-starvation of thousands of workmen—involve a serious inroad upon the nation's wealth. This perpetual liability to a disagreement between the parties to a bargain is a necessary accompaniment of freedom of contract. We have already pointed out that if it is thought desirable that the parties to a bargain should be free to agree or not to agree, it is inevitable that, human nature being as it is, there should now and again come a deadlock, leading to that trial of strength which lies behind all negotiations between free and independent contracting parties. The Trade Union Method of Collective Bargaining, though by its machinery for industrial diplomacy it may reduce to a minimum the occasions of industrial war, can never, as we have seen, altogether prevent its occurrence. We need not dwell any further upon this capital drawback of this particular Method of industrial regulation, as it is one on which both public opinion and economic authority are convinced, and of which, in our judgment, they take even an exaggerated view.

[1] The reports on the Strikes and Lock-outs of the year, which have been annually published by the Labor Department of the Board of Trade since 1888, and by various American State Governments, afford a valuable picture of the number and variety of these disputes.

The use by the Trade Unions of the Method of Legal Enactment has the great economic merit of avoiding all the waste and friction that we have been describing. Whatever may be the result of a new Factory Act, it is not bought at the cost of a strike or a lock-out. Even when a new enact· ment is supremely distasteful to both employers and operatives, as in the case of the Truck Act of 1896, there is no cessation or interruption of the nation's industry. All that happens is that employers and workmen importune their members of Parliament, and go on deputations to the Home Secretary, to beg for an amendment or a repeal of the obnoxious law. The regulations themselves, like the clauses of the Truck Act which are complained of, may be irksome, useless, or economically injurious, but the method by which they have been obtained and enforced has the inestimable merit of peacefulness.

The case of the Truck Act of 1896 supplies an instance of a corresponding drawback of the Method of Legal Enactment. An Act of Parliament is hard to obtain, and hard to alter. It is therefore probable that an industry has to go on for some years without the regulation which would be economically advantageous to it, or to endure for some time an obsolete regulation which could advantageously be amended. This want of elasticity to meet changing circumstances is specially noticeable in our legislative machinery of the present day, when the one central legislature is patently incapable of coping with the incessant new applications of law required by a complicated society. It would be interesting to ask whether this defect is inherent in the Method of Legal Enactment. If the principle of regulating the conditions of employment were definitely adopted by Parliament, there does not seem any impossibility in the rules themselves being made and amended by the fiat—carrying with it the force of law—of an executive department, a local authority, or a compulsory arbitration court for the particular industry.[1] But

[1] The ordinances of the craft-gilds, the by-laws of the mediæval town councils, and the fixing of rates of wages by the justices are familiar examples of law

though a community which believed in regulating the conditions of employment by law would be able greatly to simplify
and develop its legislative machinery, the making and amending of legally enforcible rules must, we believe, necessarily
be a more stiff and cumbrous process than the concluding
or modifying a voluntary trade agreement by a joint committee. If, therefore, it be desirable that the Regulation
itself, or the stringency with which it is interpreted or applied,
should be constantly shifted upwards or downwards, according to the changing circumstances of the day, or the relative
positions of employers and workmen, the Method of Collective
Bargaining has undoubtedly a great advantage over the
Method of Legal Enactment.

So far, therefore, the Method of Legal Enactment is
superior in the characteristics of peacefulness and absence
of preliminary friction, whilst in the qualities of elasticity,
promptness of attainment, and facility of alteration, the
Method of Collective Bargaining holds the field. When we
come to the effectiveness of the Regulation—that is to say,
the rigidity, impartiality, and universality with which it is
applied—the issue is more open to doubt. In our analysis
of the economic effects of the Common Rule, we have seen
how important it is that it should really be co-extensive with
the industry in any community. It will clearly make all the
difference to the economic effect of a reduction of hours or
an advance in costly sanitary comforts, whether all competing

making, which, though they were open to many other objections, were lacking
neither in promptitude nor elasticity. "The substance no less than the form of
the law would, it is probable, be a good deal improved if the executive government of England could, like that of France, by means of decrees, ordinances, or
proclamations having the force of law, work out the detailed application of the
general principles embodied in the Acts of the legislature" (A. V. Dicey, *The
Law of the Constitution*, ch. i.; H. Sidgwick, *Principles of Politics*, ch. xxii. p.
433). Already, a large amount of our legislation is made in the form of "rules"
or "orders" by executive departments, sometimes under a general authority given
by statute, and only nominally laid before Parliament, sometimes by mere
executive authority; see, for instance, the eight volumes of *Statutory Rules and
Orders* (London, 1897) in force having the authority of law. It is probable that
the increasing incapacity of the House of Commons to cope with its work will
lead to a silent extension of this practice. We shall, in fact, be saved by the
Royal Prerogative !

employers are equally subjected to the regulation, or whether this is enforced only on particular establishments or particular districts. At first sight it would seem that this is an overwhelming argument in favor of the law. In our own country at the present day factory legislation applies uniformly from one end of the kingdom to another. If it is properly drafted and really intended to work, it will be conscientiously and impartially enforced by the Home Office. But unfortunately, though the machinery for enforcing the regulations is, in the United Kingdom, exceptionally efficient, the regulations themselves are still very imperfect. Outside the textile and mining industries, it is not too much to say that they have generally been drafted or emasculated by ministers or legislators yielding to popular pressure, but themselves opposed, in principle, to any interference with the employer's " freedom of enterprise." Our Labor Code contains many " bogus " clauses, which were, by their authors, never intended to be applied, and which the most zealous Factory Inspectors are unable to enforce. On the other hand, the regulations which are secured in Collective Bargaining by the shrewd and experienced officials of a powerful Trade Union, are, from the outset, intended to work, and, when the trade is completely organised, they are enforced with an unrelenting and detailed exactitude unknown to the Factory Inspector or the magistrate's court. But whereas the law, however imperfect, applies equally to all firms and to all districts, it is rare, as we have seen, for a Trade Union to secure a " National Agreement," and still more unusual for the whole trade to be so well organised as to be able to enforce any uniform terms upon all the employers. The usual result is that, though the workmen enforce their Regulations on " society shops " in " good " Trade Union towns with more than the severity of the law of the land, there are numerous establishments, and sometimes whole districts, over which the Trade Union has absolutely no control.

Finally we have the question—to the statesman, as we have seen, of vital importance—whether one or other Method is best calculated to prevent industrial parasitism. From the point of view of the community, it is essential that every industry should afford, to every person employed, at least the National Minimum of sanitation and safety, leisure and wages, in order to prevent any particular trade from getting a virtual " bounty" from the community, in the form either of partially supported labor, or of successive relays of workers deteriorated in their use. Only under these conditions, as we have seen, has the nation any assurance that its industry will flow into those channels in which its capital, brains, and manual labor will be applied to the greatest economic advantage, and produce the greatest " National Dividend." Now, it is an inherent defect of any sectional action by particular Trade Unions that its success will depend, not on the real necessities of the workers, but on their strategic position. Under the Method of Collective Bargaining the provisions for Sanitation and Safety would differ from trade to trade, not according to the unhealthiness or danger of the process, but according to the capacity of the workers for organisation, the ability of their leaders, the magnitude of their " war-chests," the relative scarcity of their labor, and the " squeezability" of their employers. Where the hours of labor are not affected by law, we find, in fact, at the present time, that they vary from trade to trade without the least reference to the average strength of the workers concerned, or the exhausting character of their labors. The London Silverworkers, the Birmingham Flint Glass Makers, and the various classes of building operatives in the Metropolis, enjoy, for instance, practically an Eight Hours' Day, whilst the outworking Sheffield Cutlers, the London Carmen, and the great race of Tailors everywhere work at least half as long again for a smaller remuneration. And, turning to the four millions of women wage-earners, we come to the paradoxical result that, wherever unregulated by law, the physically weakest class in the world of labor is forced to work the longest hours for the least adequate subsistence. It is clear that the National Minimum, whether with regard to sanitation or safety, leisure or wages, cannot be secured, in the cases in which it is most required, otherwise than by law.[1]

We see, therefore, that if, for the moment, we leave out of account the Regulations themselves, the Method of Legal Enactment has, where it can be employed, a considerable balance of economic advantages over the Method of Collective Bargaining. It has, to begin with, the great merit of avoiding all stoppages of industry and of causing the minimum of economic friction. In our own country, at any rate, a Regulation enforced by Legal Enactment will be more uniformly and impartially applied throughout an industry as a whole than is ever likely to be the case with a Regulation enforced by Collective Bargaining. Its greatest drawback is the cumbrousness of the machinery that must be set in motion, and the consequent difficulty in quickly adapting the Regulations to new circumstances. Hence the Method of Legal Enactment is best adapted for those Regulations which are based on permanent considerations, such as the health and efficiency of the workers. The minimum requirements of Sanitation and Safety need no sudden modifications. Much the same argument applies to the fixing of the Normal Day and even of a minimum of wages, calculated so as to

---

[1] Even when a Trade Union uses the Method of Legal Enactment for its own benefit, it usually secures advantages for weaker classes. Thus, the adult male cotton-spinners, in getting shorter hours and improved sanitation for themselves, have secured identical conditions for the comparatively weak women ringspinners of Lancashire, and for the practically unorganised women employed to assist at mule-spinning in the mills of Glasgow. And this uniformity of regulation, initiated by the 19,000 male spinners, has not only been extended to all the 300,000 workers in cotton-mills, whether spinners, weavers, beamers, twisters, or card-room hands, but also to the 200,000 factory operatives in the competing products of the woollen, linen, and silk trades. Finally, whilst the 500,000 operatives in the textile trades thus already work under identical legal conditions, there is a constant tendency, in every amendment of the Factory Acts, to approximate to this " textile " standard the regulations applying to the hours and sanitation of all the other industries of the country. In short, when Parliament has to determine the conditions of employment, it tends necessarily, whatever the trade, to base its action on one and the same common assumption —on the necessity of securing to every class of workers at least the minimum requirements of health and efficiency.

prevent any class of workers from being driven down below
the standard of healthy subsistence. These are all matters
of physiological science. The Method of Legal Enactment
is, in fact, economically the most advantageous way of enforcing all Regulations based on the Doctrine of a Living
Wage.[1]

But the Method of Collective Bargaining has also its
legitimate sphere. In our analysis of the economic characteristics of the Common Rule, we have pointed out how
essential it is, in the interests of each particular trade, and
also in those of the community as a whole, that no section
of workers should remain content with the National Minimum
secured by law, and that each trade should be perpetually
trying to force up its own Standard of Life so as to stimulate
to the utmost the forces of Functional Adaptation and the
Selection of the Fittest within the occupation. The several
sections of workers show no backwardness in demanding
all that they can get, and they often desire, as we have
seen, to get the law on their side. But if the Doctrine
of Vested Interests is abandoned, there are many reasons
which will prevent the use of the Method of Legal Enactment for obtaining what we may call this sectional " Rent of
Ability," or " Rent of Opportunity." If, indeed, the workers
in any particular trade could prove to the representatives of

---

[1] In support of this view we are glad to be able to quote an editorial of the
Times in the palmy days of that great organ of English public opinion. Referring to the movement in favor of shortening the hours of labor of shop
assistants, its leading article of the 11th November 1846 observed : " Now we
would humbly suggest that, after all, an Act of Parliament would be the most
short and certain mode of effecting the proposed object. It would be universal
in its operation. It would admit of no partial exceptions or favoritisms. It
would be binding on all. It would be, we think, desired by all who hope to be
benefited by the change. A master who, out of spite, obstinacy, or the spirit of
martyrdom, would kick at a speech, or remain obdurate to a sermon, would bow
before the majesty of the law. There is more eloquence in a tiny penal clause
imposing a fine of £5 than in the graceful benevolence of Lord John Manners
or the historical résumés of Dr. Vaughan. No man would resist it often, or
resist it long. . . . Let the young men and women . . . appeal to Parliament
to ratify by its fiat that principle which should be the boast and the mission
of every Legislature—to protect the poor from contumely and the weak from
oppression.'

the whole community that their task required for its proper fulfilment more than ordinary leisure and income, there is no reason why they should not ask to have these exceptional conditions embodied in a new Common Rule and secured by law. But the attempts of the different trades to force up their wages and other conditions above the National Minimum, must, as we have learnt, be purely experimental. In so far as any rise in the level of the Common Rule results in an increase in the efficiency of the industry, each Trade Union can safely push its own interests. But any such attempt will be dependent for success on forces which cannot be foreseen, and many of which are unconnected with the efficiency of the manual workers themselves. The rapidity of industrial invention in the particular trade, the extent to which it is recruited by additional brain-workers, the ease with which new capital can be obtained, will determine how far and how quickly the Trade Union can, by raising its Common Rule, stimulate increased efficiency and concentrate the business in its most advantageous centres. And there is also another direction in which, under a system of private enterprise, a Trade Union may successfully push its members' claims. In our chapter on " The Higgling of the Market " we have seen how nearly every section of capitalists throws up its own bulwark against the stream of pressure, in order to enjoy its own particular pool of profit. A legal monopoly or exclusive concession, a ring or syndicate, will secure for the capitalists of the trade exemption from competition and exceptional gains. The same result occurs whenever there is a sudden rush of demand for a new product, or a sudden cheapening of production. If the wage-earners in these trades are strongly organised, they can extract some part of these exceptional profits, which the employers will concede if they are threatened with a complete stoppage of the industry. From the point of view of the community there is no reason against this " sharing of the plunder," as the expenditure of the workmen's share, distributed over thousands of families, is quite as likely to be socially advantageous as that of the swollen incomes of a comparatively small number of newly-enriched employers.[1]

For these and all other kinds of " Rent of Opportunity," the law is obviously quite inapplicable. In short, for everything beyond the National Minimum, and the technical interpretation of this to secure to each trade the conditions necessary for efficient citizenship, the wage-earners must rely on the Method of Collective Bargaining.

[1] But here again we must remind the reader that the Trade Union cannot, by any Common Rule, trench upon the exceptional profits of particular firms. Patents and Trade Marks, advertising specialities and proprietary articles are therefore beyond its reach. It is only when, as in the case of the Birmingham Alliances, the swollen profits extend over the whole industry that the Trade Union can effectively insist on sharing the plunder. And it so happens that in these cases the wage-earners are seldom sufficiently well organised even to defend their own position. When the enlarged profits of the trade arise from a sudden rush of demand or a sudden cheapening of production, it is usually a question (as in the case of the sewing-machine and the bicycle) of a new product or a new process, produced by workers who, newly gathered together, are unprotected by effective combination. Accordingly, though the wage-earners in exceptionally profitable industries often obtain continuous employment, and a slight rise of wages, they practically never secure any appreciable share of the " pools of profit " that we have described. Thus whilst the brewers, wholesale provision merchants, patent medicine proprietors, soap and pill advertisers, wholesale clothiers, sewing-machine makers, bicycle and pneumatic tyre manufacturers, and the mineral water merchants have all during the past eight years been making colossal profits, the wage-earners employed in these trades, who are almost entirely unorganised, stand, on the whole, rather below than above the average of the kingdom. In many of these cases the conditions of the wage-earners have remained actually below the level of " a Living Wage."

CHAPTER IV

TRADE UNIONISM AND DEMOCRACY

IT might easily be contended that Trade Unionism has no logical or necessary connection with any particular kind of state or form of administration. If we consider only its fundamental object——the deliberate regulation of the conditions of employment in such a way as to ward off from the manual-working producers the evil effects of industrial competition——there is clearly no incompatibility between this and any kind of government. Regulations of this type have existed, as a matter of fact, under emperors and presidents, aristocracies and democracies. The spread of the Industrial Revolution and the enormous development of international trade have everywhere brought the evils of unregulated competition into sensational prominence. The wise autocrat of to-day, conversant with the latest results of economic science, and interested in the progressive improvement of his state, might, therefore, be as eager to prevent the growth of industrial parasitism as the most democratic politician. Hence, we can easily imagine such an autocrat enforcing a National Minimum, which should rule out of the industrial system all forms of competition degrading to the health, intelligence, or character of his people. The rapid extension of factory legislation in semi-autocratic countries during recent years indicates that some inkling of this truth is reaching the minds of European bureaucracies. What is distrusted in modern Trade Unionism is not its object, nor even its devices, but its structure and its methods. When workmen meet together to discuss their grievances— still more, when they form associations of national extent, raise an independent revenue, elect permanent representative committees, and proceed to bargain and agitate as corporate bodies—they are forming, within the state, a spontaneous democracy of their own. The autocrat might see in this industrial democracy nothing more hostile to his supremacy in the state than the self-government of the village or the co-operative store. It is, we imagine, on this view that the Czar of All the Russias regards with complacency the spontaneous activity of the Mir and the Artel. More usually, however, the autocrat distrusts the educational influence of even the most subordinate forms of self-government. And when the association is national in extent, composed exclusively of one class, and untrammelled by any compulsory constitution, his faith in its objects or his tolerance for its devices becomes completely submerged beneath his fear of its apparently revolutionary organisation.[1] Hence, though European autocracies may greatly extend their factory legislation, and might even, on the advice of the economists or in response to the public opinion of the wage-earning class, deliberately enforce a National Minimum of education, sanitation, leisure, and wages, they are not likely to encourage that pushing forward of the Common Rules of each section by the method of Collective Bargaining, which is so characteristic of British Trade Unionism, and upon which, as we have seen, the maximum productivity of the community as a whole depends.[2]

The problem of how far Trade Unionism is consistent with autocratic government—important to the continental student—is not of practical concern to the Anglo-Saxon.

---

[1] In this respect, the old-fashioned Liberal stood at the opposite pole from the autocrat. What he liked in Trade Unionism was the voluntary spontaneity of its structure and the self-helpfulness of its methods ; even when he disbelieved in the possibility of its objects, and disliked its devices.

[2] It would seem to follow that, if we could suppose other things to be equal, an autocracy would not attain so great a national wealth-production as a democracy.

In the English-speaking world institutions which desire to maintain and improve their position must at all hazards bring themselves into line with democracy. The wise official who has to function under the control of a committee of management, carefully considers its modes of action and the interests and opinions of its members, so that he may shape and state his policy in such a way as to avoid the rejection of the measure he desires. In the same way each section of Trade Unionists will have to put forward a policy of which no part runs counter to the interests and ideals of the bulk of the people. Believing, as we do, in the social expediency both of popular government, and of a wisely directed Trade Unionism for each class of producers, we shall end our work by suggesting with what modifications and extensions, and subject to what limitations, British Trade Unionism can best fulfil its legitimate function in the modern democratic state. At this point, therefore, we leave behind the exposition and analysis of facts, and their generalisation into economic theory, in order to pass over into precept and prophecy.

We see at once that the complete acceptance of democracy, with its acute consciousness of the interests of the community as a whole, and its insistence on equality of opportunity for all citizens, will necessitate a reconsideration by the Trade Unionists of their three Doctrines—the abandonment of one, the modification of another, and the far-reaching extension and development of the third.[1] To begin with the Doctrine of Vested Interests, we may infer that, whatever respect may be paid to the "established expectations" of any class, this will not be allowed to take the form of a resistance to inventions, or of any obstruction of improvements in industrial processes. Equitable consideration of the interests of existing workers will no doubt be more and more expected, and popular governments may even adopt Mill's suggestion of making some provision for operatives displaced by a new machine. But this con-

[1] See Part II chap. xiii. "The Assumptions of Trade Unionism."

sideration and this provision will certainly not take the form of restricting the entrance to a trade, or of recognising any exclusive right to a particular occupation or service. Hence the old Trade Union conception of a vested interest in an occupation must be entirely given up—a change of front will be the more easy in that, as we have seen,[1] no union is now able to embody this conception in a practical policy.

Coming now to the Doctrine of Supply and Demand, we see that any attempt to better the strategic position of a particular section by the Device of Restriction of Numbers will be unreservedly condemned. Not only is this Device inconsistent with the democratic instinct in favor of opening up the widest possible opportunity for every citizen, but it is hostile to the welfare of the community as a whole, and especially to the manual workers, in that it tends to distribute the capital, brains, and labor of the nation less productively than would otherwise be the case.[2] Trade Unionism has, therefore, absolutely to abandon one of its two Devices. This throwing off of the old Adam of monopoly will be facilitated by the fact that the mobility of modern industry has, in all but a few occupations, already made any effective use of Restriction of Numbers quite impracticable.[3] Even if, in particular cases, the old Device should again become feasible, those Trade Unions which practised it would be placing themselves directly in antagonism to the conscious interests of the remainder of their own class, and of the community as a whole. And in so far as industry passes from the hands of private capitalists into the control of representatives of the consumers, whether in the form of voluntary co-operative societies,[4] or in that of

[1] Part II. chaps. x. and xi. " The Entrance to a Trade " and " The Right to a Trade."

[2] See Part III. chap. iii. " The Economic Characteristics of Trade Unionism," under the heading " The Device of Restriction of Numbers."

[3] See Part II. chap. x. " The Entrance to a Trade."

[4] Here and elsewhere in this chapter we mean by co-operative societies the characteristic British type of associations of consumers, who unite for the purpose of carrying on, by salaried service, the manufacture and distribution of the commodities they desire. This form of co-operative society—the " store " and

the municipality or the central government, any interference with freedom to choose the best man or woman for every vacancy, more and more consciously condemned by public opinion, will certainly not be tolerated.

But the manipulation of the labor market to the advantage of particular sections does not always take the form of a limitation of apprenticeship, or any Restriction of Numbers. Among the Cotton-spinners the piecers, and among the Cotton-weavers the tenters, are engaged and paid by the operatives themselves, whose earnings are accordingly partly made up of the profit on this juvenile labor. It therefore suits the interest of the adult workers, no less than that of the capitalist manufacturers, that there should be as little restriction as possible on the age or numbers of these subordinate learners : the Cotton-spinners, in fact, as we have more than once mentioned, go so far as to insist on there being always ten times as many of them as would suffice to recruit the trade. In this parasitic use of child-labor, the Cotton Operatives are sharing with the manufacturers what is virtually a subsidy from the community as a whole. The enforcement of a National Minimum would,

the "wholesale," together with their adjunct, the Co-operative Corn Mill— accounts for nineteen-twentieths of the capital, practically all the distributive trade, and three-fourths of the aggregate production of the British Co-operative Movement (*Third Annual Report of the Labour Department of the Board of Trade*, C. 8230, 1896, pp. 25-48). Though the commodities and services supplied by voluntary associations of consumers will vary from time to time, we regard this type of co-operative society as a permanent element in the democratic state. However widely we may extend the scope of central or local government, there will always be a place for voluntary associations of consumers to provide for themselves what the public authority either cannot or will not supply. The other type of organisation known as a co-operative society, the association of producers, or so-called "productive society," stands in a very different position. We see no future for this in the fully-developed democratic state. In its original ideal form of a self-governing association of manual workers, it seems to us (besides being open to grave objections) to have been made impossible by the Great Industry, whilst the subsequent forms known as "co-partnership" appear to us to be incompatible with Trade Unionism, and the indispensable maintenance of the Common Rule. See *The Co-operative Movement in Great Britain* (2nd edition, London, 1894), and *The Relationship between Co-operation and Trade Unionism* (Co-operative Union pamphlet, Manchester, 1892), both by Mrs. Sidney Webb.

as we have seen,[1] involve such a raising of the minimum age, both for half and whole time employment, as would put a stop to this particular expression of corporate self-help.

Thus, the Doctrine of Supply and Demand will have to manifest itself exclusively in the persistent attempts of each trade to specialise its particular grade of skill, by progressively raising the level of its own Common Rules. In so far as this results in a corresponding increase in efficiency it will, as we have shown,[2] not only benefit the trade itself, but also cause the capital, brains, and labor of the community to be distributed in the most productive way. And the demands of each grade will, in the absence of any Restriction of Numbers or resistance to innovations, be automatically checked by the liberty of the customer to resort to an alternative product and the absolute freedom of the directors of industry to adopt an alternative process, or to select another grade of labor. Thus, the permanent bias of the manual worker towards higher wages and shorter hours of labor is perpetually being counteracted by another——his equally strong desire for continuity of employment. If the Common Rule in any industry at any time is pressed upward further or more quickly than is compensated for by an equivalent advance in the efficiency of the industry, the cost of production, and, therefore, the price, will be raised, and the consumers' demand for that particular commodity will, in the vast majority of cases, be thereby restricted. The rise of wages will, in such a case, have been purchased at the cost of throwing some men out of work. And though the working-class official cannot, any more than the capitalist or the economist, predict the effect on demand of any particular rise of wages, even the most aggressive members of a Trade Union discover, in an increase of the percentage of unemployed colleagues whom they have to maintain, an unmistakable and imperative check upon any repeti-

---

[1] Part III. chap. iii. " The Economic Characteristics of Trade Unionism."
[2] *Ibid.* under the heading " The Effect of the Sectional Application of the Common Rule on the Distribution of Industry."

tion of an excessive claim. How constantly and effectively this check operates on the mind of the Trade Union officials can be realised only by those who have heard their private discussions, or who have watched the silent postponement of cherished aims by particular unions. It is not fear of the employers' strength, or lack of desire for shorter hours that is (1897) preventing the Cotton Operatives from using their power to obtain an eight hours' day or a rise in their piecework rates, but the ever-present dread, quickened by the sight of unemployed spinners and weavers on short-time, of driving away some of the trade of Lancashire. Paradoxical as it may seem, the sins of the Trade Unions in this respect would tend to be those of omission rather than those of commission. Whether with regard to sanitation, hours, or wages, each Trade Union would, in its fear of encouraging new inventions, be apt to stop short in its claims at an earlier point than the fullest efficiency demanded, rather than push ever onward the specialisation of its craft, at the cost of seeing some part of it, to the common advantage, superseded by another process.[1]

So far democracy may be expected to look on complacently at the fixing, by mutual agreement between the directors of industry and the manual workers, of special rates of wages for special classes. But this use of the Method of Collective Bargaining for the advantage of particular sections—this " freedom of contract " between capitalists and wage-earners—will become increasingly subject to the fundamental condition that the business of the community must not be interfered with. When in the course of bargaining there ensues a deadlock [2]—when the workmen strike, or the employers lock out—many other interests are affected than those of the parties concerned. We may accordingly expect that, whenever an industrial dispute reaches a certain

---

[1] See Part II. chap. viii. " New Processes and Machinery."

[2] See Part II. chap. ii. " The Method of Collective Bargaining," chap. iii. ' Arbitration," and chap. iv. " The Method of Legal Enactment."

magnitude, a democratic state will, in the interests of the community as a whole, not scruple to intervene, and settle the points at issue by an authoritative fiat. The growing impatience with industrial dislocation will, in fact, where Collective Bargaining breaks down, lead to its supersession by some form of compulsory arbitration ; that is to say, by Legal Enactment.[1] And when the fixing of the conditions on which any industry is to be carried on, is thus taken out of the hands of employers and workmen, the settlement will no longer depend exclusively on the strategic position of the parties, or of the industry, but will be largely influenced by

[1] In this connection, the provisions of the New Zealand Industrial Conciliation and Arbitration Act, drafted and carried through by the Hon. W. P. Reeves, are highly significant. By this Act (No. 14 of 1894, slightly amended by No. 30 of 1865 and No. 57 of 1896) there is created a complete system of industrial tribunals for dealing, from the standpoint of the public interest, not only with the interpretation and enforcement of collective agreements expressly made subject to them ; but also with industrial disputes of every kind. There is, first, in each district a Board of Conciliation, consisting in equal numbers of members elected by the employers' and workmen's associations respectively, with an impartial chairman chosen by the Board from outside itself. Any party to an industrial dispute—that is to say, an association of employers or of workmen, or one or more employers though not associated—may bring the quarrel before the Board, which is thereon required, whether the other party consents or not, to inquire into the dispute, and do its best to promote a settlement. If conciliation fails the Board is then required, within two months of the first application to it, to " decide the question according to the merits and substantial justice of the case." So far, the system is merely one of Compulsory Arbitration, with a formal award which the parties are not bound to accept. But the Board may, if it thinks fit, refer any unsettled dispute, with or without its own decision on its merits, to the central Court of Arbitration, consisting of three members appointed by the Governor, two on the nomination respectively of the associations of employers and employed, and one, who presides, from among the Judges of the Supreme Court. If the local Board does not so remit the case, any party to it may require the Board's report to be referred to the Court. The Court is thereupon required to investigate the dispute in the most complete manner, with or without the assent of any of the parties, and with all the powers of a court of justice. Its award is, in all cases, nominally binding on the associations or persons specified therein, for the period (not exceeding two years) named ; and any award which refers to an association is binding not only upon all those who are members at the date of the award, but also upon all those who subsequently join during its continuance. But though the award is nominally binding, it is within the discretion of the Court whether it shall be legally enforcible. The Court may, if it thinks fit, either at once, or, on the application of any of the parties, subsequently, file its award in the Supreme Court office, when it becomes, by leave of the Court, enforcible as if it were a judgment of the Supreme Court. The award may include an order to pay costs and

the doctrine of a living wage. The Trade Union official would then have to prove that the claims of his clients were warranted by the greater intensity of their effort, or by the rareness of their skill in comparison with those of the lowest grade of labor receiving only the National Minimum ; whilst the case of the associated employers would have to rest on a demonstration, both that the conditions demanded were unnecessary, if not prejudicial, to the workmen's efficiency, and that equally competent recruits could be obtained in sufficient numbers without the particular "rent of ability," demanded by the Trade Union over and above the National Minimum.

expenses, and penalties for its breach, not exceeding £10 against an individual workman or £500 against an association or an individual employer. The decision of the Court of Arbitration, acting by a majority of its members, may, therefore, at its discretion, be made part of the law of the land. When a dispute has once been brought before a Board or the Court, "any act or thing in the nature of a strike or lock-out" is expressly prohibited, and would presumably be punishable as contempt.

During the three years that this Act has been in force, there have been altogether sixteen labor disputes, and it has been successfully applied to every one of them, half being settled by the Boards of Conciliation and half by the Court of Arbitration. The awards have been uniformly well received by the parties, and appear to have been generally obeyed. Several of them were filed in the Supreme Court, and have thus obtained the force of law. So far the Act has been entirely successful in preventing the dislocation of industry. This success is no doubt largely due to the general support given by public opinion in the Colony to the principle of arbitration. There is at present no provision enabling the Boards or the Court to deal with a dispute, however disastrous to the public welfare, in which none of the parties request its intervention. And as there has been as yet no refusal to obey any of the awards, the actual process of enforcement has not been tested in the law courts. It has been suggested that an obstinate employer, refusing to join any association, and employing only non-unionists, might escape jurisdiction by declining to recognise (and therefore having no quarrel with) any Trade Union. Such a case occurred in South Australia, where a less ably drafted Act on somewhat the same lines as that of New Zealand is in force. The point was, however, not judicially decided ("Quelques Expériences de Conciliation par l'Etat en Australie," by Anton Bertram in *Revue d'Économie Politique*, 1897). In the present state of public opinion in New Zealand, this or any other evasion of the law would be very narrowly viewed by the judges, and any flaw discovered would be promptly cured by an amending Act. The Board or Court might easily be empowered to deal, on its own initiative, with any dispute that it considered injurious to the community, and also to take cognisance, as a dispute, of any wholesale dismissal of workmen, or of any explicit refusal to employ members of a duly registered association.

It is accordingly on the side of the Doctrine of a Living Wage that the present policy of Trade Unionism will require most extension. Democratic public opinion will expect each trade to use its strategic position to secure the conditions necessary for the fulfilment of its particular social function in the best possible way—to obtain, that is to say, not what will be immediately most enjoyed by the "average sensual man," but what, in the long run, will most conduce to his efficiency as a professional, a parent, and a citizen. This will involve some modification of Trade Union policy. Powerful Trade Unions show no backwardness in exacting the highest money wages that they know how to obtain ; but even the best organised trades will at present consent, as a part of their bargain with the employer, to work for excessive and irregular hours, and to put up with unsafe, insanitary, indecent, and hideous surroundings.[1] In all the better-paid crafts in the England of to-day, shorter and more regular hours, greater healthfulness, comfort, and refinement in the conditions of work, and the definite provision of periodical holidays for recreation and travel, are, in the interests of industrial and civic efficiency, more urgently required than a rise in the Standard Rate. Such an application of the Doctrine of a Living Wage will involve, not only a growth of deliberate foresight and self-control among the rank and file, but also a development of capacity in the Civil Service of the Trade Union movement. To haggle over an advance in wages is within the capacity of any labor leader ; to suggest to the employer and the legislature the "special rules" calculated to ensure the maximum comfort to the operatives, and cause the minimum cost and inconvenience to the industry, demands a higher degree of technical expertness.[2]

Nor is it enough for each trade to maintain and raise its own Standard of Life. Unless the better-paid occupations are to be insidiously handicapped in the competition for the

---

[1] See Part II. chap. vi. "The Normal Day," and chap. vii. "Sanitation and Safety."

[2] See Part II. chap. vii. "Sanitation and Safety."

home and foreign market, it is, as we have demonstrated,[1] essential that no one of the national industries should be permitted to become parasitic by the use of subsidised or deteriorating labor. Hence the organised trades are vitally concerned in the abolition of "sweating" in all occupations whatsoever, whether these compete with them for custom by manufacturing for the same demand, or for the means of production by diverting the organising capacity and capital of the nation. And this self-interest of the better-paid trades coincides, as we have seen, with the welfare of the community, dependent as this is on securing the utmost development of health, intelligence, and character in the weaker as well as in the stronger sections. Thus we arrive at the characteristic device of the Doctrine of a Living Wage, which we have termed the National Minimum—the deliberate enforcement, by an elaborate Labor Code, of a definite quota of education, sanitation, leisure, and wages for every grade of workers in every industry.[2] This National Minimum the public opinion of the democratic state will not only support, but positively insist on for the common weal. But public opinion alone will not suffice. To get the principle of a National Minimum unreservedly adopted ; to embody it in successive Acts of Parliament of the requisite technical detail ; to see that this legislation is properly enforced ; to cause the regulations to be promptly and intelligently adapted to changes in the national industry, requires persistent effort and specialised skill. For this task no section of the community is so directly interested and so well-equipped as the organised trades, with their prolonged experience of industrial regulation and their trained official staff. It is accordingly upon the Trade Unions that the democratic state must mainly rely for the stimulus, expert counsel, and persistent watchfulness, without which a National Minimum can neither be obtained nor enforced.

[1] Part III. chap. iii. "The Economic Characteristics of Trade Unionism" under the heading "Parasitic Trades."
[2] *Ibid.* under the heading "The National Minimum."

This survey of the changes required in Trade Union policy leads us straight to a conclusion as to the part which Trade Unionism will be expected to play in the management of the industry of a democratic state. The interminable series of decisions, which together make up industrial administration, fall into three main classes. There is, first, the decision as to what shall be produced—that is to say, the exact commodity or service to be supplied to the consumers. There is, secondly, the judgment as to the manner in which the production shall take place, the adoption of material, the choice of processes, and the selection of human agents. Finally, there is the altogether different question of the conditions under which these human agents shall be employed — the temperature, atmosphere, and sanitary arrangements amid which they shall work, the intensity and duration of their toil, and the wages given as its reward.

To obtain for the community the maximum satisfaction it is essential that the needs and desires of the consumers should be the main factor in determining the commodities and services to be produced. Whether these needs and desires can best be ascertained and satisfied by the private enterprise of capitalist profit-makers, keenly interested in securing custom, or by the public service of salaried officials, intent on pleasing associations of consumers (as in the British Co-operative Movement) or associations of citizens (the Municipality or the State), is at present the crucial problem of democracy. But whichever way this issue may be decided, one thing is certain, namely, that the several sections of manual workers, enrolled in their Trade Unions, will have, under private enterprise or Collectivism, no more to do with the determination of what is to be produced than any other citizens or consumers. As manual workers and wage-earners, they bring to the problem no specialised knowledge, and as persons fitted for the performance of particular services, they are even biassed against the inevitable changes in demand which characterise a progressive community.[1] This is even more the case with regard to the second department of industrial administration —the adoption of material, the choice of processes, and the selection of human agents. Here, the Trade Unions concerned are specially disqualified, not only by their ignorance of the possible alternatives, but also by their overwhelming bias in favor of a particular material, a particular process, or a particular grade of workers, irrespective of whether these are or are not the best adapted for the gratification of the consumers' desires. On the other hand, the directors of industry, whether thrown up by the competitive struggle or deliberately appointed by the consumers or citizens, have been specially picked out and trained to discover the best means of satisfying the consumers' desires. Moreover, the bias of their self-interest coincides with the object of their customers or employers—that is to say, the best and cheapest production. Thus, if we leave out of account the disturbing influence of monopoly in private enterprise, and corruption in public administration, it would at first sight seem as if we might safely leave the organisation of production and distribution under the one system as under the other to the expert knowledge of the directors of industry. But this is subject to one all-important qualification. The permanent bias of the profit-maker, and even of the salaried official of the Co-operative Society, the Municipality, or the Government Department, is to lower the expense of production. So far as immediate results are concerned, it seems equally advantageous whether this reduction of cost is secured by a better choice of materials, processes, or men, or by some lowering of wages or other worsening of the conditions upon which the human agents are employed. But the democratic state is, as we have seen,[2] vitally interested in upholding the highest possible Standard of Life of all its citizens, and especially of the manual workers who form four-fifths of the whole. Hence the bias of the directors of industry in favor

---

[1] See Part II. chap. ix. " Continuity of Employment."
[2] See Part III. chap. iii. " The Economic Characteristics of Trade Unionism."

of cheapness has, in the interests of the community, to be perpetually controlled and guided by a determination to maintain, and progressively to raise, the conditions of employment.

This leads us to the third branch of industrial administration—the settlement of the conditions under which the human beings are to be employed. The adoption of one material rather than another, the choice between alternative processes or alternative ways of organising the factory, the selection of particular grades of workers, or even of a particular foreman, may affect, for the worse, the Standard of Life of the operatives concerned. This indirect influence on the conditions of employment passes imperceptibly into the direct determination of the wages, hours, and other terms of the wage contract. On all these matters the consumers, on the one hand, and the directors of industry on the other, are permanently disqualified from acting as arbiters. In our chapter on " The Higgling of the Market "[1] we described how in the elaborate division of labor which characterises the modern industrial system, thousands of workers co-operate in the bringing to market of a single commodity; and no consumer, even if he desired it, could possibly ascertain or judge of the conditions of employment in all these varied trades. Thus, the consumers of all classes are not only biassed in favor of low prices : they are compelled to accept this apparent or genuine cheapness as the only practicable test of efficiency of production. And though the immediate employer of each section of workpeople knows the hours that they work and the wages that they receive, he is precluded by the stream of competitive pressure, transmitted through the retail shopkeeper and the wholesale trader, from effectively resisting the promptings of his own self-interest towards a constant cheapening of labor. Moreover, though he may be statistically aware of the conditions of employment, his lack of personal experience of those conditions deprives him of any real knowledge of their effects. To the brain-working captain

[1] Part III. chap. ii.

of industry, maintaining himself and his family on thousands a year, the manual-working wage-earner seems to belong to another species, having mental faculties and bodily needs altogether different from his own. Men and women of the upper or middle classes are totally unable to realise what state of body and mind, what level of character and conduct result from a life spent, from childhood to old age, amid the dirt, the smell, the noise, the ugliness, and the vitiated atmosphere of the workshop ; under constant subjection to the peremptory, or, it may be, brutal orders of the foreman ; kept continuously at laborious manual toil for sixty or seventy hours in every week of the year ; and maintained by the food, clothing, house-accommodation, recreation, and family life which are implied by a precarious income of between ten shillings and two pounds a week. If the democratic state is to attain its fullest and finest development, it is essential that the actual needs and desires of the human agents concerned should be the main considerations in determining the conditions of employment.[1] Here, then, we find the special function of the Trade Union in the administration of industry. The simplest member of the working-class organisation knows at any rate where the shoe pinches. The Trade Union official is specially selected by his fellow-workmen for his capacity to express the grievances from which they suffer, and is trained by his calling in devising remedies for them. But in expressing the desires of their members, and in insisting on the necessary reforms, the Trade Unions act within the constant friction-brake supplied by the need of securing employment. It is always the consumers, and the consumers alone, whether they act through profit-making entrepreneurs or through their own salaried officials, who determine how many of each particular grade of workers they care to employ on the conditions demanded.[2]

Thus, it is for the consumers, acting either through

[1] See Part II. chap. v. "The Standard Rate," and chap. iii. "Arbitration."
[2] This was the conclusion also of Fleeming Jenkin's mathematical analysis of abstract economics. "It is the seller of labor who determines the price, but it is

capitalist entrepreneurs or their own salaried agents, to decide
what shall be produced.   It is for the directors of industry,
whether profit-makers or officials, to decide how it shall be
produced, though in this decision they must take into account
the objections of the workers' representatives as to the effect
on the conditions of employment.   And, in the settlement of
these conditions, it is for the expert negotiators of the Trade
Unions, controlled by the desires of their members, to state
the terms under which each grade will sell its labor.   But
above all these, stands the community itself.   To its elected
representatives and trained Civil Service is entrusted the duty
of perpetually considering the permanent interests of the State
as a whole.   When any group of consumers desires something
which is regarded as inimical to the public wellbeing—for
instance, poisons, explosives, indecent literature, or facilities
for sexual immorality or gambling—the community prohibits
or regulates the satisfaction of these desires.   When the
directors of industry attempt to use a material, or a process,
which is regarded as injurious—for instance, food products
so adulterated as to be detrimental to health, ingredients
poisonous to the users, or processes polluting the rivers or the
atmosphere—their action is restrained by Public Health Acts.
And when the workers concerned, whether through ignorance,
indifference, or strategic weakness, consent to work under
conditions which impair their physique, injure their intellect,
or degrade their character, the community has, for its own
sake, to enforce a National Minimum of education, sanitation,
leisure, and wages.   We see, therefore, that industrial administration is, in the democratic state, a more complicated matter
than is naïvely imagined by the old-fashioned capitalist,
demanding the " right to manage his own business in his own
way."   In each of its three divisions, the interests and will of
one or other section is the dominant factor.   But no section

---

the buyer who determines the number of transactions.   Capital settles how many
men are wanted at given wages, but labor settles what wages the man shall
have."—" Graphic Representation of the Laws of Supply and Demand," by
Fleeming Jenkin, in *Recess Studies* (Edinburgh, 1870), p. 184.

wields uncontrolled sway even in its own sphere. The State is a partner in every enterprise. In the interests of the community as a whole, no one of the interminable series of decisions can be allowed to run counter to the consensus of expert opinion representing the consumers on the one hand, the producers on the other, and the nation that is paramount over both.[1]

It follows from this analysis that Trade Unionism is not merely an incident of the present phase of capitalist industry, but has a permanent function to fulfil in the democratic state.

[1] Some of the ablest Trade Union officials have already arrived at practically this analysis. Thus, the last annual report of the Amalgamated Society of Engineers, written by Mr. George Barnes, the new General Secretary, contains an interesting exposition of the modern Trade Union view as to the respective functions of the employers and the workmen in industrial administration. The interest of the wage-earners and that of the community are, it is argued, identical, "inasmuch as it is of public importance that a high standard of wages, and therefore a high purchasing power, should be maintained. The employer, on the other hand, claims absolute freedom to exercise authority in the selection and placing and paying of workmen, because he says he provides the machinery and plant. But he forgets that this freedom in the conduct generally of business has long since been taken away from him, and that he now only has liberty to conduct industrial enterprise in accordance with public opinion, as embodied in Parliamentary enactment and the pressure of Trade Unionism. As a result of these humanising influences, hours of labor have been reduced, boy-labor curtailed, machinery fenced, and workshops cleansed. In short, competition has been forced up to a higher plane with immense advantage to the commonweal, so that the employer's plea ' to do what he likes with his own ' is somewhat out of date, and cannot be sustained. We are willing, however, to admit that in certain directions both employer and employed should have freedom of action. Our society, for instance, has never questioned the right of the employer to terminate contracts, to select and discriminate between workmen, and to pay according to merit or skill. But it has stipulated, and has a right to stipulate, for the observance of a standard or minimum wage as a basis. And if, as has been stated by the Employers' Council, the introduction of machinery has simplified production, and widened the difference as between the skill of the machine and the hand operative, then the wage of the handicraftsmen should be proportionately increased. The introduction of machinery increases as well as simplifies production, and here, surely, is sufficient gain for the employer and the purchaser, without trenching upon the wage of the worker, whose needs remain the same whether tending a machine or using his tools by hand. Upon this ground we base our claim, but, convinced as we are that this, like most other questions, must ultimately be settled in accord with the common interest, and believing as we do in the wisdom contained in the utterance of the late Lord Derby that ' the greatest of all interests is peace,' we are willing to leave the matter to the arbitrament of a public and impartial authority, aided by technical knowledge from each side."—*Amalgamated Society of Engineers, Forty-Sixth Annual Report* (London, 1897), pp. vi.-vii.

Should capitalism develop in the direction of gigantic Trusts, the organisation of the manual workers in each industry will be the only effective bulwark against social oppression. If, on the other hand, there should be a revival of the small master system, the enforcement of Common Rules will be more than ever needed to protect the community against industrial parasitism.[1] And if, as we personally expect, democracy moves in the direction of superseding both the little profit-maker and the Trust, by the salaried officer of the Co-operative Society, the Municipality, and the Government Department, Trade Unionism would remain equally necessary. For even under the most complete Collectivism, the directors of each particular industry would, as agents of the community of consumers, remain biassed in favor of cheapening production, and could, as brainworkers, never be personally conscious of the conditions of the manual laborers. And though it may be assumed that the community as a whole would not deliberately oppress any section of its members, experience of all administration on a large scale, whether public or private, indicates how difficult it must always be, in any complicated organisation, for an isolated individual sufferer to obtain redress against the malice, caprice, or simple heedlessness of his official superior. Even a whole class or grade of workers would find it practically impossible, without forming some sort of association of its own, to bring its special needs to the notice of public opinion, and press them effectively upon the Parliament of the nation. Moreover, without an organisation of each grade or section of the producers, it would be difficult to ensure the special adaptation to their particular conditions of the National Minimum, or other embodiment of the Doctrine of a Living Wage, which the community would need to enforce ; and it would be impossible to have that progressive and experimental pressing upward of the particular Common Rules of each class, upon which, as we have seen, the maximum productivity of the nation depends. In short, it is essential

[1] See Part II. chap. xii. "The Implications of Trade Unionism."

that each grade or section of producers should be at least so well organised that it can compel public opinion to listen to its claims, and so strongly combined that it could if need be, as a last resort against bureaucratic stupidity or official oppression, enforce its demands by a concerted abstention from work, against every authority short of a decision of the public tribunals, or a deliberate judgment of the Representative Assembly itself.

But though, as industry passes more and more into public control, Trade Unionism must still remain a necessary element in the democratic state, it would, we conceive, in such a development, undergo certain changes. The mere extension of national agreements and factory legislation has already, in the most highly regulated trades, superseded the old guerilla warfare between employers and employed, and transformed the Trade Union official from a local strike leader to an expert industrial negotiator, mainly occupied, with the cordial co-operation of the secretary of the Employers' Association and the Factory Inspector, in securing an exact observance of the Common Rules prescribed for the trade. And as each part of the minimum conditions of employment becomes definitely enacted in the regulations governing the public industries, or embodied in the law of the land, it will tend more and more to be accepted by the directors of industry as a matter of course, and will need less and less enforcement by the watchful officials concerned.[1] The Trade Union function of constantly maintaining an armed resistance to attempts to lower the Standard of Life of its members may be accordingly expected to engage a diminishing share of its attention. On the other hand, its duty of perpetually striving to raise the level of its Common Rules, and thereby increasing the specialised technical efficiency of its craft, will remain unabated. We may therefore expect that, with the progressive nationalisation or municipalisation of public services, on the one hand, and the spread of the Co-operative movement on the other, the Trade Unions of the workers

[1] See Part II. chap. iv. "The Method of Legal Enactment."

thus taken directly into the employment of the citizen-consumers will more and more assume the character of professional associations. Like the National Union of Teachers at the present day, they may even come to be little concerned with any direct bargaining as to sanitation, hours, or wages, except by way of redressing individual grievances, or supplying expert knowledge as to the effect of proposed changes. The conditions of employment depending on the degree of expert specialisation to which the craft has been carried, and upon public opinion as to its needs, each Trade Union will find itself, like the National Union of Teachers, more and more concerned with raising the standard of competency in its occupation, improving the professional equipment of its members, "educating their masters" as to the best way of carrying on the craft, and endeavoring by every means to increase its status in public estimation.[1]

So far our review of the functions of Trade Unionism in the democratic state has taken account only of its part in industrial organisation. But the Trade Unions are turned also to other uses. At present, for instance, they compete with the ordinary friendly societies and industrial insurance companies in providing money benefits in cases of accident, sickness, and death, together with pensions for the aged.[2] This is the side of Trade Unionism which commonly meets with the greatest approval, but it is a side that, in our opinion, is destined to dwindle. As one class of invalids after another is taken directly under public care, the friendly benefits provided by the Trade Unions will no longer be necessary to save their members from absolute destitution.

---

[1] The industry with which the National Union of Teachers is mainly concerned—elementary school-keeping—has, within a couple of generations, entirely passed out of the domain of profit-making into that of a public service. The Union (established 1870, membership at end of 1896, 36,793) has thus grown up under a Collectivist organisation, and a comparison between its functions and those of the manual workers' Trade Unions is full of interest and significance. Its admirably compiled and elaborate *Annual Reports* afford constant illustrations of the above inferences.

[2] See Part II. chap. i. "The Method of Mutual Insurance."

With any general system of compensation for industrial accidents, provided or secured by the state itself, the costly "accident benefit" hitherto given by Trade Unions will become a thing of the past. The increasing use in sickness of hospitals and convalescent homes, the growing importance of isolation and skilled nursing, and the gratuitous provision in public institutions of the highest medical skill—adopted for reasons of public health—will incidentally go far to relieve working-class families of the intolerable strain of periods of bodily incapacity.[1] Any Government scheme of Old Age Pensions, such, for instance, as that proposed by Mr. Charles Booth, would absolve the Trade Unions from their present attempts, in the form of superannuation benefit, to buy off the undercutting of the Standard Rate of wages by their aged members. It is not that State provision against the absolute destitution caused by accident, sickness, or old age, will supersede, or even diminish, individual saving. On the contrary, it is one of the grounds on which Mr. Charles Booth and others advocate these measures,[2] that the state pension, by ensuring something to build on, will positively stimulate thrift. But this supplementary saving, to provide the little comforts and amenities beyond the state allowance, will, in our opinion, not be made through the Trade Union. As the manual workers advance in intelligence and foresight,

[1] There is no reason why the burial of the dead should not—to the great economic advantage of all concerned—become a public service and a common charge. Probably a majority of all the funerals in the United Kingdom already take place at the public expense, and the provision of burial grounds, once a common form of profit-making enterprise, is becoming almost exclusively a public function. In Paris, as is well known, the service of burial is performed by a strictly regulated and licensed monopolist corporation, virtually public in character.

[2] On Old Age Pensions, see "The Reform of the Poor Law," by Sidney Webb in *Contemporary Review*, July 1890, republished as Fabian Tract No. 17, March 1891 ; the paper on "Enumeration and Classification of Paupers, and State Pensions for the Aged," by Charles Booth, read before the Statistical Society, December 1891, and republished as *Pauperism, a Picture and Endowment of Old Age, an Argument* (London, 1892) ; and *Pensions and Pauperism*, by the Rev. J. Frome Wilkinson (London, 1892). These proposals must be distinguished from schemes of insurance, or making the poor provide their own pension, as to which see Part II. chap. xii. "The Implications of Trade Unionism."

they will more and more realise that a Trade Union, however honestly and efficiently administered, is, of necessity,
financially unsound as a friendly society. Hitherto the
actuarial defects of the friendly society side of Trade
Unionism have been far outweighed by the adventitious
advantages which it brought to the organisation in attracting recruits, rolling up a great reserve fund, and ensuring
discipline. But in the democratic state these adventitious
aids will no longer be necessary. The Trade Union will be
a definitely recognised institution of public utility to which
every person working at the craft will be imperatively expected, even if not (as is already the case with regard to the
appointment of a checkweigher),[1] legally compelled to contribute. With Trade Union membership thus virtually or
actually compulsory, Trade Union leaders will find it convenient to concentrate their whole attention on the fundamental purposes of their organisation, and to cede the mere
insurance business to the Friendly Societies. Thus, with the
complete recognition of Trade Unionism as an essential
organ of the democratic state, the Friendly Societies and
Mutual Insurance Companies, confining themselves to the
co-operative provision of larger opportunities and additional
amenities to the aged, sick, or injured workman, will be
relieved from the competition of actuarially defective trade
societies, and may therefore be expected to expand and consolidate their own position as an indispensable part of social
organisation.

To this decay of the friendly society side of Trade
Unionism there will probably be one exception. In the
democratic state the evil effects of the alternate expansions
and contractions of demand will doubtless be mitigated by
the increasing regulation and concentration of industry, if
not also, as some would say, by the substitution, for the
speculative middleman, of the salaried official of the consumers. But the inevitable fluctuations in the consumers'

---

[1] See Part II. chap. ii. "The Method of Collective Bargaining," and chap. v.
"The Standard Rate."

own tastes, together with the vicissitudes of harvests, will at all times leave some workmen in some trades or in some districts temporarily unemployed. Hence the Out of Work Benefit, or Donation, will form a permanent feature of the democratic state. This provision for temporarily unemployed craftsmen,—to be carefully distinguished from persons falling below the standard of the National Minimum, or the unemployable—can, as we have suggested, be best administered by the Trade Union. Even when, as in times of severe depression, or in cases of supersession by a new invention, some assistance of the temporarily unemployed is given from public funds, it will probably be most economical for it to take the form of a capitation grant to the Trade Union, so calculated that the allowance to each unemployed member is shared between the government and the distributing association.

But whilst Trade Unionism may be expected to lose some of its present incidental functions, we suggest that the democratic state will probably find it new duties to fulfil. For most of the purposes of government, including registration, taxation, the general education of the young, and the election of representatives, the classification of the citizens into geographical districts according to their place of abode is, no doubt, the most convenient form. But there are other purposes for which the geographical organisation may usefully be supplemented by an organisation according to professional occupations. The technical instruction of our craftsmen would, for instance, gain enormously in vigor and reality if the Trade Unions were in some way directly associated with the administration of the technological classes relating to their particular trades. Even now Trade Union committees sometimes render admirable service by watchful supervision of trade classes, by suggestion and criticism, and by practically requiring their apprentices to attend. And once it becomes clearly understood all round that the object of Technical Education is not, by increasing the number of craftsmen, to lower wages, but, by increasing the competence of those who have already entered the various trades, positively to raise their Standard of Life, the Trade Unions and the community as a whole will be seen to have an identical interest in the matter.   There is, in fact, no reason why a Trade Union should not be treated as a local administrative committee of the Technical Education Authority, and allowed, under proper supervision, to conduct its own technological classes with public funds.[1]   In other directions, too, such as the compilation of statistics relating to particular occupations, and the dissemination of information useful to members of particular crafts, the democratic state will probably make increasing use of Trade Union machinery.

Finally, there is the service of counsel.   On all issues of industrial regulation, whether in their own or other trades, the Trade Union officials will naturally assume the position of technical experts, to whom public opinion will look for guidance.   But industrial regulation is not the only matter on which a democratic state needs the counsels of a working-class organisation.   Whenever a proposal or a scheme touches the daily life of the manual-working wage-earner, the representative committees and experienced officials of the Trade Union world are in a position to contribute information and criticism, which are beyond the reach of any other class.   They are, of course, ignorant, if not incapable, of the complications and subtilties of the law.   Their suggestions are one-sided and often impracticable, and their opinion can never be accepted as decisive.   But whenever a minister has to deal with such questions as the Housing of the People or the Regulation of the Liquor Traffic, the administration of the law by magistrates or county-court judges, the un-

---

[1] There seems much to be said for combining trade classes with the provision for the temporarily unemployed.   A large proportion of the unemployed printers, for instance, who hang about the office of the London Society of Compositors waiting for a "call" from an employer, are very indifferent workmen, often young men who have "picked up" the trade without any really educational apprenticeship.   There would be much advantage if their Out of Work Donation were made conditional on their spending the idle time in perfecting themselves at their craft.

employed or the unemployable, the working of the Education
Acts and the Poor Law, or, to pass into quite another
department of the public service, the organisation of
popular recreation and amusement, he will find himself
obliged, if he wishes to make his legislation or administration genuinely successful, to discover the desires and needs
of the manual workers, as represented by the committees
and officials whom they elect.

This examination of the function of Trade Unionism
brings us face to face with its inherent limitations. Trade
Unionism, to begin with, does not furnish any complete
scheme of distribution of the community's income. The
Device of the Common Rule, can, by its very nature, never
reach any other part of the product than the minimum
applicable to the worst as well as to the best establishment
for the time being in use. It leaves untouched, as we have
shown,[1] all that large proportion of the aggregate income
which is the equivalent of the differential advantages of the
various factors of production above the marginal level,
whether their superiority lies in soil or site, machinery or
organisation, intellect or physical strength. In short, as
between different localities, different establishments, or
different individuals, Trade Unionism leaves unaffected
everything in the nature of economic rent. And even if we
imagine each branch of productive industry throughout the
community to be amalgamated into a single capitalist trust
or government department, each grade or section of manual
workers would find itself receiving, not an aliquot part of the
total produce, but a wage depending either on the minimum
necessary for the efficient fulfilment of its particular function,
or, for all the grades above the National Minimum, upon the
degree of technical specialisation, and therefore of relative
scarcity, to which it had brought its particular service. The
disposal of the balance of the product—the administration,
that is to say, of the rent of land and capital—must, under

[1] Part III. chap. iii. "The Economic Characteristics of Trade Unionism,"
under the heading "The Device of the Common Rule."

any system of society, fall to the owners of the material instruments of production.

Now, Trade Unionism has no logical connection with any particular form of ownership of land and capital, and the members of British Trade Unions are not drawn, as Trade Unionists, unreservedly either towards Individualism or towards Collectivism. Certain sections of the Trade Union world, as we have pointed out in our chapter on "The Implications of Trade Unionism,"[1] find that they can exact better terms from the capitalist employer than would be likely to be conceded to them by a democratic government department. Other sections, on the contrary, see in the extension of public employment the only remedy for a disastrous irregularity of work and all the evils of sweating. This divergence of immediate interests between different sections of producers will inevitably continue. But the nationalisation or municipalisation of any industry—the taking over of the telephones, ocean cables, railways, or mines by the central government, or the administration of slaughter-houses, tramways, river steamboats, or public-houses by the Town Council—has to be determined on wider issues than the sectional interests of the wage-earners employed. It is in their capacity of citizens, not as Trade Unionists, that the manual workers will have to decide between the rival forms of social organisation, and to make up their minds as to how they wish the economic rent of the nation's land and capital to be distributed. And though, in this, the most momentous issue of modern democracy, the manual workers will be influenced by their poverty in favor of a more equal sharing of the benefits of combined labor,[2] they will, by their Trade Unionism, not be biassed in favor of any particular scheme of attaining this result outside their own Device of the Common Rule. And when we pass from the ownership of the means

[1] Part II. chap. xii.

[2] "The social problem of the future we considered to be, how to unite the greatest individual liberty of action with a *common ownership in the raw material of the globe, and an equal participation of all in the benefits of combined labor.*"— John Stuart Mill, *Autobiography* (London, 1879), p. 232.

of production and the administration of industry to such practical problems as the best form of currency or the proper relation between local and central government, or to such vital questions as the collective organisation of moral and religious teaching, the provision for scholarship and science and the promotion of the arts—not to mention the sharper issues of "Home Rule" or foreign affairs—the members of the Trade Union world have no distinctive opinion, and their representatives and officials no special knowledge. We may therefore infer that the wage-earners will, in the democratic state, not content themselves with belonging to their Trade Union, or even to any wider organisation based on a distinction of economic class. Besides their distinctive interests and opinions as wage-earners and manual workers, they have others which they share with persons of every grade or occupation. The citizen in the democratic state, enrolled first in his geographical constituency, will take his place also in the professional association of his craft ; but he will go on to combine in voluntary associations for special purposes with those who agree with him in religion or politics, or in the pursuit of particular recreations or hobbies.

These considerations have a direct bearing on the probable development of Trade Union structure. In the first part of this work we described[1] how, in spite of historical tradition, in spite of crude ideas of democracy suited only to little autonomous communities, and in spite of a strong prejudice in favor of local exclusiveness, the Trade Union world has, throughout its whole history, manifested an overpowering impulse to the amalgamation of local trade clubs into national unions, with centralised funds and centralised administration. The economic characteristics of Trade Unionism revealed to us the source of this impulse in the fundamental importance to each separate class of operatives that its occupation should

[1] Part I. chap. i. "Primitive Democracy," chap. ii. "Representative Institutions," chap. iii. "The Unit of Government."

be governed by its own Common Rules, applicable from one end of the kingdom to the other. This centralisation of administration, involving the adoption of a national trade policy, and, above all, the constant levelling-up of the lower-paid districts to the higher standard set in more advantageous centres, requires, it is clear, the development of a salaried staff, selected for special capacity, devoting their whole attention to the commercial position and technical details of the particular section of the industry that they represent, and able to act for the whole of that section throughout the nation. It is, as we saw in our chapter on "The Method of Collective Bargaining," [1] because of the absence of such a staff that so few of the Trade Unions of the present day secure national agreements, or enforce with uniformity such Common Rules as they obtain. The Trade Union of the future will, therefore, be co-extensive with its craft, national in its scope, centralised in its administration, and served by an expert official staff of its own.

This consolidation of authority in the central office of the national union for each craft will be accompanied by an increased activity of the branches. In our description of Trade Union Structure,[2] we saw that the crude and mechanical expedients of the Initiative and the Referendum were being steadily replaced, for all the more complicated issues of government, by an organic differentiation of representative institutions. So long as a union was contented with Government by Referendum all that was necessary was an ambulatory ballot-box by which an unemployed member collected "the voices" of each factory or each pit. When a representative is appointed, the branch meeting affords the opportunity for ascertaining the desires of his constituents, impressing upon them his own advice, and consulting with them in any emergency. The branch thus becomes the local centre of the union's intellectual life. At the same time it retains and even extends its

[1] Part II. chap. ii.
[2] Part I. chap. i. "Primitive Democracy," and chap. ii. "Representative Institutions."

functions as a jury or local administrative committee. For even if the Trade Union gradually discards its purely " friendly " benefits, the branch will have to administer the all-important Out of Work Donation, supplemented, as this may be, by a grant from public funds. And with the increasing use which the democratic state may make of Trade Union machinery, it will be the branch, and not the central office, that will be charged with conducting technical classes, collecting statistics, or disseminating information. Finally, when the Trade Union world desires to make use of the Method of Legal Enactment,[1] or to supervise the conditions of employment granted by local governing bodies, the network of branches pervading every district affords, as we have seen, the only practicable way of superposing an organisation by constituencies on an organisation by trades.

There is one direction in which the branch (or, in the larger centres, the district committee representing several branches) will find this increase of work accompanied by a decrease of autonomy. The central executive and the salaried officials at the head office of each craft will be principally occupied in securing national minimum conditions of employment throughout the country. It will be for the branches and their district committees to be constantly considering the particular needs and special opportunities of their own localities. But the fact that the cost of any " advance movement " falls upon the funds of the union as a whole makes it imperative that no dispute should be begun, and even that no claim should be made, until the position has been carefully considered by the central executive representing the whole society. This precept of democratic finance is made more imperative by every consolidation of the forces of capital. It is obvious that if the demand of the branches in one town for an advance of wages or reduction of hours is liable to be met by a lockout of the whole trade throughout the country, a union which permits its local branches to involve it in war at

[1] See Part II. chap. iv. " The Method of Legal Enactment."

their own uncontrolled discretion simply courts disaster. In matters of trade policy the branches or district committees, whilst undertaking even more of the work of supervision, local interpretation, and suggestion, must definitely give up all claim to autonomy.[1]

The need for centralisation of authority, as an inevitable consequence of centralisation of funds, is not the only lesson in structure that the Trade Unions have derived from their experience, or will learn as they realise their full function in the democratic state. In our chapter on " Inter-Union Relations "[2] we pointed out that the amalgamation of different sections into a single society may easily be carried too far. The formation of a central fund, filled by equal contributions from all the members, inevitably leads to equality of franchise and government by the numerical majority. So long as the interests of all the members are fairly identical, this majority rule, where efficient representative machinery has been developed, is the most feasible contrivance for uniting administrative efficiency with popular control. But whenever the association contains several distinct classes of workers, having different degrees of skill, divergent standards of expenditure, and varying needs and opportunities, experience shows that any scheme of equalised finance and centralised administration produces, even with the best democratic machinery, neither efficiency nor the consciousness of popular control, and hence is always in a condition of unstable equilibrium. The several minorities, keenly alive to their separate requirements and opportunities, are always feeling themselves thwarted in pushing their own interests, and deprived of any effective control over the conditions of their own lives. In voluntary associations the result is a perpetual tendency to secession, each distinct section aiming at Home Rule by setting up for itself as a separate national union. This limitation on the process of amalgamation, arising out of the conditions of democratic

---

[1] See Part I. chap. iii. " The Unit of Government."
[2] Part I. chap. iv.

structure, is fortified, as we can now see, by economic considerations.[1] The largest income for the wage-earners, and the highest efficiency of industry, will, as we have pointed out, be secured not by any uniform wage for manual labor as such, or for all the operatives in any industry, but by each distinct section of workers using the Device of the Common Rule to raise to the utmost its own conditions of employment. This persistent pushing forward of each class of operatives, constantly imperilled, as it must be, by a rise in the price of the product and a diminution of demand for some particular section of labor, can be undertaken, it will be obvious, only at the risk and cost of that section, and therefore, in practice, on its own initiative, untrammelled by the votes of other sections. We may therefore expect, in the democratic state, not a single association of the whole wage-earning class, nor yet a single amalgamated union for each great industry, but separate organisations for such of the various sections of producers as are so far specialised from others as to possess and require separate Common Rules of their own.

These separate national organisations will, however, clearly have many interests in common. In such matters as cubic space, ventilation, temperature, sanitary conveniences, precautions against fire, fencing of machinery, and, last but by no means least, the fixing and distribution of the Normal Day, the conditions of employment must, in the majority of manufacturing industries, be identical for all the grades of labor in each establishment. Even for Collective Bargaining they must necessarily develop some federal machinery for concerting identical demands upon their common employers, and for supporting them by joint action. Moreover, as we have pointed out, in all questions of this sort, the democratic state will be influenced in the main by the Doctrine of a Living Wage, and they will accordingly tend more and more to be settled on physiological grounds and enforced by the Method of Legal Enactment. It is unnecessary

[1] Part III. chap. iii. "The Economic Characteristics of Trade Unionism."

to repeat that for any effective use of this Method in a Parliamentary community, organisation by crafts is practically useless, unless it is supplemented by a geographical organisation by constituencies. Hence we see rising in the Trade Union world not only federal action among groups employed in one establishment, such as the joint committees of the building trades, but also such political federations as the United Textile Factory Workers' Association, the local Trades Councils, and the Trade Union Congress. But the economic analysis of the Common Rule has shown us that there is a third, and even more important, reason for this federal action between different trades. It will, as we have seen, be a primary duty of the Trade Unions in the democratic state to maintain and progressively to raise, not their own Common Rules alone, but also the National Minimum for the whole wage-earning class. To the national amalgamation of each section, and the federal union of the different sections in each great industry, there must be added a federation of the whole Trade Union world.

Our vision of the sphere of Trade Unionism in the democratic state does more than explain the development of the Trade Union world into a hierarchy of federations. It gives us also its political programme. The weakness and inefficiency of the existing Trades Councils and Trade Union Congress spring, as we have pointed out, not only from their extremely imperfect structure, but also from an entire misapprehension of their proper function.[1] In spite of the fact that Trade Unionists include men of all shades of political opinion, — Conservatives from Lancashire, Liberals from Scotland, Socialists from London and Yorkshire, — the federal organisations of the British Trade Unions of to-day are perpetually meddling with wide issues of general politics, upon which the bulk of their constituents have either no opinions at all, or are marshalled in the ranks of one or another of the political parties. Resolutions abolishing the House of Lords, secularising education,

[1] See Part II. chap. iv. "The Method of Legal Enactment."

rehabilitating silver, establishing a system of peasant
proprietorship, enfranchising leaseholds, or "nationalising
the means of production, distribution, and exchange,"—
questions in which the Trade Unionists, as such, are not more
interested, not better informed, nor yet more united than
other citizens, — find a place on Trade Union agendas,
and either get formally passed through sheer indifference, or
become the source of discord, recrimination, and disruption.
This waste of time and dissipation of energy over extraneous
matters arises, we think, mainly from the absence of any
clearly conceived and distinctive Trade Union programme.
In the democratic state of the future the Trade Unionists
may be expected to be conscious of their own special
function in the political world, and to busy themselves
primarily with its fulfilment. First in importance to every
section we put the establishment of a National Minimum of
education, sanitation, leisure, and wages, its application to all
the conditions of employment, its technical interpretation to
fit the circumstances of each particular trade, and, above all,
its vigorous enforcement, for the sake of the whole wage-
earning world, in the weak trades no less than in those more
able to protect themselves. But the systematic rehandling
of the Factories and Workshops, Mines, Railways, Shops, and
Merchant Shipping Acts, which is involved in this conception
of a National Minimum, will, as we have explained, only
secure the base of the pyramid. Upon this fundamental
ground level each separate craft will need to develop such
technical regulations of its own as are required to remove any
conditions of employment which can be proved to be actually
prejudicial to the efficiency of the operatives concerned. On
all these points, as we have seen, the claim of any particular
section for the help of the law may not only advantageously
be supported by all the other trades, but may also profitably
be conceded by the representatives of the community. And
since the utmost possible use of the Method of Legal Enactment will, as we have seen, still permanently leave a large
sphere for the Method of Collective Bargaining, there must

be added to the political programme of the federated unions all that we have described as the Implications of Trade Unionism.[1]   The federal executive of the Trade Union world would find itself defending complete freedom of association, and carefully watching every development of legislation or judicial interpretation to see that nothing was made criminal or actionable, when done by a Trade Union or its officials, which would not be criminal or actionable if done by a partnership of traders in pursuit of their own gain.   And the federal executive would be on its guard, not only against a direct attack on the workmen's organisations, but also against any insidious weakening of their influence. It would insist on the legal prohibition of all forms of truck, or deductions from wages, including fines, loom-rent, and payments to national insurance funds or employers' benefit societies.   Above all, it would resist any attempt on the part of the employer to transform the workman's home into a workshop, and thus escape the responsibility for the carrying out of the conditions of employment embodied in the law of the land   With a programme of this kind, the federal executive would find itself backed by the whole force of the Trade Union world, which would thus contribute to the councils of the nation that technical knowledge and specialist experience of manual labor without which the regulation of industry can become neither popular nor efficient.

The student of political science will be interested in considering what light the experience of the workmen's organisations throws upon democracy itself. The persistence of Trade Unionism, and its growing power in the state, indicates, to begin with, that the very conception of democracy will have to be widened, so as to include economic as well as political relations. The framers of the United States constitution, like the various parties in the French Revolution of 1789, saw no resemblance or analogy between the personal power which they drove from the castle, the altar, and the throne, and that which they left

---

[1] Part II. chap. xii. and Appendix I. as to the legal position.

unchecked in the farm, the factory, and the mine. Even at the present day, after a century of revolution, the great mass of middle and upper-class "Liberals" all over the world see no more inconsistency between democracy and unrestrained capitalist enterprise, than Washington or Jefferson did between democracy and slave-owning. The "dim, inarticulate" multitude of manual-working wage-earners have, from the outset, felt their way to a different view. To them, the uncontrolled power wielded by the owners of the means of production, able to withhold from the manual worker all chance of subsistence unless he accepted their terms, meant a far more genuine loss of liberty, and a far keener sense of personal subjection, than the official jurisdiction of the magistrate, or the far-off, impalpable rule of the king. The captains of industry, like the kings of yore, are honestly unable to understand why their personal power should be interfered with, and kings and captains alike have never found any difficulty in demonstrating that its maintenance was indispensable to society. Against this autocracy in industry, the manual workers have, during the century, increasingly made good their protest. The agitation for freedom of combination and factory legislation has been, in reality, a demand for a "constitution" in the industrial realm. The tardy recognition of Collective Bargaining and the gradual elaboration of a Labor Code signifies that this Magna Carta will, as democracy triumphs, inevitably be conceded to the entire wage-earning class. "One thing is clear," wrote, in 1869, a hostile critic ; "the relation between workmen and their employers has permanently changed its character. The democratic idea which rules in politics has no less penetrated into industry. The notion of a governing class, exacting implicit obedience from inferiors, and imposing upon them their own terms of service, is gone, never to return. Henceforward, employers and their workmen must meet as equals."[1] What has not been so obvious to middle-class observers is the necessary condition of this

---

[1] *Trade Unionism*, by James Stirling (Glasgow, 1869), p. 55.

equality. Individual Bargaining between the owner of the means of subsistence and the seller of so perishable a commodity as a day's labor must be, once for all, abandoned. In its place, if there is to be any genuine "freedom of contract," we shall see the conditions of employment adjusted between equally expert negotiators, acting for corporations reasonably comparable in strategic strength, and always subject to and supplemented by the decisions of the High Court of Parliament, representing the interests of the community as a whole. Equality in industry implies, in short, a universal application of the Device of the Common Rule.[1]

Besides the imperative lesson that political democracy will inevitably result in industrial democracy, Trade Unionism affords some indications as to the probable working of democratic institutions. We notice, in the first place, that the spontaneous and untrammelled democracies of the workmen show neither desire for, nor tendency to, "one dead level" of equality of remuneration or identity of service. On the contrary, the most superficial study of the Trade Union world makes the old-fashioned merging of all the manual workers into the "laboring class" seem almost ludicrous in its ineptitude. Instead of the classic economist's categories

[1] We attribute to an imperfect appreciation of the change of status many industrial disputes, and a large proportion of the resentment of working-class pretensions manifested by the brain - working and propertied classes. The employer cannot rid himself of the idea that he has bought the whole energy and capacity of the operative within the hours of the working day, just as the slave-owner had bought the whole capacity of his slaves for life. The workman, on the other hand, regards himself as hired to co-operate in industry by performing a definite task, and feels himself defrauded if the employer seeks to impose upon him any extra strain or discomfort, or any different duty, not specified in the bargain. A similar misunderstanding lingers as to social relations. The capitalist is very fond of declaring that labor is a commodity, and the wage contract a bargain of purchase and sale like any other. But he instinctively expects his wage-earners to render him, not only obedience, but also personal deference. If the wage contract is a bargain of purchase and sale like any other, why is the workman expected to touch his hat to his employer, and to say "sir" to him without reciprocity, when the employer meets on terms of equality the persons (often actually of higher social rank than himself) from whom he buys his raw material or makes the other bargains incidental to his trade?

of " the capitalist " and " the laborer," we see Trade Unionism
adopting and strengthening the almost infinite grading of
the industrial world into separate classes, each with its own
corporate tradition and Standard of Life, its own specialised
faculty and distinctive needs, and each therefore exacting its
own " Rent of Opportunity " or " Rent of Ability." And
when we examine the indirect effect of the Trade Union
Device of the Common Rule in extinguishing the Small
Master system and favoring the growth of the Great
Industry,[1] we realise how effectively Trade Unionism extends
a similar grading to the brain-working directors of industry.
In place of the single figure of the " capitalist entrepreneur " we
watch emerging in each trade a whole hierarchy of specialised
professionals, — inventors, designers, chemists, engineers,
buyers, managers, foremen, and what not,—organised in
their own professional associations,[2] and standing midway
between the shareholder, taxpayer, or consumer, whom they
serve, and the graded army of manual workers whom they
direct. Nor does this progressive specialisation of function
stop at economic relations. The internal development of
the Trade Union world unmistakably indicates that division
of labor must be carried into the very structure of democracy.
Though the workmen started with a deeply-rooted conviction
that " one man was as good as another," and that democracy
meant an "equal and identical " sharing of the duties of government, as well as of its advantages, they have been forced to
devolve more and more of " their own business " on a specially
selected and specially trained class of professional experts.
And in spite of the almost insuperable difficulties which

[1] Part III. chap. iii. "The Economic Characteristics of Trade Unionism."

[2] It is not commonly realised how numerous and how varied are these professional associations. Besides the obvious instances oi the three "learned
professions," organisations of this kind now exist among all grades of brain-
workers in almost every department of social life. Not to speak of the architects, surveyors, engineers, actuaries, and accountants, we have such associations
as those of the Gasworks Managers, Colliery Managers, School Board Clerks,
Sanitary Engineers, Sanitary Inspectors, Medical Officers of Health, Inspectors
of Weights and Measures, different varieties of Foremen and Managers, and even
Ships' Clerks. No study of these professional associations, or of their extensive
Common Rules, has yet been made.

representative institutions present to a community of un-leisured manual workers, we find union after union abandon-ing the mechanical devices of the Referendum and the Initiative, and gradually differentiating, for the sake of the efficient administration of its own affairs, the Representative from the Civil Servant on the one hand and the Elector on the other. In short, whilst Trade Unionism emphasises the classic dictum of Adam Smith that division of labor increases material production, it carries this principle into the organ-isation of society itself. If democracy is to mean the com-bination of administrative efficiency with genuine popular control, Trade Union experience points clearly to an ever-increasing differentiation between the functions of the three indispensable classes of Citizen-Electors, chosen Representa-tives, and expert Civil Servants.[1]

Thus we find no neat formula for defining the rights and duties of the individual in society. In the democratic state every individual is both master and servant. In the work that he does for the community in return for his subsistence he is, and must remain, a servant, subject to the instructions and directions of those whose desires he is helping to satisfy. As a Citizen-Elector jointly with his fellows, and as a Con-sumer to the extent of his demand, he is a master, determining, free from any superior, what shall be done. Hence, it is the supreme paradox of democracy that every man is a servant in respect of the matters of which he possesses the most intimate knowledge, and for which he shows the most expert proficiency, namely, the professional craft to which he devotes his working hours ; and he is a master over that on which he knows no more than anybody else, namely, the general interests of the community as a whole. In this paradox, we suggest, lies at once the justification and the strength of democracy. It is not, as is commonly asserted by the superficial, that Ignorance rules over Knowledge, and Medio-crity over Capacity. In the administration of society Know-ledge and Capacity can make no real and durable progress

[1] See Part I. chaps. i. to iv. " Trade Union Structure."

except by acting on and through the minds of the common human material which it is desired to improve. It is only by carrying along with him the "average sensual man," that even the wisest and most philanthropic reformer, however autocratic his power, can genuinely change the face of things. Moreover, not even the wisest of men can be trusted with that supreme authority which comes from the union of knowledge, capacity, and opportunity with the power of untrammelled and ultimate decision. Democracy is an expedient—perhaps the only practicable expedient—for preventing the concentration in any single individual or in any single class of what inevitably becomes, when so concentrated, a terrible engine of oppression. The autocratic emperor, served by a trained bureaucracy, seems to the Anglo-Saxon a perilously near approach to such a concentration. If democracy meant, as early observers imagined, a similar concentration of Knowledge and Power in the hands of the numerical majority for the time being, it might easily become as injurious a tyranny as any autocracy. An actual study of the spontaneous democracies of Anglo-Saxon workmen, or, as we suggest, of any other democratic institutions, reveals the splitting up of this dangerous authority into two parts. Whether in political or in industrial democracy, though it is the Citizen who, as Elector or Consumer, ultimately gives the order, it is the Professional Expert who advises what the order shall be.[1]

[1] It is here that we discover the answer to Carlyle's question, " How, in conjunction with inevitable Democracy, indispensable Sovereignty is to exist : certainly it is the hugest question ever heretofore propounded to Mankind " (*Past and Present*, Book IV. chap. i. p. 311 of 1843 edition). The student of Austin will probably find, in the industrial democracy of the future, that Sovereignty, in the old sense, is as hard to discover as it already is in the political democracies of to-day (see Professor D. G. Ritchie, *Darwin and Hegel*, London, 1893). Whatever sphere may be allotted to private ownership of land and capital, this will no more carry with it uncontrolled power to fix the conditions of industry, than kingship does of fixing the conditions of citizenship. In modern conceptions of society the old simple division into Sovereign and Subject is entirely superseded by a complex differentiation of social structure and function.

More interesting, perhaps, in the present connection, is Auguste Comte's famous proposal to separate Social Knowledge from Social Power—to differentiate

It is another aspect of this paradox that, in the democratic state, no man minds his own business. In the economic sphere this is a necessary consequence of division of labor ; Robinson Crusoe producing solely for his own consumption, being the last man who minded nothing but his own business. The extreme complication brought about by universal production for exchange in itself implies that every one works with a view to fulfilling the desires of other people. The crowding together of dense populations, and especially the co-operative enterprises which then arise, extend in every direction this spontaneous delegation to professional experts of what the isolated individual once deemed " his own business." Thus, the citizen in a modern municipality no longer produces his own food or makes his own clothes ; no longer protects his own life or property ; no longer fetches his own water; no longer makes his own thoroughfares, or cleans or lights them when made ; no longer removes his own refuse or even disinfects his own dwelling. He no longer educates his own children, or doctors and nurses his own invalids. Trade Unionism adds to the long list of functions thus delegated to professional experts the settlement of the conditions on which the citizen will agree to co-operate in the national service. In the fully-developed democratic state, the Citizen will be always minding other people's business. In his professional occupation he will, whether as brain-worker or manual laborer, be continually striving to fulfil the desires of those whom he serves, whilst, as an Elector, in his parish

a class of highly-educated Priests, possessing no authority, from the Administrators, wielding uncontrolled authority under the constant moral influence of this Spiritual Power. This proposal, though embodied in a fantastic form, seems at first sight to approximate to that separation between Expert Knowledge and Ultimate Control which we regard as a necessary condition of Liberty. In reality, however, it would secure no such separation. The Administrators, highly educated, specialised, and constantly acting on affairs, would possess both Knowledge and Power, and would be irresistible. Comte's proposed differentiation is much more that between two separate classes of Experts—the men of pure science, investigating and discovering, and the practical men of action, applying to the affairs of daily life the generalisations of science. In democracy, these two classes of Experts, both absolutely essential to progress, are neither of them entrusted with ultimate decision.

or his co-operative society, his Trade Union or his political
association, he will be perpetually passing judgment on issues
in which his personal interest is no greater than that of his
fellows.

If, then, we are asked whether democracy, as shown by
an analysis of Trade Unionism, is consistent with Individual
Liberty, we are compelled to answer by asking, What is
Liberty? If Liberty means every man being his own
master, and following his own impulses, then it is clearly
inconsistent, not so much with democracy or any other
particular form of government, as with the crowding together
of population in dense masses, division of labor, and, as we
think, civilisation itself. What particular individuals, sections, or classes usually mean by " freedom of contract,"
" freedom of association," or " freedom of enterprise " is freedom of opportunity to use the power that they happen to
possess ; that is to say, to compel other less powerful people
to accept their terms. This sort of personal freedom in a
community composed of unequal units is not distinguishable
from compulsion. It is, therefore, necessary to define Liberty
before talking about it, a definition which every man will
frame according to his own view of what is socially desirable.
We ourselves understand by the words " Liberty " or " Freedom," not any quantum of natural or inalienable rights, but
such conditions of existence in the community as do, in
practice, result in the utmost possible development of faculty
in the individual human being.[1] Now, in this sense democracy is not only consistent with Liberty, but is, as it seems
to us, the only way of securing the largest amount of it. It
is open to argument whether other forms of government may
not achieve a fuller development of the faculties of particular
individuals or classes. To an autocrat, untrammelled rule over
a whole kingdom may mean an exercise of his individual
faculties, and a development of his individual personality, such
as no other situation in life would afford. An aristocracy, or

---

[1] " Liberty, in fact, means just so far as it is realised, the right man in the
right place."—Sir John Seeley, *Lectures and Essays*, p. 109.

government by one class in the interests of one class, may conceivably enable that class to develop a perfection in physical grace or intellectual charm attainable by no other system of society. Similarly, it might be argued that, where the ownership of the means of production and the administration of industry are unreservedly left to the capitalist class, this " freedom of enterprise " would result in a development of faculty among the captains of industry which could not otherwise be reached. We dissent from all these propositions, if only on the ground that the fullest development of personal character requires the pressure of discipline as well as the stimulus of opportunity. But, however untrammelled power may affect the character of those who possess it, autocracy, aristocracy, and plutocracy have all, from the point of view of the lover of liberty, one fatal defect. They necessarily involve a restriction in the opportunity for development of faculty among the great mass of the population. It is only when the resources of the nation are deliberately organised and dealt with for the benefit, not of particular individuals or classes, but of the entire community ; when the administration of industry, as of every other branch of human affairs, becomes the function of specialised experts, working through deliberately adjusted Common Rules ; and when the ultimate decision on policy rests in no other hands than those of the citizens themselves, that the maximum aggregate development of individual intellect and individual character in the community as a whole can be attained.

For our analysis helps us to disentangle, from the complex influences on individual development, those caused by democracy itself. The universal specialisation and delegation which, as we suggest, democratic institutions involve, necessarily imply a great increase in capacity and efficiency, if only because specialisation in service means expertness, and delegation compels selection. This deepening and narrowing of professional skill may be expected, in the fully-developed democratic state, to be accompanied by a growth in culture of which our present imperfect organisation gives us no adequate idea. So long as life is one long scramble for personal gain—still more, when it is one long struggle against destitution—there is no free time or strength for much development of the sympathetic, intellectual, artistic, or religious faculties. When the conditions of employment are deliberately regulated so as to secure adequate food, education, and leisure to every capable citizen, the great mass of the population will, for the first time, have any real chance of expanding in friendship and family affection, and of satisfying the instinct for knowledge or beauty. It is an even more unique attribute of democracy that it is always taking the mind of the individual off his own narrow interests and immediate concerns, and forcing him to give his thought and leisure, not to satisfying his own desires, but to considering the needs and desires of his fellows. As an Elector—still more as a chosen Representative—in his parish, in his professional association, in his co-operative society, or in the wider political institutions of his state, the "average sensual man" is perpetually impelled to appreciate and to decide issues of public policy. The working of democratic institutions means, therefore, one long training in enlightened altruism, one continual weighing, not of the advantage of the particular act to the particular individual at the particular moment, but of those "larger expediencies" on which all successful conduct of social life depends.

If now, at the end of this long analysis, we try to formulate our dominant impression, it is a sense of the vastness and complexity of democracy itself. Modern civilised states are driven to this complication by the dense massing of their populations, and the course of industrial development. The very desire to secure mobility in the crowd compels the adoption of one regulation after another, which limit the right of every man to use the air, the water, the land, and even the artificially produced instruments of production, in the way that he may think best. The very discovery of improved industrial methods, by leading to specialisation, makes manual laborer and brain-worker alike dependent on the rest of the community for the means of subsistence, and subordinates them, even in their own crafts, to the action of others. In the world of civilisation and progress, no man can be his own master. But the very fact that, in modern society, the individual thus necessarily loses control over his own life, makes him desire to regain collectively what has become individually impossible. Hence the irresistible tendency to popular government, in spite of all its difficulties and dangers. But democracy is still the Great Unknown. Of its full scope and import we can yet catch only glimpses. As one department of social life after another becomes the subject of careful examination, we shall gradually attain to a more complete vision. Our own tentative conclusions, derived from the study of one manifestation of the democratic spirit, may, we hope, not only suggest hypotheses for future verification, but also stimulate other students to carry out original investigations into the larger and perhaps more significant types of democratic organisation.

APPENDICES

APPENDICES

APPENDIX I

THE LEGAL POSITION OF COLLECTIVE BARGAINING [1]

SINCE 1824-25, when Collective Bargaining with respect to wages and hours was made lawful, and especially since 1871-75, when this right of combined action was extended to all other conditions of employment, the controversy as to the precise legal position of this method of Trade Unionism has turned upon its various incidents. The points at issue have been continually shifting, according as the lawyers have dealt with the different forms of pressure that combination incidentally exercises on other parties. For half a century after the repeal of the Combination Acts in 1824-25, the question seems, in the minds of judges and legislators, always to have been muddled up with that of physical violence. Because angry strikers here and there committed assaults, it was habitually assumed that Trade Unionism practically depended upon, and inevitably involved, personal molestation of one sort or another. With such an assumption any exact discrimination between various forms of compulsion was not to be looked for. This confusion has now been cleared away, so far at least as the judges are concerned. In 1867 Professor Beesly incurred great odium in his own class for pointing out that "a Trade Union murder was neither better nor worse than any other murder." To-day, as Sir Frederick Pollock observes, "there is no doubt that assault and battery, unlawful wounding, riot, unlawful assembly, and other open offences against the Queen's peace, are *equally* offences, whether committed in the course of any trade dispute, or by members of any trade combination, or not."[2] Trade Unionists have, on this point, never asked for any other version of the law.

The confusion of mind just described often led judges and

[1] See Part II. chap. ii. "The Method of Collective Bargaining.

[2] Memorandum in Appendix to Report of the Royal Commission on Labor, C. 7063.

magistrates, down to 1891, to regard as a criminal offence, under the head of "intimidation," any threat or warning uttered by a Trade Unionist to an employer or a non-unionist, even if the consequences alluded to were of the most peaceful kind. This interpretation of the statutes has always been resented by the workmen, and was, in 1891, authoritatively overruled. The point in controversy was, in what the statutory offence of intimidation consisted. "Must intimidation be a threat of something which, if executed, would be a criminal offence against person or tangible property? Or does it include the threat of doing that which would be civilly, though not criminally, wrongful? Or, lastly, can it include the announcement of an intent to do or cause to be done something which, without being in itself wrongful, is capable of putting moral compulsion on the person threatened? A specially constituted Court of Queen's Bench Division, proceeding on the intention of Parliament as shown by the Trade Union Act of 1871 as well as in the Act of 1875, has pronounced the first of these interpretations to be the correct one."[1] "Intimidation" is thus authoritatively narrowed down to a threat of committing a criminal offence against person or tangible property.

So far as violence and intimidation are concerned, the issues have, therefore, been completely settled to the satisfaction of the Trade Unionists. However adverse may be the judicial bias against Trade Unionism, however injurious the judges may think its action, it is now determined that nothing is a criminal offence when done in pursuance of a trade combination, which would not be a criminal offence if done in pursuance of the most conservative or respectable of associations. This can hardly be said to be yet the case with regard to those breaches of public order which are summarily dealt with by the magistrate. It is difficult for any trade dispute to take place, except in the most highly organised unions, without the workmen laying themselves open to such accusations as "obstructing the thoroughfare," or the vague charge of committing acts of annoyance. Contraventions of this kind are committed every day by all sorts and conditions of men, from the excited crowds of stockbrokers in the City down to the gatherings round street-corner preachers. Whether or not they are made the subject of police prosecution, and punished by the magistrate, depends, partly on the magnitude of the offence, but much more on the view taken by the authorities as to the objects of the gathering.

[1] Memorandum in Appendix to Report of the Royal Commission on Labor, C. 7063; see also Gibson *v.* Lawson and Curran *v.* Treleaven, 1891, 2 Q.B. 545; *Law Quarterly Review*, January 1892, p. 7.

This brings us to the subject of "picketing," which has attracted much more public attention than it deserves.[1] Since 1875 it is clear that workmen are within their legal rights in declining, by concerted action, to enter into contracts of service with a particular employer, or of withdrawing themselves from his service on the termination of their engagements, or after the prescribed notice. The strike, that is to say, is definitely made lawful. The strikers have the same right as any one else to communicate the fact that a strike is in progress to any workmen who are unaware of it, and also to address peaceful persuasions or exhortations to such workmen. It is often forgotten that "picketing" in this sense was specially and expressly legalised by the Act of 1875. "Attending at or near the house or place where a person resides, or works, or carries on business, or happens to be, or the approach to such house or place, in order merely to obtain or communicate information shall not," declares the statute, "be deemed watching or besetting," however annoying such a practice may be to the employer whose objects are defeated thereby. The practice of picketing has, therefore, received explicit legislative sanction, and any acts committed by Trade Union pickets ought not to be regarded as offences, unless they would equally have been so regarded if they had been committed in pursuance of some admittedly laudable object, such, for instance, as dissuading men from excessive drinking or women from prostitution. This, however, the average magistrate seldom understands. He habitually assumes that strikes, though not criminal, are morally reprehensible; and he chooses, in defiance of the intention of Parliament, to consider the moral suasion of the most peaceful picketing as an unwarranted interference with personal liberty. He is, therefore, often led to regard as criminal, when perpetrated by Trade Unionists, acts of obstruction or annoyance, which would be over-

[1] A clear definition and full description of picketing, from the pen of Mr. Henry Crompton, will be found in the *History of Trade Unionism*, p. 262; see also the article by Mr. George Howell in the *Contemporary Review*, September 1877, and his *Conflicts of Labour and Capital*, 2nd edition (London, 1890). It is interesting to learn from Dr. Gross that "picketing is not a modern invention. In 1614 the Company of Mercers and Ironmongers of Chester ordered T. Aldersey (who had married the niece of an ironmonger) to shut up his shop. He refused, 'soe daie by daie two others (of their Company) walked all daie before the said shop and did forbidd and inhibitt all that came to the said shopp for buyinge any wares there, and stopped such as came to buy wares there.' The Mayor ordered them to depart 'upon their oathe'; they answered that they were sworn to their Company; and so 'they walked and remayned and plaied their wilfull parte.'"—Harl. MS. Brit. Mus. 2054, ff. 89-90, cited in *The Gild Merchant*, vol. i. p. 36 *note*.

looked in the religious propagandist, the tract distributor, the street hawker, the organ-grinder, a football crowd, or a Salvation Army procession.   Such a partial exercise of the necessary magisterial discretion is unjust.

The picketing thus sanctioned by Act of Parliament is, of course, strictly limited in character.   In this respect, however, Trade Union picketing stands in exactly the same position as any other inform-ing or persuading, such, for instance, as a group of temperance advocates might use to induce men not to enter a public-house.   It must, to begin with, not create any breach of public order, or obstruc-tion of the thoroughfare—matters to be dealt with by the police irrespective of the objects or motives of the persons concerned.   It must not infringe the statutory prohibition of "watching or besetting" with a view to compulsion,[1] from which, as we have mentioned, picketing for the purpose merely of obtaining or communicating information is expressly excluded.   Finally, Trade Union picketing, like the action of any other group of people acting in concert for the most laudable object, is subject to the vague and indeterminate limits of the law of criminal conspiracy.

But the whole controversy as to violence and intimidation, in connection with Trade Unionism, has really passed out of date. The serious crimes which disgraced the workmen's combinations in Dublin and Glasgow at the beginning of this century, and which lasted in Sheffield down to 1867, have been for many years entirely unknown.   Individual workmen still commit assaults when their blood is up, in connection with Trade Union as with all other disputes.   So far as Trade Unionism itself is concerned, we do not think that any fair-minded student would hesitate to conclude that, especially for the last thirty years, so far from inciting to or causing crime, it has exercised a wonderful restraining influence.   The more strongly organised is the union, the more efficacious is this influence for peace.   The most powerful unions of the present day, the most exacting in their demands on the employers, have gone a stage farther, and have laid aside the whole system of picketing, with its intangible annoyance and easy transition into breaches of public order.   In the great five months' strike of the Cotton-spinners

---

[1] " Every person who, *with a view to compel any other person to abstain from doing or to do any act* which such other person has a legal right to do or abstain from doing, wrongfully and without legal authority . . . watches or besets the house or other place where such other person resides or works or carries on business or happens to be, or the approach to such house or place," shall on conviction . . . be liable to a penalty of £20 or three months' imprisonment.— Sec. 7 of Conspiracy and Law of Property Act, 1875.

in 1893, and in the gigantic stoppage of the Miners' Federation in 1894, practically no "pickets" were posted or needed. "It is not worth the risk, trouble, or expense," writes a leading Trade Union official, "of resorting to the practice. . . . Every wage-earner is able to read and write, and discern the difference between right and wrong; and with the assistance of the public press a full knowledge can be gained as to the reasons why a strike takes place. Hence no one is required to hang about a workshop where a strike is going on for the supposed purpose of giving information to persons who may desire to apply for work on the employer's conditions."[1] Picketing, in fact, is a mark not of Trade Unionism, but of its imperfection. With such completely organised trades as the Cotton Operatives and the Boilermakers, and, in many districts, the Coalminers, compulsory Trade Unionism leaves practically no competent workman outside the combination. The weak-kneed member is kept loyal to his union by a far more effective sanction than having to run the gauntlet of the pickets. In this, as in other respects, the very completeness of the compulsion renders its forms both strictly lawful and absolutely impalpable.

There remains the elastic and indeterminable law of criminal conspiracy, the limits of which, never yet defined with any precision, seem at the present moment (October 1897) more than usually uncertain. A combination in itself lawful, but contemplating any act in itself criminal, whether as an end or as a means, is certainly a criminal conspiracy, even if its main object or general purpose be lawful and laudable. On the other hand, the mere act of combination, for a purpose not forbidden by law, not contemplating any criminal act, and not violating any actionable private right, is, however objectionable it may be to other people, certainly not criminal in the United Kingdom, though such a combination would be criminal, if formed without express authority, in many foreign countries. The case in doubt is that in which a combination for lawful purposes, contemplating and using only lawful means, violates some actionable private right. Such a combination, besides giving ground for a civil action, might, in the opinion of some authorities, be indictable as a criminal conspiracy, if the private right is one in which the public has a sufficient interest.[2] So long as this view is

---

[1] *Cotton Factory Times*, 8th October 1896.

[2] Sir W. Erle, *The Law relating to Trade Unions* (London, 1869), p. 32 ; R. S. Wright, *The Law of Criminal Conspiracies and Agreements* (London, 1873); and the incidental observations of the law lords in the case of the Mogul Steamship Company *v.* M'Gregor, Gow, & Co., Appeal Cases, 1892 ; see also House of Commons Return, No. 217 of 1897, " the Judges' Opinions."

not definitely negatived, there will always be danger, especially in periods of reaction, of the law of criminal conspiracy being invoked and enforced against any association which is unpopular, or against which the judges or the governing classes are prejudiced. Trade Unionists have, until lately, thought themselves specially protected against any such application of the criminal law by sec. 3 of the Act of 1875, which enacts that "an agreement or combination by two or more persons to do or procure to be done any act in contemplation or furtherance of a trade dispute between employers and workman shall not be indictable as a conspiracy, if such act committed by one person would not be punishable as a crime." This seems clear enough, but the judges have lately been exhibiting a disposition to narrow the scope of the section in such a way as to bring many ordinary incidents of a strike once more within danger of the criminal law. In connection with the civil actions of Temperton *v.* Russell, 1893, 1 Q.B. 715; J. Lyons & Son *v.* Wilkins, 1896, 1 Ch. 811; and Flood *v.* Jackson, various judges expressed the opinion that unless the acts complained of were done in contemplation or in furtherance, not of a trade dispute at large, but of one between the particular parties bringing pressure to bear on the one hand, and the parties on whom pressure was borne on the other, they might be indictable as a criminal conspiracy. There is still so much ignorance of, and prejudice against even the ordinary Trade Union action in industrial disputes that any such whittling away of the Trade Union charter of 1875, if upheld by the judges, may possibly mean that the workmen will need to fight the whole battle for freedom over again.

Failing the criminal law, the employers have lately turned to a new weapon against the workmen's combinations. Though a Trade Union cannot itself be proceeded against,[1] its officers are, of course, like every one else, personally liable to be sued for damages if they commit an actionable wrong against any individual. Here we must discriminate between the breaking of a contract, and the mere refusal to enter into one. If a workman breaks his contract of service (as, for instance, by leaving his work without giving the notice agreed upon) he can be sued by the employer, and made to pay damages. This remedy is frequently used by coalowners against miners who have gone impetuously on strike. Trade Union executives are always warning their members against such breaches of contract; and

---

[1] So strong is still the legal feeling against Trade Unionism that, in 1896, a judge of the High Court was capable, in flat defiance of the Trade Union Act of 1871, of making a Trade Union a party to a suit, and attaching its corporate funds for damages. It cost the workmen a large sum in costs to get this injustice overruled by the Court of Appeal (Warnham *v.* Stone).

there is no real grievance in the fact that a Trade Union official, who urges workmen to break their contracts, renders himself personally liable to be sued by the employer for the damage that results from his advice to the men to violate agreements that they have entered into.

The bias of the judges against Trade Unionism is, however, still so strong that they have recently forged a new weapon for the employers' use. It may be admitted, as both law and justice, that a Trade Union official should be held personally liable for damages, if he persuades men to do, to the detriment of a third party, an unlawful act. It is an entirely different thing when he merely persuades them to do what is admittedly within their rights, even though the exercise of these rights should cause damage to a third party. In the case of Temperton *v.* Russell,[1] the officers of the unions of various building trades, and of a joint committee of such trades, in the town of Hull, were held liable in damages to an employer, merely for having persuaded workmen not to renew their engagements, this being admittedly within the workmen's rights, and coercion or intimidation of the workmen not being alleged. According to this decision a combination of workmen to leave a particular firm, at the expiration of their contracts, and after due notice, may render the members of that combination liable to be individually and personally sued for damages. The judges have even gone a step farther. In Flood *v.* Allen, the District Delegate of the Boilermakers had informed an employer with perfect politeness and courtesy, that the members of his union would not renew their engagement with him, if he continued to employ two Shipwrights on certain iron work. The employer thereupon preferred to exercise his legal right to dispense, after due notice, with the services of these two workmen, who then brought an action for damages against the District Delegate and members of the Executive Committee of the Boilermakers' Trade Union. The Court of Appeal held that no conspiracy to procure their discharge had been proved. But the Court decided that it was an actionable wrong for even a single person "maliciously" to procure the discharge of workmen to their detriment, and the Boilermakers' District Delegate was accordingly cast in damages.

Both these cases turned upon the question of motive. If a trader, for his own profit, induces a customer without breach of contract to dispense with the services of his rivals, and transfer the custom to himself, the rivals have clearly no remedy at law. In the

[1] 1 Q.B. 1893, 715.

case of the Mogul Steamship Company *v.* M'Gregor, Gow, & Co.[1] it was decided that even a combination of traders, seeking, for their own profit, to exclude a particular rival from trade, and thus ruin him, was not actionable. In the case of Temperton *v.* Russell the same argument was incidentally upheld. "This is a perfectly free country," said Mr. Justice Chitty, "and people have a right to trade and to carry on competition to the very utmost limit. People may advance their own trade by every possible effort. They may hold out such inducements to trade with them that people will withdraw their custom from others and give it to them, and they may combine to do that; and if the purpose of the combination is in (the opinion of the jury) primarily to subserve their own trade, if as an incident of that they hurt other people, they have done no wrong for which an action can be maintained." To any one acquainted with the objects and methods of Trade Unionists, it would be clear enough that their refusal to work with particular employers or particular workmen was "primarily to subserve their own trade," and according to the present law of England, no more an actionable wrong than the concerted attempt of a capitalist ring to oust rivals from business, or bring them to terms. But by a series of wire-drawn distinctions, the judges succeeded in putting Trade Unionism outside the pale. The Trade Union officials who were sued were admittedly not acting with a view to their own personal gain, and hence, in the eye of the law, their action, though absolutely impersonal, was technically "malicious." This absence of the only motive that the law would recognise as a justification would not have mattered, had the judges been willing to see that (the Trade Union officials being also members of their society) they acted as members of a combination having a clear joint interest at stake. If the combination in question had (even if legally incorporated) been one of traders aiming at increasing their profits, the agents would not have been liable for the damage that they, in pursuit of the advantage of the combination, and within the scope of its own legal rights, incidentally did to a third party. But because the combination was a Trade Union, not aiming at commercial profit, the judges refused to recognise that its members had any adequate lawful motive for jointly exercising their admitted rights, by their duly appointed agent, to the incidental detriment of other persons.[2] The judges, in

---

[1] *Law Reports*, 23 Q.B.D. 598; A.C. 1892, 38.

[2] A corresponding distinction seems to have been made in the United States with regard to "sympathetic strikes" or combinations to boycott. A strike for the strikers' own benefit is legal, because they have what the law regards as a legitimate motive, namely, that of bettering their own condition. But in a sympathetic strike or boycott "there can be no possible intention of benefiting

fact, though conceding that the workmen were not acting from spite or malice in the ordinary sense and that their motives might be "laudable, meritorious, and philanthropic," for the ultimate benefit of their own class, and even of mankind, failed to perceive that their intention of increasing their own wages, and of reducing the burden cast upon them by their own unemployed members by getting these employed instead of the Shipwrights, constituted as real, immediate, and direct a pecuniary interest as the trader's hope of profit.[1]

Unless these decisions are overruled, Trade Unionists will have to fight over again the battle for the right of combination which was believed to have been won in 1875. Collective Bargaining will become impossible if, whenever Trade Unionists are warned not to accept employment from a particular firm for any reason whatsoever, the Trade Union officials can be harassed by writs, cast in damages, and driven into bankruptcy. Unfortunately, the present generation of Trade Unionists, not excluding the responsible officials, are not alive to the gravity of the legal situation. They will presently find, if we are not mistaken, that the argument of the Court of Appeal can be applied much farther than has yet appeared. The most peaceful picketing may become unlawful and can be stopped by injunction, if the employer merely issues a writ claiming damages against a Trade Union official for withdrawing the workmen. In one case[2] already an aggrieved employer has actually induced the Courts to issue an injunction against picketing as such, as if this were any more illegal than abstaining from purchasing. But this is not all. There is always the possibility of the vague and elastic law of libel being brought to bear on Collective Bargaining. If the judges hold that the ordinary objects of Trade Unionism do not amount to such a motive for the exercise of actual personal rights, as will take that exercise out of the character of "legal malice," the mere announcement to the members of a Union, in its official circular, that a particular firm is a "closed house," where Trade Unionists are advised not to work, may lead to an action for damages by the firm in question (see Trollope's case, 72 L.T. 342); and any expression in which a jury chooses to find an innuendo may lead to an adverse verdict.

the conspirators but at best a desire to help their fellow-workmen; and the law does not yet recognise altruism to this extent !"—*Labor in its Relations to Law*, by F. J. Stimson, p. 92 (New York, 1895), and the *Handbook to the Labor Law of the United States* (New York, 1896), by the same author.

[1] "The principle of acknowledging every man's right to trade freely has been applied by the Courts in a sense which has accorded to combined capitalists a privilege not granted to the Trade Union."—The Hon. A. Lyttelton, "The Law of Trade Combinations," in *A Policy of Free Exchange*, p. 291.

[2] J. Lyons & Son *v.* Wilkins, 1896, 1 Ch. 811.

The decisions to which we have referred, though they amount at present to an authoritative statement of the law, have excited animadversion among lawyers ; and some jurists of eminence, such as Sir Frederick Pollock, have expressed doubts whether they will be upheld by the House of Lords. The law lords themselves are known to be sharply divided on the question, and their judgment is still withheld owing to this difference of opinion. The philosophy of the question appears to us to be simple. If the community thinks it desirable to let the conditions of labor be settled by bargaining, each party must be left to be the judge of what is for its own interest, and to seek that interest by combination, even to the detriment of others. It is a mockery of justice, on the one hand, to accord to workmen, in order that they may exact better terms from their employers, the abstract right of combining to refuse to work ; and, on the other hand, to cast them in damages when they lawfully and peacefully exercise that right to the detriment of the other party to the bargain, or even third persons. Trade Unionists, it is clear, must be accorded, in the domain of civil procedure, what has long since been conceded to them in criminal law. If a workman is allowed the option, to the detriment of his employer, of refusing to continue in his service unless certain conditions are granted ; if, moreover, this option extends to freedom to refuse to work with unpopular associates, it is impossible, now that the right of combination has been unreservedly conceded by Parliament, to prevent the same option being collectively exercised by the combination of workmen acting through their duly appointed agents. The fact that this use of the right of combination causes pecuniary damage to the employer, or to other persons, whether customers, employers, or workmen, is no more argument against it than the corresponding fact that a gigantic modern enterprise seriously reduces the profits of the middleman, ruins its smaller rivals, and finally raises the price to the consumer. It may well be that combinations of workmen, or combinations of capitalists, lawfully and peacefully pursuing what they conceive to be their own corporate or class interest, will insist on terms in their bargains which are detrimental, not only to other parties, but also to the common weal. In that case the remedy is not to shackle one of the contracting parties by civil liabilities to individuals who may feel aggrieved by the exercise of the right, but to protect the community from such consequences of legal freedom of contract by definitely prescribing, by Factory Act or otherwise, any conditions of employment or trade that are deemed necessary in the public interest.

APPENDIX II[1]

THE BEARING OF INDUSTRIAL PARASITISM AND THE POLICY OF A
NATIONAL MINIMUM ON THE FREE TRADE CONTROVERSY

THE existence of parasitic trades supplies the critic of international Free Trade with an argument which has not yet been adequately met. To the enlightened patriot, ambitious for the utmost possible development of his country, it has always seemed a drawback to Free Trade, that it tended, to a greater or lesser extent, to limit his fellow-countrymen's choice of occupation. Thus, one community, possessing great mineral wealth, might presently find a large proportion of its population driven underground; another might see itself doomed to become the mere stock-yard and slaughter-house of the world; whilst the destiny of a third might be to have its countryside depopulated, and the bulk of its citizens engaged in the manufacture, in the slum tenements of great cities, of cheap boots and ready-made clothing for the whole habitable globe. To this contention the answer has usually been that the specialisation of national function, whilst never likely to be carried to an extreme, was economically advantageous all round. Such a reply ignores the possibility of industrial parasitism. If unfettered freedom of trade ensured that each nation would retain the industry in which its efficiency was highest, and its potentialities were greatest, this international "division of labor" might be accepted as the price to be paid for getting every commodity with the minimum of labor. But under unfettered freedom of competition there is, as we have seen, no such guarantee. Within a trade, one district may drive all the rest out of the business, not by reason of any genuine advantage in productive efficiency, but merely because the workers in the successful district get some aid from the rates or from other sources. Within a community, too, unless care be

[1] See Part III. chap. iii. "The Economic Characteristics of Trade Unionism."

taken to prevent any kind of parasitism, one trade or one process may flourish and expand at the expense of all the rest, not because it is favored by natural advantages or acquired capacity, but merely by reason of some sort of "bounty." Under Free Trade the international pressure for cheapness is always tending to select, as the speciality of each nation in the world-market, those of its industries in which the employers can produce most cheaply. If each trade were self-supporting, the increased efficiency of the regulated trades would bring these easily to the top, notwithstanding (or rather, in consequence of) the relatively high wages, short hours, and good sanitary conditions enjoyed by their operatives. If, however, the employers in some trades can obtain labor partially subsisted from other sources, or if they are free to use up in their service not only the daily renewed energy, but also the capital value of successive relays of deteriorating workers, they may well be able to export more cheaply than the self-supporting trades, to the detriment of these, and of the community itself. And this, as we have seen, is the direct result of the very freedom of Individual Bargaining on which the Free Traders rely. Indeed, if we follow out to its logical conclusion the panacea of unlimited freedom of competitive industry both within the country and without, we arrive at a state of things in which, out of all the various trades that each community pursues, those might be "selected" for indefinite expansion, and for the supply of the world-market, in which the employers enjoyed the advantage of the greatest bounty; those, for instance, which were carried on by operatives assisted from other classes, or, still worse, those supplied with successive relays of necessitous wage-earners standing at such a disadvantage in the sale of their labor that they obtained in return wages so low and conditions so bad as to be positively insufficient to maintain them permanently in health and efficiency. Instead of a world in which each community devoted itself to what it could do best, we should get, with the "sweated trades," a world in which each community did that which reduced its people to the lowest degradation. Hence the Protectionist is right when he asserts that, assuming unfettered individual competition within each community, international free trade may easily tend, not to a good, but to an exceedingly vicious international division of labor.

This criticism is not dealt with, so far as we are aware, in any of the publications of the Cobden Club, nor by the economic defenders of the Free Trade position. Thus, Professor Bastable, in his lucid exposition of *The Theory of International Trade* (2nd edition, London, 1897), assumes throughout that the prices of commodities in the home market, and thus their relative export, will vary according to the actual "cost of production," instead of merely according to their "expenses of production," to the capitalist entrepreneur. Yet it is evidently not the sum of human efforts and sacrifices involved in the production that affects the import or export trade, but simply the expenses that production involves to the capitalist. This absence of any reference to the possibility of the cheapness being due to underpaid (because subsidised or deteriorating) labor, enables Professor Bastable optimistically to infer (p. 18) that "the rule is that each nation exports those commodities for the production of which it is specially suited." Similarly Lord Farrer, in *The State in its Relation to Trade* (London, 1883), when stating the argument against Protection, simply assumes (p. 134) that the industry for which the country is specially suited pays higher wages than others. "One thing is certain, viz. that we cannot buy the French or Swiss ribbons without making and selling something which we can make better and cheaper than ribbons, and which *consequently* brings more profit to our manufacturer, *and better wages to our workmen.*" And Mr. B. R. Wise, seeking in his *Industrial Freedom* to revise and restate the Free Trade argument in the light of practical experience, is driven to warn his readers that "it cannot be too often repeated that the competition of abstract political economy —that competition through which alone political economy has any pretension to the character of a science—is a competition between equal units," . . . and nothing could be further from the truth than to suppose that "free competition" in the labor market bore any resemblance to the competition between equal units that the current expositions of Free Trade theory required.[1]

But though the existence of parasitic trades knocks the bottom out of the argument for *laisser faire*, it adds no weight to the case for a protective tariff. What the protectionist is concerned about is the contraction of some of his country's industries; the evil revealed by our analysis is the expansion of certain others. The advocate of a protective tariff aims at excluding imports; the opponent of "sweating," on the other hand, sees with regret the rapid growth of particular exports, which imply the extension within the country of its most highly subsidised or most parasitic industries. Hence, whatever ingenious arguments may be found in favor of a protective tariff,[2] such a remedy fails altogether to cope with this

[1] B. R. Wise, *Industrial Freedom* (London, 1882), pp. 13, 15.
[2] For any adequate presentment of the case against international free trade, the student must turn to Germany or the United States, notably to Friedrich List, *The National System of Political Economy*, published in Germany in 1841, and

particular evil. If the expansion of the industries which England pursues to the greatest economic advantage—say, for instance, coal mining and shipbuilding, textile manufacture and machine-making —is being checked, this is not because coal and ships, textiles and machinery are being imported into England from abroad, but because other less advantageous industries within England itself, by reason of being favored with some kind of bounty, have secured the use of some of the nation's brains and capital, and some of its export trade. This diversion would clearly not be counteracted by putting an import duty on the small and exceptional amounts of coal and shipping, textiles and machinery that we actually import, for this would leave unchecked the expansion of the subsidised trades, which, if the subsidy were only large enough, might go on absorbing more and more of the nation's brains and capital, and more and more of its export trade. To put it concretely, England might find its manufactures and its exports composed, in increasing proportions, of slop clothing, cheap furniture and knives, and the whole range of products of the sweated trades, to the detriment of its present staple industries of cotton and coal, ships and machinery In the same way, every other country might find its own manufactures and its own exports increasingly made up of the products of its own parasitic trades. In short, the absolute exclusion by each country of the imports competing with its own products would not, any more than Free Trade itself, prevent the expansion within the country of those industries which afforded to its wage-earners the worst conditions of employment.[1]

A dim inkling of this result of international competition is at the back of recent proposals for the international application of the Device of the Common Rule. During the past seven years statesmen have begun to feel their way towards an international uniformity of factory legislation, so as to make all cotton mills, for instance, work identical hours, and workmen are aspiring to an international

translated by Sampson Lloyd (London, 1885) and the works of H. C. Carey. The arguments of List and Carey were popularised in America by such writers as Professor R. E. Thompson, *Political Economy with Especial Reference to the Industrial History of Nations* (Philadelphia, 1882), H. M. Hoyt, *Protection and Free Trade the Scientific Validity and Economic Operation of Defensive Duties in the United States*, 3rd edition (New York, 1886); whilst another line has been taken by Francis Bowen, *American Political Economy*. The whole position has been restated by Professor Patten, in *The Economic Basis of Protection* (Philadelphia, 1890), and other suggestive works which deserve more attention in England.

[1] It is unnecessary to notice the despairing suggestion that a protective duty should be placed on the products of the sweated trades themselves. But these,

Trade Unionism, by means of which, for example, the coalminers, cotton-operatives, glass-workers, or dock-laborers of the world might simultaneously move for better conditions. If, indeed, we could arrive at an International Minimum of education and sanitation, leisure and wages, below which no country would permit any section of its manual workers to be employed *in any trade whatsoever*, industrial parasitism would be a thing of the past. But internationalism of this sort—a "zollverein based on a universal Factory Act and Fair Wages clause"—is obviously Utopian. What is not so generally understood, either by statesmen or by Trade Unionists, is that international uniformity of conditions *within a particular trade*, which is all that is ever contemplated, would do little or nothing to remedy the evil of industrial parasitism. In this matter, as in others, a man's worst foes are those of his own household. Let us imagine, for instance, that, by an international factory act, all the cotton mills in the world were placed upon a uniform basis of hours and child-labor, sanitation and precautions against accidents. Let us carry the uniformity even a stage further, and imagine what is impossible, an international uniformity of wage in all cotton mills. All this would in no way prevent a diversion of the nation's brains and capital away from cotton manufacture to some other industry, in which, *by reason of a subsidy or bounty*, the employer stood at a greater relative advantage towards the home or foreign consumer. The country having the greatest natural advantages and technical capacity for cotton manufacture would doubtless satisfy the great bulk of the world's demand for cotton goods. But, if there existed within that same country any trades carried on by parasitic labor, or assisted by any kind of bounty, it would obtain less of the cotton trade of the world than would otherwise be the case ; the marginal business in cotton would tend to be abandoned to the next most efficient country, in order that some brains and capital might, to the economic loss of the nation and of the world, take advantage of the subsidy or bounty.[1] We see,

as we have seen (if they are really parasitic industries like the wholesale clothing manufacture, and not merely self-supporting but unprogressive industries like English agriculture), will usually be exporting trades, not subject to the competition of foreign imports. Merely to put an import duty on the odds and ends of foreign-made clothing or cheap knives that England imports would in no way strengthen the strategic position, as against the employer, of the sweated outworkers of East London or Sheffield, or render the respectable young women of Leeds less eager to be taken on at a pocket-money wage in the well-appointed clothing factories of that city.

[1] This hypothetical case is, we believe, not unlike the actual condition of the cotton manufacture in the United Kingdom at the present time, in spite of the absence of international uniformity.

therefore, that even an international uniformity of conditions within a particular trade would not, in face of industrial parasitism at home, prevent the most advantageously situated country from losing a portion of this uniformly regulated trade.   The parasitic trades have, in fact, upon the international distribution of industry, an effect strictly analogous to that which they have upon the home trade.   By ceding as a bribe to the consumer the bounty or subsidy which they receive, they cause the capital, brains, and labor of the world to be distributed, in the aggregate, in a less productive way than would otherwise have been the case.

We can now see that the economists of the middle of the century only taught, and the Free Trade statesmen only learnt, one-half of their lesson.   They were so much taken up with the idea of removing the fiscal barriers between nations that they failed to follow up the other part of their own conception, the desirability of getting rid of bounties of every kind.   M'Culloch and Nassau Senior, Cobden and Bright, realised clearly enough that the grant of money aid to a particular industry out of the rates or taxes enabled that industry to secure more of the nation's brains and capital, and more of the world's trade, than was economically advantageous.   They even understood that the use of unpaid slave labor constituted just such a bounty as a rate in aid of wages.   But they never clearly recognised that the employment of children, the overwork of women, or the payment of wages insufficient for the maintenance of the operative in full industrial efficiency stood, economically, on the same footing.   If the object of " Free Trade " is to promote such a distribution of capital, brains, and labor among countries and among industries, as will result in the greatest possible production, with the least expenditure of human efforts and sacrifices, the factory legislation of Robert Owen and Lord Shaftesbury formed as indispensable a part of the Free Trade movement as the tariff reforms of Cobden and Bright.   "During that period," wrote the Duke of Argyll of the nineteenth century,[1] "two great discoveries have been made in the Science of Government : the one is the immense advantage of abolishing restrictions upon Trade ; the other is the absolute necessity of imposing restrictions on labor. . . . And so the Factory Acts, instead of being excused as exceptional, and pleaded for as justified only under extraordinary conditions, ought to be recognised as in truth the first legislative recognition of a great Natural Law, quite as important as Freedom of Trade, and which, like this last, was yet destined to claim for itself wider and wider application."

[1] *The Reign of Law* (London, 1867), pp. 367, 399.

Seen in this light, the proposal for the systematic enforcement, throughout each country, of its own National Minimum of education, sanitation, leisure, and wages, becomes a necessary completion of the Free Trade policy. Only by enforcing such a minimum on all its industries can a nation prevent the evil expansion of its parasitic trades being enormously aggravated by its international trade. And there is no advantage in this National Minimum being identical or uniform throughout the world. Paradoxical as it may seem to the practical man, a country enforcing a relatively high National Minimum would not lose its export trade to other countries having lower conditions, any more, indeed, than a country in which a high Standard of Life spontaneously exists, loses its trade to others in which the standard is lower. If the relatively high National Minimum caused a proportionate increase in the productive efficiency of the community, it would obviously positively strengthen its command of the world market. But even if the level of the National Minimum were, by democratic pressure, forced up farther or more rapidly than was compensated for by an equivalent increase in national efficiency, so that the expenses of production to the capitalist employer became actually higher than those in other countries, this would not stop (or even restrict the total of) our exports. " General low wages," emphatically declare the economists, " never caused any country to undersell its rivals, nor did general high wages ever hinder it from doing so."[1] So long as we continued to desire foreign products, and therefore to import them in undiminished quantity, enough exports would continue to be sent abroad to discharge our international indebtedness. We should, it is true, not get our tea and foodstuffs, or whatever else we imported, so cheaply as we now do ; the consumer of foreign goods would find, indeed, that these had risen in price, just as English goods had. If we ignore the intervention of currency, and imagine foreign trade to be actually conducted, as it is virtually, by a system of barter, we shall understand both this rise of price of foreign goods, and the continued export of English goods, even when they are all dearer than the corresponding foreign products. For the English importing firms, having somehow to discharge their international indebtedness, and finding no English products which they can export at a profit, will be driven to export some even at a loss—a loss which, like the item of freight or any other expense of carrying on their business, they will add to the price charged to the consumer of foreign imports. They will, of course, select for export

---

[1] J. S. Mill, *Principles of Political Economy*, Book III. chap. xxv. § 4, p. 414 of 1865 edition.

those English products on which the loss is least—that is to say, those in which England stands at relatively the greatest advantage, or, what comes to the same thing, the least disadvantage. Therefore, if the rise in the expense of English production were uniform, not only the total, but also the distribution of our exports would remain unaffected. The foreign consumer, by reason of the cheapness of production of his own goods, will then be getting English-made goods at a lower price than would otherwise be the case—it may be, even a lower price than the Englishman is buying them at in his own country—just as the Englishman at the present time buys American products in London at the comparatively low level of English prices, and sometimes actually cheaper than they are sold at in New York. For this process of exporting at an apparent loss, as a set-off against a profitable import trade, actually takes place, now in one country, now in another.[1] It sometimes happens that the same firm of merchants both exports and imports : more usually, however, the compensatory process is performed through the banking houses, and manifests itself in those fluctuations of the foreign exchanges, which, though clear enough to the eye of the practical financier and the economist, shroud all the processes of international exchange from the ordinary man by a dense veil of paradox.

The practical check to a rise in the National Minimum comes, indeed, not from the side of international trade, but, as we have already explained, from the home taxpayer and the home consumer. Every rise in the National Minimum not compensated for by some corresponding increase in the efficiency with which the national industry was carried on would imply an increase in the number of the unemployable, and thus in the Poor Rate or other provision for their maintenance ; and every increase in the expenses of production would be resented as a rise in price by the bulk of the population. The lowlier grades of labor, employing a majority of the citizens, would clearly benefit by the improvement which the rise would cause in their own conditions. Other grades of producers, including the brain-working directors of industry, would find their own "rent" of specialised or otherwise exceptional faculty undiminished, even if they had to pay away more of it in taxes and higher prices. The great and growing army of officials on fixed incomes would loudly complain of the increased cost of living, which would presently be met by a rise in salaries. But the real

---

[1] When, for instance, the export of gold is prohibited, or when all the gold has already been sent away ; or when, for any reason, less expensive ways of discharging a balance of indebtedness do not exist.—See Goschen's *Theory of the Foreign Exchanges*, or Clare's *A.B.C. of the Foreign Exchanges*.

sufferers would be the *rentier* class, existing unproductively on their investments. These persons would be hit both ways : they would find themselves, by increased taxation, saddled with most of the cost of the unemployable, and by higher prices, charged with at least their share of the increase in the nation's wage-bill. Such a practical diminution in the net income of the dividend-receiving classes would, from Ricardo down to Cairnes, have been supposed to correct itself by a falling off in their rate of saving, and therefore, as it was supposed, in the rate of accumulation of additional capital. This, as we have seen, can no longer be predicted, even if we cannot yet bring ourselves to believe, with Sir Josiah Child and Adam Smith, that the shrinking of incomes from investments would actually quicken production and stimulate increased accumulation. What it might conceivably do would be to drive the *rentier* class to live increasingly abroad, with indirect consequences which have to be considered.

We have hitherto left on one side the possible migration of capital from a country, in which the National Minimum had been unduly raised, to others in which labor could be hired more cheaply. This is hindered, to an extent which we do not think is sufficiently appreciated, by the superior amenity of English life to the able business man. So long as our captains of industry prefer to live in England, go abroad with reluctance even for high salaries, and return to their own country as soon as they possibly can, it will pay the owners of capital to employ it where this high business talent is found. The danger to English industrial supremacy would seem to us, therefore, to lie in any diminution of the attractiveness of life in England to the able brain-working Englishman. An increase in the taxation of this class, or a rise in the price of the commodities they consume, is not of great moment, provided that facilities exist for them to make adequate incomes ; and these rewards of exceptional talent are, it will be remembered, in no way diminished by the Device of the Common Rule. But any loss of public consideration, or any migration of their *rentier* friends or relations, might conceivably weaken their tie to England, and might, therefore, need to be counter-acted by some increase in their amenities or rewards.[1] Our own opinion is that this increased amenity, and also this increased reward of exceptional ability, would actually be the result of a high National Minimum. It is difficult for the Englishman of to-day to form any

[1] It would be interesting to inquire how far the fatal "absenteeism" of Ireland's men of genius has been caused or increased by the reduction of Dublin from the position of a wealthy and intellectual capital to that of a second-rate provincial town.

adequate idea of how much pleasanter English life would be if we were, once for all, rid of the slum and sweating den, and no class of workers found itself condemned to grinding poverty; if science had so transformed our unhealthy trades that no section of the population suffered unnecessarily from accident or disease; and if every grade of citizens was rapidly rising in health, intelligence, and character.

It follows that each community is economically free, without fear of losing its foreign trade, to fix its own National Minimum, according to its own ideas of what is desirable, its own stage of industrial development, and its own customs of life. The course and extent of international trade—if we imagine all fiscal barriers to be removed, and all bounties to be prevented—is, in fact, determined exclusively by the desires of the world of consumers, and the actual faculties and opportunities of the producers in the different countries; not by the proportion in which each nation chooses to share its National Dividend between producers and property-owners. Each community may, therefore, work out its own salvation in the way it thinks best. The nation eager for progress, constantly raising its National Minimum, will increase in productive efficiency, and steadily rise in health and wealth. But it will not thereby interfere with the course chosen by others. The country which honors Individual Bargaining may reject all regulation whatsoever, and let trade after trade become parasitic; but it will not, by its settling down into degradation, gain any aggregate increase in international trade, or really undermine its rivals.[1] Finally, the nation which prefers to be unprogressive, but which yet keeps all its industries self-supporting, may, if circumstances permit its stagnation, retain its customary organisation, and yet continue to enjoy the same share in international commerce that it formerly possessed.

[1] Let us suppose, for instance, that the capitalists in the United States so far strengthen their position as to put down all combinations of the wage-earners, annul all attempts at factory legislation, and, in fact, prohibit every restriction on Individual Bargaining as a violation of the Constitution. The result would doubtless be a proletarian revolution. But assuming this not to occur, or to be suppressed, and the rule of the Trusts to be unchecked, we should expect to see the conditions of employment in each trade fall to subsistence level, and with the advance of population, stimulated by this hopeless poverty, even below the standard necessary for continued efficiency. The entire continent of America might thus become parasitic, and successive generations of capitalists, served by a hierarchy of brain-working agents, might use up for their profit successive generations of degenerate manual toilers, until these were reduced to the level of civilisation of the French peasants described by La Bruyére. But the total international trade of America would not be thereby increased; on the contrary, it would certainly be diminished as the faculties of the nation declined.

APPENDIX III[1]

SOME STATISTICS BEARING ON THE RELATIVE MOVEMENTS OF THE
MARRIAGE AND BIRTH-RATES, PAUPERISM, WAGES, AND THE
PRICE OF WHEAT.

In connection with the relation of the number of births to the
number of marriages, and the connection of one or both of these
with the price of wheat, the amount of pauperism, or the rate of
wages, the following diagram and table may be of interest.

We have placed side by side the number of persons, per thousand
of the population in England and Wales, who were married or born
in each year from 1846 to 1895 inclusive; the number simultaneously in receipt of Poor Law relief on one day in each of the
years 1849 to 1895 inclusive; and the average recorded price of
wheat per imperial quarter for each year from 1846 to 1896. These
are the ordinary statistics of the Registrar-General's Reports. To
them we have added the weekly wages from 1846 to 1896 actually
paid to the engineman at a small colliery in the Lothians, taken
from the colliery books. Where the rate was altered during any
year, the average of the fifty-two weekly rates of that year has been
calculated. We have also added columns showing the Trade Union
Standard Rate for Stonemasons in Glasgow from 1851 to 1896,
averaged in the same manner, and that for Compositors in London
from 1846 to 1896, the latter (the "Stab" or time wages) changing
so rarely that it has been taken as constant for each year. And in
order to give some rough idea of the amount of real wages, to which
these money wages have been equivalent, we have in each case
reckoned out the "wages in wheat," the amount of wheat that the
Lothians Engineman, the Glasgow Stonemason, and the London
Compositor could have purchased each year with a full week's wages.
This does not, of course, express the "real wages" with any precision,

[1] See Part III. chap. i. "The Verdict of the Economists."

for whilst the price of wheat has moved predominantly in one direction, the amount paid by the workmen for meat and house-rent has certainly moved considerably in the other. It must be remembered, too, that no allowance has been made for "lost time," periods of unemployment, and other deductions. The wages of the Engineman are practically continuous throughout the year. The Stonemason, on the other hand, is necessarily idle in the months of frost, and probably loses more, even in the summer, by deductions of one kind and another, than he gains by "overtime." The London Compositor may be either employed with great constancy, or be intermittently out of work. It does not seem possible to ascertain whether these irregularities are greater or less than in past times. Nor can it be assumed with certainty that the wages at different periods represent a payment for the same labor. The work of the Stonemason and the Compositor is, perhaps, not essentially different to-day from that of the corresponding classes fifty years ago ; the higher standard of speed and intensity now required being set off against the reduction of the weekly hours. On the other hand, the development of steam engines, and the increased speed and complexity of their working, have transformed the Engineman into a skilled and responsible mechanic, who is now claiming to be a certificated professional.

The diagram and table of figures have been prepared by Mr. F. W. Galton :—

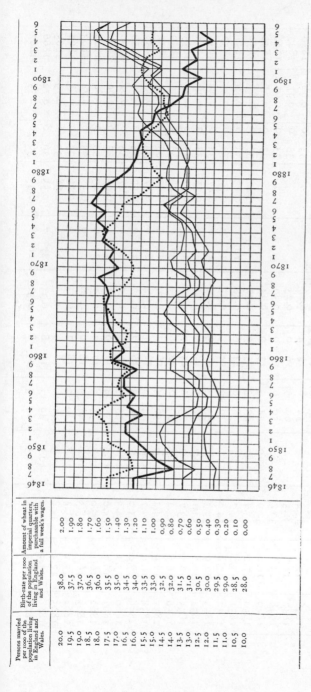

Persons married per 1000 of the population living in England and Wales.	Birth-rate per 1000 of the population living in England and Wales.	Amount of wheat in imperial quarters, purchasable with a full week's wages.
20.0	38.0	2.00
19.5	37.5	1.90
19.0	37.0	1.80
18.5	36.5	1.70
18.0	36.0	1.60
17.5	35.5	1.50
17.0	35.0	1.40
16.5	34.5	1.30
16.0	34.0	1.20
15.5	33.5	1.10
15.0	33.0	1.00
14.5	32.5	0.90
14.0	32.0	0.80
13.5	31.5	0.70
13.0	31.0	0.60
12.5	30.5	0.50
12.0	30.0	0.40
11.5	29.5	0.30
11.0	29.0	0.20
10.5	28.5	0.10
10.0	28.0	0.00

Dotted line .... Persons married per 1000 of the population living in England and Wales.

Thick Black line —— Birth-rate per 1000 of the population living in England and Wales.

Thin Black lines —— Highest line.—Average number of quarters of wheat purchasable with the weekly wages of a London Compositor, calculated at the Standard Trade Union Rate.

Middle line.—Average number of quarters of wheat purchasable with the weekly wages of a Glasgow Stonemason, calculated at the Standard Trade Union Rate.

Lowest line.—Average number of quarters of wheat purchasable with the actual weekly earnings of an Engineman at a Colliery in the Lothians.

[To face page 874.]

Year.	Quarters of wheat purchasable with wages of Compositor London per week.	Standard Rate of wages of Compositors London per week.		Quarters of wheat purchasable by the wages of Stonemason Glasgow per week.	Average Standard Rate of wages per week of Stonemasons in Glasgow.		Quarters of wheat purchasable with the Engineman's wages per week.	Average weekly wages of Engineman in a colliery in the Lothians.		Average recorded price of wheat per quarter in England and Wales.		Average number to 1000 persons living in receipt of Poor Law Relief England and Wales.	Persons born per 1000 of population living England and Wales.	Persons married per 1000 of population living England and Wales.	Year.
		s.	d.		s.	d.		s.	d.	s.	d.				
1846	0.60	33	0	...	...		0.26	14	4	54	8	...	33.8	17.2	1846
1847	0.47	33	0	...	...		0.23	16	0	69	9	...	31.5	15.8	1847
1848	0.65	33	0	...	...		0.30	15	0	50	6	...	32.4	15.9	1848
1849	0.75	33	0	...	...		0.34	15	0	44	3	62.0	32.9	16.2	1849
1850	0.82	33	0	...	...		0.37	15	0	40	3	56.7	33.4	17.2	1850
1851	0.86	33	0	0.53	20	6	0.38	14	6	38	6	52.4	34.2	17.2	1851
1852	0.81	33	0	0.50	20	6	0.35	14	5	40	10	53.0	34.2	17.4	1852
1853	0.62	33	0	0.47	25	0	0.27	14	3	53	3	48.2	33.3	17.9	1853
1854	0.46	33	0	0.35	25	0	0.21	15	0	72	5	46.4	34.1	17.2	1854
1855	0.44	33	0	0.33	25	0	0.21	15	7	74	8	47.7	33.7	16.2	1855
1856	0.48	33	0	0.43	30	0	0.24	16	8	69	2	48.2	34.4	16.7	1856
1857	0.59	33	0	0.42	23	9	0.29	16	2	56	4	44.6	34.4	16.5	1857
1858	0.75	33	0	0.57	25	0	0.34	15	1	44	2	44.7	33.7	16.0	1858
1859	0.75	33	0	0.57	25	0	0.37	16	3	43	9	41.5	35.0	17.0	1859
1860	0.62	33	0	0.47	25	0	0.32	17	0	53	3	40.1	34.3	17.1	1860
1861	0.60	33	0	0.43	23	9	0.31	17	0	55	4	41.9	34.6	16.3	1861
1862	0.60	33	0	0.43	23	9	0.31	17	2	55	5	46.7	35.0	16.1	1862
1863	0.74	33	0	0.53	23	9	0.40	18	0	44	9	48.0	35.3	16.8	1863
1864	0.82	33	0	0.59	23	9	0.45	18	2	40	2	43.8	35.4	17.2	1864
1865	0.79	33	0	0.68	28	6	0.43	18	0	41	10	41.9	35.4	17.5	1865
1866	0.72	36	0	0.55	27	7	0.35	17	8	49	11	40.5	35.2	17.5	1866
1867	0.55	36	0	0.45	28	8	0.31	19	8	64	5	42.5	35.4	16.5	1867

1	2	3	4	5	6	7	8	9	10	11	12	13	14	15	16
1868	0.56	0	36	0.45	8	28	0.28	9	17	9	63	43.6	35.8	16.1	1868
1869	0.75	0	36	0.57	7	27	0.40	4	19	2	48	43.4	34.8	15.9	1869
1870	0.77	0	36	0.59	7	27	0.43	0	20	10	46	43.5	35.2	16.1	1870
1871	0.64	0	36	0.49	7	27	0.35	0	20	8	56	41.6	35.0	16.7	1871
1872	0.63	0	36	0.52	9	29	0.41	4	23	0	57	36.9	35.6	17.4	1872
1873	0.61	0	36	0.54	10	31	0.49	11	28	8	58	33.9	35.4	17.6	1873
1874	0.65	0	36	0.61	0	34	0.54	0	30	8	55	31.5	36.0	17.0	1874
1875	0.80	0	36	0.80	1	36	0.66	8	29	2	45	29.7	35.4	16.7	1875
1876	0.78	0	36	0.87	4	40	0.61	2	28	2	46	27.5	36.3	16.5	1876
1877	0.63	0	36	0.71	4	40	0.50	6	28	9	56	27.0	36.0	15.7	1877
1878	0.77	0	36	0.59	7	27	0.67	0	31	5	46	27.3	35.6	15.2	1878
1879	0.82	0	36	0.58	6	25	0.62	5	27	0	43	29.0	34.7	14.4	1879
1880	0.81	0	36	0.61	6	25	0.61	10	26	4	44	28.4	34.2	14.9	1880
1881	0.79	0	36	0.66	7	27	0.58	3	26	4	45	28.2	33.9	15.1	1881
1882	0.80	0	36	0.77	9	29	0.58	3	25	1	45	27.2	33.8	15.5	1882
1883	0.86	0	36	0.83	10	31	0.62	9	25	7	41	26.7	33.5	15.5	1883
1884	1.01	0	36	0.91	9	29	0.72	9	26	8	35	26.0	33.6	15.1	1884
1885	1.10	0	36	0.96	9	29	0.80	2	26	10	32	26.0	32.9	14.5	1885
1886	1.16	0	36	0.92	9	29	0.85	3	26	0	31	26.6	32.8	14.2	1886
1887	1.11	0	36	0.93	9	29	0.81	3	25	6	32	26.2	31.9	14.4	1887
1888	1.13	0	36	1.04	9	29	0.80	4	26	10	31	26.0	31.2	14.4	1888
1889	1.21	0	36	1.00	10	30	0.90	11	31	9	29	25.0	31.1	15.0	1889
1890	1.13	0	36	0.89	10	31	1.00	10	33	11	31	23.8	30.2	15.5	1890
1891	1.03	0	38	1.16	11	32	0.90	2	33	0	37	22.8	31.4	15.6	1891
1892	1.26	0	38	1.37	1	35	1.10	3	32	3	30	22.7	30.5	15.4	1892
1893	1.44	0	38	1.58	1	36	1.25	10	33	4	26	23.2	30.8	14.7	1893
1894	1.66	0	38	1.61	1	36	1.48	10	33	10	22	23.4	29.6	15.1	1894
1895	1.65	0	38	1.61	2	37	1.44	3	33	1	23	24.3	30.4	15.0	1895
1896	1.45	0	38	1.46	3	38	1.27	3	33	2	26	...	...	...	1896

APPENDIX IV

A SUPPLEMENT TO THE BIBLIOGRAPHY OF TRADE UNIONISM

THE following list of publications bearing on Trade Unionism and combinations of workmen has no special connection with the present work, and must be regarded merely as a supplement to the list, forty-four pages in length, which formed Appendix VI. of the *History of Trade Unionism*. It has been prepared in the same manner as the original list. It accordingly omits all Parliamentary Papers, for which the student should consult the excellent classified catalogues issued by Messrs. P. S. King and Son of Westminster; it omits all local histories and records mentioned in the bibliography appended to vol. i. of *The Gild Merchant* by Dr. Gross; and it makes no attempt to include ordinary economic works on the one hand, or trade histories on the other. As before, we have given the reference number in the British Museum catalogue, whenever we have been able to find a copy of the work in that invaluable storehouse, and we have mentioned other libraries only when no copy could be discovered at the British Museum.

For the present work, even more than for the *History of Trade Unionism*, we have had to go, not to any regularly published books, but to the voluminous internal literature of the Trade Unions themselves, of which hundreds of publications are issued annually. These are still seldom collected or preserved by public libraries, though they afford most valuable material to the student of sociology. The British Library of Political Science (10 Adelphi Terrace, Strand, London; director, Professor W. A. S. Hewins) has now been established for the express purpose of collecting these and other materials for sociological inquiry. Our own considerable collection of manuscript extracts and printed documents relating to Trade Unionism, comparatively few of which are mentioned in the following list, has now been deposited in this library, where it can be consulted by any student.

BIBLIOGRAPHY

ABERDEEN, Papers relating to the Trades of, 1777-1818.   Aberdeen Pub. Lib.
—— Report on the affairs of the Guildry of. *Aberdeen*, 1836. 8vo.
                                                         Aberdeen Pub. Lib.
AGRICULTURAL and General Laborers, Federal Union of. Report to the
    Trade Societies and general public of the United Kingdom. *London*, [1874].
    8vo.   Brit. Lib. Pol. Science.
AKROYD, EDWARD.   On the present attitude of Political Parties.   *London*
    [*Leeds printed*], 1874. 8vo.   8138 g.
ALLEN, THOMAS. The history and antiquities of London, Westminster, South-
    wark and parts adjacent. *London*, 4 vols. 8vo. 1827-1829.   2065 a.
ANSIAUX, M. Heures de travail et salaires, etc. *Paris*, 1896. 8vo.
                                                                08276 k. 1.
—— Rapport sur la journée de huit heures de travail. Société d'études sociales
    et politiques. *Bruxelles*, 1897. 8vo.   Brit. Lib. Pol. Science.
ANSTIE, J. [Chairman to the General Wool Meeting in the year 1788]. Obser-
    vations on the importance and necessity of introducing improved machinery
    into the Woollen Manufactory, etc. *London*, 1803. 8vo.   1138 i. 2 (2).
APPEAL, an, to Manufacturers on the present state of Trade, etc. *Birmingham*,
    1795. 8vo.   T. 1467 (16).
—— an, to the Editors of the *Times* in behalf of the Working Classes, etc.
    London, 1845. 8vo.   1390 g. 21.
APPLEGARTH, R.   Compulsory attendance at school.   Reprinted from the
    Sheffield Independent. [*London*, 1874 ?] 8vo.   Brit. Lib. Pol. Science.
APPRENTICE LAWS. Resolutions of the Master Manufacturers and Tradesmen
    of the cities of London and Westminster on the Statute 5 Eliz. c. 4. [*Lon-
    don*, 1814.] fol.   1882 d. 2.
ARBITRATION between the North-Eastern Railway Company and their work-
    men at Newcastle-on-Tyne and Gateshead, December 1889, Shorthand
    notes of the. R. Spence Watson, arbitrator. MS., 213 pp. fol.
                                                         Newcastle-on-Tyne Lib.
ASHLEY, W. J.   The Railroad Strike of 1894. [American Economic Associa-
    tion.] *Cambridge, Mass.*, 1895. 8vo.   Brit. Lib. Pol. Science.
ASHWORTH, HENRY. An inquiry into the origin, progress, and results of the
    strike of the Operative Cotton-spinners of Preston. *Manchester*, 1838.
                                                                Foxwell Coll.

B. P. GENT.   A help to magistrates and ministers of justice ; also a guide to
    Parish and Ward officers, etc. *London*, 1700. 12mo.
                                                       Brit. Lib. Pol. Science.

BALMFORTH, OWEN. Huddersfield, past and present. *Huddersfield*, 1894. 8vo.   Brit. Lib. Pol. Science.

BANKS, THOMAS. A short sketch of the Cotton Trade of Preston for the last sixty-seven years. [*Preston*] 1888. 8vo.   Brit. Lib. Pol. Science.

BARRISTER, A. Observations upon the law affecting Combinations and Trades Unions, and upon the Trades Union Bill. By a barrister. *London*, 1869. 8vo.   Brit. Lib. Pol. Science.

BARTON, JOHN. Observations on the circumstances which influence the condition of the laboring classes. *London*, 1817. 8vo.   8275 c.

—— A letter to the Rt. Hon. the Marquis of Lansdowne, etc. *Lambeth*, 1839. 8vo.   8247 bbb. 41.

BATT, W. S. The Ship Constructive Association, Portsmouth. Presidential address . . . . at the first annual general meeting, ... 24th April 1884. *Portsea*, 1884. 8vo.   Brit. Lib. Pol. Science.

—— The Ship Constructive Association, Devonport. Address by W. S. B. . . . . at Devonport, 5th December 1884. *Devonport*, 1884. 8vo.   Brit. Lib. Pol. Science.

BAYES, W. Remarks upon Archbishop Whately's letter on Medical Trades-Unions. *London*, 1863. 8vo.   7390 aaa.

BECHTLE, OTTO. Die Gewerkvereine in der Schweiz. *Jena*, 1887. 4to. In Elster, L. Staatswissenschaftliche Studien, etc. Bd. 2, Heft 1, 1887, etc.   8207 h.

BIRKS, JAMES. Trades Unionism ; a criticism and a warning, etc. Reprinted from the *Newcastle Weekly Chronicle*. *West Hartlepool*, 1894. 8vo.   08275, ee 21 (12).

BIRMINGHAM and National Trades' Defence Association, Rules of. [*Birmingham*, 1862.] 8vo.   T.U.

—— TOWN COUNCIL. Reduction of wages in the Public Works department. Report of the debate in the Council on 4th January 1881. *Birmingham*, 1881. 8vo.   Brit. Lib. Pol. Science.

BONWICK, JAMES. Romance of the wool trade. *London*, 1887. 8vo.   8229 c. 32.

Second edition. *London*, 1893. 8vo.   08227 g. 46.

BOOK OF TRADES, The, or library of the useful arts. Fourth edition. *London*, 1811. Three pts. 12mo.   7942 a. 55.

—— —— Sixth edition. *London*, 1815. 3 pts. 16mo.   7943 a. 3.

BOOKBINDERS. Articles of the Friendly Society of Journeymen Bookbinders of London and Westminster. MS. 24th March 1820. *Printed, London*, 1828.   Foxwell Coll.

—— Day-working Society of, London. Report of the Advisory Committee appointed to the duty of preparing a list of the Jaffray collection of trade documents pursuant to a resolution of the lodge, July 1882. *London*, [1883]. 8vo.   National Liberal Club Lib.

—— Account of receipts and expenditure of the dispute in the Metropolitan bookbinding trade, October 1891 to December 1892. *London*, 1893. fol.   Brit. Lib. Pol. Science.

BOULTON, S. B. The genesis of a Conciliation Act. [Reprinted from the *Chamber of Commerce Journal*, September 1896.] *London*, 1896. 8vo.   Brit. Lib. Pol. Science.

BRADFORD. Protest of the Bradford Short-time Committee against the proceedings of Mr. Richards, the Factory Inspector. *Bradford*, 1835.   Foxwell Coll.

BRASSWORKERS. Breeden *v.* Noon. An important point of law to workmen. [Report of the trial of, etc.] *Birmingham,* 1890. 4to.
Brit. Lib. Pol. Science.

—— *The Brassworkers' Year-book,* No. 1 for 1895. Issued by the National Society of Amalgamated Brassworkers. *Birmingham,* 1895. 8vo.
Brit. Lib. Pol. Science.

BRICKLAYERS. Operative Bricklayers' Society. Metropolitan Central Strike Committee's report, from 11th April to 15th November 1892. *London,* 1892. 8vo.
Brit. Lib. Pol. Science.

BRIEF STATE, a, of the inland or home trade of England ; and of the oppressions it suffers, and the dangers which threaten it from the invasion of hawkers, pedlars, and clandestine traders of all sorts. *London,* 1730. 8vo.
Guildhall Lib., catalogued under *Trade.*

BROADHURST, J. Political Economy. *London,* 1842. 8vo. 1138, h. 6.

BRUSHMAKERS. A List of Prices agreed upon between the Masters and Journeymen Brush Manufacturers in London, Friday 15th March 1805. *London,* 1805. 8vo.
T.U.

—— A List of Prices agreed upon between the Masters and Journeymen Brushmakers in Sheffield on the 17th June 1825. *Sheffield,* 1825. 8vo.
Brit. Lib. Pol. Science.

—— The Half-Yearly Returns of the Society of Journeymen Brushmakers, with an accurate list of the names of every tramp relieved from the 8th December 1828 to the 8th June 1829, etc. *London,* 1829. 8vo.
Brit. Lib. Pol. Science.

BUCKLEMAKERS. Appeal from the Buckle Trade of London and Westminster to the Royal conductors of fashion. *London* [1792]. 8vo. 1044 h. 28 (5).

BULLEY, A. A., and Whitley, M. Women's Work, etc. [Social Questions of To-day series, vol. 13.] 1894. 8vo. 08276 e.

BUILDERS. The Builders' Price Book, containing a correct list of the prices allowed by the most eminent surveyors in London to the several artificers concerned in building. [Collected by an experienced surveyor.] *London* [N.D.] 8vo. 1029 i. 6 (3).

BUILDING TRADES. [London.] The Strike, Trade Rules, Conduct of the Masters, etc. Case prepared at the request of the Building Trades Conference by Mr. W. P. Roberts, solicitor, and opinion of Mr. Edwin James, Q.C., and Mr. Gordon Allan. *London,* 1859. 8vo. T.U.

—— Report of preliminary conference on National Federation of the Building Industry. Held at . . . London, 7th and 8th August 1895. *London,* 1895. 8vo.
Brit. Lib. Pol. Science.

—— Birmingham Master Builders' Association. Reports and statement of accounts, 1884, etc. (In progress) *Birmingham,* 1885, etc. fol. 8282 h.

BUILDING TRADES GAZETTE, THE NATIONAL. A monthly journal. No. 1. September 1895. 4to. Issued by the London Building Trades Federation.
B.M. (P.P.)

BUILDING TRADES NEWS, THE. A monthly journal issued by the London Building Trades' Federation. No. 1. September 1894. 4to. etc.
B.M. (P.P.)

[BURN, J. DAWSON.] A Glimpse at the Social Condition of the Working Classes during the early part of the present century, etc. *London* [1868]. 8vo.
8282 aa. 39.

BURNLEY, JAMES. The history of wool and wool-combing. *London,* 1889. 8vo. 2251 e. 13.

C. W. and M[ATHER] R[ALPH]. An impartial representation of the case of the poor Cotton-spinners in Lancashire, etc., with a mode proposed to the Legislature for their relief, etc. *London*, 1780. 8vo. 523 g. 23 (2).

CABINETMAKERS. The prices of Cabinet work, with tables and designs, etc. *London*, 1797. 4to. Birmingham Library.

—— A Supplement to the London Cabinetmakers' Price Book of 1797, as agreed to in Birmingham, 1803. *Birmingham*, 1803. 4to.
Birmingham Library.

—— No. 1 Supplement to the Cabinetmakers' London book of prices, by George Atkinson and William Somerville. *London*, 1805. 4to. 712 k. 14.

—— The Edinburgh Book of Prices for Manufacturing Cabinet Work, etc. *Edinburgh*, 1805. 8vo. Foxwell Coll.

—— The Portable Desk makers' and Cabinet small workers' London Book of prices, as settled at an adjourned meeting of the trade, 1st September 1806. *London* [printed for the Society], 1806. 8vo. 7942 c. 29.

—— Articles of agreement made between the members of the Society of Cabinetmakers... in Birmingham. *Birmingham*, 1808. 8vo. Birmingham Library.

—— The London Cabinetmakers' Book of Prices for extensible dining tables. By a Committee. *London*, 1815. 4to. 712 R. 14.

—— Supplement to the Cabinetmakers' [of Edinburgh] Book of Prices, etc. *Edinburgh*, 1825. 8vo. Foxwell Coll.

—— The London Cabinetmakers' Book of Prices for work not provided for in the Union Book. By a Committee. *London*, 1831. 4to. 712 r. 15.

CALICO PRINTERS. Considerations addressed to the Journeymen, by one of their Masters. *Manchester*, 1815. Manchester Library.

—— Rules for the conducting of the Union Society of Printers, Cutters, and Drawers in Lancashire, Cheshire, Derbyshire, etc. *Manchester*, 1813.
Manchester Library.

—— Report of the Calico Printers' Committee on Wages. *Manchester*, 1831. 12 pp. Manchester Library.

CARPENTERS. The Carpenters and Joiners *vade mecum* and faithful guide, or an authentic book of rates or prices, etc. *London*, 1776. 8vo. 1029 i. 6 (5).

—— The London Standard, or a concise and comprehensive list of Carpenters' and Joiners' prices, etc. Duly considered and adjusted by a considerable and respectable number of masters. *London* [printed for the Society of Master Carpenters], 1778. 8vo. 1029 i. 6 (4).

—— Prices of Carpenters' and Joiners' work for the present year. *London*, 1801. 8vo. 1029 k. 14.

—— The Journeymen Carpenters' and Joiners' guide to the price of labor. Published by order of the Trade. *London*, 1811. Foxwell Coll.

—— Laws and Regulations of the Joiners' Protective Society. Instituted 15th February 1832, and remodelled 20th May 1842. *Glasgow*, 1842. 8vo.
Brit. Lib. Pol. Science.

—— Rules and Regulations of the Friendly Society of Operative House Carpenters and Joiners, as revised and agreed to . . . 1836. *London*, 1836. 8vo. Brit. Lib. Pol. Science.

—— 1837. Do.

—— 1838. Do.

—— 1840. Do.

—— 1859. Do.

—— Balance-sheet of the Operative Carpenters and Joiners of Manchester and vicinities Lock-out from 10th May to 6th November 1866. *Manchester*, 1866. *S.sh. fol.* Brit. Lib. Pol. Science.

CARTERS. Report of the Proceedings and Transactions of the Glasgow Carters' Committee. *Glasgow*, 1835. Mitchell Library, Glasgow.

CARTWRIGHT, Dr., Memoir of the Life of. MS. 1843, in Devonshire Collection. Derby Library.

CHAIRMAKERS, etc. The London Chairmakers' and Carvers' book of prices for workmanship. *London*, 1802. 4to. 558 b. 20 (2).

—— Supplement to the London Chairmakers' and Carvers' book of prices. *London*, 1808. 4to. 558 b. 20 (3).

—— Second Supplement to the London Chairmakers' and Carvers' book of prices . . . by a Committee of Master Chair Manufacturers and Journeymen. *London*, 1811. 4to. 712 k. 16.

CHESTER, G. J. The voice of blood crying from the ground. A sermon on the late alleged trade outrage. *Sheffield* [1861]. 8vo. 4277 aaa. 14.

CHEVALIER, É. Les salaires aux xixᵉ siècle. *Paris*, 1887. 8vo.
08228 h. 10.

CHICAGO. Report of the Chicago Strike of June-July 1894. By the United States Strike Commission. *Washington*, 1894. 8vo.
Brit. Lib. Pol. Science.

—— Eugene *v.* Debs and others. Report of the case of, in the Supreme Court of the United States. *Chicago* [1894]. 8vo. [By C. S. Darrow, counsel for petitioners]. Brit. Lib. Pol. Science.

CHITTY, J. A practical Treatise on the law relative to apprentices and journeymen, and to exercising trades. *London*, 1812. 8vo.
6325 aaa. 15.

CLELAND, Dr. J. Former and present state of Glasgow. [Glasgow Stat. Soc.] *Glasgow*, 1836. Mitchell Lib., Glasgow.

CLERKS. The necessity for a National Union of. *London*, N.D. 8vo.
Brit. Lib. Pol. Science.

COACHMAKERS. Rules of the Coachmakers' Society. Wisbech, Isle of Ely. Instituted 1st May 1827. *Wisbech*, 1835. 8vo. T.U.

—— United Kingdom Society of. Appeal from the delegate meeting assembled at Leeds, June 1848, to the Coachmakers of the three kingdoms. [*Leeds*] 1848. 8vo. T.U.

COALHEAVERS. The Coalheavers' Case [a petition to the House of Commons]. *S.sh. fol.* 1764. 214 i. 3 (68).

COBBETT, W. Cobbett's *Weekly Register*, Saturday, 14th April 1821. No. 2 vol. 39. To the Stocking-weavers of Leicestershire, Nottinghamshire, and Derbyshire, etc. Nottingham Free Library.

CONCILIATION, de la, et de l'Arbitrage dans les conflits collectifs entre patrons et ouvriers en France et a l'étranger. Office du Travail. *Paris*, 1893. 4to.
Brit. Lib. Pol. Science.

—— in Trade disputes. *Newcastle Leader* Extra. *Newcastle-on-Tyne*, 1894. 4to. Brit. Lib. Pol. Science.

COOPERS, Incorporation of, Glasgow. List of Office Bearers 1890-91, and abstract of accounts for year 1889-90. *Glasgow*, 1870. 8vo.
Brit. Lib. Pol. Science.

COTTON TRADE. The Cotton-weavers' New Act [of 1800] passed in consequence of two petitions presented to the House of Commons, etc. Printed for the use of the petitioners. *Manchester*, 1800. 8vo.
Manchester Library.

—— An abstract of the Cotton-weavers' Amended New Act [1804]. By order of the Select Committee of Weavers in Bolton. *Bolton*, 1804. 8vo.
Manchester Library.

COTTON TRADE. Rules for governing the Union of Weavers associated for the purpose of obtaining a proper remuneration for their industry, etc. *Manchester*, 1824.   Manchester Library.

—— Manual Labor *versus* Machinery. By the member for Lanarkshire. *London*, 1834. 8vo. 47 pp.   Manchester Library.

—— Report of Deputation to the Right Hon. H. Matthews, Q.C., M.P., 27th January 1887, in regard to Factory and Workshop Inspection. Also, Report of Joint Interview of employers and employed with the Right Hon. the Marquis of Salisbury, P.C., K.G., 28th January 1887, with reference to the Limited Liability Acts. *Accrington*, 1887. 8vo.
Brit. Lib. Pol. Science.

—— Weaving. Names of firms and number of looms in the districts comprising the Northern Counties' Amalgamated Associations of Weavers. [*Accrington*] 1888. 4to.   Brit. Lib. Pol. Science.

—— Weaving. Report of the Special Committee [of the Town Council of Blackburn] appointed to inquire into the subject of steaming in weaving sheds. *Blackburn*, 1888. fol.   Brit. Lib. Pol. Science.

—— List of private firms and Spinning companies in each district comprising the Oldham Province, etc. *Oldham*, 1889. 8vo.
Brit. Lib. Pol. Science.

—— Sir Henry James and the textile workers. Presentation at . . . Bury. *Bury* [1892]. 8vo.   Brit. Lib. Pol. Science.

—— Report of the Proceedings of the first International Textile Congress, held at Manchester, July 1894. *Manchester* [1894]. 8vo.
Brit. Lib. Pol. Science.

—— Report of the Second International Congress of Textile Workers, held in Ghent, Belgium, August 1895. *Ghent*, 1895. 8vo.
Brit. Lib. Pol. Science.

—— Report of the Case of Andrew Harris *v.* The Preston Weavers' Association Judgment. *Preston*, 1895. 8vo.   Brit. Lib. Pol. Science.

—— Division list of M.P.'s who voted for and against the imposition of the Indian Import Duties, etc. Issued by the United Textile Factory Workers' Association. *Manchester*, 1895. fol.   Brit. Lib. Pol. Science.

—— Indian Import Duties. Issued by the United Textile Factory Workers' Association. *Manchester*, 1896. 8vo.   Brit. Lib. Pol. Science.

—— Weaving. Steaming in Weaving sheds. Demonstration of Blackburn Weavers. *Blackburn*, N.D. 8vo.   Brit. Lib. Pol. Science.

CROSBY, B. Crosby's Builders' new Price Book. *London*, 1806, etc. [annually to 1854-55]. 8vo.   P.P. 2491 m.

DANBY, J. Des grèves ouvrières. *Bruxelles*, 1884. 8vo.
Brit. Lib. Pol. Science.

DAVIS, C. T. Labor and Wages. *Washington*, 1878. 8vo. 8275 dd 6 (2).

—— H. F. A. The Law and Practice of Friendly Societies and Trades Unions under the Friendly Societies Act 1875, the Trades Union Act 1871, and the Conspiracy and Protection of Property Act 1875, etc. *London*, 1876. 8vo.
6376 bb.

DAVIES, THOMAS. Prize Essay on the evils which are produced by late hours of business, etc. *London*, 1843. 8vo.   8276 c. 61.

—— Prize Essay on the evils which are produced by late hours of business, etc. 13th ed. *London*, 1844. 8vo.   8282 c. 36.

DECHESNE, L. La grève contre le tissage à deux métiers dans l'industrie lainière de Verviers en 1895-1896. *Verviers*, 1897. 8vo. Brit. Lib. Pol. Science.

DEFENCE of the Working Classes, in reply to an article in Chambers's *Edinburgh Journal*, entitled "Strikes, their Statistics." *London*, N.D. 8vo.
Foxwell Coll.

DEHN, P. Arbeiterschutzmassregeln gegen Unfall- und Krankheitsgefahren. *Berlin*, 1882. 8vo. 8277 f. 16 (12).

DELONEY, THOMAS. The History of John Winchcomb, usually called Jacke of Newberie, the famous clothier. [Edited by J. O. Halliwell]. *London*, 1859. 4to. 12612 g. 19.

DEW, GEORGE. Government and municipal contracts fair wages movement. A brief history. *London*, 1896. 8vo. Brit. Lib. Pol. Science.

DOCK Laborers' Strike 1889, the Great, Manifesto and Statement of Accounts. An epitomised history. *London*, 1889. Large 8vo. Brit. Lib. Pol. Science.

DOHERTY, JOHN. A letter to the members of the National Association for the protection of labor. *Manchester*, 1831. 24 pp. Foxwell Coll.

DOXFORD, W. T. [Engineer and Shipbuilder]. Memorandum of proposed evidence to be given before the Royal Commission on Labor, by W. T. D. . . . *re* the Board of Conciliation for the Wear Shipbuilding Trade. fol. N.D. or imprint. [1892 ?]. Brit. Lib. Pol. Science.

DRAGE, GEOFFREY. The Labor Problem. *London*, 1896. 8vo. 08277 h. 18.

—— The Unemployed. *London*, 1894. 8vo. 08275 ee. 5.

DRURY, JOHN. Reply of the Committee of the General United Grinding Branches of Sheffield and its vicinity to Earl Fitzwilliam's speech delivered at the Cutlers' Feast, 1844. *Sheffield*, 1844. 8vo. Sheffield Library.

DUBLIN. Committee on Combinations. Letter to the Committee lately appointed on combinations. By a workman and employer. *Dublin*, 1827. 8vo. 8146 bb. 34 (7).

—— Letter to employer and employed. By a manufacturer. *Dublin*, 1827. 8vo. 8146 bb 34 (7).

—— Collection of documents relating to the trade clubs of Builders, Shoemakers, Smiths, Tailors, and Weavers, etc. in Dublin. *Circa* 1720 etc. 839 m 23 and 1890 e 5.

DUNSFORD, MARTIN. Historical Memoirs of the town and parish of Tiverton in the County of Devon, etc. *Exeter*, 1790. 8vo. 2066 d. (1).

DYER, H. The evolution of industry. *London*, 1895. 8vo. 08277 h. 1.

EDINBURGH. Collection of documents relating to the Edinburgh Trades Societies' Agitation for Reform in 1830-1832. 808 m. 16.

—— Chamber of Commerce and Manufactures. Memorandum on Strikes and Labor Disputes. *Edinburgh*, 1890. fol. Brit. Lib. Pol. Science.

EMPLOYERS' Liability, Past and Prospective Legislation, with special reference to "Contracting-Out," etc. Reprinted from *The Sun. London*, 1896. 4to.
Brit. Lib. Pol. Science.

—— The Workers' Tragedy, etc. Reprinted from the *Daily Chronicle. London*, 1897. 4to. Brit. Lib. Pol. Science.

ENGINEERS. The Laws of the Friendly Society of Operative Metal Workers. *London*, 1834. 16 pp. Foxwell Coll.

—— Rules of the private donation fund of the Steam-engine Makers' Society. *Manchester*, 1848. 6to. Foxwell Coll.

—— Amalgamated Society of Engineers. Balance Sheet and List of Subscribers to the Newton testimonial. *London*, 1862. 8vo. Brit. Lib. Pol. Science.

—— Sheffield Strike of Engineers. Balance Sheet for the 7th week, ending 18th August 1873. *Sheffield*, 1873. 8vo. Brit. Lib. Pol. Science.

ENGINEERS. Amalgamated Society of Engineers. Rules of the Society from 1847 to 1892. Reprinted 1892. *London*, 1892. 4to. Brit. Lib. Pol. Science.
—— Amalgamated Society of Engineers. Report of the Executive Council on the Financial Position of the Society, with statistics and diagrams. *London*, 1895. 8vo. Brit. Lib. Pol. Science.
—— Amalgamated Society of Engineers. Statistics of Rates of Wages and Lists of Corresponding Officers, etc. 1895. *London*, 1895. Oblong 8vo.
Brit. Lib. Pol. Science.
—— Amalgamated Society of Engineers. Report, *re* the Government and Fair Contracts. *London*, 1895. 8vo. T.U.
—— Amalgamated Society of Engineers. Report on Dockyard Administration. *London*, 1895. 8vo. Brit. Lib. Pol. Science.

ENQUIRY, an, into the management of the poor. [Anon.] *London*, 1767. 8vo.
104 n. 28.
—— an [into the causes of poverty, etc., Anon.]. *London* [1795 ?] 8vo.
8275 d. 1 (1).
—— an, into the state of the manufacturing population. [Anon.] *London*, 1831. 8vo. T. 1351 (13).
ENTICK, J. A new and accurate history and survey of London, etc. 4 vols. *London*, 1766. 8vo. 290 f. 22-25.

FACTORY ACTS. Answers to certain objections made to Sir Robert Peel's Bill, etc. *Manchester*, 1819. 8vo. Foxwell Coll.
FELKIN, W. Facts and calculations illustrative of the present state of the Bobbin Net Trade. *Nottingham*, 1831. 8vo. Nottingham Library.
—— Remarks upon the importance of an inquiry into the amount and appropriation of wages by the working classes. *London*, 1837. 8vo.
Nottingham Library.
—— An account of the Machine-wrought Hosiery Trade. [A paper read before the British Association 18th September 1844.] *Reprinted. London*, 1845. 8vo. Nottingham Library.
FERRARIS, C. F. Gli infortuni sue lavoro, e la legge. *Roma*, 1897. 8vo.
Brit. Lib. Pol. Science.
—— Il materismo storico e lo stato. *Palermo*, 1897. 8vo.
Brit. Lib. Pol. Science.
FIELDEN, S. The Turn-out of the Master Mechanics. A letter to the *Times*. *Bolton*, 1852. 8vo. Manchester Library.
FOUCCROULLE, G. Les Conseils de Conciliation. *Bruxelles*, 1894. 8vo.
Brit. Lib. Pol. Science.
FOX, Stephen N., and Black, Clementina. The Truck Acts—what they do and what they ought to do. *London*, 1894. 8vo. 08282 g. 5 (7).
FRANKENSTEIN, K. Der Arbeiterfrage in der Deutschen Landwirthschaft. *Berlin*, 1893, 8vo. 08276 k. 22.
—— Der Arbeiterschutz, seine Theorie und Politik. *Leipzig*, 1896. 8vo.
8009 k.
FREE LABOR CONFERENCE, verbatim report of the, held . . . June 1894. *London*, 1894. 8vo. Brit. Lib. Pol. Science.
FREE LABOUR GAZETTE, THE. The organ of the National Free Labor Association. *London* (weekly), 1895-1896, etc. fol. Brit. Lib. Pol. Science.
FRENCH POLISHERS. Alliance and West-end Metropolitan. Guide to members in search of employment, of firms paying the minimum rate of wages and over. *London*, 1889. 8vo. 8247 a. 54.

FRIENDLY Societies. Collection of Rules of, etc.
Manchester Library (368-372.)

GALTON, F. W. (Editor). Workers on their Industries. *London*, 1894. 8vo.
08275 e. 26.
—— Select documents illustrating the history of Trade Unionism. I. The Tailoring Trade. *London*, 1896. 8vo. 08207 f.
GIBSON *v.* LAWSON. Report of the proceedings in the Supreme Court of Judicature. *Gateshead [printed]*, 1891. 8vo. Brit. Lib. Pol. Science.
GILBERT, J. T. Calendar of Ancient Records of Dublin in the possession of the municipal corporation of that city. *Dublin*, 1889, etc. 8vo.
10390 i. (In progress.)
GIRDLESTONE, C. The South Staffordshire colliery district. Its evils and their cure. *London [Stourbridge, printed]*, 1855. 8vo. 8282 d. 28.
—— A Letter to the . . . Bishop of London . . . in reference to the meeting of the landowners and employers of labor in the metropolis, holden on . . . 29th April 1863. *London* [1863]. 8vo. 4107 bb. 41.
GLASGOW. Address of the United Trades Committee appointed in aid of the Miners, to the various organised bodies in Scotland and elsewhere. *Glasgow*, 1856. 4to. Brit. Lib. Pol. Science.
GLASS BOTTLE MAKERS. Answers to the Schedule of Questions issued by the Royal Commission on Labor. [Reprinted from C. 6795–ix.]. *Castleford*, 1892. 8vo. Brit. Lib. Pol. Science.
—— Minutes of evidence taken before the Royal Commission on Labor. [Reprinted from C. 6894–ix.]. *Castleford*, 1893. 8vo.
Brit. Lib. Pol. Science.
—— Fifth Report of the International Union of. *London*, 1893. 8vo.
Brit. Lib. Pol. Science.
—— A Report of Conference of the Yorkshire Glass Bottle Manufacturers and the Glass Bottle Makers on the Wages Question, etc. 1893. 8vo.
Brit. Lib. Pol. Science.
—— A Report of the Rates of Wages, Lists of Numbers, Rates of overwork and working regulations of the Glass Bottle Makers of G. B. and I. for 1895. *[Castleford]*, 1895. 60 pp. 8vo. Brit. Lib. Pol. Science.
GLASSMAKERS. Articles, Rules, Orders, and Regulations of the Friendly Society of Glassmakers. . . . Lemington. Established 10th January 1789. *Newcastle*, 1829. 8vo. 8275 bb. 4.
—— An earnest appeal from the furnace, by a bottle hand to his fellow-workmen, etc. *London*, [1856]. 8vo. 8435 a. 108 (2).
GLOTIN, HYACINTHE. Étude historique, juridique et économique sur les syndicats professionels. *Paris*, 1892. 8vo. 5406 de. 10.
GOVERNMENT SERVANTS. Statement by the extra out-door officers of the Port of London, with reference to their hours of work, pay, and general conditions. *London* [1890]. fol. Brit. Lib. Pol. Science.
—— Statement of grievances of Government Employees, submitted to the Parliamentary Committee of the Trades Union Congress, January 1895. *London*, 1895. 8vo. Brit. Lib. Pol. Science.
GRAND National Consolidated Trades Union of Great Britain and Ireland, Rules and Regulations of the, etc. *London*, 1834. 8vo. Brit. Lib. Pol. Science.
GREEN, C. H. Employers' Liability, its History, Limitations, and Extension. *London*, 1897. 8vo. Brit. Lib. Pol. Science.
—— J. L. The rural industries of England. *London*, 1895. 8vo.
08276 g. 73.

GREG, W. R.   Essays on political and social science, etc.   2 vols.   *London*, 1853.   8vo.   2238 c. 8.

GUTTERIDGE, J. R.   The disease and the remedy.   An essay on the present state of the working classes ; including a true description of the degraded character of our railway laborers.   *London*, 1852.   12mo.
8275 a. 61 (10).

―― J.   Lights and shadows in the life of an artisan.   *Coventry*, 1893.   8vo.
10827 aaa. 45.

HALE, W.   A letter to Samuel Whitbread, Esq., M.P., containing observations on the distresses peculiar to the poor of Spitalfields, etc.   *London*, 1816.   8vo.
1103 h. 30.

―― An address to the manufacturers of England on the causes which have led to the unparalleled calamities of our manufacturing poor.   *London*, 1826.   12mo.
T. 1131 (13).

HALL, LEONARD.   The old and new Unionism.   *Manchester*, 1894.   8vo.
Brit. Lib. Pol. Science.

HALLAM, W.   Miners' Leaders.   Thirty portraits and biographical sketches.   *London*, [1894].   8vo.   10803 aaa. 33.

HARDING, W.   The history of Tiverton.   2 vols.   *Tiverton*, 1845-47.   8vo.
2066 b.

HARRISON, FREDERIC.   Workmen and the Law of Conspiracy.   [Tracts for Trades Unionists, No. 2].   *London*, 1874.   8vo.   8282 cc. 1.

HERKNER, H.   Die sociale Reform als Gebot des wirtschaftlichen Fortschrittes.   *Leipzig*, 1891.   8vo.   Brit. Lib. Pol. Science.

―― Die Arbeiterfrage.   *Berlin*, 1894.   8vo.   08276 i. 40.

HOLLAND, JOHN.   The history and description of fossil fuel, the collieries and coal trade of Great Britain.   *London*, 1835.   8vo.   726 i. 40.

―― 2nd edition.   *London*, 1841.   8vo.   726 i. 14.

HOLROYD, J. B. [Earl of Sheffield].   Observations on the manufactures, trade, and present state of Ireland.   2 parts.   *London*, 1785.   8vo.
Many other editions.   1102 h. 14 (5).

HOOLE, H.   A letter to the Rt. Hon. Lord Viscount Althorp, M.P., in defence of the Cotton Factories of Lancashire.   *Manchester*, 1832.   8vo.
Foxwell Coll.

―― A Report of the proceedings on the conviction of Benjamin Taylor, John Ball, W. Rutherford, and James Snow, part of the Framework Knitters' Committee.   *Nottingham*, 1821.   Nottingham Library.

―― A statement of prices for making and repairing stocking-frames, etc. June 1838.   *Derby*, 1838.   Nottingham Library.

―― The Framework Knitters' Trial, in the Exchequer Chamber, before fifteen judges of the land.   Archer *v.* James, Channer *v.* Cummings, and the Truck Act, etc.   *Nottingham*, 1861.   Nottingham Library.

HOWITT, W.   The rural life of England.   2 vols.   *London*, 1838.   8vo.
2366 c. 9.

―― The Rural and Domestic Life of Germany, etc.   *London*, 1842.   8vo.
2364 e. 6.

INGLIS, J.   [Engineer and Shipbuilder].   Memorandum on the apprentice question.   Presented to the Royal Commission on Labor.   *Glasgow*, 1892.   fol.   Brit. Lib. Pol. Science.

―― Memorandum of evidence proposed to be given before the Royal Commission on Labor . . . on demarcation of work, and on picketing.   *Glasgow*, N.D.   Fol.   Brit. Lib. Pol. Science.

INGLIS, J The Apprentice Question. *Glasgow*, 1894. Brit. Lib. Pol. Science.
INSTRUCTIONS for masters, traders, laborers, etc. In four parts, to masters, traders, and laborers; apprentices and servants; youth; and children. *London*, 1699. 12mo. 8410 b. 38.
—— Another edition. *London*, 1718. 12mo. 8410 aa. 33.
IRELAND. A Digest of the evidence taken before Select Committees of the two Houses of Parliament appointed to inquire into the state of Ireland, 1824-25. *London*, 1826. Haliday Tracts, vol. 1335. Royal Irish Academy.
IRON and STEEL WORKERS. South Wales. Memorandum of agreement [between employers and workmen, as to joint Board and Sliding Scale for the Industry]. *Cardiff*, 1890. fol. Brit. Lib. Pol. Science.
—— South Wales. Memorandum of agreement [between employers and workmen as to joint Board and Sliding Scale for the industry]. *Ebbw Vale*, 1893. fol. Brit. Lib. Pol. Science.
IRONMOULDERS OF SCOTLAND, Associated Society of, Evidence before the Labor Commission, June 1892. *Glasgow*, 1892. 8vo.
  Brit. Lib. Pol. Science.
IRON TRADE, North of England. Report of arbitration case before Messrs. Williams and Mundella, February and March 1876. From the *Ironworkers' Journal*, in the volume of MS. etc. relating to arbitration in the Iron Trades, in the Newcastle-on-Tyne Library.
—— —— Board of Arbitration and Conciliation. Report of discussion before the arbitrator at Darlington, July 1877. *Darlington*, 1877. 4to. 26 pp. Newcastle-on-Tyne Library.
—— —— Board of Arbitration and Conciliation. Report of discussion before the arbitrator at Darlington, April 1878. *Darlington*, 1878. 15 pp. 4to.
  Newcastle-on-Tyne Library.
—— —— Board of Arbitration and Conciliation. Arbitration proceedings at Darlington on the Wages Question. December 1878. *Darlington*, 1879. 19 pp. 4to. Newcastle-on-Tyne Library.
—— —— Board of Arbitration and Conciliation. Report of discussions before the arbitrator at Darlington, August and October, 1879. *Darlington*, 1879. 21 pp. 4to. Newcastle-on-Tyne Library.
—— —— Board of Arbitration and Conciliation. Report of Board meeting held in Darlington, May 1880, to hear Mr. Waterhouse's explanation, etc. *Darlington*, 1880. 12 pp. 8vo. Newcastle-on-Tyne Library.
—— —— Board of Arbitration and Conciliation. Claim by the workmen in plate and sheet mills for a return of the $7\frac{1}{2}$ per cent (special) reduction, 27th November 1880. *Darlington*, 1881. 29 pp. 8vo.
  Newcastle-on-Tyne Library.
—— —— Board of Arbitration and Conciliation. Presentation to Mr. David Dale, J.P. at Darlington, 4th October 1881. *Darlington*, 1881. 12 pp. 8vo. Newcastle-on-Tyne Library.
—— —— Board of Arbitration and Conciliation. Report of discussions before the arbitrator at Middlesbrough, April 1882. *Darlington* [*printed*]. 24 pp. 4to. Newcastle-on-Tyne Library.
—— —— Board of Arbitration and Conciliation. Report of discussion before the arbitrator at Middlesbrough. November 1882. *Darlington* [*printed*] 1882. 11 pp. 4to. Newcastle-on-Tyne Library.
—— —— Board of Conciliation and Arbitration. Rules, By-laws, and Instructions. *Middlesbrough*, 1883. 8 pp. 8vo.
  Newcastle-on-Tyne Library.
—— —— Board of Conciliation and Arbitration. Report of discussion before

the Arbitrator at Newcastle, 4th January 1884. *Darlington* [*printed*] 1884. 20 pp. 4to. Newcastle-on-Tyne Library.

IRON TRADE, North of England. Board of Conciliation and Arbitration. Report of discussion before the arbitrator at Newcastle, April 1884. *Darlington.* [*printed*] 1884. 14 pp. 4to. Newcastle-on-Tyne Library.

—— —— Board of Conciliation and Arbitration. Report of discussion before the arbitrator at Newcastle, November 1884. *Darlington* [*printed*] 1885. 17 pp. 4to. Newcastle-on-Tyne Library.

—— —— Board of Conciliation and Arbitration. Wages arbitration before R. S. Watson, Esq., LL.D. Court held at Newcastle-on-Tyne, October 1885. *Darlington* [*printed*] 1885. 23 pp. 4to. Newcastle-on-Tyne Library.

—— —— Board of Conciliation and Arbitration. Wages arbitration before R. S. Watson, Esq., LL.D. Court held at Newcastle-on-Tyne, November 1888. *Darlington* [*printed*] 1888. 12 pp. 4to. Newcastle-on-Tyne Library.

—— —— Statement showing the average net selling price of manufactured iron and the relative wages [for puddling] from 1876 to 1885. fol.
Newcastle-on-Tyne Library.

—— —— Description of the Consett Iron Works. *Newcastle-on-Tyne*, 1893. 8vo. Brit. Lib. Pol. Science.

IRWIN, M. H. The conditions of women's work in laundries, etc. *Glasgow*, 1894. fol. Brit. Lib. Pol. Science.

—— Women's employment in shops. Report of an inquiry conducted for the National Federal Council of Scotland for Women's Trades. *Glasgow*, 1896. fol. Brit. Lib. Pol. Science.

—— Home work amongst women. Report of an inquiry conducted for the Glasgow Council for Women's Trades. *Glasgow* [1897]. fol.
Brit. Lib. Pol. Science.

ITHURIEL. First prize essay on Trades Unions. *Glasgow*, 1875. 8vo.
Brit. Lib. Pol. Science.

JACKSON, S. and Milner, J. The evidence of, on the state of Trade in Sheffield, given before the Royal Commission on Manufacturers, 1833. *Sheffield*, 1833. 8vo. Sheffield Library.

JEANS, J. S. Conciliation and arbitration in labor disputes, etc. *London*, 1894. 8vo. 08276 f. 81.

JEFFREY, F. [afterwards Lord]. Substance of the speech of . . . at the public dinner given at Edinburgh to Joseph Hume, Esq., M.P., 18th November 1825. *Edinburgh*, 1825. 8vo. Brit. Lib. Pol. Science.

JOURDAN, F. S. De l'Assurance obligatoire contre les accidents du travail en Allemagne. *Paris*, 1894. 8vo. Brit. Lib. Pol. Science.

JUBB, SAMUEL. The history of the shoddy trade, etc. *London* [*Batley printed*] 1860. 12mo. 7943 b. 5.

JUSTITIA, M. [pseud. *i.e.* John Frearson]. The relative rights and interests of the employer and the employed discussed, etc. *London*, 1855. 8vo.
8276 b. 35.

—— —— An essay . . . showing how the surplus funds of the Amalgamated Society of Engineers may be practically applied to associated productive purposes. *London* [1855]. 8vo. 8226 a. 63 (2).

KATZENSTEIN, L. Die Lohnfrage unter dem Englischen Submissionswesen. *Berlin*, 1896. 8vo. Brit. Lib. Pol. Science.

KAUTSKY, K. Das Erfurter Programm. *Stuttgart*, 1892. 8vo.
Brit. Lib. Pol. Science.

KAY, J. P.   The moral and physical condition of the working classes employed in the cotton manufacture in Manchester. *London*, 1832. 8vo.
8276 de 13. (10).

KEUFER, A.   Rapport tendant à rechercher les moyens de parer aux funestes conséquences du système actuel des adjudications. [Pour la Fédération Française des travailleurs du libre]. *Paris*, 1896. 8vo.   Brit. Lib. Pol. Science.

LABOUR AND THE POOR.   Extracts reprinted from the *Morning Chronicle*, 1850. *London*, 1850. 8vo.   8276 de. 14.

LABOUR JOURNAL, the official organ of the Hull, Grimsby, and Goole Trades Councils. Monthly, 1894-1896. 4to.   Brit. Lib. Pol. Science.

LANGFORD, J. A.   A century of Birmingham life. 2 vols. *Birmingham*, 1868. 8vo.   2368 e.

LAW of Intimidation, The.   What does it mean? Reprinted from the *Western Daily Mercury*. *Plymouth*, 1890. 8vo.   Brit. Lib. Pol. Science.

LAWS Concerning Trade and Tradesmen. *London*, 1712. 12mo.
Brit. Lib. Pol. Science.

LECKY, W. E. H.   Democracy and liberty. 2 vols. *London*, 1896. 8vo.
2238 cc. 15.

LETTER, a, to the members in Parliament on the present state of the coinage. With proposals etc. *London*, 1771. 8vo.   T. 933 (15).

—— a, to a member of Parliament on the importance of liberty etc. *London*, 1745. 8vo.   Foxwell Coll.

LEVASSEUR, E.   Histoire des classes ouvrières en France, etc. 2 vols. *Paris*, 1859. 8vo.   2240 d. 7.

—— Les corporations et la liberté du travail [cours d'économie industrielle, etc. Association Polytechnique de Paris]. *Paris*, 1866, etc. 8vo.   ac. 4417.

LEVY, J. H.   The economics of labor remuneration. *London* [1894], 8vo.
08275 ee. 21 (14).

LLOYD, H. D.   Wealth against commonwealth. *London*, 1894. 8vo.
8282 cc. 46.

LOCH, D.   Letters concerning the trade and manufactures of Scotland, particularly the woollen and linen manufactures. Second edition with large additions. *Edinburgh*, 1774. 4to.   8246 g. 7.

—— Third Edition. *Edinburgh*, 1774. 8vo.   8247 b. 32.

—— Fourth Edition. *Edinburgh*, 1775. 4to.   8246 g. 8.

—— Essays on the trade, commerce, manufactures, and fisheries of Scotland, etc. 3 vols. *Edinburgh*, 1778-79. 12m.   8227 aa. 42.

LONDON.   The privileges of the free artificers of the city of London defended; in an appeal to the committee appointed to receive the complaints of the masters of the several manufactures in the city against their journeymen. *London*, N.D. [1750?]. 8vo.   Guildhall Lib. [catalogued under Free].

LONDON Trades Council, The.   Report of the deputation to the London School Board relative to the printing contract, October 1886. *London*, 1886. 8vo.
Brit. Lib. Pol. Science.

LOWELL, J. S.   Industrial Arbitration and conciliation, etc. *New York*, 1893. 8vo.   08276 g. 57.

MACDONNELL, G. P.   The industrial future and the prospects of the working classes. *London*, 1886. 8vo.   4018 c.

MACILWAINE, J. H.   [Engineer and Shipbuilder]. Memorandum of evidence proposed to be given before the Royal Commission on Labor, by, . . . on strikes, overtime, apprentices, hours of labor, demarcation of work, fluctuations of wages, etc. fol. N.D.   W. Coll.

MAHAIM, E.   Études sur l'association professionelle.   *Liège*, 1891.   8vo.
Brit. Lib. Pol. Science.

—— Les syndicats professionnels.   *Bruxelles* [1892 ?].   8vo.
Brit. Lib. Pol. Science.

MANCHESTER.   A collection of police documents relating to Manchester.
Circa 1780 etc.   fol. 1856.   Manchester Library.

—— The chief constable's accounts, 1854 etc.   Manchester Library.

MANN, T.   What a compulsory eight hour working day means to the workers.
London [1886].   8vo.   Brit. Lib. Pol. Science.

—— Presidential address.   [To the delegate meeting of the Dockers' Union at
Hull, 1892].   *London* [1892].   8vo.   Brit. Lib. Pol. Science.

—— and Tillett, B.   The new Trade Unionism.   A reply to Mr. George
Shipton.   *London* [1892].   8vo.   8282 cc. 47 (3).

MARTIN, R.   Die Ausschliessung der verheirateten Frauen aus der Fabrik.
Eine Studie an der Textil-Industrie.   *Tübingen*, 1897.   8vo.
Brit. Lib. Pol. Science.

MARTINEAU, Harriet.   On the tendency of sticks and strikes to produce low
wages.   *London*, 1834.   Brit. Lib. Pol. Science.

MARTIN-SAINT-LEON, E.   Histoire des corporations de métiers, etc.   *Paris*,
1897.   8vo.   W. Coll.

MATHER, W.   The forty-eight hours' week.   A year's experiment and its results
at the Salford Iron Works, Manchester.   *Manchester*, 1894.   8vo.
8282 ff. 12 (14).

—— A reply to some criticisms on Mr. Mather's report of a year's trial of the
forty-eight hours' week.   *London*, 1894.   8vo.   8282 ff. 12 (15).

MINERS.   Report of the proceedings at a public meeting held at the London
Tavern, 24th February 1818, to take into consideration the best means of
alleviating the condition of the distressed miners in different parts of the
kingdom.   8276 ee. 60.

—— Miners' wages and price of furnace coal for the last twenty years.   *Tipton*,
1884.   *S.sh. fol.*   Issued by the West Bromwich etc. Amalgamated Association of Miners.   Brit. Lib. Pol. Science.

—— South Staffordshire and East Worcestershire Coal and Ironstone Miners'
Wages Board and Sliding Scale Agreement.   [*Dudley*] 1890.   Fol.
Brit. Lib. Pol. Science.

—— The Royal Commission on mining royalties.   Evidence of Mr. S. Woods.
Reprinted from the *Wigan Observer*, 16th May 1891.   *Wigan*, 1891.   4to.
Brit. Lib. Pol. Science.

—— Durham Coal Trade Arbitration Cokemen, 1891.   *Newcastle-on-Tyne*,
1891, 352 pp.   8vo.   Dr. R. S. Watson's Collection, Newcastle-on-Tyne.

—— Derbyshire Miners' Association.   A Report by Dr. J. Court of the Examination of the eyes of coal miners working in collieries in Derbyshire using both
safety lamps and naked lights.   *Chesterfield*, 1891.   8vo.   Brit. Lib. Pol. Science.

—— Minutes, Circular Reports, etc., of the Durham County Mining Federation
Association.   Vol. II.   From 1891 to 1894.   *Durham*, 1894.   8vo.
Brit. Lib. Pol. Science.

—— Northumberland Miners' Gala, July 7th, 1894.   Speeches by members of
Parliament.   Address by the Bishop of Durham.   *Newcastle*, 1894.   8vo.
Brit. Lib. Pol. Science.

—— Miners' Conciliation Board.   Minutes of proceedings at a Joint Conference.
. . . Tuesday, 3rd April 1894.   Lord Shand in the Chair.   [No imprint.
N.D.].   8vo.   Brit. Lib. Pol. Science.

—— Board of Conciliation for the Durham Coal Trade.   Report of proceedings

30th April and 1st May 1895. The Rt. Hon. Lord Davey in the Chair. *Newcastle-on-Tyne*, 1895. 8vo. Brit. Lib. Pol. Science.

MINERS. Board of Conciliation for the Durham Coal Trade. Report of proceedings 23rd September and 4th October 1895. The Rt. Hon. Lord Davey in the Chair. *Durham*, 1896. 8vo. Brit. Lib. Pol. Science.

—— The Sixth International Miners' Congress. Held at . . . Paris, June 1895. Report of Proceedings. *London*, 1895. 8vo.

Brit. Lib. Pol. Science.

—— Miners' Federation of Great Britain. Report on Mines Eight Hours' Bill. *London*, 1895. 8vo. Brit. Lib. Pol. Science.

—— Mines Eight Hours' Bill. Report of a deputation to the Most Hon. the Marquis of Salisbury, K.G., and the Right Hon. Arthur J. Balfour, M.P., 14th March 1895. *London*, 1895. 8vo. Brit. Lib. Pol. Science.

—— The Blackwell Colliery Company's Coals and their treatment. Reprinted from *Coal and Iron*, 10th February 1896. *London*, 1896. 8vo.

Brit. Lib. Pol. Science.

MORTIMER, T. The universal director; or the nobleman and gentleman's true guide to the masters and professors of the liberal and polite arts and sciences, and of the mechanic arts manufactures and trades, established in London, etc. *London*, 1743. 8vo. Guildhall Lib.

—— Another copy. *London*, 1763. 8vo. 10349 c. 3.

MOSES, E. and Son. The growth of an important branch of British industry. The ready-made clothing system. *London*, 1860. 8vo. 8244 b. 29.

MUSÉE SOCIAL, LE (PARIS). See the valuable series of "circulars" published since January 1896 on the principal events in the Labor Movement.

Brit. Lib. Pol. Science.

NARRATIVE and exposition of the origin, progress, principles and objects of the General Association for the purpose of benefiting the manufacturing and agricultural laborers. *London*, 1828. 8vo. Foxwell Coll.

NASH, VAUGHAN. Trade Unionists and co-operation. *London*, N.D. 8vo.

Brit. Lib. Pol. Science.

NEVE, R. The city and country purchaser and builder's dictionary; or the compleat builder's guide. *London*, 1703. 8vo. 7820 bb.
Several other editions.

NEVILL, JOHN. Seasonable Remarks on the Linen Trade of Ireland. *Dublin*, 1783. Haliday Tracts, vol. 461, Royal Irish Academy, Dublin.

NEWBIGGING, T. Lancashire characters and places. *Manchester*, 1891. 8vo. 10360 d. 26.

NIELD, D. Addresses to the different classes of men in the parish of Saddleworth. 1795. 8vo. Foxwell Coll.

NORTHHOUSE, W. S. Coal Combination, etc. *London*, 1839. 8vo. 8282 dd. 20 (3).

NOTTINGHAM Date Book, The. *Nottingham*, 1880. Foxwell Coll.

NUNQUAM [R. BLATCHFORD]. The living wage. *London*, 1894. 8vo.

Brit. Lib. Pol. Science.

OASTLER, R. Sketch of the life and opinions of R. O. *Leeds*, 1838. 8vo.

Brit. Lib. Pol. Science.

OLDROYD, M. A living wage. [*London*], 1894. 8vo.

Brit. Lib. Pol. Science.

OLIVER, G. History of the Holy Trinity Guild at Sleaford, etc. *Lincoln*, 1837. 8vo. 4784 d. 23.

OLIVER, T. A new picture of Newcastle-on-Tyne. *Newcastle*, 1831. 12mo.
796 b. 31.

PAGAN, J. Glasgow past and present. [Edited by J. P.]. *Glasgow*, 1851 etc. 8vo. 10370 e.
Various other editions.

PARE, W. The claims of capital and labour, etc. *London*, 1854. 8vo.
8206 b. 7.

PEEL, F. The risings of the Luddites, Chartists, and Plug-drawers. *Brighouse*, 1895. 8vo. Brit. Lib. Pol. Science.

PERCIVAL, T. A letter to a friend occasioned by the late disputes between the checkmakers of Manchester and their weavers. *Halifax*, 1758.
Manchester Library.

PERCY, S. and R. London : or interesting memorials of its rise, progress, and present state. 3 vols. *London*, 1823. 12mo. 578 a. 18.

PHILLIPS, W. A. Labor, land, and law ; a search for the missing wealth of the working poor. *New York*, 1886. 12mo. 08277 ff. 5.

PICKARD, B. and Hartford, E. Labor questions. Speeches to the Eighty Club. *London* [1894]. 8vo.

PIDGEON, D. An engineer's holiday, etc. 2 vols. *London*, 1882. 8vo.
10025 bbb. 4.

PLAN of a relieving fund for the prevention of future encroachments and reductions of wages. Printed by order of the meeting on Platt Hill. July 6th, 1795. 8vo. Foxwell Coll.

—— A practicable and eligible, to secure the rights and privileges of mechanics ; with proper directions for the journeymen whereby they may get an advancement in their wages without loss of time or hindrance of business, etc. *London*, 1776. 8vo. 1029 i. 6. (6).

PLASTERERS. List of prices agreed to at a general meeting of Master Plasterers. *London*, 1796. 8vo. 1029 k. 14.

PLAYFAIR, W. A letter to the Right Honourable and Honourable the Lords and Commons of Great Britain on the advantages of apprenticeships. *London*, 1814. 8vo. Brit. Lib. Pol. Science.

PLUMER, T. Speech of T. P. addressed to the Committee of the House of Commons [on the Woollen Trade], 1803. 1803. 8vo. Foxwell Coll.

POSTMEN. The postmen's case for inquiry. *London* [1894]. 8vo.
Brit. Lib. Pol. Science.

POTTERS. Articles of the Potters' Independent Friendly Society. *Newcastle*. 1837. 8vo. 8275 bb. 4.

POWELL, J. A letter . . . on the general influence of large establishments of apprentices, etc. *London*, 1819. 8vo. Brit. Lib. Pol. Science.

PRICE, JOHN. [Engineer and Shipbuilder]. Memorandum on the demarcation of work, also on overtime and freedom of labor. Presented to the Royal Commission on Labor. *Glasgow*, 1892. Fol. W. Coll.

PRINTERS. The brotherly meeting of the masters and workmen - printers. Begun 25th November, 1621 . . . and hath been continued . . . to this present fourth of May, 1680. *London*, 1680. *S.sh. fol.* 1871 e. 9 (57).

—— An Account of the Rise and Progress of the dispute between the Masters and Journeymen Printers exemplified in the trial at large, etc. *London*, 1799.
Foxwell Coll.

—— Address of the Compositors of Edinburgh to the Master Printers, at a General Meeting of the Compositors of this City under authority of the Sheriff. *Edinburgh*, 1803. Foxwell Coll.

PRINTERS, Edinburgh. Memorial for the Compositor Printers, 28th Feb. 1804.
Foxwell Coll.

—— —— Additional Memorial for the Compositor Printers, 12th May 1804.
Foxwell Coll.

—— —— Report in the Process, by Robert Bell, 20th November 1804.
Foxwell Coll.

—— —— The Petition of David Ramsay for the Master Printers, 23rd Jan.
1805. Foxwell Coll.

—— —— Answers for the Compositors to the Petition of the Master Printers,
9th February 1805. Foxwell Coll.

—— Scale of Compositors' Prices agreed to by the Master Printers in Glasgow,
1st May 1815. *Glasgow*, 1815. *S.sh.* 8vo. Brit. Lib. Pol. Science.

—— Rules and Regulations of the London Union of Compositors. *London*
[1840]. 12mo. Brit. Lib. Pol. Science.

—— London Society of Compositors. Report of the Committee on the System
of working adopted in each Office. *London*, 1891. 8vo.
Brit. Lib. Pol. Science.

—— Memorandum of Agreement between the Economic Printing and Publishing Company, Limited, and the London Society of Compositors, *London*,
1892. 8vo. Brit. Lib. Pol. Science.

—— London Society of Compositors and Government Printing Contracts.
London, 1894. 8vo. Brit. Lib. Pol. Science.

—— London Society of Compositors. [Report on] forty-eight hour working
week and Federation. *London*, 1894. 8vo. Brit. Lib. Pol. Science.

—— London Society of Compositors and the Linotype. *London*, 1894. 8vo.
Brit. Lib. Pol. Science.

—— Printing Trades' Federation, The. An appeal for justice to the delegates
of the London Trades Council, *re* the Salvation Army. *London*, 1895.
8vo. Brit. Lib. Pol. Science.

—— London Society of Compositors. Provisional Agreement *re* Machine
Scale. *London*, 1896. 8vo. Brit. Lib. Pol. Science.

—— Fédération Française des travailleurs du livre, fondée en 1881. Statuts
modifiés au congrès typographique de Marseilles, Septembre 1895. *Paris*,
1896. 8vo. Brit. Lib. Pol. Science.

PROCEEDINGS of the Third Congress of the Association of all classes of all
Nations, held in Manchester, May 1838. [*Manchester*], 1838. 8vo.
Foxwell Coll.

RAAIJMAKERS, C. Verzekering tegen Werkloosheid. *Amsterdam*, 1895. 8vo.
Brit. Lib. Pol. Science.

RENAULT, C. Histoire des grèves. *Paris*, 1887. 12mo. 08275 e. 13.

RICHARDSON, M. A. Descriptive companion through Newcastle-upon-Tyne
and Gateshead. *Newcastle*, 1838. 8vo. 10352 aaa. 12.
Various other editions.

—— E. The National Agricultural Laborers' Union Melody Book. Original
Hymns and Songs. *Aylesbury*, 1874. 32mo. 11647 a. 80 (8).

—— J. L. C. Employment of females and children in factories and workshops, etc. *Dunedin* [*New Zealand*] 1881. 8vo. 8275 cc. 15 (4).

RICHMOND, A. B. Narratives of the condition of the manufacturing population
and the proceedings of Government which led to the State trials in Scotland
. . . for administering unlawful oaths in 1817, etc. *London* [*printed*] *Glasgow*, 1825. 8vo. 809 h. 13.

RICHMOND, A. B. Trial for libel, etc., Richmond v. Simpkin Marshall and others. [*Glasgow*, 1834?]. 8vo. 8135 bb. (2).

ROCHETIN, E. La Caisse Nationale de prévoyance ouvrière, et l'intervention de l'État, etc. *Paris*, 1894. 12mo. 08275 f. 16.

——— Les Assurances ouvrières mutualités contre la maladie, l'incendie et le chômage. *Paris*, 1896. 8vo. 08275 e. 46.

ROGERS, F. The art of bookbinding, etc. *London*, 1894. 8vo. Pam. 94.

ROLLE, John. The trader's safeguard, etc. *London*, 1822. 12mo. 515 b. 28.

ROMILLY, Sir S. Memoirs of the life of, etc. 3 vols. *London*, 1840.
 1130 d. 39.
 Other editions.

ROPEMAKERS' Friendly Society, Articles and Regulations of the Associated, Glasgow, Instituted 11th September 1824. *Glasgow*, 1837. 8vo.
 Brit. Lib. Pol. Science.

ROUSIERS, P. de. La question ouvrière en Angleterre. *Paris*, 1895. 8vo.
 08275 ee. 40.

——— English edition, translated by F. L. D. Herbertson. *London*, 1896. 8vo. 108277 h. 14.

——— [Editeur]. Le Trade Unionisme en Angleterre, etc. *Paris*, 1896. 8vo.
 Brit. Lib. Pol. Science.

SCHMID, C. A. Beiträge zur Geschichte der gewerblichen Arbeit in England wahrend der letzten 50 Jahre. In Elster L. staatswissenschaftliche Studien, etc. *Jena*, 1896. 8vo. 8207 h.

SCHMOLE, J. Die socialdemokratischen Gewerkschaften in Deutschland, seit dem Erlasse des Socialisten-Gesetzes. *Jena*, 1896. 8vo.
 Brit. Lib. Pol. Science.

SCHMOLLER, G. Zur Geschichte der Deutschen Kleingewerbe im 19. Jahrhundert. *Halle*, 1870. 12mo. 8244 bb. 36.

——— Jahrbuch für Gesetzgebung Verwaltung und Volkswirtschaft. *Leipzig*, 1871, etc. (continued). P.P. 1385 e.

SCHOENHOF, J. Wages and trade in manufacturing industries in America and in Europe. *New York*, 1884. 8vo. 8275 cc. 14 (7)

——— The industrial situation and the question of wages. *New York and London*, 1885. 8vo. 8275 bbb. 50.

——— The economy of high wages. *New York and London*, 1892. 8vo.
 08276. f. 66.

SCHULZE-GAEVERNITZ, G. von. The Cotton Trade in England and on the Continent. Tr. *London*, 1895. 8vo. W. Coll.

SCHWIEDLAND, E. Kleingewerbe und Hausindustrie in Osterreich. 2 vols. *Leipzig*, 1894. 8vo. Brit. Lib. Pol. Science.

——— Vorbericht über eine gesetzliche Regelung der Heimarbeit. *Vienna*, 1896. 4to. Brit. Lib. Pol. Science.

——— Un projet de loi français sur de soi-disant Conseils de Conciliation. *Paris*, 1896. 8vo. Brit. Lib. Pol. Science.

SCOTTISH Trades Union Congress, Report of the First Annual. Held in . . . Glasgow, March 1897. *Glasgow*, 1897. 8vo. Brit. Lib. Pol. Science.

SEAMEN. Evidence in favor of the seamen given by J. Beveridge of North Shields before a Select Committee of the House of Commons, 10th July 1825. *North Shields*, 1826. 8vo. 8275 bb. 4.

——— Representation of Seamen on Pilotage Boards, the. A paper read at the Seamen's Congress, Cardiff, 1889. 1889. 8vo. Brit. Lib. Pol. Science.

SEILHAC, L. de. La grève de Carmaux et la verrerie d'Albi. *Paris*, 1897.
8vo. Brit. Lib. Pol. Science.
SERIOUS Considerations addressed to British laborers and mechanics at the
present crisis. *London*, 1803. 8vo. 104 g. 44 (17)
SETTLE, A. The meaning of the labor movement. *Manchester*, 1893. 8vo.
Brit. Lib. Pol. Science.
SEVERN, M. The miner's evangel. A text-book for all manual workers.
Pontypridd, 1895. 8vo. Brit. Lib. Pol. Science.
SHIPBUILDING TRADES. The shipwrights' vade mecum, etc. *London*, 1805.
8vo. 716 d. 24.
—— of the River Thames. A scale of prices for job work on old ships, care-
fully arranged and compiled [by a committee of journeymen]. *London*, 1825.
8vo. Brit. Lib. Pol. Science.
—— Conference on Apprentice Question held at Newcastle-on-Tyne, 18th
May 1893, between members of the Employers' Federation of the Shipbuilding
and Engineering Trades and the Representatives of the Boilermakers' and Iron
and Steel Shipbuilders' Society. *Newcastle*, 1893. 8vo.
Brit. Lib. Pol. Science.
—— Minutes of Line of Demarcation Joint Committee of Shipwrights and
Joiners, which met on Monday 2nd October 1893, and following days.
Glasgow, 1894. Large 8vo. 285 pp. Brit. Lib. Pol. Science.
—— Employers' Handbook in the Shipbuilding and Engineering Trades at
Newcastle-on-Tyne, 1894. *Newcastle*, 1894, Sm. 8vo.
—— Agreements between the Employers' Association and the Boilermakers and
Iron and Steel Shipbuilders' Society. *Newcastle*, 1894. 8vo.
Brit. Lib. Pol. Science.
SHIRLEY, S. Our national sinews, etc. *London* [1855]. 8vo. 8276, A. 65.
SHOEMAKERS, Dublin. A poem in honor of the Loyal Society of Journeymen
Shoemakers who are to dine at the Castle, in Castle Street, on Monday, 25th
October 1725. By R. Ashton. *Dublin*, 1725. *S.sh. fol.* 839 m. 23 (88).
—— A poem in honor of the Loyal Society of Journeymen Shoemakers, etc.
By R. Ashton. *Dublin*, 1726. *S.sh. fol.* 839 m. 23 (155).
—— A dialogue between a brogue maker and the journeymen shoemakers.
Dublin, N.D. [1730 ?]. *S.sh. fol.* 839 m. 23 (101).
—— Articles of the Journeymen of the City of Edinburgh. Established 1727.
Edinburgh, 1778. 8vo. Foxwell Coll.
—— London Statement of Wages. Established 1st May 1812. *London*, 1812.
16 pp.
SILK manufacture. Reasons for renewing the office of Silk Dyeing.
816 m. 12 (96).
—— Weavers. The case of the Silk and Worsted Weavers in a letter to a
member of Parliament. *Dublin*, 1749. 8 pp. Haliday tracts. Vol. 221.
Roy. Irish Academy.
—— An account of the proceedings of the Committee of the Journeymen Silk-
weavers of Spitalfields in the legal defence of the Acts of Parliament granted to
their trade. *London*, 1823. 67 pp.
—— Rules and regulations adopted by the Macclesfield Silk Trade Board, etc.
Macclesfield, 1849. 136 pp. 8vo. 1400 b. 35.
SIX Prize essays on labor and wages. *Leicester*, 1849. Manchester Library.
SMART, H. R. Trade Unionism and politics. *Manchester*, 1893. 8vo.
Brit. Lib. Pol. Science.
—— Miners' wages and the sliding scale. *Glasgow*, 1894. 8vo.
8282 ff. 12 (17).

SMART, W.   On women's wages.   *Glasgow*, 1892.   8vo.   Brit. Lib. Pol. Science.
—— Studies in Economics.   *London*, 1895.   8vo.
SMITH, E. J.   The new Trades Combination movement.   Its principles and
methods.   *Birmingham*, 1895.   8vo.   Brit. Lib. Pol. Science.
—— J. T.   Nollekens and his times, etc.   2 vols.   *London*, 1828.   8vo.
Various other editions.   2032 b.
STRIKE or Legislate?   An appeal to Trade Unionists.   *Liverpool*, 1894.   Leaf-
let.   8vo.   Brit. Lib. Pol. Science.
SYKES, J.   Local Records . . . of Durham and Northumberland, etc.   *Newcastle*,
1824.   8vo.   797 g. 26.
Various other editions.

TAILORS [London].   A true account of the case between the Worshipful the
Master, Wardens, and Court of Assistants of the Company of Merchant
Taylors of the City of London, and the Master Working Taylors, freemen of
this city, and members also of the said Company.   *London*, 1687.   *S.sh.
fol.*   Guildhall Library.
—— The case of the Master Cutting Taylors and all other Master Workers duly
qualified in the Taylory trade within the cities of London and Westminster,
etc.   *London*, N.D. 1702-1714.   *S.sh. fol.*   Guildhall Library.
—— The Tailors.   A tragedy for warm weather ; in three acts.   As it is performed at the Theatre Royal in the Haymarket.   *London*, 1778.   8vo.
                                                                                 643 e. 8 (2).
—— An appeal to the Operative Tailors of Scotland.   By a fellow-workman.
N.D. 1880.   8vo.   Brit. Lib. Pol. Science.
—— Tailors, Woollen-drapers, etc.   See the collection of documents relating to
these trades.   816 m. 14.
TAYLOR, Wm.   An answer to Mr. Carlile's Sketches of Paisley.   *Paisley*, 1809.
                                                                         Mitchell Library, Glasgow.
—— W. C.   Notes of a tour in the manufacturing districts of Lancashire, etc.
London, 1842.   8vo.   792 b. 4.
TEMPERTON *v.* Russell and others, The case of, an examination of its bearing
upon the rights of combination, etc.   *London*, 1895.   8vo.   Brit. Lib. Pol. Science.
THACKRAH, C. T.   The effects of the principal arts, etc.   *Leeds*, 1831.   8vo.
                                                                                 1039 l. 28.
THOM, W.   Rhymes and recollections of a handloom weaver.   *London. Aber-
deen* [*printed*], 1844.   8vo.   1465 c. 49.
Other editions.
TILLETT, B.   Address on man's individual responsibility.   *London*, 1892.
8vo.   Brit. Lib. Pol. Science.
—— The help yourself gospel ; or, the New Trades Unionism.   *Dundee*
[*printed*], N.D.   8vo.   Brit. Lib. Pol. Science.
—— The legislature and labour.   An address.   *Cardiff* [*printed*], N.D.   8vo.
                                                                 Brit. Lib. Pol. Science.
TRADE Unionism, the tyranny of.   Reprinted from the *Globe.*   *London*, 1894.
8vo.   Brit. Lib. Pol. Science.
TRADES Union Congress.   Parliamentary Committees' Report on the Employers'
Liability Bill.   *London*, 1894.   8vo.   Brit. Lib. Pol. Science.
—— Parliamentary Committee, the Report of Important Deputations to Cabinet
Ministers.   13th, 14th, and 15th November 1895.   *London*, 1895.   8vo.
                                                                 Brit. Lib. Pol. Science.
TURGOT, A. R. J.   Œuvres . . . Nouvelle édition classée par ordre de matières
etc.   Par E. Daire.   Two vols.   *Paris*, 1844.   8vo.   1390 k. 5-6.

TYLOR, L. Old Age Allowances. [The Central Association for dealing with distress caused by mining accidents.] *Cardiff*, 1895. 4to.
Brit. Lib. Pol. Science.

UNEMPLOYMENT. Report of the committee appointed at a public meeting at the city of London Tavern, 2nd May 1826, to relieve the manufacturers, etc. *London* [1829], by W. H. Hylett. Foxwell Coll.
—— Rapport sur la question du chômage présente au nom de la commission permanente. *Paris*, 1896, 4to. Brit. Lib. Pol. Science.
UNITED Kingdom Alliance of Organised Trades. Rules for the government of the, as adopted at the Conference held in Manchester. *January* 1867. *Sheffield* [*printed*], 1867. 8vo. Brit. Lib. Pol. Science.
UPHOLSTERERS, London West End Trade Society. Report of the committee on Co-operative Production, appointed November 1894. *London*, 1895. 8vo.
Brit. Lib. Pol. Science.

VALERA, P. L'insurregione chartista in Inghilterra. *Milano*, 1895. 8vo.
9525 aaa. 27.
VANDERVELDE, E. DE. Enquêtes sur les associations professionelles d'artisans et ouvriers en Belgique. 2 vols. *Bruxelles*, 1891. 8vo. Brit. Lib. Pol. Science.
VOICE from the aliens, a, about the anti-alien resolution of the Cardiff Trades Union Congress. *London* [1896]. 8vo. Brit. Lib. Pol. Science.
VOLTA, R. D. Le forme del salario. *Firenze*, 1893. 8vo. 08275 f. 18.
—— Le coalezioni industriali. *Firenze*, 1894. 8vo. Brit. Lib. Pol. Science.

WARD, BENJAMIN. The state of the woollen manufacture considered, etc. *London*, 1731. 8vo. 1139 i. 2.
—— JOHN. The Borough of Stoke-upon-Trent. *London*, 1843. 8vo.
1302 l. 1.
—— W. G. Capital and Labor. *Nottingham*, 1874. 8vo. 8277 bbb. 5.
WATERMEN. The case of the keelmen of Newcastle, etc. [*London*, 1712?] *S.sh. fol.* 8223 e. 9 (31).
—— The case of the poor skippers and keelmen of Newcastle, truly stated, etc. [*London*, 1712?] *S.sh. fol.* 8223 e. 9 (32).
—— A farther case relating to the poor keelmen of Newcastle. [*London*, 1712?] fol. 8223 e. 9 (32).
—— Warning to the keelmen [of Newcastle] by the Magistrates. [Against a strike and Riots]. *Newcastle*, 1822 *S.sh. fol.* 1879 b. 2.
—— Lightermen's work and wages. Arbitration by Lord Brassey, K.C.B. Award . . . of the umpire, etc. *London*, 1889. fol. Brit. Lib. Pol. Science.
—— The award and conditions of service under which the lightermen. . . . of the River Humber met work. The award of E. N. Hill and J. D. Welch, arbitrators. *Hull* [1890]. 12mo. Brit. Lib. Pol. Science.
—— Report of a Conference between Representatives of the Association of Master Lightermen and of the Amalgamated Society of Watermen to consider Lord Brassey's award, etc. *London*, 1889. 8vo. T.U.
WATTS, J. The catechism of wages and capital, London. *Manchester* [*printed*], 1867. 12mo. 8206 a. 38 (5).
—— The working man : a problem. *Manchester* [1875]. 8vo.
8276 aa. 38 (5).
WAUGH, MANSIE, Tailor in Dalkeith. The life of, written by himself. [by D. M. Moir]. *Edinburgh*, 1828. 12mo. N. 550.
WEILER, J. La conciliation industrielle et le role des meneurs. *Bruxelles*, 1892. 8vo. Brit. Lib. Pol. Science.

WEILER, J. Vivons-nous sur un volcan? *Bruxelles*, 1893. 8vo. Brit. Lib. Pol. Science.
—— L'esprit d'autorité et la conciliation industrielle. *Bruxelles*, 1894. 8vo.
Brit. Lib. Pol. Science.
WHITE, G. A digest of the minutes of evidence taken before the committee on Artisans and Machinery. *London*, 1824. 8vo. 1044 h. 16.
—— Abstract of the Acts repealing the laws against combinations of workmen, etc. *London*, 1824. 8vo. 8275 b.
WHITE SLAVERY. A collection of pamphlets on the Factory Acts, Poor Law, etc., 1818 to 1837. 16 vols. Foxwell Coll.
WOLF, J. Sozialismus und Kapitalistiche gesellschaftsordnung, etc. *Stuttgart*, 1892. 8vo. Brit. Lib. Pol. Science.
WOLFF, H. W. Employers' Liability, what ought it to be? *London*, 1897. 8vo. 8276 d. 65.
WOOLLEN TRADES. [A collection of tracts upon wool and the woollen trade]. *London*, 1782-1818. 8vo. B. 547.
—— A copy of some of the reasons formerly offered by the Gloucestershire clothers to show the true cause of the decay of the Worcester trade. N. D.
Foxwell Coll.
—— An abstract of the grievances of trade which oppress our poor. Humbly offered to the Parliament. *London*, 1694. 8vo. 104 g. 44.
—— Articles of agreement made, concluded, and agreed upon by the Royal Society of Worsted Weavers in the city of Norwich and county of the same, 23rd Nov. 1717. Corrected and amended, 12th Feb. 1725-26. *Norwich*, 1826.
—— Articles of agreement made, concluded, and agreed upon by the Royal Society of Worsted Weavers in the city of Norwich and county of the same. 23rd Nov. 1717. Corrected and amended 12th Feb. 1725-26.
—— Verses addressed by the Union of Trowbridge to their brother operatives. *Trowbridge, S.sh. fol.* N.D. 772 i. I (21).
—— The case of the weavers of the city of Coventry. [*Coventry*, 1720?] fol.
357 b. 3 (108).
—— The Procurator Fiscal *v.* the Woolcombers of Aberdeen, 1762.
Foxwell Coll.
—— Considerations on the woollen manufactory of Ireland. By a friend to Ireland. *Dublin*, 1785. Foxwell Coll.
—— Considerations upon a Bill now before Parliament for repealing (in substance) the whole code of laws respecting the woollen manufactures of Great Britain, etc. [By the clothworkers or shearmen of the counties of Wilts, Somerset, York, and Gloucester]. *London*, 1803. 8vo. 1102 i. 89.
—— Observations on woollen machinery, 1803. Foxwell Coll.
—— An address to the inhabitants of Rochdale and its vicinity on the subject of the present differences between the weavers and their employers. *Rochdale*, 1829. 12 pp. Foxwell Coll.
—— Two letters of G. Poulett Scrope, M.P., to the chairman of the central committee of the Handloom Worsted Weavers of the West Riding of York, with their answers to the same. *Bradford*, 1835. Foxwell Coll.
—— The miseries of the miserable, or, an essay towards laying open the decay of the fine woollen trade, and the unhappy condition of the poor Wiltshire manufacturers. By a gentleman of Wilts, 1739. Manchester Library.
—— A vindication of the Broad Cloth Weavers, being the journeymen's answer to Mr. Textor's letter in the sixteenth Censor. *Dublin*, 1749. 8 pp. Haliday Tracts, vol. 221. Roy. Irish Academy.
WOMEN'S WORK. Report of investigations into the conditions of. Women's Co-operative Guild. *Manchester*, 1896. 8vo. Brit. Lib. Pol. Science.

INDEX

ABATTOIRS, municipal, ii. 788
Aberdeen, combinations in, 336
Abinger, Lord, 367
Abraham, May (Mrs. Tennant), 329, 350
Absentee employers, 296
Abstinence, ii. 623
Accident benefit, 152, 170
Accidents, long indifference to, 355; working rules against, 358; lead to agitation for Employers' Liability, 368; frequency of, 374, 376; compensation for, 378, 388, 390; inquiry into, 378, 384, 390
Accumulation of capital, causes influencing the, ii. 610-632, 871
Accumulative vote in Coalminers' conferences, 45; at Trade Union Congress, 277; absence of, in Federation of Engineering Trades, ii. 523
Act of God, 356, 379
Activities in relation to wants, ii. 697, 704
Acton, Lord, 59
Actuarial difficulties of competing unions, 113; increased by Direct Legislation, 61, 115; affected by legal position of Trade Unionism, 154; not yet properly studied, 156
Administration, at first by whole body of members, 3; in times of war by secret committees, 9; by general mass meetings, 10; by a governing branch, 12; by specialised officers, 16, 27; by a Cabinet, 30, 39, 43; by a Representative Executive, 47; need for specialisation of, 59; progressive centralisation of, 88-103; function of the branch in, 100
Admiralty dockyards, ii. 554; analogy to Wage Fund of, 605; minimum wage of, 775

Adulteration Acts, ii. 734
Aged, Trade Union provision for the, 152-172; allowed to work below Standard Rate, 165; compulsory insurance for, objected to, ii. 529; pensions for, not objected to, 827
Agricultural land, exhaustion of, ii. 752
Agriculture, excluded from Workmen's Compensation Act, 388; yearly hirings in, 431; supplied idea of Wage Fund, ii. 605; decay of, 761; a Poor Law industry, 788
Alexander the Coppersmith, ii. 564
Alien immigrants, desire for exclusion of, 252; effect of, ii. 744
Allan, William, 110, 133, 134, 167, 170
Alliances, the Birmingham, ii. 577, 665, 806
Altrincham Stonemasons, 78
"Amalgamated," for societies so termed, see under the respective trades
Amalgamated Engineers' Monthly Journal, 133; ii. 514, 515, 524, 563
Amalgamation, attractiveness of, 109; in the building trades, 109; among the Coalminers, 109; among the Clothworkers, 109; among the Engineers, 110; difficulties as to basis of, 111; objections to, 110, 128; gradual differentiation of, from federation, 129-141; of trade and friendly benefits, 157
America, early use of Referendum in, 19; boot and shoe factories in, 398, 413; trusts in, 448; ii. 582, 709; nail mills in, 754; possible future of, 872
Andrew, Samuel, 449
Annual election, of officers, 16; advocated as democratic, 36; leads to permanence of tenure, 16, 50;

THE END